...vent to the National ...useum of Nature and ...cience in Ueno the ...her day and saw a ...rannosaurus. It was so cool. If I weren't a manga artist, I think I would've been a Hercules beetle or a Tyrannosaurus. That's how much I love them.

—Tite Kubo, 2009

BLEACH is author Tite Kubo's second title. Kubo made his debut with *ZOMBIEPOWDER.*, a four-volume series for *WEEKLY SHONEN JUMP*. To date, *BLEACH* has been translated into numerous languages and has also inspired an animated TV series that began airing in the U.S. in 2006. Beginning its serialization in 2001, *BLEACH* is still a mainstay in the pages of *WEEKLY SHONEN JUMP*. In 2005, *BLEACH* was awarded the prestigious Shogakukan Manga Award in the *shonen* (boys) category.

BLEACH
3-in-1 Edition

SHONEN JUMP Manga Omnibus Edition Volume 14
A compilation of the graphic novel volumes 40–42

STORY AND ART BY
TITE KUBO

English Adaptation/Lance Caselman
Translation/Joe Yamazaki
Touch-up Art & Lettering/Mark McMurray
Design - Manga Edition/Kam Li, Yukiko Whitley
Design - Omnibus Edition/Fawn Lau
Editor - Manga Edition/Alexis Kirsch
Editor - Omnibus Edition/Pancha Diaz

BLEACH © 2001 by Tite Kubo. All rights reserved.
First published in Japan in 2001 by SHUEISHA Inc., Tokyo.
English translation rights arranged by SHUEISHA Inc.

The stories, characters and incidents mentioned in this publication are entirely fictional.

No portion of this book may be reproduced or transmitted in any form or by any means
without written permission from the copyright holders.

Printed in the U.S.A.

Published by VIZ Media, LLC
P.O. Box 77010
San Francisco, CA 94107

10 9 8 7 6 5 4 3 2 1
Omnibus edition first printing, February 2016

NEWPORT PUBLIC LIBRARY
NEWPORT, OREGON 97365

www.viz.com

PARENTAL ADVISORY
BLEACH is rated T for Teen and is
recommended for ages 13 and up. This
volume contains fantasy violence.
ratings.viz.com

THE WORLD'S
MOST POPULAR MANGA
SHONEN JUMP
www.shonenjump.com

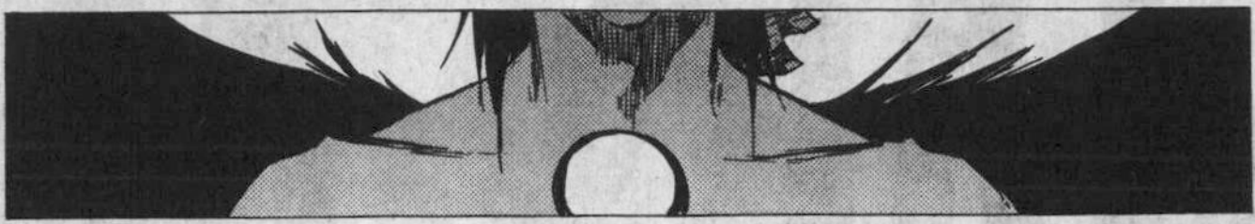

Envious because I have a heart

Gluttonous because I have a heart

Greedy because I have a heart

Prideful because I have a heart

Slothful because I have a heart

Wrathful because I have a heart

Because I have a heart

I lust for all that you are

BLEACH 40 THE LUST

Shonen Jump Manga

STARS AND

Ichigo Kurosaki

Ulquiorra

★ plot

When high school student Ichigo Kurosaki meets Soul Reaper Rukia Kuchiki his life is changed forever. Soon Ichigo is a soul-cleansing Soul Reaper too, and he finds himself having adventures, as well as problems, that he never would have imagined. Now Ichigo and his friends must stop renegade Soul Reaper Aizen and his army of Arrancars from destroying the Soul Society and wiping out Karakura as well.

The battle finally begins! The Thirteen Court Guard Companies head to Karakura while Ichigo remains in Hueco Mundo to fight Ulquiorra. As Orihime watches, the fight goes back and forth. Who will come out on top?!

BLEACH ALL

井上織姫

Orihime Inoue

STORIES

BLEACH 40

THE LUST

Contents

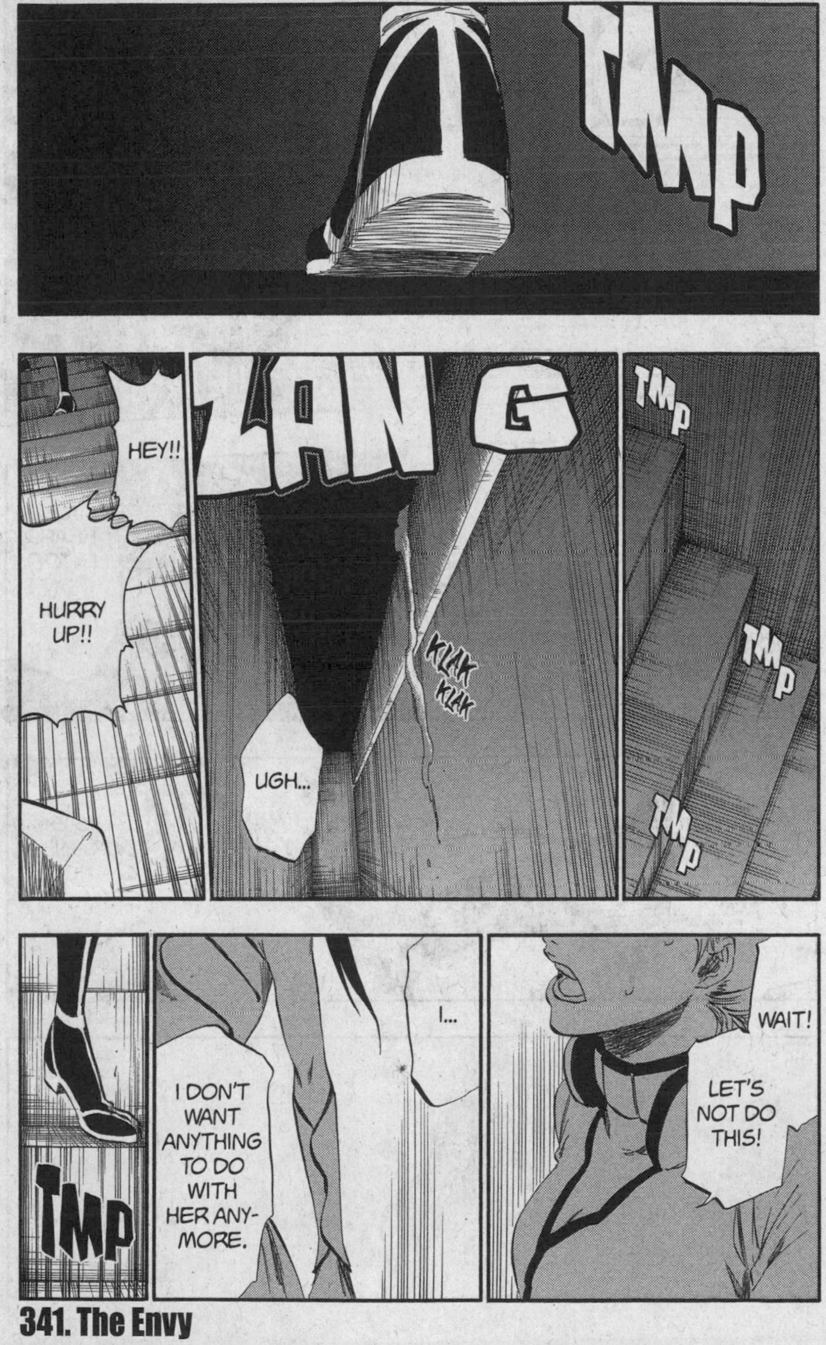
TMP
TMP
TMP
TMP
ZANG
KLAK KLAK
UGH...
HEY!!
HURRY UP!!
WAIT!
LET'S NOT DO THIS!
I...
I DON'T WANT ANYTHING TO DO WITH HER ANY-MORE.
TMP

341. The Envy

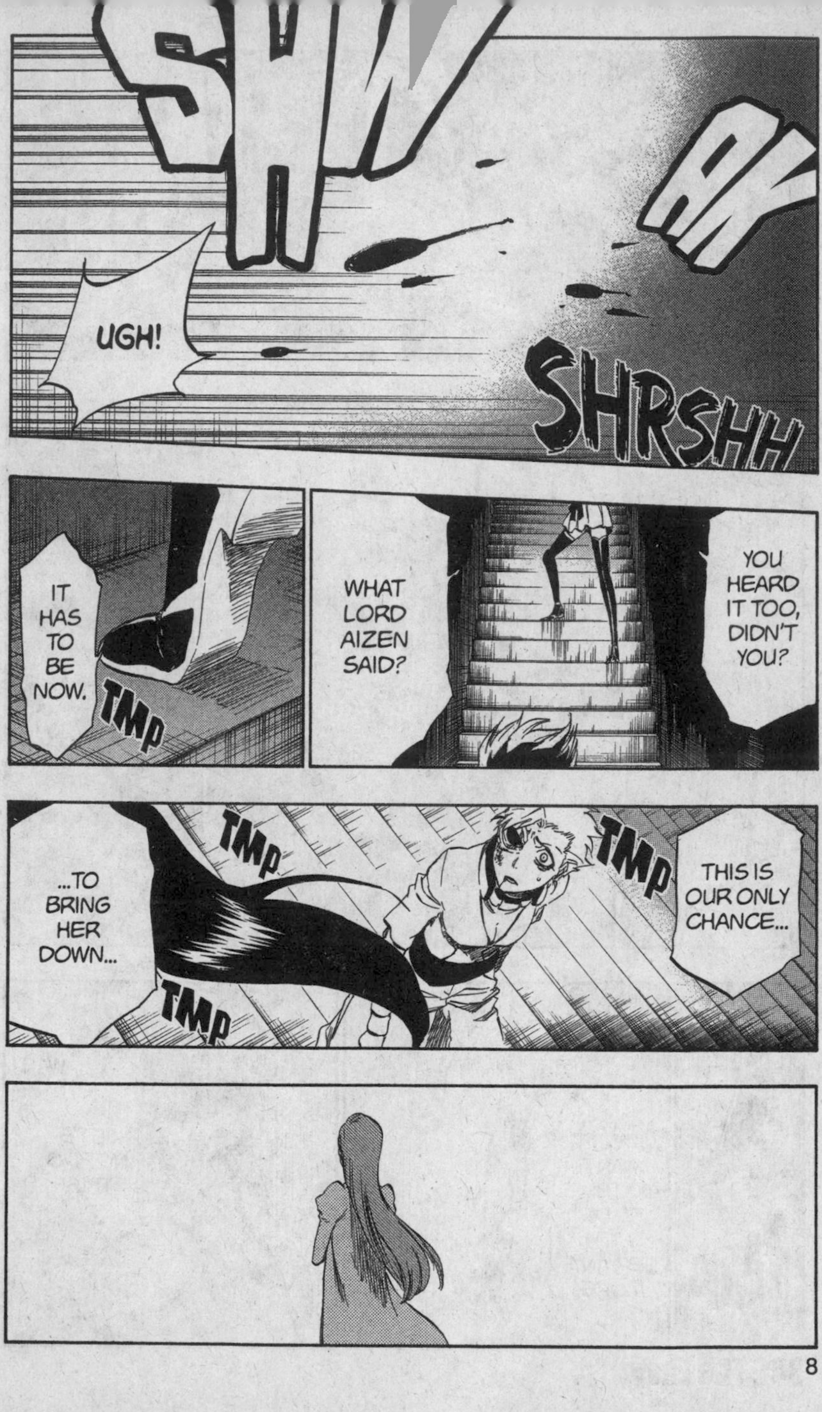
SHWAY
UGH!
SHRSHH
YOU HEARD IT TOO, DIDN'T YOU?
WHAT LORD AIZEN SAID?
IT HAS TO BE NOW.
TMP
THIS IS OUR ONLY CHANCE...
TMP
TMP
...TO BRING HER DOWN...
TMP

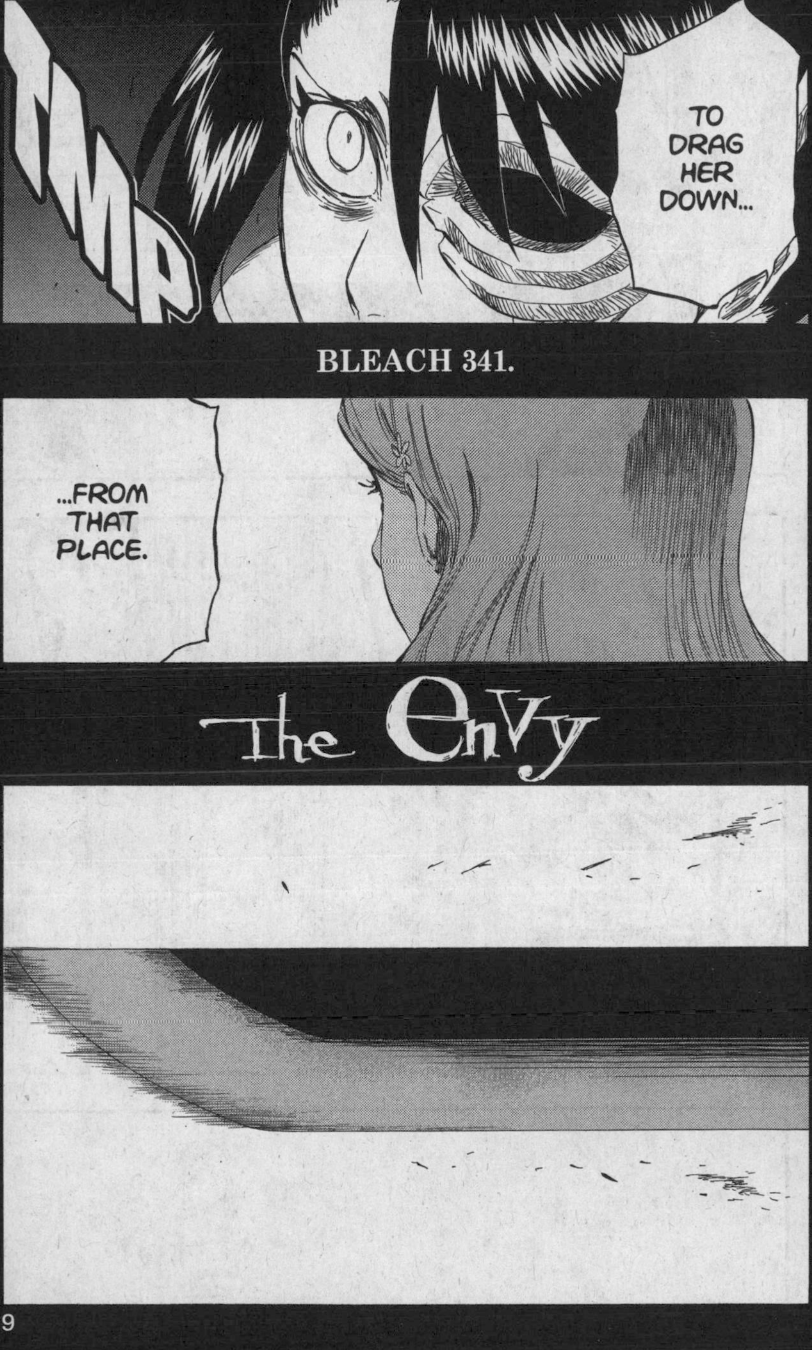
TO DRAG HER DOWN...
TMP
BLEACH 341.
...FROM THAT PLACE.
The Envy

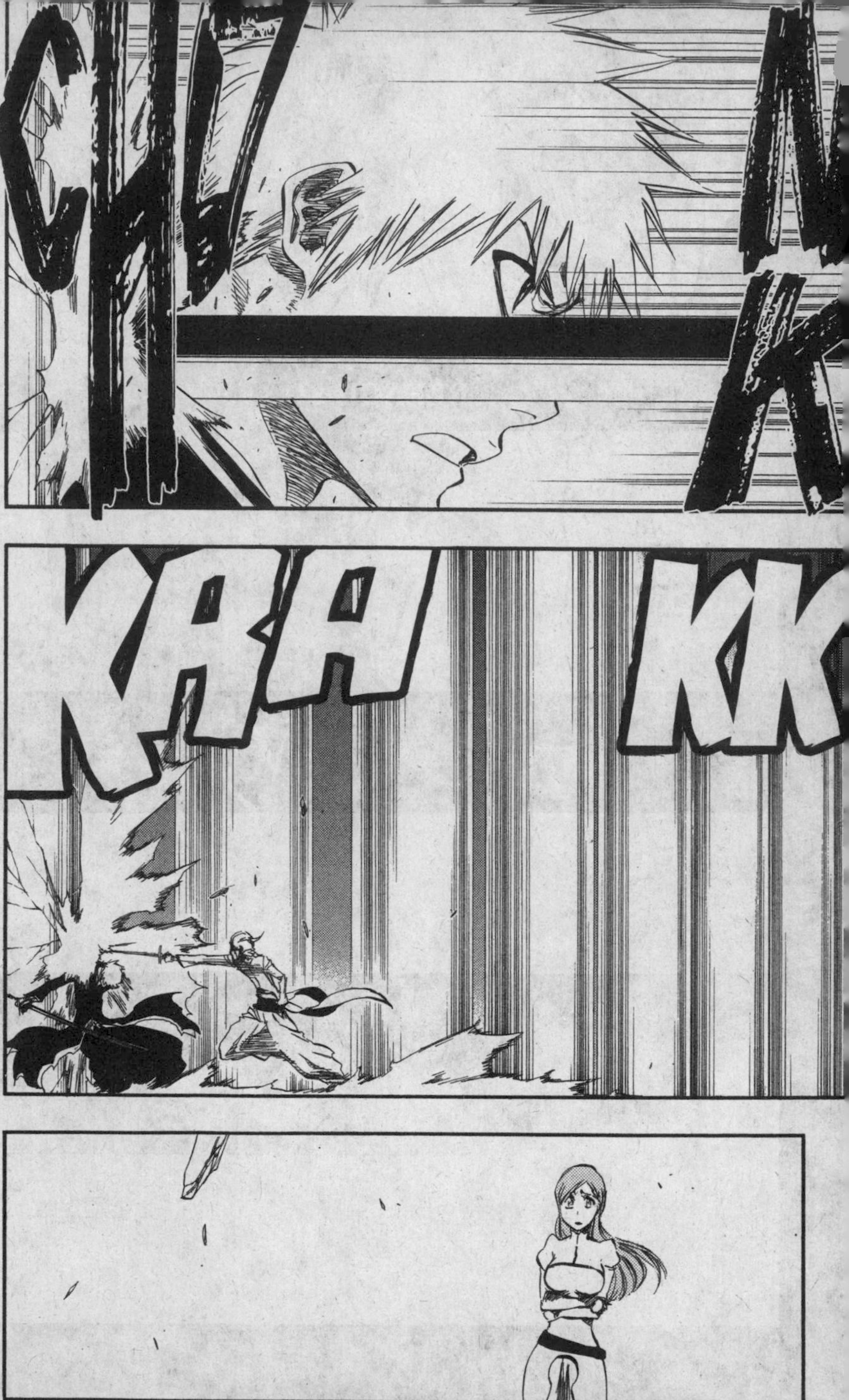
CHI
KRA
KK

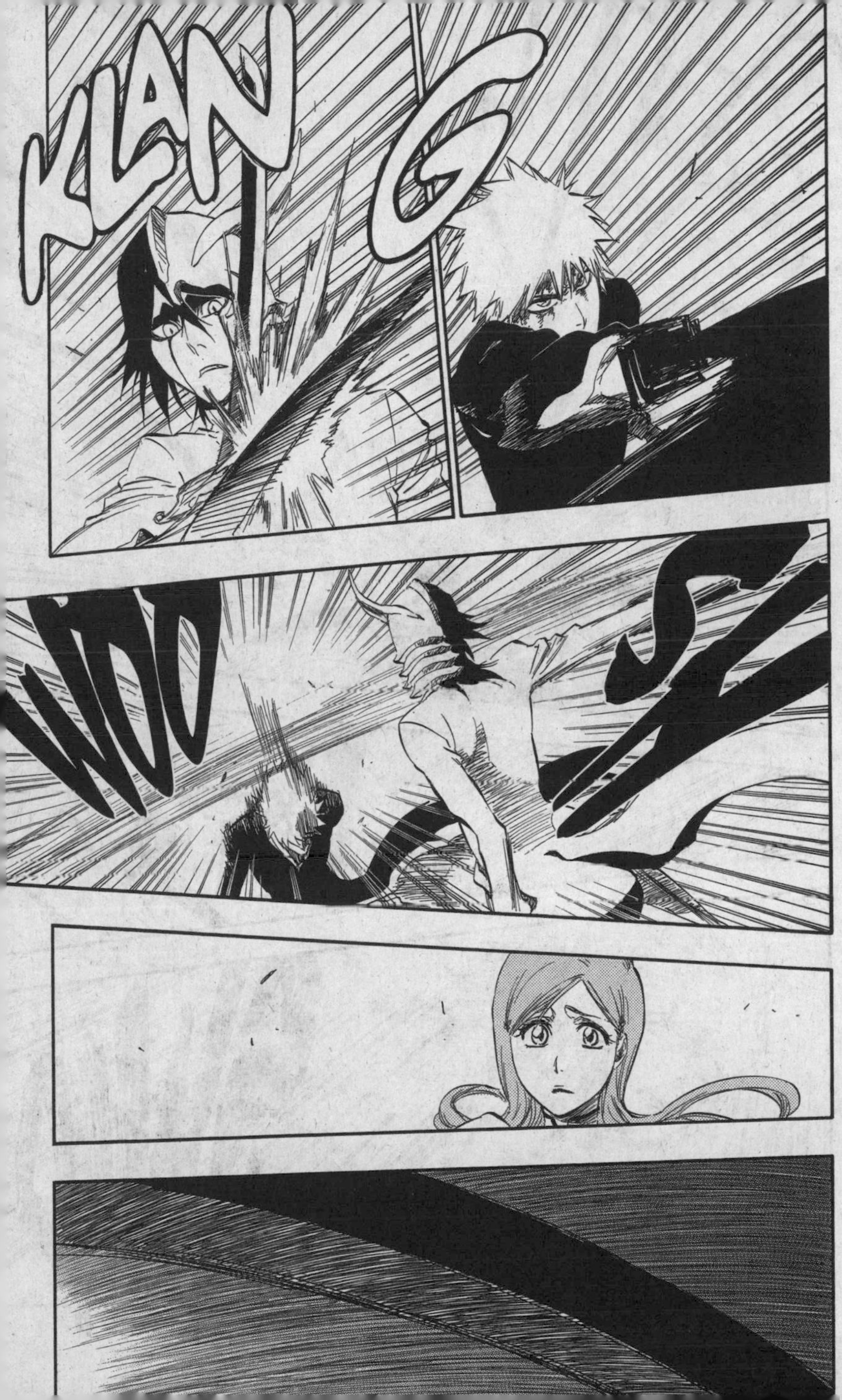
KLANG
WOOSH

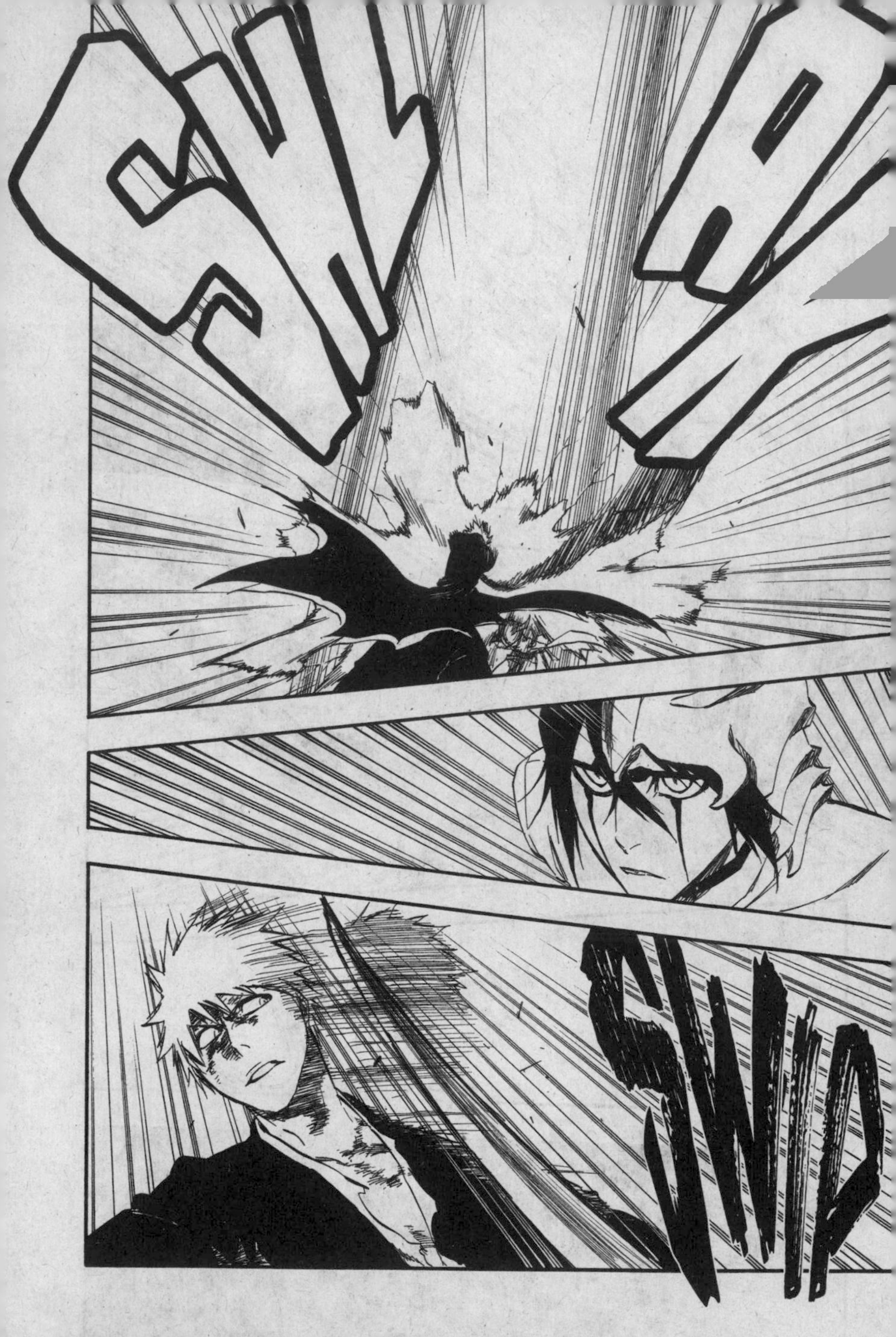
SWIP

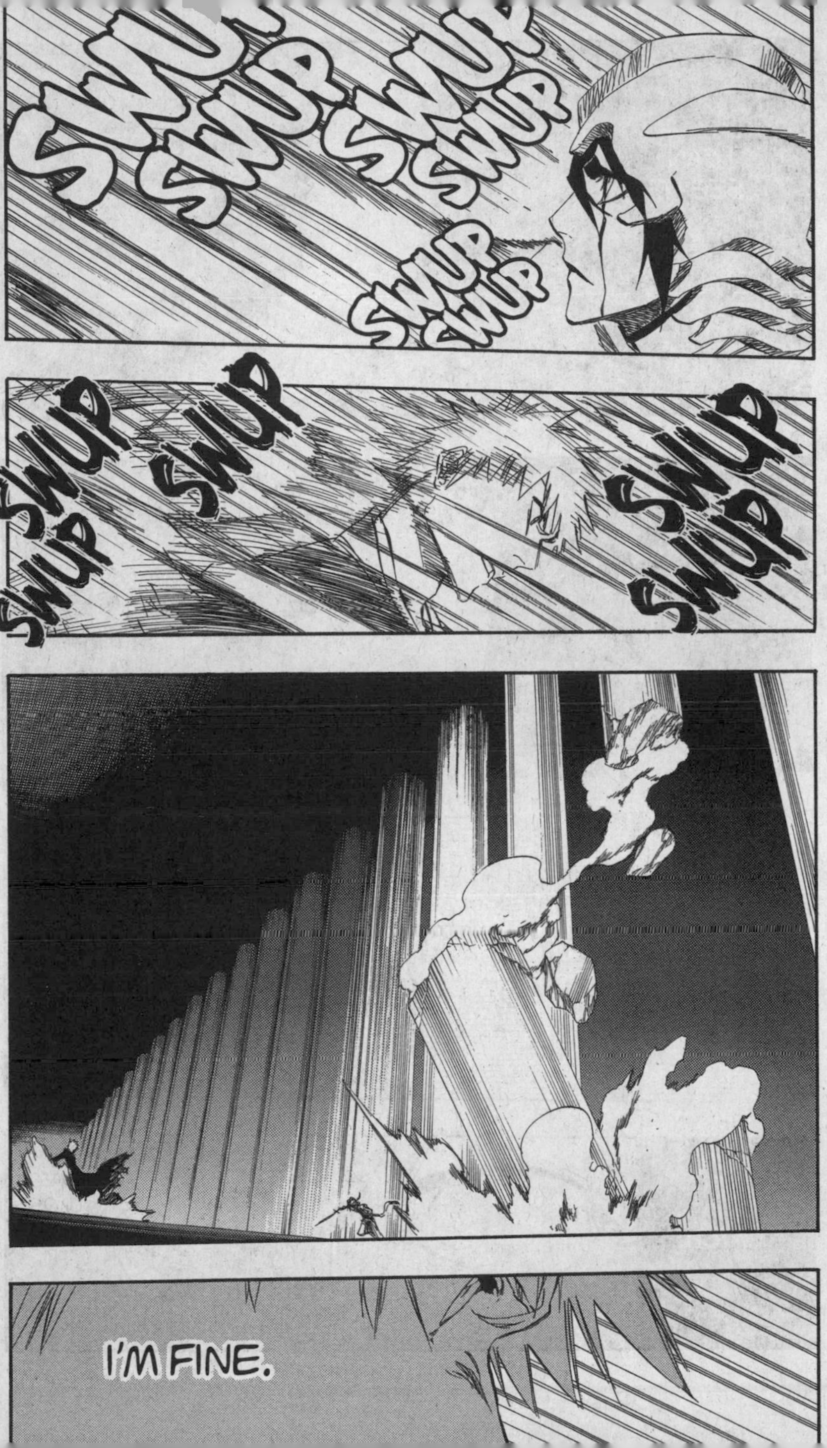
SWUP
SWUP
SWUP
SWUP
SWUP
SWUP
SWUP
SWUP
SWUP
SWUP
SWUP
SWUP
I'M FINE.

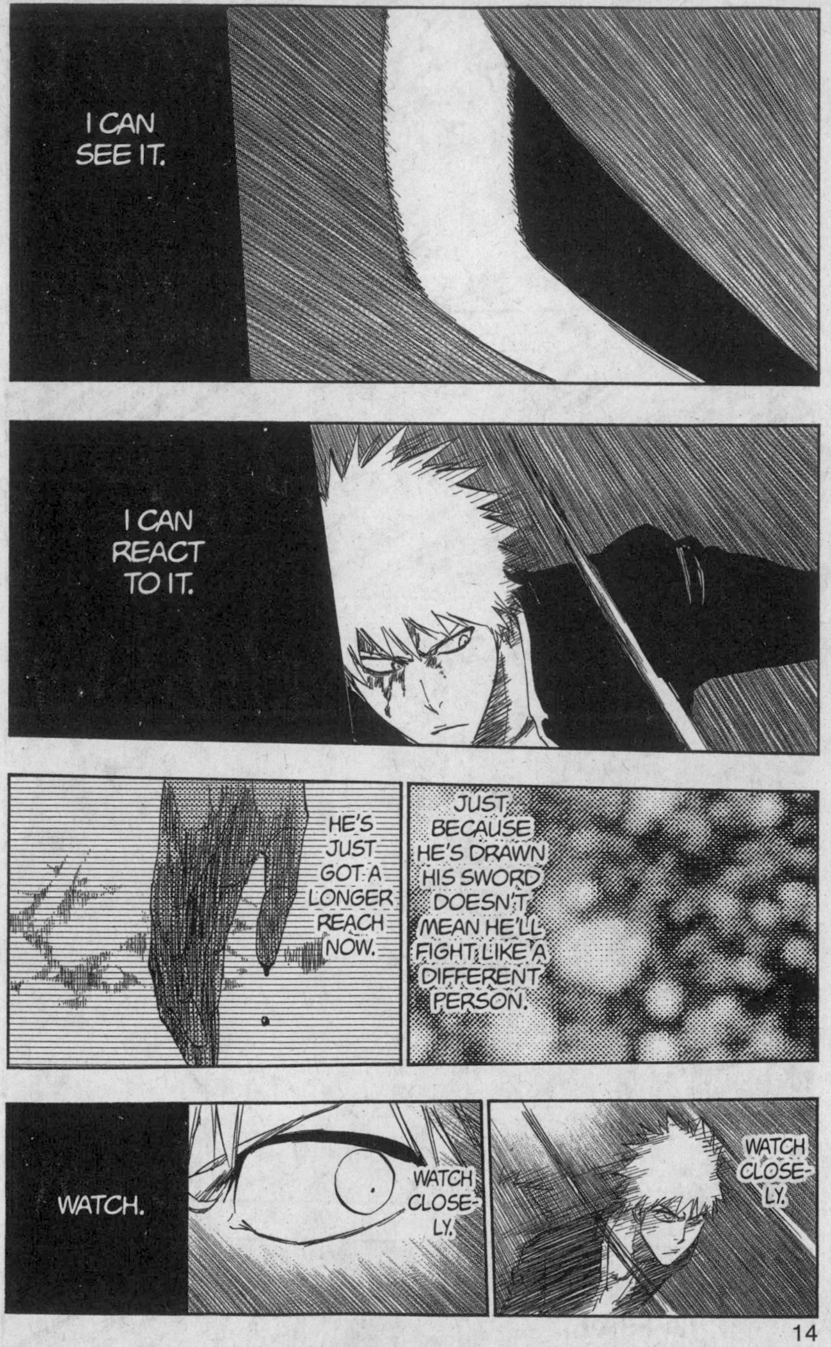
I CAN SEE IT.
I CAN REACT TO IT.
JUST BECAUSE HE'S DRAWN HIS SWORD DOESN'T MEAN HE'LL FIGHT LIKE A DIFFERENT PERSON.
HE'S JUST GOT A LONGER REACH NOW.
WATCH CLOSE-LY.
WATCH CLOSE-LY.
WATCH.

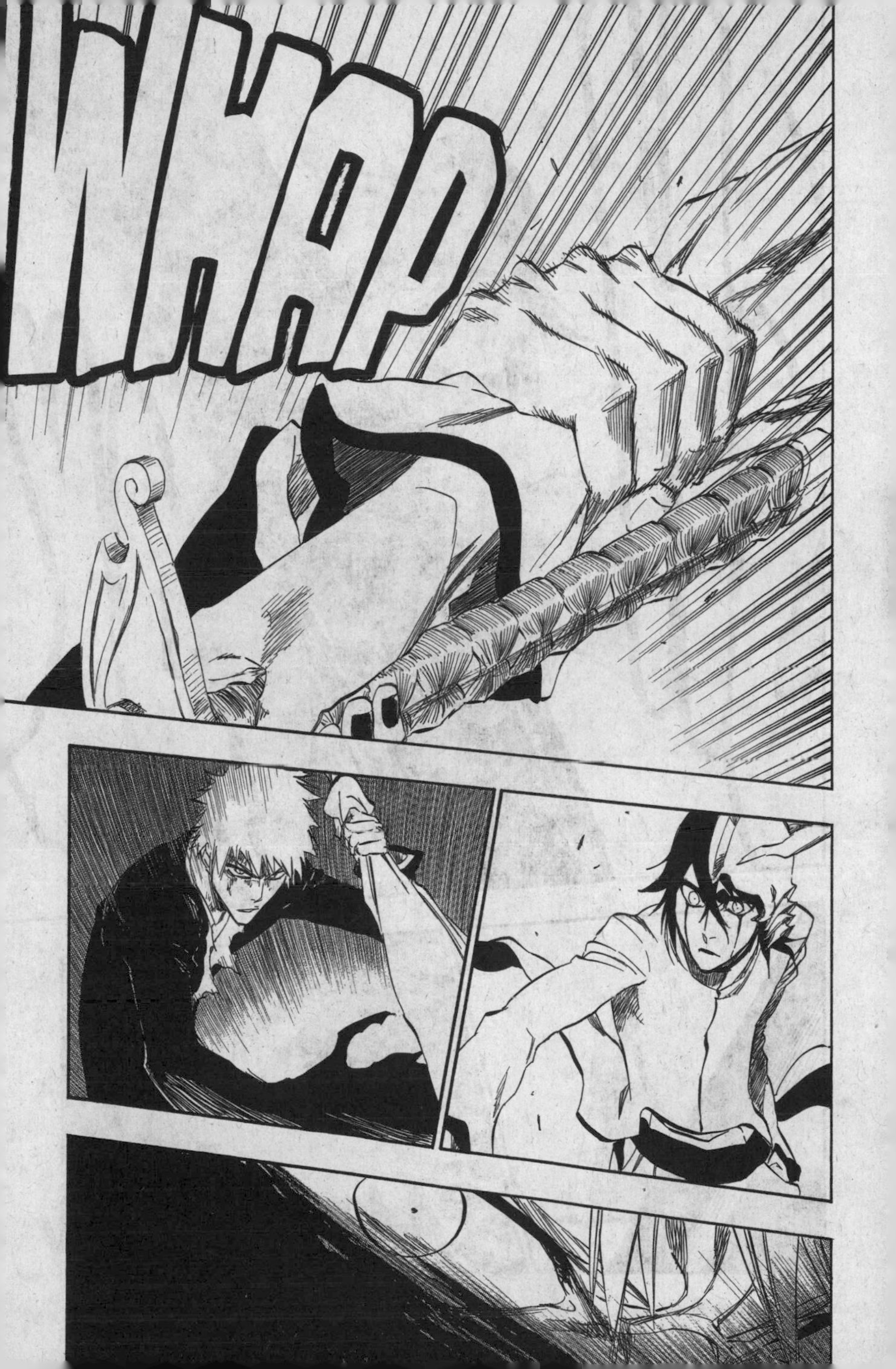
WHAP

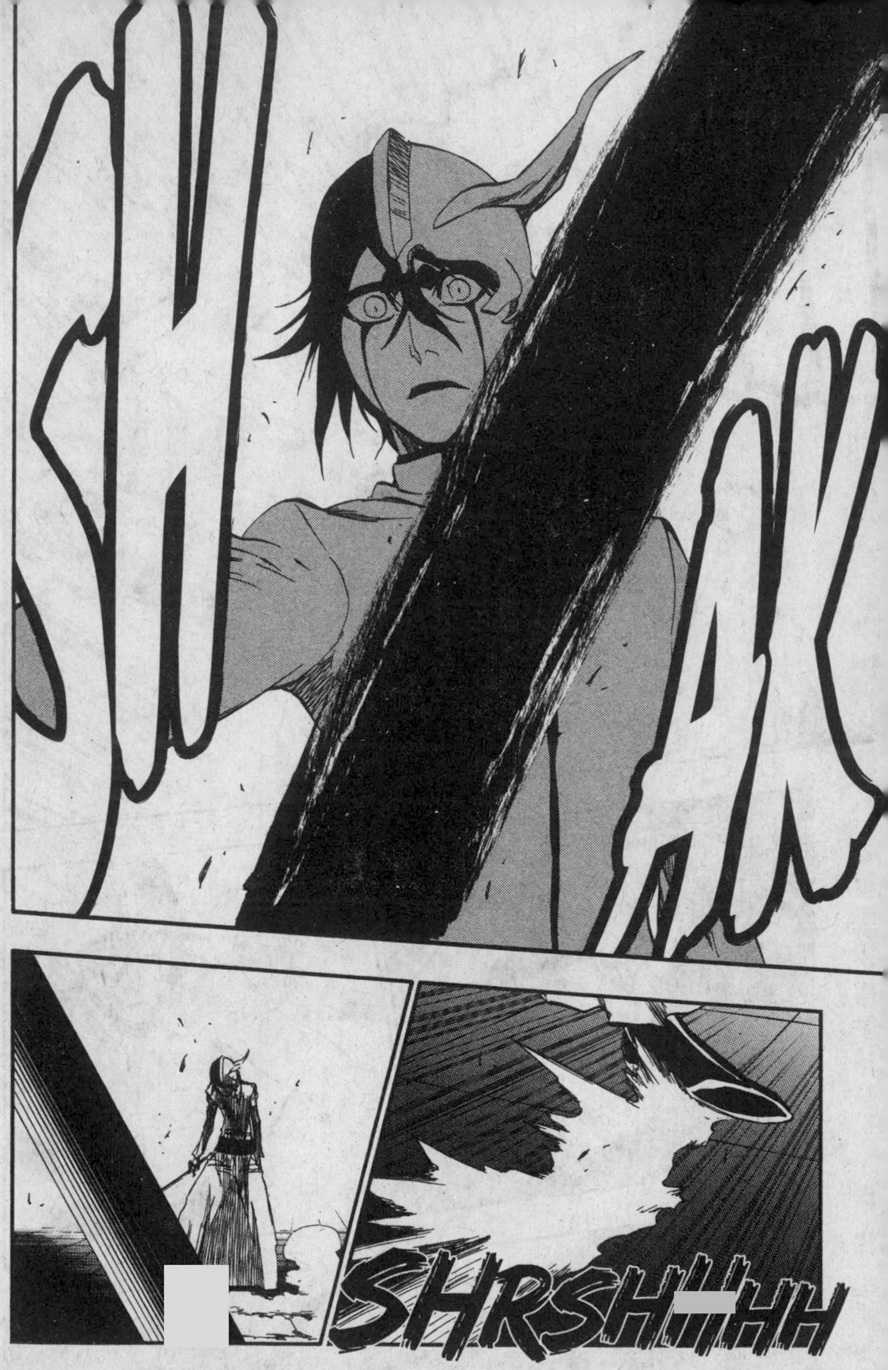
SHAK
SHRSHHH

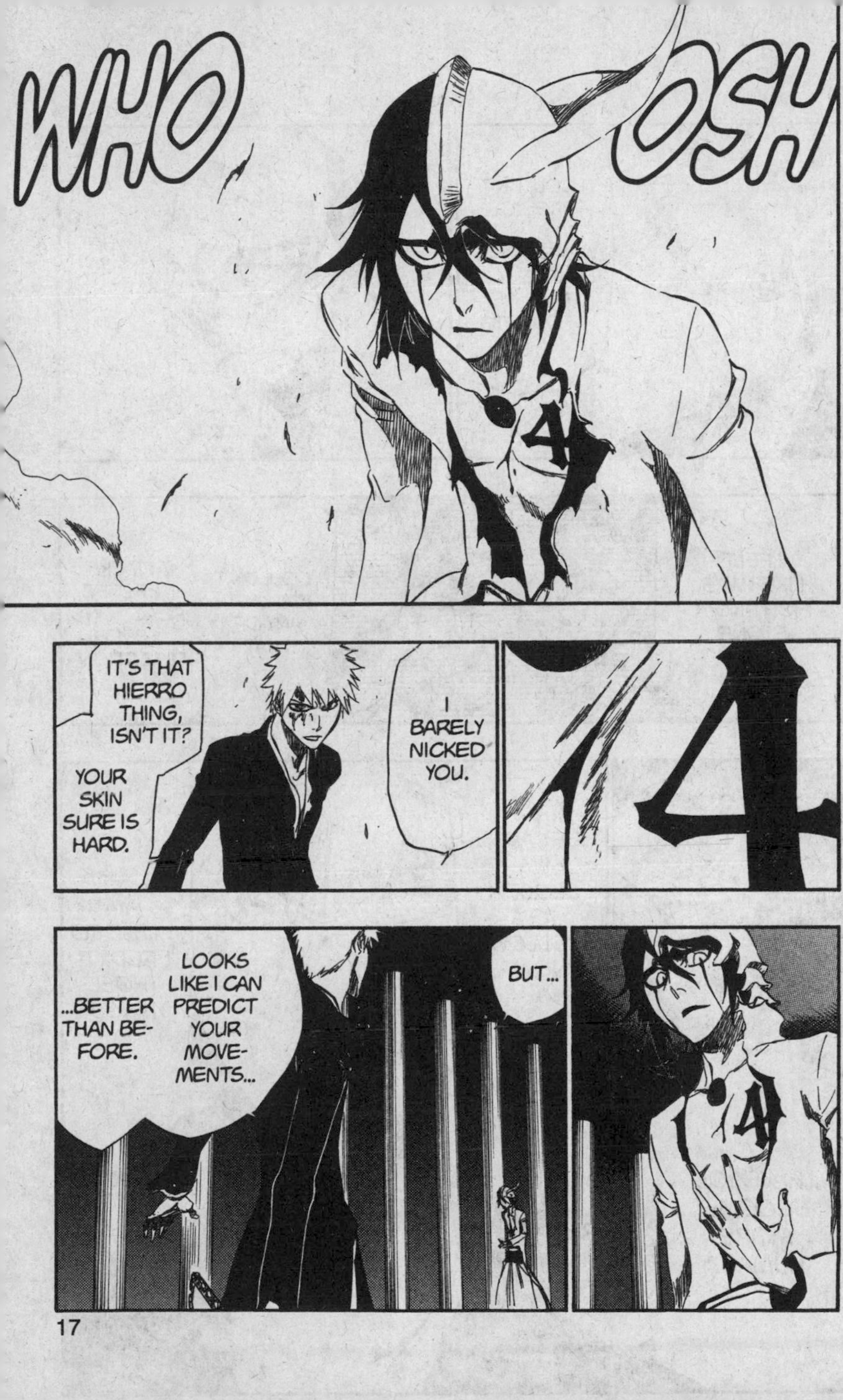
WHOOSH
I BARELY NICKED YOU.
IT'S THAT HIERRO THING, ISN'T IT?
YOUR SKIN SURE IS HARD.
BUT...
LOOKS LIKE I CAN PREDICT YOUR MOVEMENTS...
...BETTER THAN BEFORE.

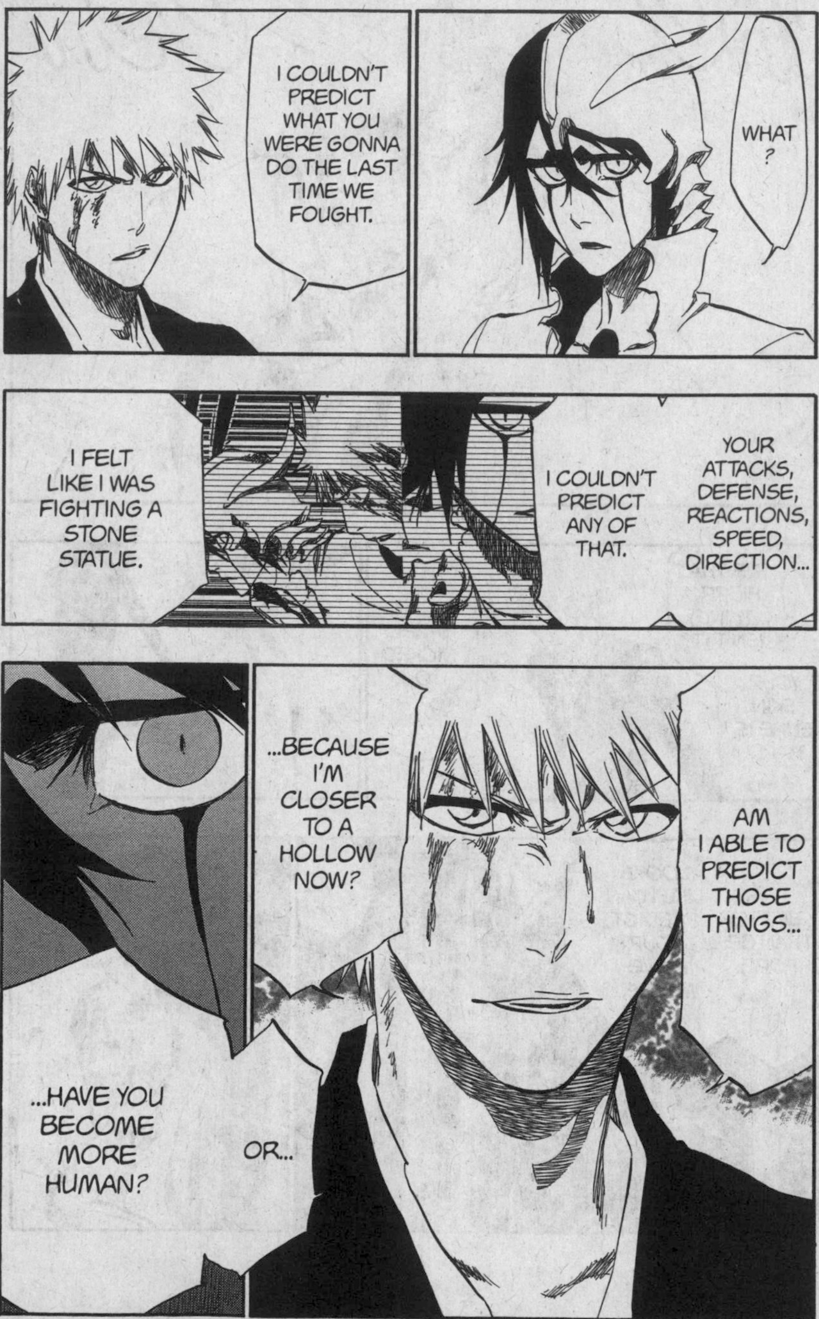
WHAT?
I COULDN'T PREDICT WHAT YOU WERE GONNA DO THE LAST TIME WE FOUGHT.
YOUR ATTACKS, DEFENSE, REACTIONS, SPEED, DIRECTION...
I COULDN'T PREDICT ANY OF THAT.
I FELT LIKE I WAS FIGHTING A STONE STATUE.
AM I ABLE TO PREDICT THOSE THINGS...
...BECAUSE I'M CLOSER TO A HOLLOW NOW?
OR...
...HAVE YOU BECOME MORE HUMAN?

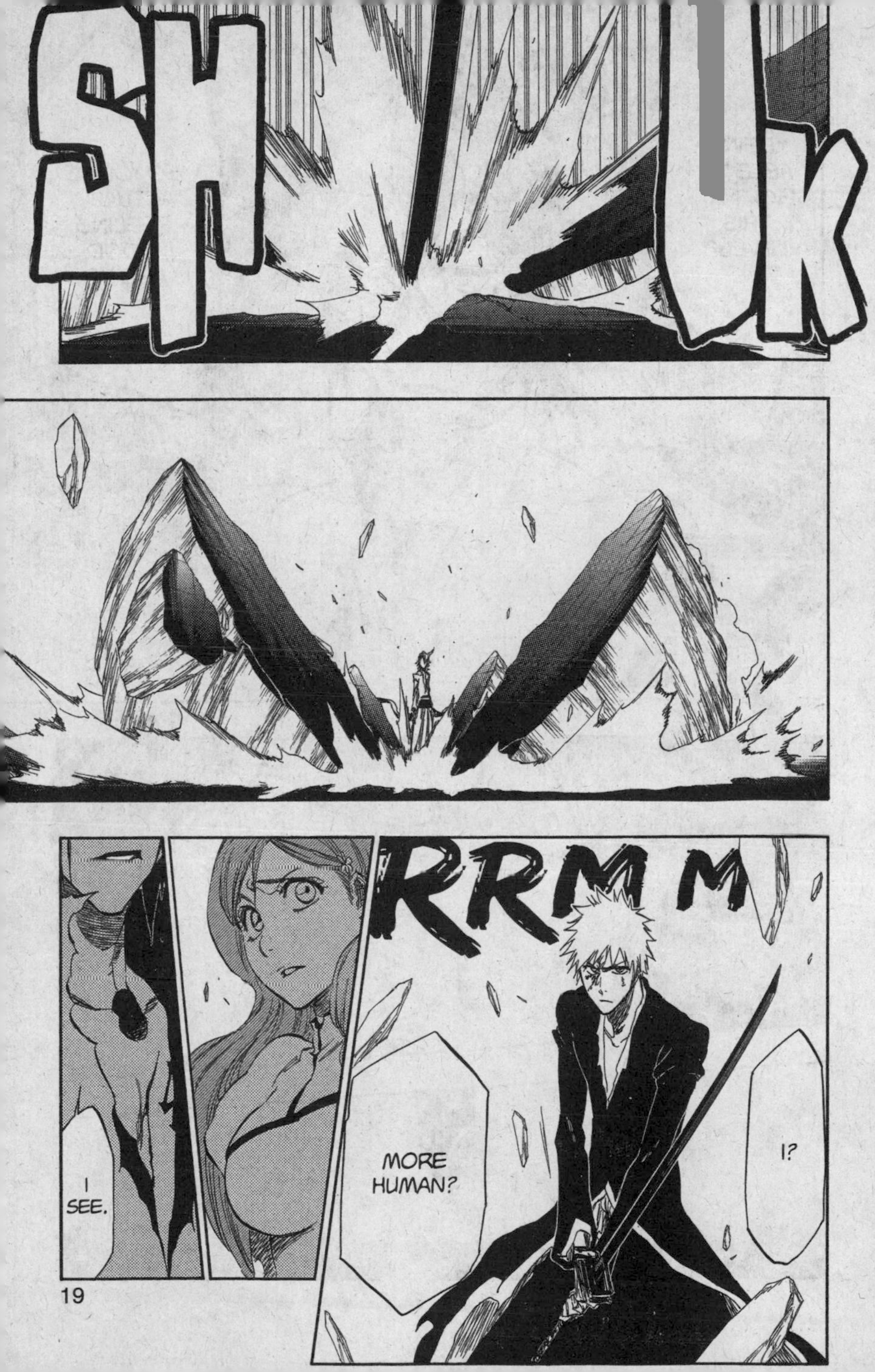
SH
K
RRMM
!?
MORE HUMAN?
I SEE.

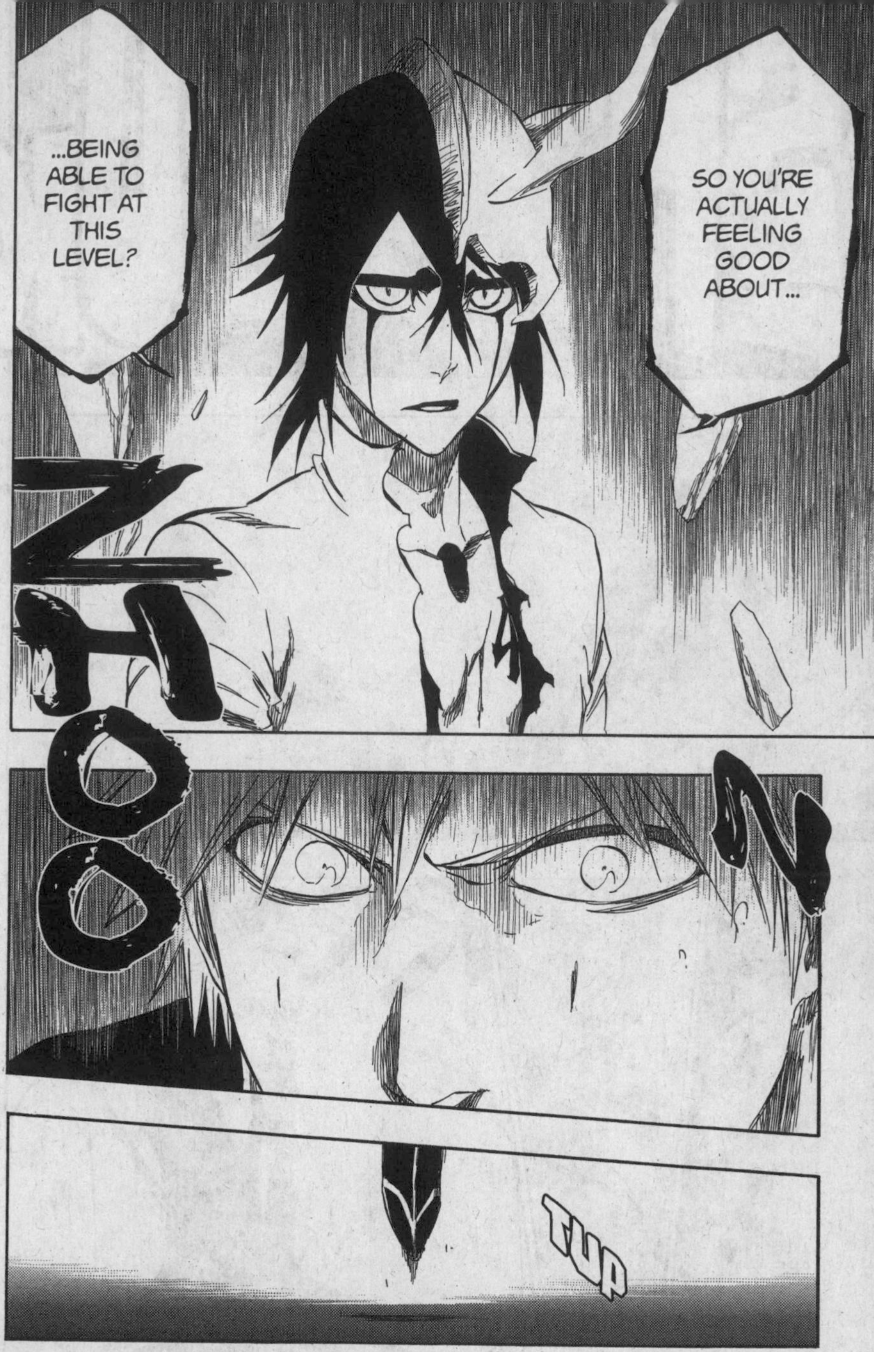
SO YOU'RE ACTUALLY FEELING GOOD ABOUT...
...BEING ABLE TO FIGHT AT THIS LEVEL?
TUP

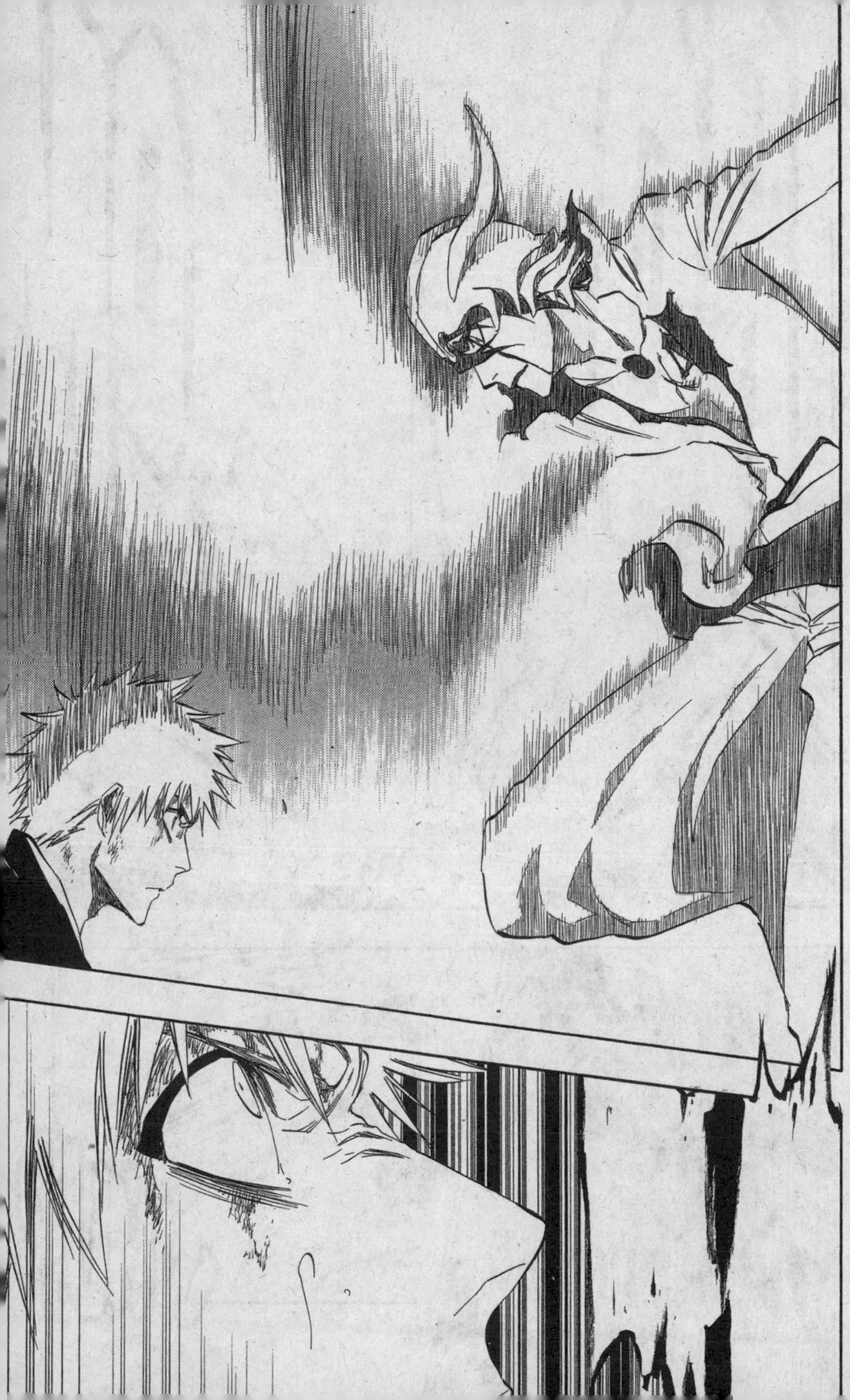

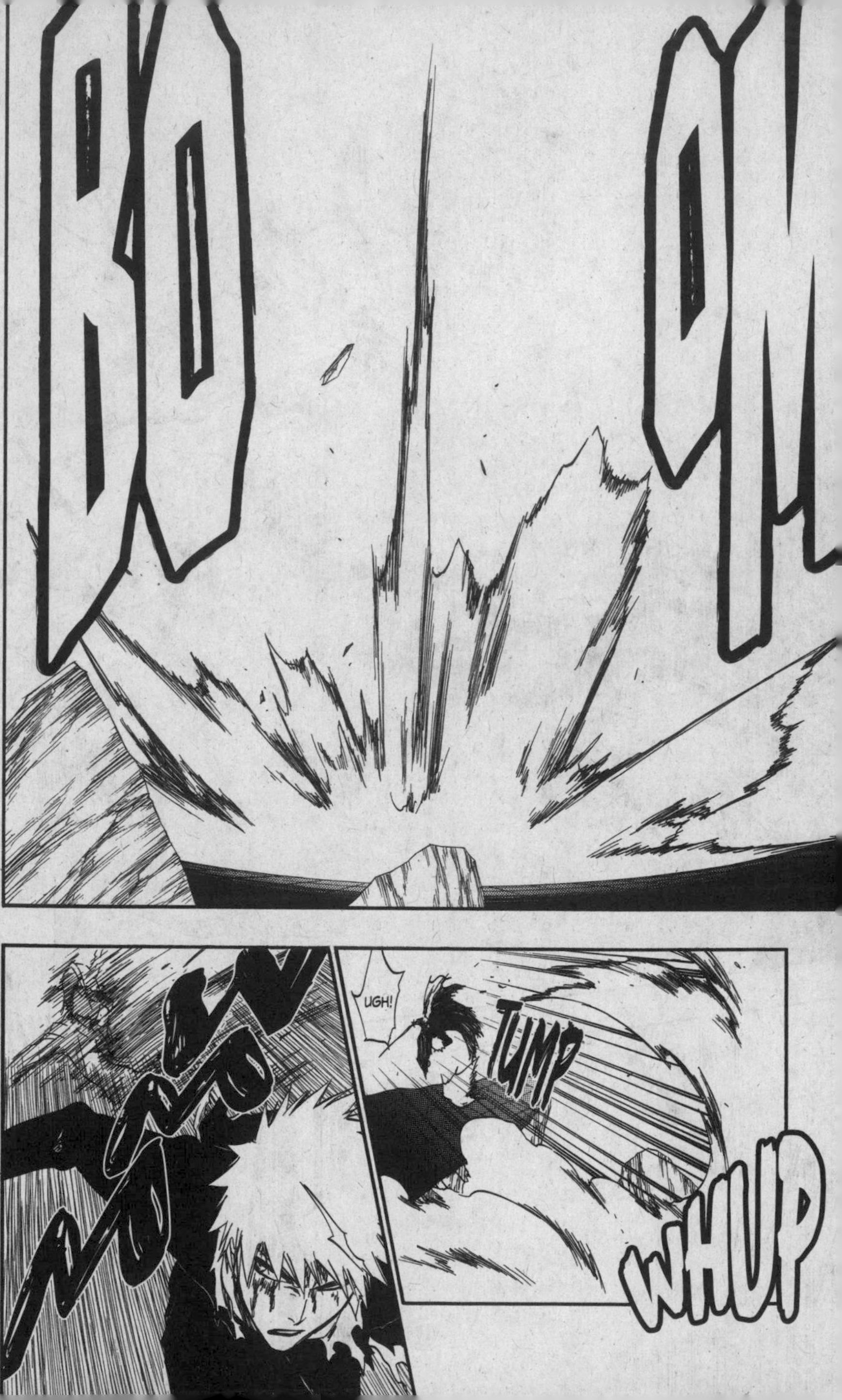
BOOM
UGH!
TUMP
WHUP

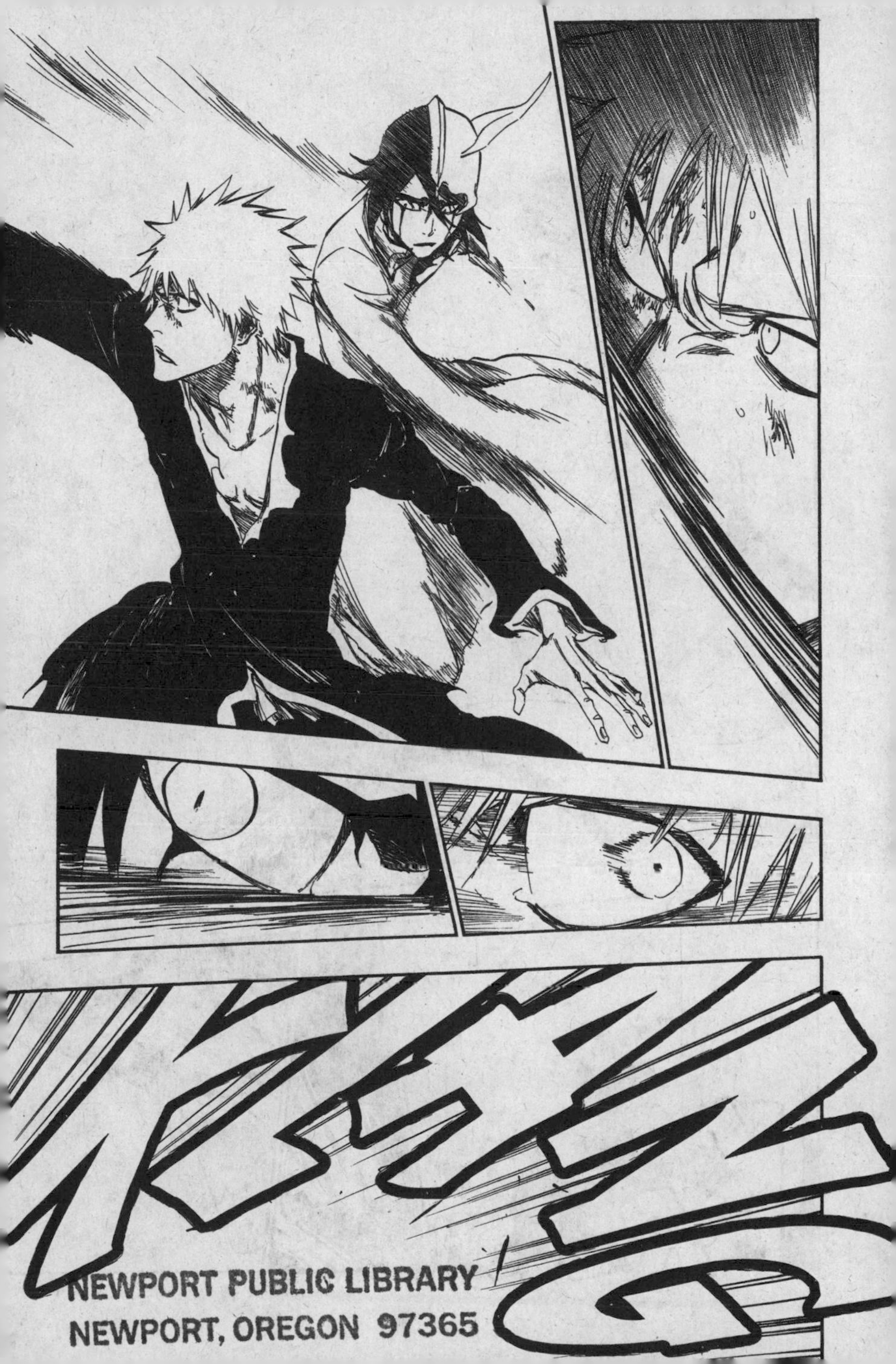

NEWPORT PUBLIC LIBRARY
NEWPORT, OREGON 97365

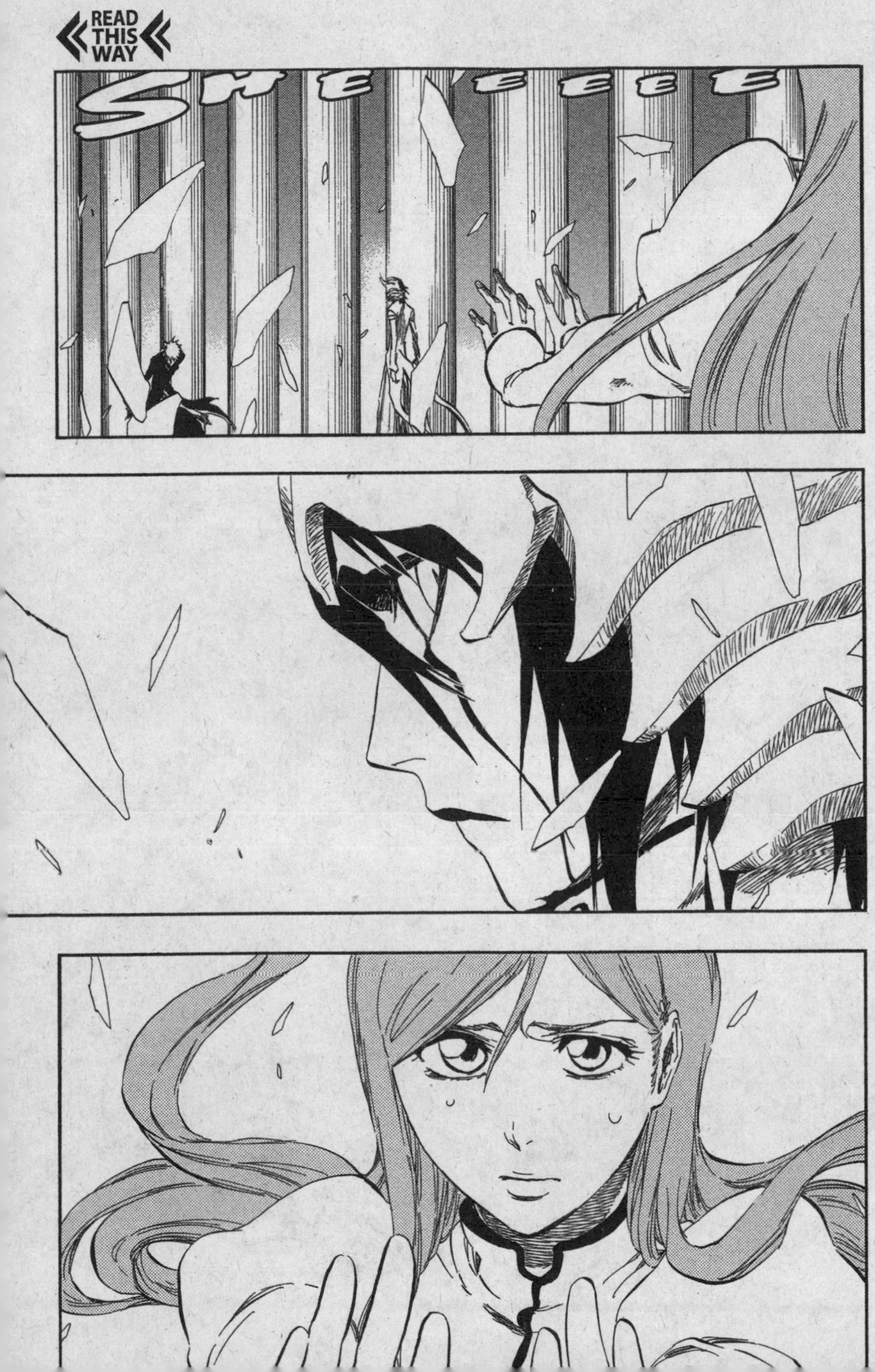
READ THIS WAY
SHEEEEE

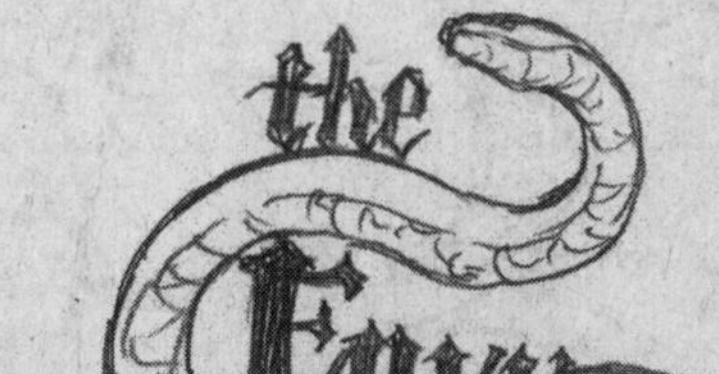
the Envy

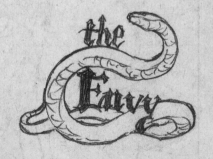

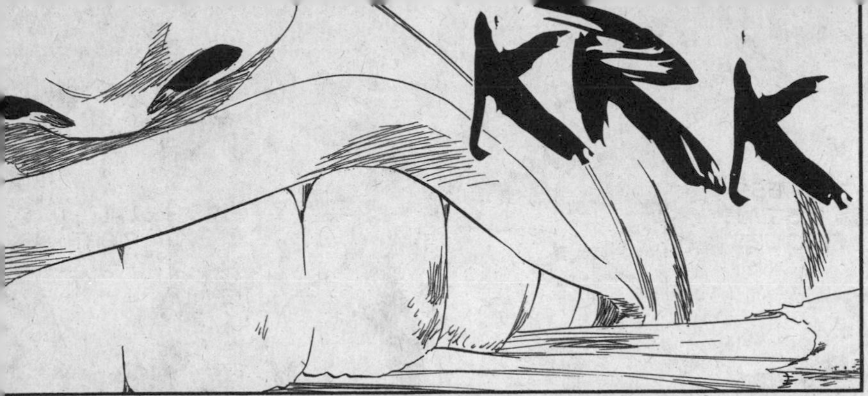
KRRK

342. The Gluttony

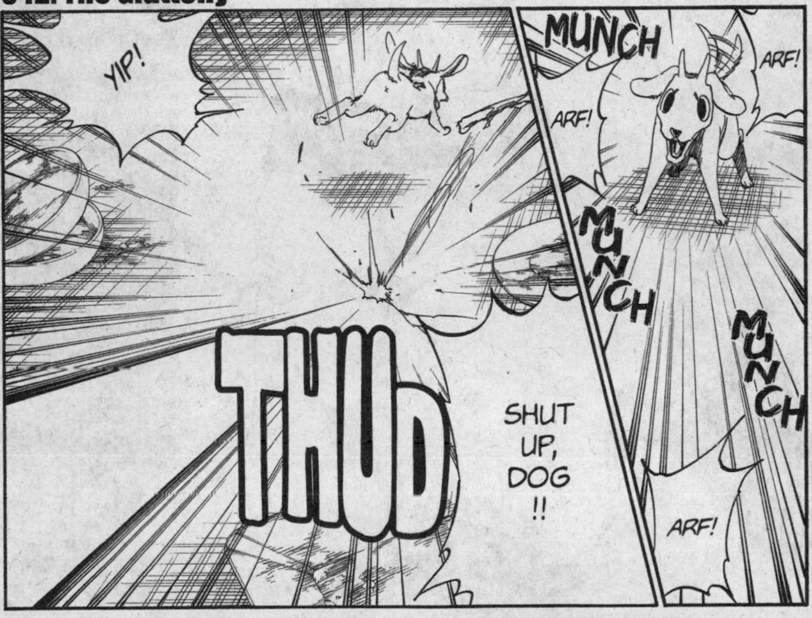
MUNCH
ARF!
ARF!
MUNCH
MUNCH
ARF!
YIP!
THUD
SHUT UP, DOG !!

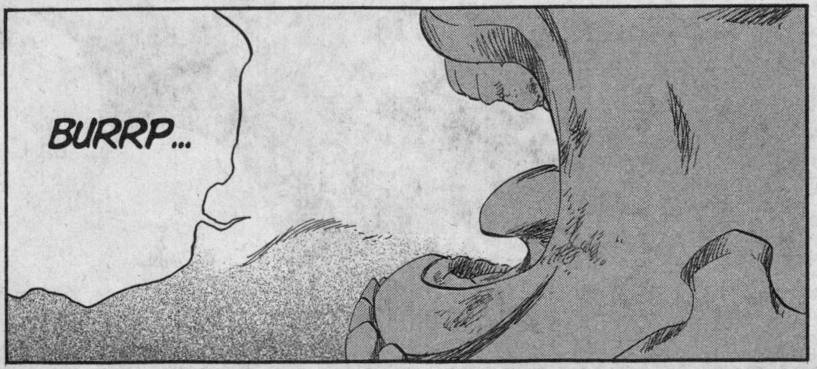
BURRP...

342. The Gluttony

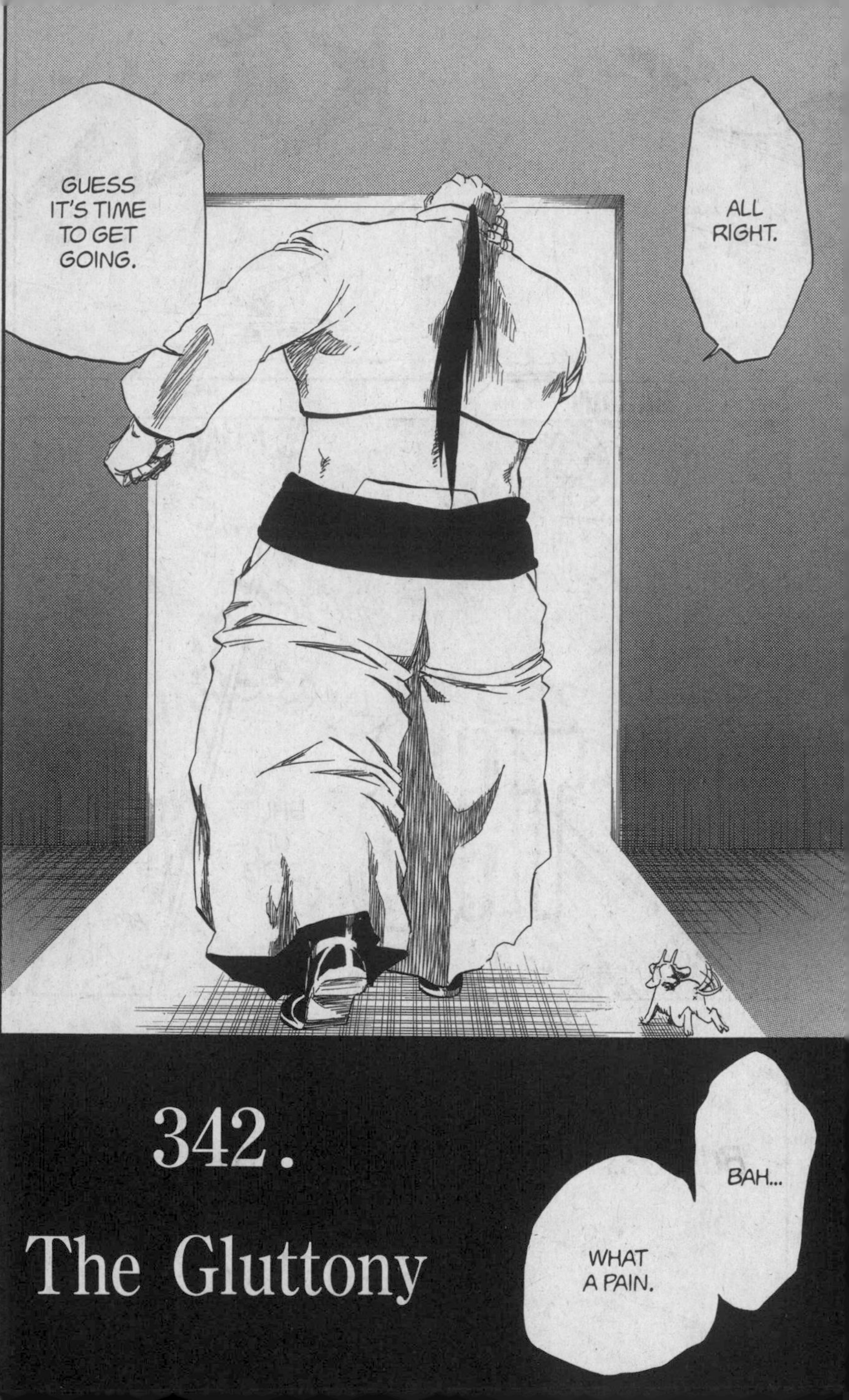
ALL RIGHT.
GUESS IT'S TIME TO GET GOING.
BAH...
WHAT A PAIN.

BLEACH

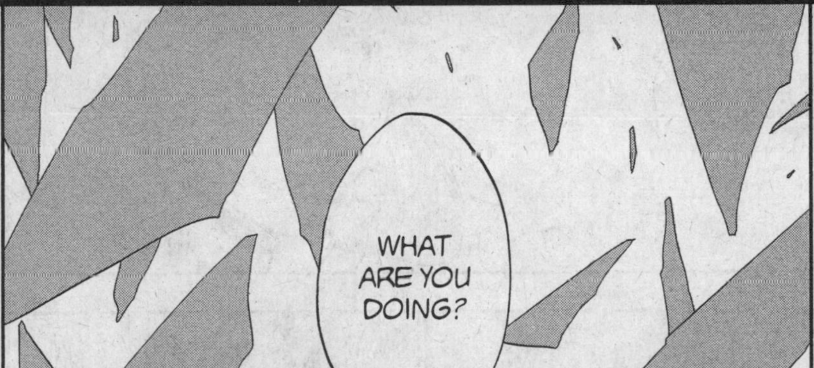
WHAT ARE YOU DOING?

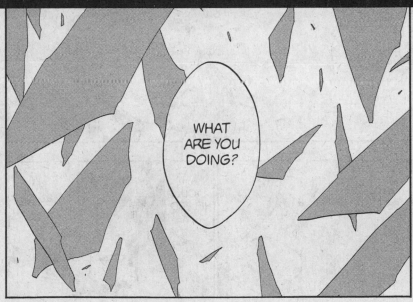

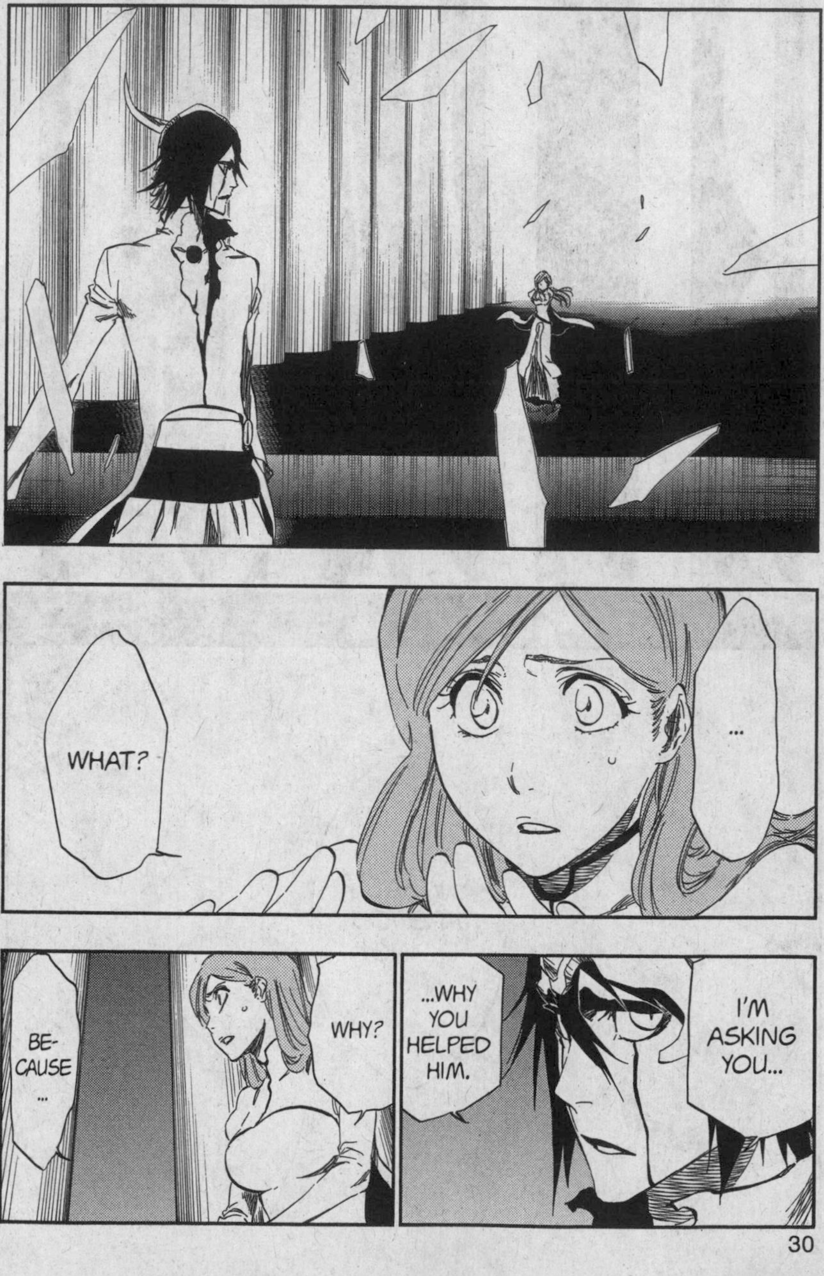
...
WHAT?
I'M ASKING YOU...
...WHY YOU HELPED HIM.
WHY?
BE-CAUSE ...

READ THIS WAY

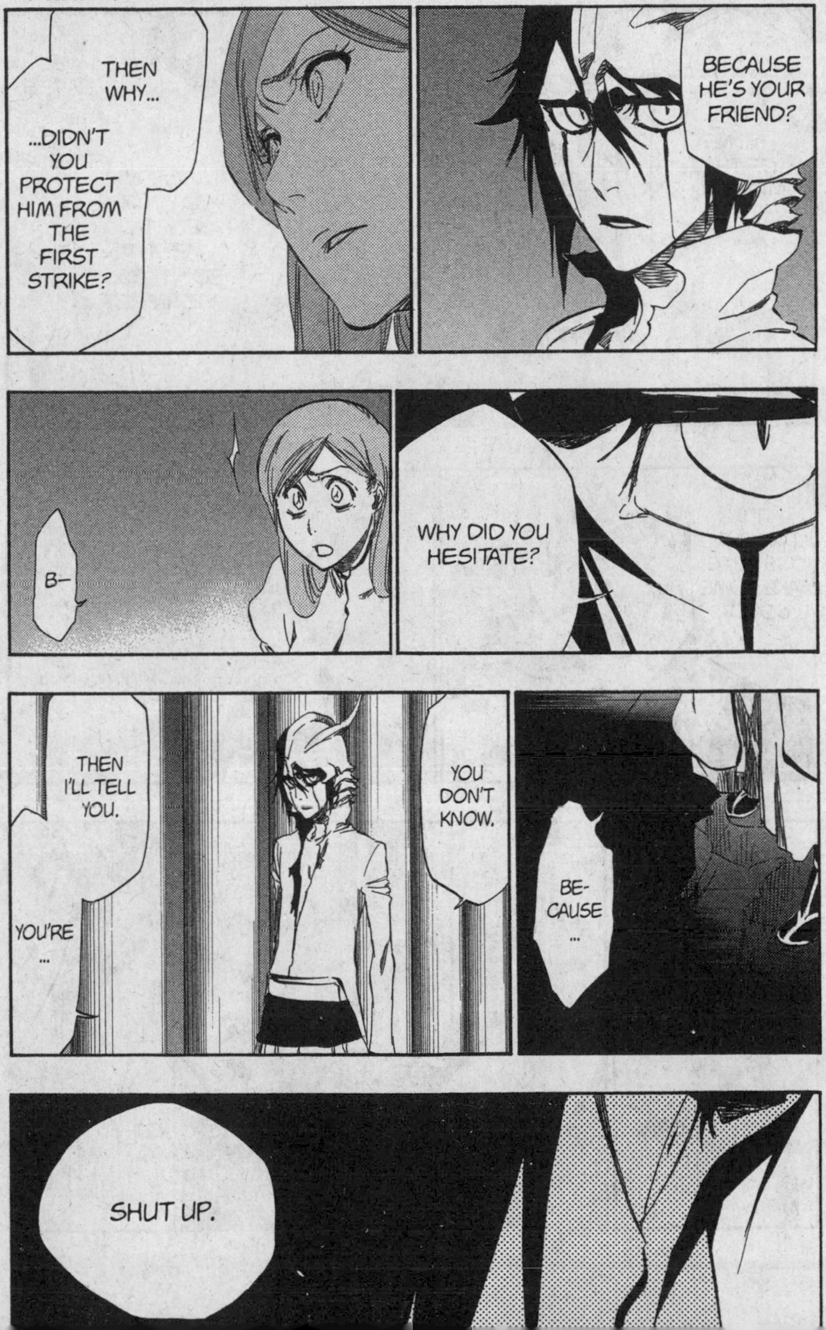
BECAUSE HE'S YOUR FRIEND?
THEN WHY...
...DIDN'T YOU PROTECT HIM FROM THE FIRST STRIKE?
WHY DID YOU HESITATE?
B—
BE-CAUSE...
YOU DON'T KNOW.
THEN I'LL TELL YOU.
YOU'RE...
SHUT UP.

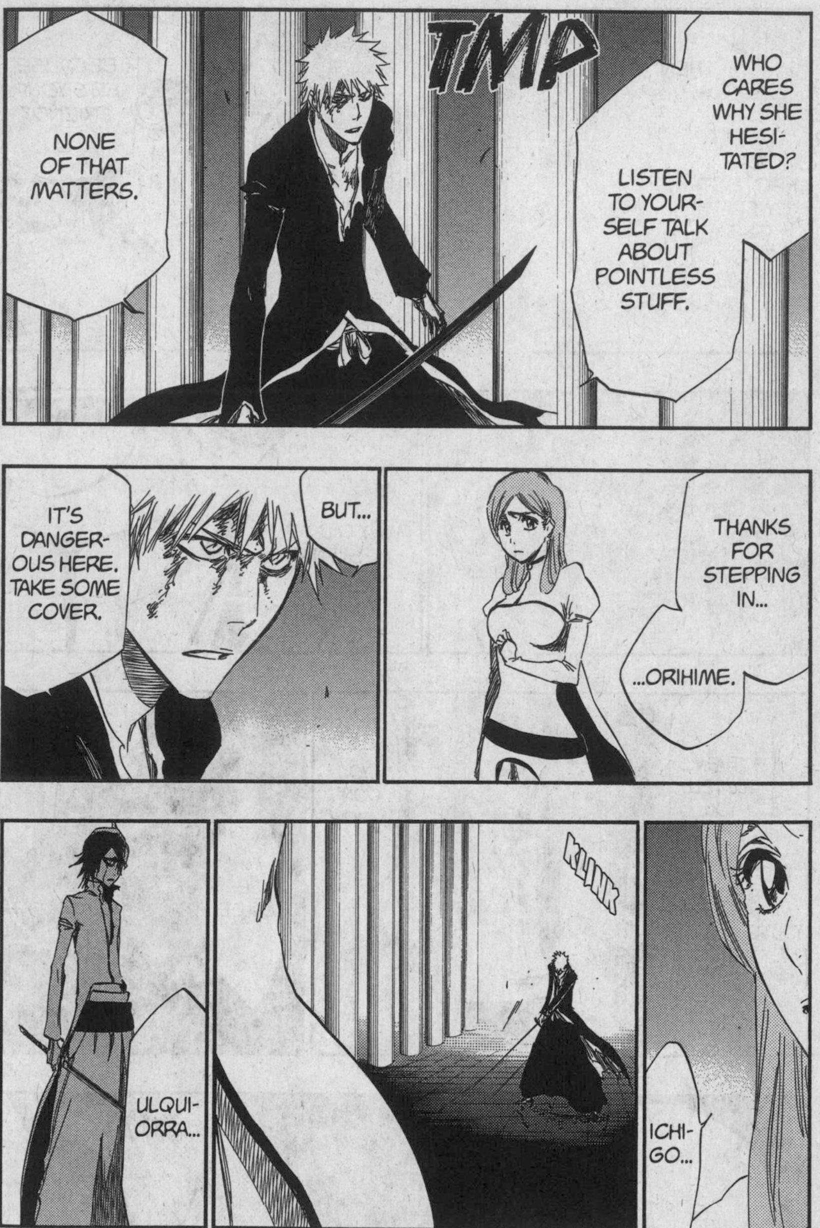
TMP
WHO CARES WHY SHE HESI-TATED?
LISTEN TO YOUR-SELF TALK ABOUT POINTLESS STUFF.
NONE OF THAT MATTERS.
THANKS FOR STEPPING IN...
...ORIHIME.
BUT...
IT'S DANGER-OUS HERE. TAKE SOME COVER.
ICHI-GO...
KLINK
ULQUI-ORRA...

READ THIS WAY

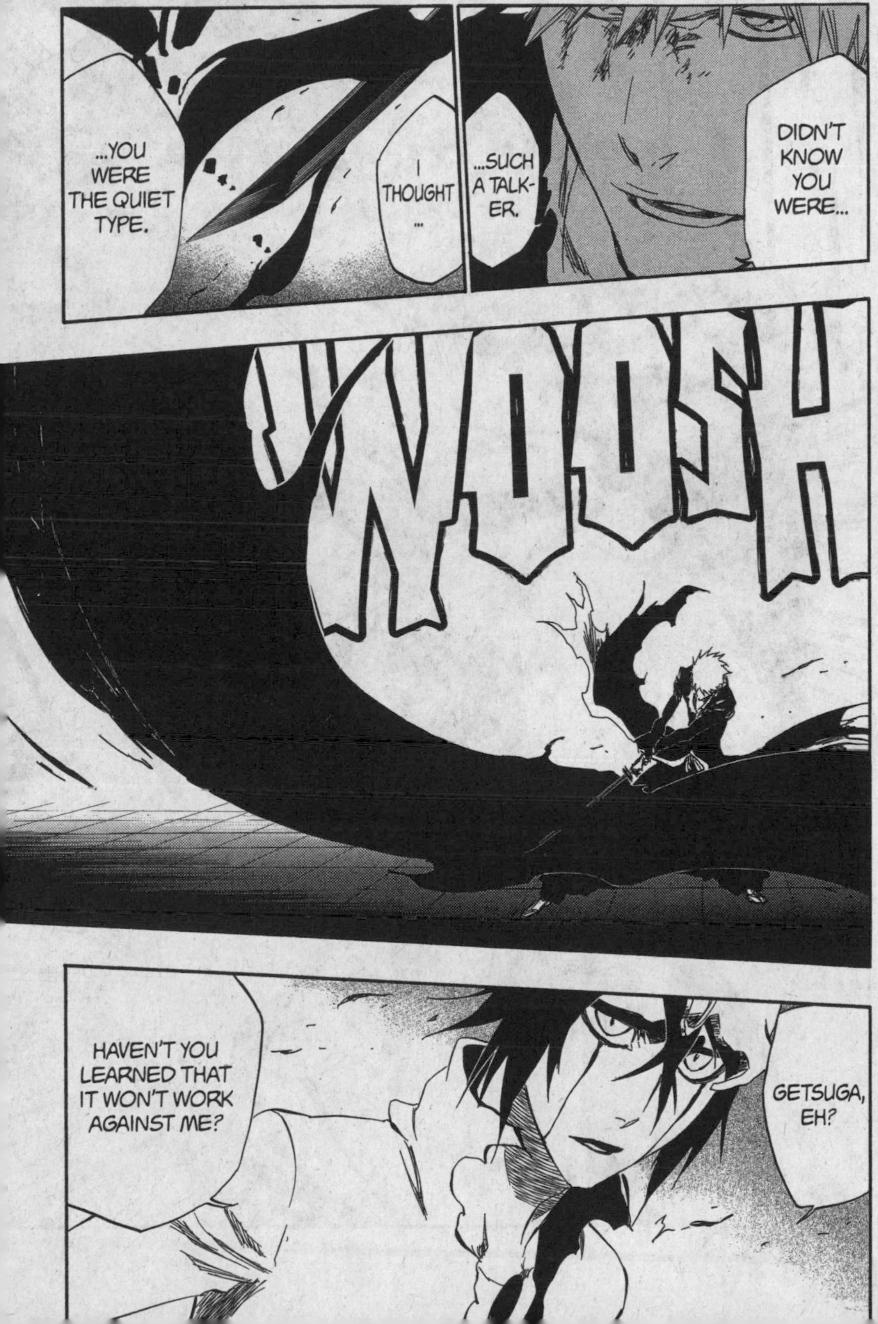
DIDN'T KNOW YOU WERE...
...SUCH A TALK-ER.
I THOUGHT ...
...YOU WERE THE QUIET TYPE.
WOOSH
GETSUGA, EH?
HAVEN'T YOU LEARNED THAT IT WON'T WORK AGAINST ME?

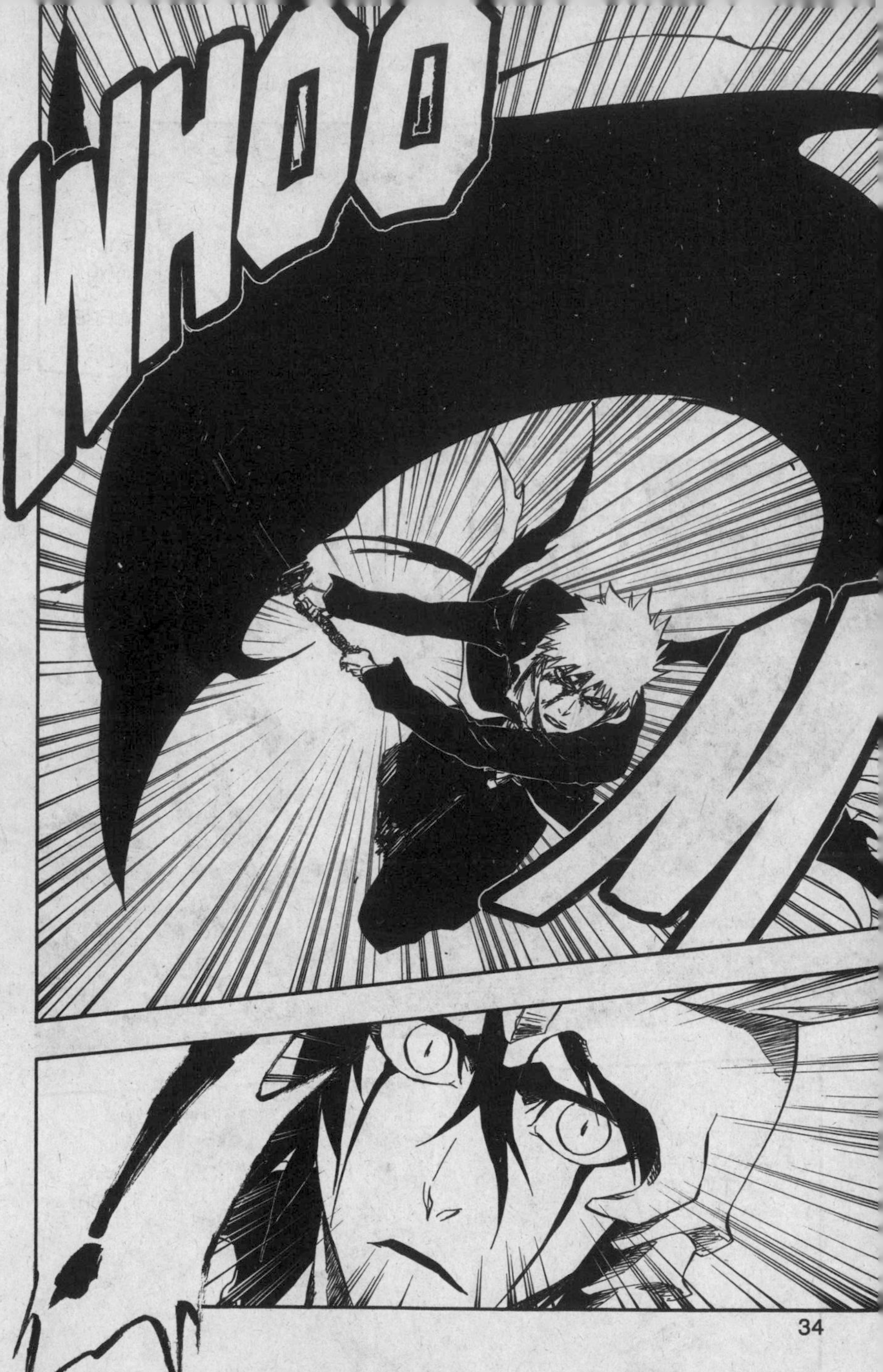
WHOOM

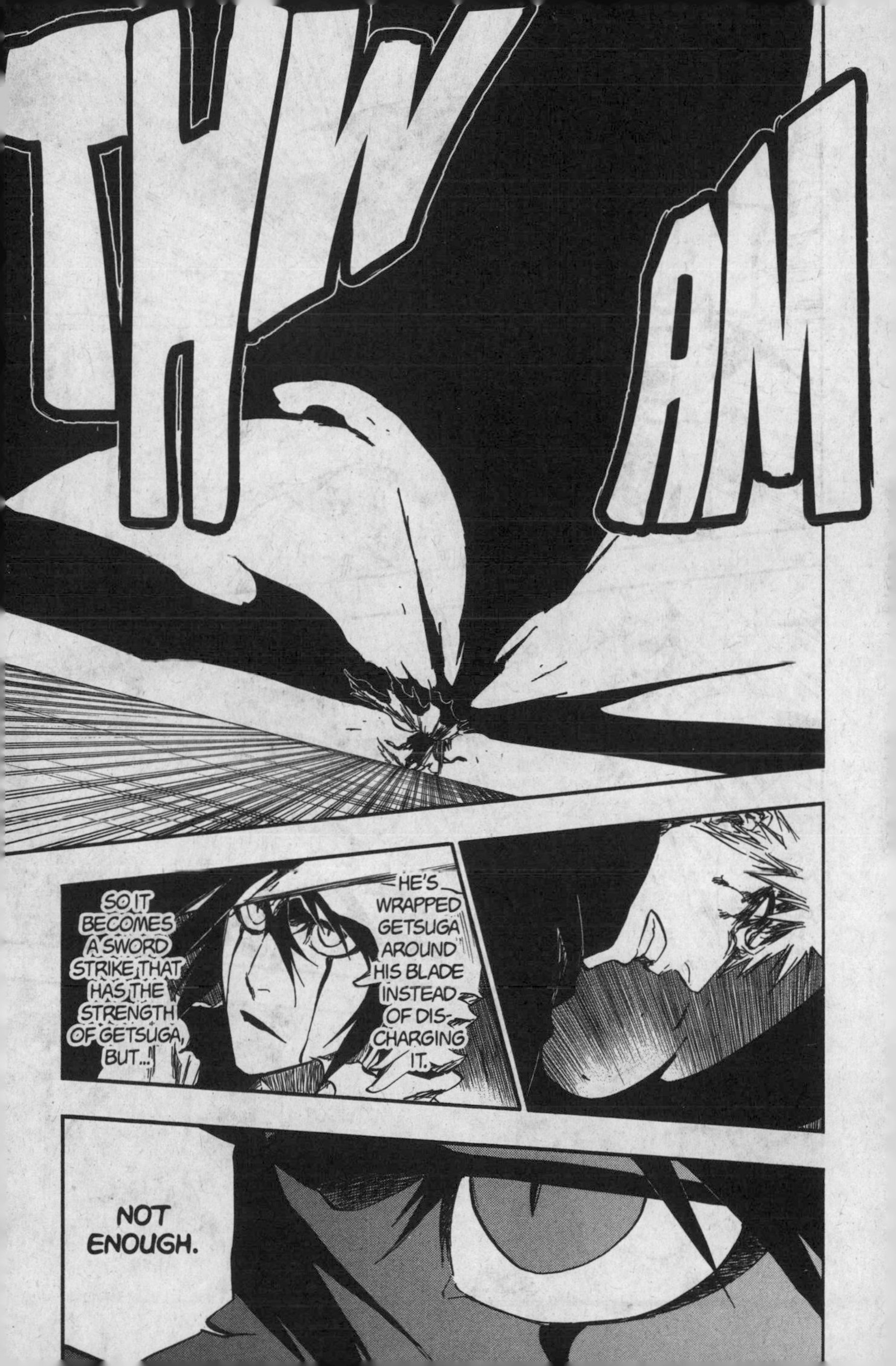
THWAM
HE'S WRAPPED GETSUGA AROUND HIS BLADE INSTEAD OF DIS-CHARGING IT.
SO IT BECOMES A SWORD STRIKE THAT HAS THE STRENGTH OF GETSUGA, BUT...
NOT ENOUGH.

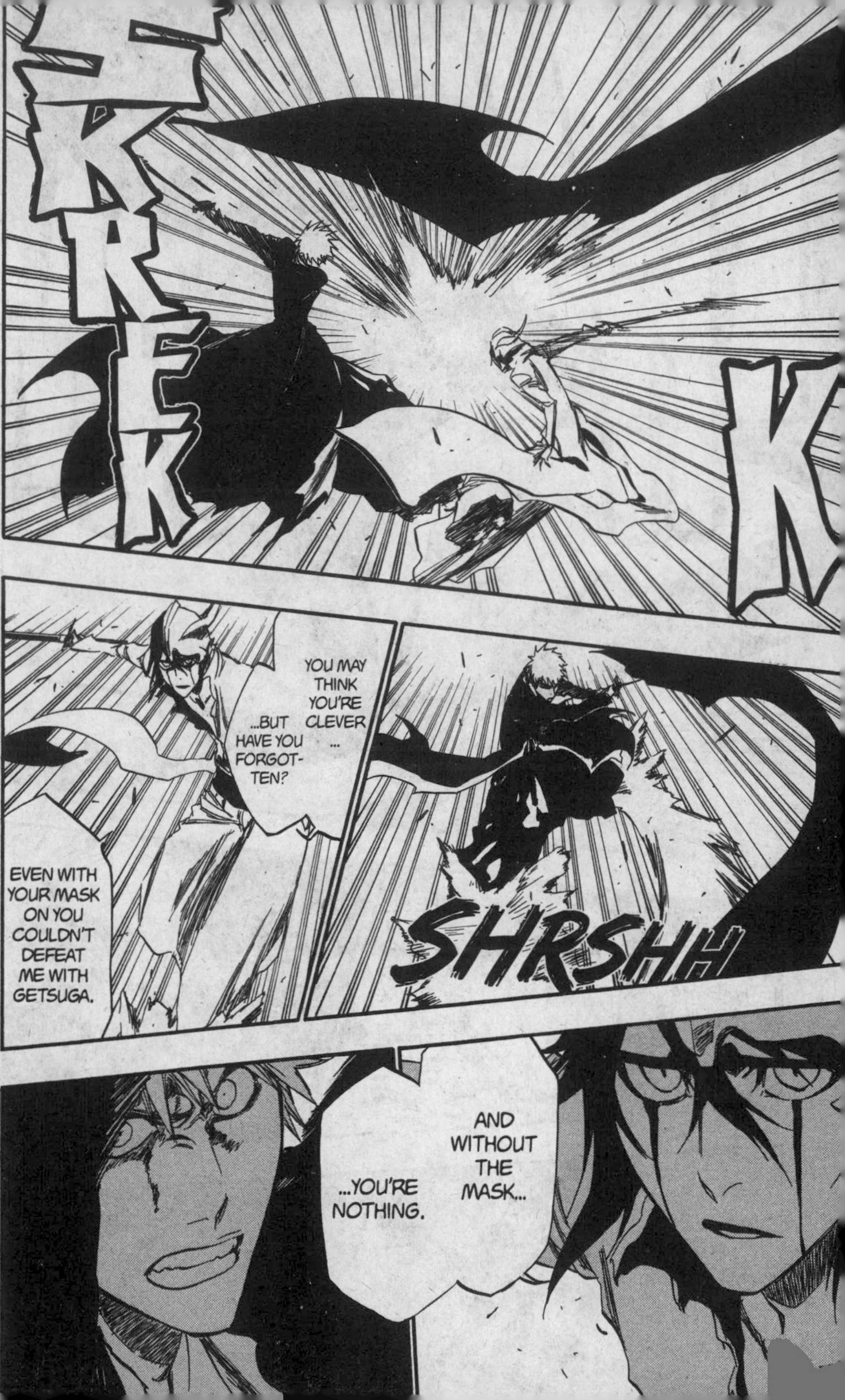
K
KREK
SHRSHH
YOU MAY THINK YOU'RE CLEVER...
...BUT HAVE YOU FORGOTTEN?
EVEN WITH YOUR MASK ON YOU COULDN'T DEFEAT ME WITH GETSUGA.
AND WITHOUT THE MASK...
...YOU'RE NOTHING.

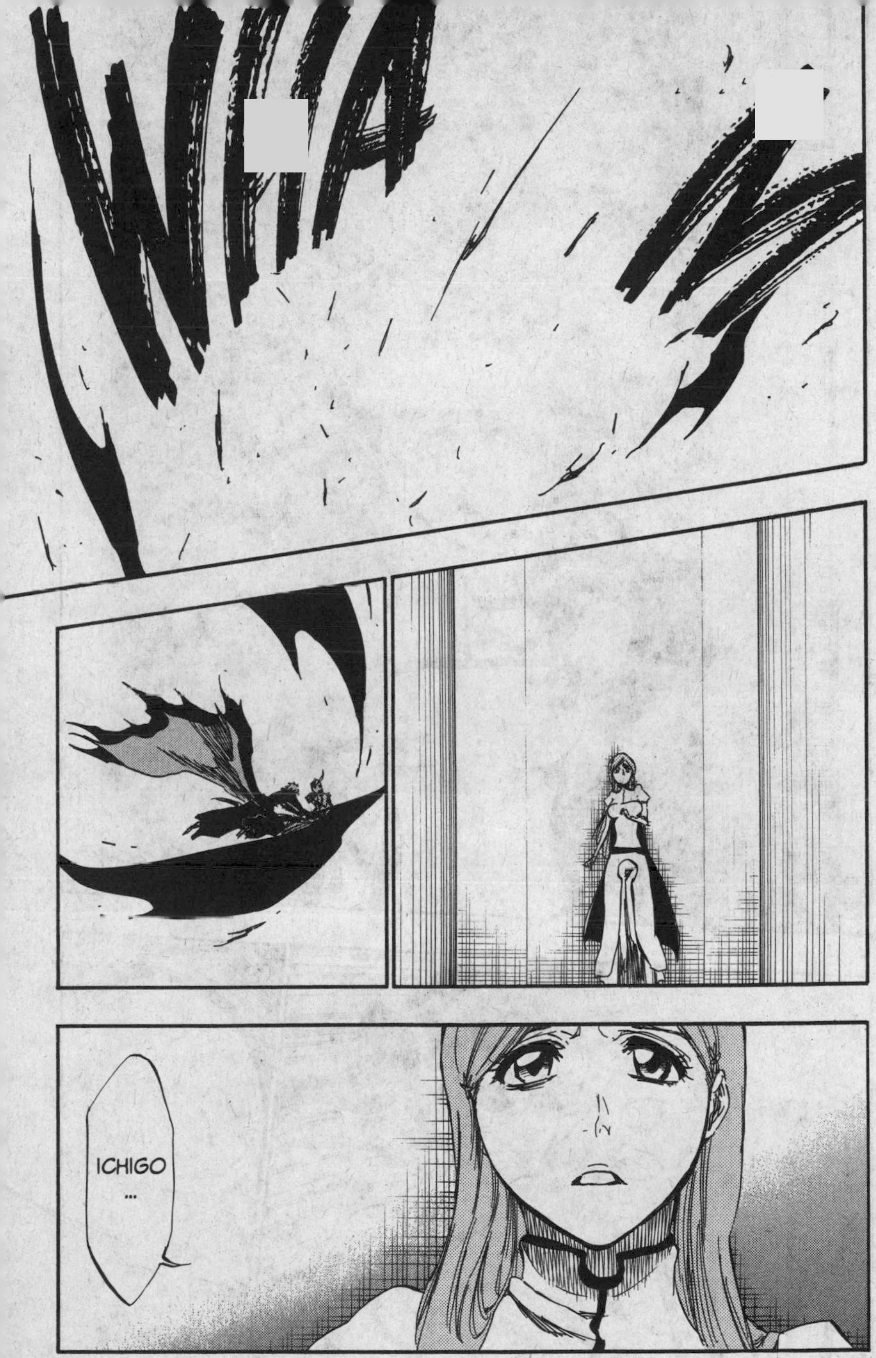
ICHIGO
...

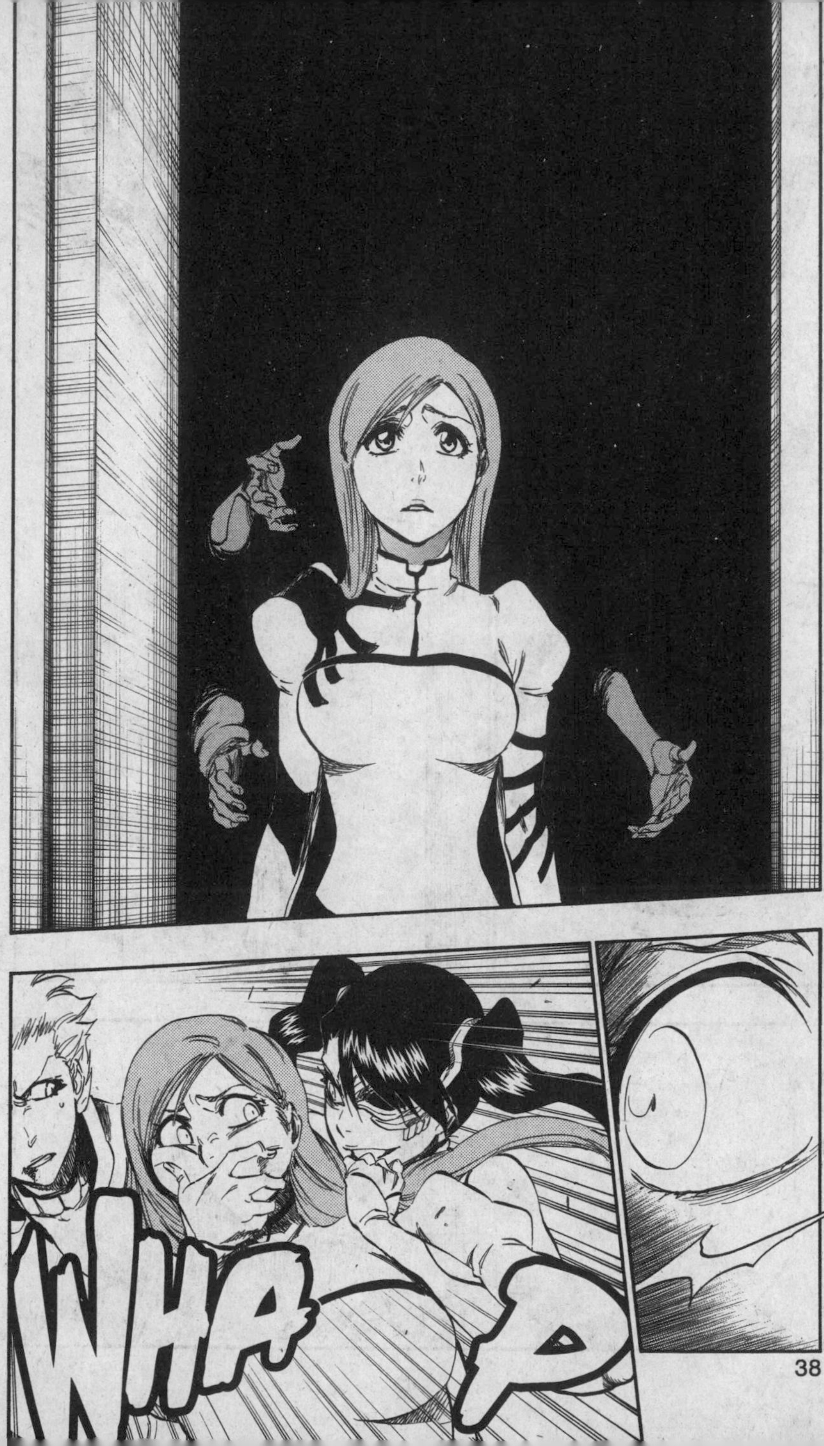
WHAP

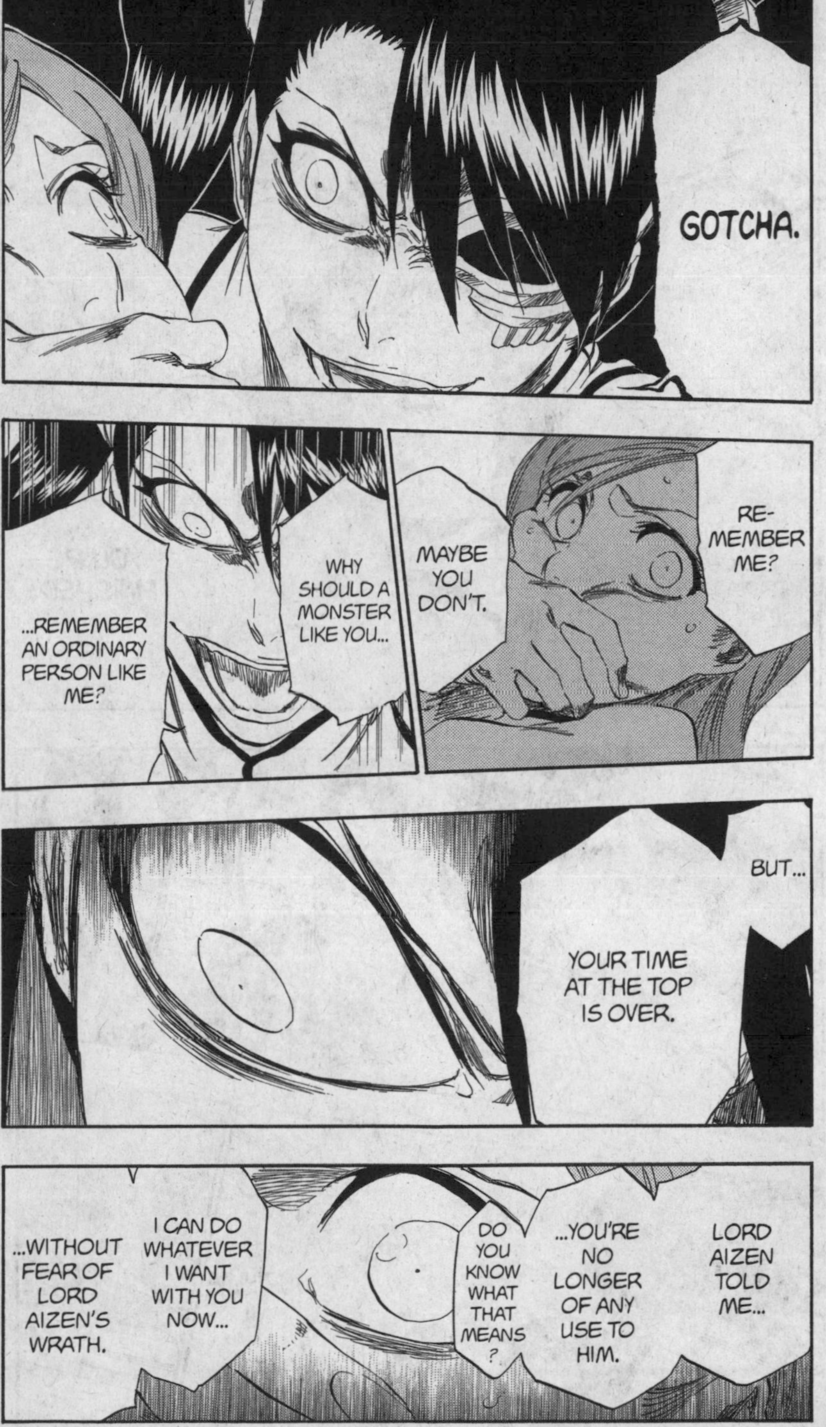
GOTCHA.
REMEMBER ME?
MAYBE YOU DON'T.
WHY SHOULD A MONSTER LIKE YOU...
...REMEMBER AN ORDINARY PERSON LIKE ME?
BUT...
YOUR TIME AT THE TOP IS OVER.
LORD AIZEN TOLD ME...
...YOU'RE NO LONGER OF ANY USE TO HIM.
DO YOU KNOW WHAT THAT MEANS?
I CAN DO WHATEVER I WANT WITH YOU NOW...
...WITHOUT FEAR OF LORD AIZEN'S WRATH.

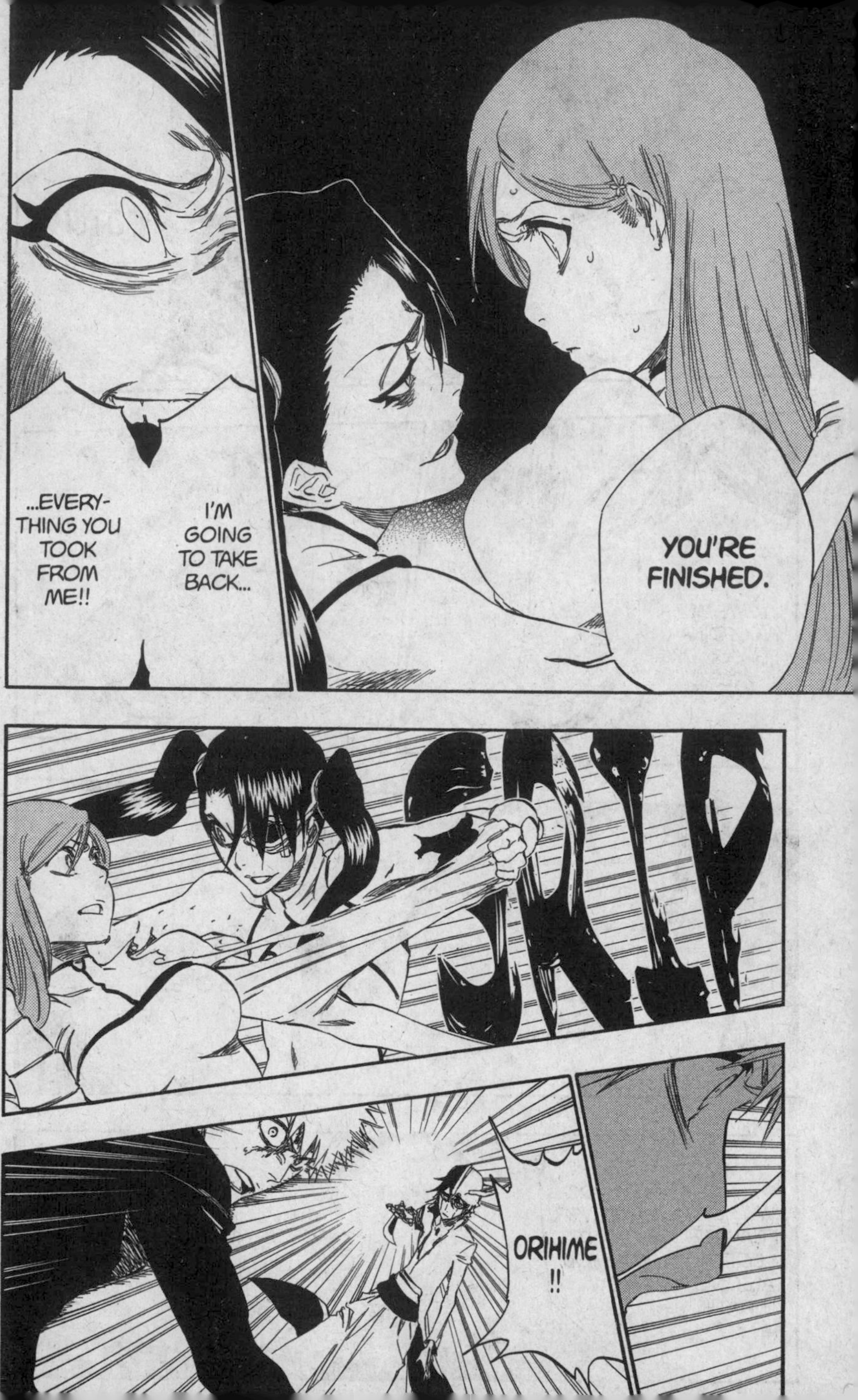
YOU'RE FINISHED.
I'M GOING TO TAKE BACK...
...EVERYTHING YOU TOOK FROM ME!!
SNIP
ORIHIME !!

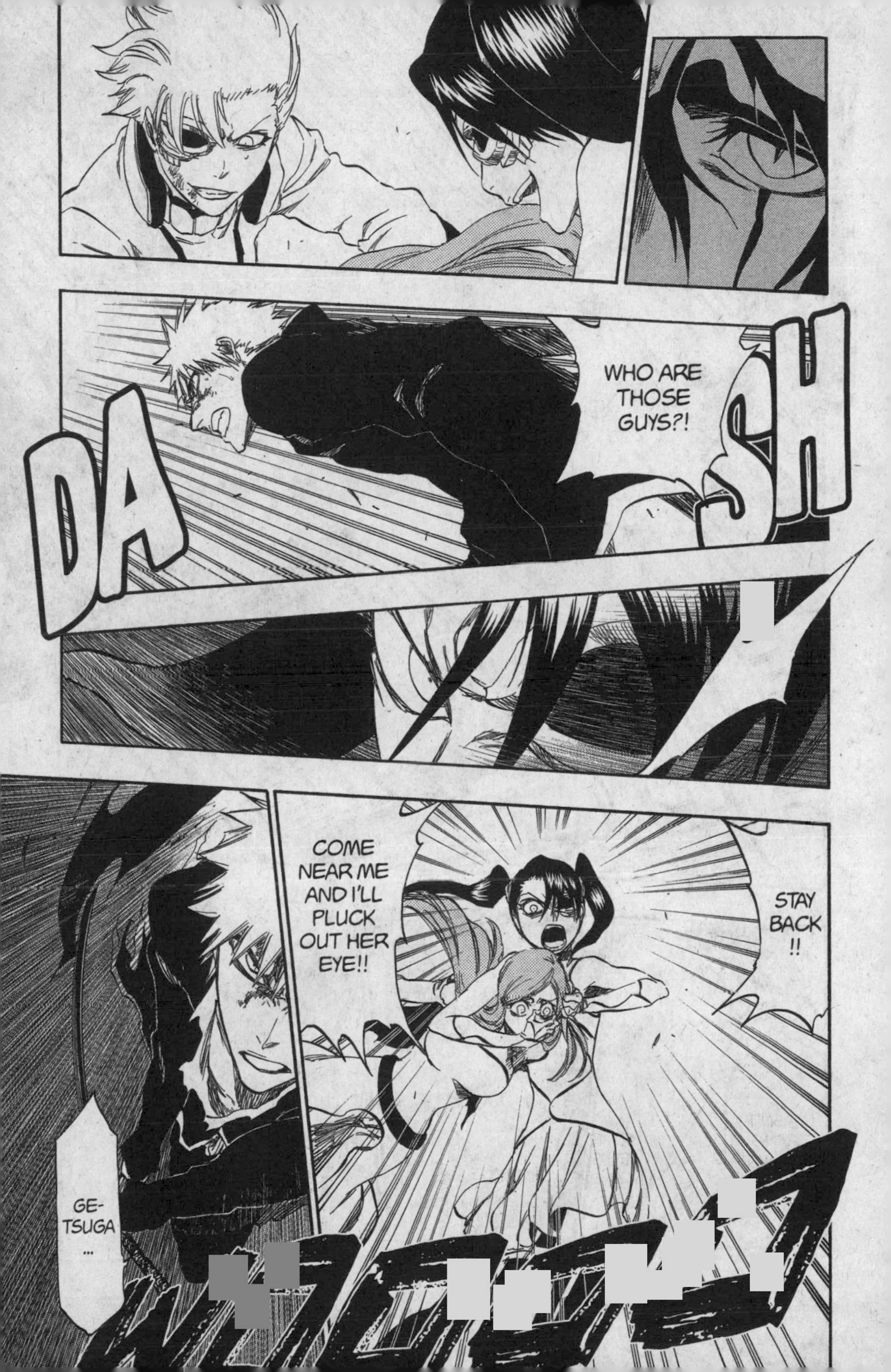
WHO ARE THOSE GUYS?!
DA
SH
STAY BACK !!
COME NEAR ME AND I'LL PLUCK OUT HER EYE!!
GE-TSUGA ...

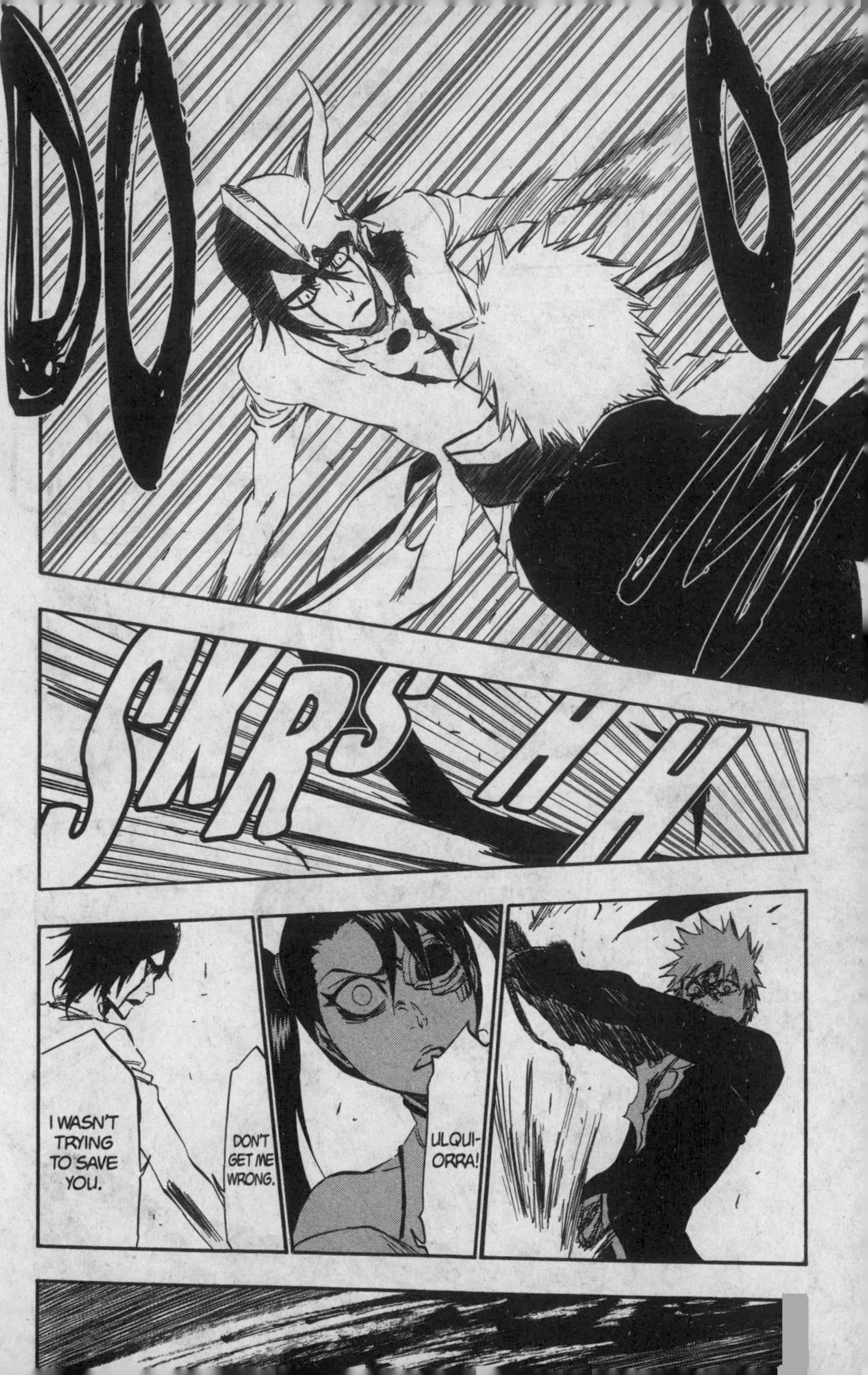
ULQUI-ORRA!
DON'T GET ME WRONG.
I WASN'T TRYING TO SAVE YOU.

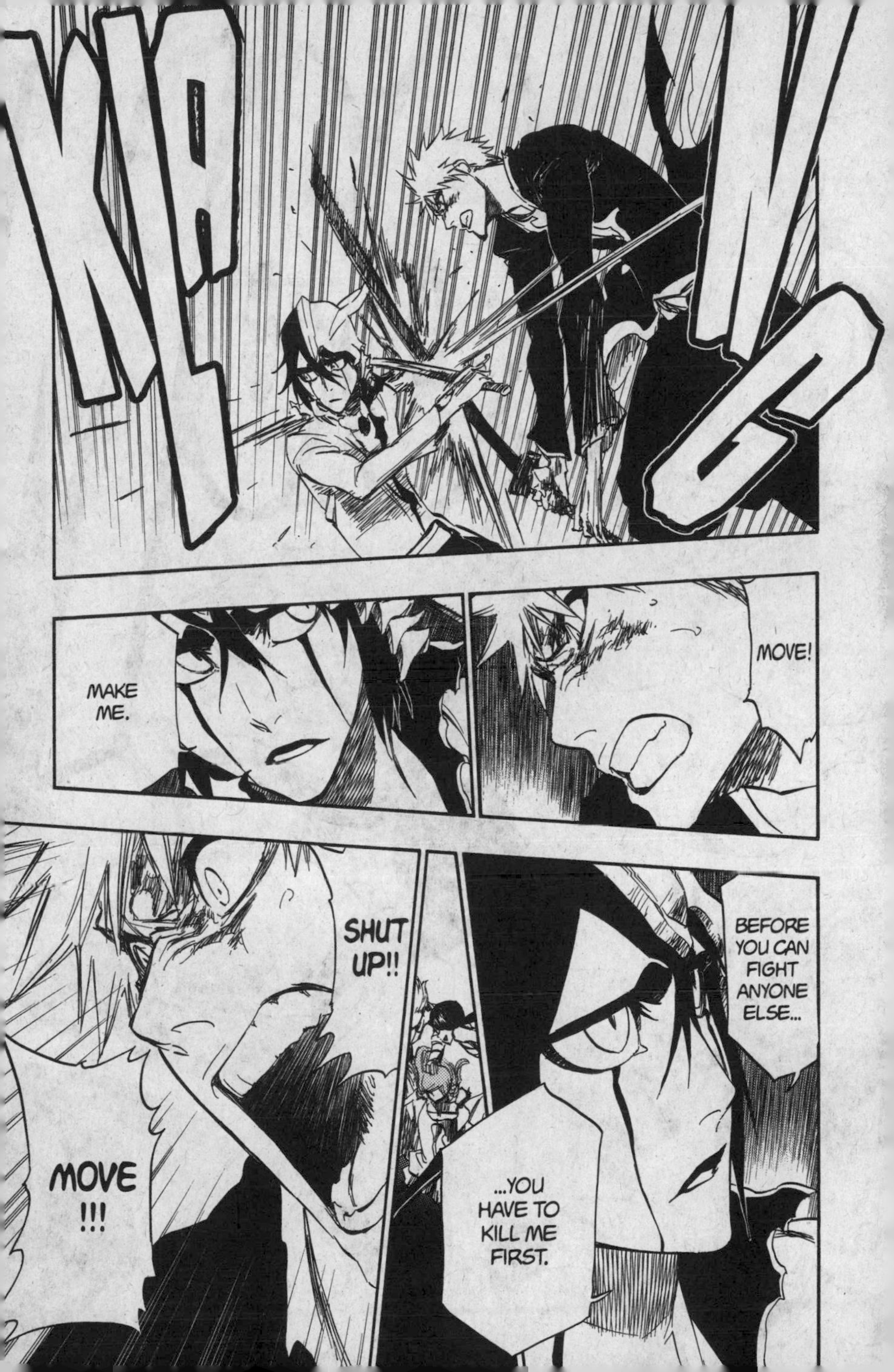
MOVE!
MAKE ME.
BEFORE YOU CAN FIGHT ANYONE ELSE...
...YOU HAVE TO KILL ME FIRST.
SHUT UP!!
MOVE !!!

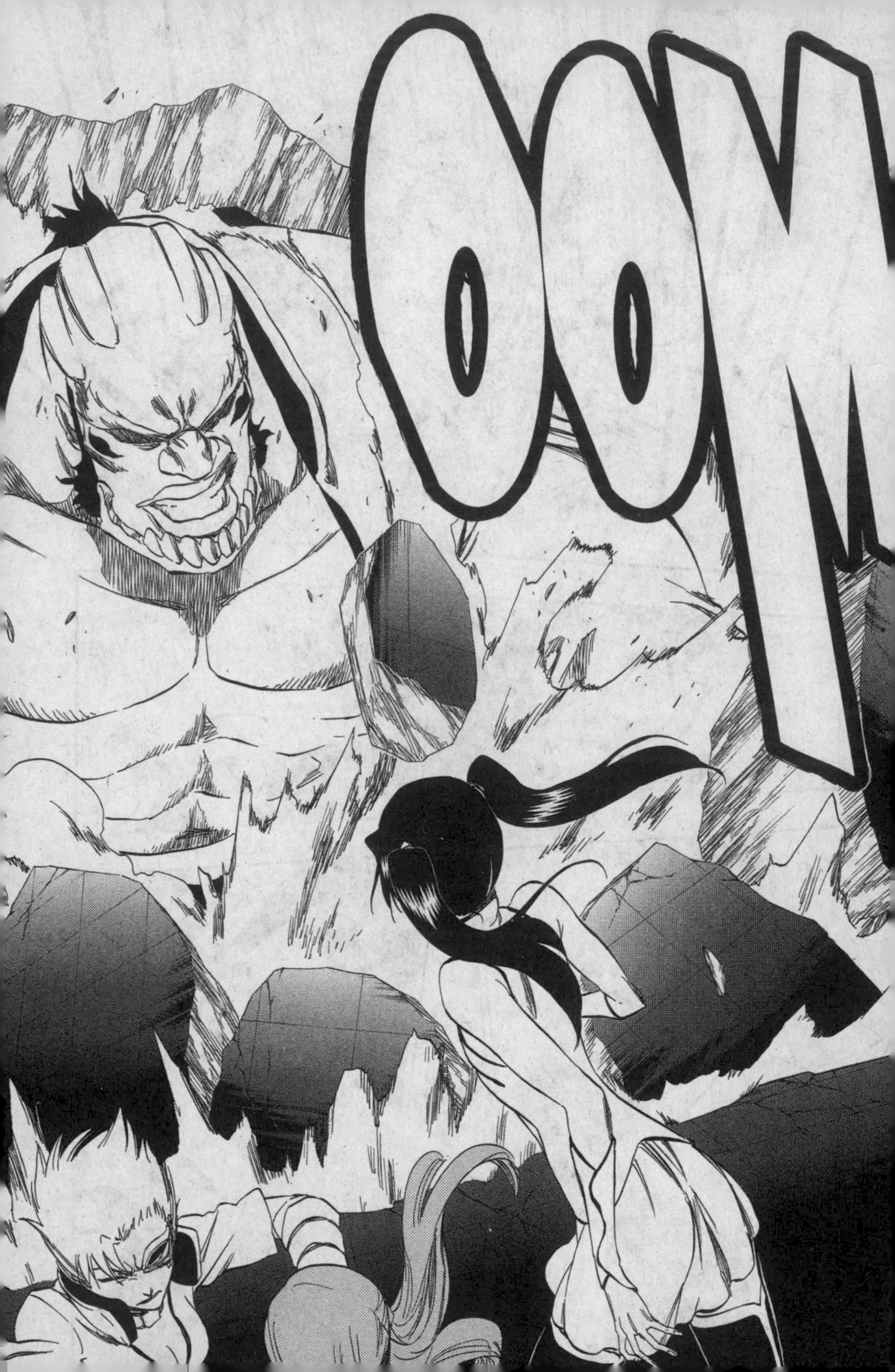
OOM

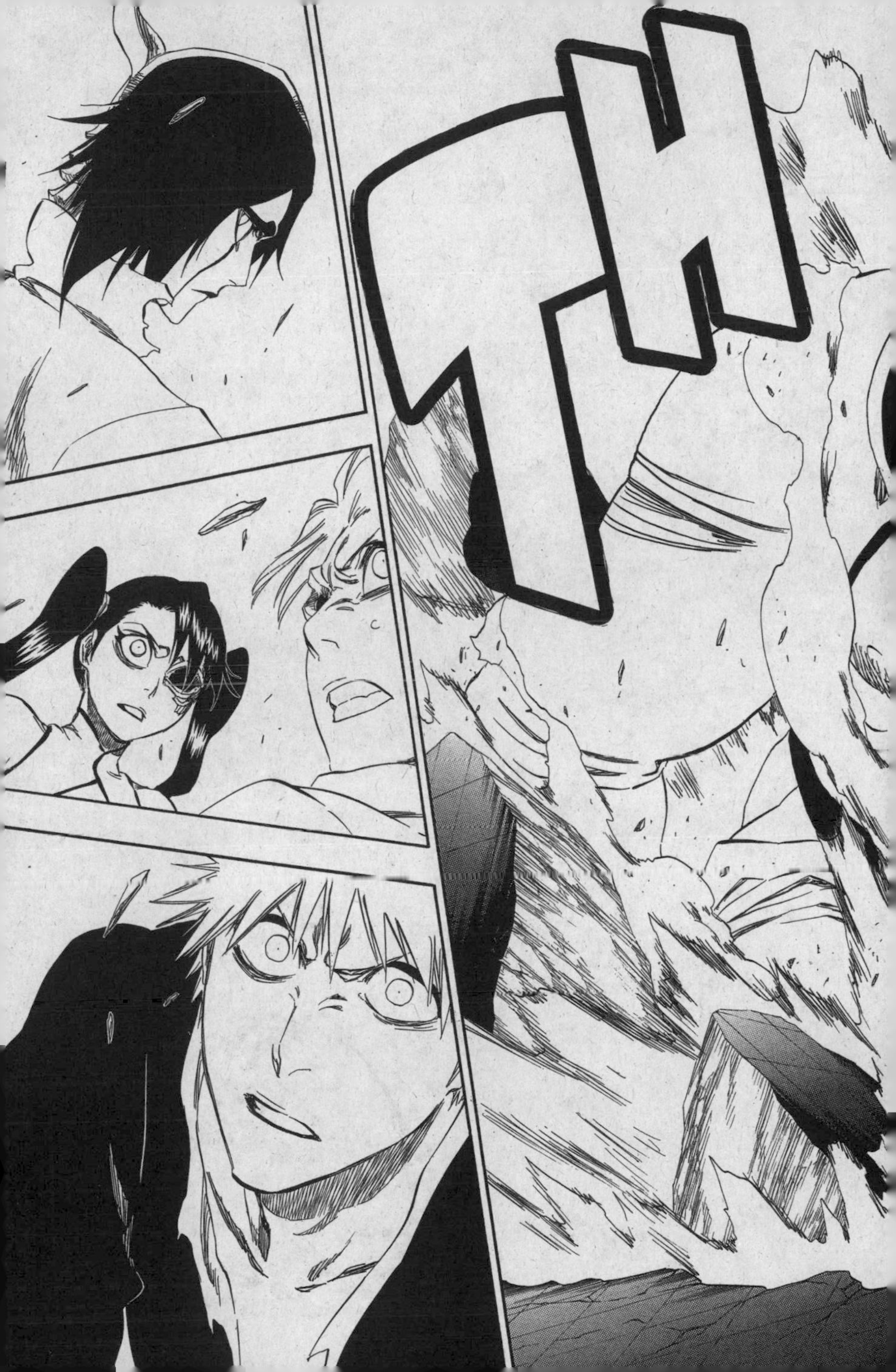
TH

The Gluttony

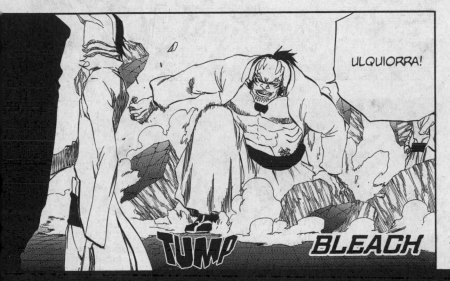

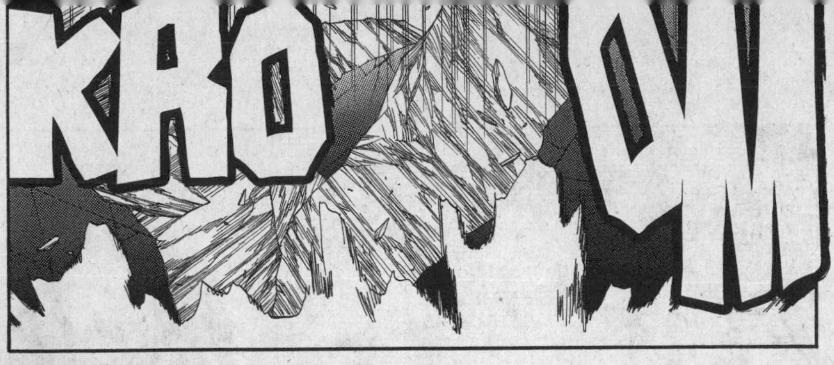
KRAOOM

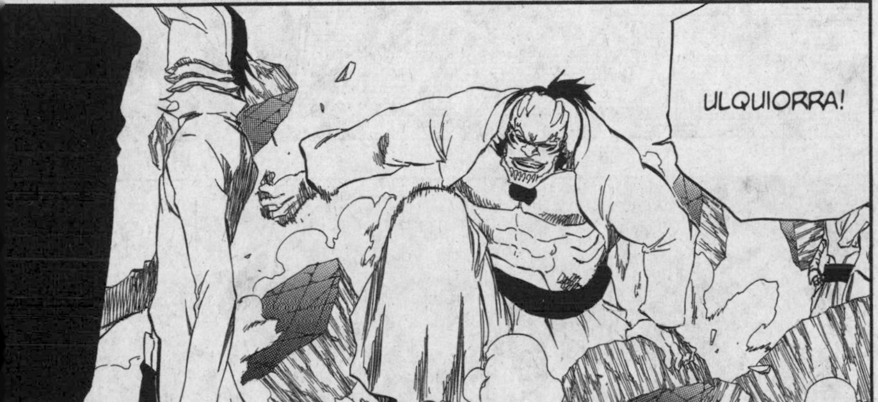
ULQUIORRA!
TUMP
BLEACH

343. The Greed

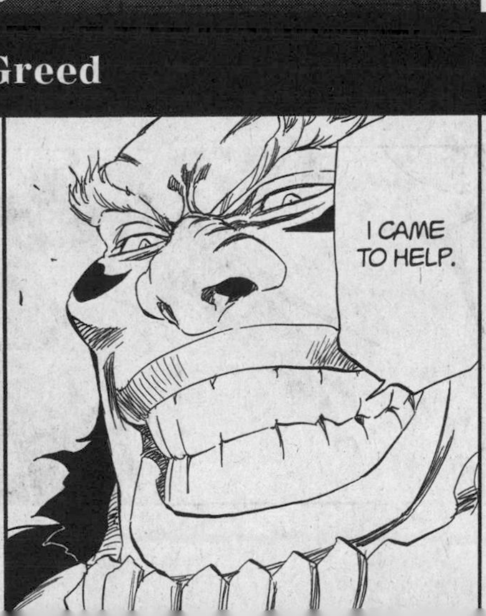
I CAME TO HELP.

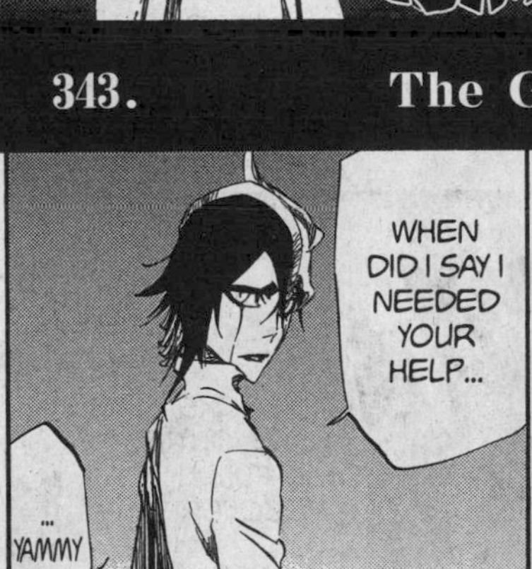
WHEN DID I SAY I NEEDED YOUR HELP...
...YAMMY?

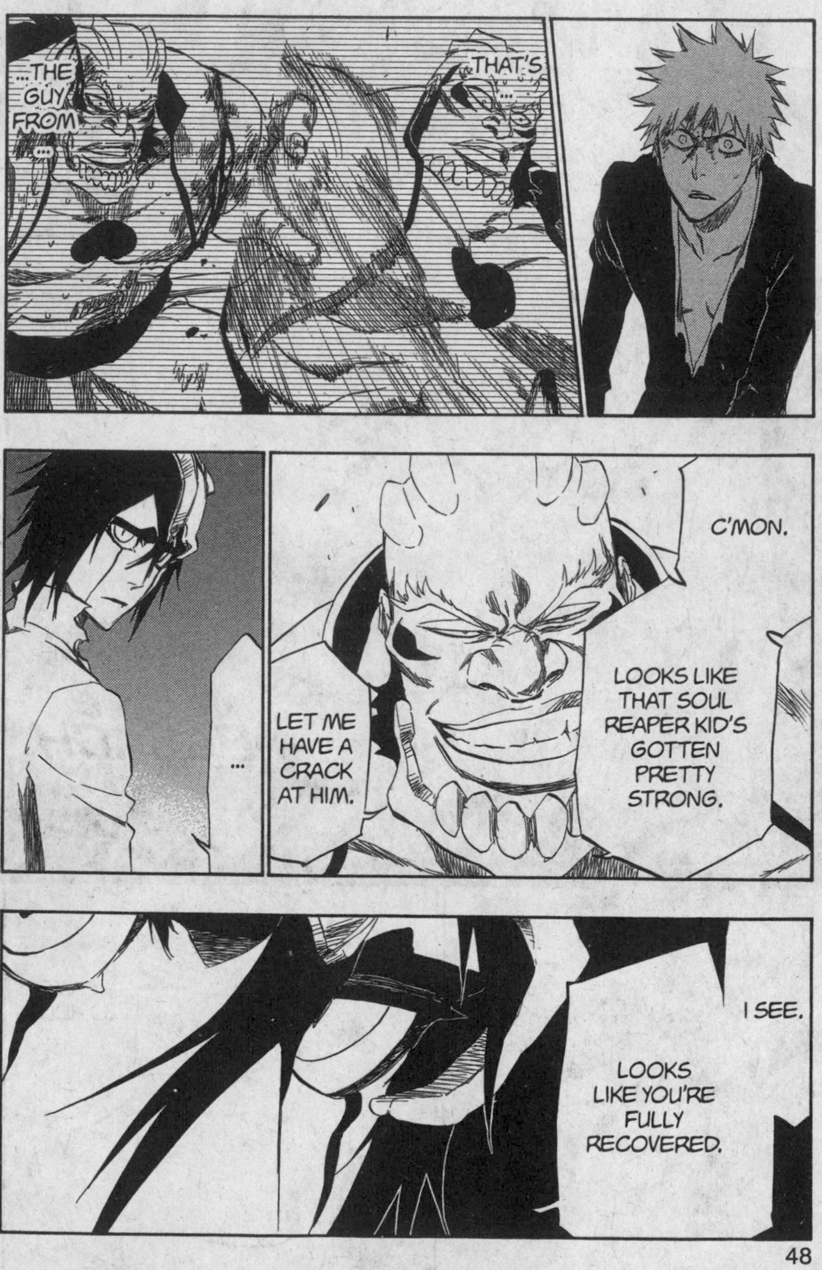
THAT'S ...
...THE GUY FROM ...
C'MON.
LOOKS LIKE THAT SOUL REAPER KID'S GOTTEN PRETTY STRONG.
LET ME HAVE A CRACK AT HIM.
...
I SEE.
LOOKS LIKE YOU'RE FULLY RECOVERED.

READ THIS WAY

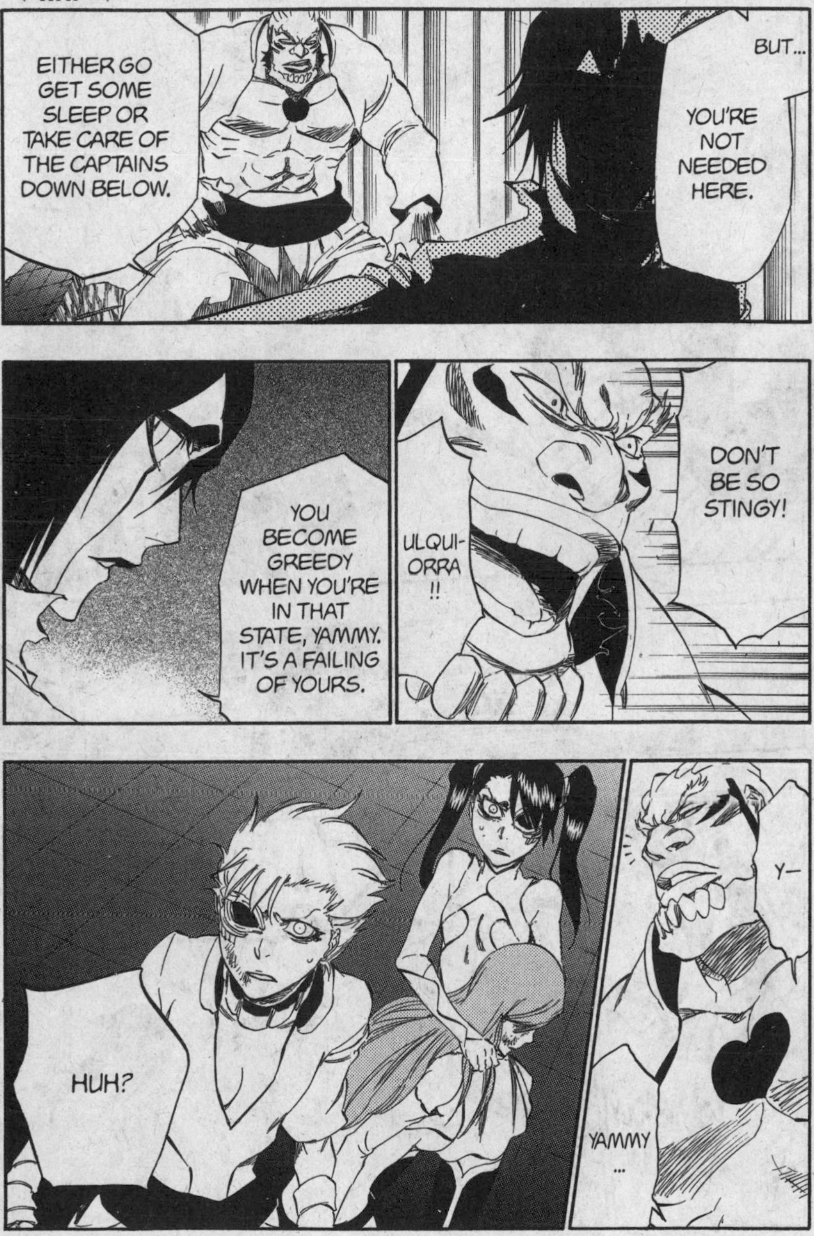
BUT...
YOU'RE NOT NEEDED HERE.
EITHER GO GET SOME SLEEP OR TAKE CARE OF THE CAPTAINS DOWN BELOW.
DON'T BE SO STINGY!
ULQUI-ORRA!!
YOU BECOME GREEDY WHEN YOU'RE IN THAT STATE, YAMMY. IT'S A FAILING OF YOURS.
Y—
YAMMY...
HUH?

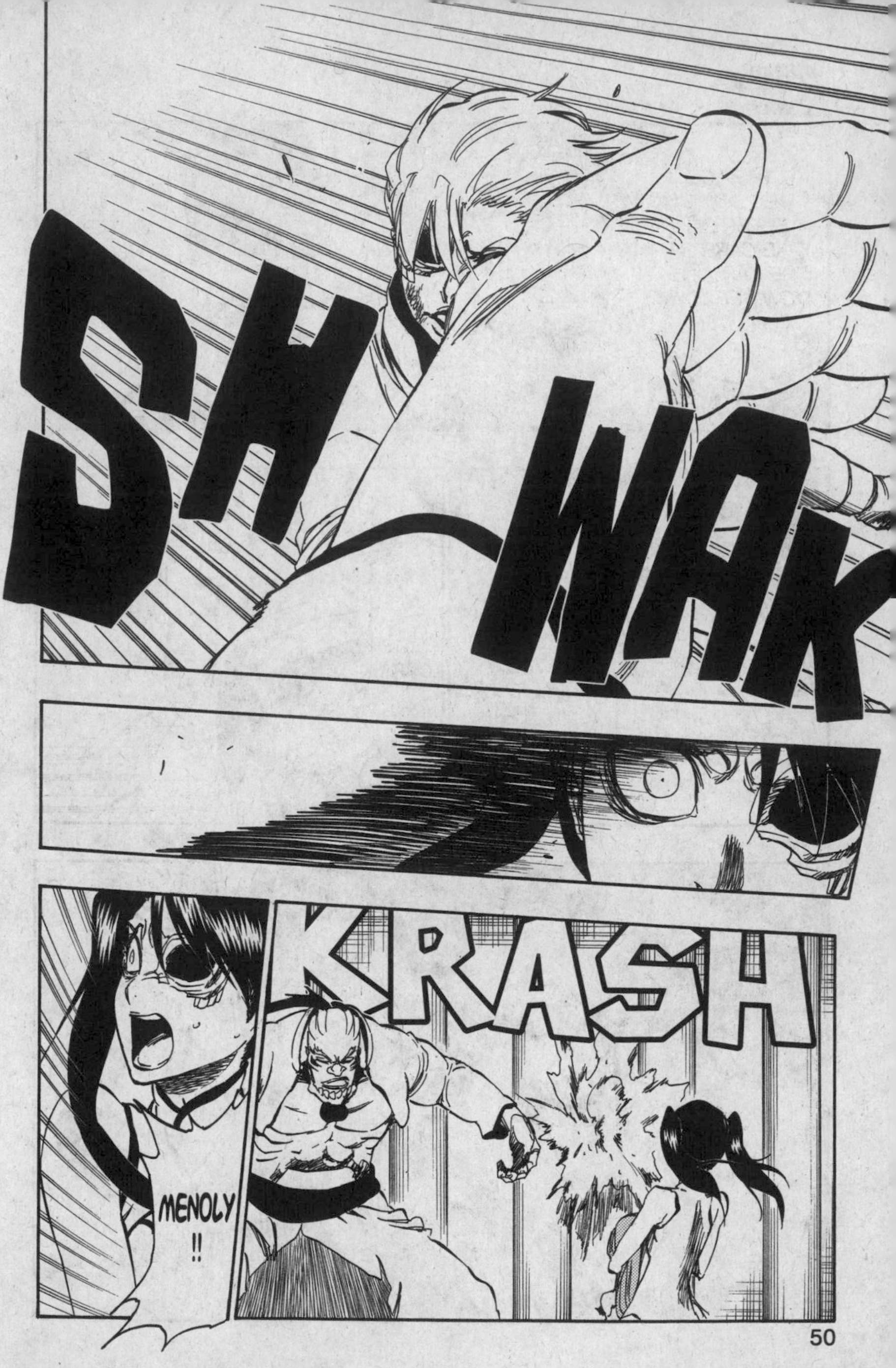
SHWAK
KRASH
MENOLY !!

READ THIS WAY

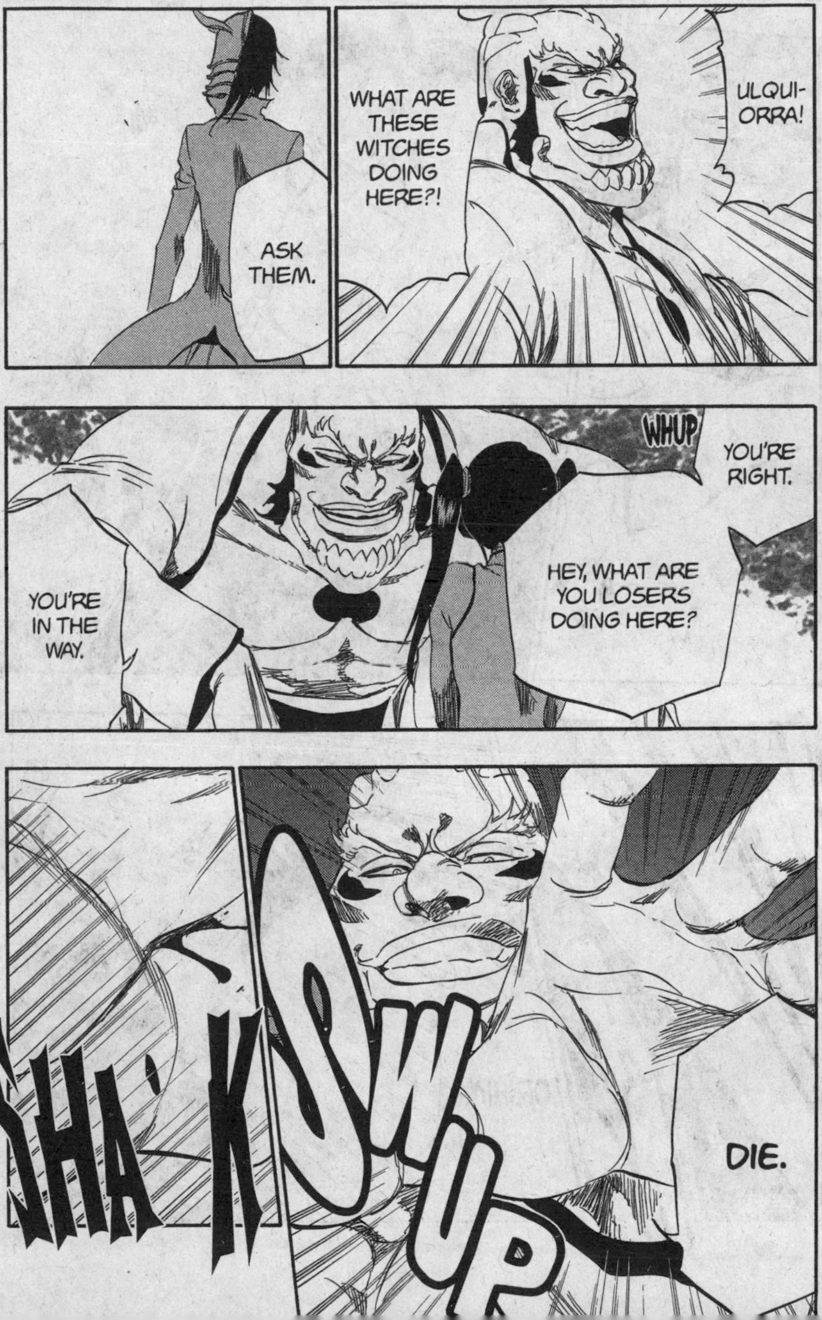
ULQUI-ORRA!
WHAT ARE THESE WITCHES DOING HERE?!
ASK THEM.
WHUP
YOU'RE RIGHT.
HEY, WHAT ARE YOU LOSERS DOING HERE?
YOU'RE IN THE WAY.
DIE.

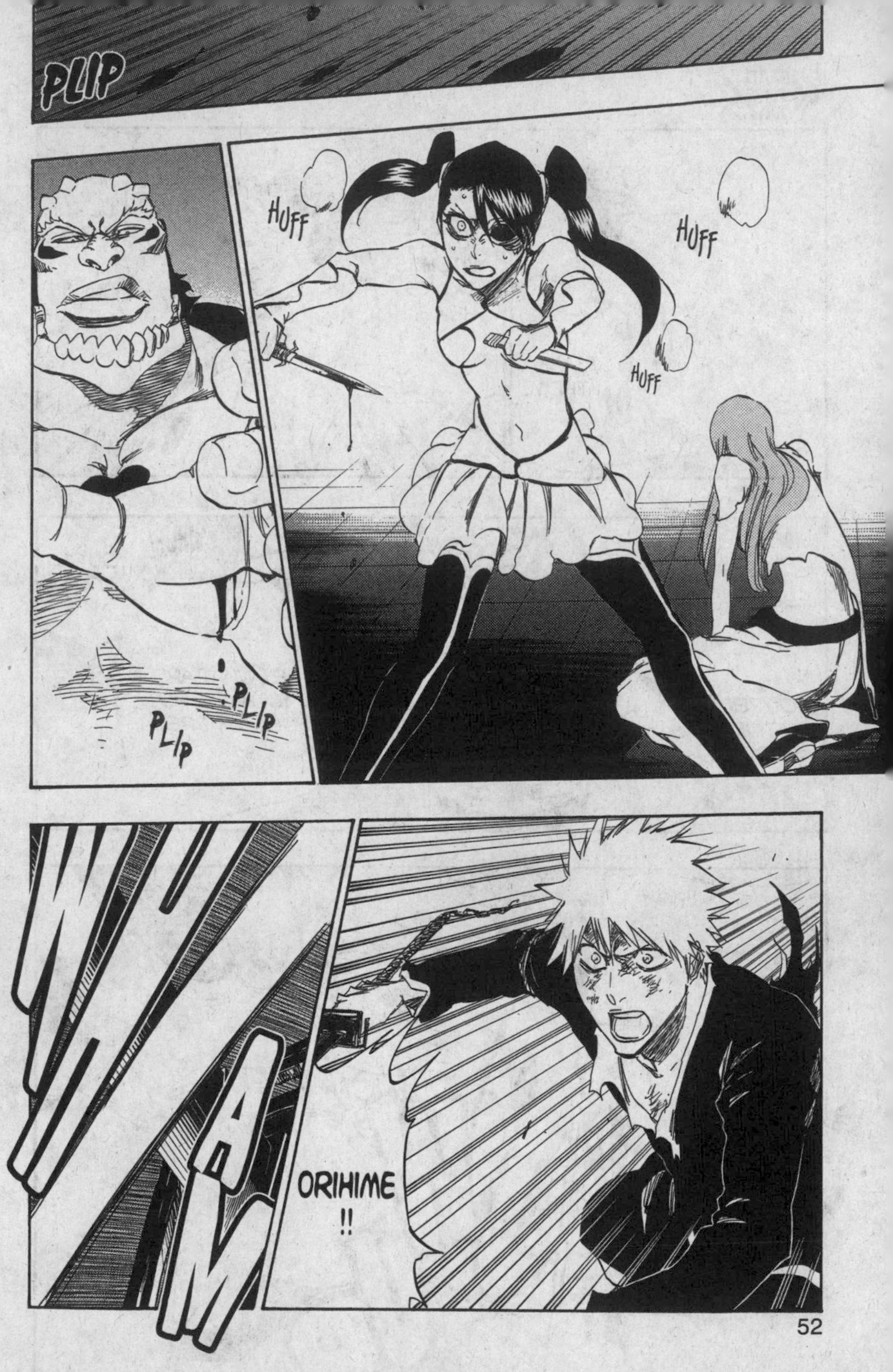
PLIP
HUFF
HUFF
HUFF
PLIP
PLIP
ORIHIME
!!
WHAM

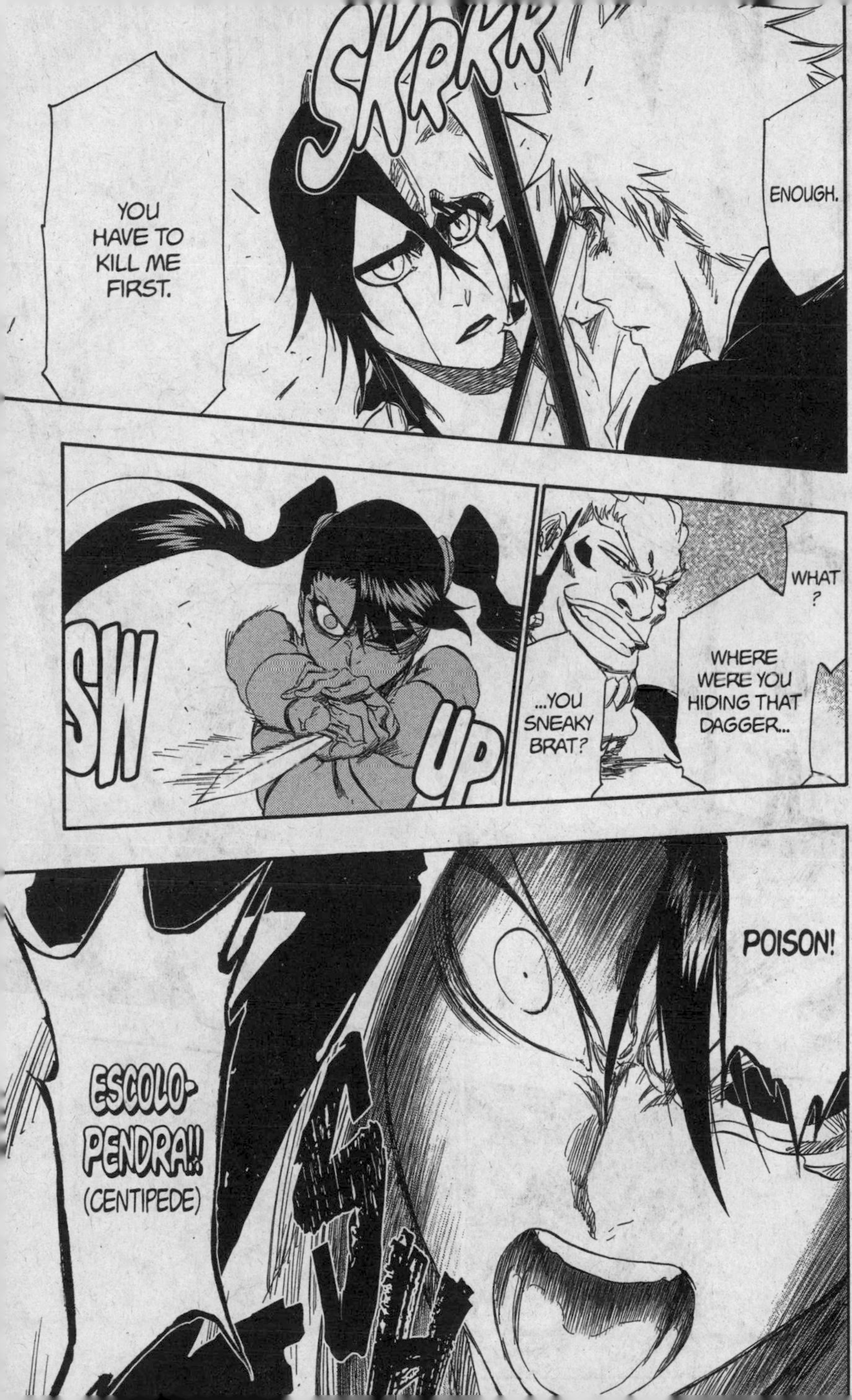

SKRKK
ENOUGH.
YOU HAVE TO KILL ME FIRST.
WHAT?
WHERE WERE YOU HIDING THAT DAGGER...
...YOU SNEAKY BRAT?
SW UP
POISON!
ESCOLO-PENDRA!!
(CENTIPEDE)

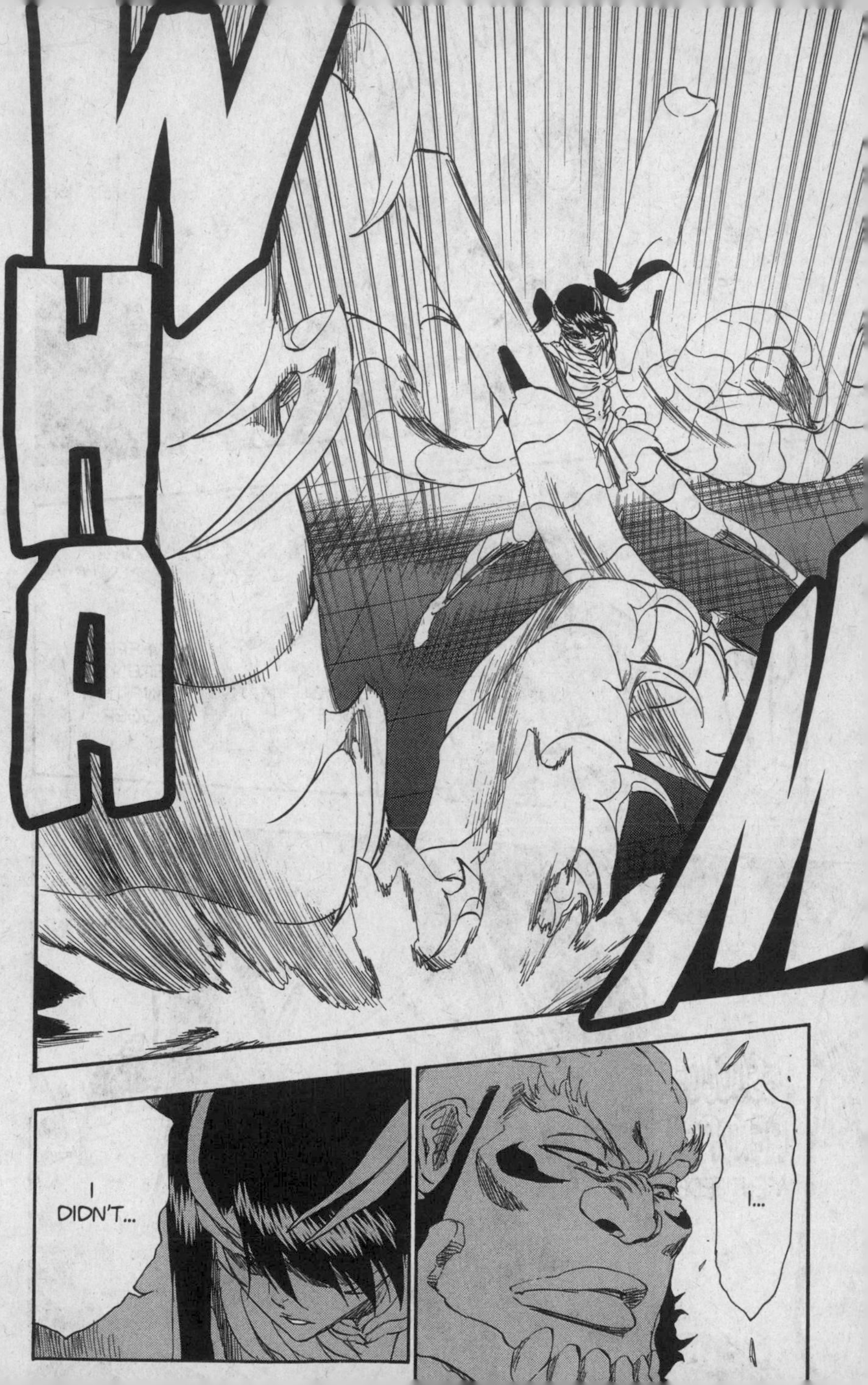
WHAM
I...
I DIDN'T...

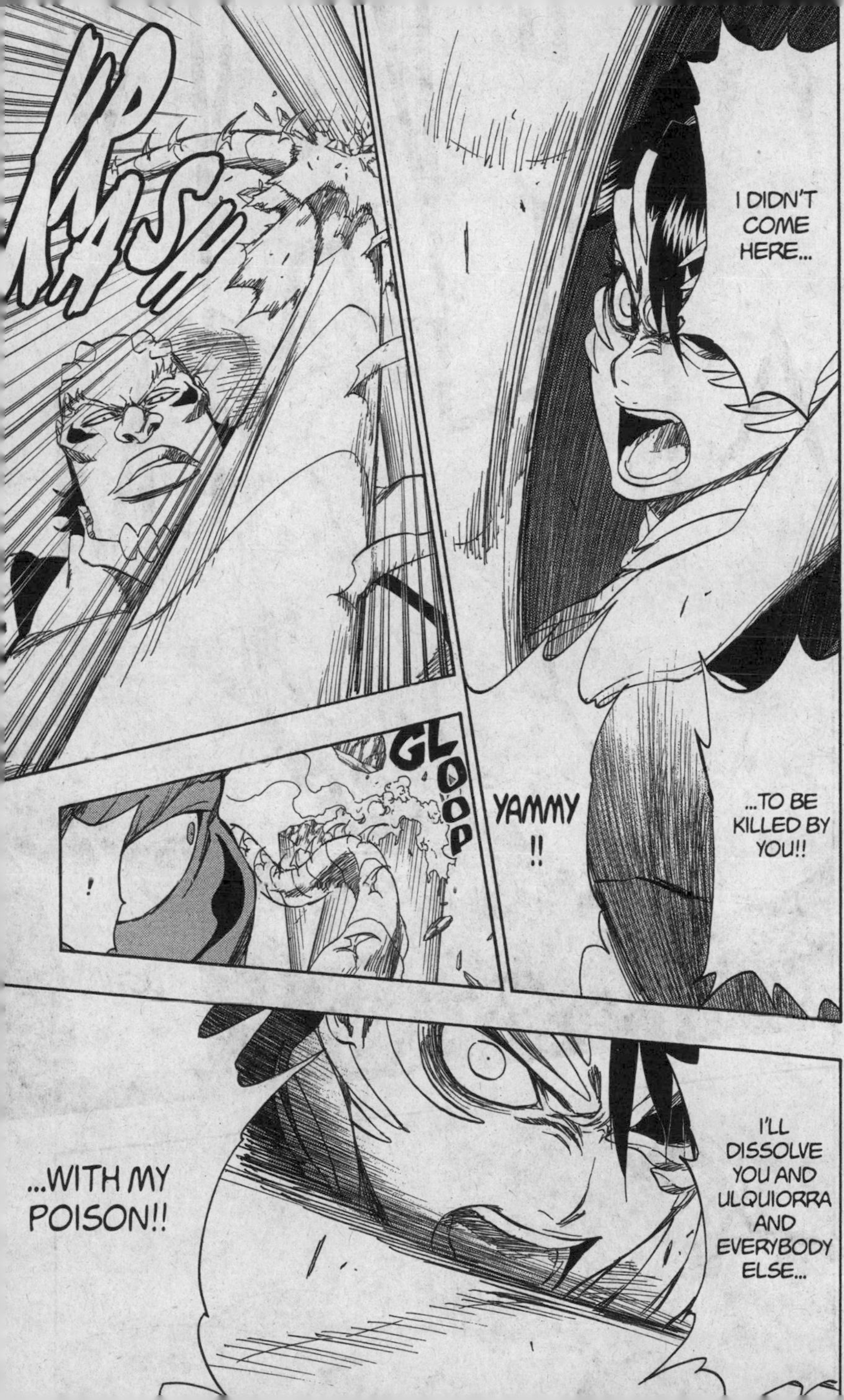

I DIDN'T COME HERE...
...TO BE KILLED BY YOU!!
YAMMY !!
WHAP
GLOOP
I'LL DISSOLVE YOU AND ULQUIORRA AND EVERYBODY ELSE...
...WITH MY POISON!!

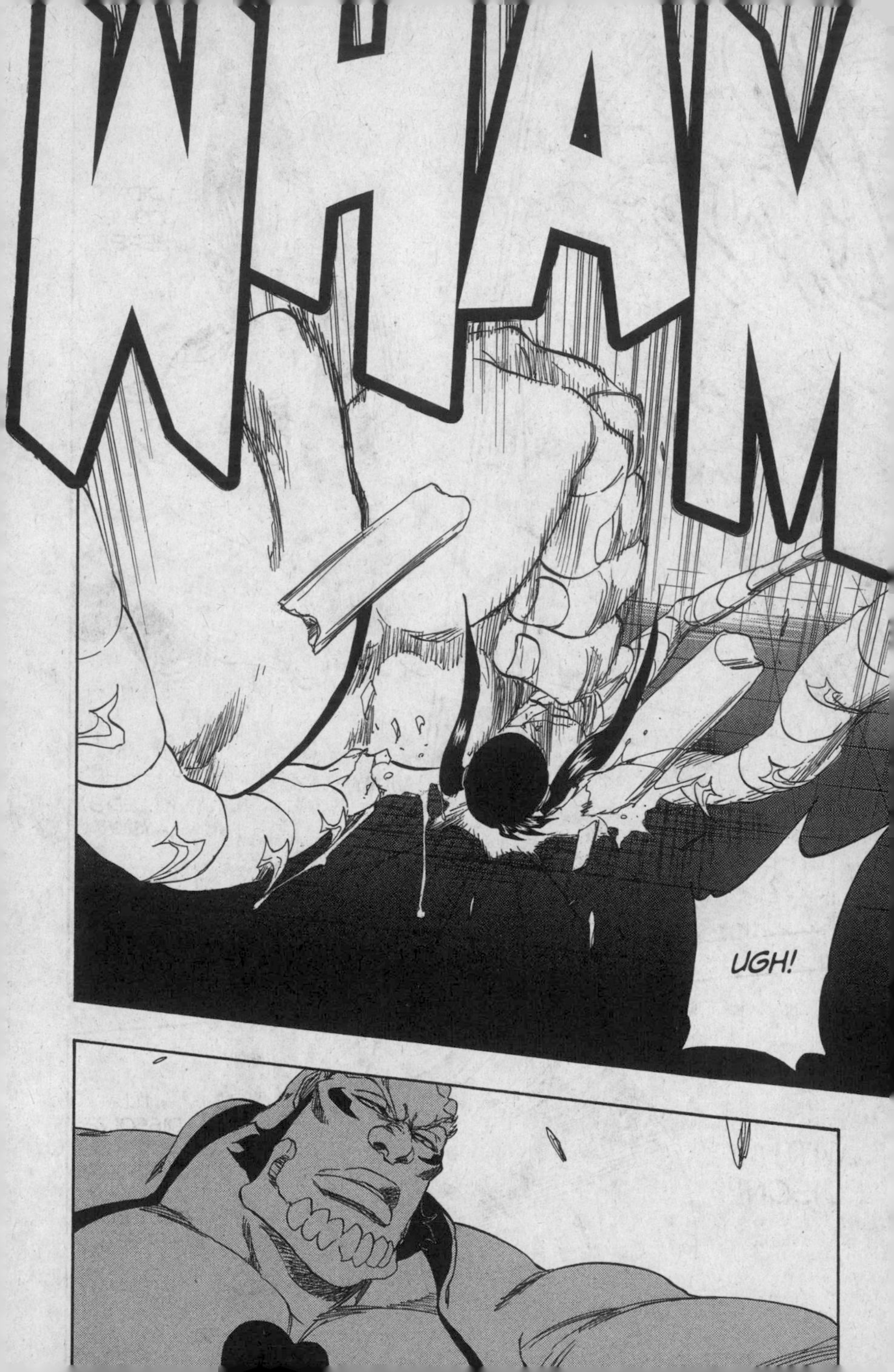
WHAM
UGH!

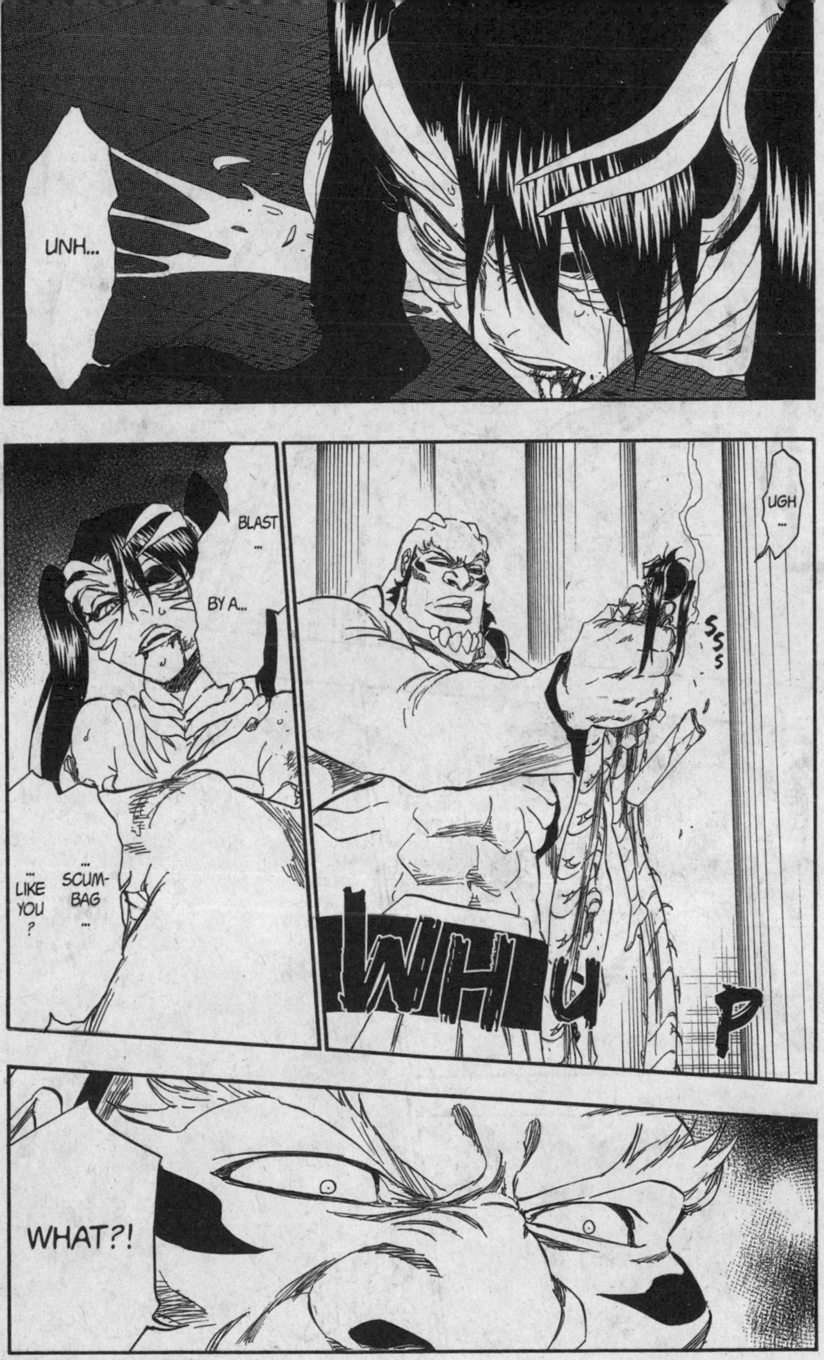
UNH...
UGH ...
SSS
WHUP
BLAST ...
BY A...
... SCUM-BAG ...
... LIKE YOU ?
WHAT?!

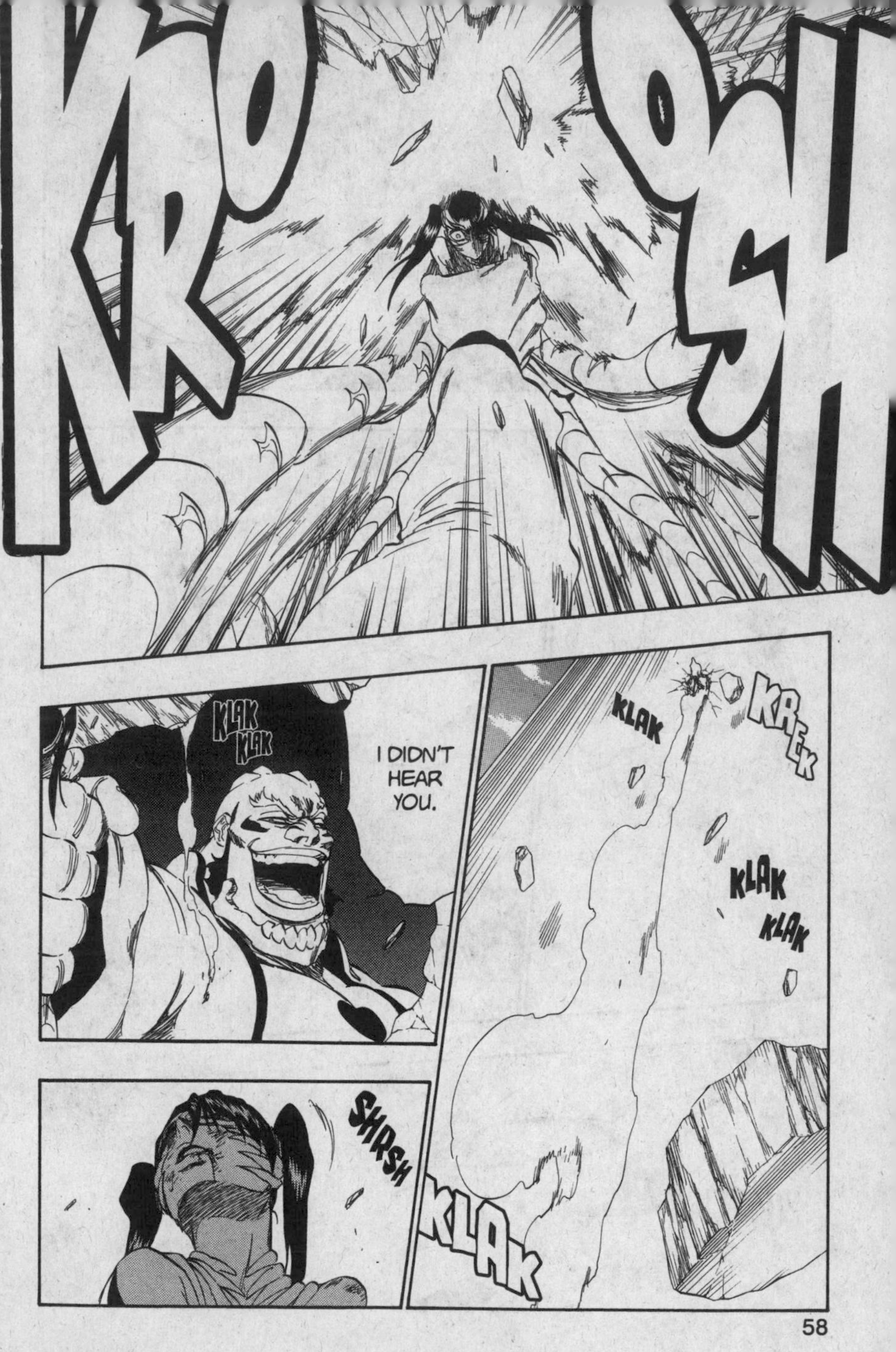
KROOSH
KLAK
KREEK
KLAK
KLAK
KLAK
KLAK
KLAK
I DIDN'T HEAR YOU.
SHRSH

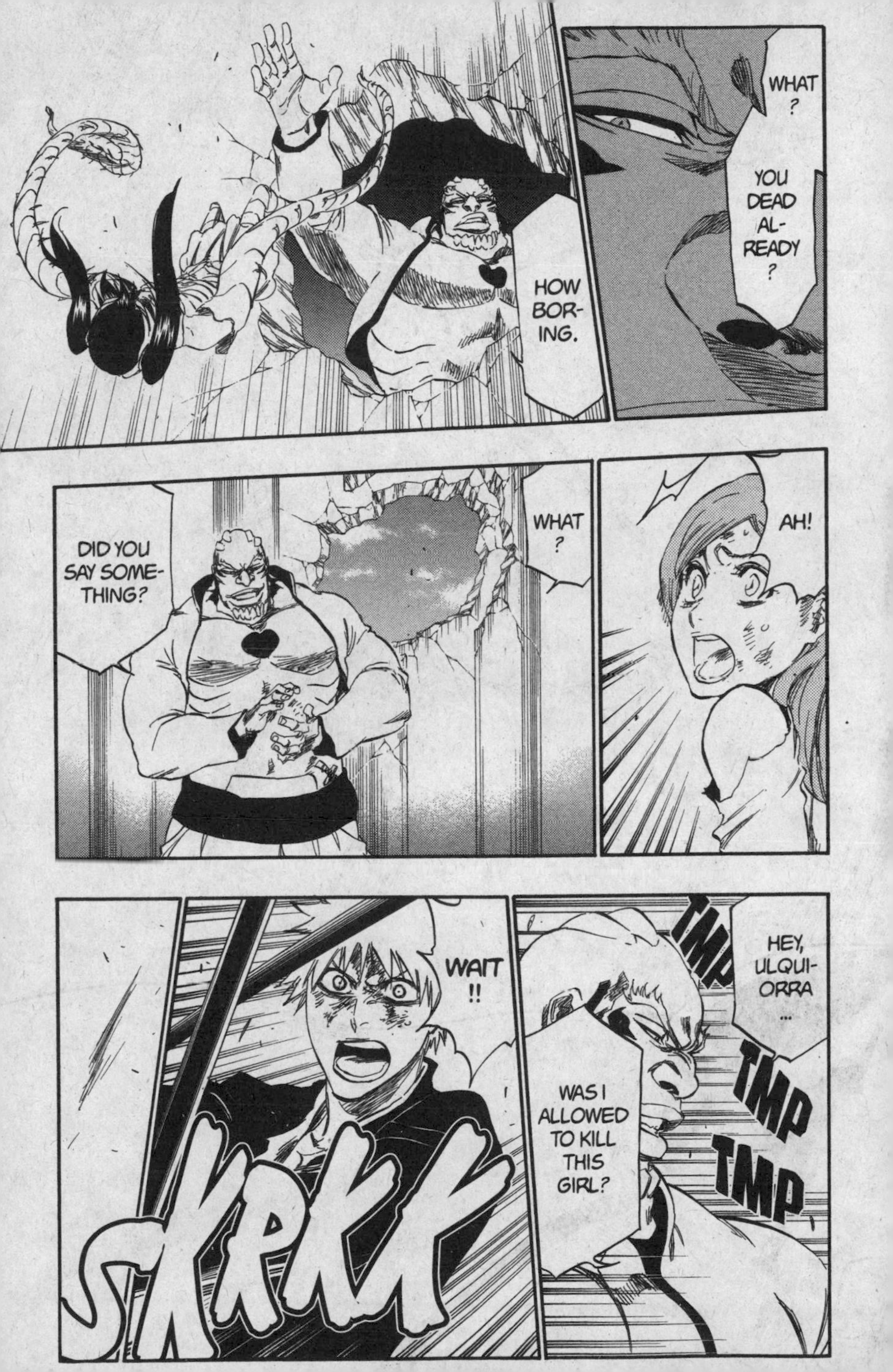
WHAT?
YOU DEAD ALREADY?
HOW BORING.
AH!
WHAT?
DID YOU SAY SOMETHING?
TMP
HEY, ULQUIORRA...
TMP
TMP
TMP
WAS I ALLOWED TO KILL THIS GIRL?
WAIT!!
SHKUK

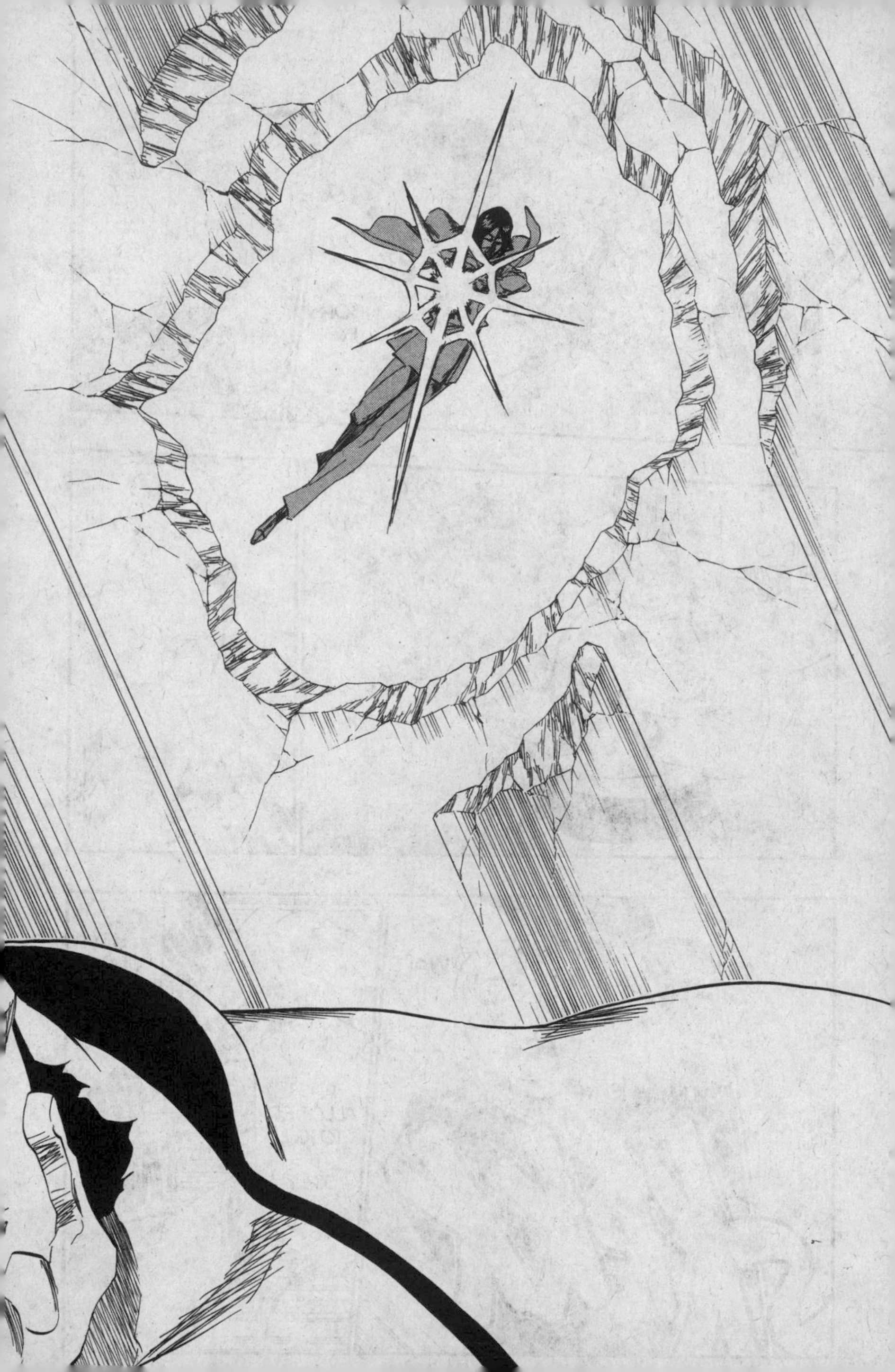

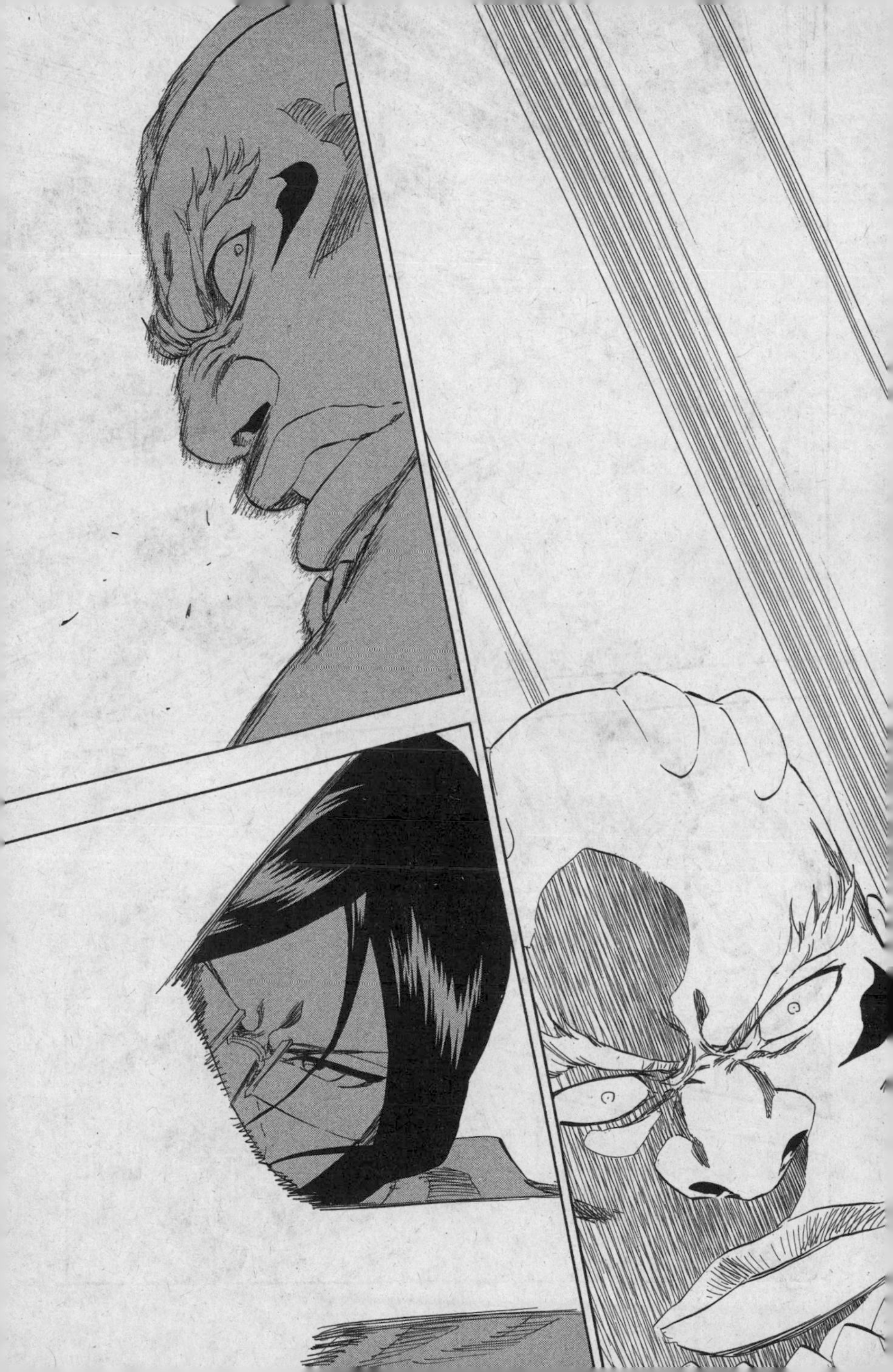

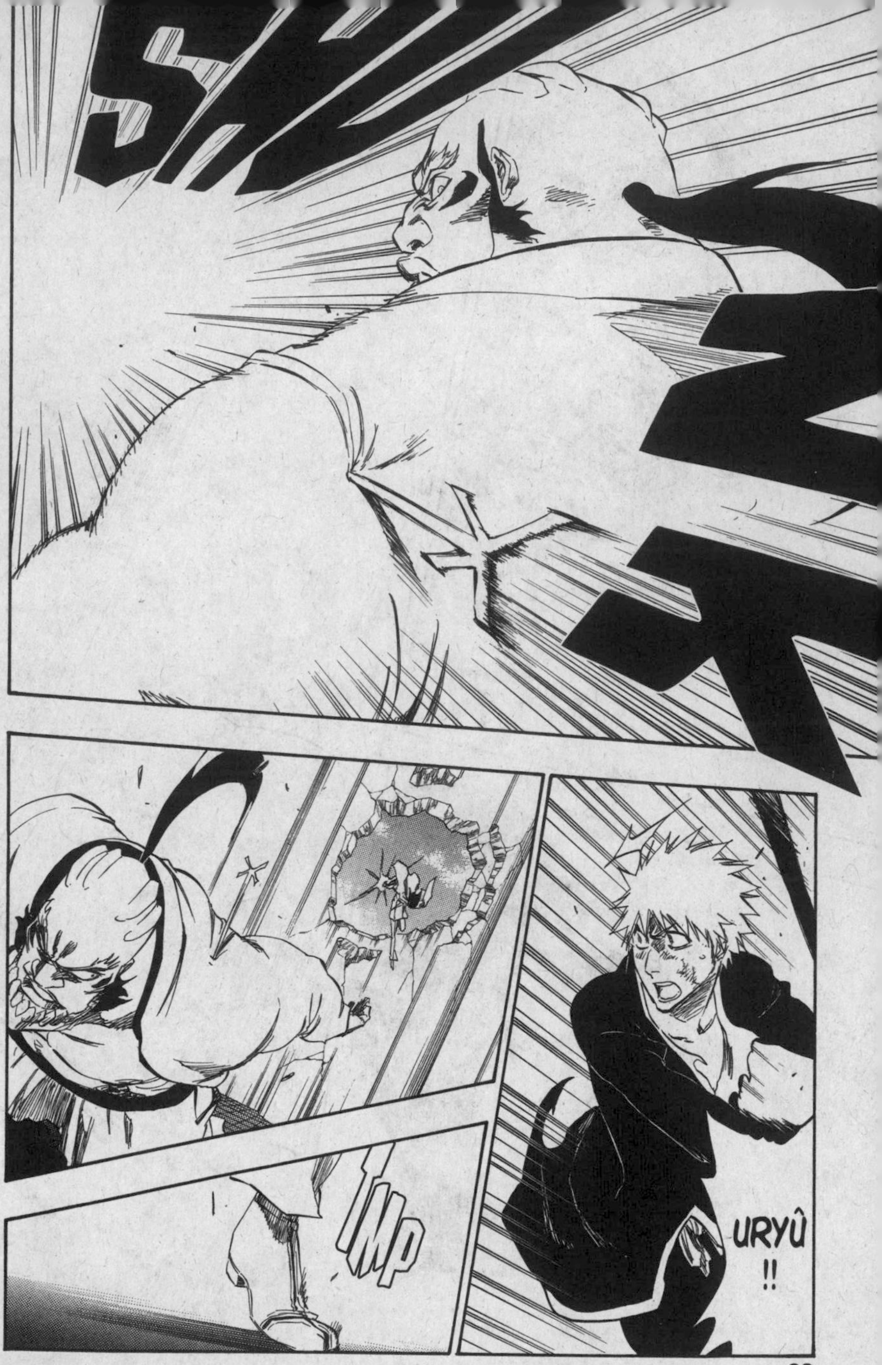
URYÛ
!!
TMP

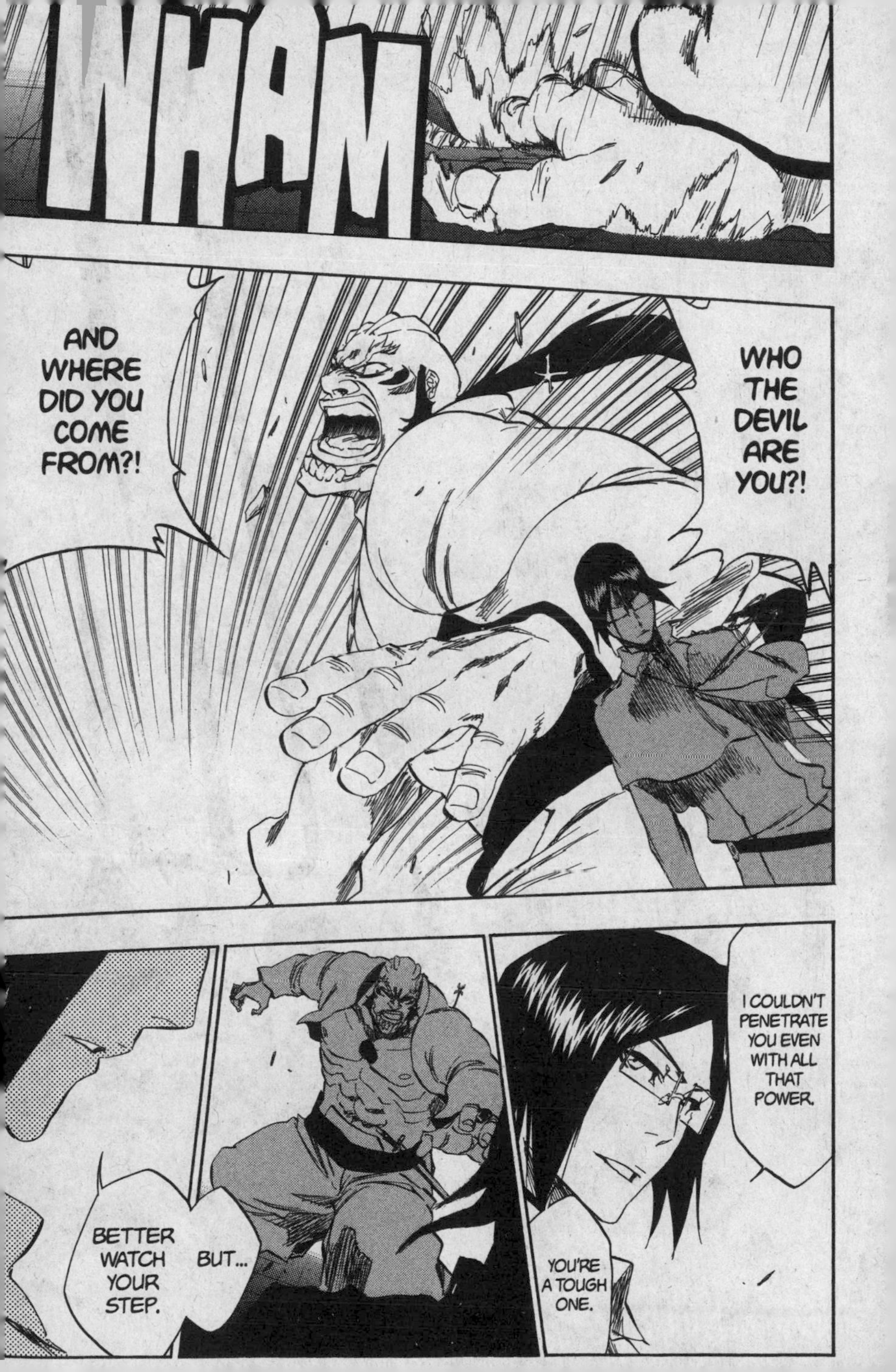
WHAM
WHO THE DEVIL ARE YOU?!
AND WHERE DID YOU COME FROM?!
I COULDN'T PENETRATE YOU EVEN WITH ALL THAT POWER.
YOU'RE A TOUGH ONE.
BUT...
BETTER WATCH YOUR STEP.

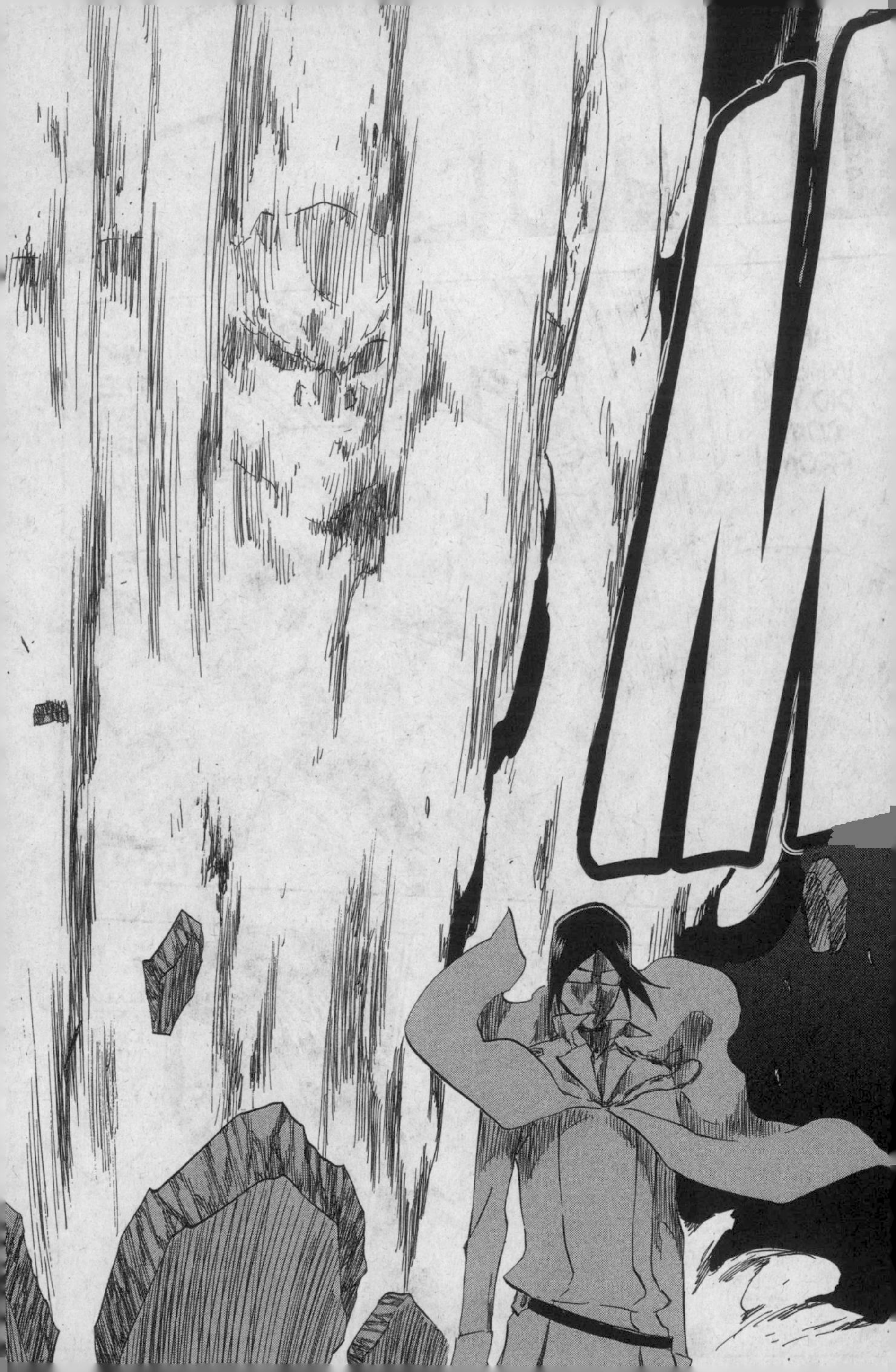

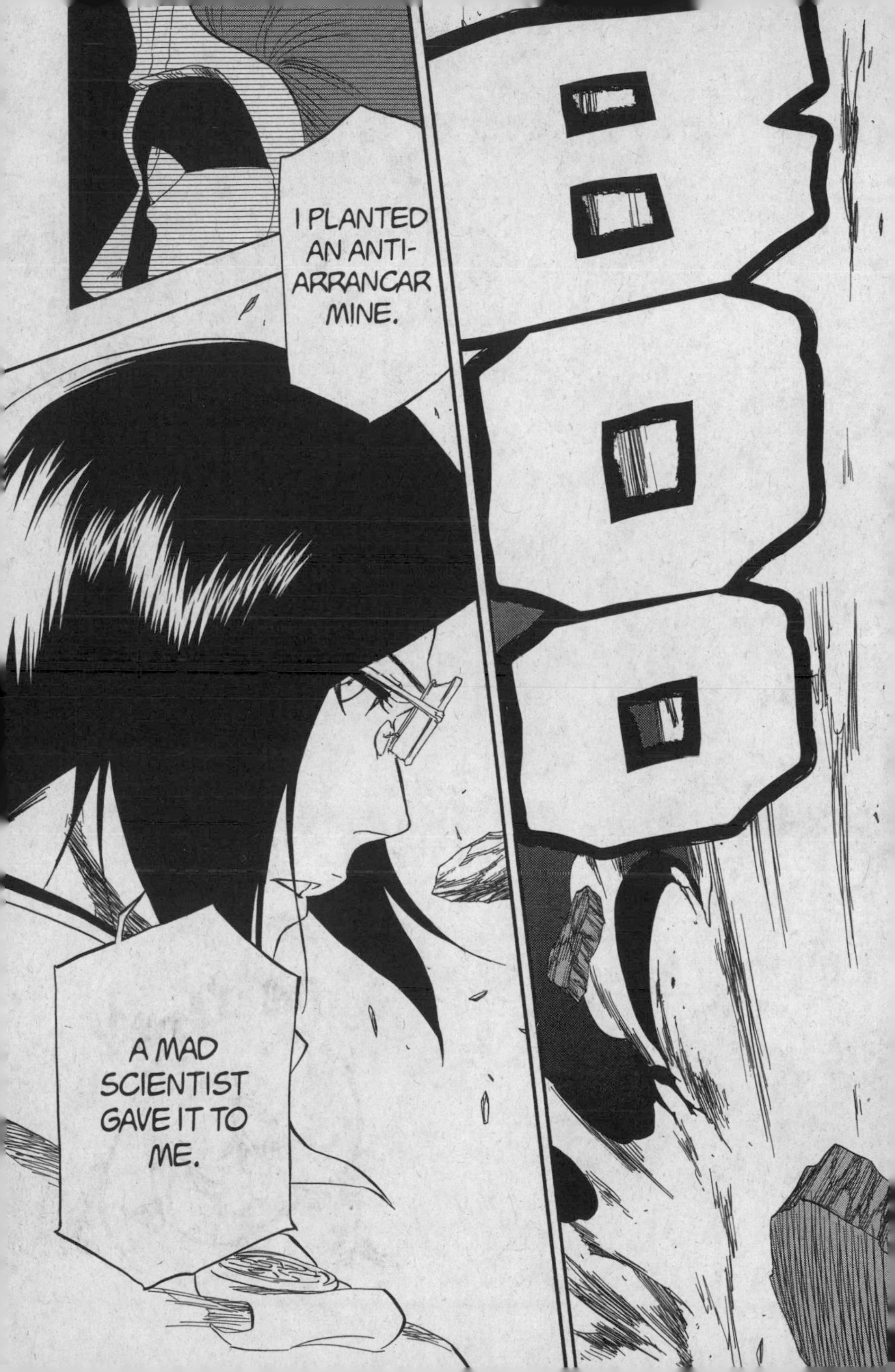
I PLANTED AN ANTI-ARRANCAR MINE.
A MAD SCIENTIST GAVE IT TO ME.

the Greed

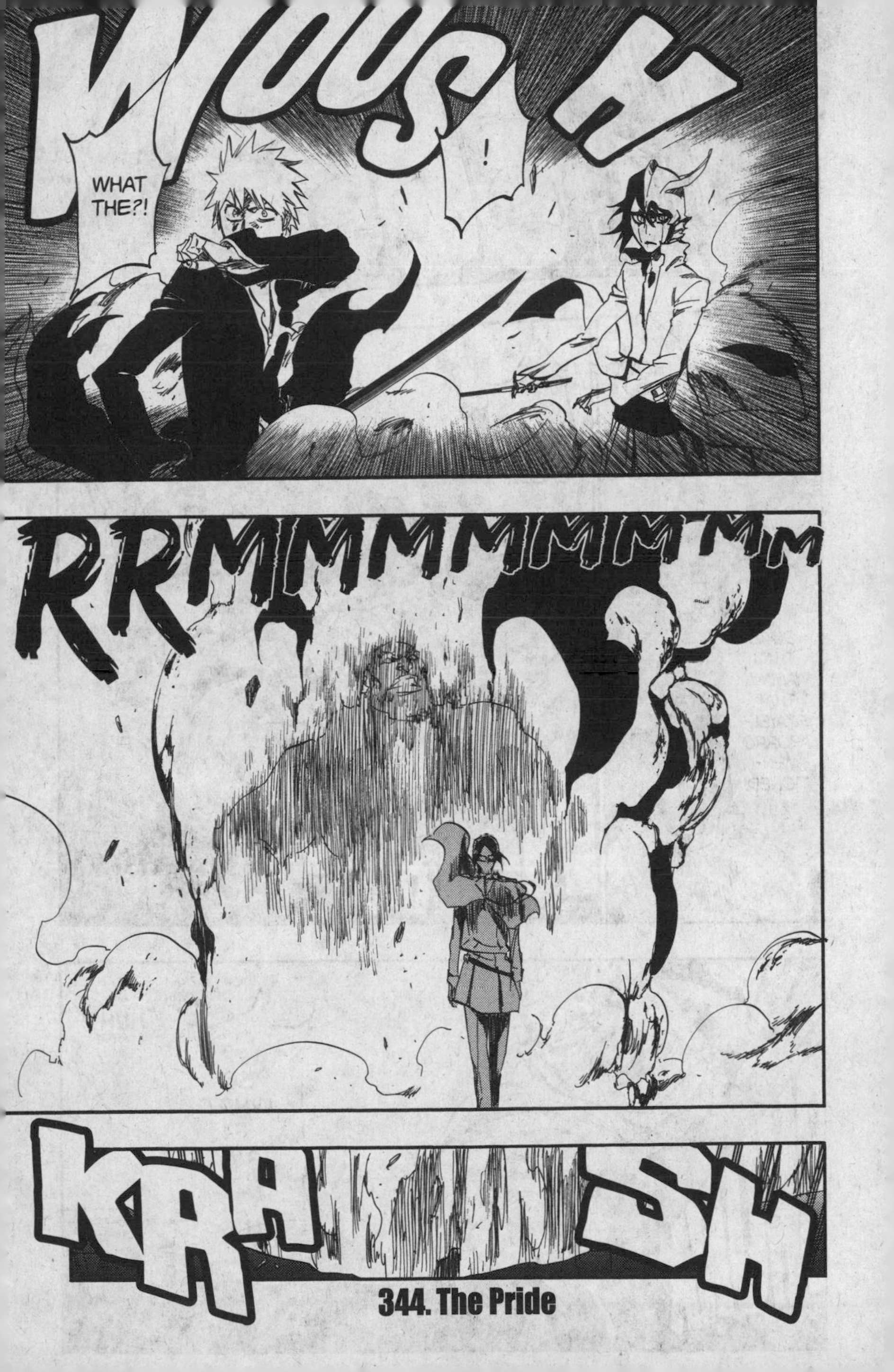
WOOSH
WHAT THE?!
!
RRMMMMMMMMM
KRAAASH

344. The Pride

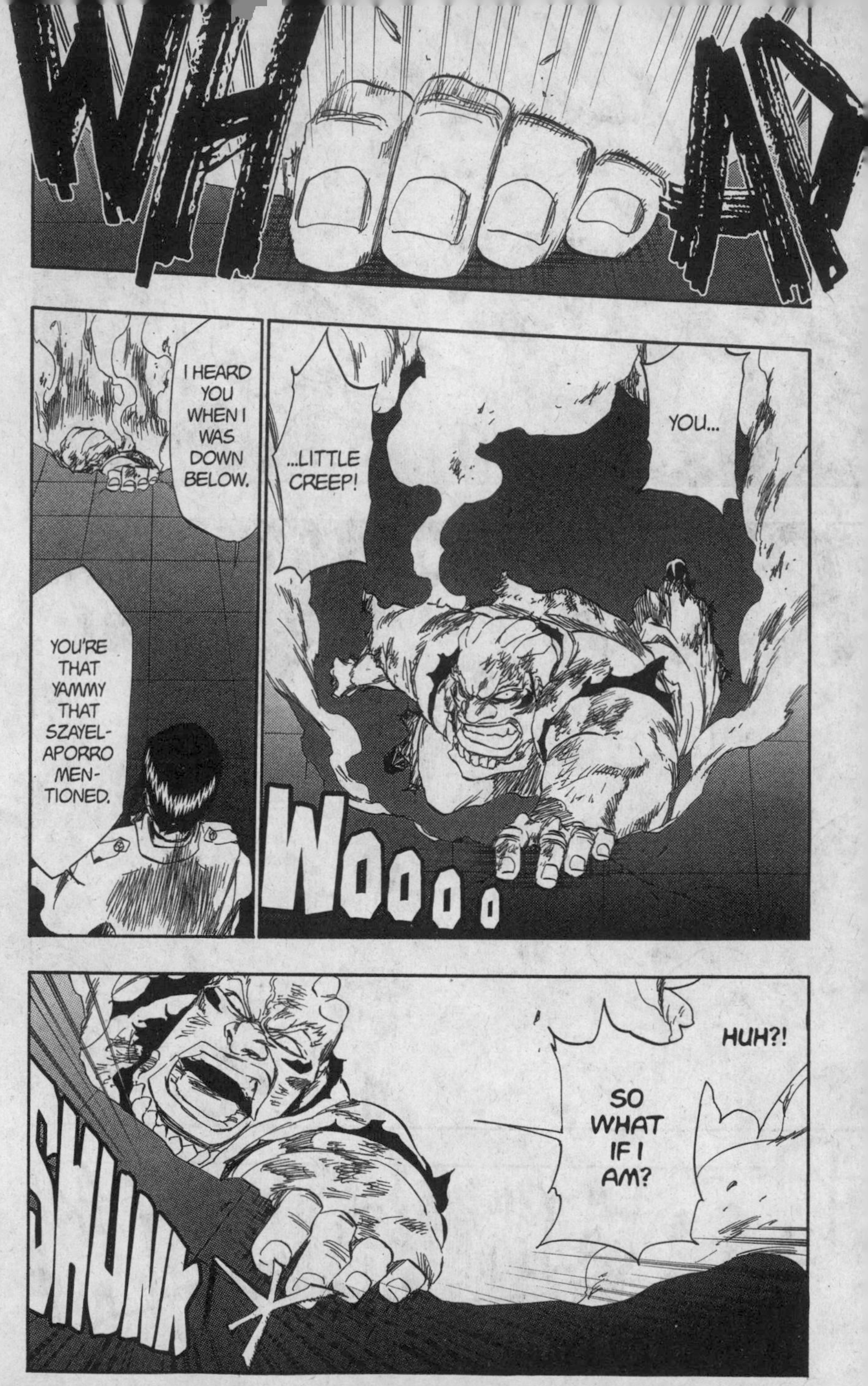
WHAD
YOU...
...LITTLE CREEP!
WOOOO
I HEARD YOU WHEN I WAS DOWN BELOW.
YOU'RE THAT YAMMY THAT SZAYEL-
APORRO MENTIONED.
HUH?!
SO WHAT IF I AM?
SHUNK

READ THIS WAY

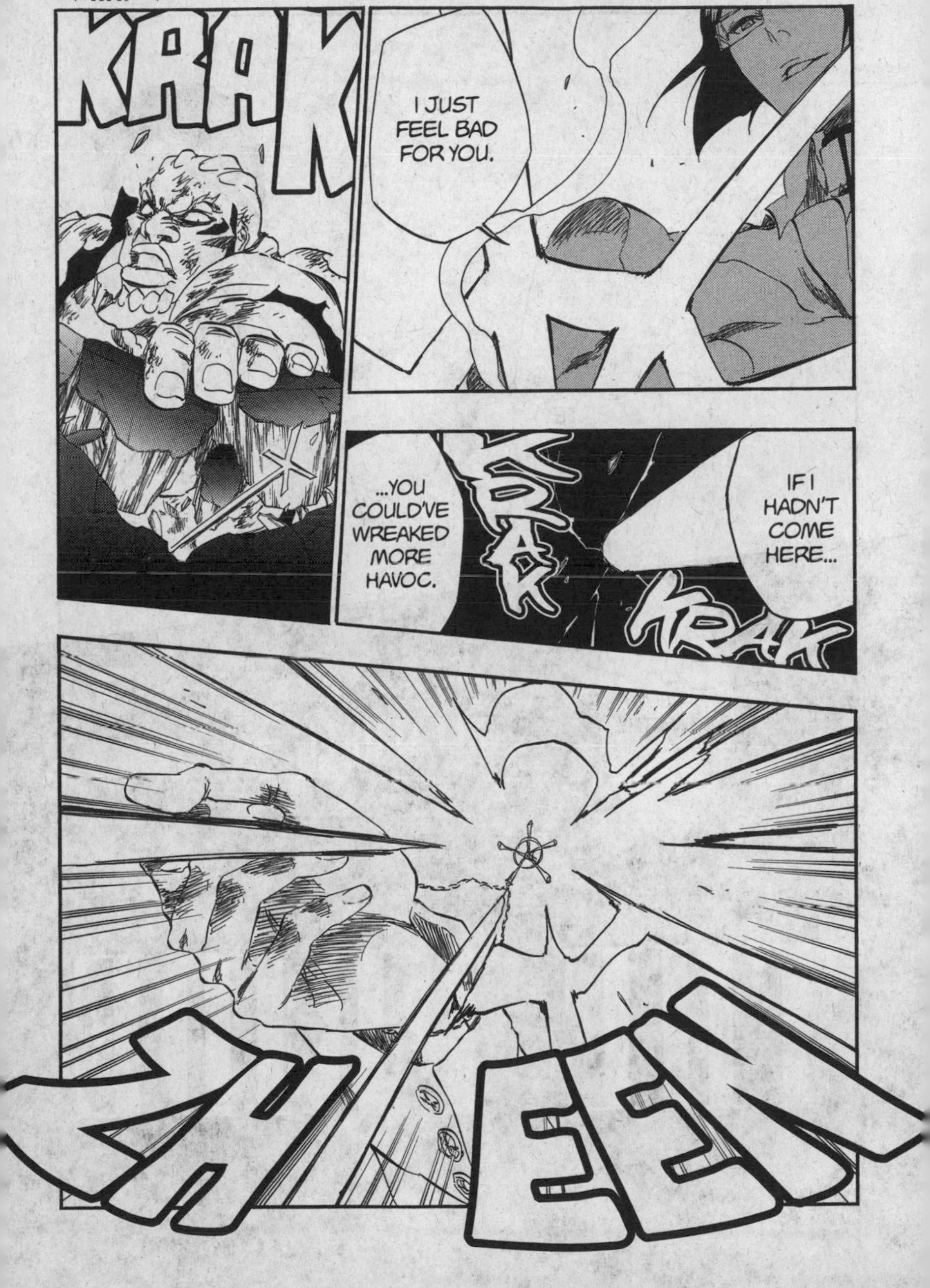

I JUST FEEL BAD FOR YOU.
IF I HADN'T COME HERE...
...YOU COULD'VE WREAKED MORE HAVOC.
KRAK
KRAK
KRAK

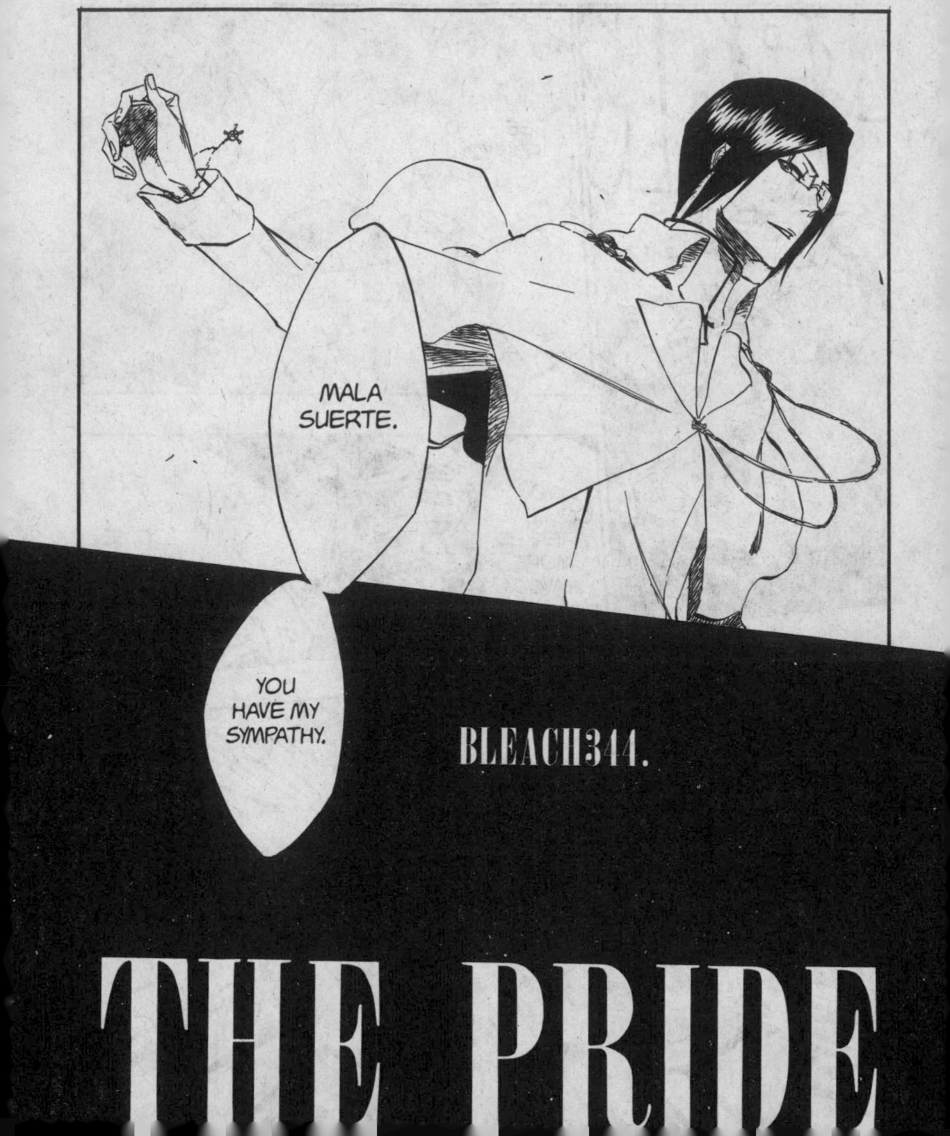
MALA SUERTE.
YOU HAVE MY SYMPATHY.
BLEACH344.
THE PRIDE

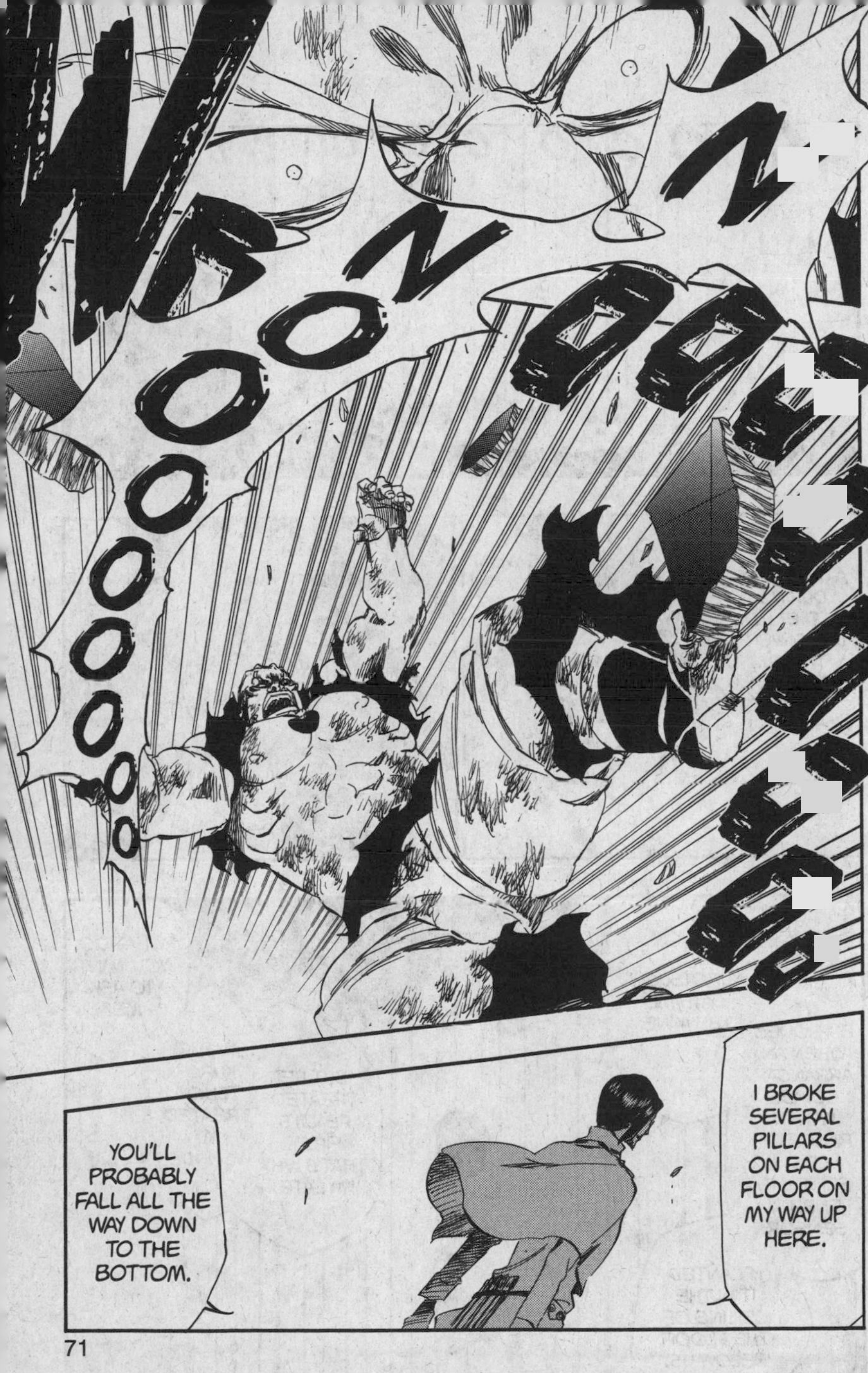
I BROKE SEVERAL PILLARS ON EACH FLOOR ON MY WAY UP HERE.
YOU'LL PROBABLY FALL ALL THE WAY DOWN TO THE BOTTOM.

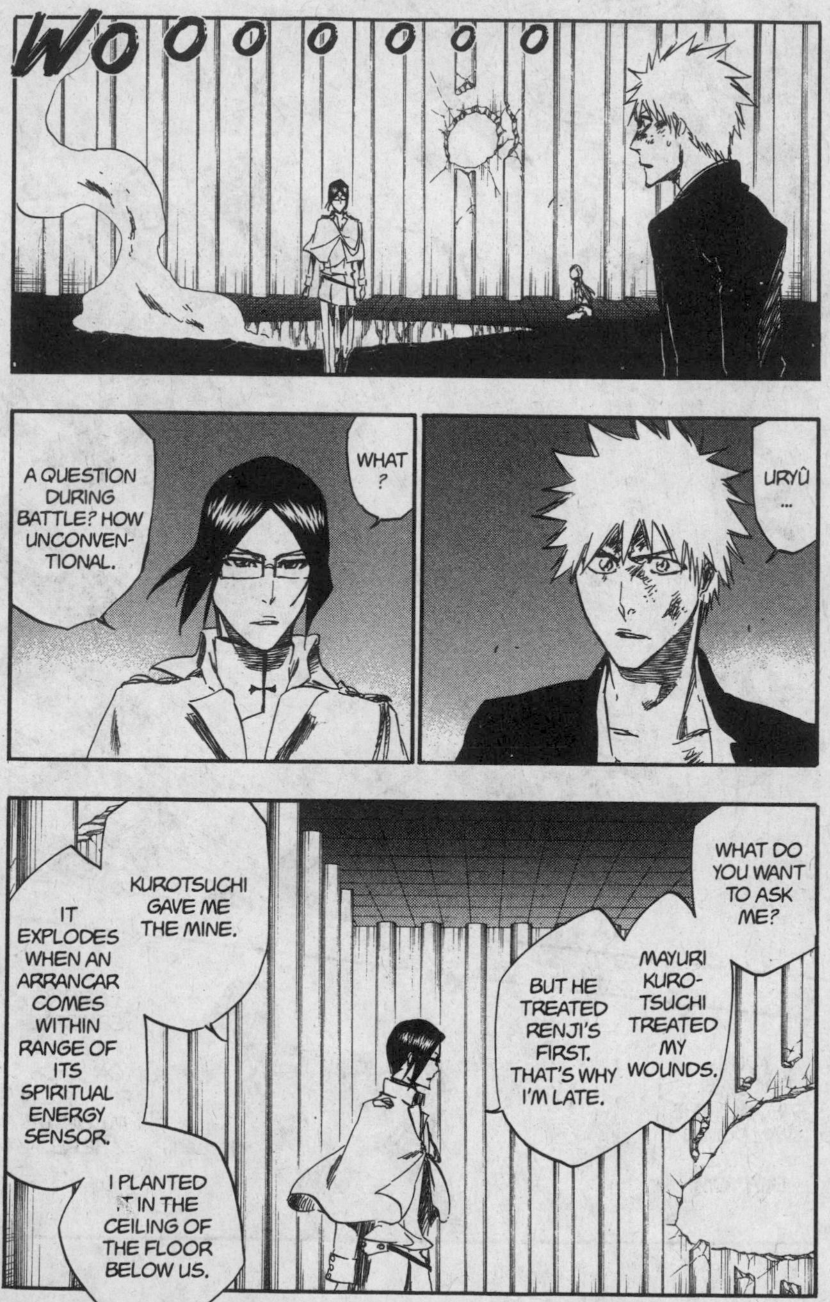
WOOOOOOO
URYÛ ...
WHAT ?
A QUESTION DURING BATTLE? HOW UNCONVENTIONAL.
WHAT DO YOU WANT TO ASK ME?
MAYURI KUROTSUCHI TREATED MY WOUNDS.
BUT HE TREATED RENJI'S FIRST. THAT'S WHY I'M LATE.
KUROTSUCHI GAVE ME THE MINE.
IT EXPLODES WHEN AN ARRANCAR COMES WITHIN RANGE OF ITS SPIRITUAL ENERGY SENSOR.
I PLANTED IT IN THE CEILING OF THE FLOOR BELOW US.

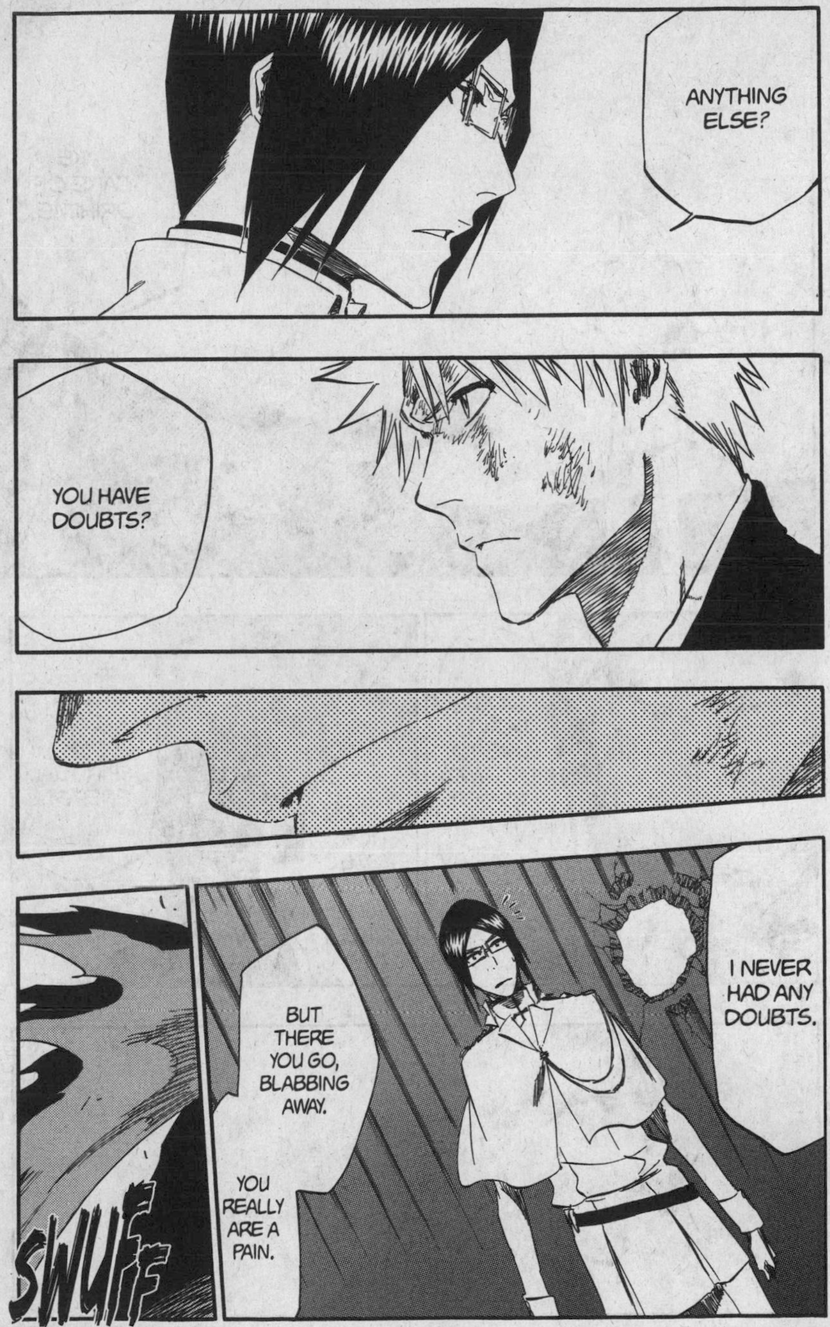
ANYTHING ELSE?
YOU HAVE DOUBTS?
I NEVER HAD ANY DOUBTS.
BUT THERE YOU GO, BLABBING AWAY.
YOU REALLY ARE A PAIN.
SWUF

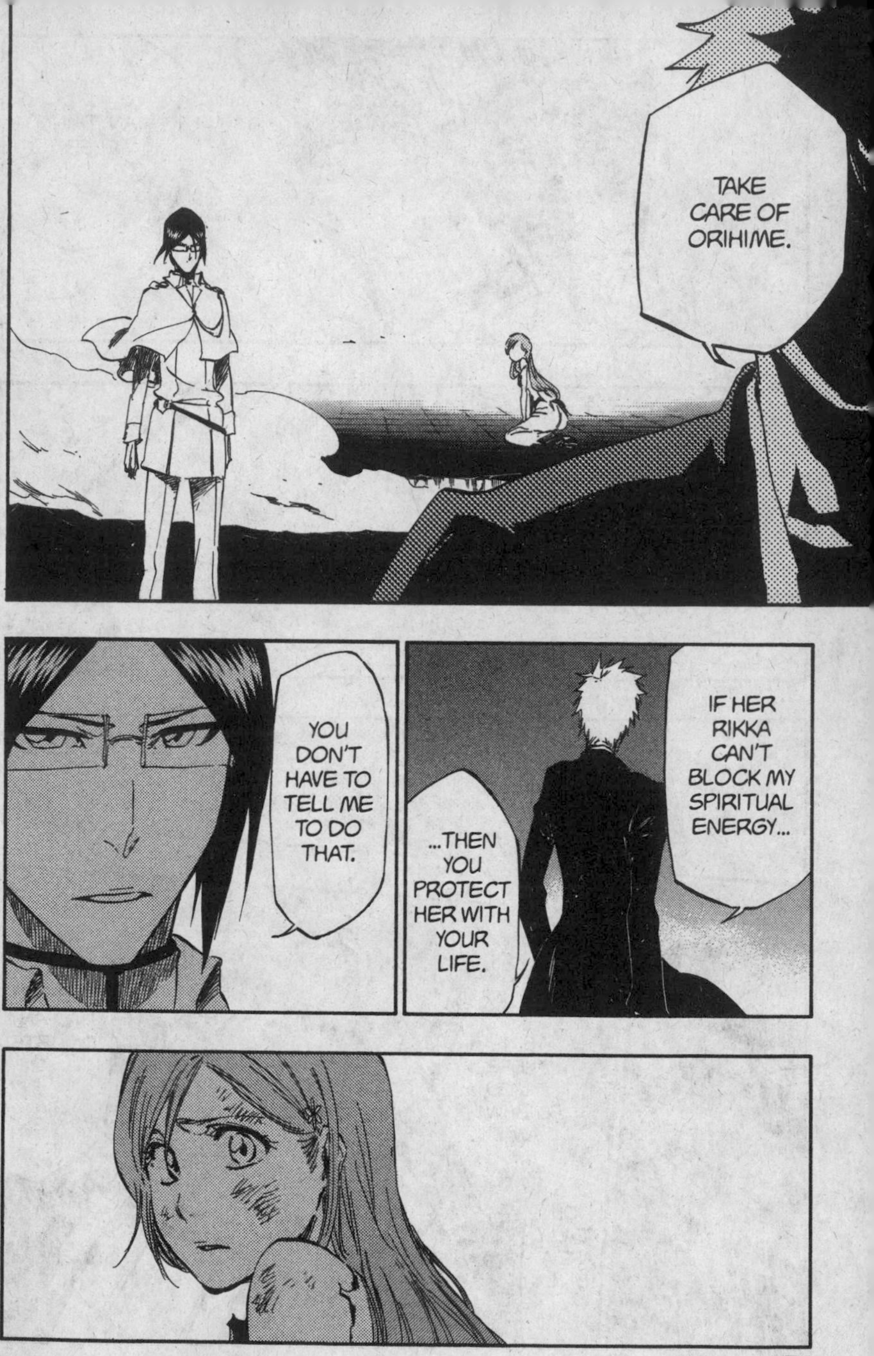
TAKE CARE OF ORIHIME.
IF HER RIKKA CAN'T BLOCK MY SPIRITUAL ENERGY...
...THEN YOU PROTECT HER WITH YOUR LIFE.
YOU DON'T HAVE TO TELL ME TO DO THAT.

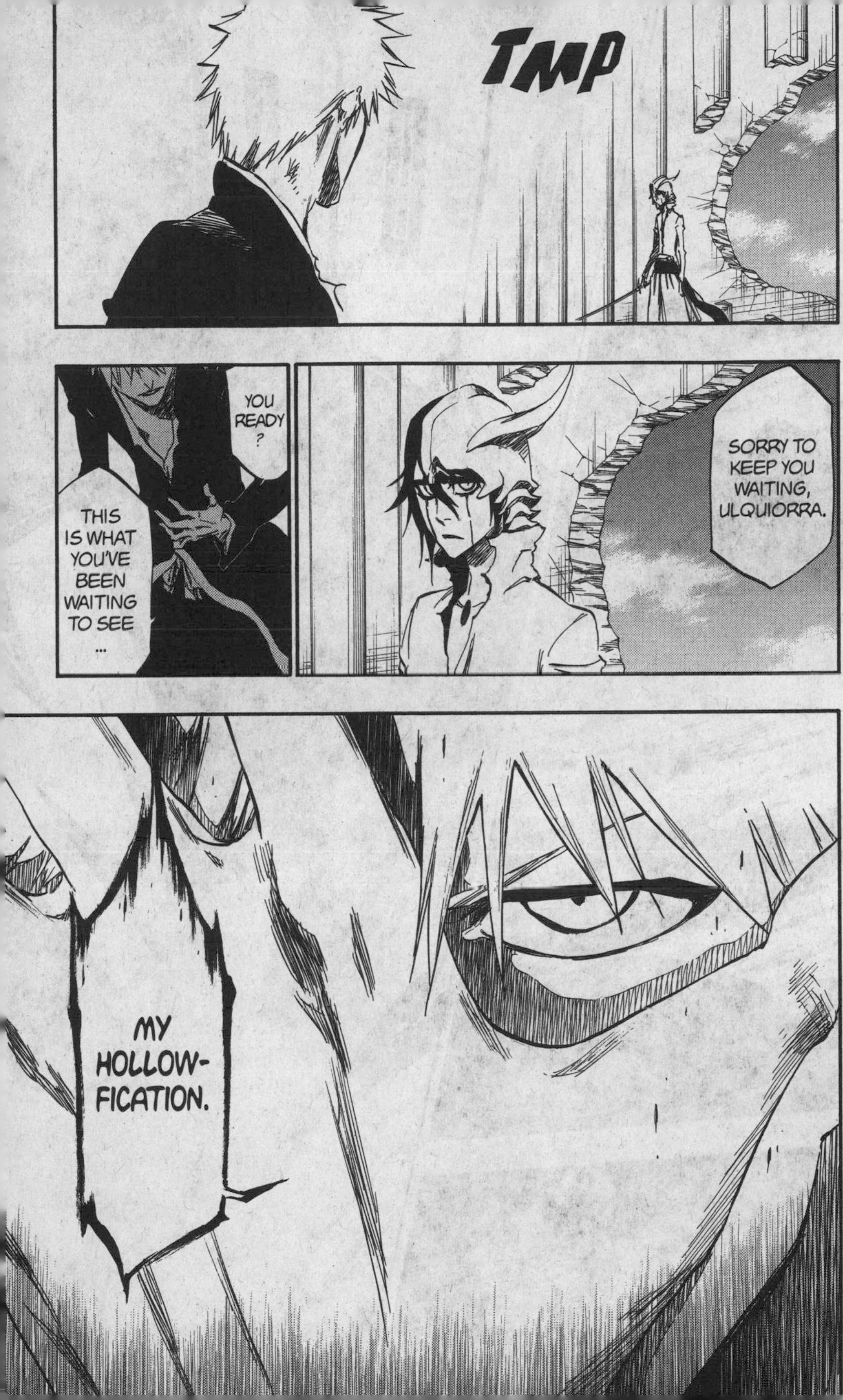
TMP
SORRY TO KEEP YOU WAITING, ULQUIORRA.
YOU READY?
THIS IS WHAT YOU'VE BEEN WAITING TO SEE...
MY HOLLOW-FICATION.

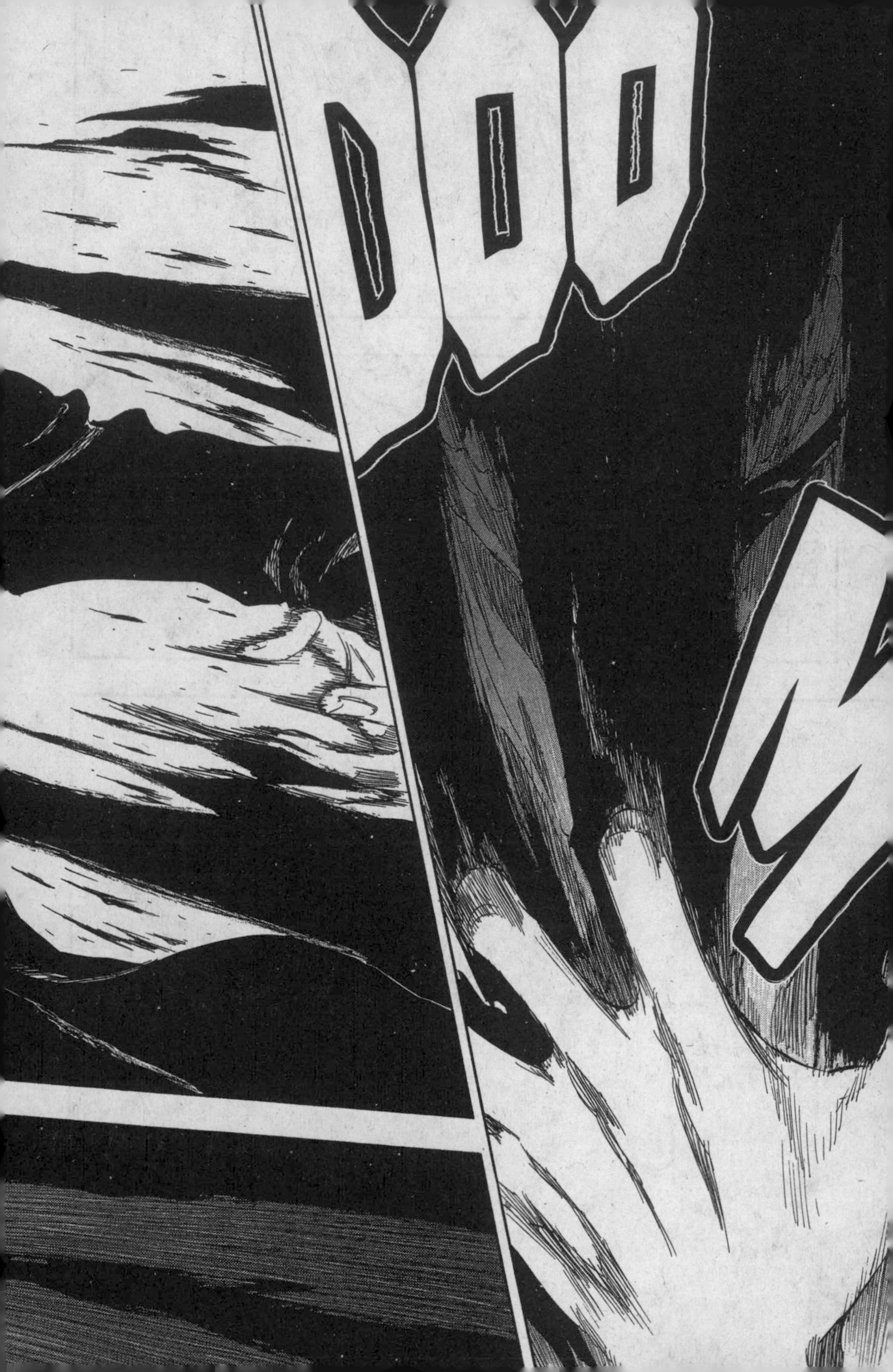

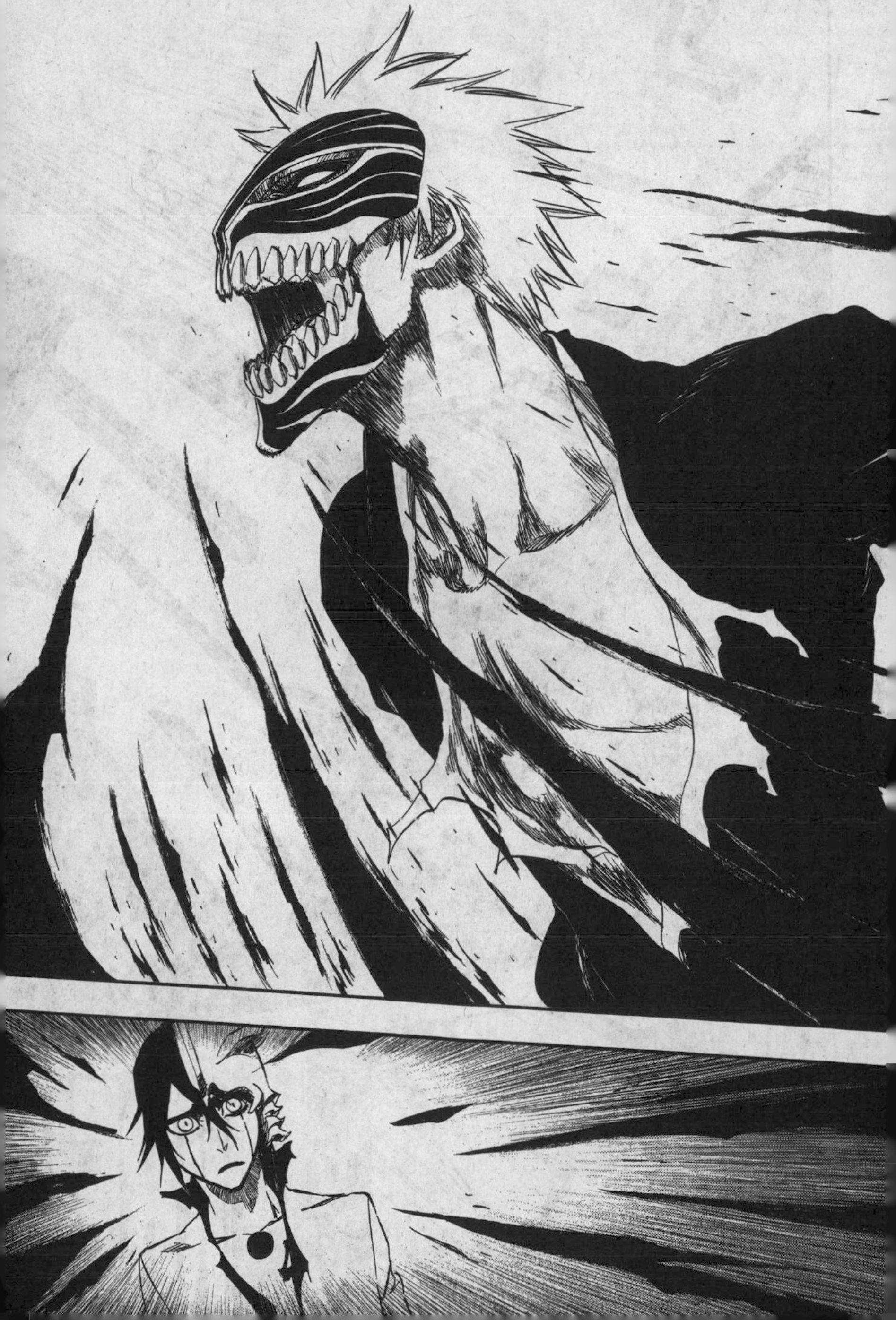

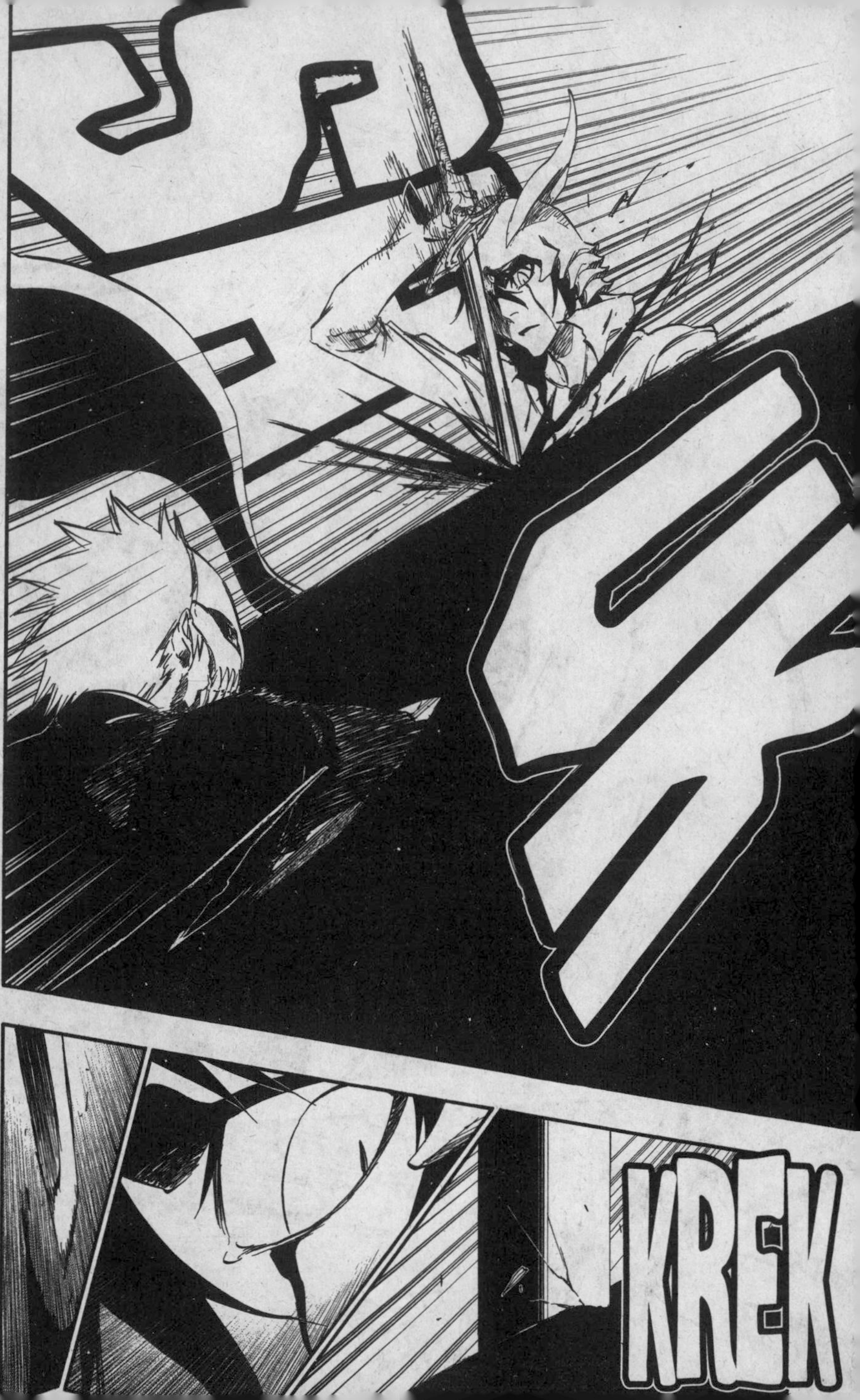
KREK

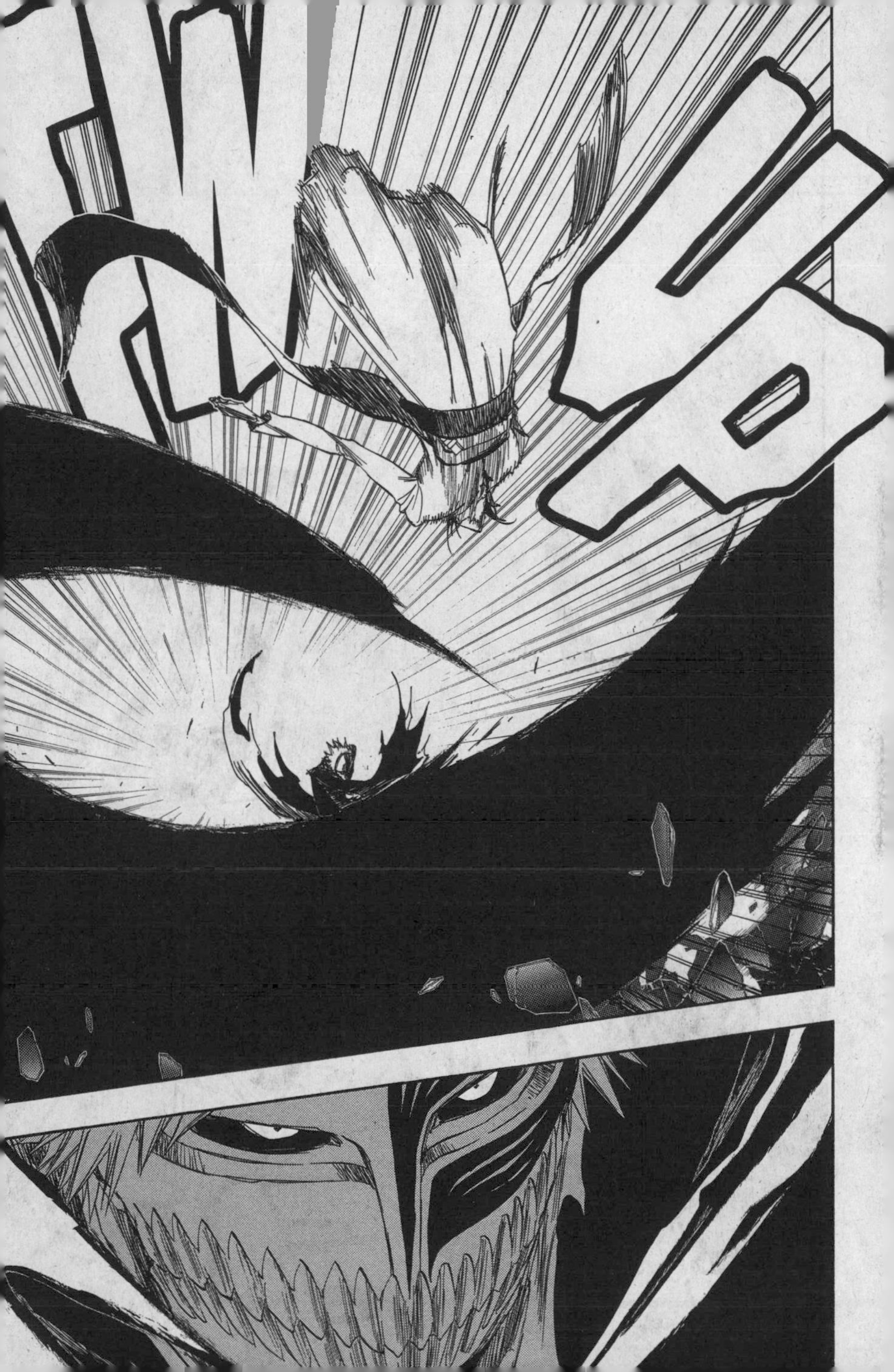

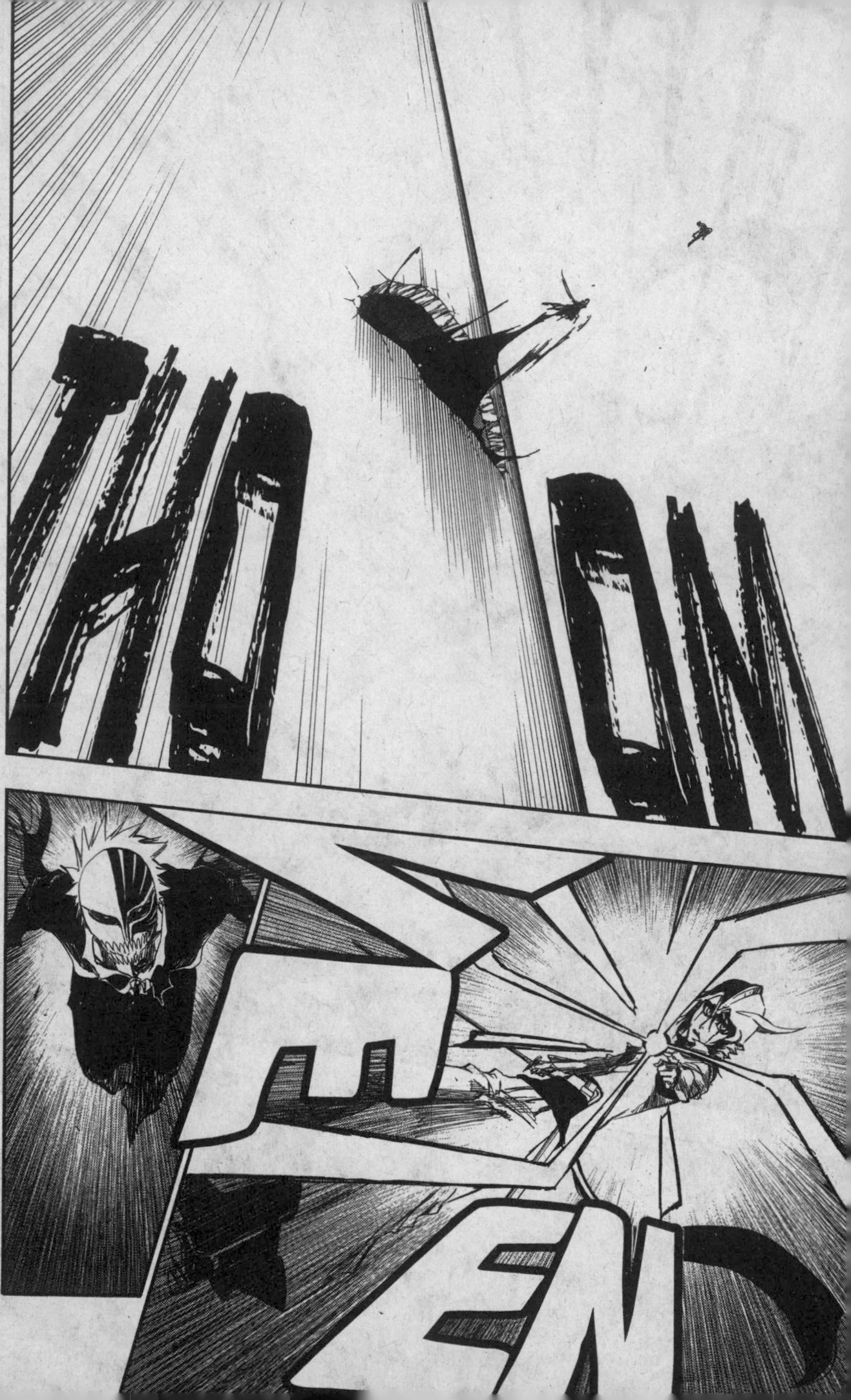
THOOM

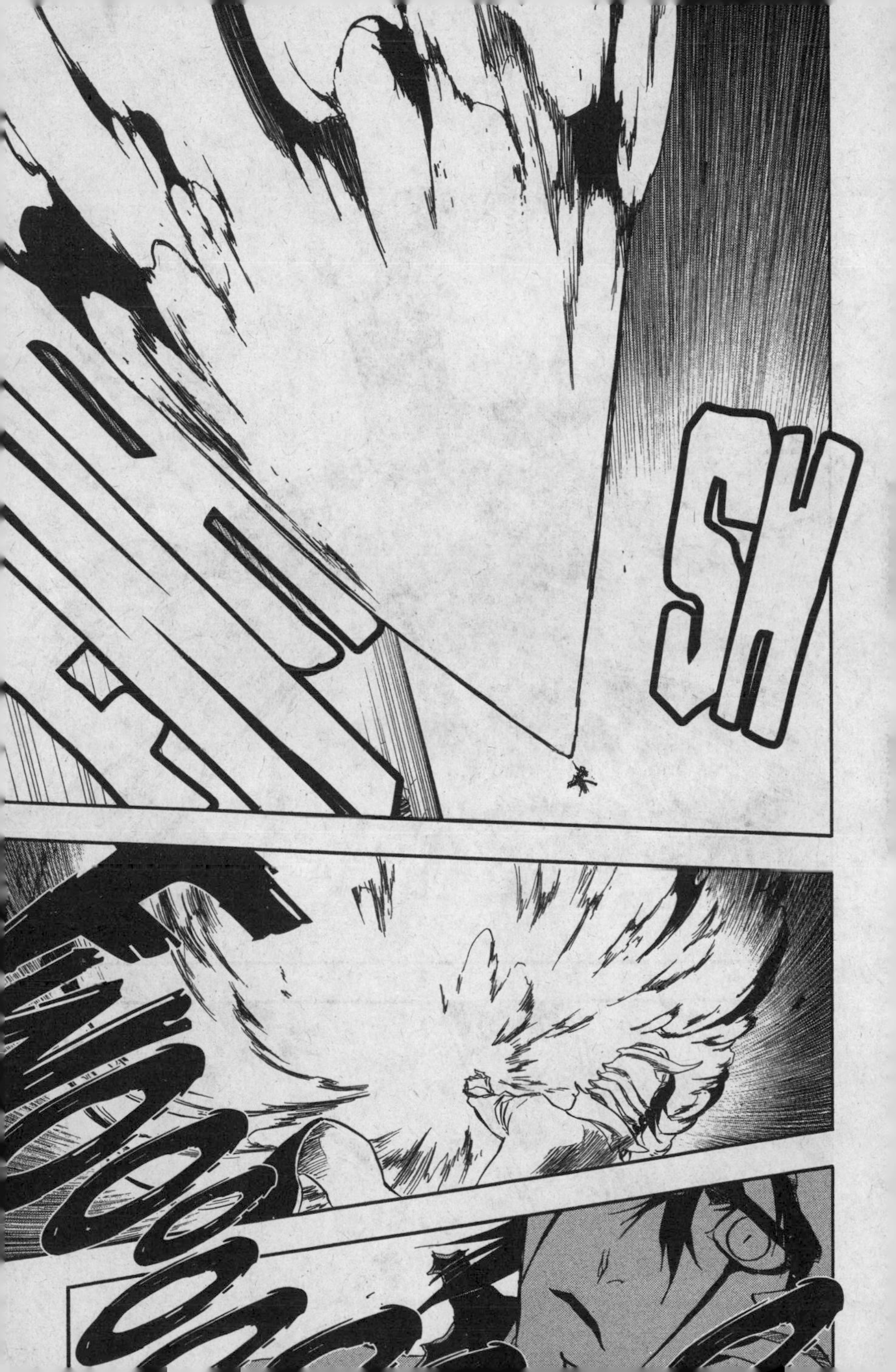
SH
FWOOOOOO

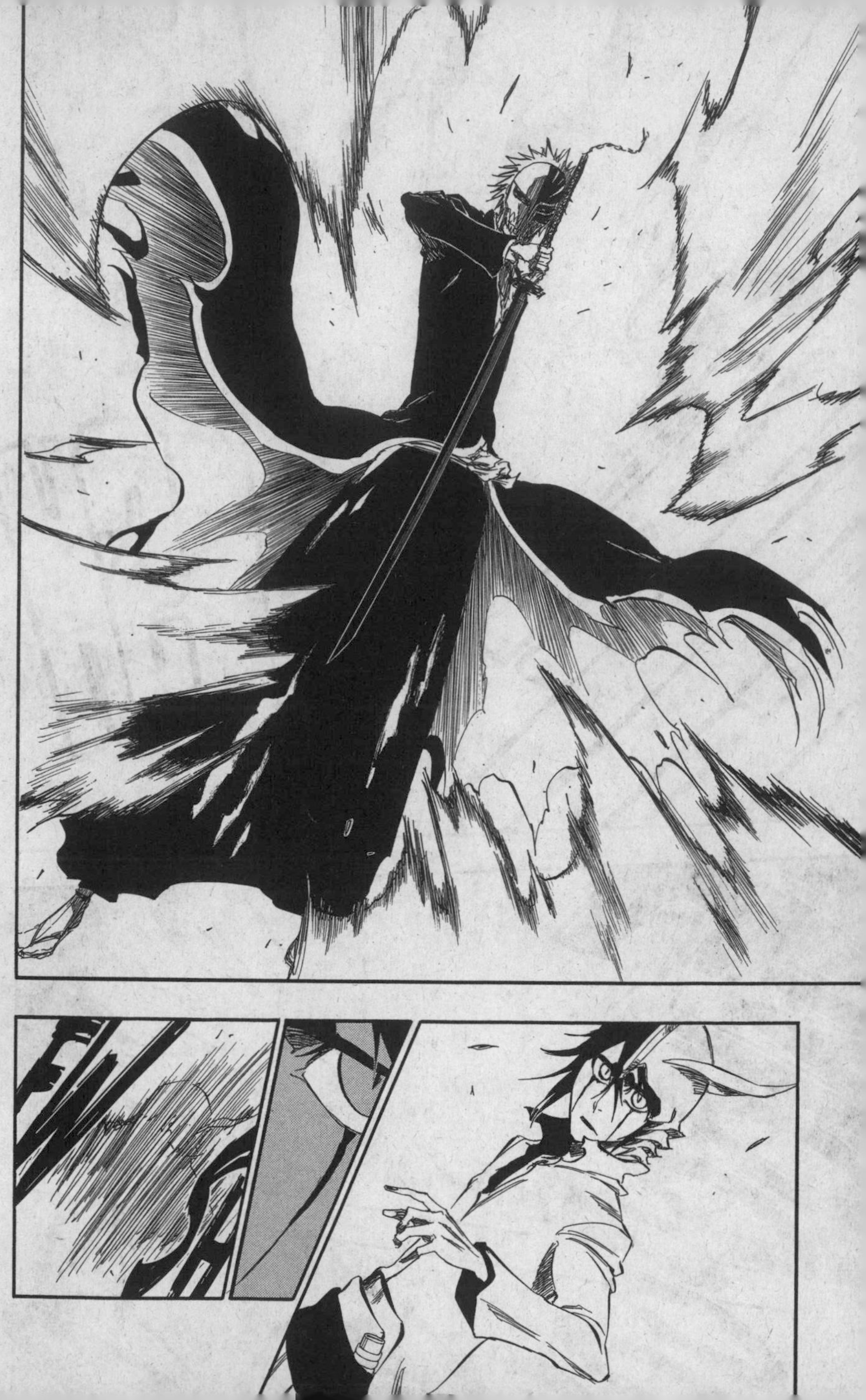

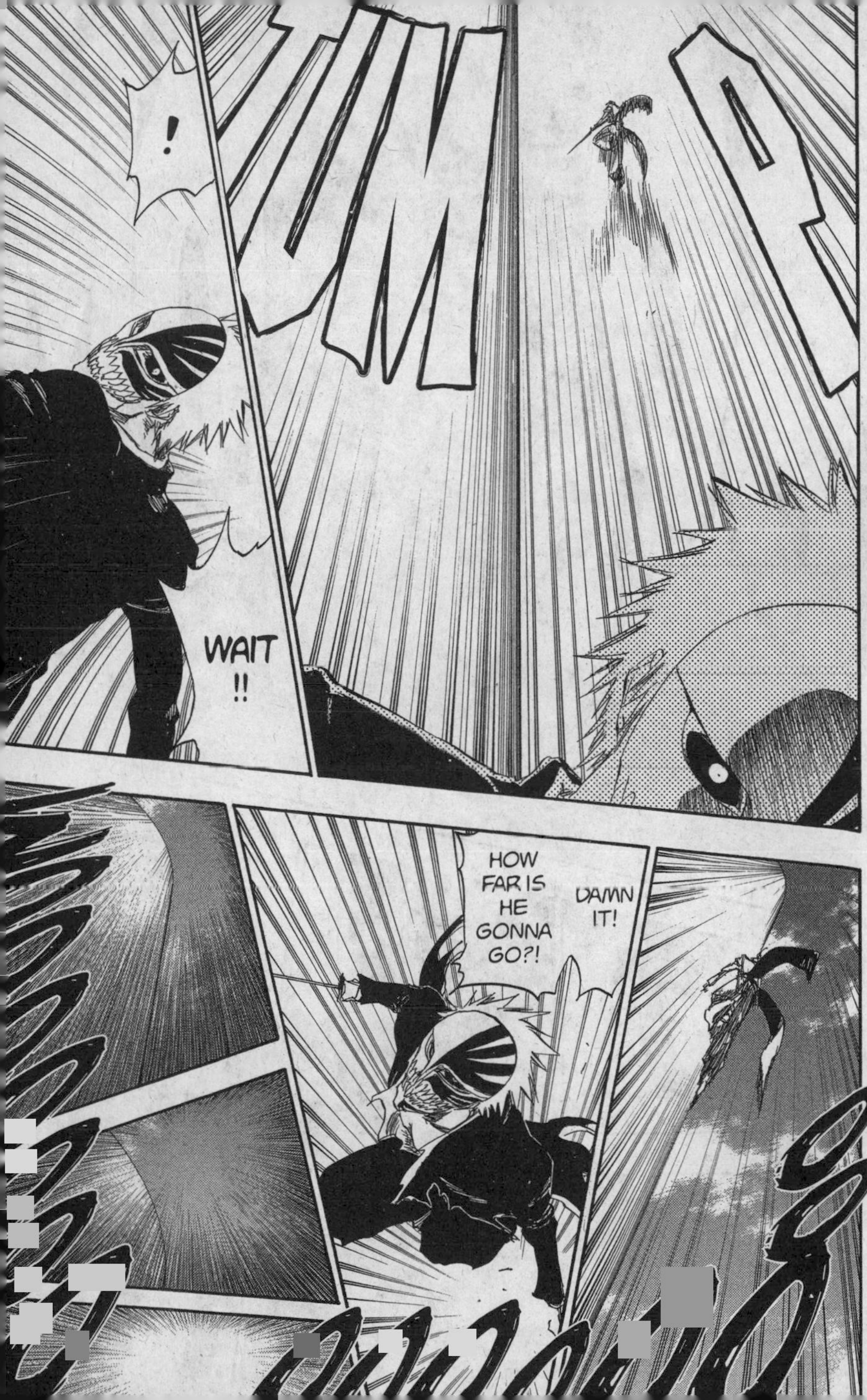
!
WAIT !!
DAMN IT!
HOW FAR IS HE GONNA GO?!

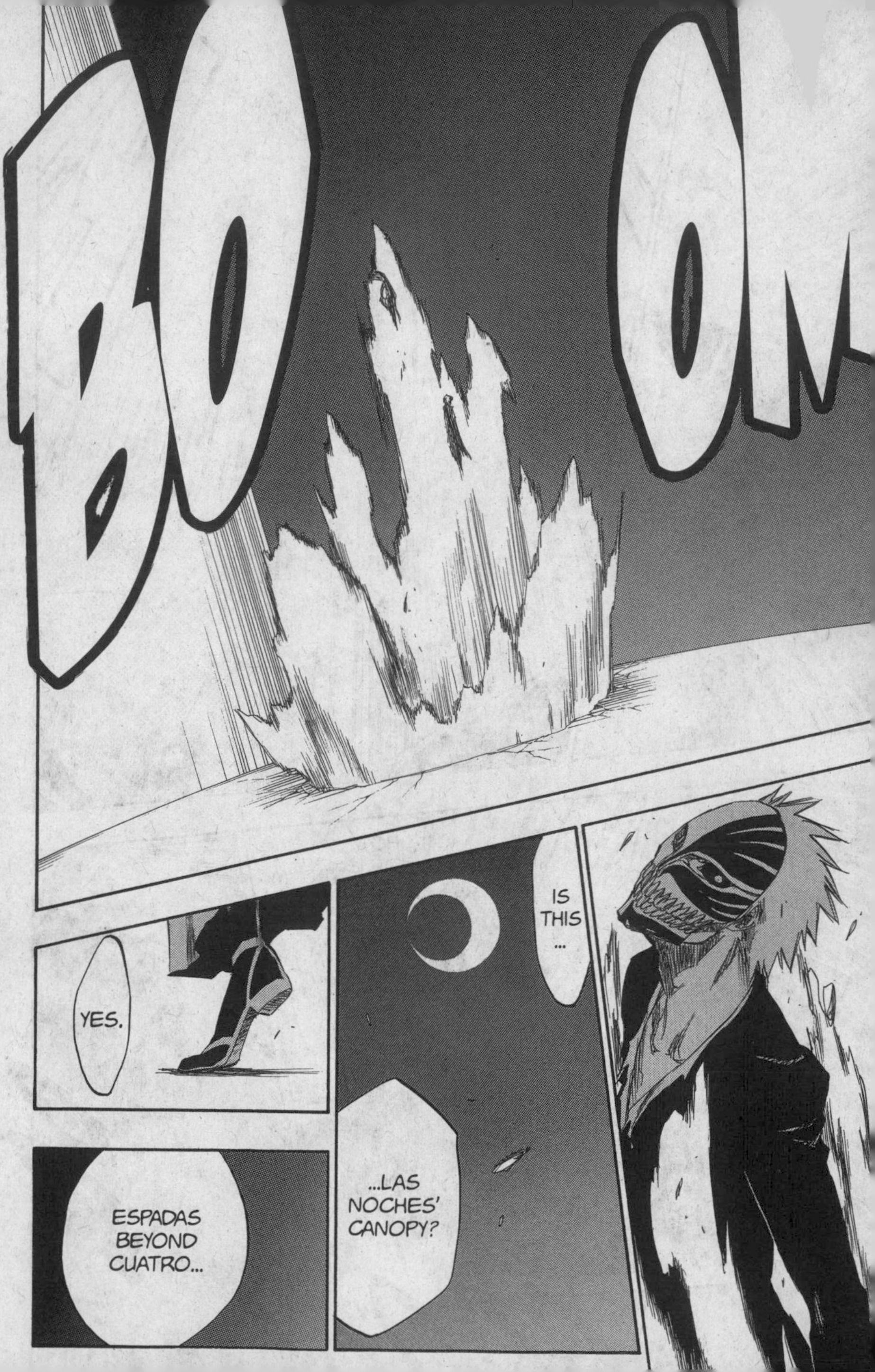
BOOM
IS THIS...
...LAS NOCHES' CANOPY?
YES.
ESPADAS BEYOND CUATRO...

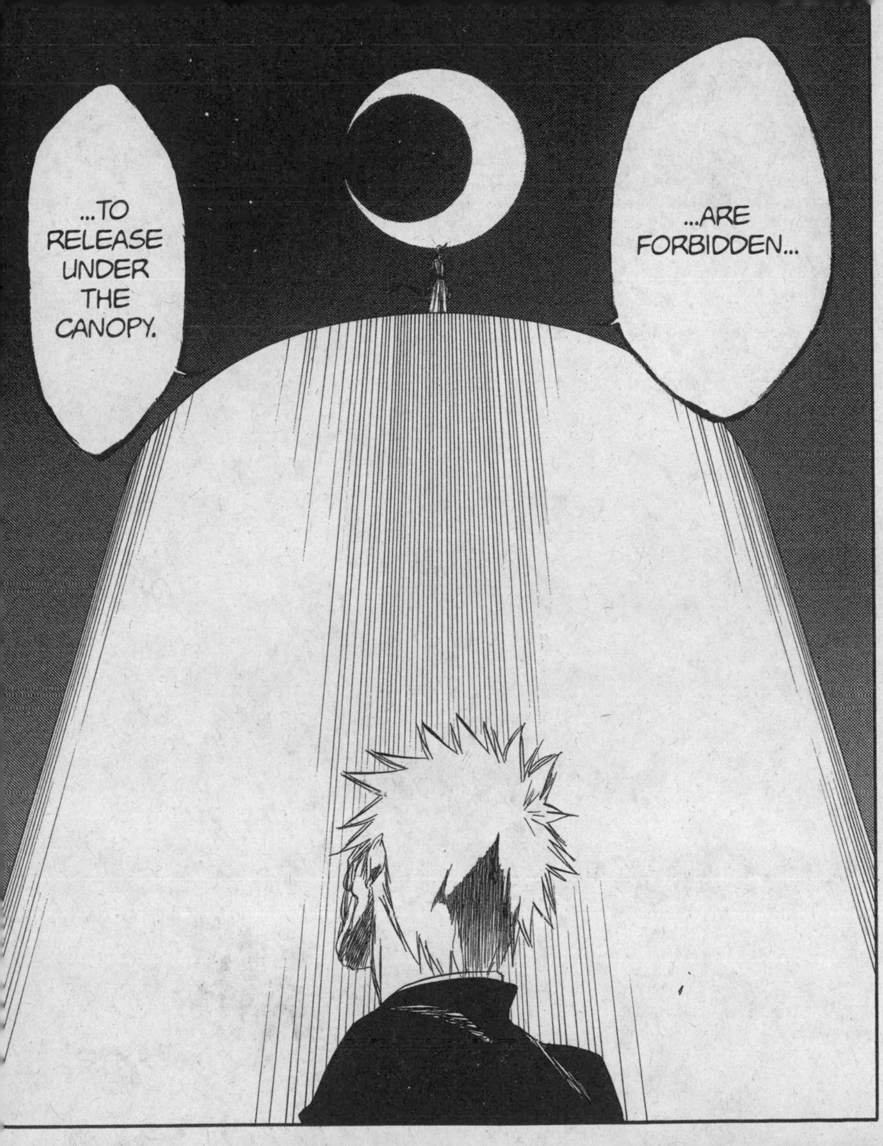
...ARE FORBIDDEN...
...TO RELEASE UNDER THE CANOPY.
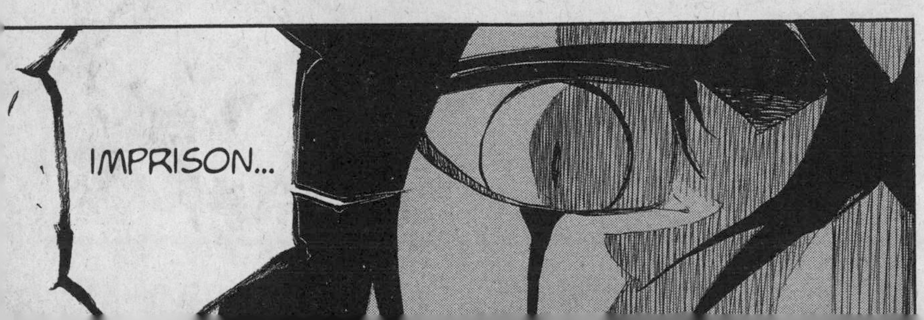
IMPRISON...

the
Pride

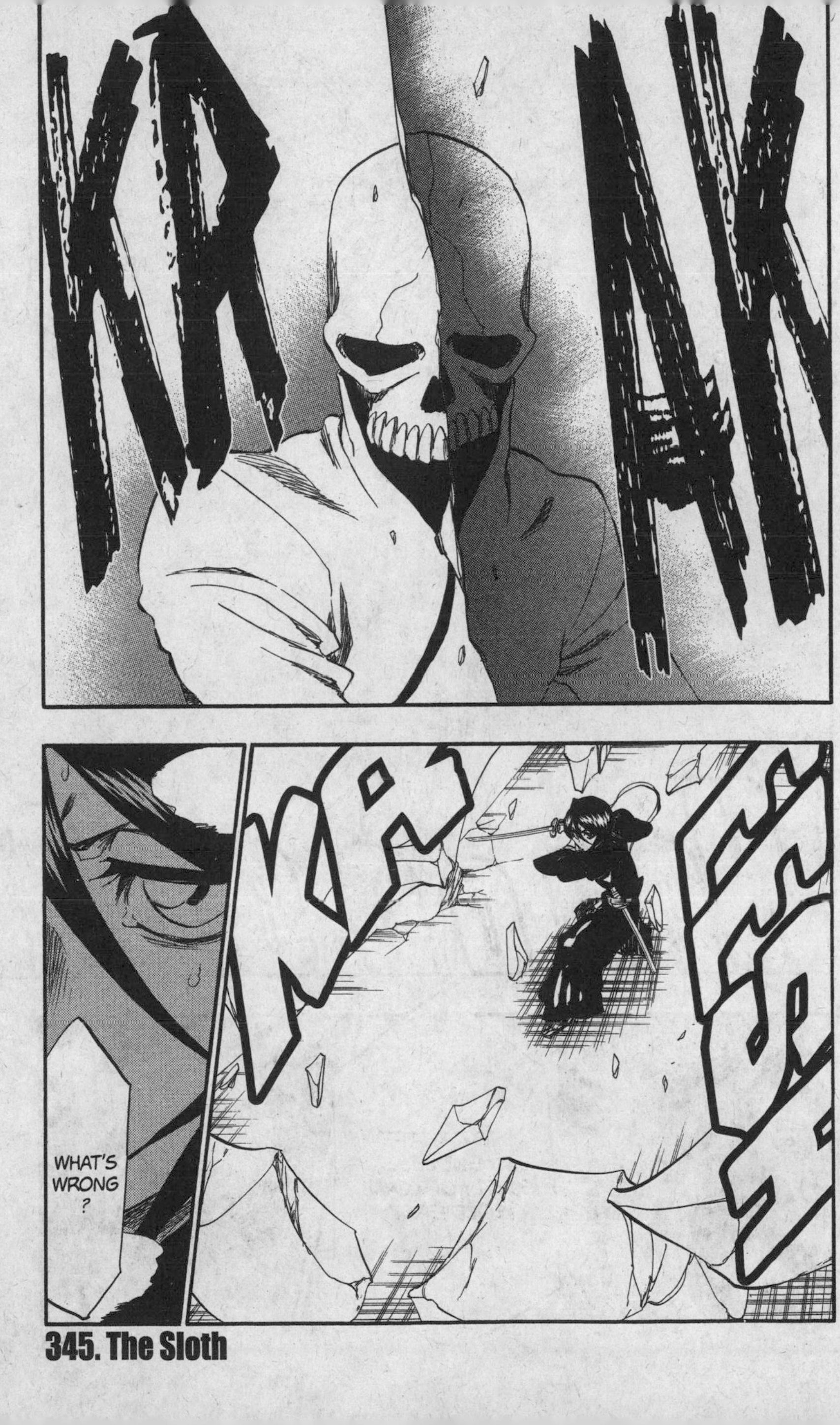
KRAK
WHAT'S WRONG?

345. The Sloth

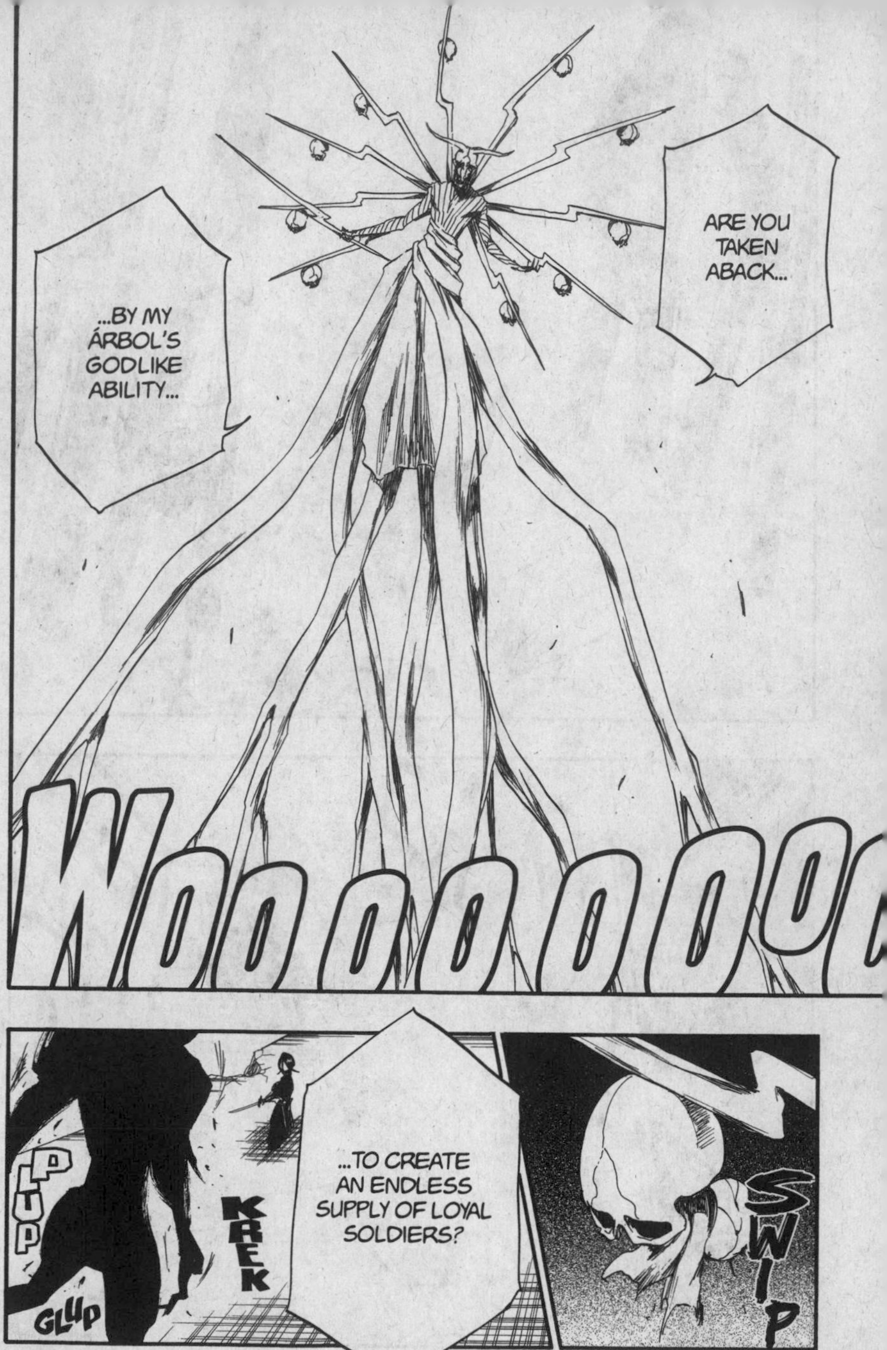
ARE YOU TAKEN ABACK...
...BY MY ÁRBOL'S GODLIKE ABILITY...
WOOOOOOO
SWIP
...TO CREATE AN ENDLESS SUPPLY OF LOYAL SOLDIERS?
KREK
LUP
GLUP

READ THIS WAY

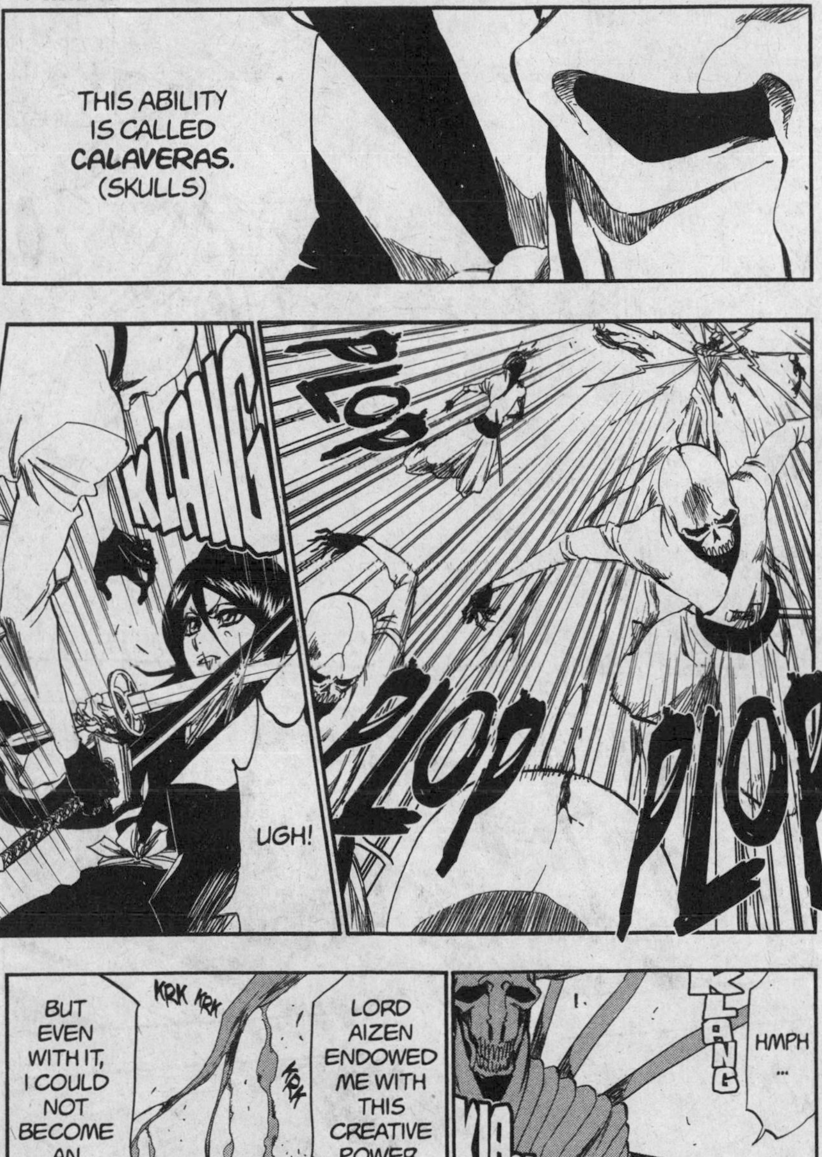

THIS ABILITY IS CALLED CALAVERAS. (SKULLS)
PLOP
PLOP
PLOP
KLANG
UGH!
KLANG
HMPH ...
KLANK
LORD AIZEN ENDOWED ME WITH THIS CREATIVE POWER.
KRK
KRK KRK
BUT EVEN WITH IT, I COULD NOT BECOME AN ESPADA.

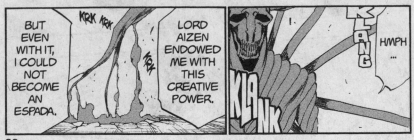

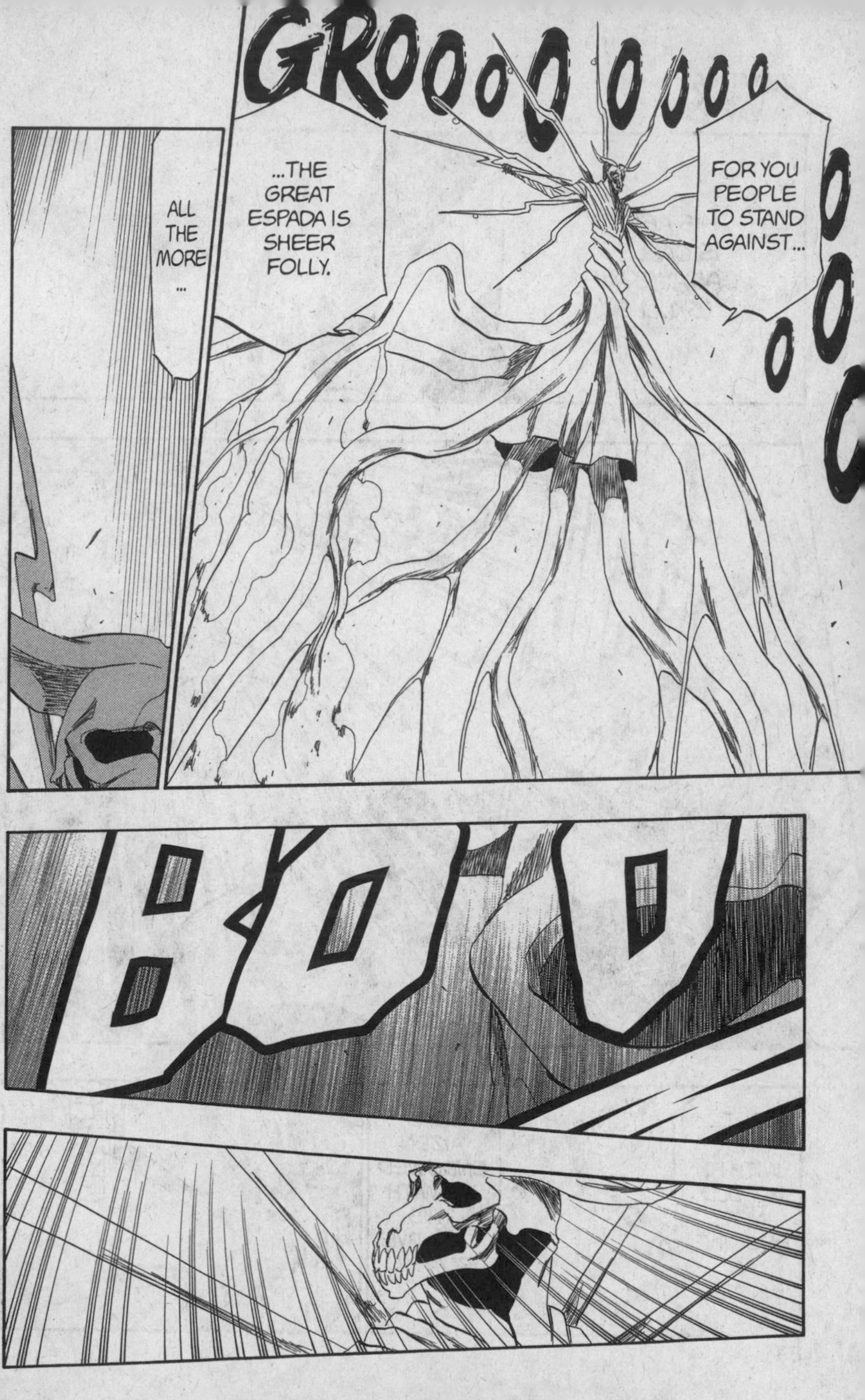
GROOOOOOOOOOOOOO
FOR YOU PEOPLE TO STAND AGAINST...
...THE GREAT ESPADA IS SHEER FOLLY.
ALL THE MORE ...

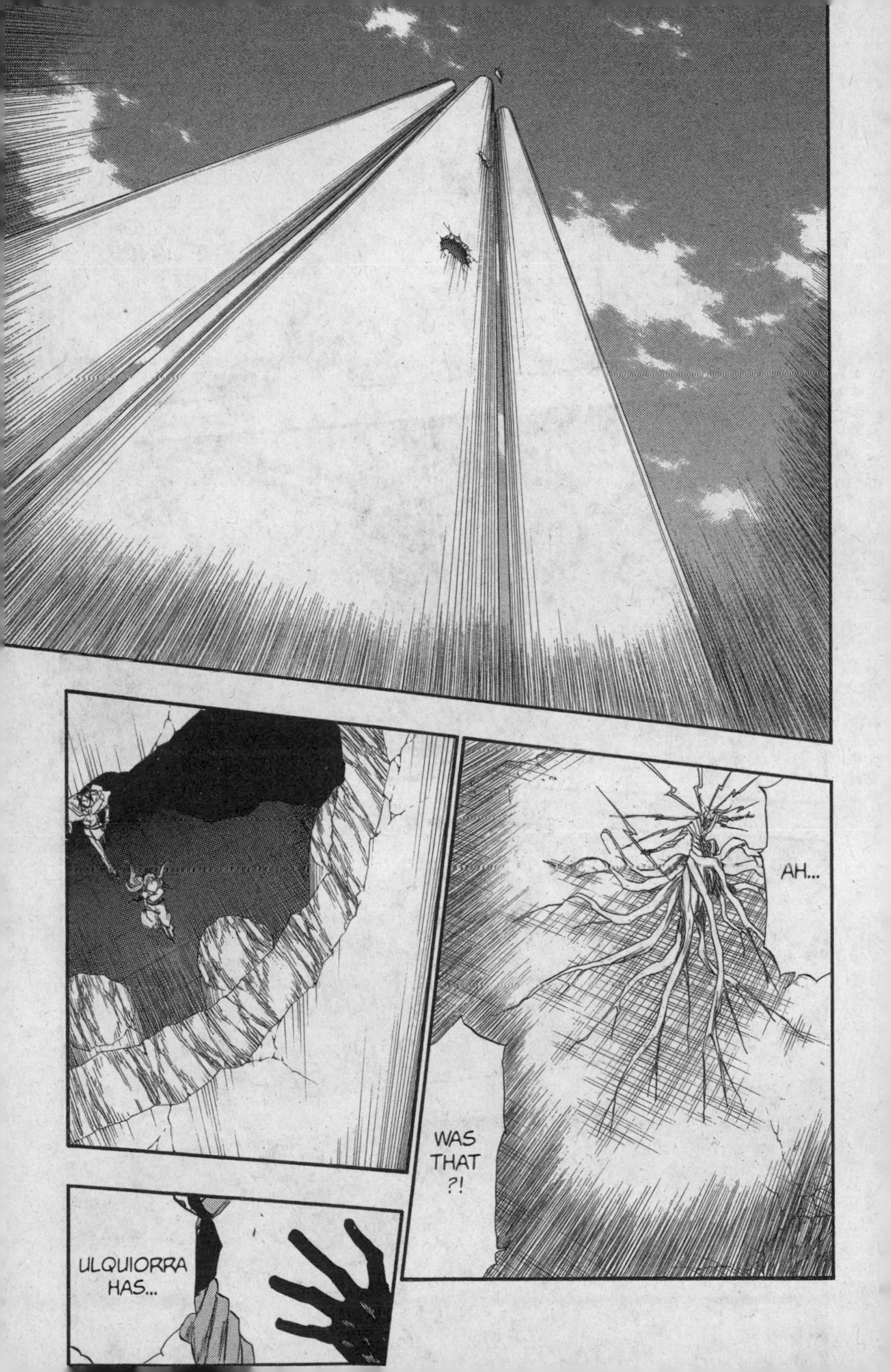
AH...
WAS THAT ?!
ULQUIORRA HAS...

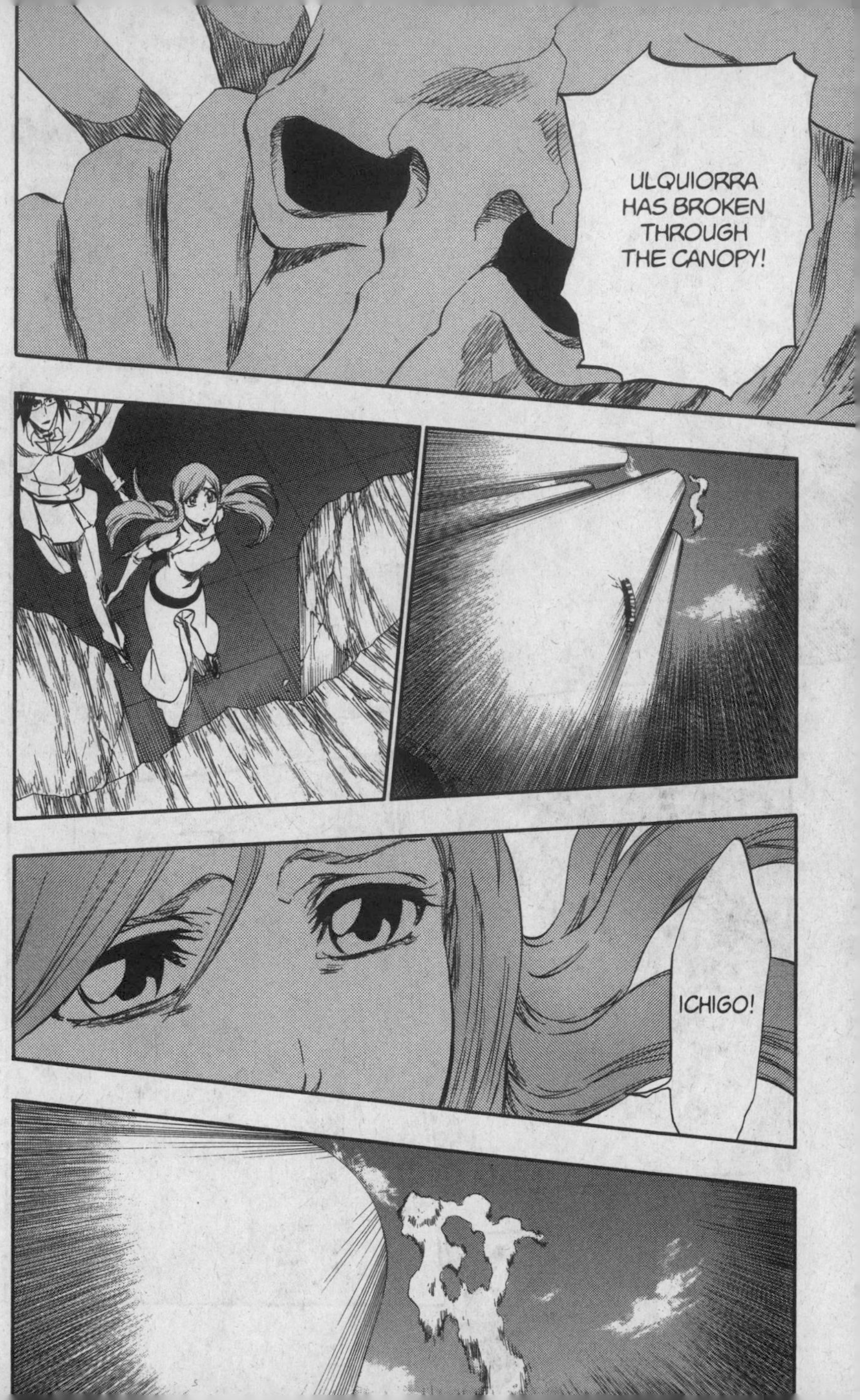
ULQUIORRA HAS BROKEN THROUGH THE CANOPY!
ICHIGO!

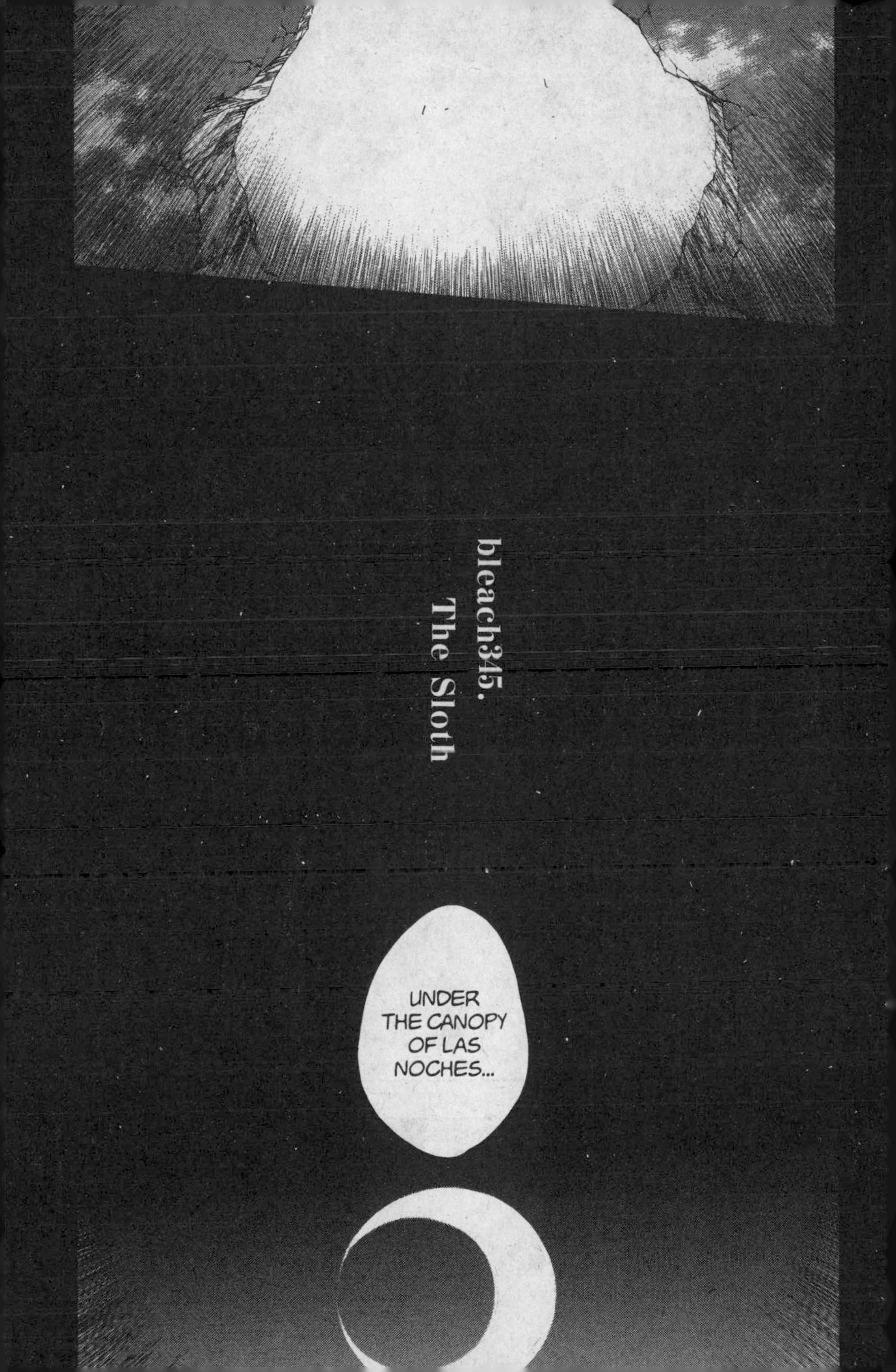
bleach345. The Sloth
UNDER THE CANOPY OF LAS NOCHES...

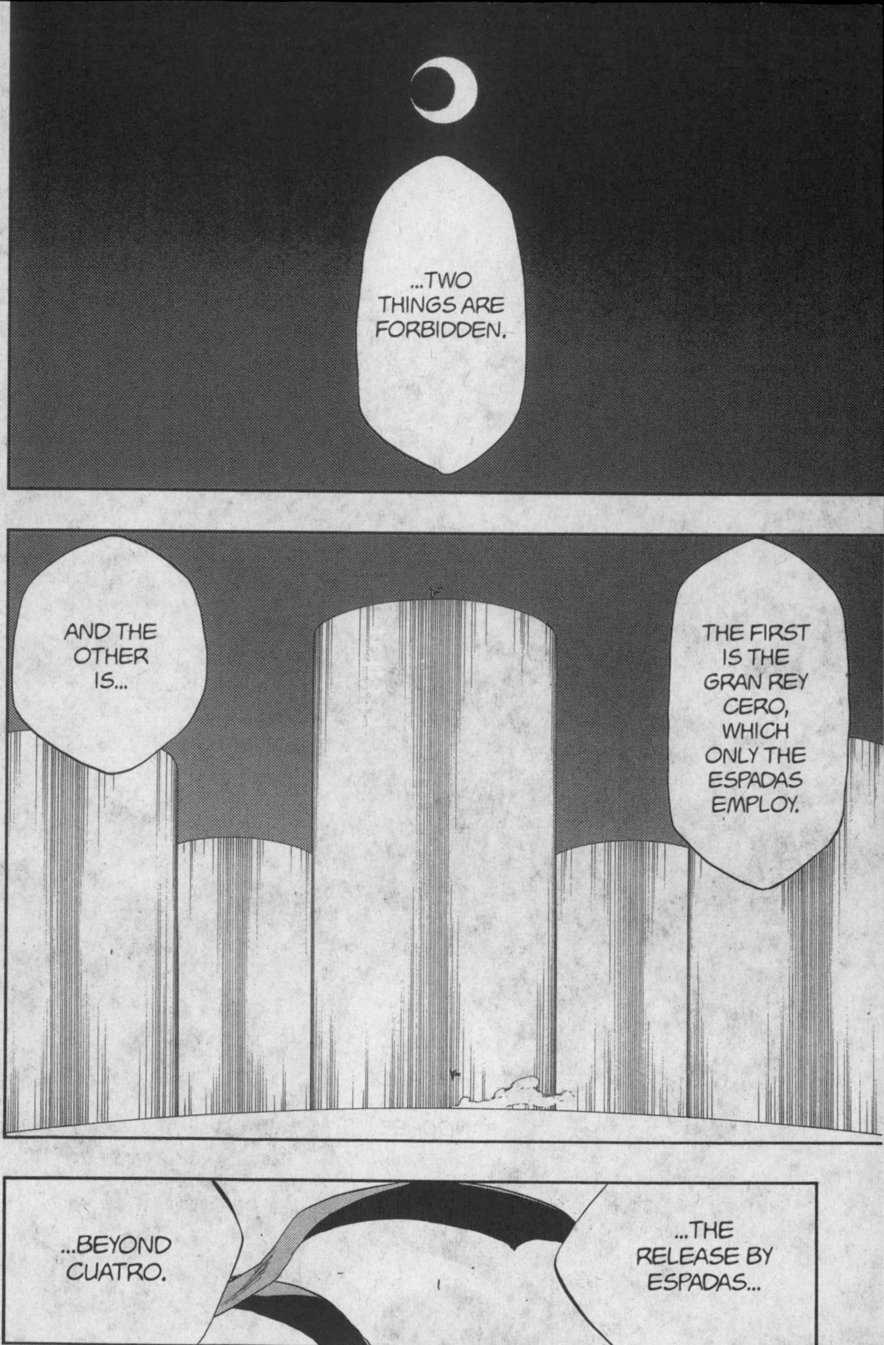
...TWO THINGS ARE FORBIDDEN.
THE FIRST IS THE GRAN REY CERO, WHICH ONLY THE ESPADAS EMPLOY.
AND THE OTHER IS...
...THE RELEASE BY ESPADAS...
...BEYOND CUATRO.

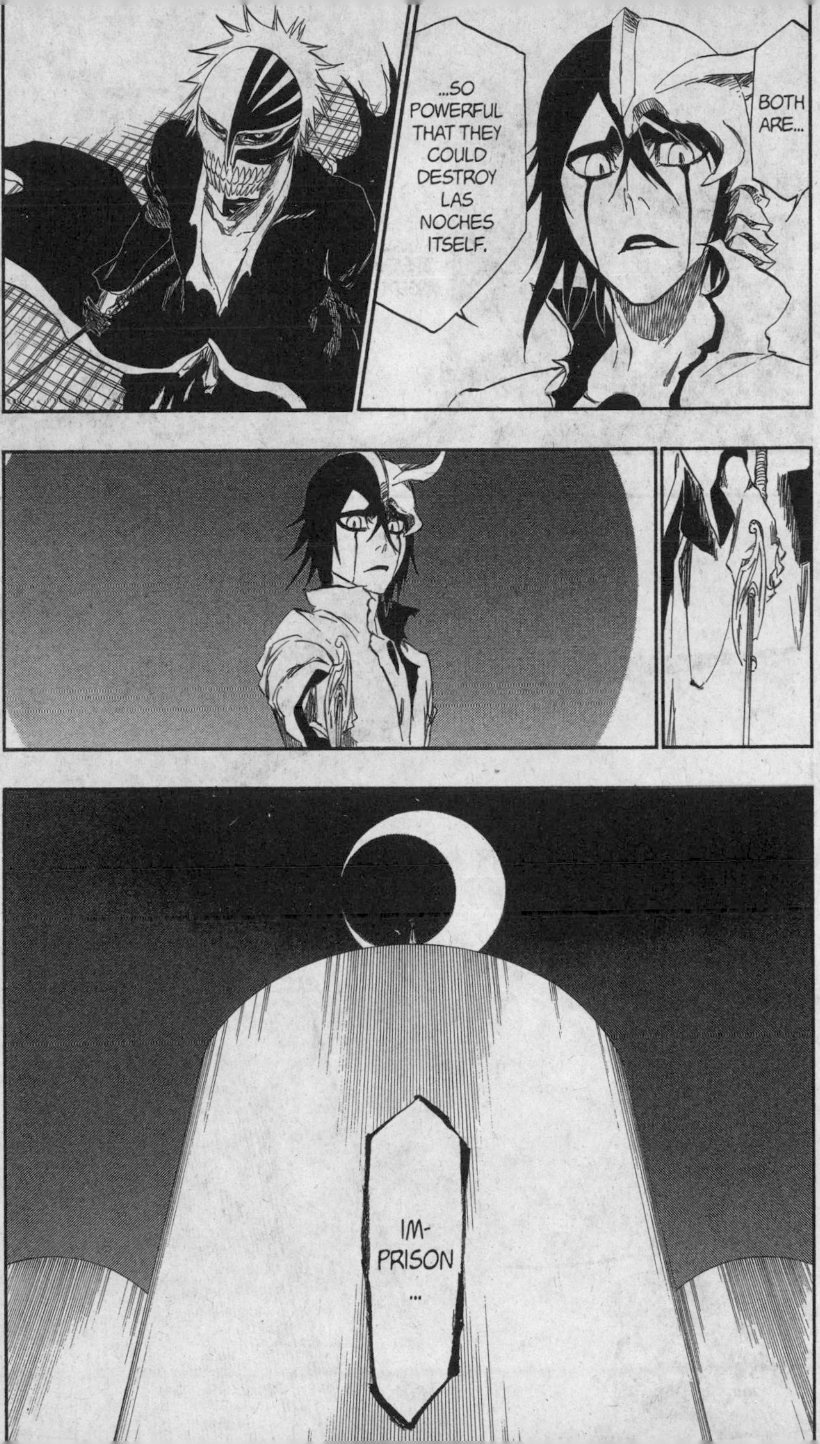
BOTH ARE...
...SO POWERFUL THAT THEY COULD DESTROY LAS NOCHES ITSELF.
IM-PRISON ...

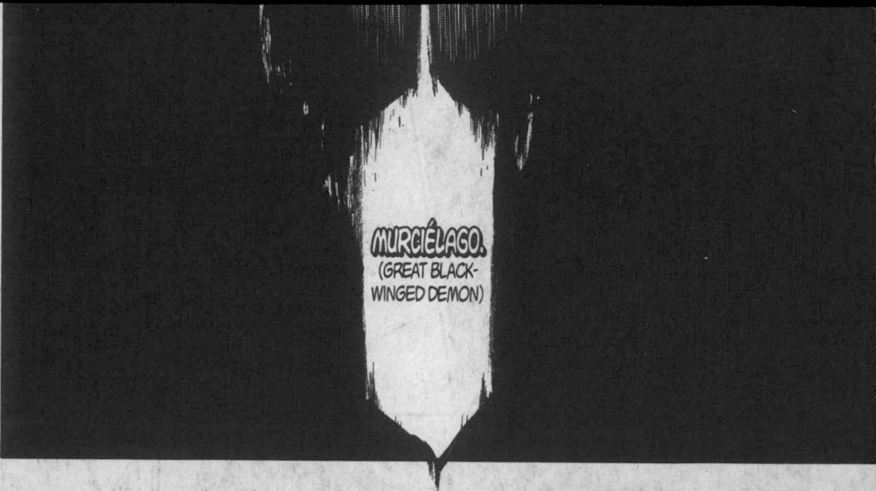
MURCIÉLAGO.
(GREAT BLACK-WINGED DEMON)
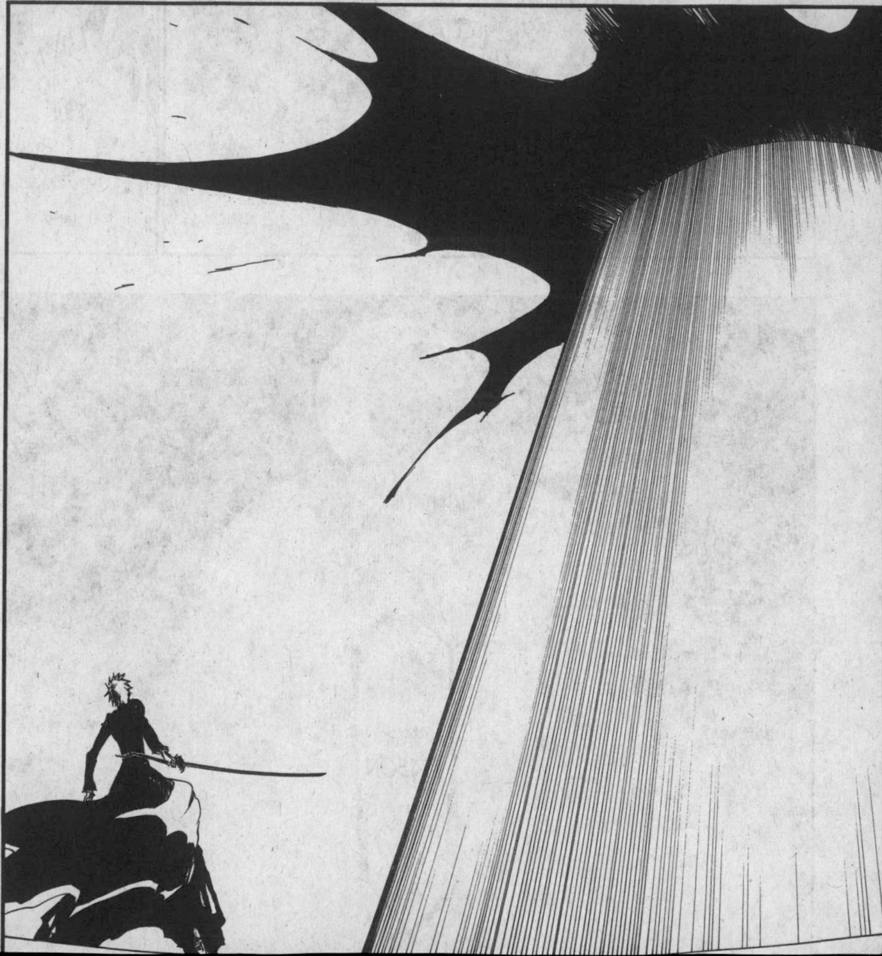

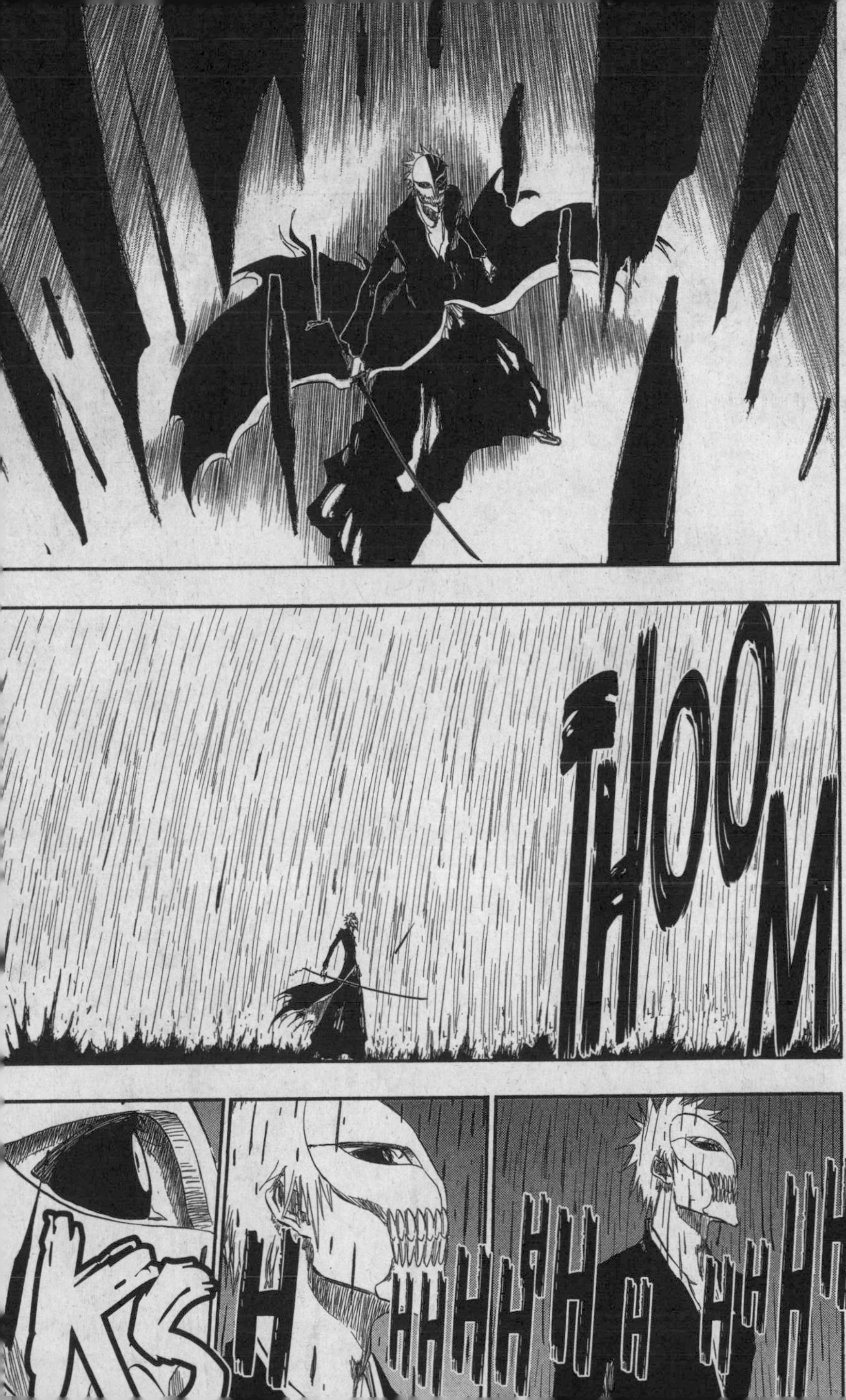
THOOM
HHHHHHHHHHHH
KSH

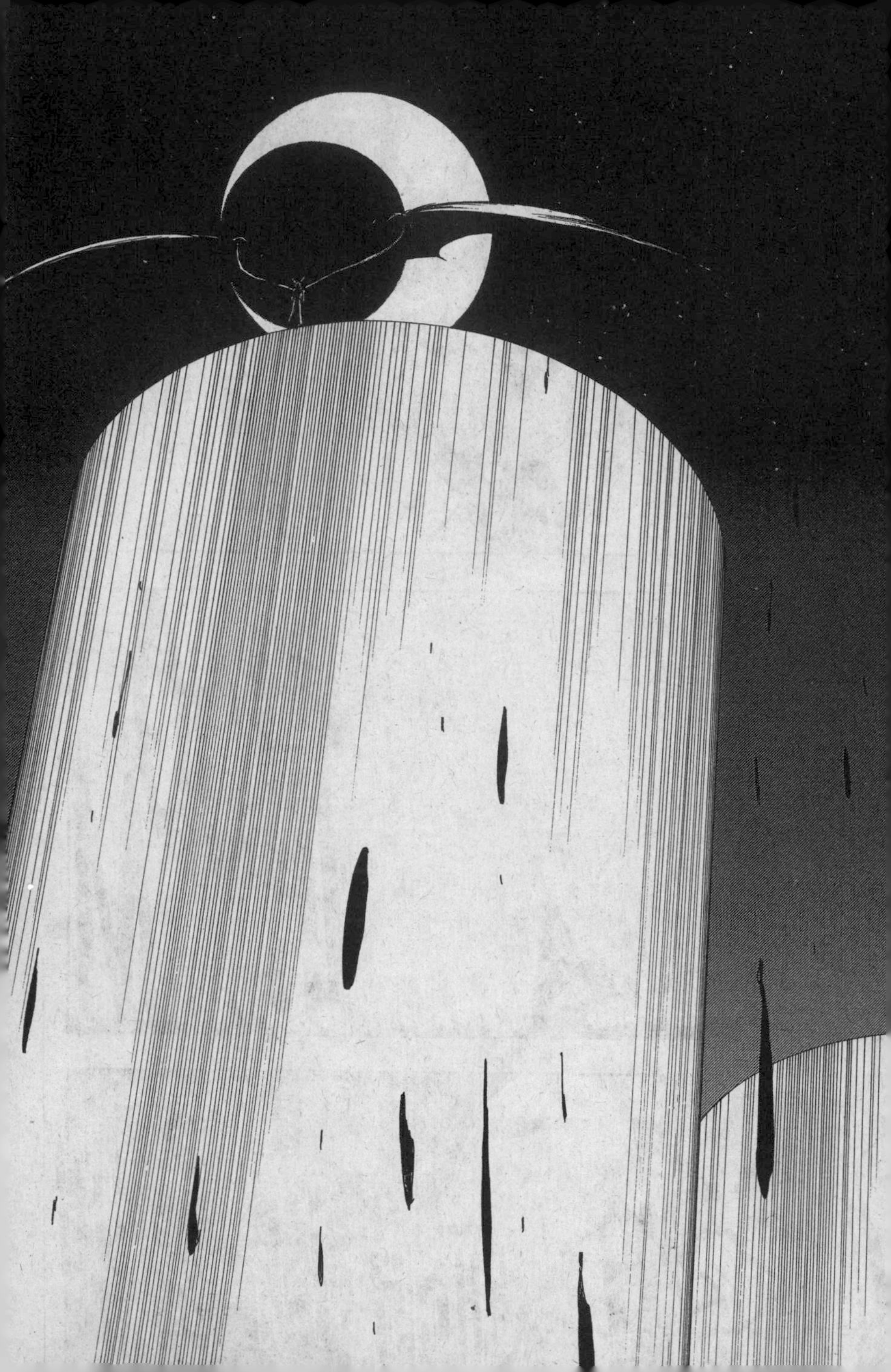

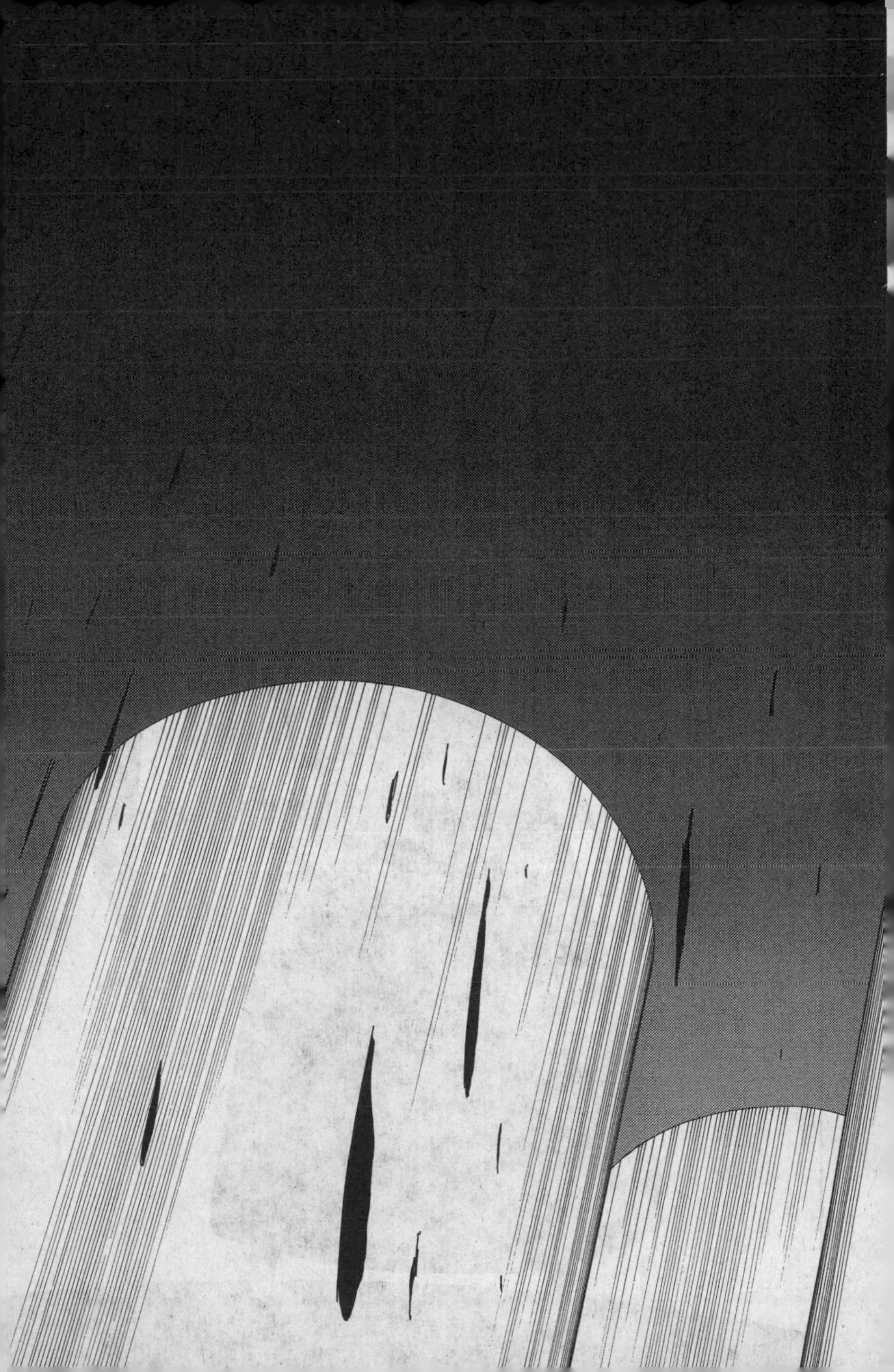

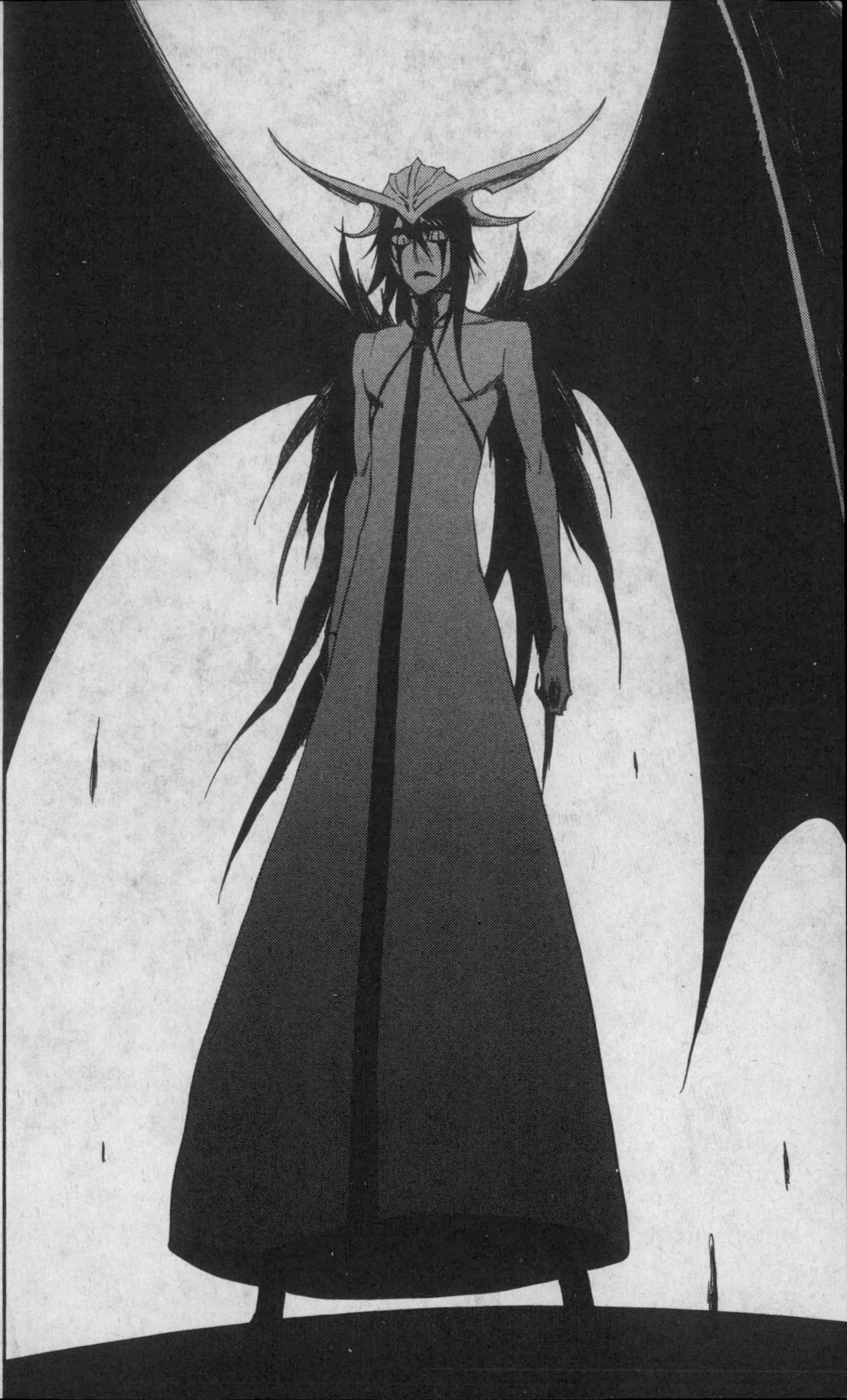

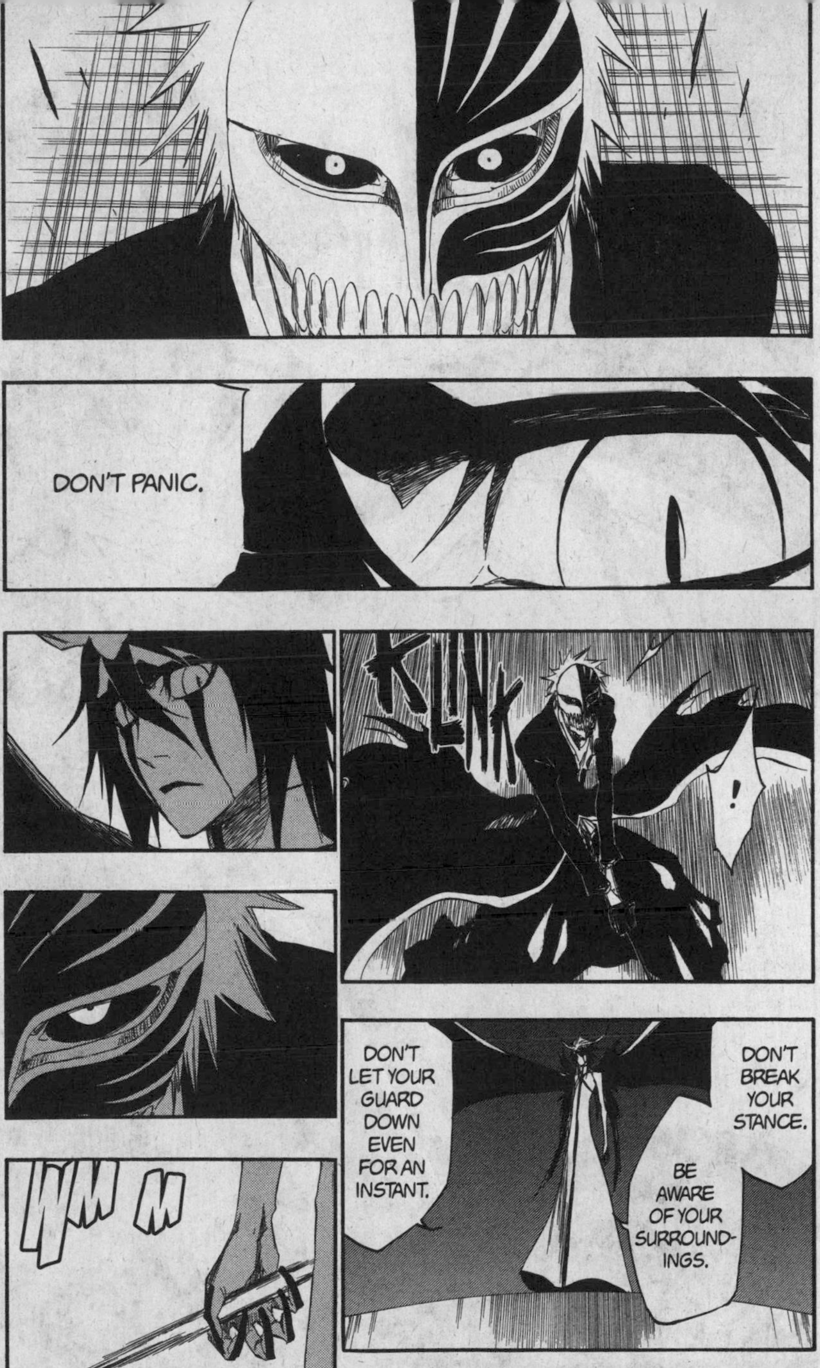
DON'T PANIC.
KLINK
!
DON'T BREAK YOUR STANCE.
DON'T LET YOUR GUARD DOWN EVEN FOR AN INSTANT.
BE AWARE OF YOUR SURROUNDINGS.

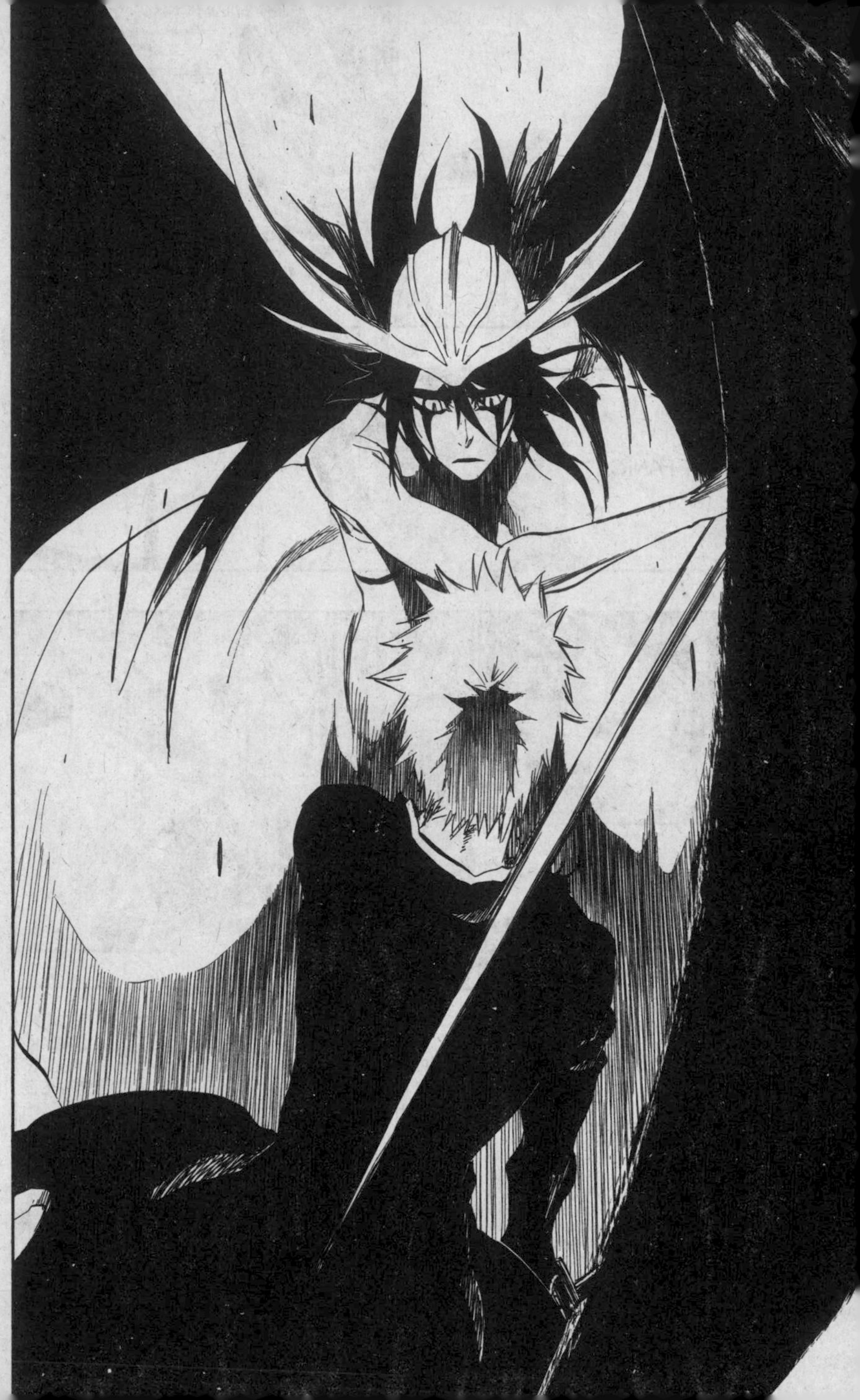

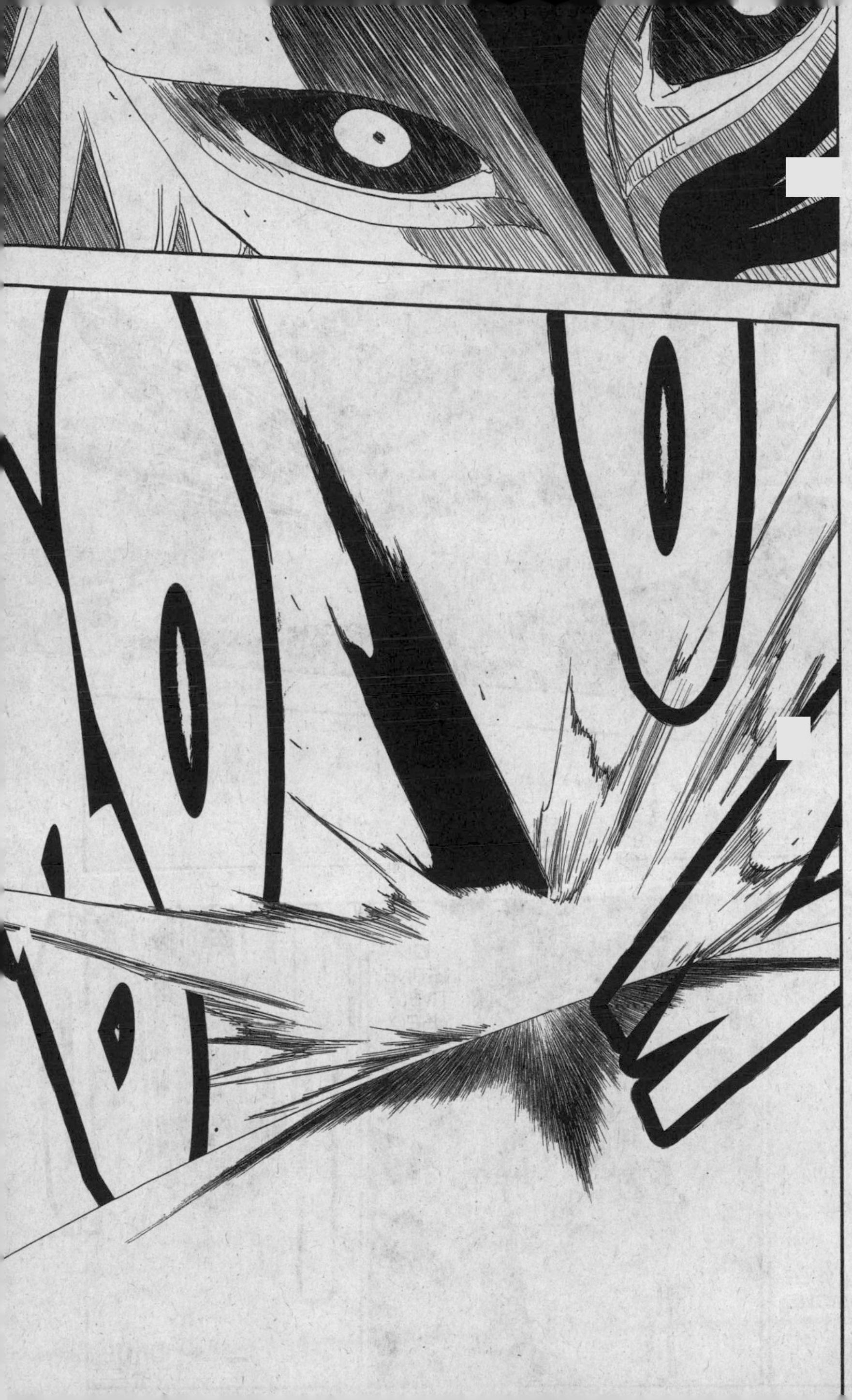

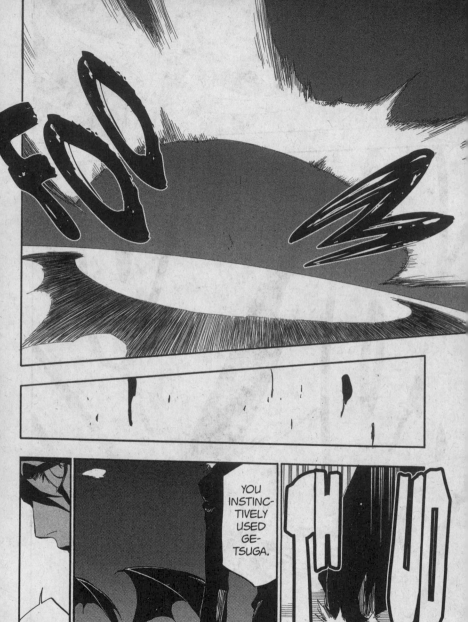

YOU INSTINCTIVELY USED GETSUGA.

A WISE MOVE.

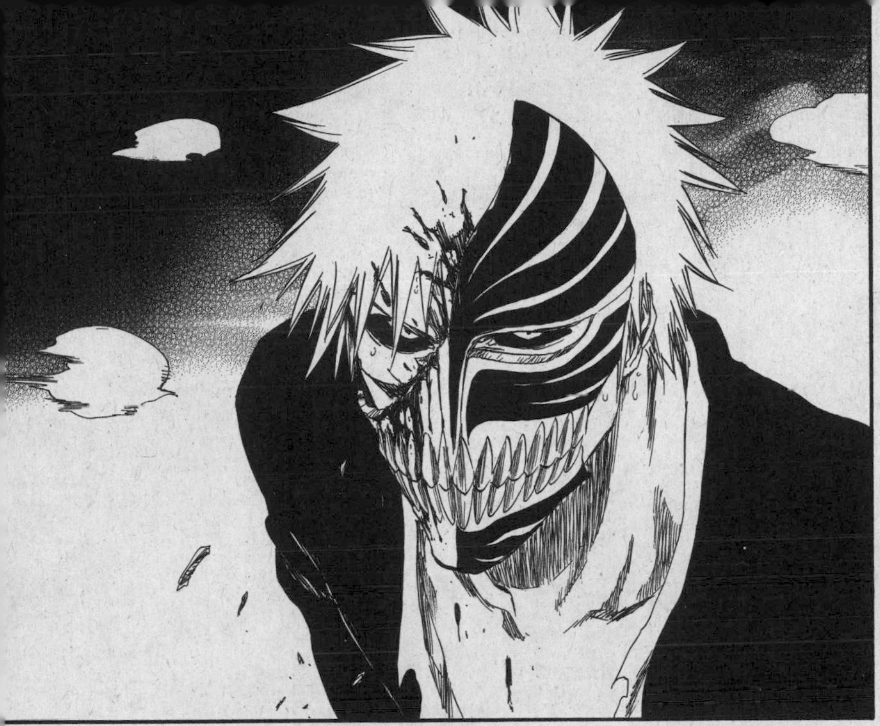

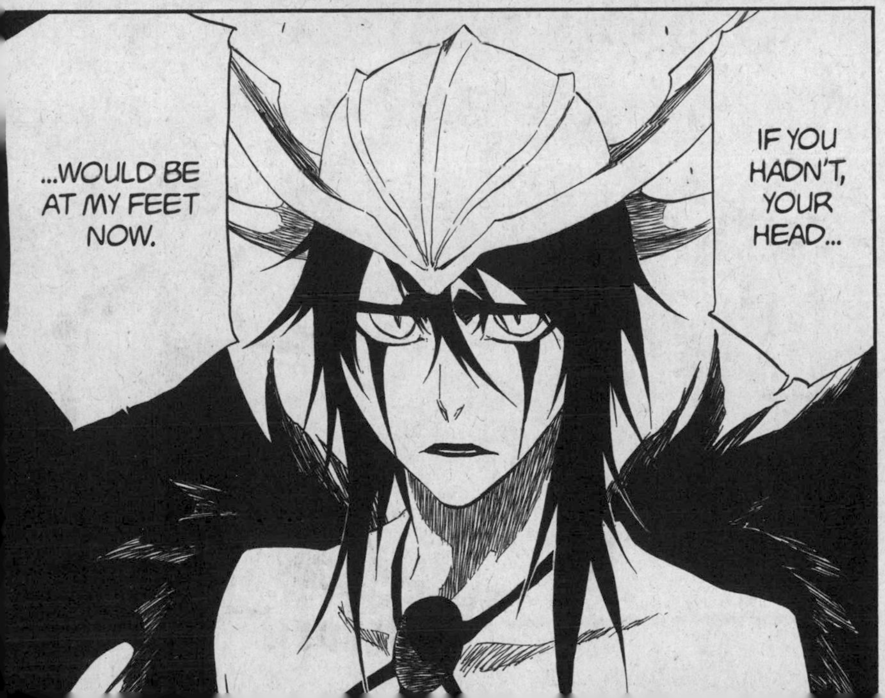
IF YOU HADN'T, YOUR HEAD...
...WOULD BE AT MY FEET NOW.

The Sloth

KLANK
POP

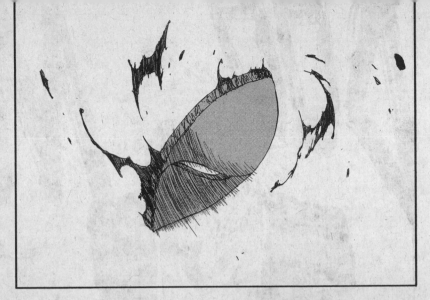

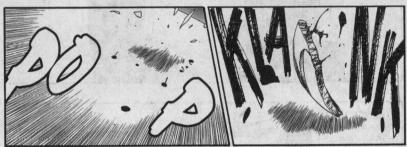

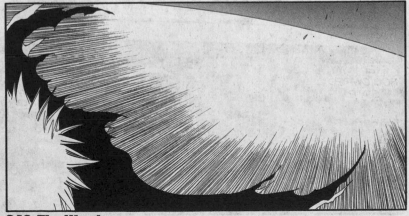

346. The Wrath

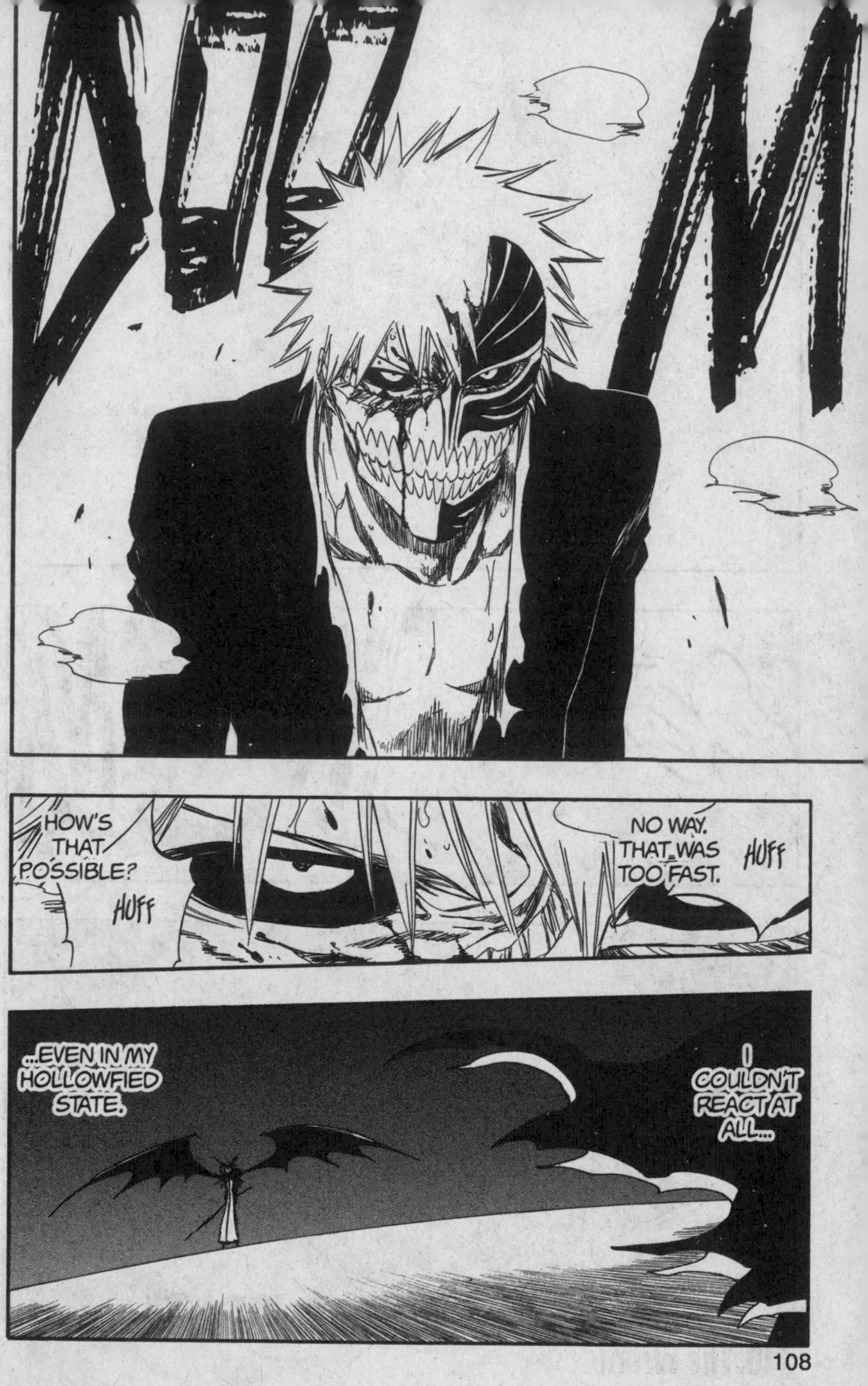
NO WAY. THAT WAS TOO FAST.
HUFF
HOW'S THAT POSSIBLE?
HUFF
I COULDN'T REACT AT ALL...
...EVEN IN MY HOLLOWFIED STATE.

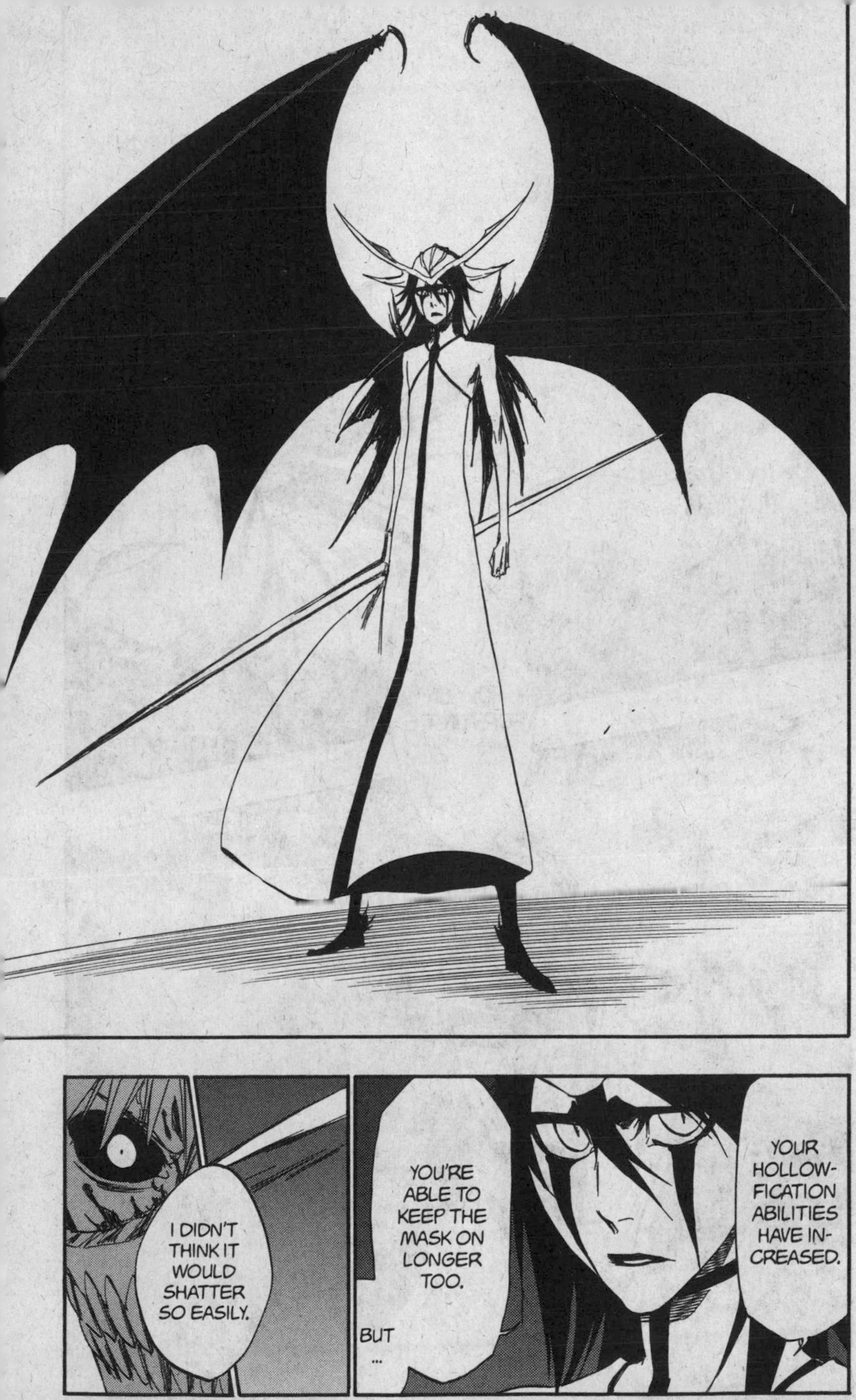
YOUR HOLLOW-FICATION ABILITIES HAVE IN-CREASED.
YOU'RE ABLE TO KEEP THE MASK ON LONGER TOO.
BUT ...
I DIDN'T THINK IT WOULD SHATTER SO EASILY.

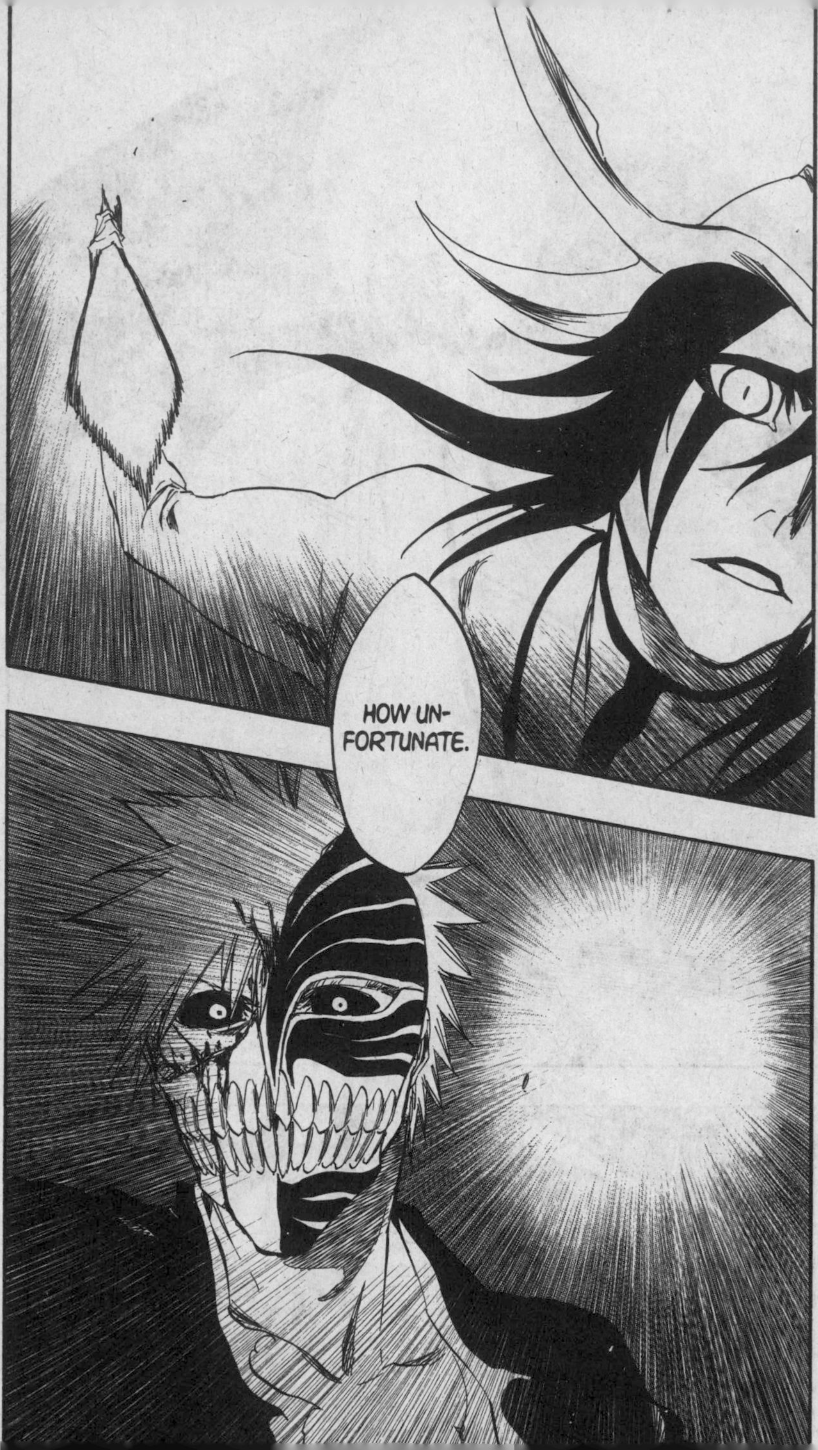
HOW UN-
FORTUNATE.

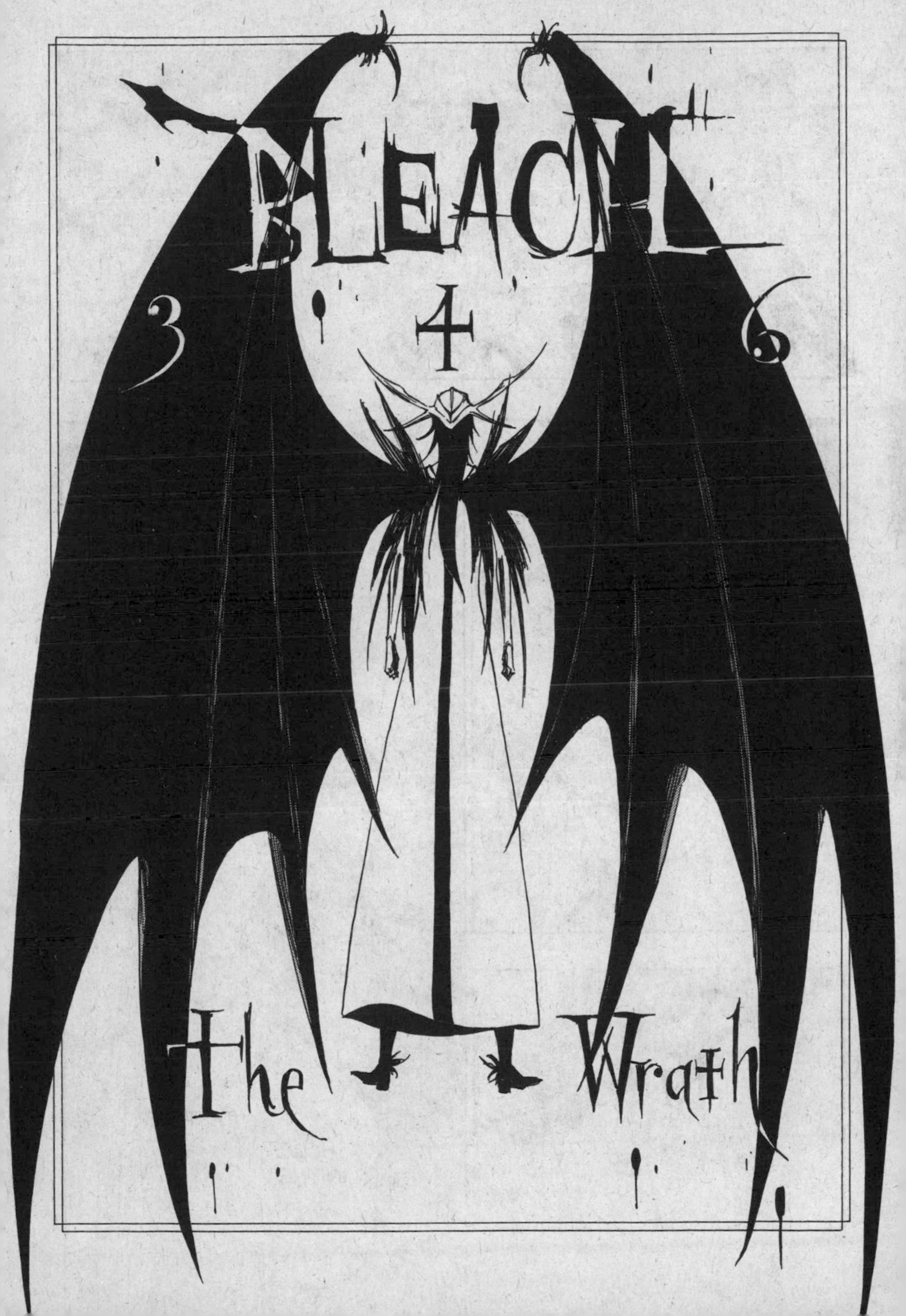
BLEACH
3
4
6
The Wrath

WOOO ooo o oo.

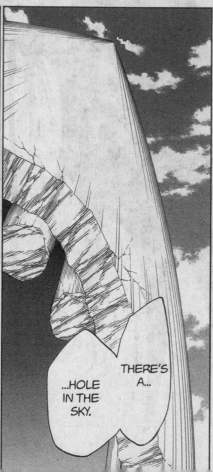

IT REALLY WAS...

...FAKE.

THERE'S A...

...HOLE IN THE SKY.

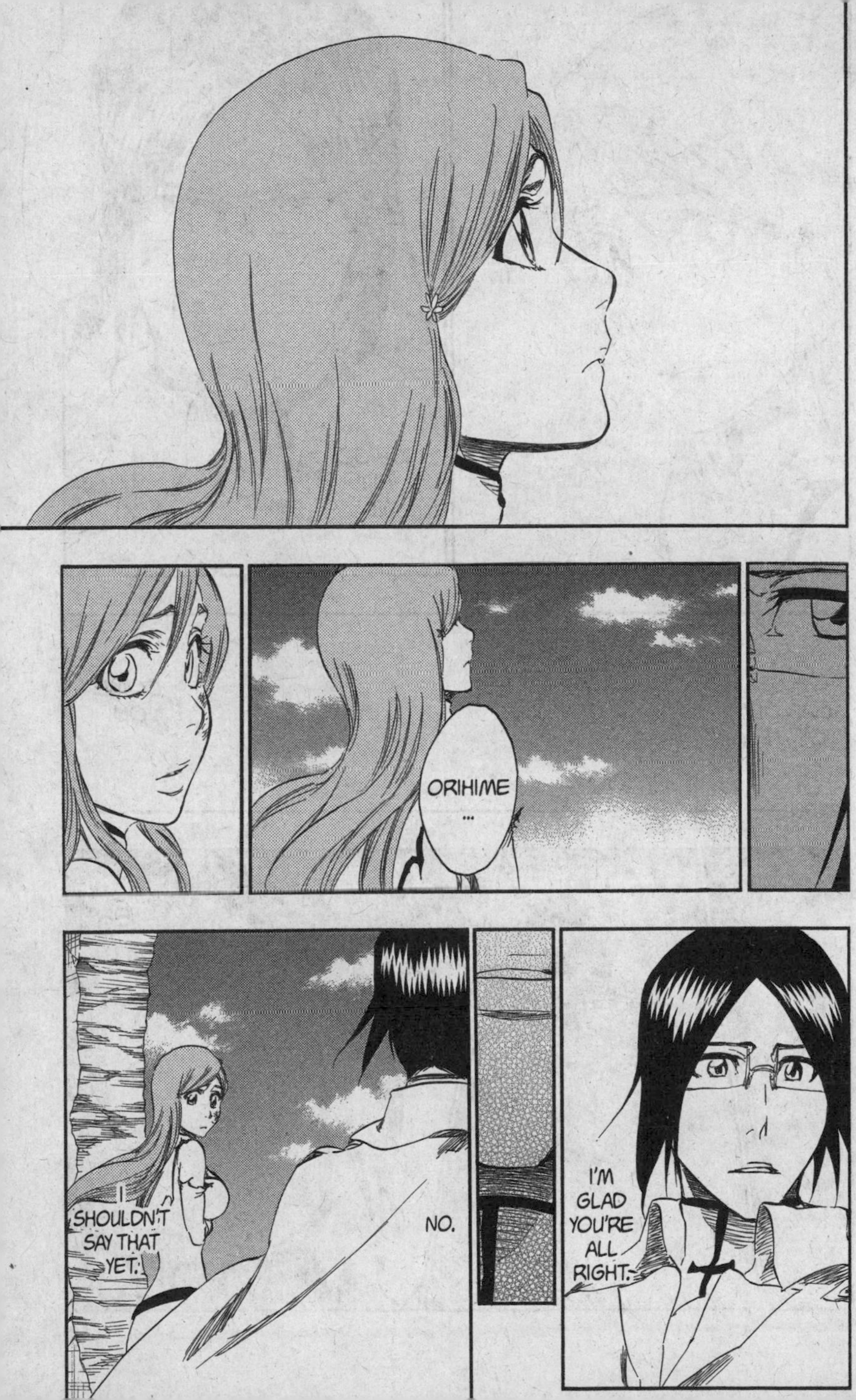
ORIHIME ...
I'M GLAD YOU'RE ALL RIGHT.
NO.
I SHOULDN'T SAY THAT YET.

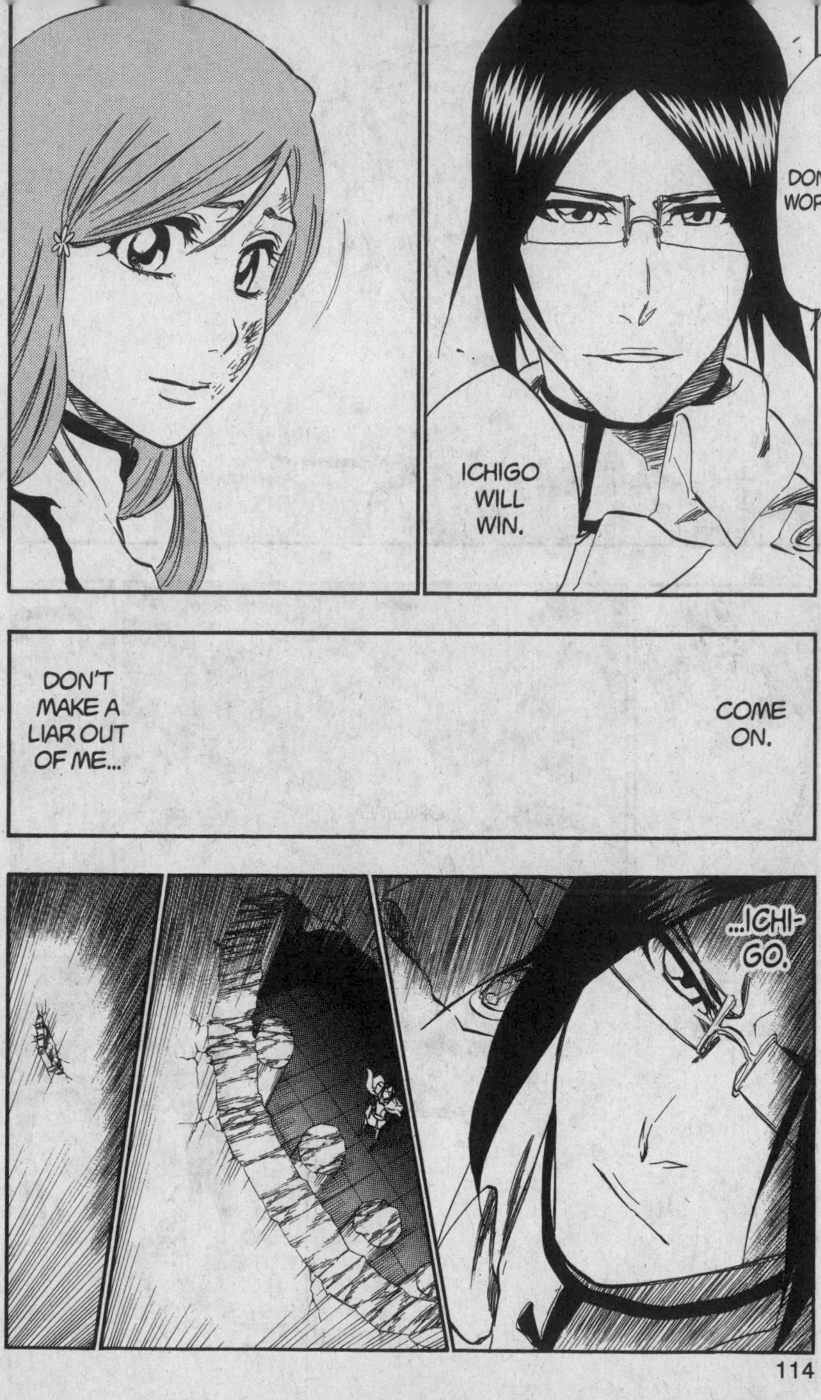
DON'T WORRY.
ICHIGO WILL WIN.
COME ON.
DON'T MAKE A LIAR OUT OF ME...
...ICHI-GO.

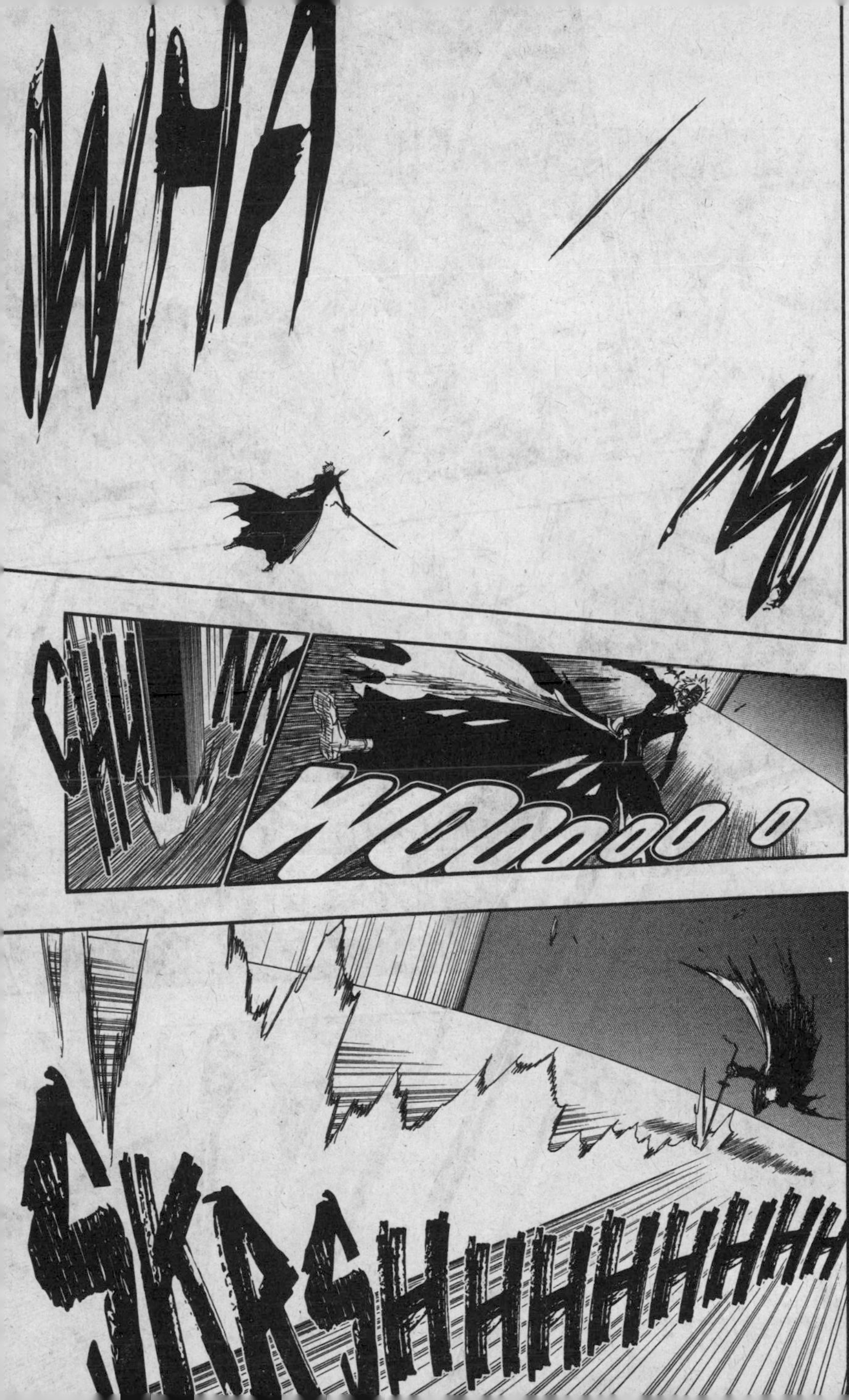
WHAM
WOOOOO O
CHUNK
SKRSHHHHHHHH

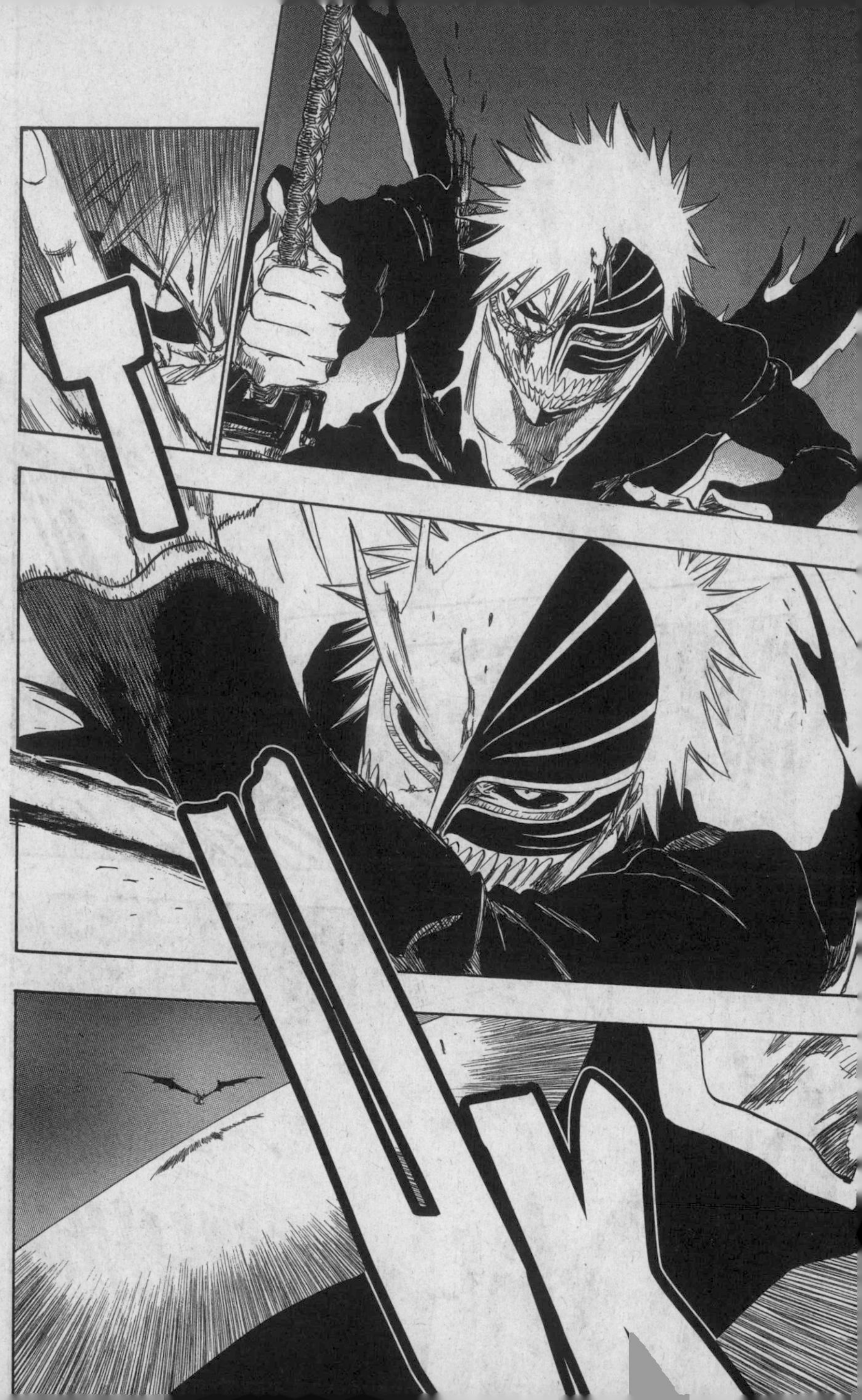

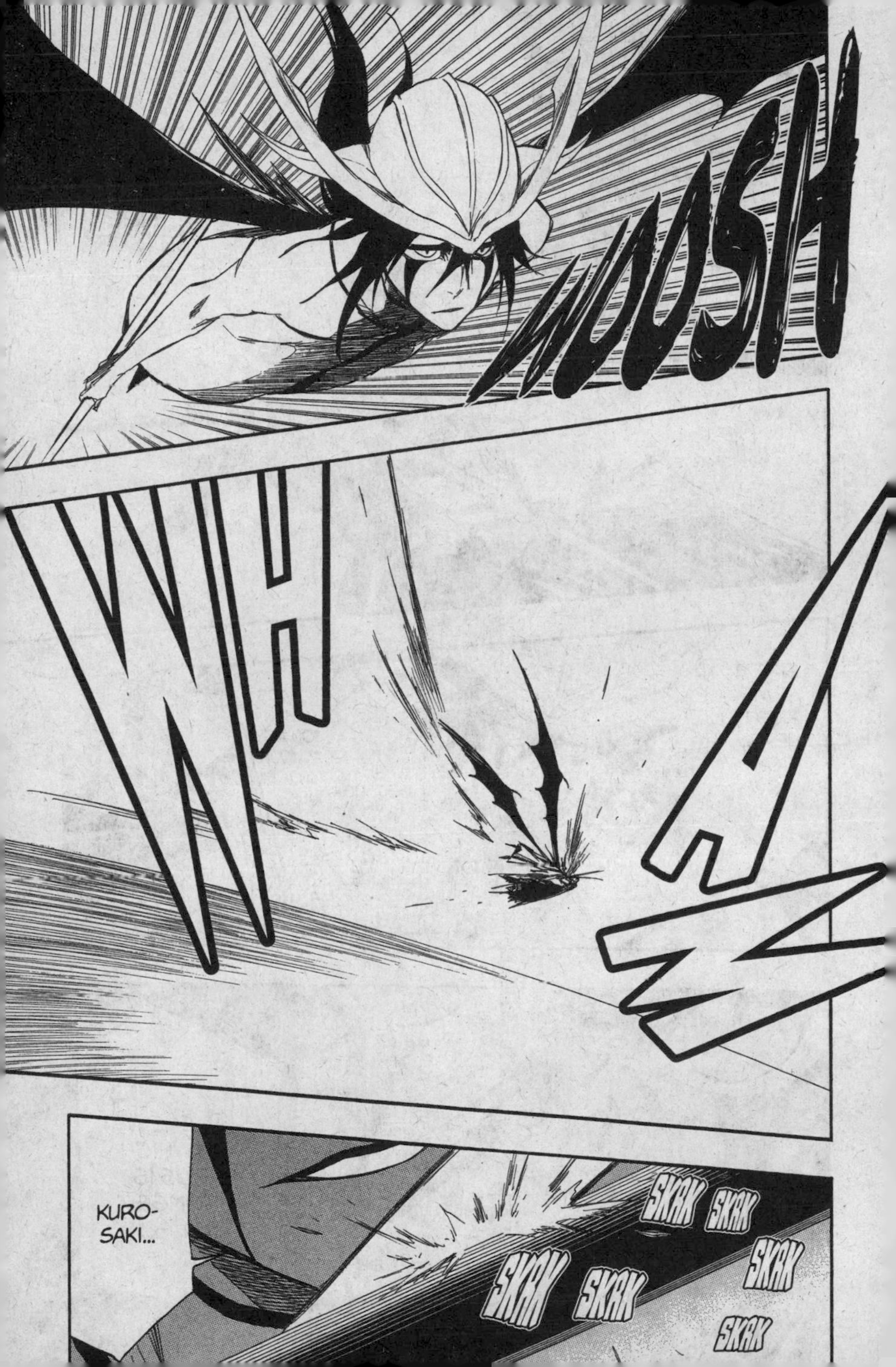
WUOSH
WHAM
KURO-SAKI...
SKRK SKRK SKRK SKRK SKRK SKRK

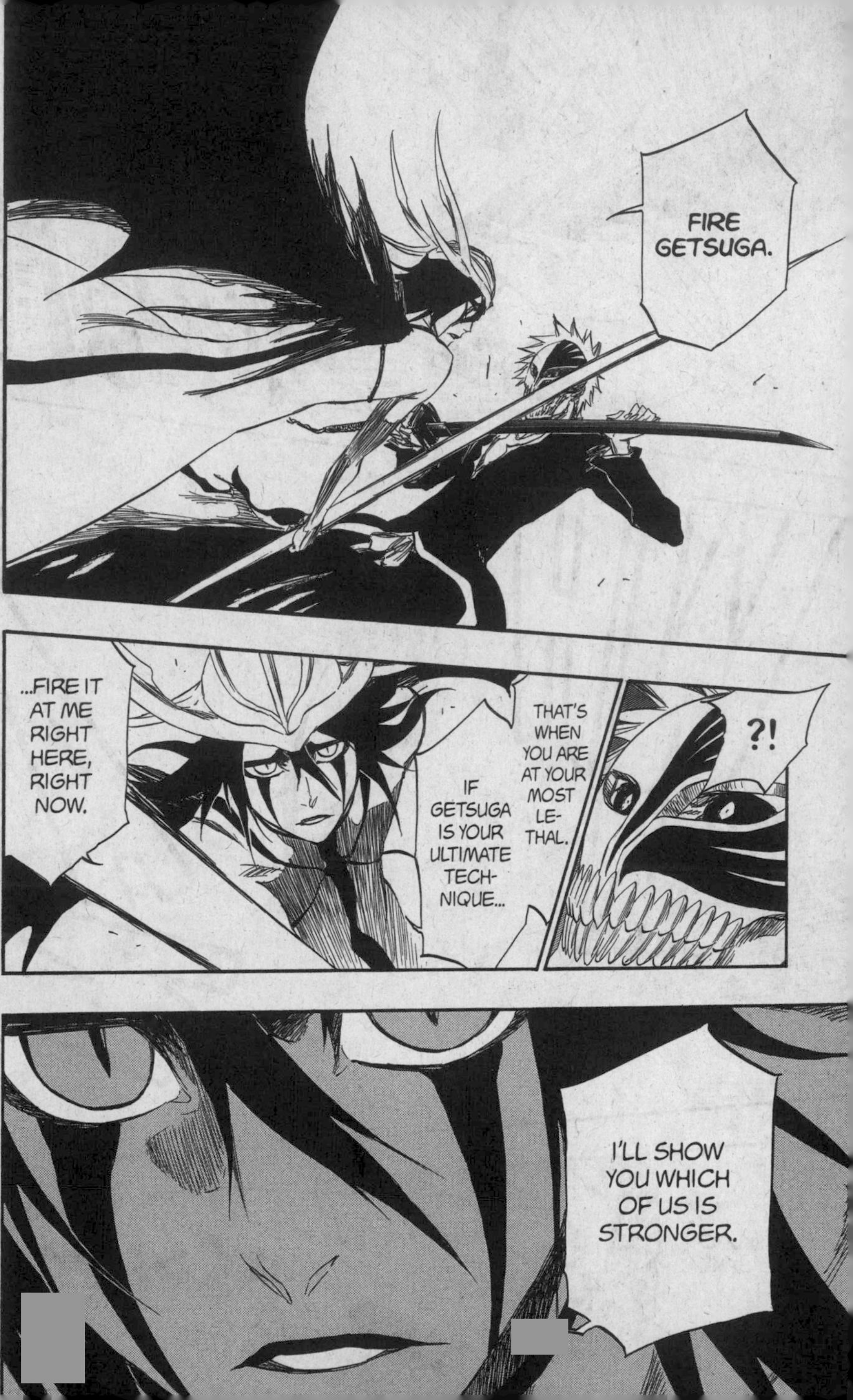
FIRE GETSUGA.
?!
THAT'S WHEN YOU ARE AT YOUR MOST LE-THAL.
IF GETSUGA IS YOUR ULTIMATE TECH-NIQUE...
...FIRE IT AT ME RIGHT HERE, RIGHT NOW.
I'LL SHOW YOU WHICH OF US IS STRONGER.

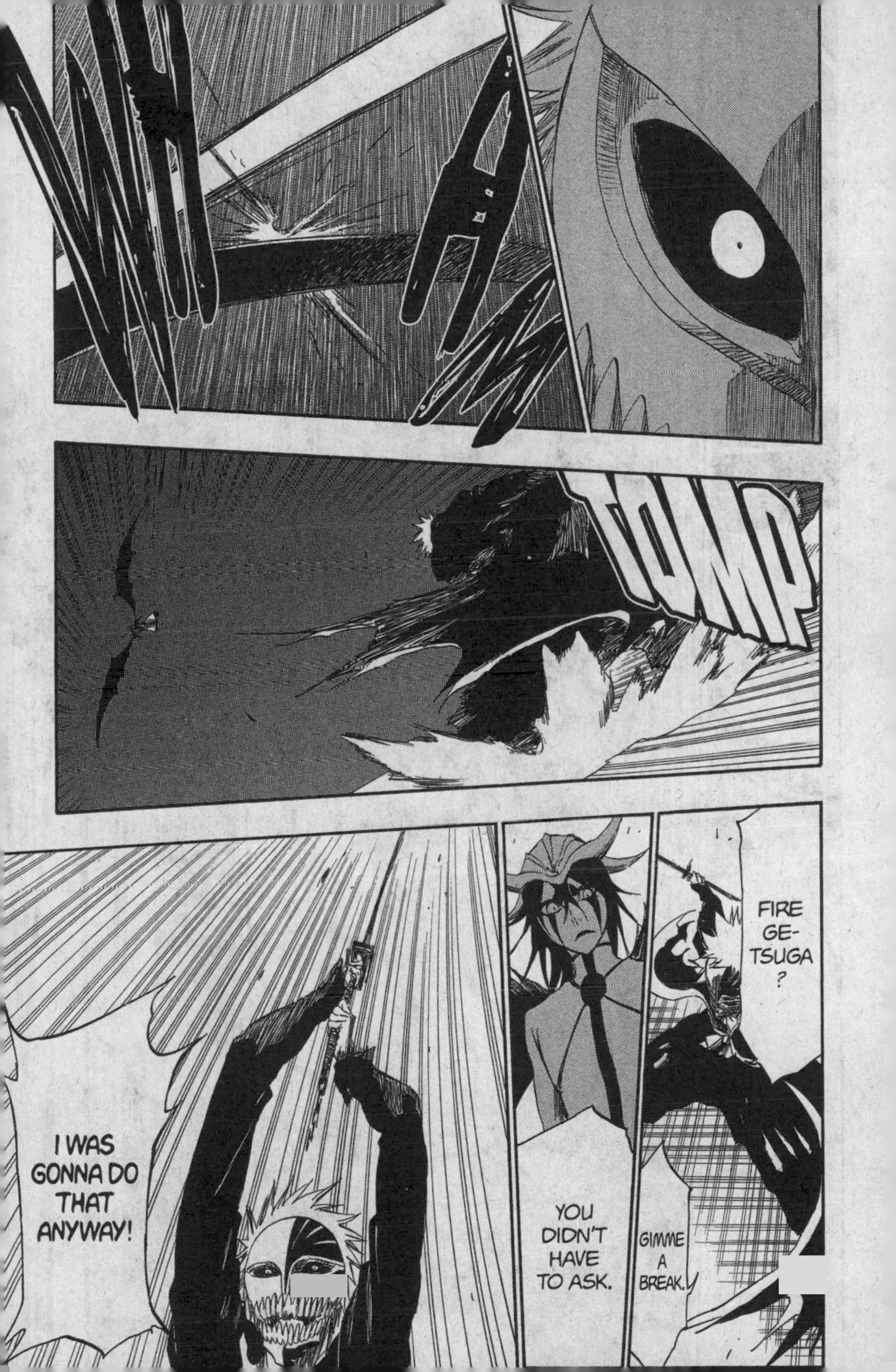
FIRE GE-TSUGA?
GIMME A BREAK.
YOU DIDN'T HAVE TO ASK.
I WAS GONNA DO THAT ANYWAY!

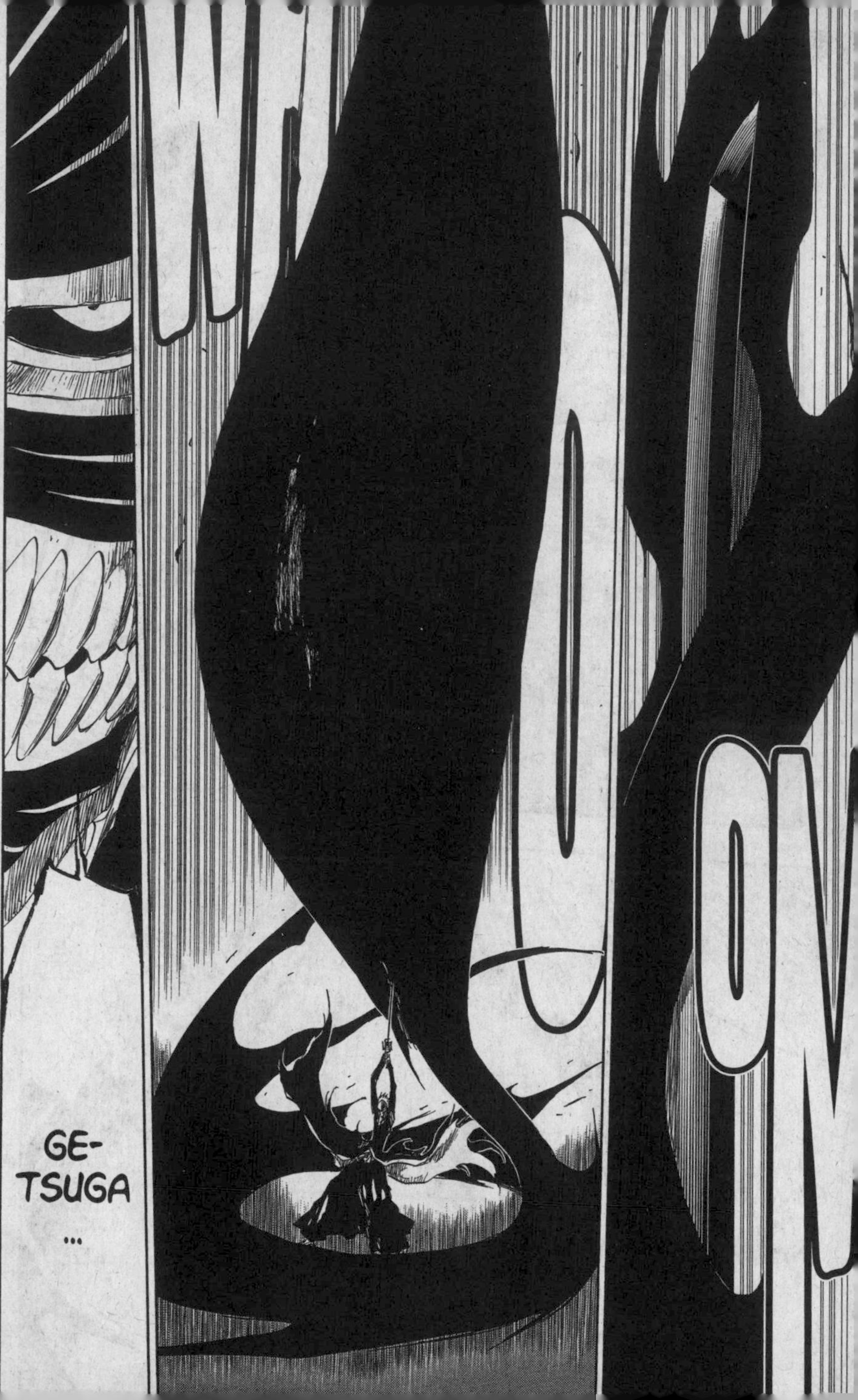
GE-
TSUGA
...

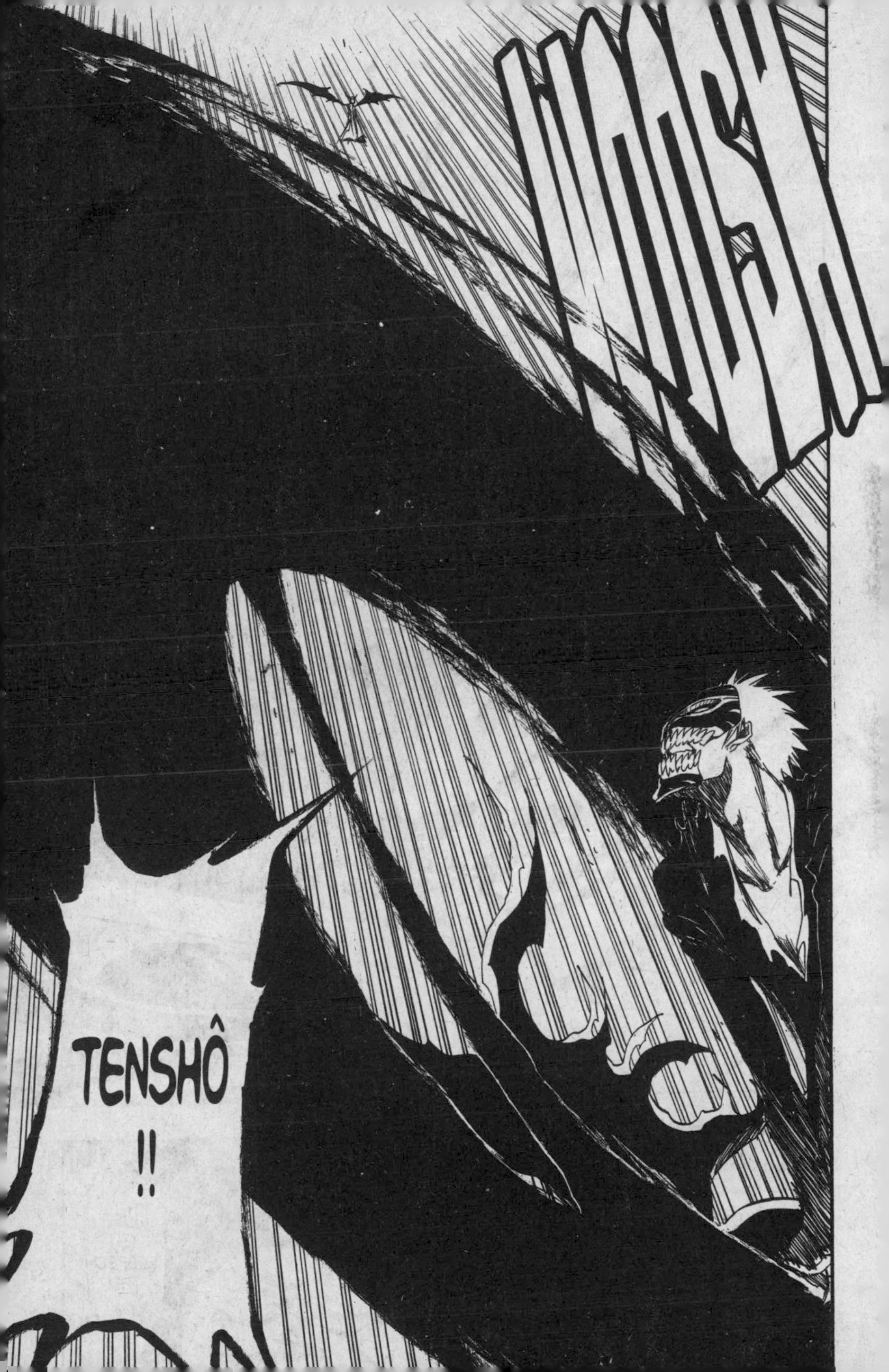
WOOSH
TENSHÔ !!

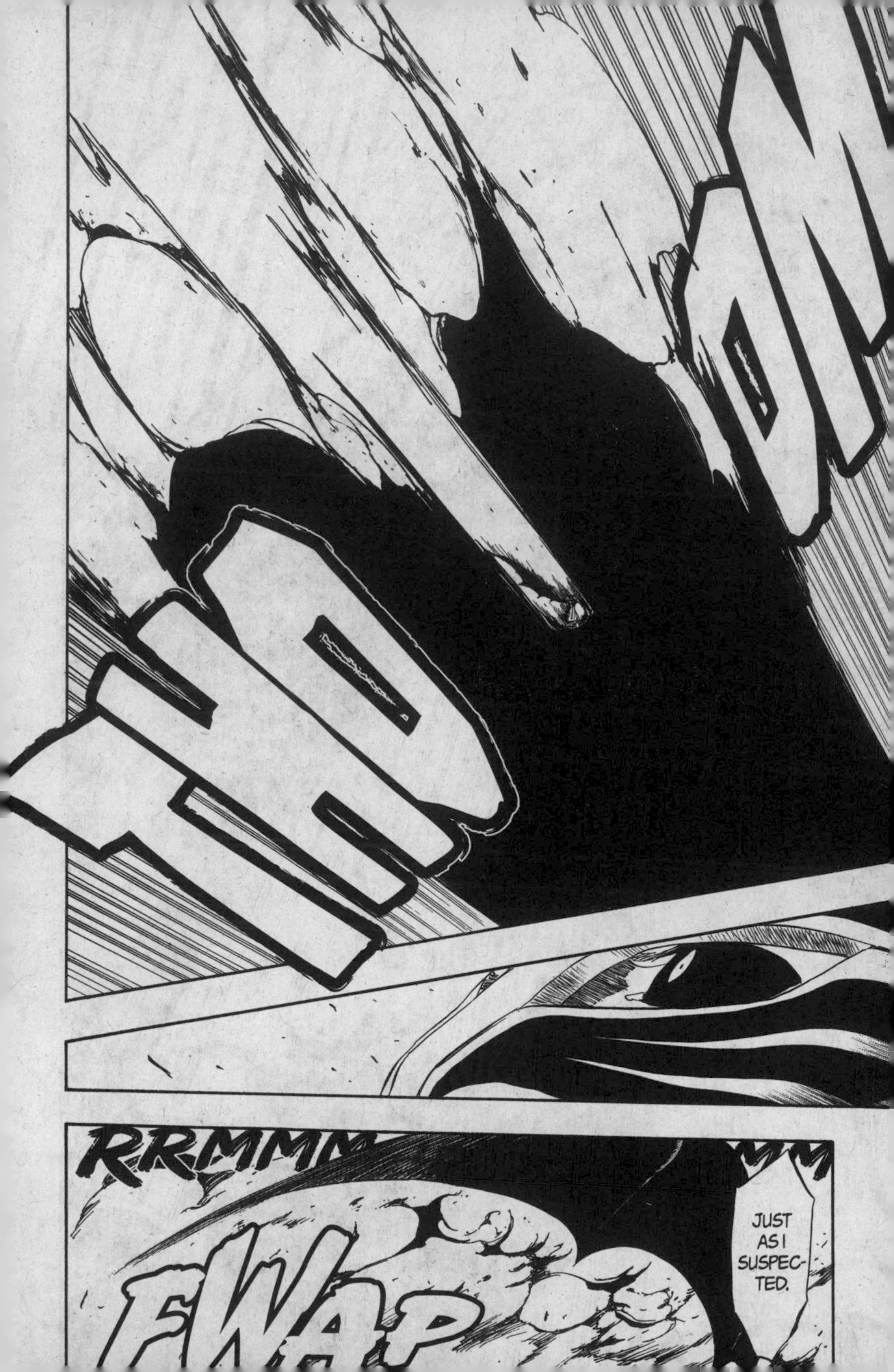
JUST AS I SUSPECTED.
FWAP

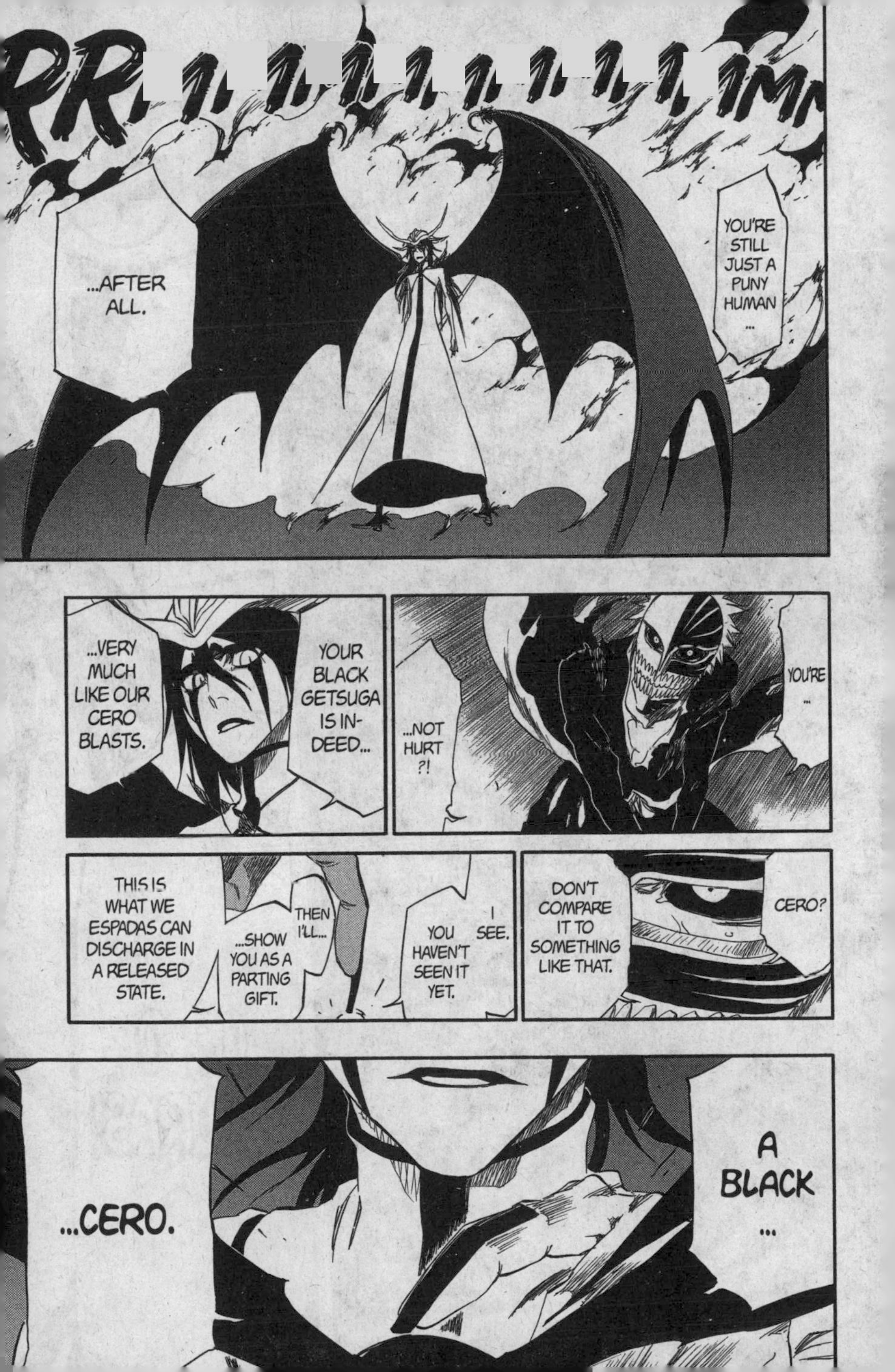
YOU'RE STILL JUST A PUNY HUMAN ...
...AFTER ALL.
YOU'RE ...
...NOT HURT ?!
YOUR BLACK GETSUGA IS IN-DEED...
...VERY MUCH LIKE OUR CERO BLASTS.
CERO?
DON'T COMPARE IT TO SOMETHING LIKE THAT.
I SEE.
YOU HAVEN'T SEEN IT YET.
THEN I'LL...
...SHOW YOU AS A PARTING GIFT.
THIS IS WHAT WE ESPADAS CAN DISCHARGE IN A RELEASED STATE.
A BLACK ...
...CERO.

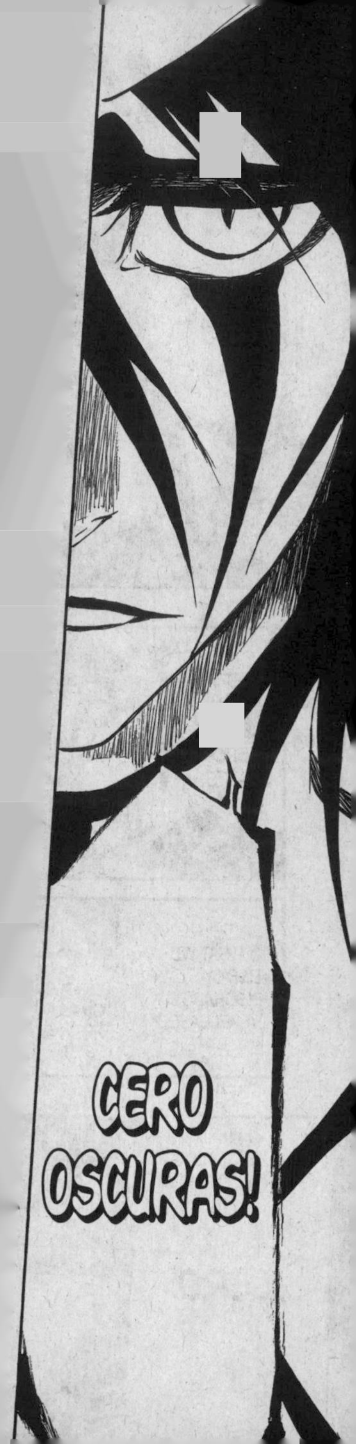
CERO OSCURAS!

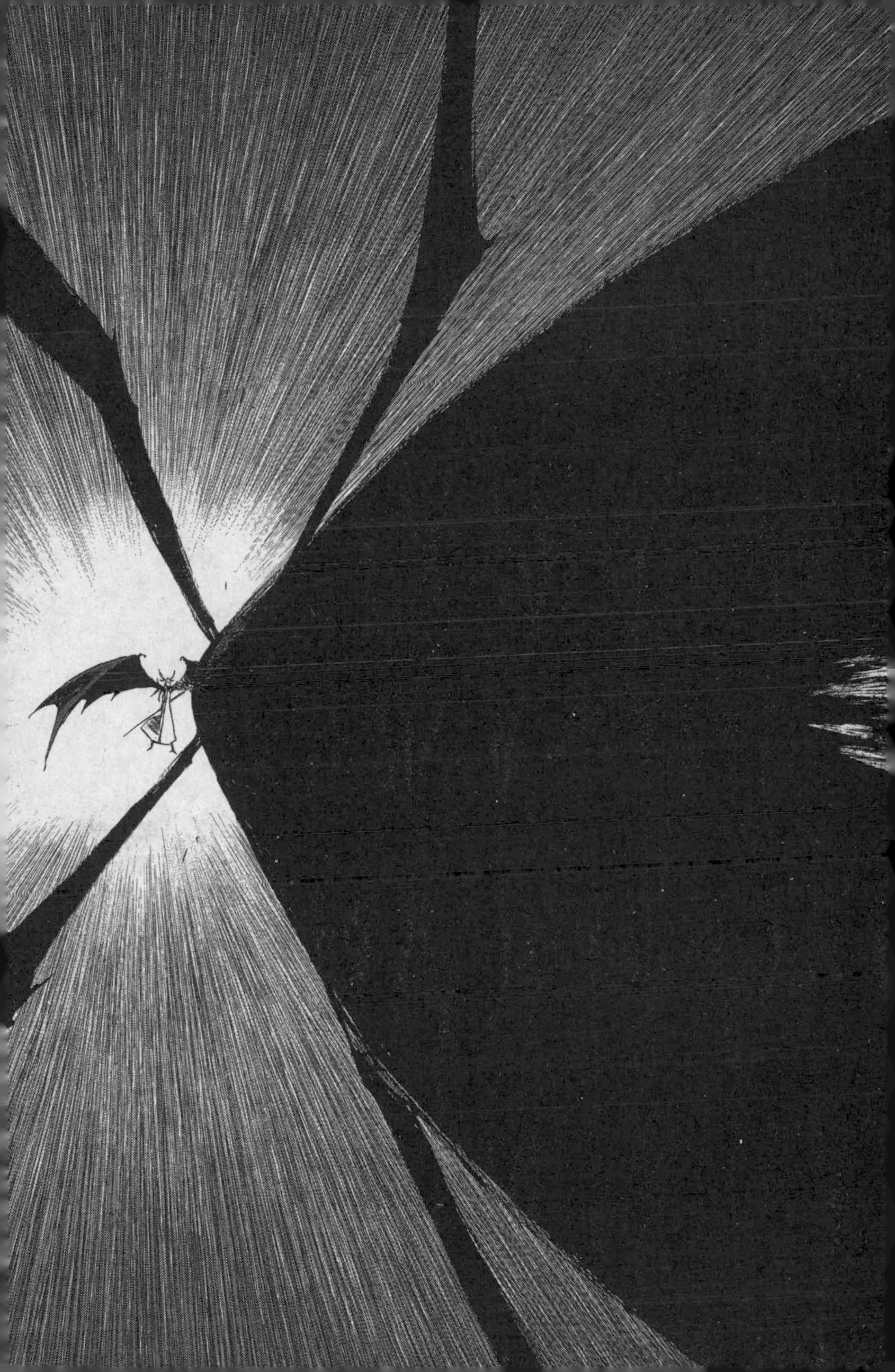

the
Wrath

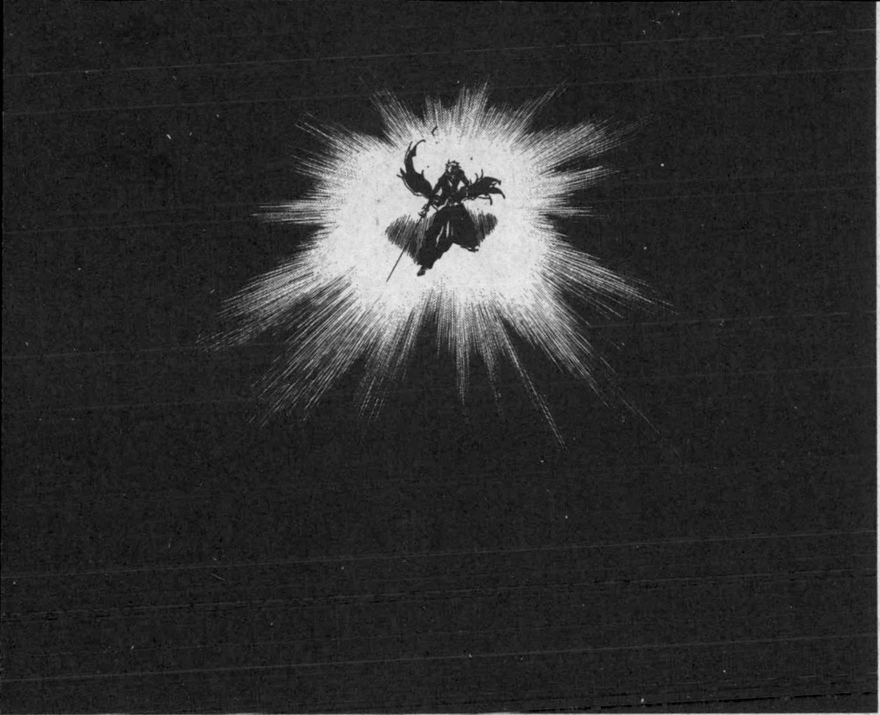

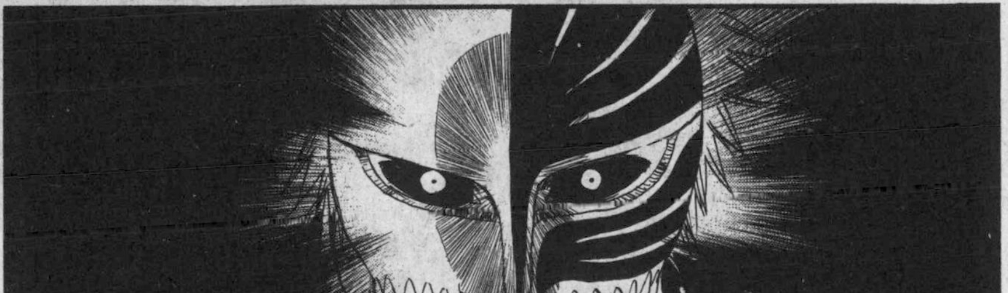

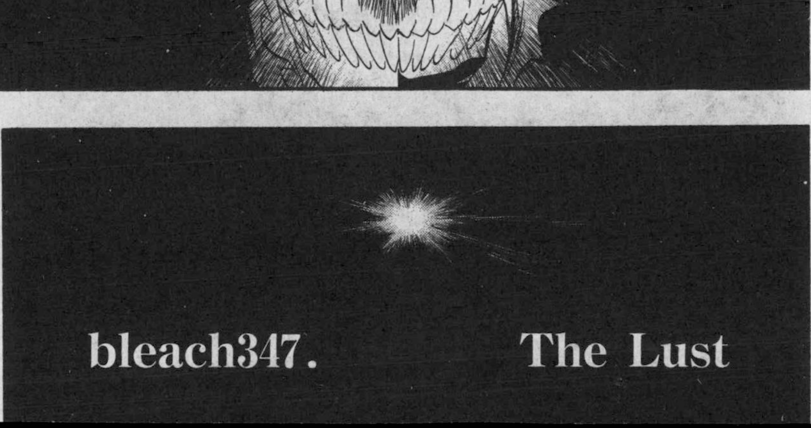
bleach347. The Lust

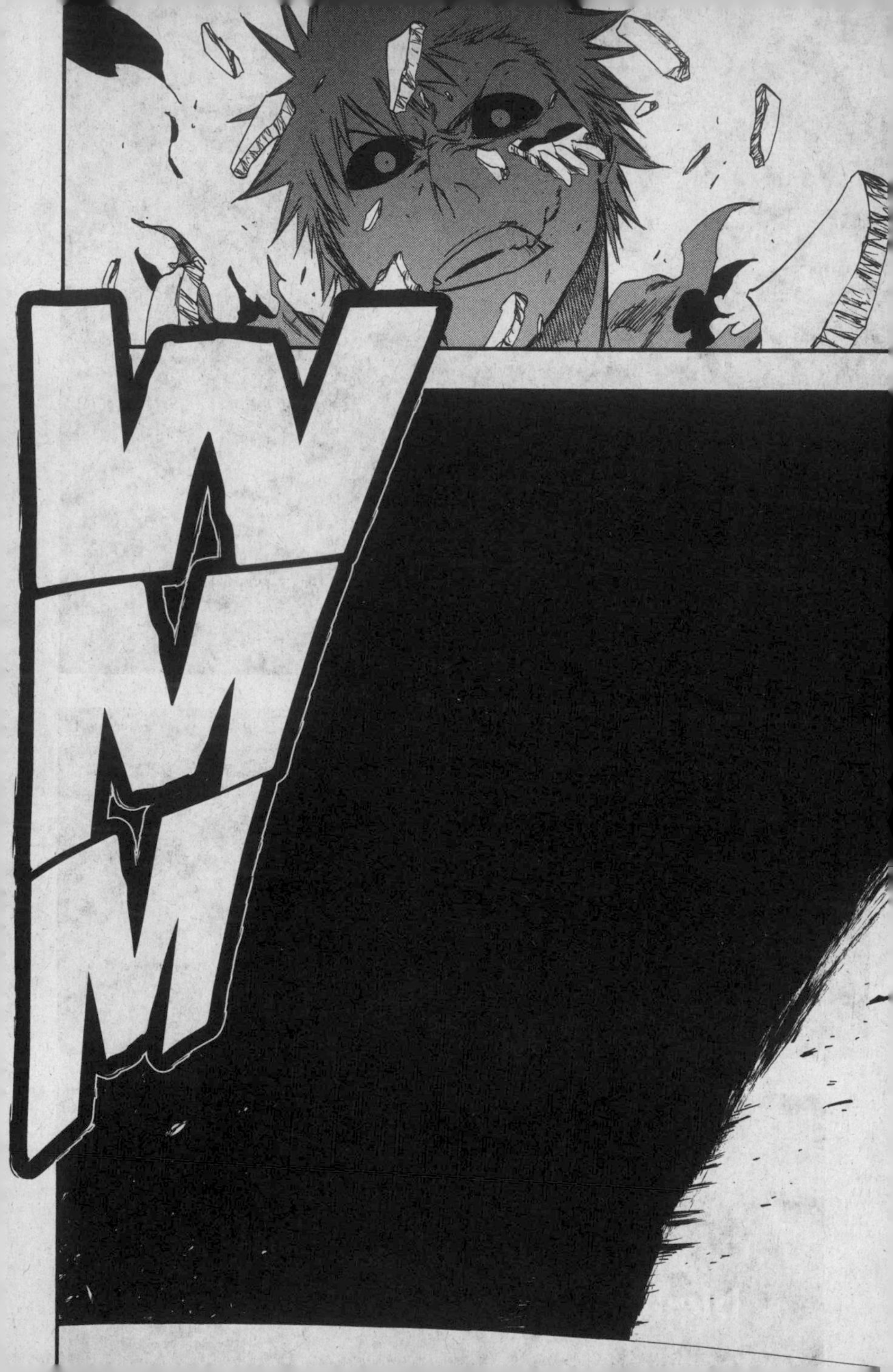
WMM

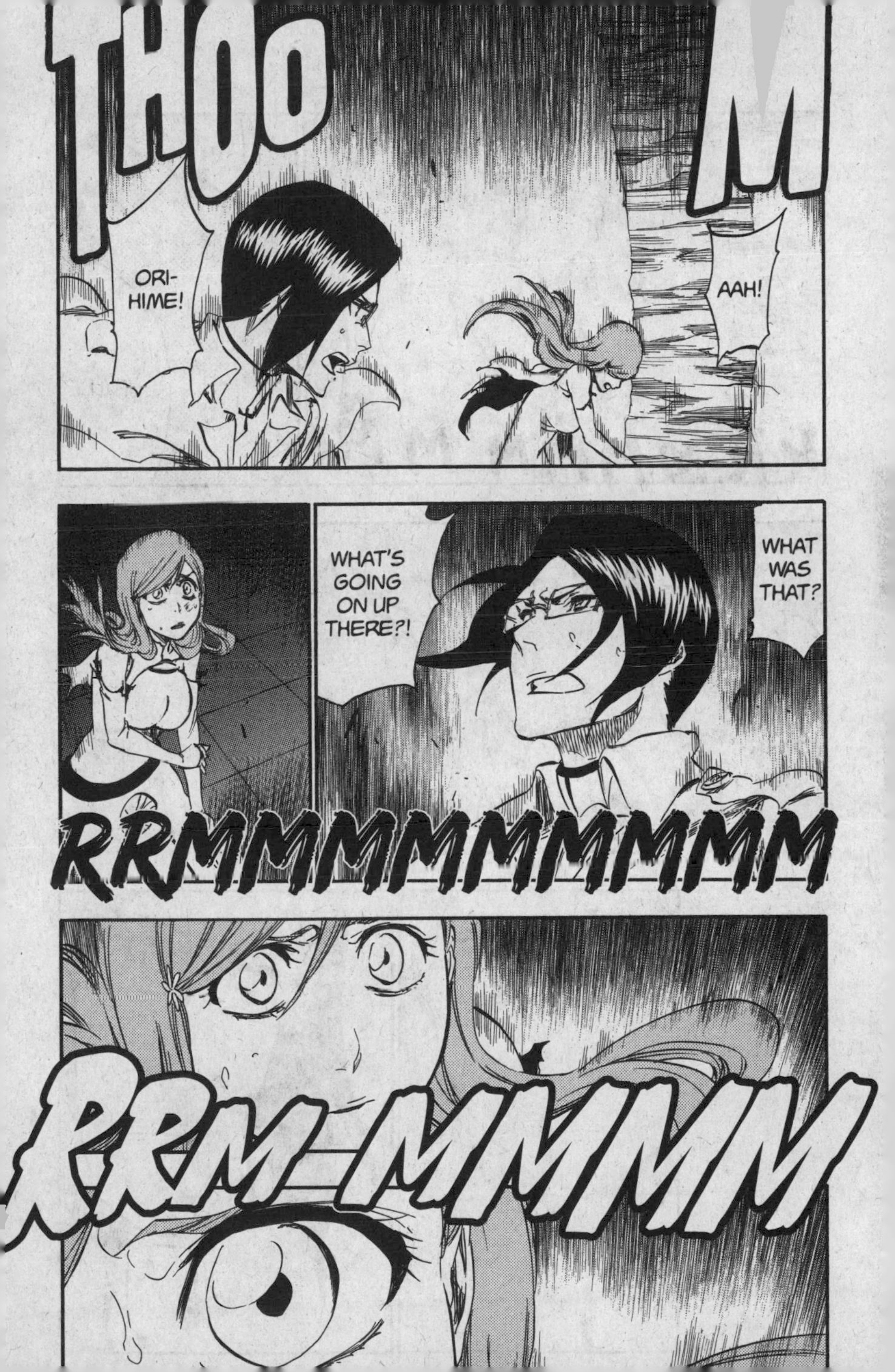
THOOM
AAH!
ORI-HIME!
WHAT WAS THAT?
WHAT'S GOING ON UP THERE?!
RRMMMMMMMMMMMM
RRM MMMM

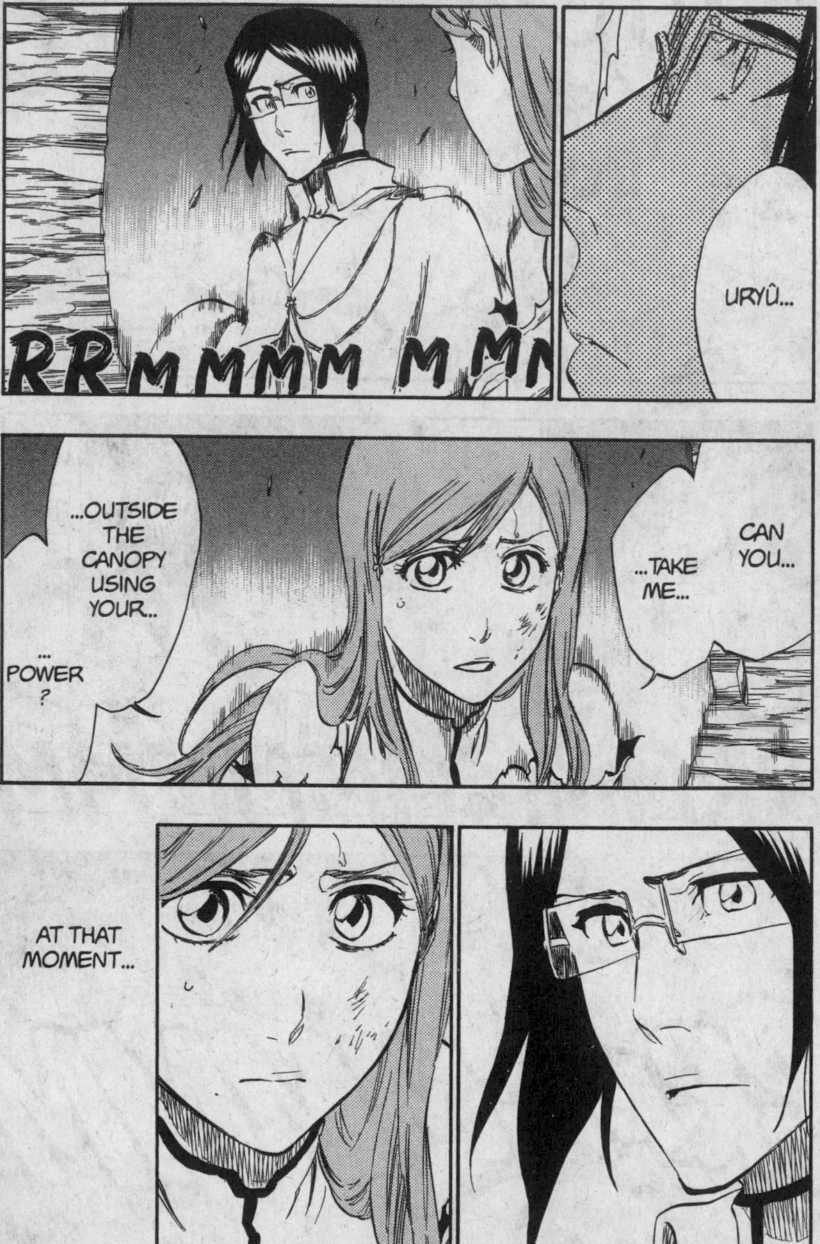
URYŪ...
RRMMMMM MMM
CAN YOU...
...TAKE ME...
...OUTSIDE THE CANOPY USING YOUR...
...POWER?
AT THAT MOMENT...

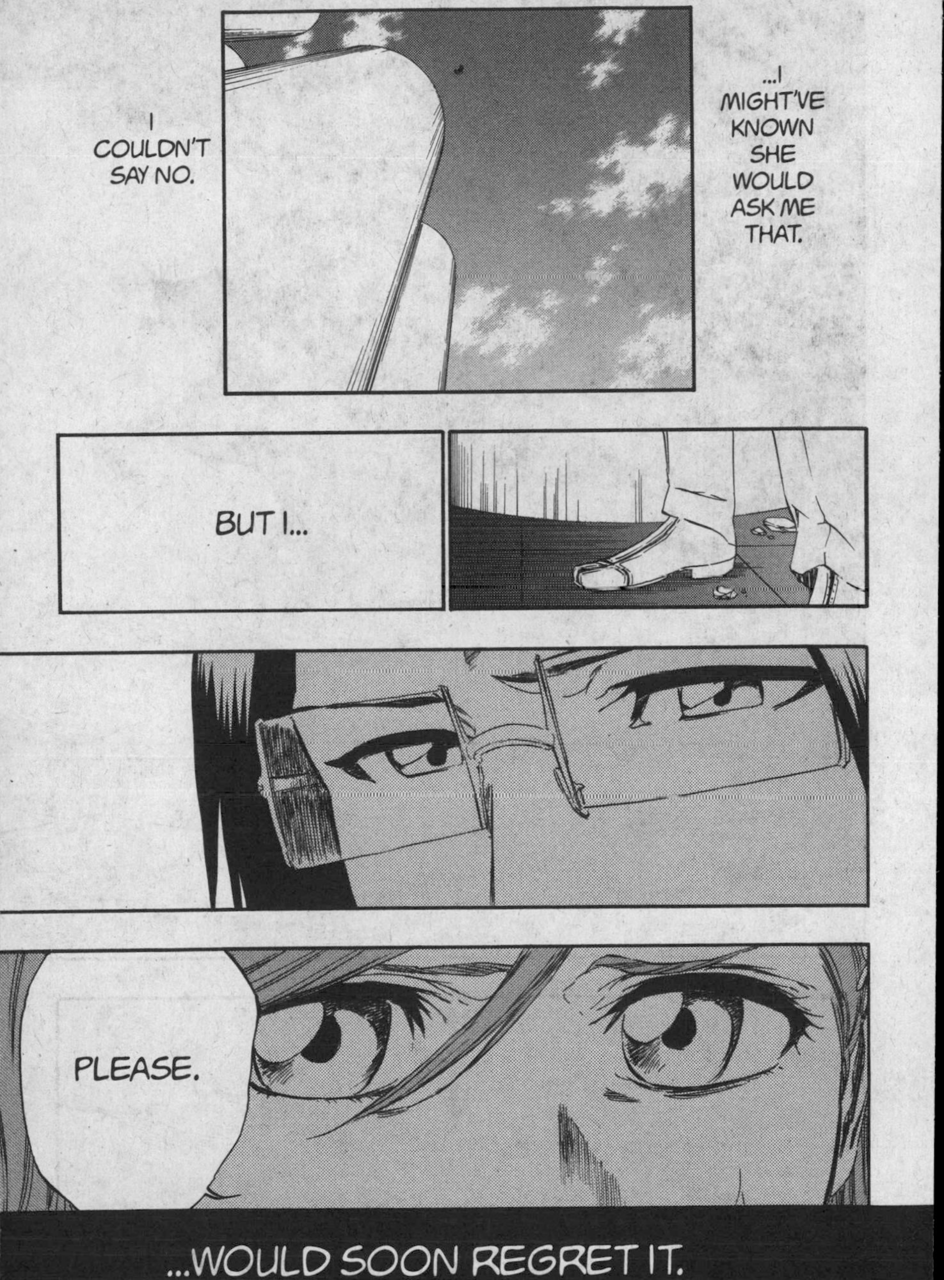
...I MIGHT'VE KNOWN SHE WOULD ASK ME THAT.
I COULDN'T SAY NO.
BUT I...
PLEASE.
...WOULD SOON REGRET IT.

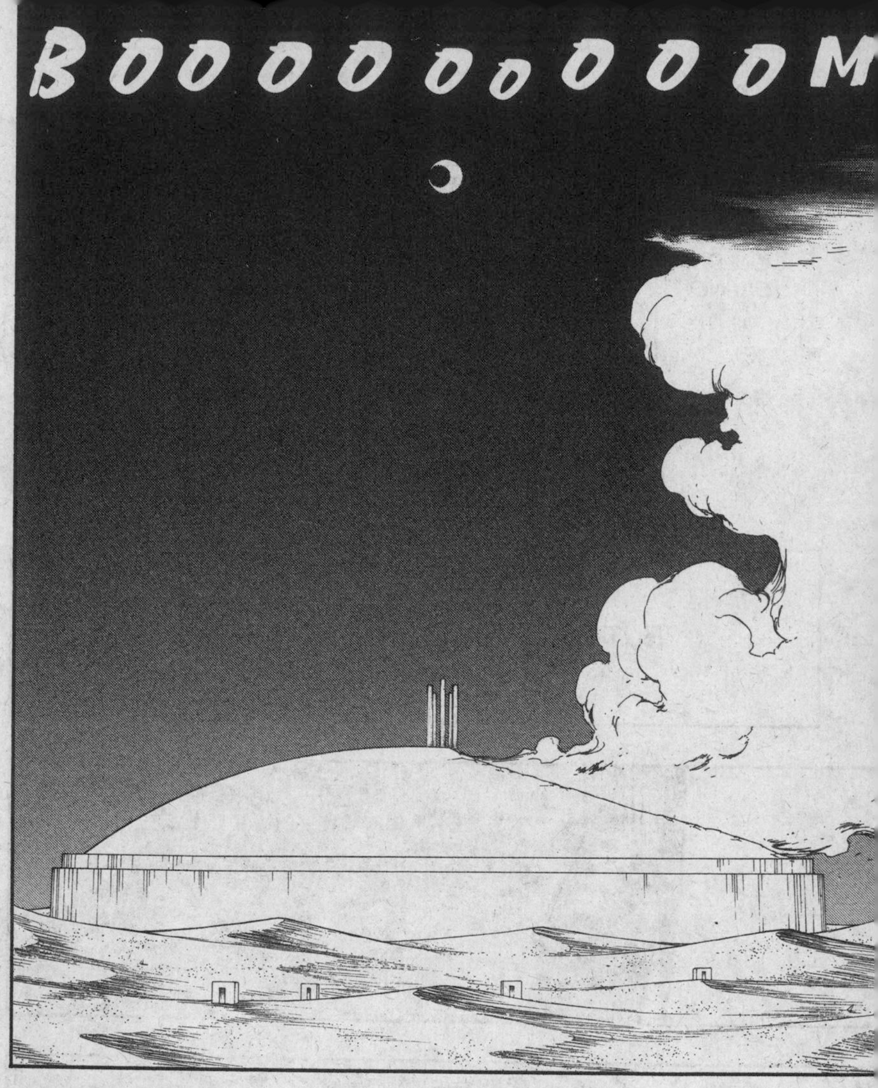
BOOOOOOOOOM
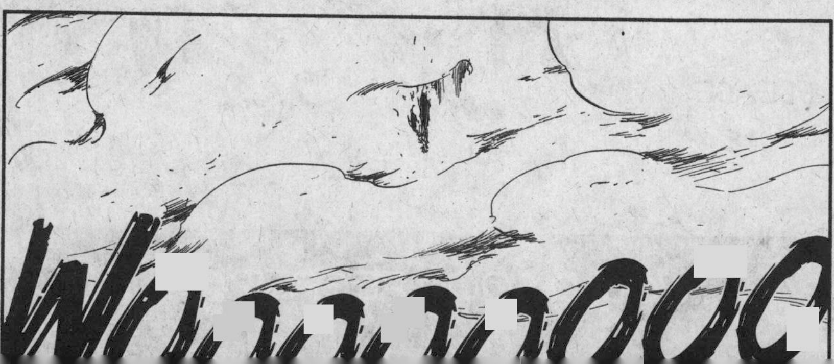

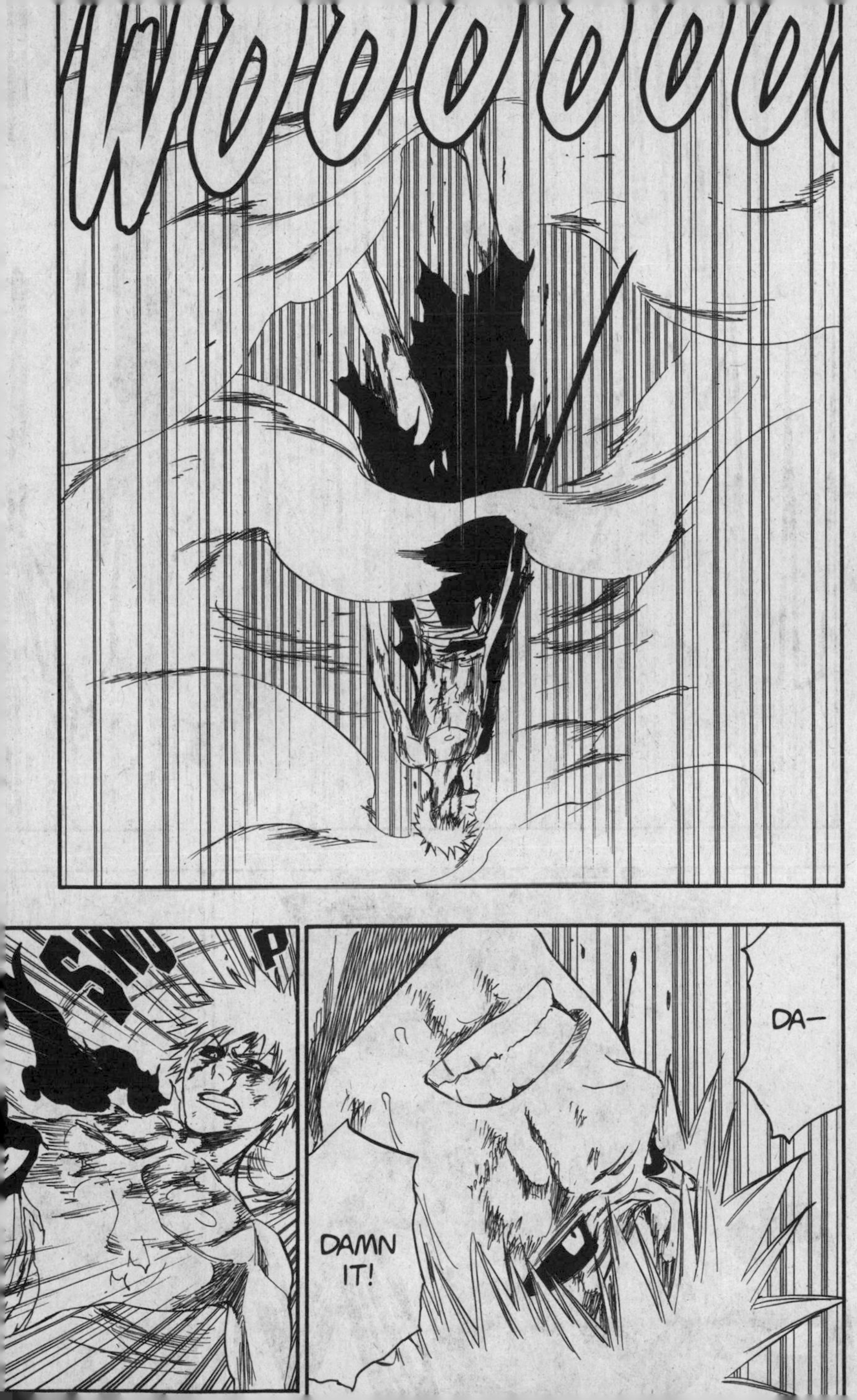
WOOOOOOO
DA-
DAMN IT!

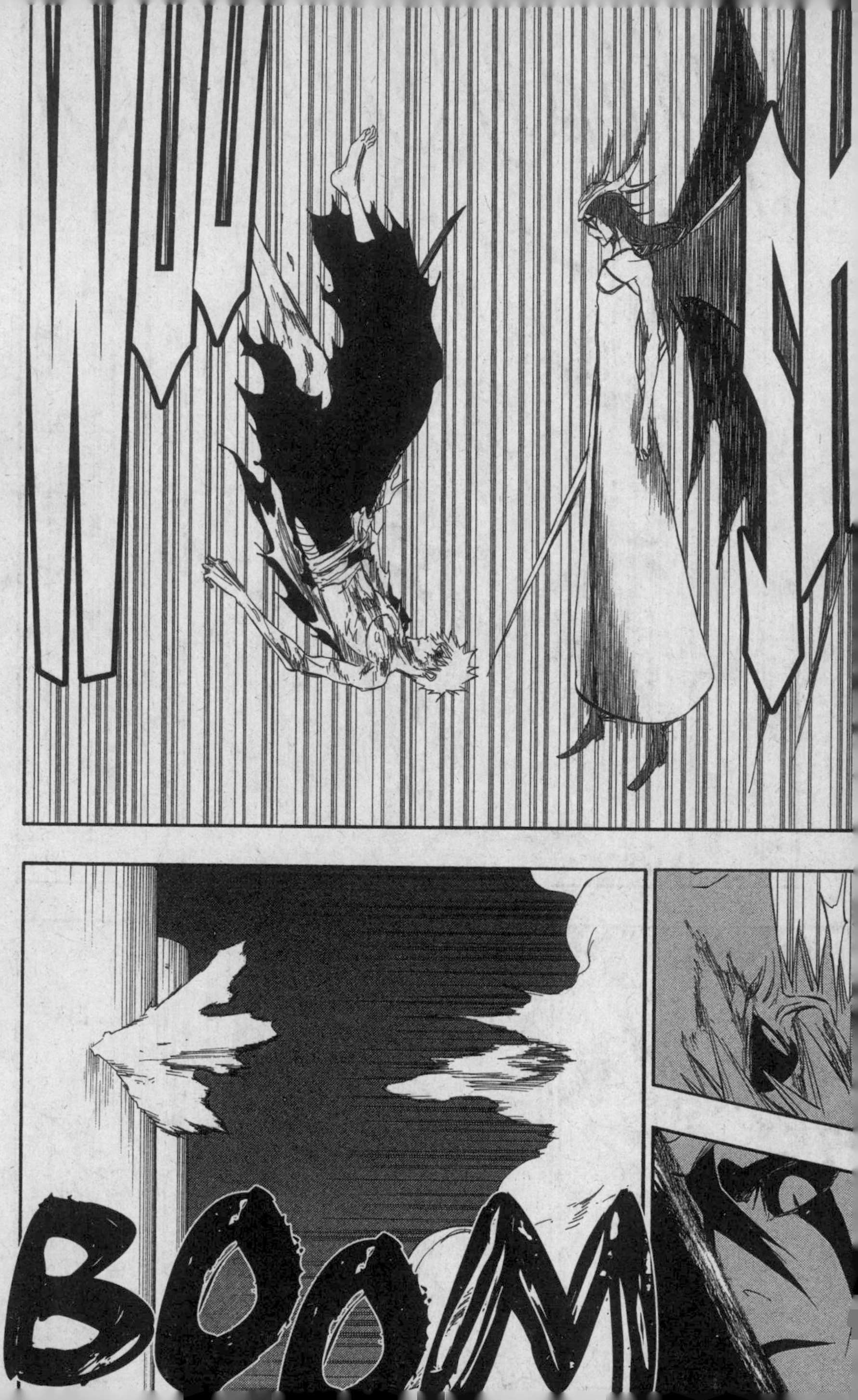
BOOM

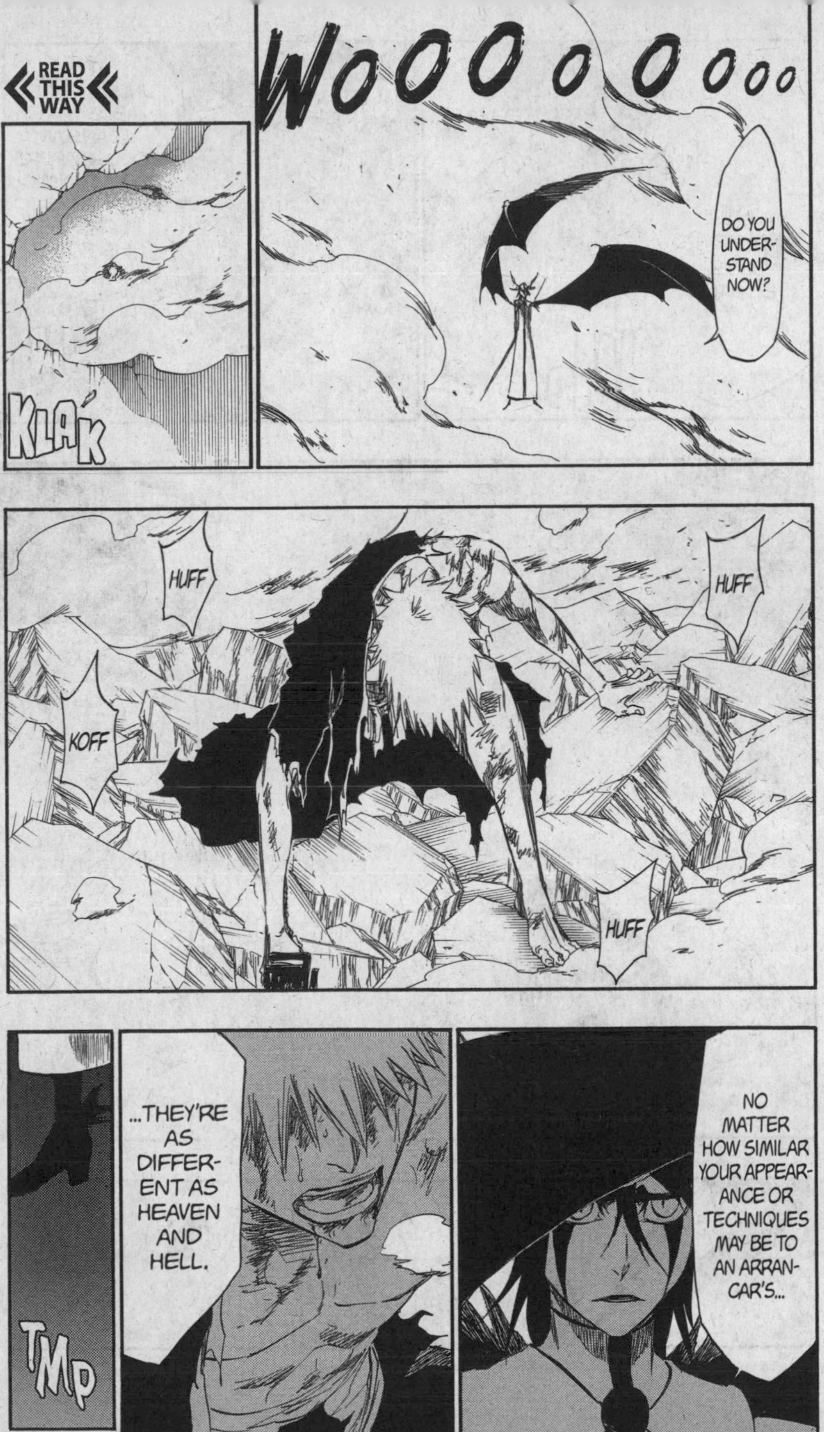
READ THIS WAY
WOOOO OOOoo
DO YOU UNDER-STAND NOW?
KLAK
HUFF
HUFF
KOFF
HUFF
NO MATTER HOW SIMILAR YOUR APPEAR-ANCE OR TECHNIQUES MAY BE TO AN ARRAN-CAR'S...
...THEY'RE AS DIFFER-ENT AS HEAVEN AND HELL.
TMP

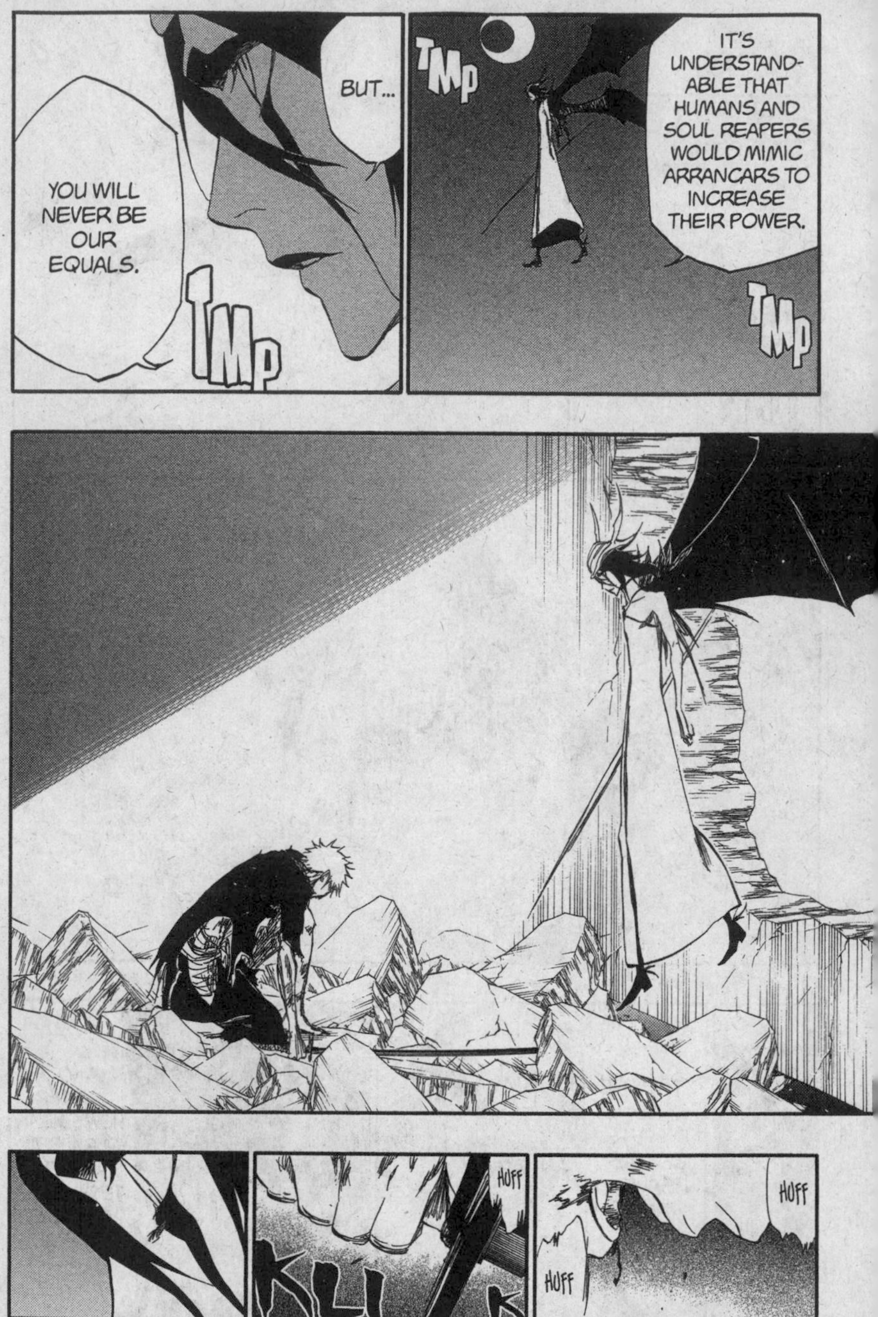
TMP
IT'S UNDERSTAND-ABLE THAT HUMANS AND SOUL REAPERS WOULD MIMIC ARRANCARS TO INCREASE THEIR POWER.
TMP
BUT...
YOU WILL NEVER BE OUR EQUALS.
TMP
HUFF
HUFF
HUFF
KLIK

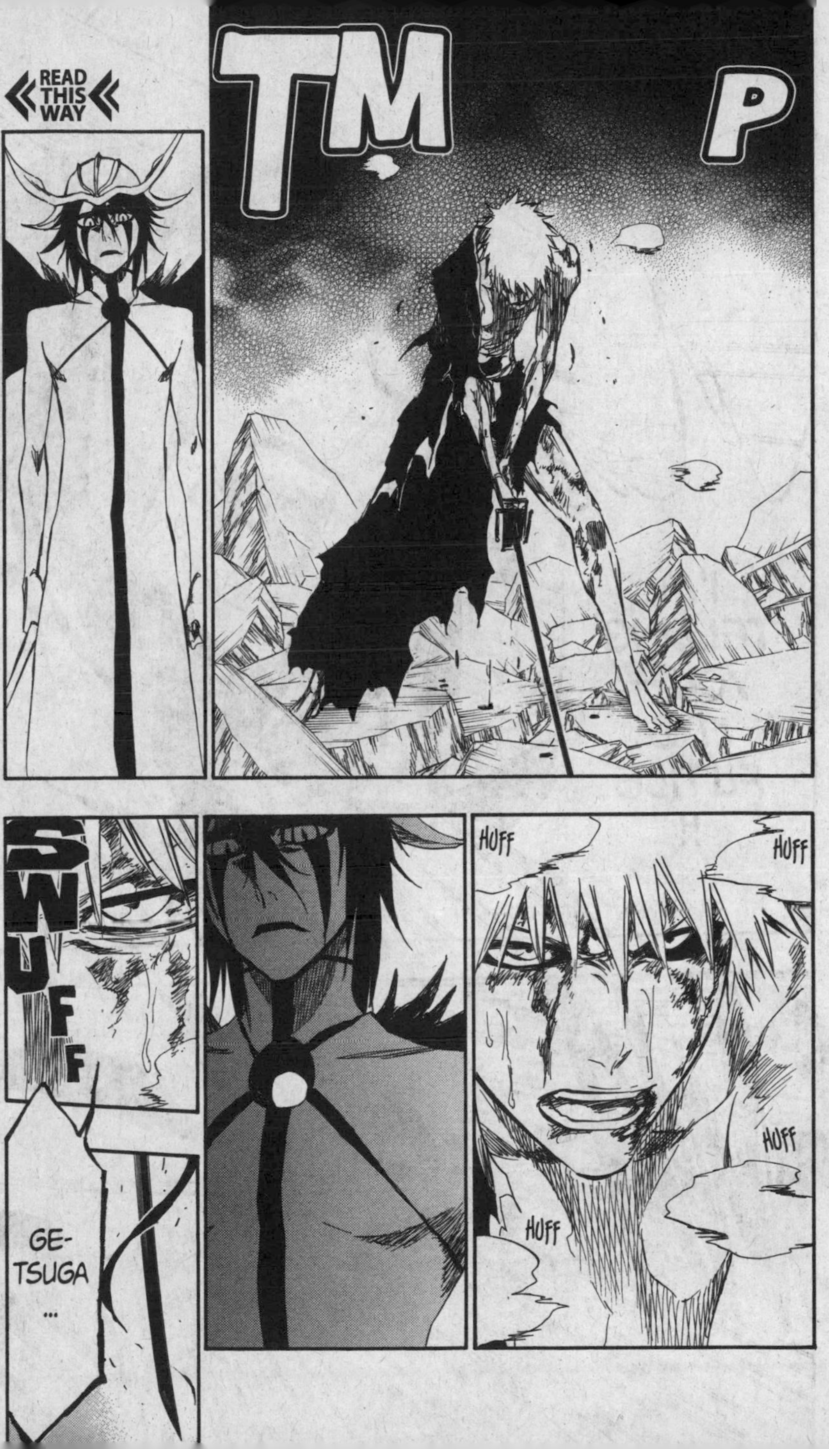
READ THIS WAY
TMP
SWUFF
HUFF
HUFF
HUFF
HUFF
GE-TSUGA ...

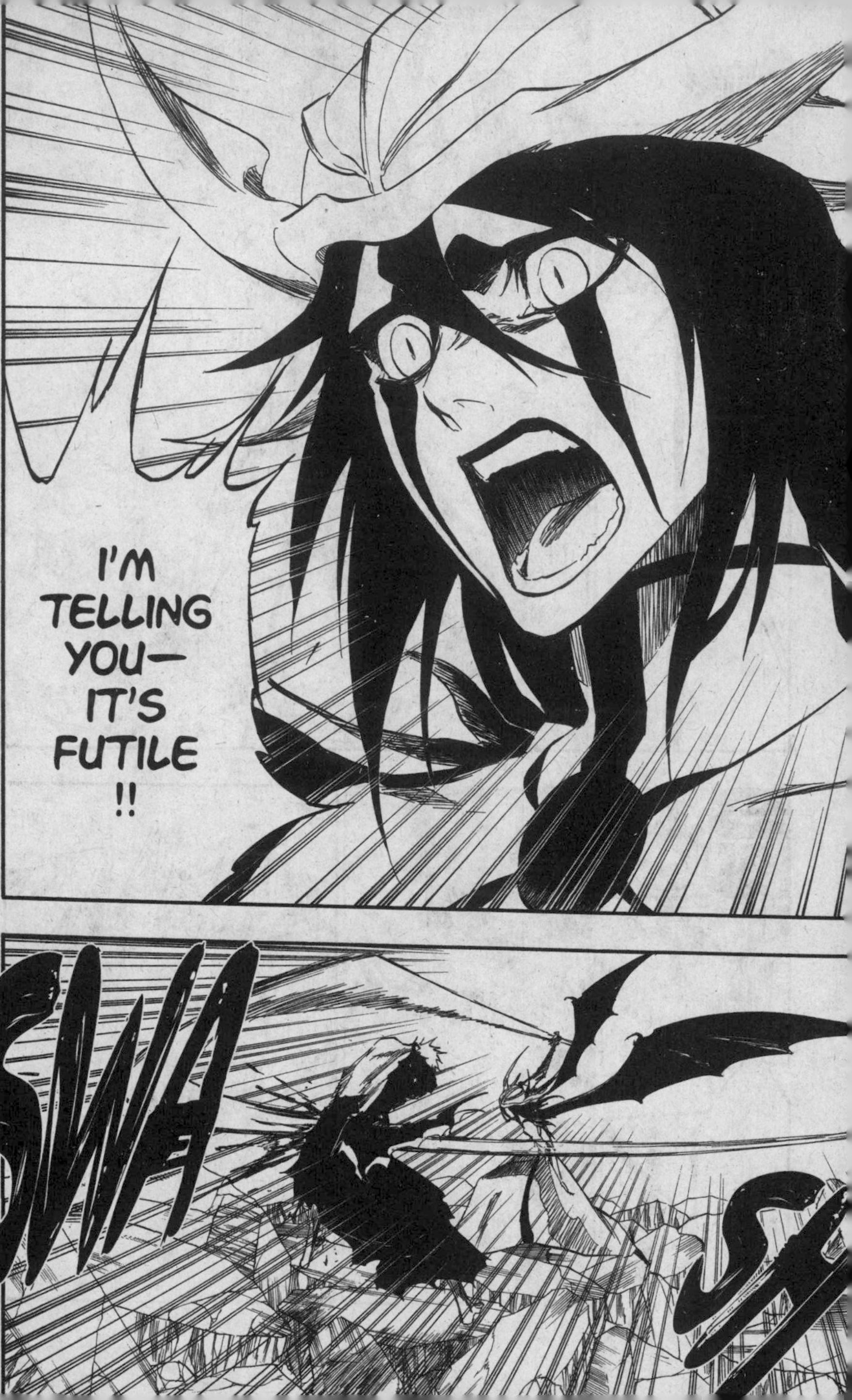
I'M TELLING YOU— IT'S FUTILE !!
SWA
SH

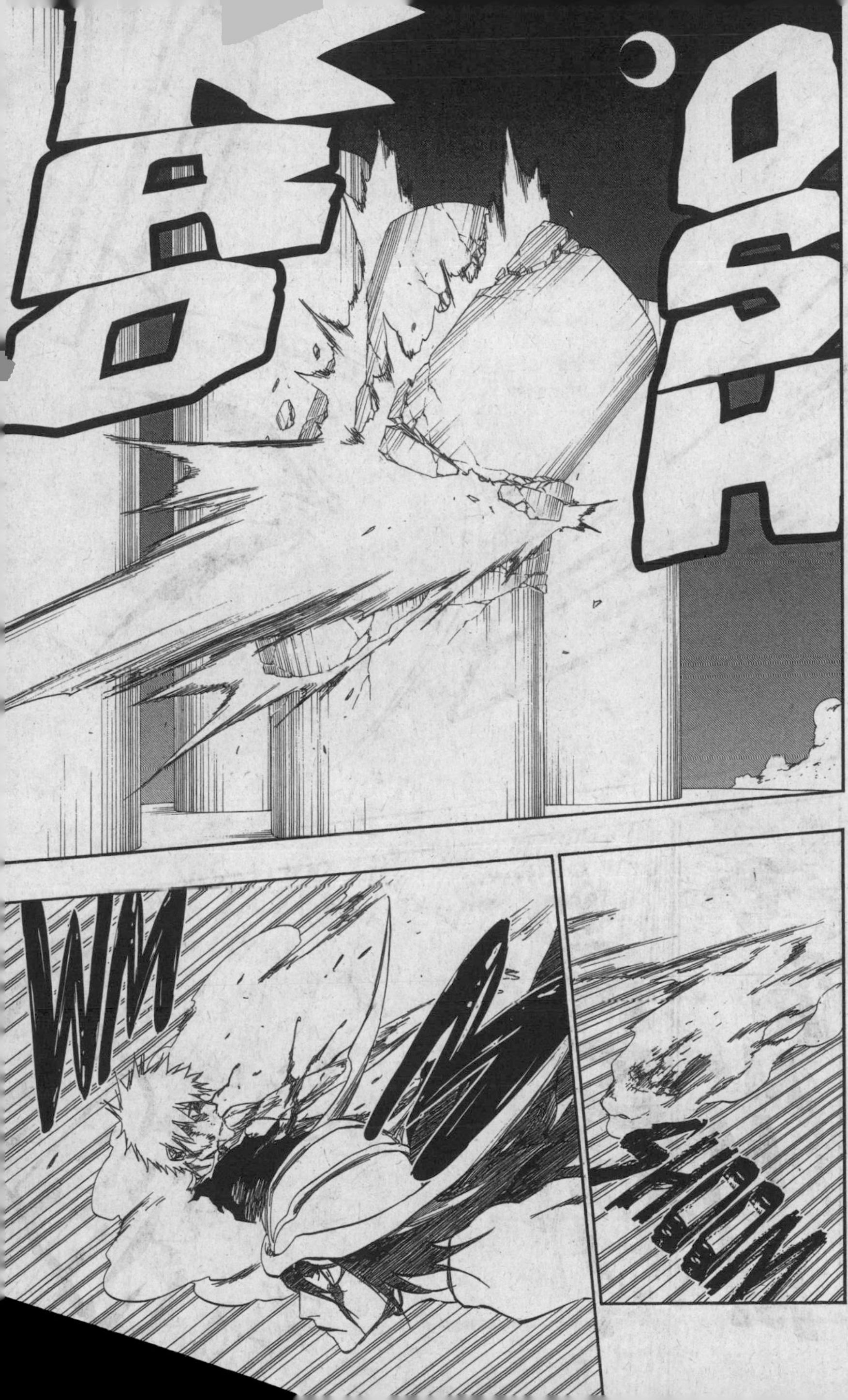
SHOOM

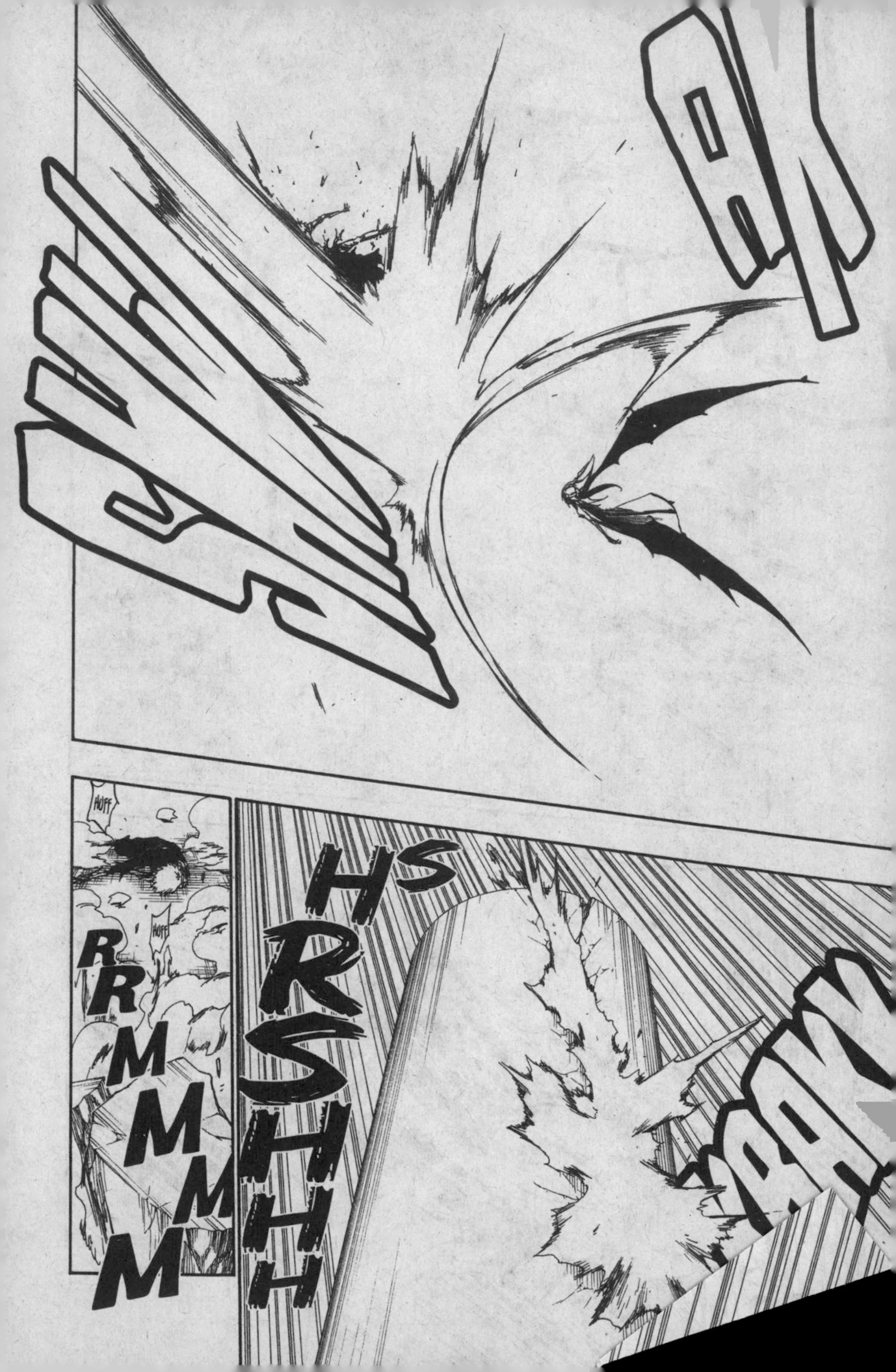
HUFF
HUFF
RRMMMM

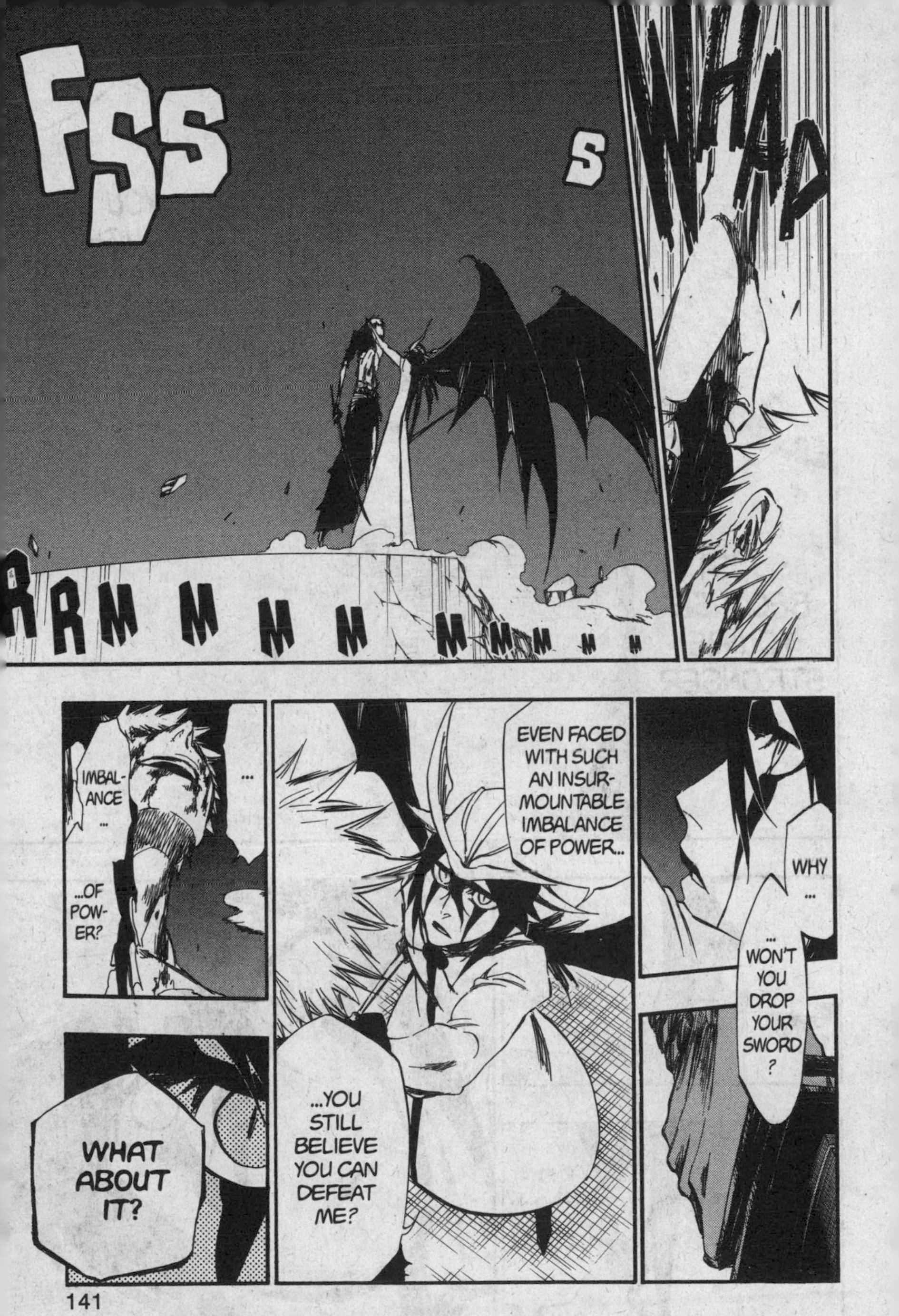
WHAD
FSS
S
RRMMMMMMMMM
WHY...
...WON'T YOU DROP YOUR SWORD?
EVEN FACED WITH SUCH AN INSURMOUNTABLE IMBALANCE OF POWER...
...YOU STILL BELIEVE YOU CAN DEFEAT ME?
...
IMBALANCE...
...OF POWER?
WHAT ABOUT IT?

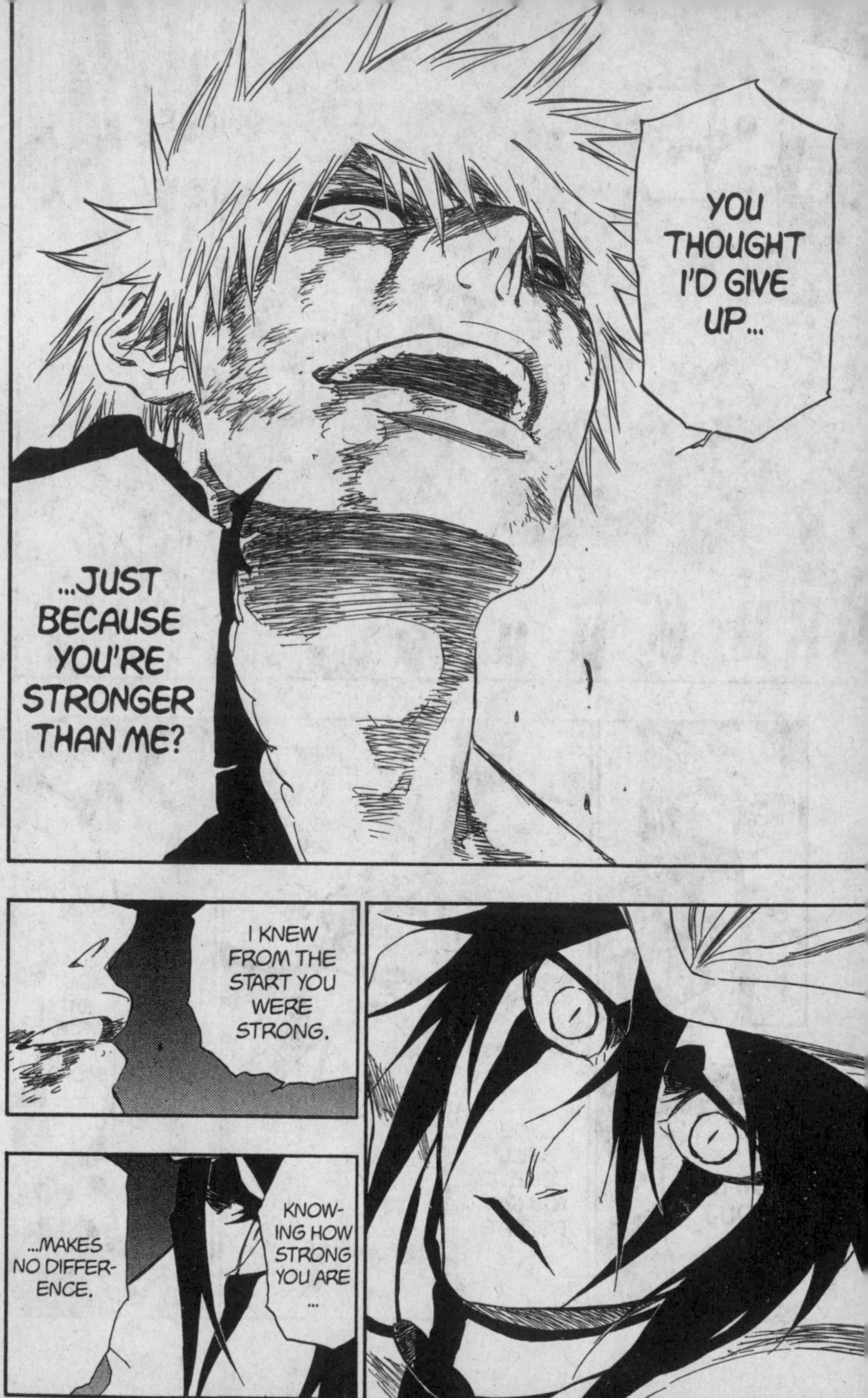
YOU THOUGHT I'D GIVE UP...
...JUST BECAUSE YOU'RE STRONGER THAN ME?
I KNEW FROM THE START YOU WERE STRONG.
KNOW-ING HOW STRONG YOU ARE ...
...MAKES NO DIFFER-ENCE.

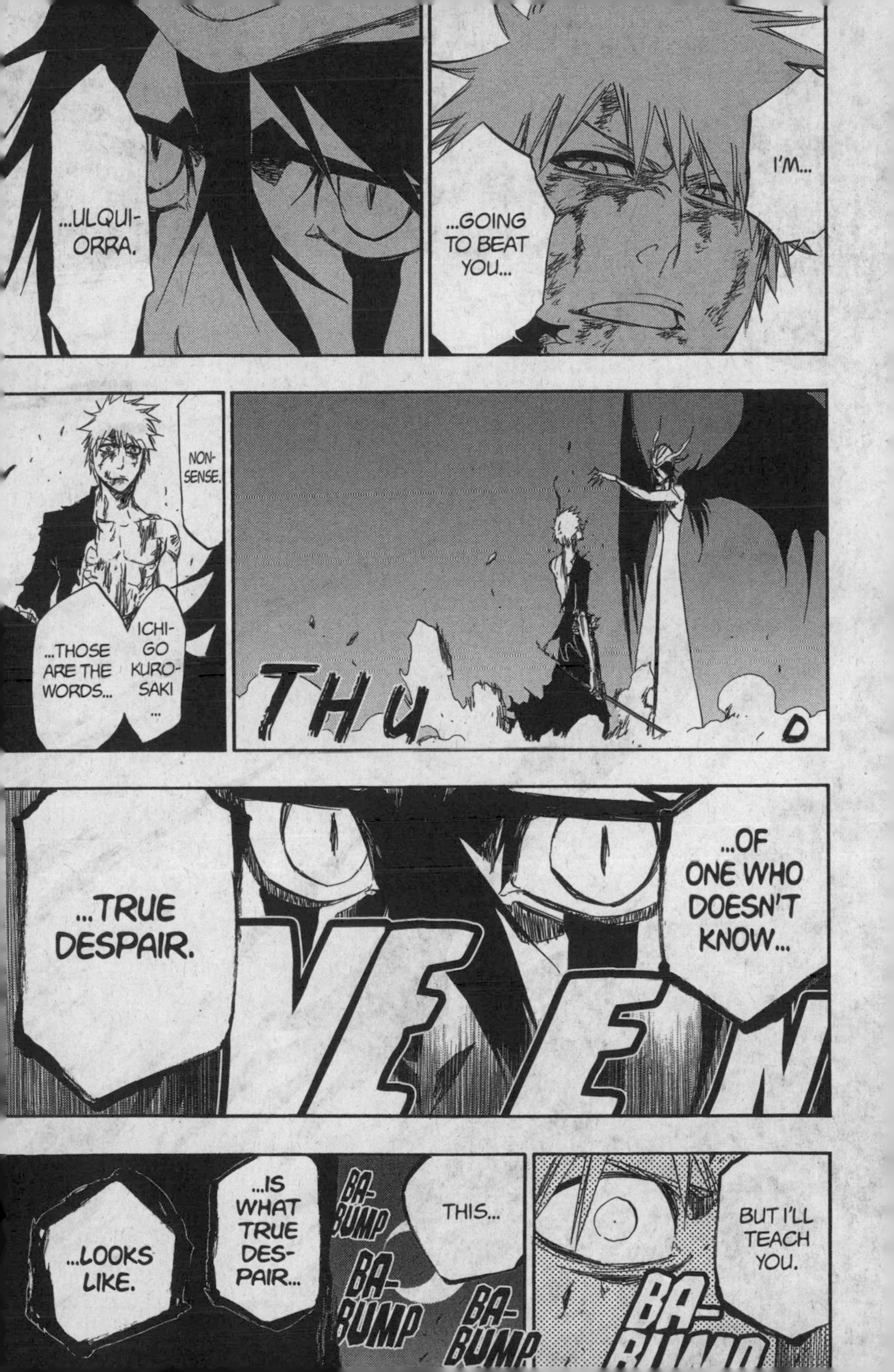
I'M...
...GOING TO BEAT YOU...
...ULQUIORRA.
THUD
NONSENSE.
ICHIGO KUROSAKI...
...THOSE ARE THE WORDS...
...OF ONE WHO DOESN'T KNOW...
VEEN
...TRUE DESPAIR.
BUT I'LL TEACH YOU.
BA-BUMP
THIS...
BA-BUMP
BA-BUMP
BA-BUMP
...IS WHAT TRUE DESPAIR...
...LOOKS LIKE.

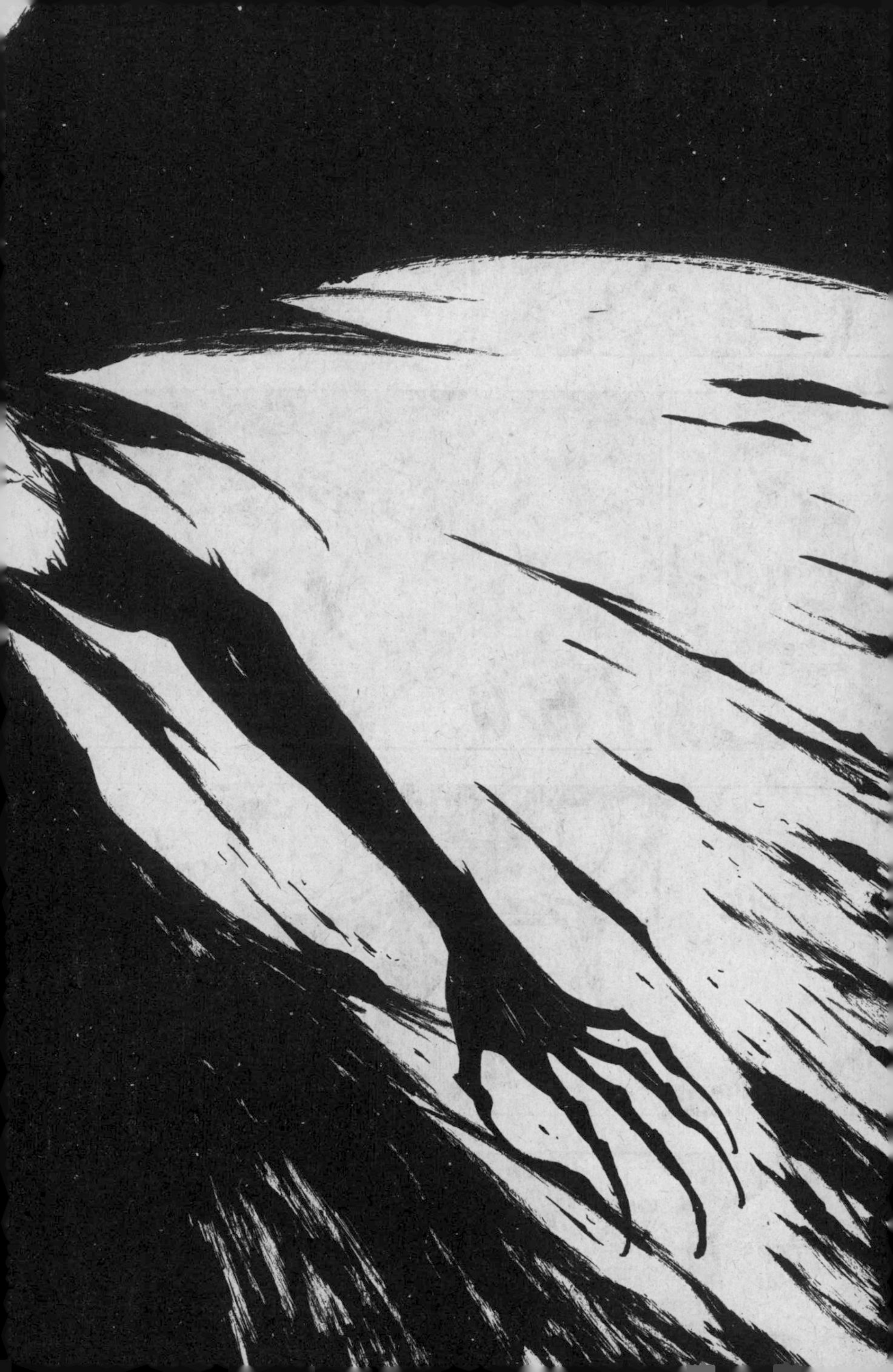

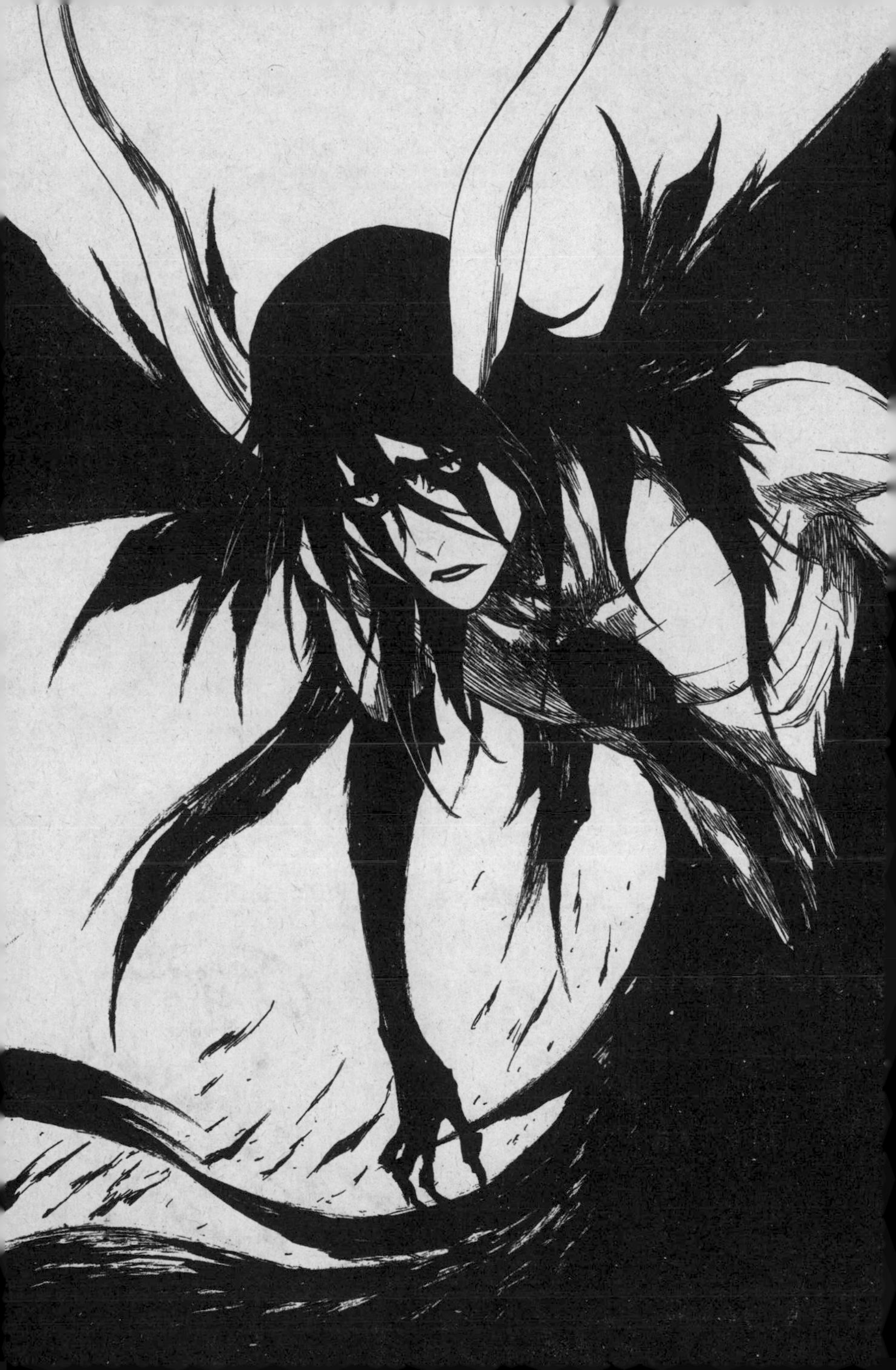

the Lust

348. The Lust 2

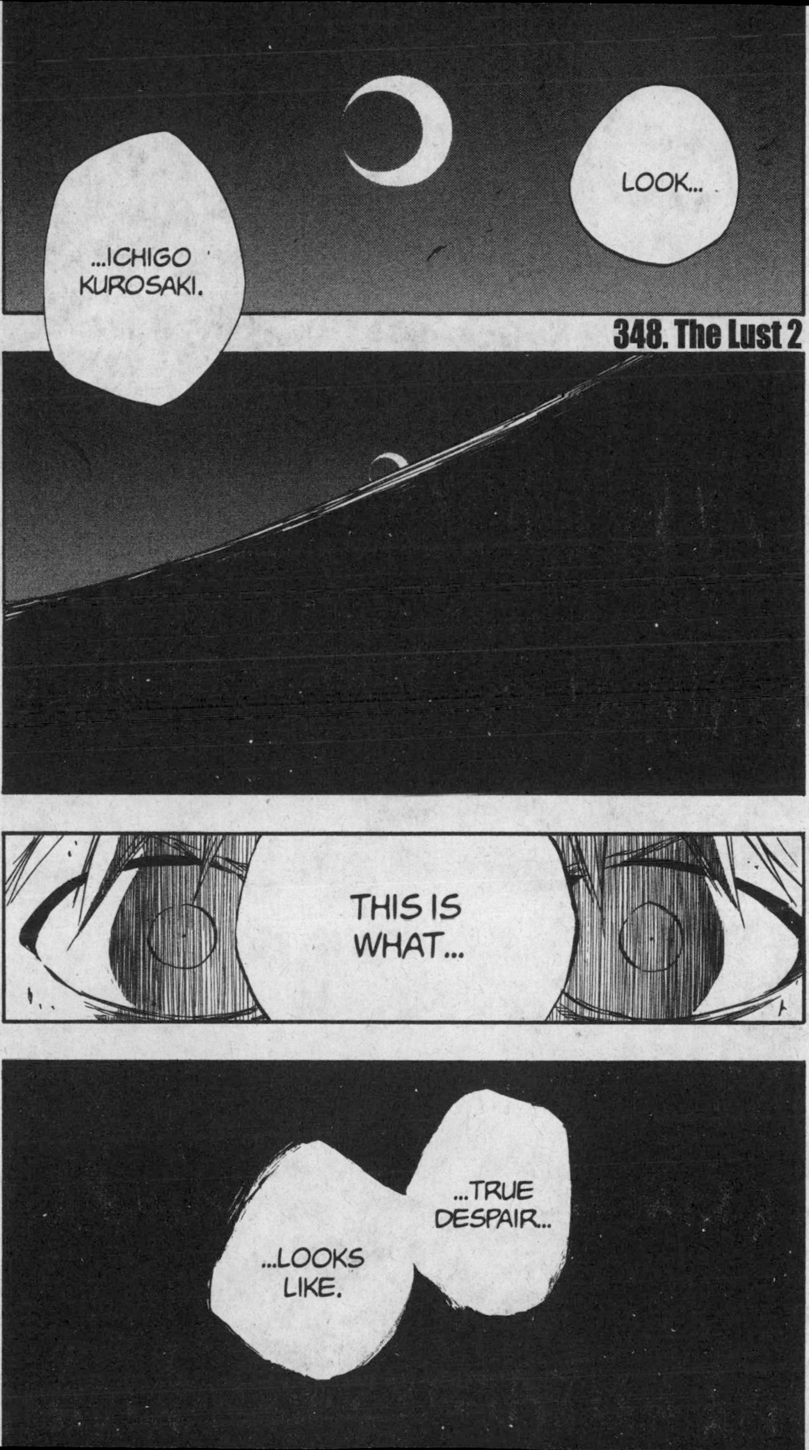
LOOK...
...ICHIGO KUROSAKI.
THIS IS WHAT...
...TRUE DESPAIR...
...LOOKS LIKE.

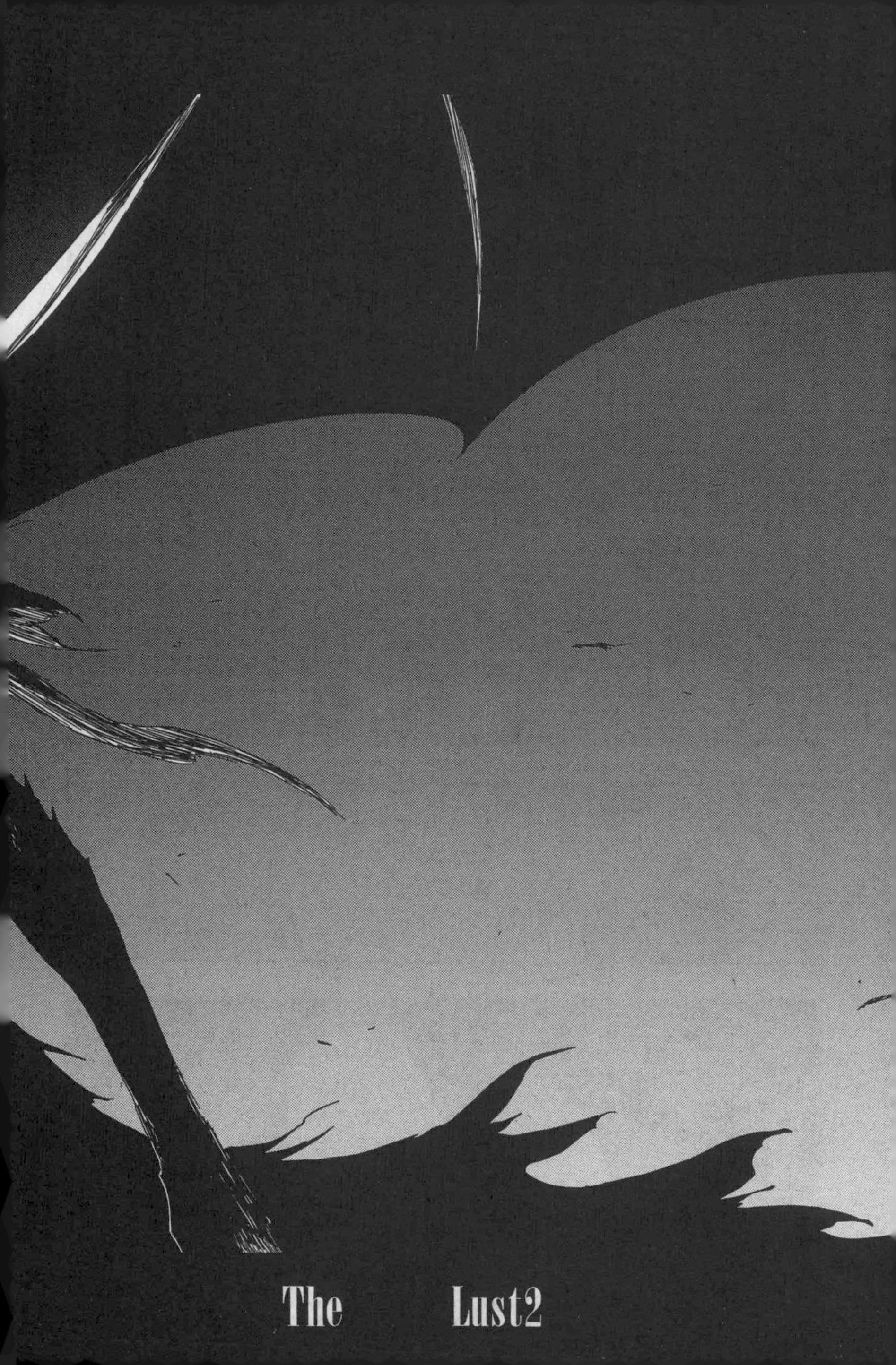
The Lust2

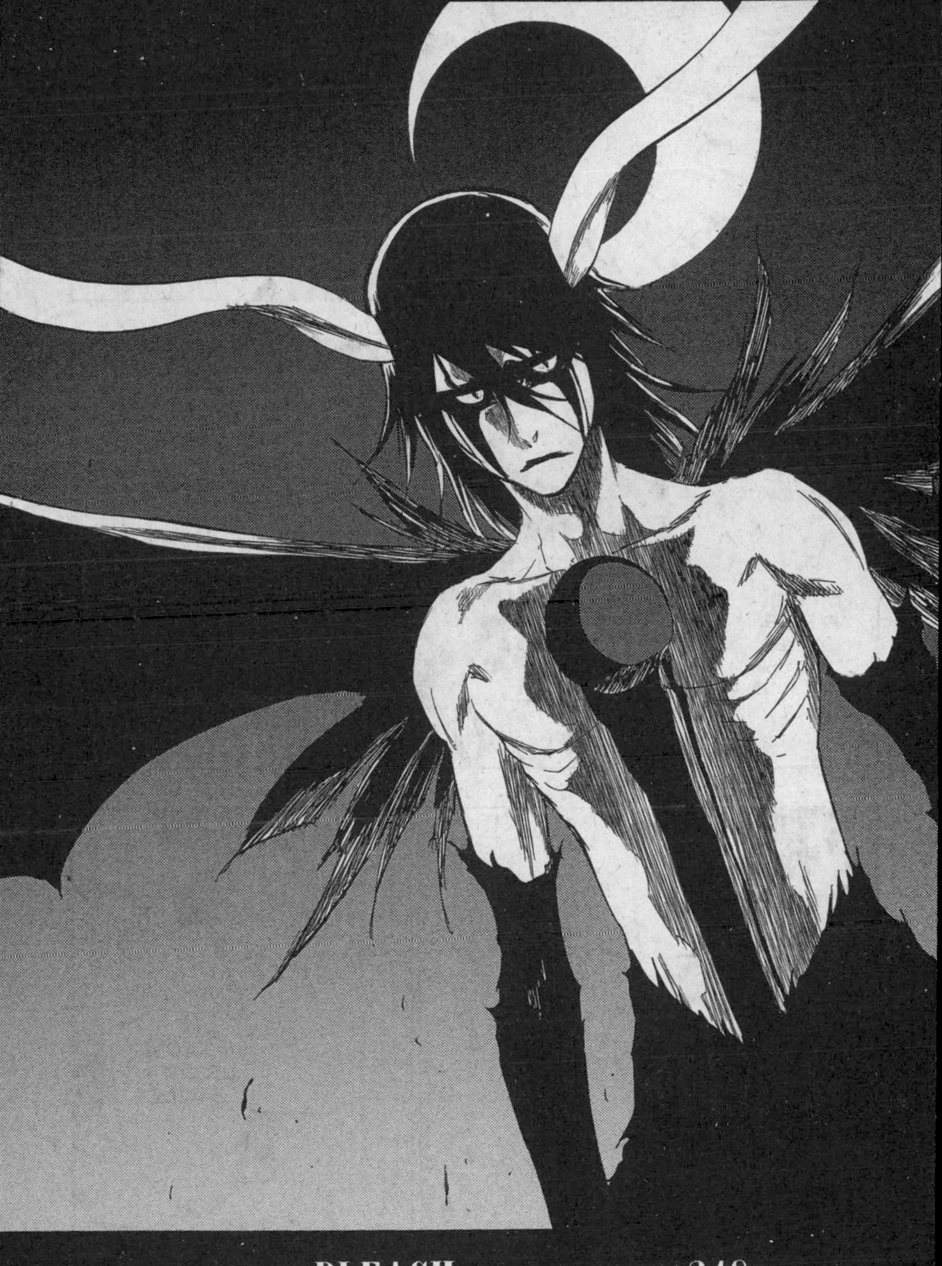

BLEACH 348.

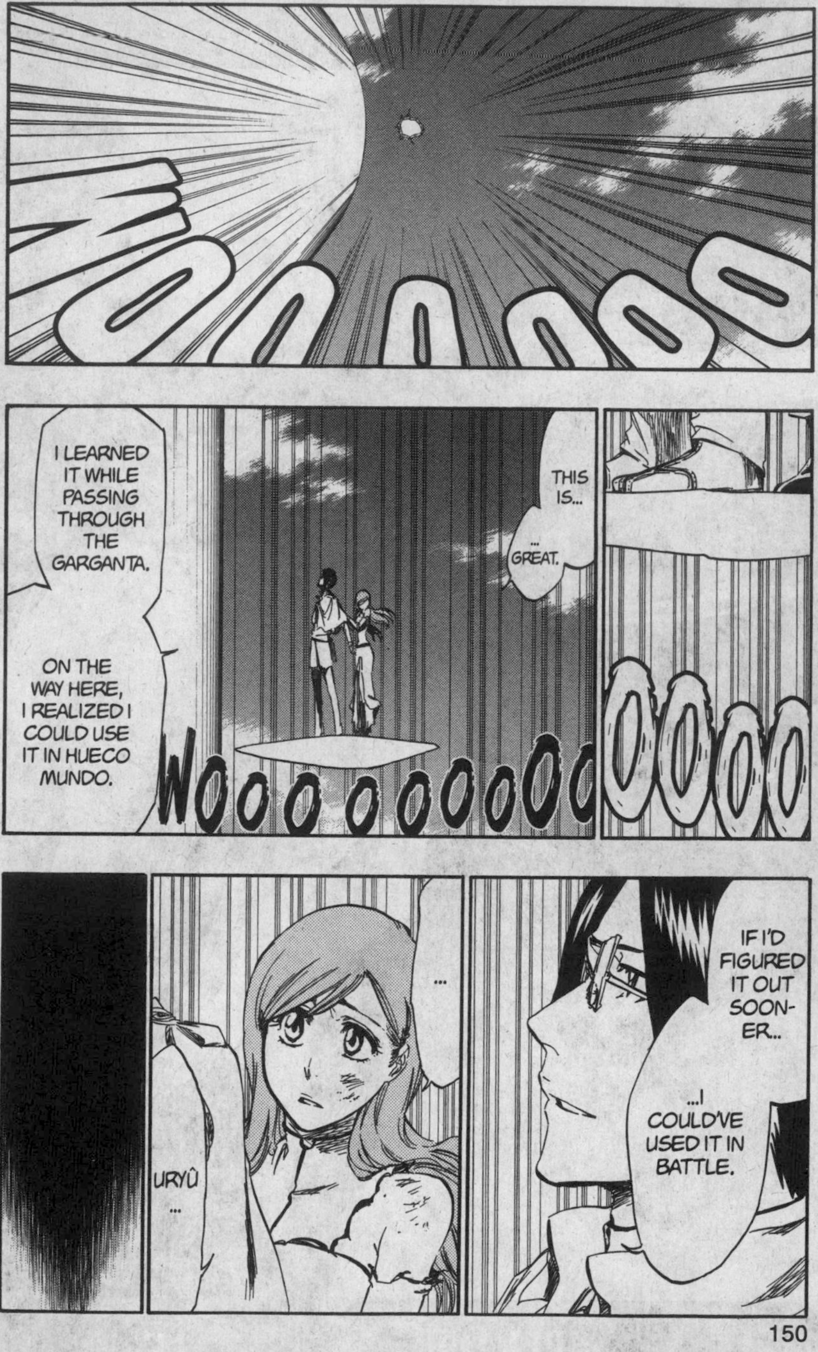
WOOOOOOO
OOOOO
THIS IS...
...GREAT.
I LEARNED IT WHILE PASSING THROUGH THE GARGANTA.
ON THE WAY HERE, I REALIZED I COULD USE IT IN HUECO MUNDO.
WOOOOOOOOO
IF I'D FIGURED IT OUT SOONER...
...I COULD'VE USED IT IN BATTLE.
...
URYÛ...

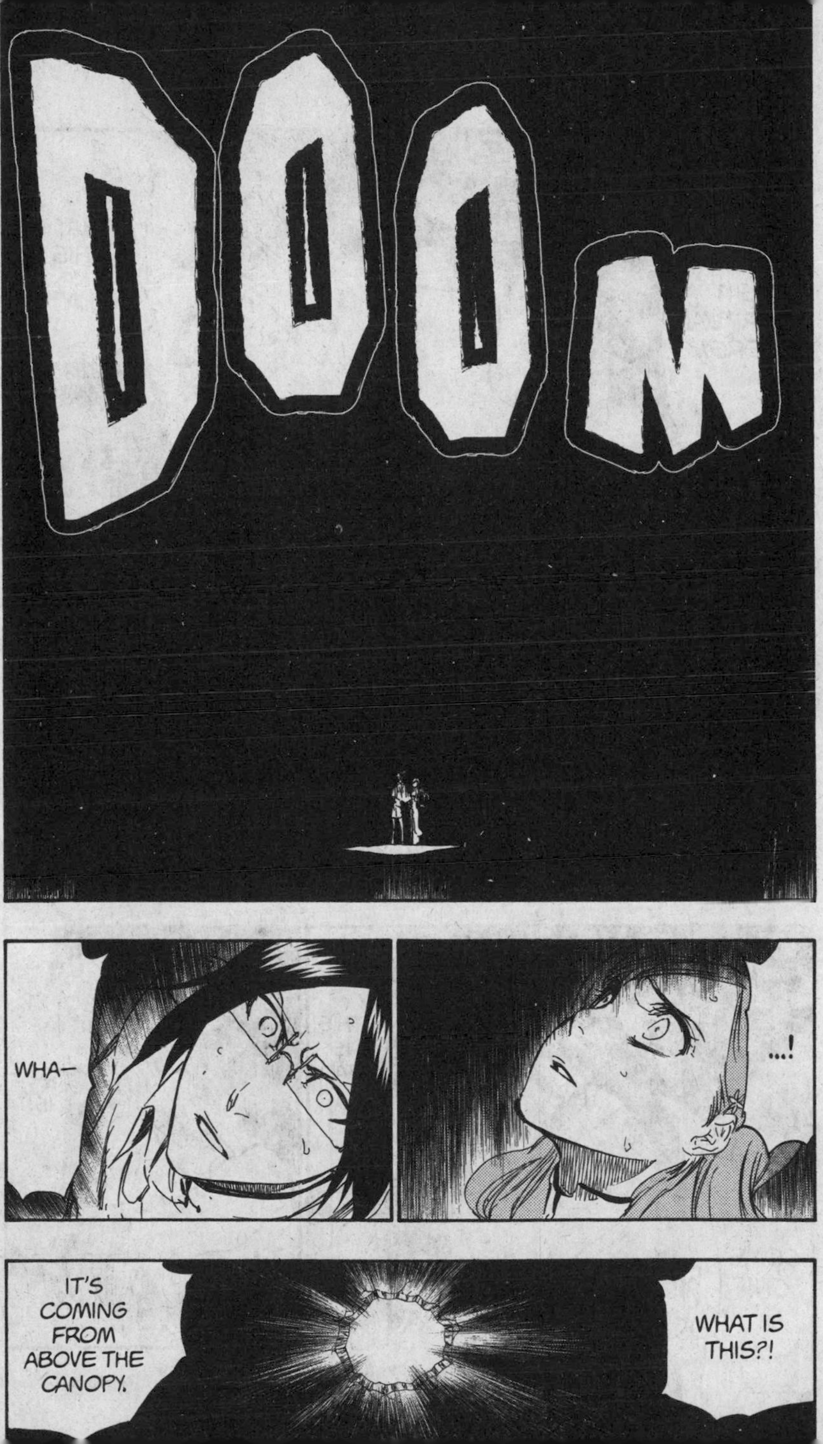
DOOM
...!
WHA—
WHAT IS THIS?!
IT'S COMING FROM ABOVE THE CANOPY.

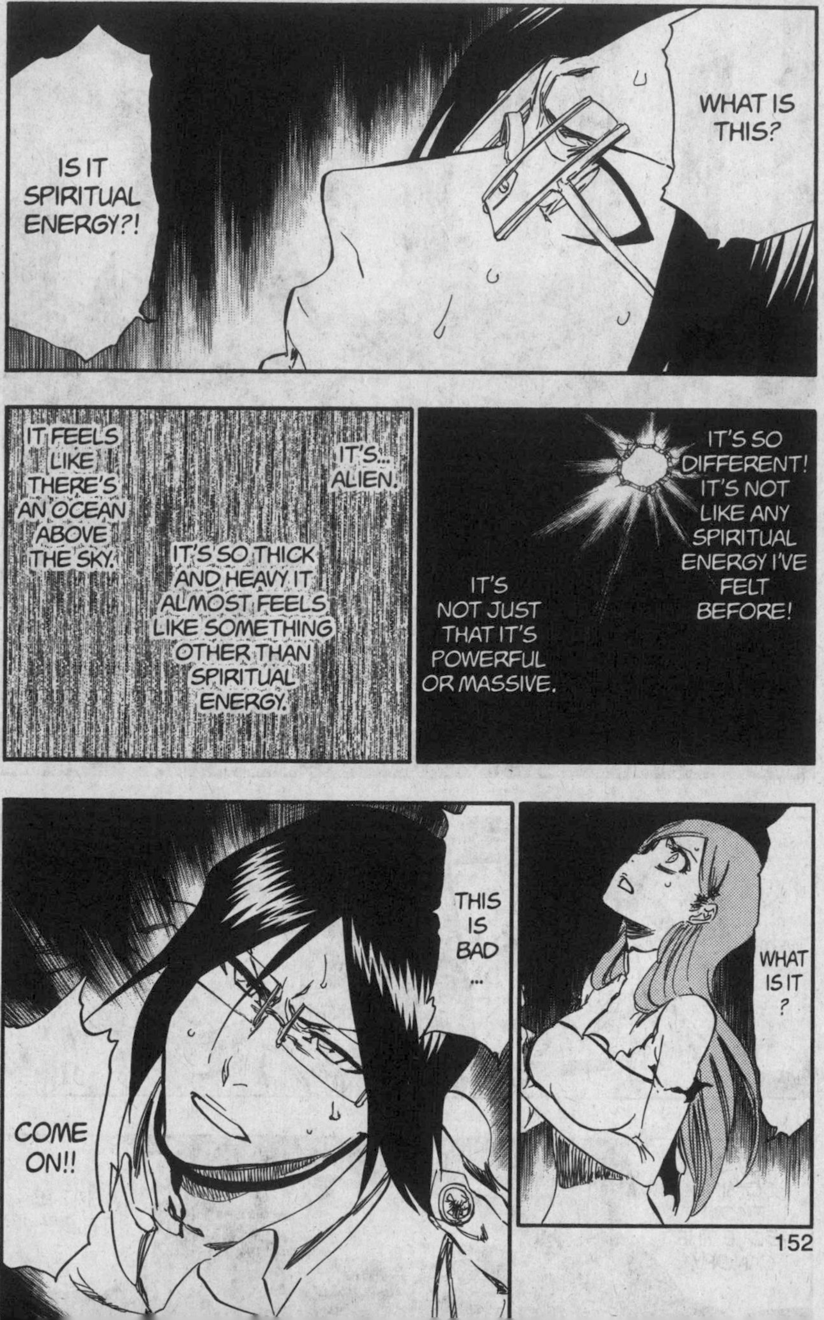
WHAT IS THIS?
IS IT SPIRITUAL ENERGY?!
IT'S SO DIFFERENT! IT'S NOT LIKE ANY SPIRITUAL ENERGY I'VE FELT BEFORE!
IT'S NOT JUST THAT IT'S POWERFUL OR MASSIVE.
IT'S... ALIEN.
IT FEELS LIKE THERE'S AN OCEAN ABOVE THE SKY.
IT'S SO THICK AND HEAVY IT ALMOST FEELS LIKE SOMETHING OTHER THAN SPIRITUAL ENERGY.
WHAT IS IT?
THIS IS BAD...
COME ON!!

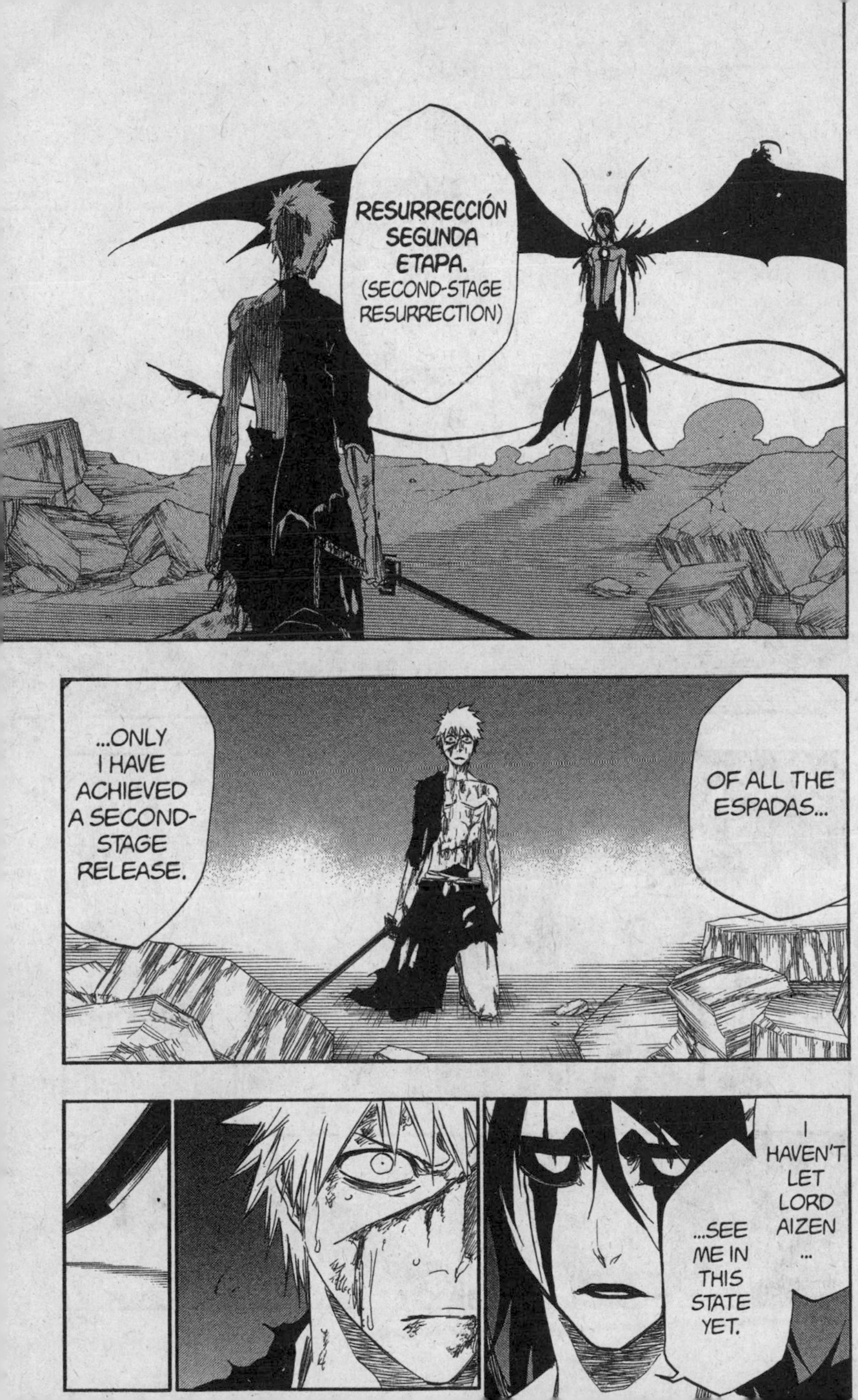
RESURRECCIÓN SEGUNDA ETAPA. (SECOND-STAGE RESURRECTION)
OF ALL THE ESPADAS...
...ONLY I HAVE ACHIEVED A SECOND-STAGE RELEASE.
I HAVEN'T LET LORD AIZEN...
...SEE ME IN THIS STATE YET.

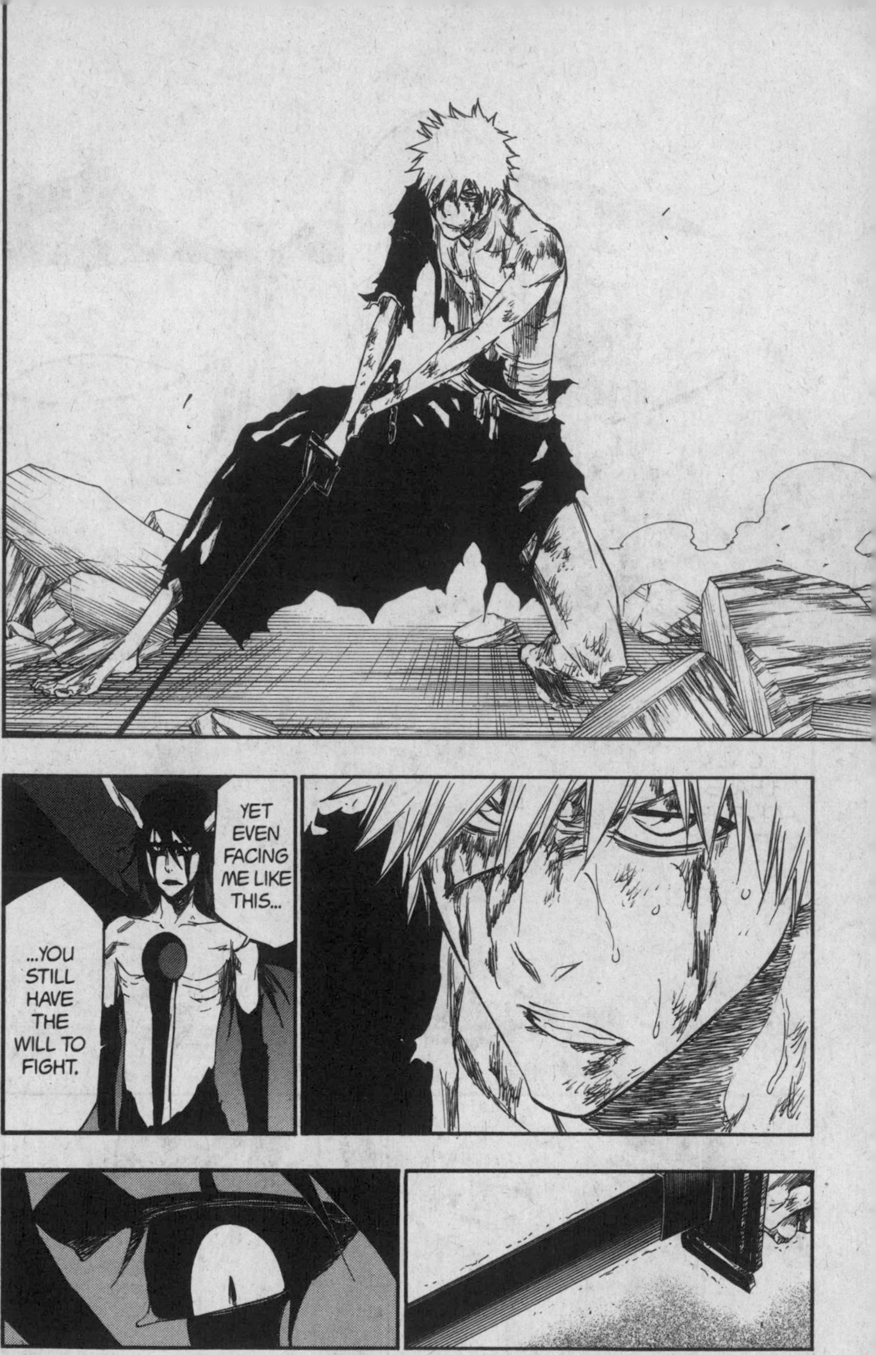
YET EVEN FACING ME LIKE THIS...
...YOU STILL HAVE THE WILL TO FIGHT.

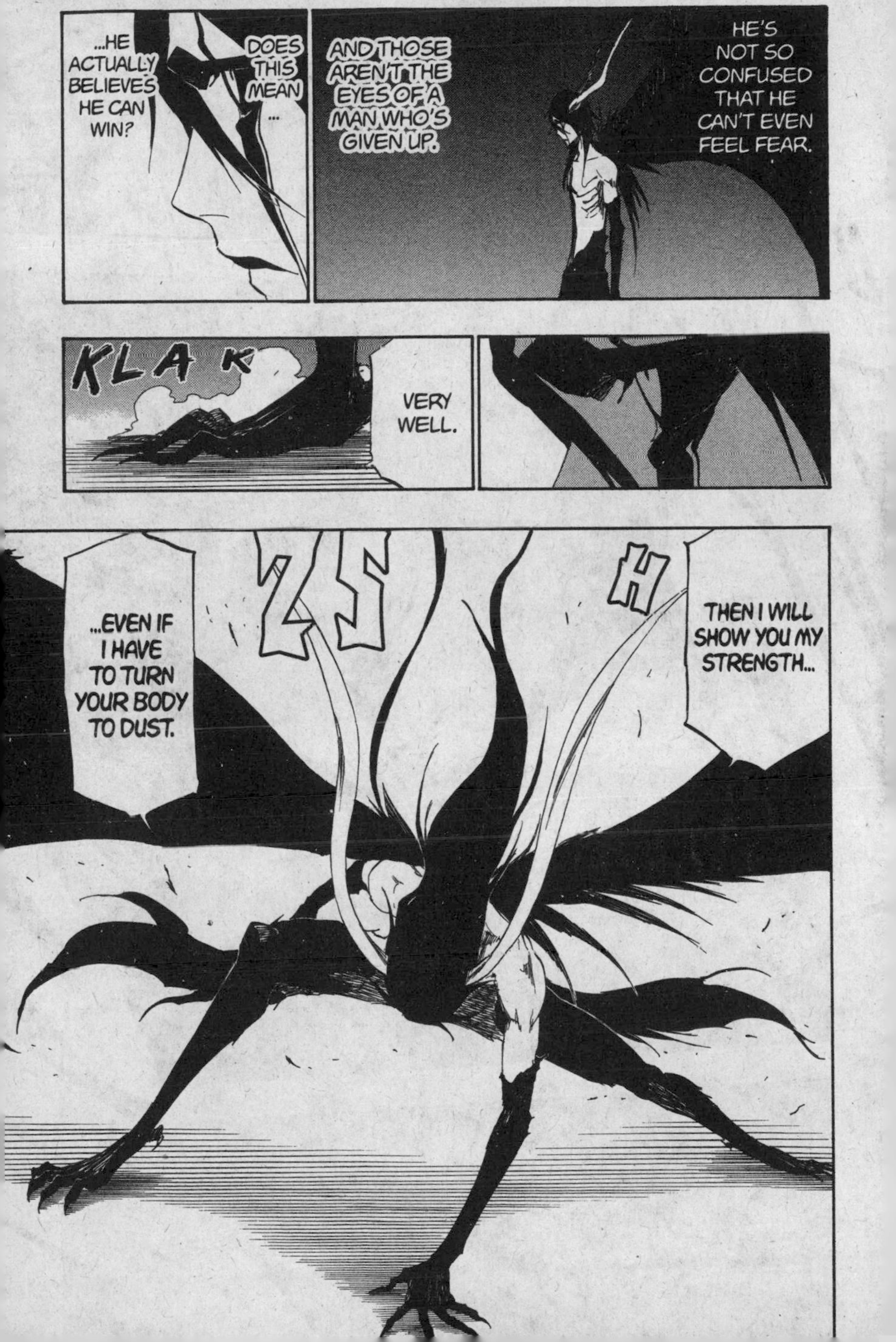
HE'S NOT SO CONFUSED THAT HE CAN'T EVEN FEEL FEAR.
AND THOSE AREN'T THE EYES OF A MAN WHO'S GIVEN UP.
DOES THIS MEAN ...
...HE ACTUALLY BELIEVES HE CAN WIN?
VERY WELL.
KLAK
THEN I WILL SHOW YOU MY STRENGTH...
ZSH
...EVEN IF I HAVE TO TURN YOUR BODY TO DUST.

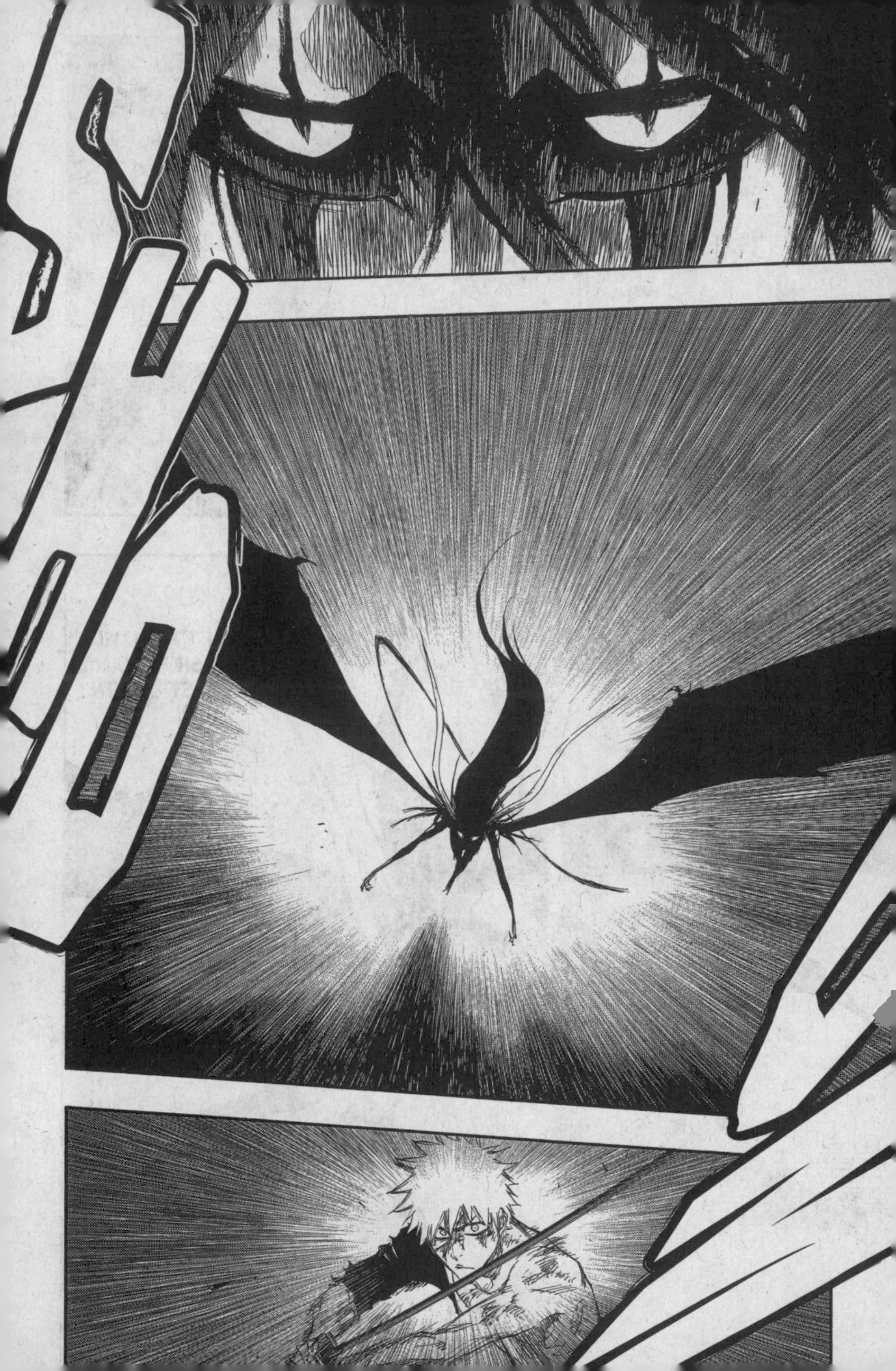

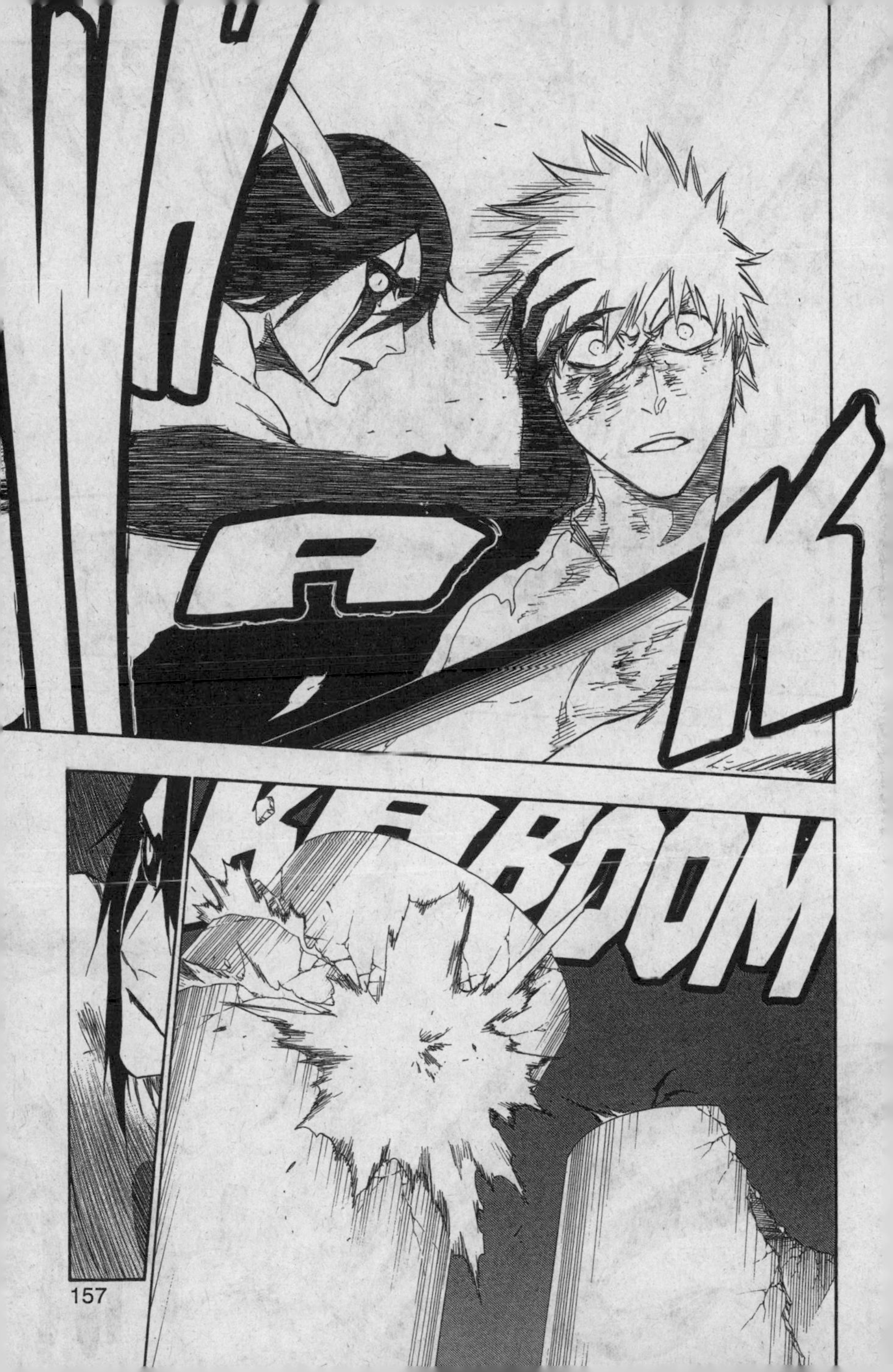

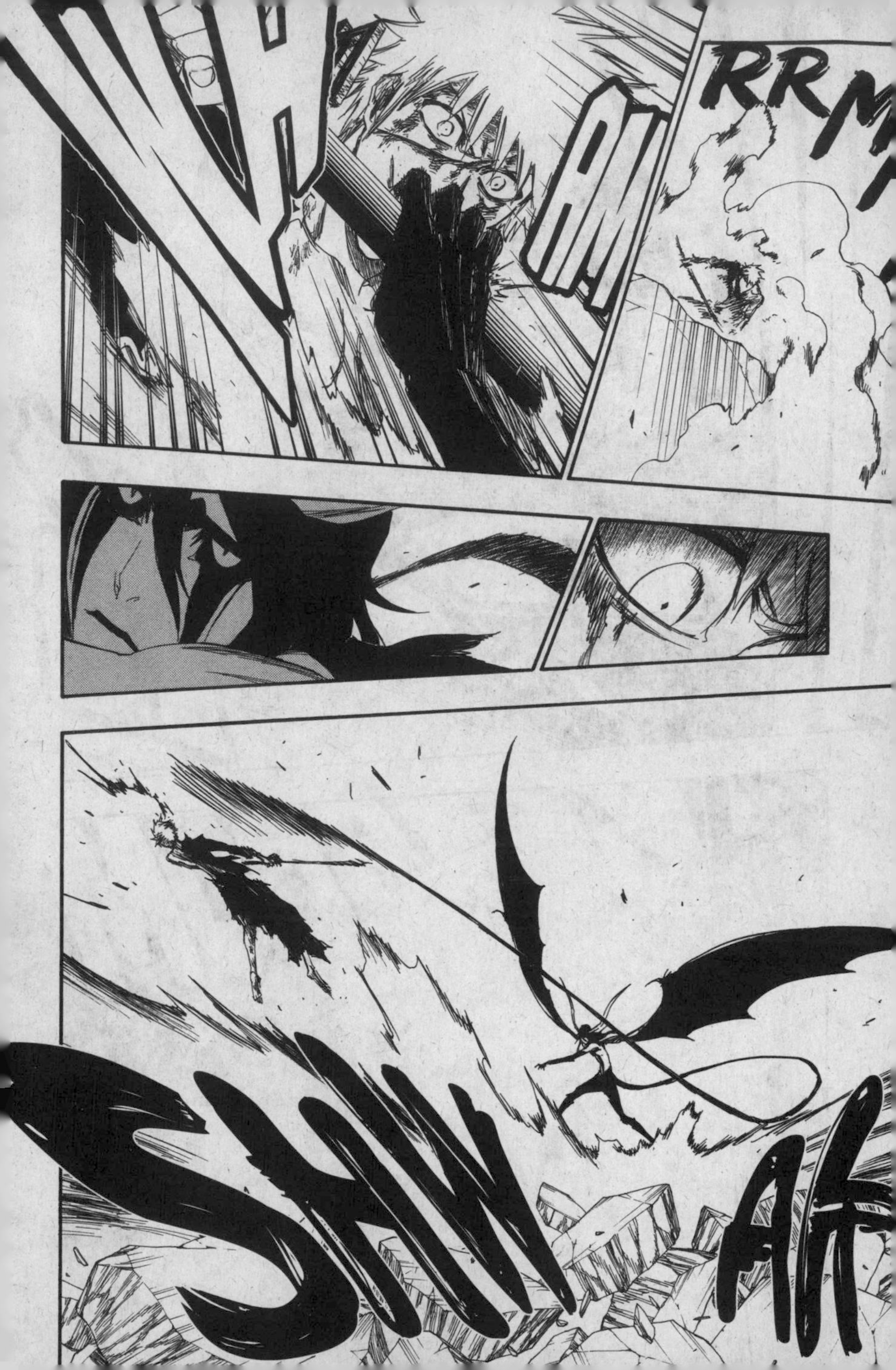
RRM

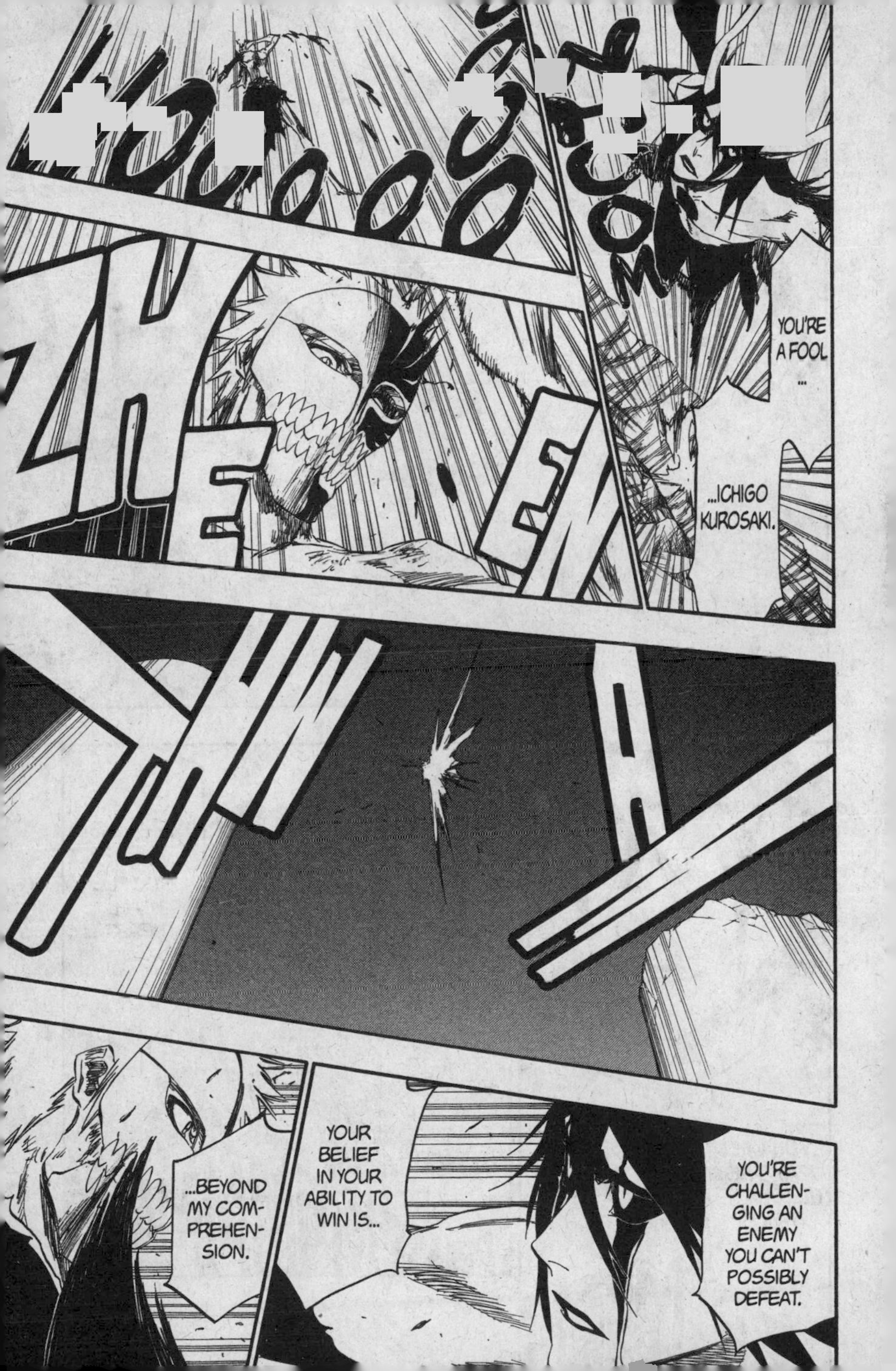
YOU'RE A FOOL ...
...ICHIGO KUROSAKI.
YOU'RE CHALLENGING AN ENEMY YOU CAN'T POSSIBLY DEFEAT.
YOUR BELIEF IN YOUR ABILITY TO WIN IS...
...BEYOND MY COMPREHENSION.

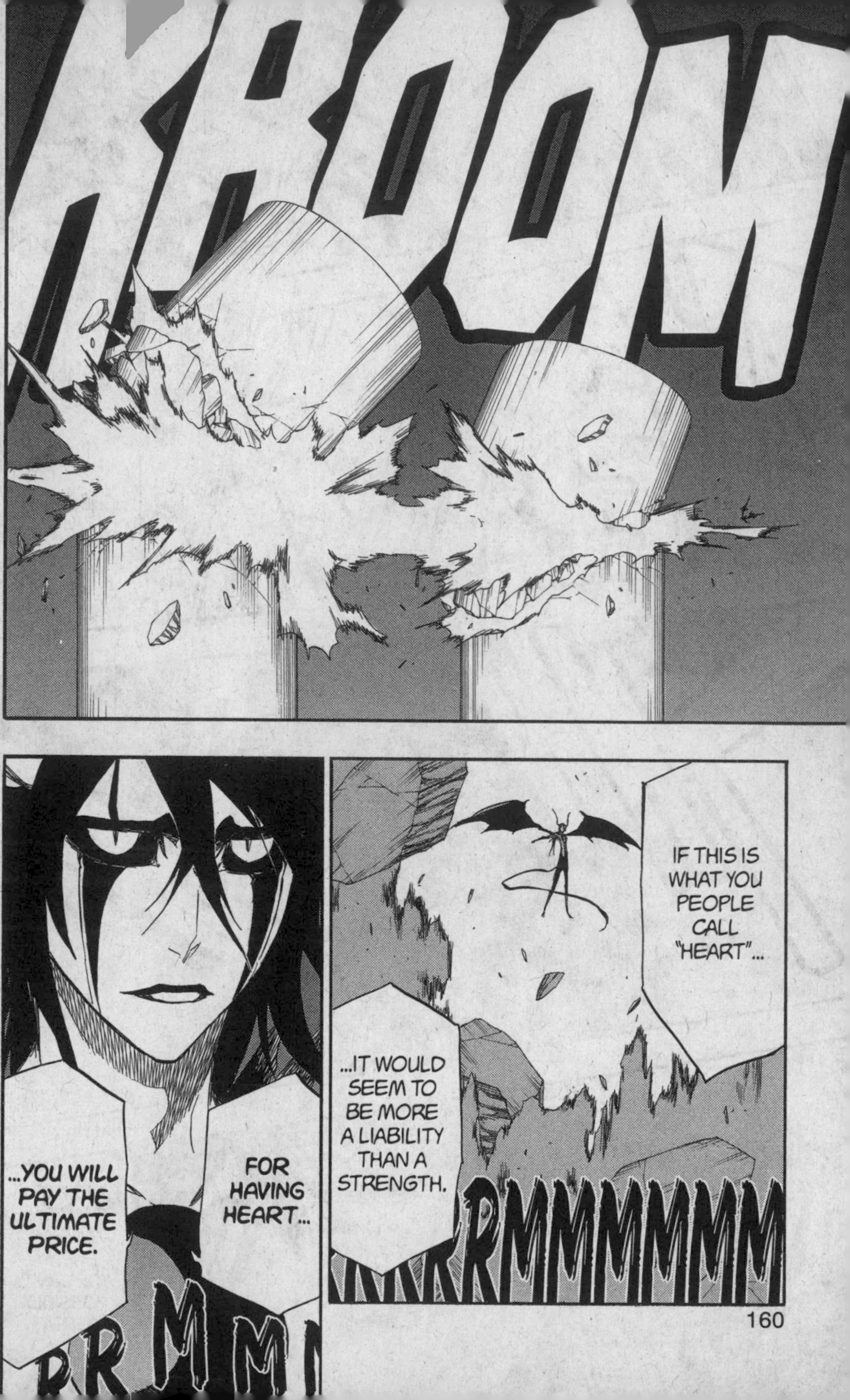
KBOOM
IF THIS IS WHAT YOU PEOPLE CALL "HEART"...
...IT WOULD SEEM TO BE MORE A LIABILITY THAN A STRENGTH.
RMMMMMMM
FOR HAVING HEART...
...YOU WILL PAY THE ULTIMATE PRICE.
DRMM

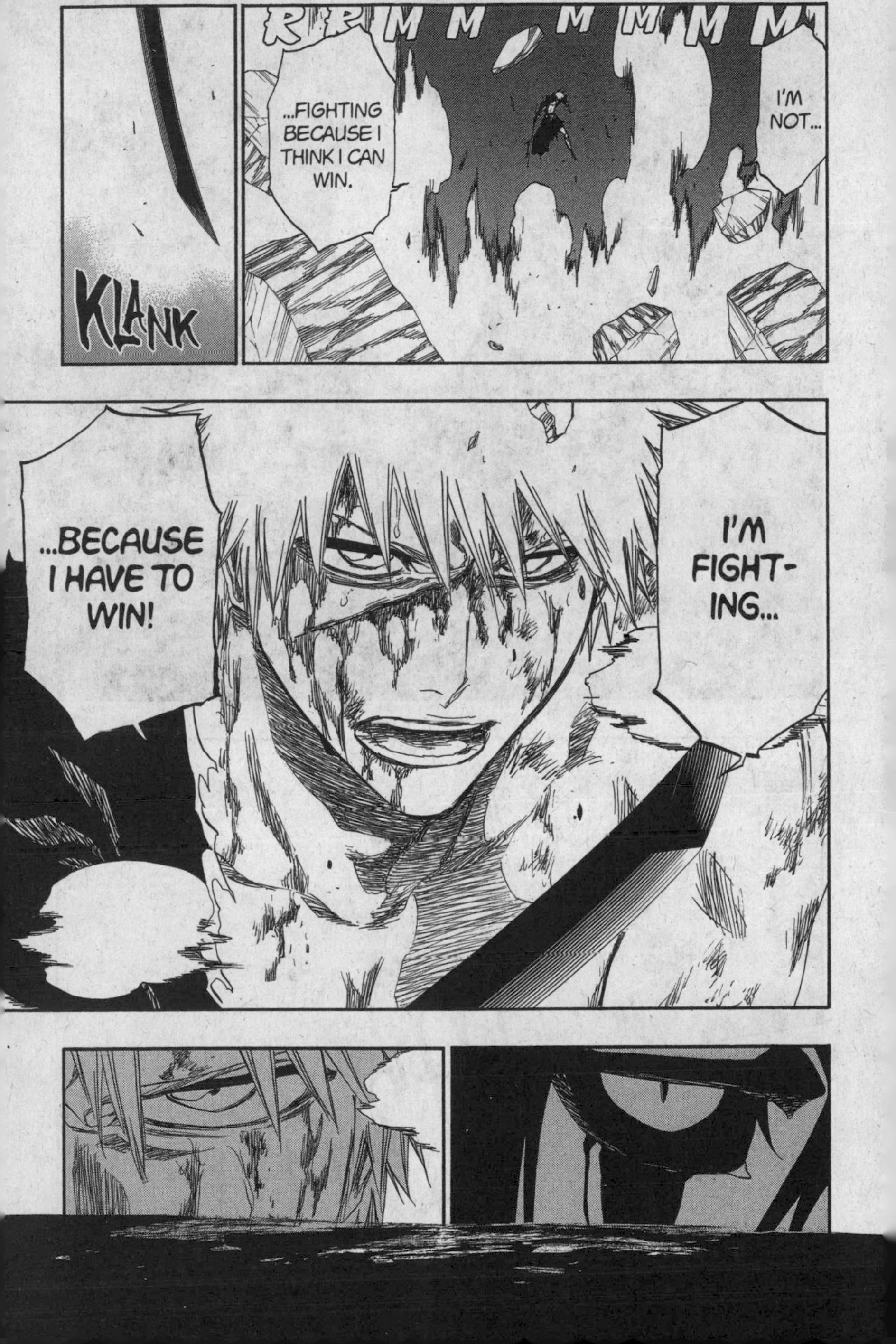
RRMMMMMMMM
I'M NOT...
...FIGHTING BECAUSE I THINK I CAN WIN.
KLANK
I'M FIGHT-ING...
...BECAUSE I HAVE TO WIN!

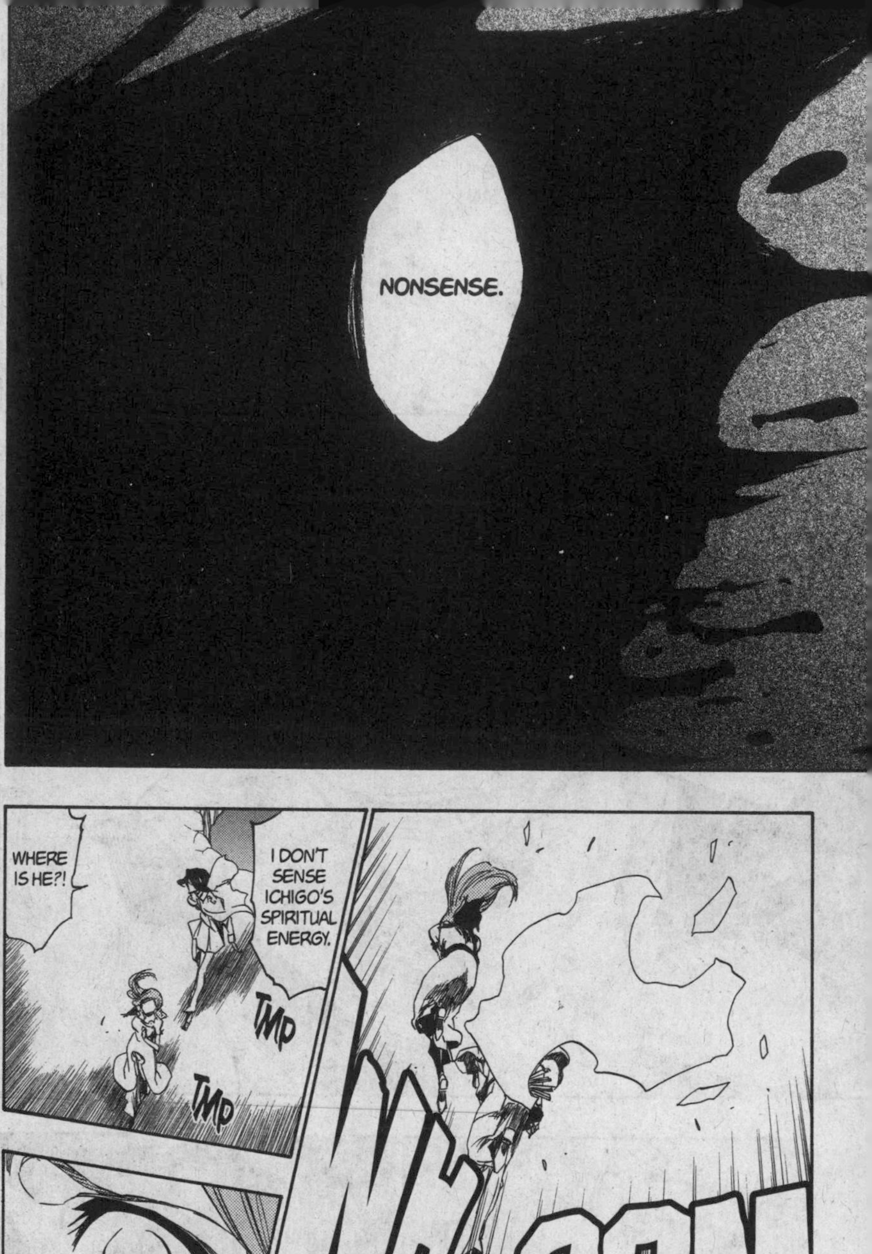
NONSENSE.
WHOOM
I DON'T SENSE ICHIGO'S SPIRITUAL ENERGY.
WHERE IS HE?!
TMP
TMP

...WOMAN.

YOU'RE
HERE...

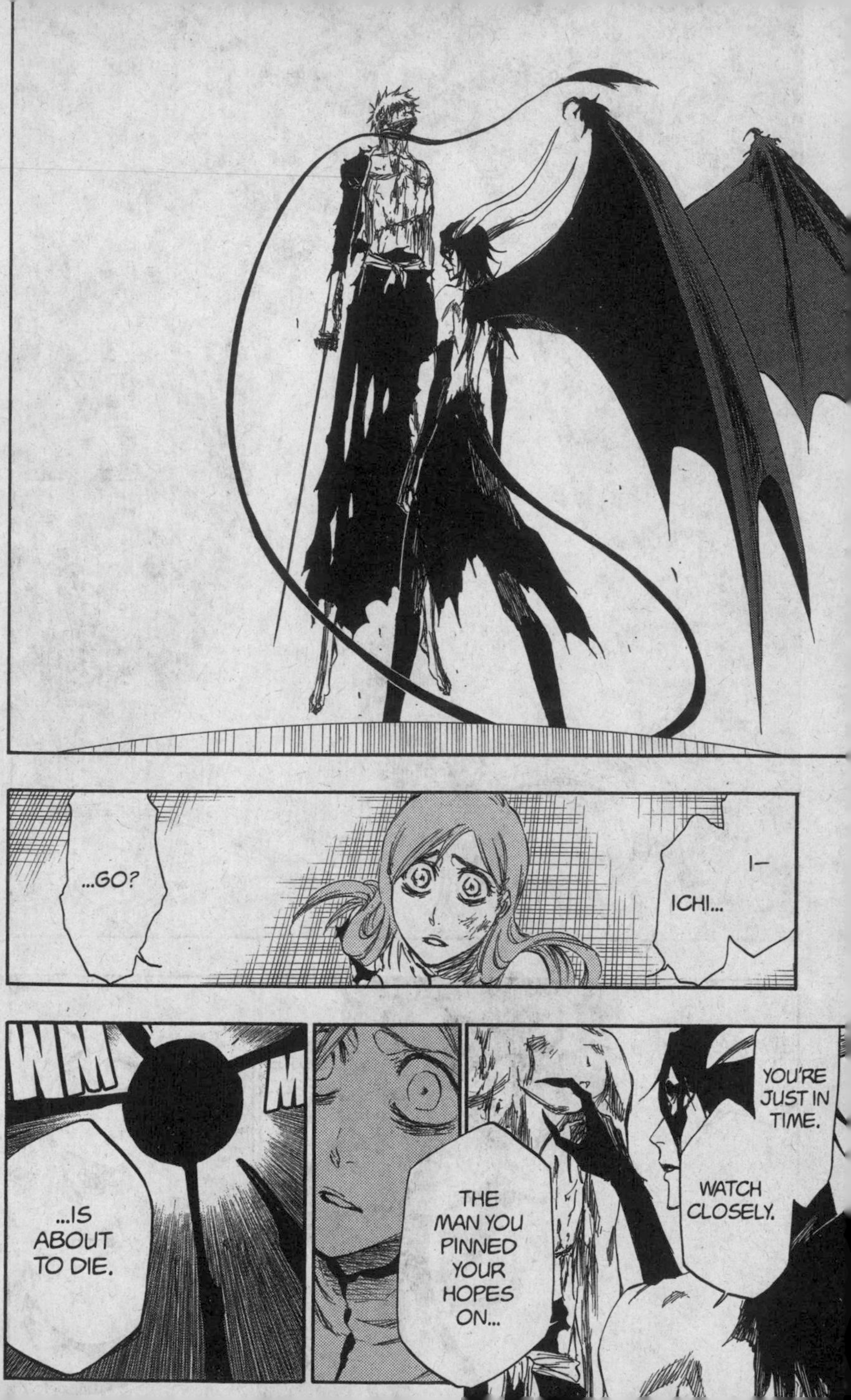
I— ICHI...
...GO?
YOU'RE JUST IN TIME.
WATCH CLOSELY.
THE MAN YOU PINNED YOUR HOPES ON...
WM M
...IS ABOUT TO DIE.

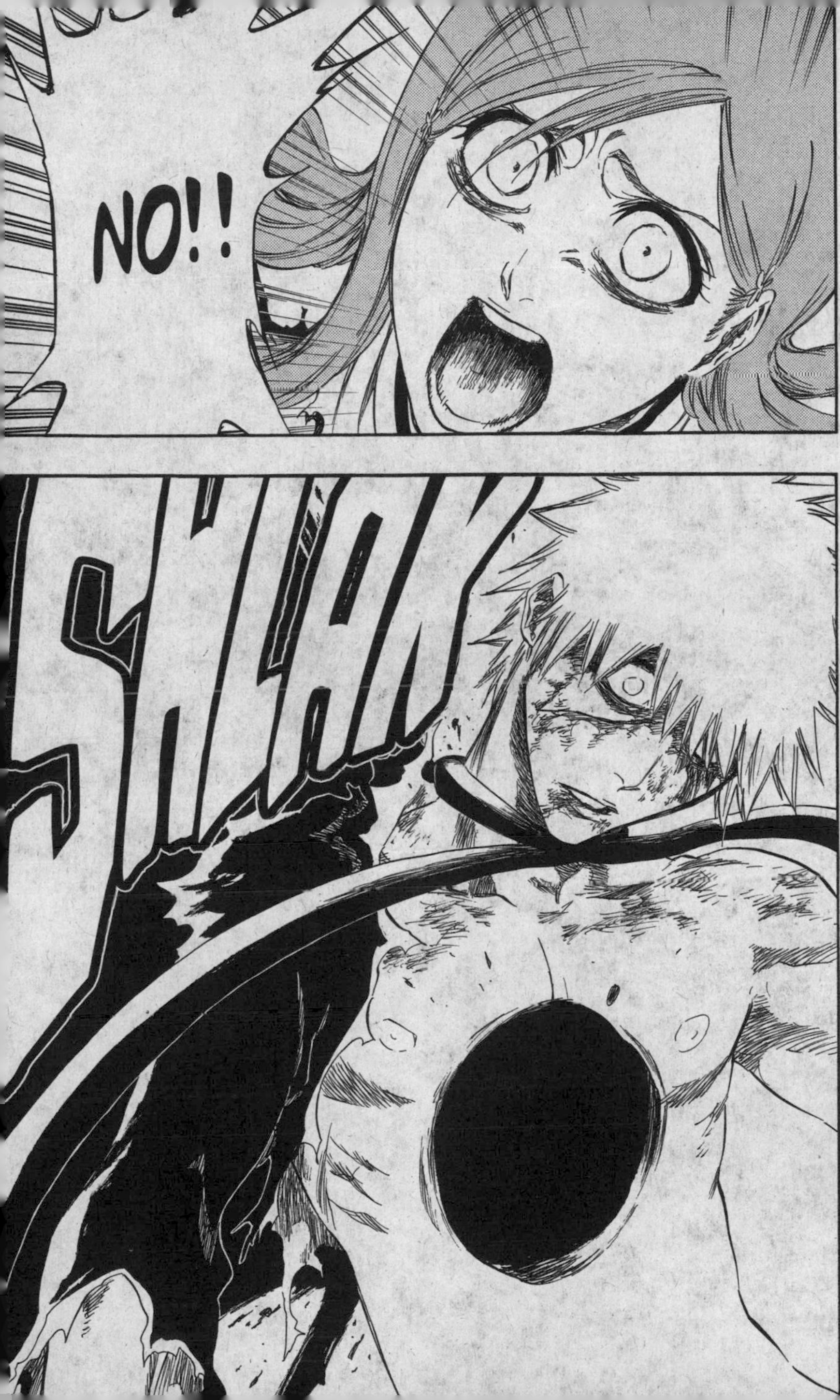
NO!!

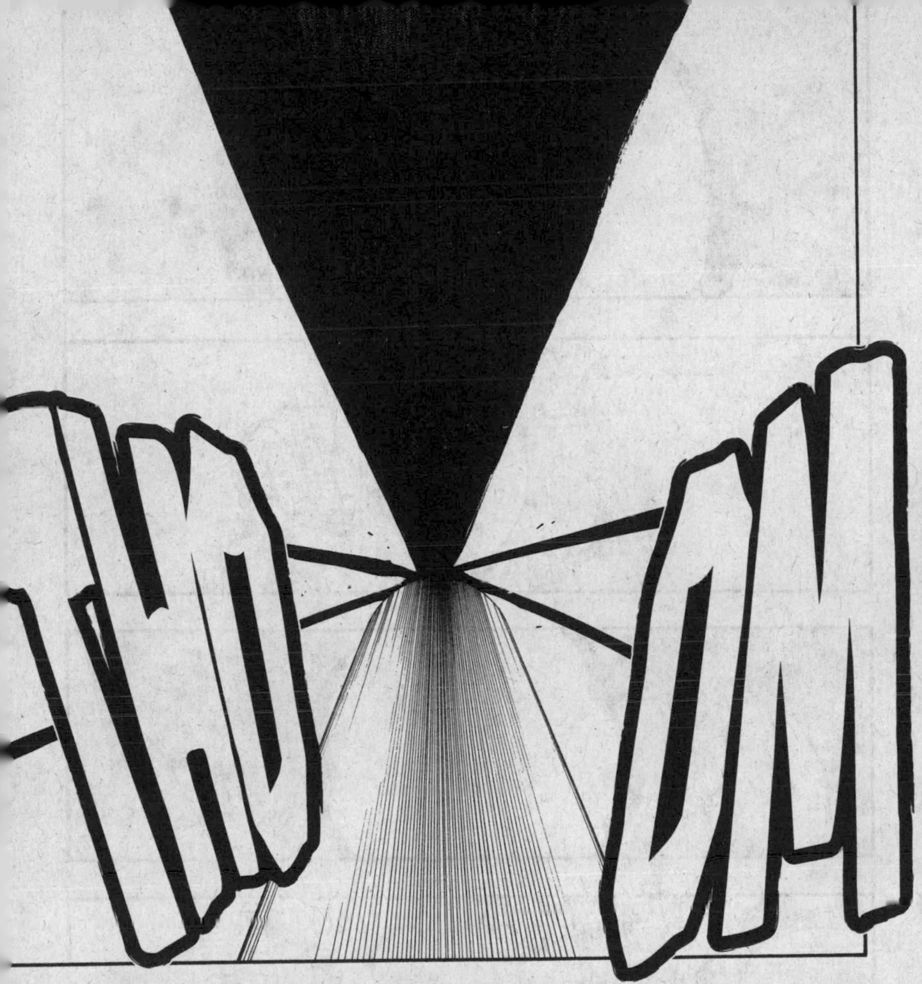
THOOM

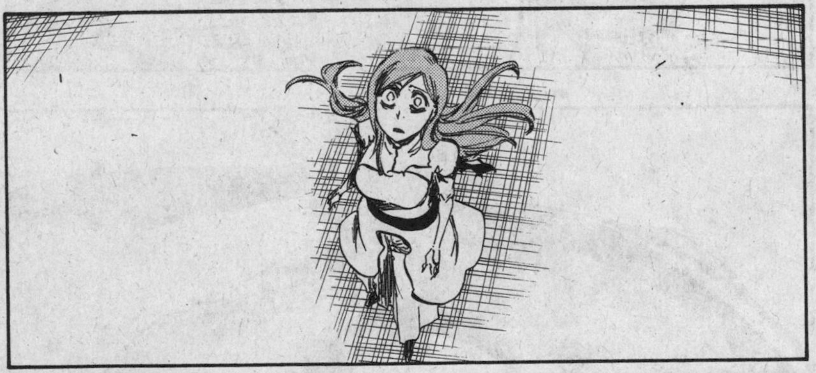

349. The Lust 3

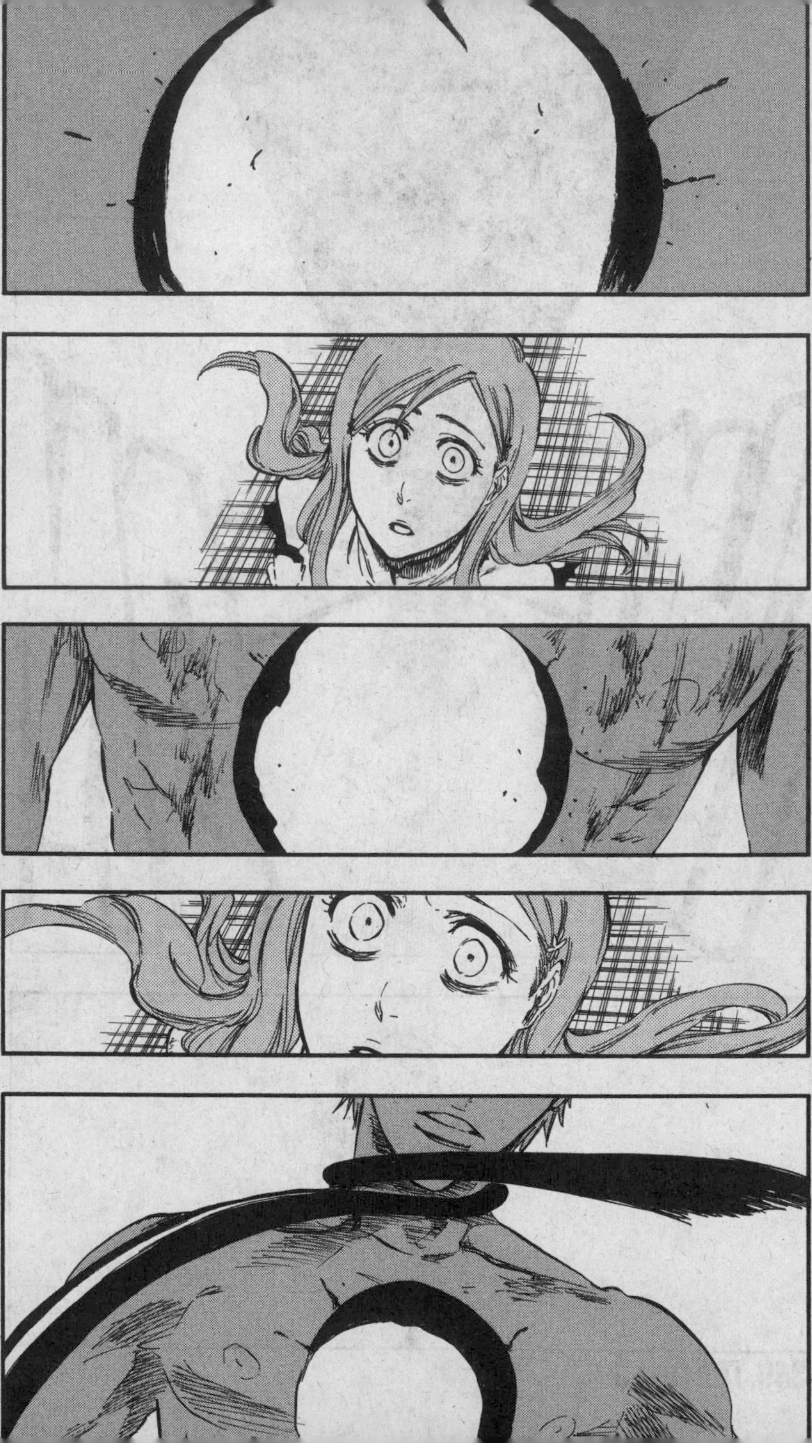

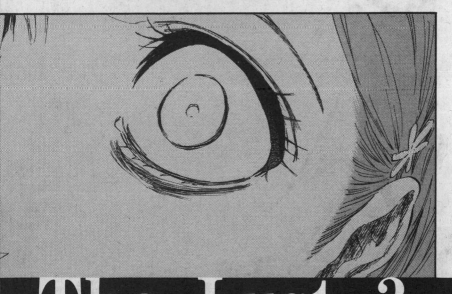

The Lust 3

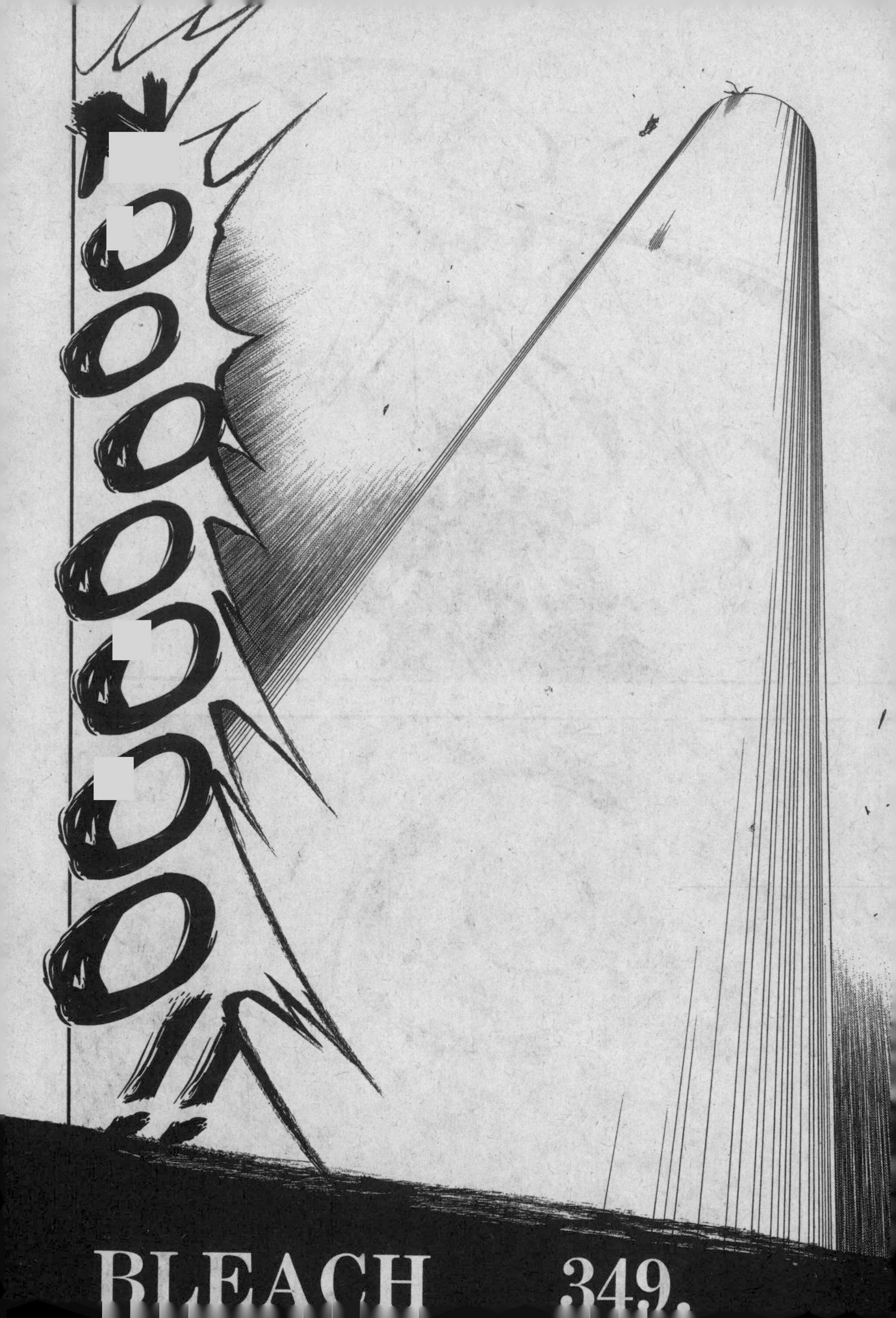
BLEACH 349.

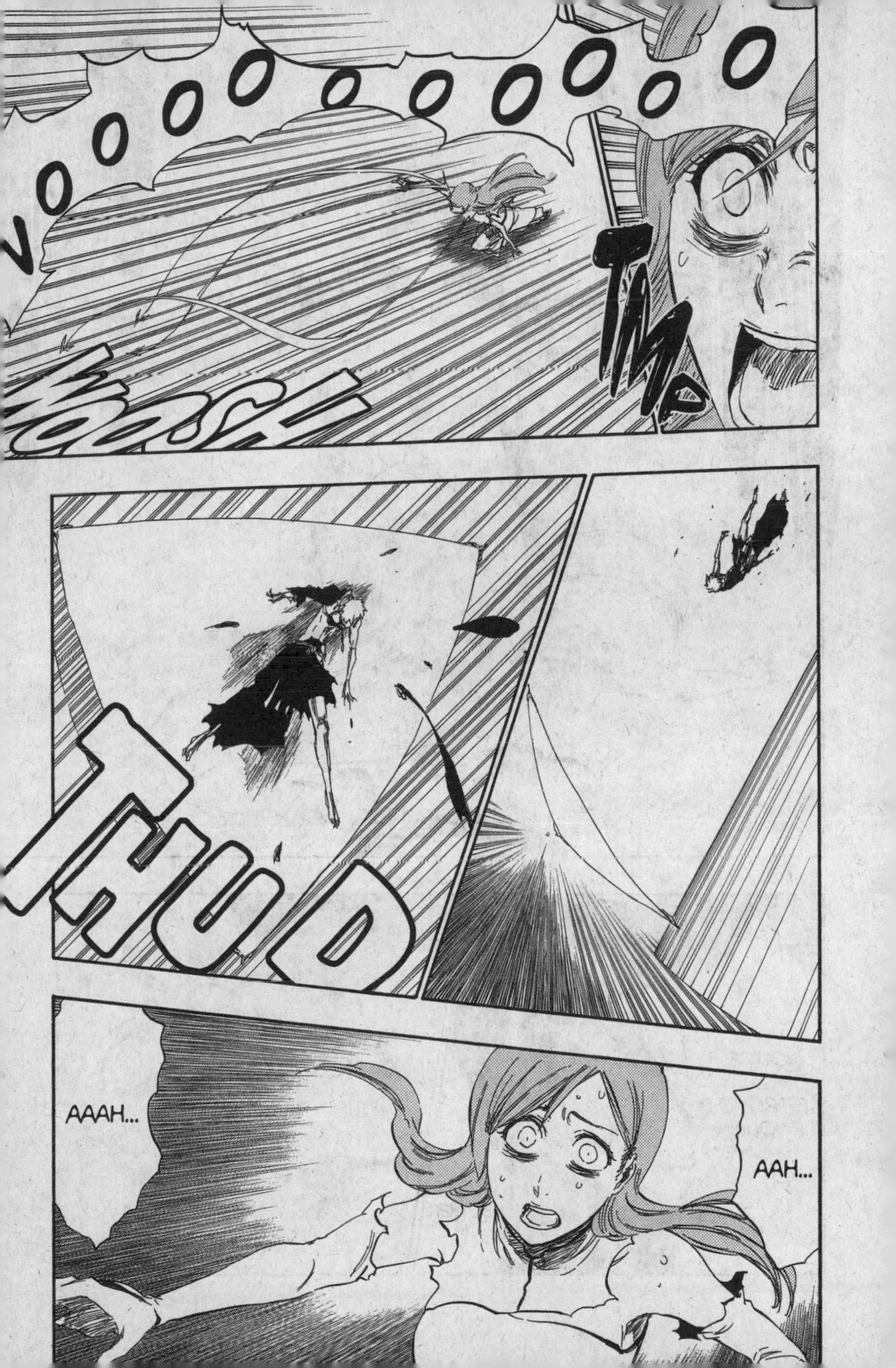
THUD
AAH...
AAAH...

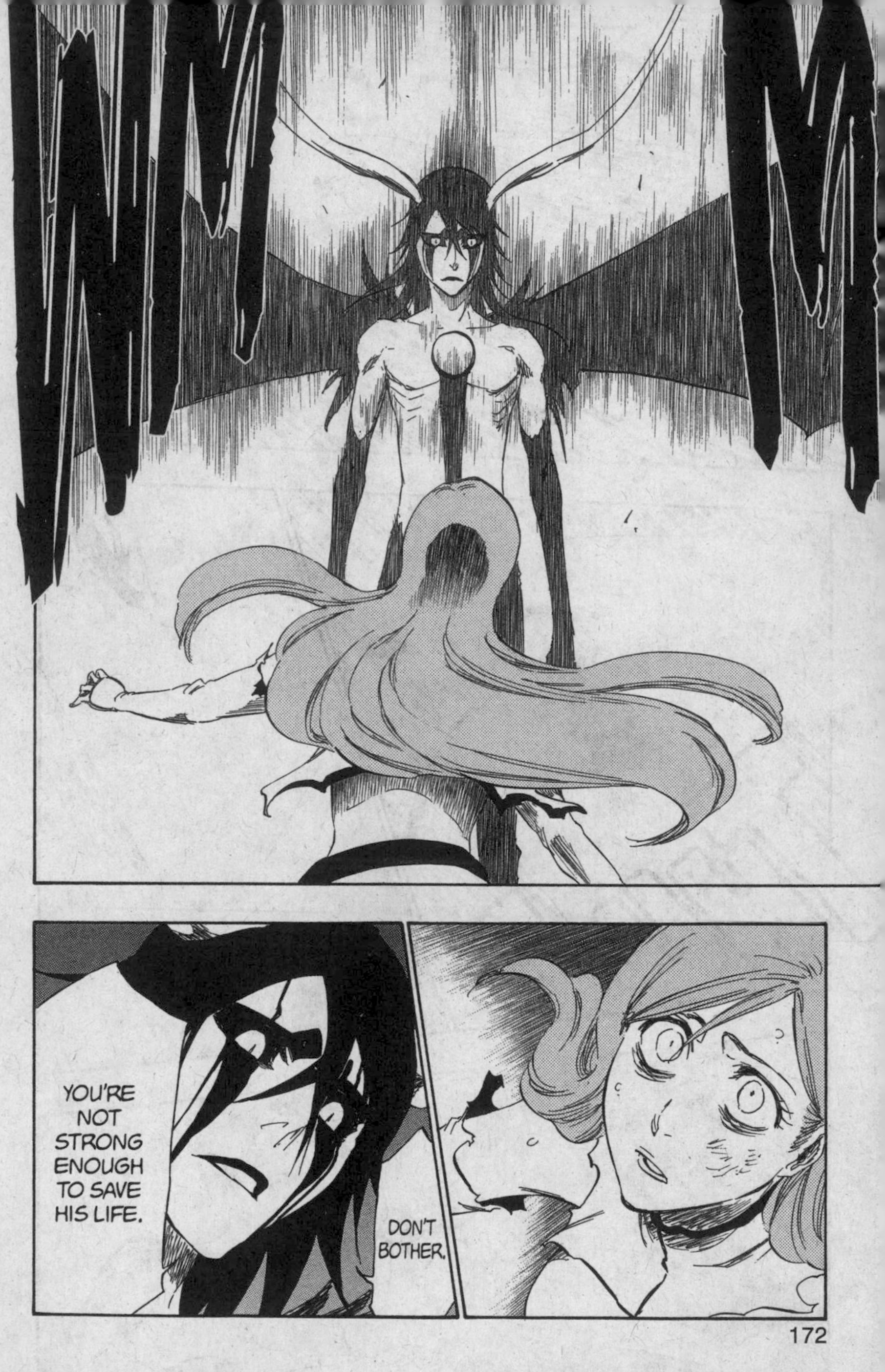
DON'T BOTHER.
YOU'RE NOT STRONG ENOUGH TO SAVE HIS LIFE.

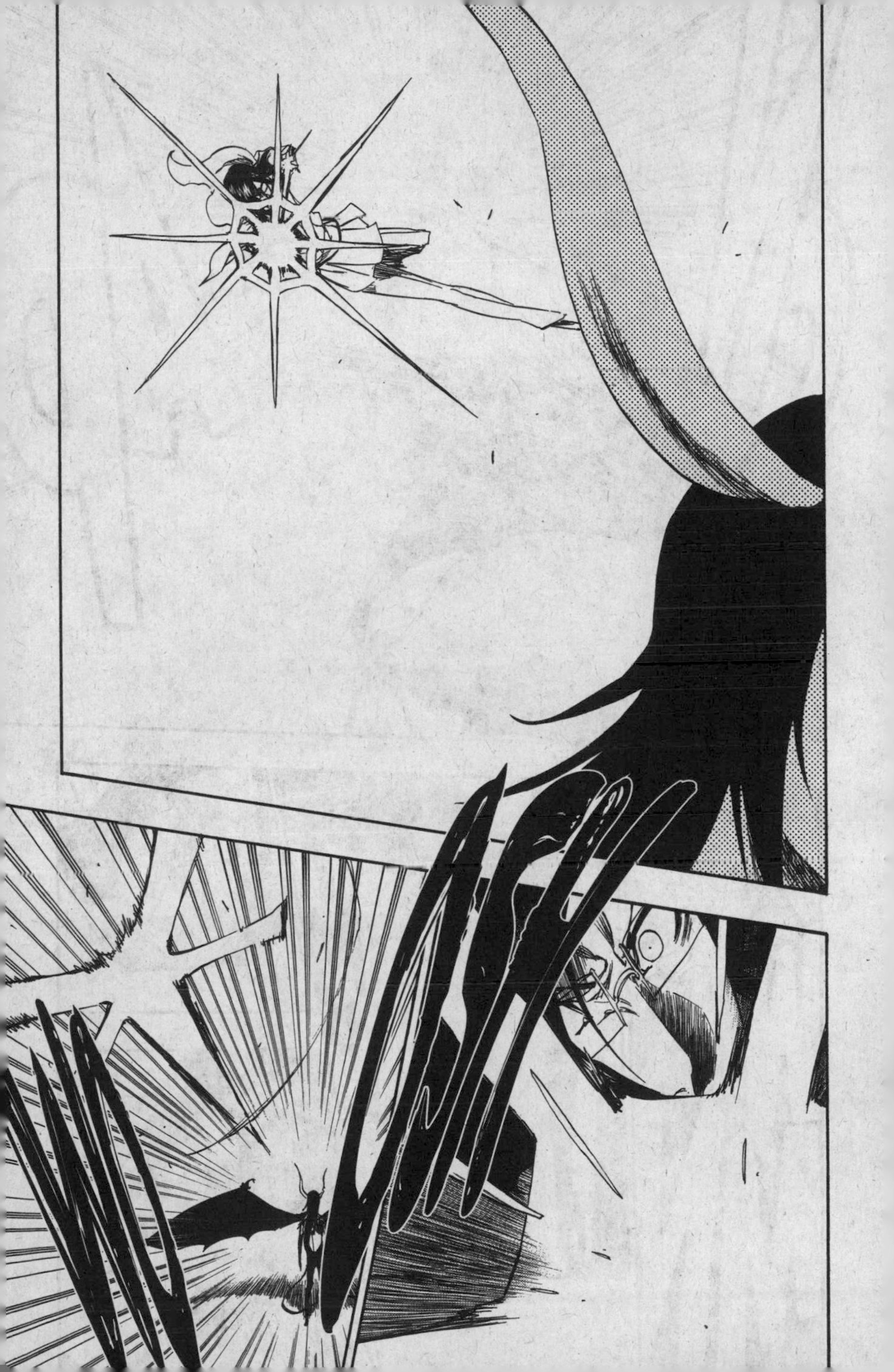

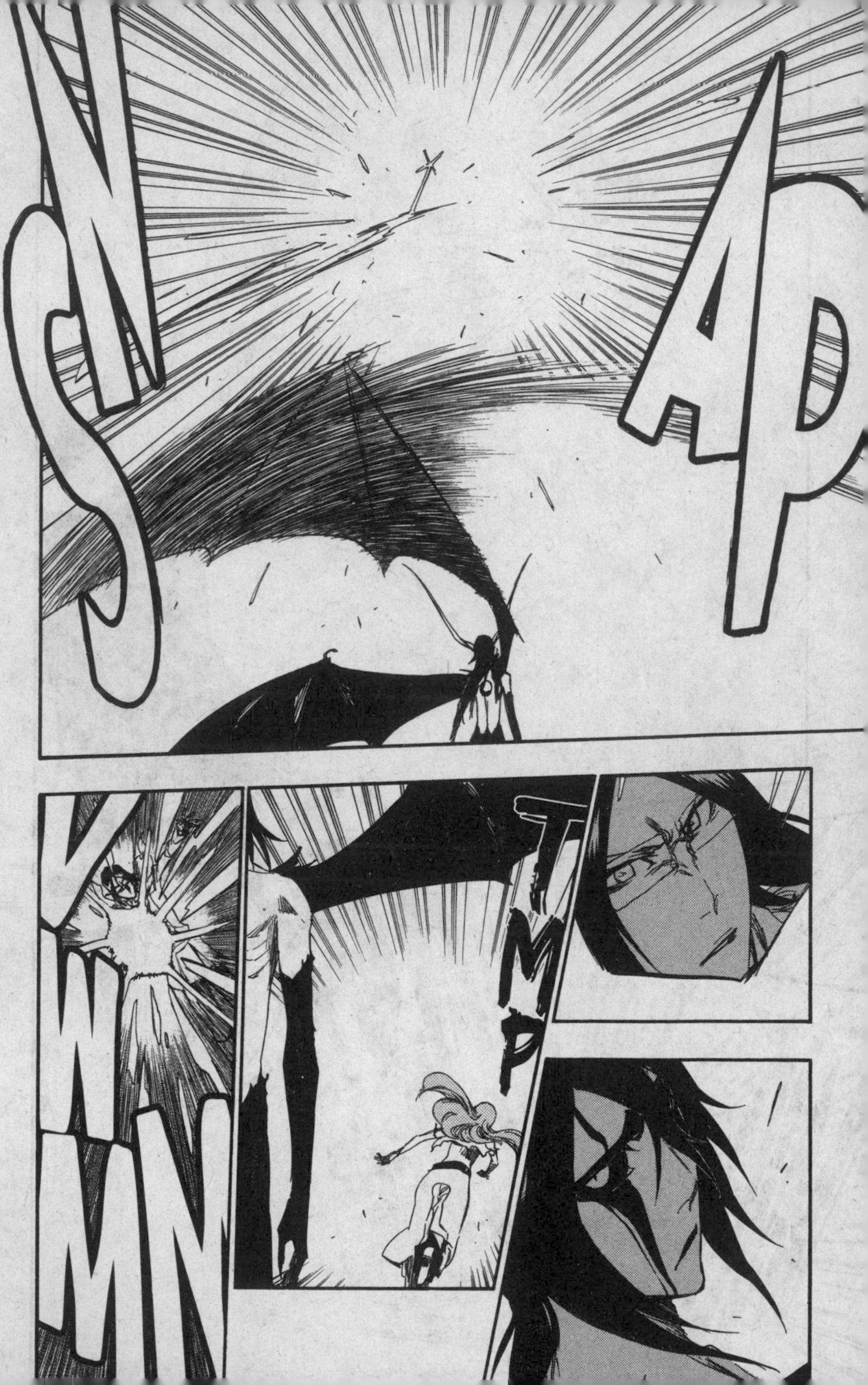
SNAP
TMP

LICHT REGEN.
(RAIN OF LIGHT)

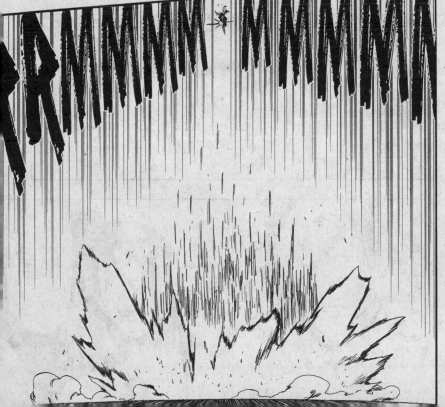

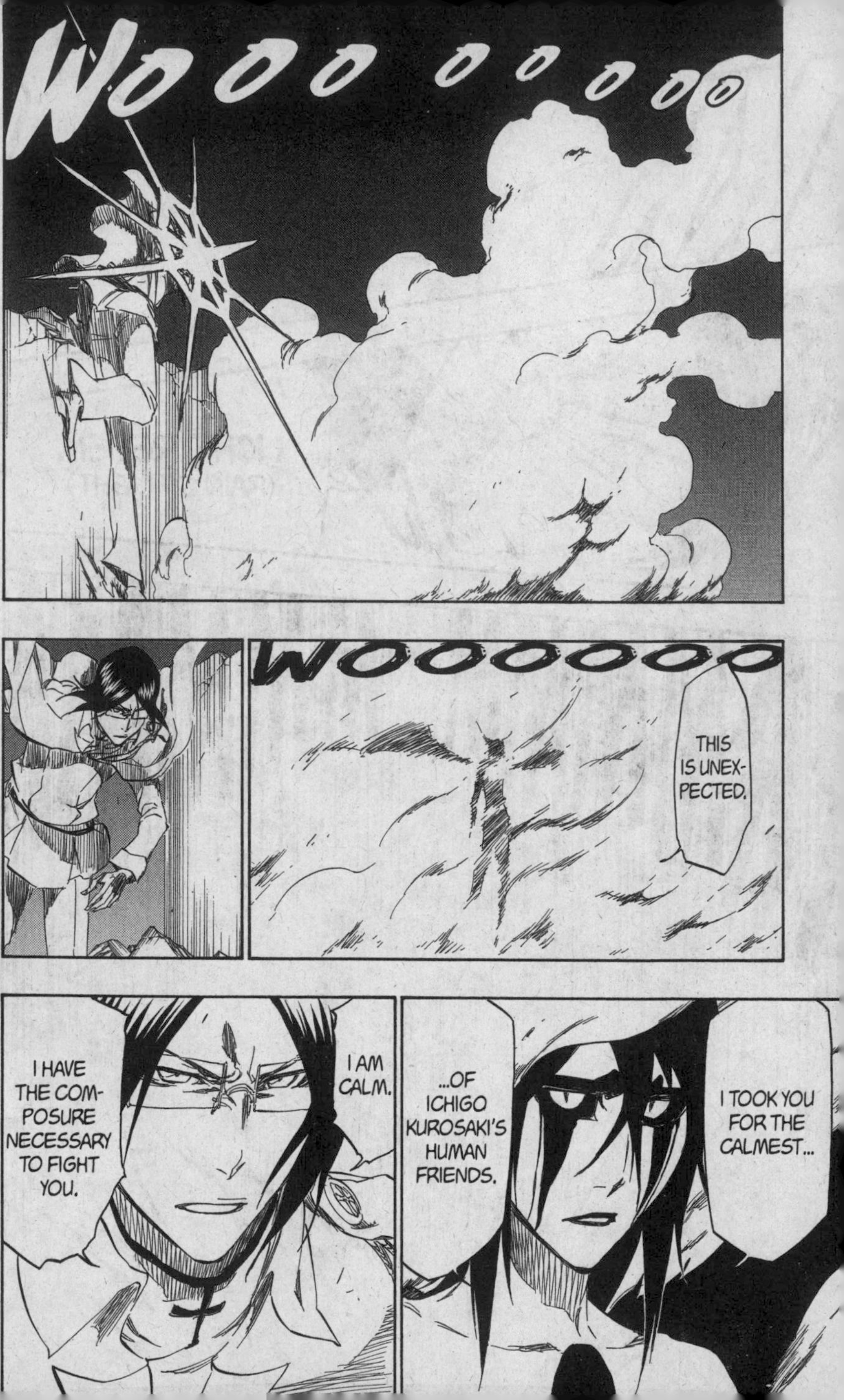
WOOOOOOOO
WOOOOOOO
THIS IS UNEXPECTED.
I TOOK YOU FOR THE CALMEST...
...OF ICHIGO KUROSAKI'S HUMAN FRIENDS.
I AM CALM.
I HAVE THE COMPOSURE NECESSARY TO FIGHT YOU.

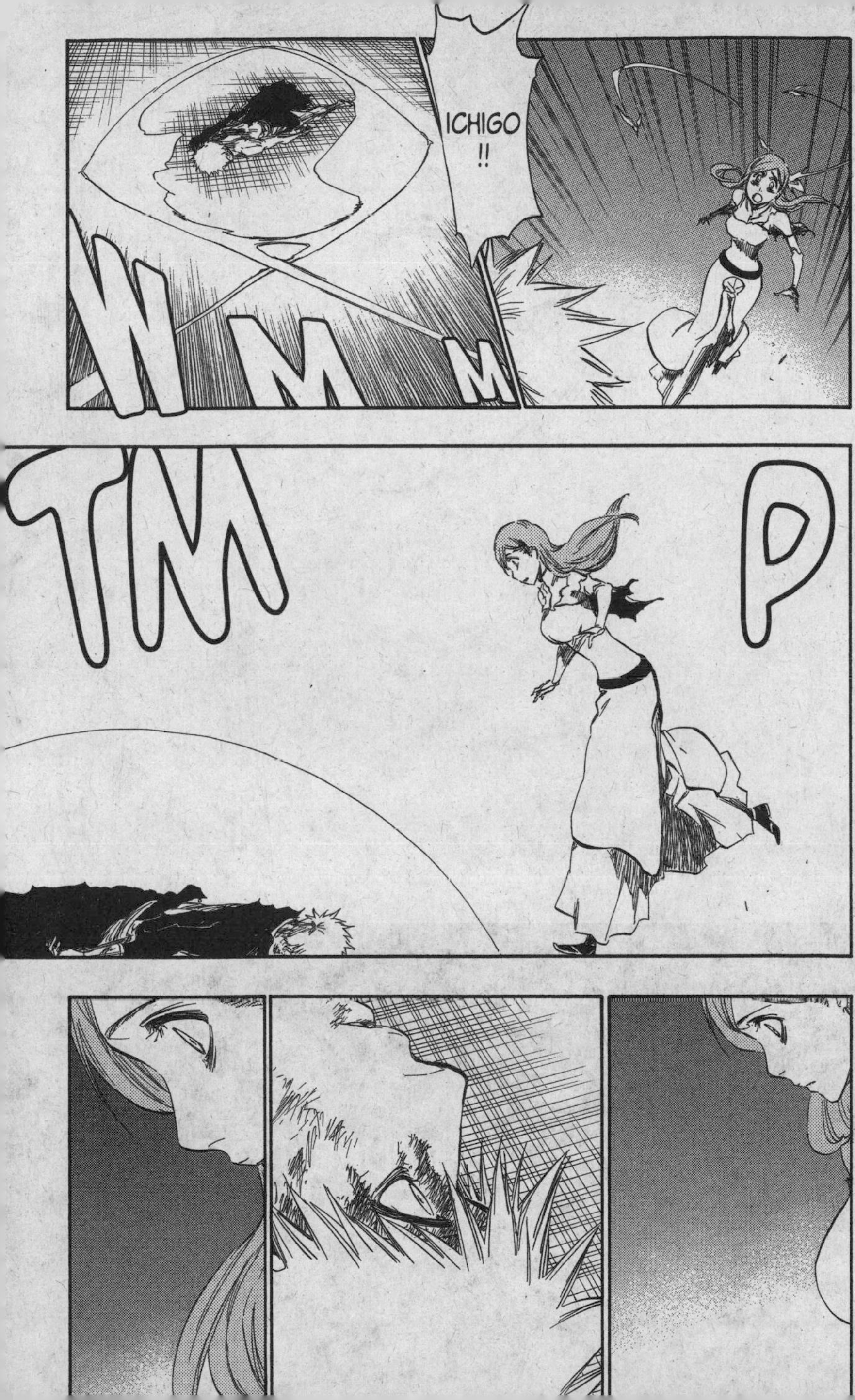
ICHIGO !!
WMM
TMP

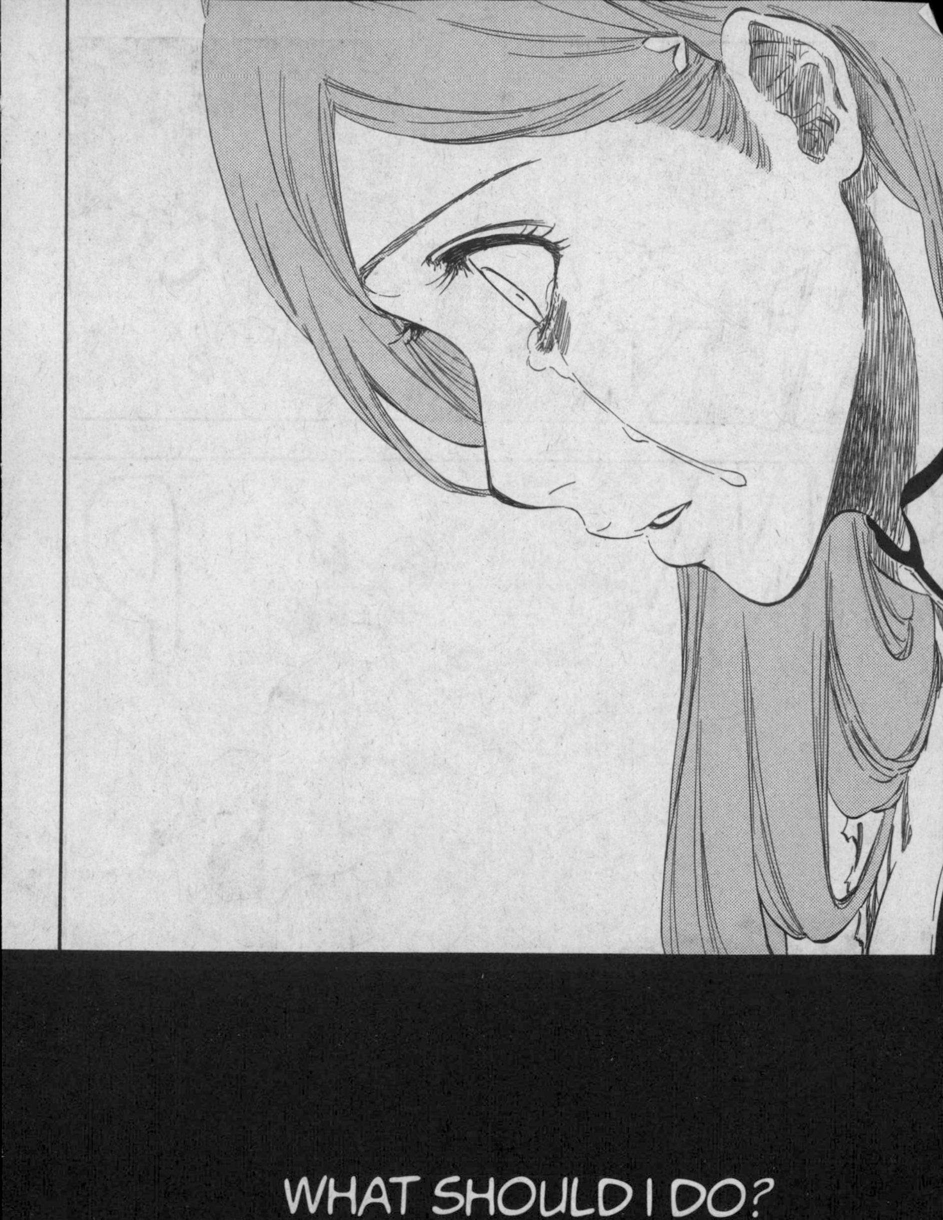

WHAT SHOULD I DO?

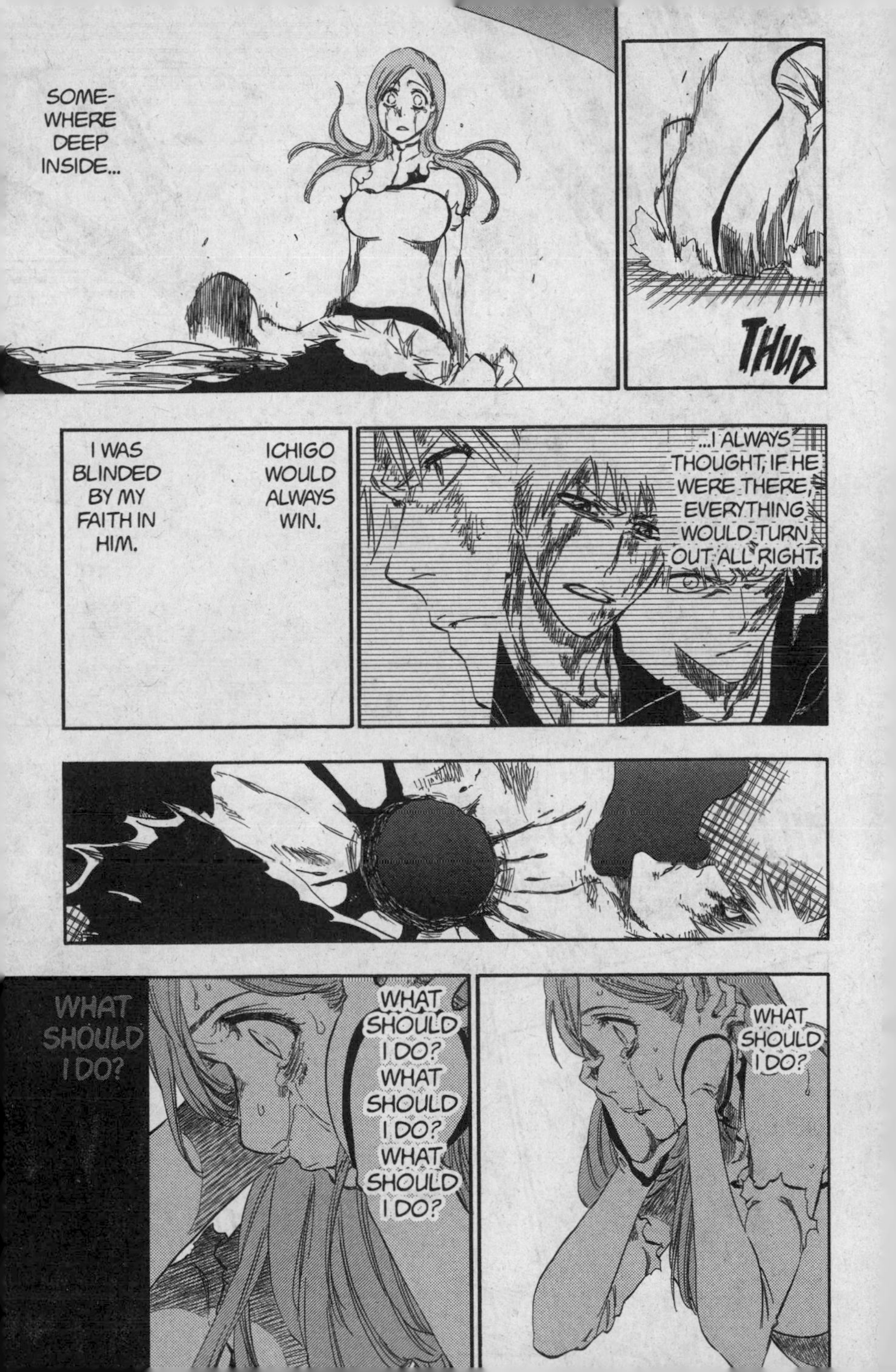
THUD
SOME-WHERE DEEP INSIDE...
...I ALWAYS THOUGHT, IF HE WERE THERE, EVERYTHING WOULD TURN OUT ALL RIGHT.
ICHIGO WOULD ALWAYS WIN.
I WAS BLINDED BY MY FAITH IN HIM.
WHAT SHOULD I DO?
WHAT SHOULD I DO? WHAT SHOULD I DO? WHAT SHOULD I DO?
WHAT SHOULD I DO?

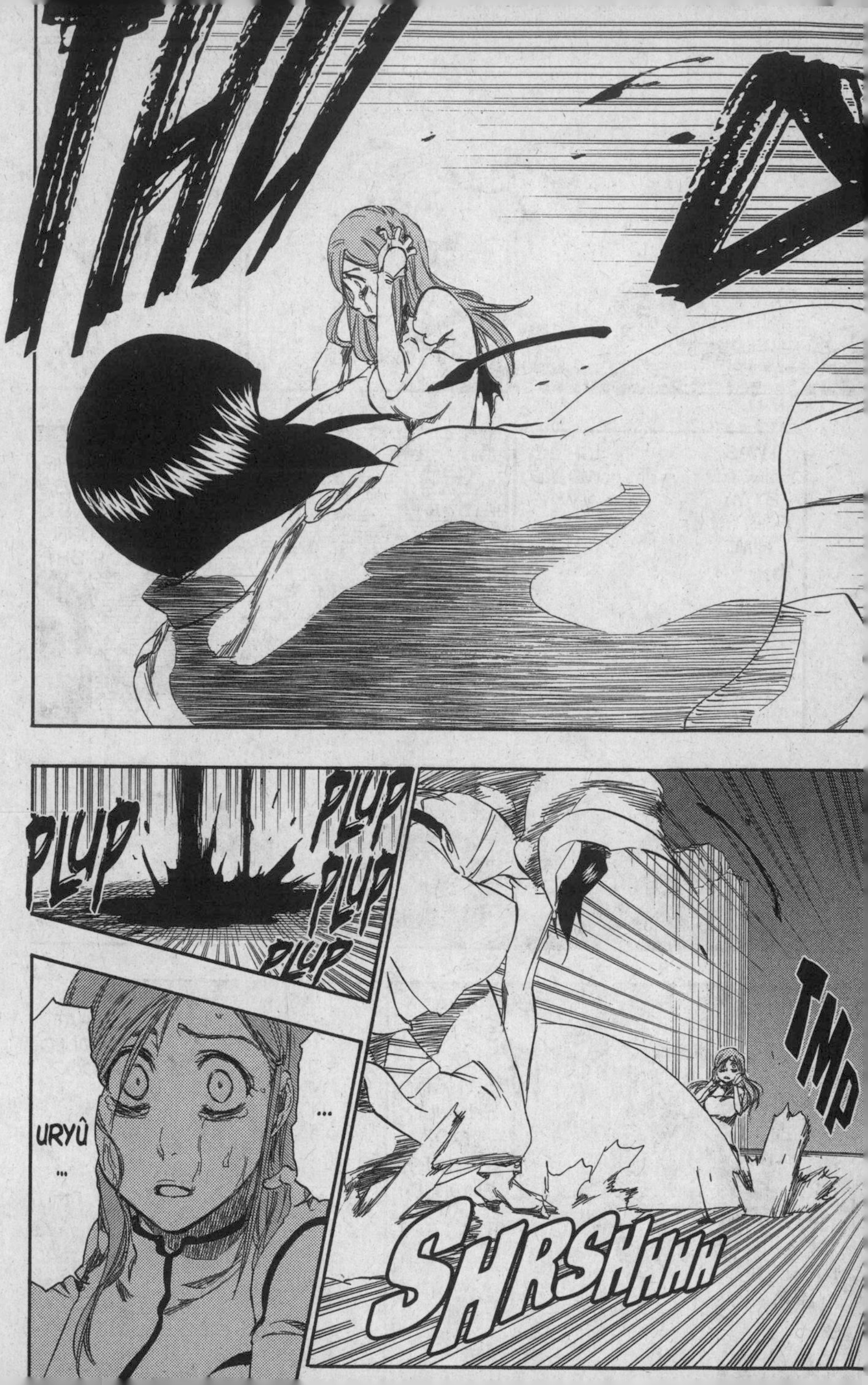
THW
D
TMP
SHRSHHHH
PLUP
PLUP
PLUP
PLUP
...
URYÛ
...

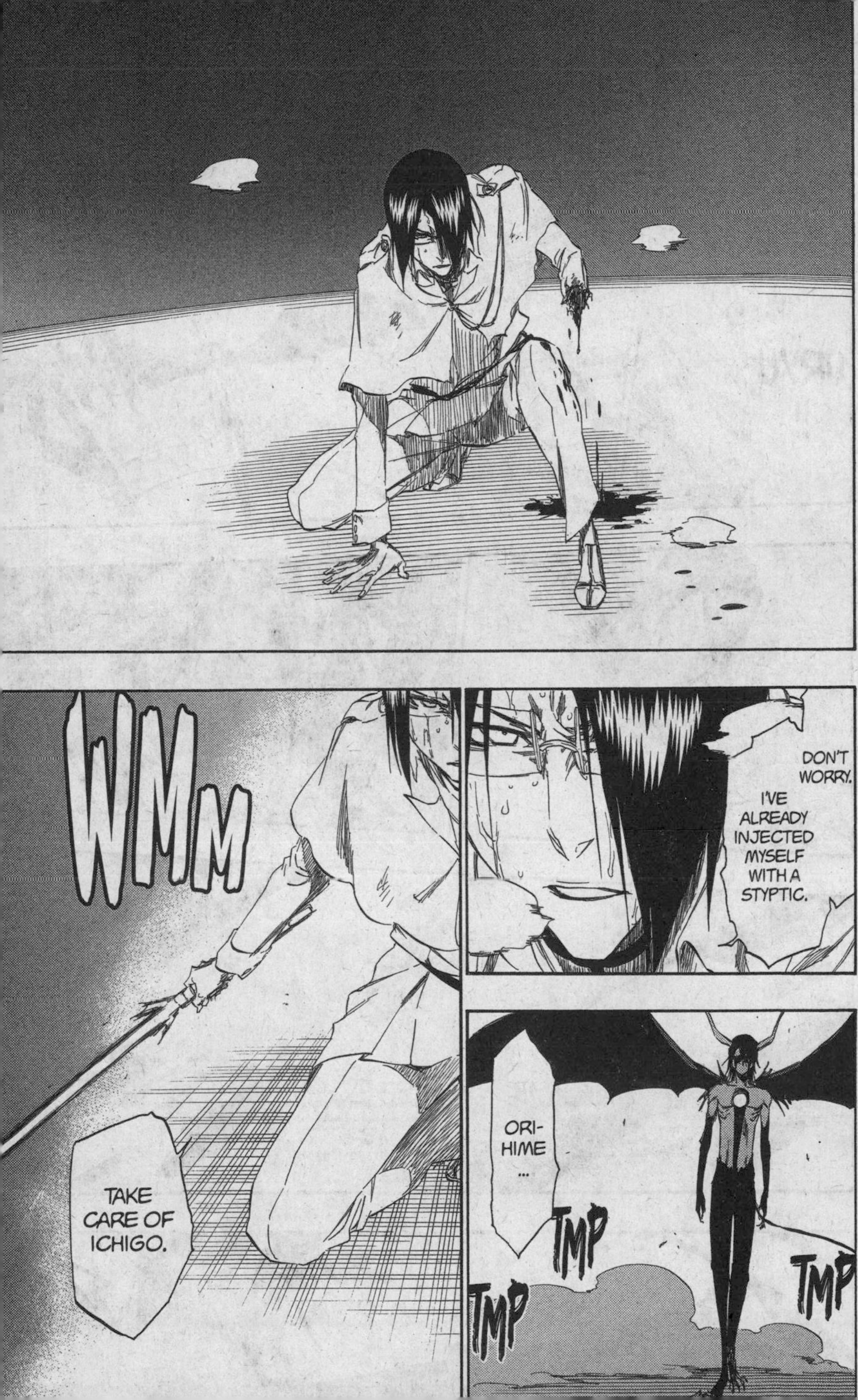
DON'T WORRY.
I'VE ALREADY INJECTED MYSELF WITH A STYPTIC.
ORI-HIME ...
TMP
TMP
TMP
WMM
TAKE CARE OF ICHIGO.

URYÛ
!!

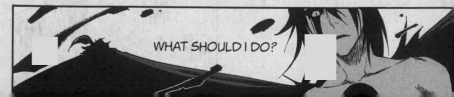

WHAT SHOULD I DO?

READ THIS WAY

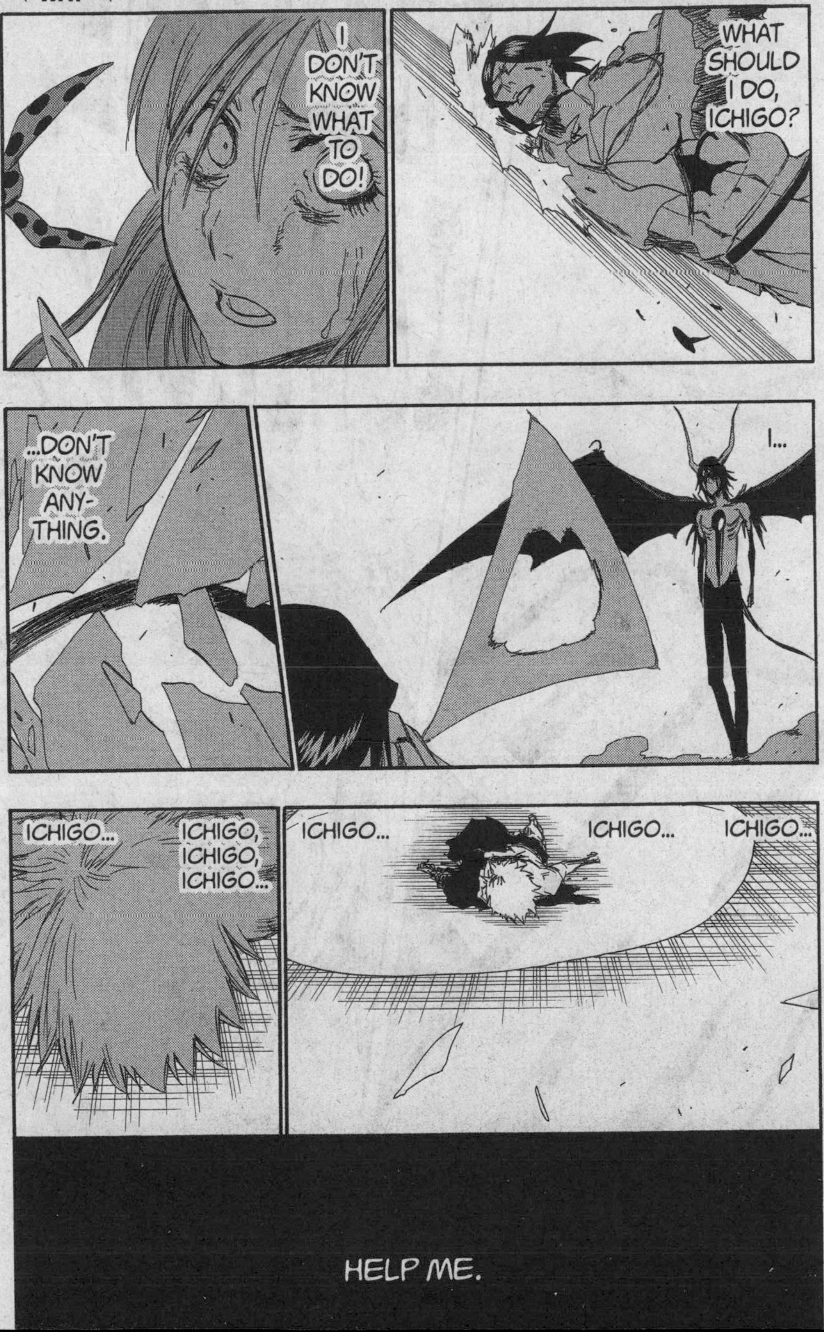
WHAT SHOULD I DO, ICHIGO?
I DON'T KNOW WHAT TO DO!
I...
...DON'T KNOW ANY-THING.
ICHIGO...
ICHIGO...
ICHIGO...
ICHIGO, ICHIGO, ICHIGO...
ICHIGO...
HELP ME.

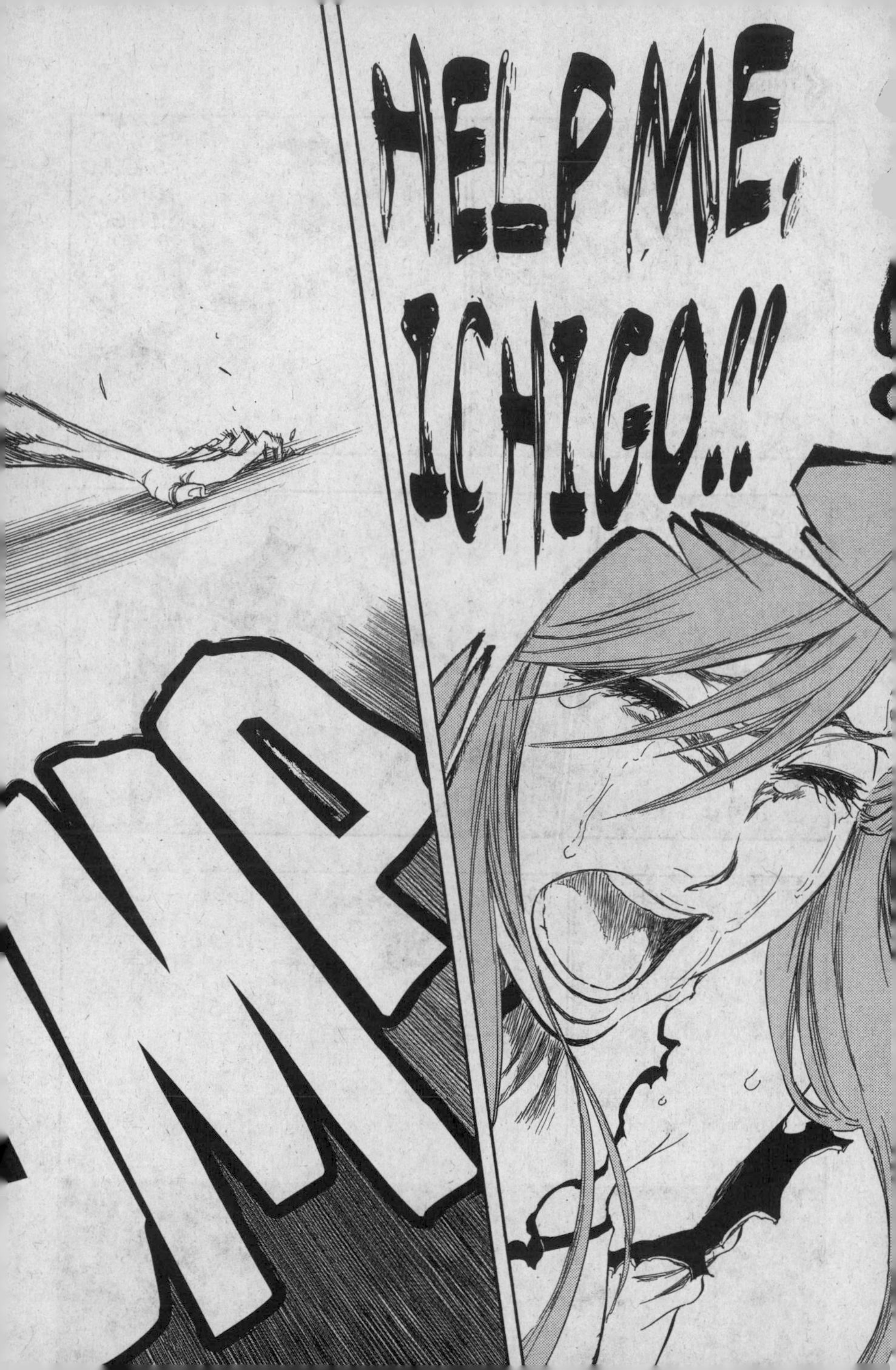
HELP ME, ICHIGO!!

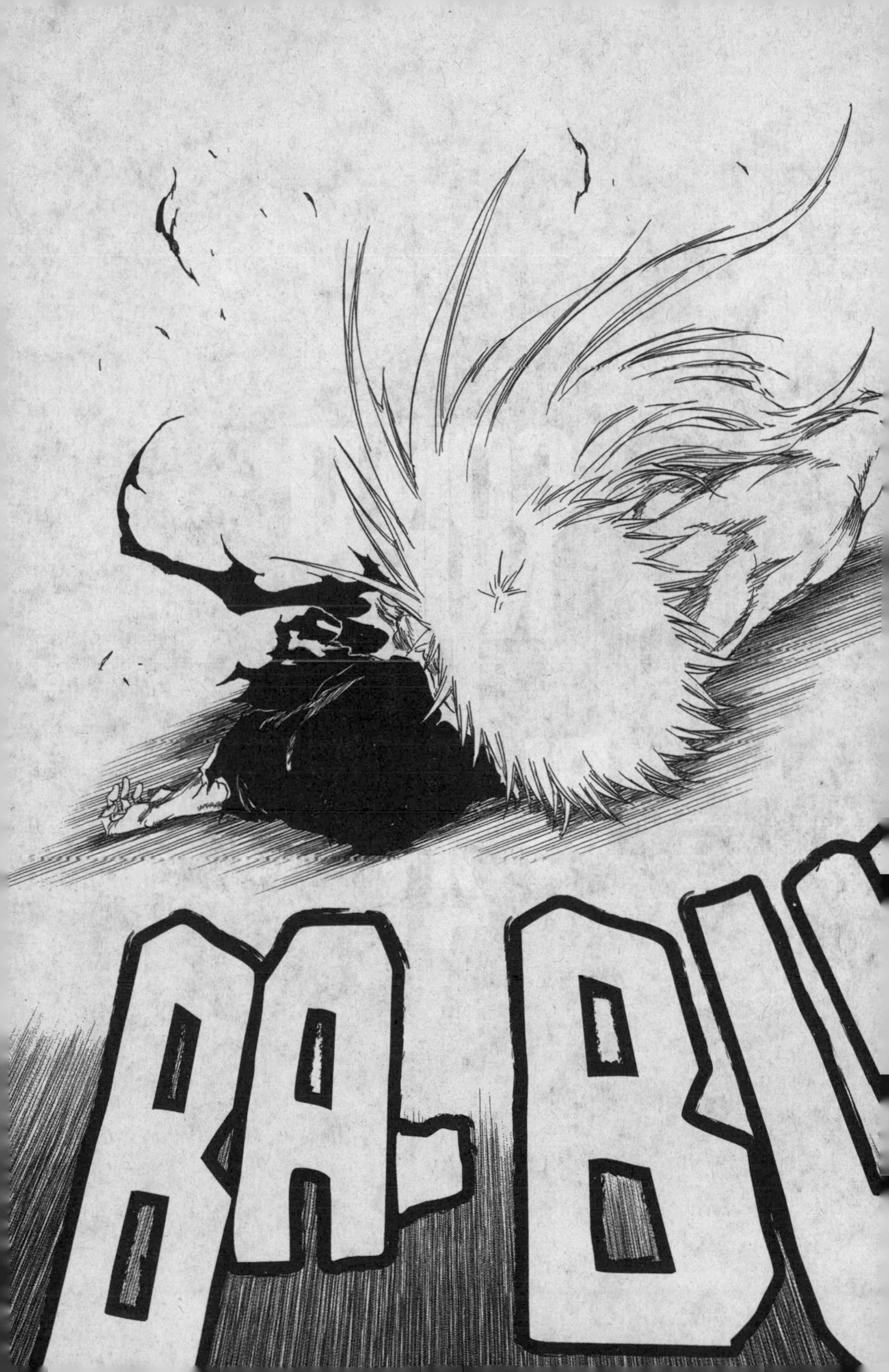
BA-B

CONTI
NUED
IN
BLEACH
41

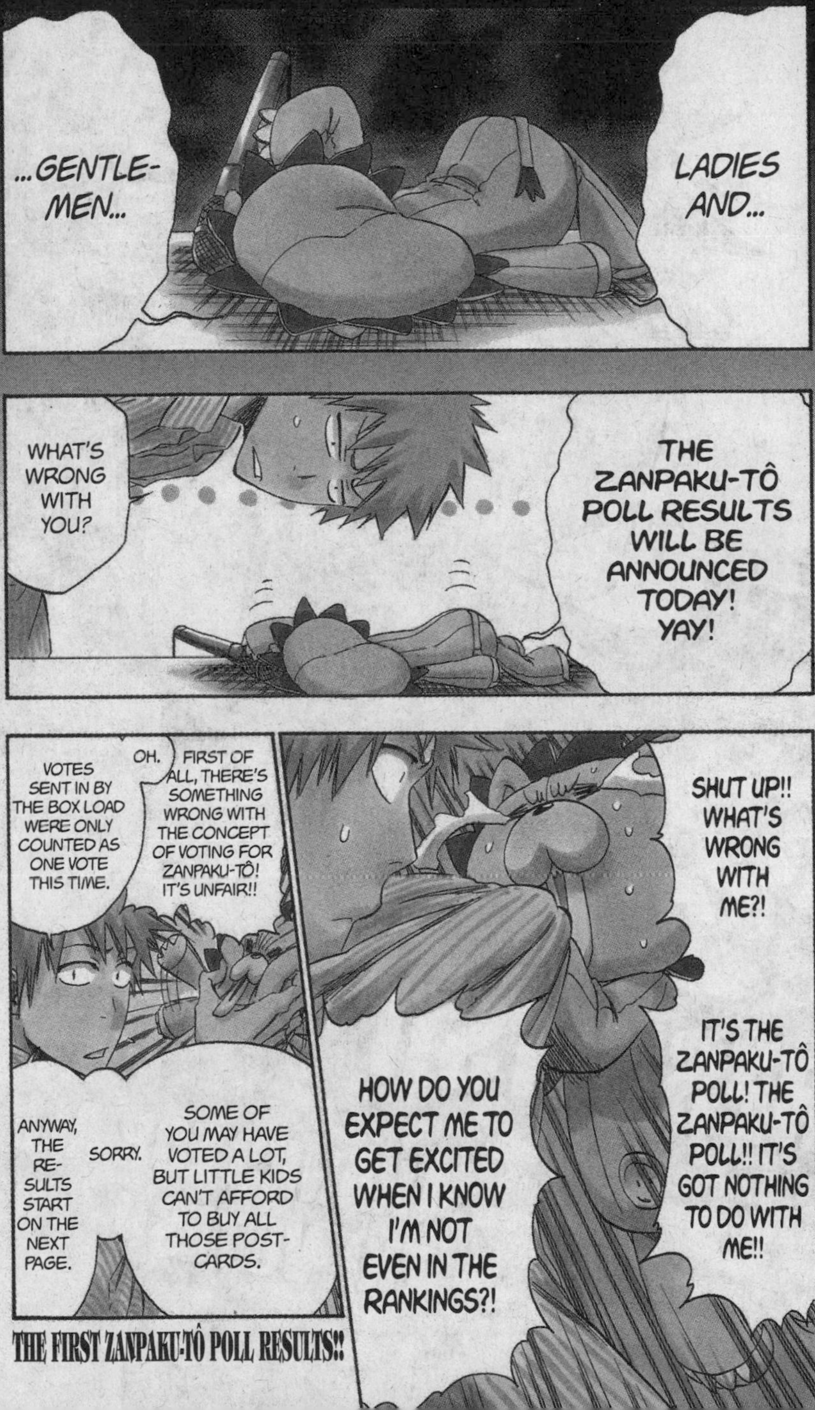
LADIES AND...
...GENTLEMEN...
THE ZANPAKU-TÔ POLL RESULTS WILL BE ANNOUNCED TODAY! YAY!
WHAT'S WRONG WITH YOU?
SHUT UP!! WHAT'S WRONG WITH ME?!
IT'S THE ZANPAKU-TÔ POLL! THE ZANPAKU-TÔ POLL!! IT'S GOT NOTHING TO DO WITH ME!!
HOW DO YOU EXPECT ME TO GET EXCITED WHEN I KNOW I'M NOT EVEN IN THE RANKINGS?!
FIRST OF ALL, THERE'S SOMETHING WRONG WITH THE CONCEPT OF VOTING FOR ZANPAKU-TÔ! IT'S UNFAIR!!
OH.
VOTES SENT IN BY THE BOX LOAD WERE ONLY COUNTED AS ONE VOTE THIS TIME.
SOME OF YOU MAY HAVE VOTED A LOT, BUT LITTLE KIDS CAN'T AFFORD TO BUY ALL THOSE POST-CARDS.
SORRY.
ANYWAY, THE RE-SULTS START ON THE NEXT PAGE.

THE FIRST ZANPAKU-TÔ POLL RESULTS!!

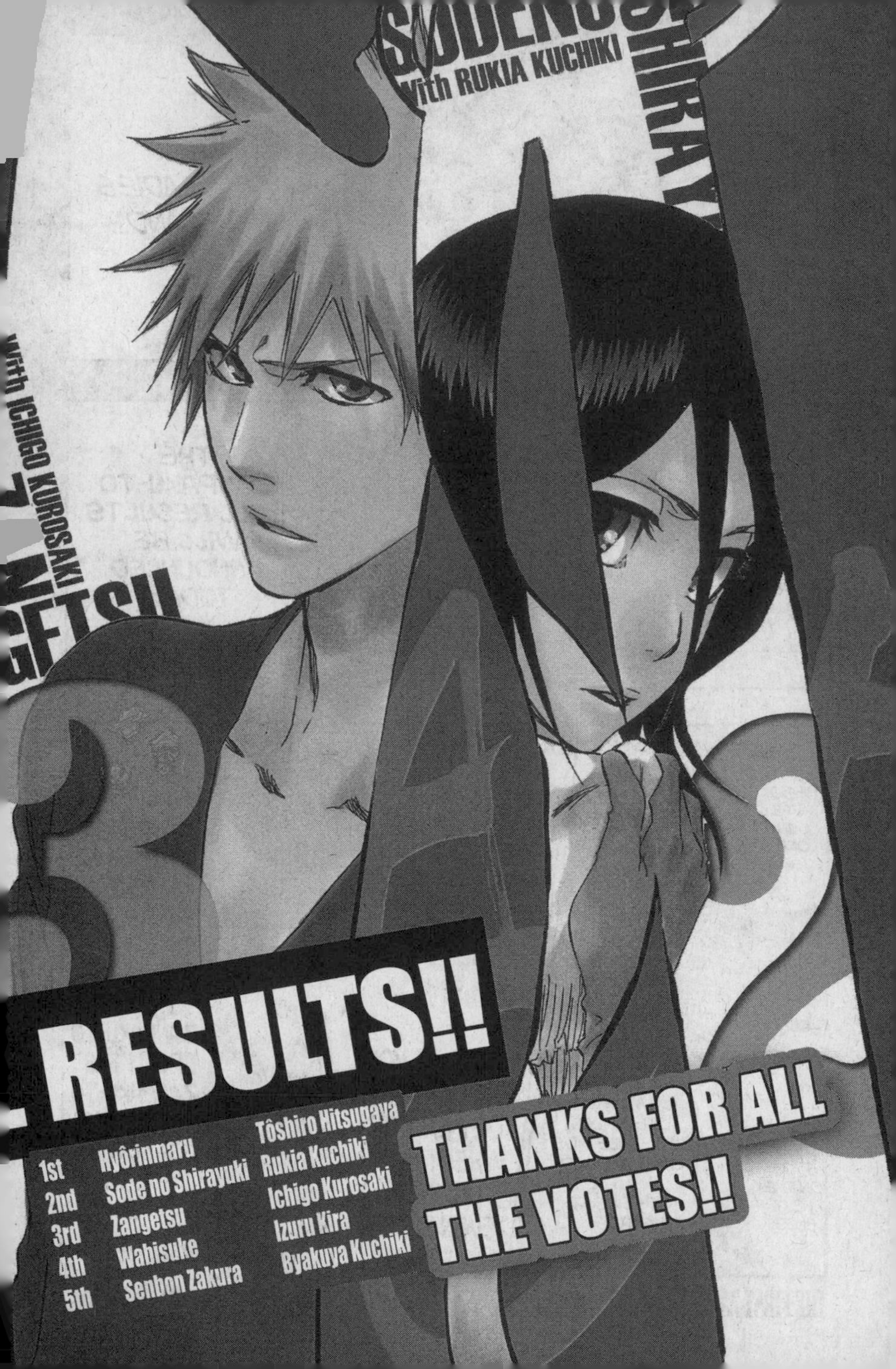
with RUKIA KUCHIKI
with ICHIGO KUROSAKI
RESULTS!!
1st Hyôrinmaru Tôshiro Hitsugaya
2nd Sode no Shirayuki Rukia Kuchiki
3rd Zangetsu Ichigo Kurosaki
4th Wabisuke Izuru Kira
5th Senbon Zakura Byakuya Kuchiki
THANKS FOR ALL THE VOTES!!

THE FIRST ZANPAKU-TÔ POL

SENBON ZAK WITH BYAKUYA KUCHIKI

ORIN MAR WITH TÔSHIRO HITSUGAYA

WABISU WITH IZURU...

6th ▶ 64th!

6th
Kazeshini (Shuhei Hisagi)
7th
Zabimaru (Renji Abarai)
8th
Shinsô (Gin Ichimaru)
9th
Pantera (Grimmjow)
10th
Tensa Zangetsu (Ichigo Kurosaki)
11th
Ginrei Kojaku (Uryû Ishida)
12th
Benihime (Kisuke Urahara)
13th
Hôzuki-maru (Ikkaku Madarame)
14th
Ruri Iro Kujaku (Yumichika Ayasegawa)
15th
Suzumebachi (Soifon)
16th
Daiguren Hyôrinmaru (Tôshiro Hitsugaya)
17th
Sôgyo Kotowari (Jushiro Ukitake)
18th
Kyoka Suigetsu (Sousuke Aizen)
Neji Bana (Kaien Shiba)
Haineko (Rangiku Matsumoto)
21st
Seeleschneider (Uryû Ishida)
22nd
Kojaku (Uryû Ishida)
23rd
Tobiume (Momo Hinamori)
La Lujuriosa (Szayelaporro)
25th
Senbon Zakura
Kageyoshi/Gôkei/Shûkei/Hakuteiken (Byakuya Kuchiki)
26th
Ashisogi Jizô (Mayuri Kurotsuchi)
27th
Fujikujaku (Yumichika Ayasegawa)
Ryûmon Hôzuki-Maru (Ikkaku Madarame)
29th
Kenpachi Zaraki's Zanpaku-tô
30th
Santa Teresa (Nnoitra)
31st
Hisago-maru (Hanataro Yamada)
32nd
Ryûjin Jakka (Shigekuni Genryûsai Yamamoto)
33rd
Katen Kyôkotsu (Shunsui Kyôraku)
Shunshun Rikka (Orihime Inoue)
Gamuza (Nelliel)
36th
Hihi-oh Zabimaru (Renji Abarai)
Mirokumaru (Senna)
38th
Tachikaze (Kensei Muguruma)
39th
Minazuki (Retsu Unohana)
40th
Suzumushi (Kaname Tôsen)
41st
Verruga (Tesla)
Tsuchi Namazu (Zennosuke Kurumadani)
43rd
Yachiru's Zanpaku-tô
Brazo Izquierda del Diablo (Yasutora Sado)
Konjiki Jizô (Mayuri Kurotsuchi)
46th
Ulquiorra's Sword
Del Toro (Ilfort)
Kokujôten Tengen Myo Oh (Sajin Komamura)
Tsunzaki Garasu (Jirôbô Ikkanzaka)
Trepadora (Luppi)
Reina De Rosas (Chuhlhourne)
52nd
Glotonería (Aaroniero)
Kotômaru (Matsuri Kudoh)
Beni-Shidare (Kenryû)
Tenra (Izuru Kira)
56th
Devorar Pluma (Abirama)
Golondrina (Cirruci)
White Zangetsu/Getsuga Tenshô (Ichigo Kurosaki)
Brujeria (Zommari)
Shinji Hirako's Zanpaku-tô
Tenken (Sajin Komamura)
Giralda (Dordoni)
64th
Asauchi
Rain Glove
Nanao Ise's eyeglasses' temple
Itegumo (Isane Kotetsu)
Tetsuzaemon Iba's Zanpaku-tô
Ulquiorra's Resurrección
Ulquiorra's eyeball
Ulquiorra's fingernails
Volcánica (Edorad)
Karin's soccer ball
Ultima (Pesche)
9th Company Shinobu Eishima's Zanpaku-tô
Brazo Derecha de Gigante (Yasutora Sado)
Águila (Abirama)
Sojiro Kusaki's Hyôrinmaru
Hôzan (Enjôji Tatsufusa)
Good Morning Ichigo!!
Gonryômaru (Chôjiro Sasakibe)
Chad's right arm that changed for the first time
Hiyori Sarugaki's Zanpaku-tô
Akei Hisagomaru (Hanataro Yamada)
Shunkô (Yoruichi Shihôin)
Hakuren (Rukia Kuchiki)
Tatsuki's fist
Pinza Aguda (Findorr)
Super Spirits Cane (Don Kannonji)
Kakushi Tsuijaku (Tsubaki/Orihime Inoue)
Uña Tirotear (Ice Ringer)
Kokyû Ryûjômaru (Fujimaru Kudoh)
Nijigasumi (Maki Ichinose)
Hinamori's "eye-glass cookie"
Desgarrón (Grimmjow)
Makimaki's Zanpaku-tô
Lanzador Verde (Nelliel)
Infinite Slick (Pesche)
Ms. Rangiku's breasts
Ryûjômaru (Matsuri Kudoh)

We decided to do a Zanpaku-tô Poll this time. A poll about Zanpaku-tô, techniques and Kidô was unprecedented, so there were some concerns, but it was interesting for those of us counting the votes to see the current stories (volumes 37 and 38) reflected in the results. As usual, non-*Bleach* things didn't count. So vote for Tôyako if you want, but we won't count it.

LOLY'S CURRENT SITUATION

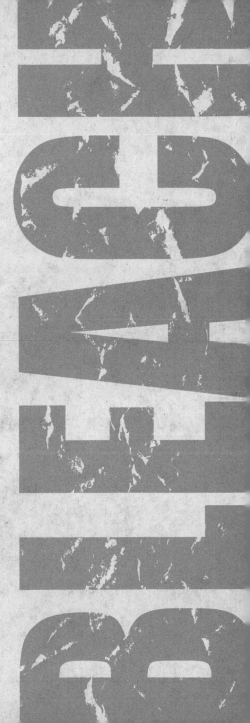

I moved. No, I had
to move. After three
years, I finally got
bored of the workspace
I loved so much. I had
never even made it to
two years in the past,
so that means I liked
this one 1.5 times more
than the others. Wait.
That's not as much
as I thought.
My new workspace is on
the 34th floor! I'm not
very good with heights,
so how many years will
I be able to stand it?!
We'll see!!

-Tite Kubo, 2009

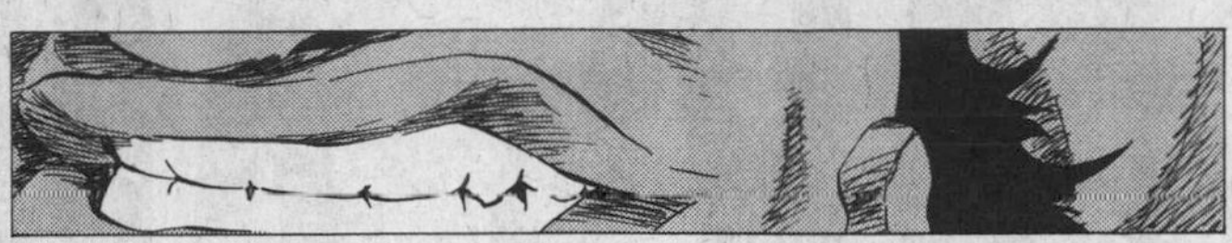

Take back what was lost
Blood, flesh, bone, and one more thing

BLEACH 41 HEART

Shonen Jump Manga

STARS AND

Ulquiorra

Orihime Inoue

Ichigo Kurosaki

plot

When high school student Ichigo Kurosaki meets Soul Reaper Rukia Kuchiki his life is changed forever. Soon Ichigo is a soul-cleansing Soul Reaper too, and he finds himself having adventures, as well as problems, that he never would have imagined. Now Ichigo and his friends must stop renegade Soul Reaper Aizen and his army of Arrancars from destroying the Soul Society and wiping out Karakura as well.

In a long-awaited clash, the Thirteen Court Guard Companies do battle with the Espadas in Karakura Town. Meanwhile in Hueco Mundo, Ichigo fights Ulquiorra to save Orihime. But after the Espada's devastating second stage release, Orihime fears this might be Ichigo's final duel.

BLEACH ALL

Rukia Kuchiki

Uryû Ishida

Yammy

STORIES

BLEACH41

HEART

Contents

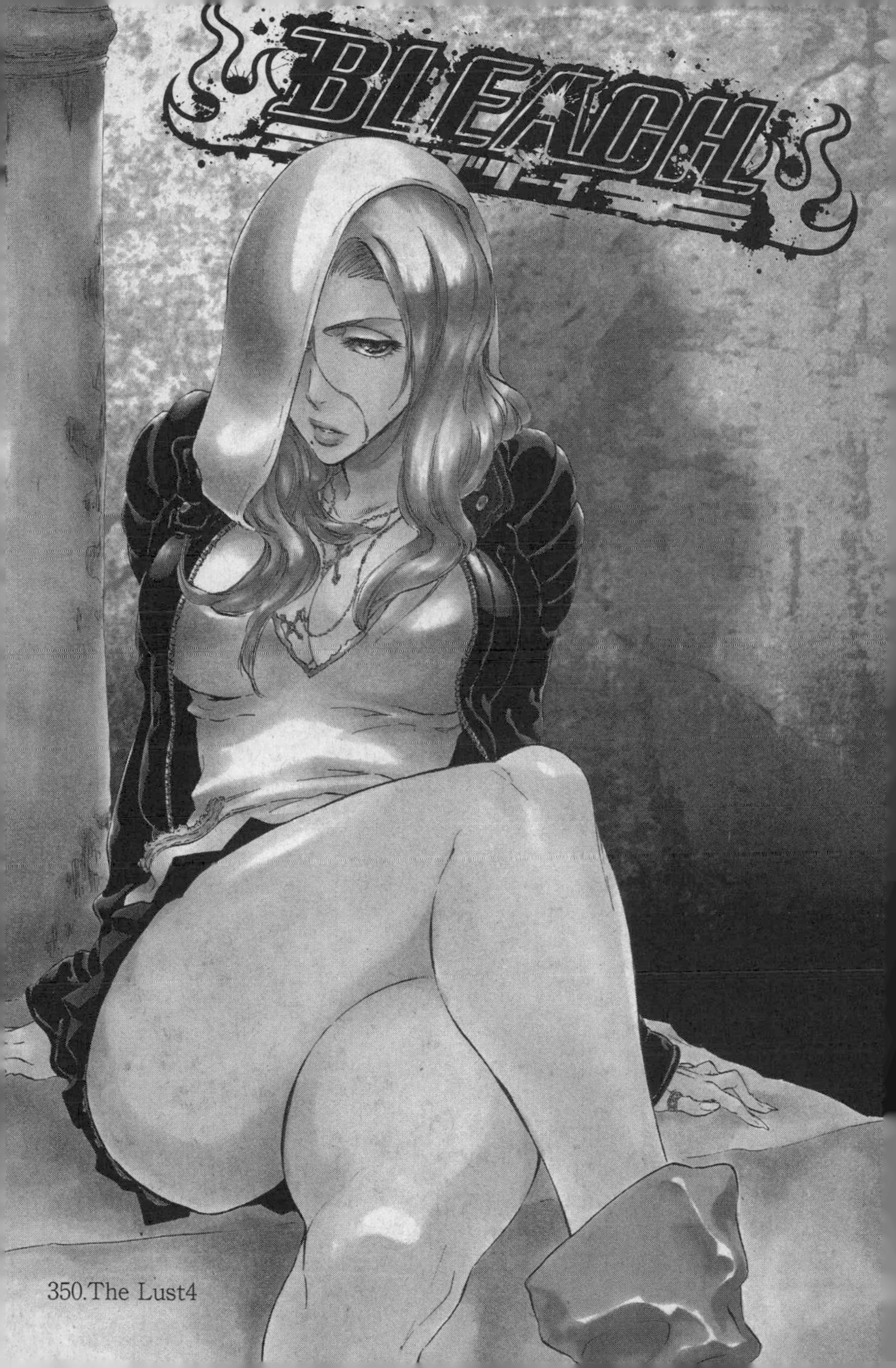
BLEACH
350.The Lust4

BLEACH
ブリーチ

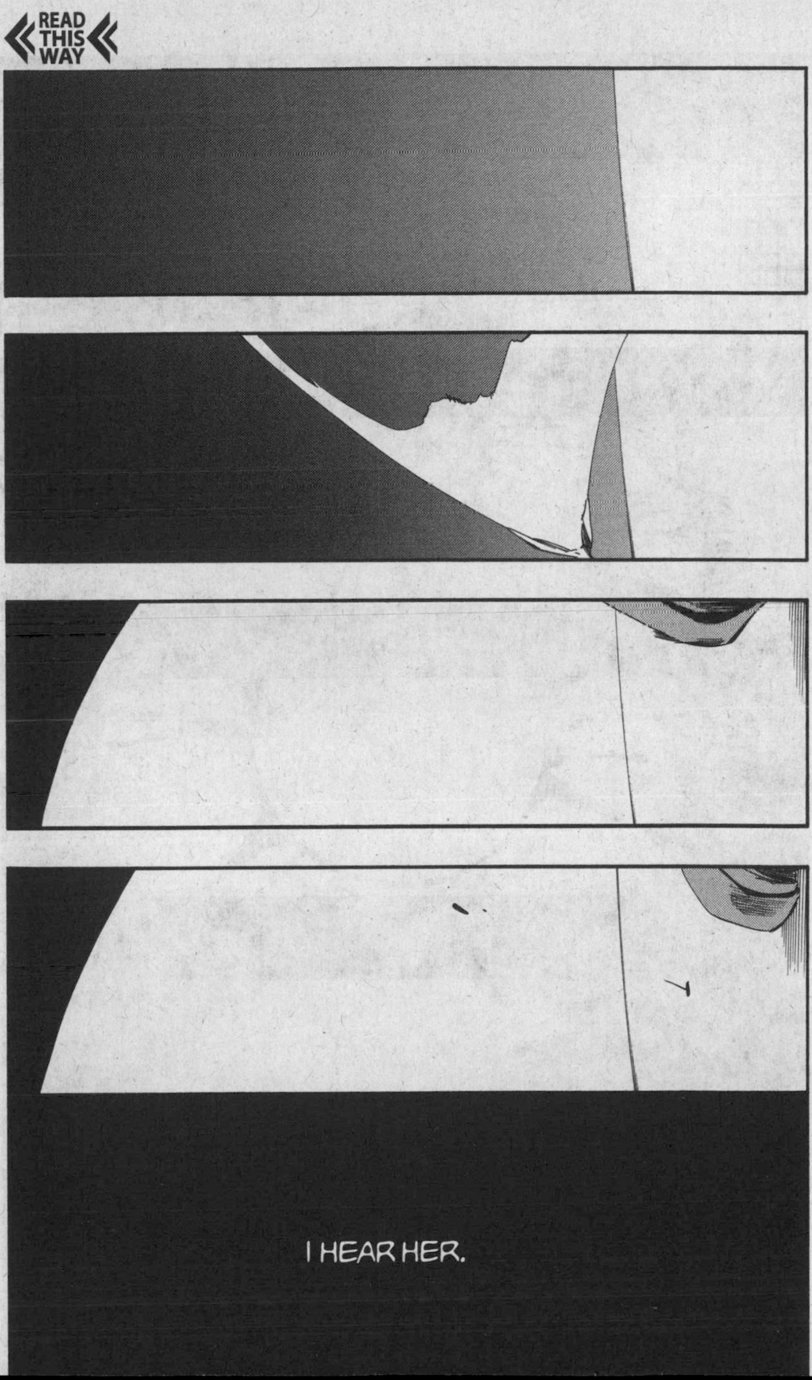
READ THIS WAY
I HEAR HER.

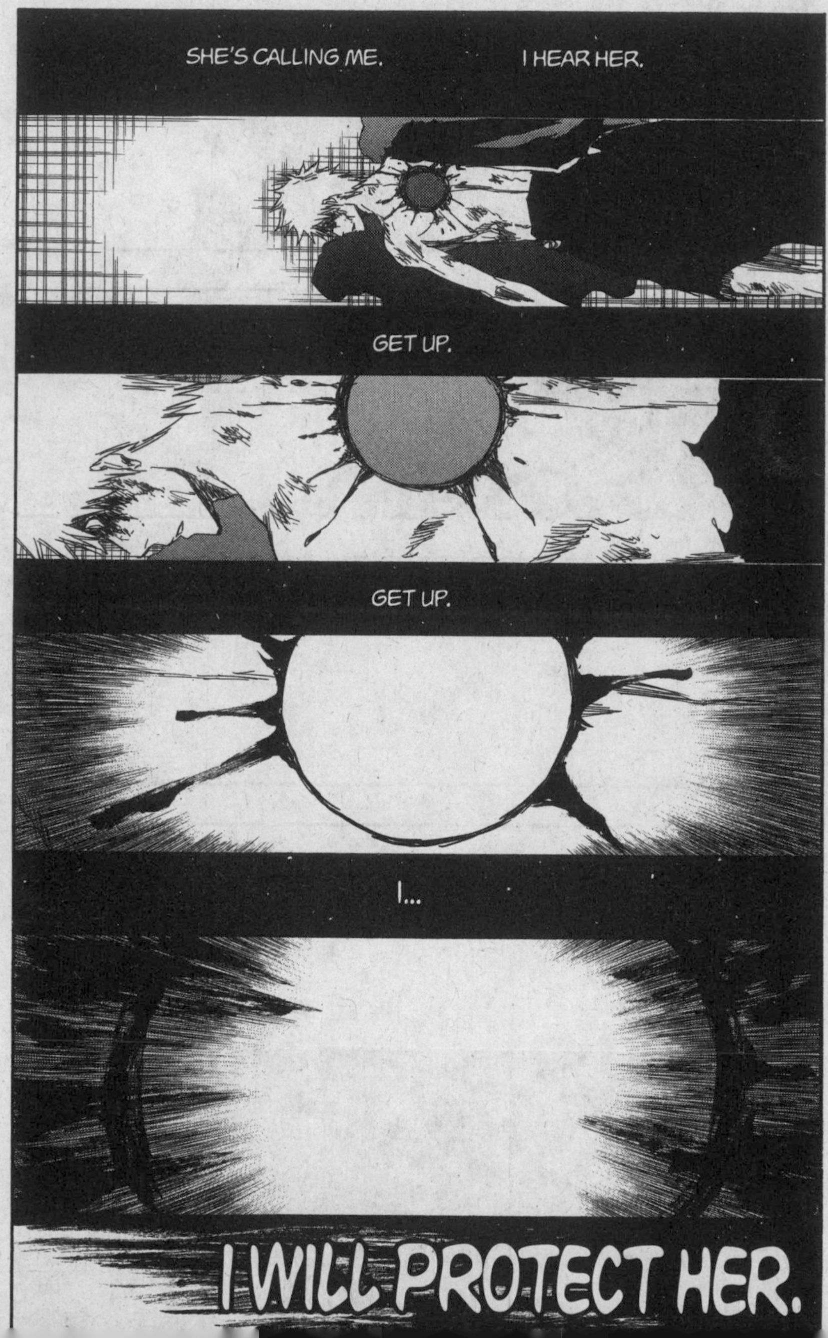
SHE'S CALLING ME.
I HEAR HER.
GET UP.
GET UP.
I...
I WILL PROTECT HER.

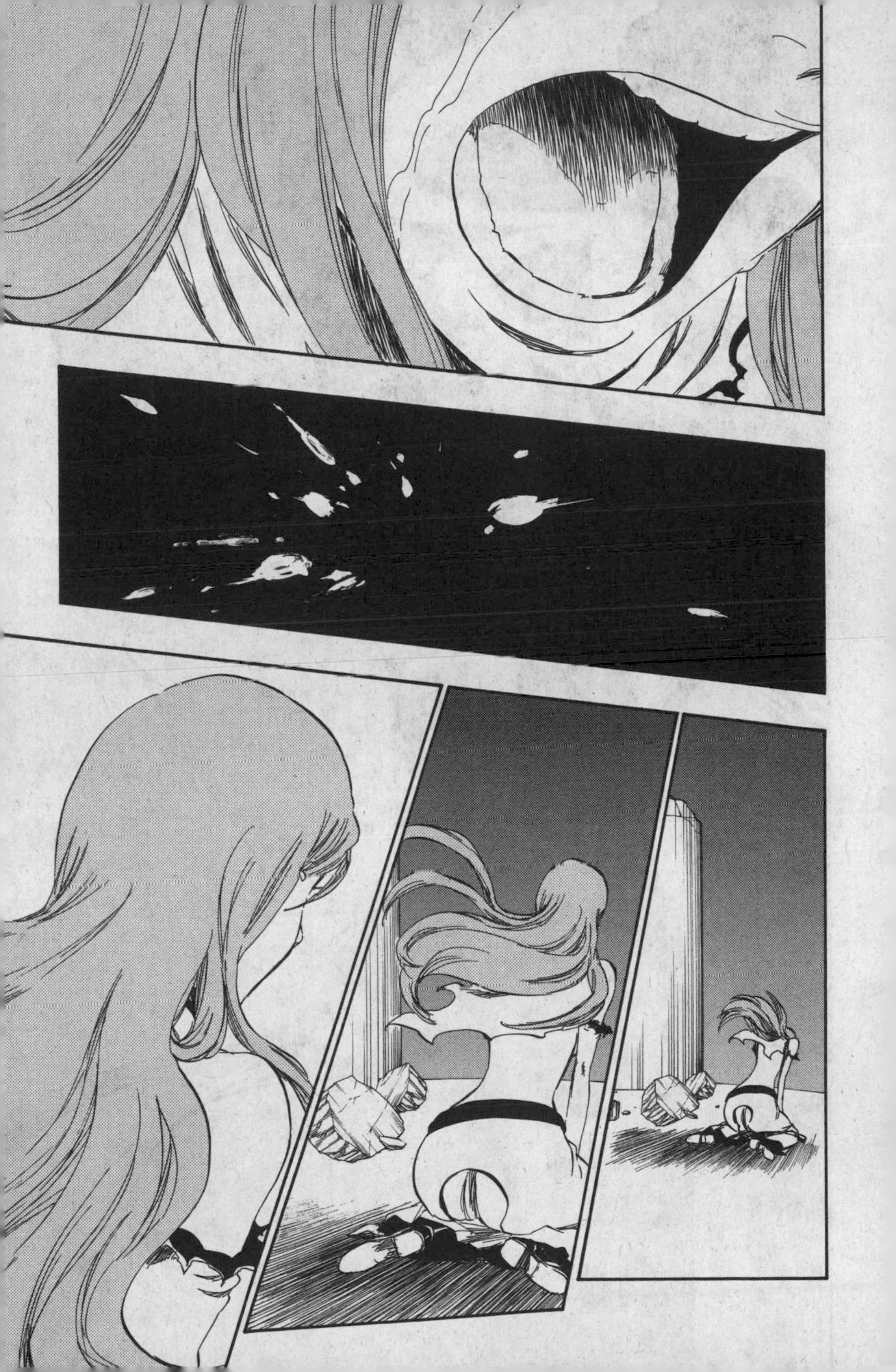

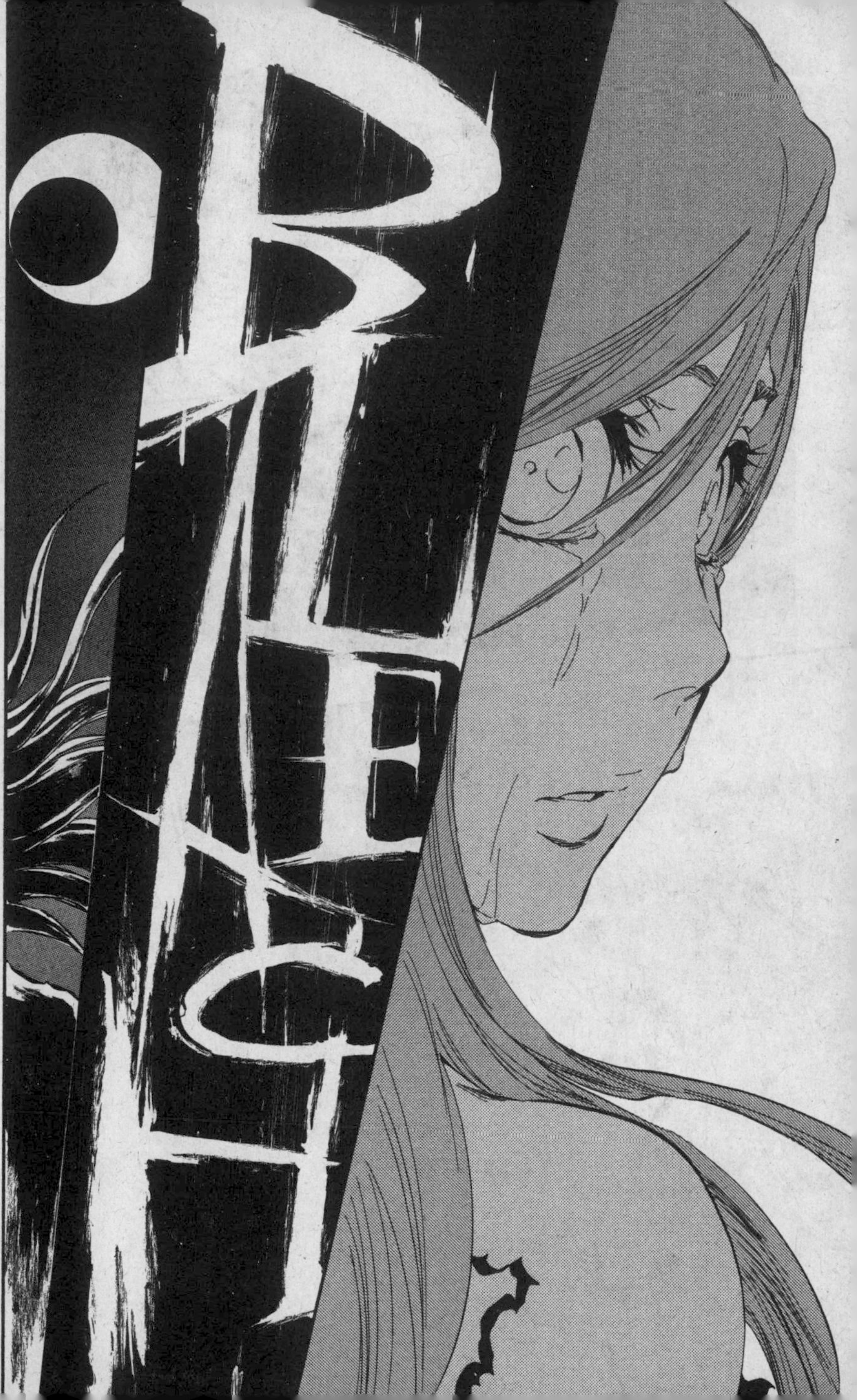

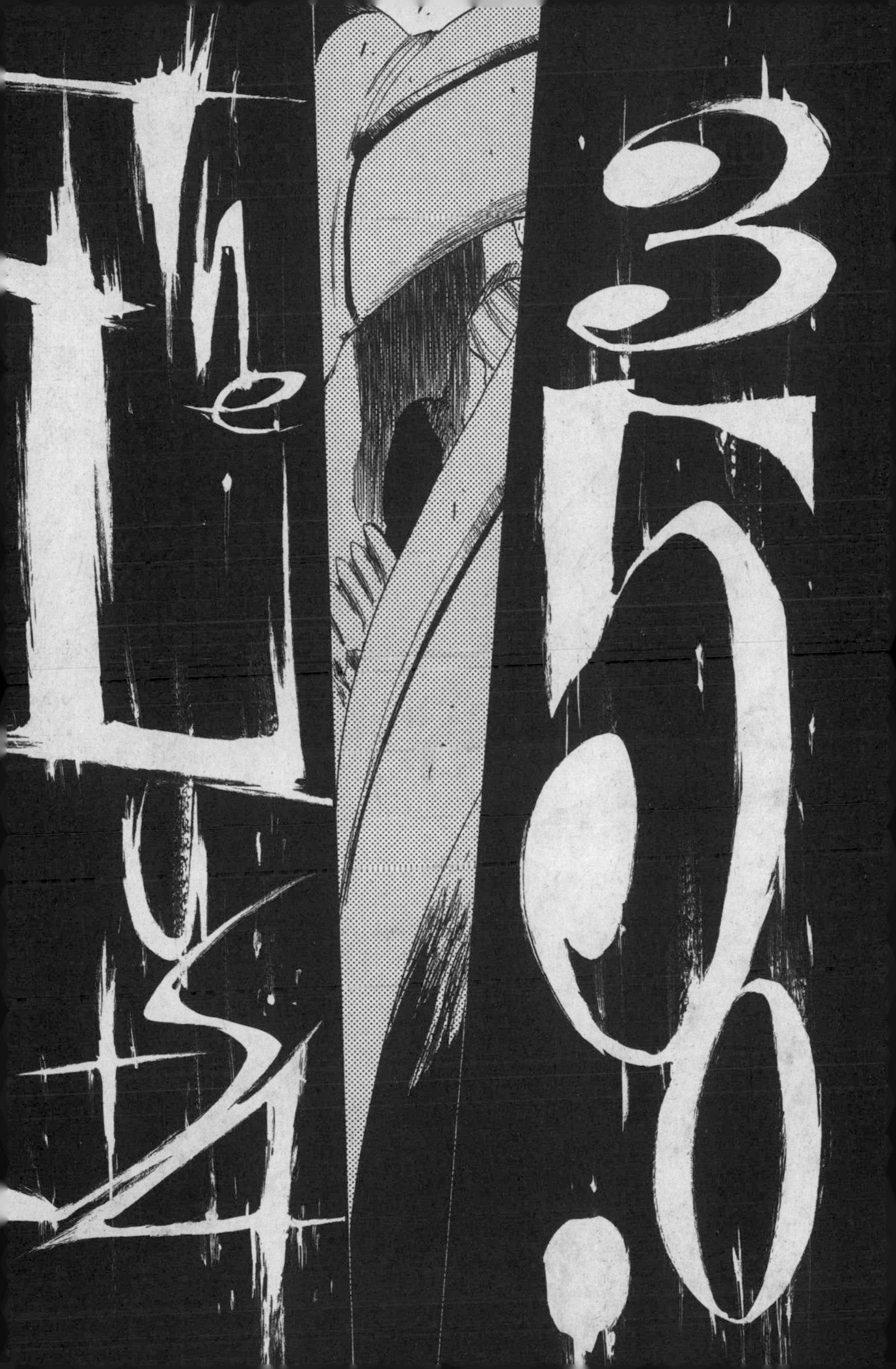

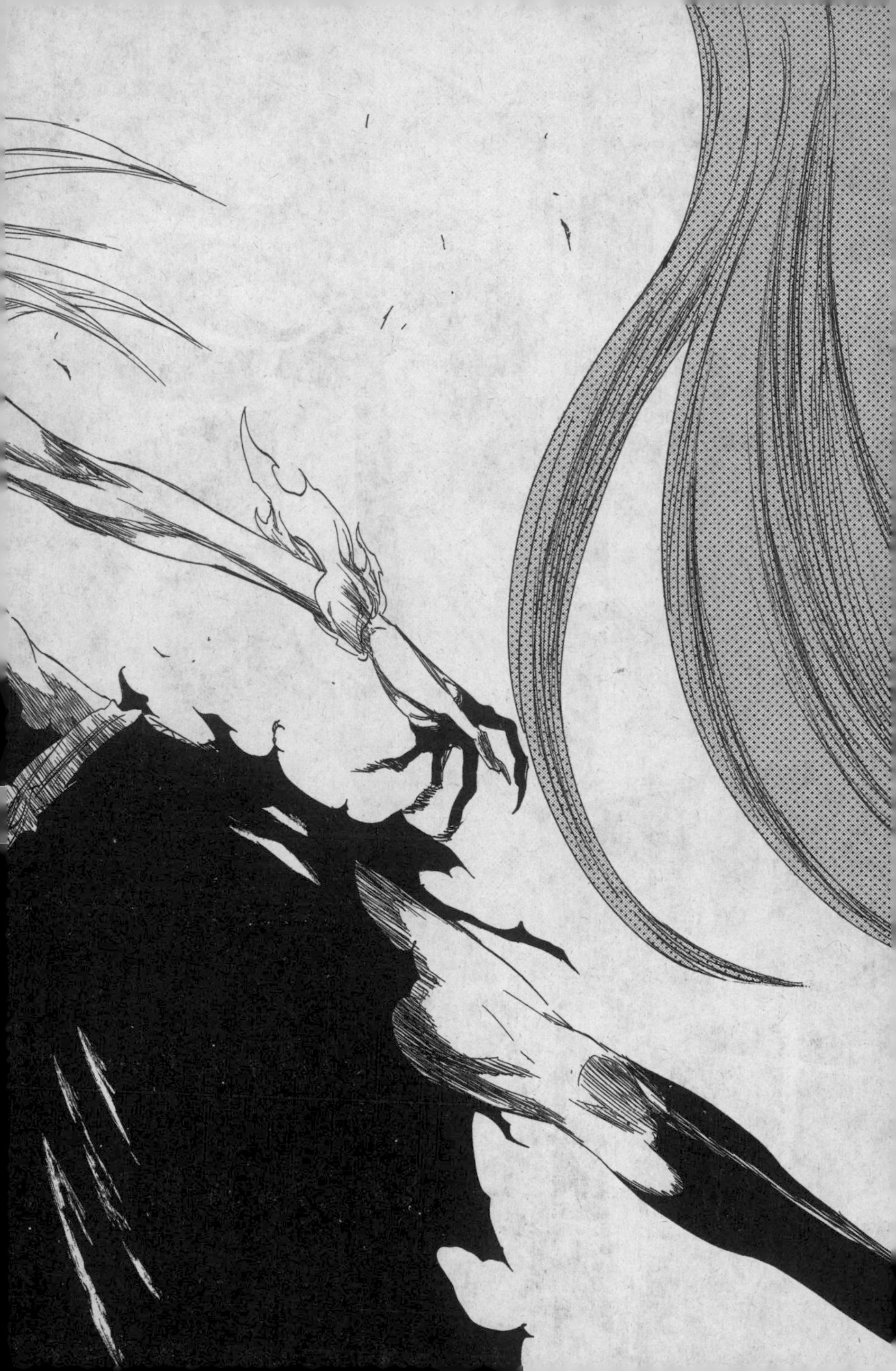

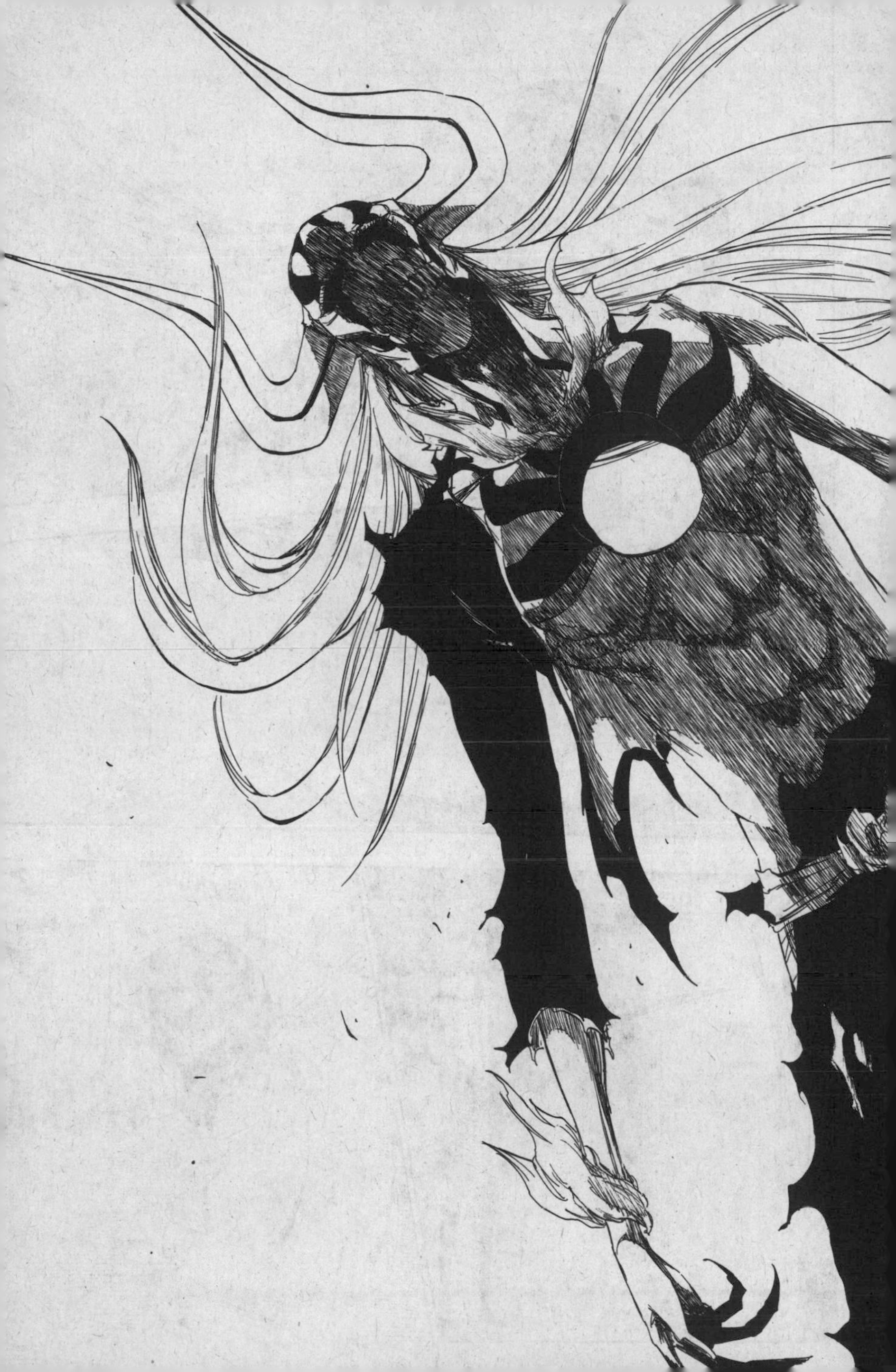

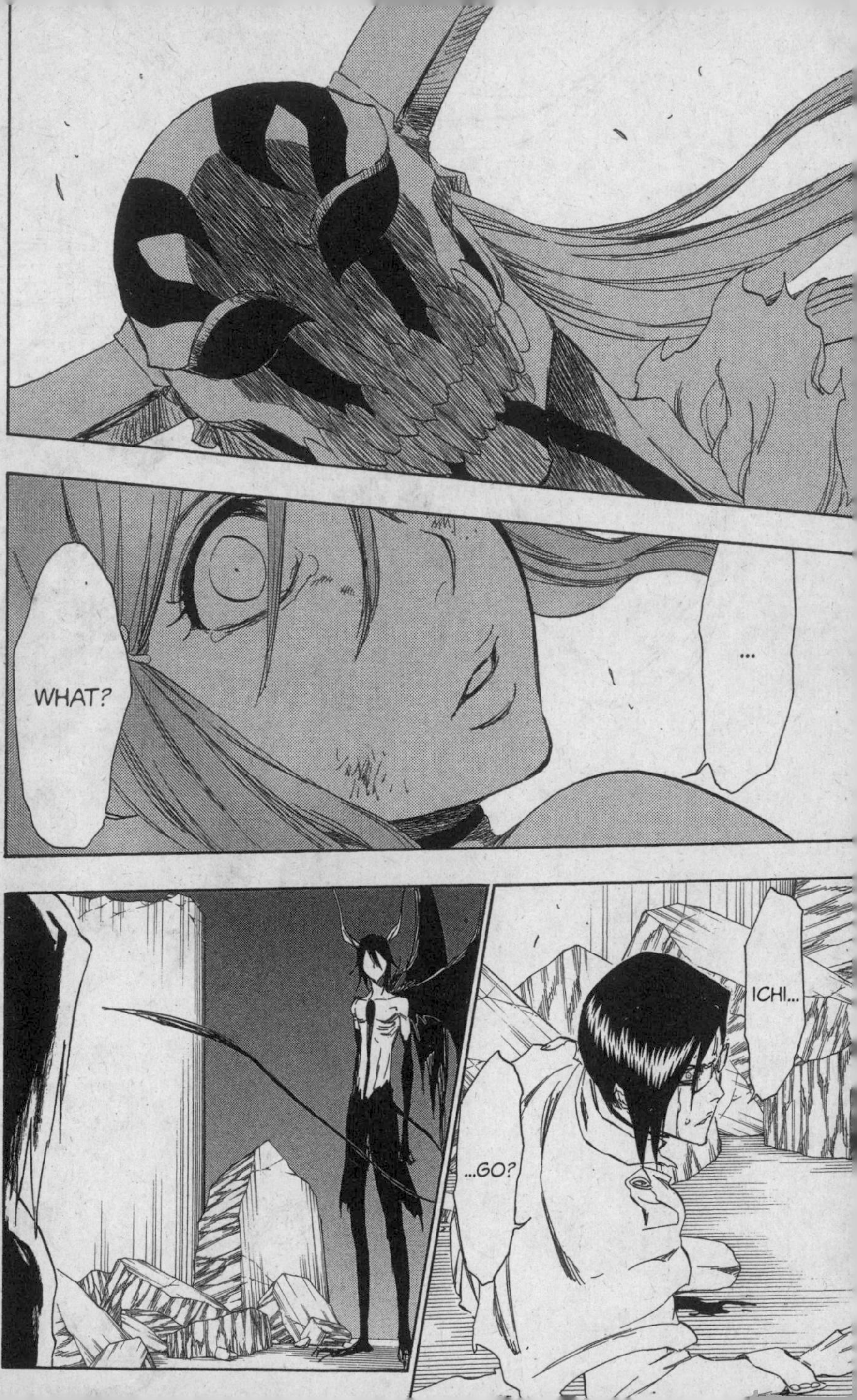
...
WHAT?
ICHI...
...GO?

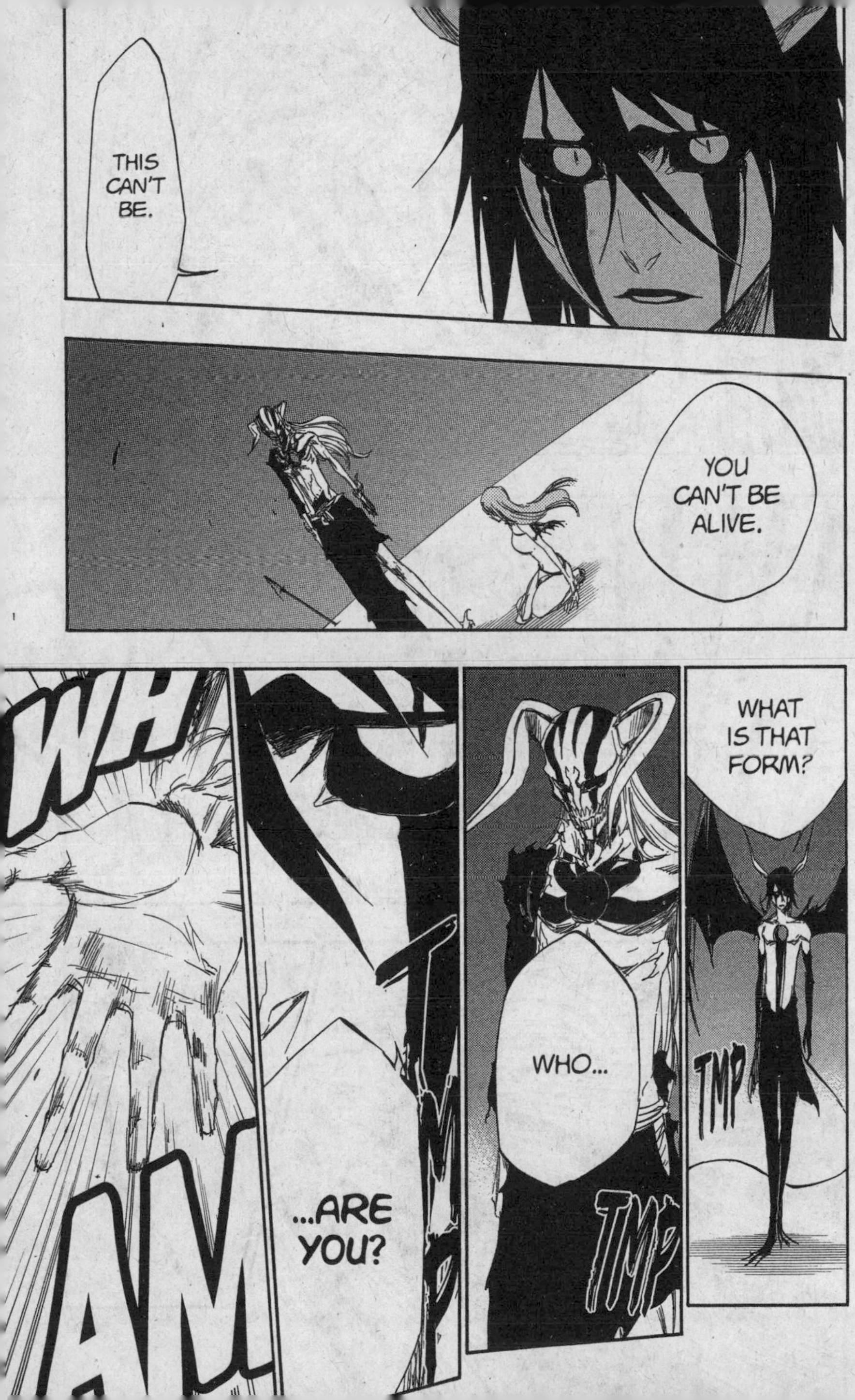
THIS CAN'T BE.
YOU CAN'T BE ALIVE.
WHAT IS THAT FORM?
TMP
WHO...
TMP
...ARE YOU?
WH
AM

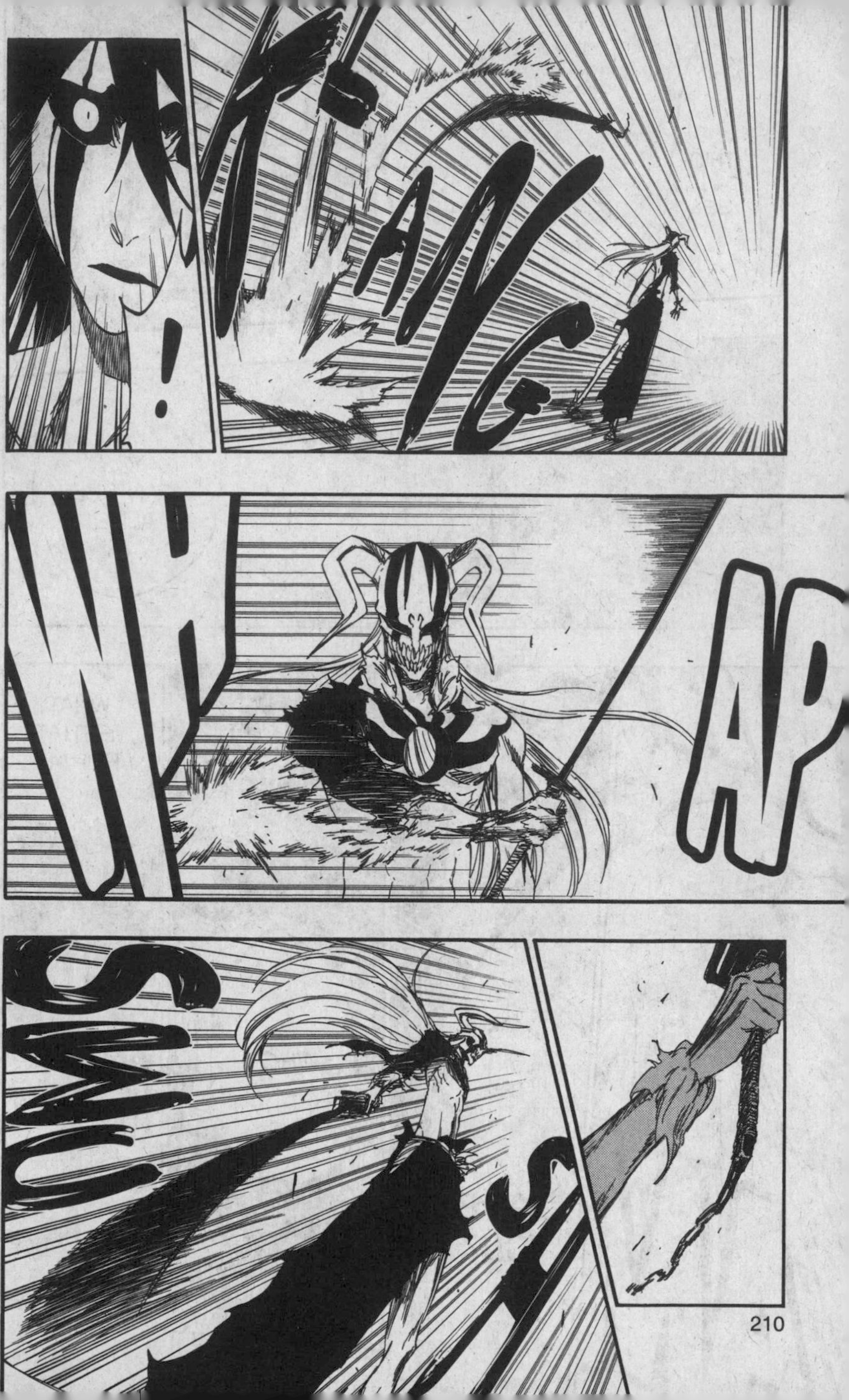
!
WHAP

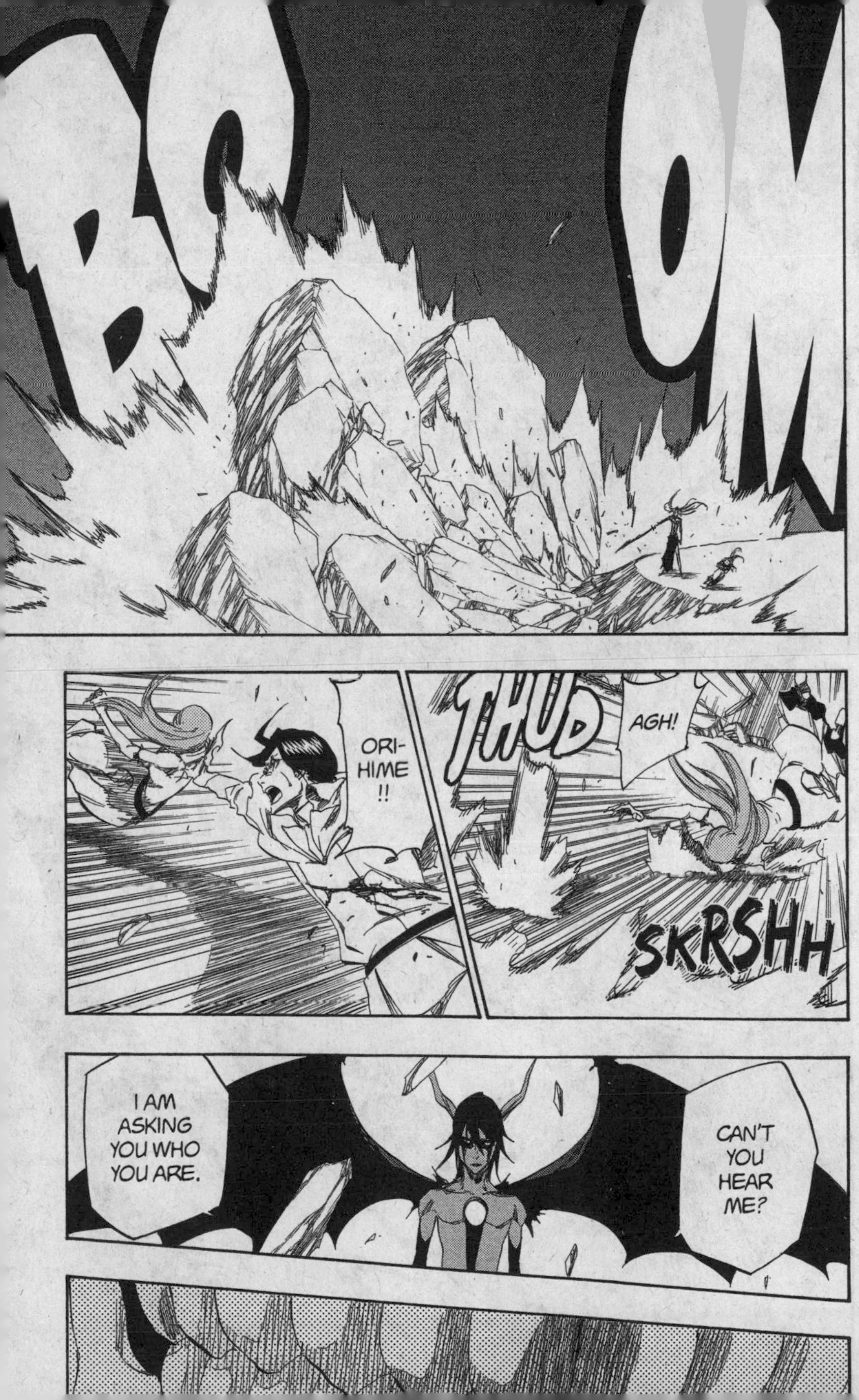
BOOM
AGH!
THUD
SKRSHH
ORI-
HIME
!!
CAN'T
YOU
HEAR
ME?
I AM
ASKING
YOU WHO
YOU ARE.

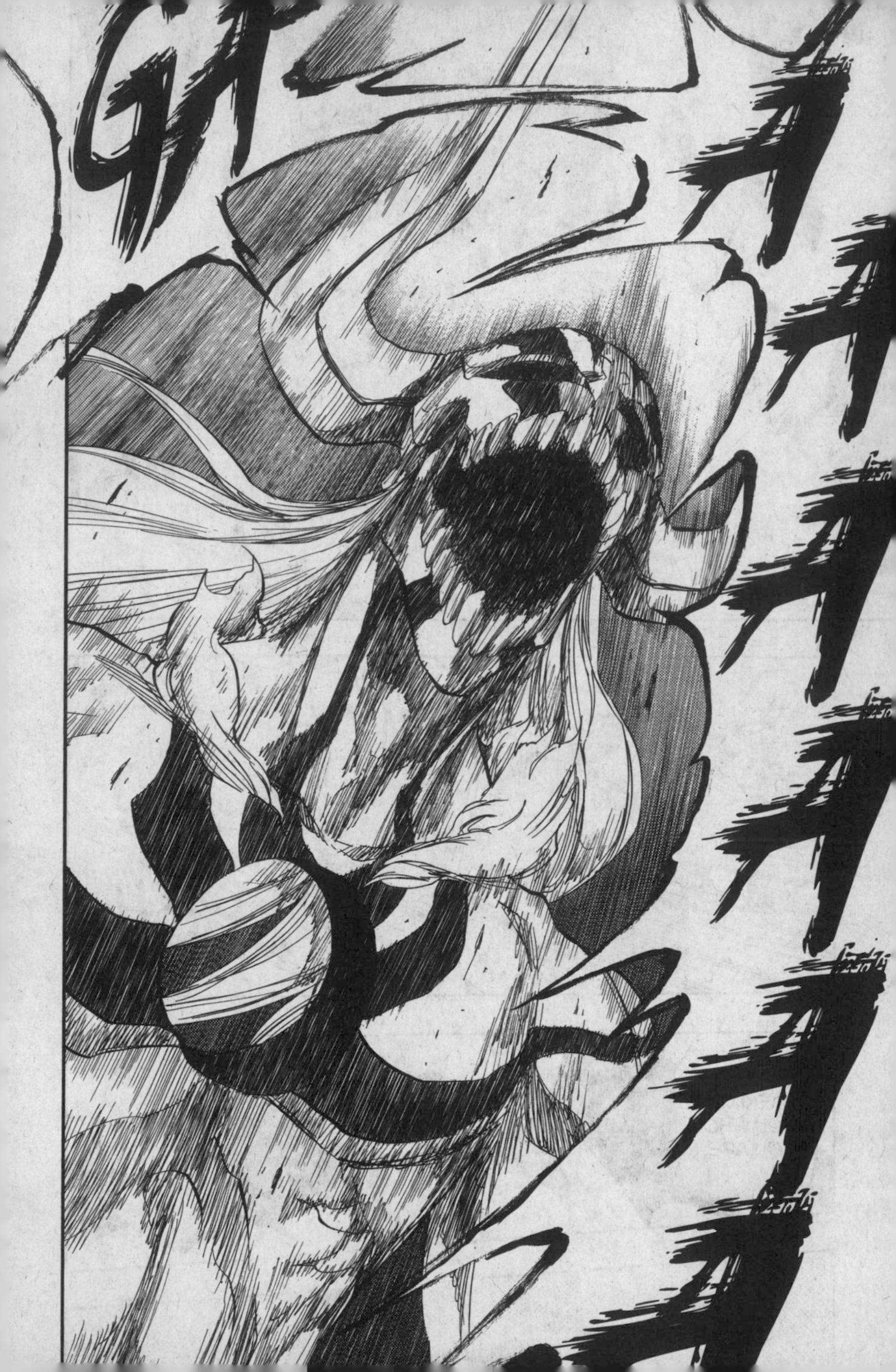

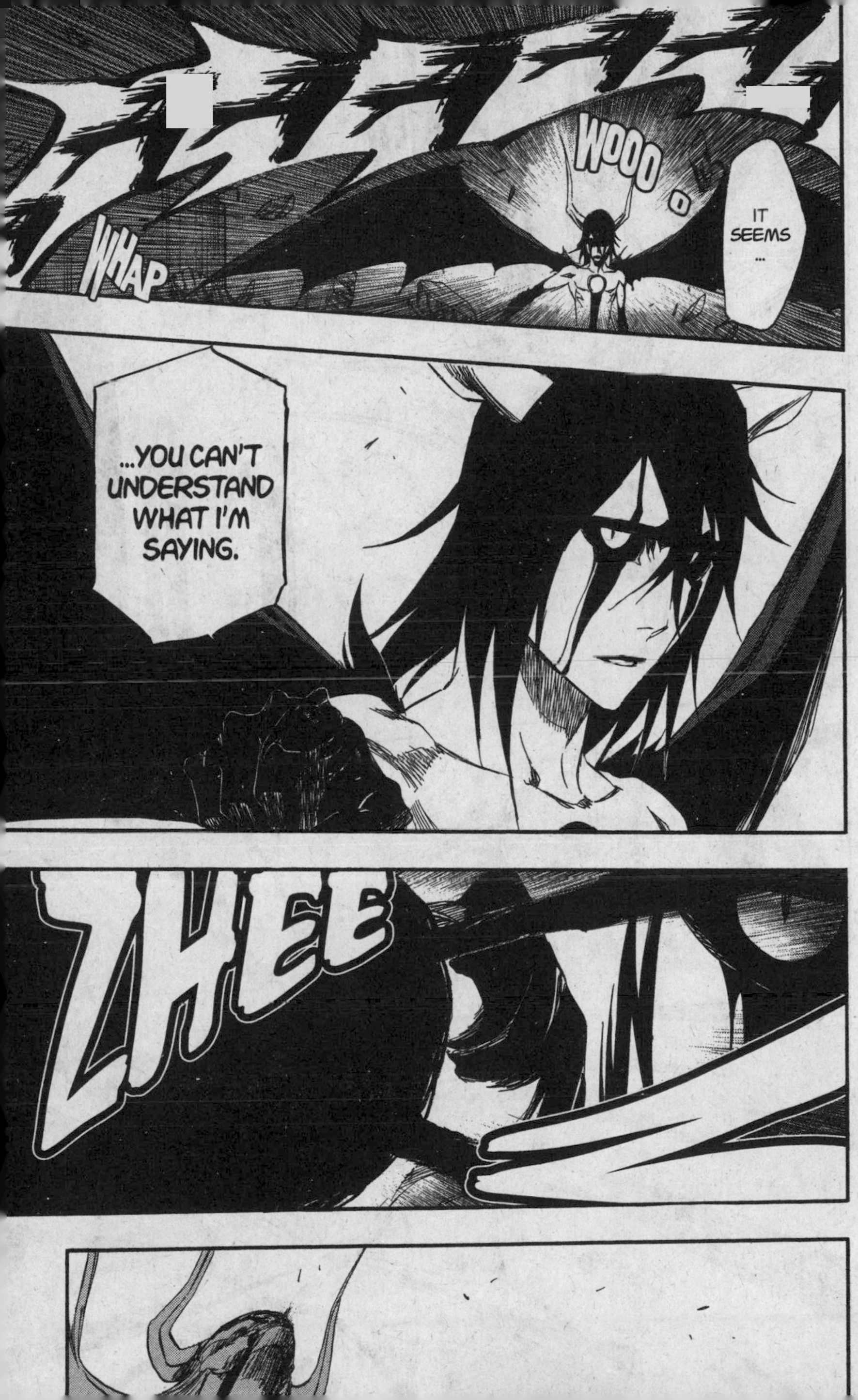
IT SEEMS ...
WOOO
WHAP
...YOU CAN'T UNDERSTAND WHAT I'M SAYING.
ZHEE

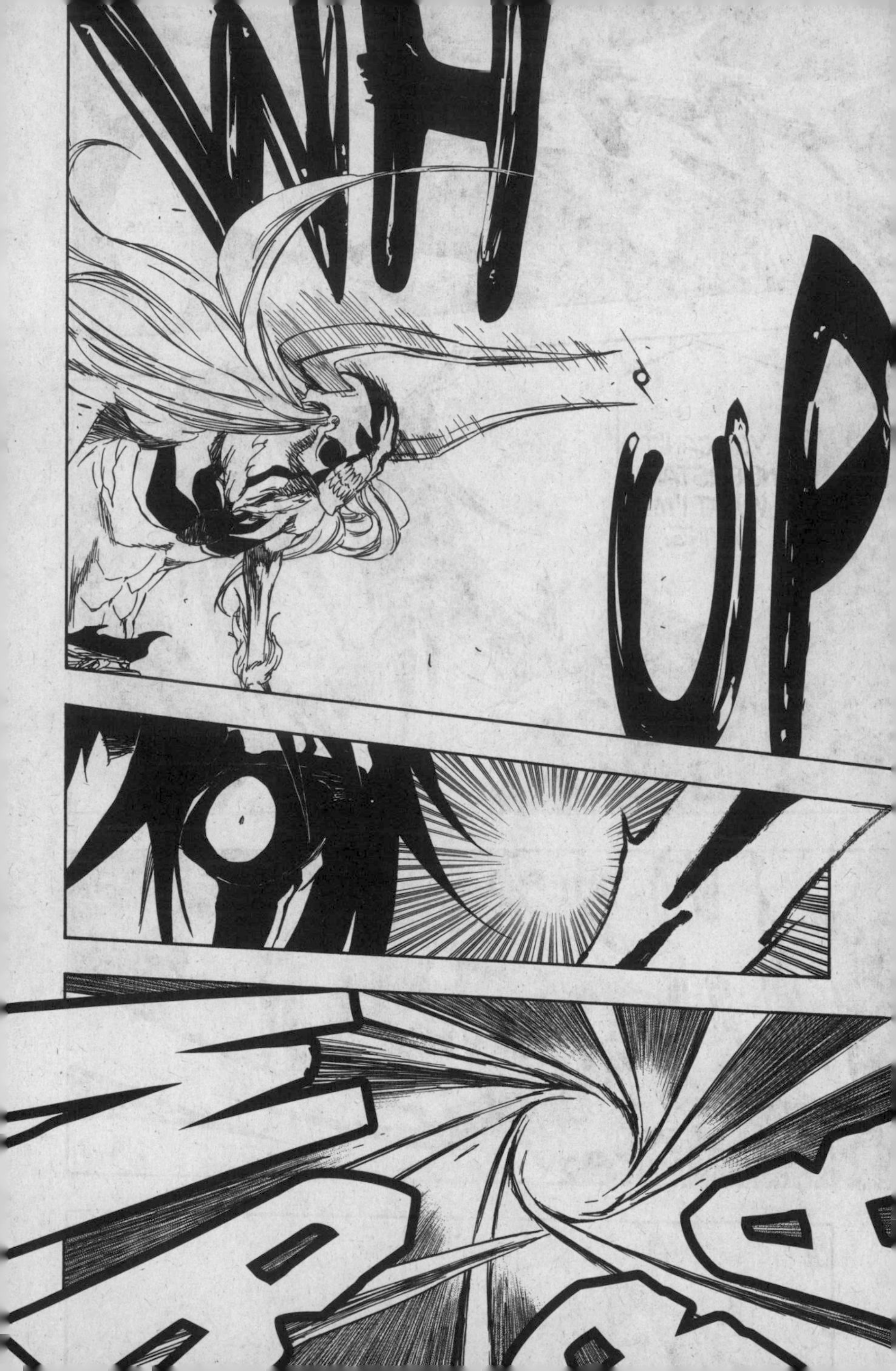
WHUP

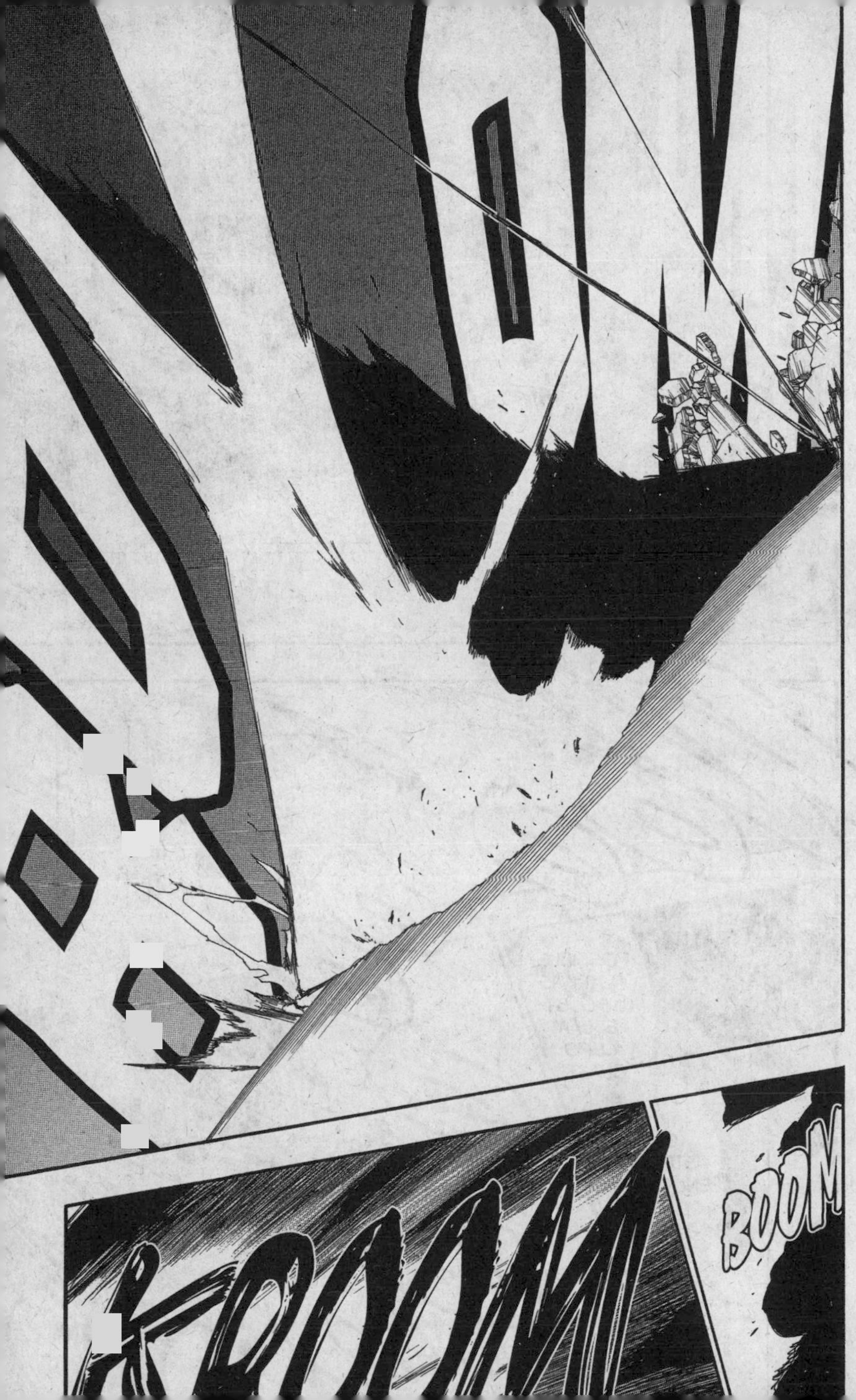
BOOM

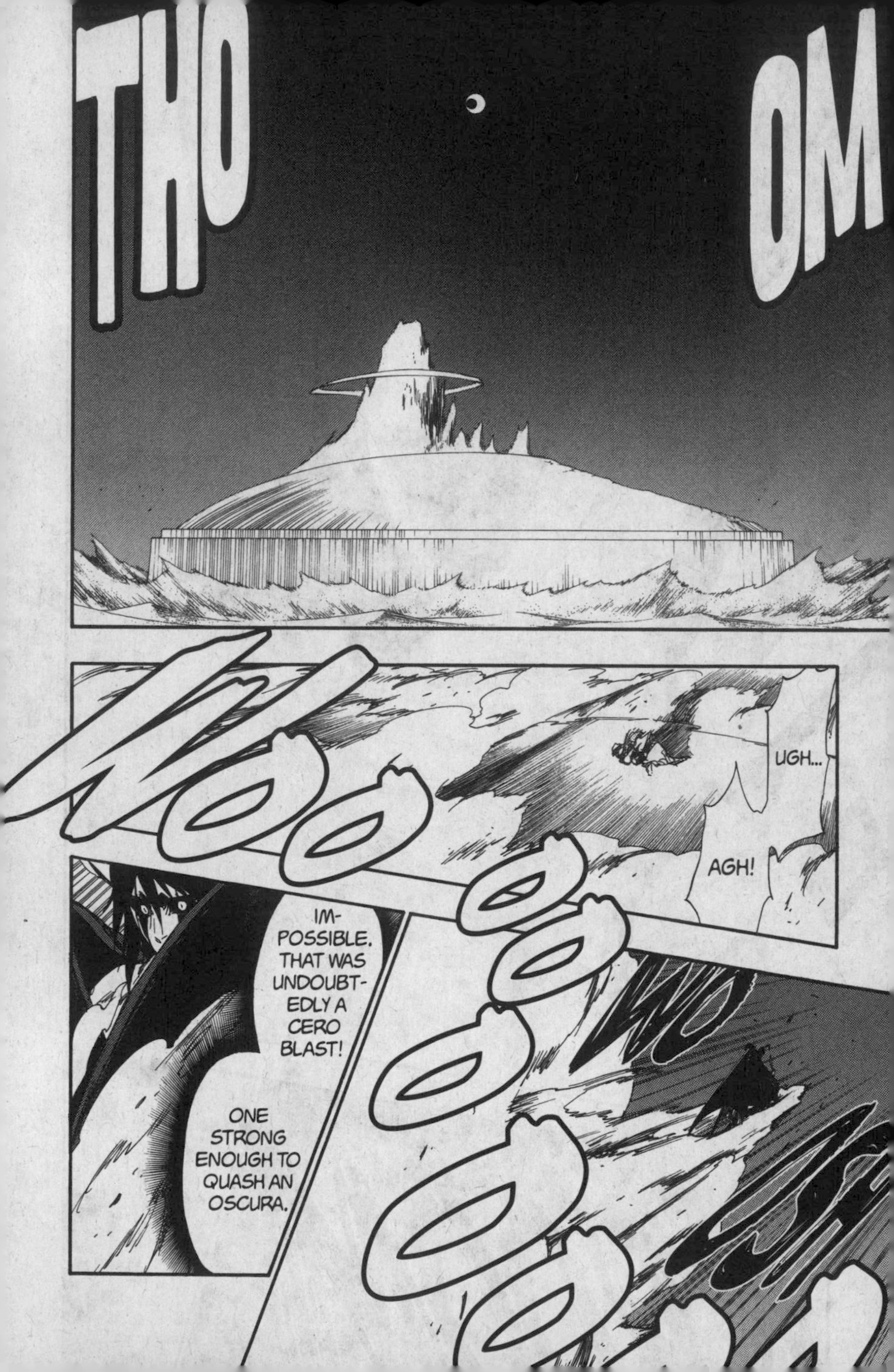
THOOM
UGH...
AGH!
IM-POSSIBLE. THAT WAS UNDOUBT-EDLY A CERO BLAST!
ONE STRONG ENOUGH TO QUASH AN OSCURA.

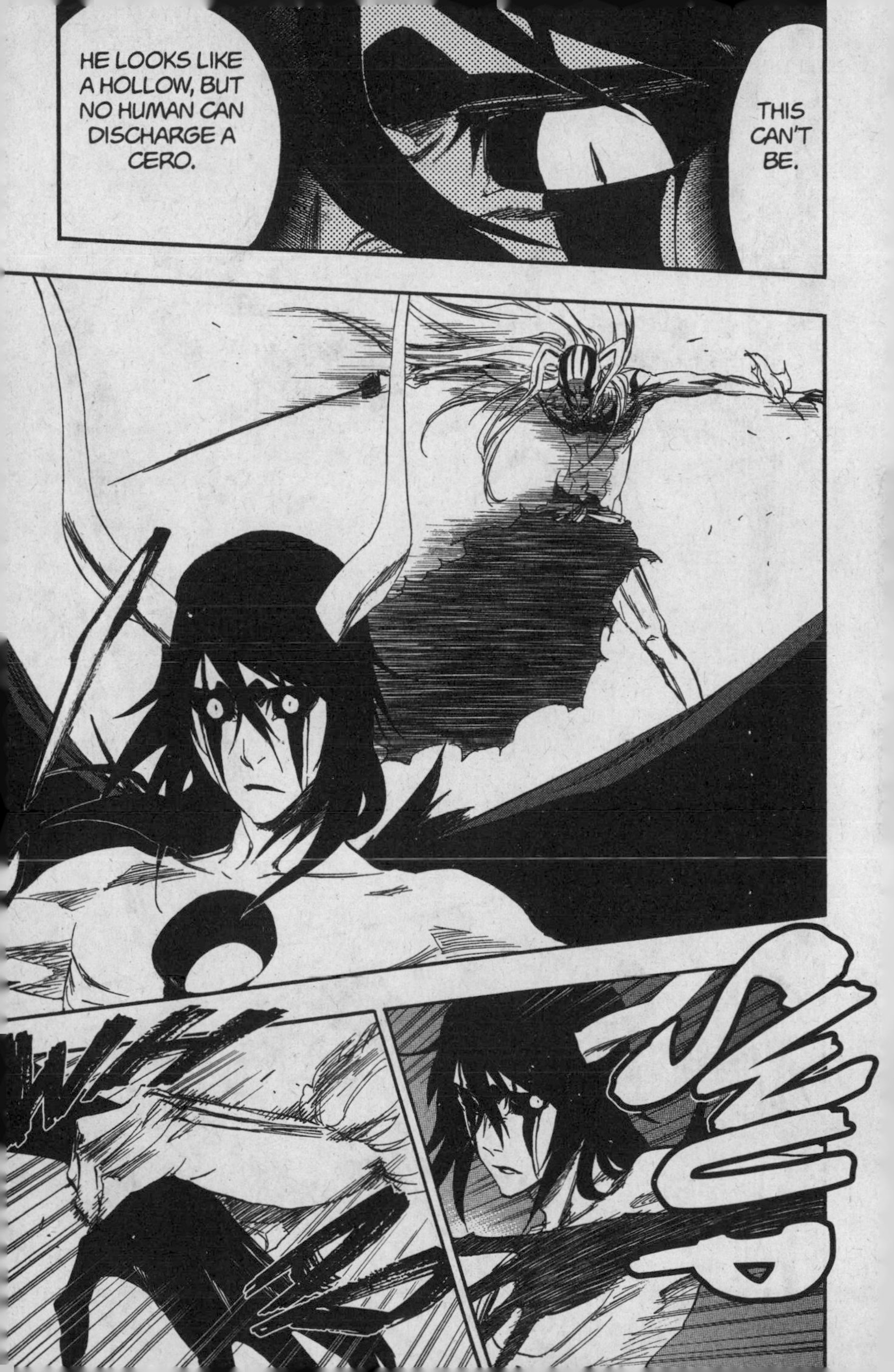
THIS CAN'T BE.
HE LOOKS LIKE A HOLLOW, BUT NO HUMAN CAN DISCHARGE A CERO.

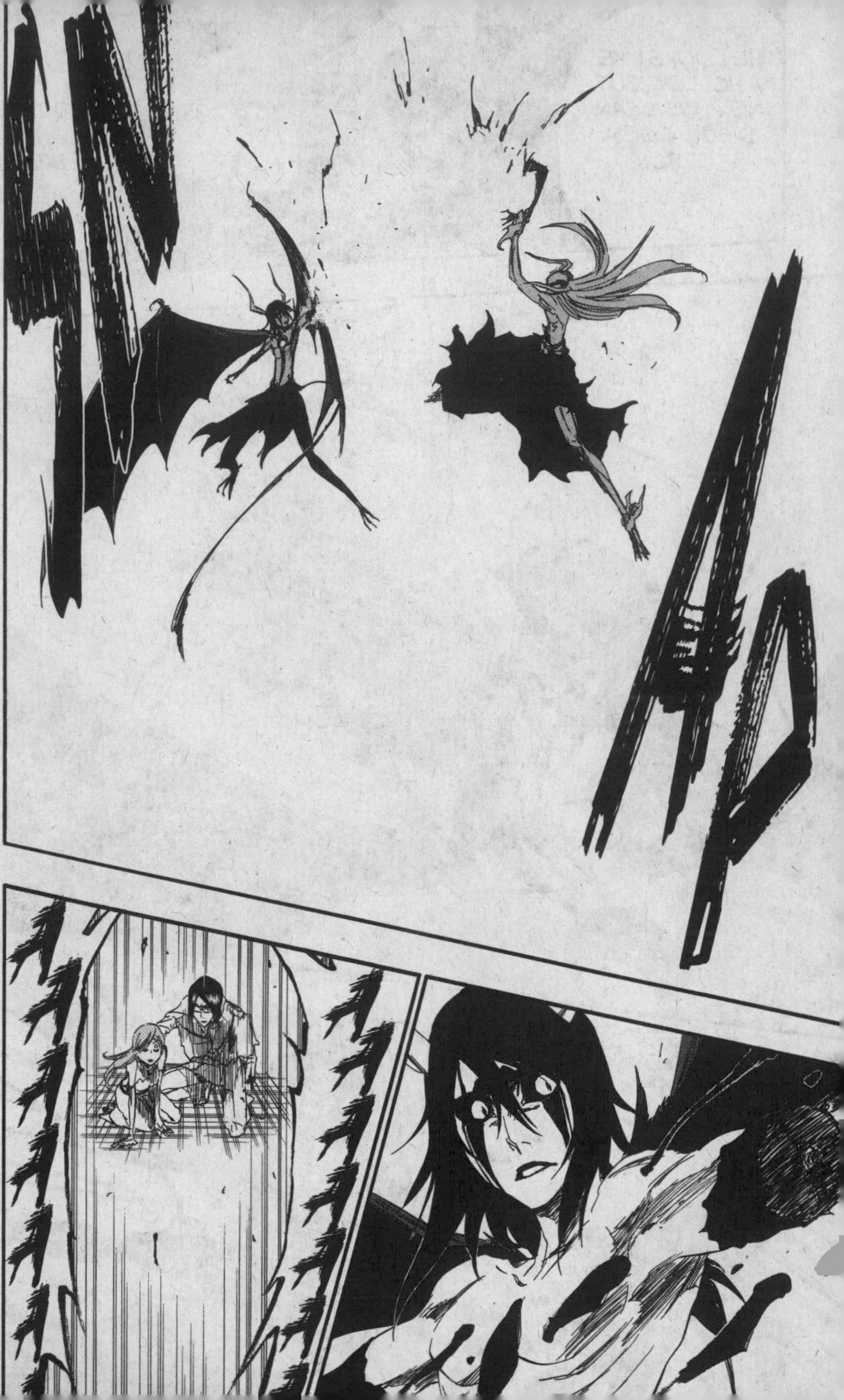

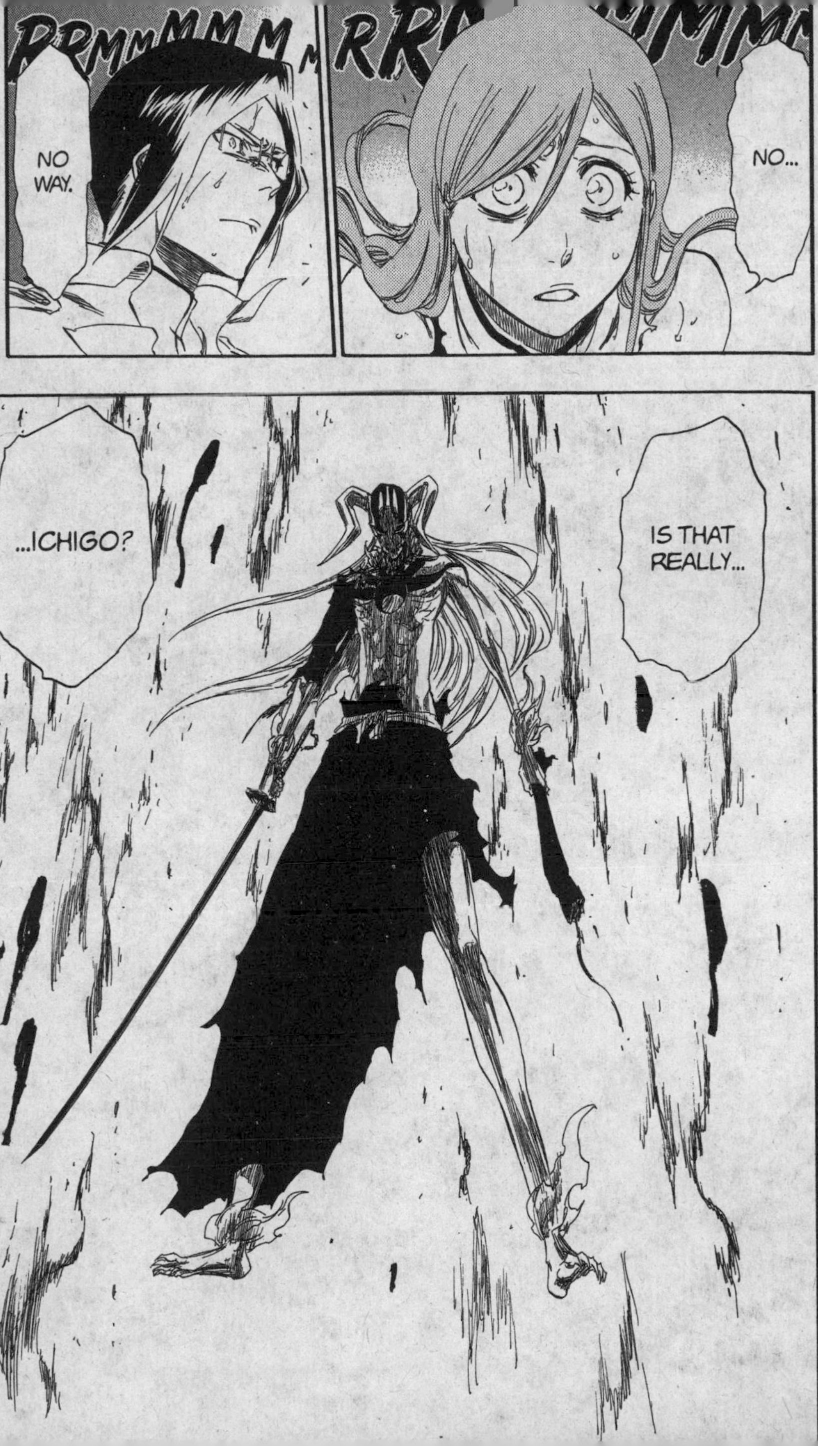
NO...
NO WAY.
IS THAT REALLY...
...ICHIGO?

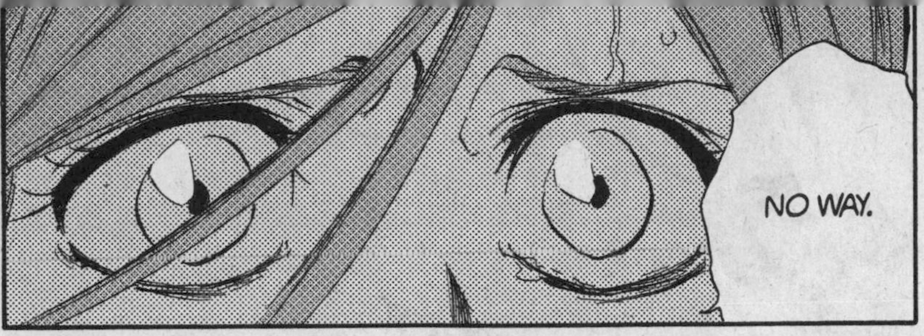
NO WAY.

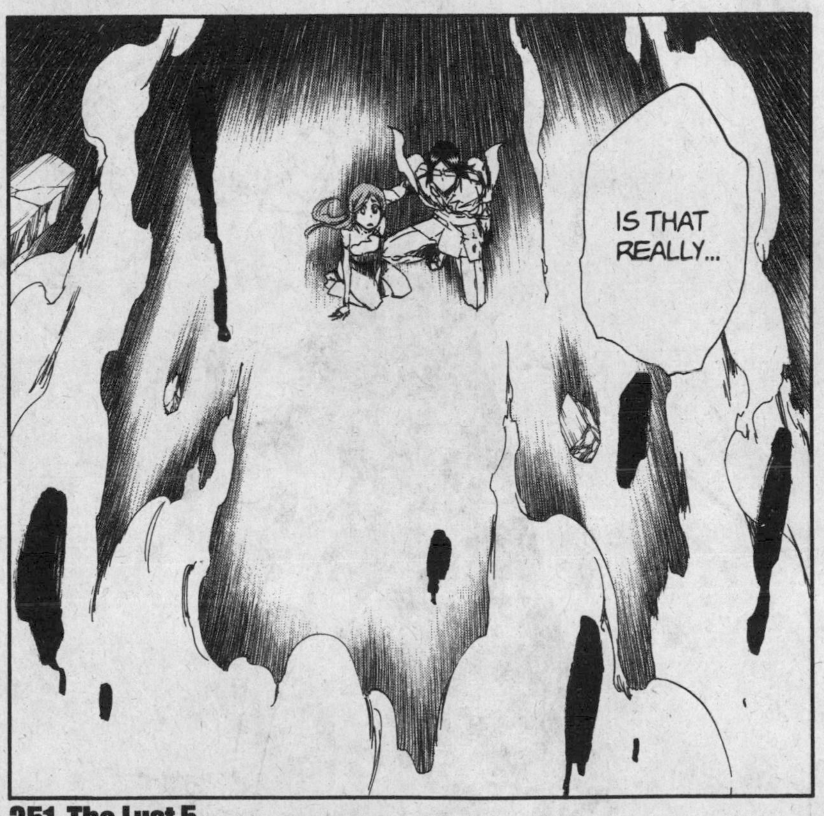
IS THAT REALLY...

351. The Lust 5

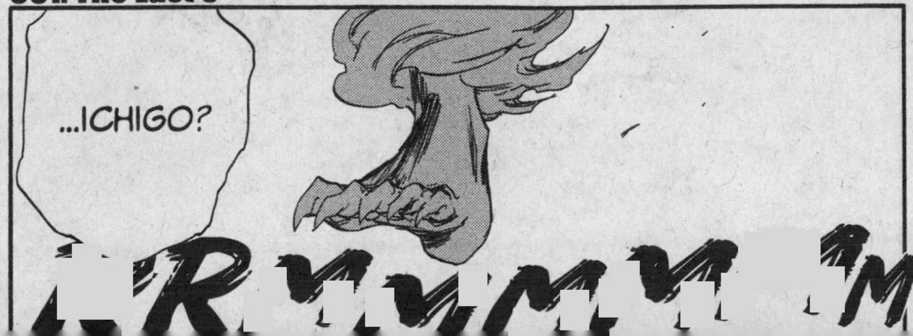
...ICHIGO?

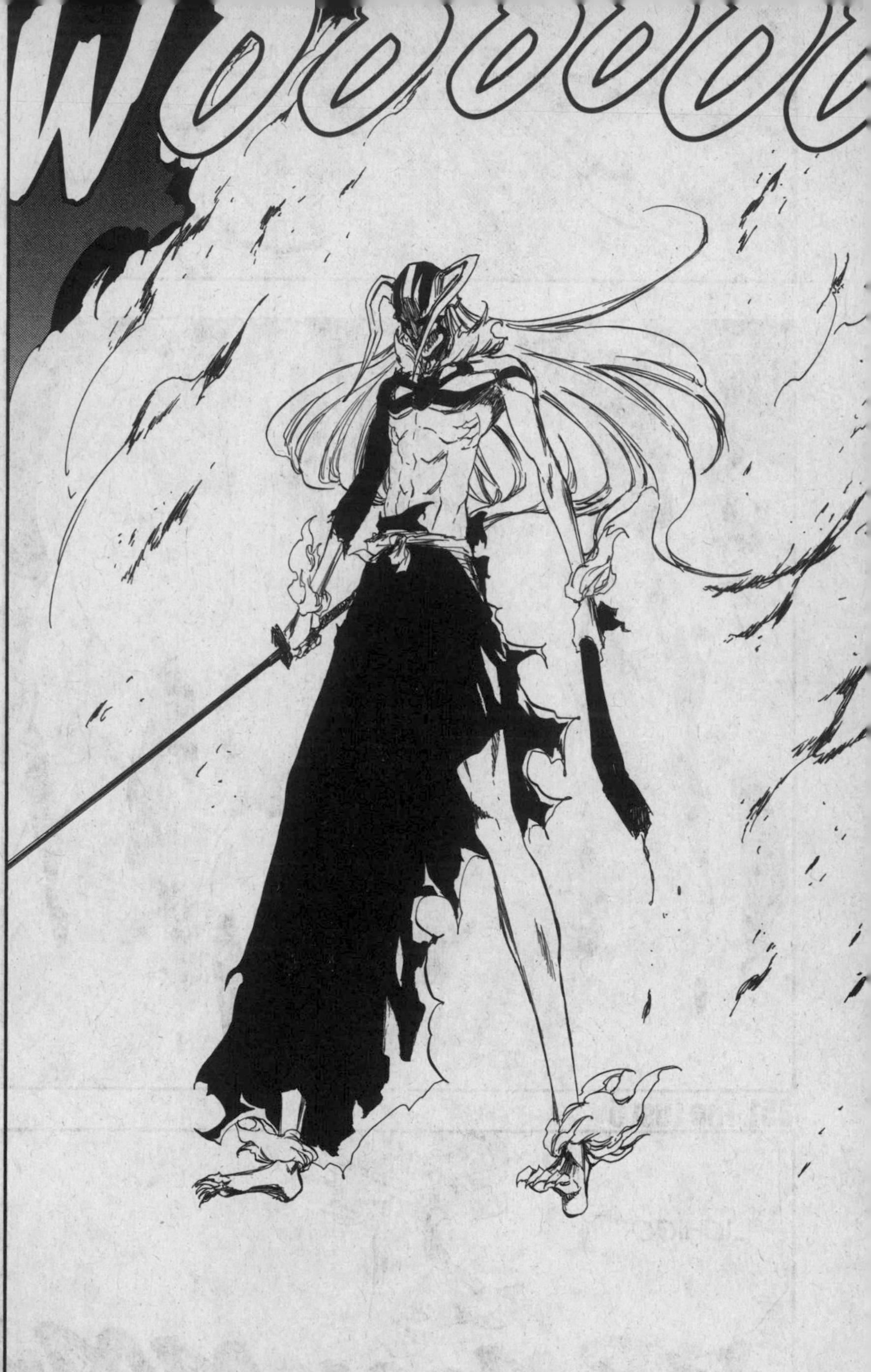
WOOOOOO

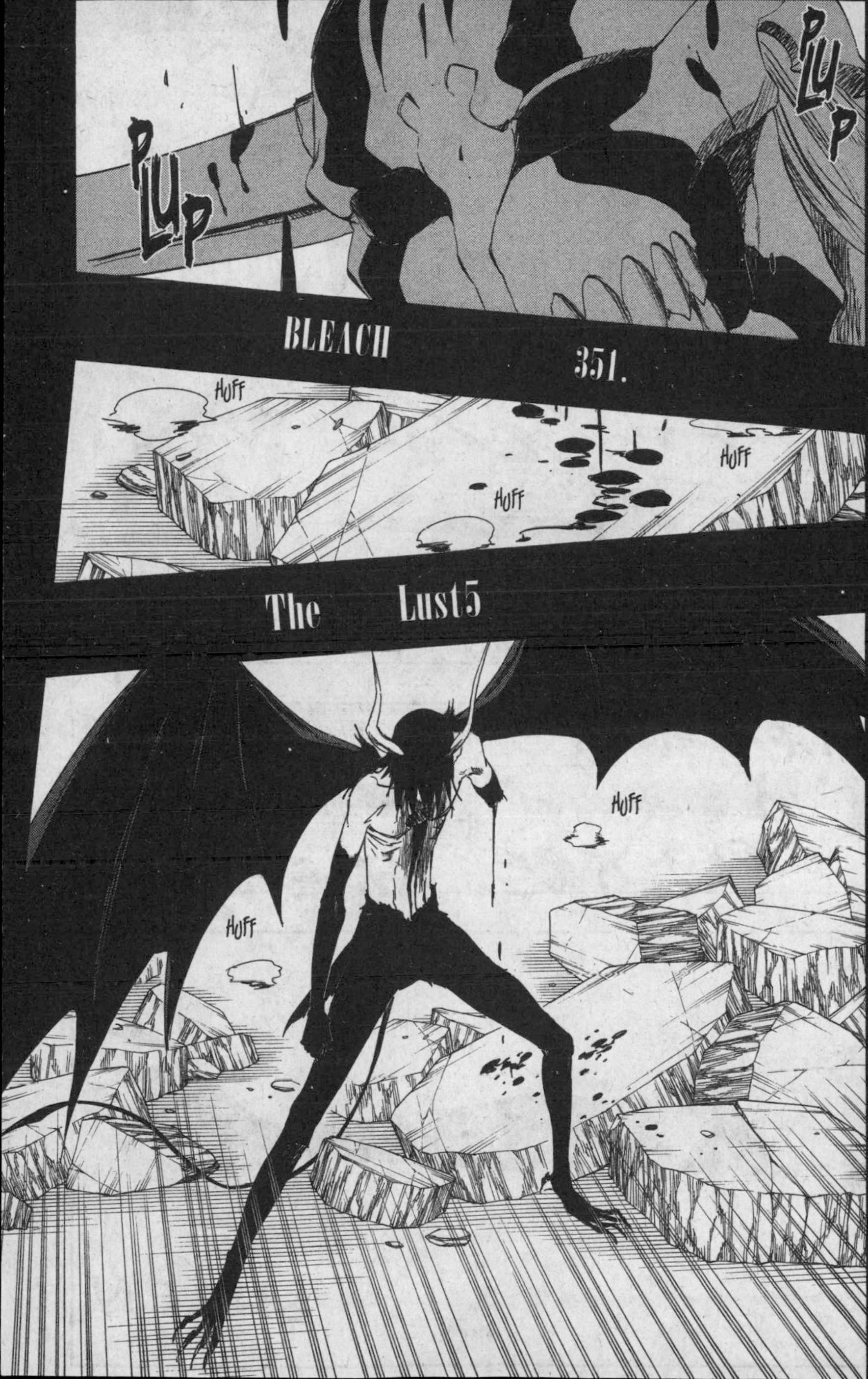
PLUP
PLUP
BLEACH 351.
The Lust5
HUFF
HUFF
HUFF
HUFF
HUFF

HUFF

SHH

AK

KREK

KREK KREK KREK KREK EK

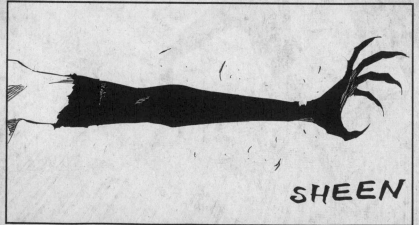

SHEEN

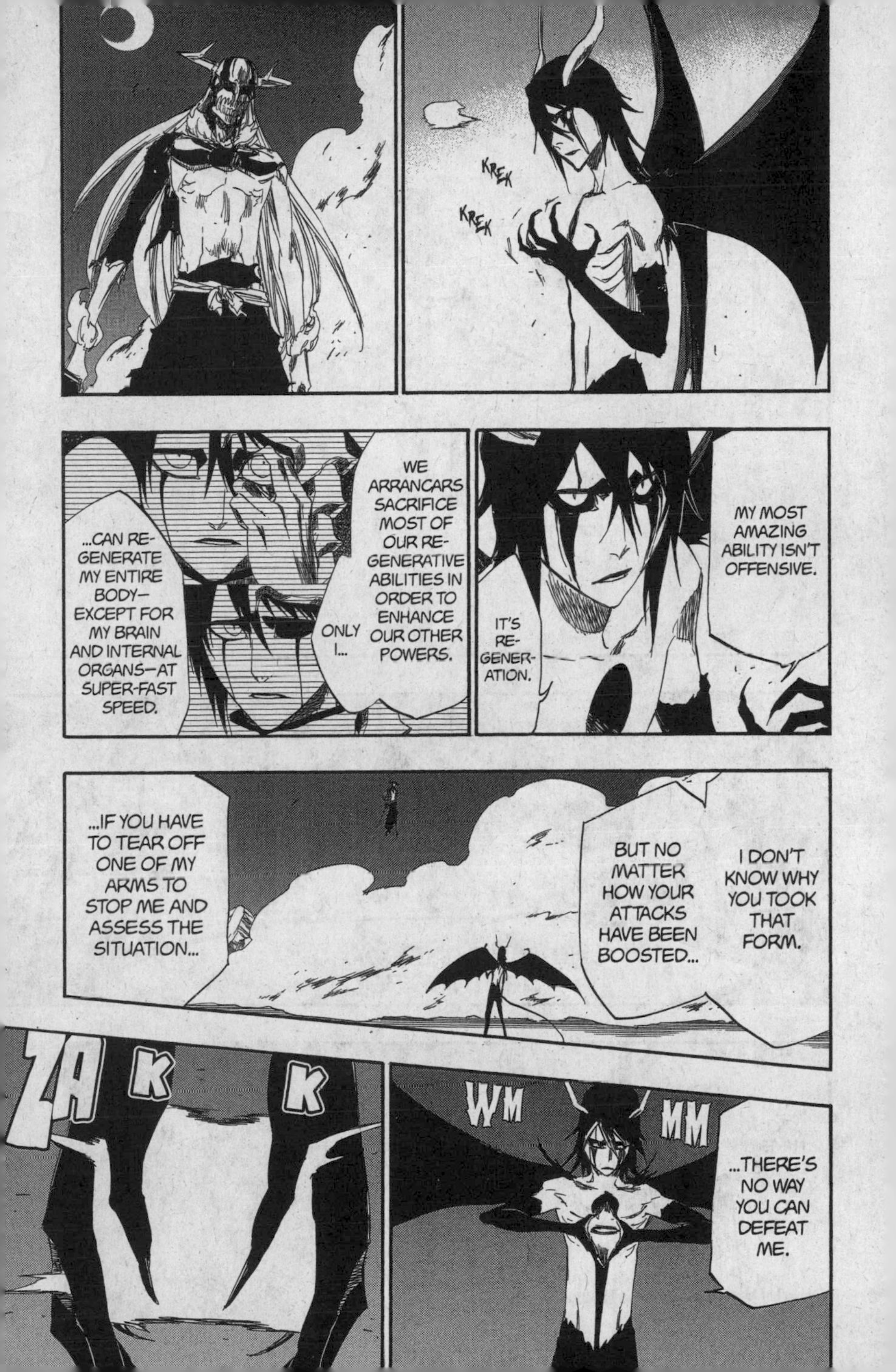
KREK
KREK
MY MOST AMAZING ABILITY ISN'T OFFENSIVE.
IT'S RE-GENERATION.
WE ARRANCARS SACRIFICE MOST OF OUR RE-GENERATIVE ABILITIES IN ORDER TO ENHANCE OUR OTHER POWERS.
ONLY I...
...CAN RE-GENERATE MY ENTIRE BODY—EXCEPT FOR MY BRAIN AND INTERNAL ORGANS—AT SUPER-FAST SPEED.
I DON'T KNOW WHY YOU TOOK THAT FORM.
BUT NO MATTER HOW YOUR ATTACKS HAVE BEEN BOOSTED...
...IF YOU HAVE TO TEAR OFF ONE OF MY ARMS TO STOP ME AND ASSESS THE SITUATION...
WM MM
...THERE'S NO WAY YOU CAN DEFEAT ME.
ZA K K

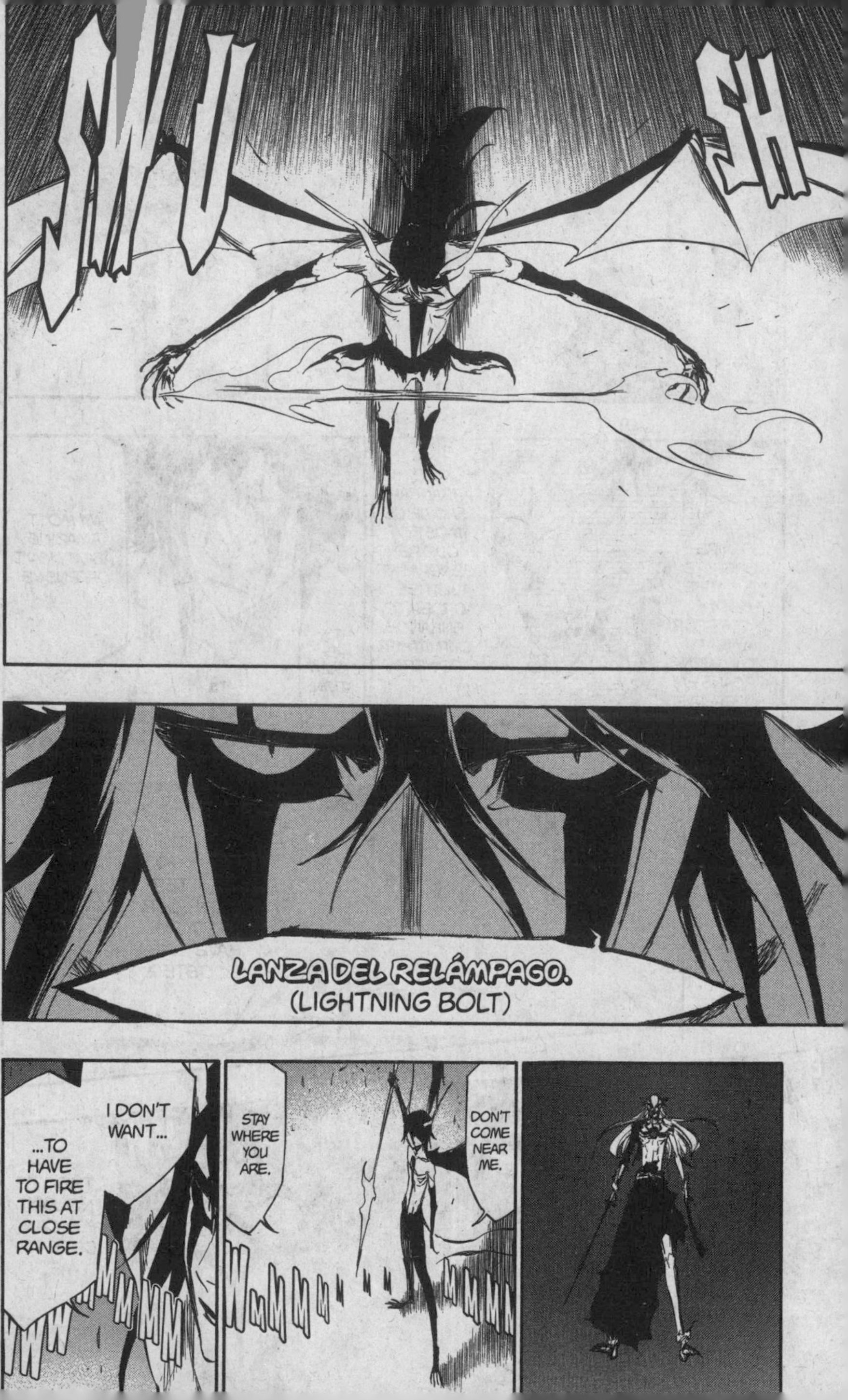
SWU
SH
LANZA DEL RELÁMPAGO.
(LIGHTNING BOLT)
DON'T COME NEAR ME.
STAY WHERE YOU ARE.
I DON'T WANT...
...TO HAVE TO FIRE THIS AT CLOSE RANGE.

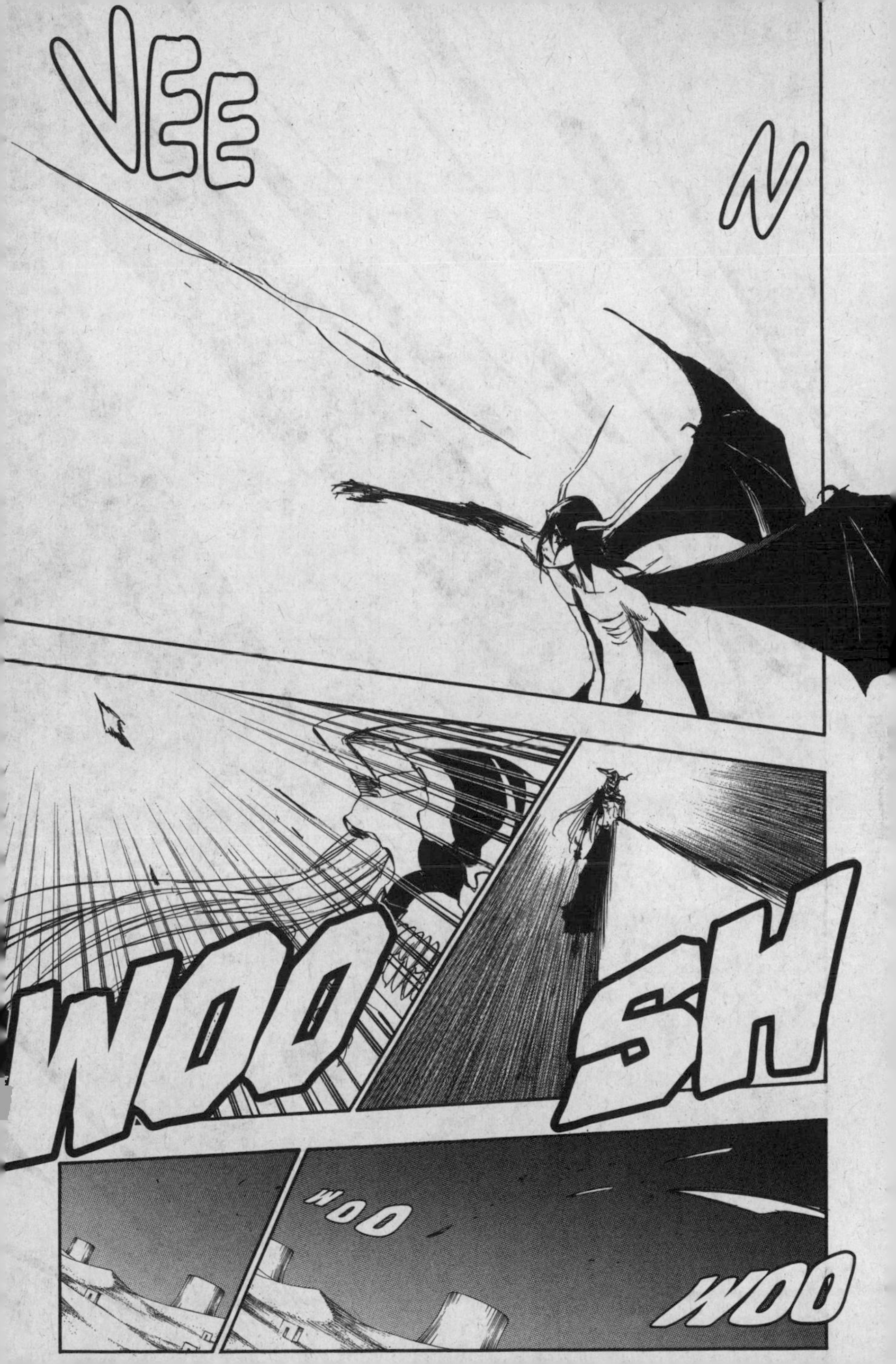
VEE
N
WOO
SH
WOO
WOO

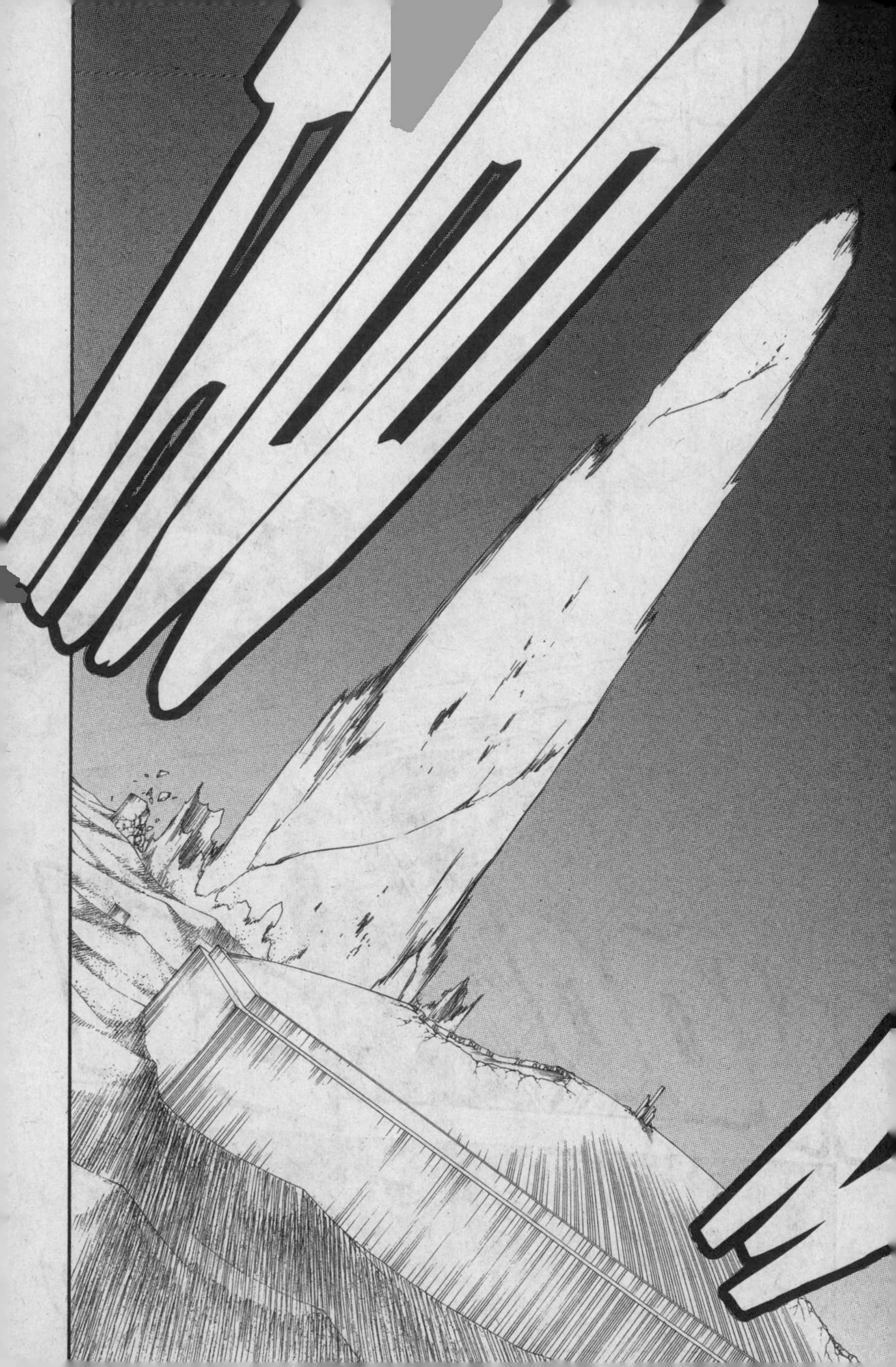

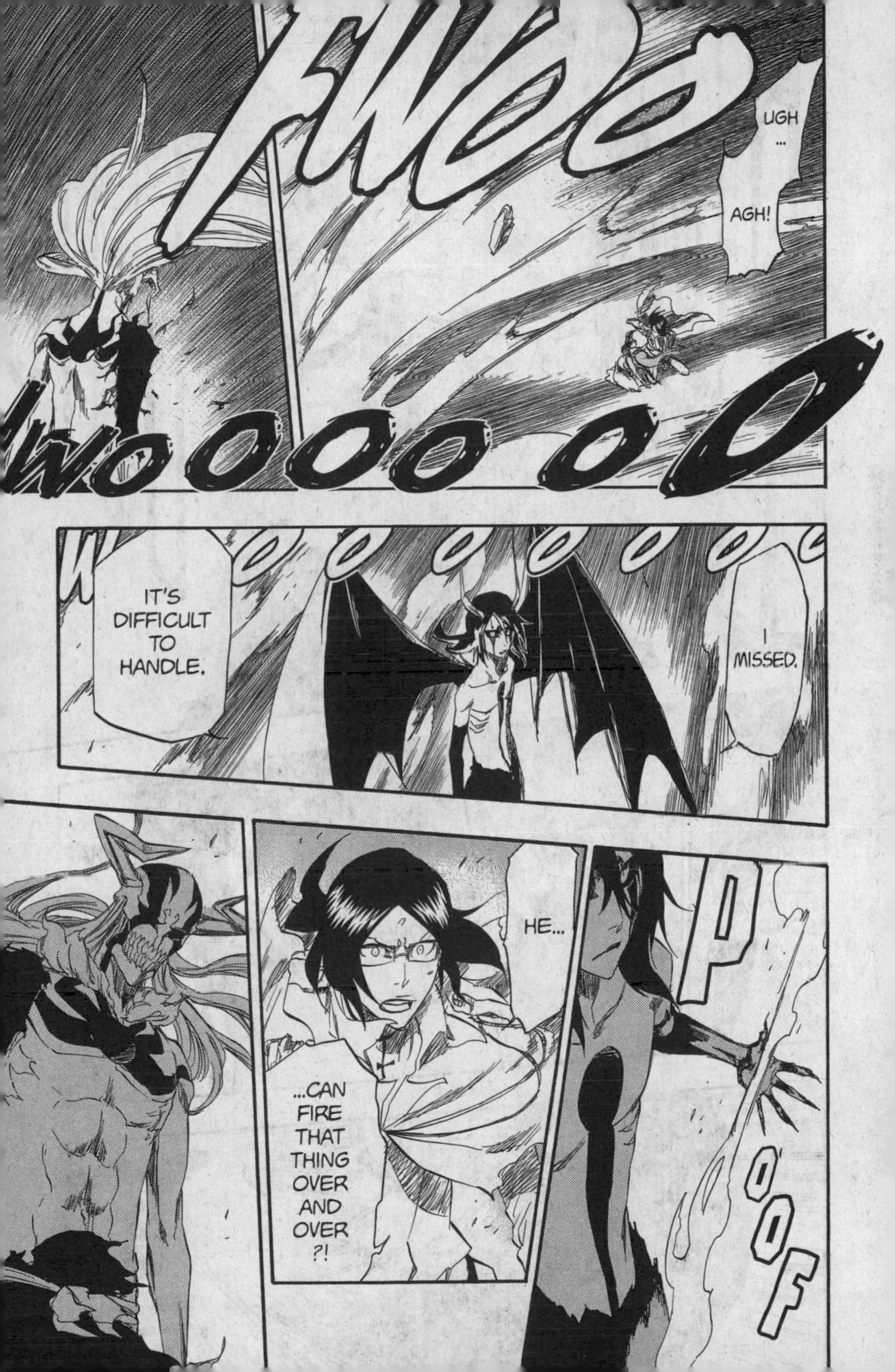
FWEE
UGH ...
AGH!
WOOOOOO
I MISSED.
IT'S DIFFICULT TO HANDLE.
POOF
HE...
...CAN FIRE THAT THING OVER AND OVER ?!

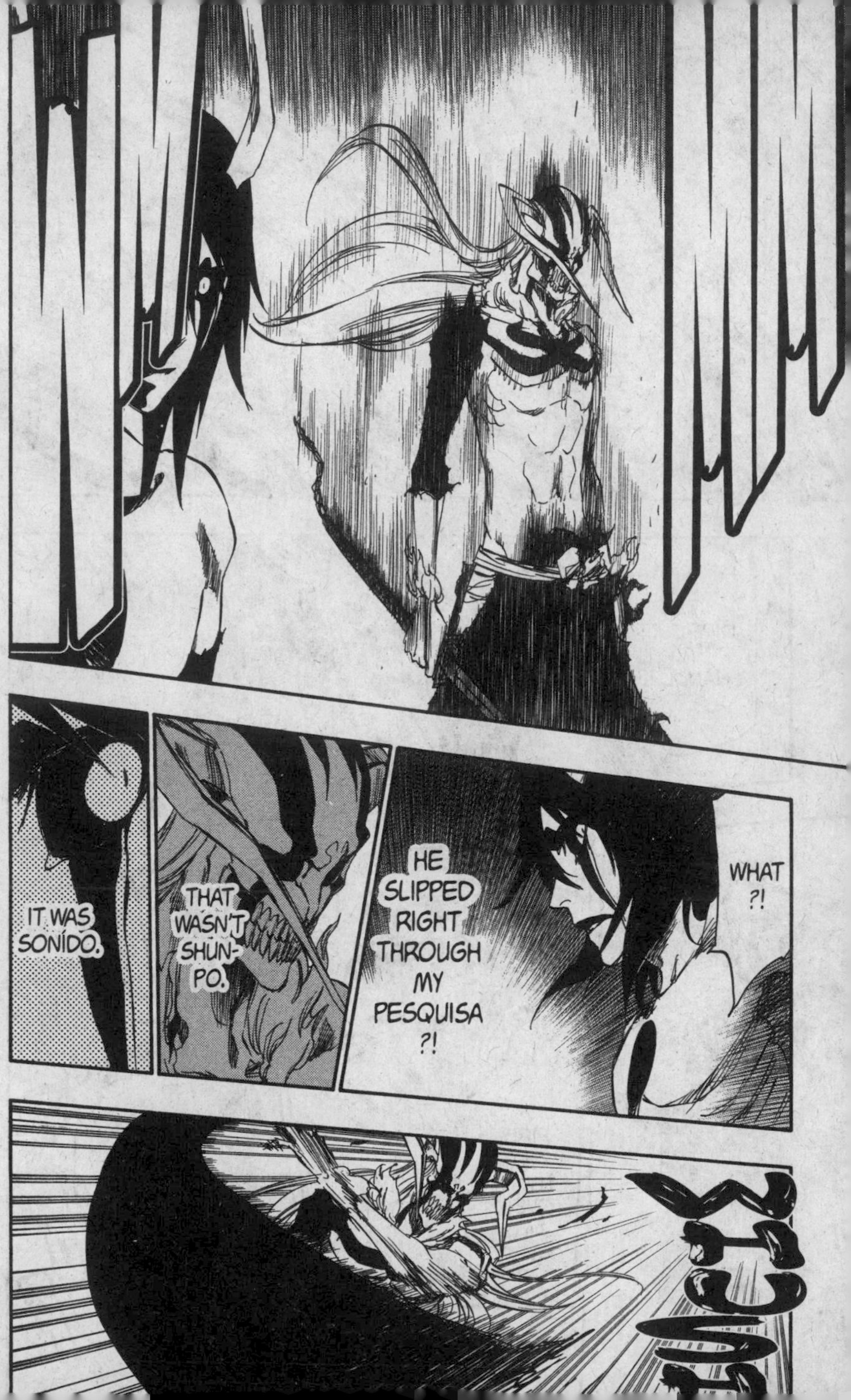
WHAT ?!
HE SLIPPED RIGHT THROUGH MY PESQUISA ?!
THAT WASN'T SHUNPO.
IT WAS SONÍDO.

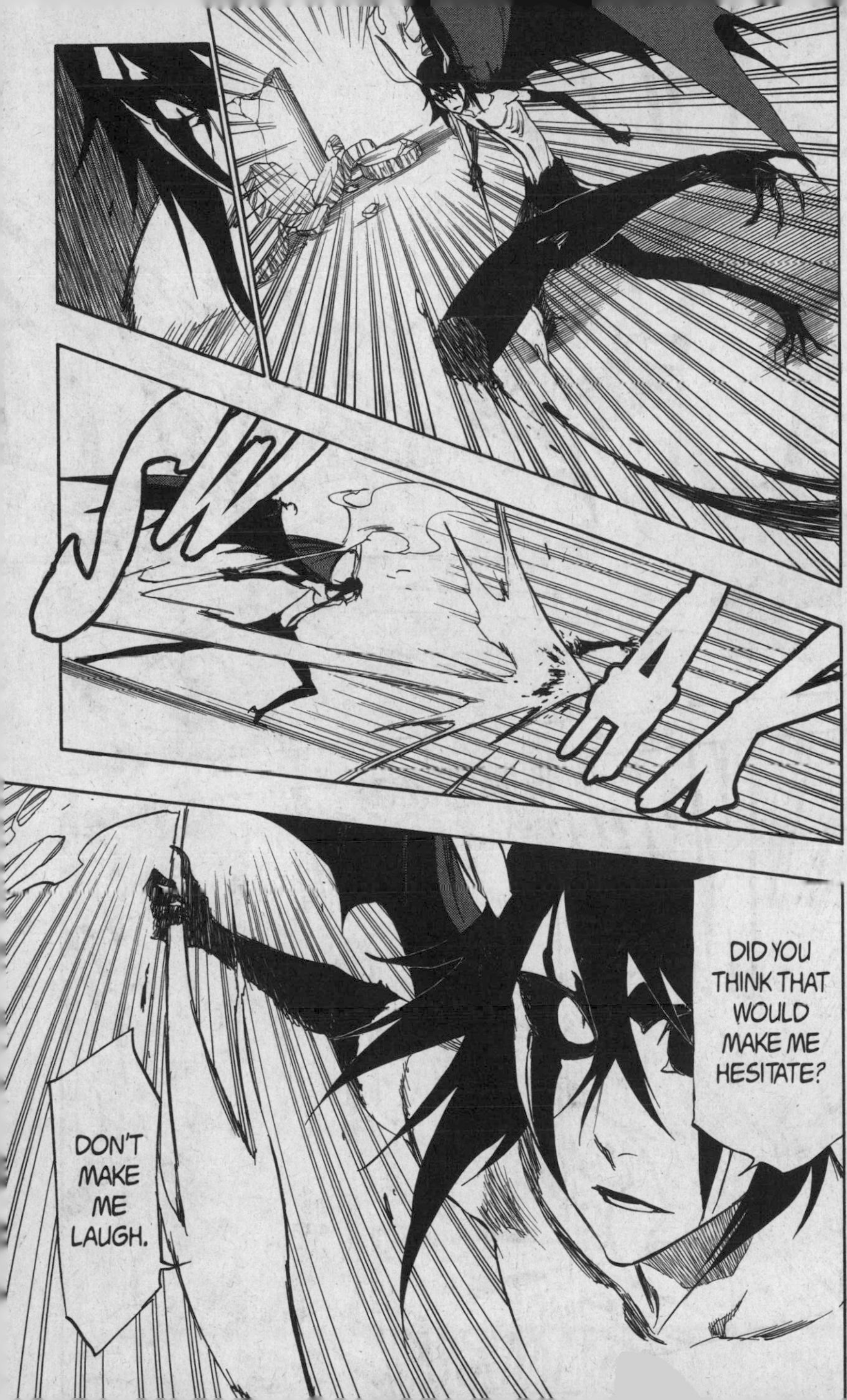
DID YOU THINK THAT WOULD MAKE ME HESITATE?
DON'T MAKE ME LAUGH.

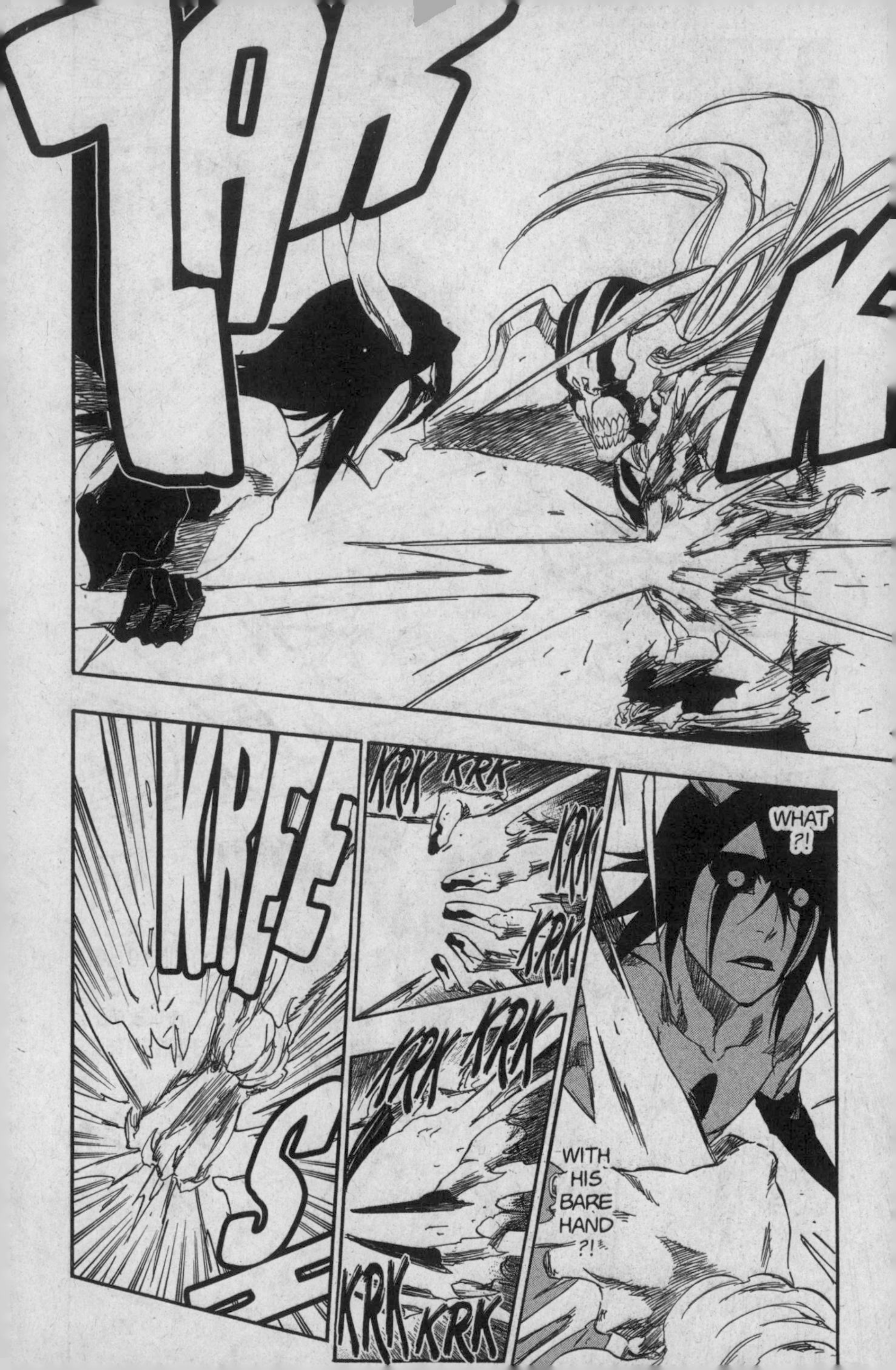

TAK
WHAT ?!
WITH HIS BARE HAND ?!
KRK KRK
KRK
KRK
KRK KRK
KRK KRK
KREE

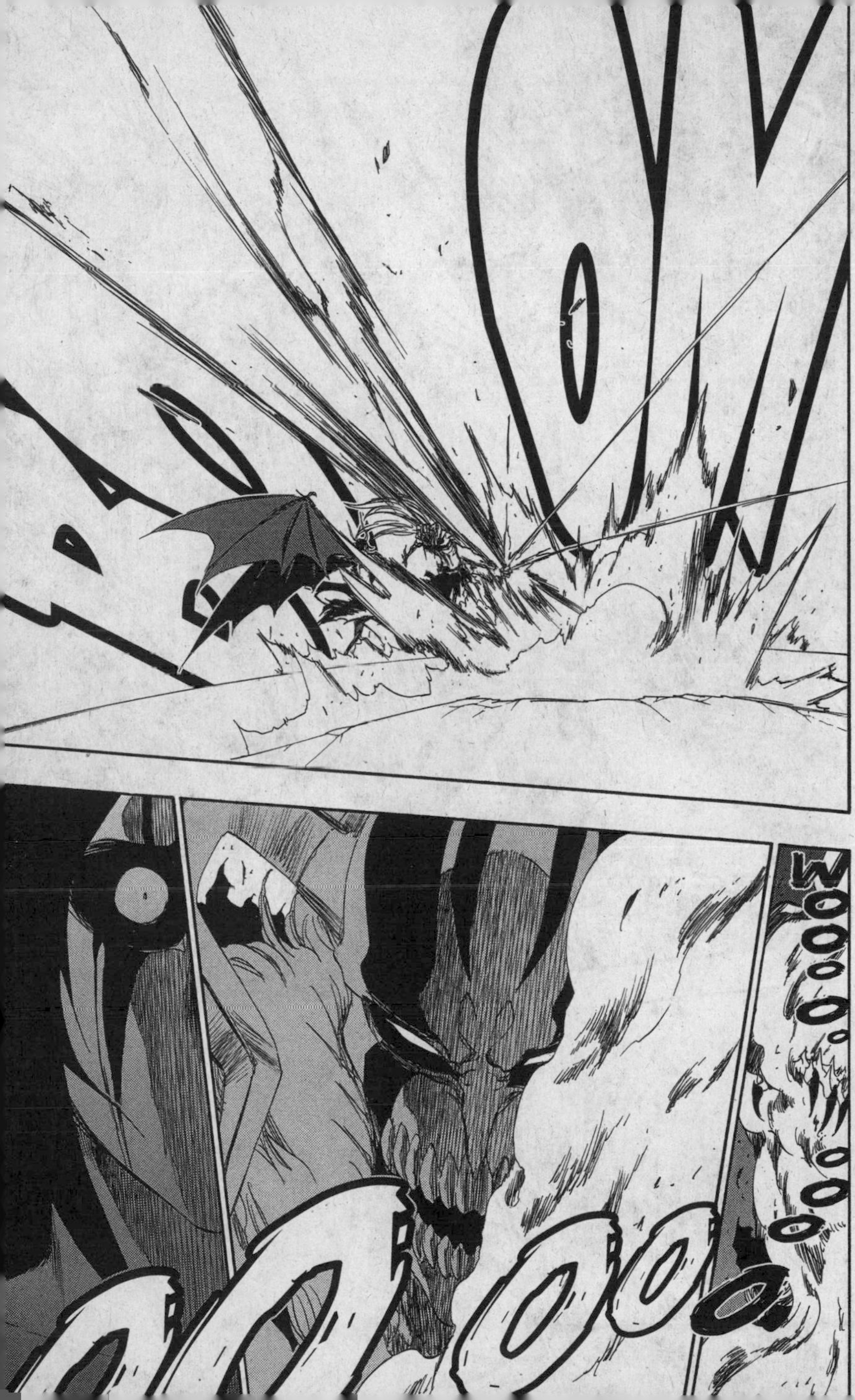
WOOOOOOOOOOOOOO

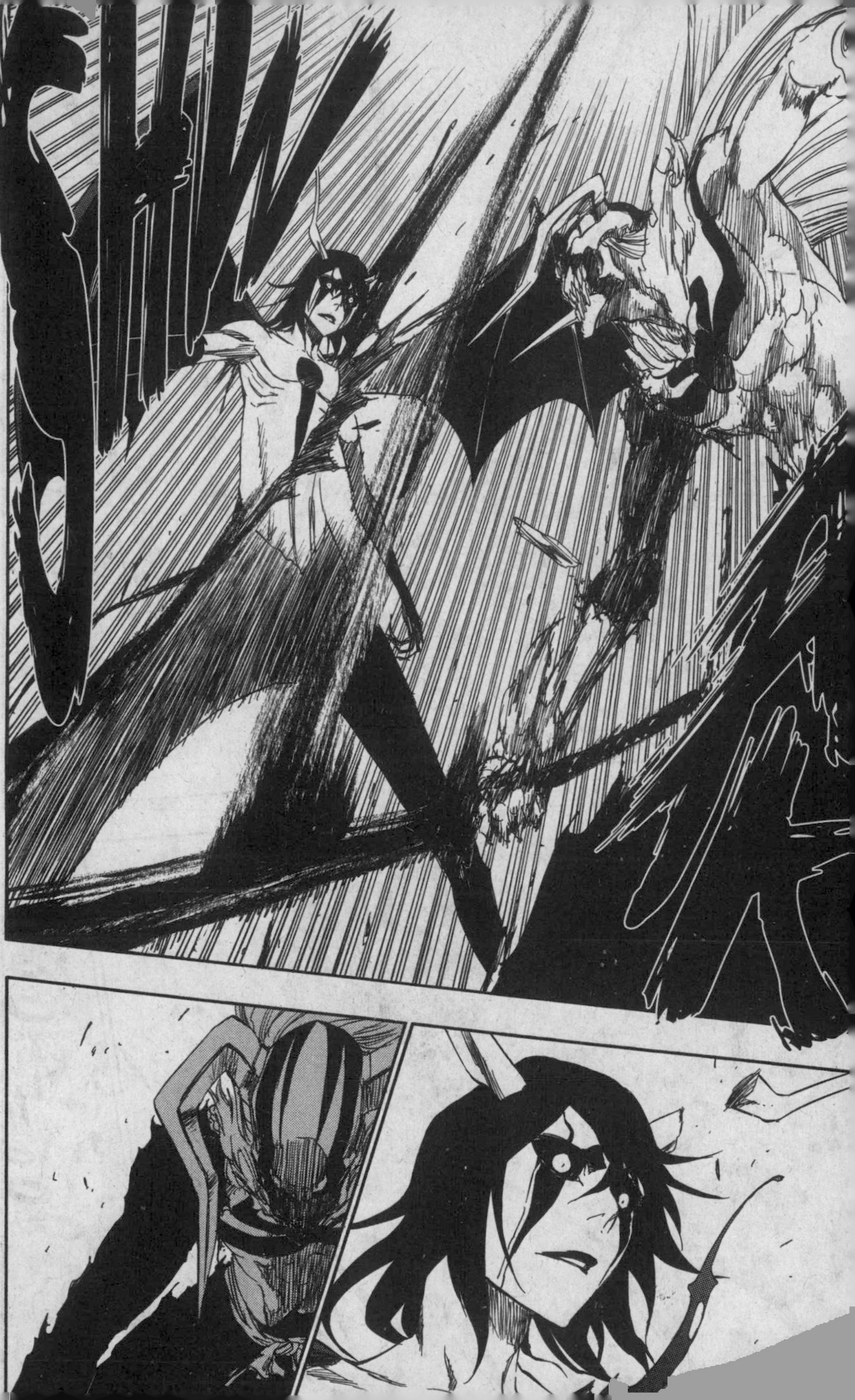

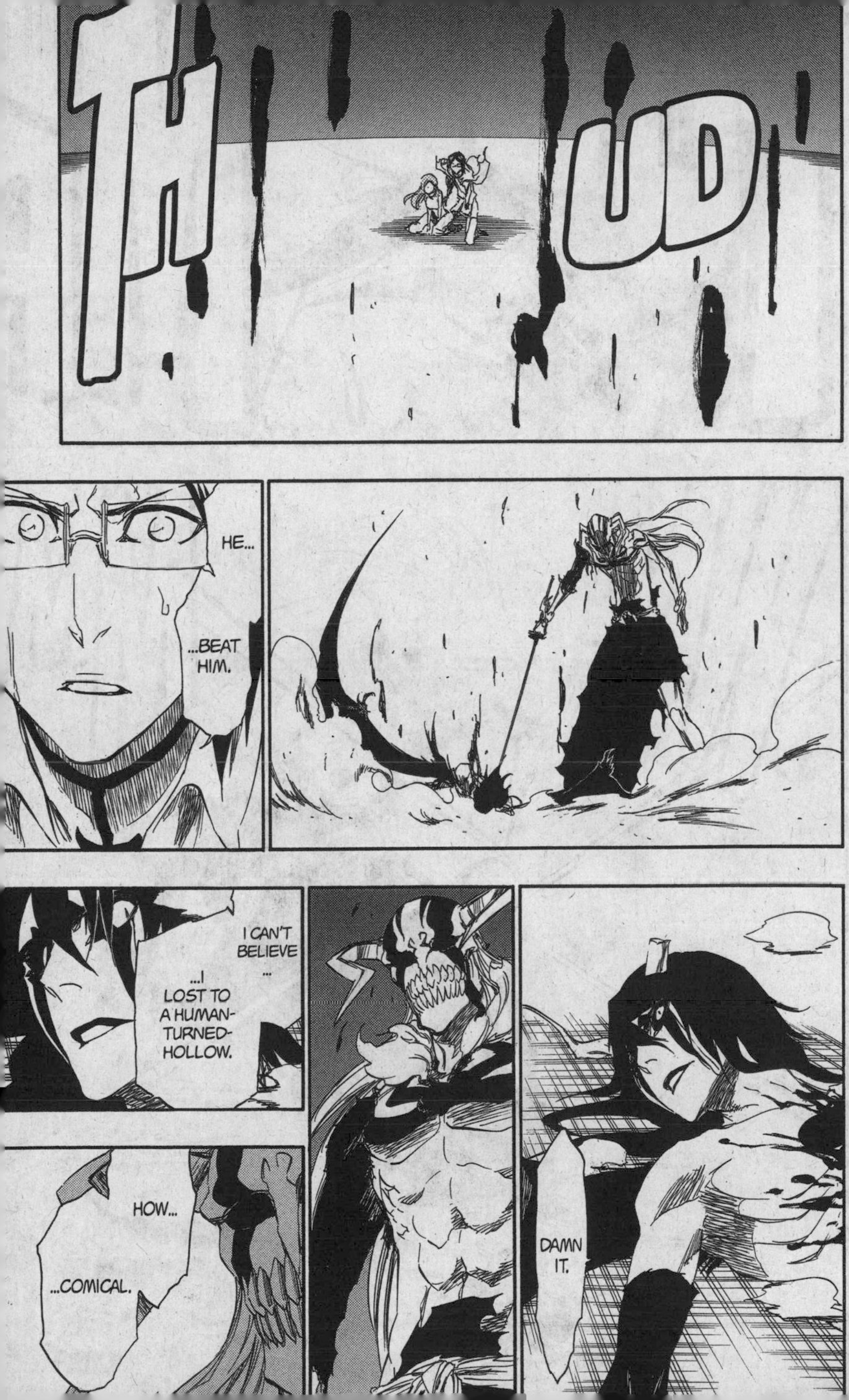
THUD
HE...
...BEAT HIM.
DAMN IT.
I CAN'T BELIEVE...
...I LOST TO A HUMAN-TURNED-HOLLOW.
HOW...
...COMICAL.

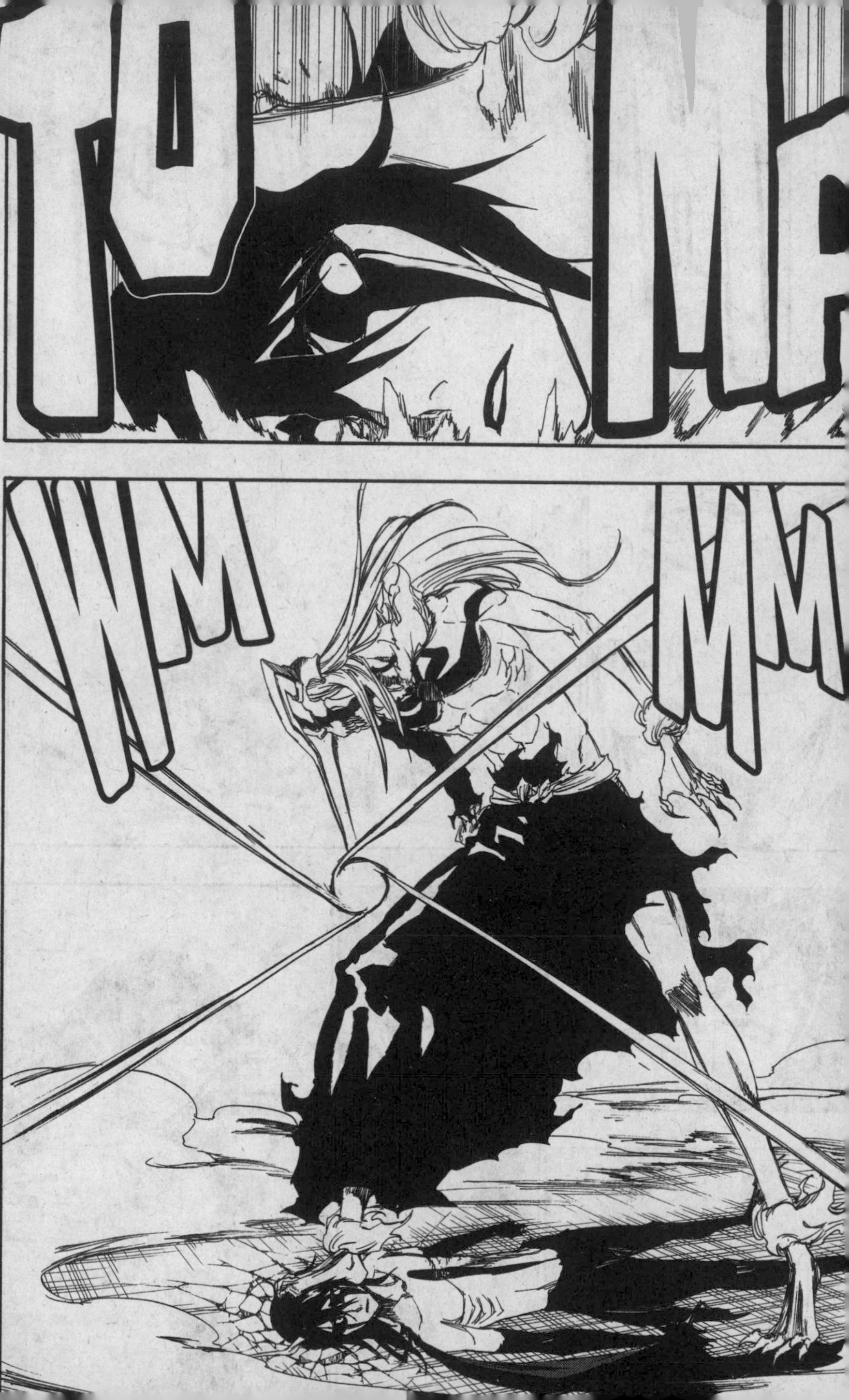
WM
MM

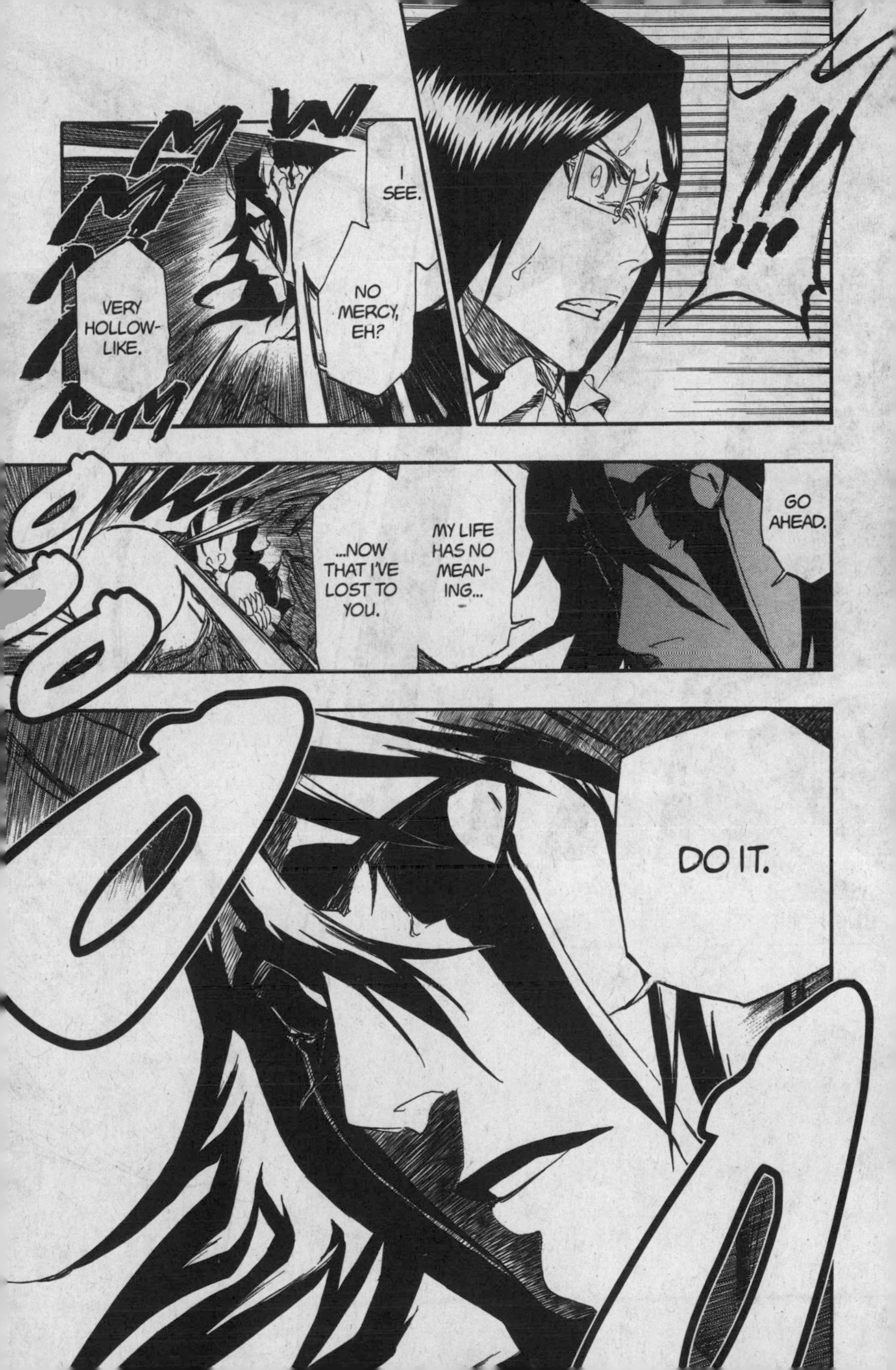
I SEE.
NO MERCY, EH?
VERY HOLLOW-LIKE.
GO AHEAD.
MY LIFE HAS NO MEANING...
...NOW THAT I'VE LOST TO YOU.
DO IT.

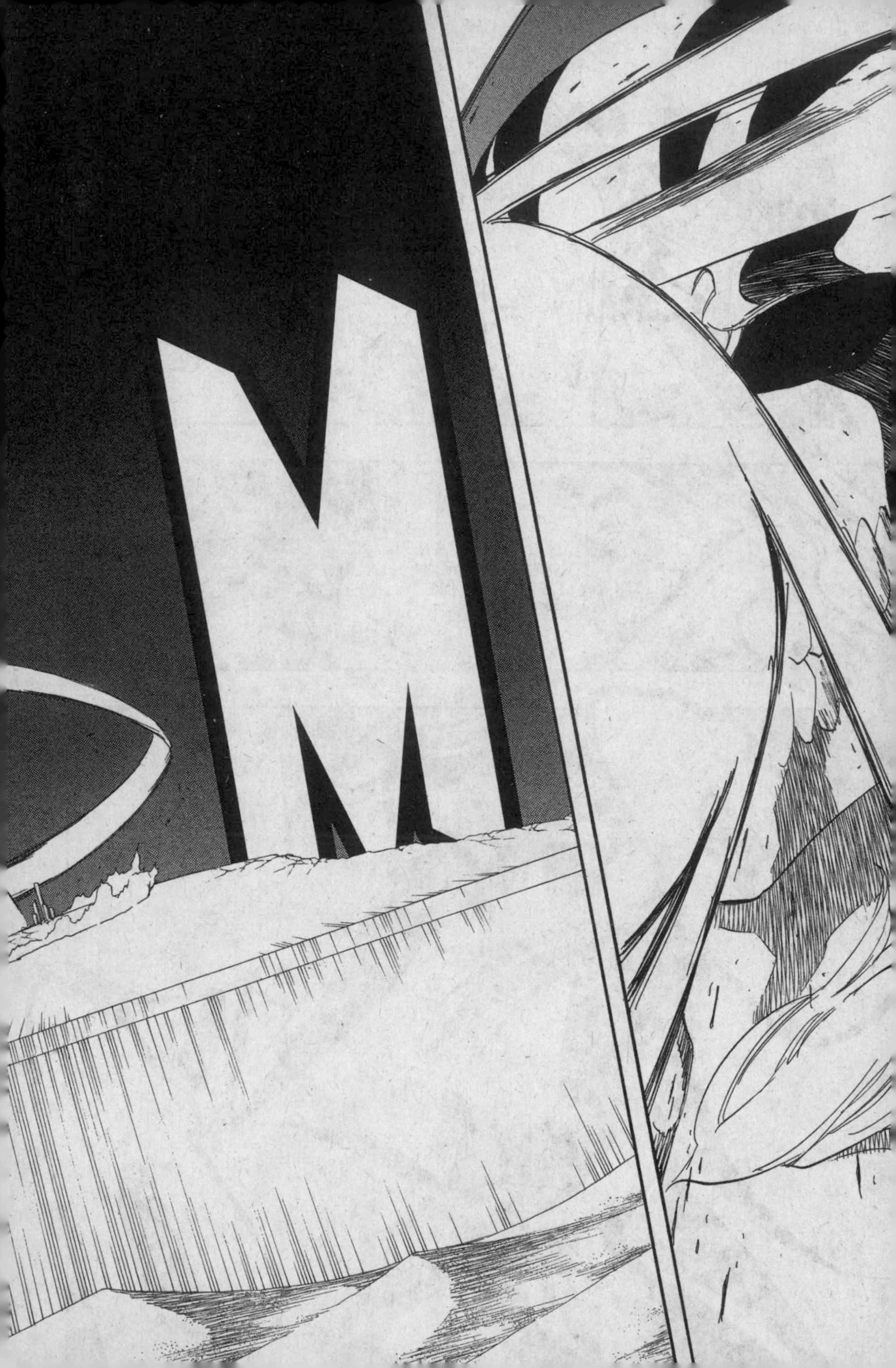
MM

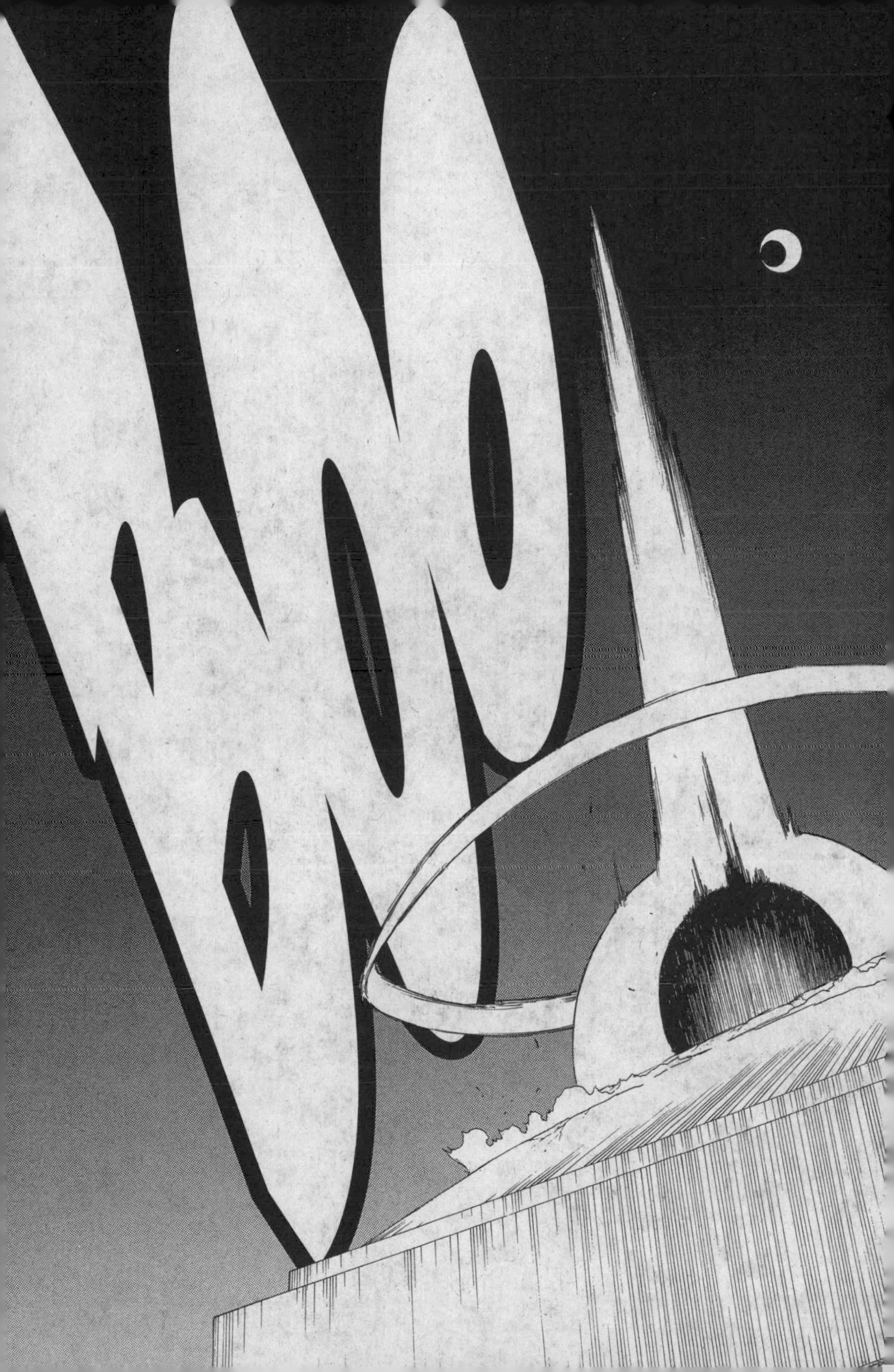

352. The Lust 6

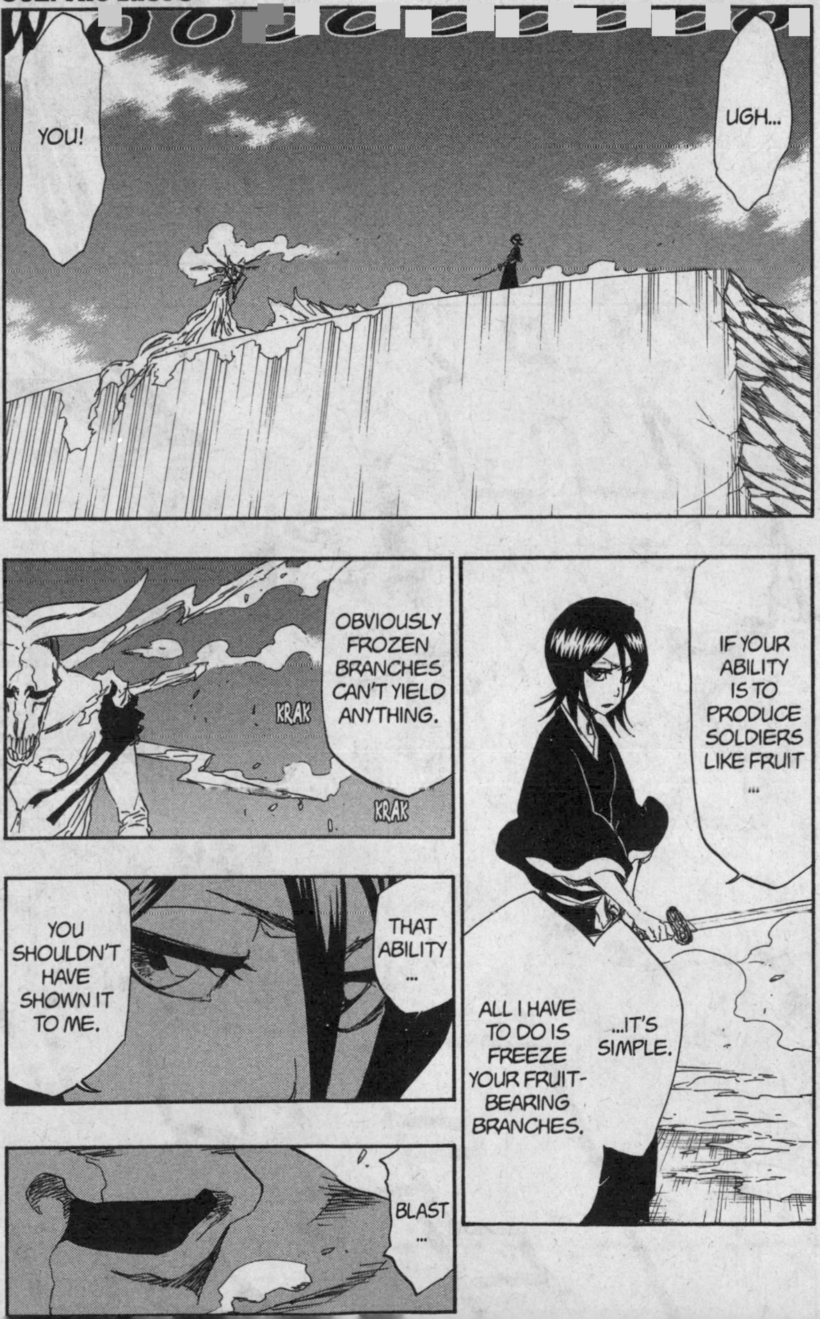
UGH...
YOU!
IF YOUR ABILITY IS TO PRODUCE SOLDIERS LIKE FRUIT ...
...IT'S SIMPLE.
ALL I HAVE TO DO IS FREEZE YOUR FRUIT-BEARING BRANCHES.
OBVIOUSLY FROZEN BRANCHES CAN'T YIELD ANYTHING.
KRAK
KRAK
THAT ABILITY ...
YOU SHOULDN'T HAVE SHOWN IT TO ME.
BLAST ...

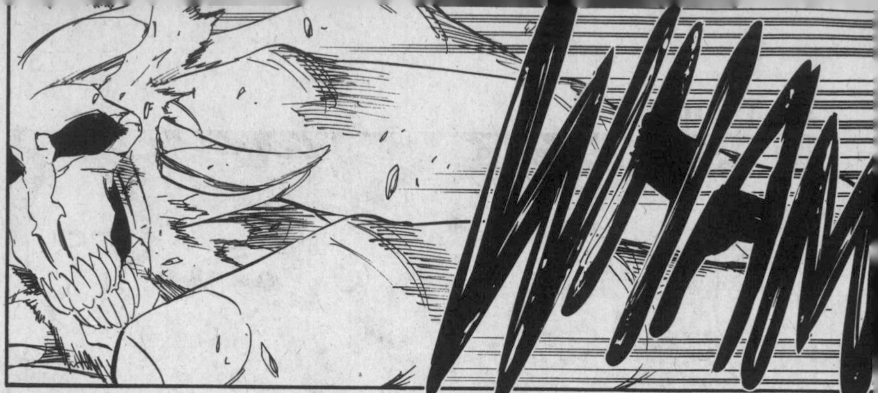
WHAM
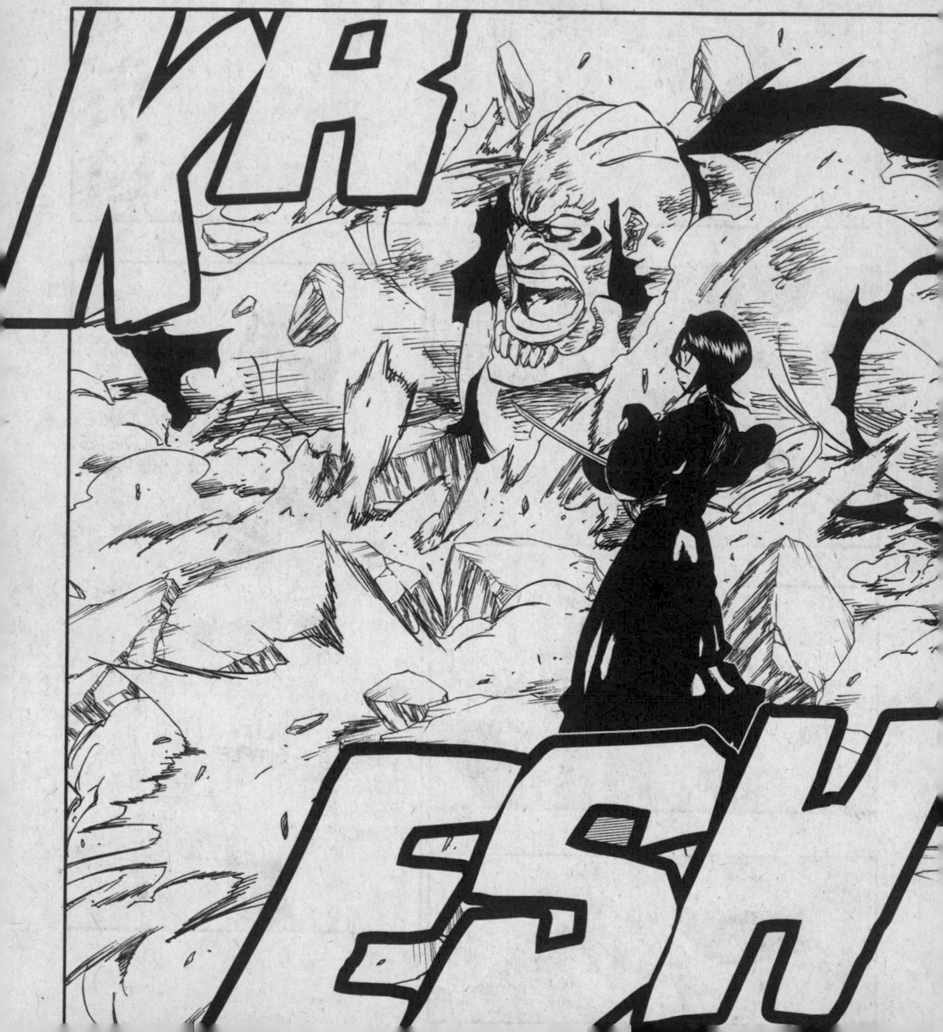

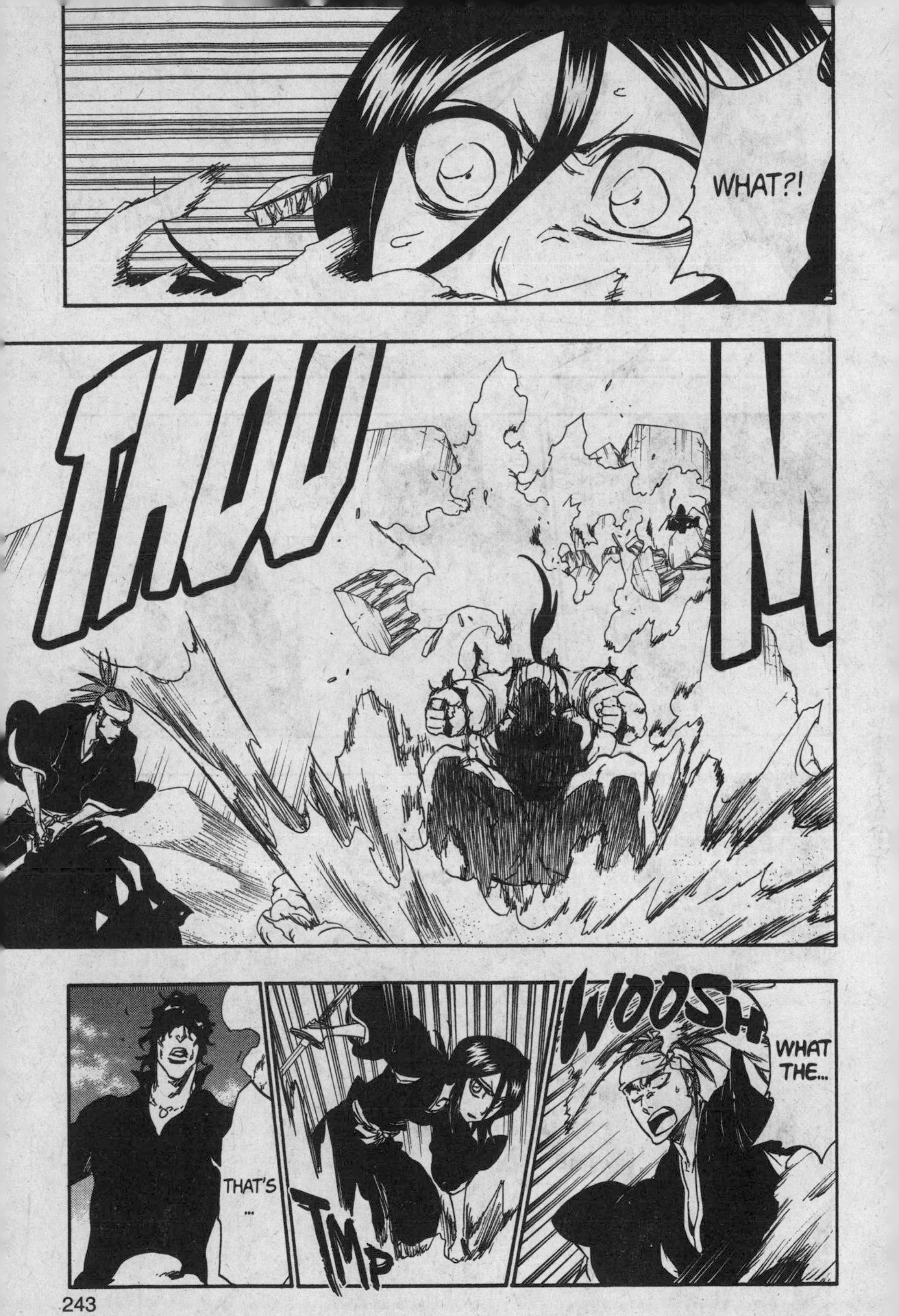
WHAT?!
THOOM
WOOSH
WHAT THE...
TMP
THAT'S ...

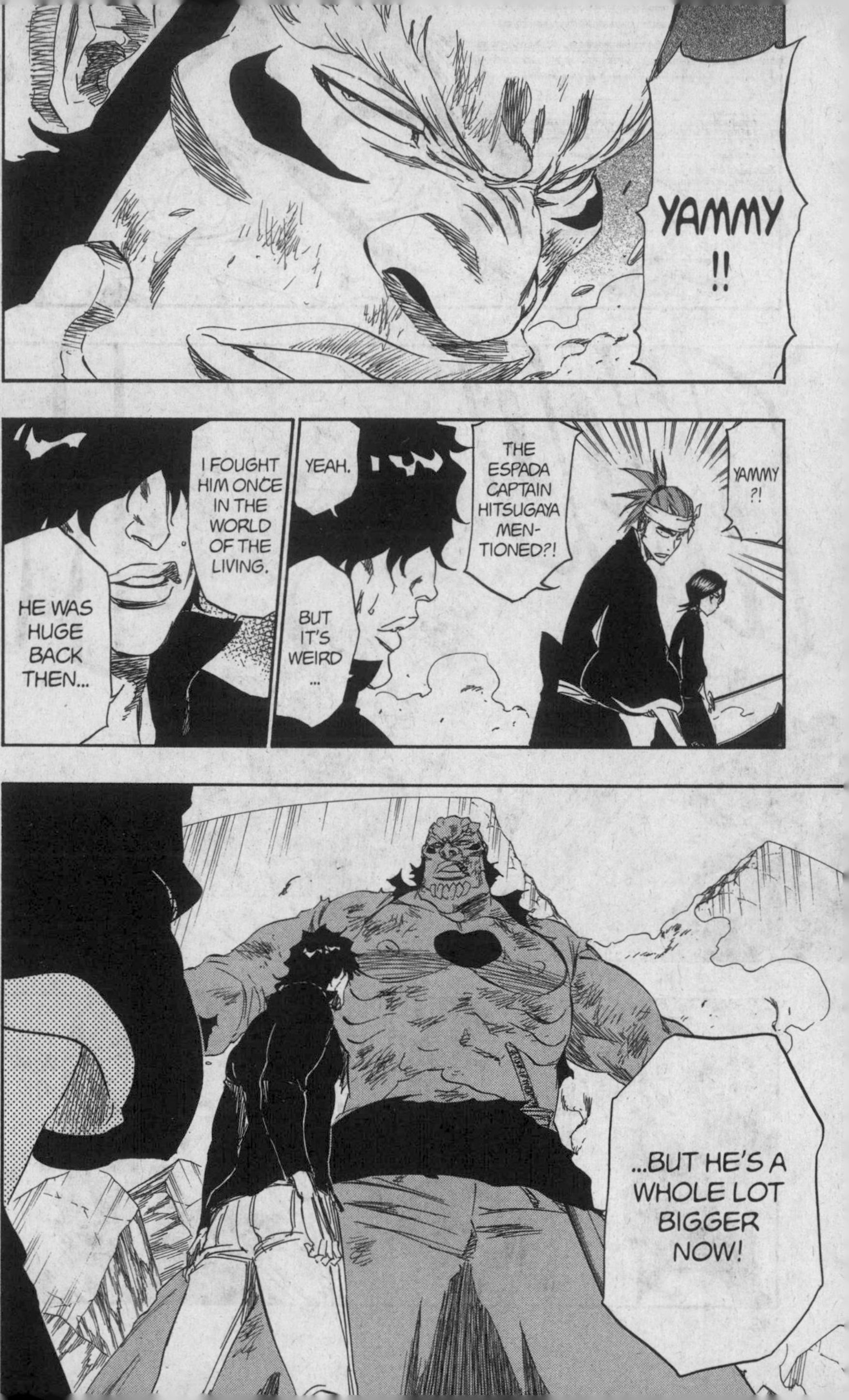
YAMMY !!
YAMMY ?!
THE ESPADA CAPTAIN HITSUGAYA MENTIONED?!
YEAH.
I FOUGHT HIM ONCE IN THE WORLD OF THE LIVING.
HE WAS HUGE BACK THEN...
BUT IT'S WEIRD ...
...BUT HE'S A WHOLE LOT BIGGER NOW!

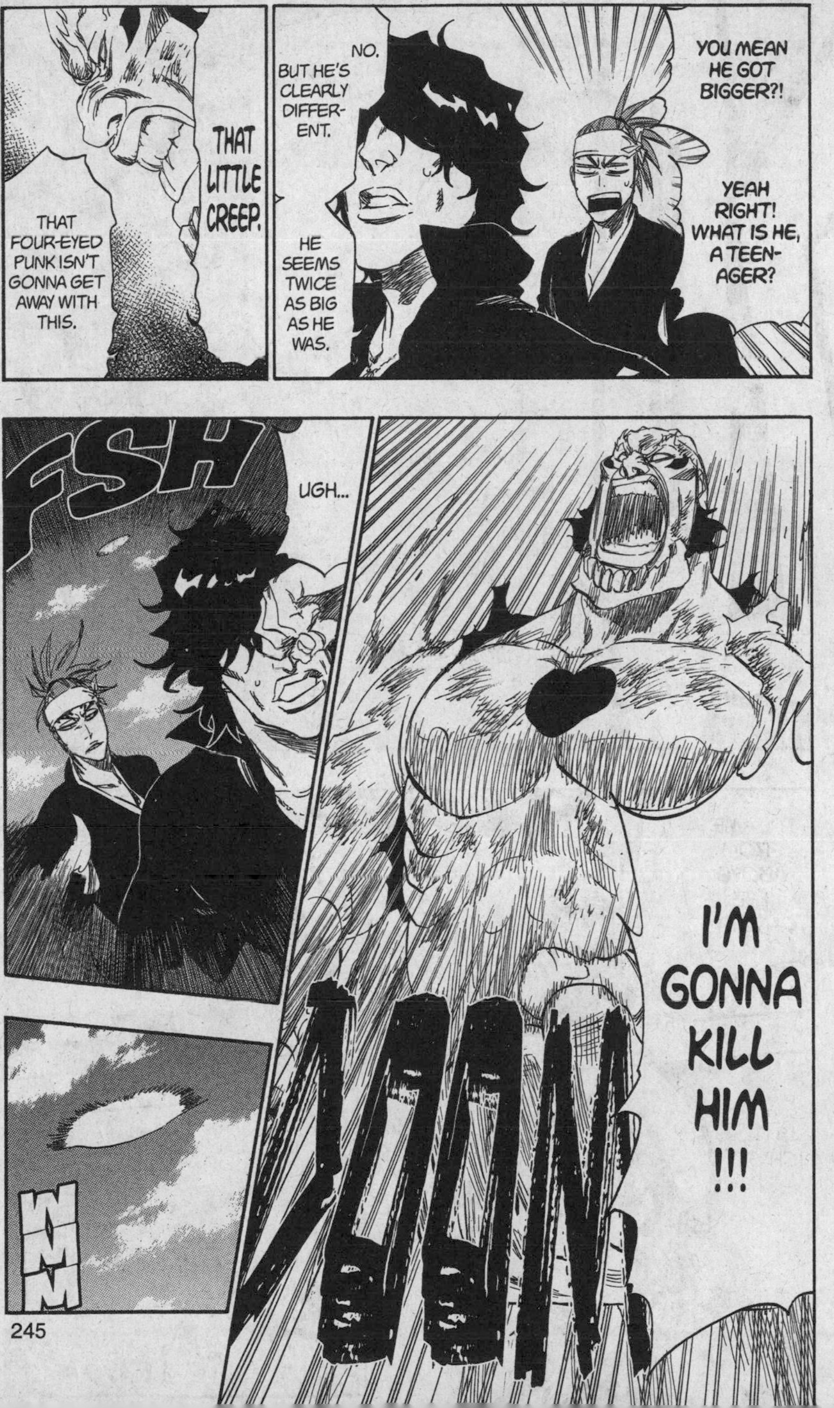
YOU MEAN HE GOT BIGGER?!
NO.
BUT HE'S CLEARLY DIFFERENT.
HE SEEMS TWICE AS BIG AS HE WAS.
YEAH RIGHT! WHAT IS HE, A TEENAGER?
THAT LITTLE CREEP.
THAT FOUR-EYED PUNK ISN'T GONNA GET AWAY WITH THIS.
I'M GONNA KILL HIM!!!
FSH
UGH...

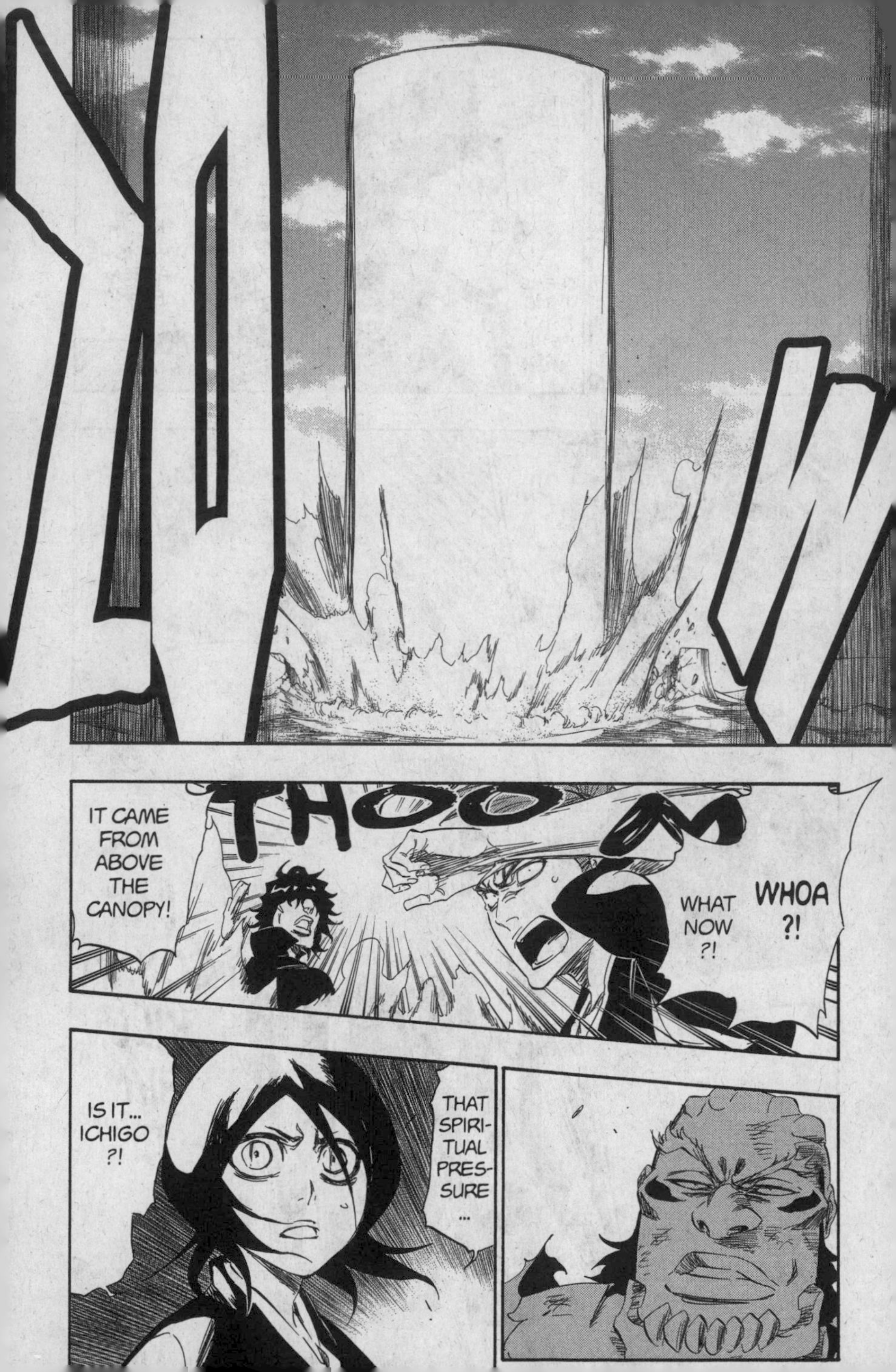
THOOM
WHOA ?!
WHAT NOW ?!
IT CAME FROM ABOVE THE CANOPY!
THAT SPIRI-TUAL PRES-SURE...
IS IT... ICHIGO ?!

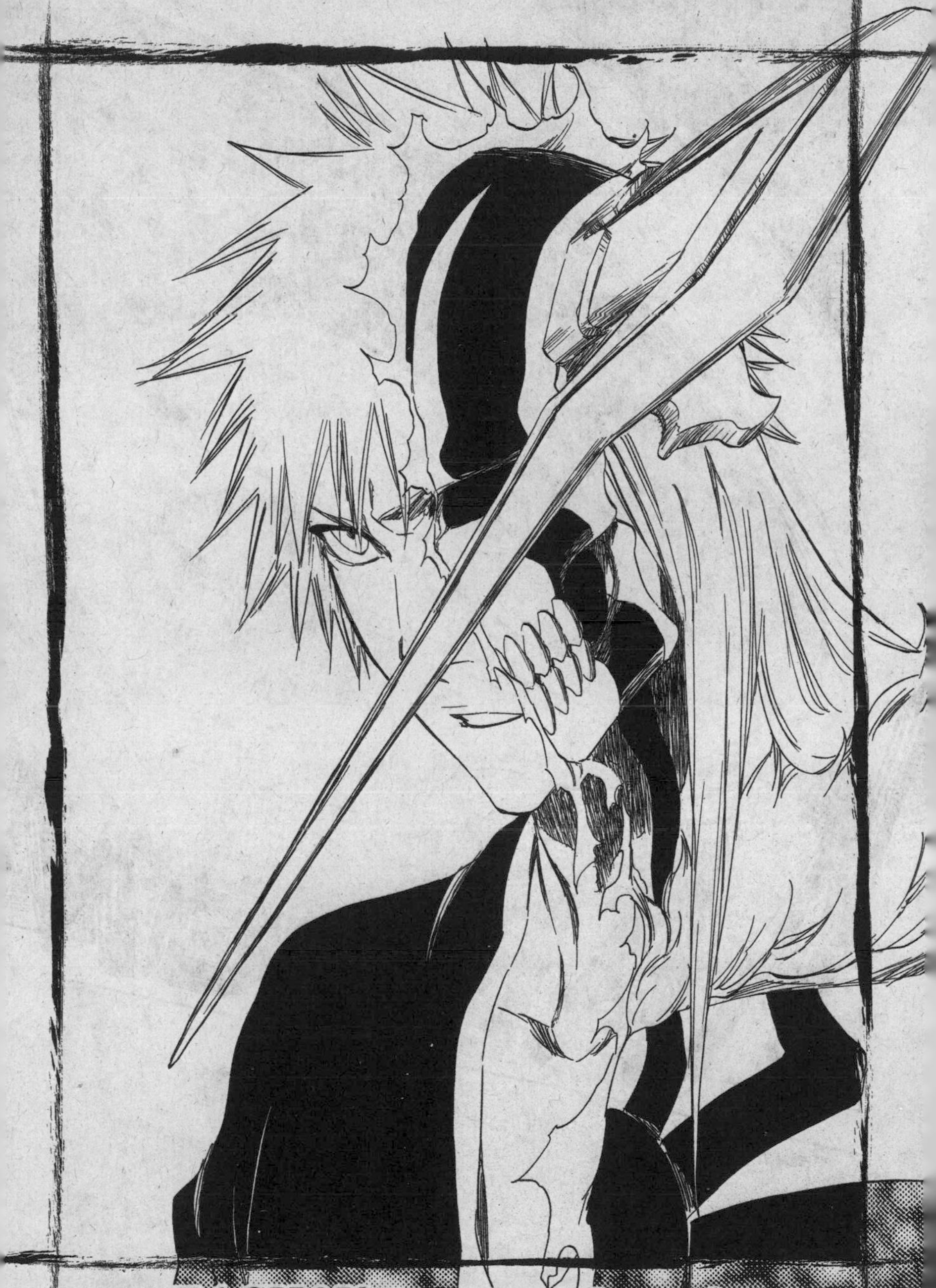

BLEACH 352. The Lust 6

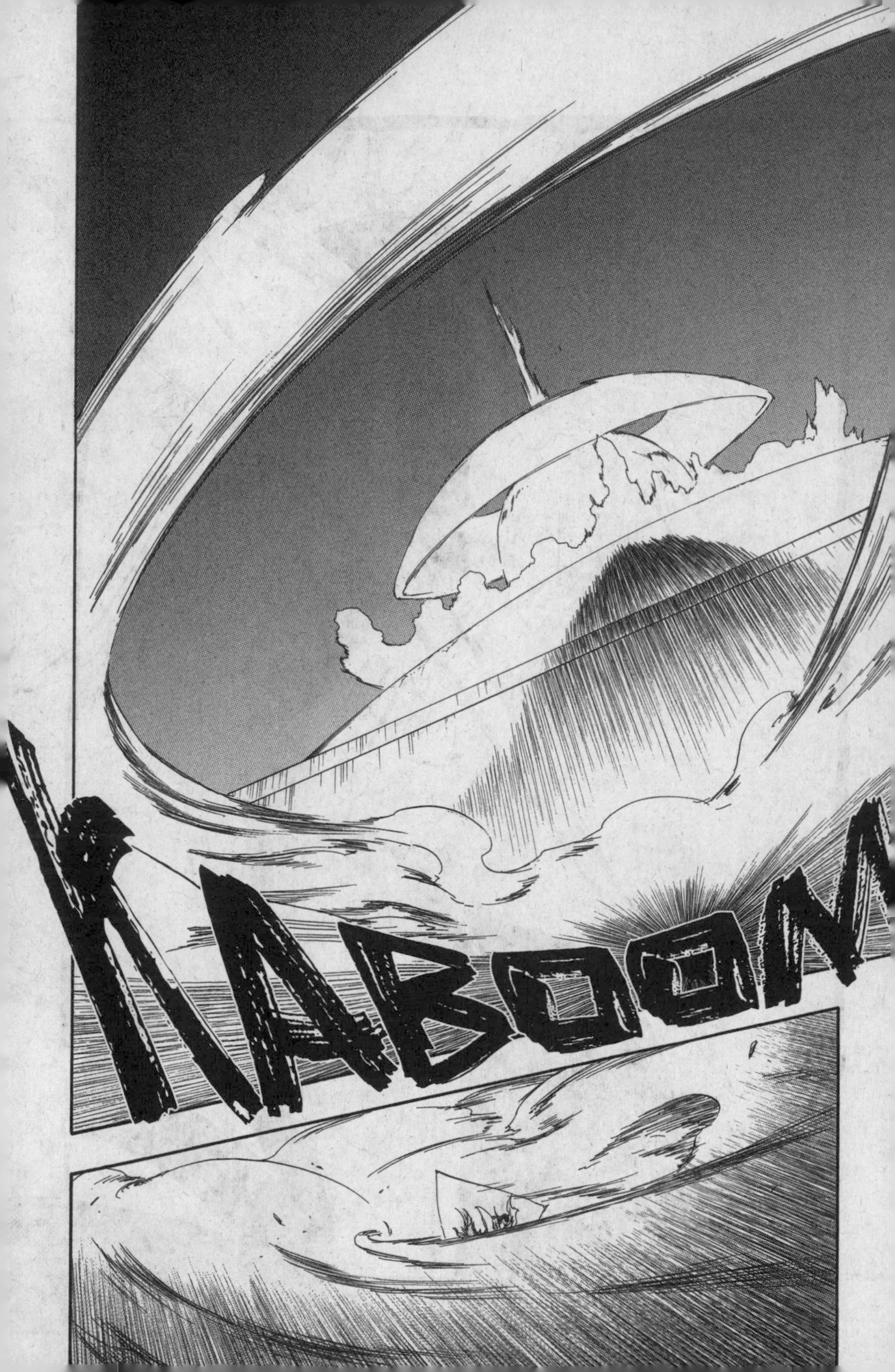
KABOOM

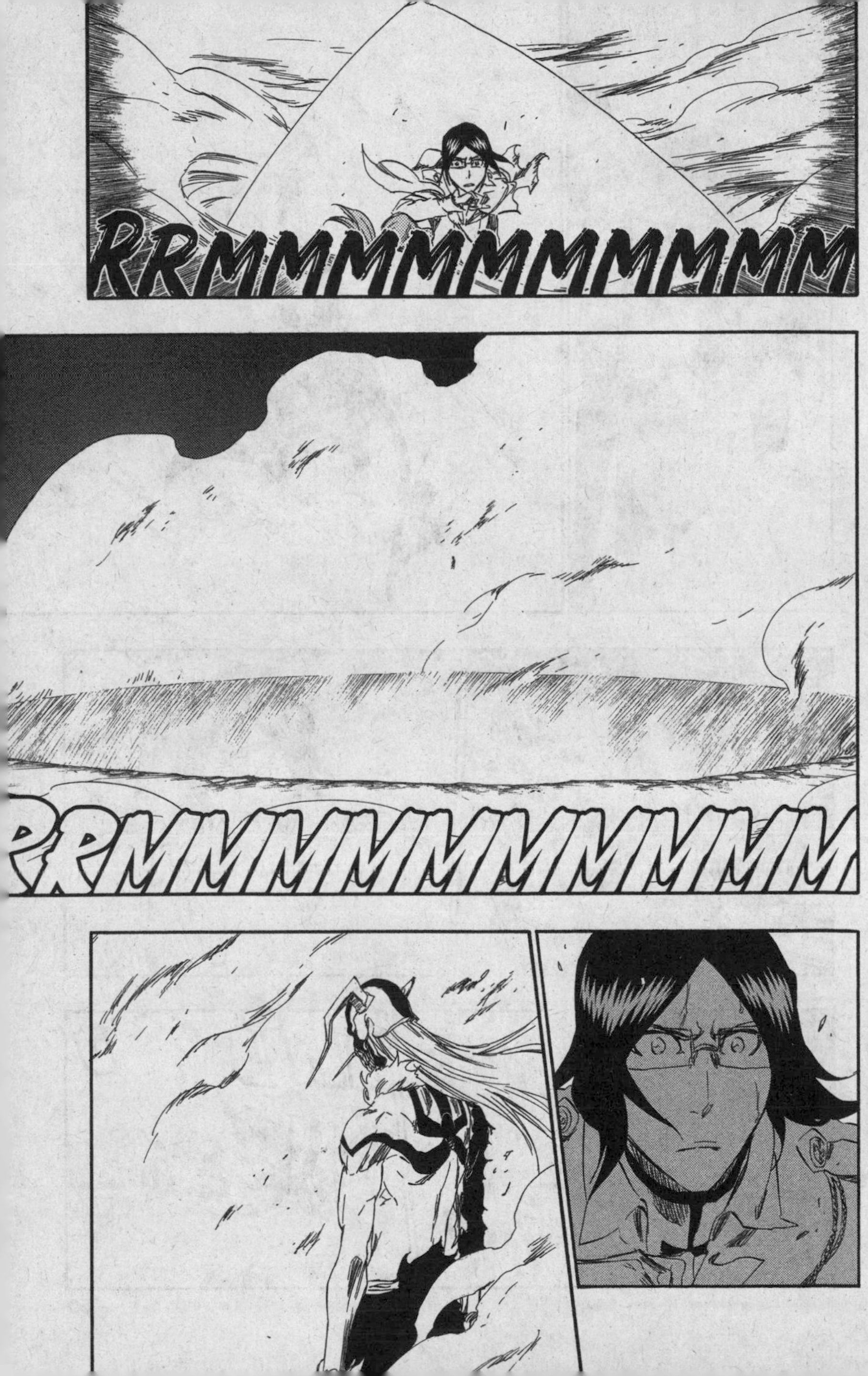
RRMMMMMMMMMMMM
RRMMMMMMMMMMMMM

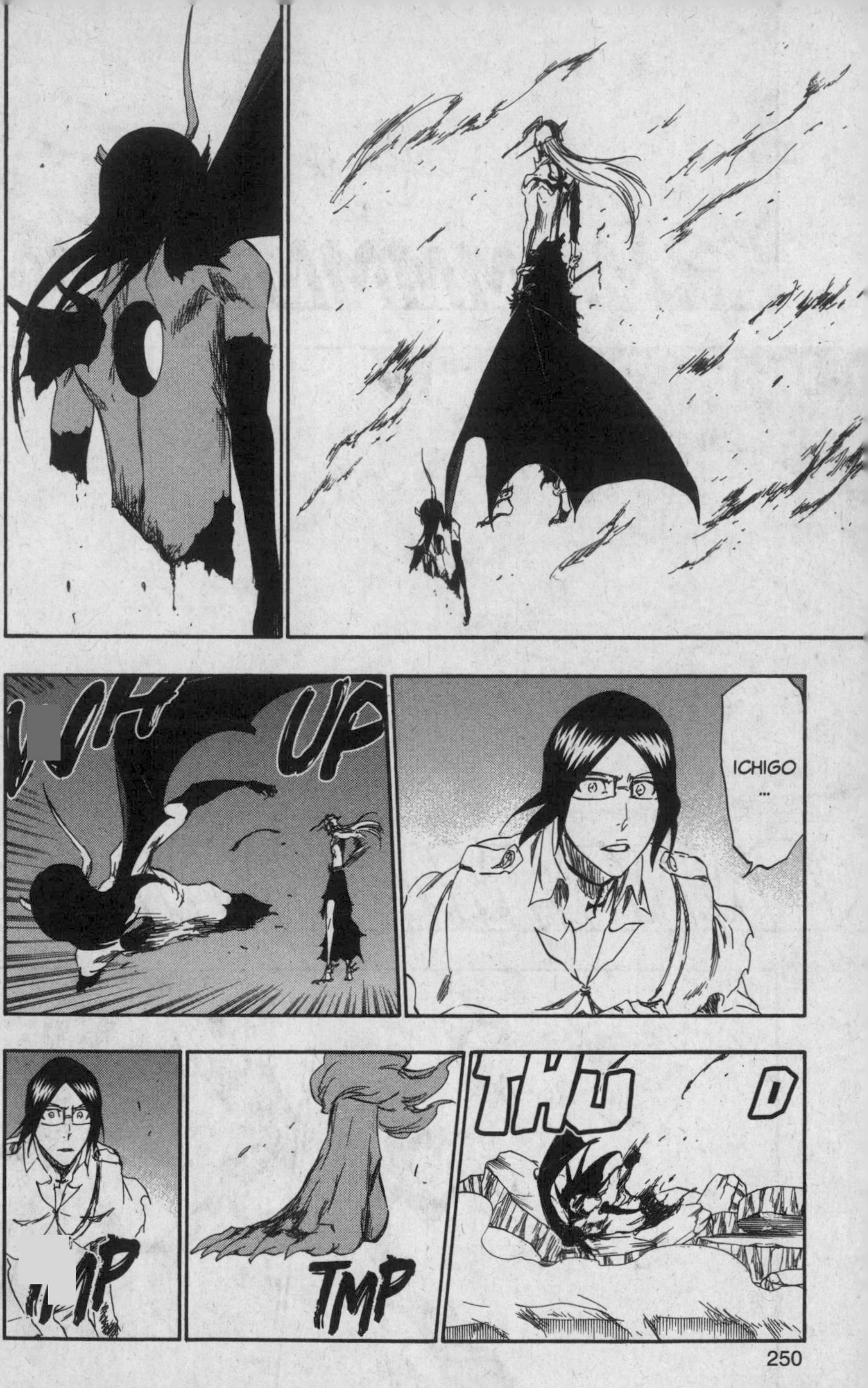
ICHIGO ...
UP
THUD
TMP

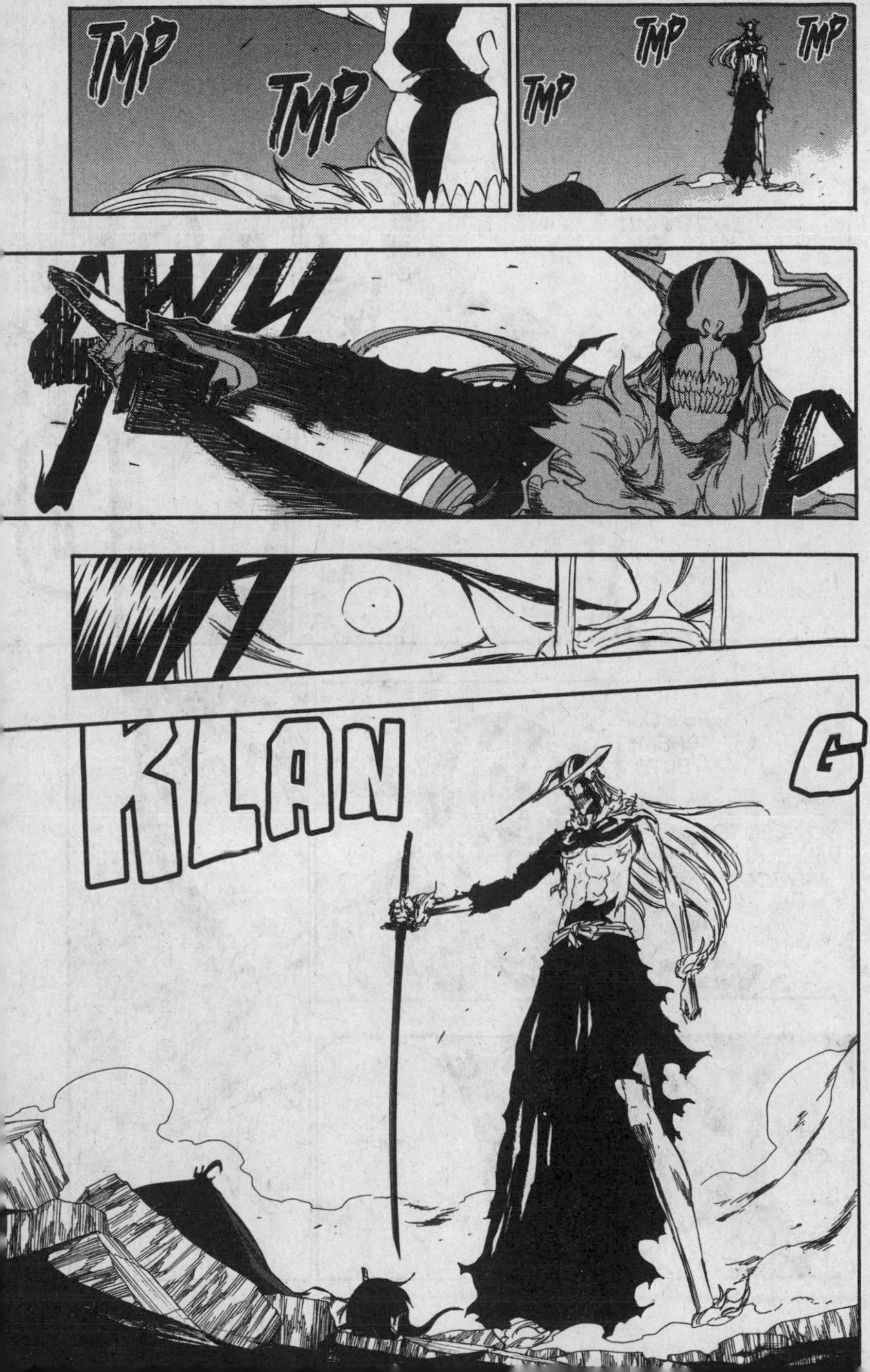
TMP
TMP
TMP
TMP
TMP
KLANG

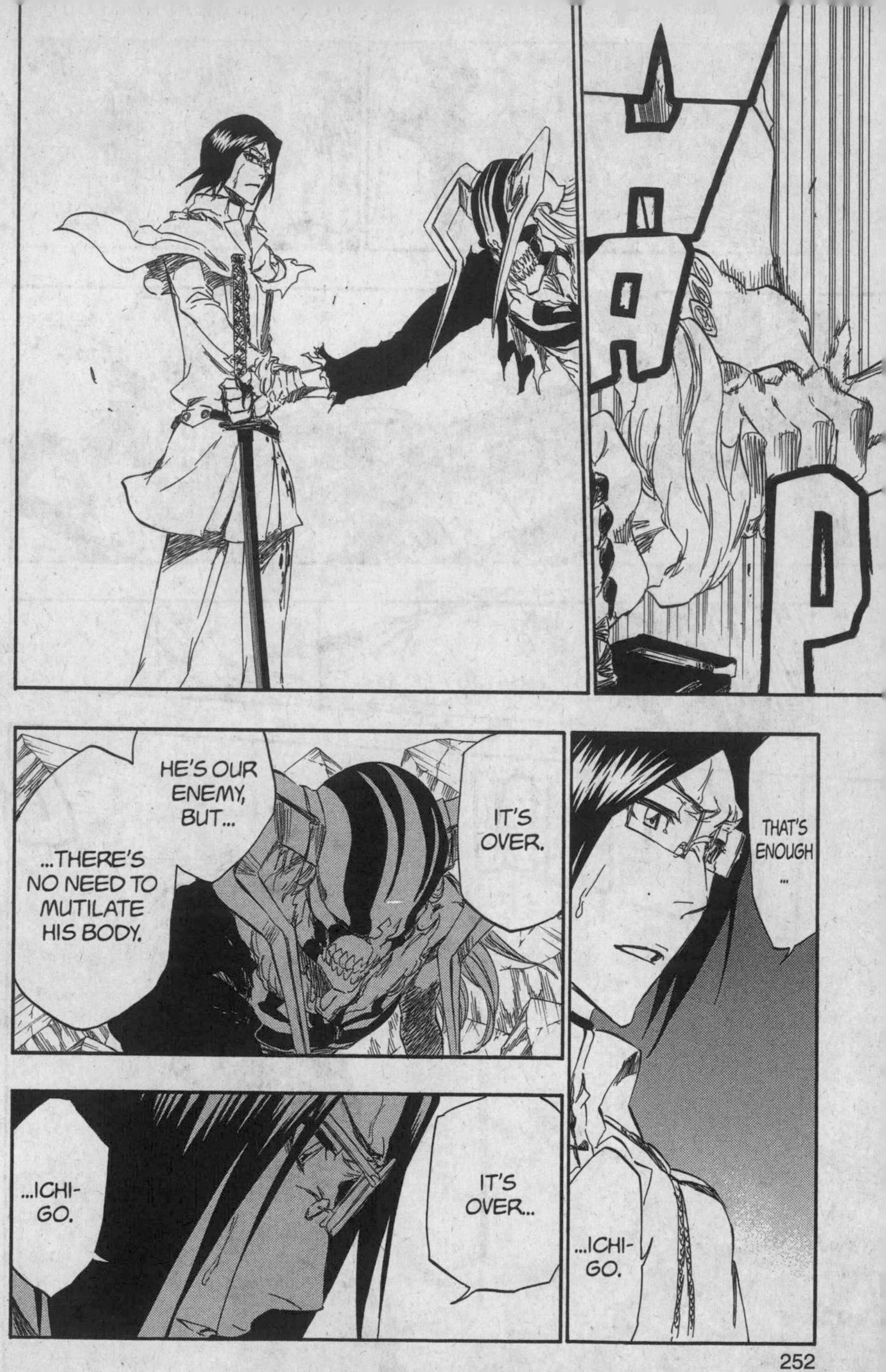

THAT'S ENOUGH...
...ICHI-GO.
IT'S OVER.
HE'S OUR ENEMY, BUT...
...THERE'S NO NEED TO MUTILATE HIS BODY.
IT'S OVER...
...ICHI-GO.

READ THIS WAY

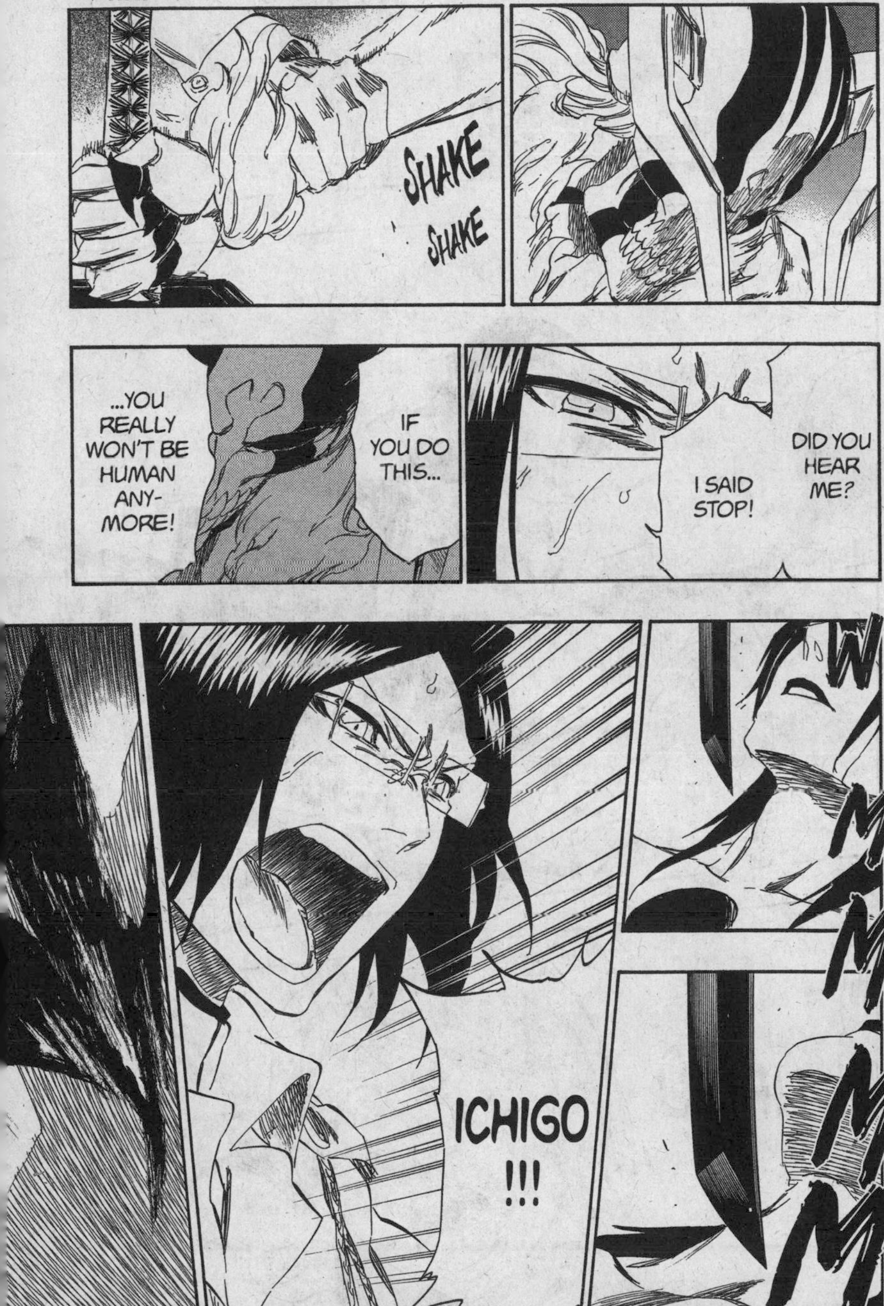
SHAKE
SHAKE
DID YOU HEAR ME?
I SAID STOP!
IF YOU DO THIS...
...YOU REALLY WON'T BE HUMAN ANYMORE!
WMMMMMMM
ICHIGO!!!

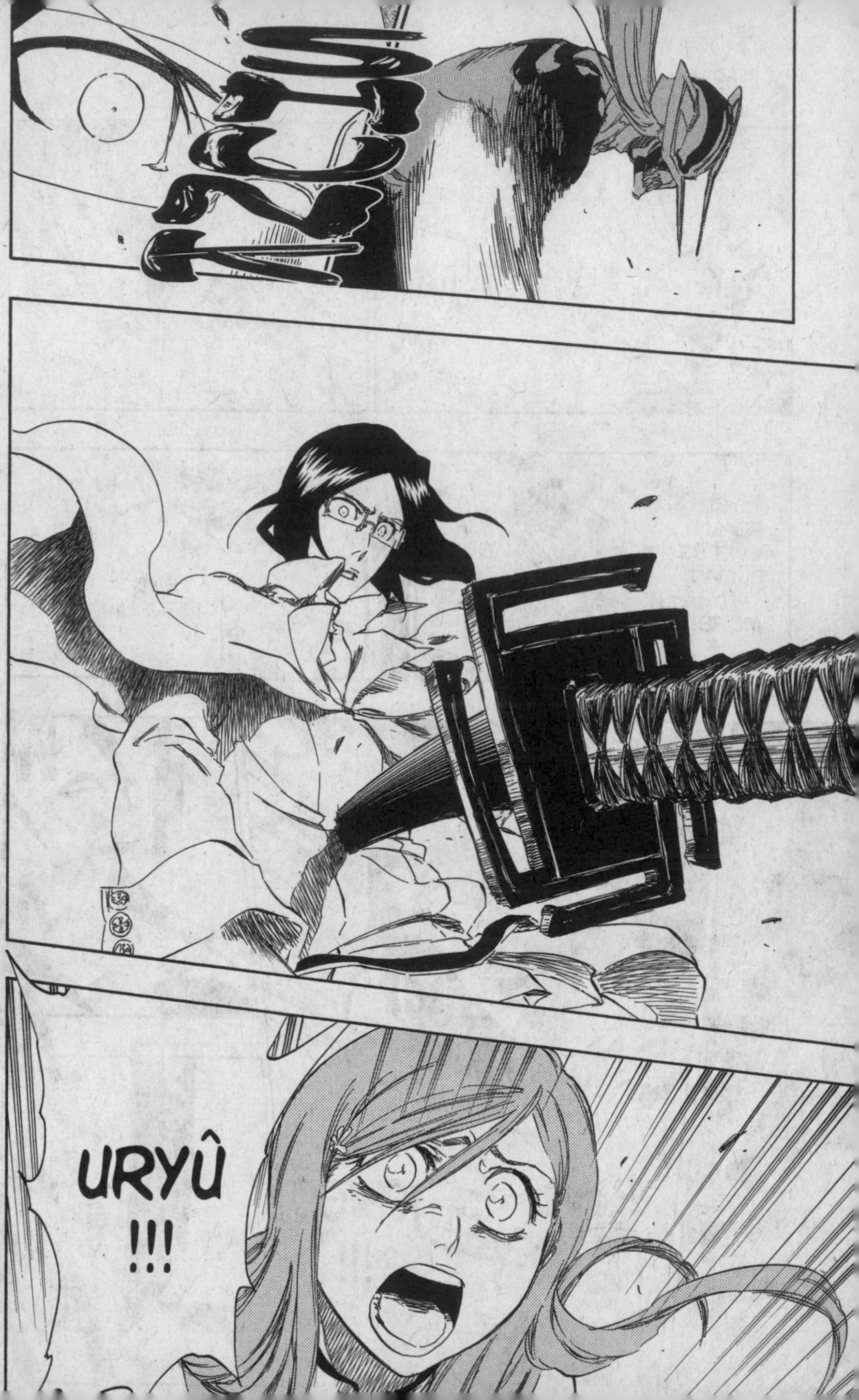
URYÛ !!!

...ECT...

I WILL...
...PROTECT...
...HER.

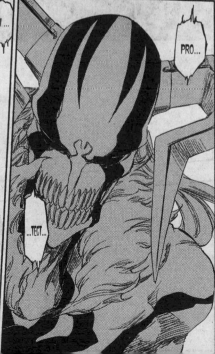
PRO...
...TECT...

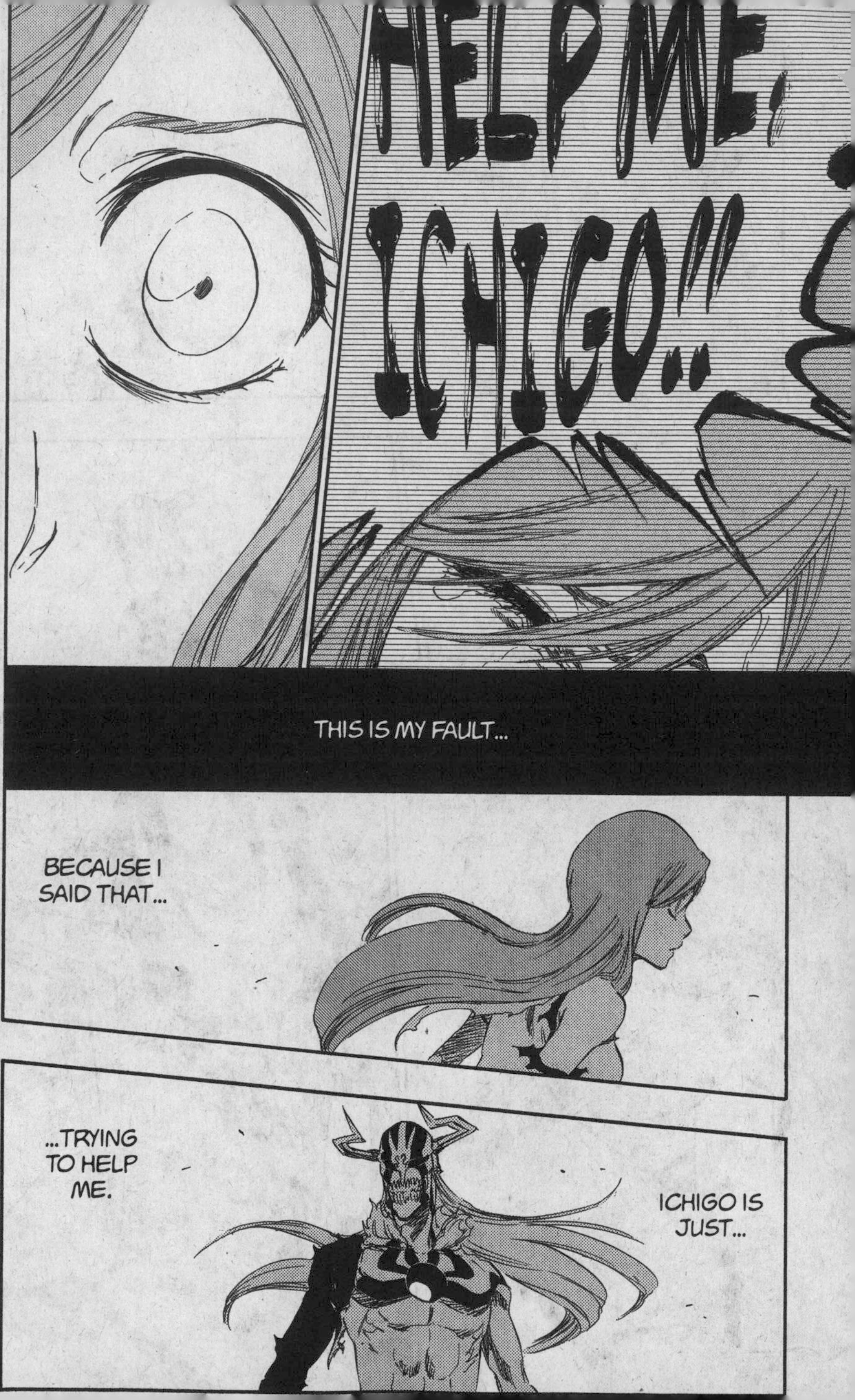
HELP ME, ICHIGO!!
THIS IS MY FAULT...
BECAUSE I SAID THAT...
ICHIGO IS JUST...
...TRYING TO HELP ME.

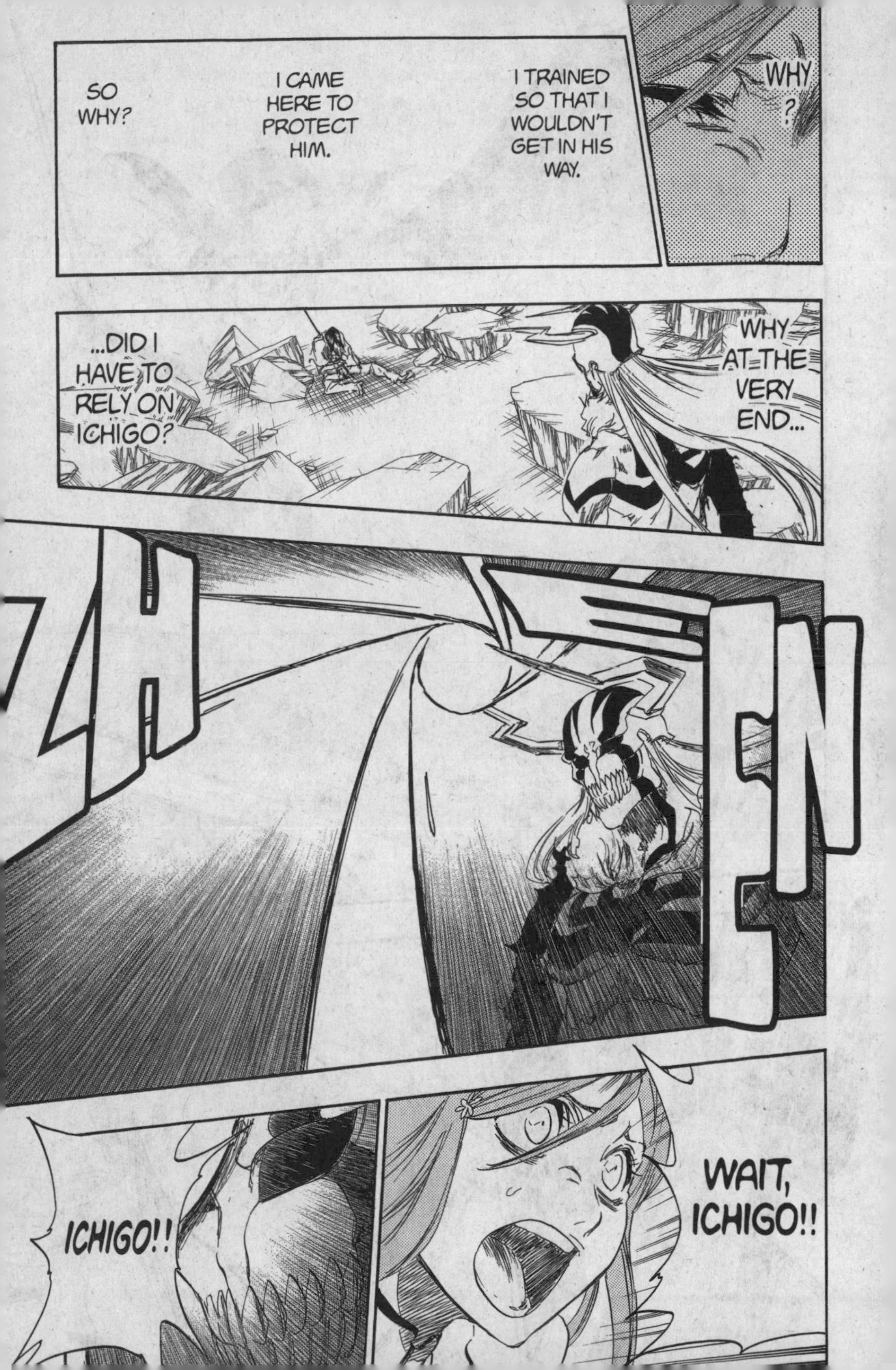
WHY?
I TRAINED SO THAT I WOULDN'T GET IN HIS WAY.
I CAME HERE TO PROTECT HIM.
SO WHY?
WHY AT THE VERY END...
...DID I HAVE TO RELY ON ICHIGO?
ZHEN
WAIT, ICHIGO!!
ICHIGO!!

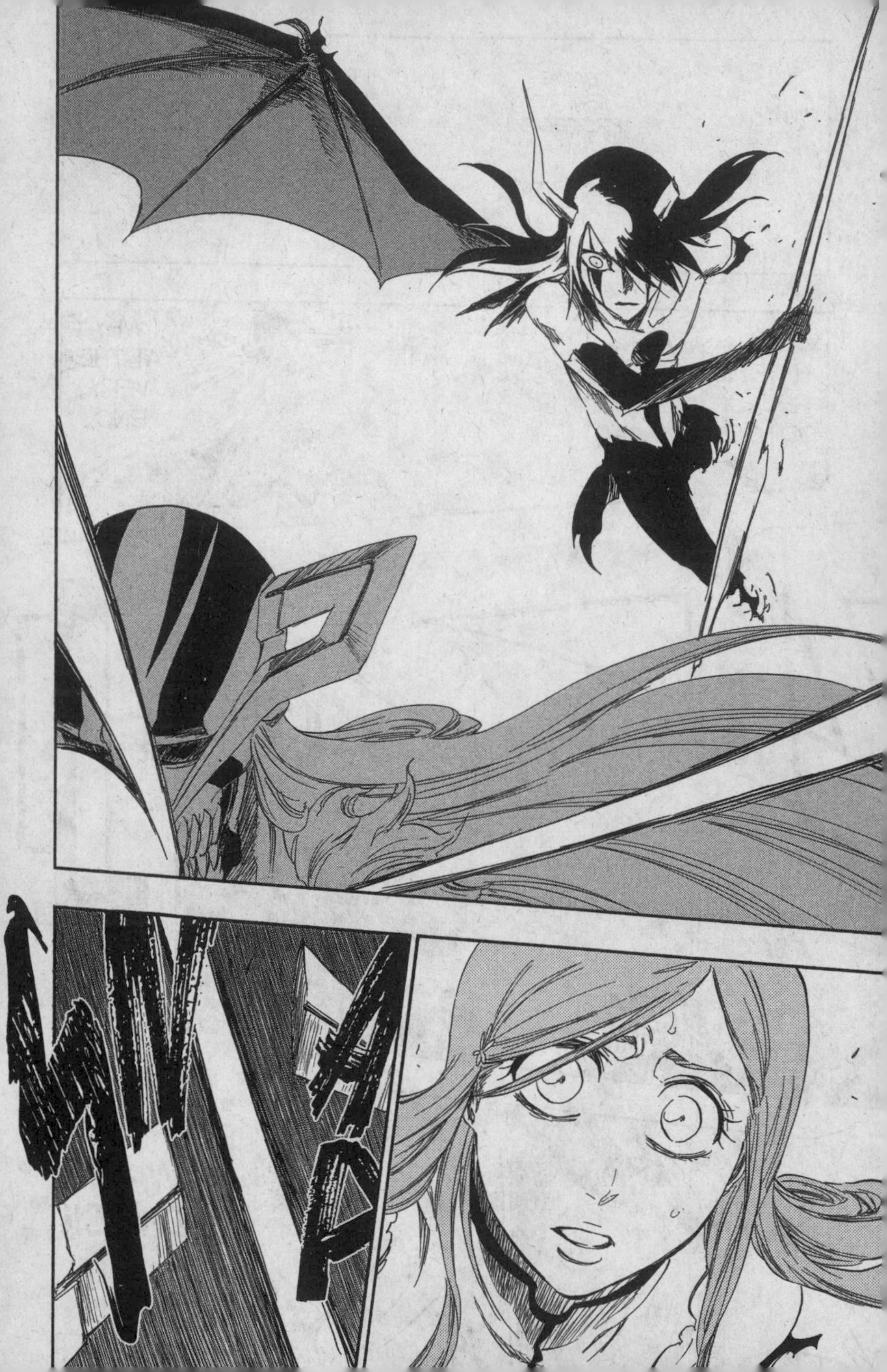

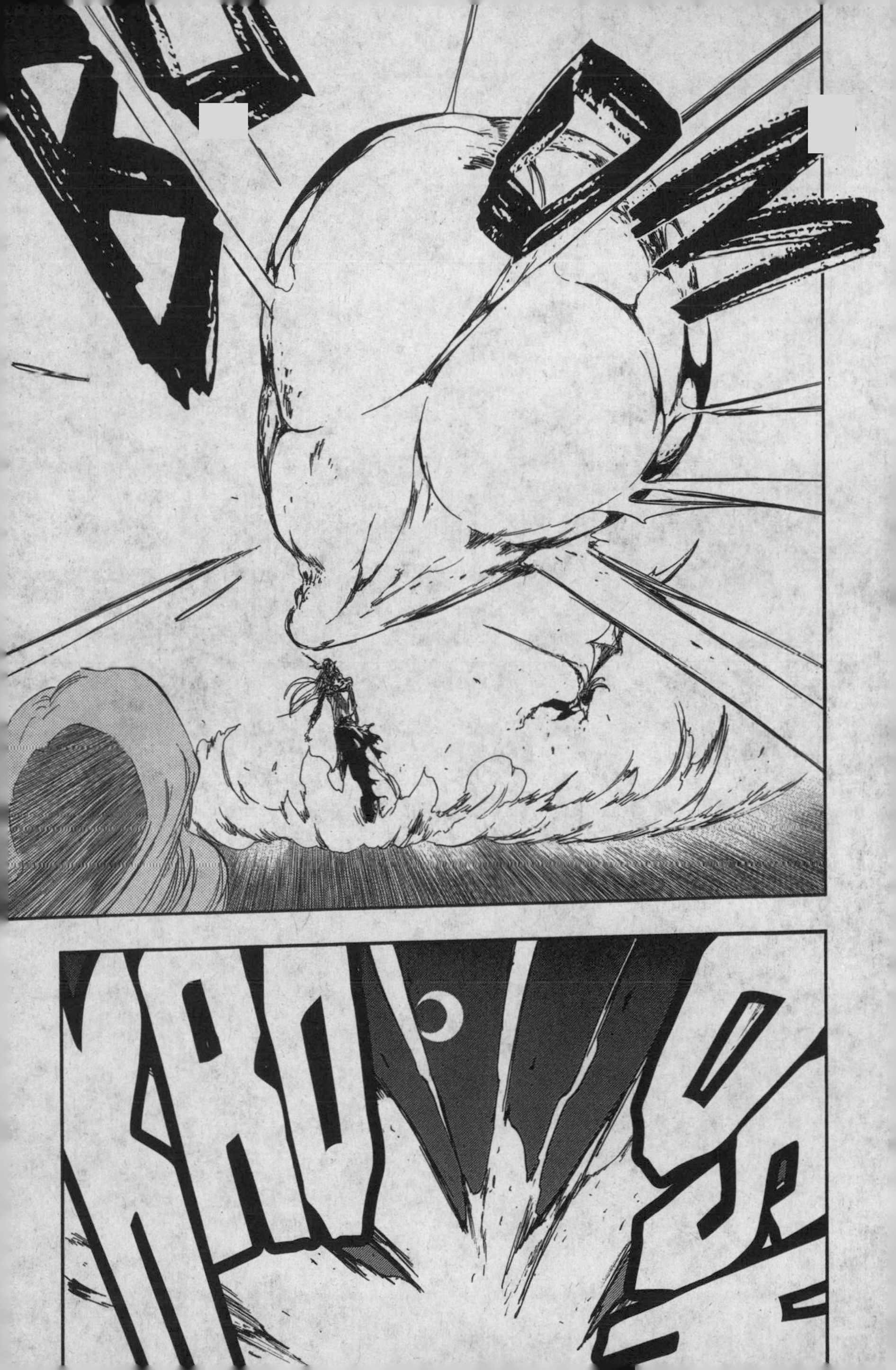

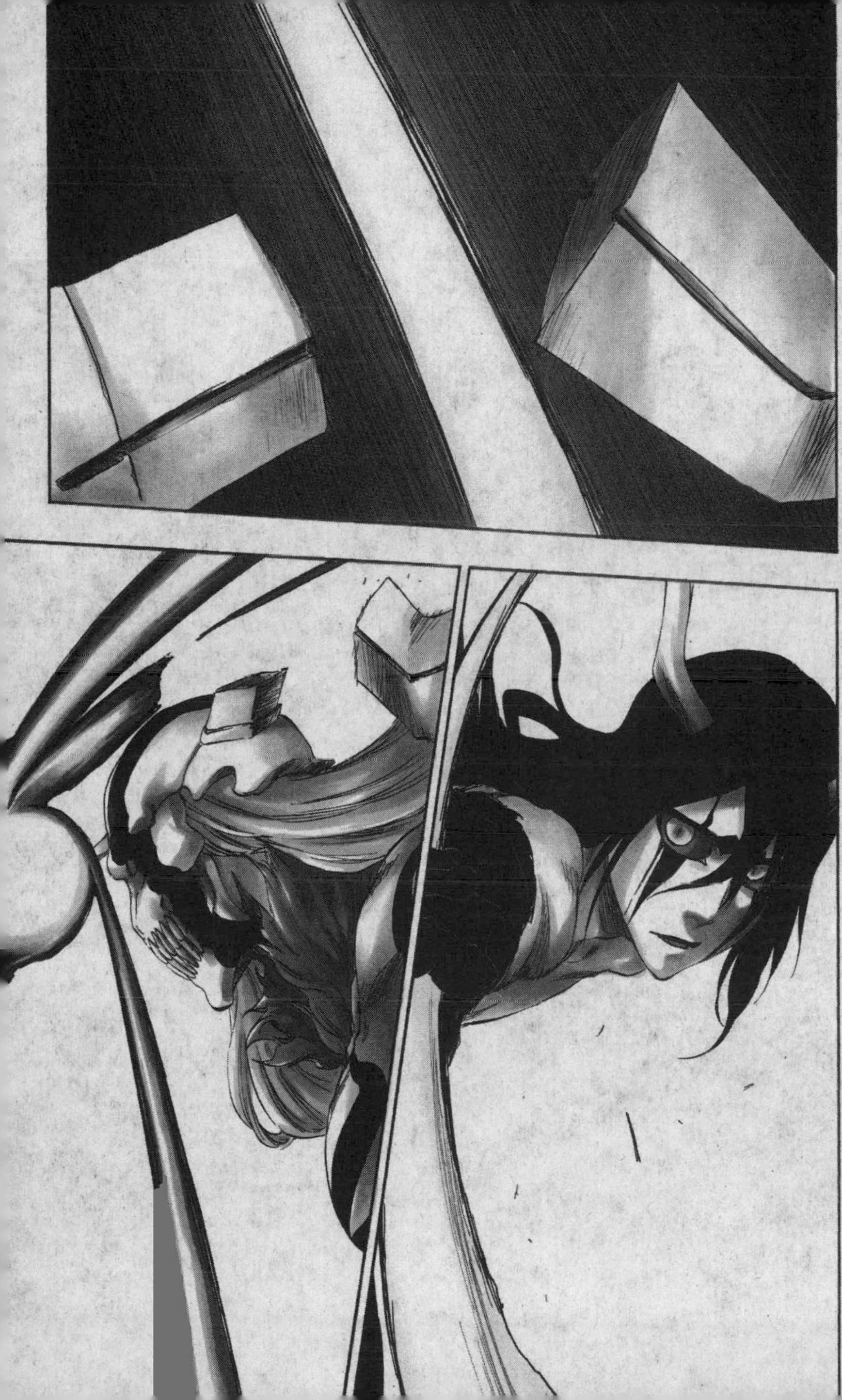

bleach353. The Ash

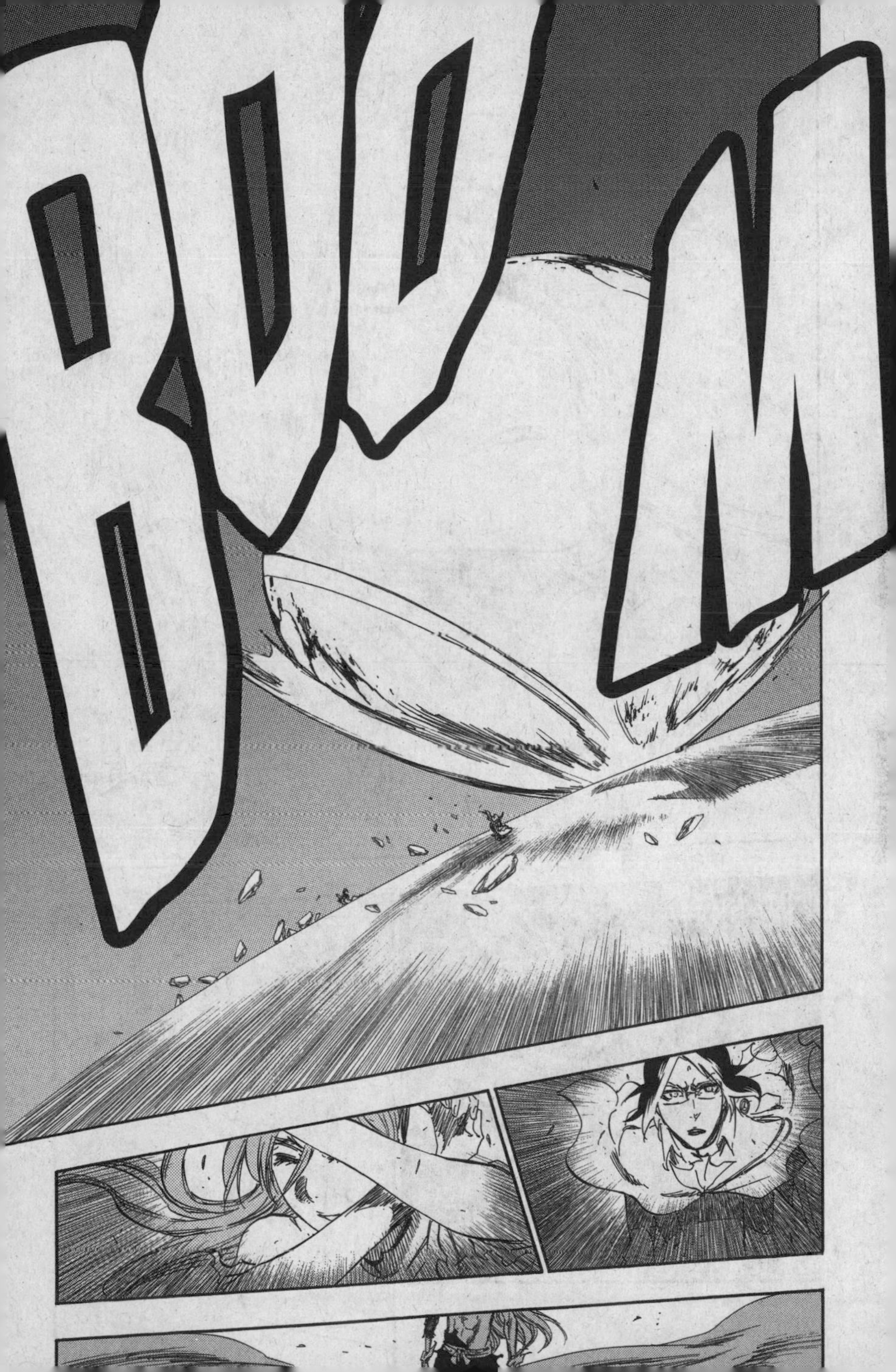
BOOM

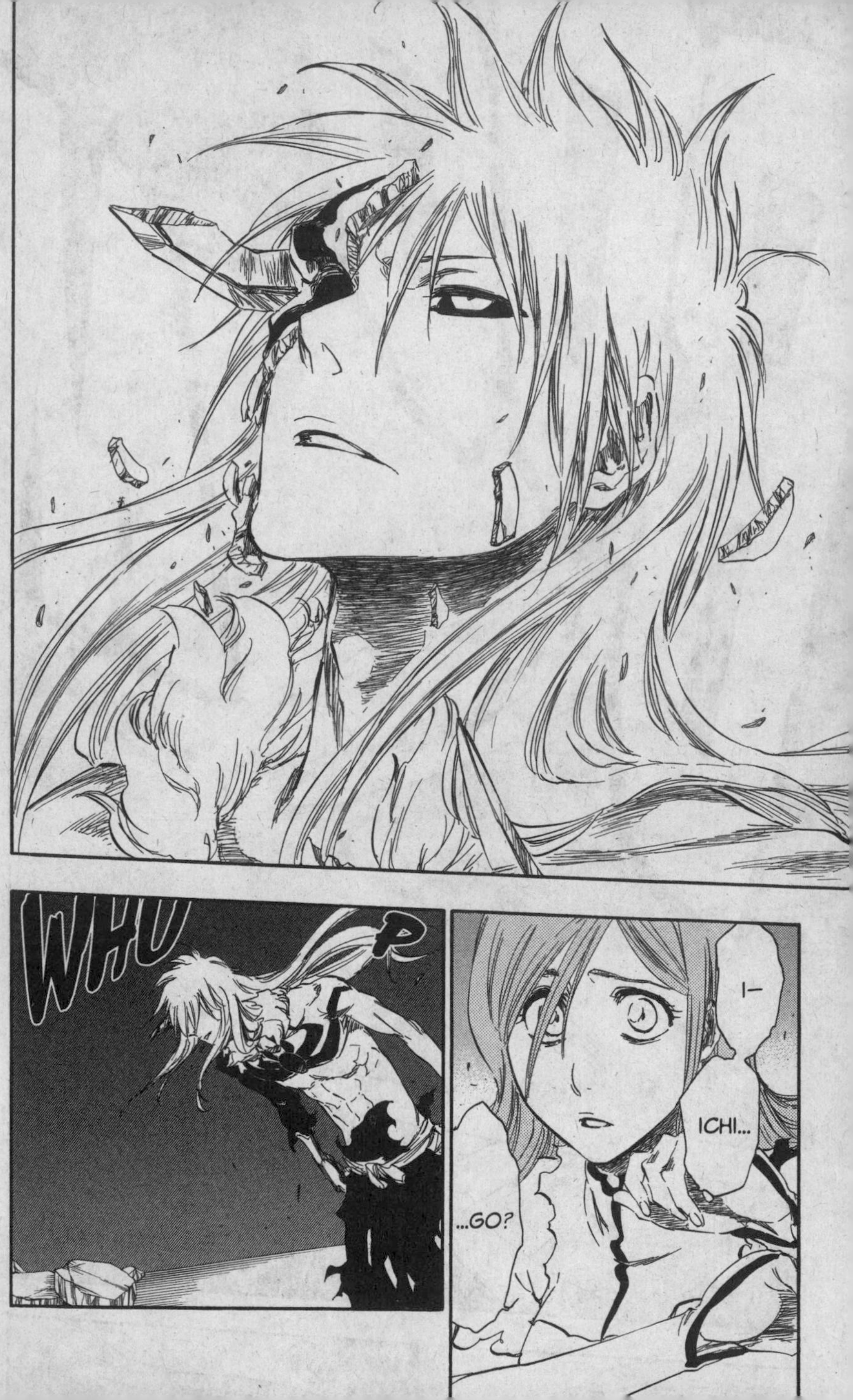
I–
ICHI...
...GO?
WHUP

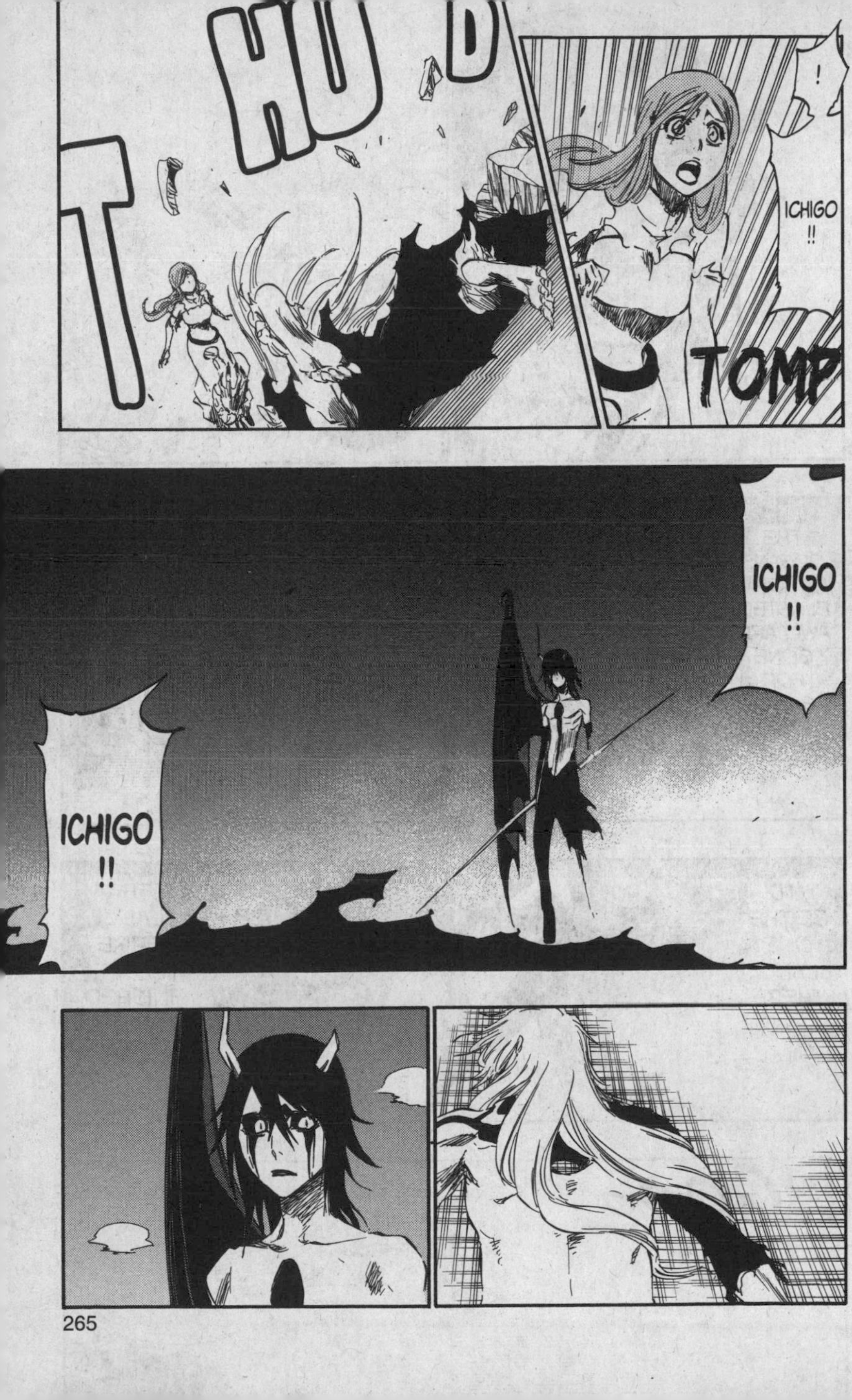
!
ICHIGO !!
TOMP
THUD
ICHIGO !!
ICHIGO !!

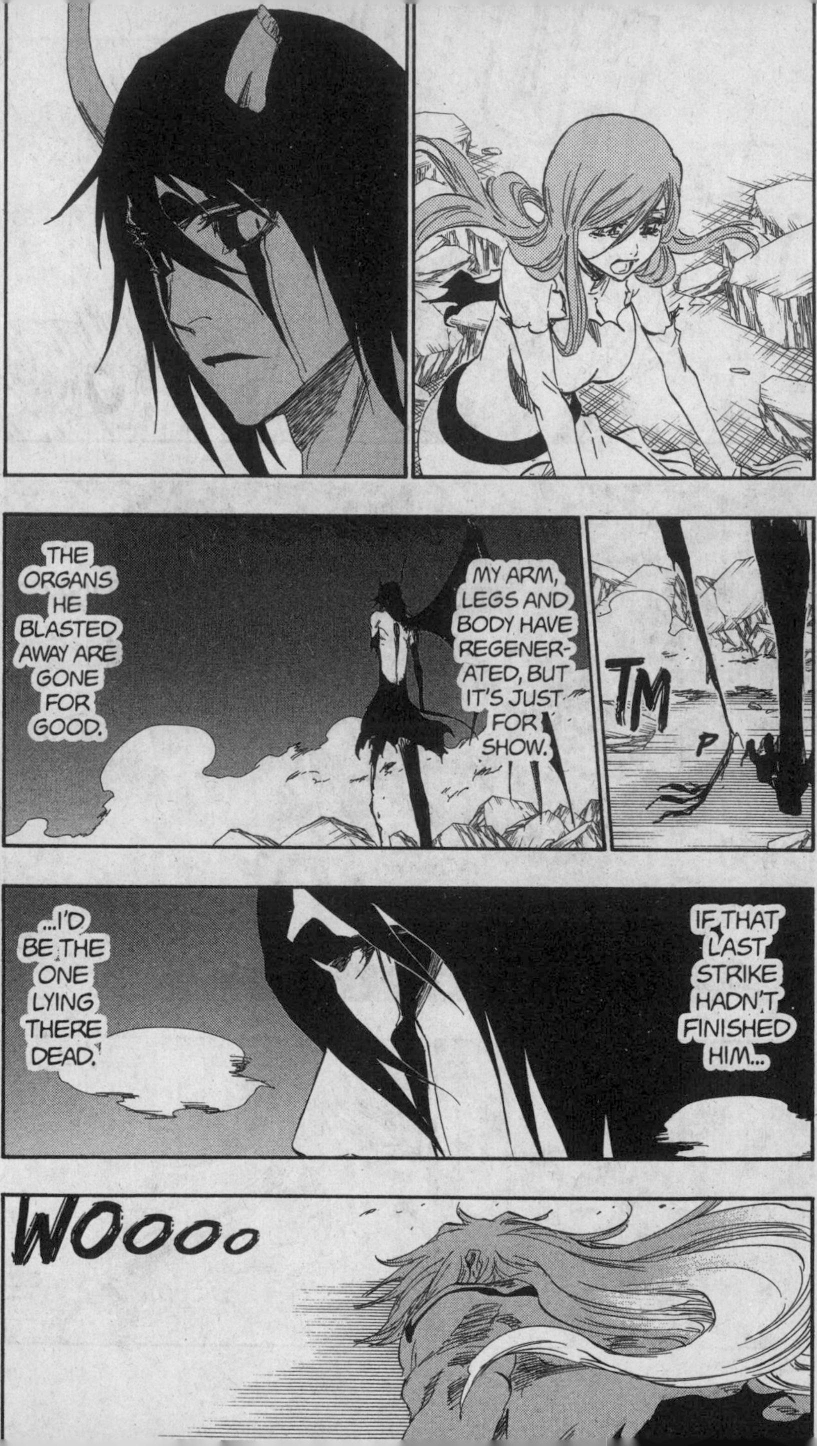
TM
P
MY ARM, LEGS AND BODY HAVE REGENERATED, BUT IT'S JUST FOR SHOW.
THE ORGANS HE BLASTED AWAY ARE GONE FOR GOOD.
IF THAT LAST STRIKE HADN'T FINISHED HIM...
...I'D BE THE ONE LYING THERE DEAD.
WOOOO

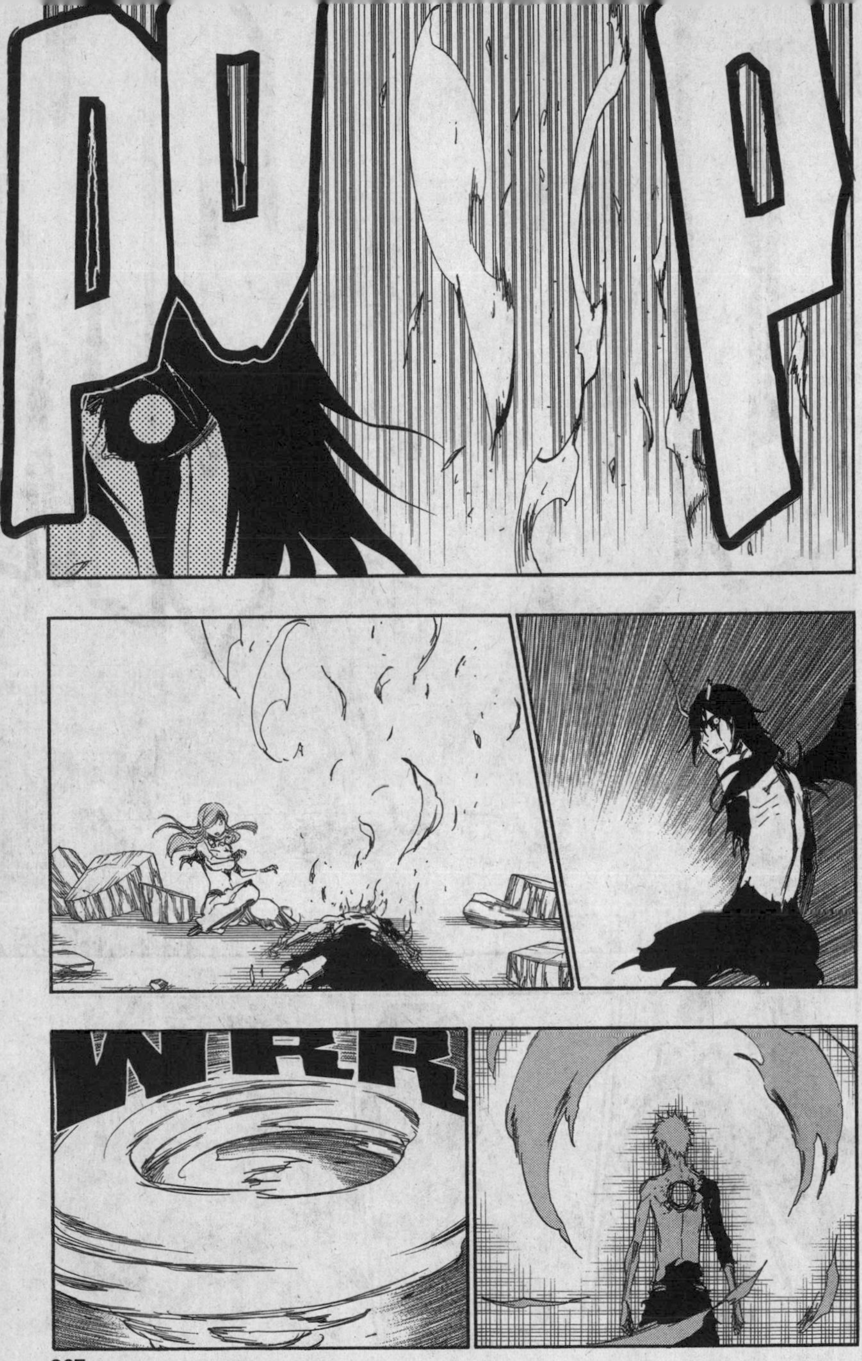
WRR

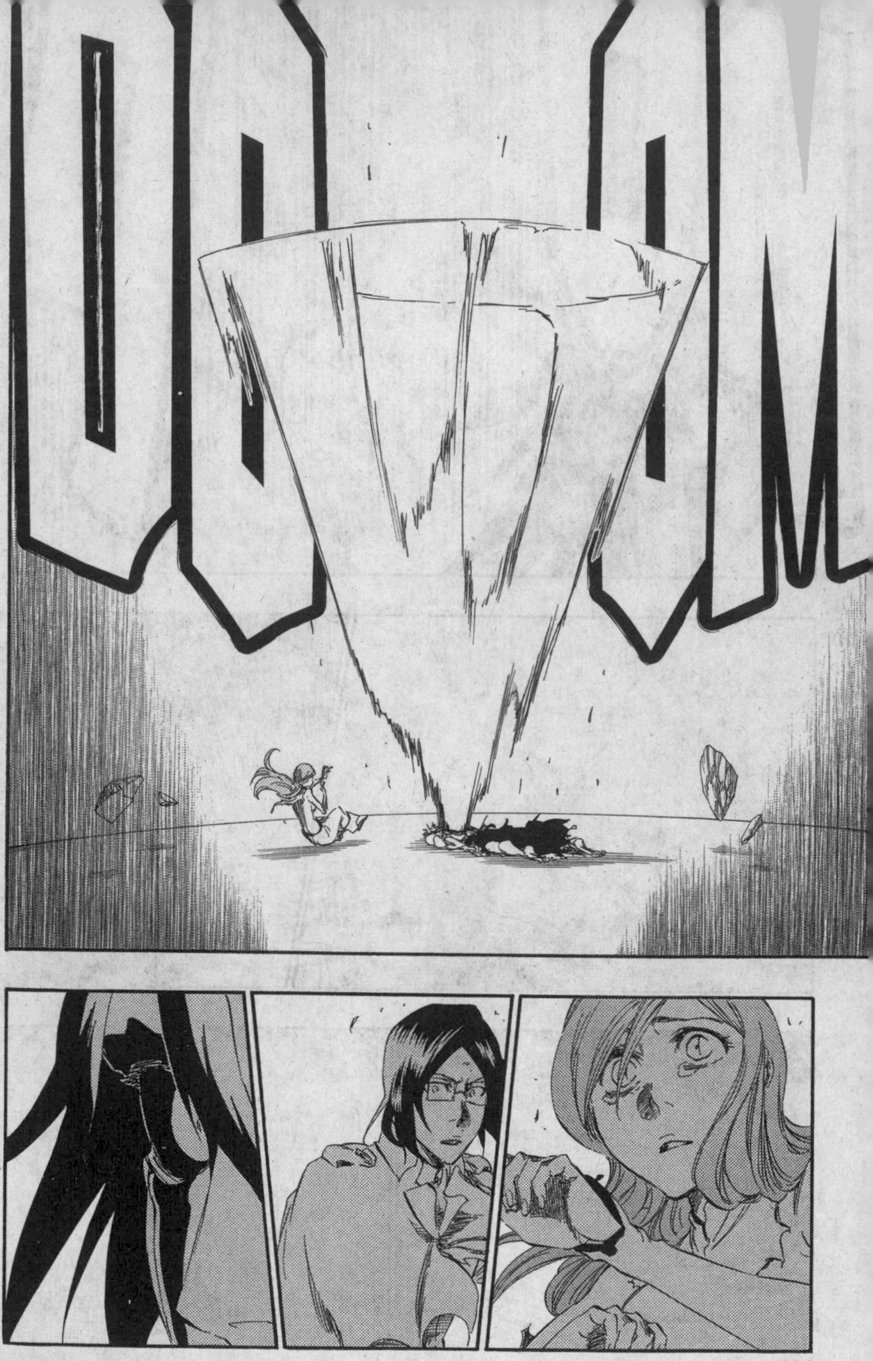
DOOM

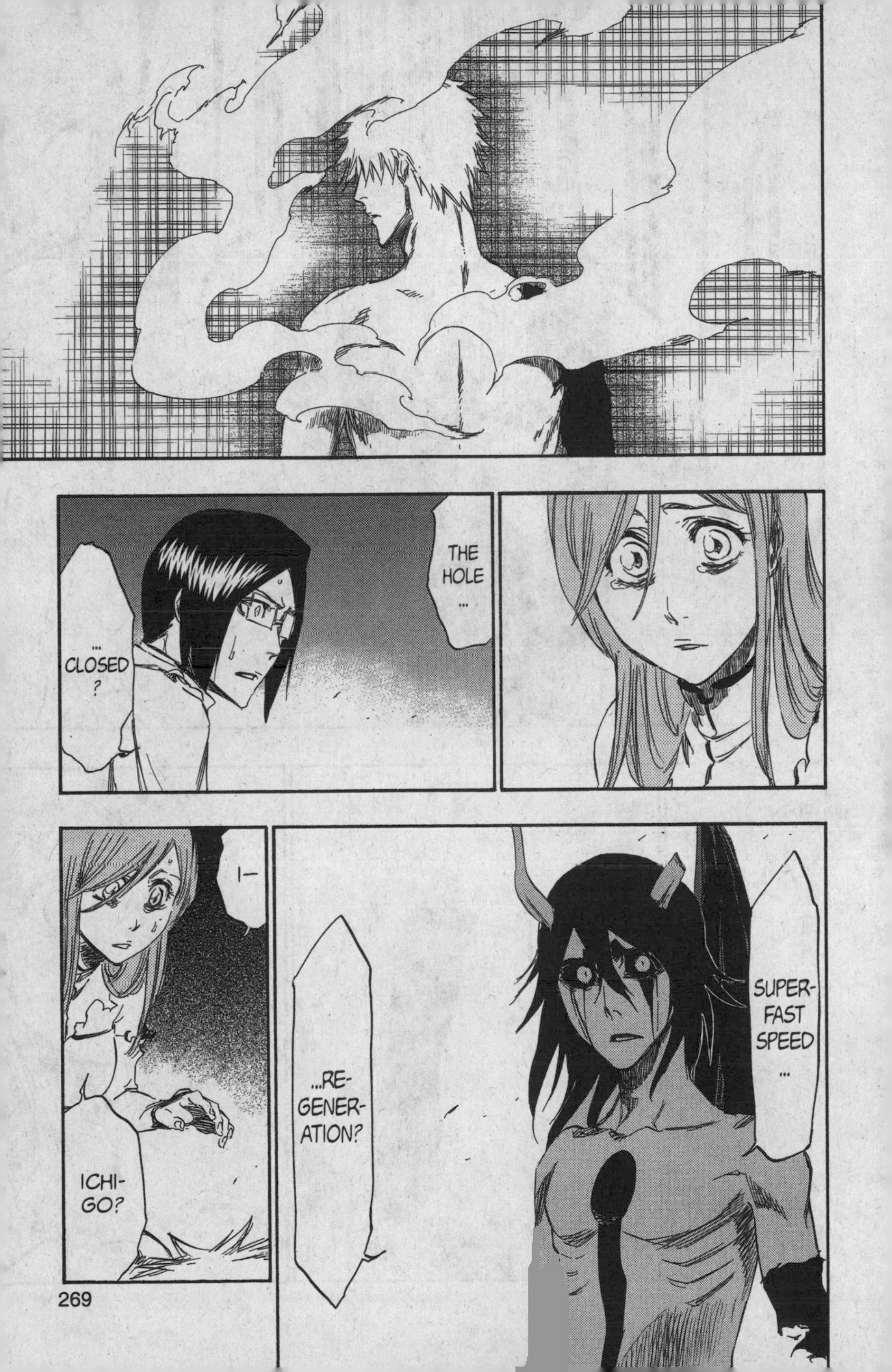
THE HOLE ...
... CLOSED ?
SUPER-FAST SPEED ...
...RE-GENERATION?
I—
ICHI-GO?

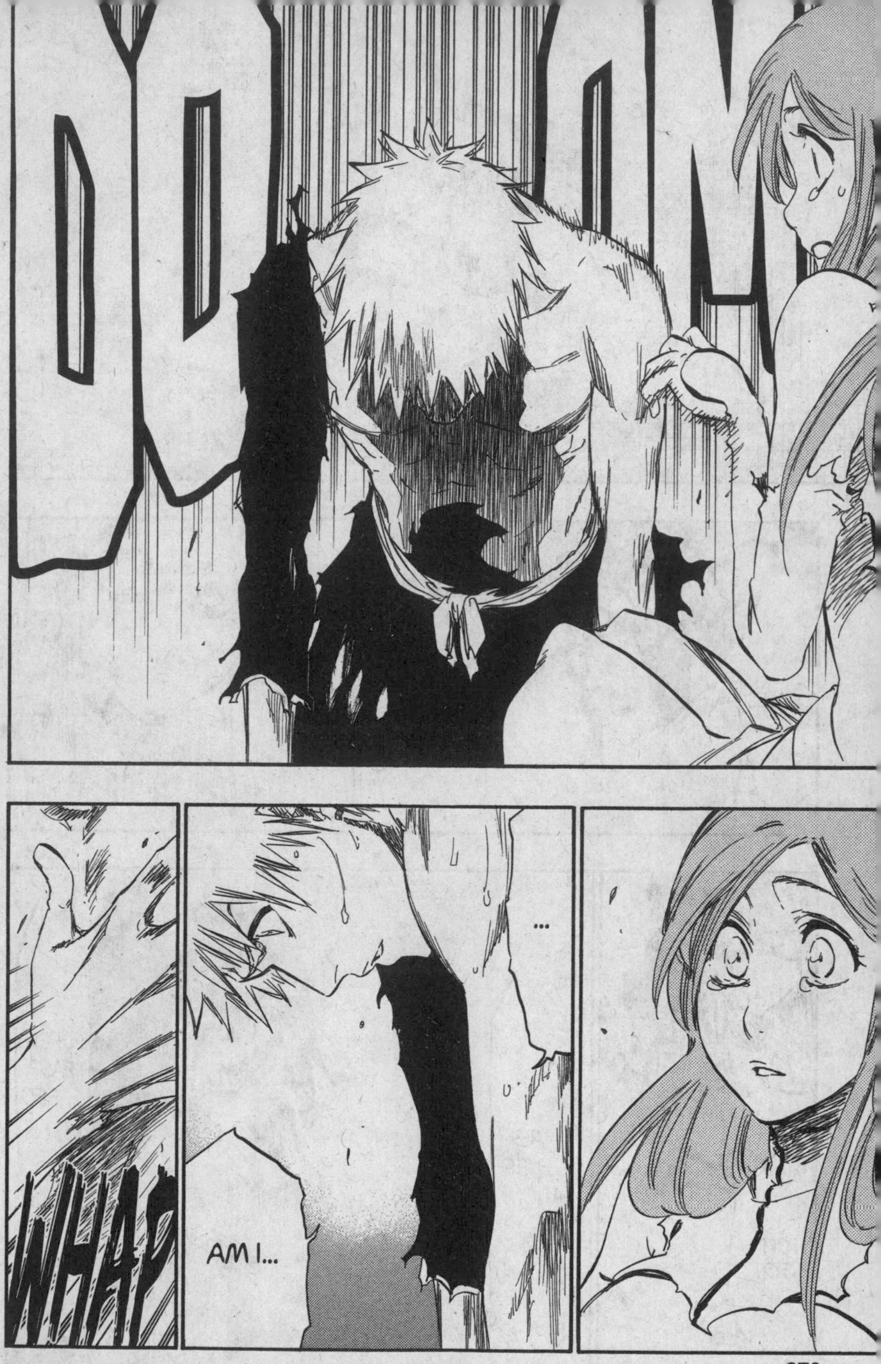
...
AM I...
WHAP

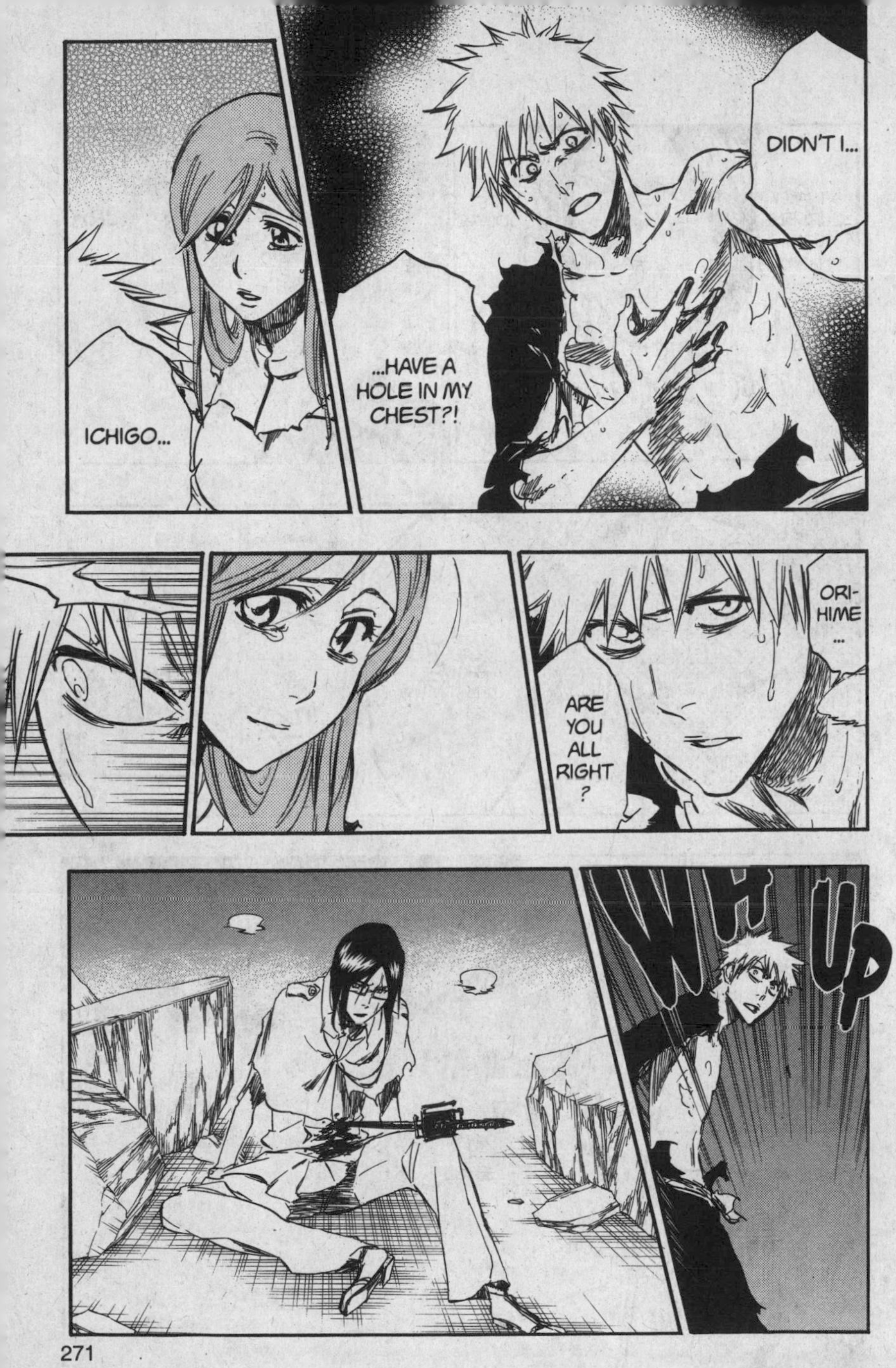

DIDN'T I...
...HAVE A HOLE IN MY CHEST?!
ICHIGO...
ORI-HIME...
ARE YOU ALL RIGHT?
WHUP

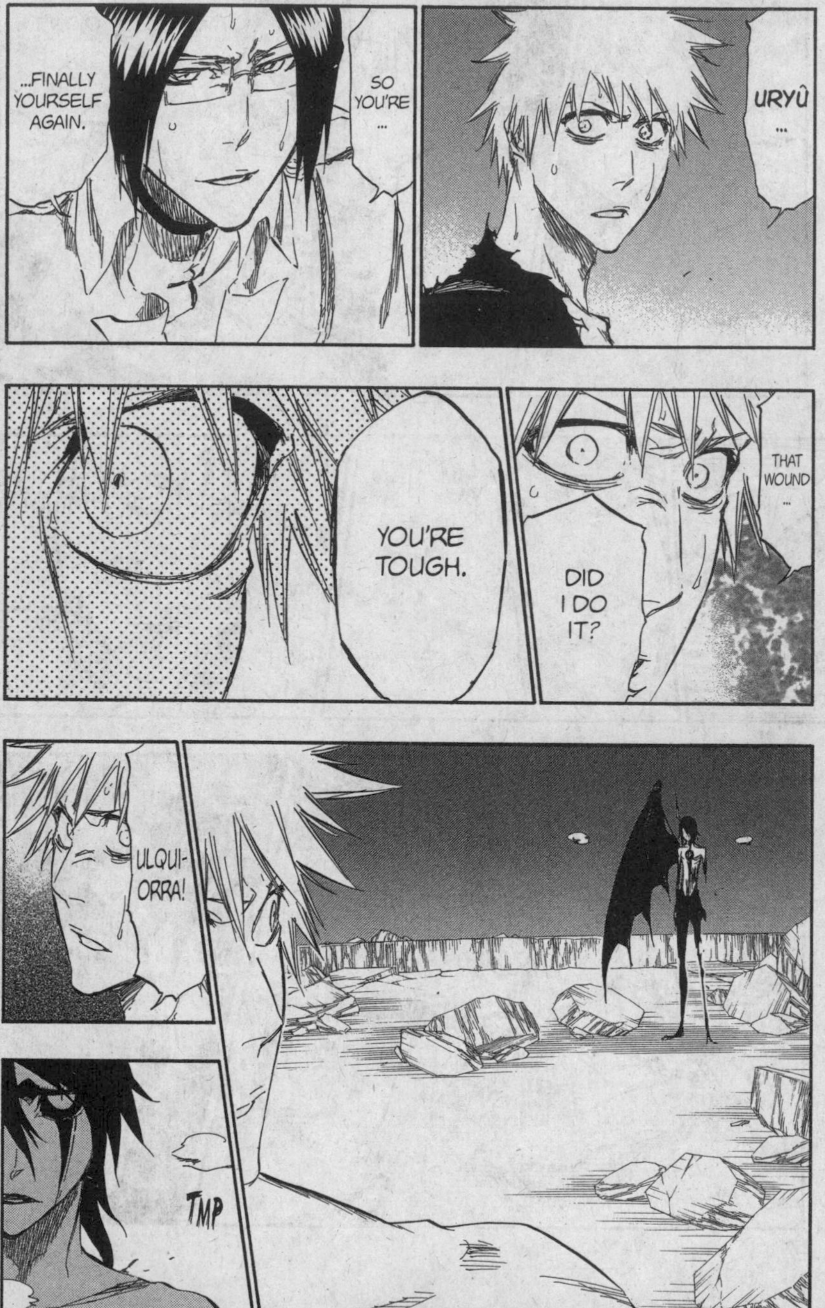
URYÛ ...
SO YOU'RE ...
...FINALLY YOURSELF AGAIN.
THAT WOUND ...
DID I DO IT?
YOU'RE TOUGH.
ULQUI-ORRA!
TMP

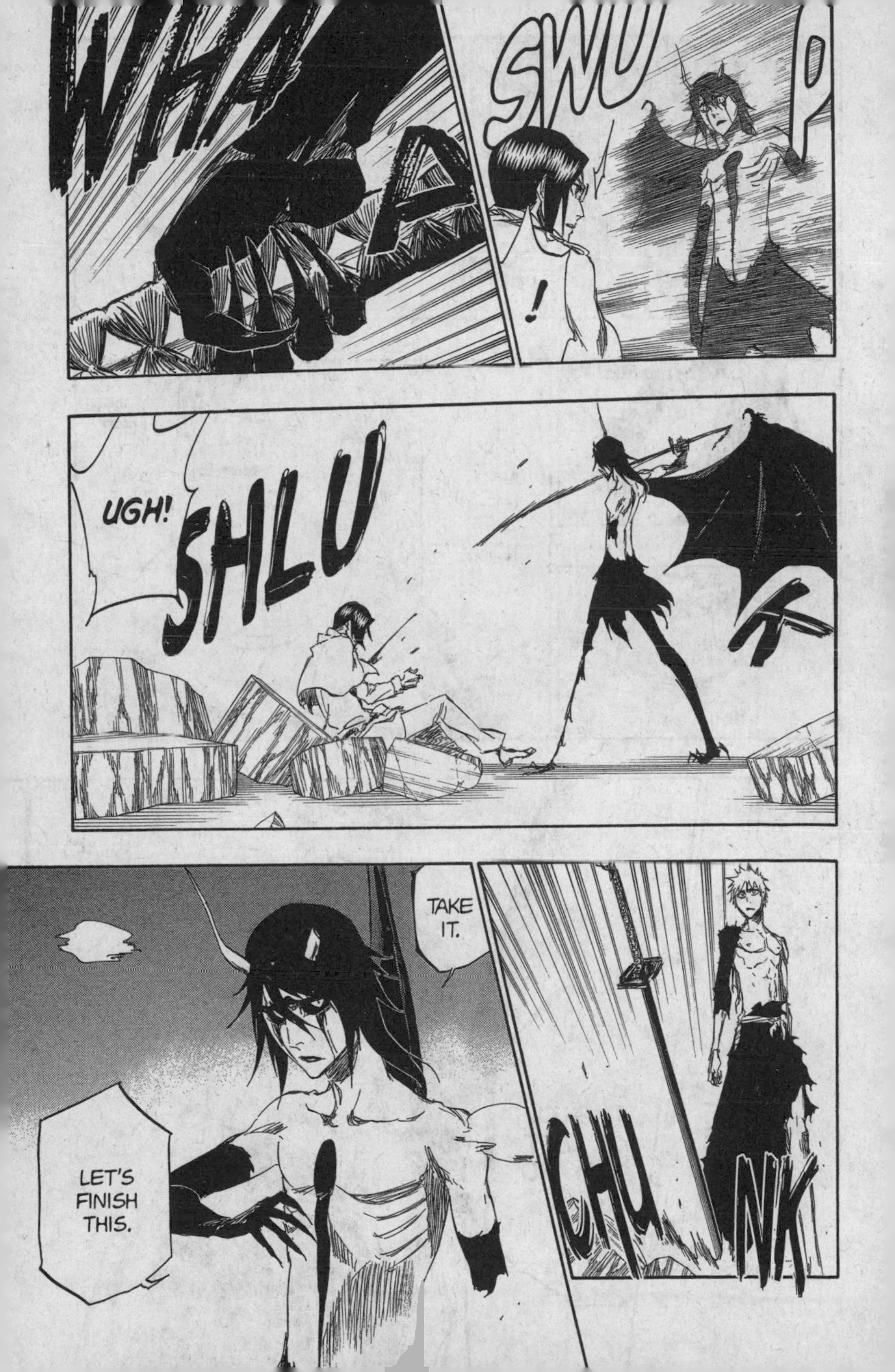
SWU
P
!
WHA
A
UGH!
SHLU
K
CHU
NK
TAKE IT.
LET'S FINISH THIS.

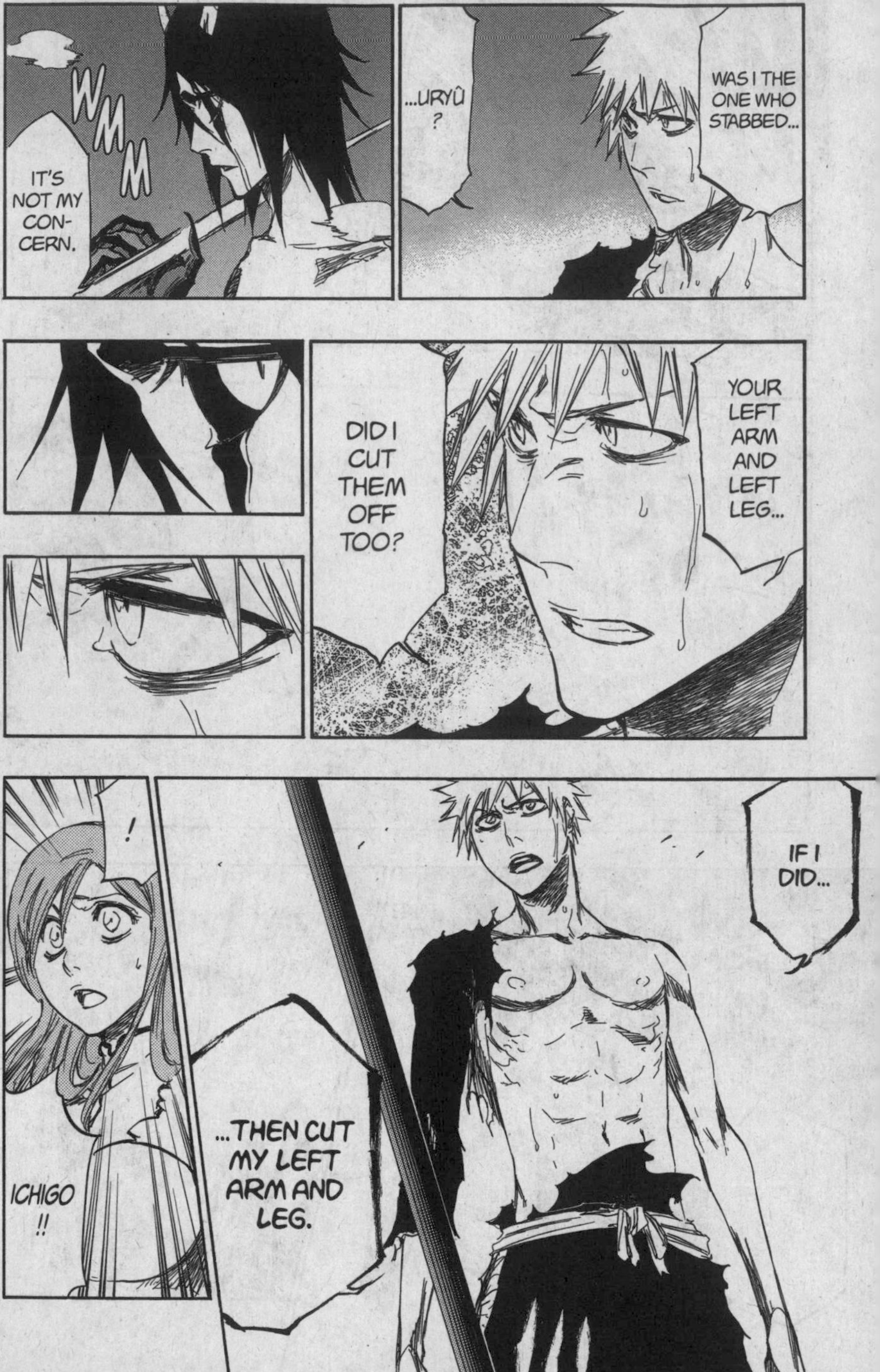
WAS I THE ONE WHO STABBED...
...URYÛ ?
WMMM
IT'S NOT MY CON-CERN.
YOUR LEFT ARM AND LEFT LEG...
DID I CUT THEM OFF TOO?
IF I DID...
...THEN CUT MY LEFT ARM AND LEG.
!
ICHIGO !!

READ THIS WAY

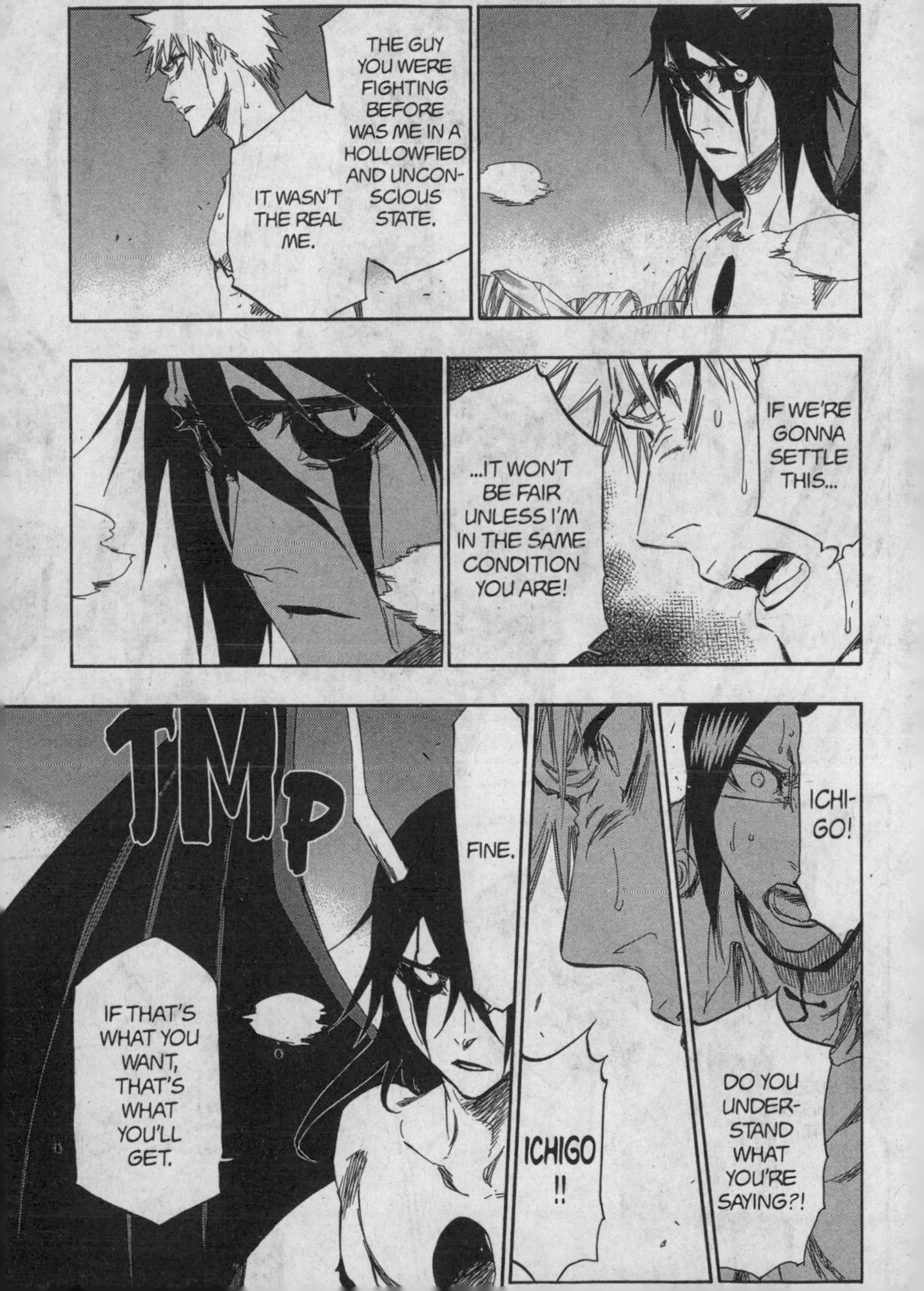
THE GUY YOU WERE FIGHTING BEFORE WAS ME IN A HOLLOWFIED AND UNCONSCIOUS STATE.
IT WASN'T THE REAL ME.
IF WE'RE GONNA SETTLE THIS...
...IT WON'T BE FAIR UNLESS I'M IN THE SAME CONDITION YOU ARE!
ICHIGO!
DO YOU UNDERSTAND WHAT YOU'RE SAYING?!
ICHIGO !!
TMP
FINE.
IF THAT'S WHAT YOU WANT, THAT'S WHAT YOU'LL GET.

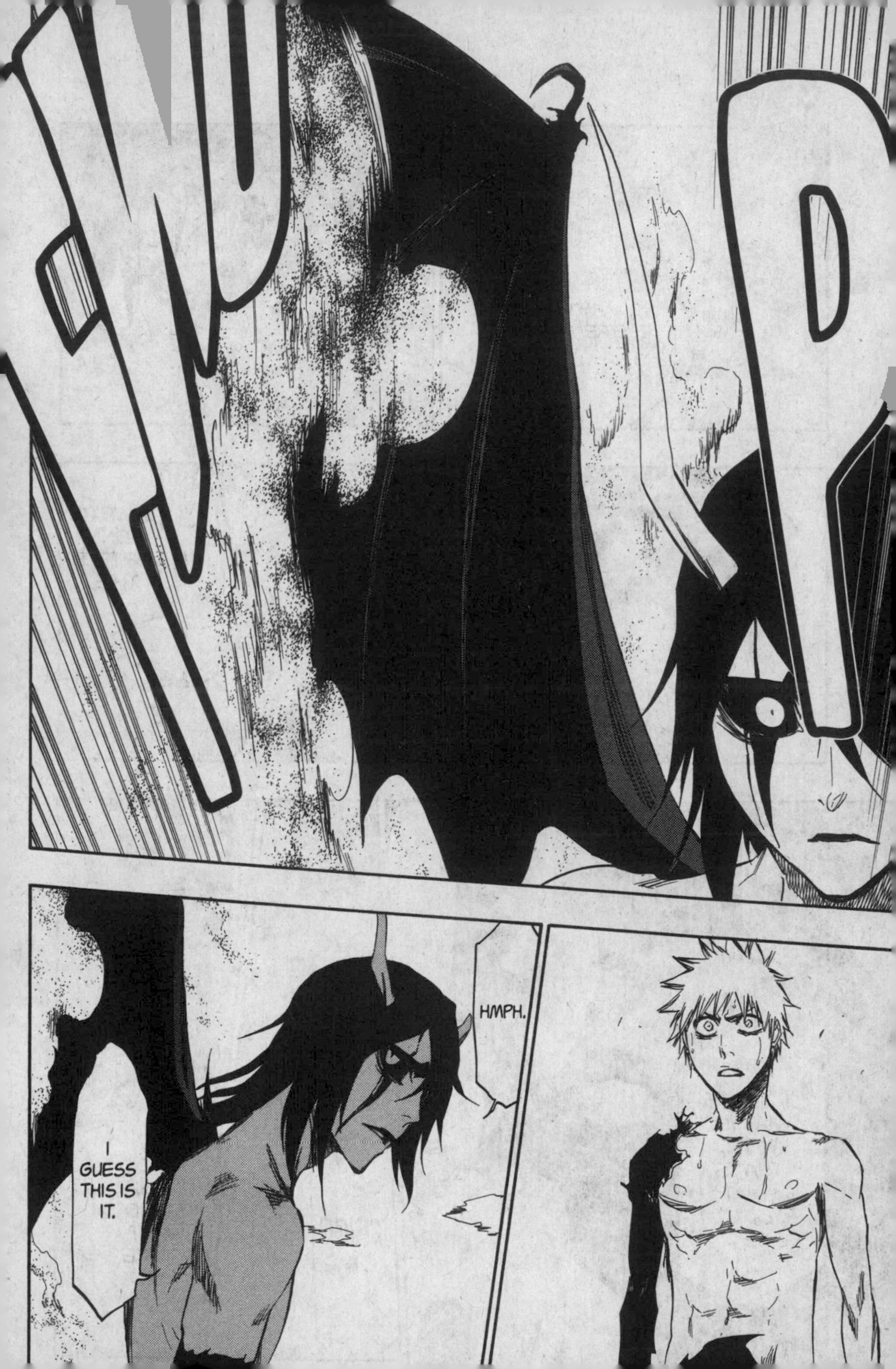
HMPH.
I GUESS THIS IS IT.

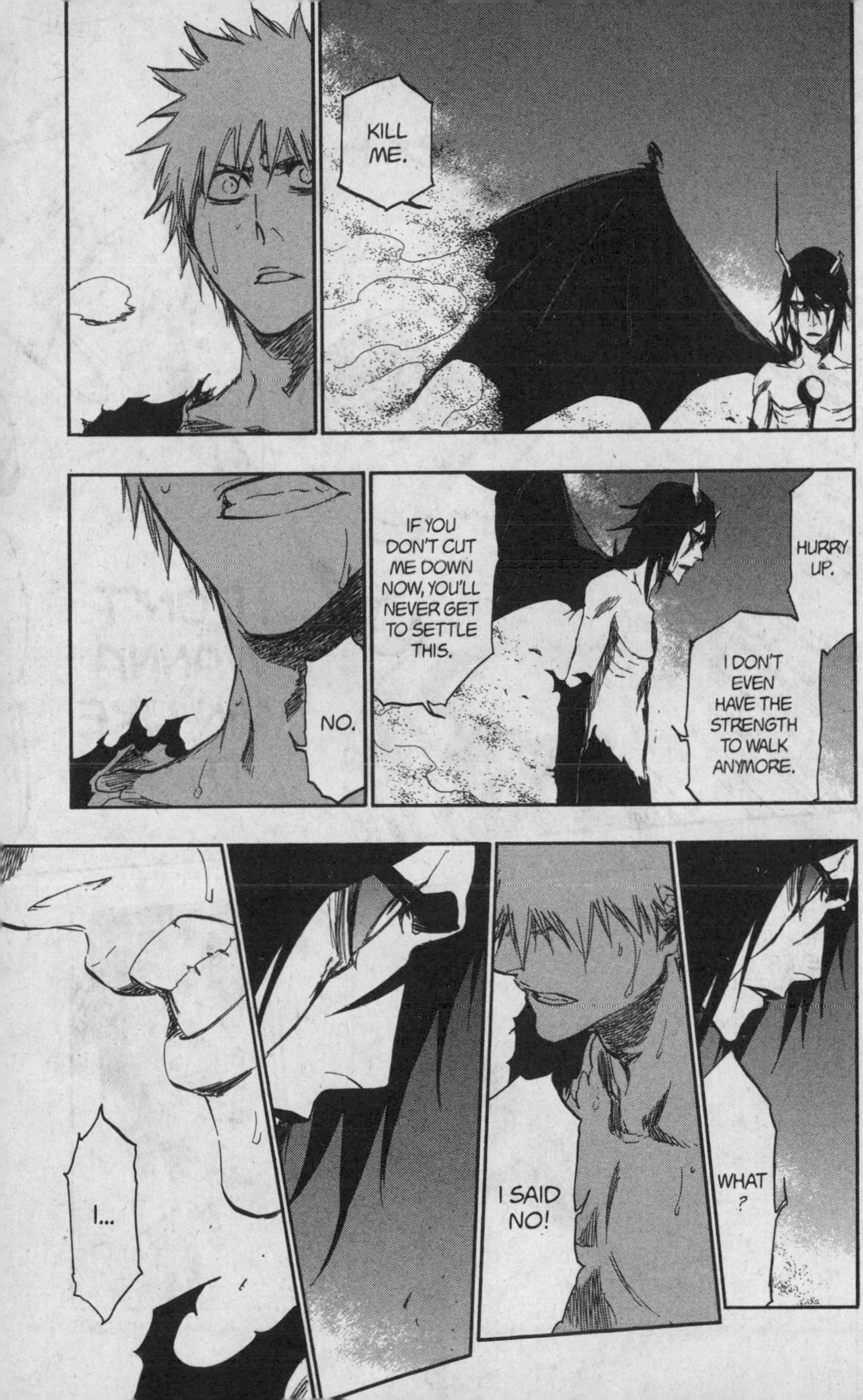
KILL ME.
HURRY UP.
I DON'T EVEN HAVE THE STRENGTH TO WALK ANYMORE.
IF YOU DON'T CUT ME DOWN NOW, YOU'LL NEVER GET TO SETTLE THIS.
NO.
WHAT?
I SAID NO!
I...

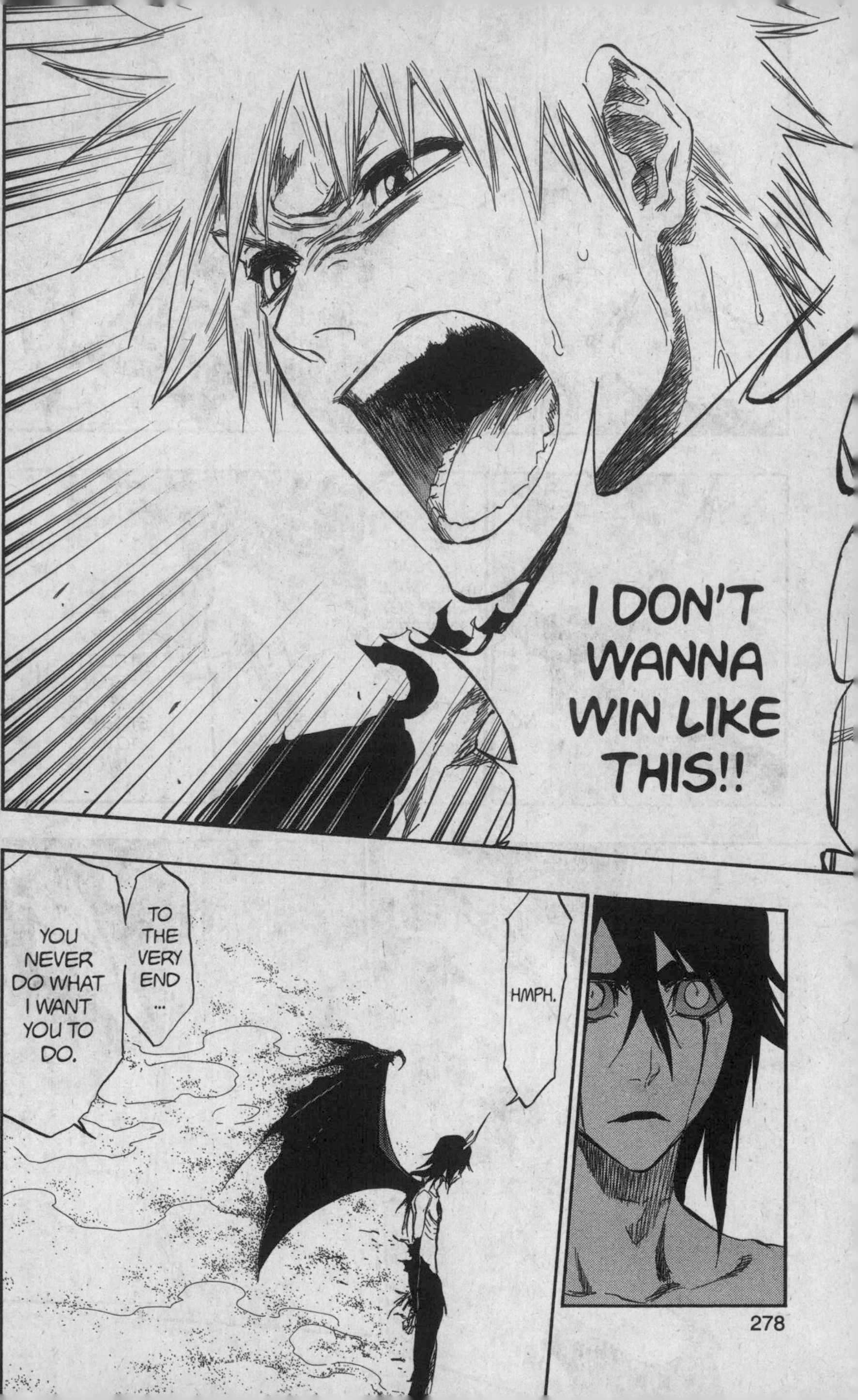
I DON'T WANNA WIN LIKE THIS!!
HMPH.
TO THE VERY END ...
YOU NEVER DO WHAT I WANT YOU TO DO.

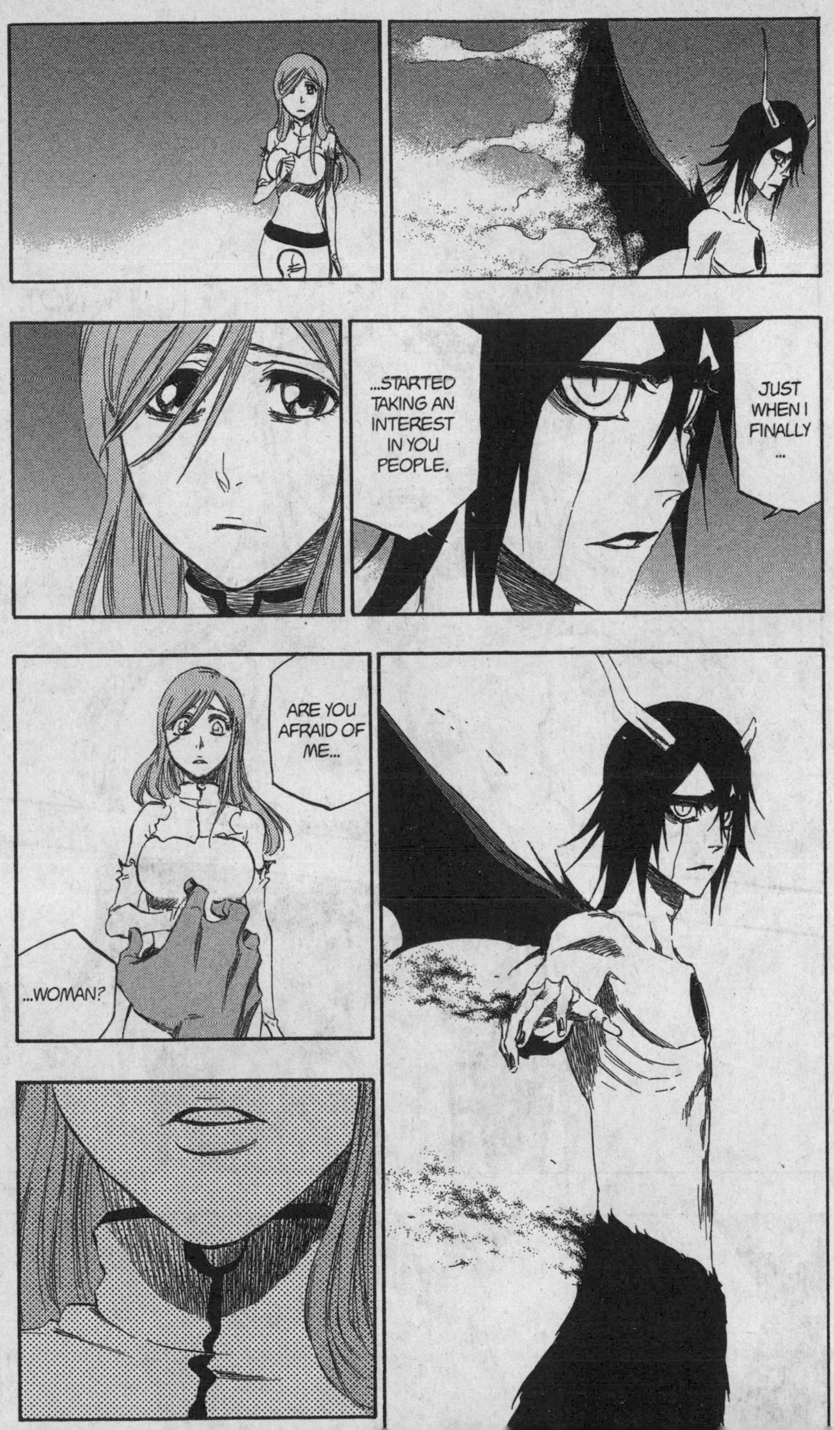
JUST WHEN I FINALLY ...
...STARTED TAKING AN INTEREST IN YOU PEOPLE.
ARE YOU AFRAID OF ME...
...WOMAN?

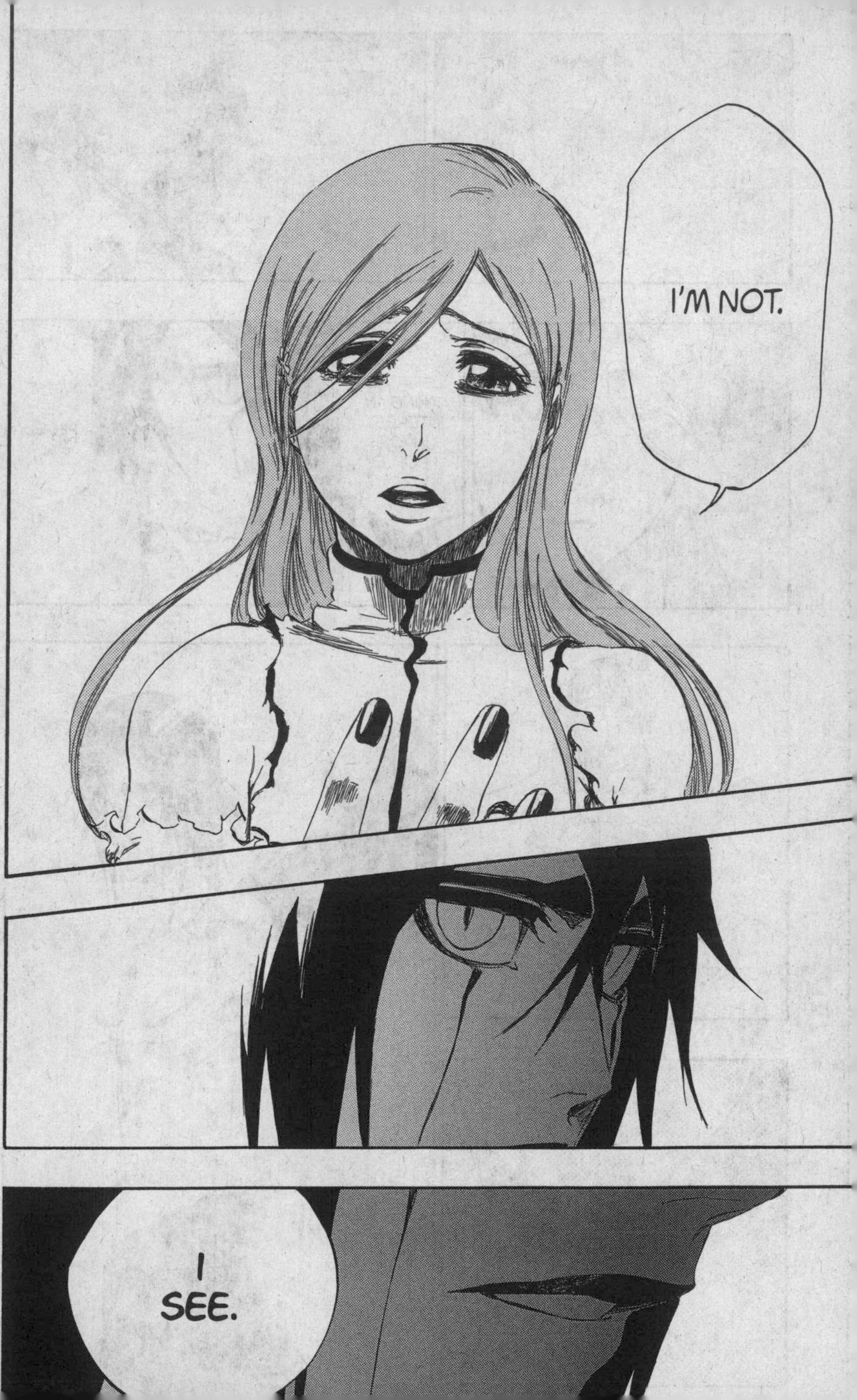
I'M NOT.
I SEE.

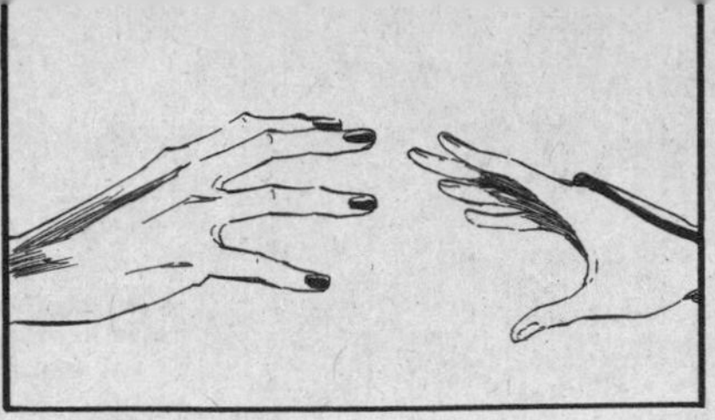

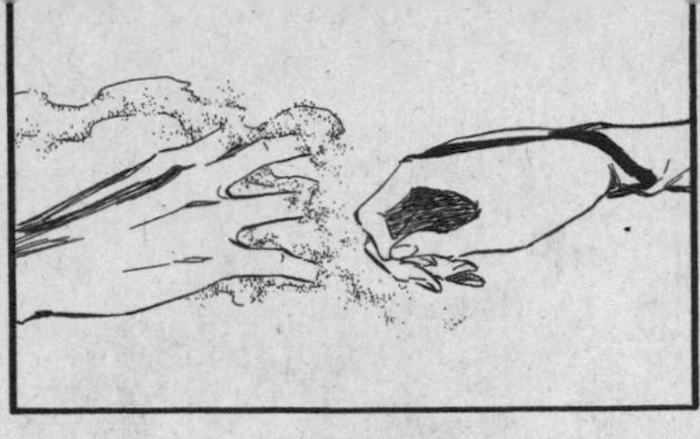

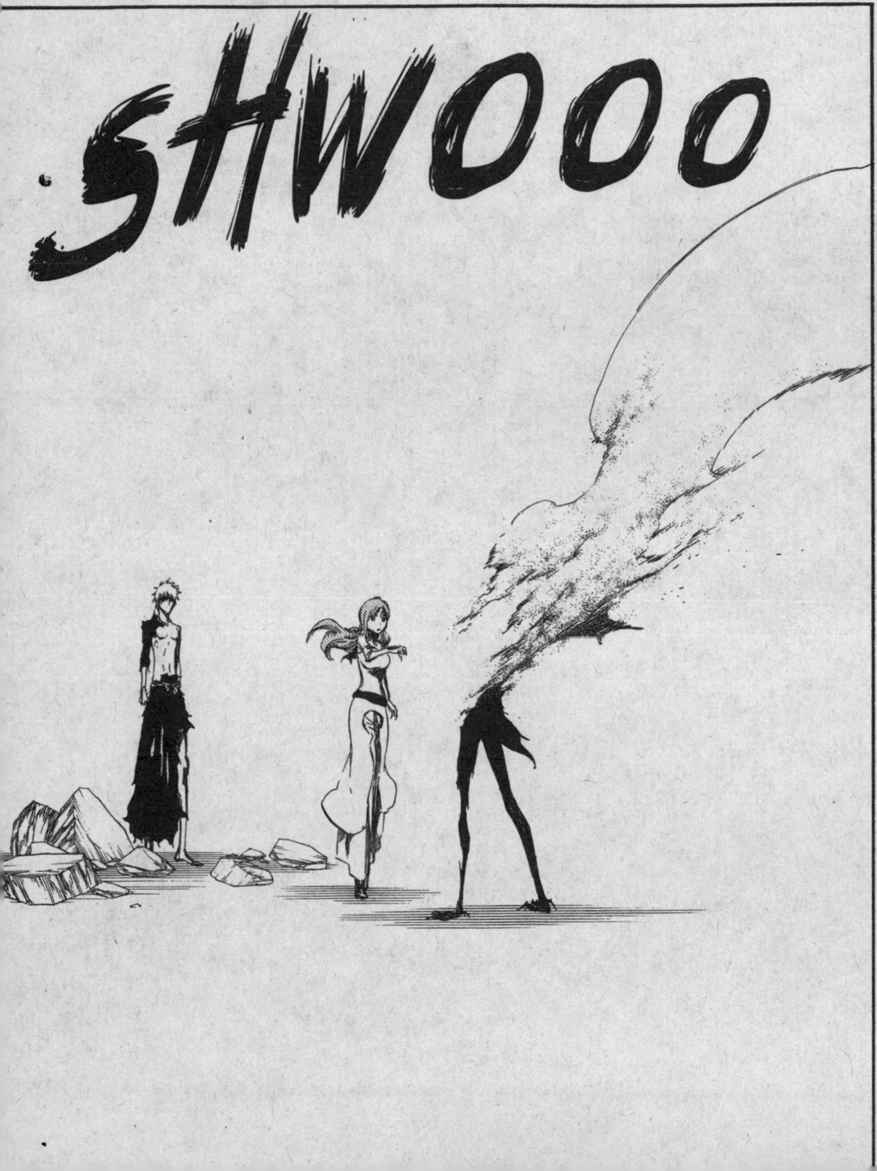
SHWOOO

354. heart

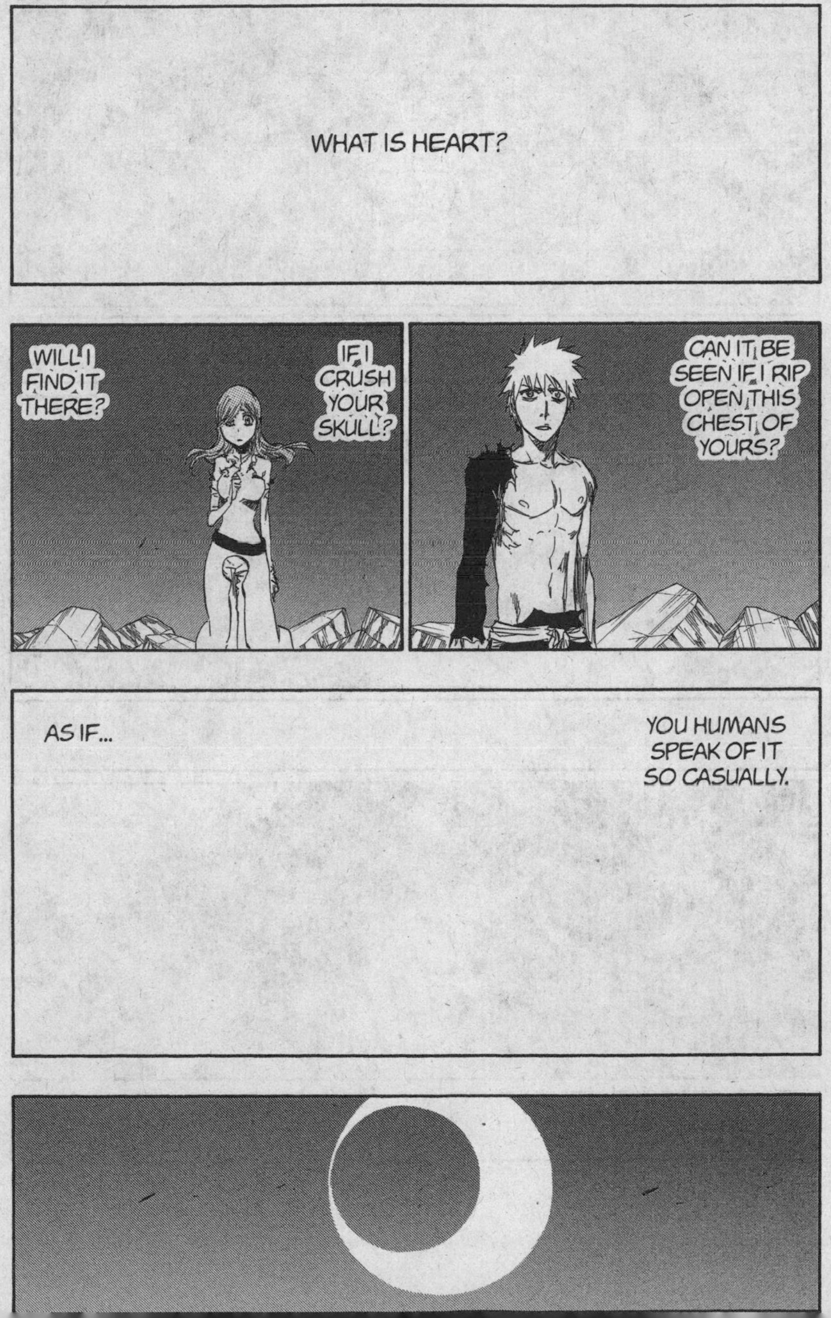
WHAT IS HEART?
CAN IT BE SEEN IF I RIP OPEN THIS CHEST OF YOURS?
IF I CRUSH YOUR SKULL?
WILL I FIND IT THERE?
YOU HUMANS SPEAK OF IT SO CASUALLY.
AS IF...

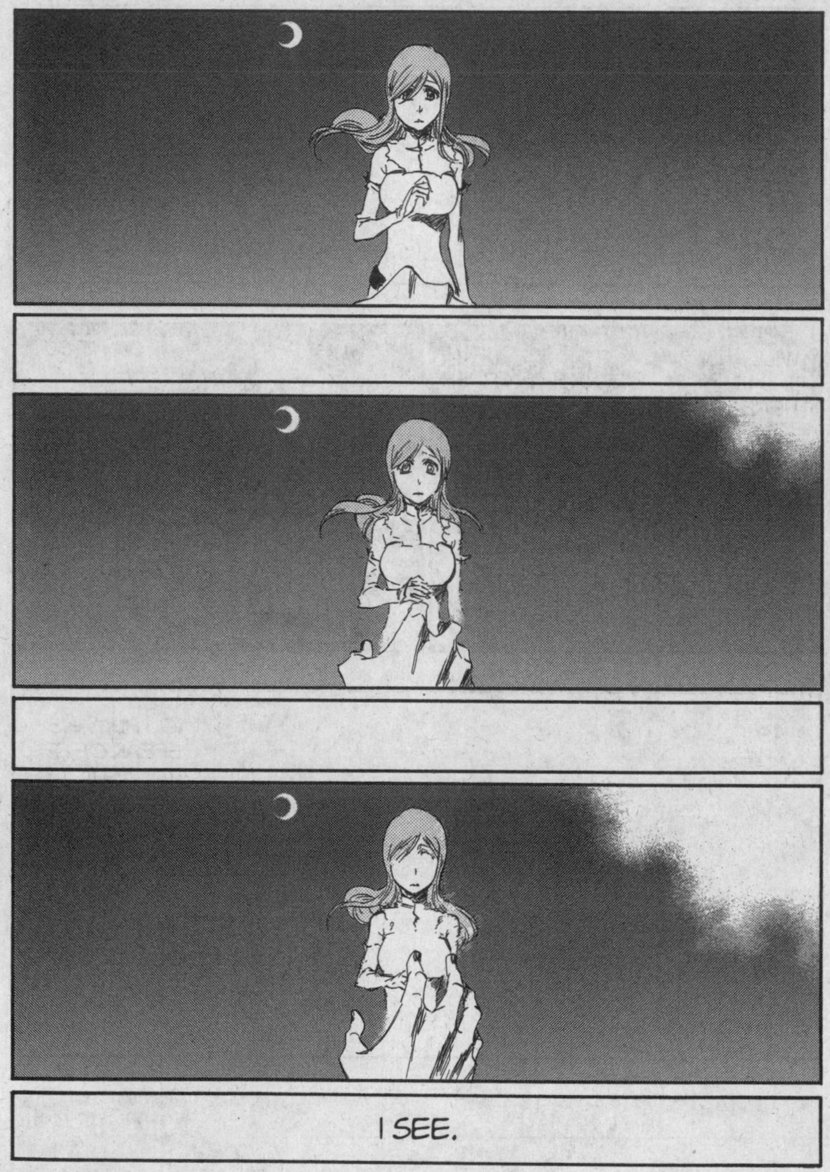
I SEE.

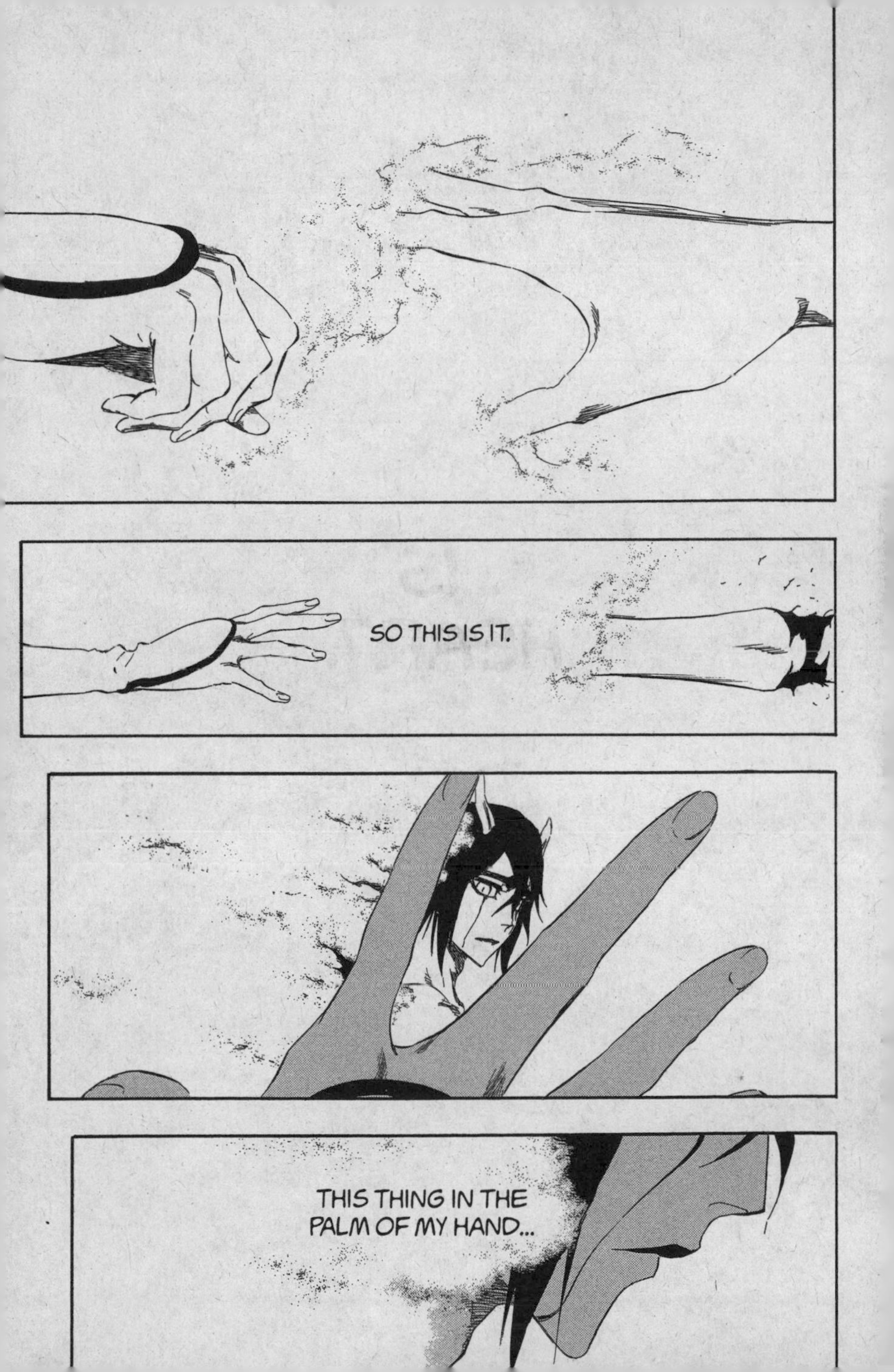
SO THIS IS IT.
THIS THING IN THE PALM OF MY HAND...

...IS
HEART.

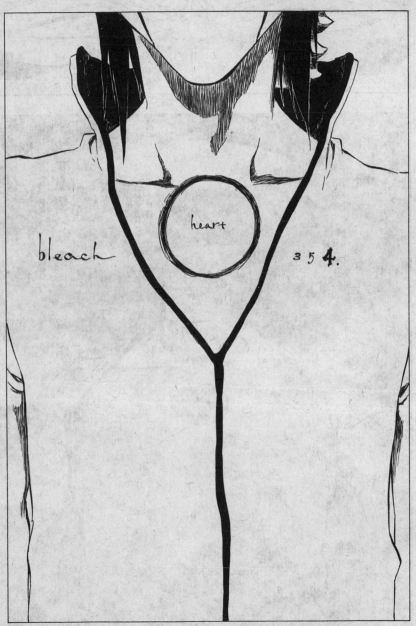

bleach   heart   3 5 4.

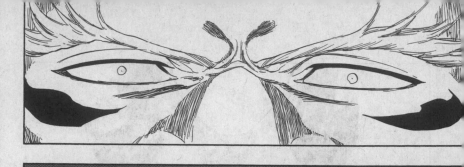

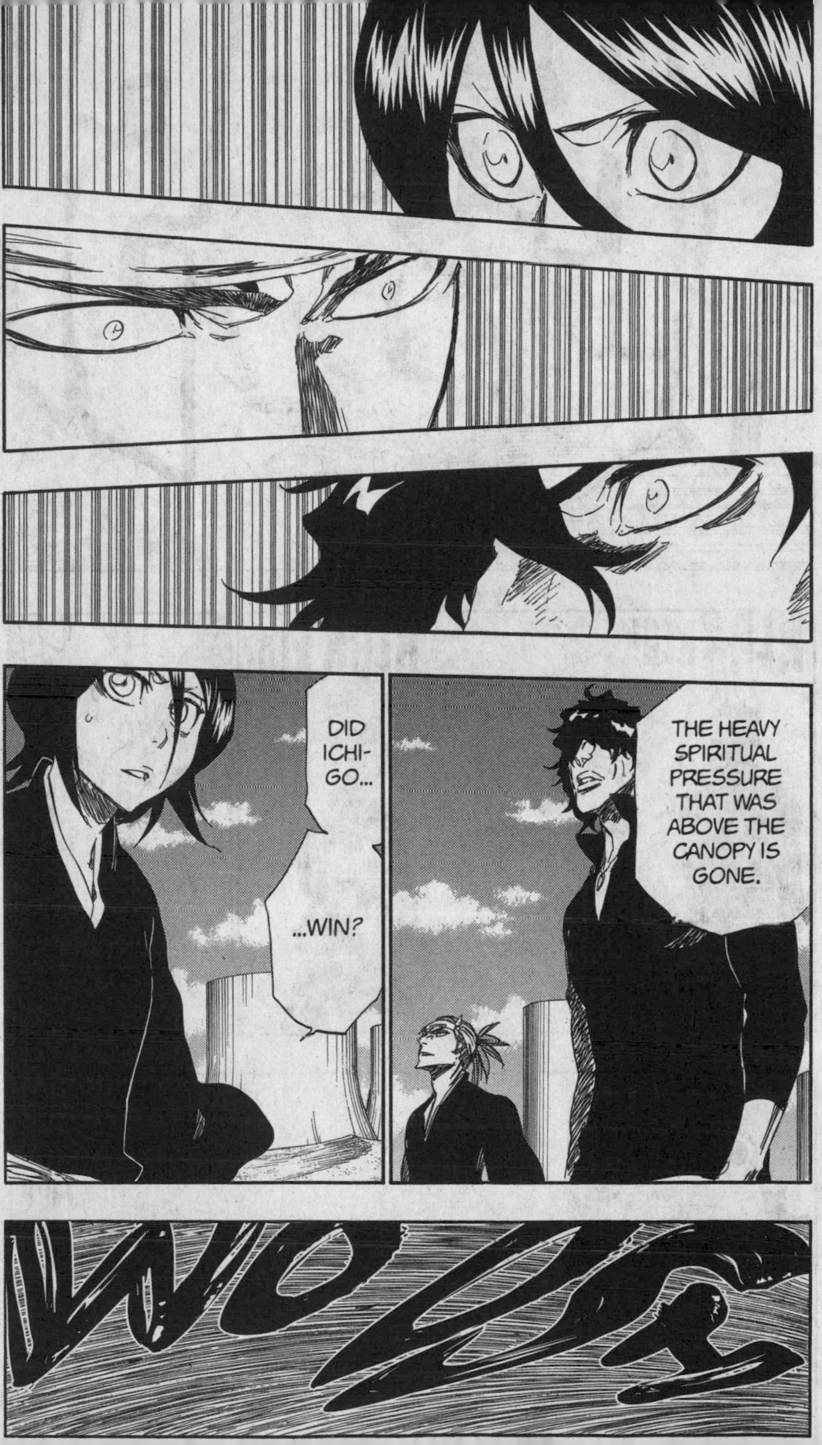
THE HEAVY SPIRITUAL PRESSURE THAT WAS ABOVE THE CANOPY IS GONE.
DID ICHIGO...
...WIN?

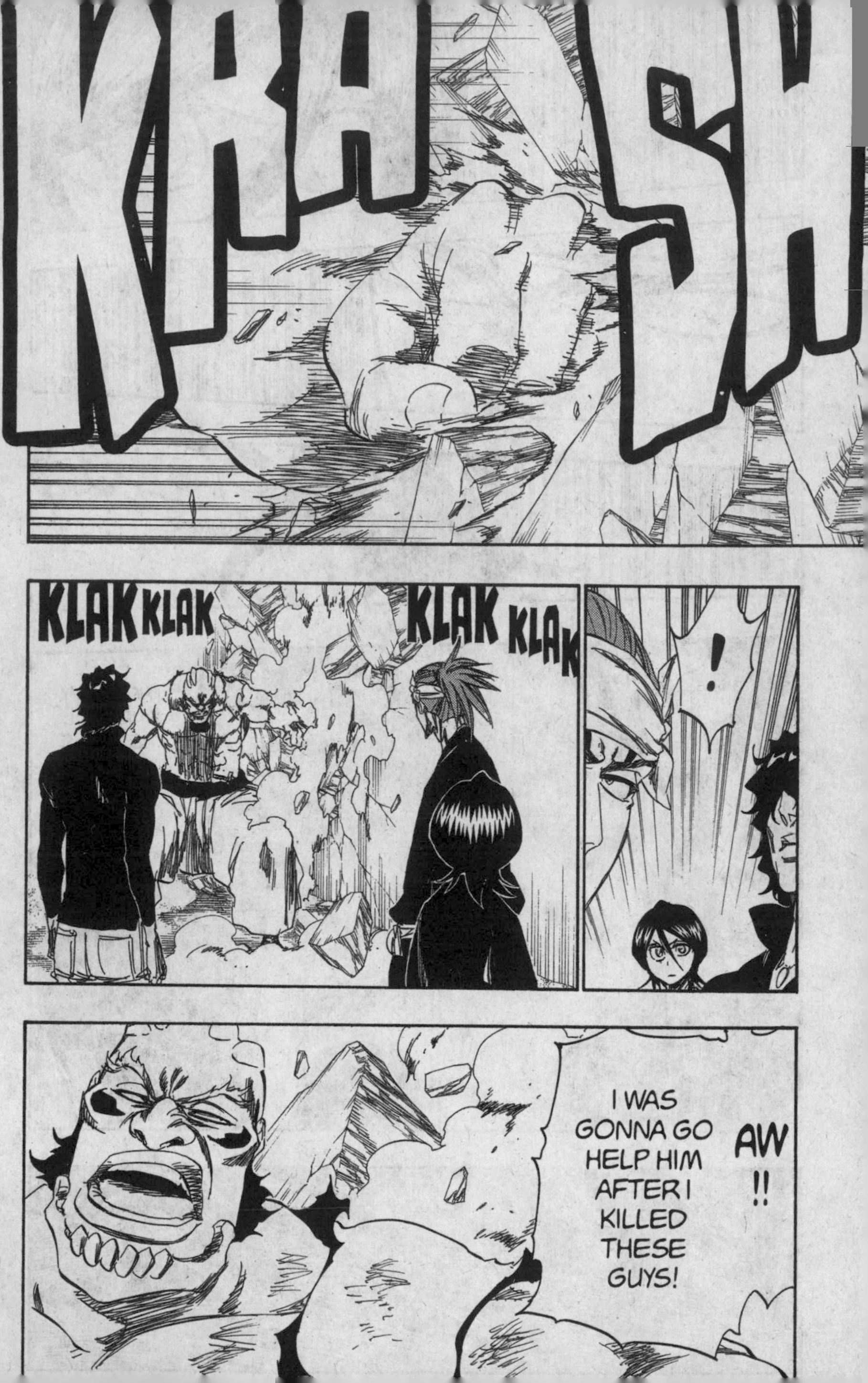
KRASH
!
KLAK KLAK
KLAK KLAK
AW!!
I WAS GONNA GO HELP HIM AFTER I KILLED THESE GUYS!

READ THIS WAY

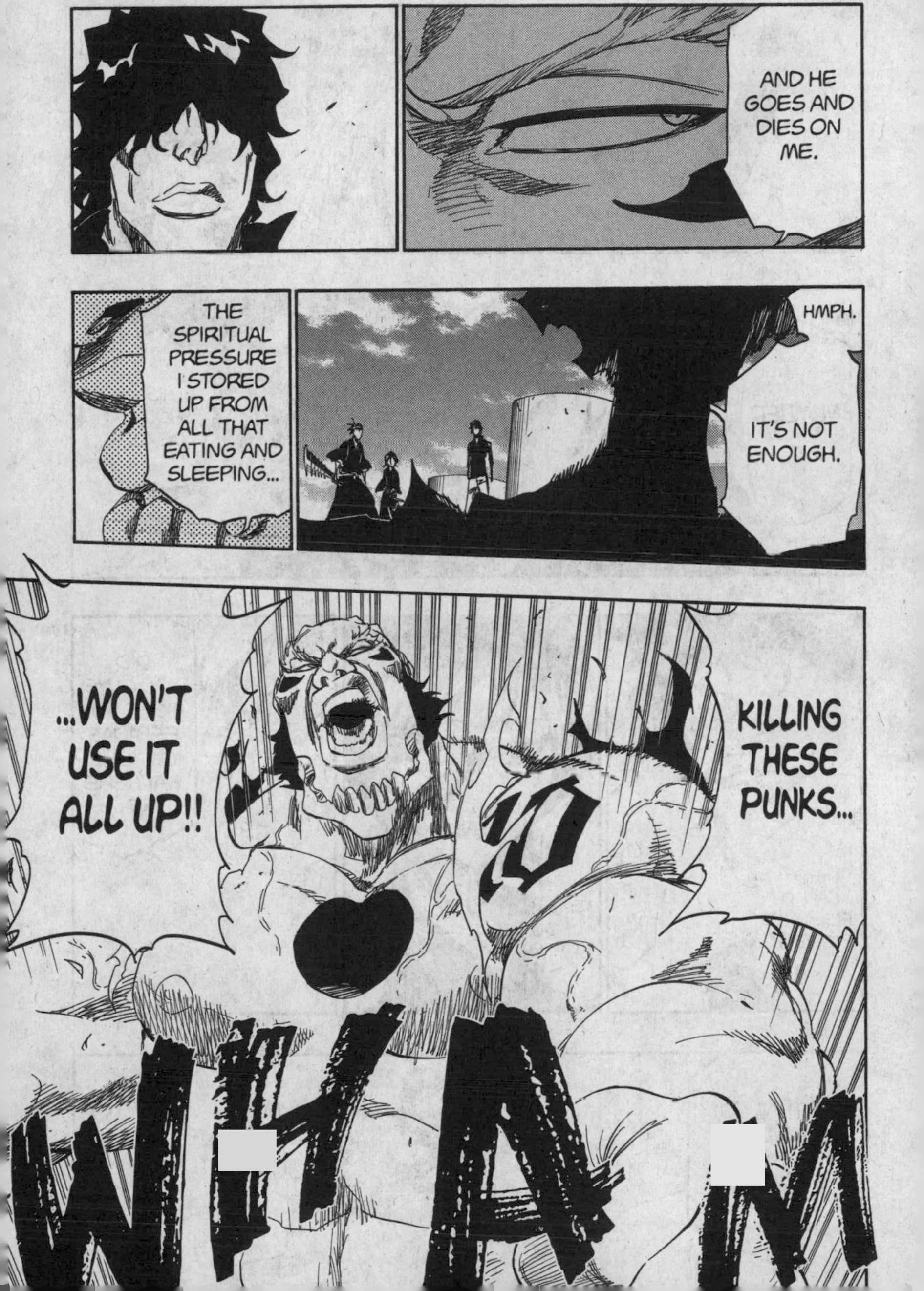
AND HE GOES AND DIES ON ME.
HMPH.
IT'S NOT ENOUGH.
THE SPIRITUAL PRESSURE I STORED UP FROM ALL THAT EATING AND SLEEPING...
KILLING THESE PUNKS...
...WON'T USE IT ALL UP!!
WHAM

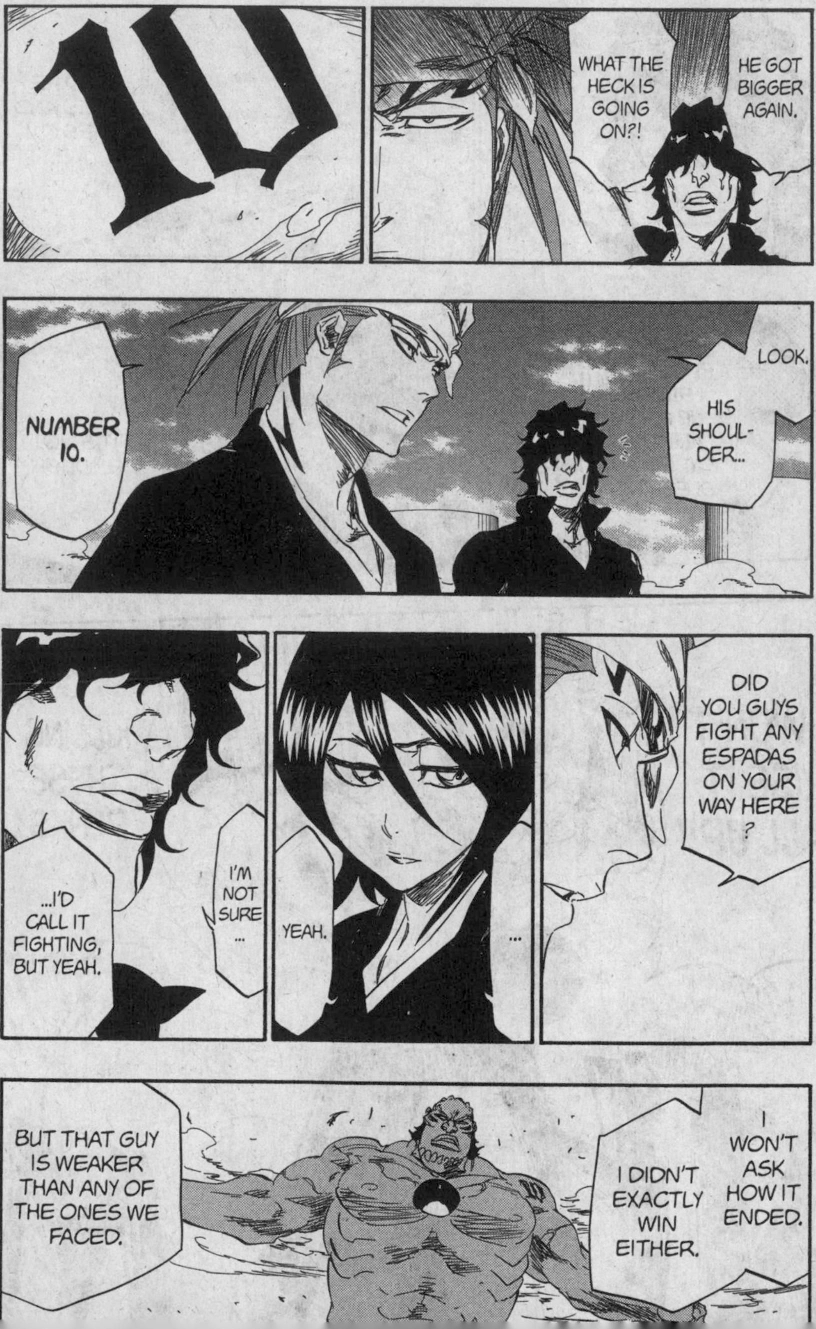
HE GOT BIGGER AGAIN.
WHAT THE HECK IS GOING ON?!
LOOK.
HIS SHOUL-DER...
NUMBER 10.
DID YOU GUYS FIGHT ANY ESPADAS ON YOUR WAY HERE?
...
YEAH.
I'M NOT SURE...
...I'D CALL IT FIGHTING, BUT YEAH.
I WON'T ASK HOW IT ENDED.
I DIDN'T EXACTLY WIN EITHER.
BUT THAT GUY IS WEAKER THAN ANY OF THE ONES WE FACED.

READ THIS WAY

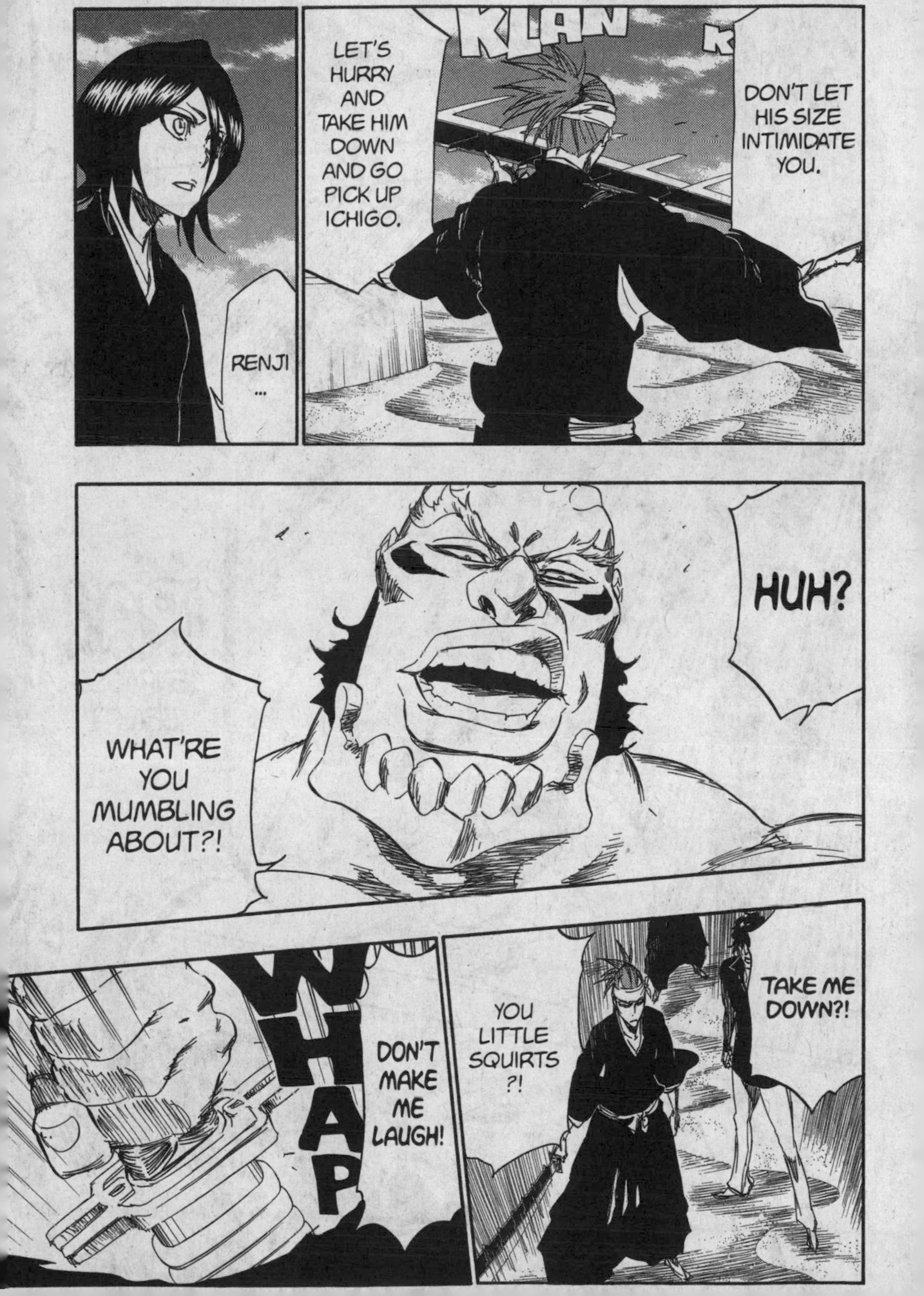
KLAN
K
DON'T LET HIS SIZE INTIMIDATE YOU.
LET'S HURRY AND TAKE HIM DOWN AND GO PICK UP ICHIGO.
RENJI ...
HUH?
WHAT'RE YOU MUMBLING ABOUT?!
TAKE ME DOWN?!
YOU LITTLE SQUIRTS?!
DON'T MAKE ME LAUGH!
WHAP

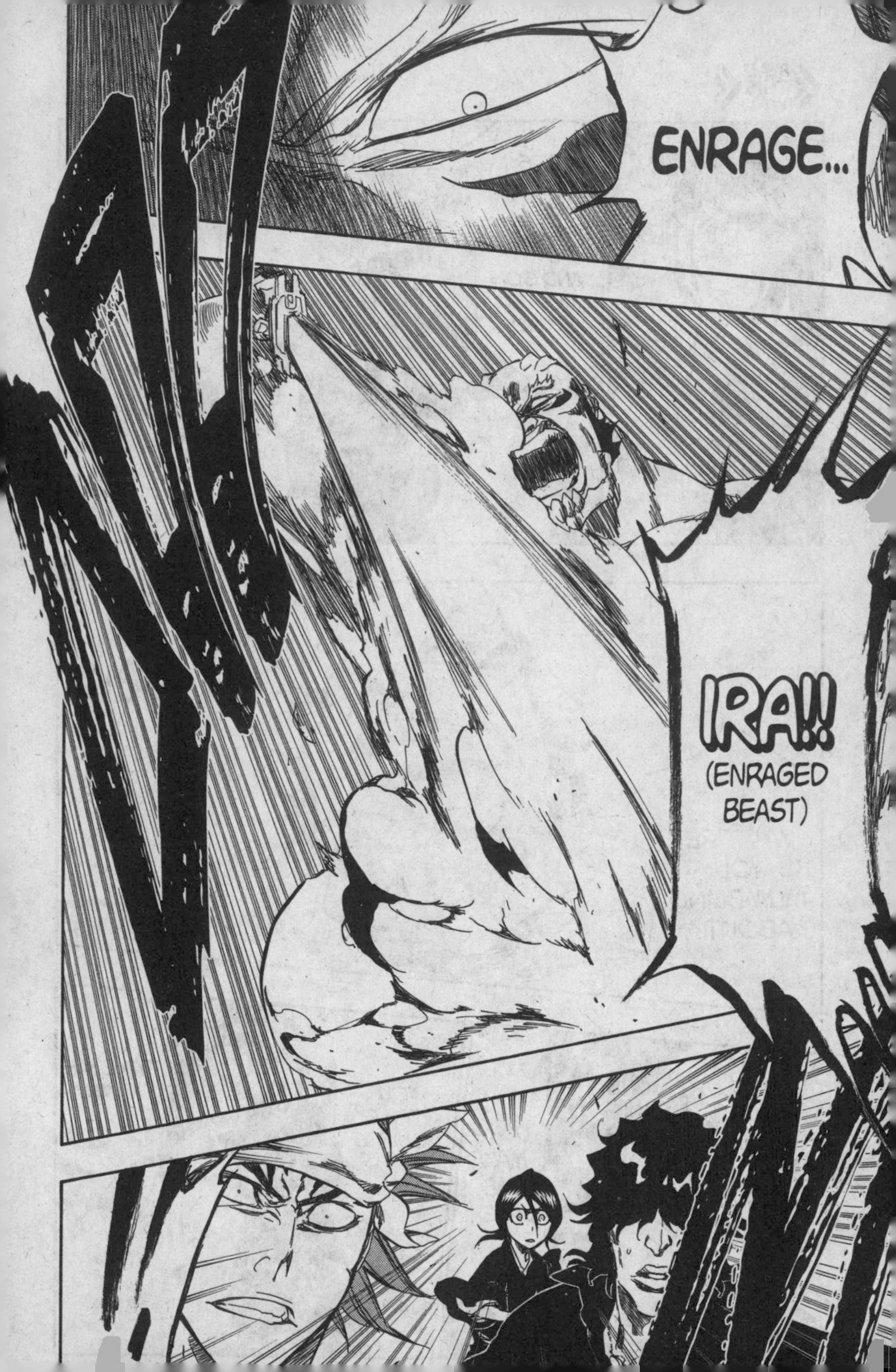
ENRAGE...
IRA!!
(ENRAGED
BEAST)

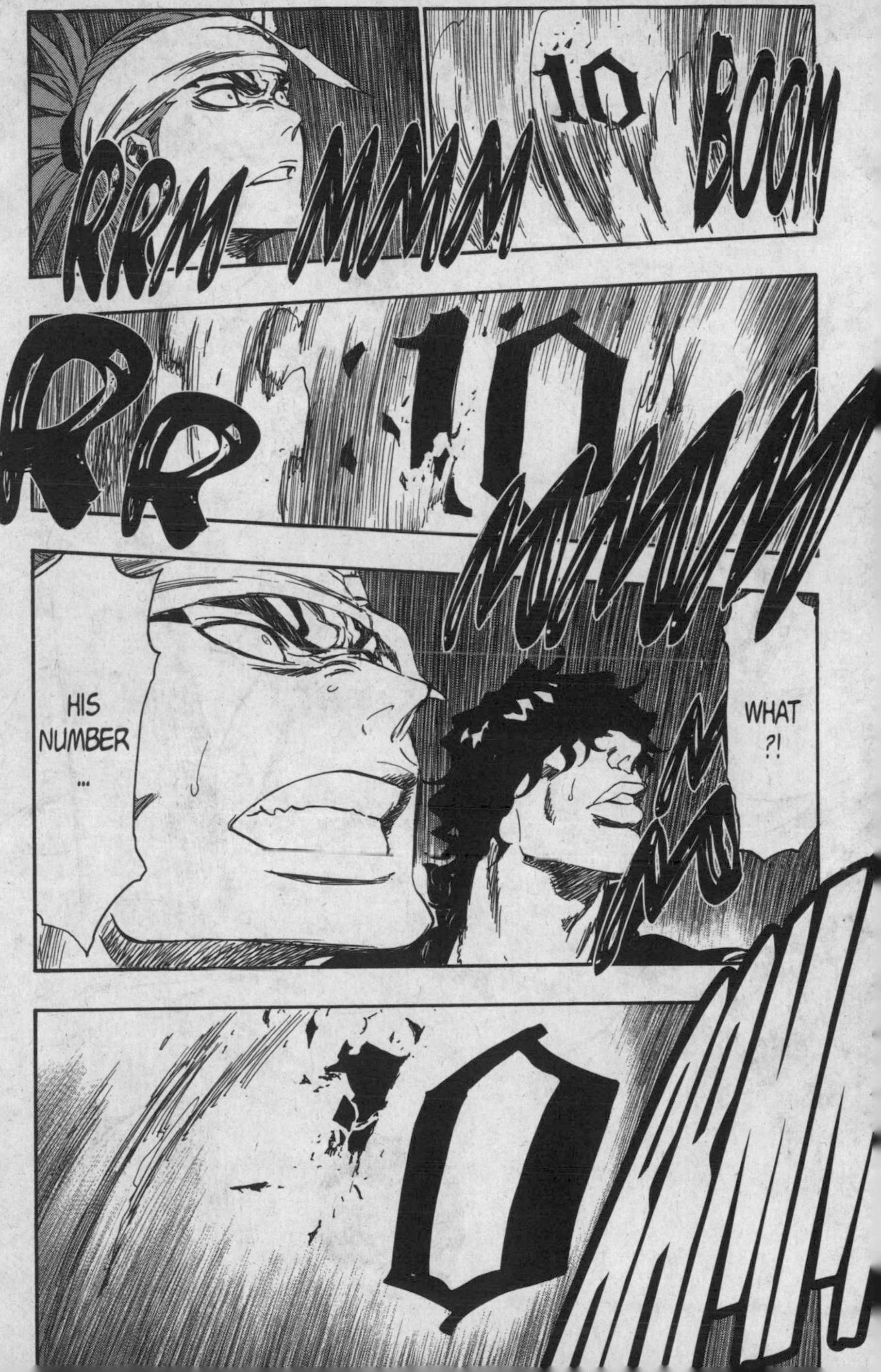
10
BOOM
RRM MMM
RR
10
WHAT ?!
HIS NUMBER ...
0

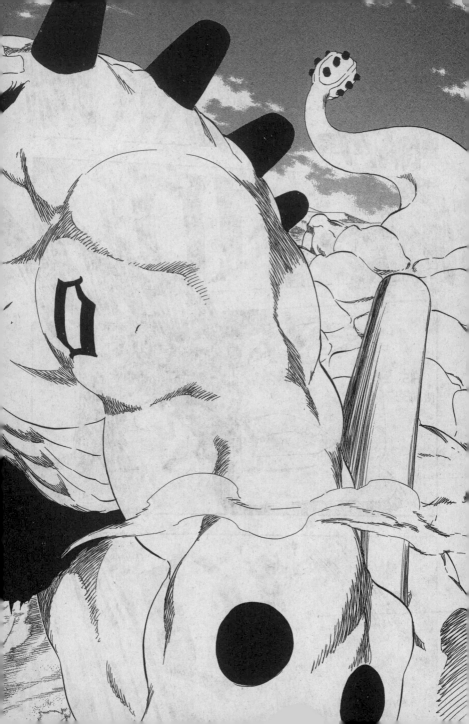

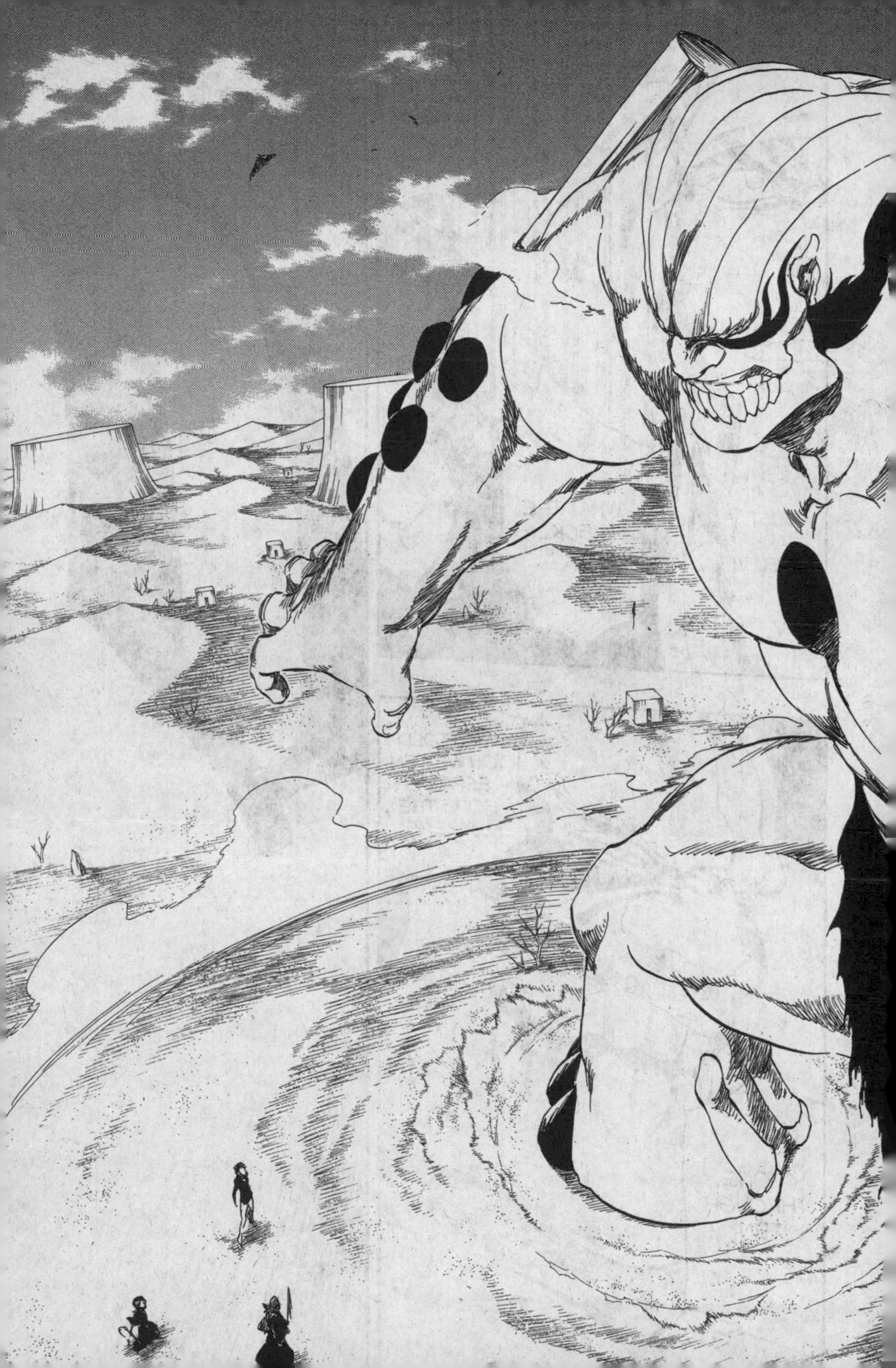

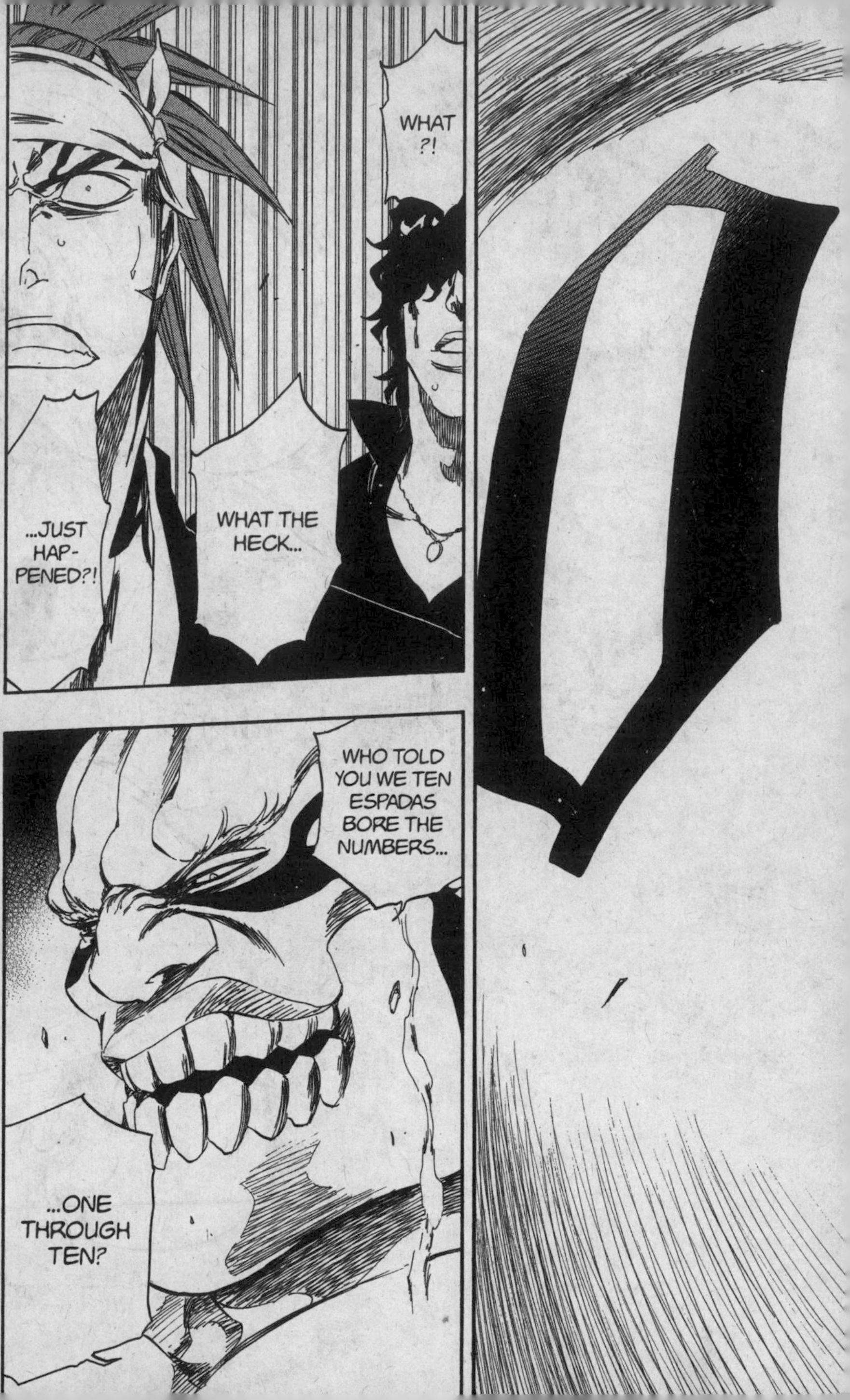
WHAT ?!
WHAT THE HECK...
...JUST HAP-PENED?!
WHO TOLD YOU WE TEN ESPADAS BORE THE NUMBERS...
...ONE THROUGH TEN?

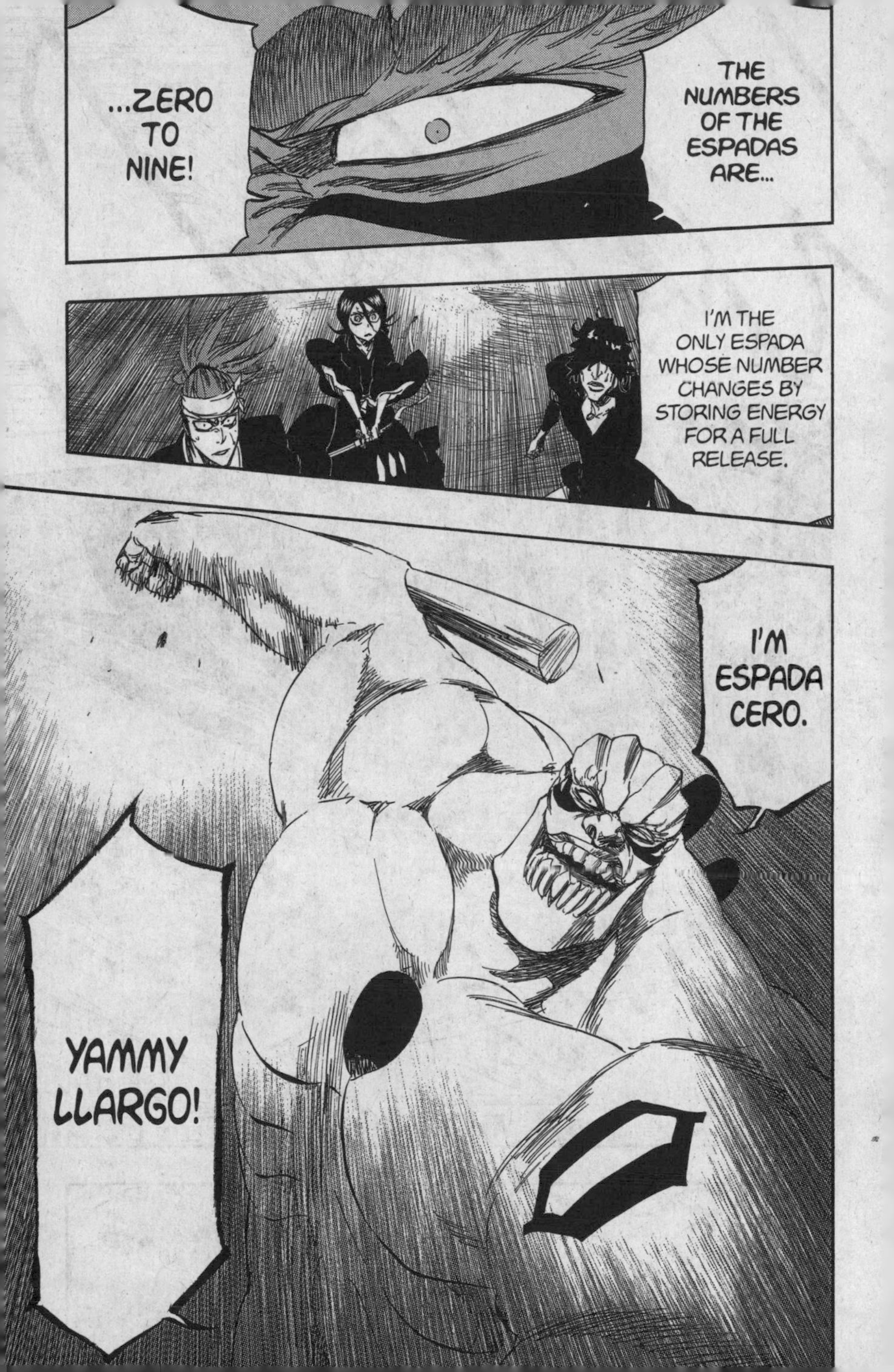
THE NUMBERS OF THE ESPADAS ARE...
...ZERO TO NINE!
I'M THE ONLY ESPADA WHOSE NUMBER CHANGES BY STORING ENERGY FOR A FULL RELEASE.
I'M ESPADA CERO.
YAMMY LLARGO!

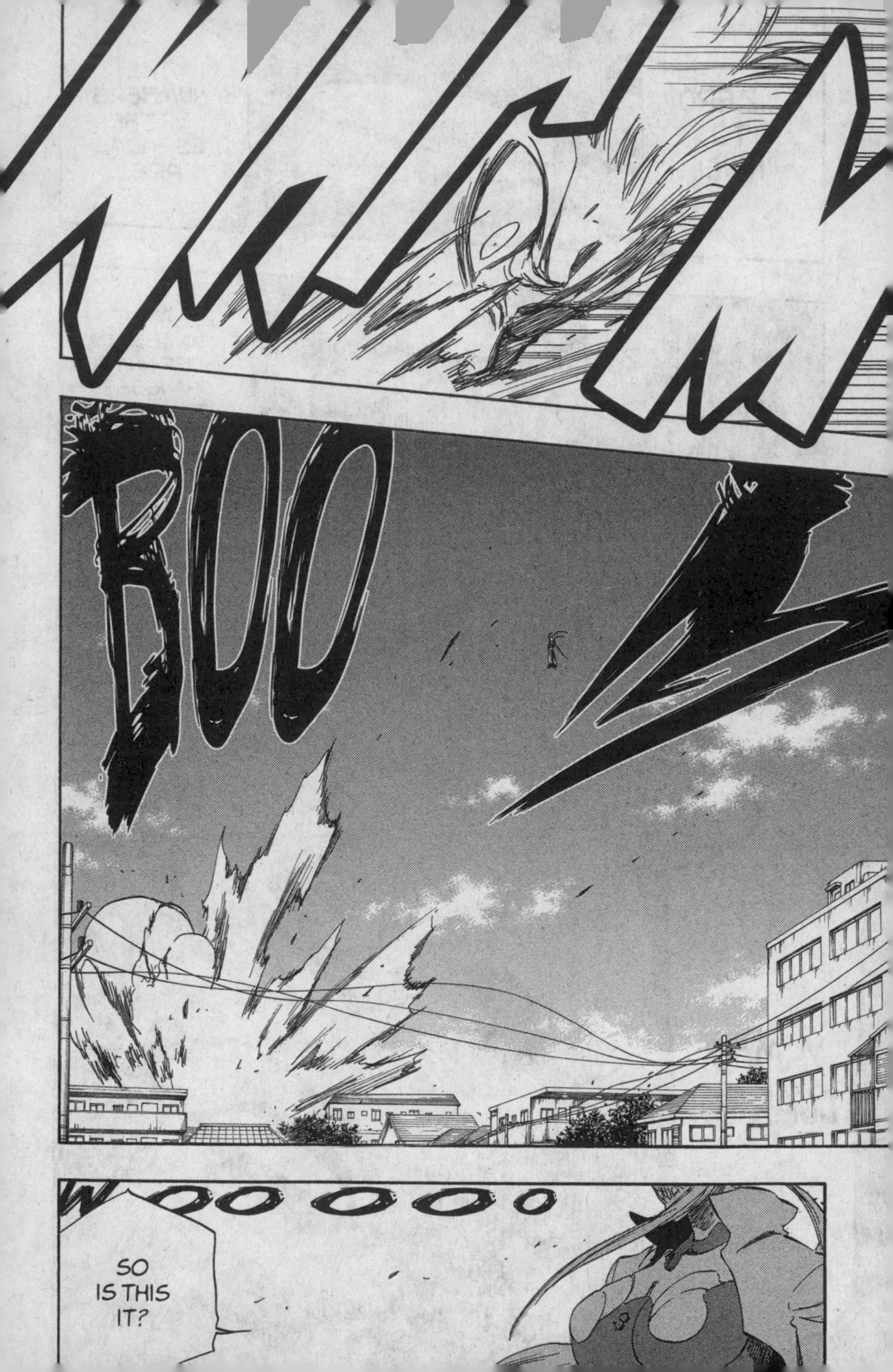
BOOM
WOOOOOO
SO IS THIS IT?

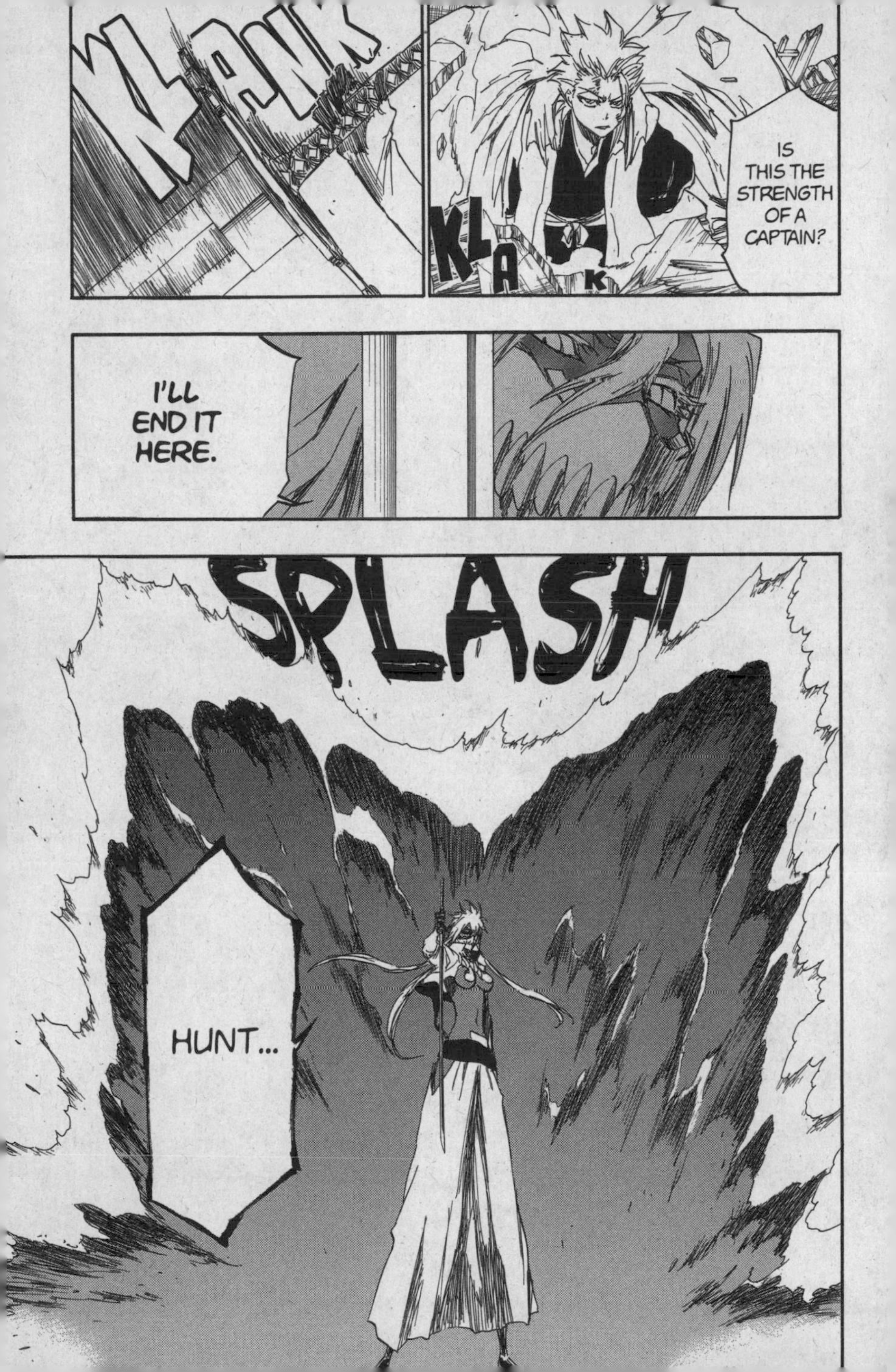
IS THIS THE STRENGTH OF A CAPTAIN?
KLAK
KLANK
I'LL END IT HERE.
SPLASH
HUNT...

See.

here

it

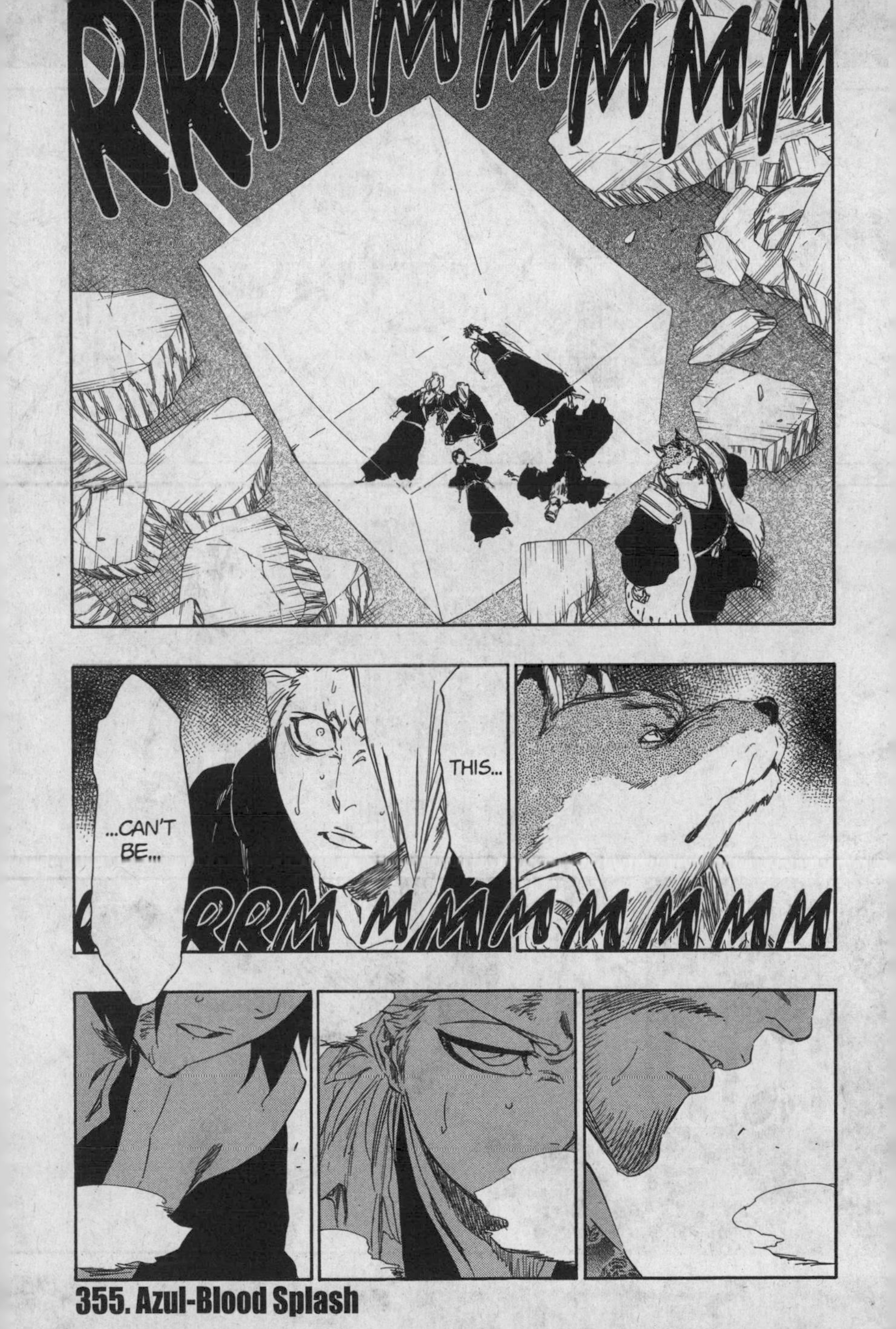
RRMMMMMMMMM
THIS...
...CAN'T BE...
RRMMMMMMMMMM

355. Azul-Blood Splash

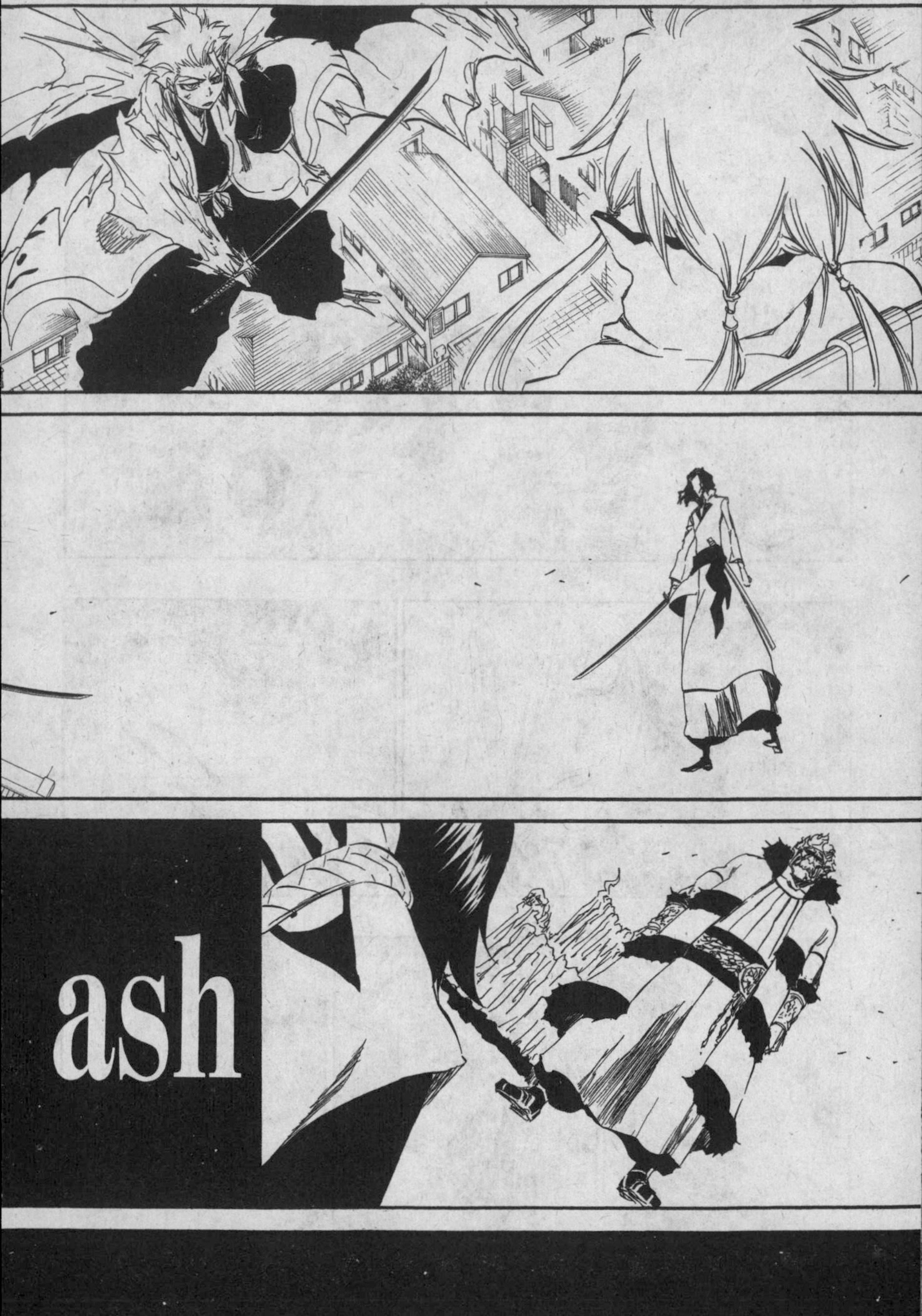
ash

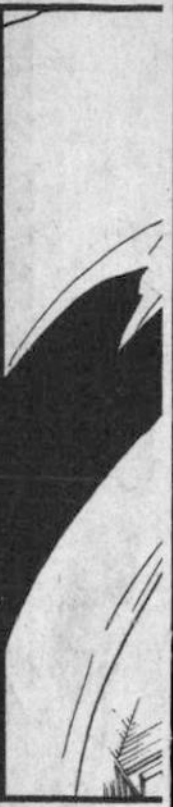

BLEACH

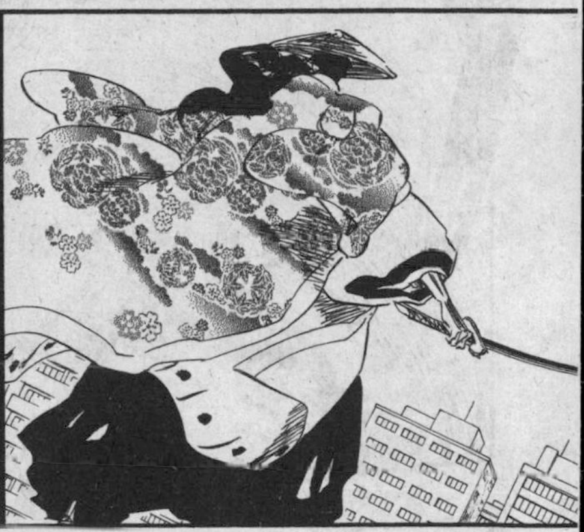

355. Azul-Blood Spl

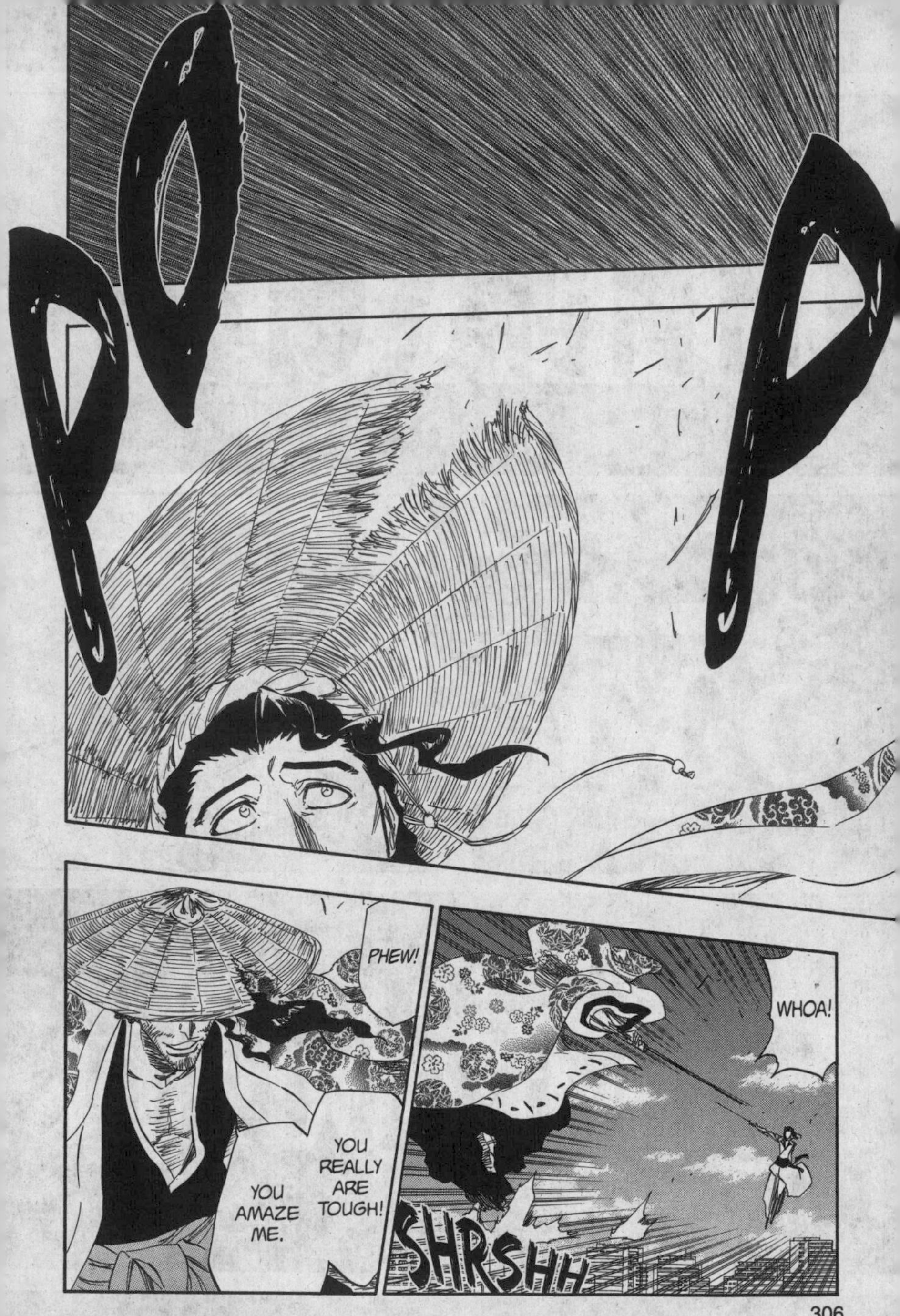
POP
WHOA!
SHRSHH
PHEW!
YOU REALLY ARE TOUGH!
YOU AMAZE ME.

READ THIS WAY

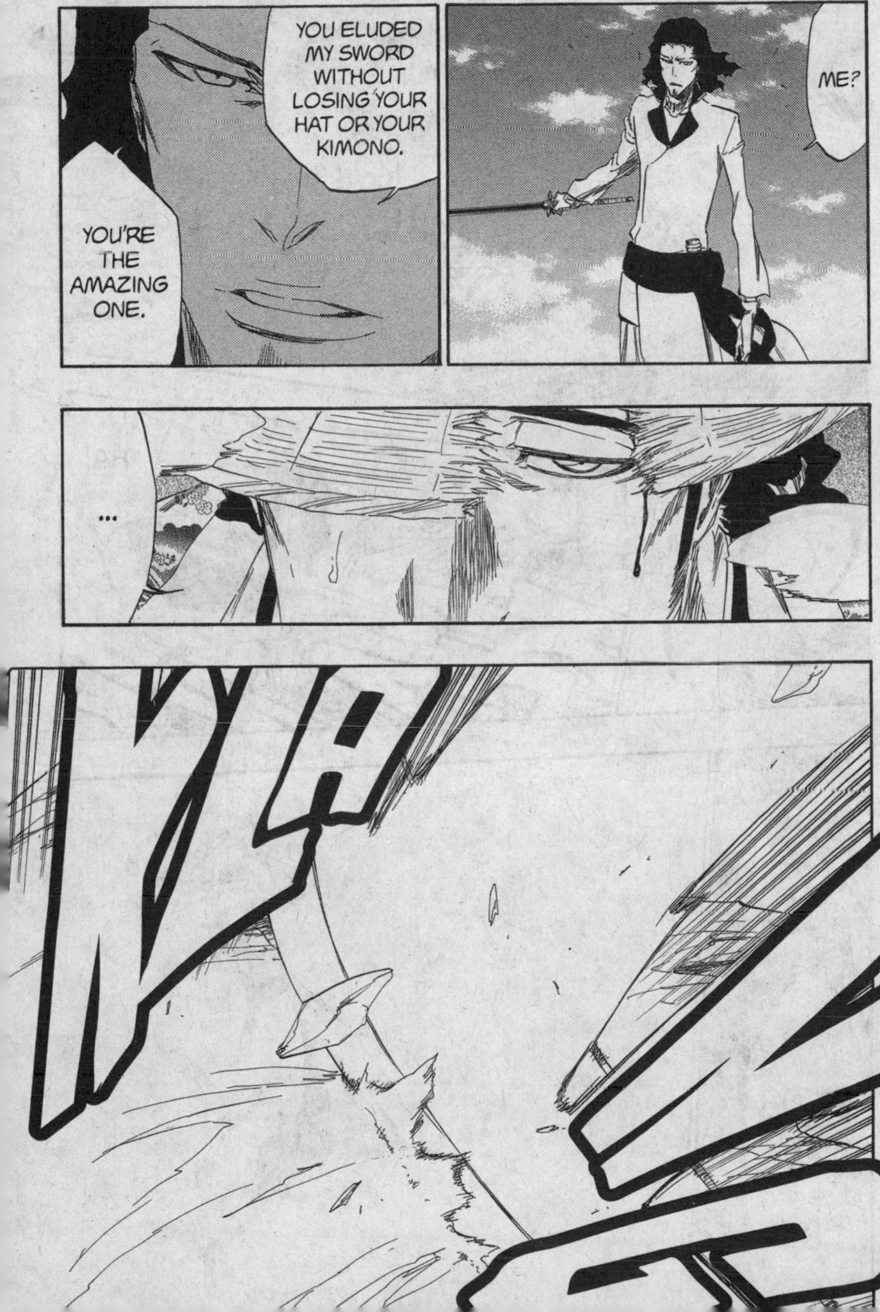
ME?
YOU ELUDED MY SWORD WITHOUT LOSING YOUR HAT OR YOUR KIMONO.
YOU'RE THE AMAZING ONE.
...

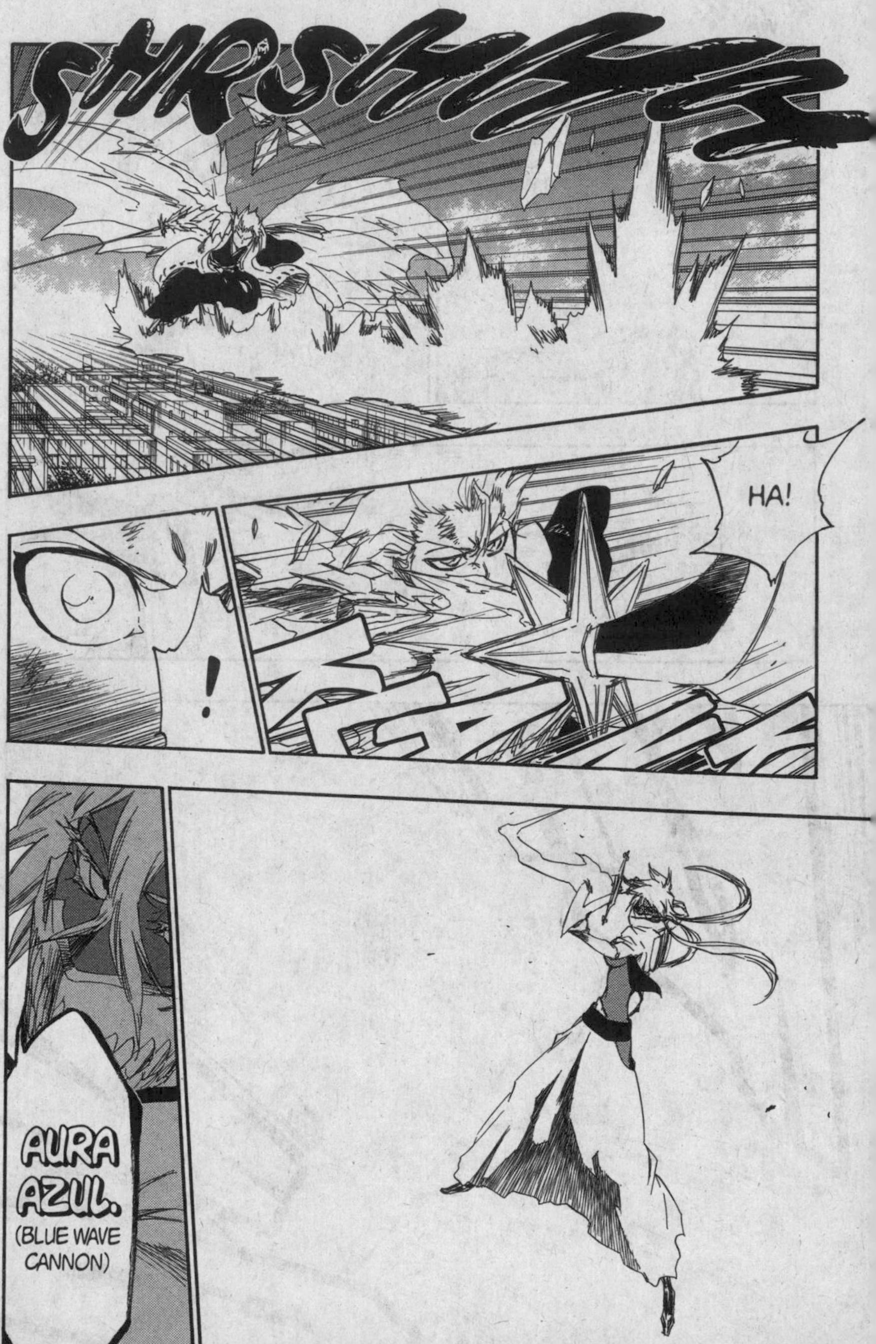
SHASHAA
HA!
!
AURA AZUL.
(BLUE WAVE CANNON)

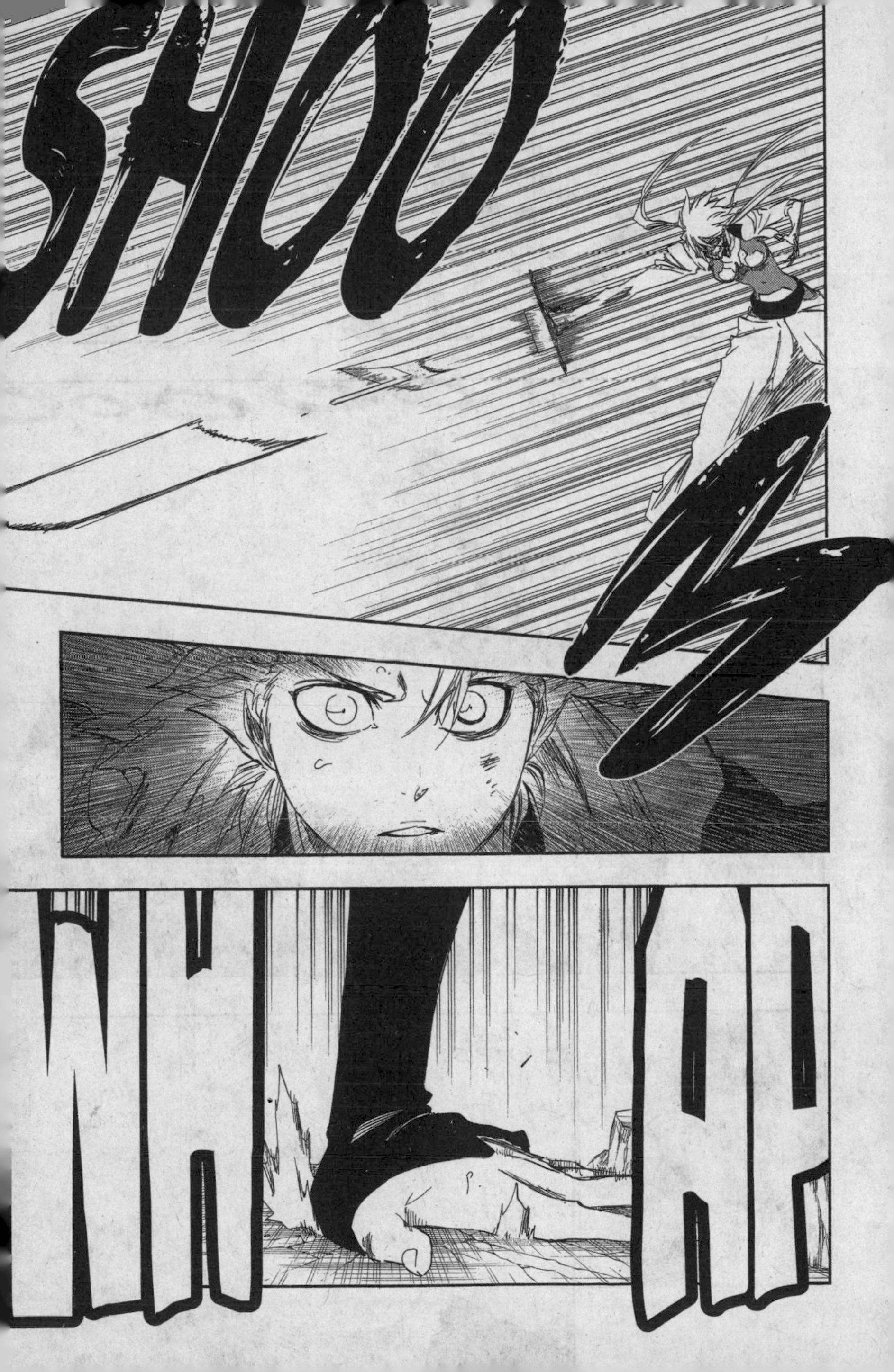
SHOO
OM
WHAP

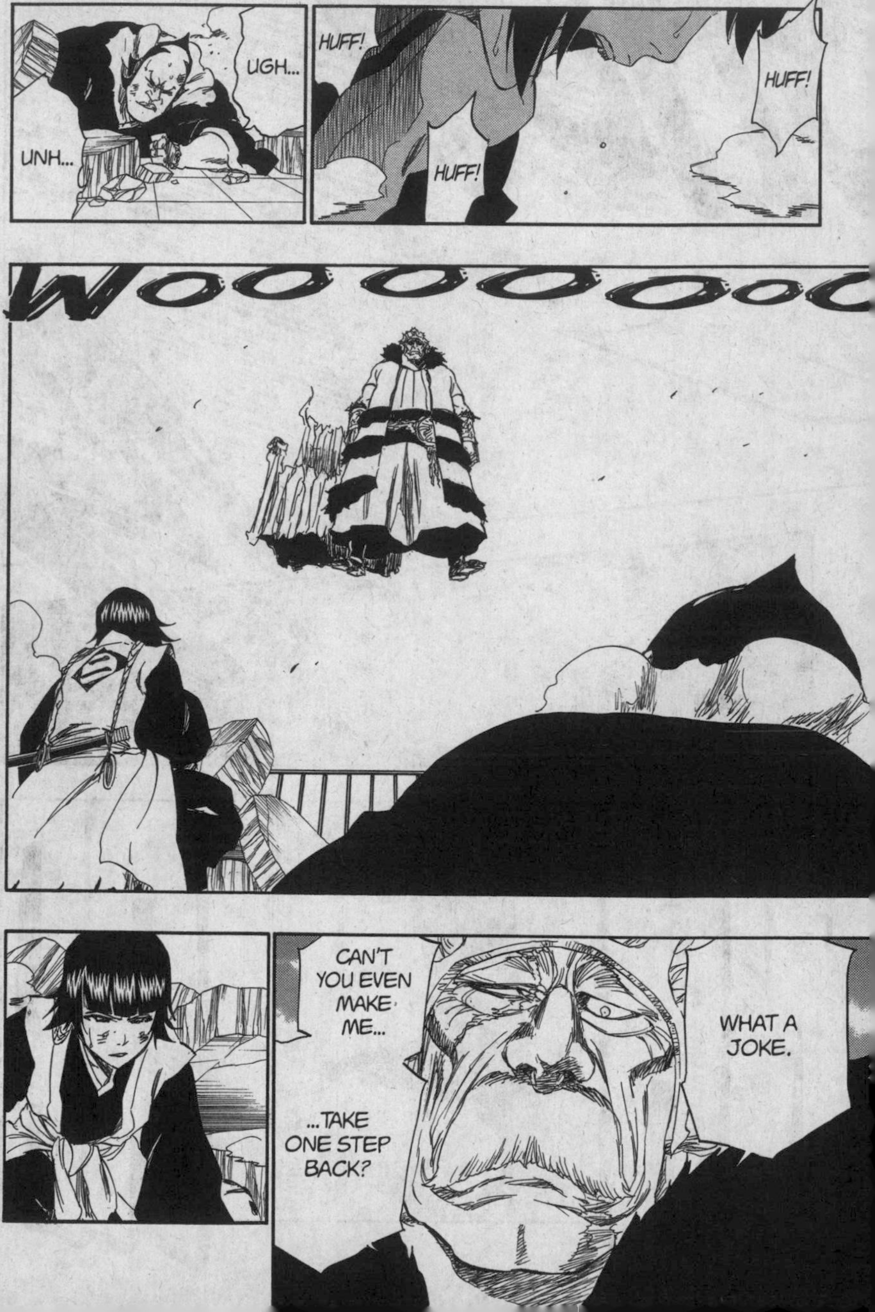
HUFF!
HUFF!
HUFF!
UGH...
UNH...
WOOOOOOC
CAN'T YOU EVEN MAKE ME...
...TAKE ONE STEP BACK?
WHAT A JOKE.

READ THIS WAY

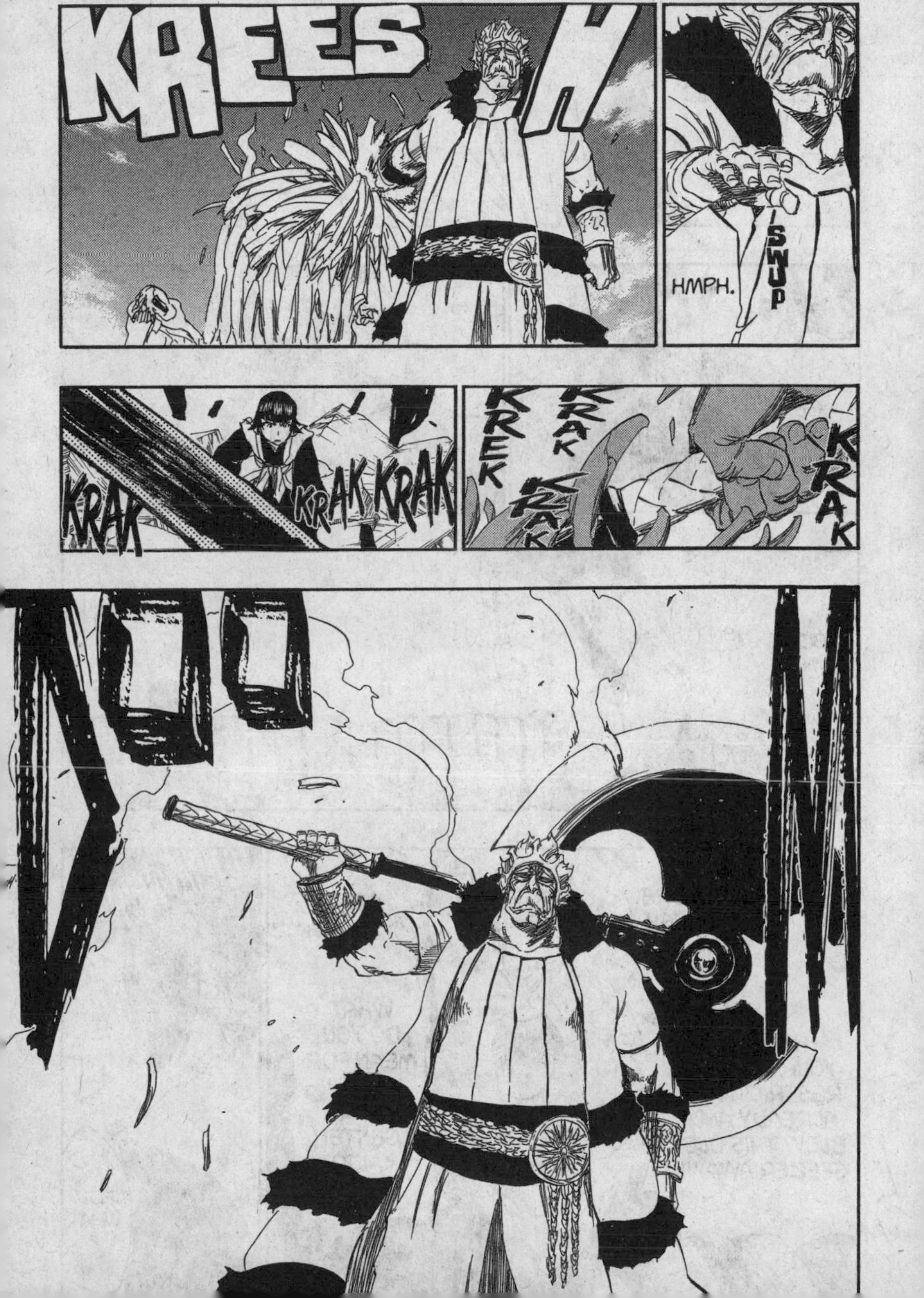
HMPH.
SWUP
KREESH
KREK
KRAK
KRAK
KRAK
KRAK
KRAK KRAK
KRAK

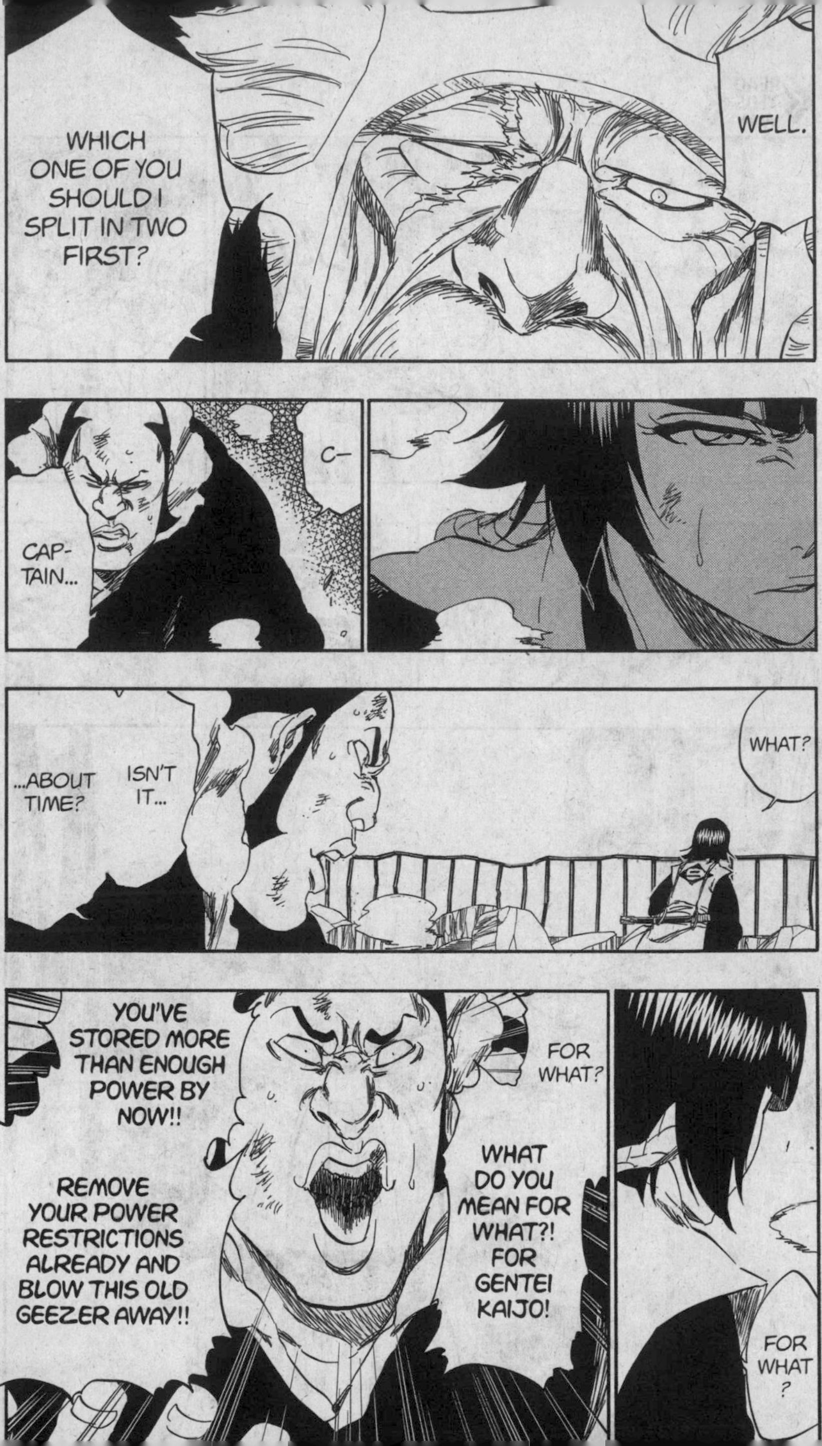
WELL.
WHICH ONE OF YOU SHOULD I SPLIT IN TWO FIRST?
C—
CAP-TAIN...
WHAT?
ISN'T IT...
...ABOUT TIME?
FOR WHAT?
FOR WHAT?
WHAT DO YOU MEAN FOR WHAT?! FOR GENTEI KAIJO!
YOU'VE STORED MORE THAN ENOUGH POWER BY NOW!!
REMOVE YOUR POWER RESTRICTIONS ALREADY AND BLOW THIS OLD GEEZER AWAY!!

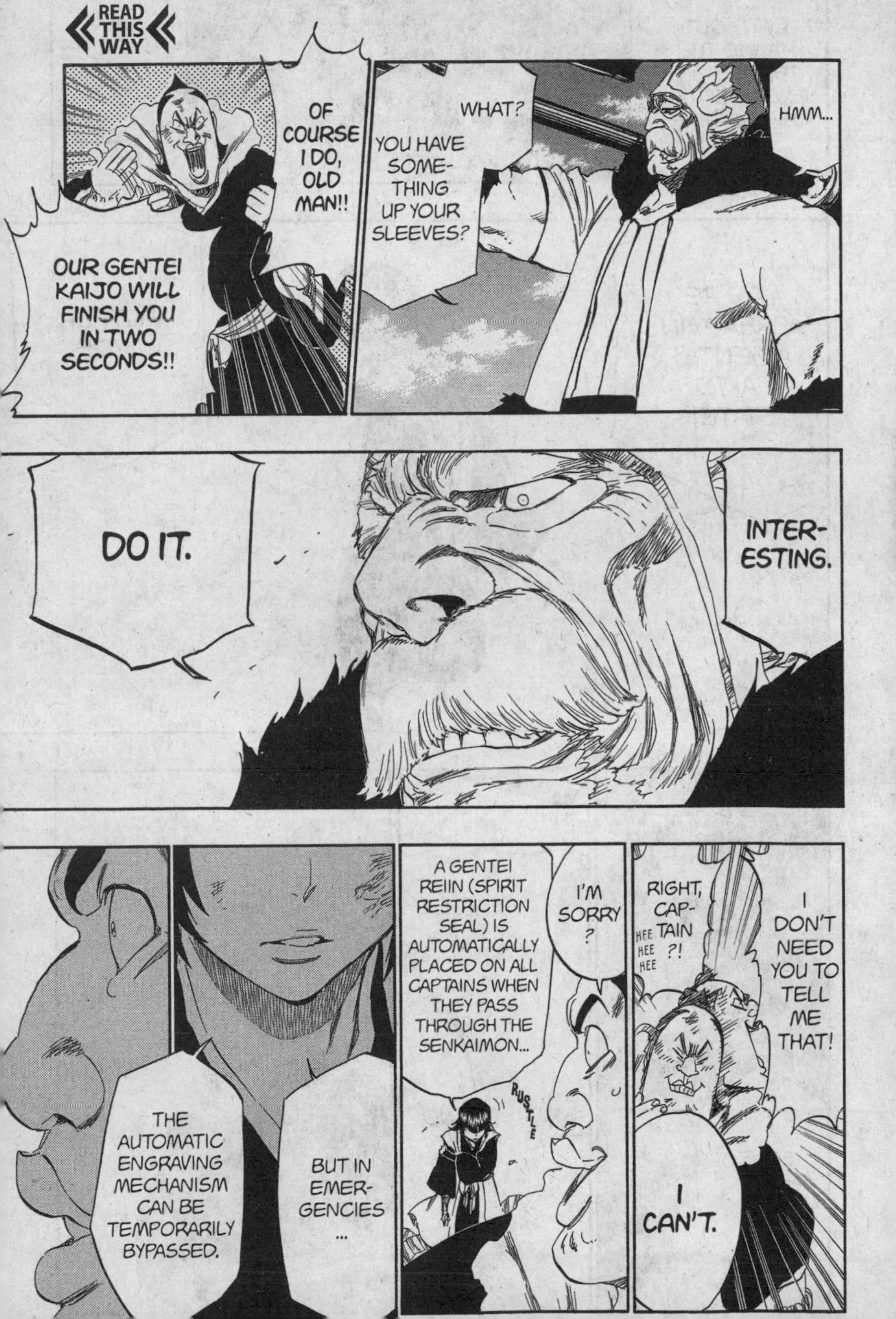
READ THIS WAY
HMM...
WHAT?
YOU HAVE SOMETHING UP YOUR SLEEVES?
OF COURSE I DO, OLD MAN!!
OUR GENTEI KAIJO WILL FINISH YOU IN TWO SECONDS!!
INTER-ESTING.
DO IT.
I DON'T NEED YOU TO TELL ME THAT!
RIGHT, CAPTAIN?!
HEE HEE HEE
I CAN'T.
I'M SORRY?
A GENTEI REIIN (SPIRIT RESTRICTION SEAL) IS AUTOMATICALLY PLACED ON ALL CAPTAINS WHEN THEY PASS THROUGH THE SENKAIMON...
RUSTLE
BUT IN EMERGENCIES...
THE AUTOMATIC ENGRAVING MECHANISM CAN BE TEMPORARILY BYPASSED.

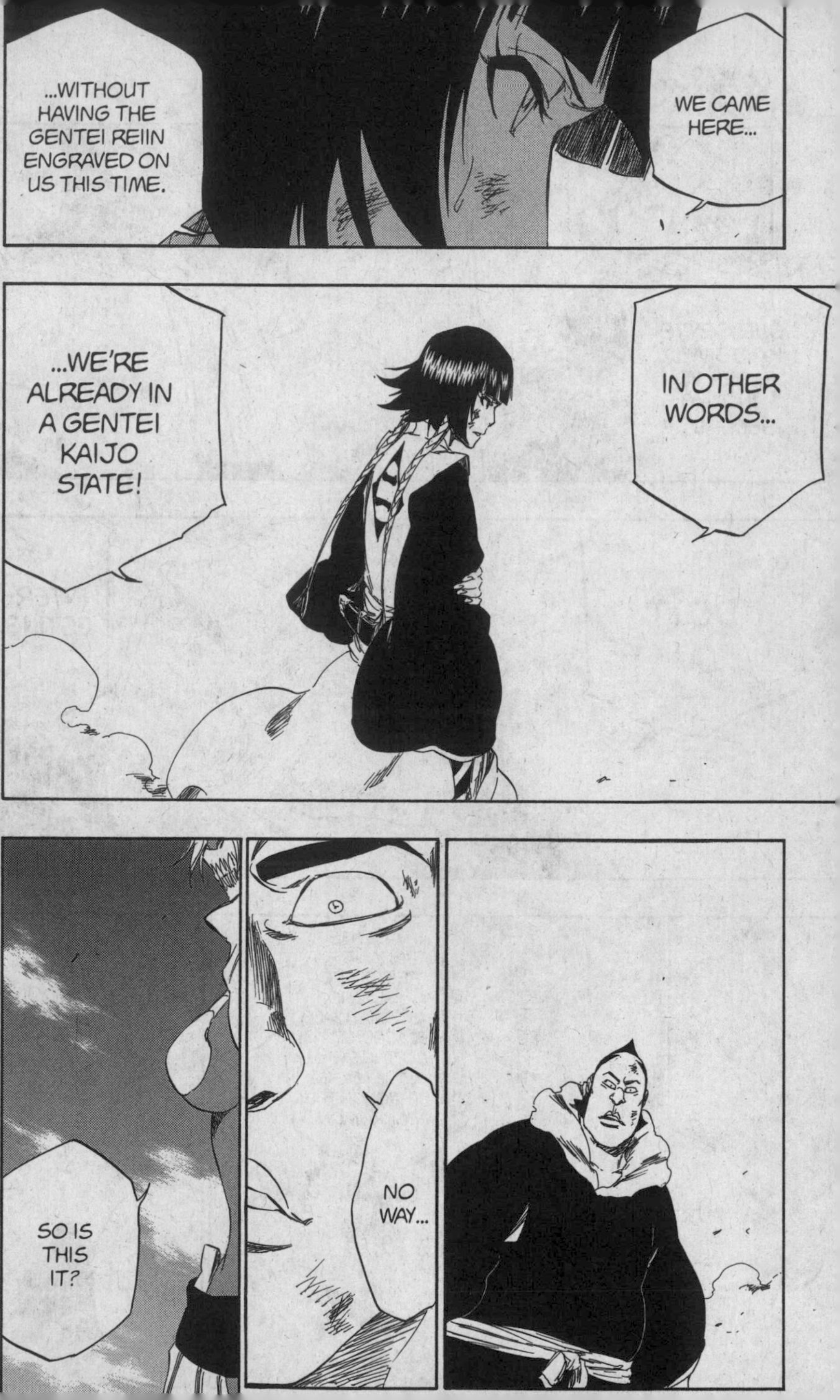
WE CAME HERE...
...WITHOUT HAVING THE GENTEI REIIN ENGRAVED ON US THIS TIME.
IN OTHER WORDS...
...WE'RE ALREADY IN A GENTEI KAIJO STATE!
NO WAY...
SO IS THIS IT?

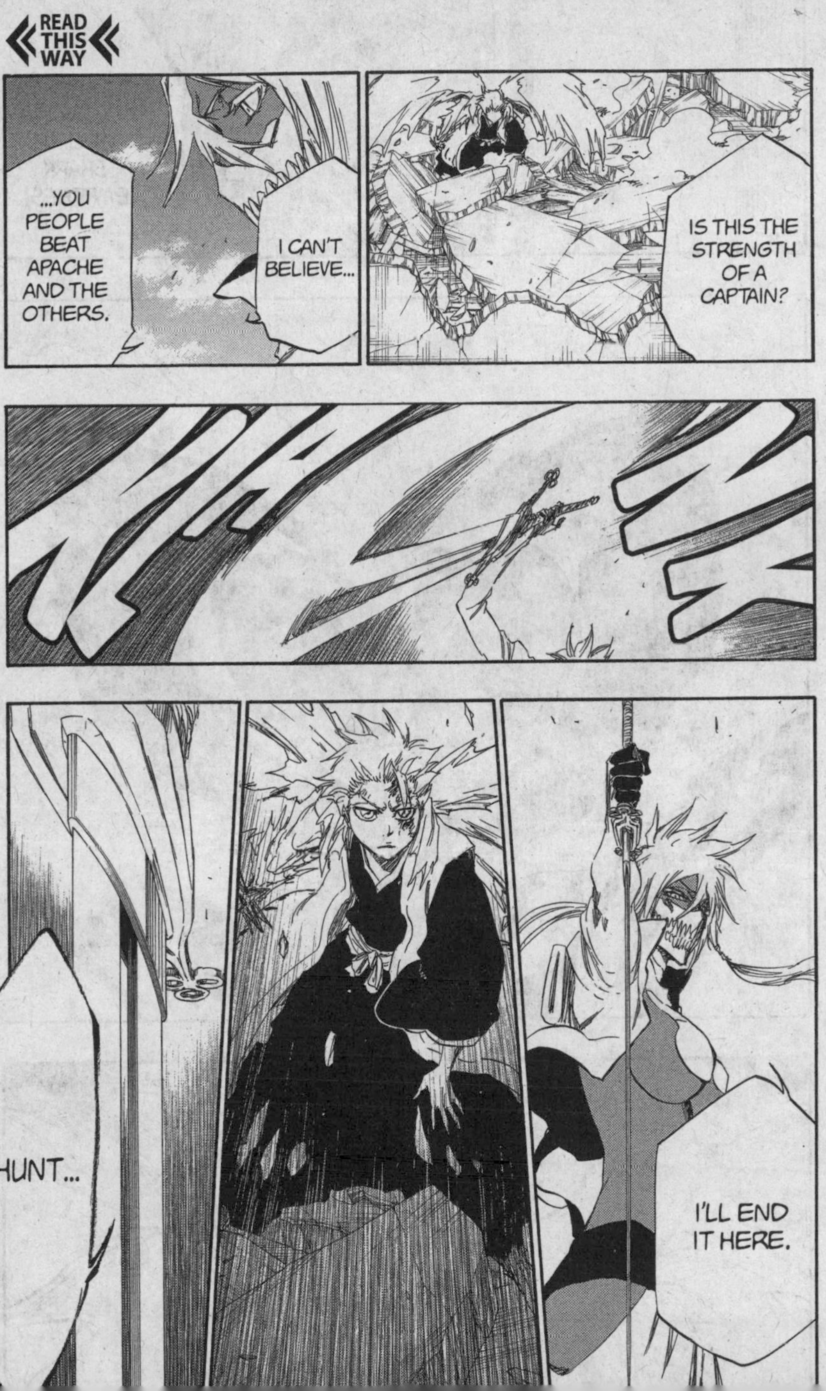
READ THIS WAY
IS THIS THE STRENGTH OF A CAPTAIN?
I CAN'T BELIEVE...
...YOU PEOPLE BEAT APACHE AND THE OTHERS.
I'LL END IT HERE.
HUNT...

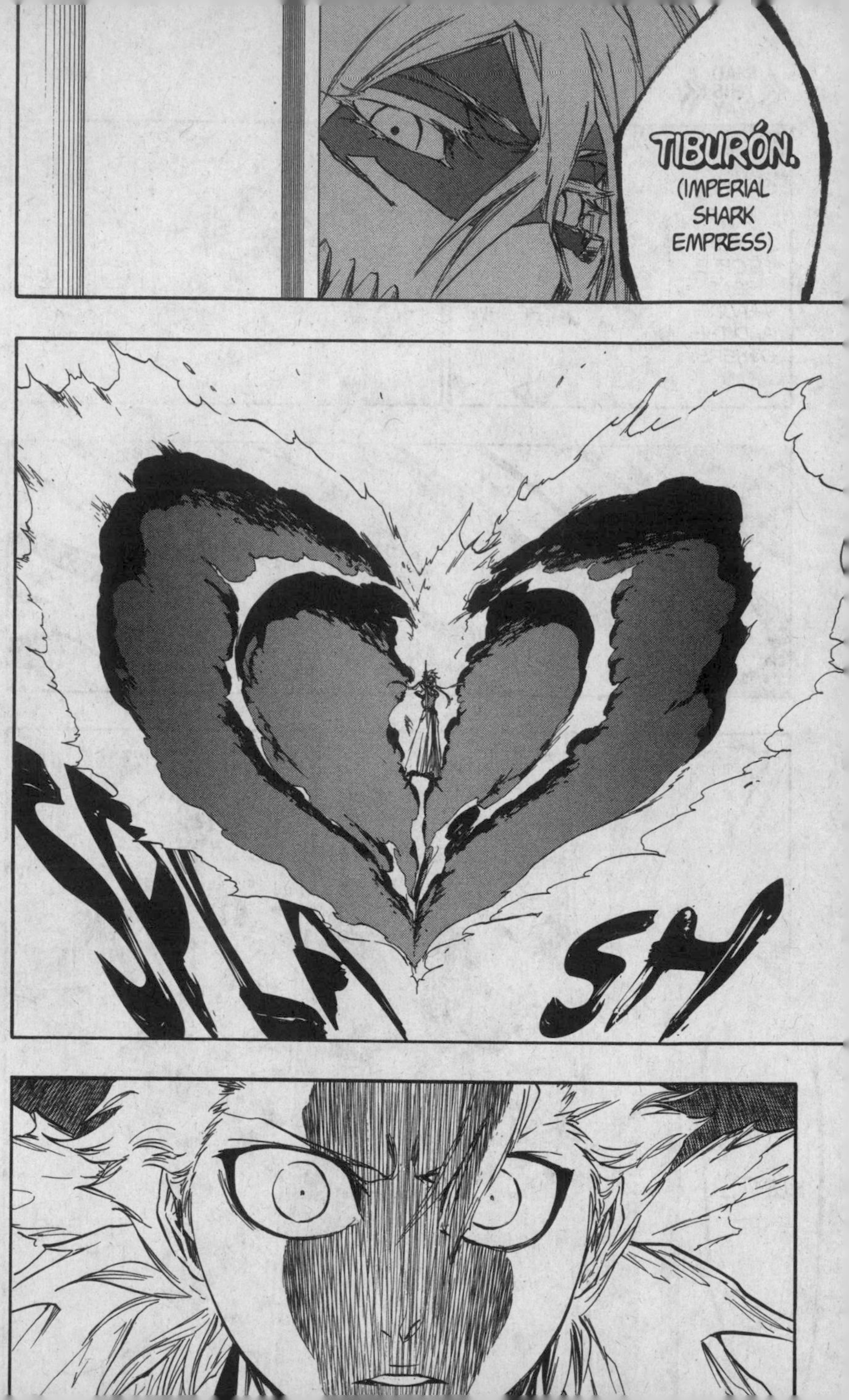
TIBURÓN.
(IMPERIAL SHARK EMPRESS)
SPLASH

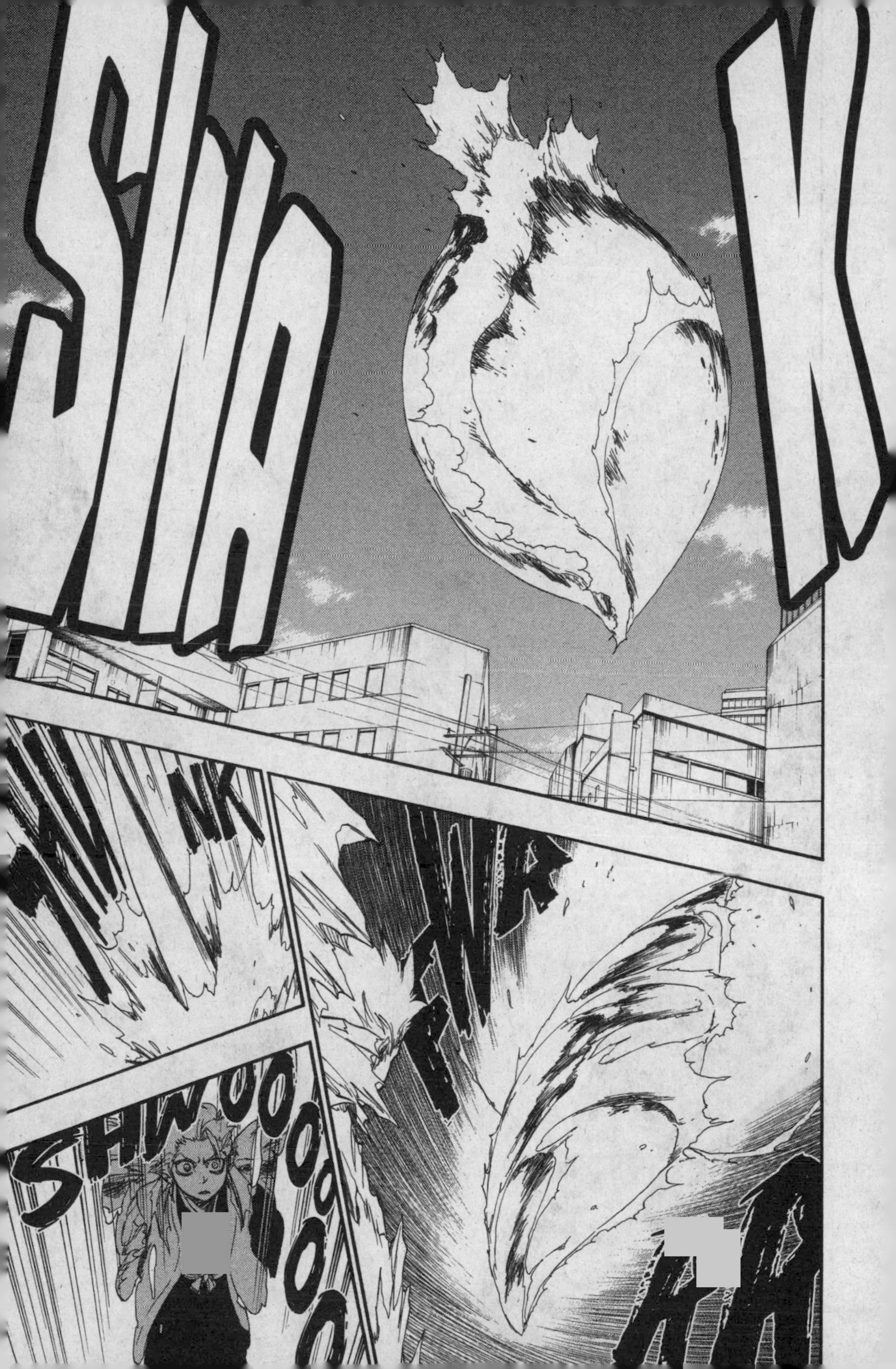

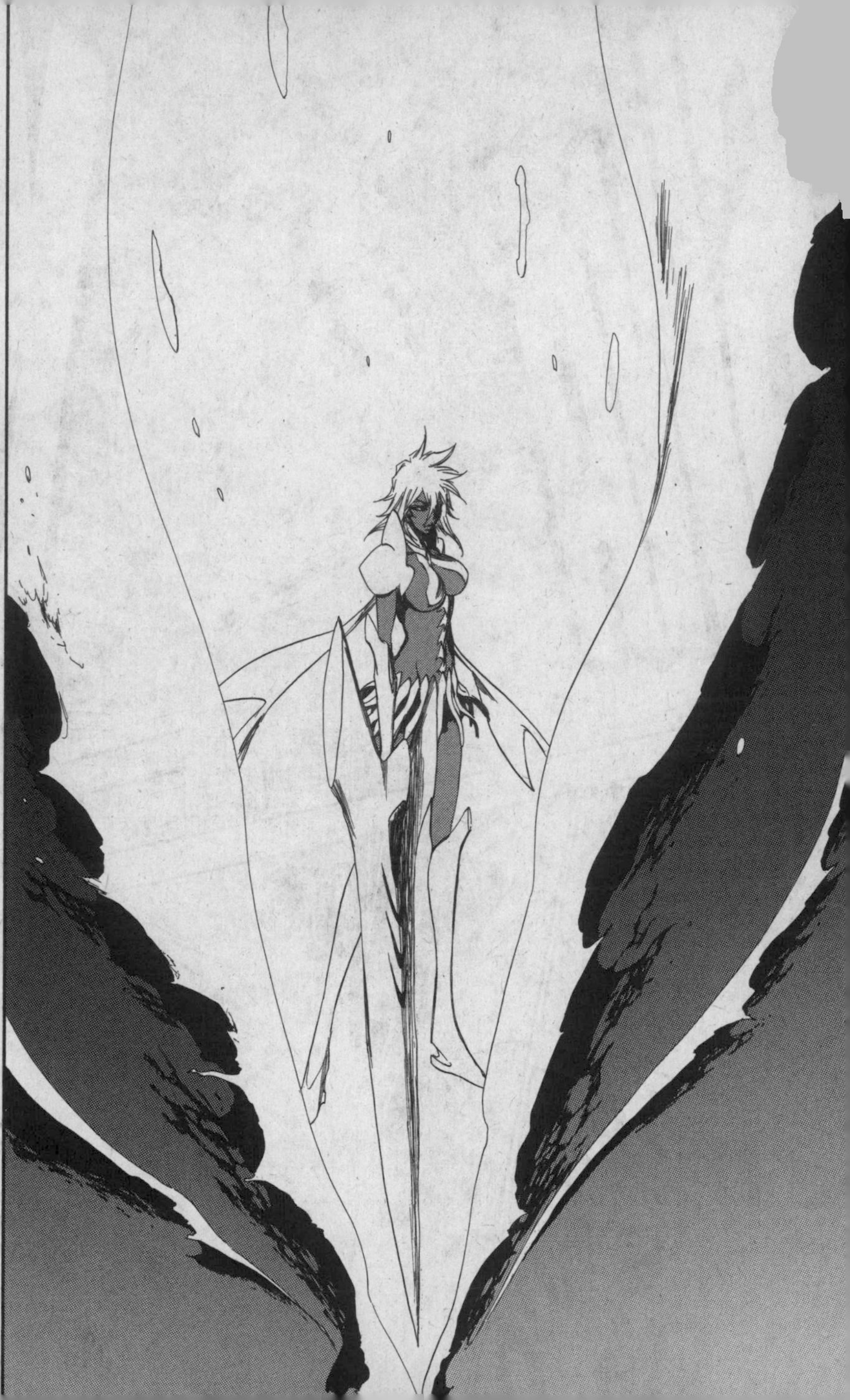

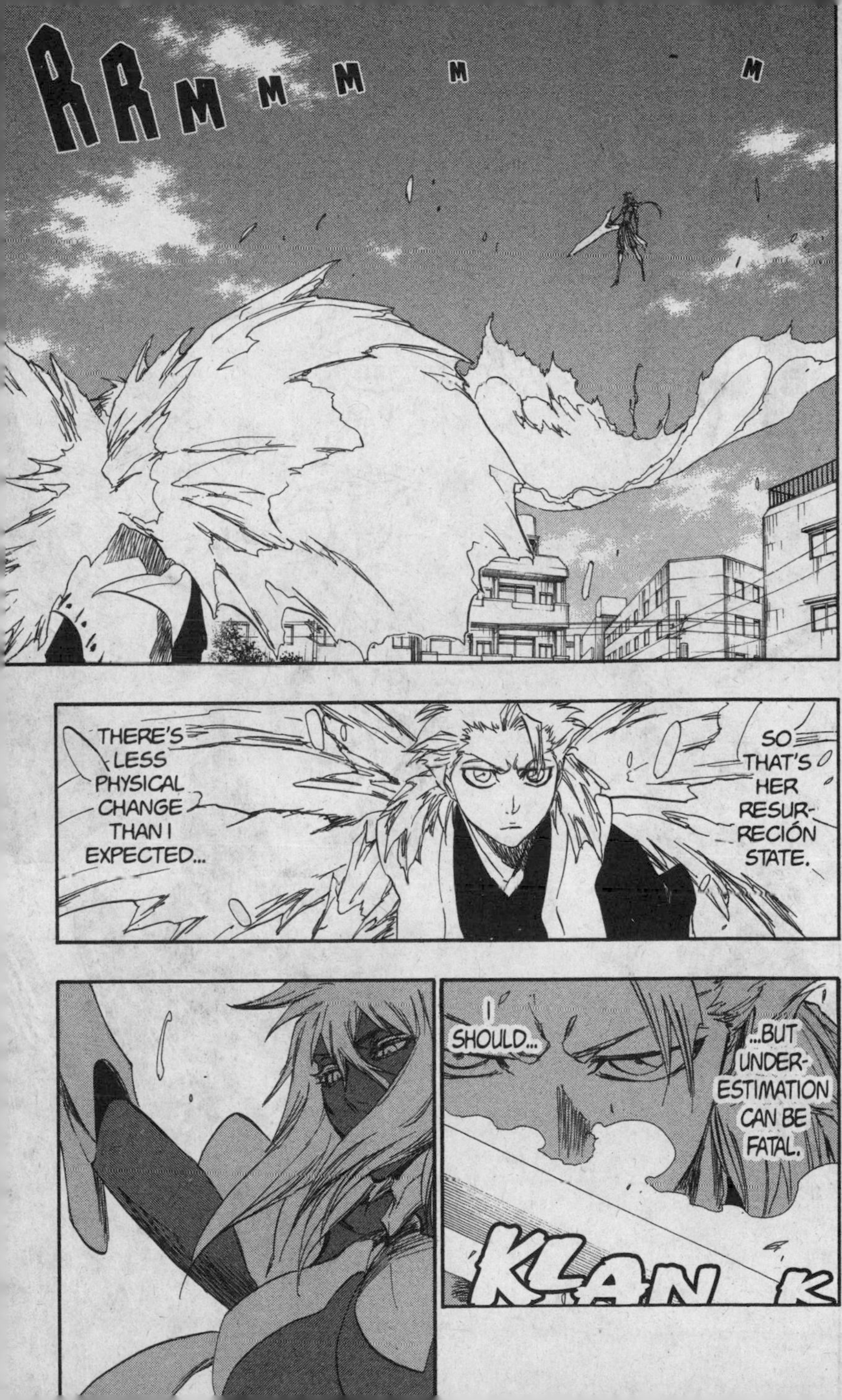
RRMMMMM
SO THAT'S HER RESURRECIÓN STATE.
THERE'S LESS PHYSICAL CHANGE THAN I EXPECTED...
I SHOULD...
...BUT UNDER-ESTIMATION CAN BE FATAL.
KLANK

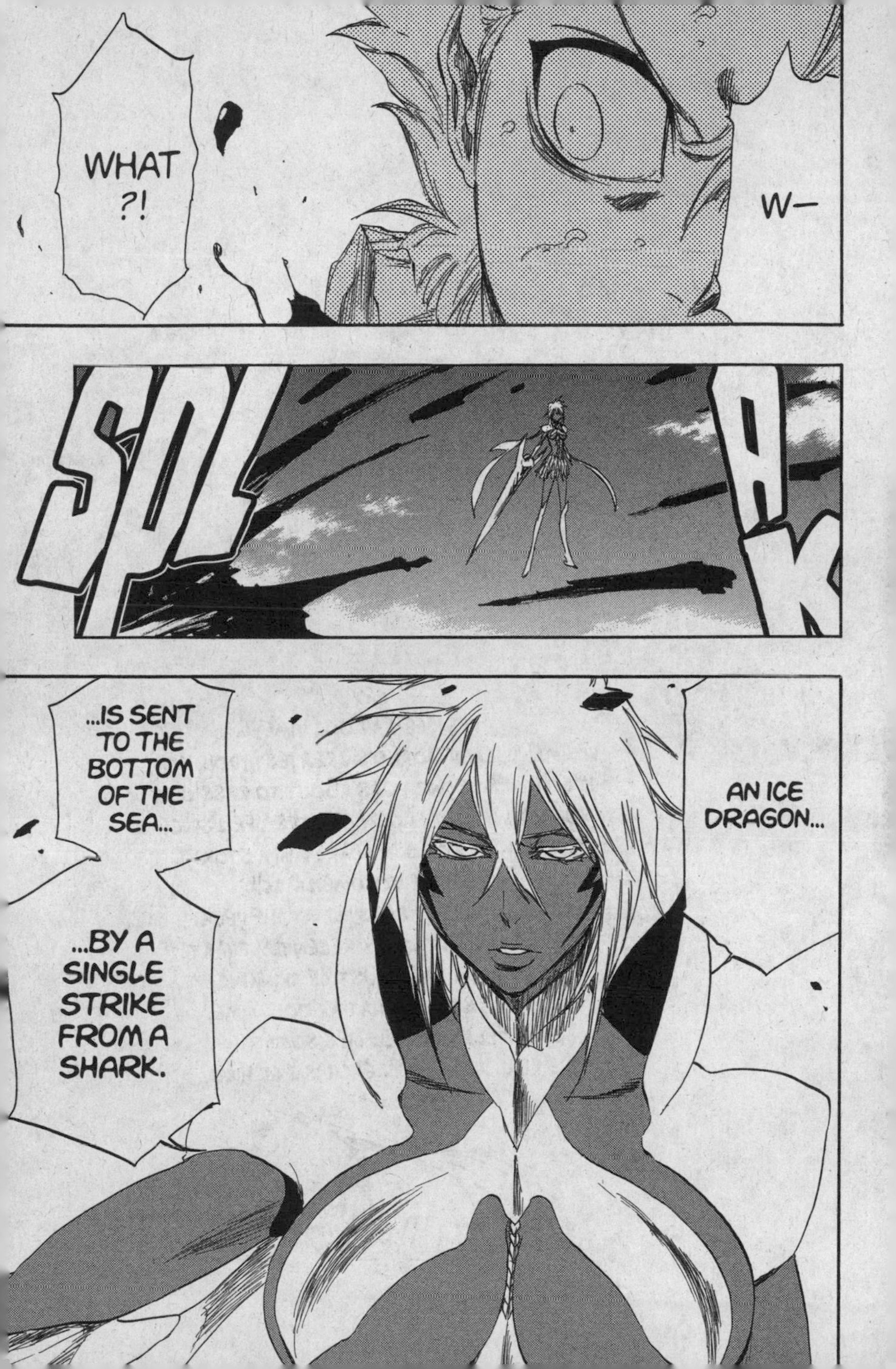
W—
WHAT ?!
SPLAK
AN ICE DRAGON...
...IS SENT TO THE BOTTOM OF THE SEA...
...BY A SINGLE STRIKE FROM A SHARK.

HEY!
IT'S BEEN A LONG TIME!
IT'S ME! BLEACH WORLD'S GREATEST IDOL, KON!!
IT'S BEEN SO LONG I WAS ABOUT TO PASS OUT.
YOU WANNA KNOW HOW LONG IT'S BEEN SINCE
SUPER IDOL KON'S APPEARED IN A STORY?
NOT SINCE VOLUME 25! 25!!
IT'S BEEN THREE YEARS!! WHAT THE HECK?!
THOSE OF YOU WHO ONLY RECENTLY STARTED
READING BLEACH MUST BE THINKING,
"HUH? WHO'S KON? WHAT A COOL NAME."
SO I'LL TELL YOU NEWBIES SOMETHING!
THE REAL HERO OF BLEACH ISN'T ICHIGO,
IT'S ME!!

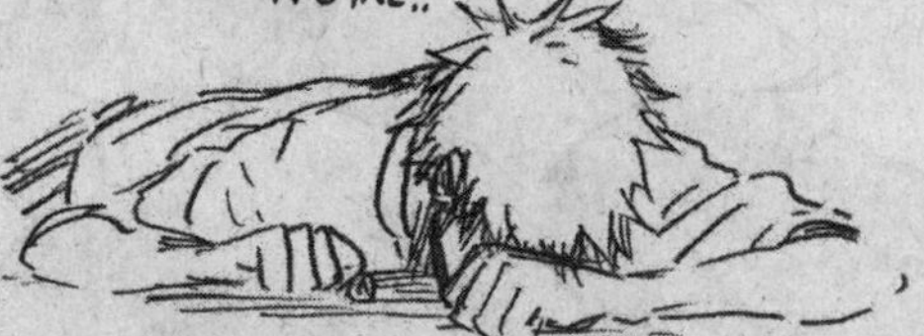

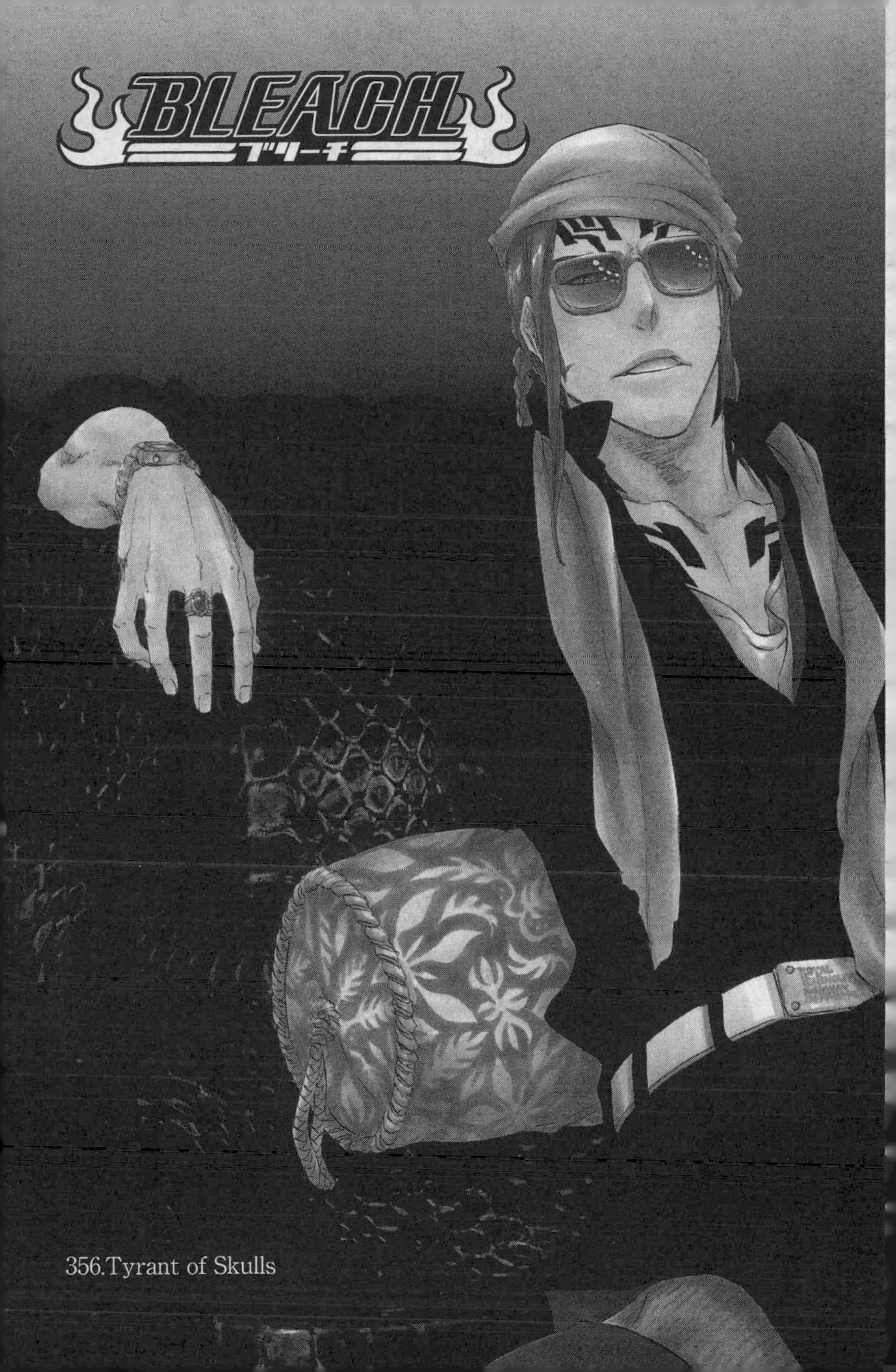
BLEACH
ブリーチ

356.Tyrant of Skulls

BLEACH
ブリーチ

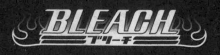

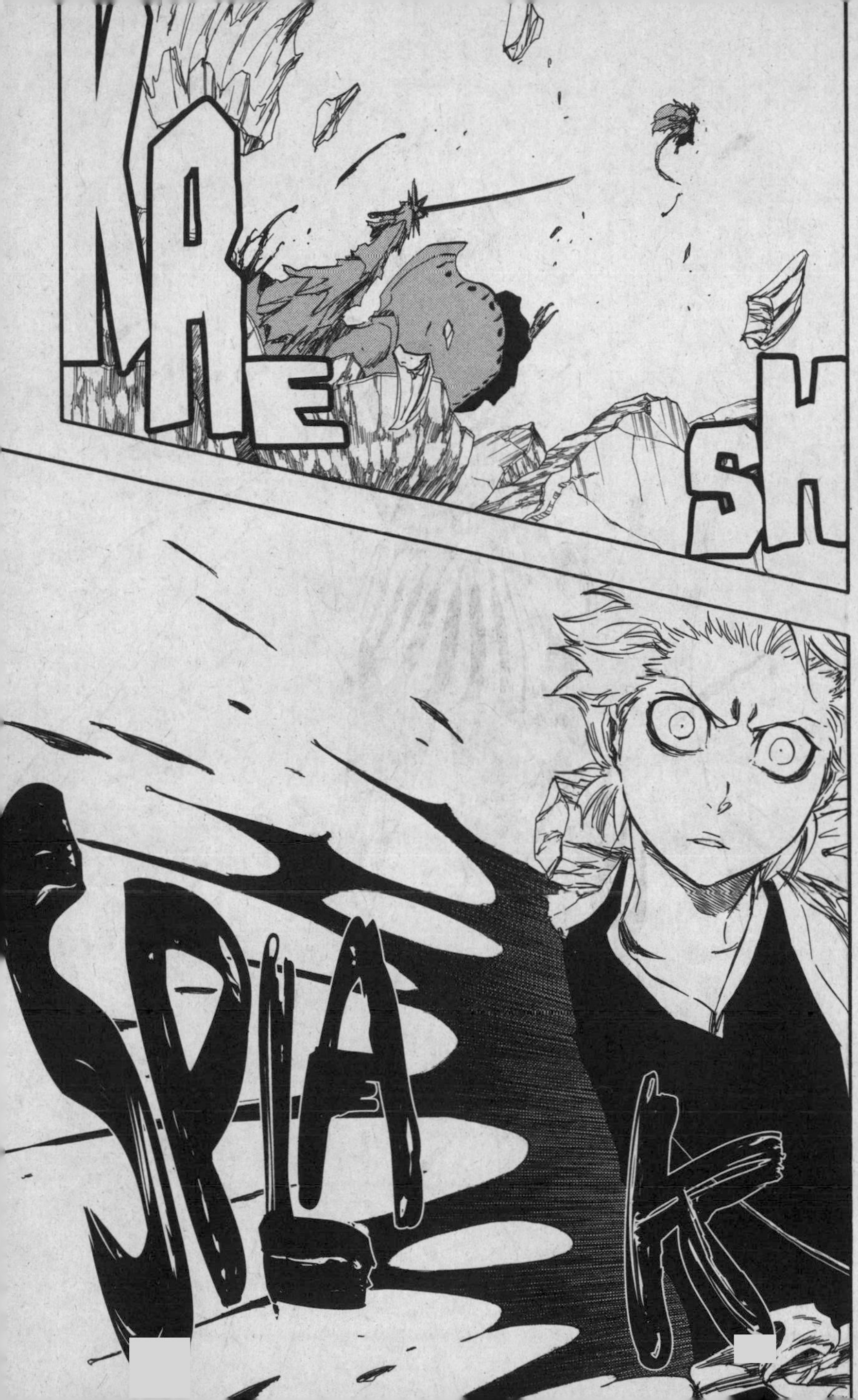

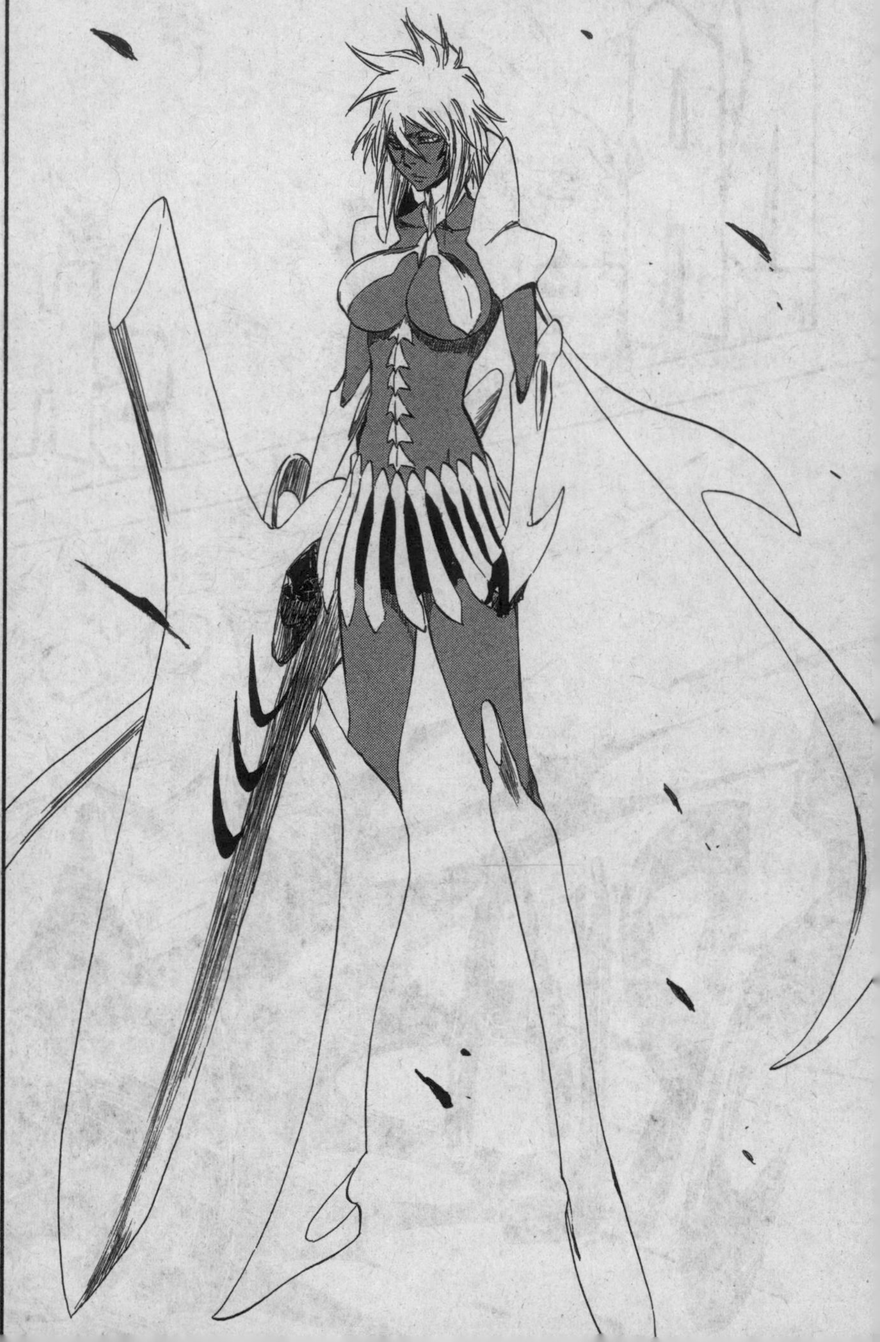

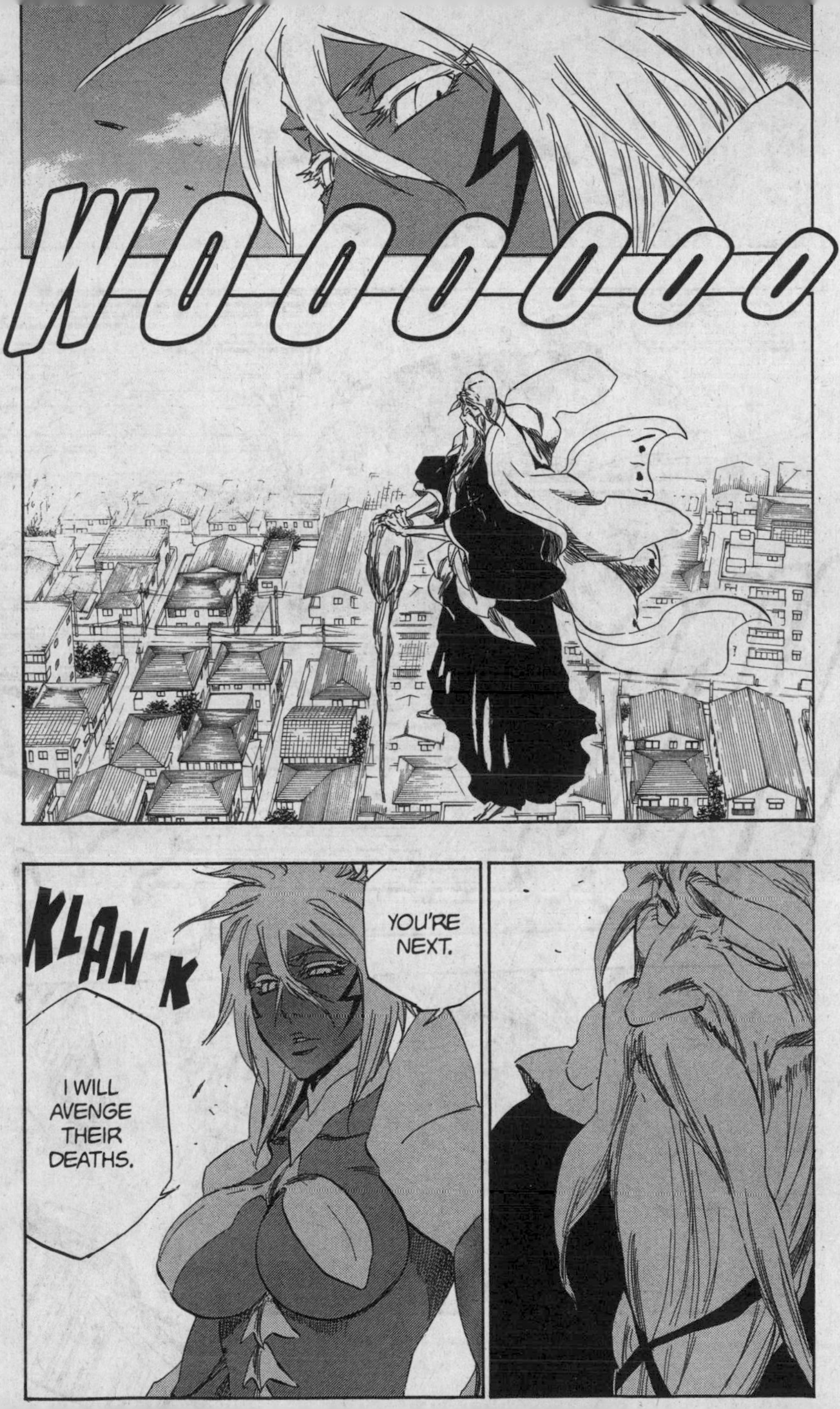
WOOOOOO
KLAN K
YOU'RE NEXT.
I WILL AVENGE THEIR DEATHS.

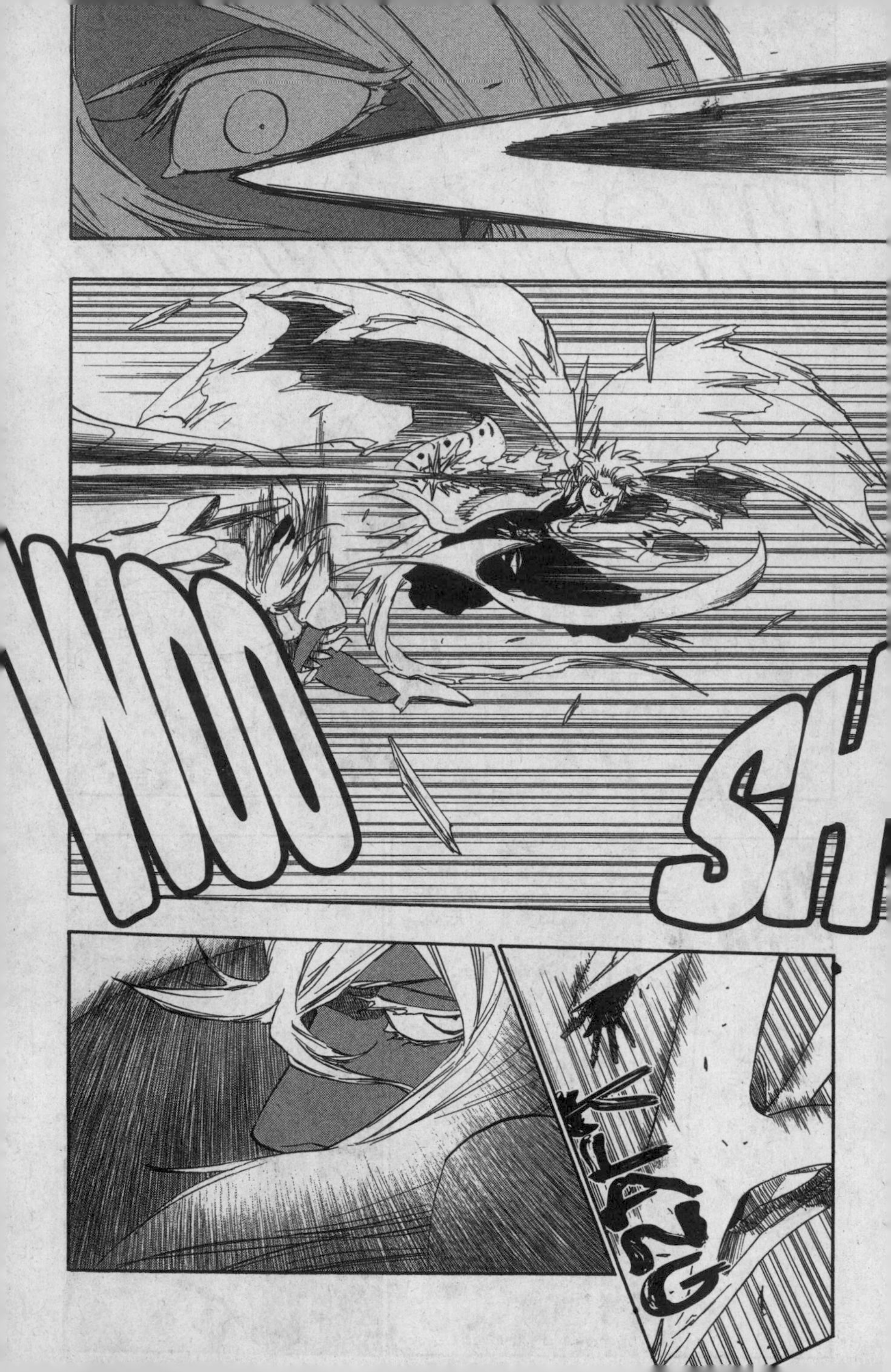
WOO
SH
KLANG

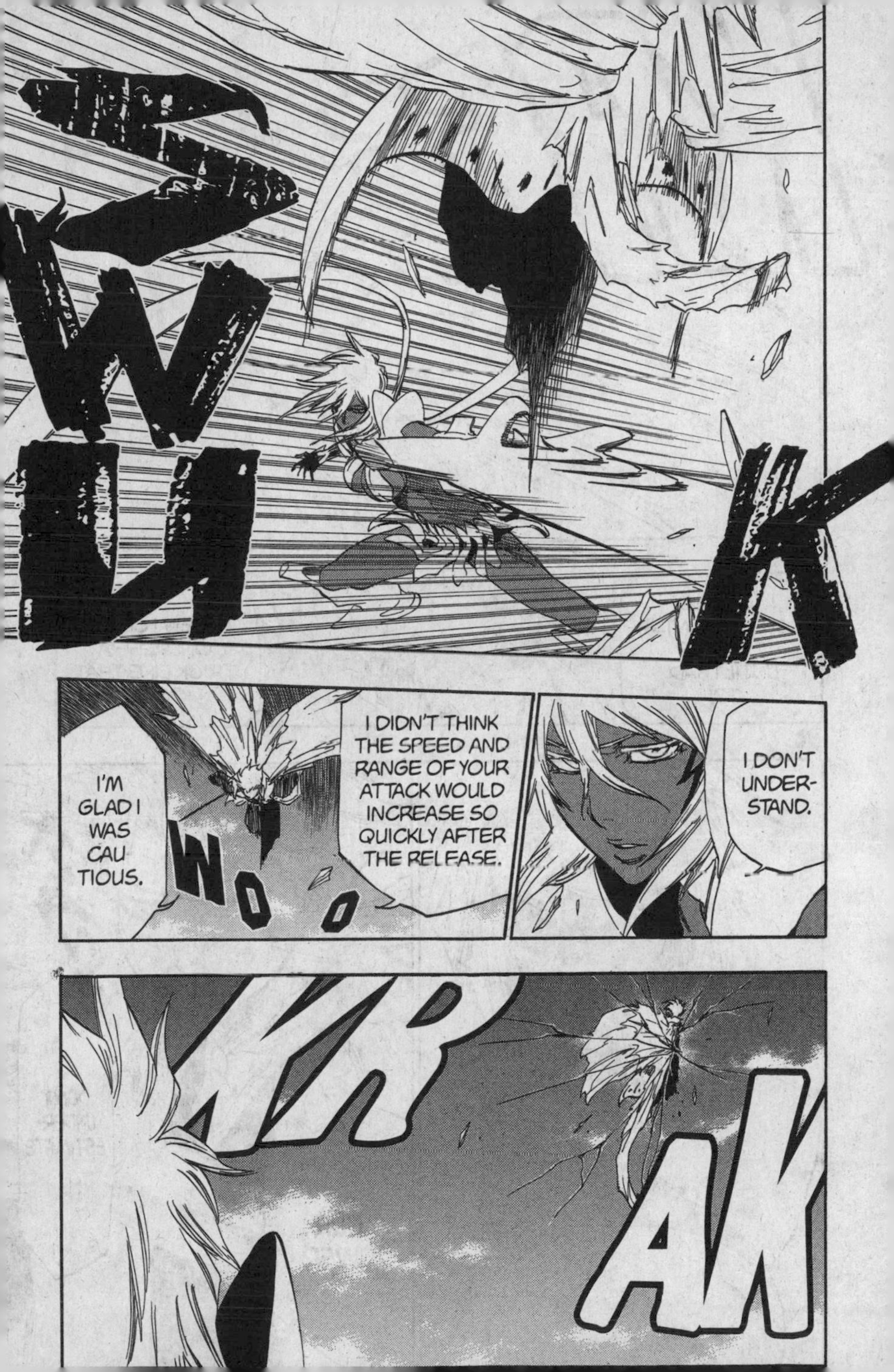
I DON'T UNDERSTAND.
I DIDN'T THINK THE SPEED AND RANGE OF YOUR ATTACK WOULD INCREASE SO QUICKLY AFTER THE RELEASE.
I'M GLAD I WAS CAUTIOUS.
KRAK

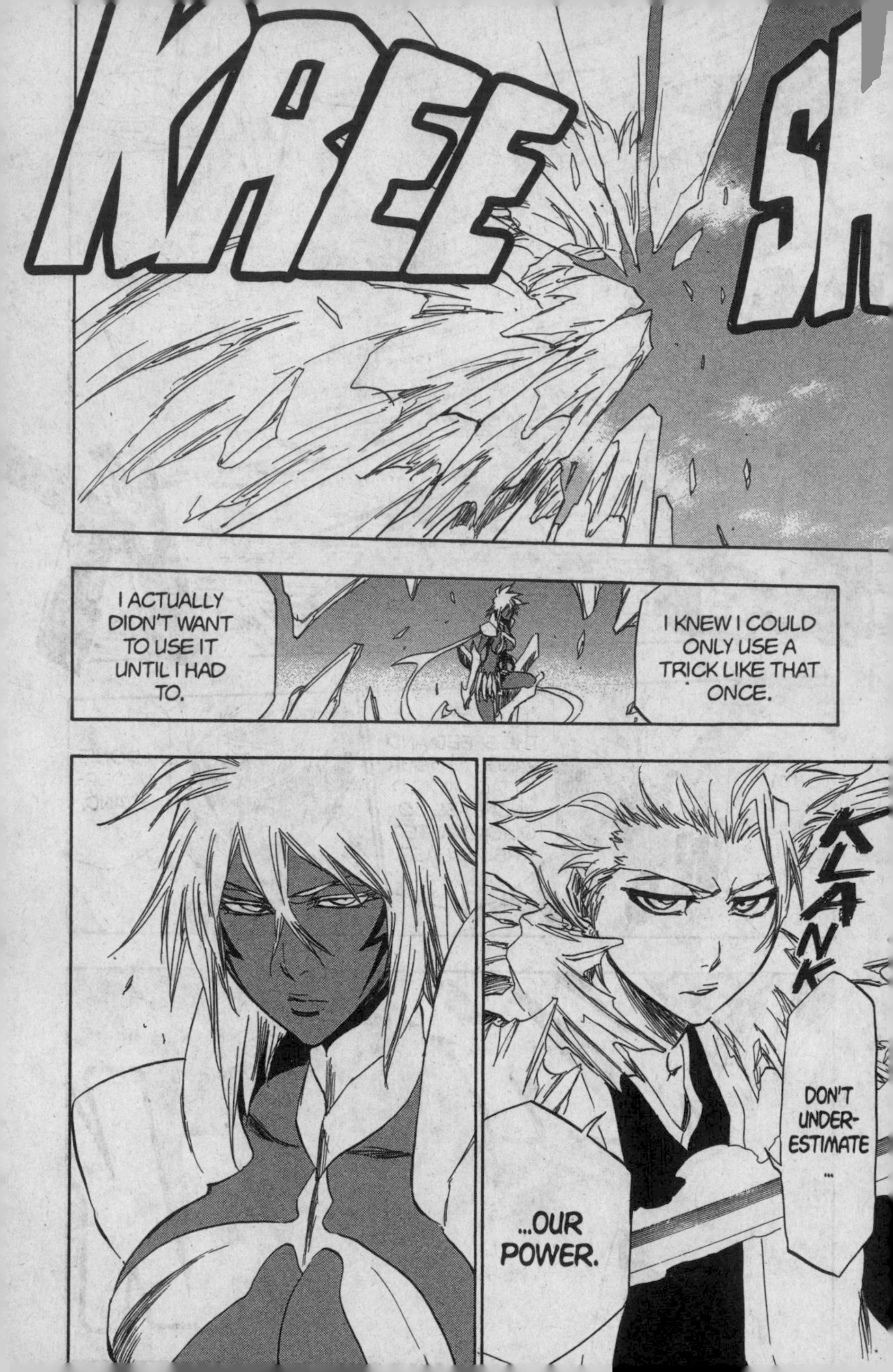
KREE
I KNEW I COULD ONLY USE A TRICK LIKE THAT ONCE.
I ACTUALLY DIDN'T WANT TO USE IT UNTIL I HAD TO.
KLANK
DON'T UNDER-ESTIMATE ...
...OUR POWER.

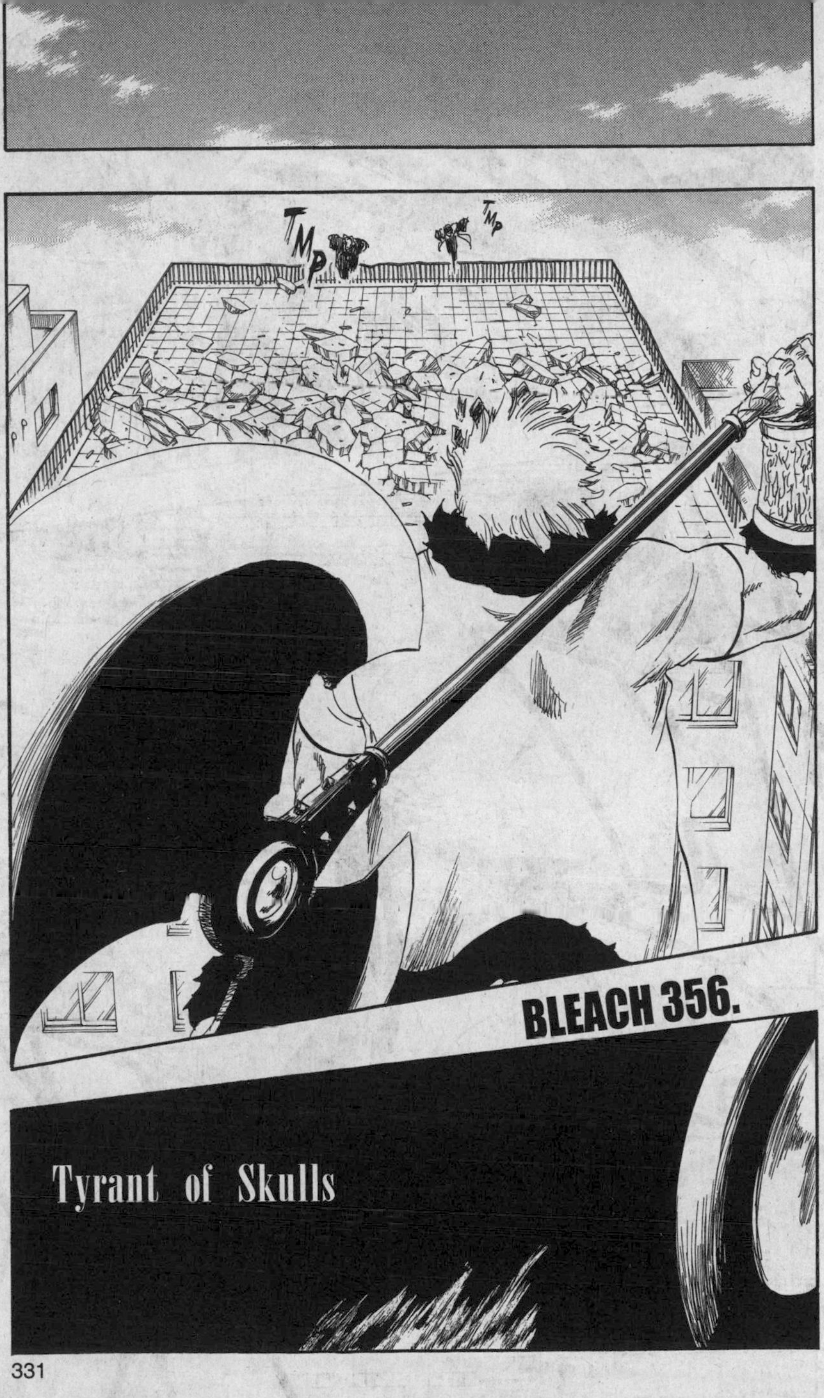
TMP
TMP
BLEACH 356.
Tyrant of Skulls

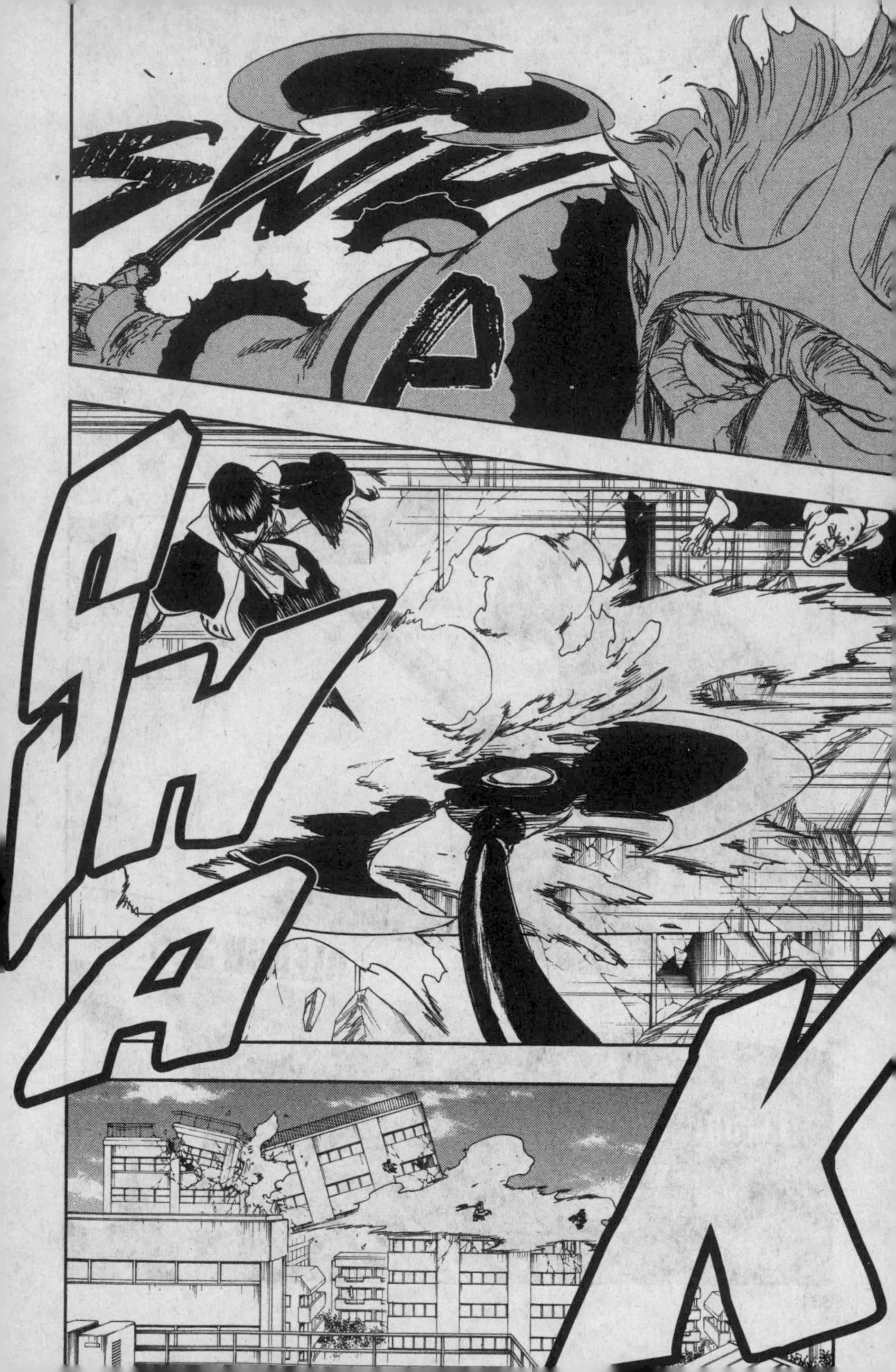
SWAK

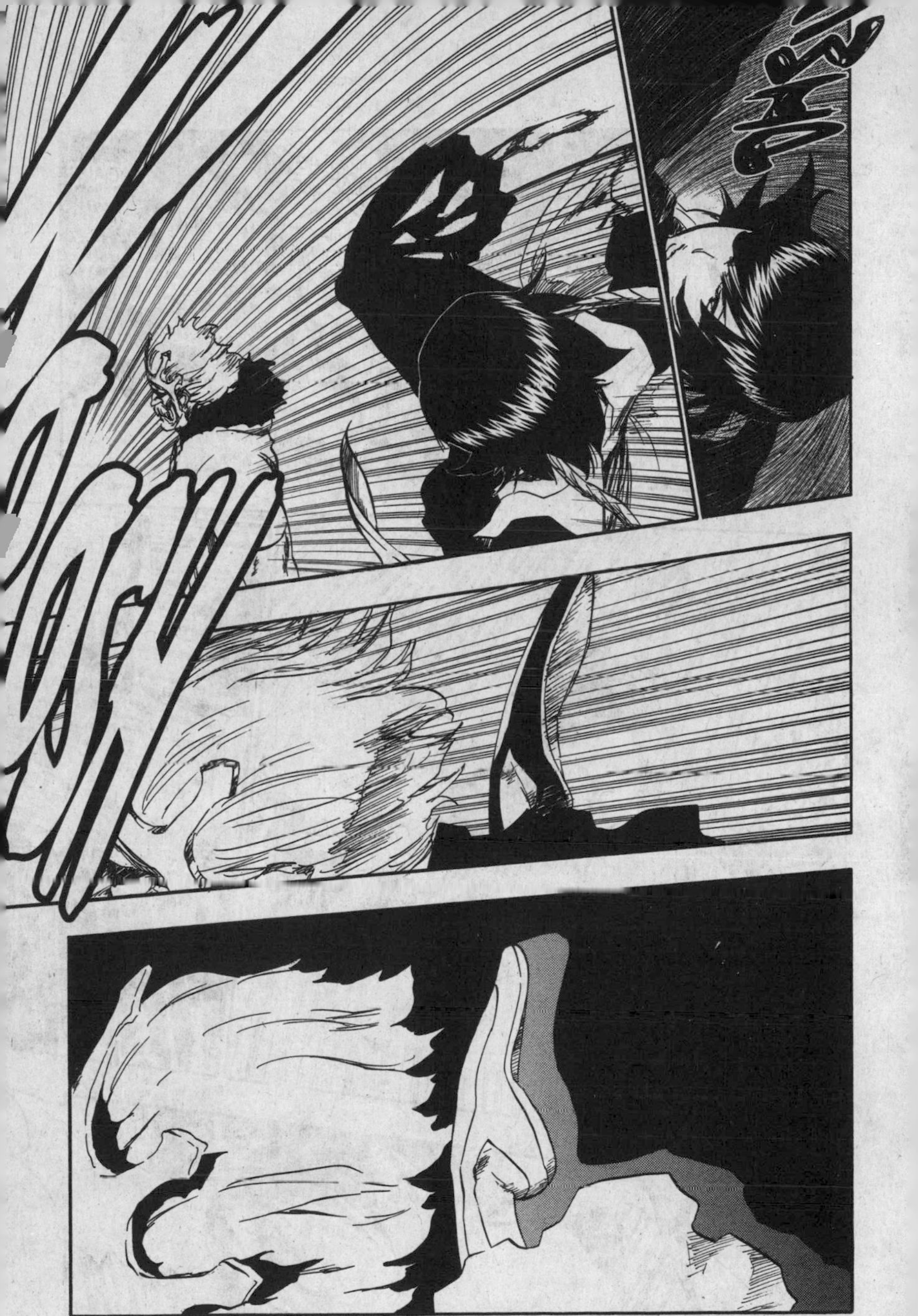

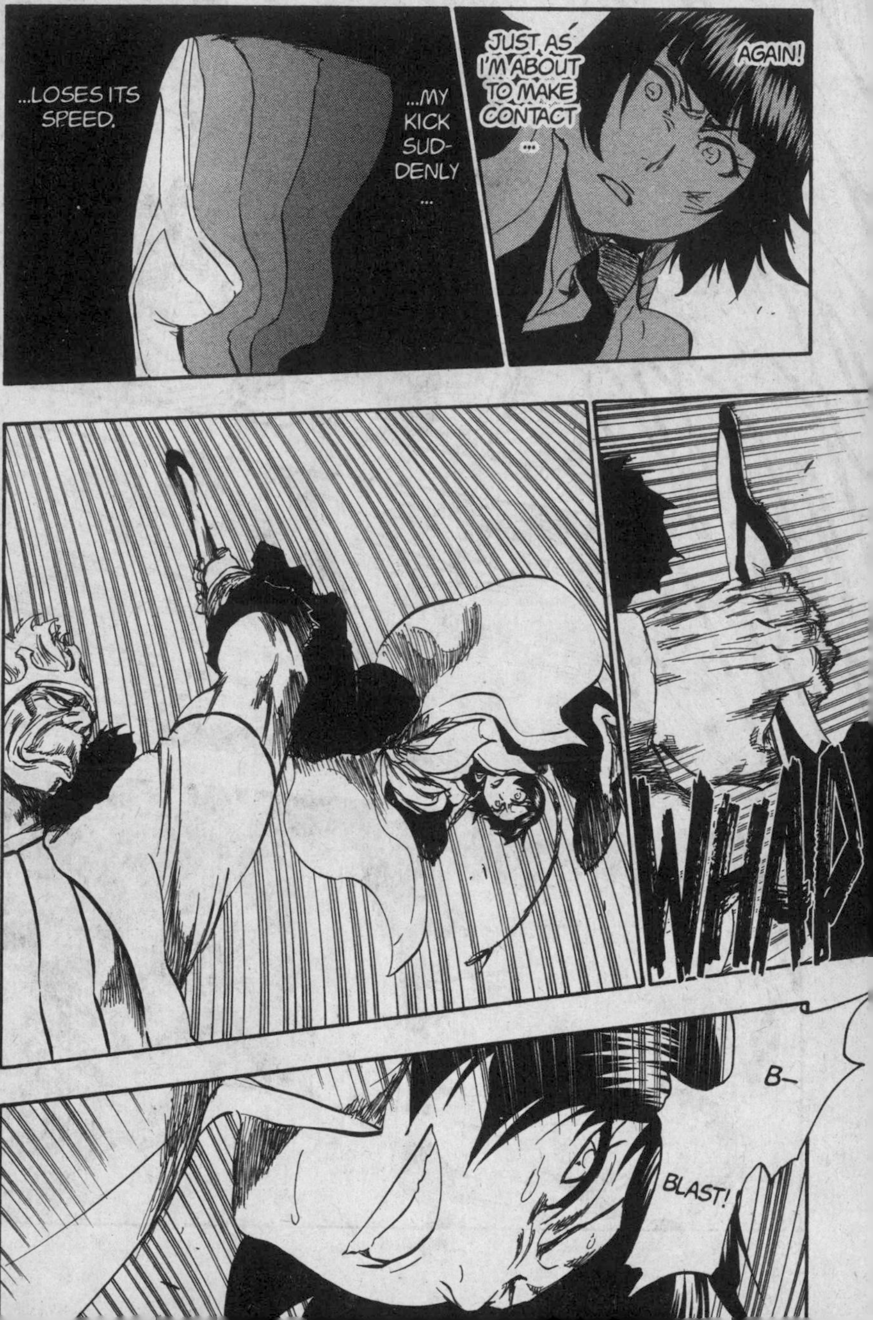
AGAIN!
JUST AS I'M ABOUT TO MAKE CONTACT...
...MY KICK SUD-DENLY...
...LOSES ITS SPEED.
WHAP
B—
BLAST!

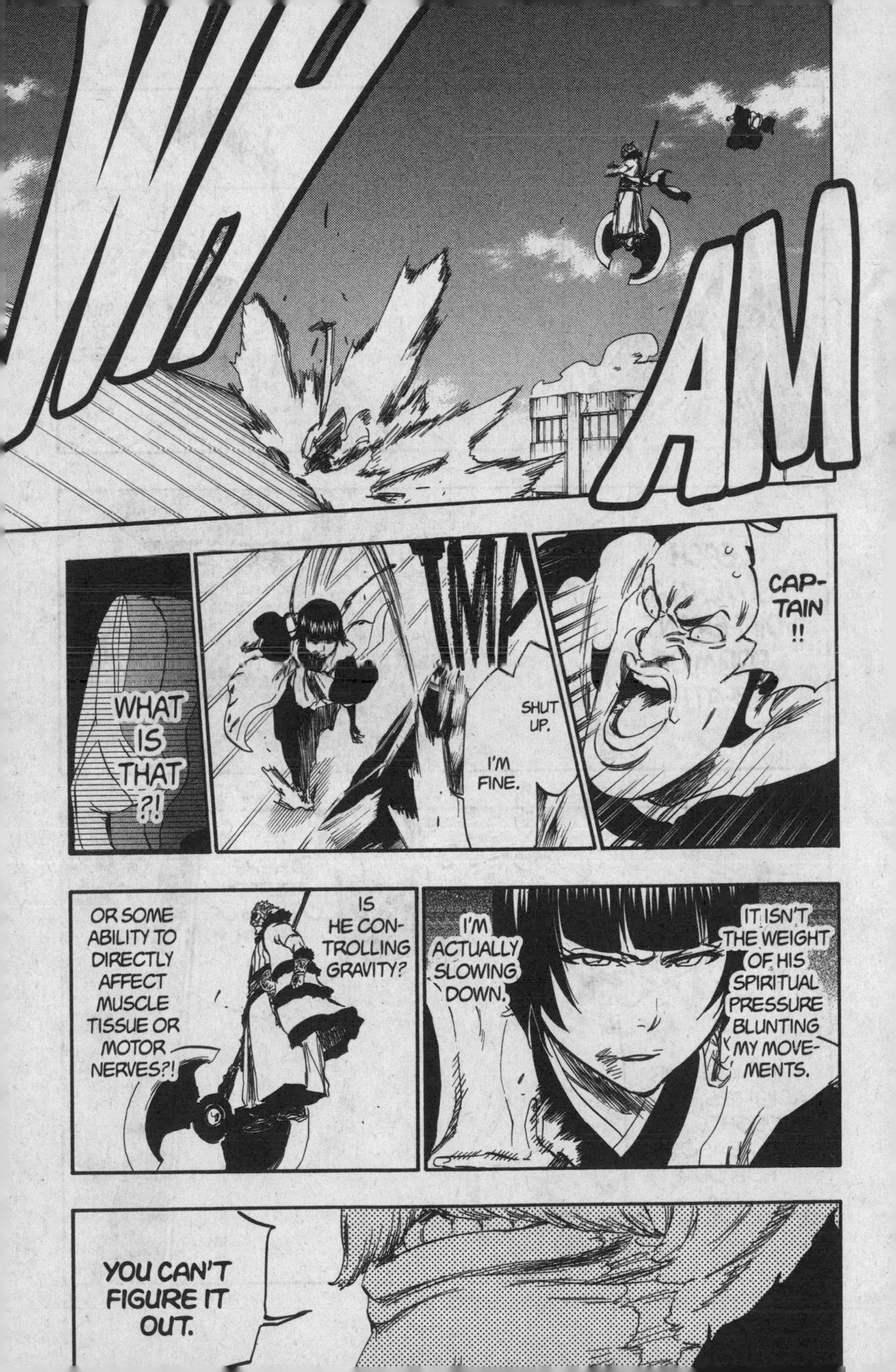
WH
AM
CAP-TAIN!!
SHUT UP.
I'M FINE.
WHAT IS THAT?!
IT ISN'T THE WEIGHT OF HIS SPIRITUAL PRESSURE BLUNTING MY MOVE-MENTS.
I'M ACTUALLY SLOWING DOWN.
IS HE CON-TROLLING GRAVITY?
OR SOME ABILITY TO DIRECTLY AFFECT MUSCLE TISSUE OR MOTOR NERVES?!
YOU CAN'T FIGURE IT OUT.

...PERPLEX-ING.

YOU MUST FIND MY POWER...

...EACH GOVERN A DIFFERENT FORM OF DEATH.

WE ESPADAS...

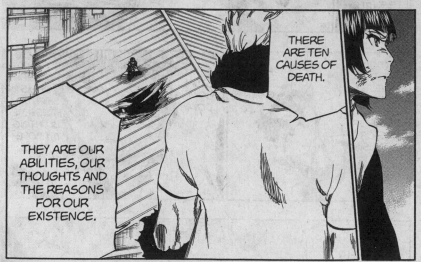

THERE ARE TEN CAUSES OF DEATH.

THEY ARE OUR ABILITIES, OUR THOUGHTS AND THE REASONS FOR OUR EXISTENCE.

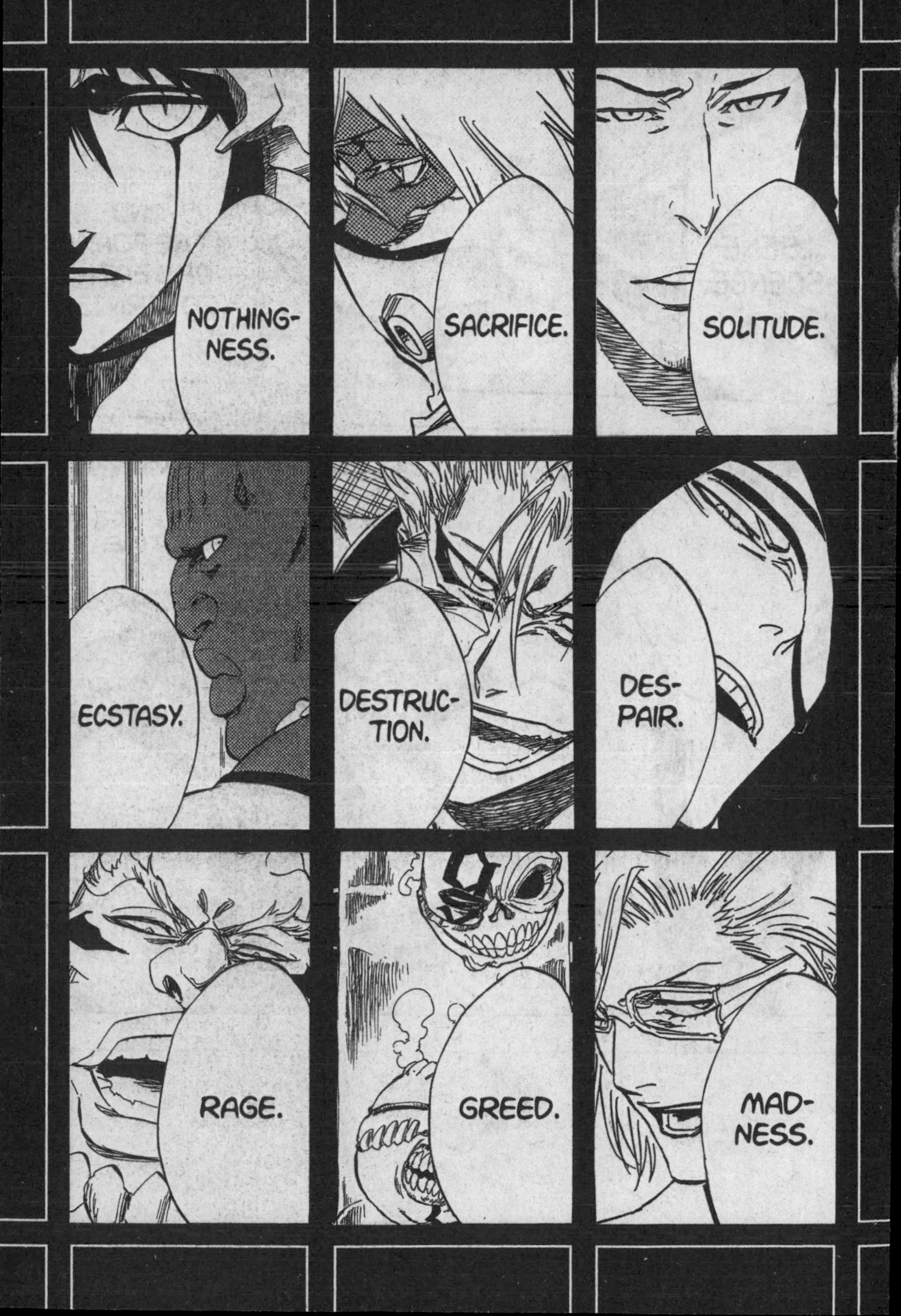
SOLITUDE.
SACRIFICE.
NOTHING-
NESS.
DES-
PAIR.
DESTRUC-
TION.
ECSTASY.
MAD-
NESS.
GREED.
RAGE.

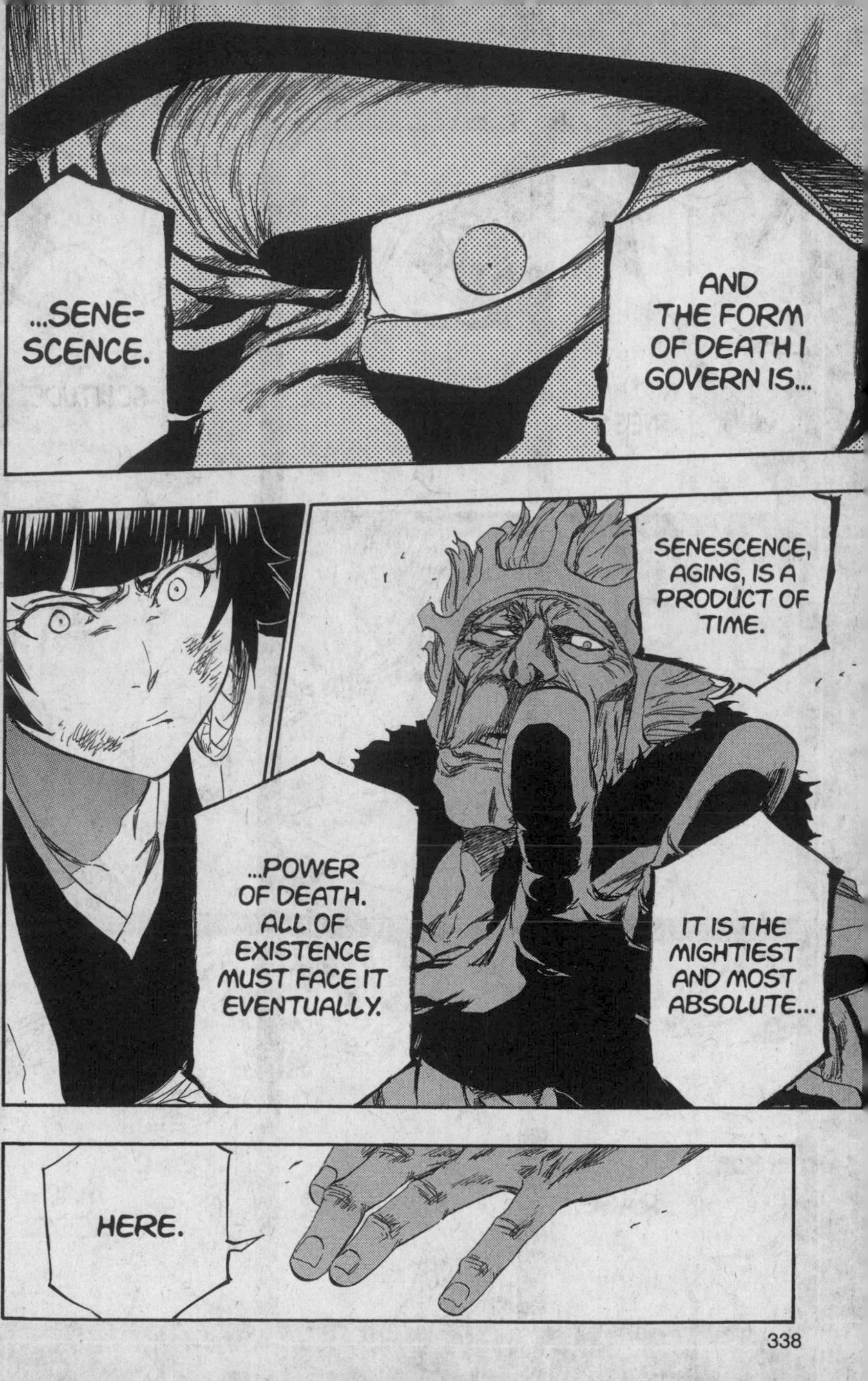
AND THE FORM OF DEATH I GOVERN IS...
...SENE-SCENCE.
SENESCENCE, AGING, IS A PRODUCT OF TIME.
IT IS THE MIGHTIEST AND MOST ABSOLUTE...
...POWER OF DEATH. ALL OF EXISTENCE MUST FACE IT EVENTUALLY.
HERE.

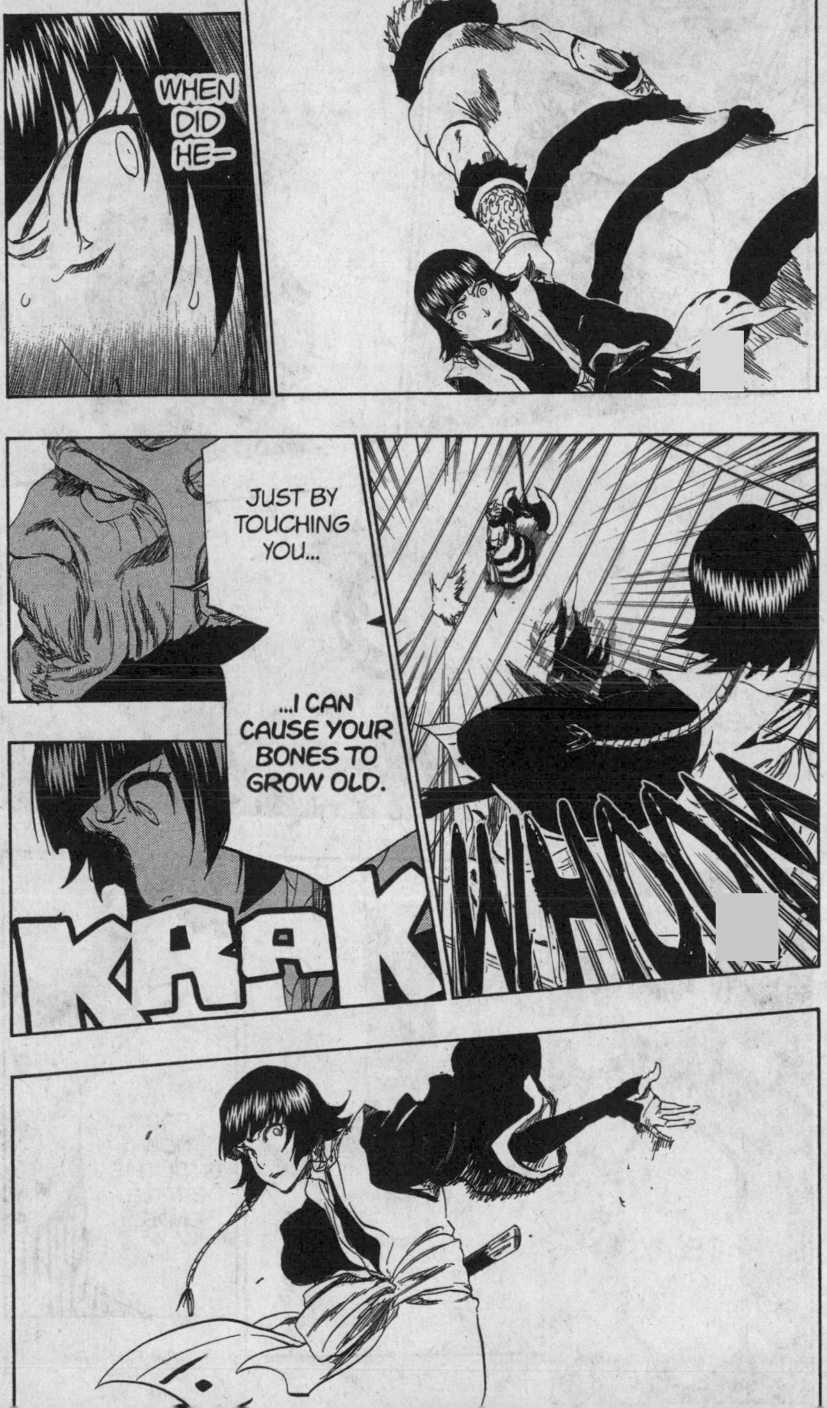
WHEN DID HE—
WHOOM
JUST BY TOUCHING YOU...
...I CAN CAUSE YOUR BONES TO GROW OLD.
KRAK

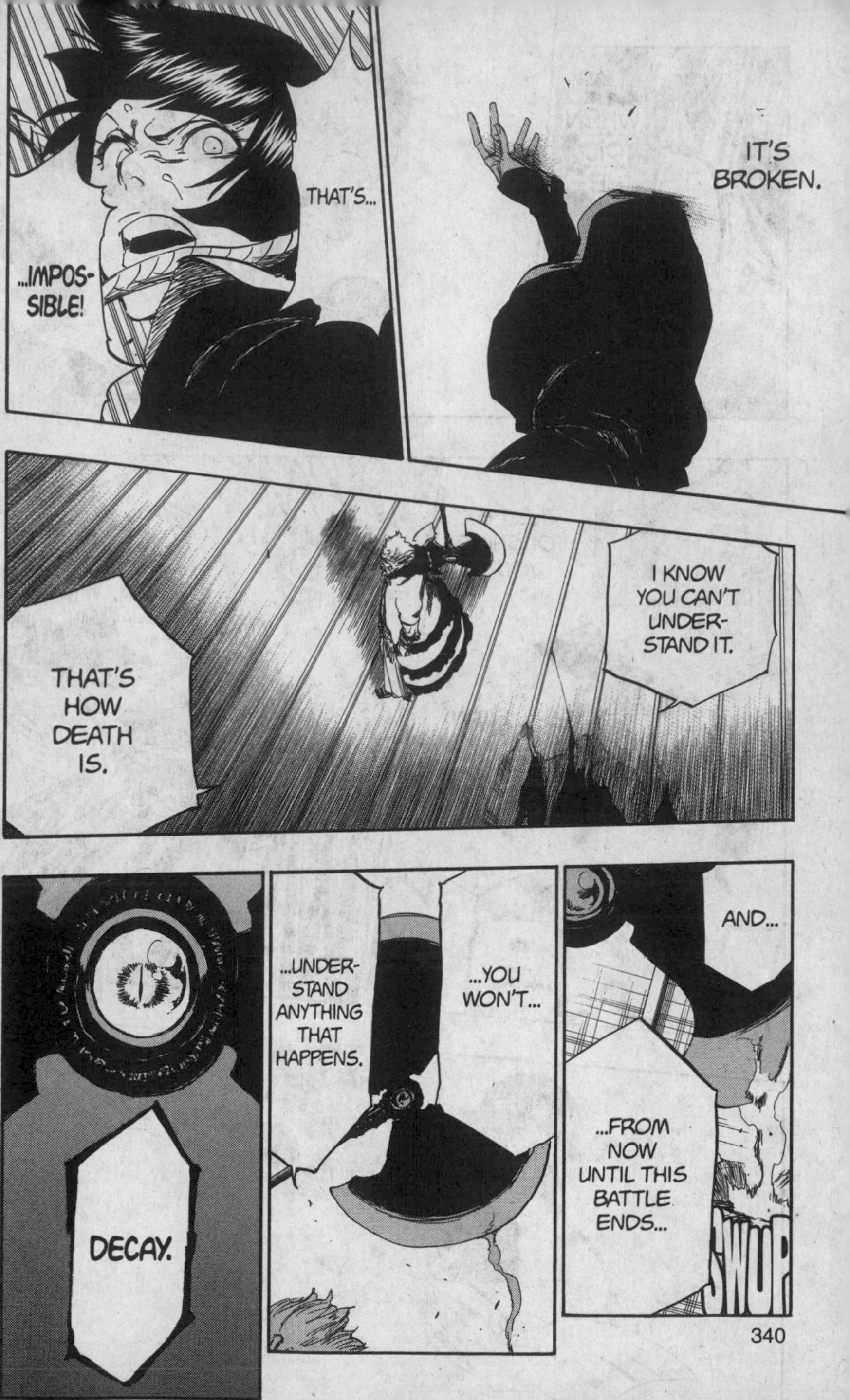
IT'S BROKEN.
THAT'S...
...IMPOS-SIBLE!
I KNOW YOU CAN'T UNDER-STAND IT.
THAT'S HOW DEATH IS.
AND...
...FROM NOW UNTIL THIS BATTLE ENDS...
SWOP
...YOU WON'T...
...UNDER-STAND ANYTHING THAT HAPPENS.
DECAY.

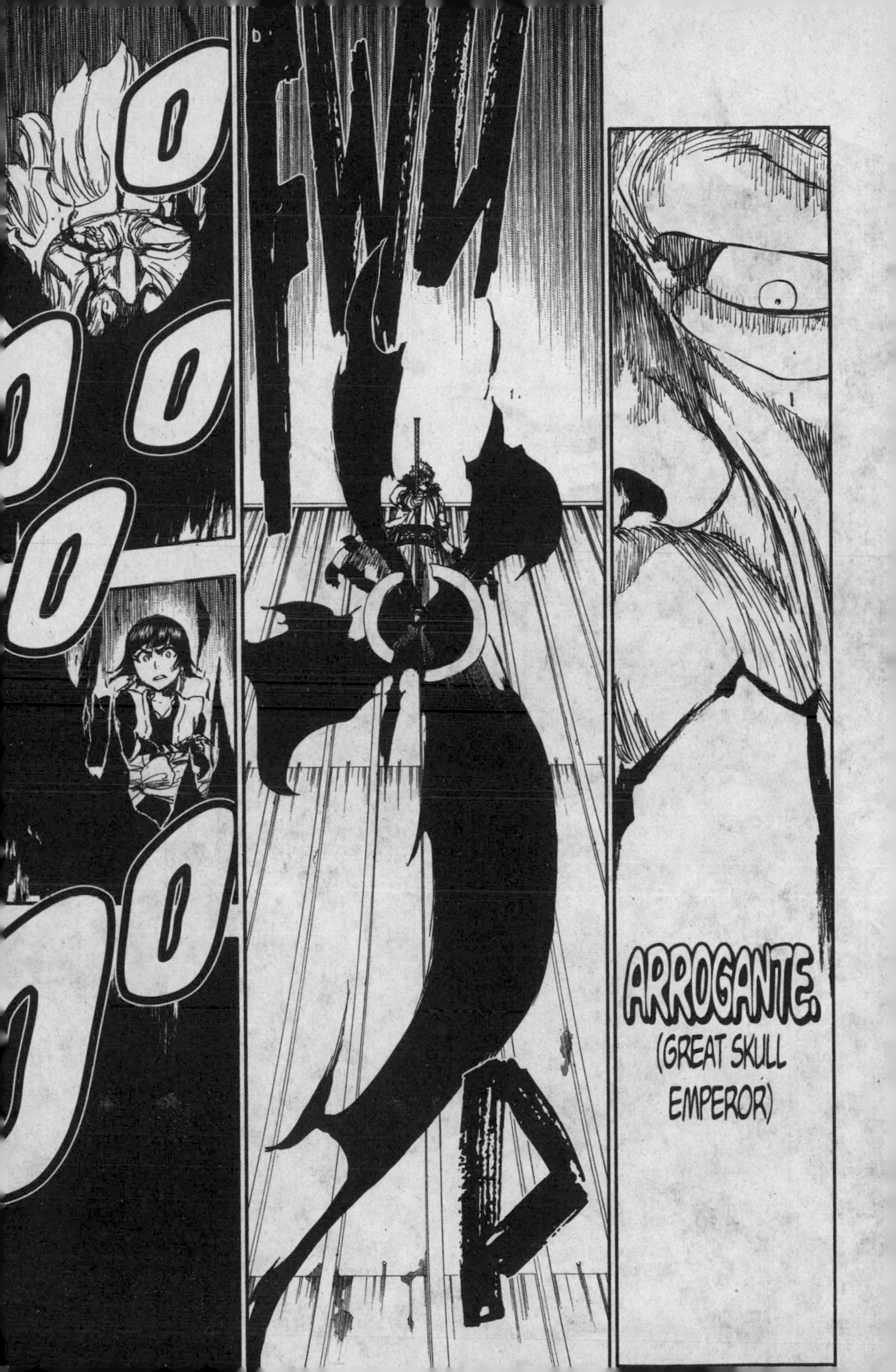
ARROGANTE.
(GREAT SKULL EMPEROR)
OOOOOOOO

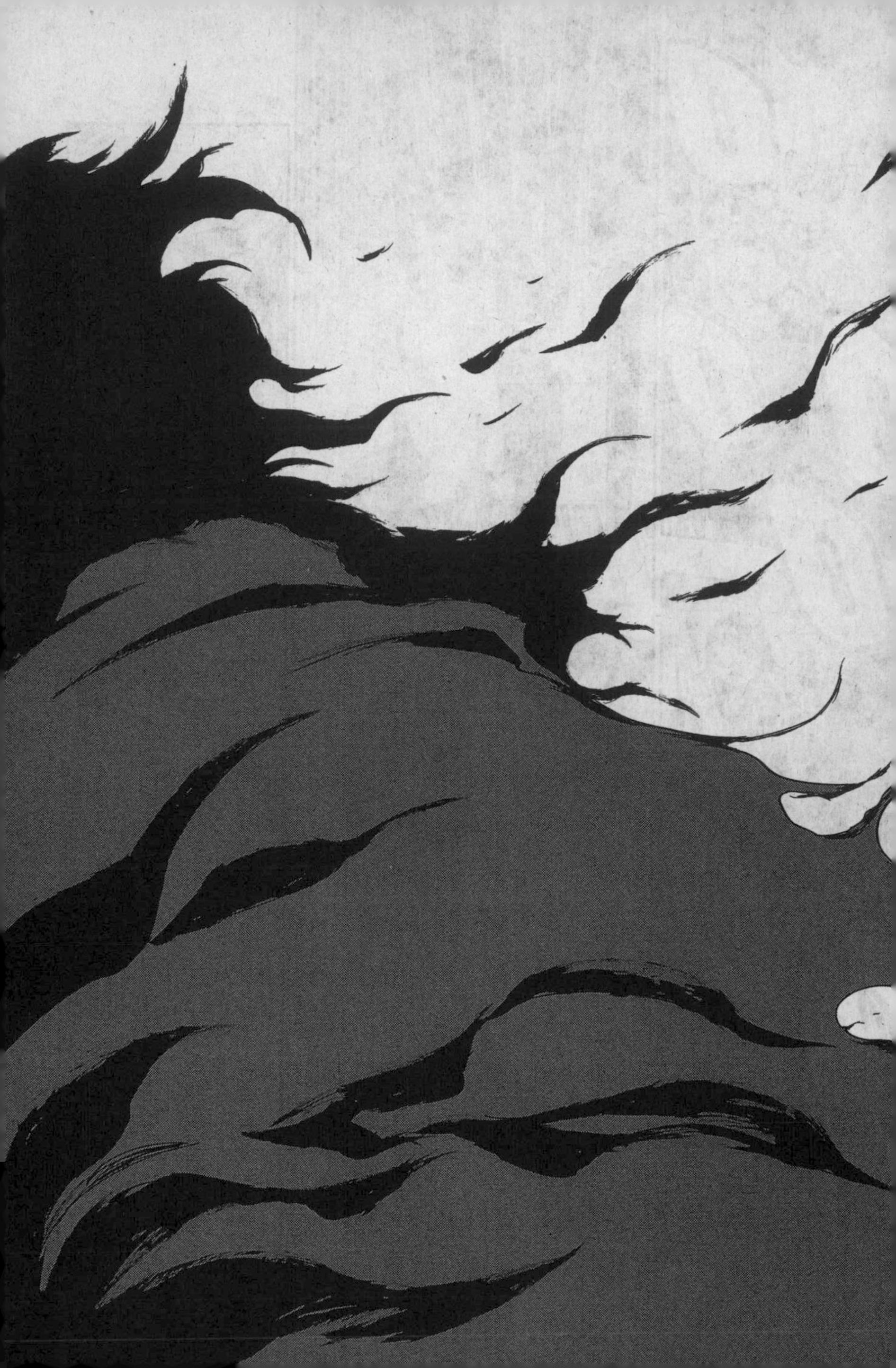

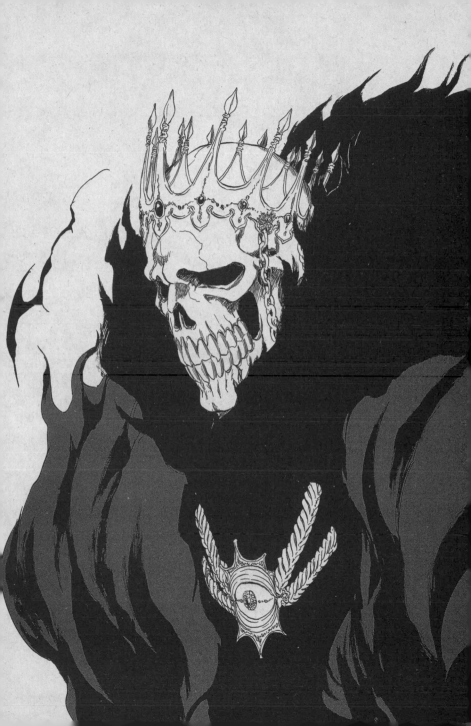

SO IT'S BEEN A LONG TIME SINCE I, THE MAIN CHARACTER AND SUPER IDOL, MADE AN APPEARANCE. LET ME EXPLAIN WHY I'M ON THE GROUND LIKE THIS.
WHILE WALKING AROUND TOWN IN ICHIGO'S BODY, I SUDDENLY GOT SLEEPY AND PASSED OUT.
THE TOWN SEEMED DIFFERENT WHEN I WOKE UP SO I DIDN'T KNOW IF I SHOULD GET UP OR NOT. SO I'M MONITORING THE SITUATION FROM THIS POSITION!
BUT IT SEEMS TO ME THIS TOWN LOOKS LIKE THE RUKONGAI I SAW A LONG TIME AGO.
YACK YACK YACK
HUH? IS SOMEBODY COMING? I HOPE IT'S A HOTTIE WITH HUGE...

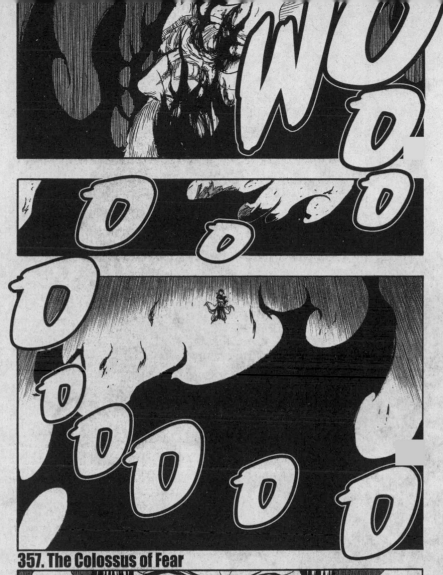

357. The Colossus of Fear

WHAT?!

W—

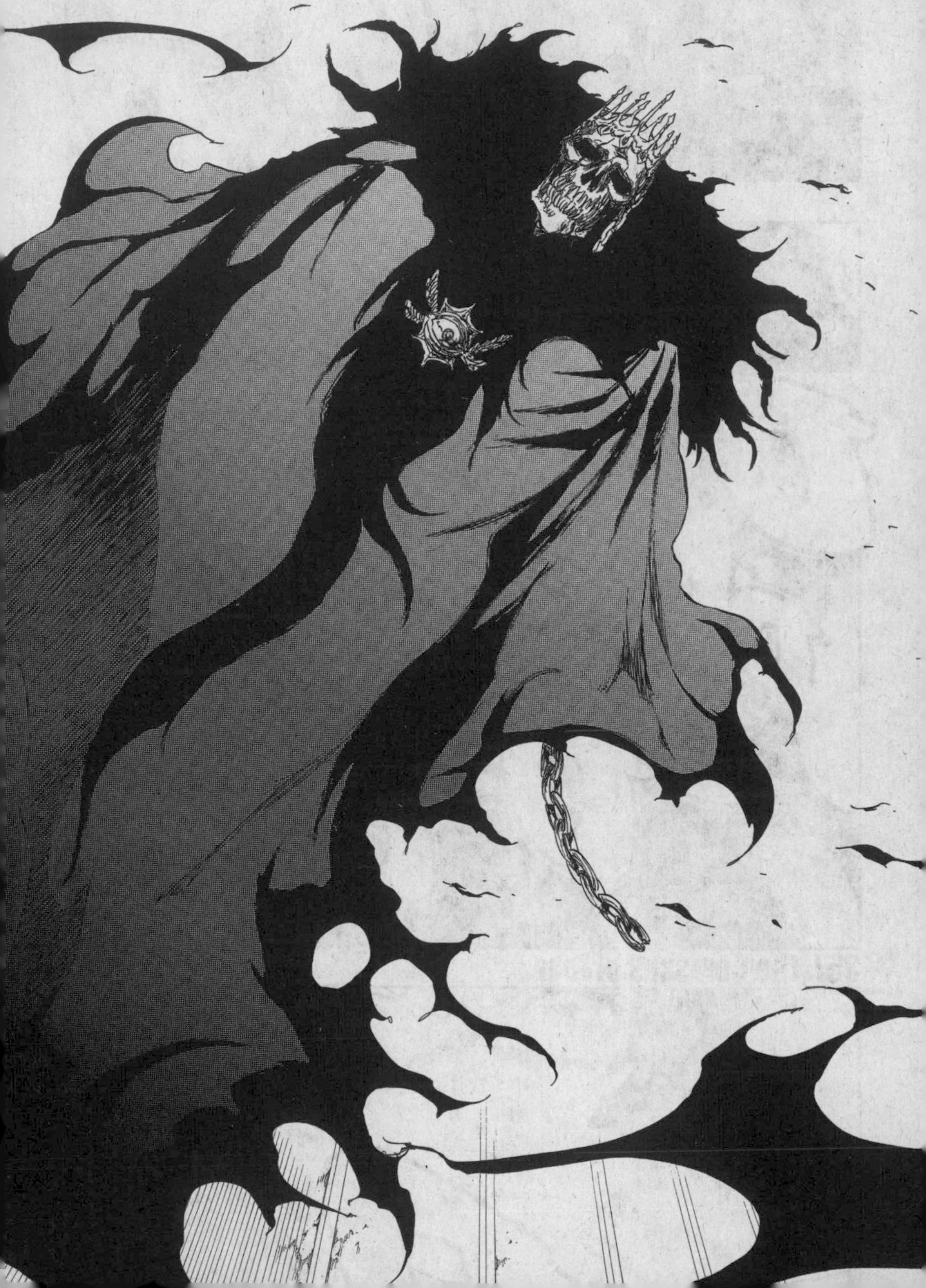

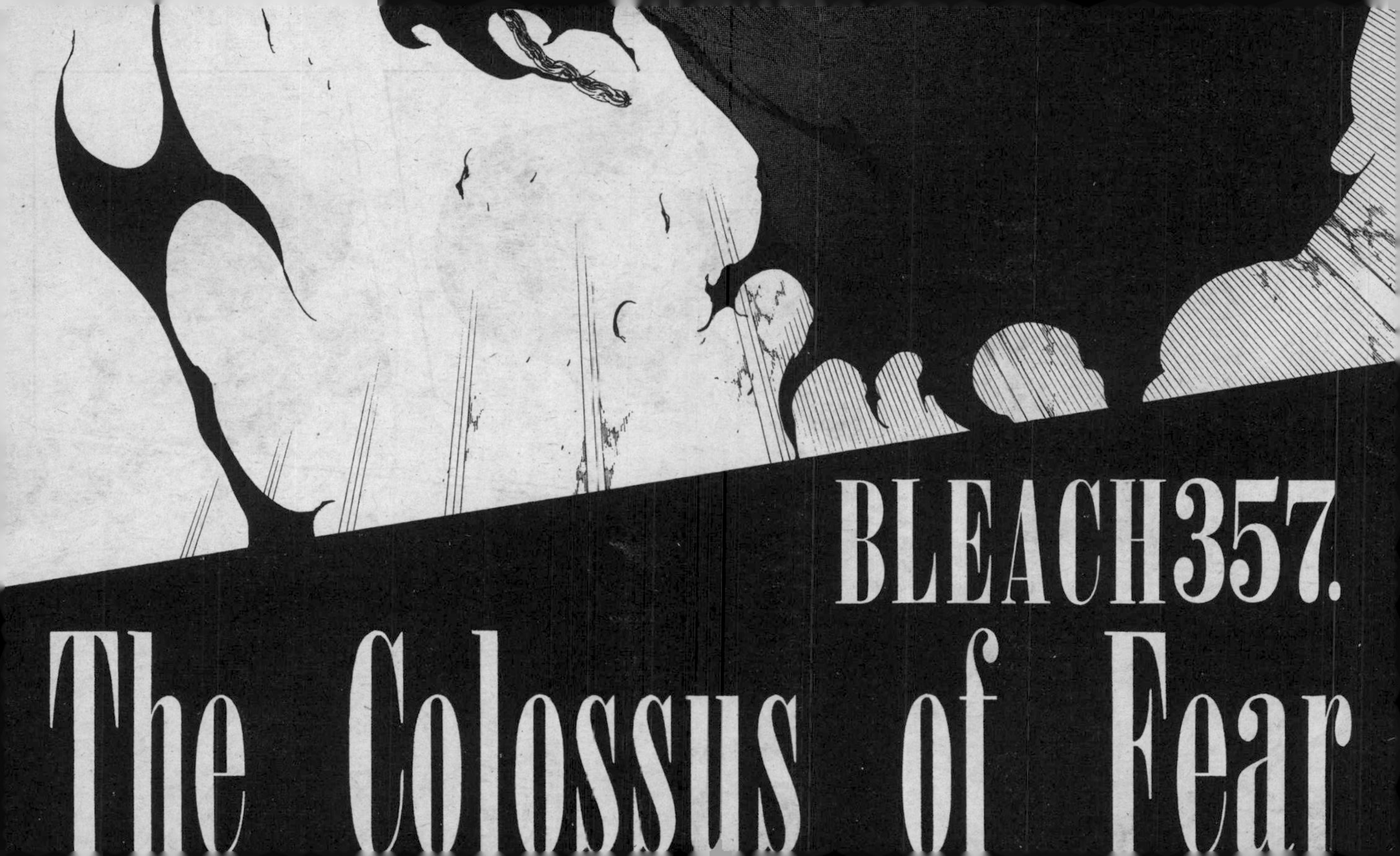
BLEACH357.
The Colossus of Fear

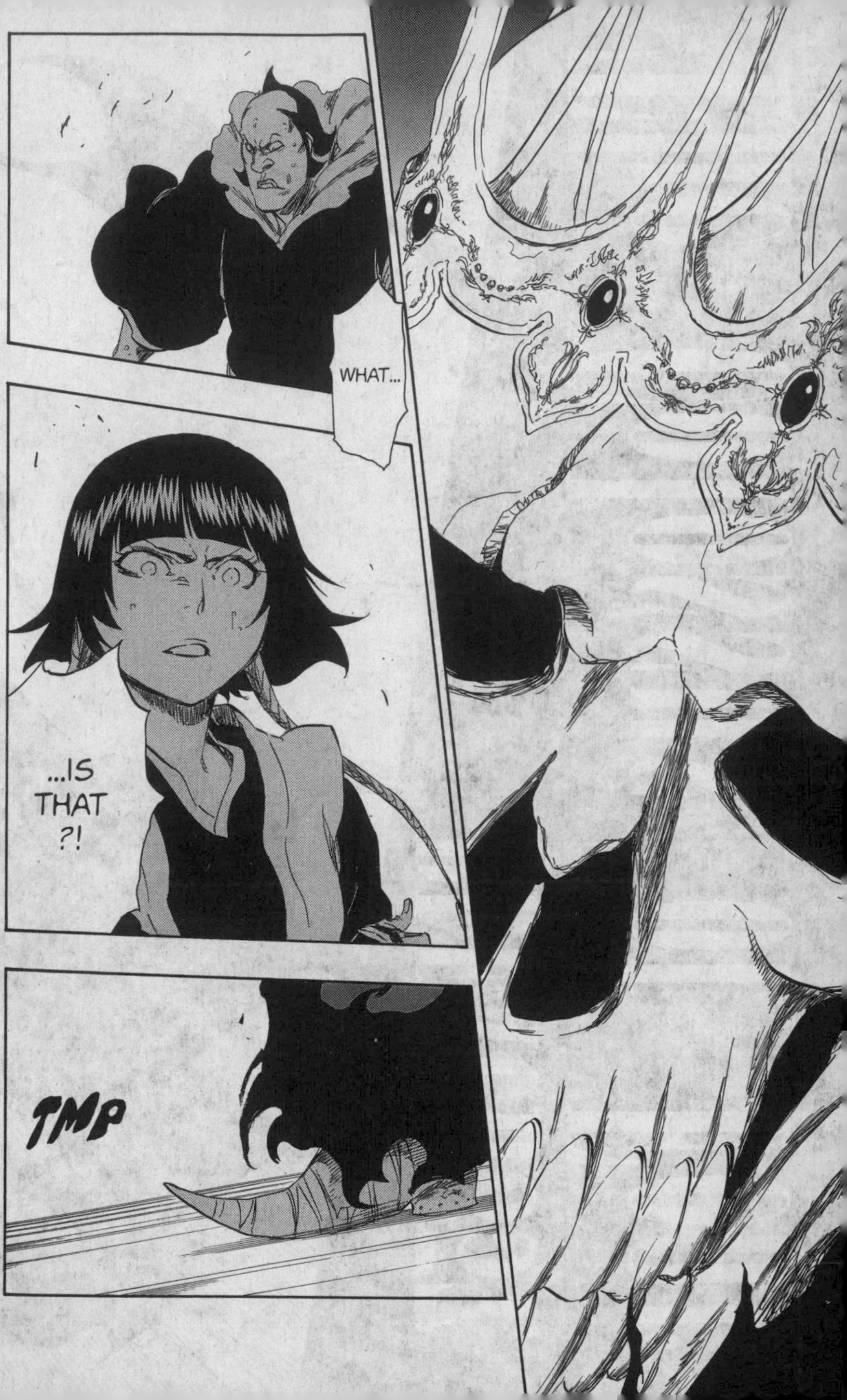
WHAT...
...IS THAT ?!
TMP

READ THIS WAY

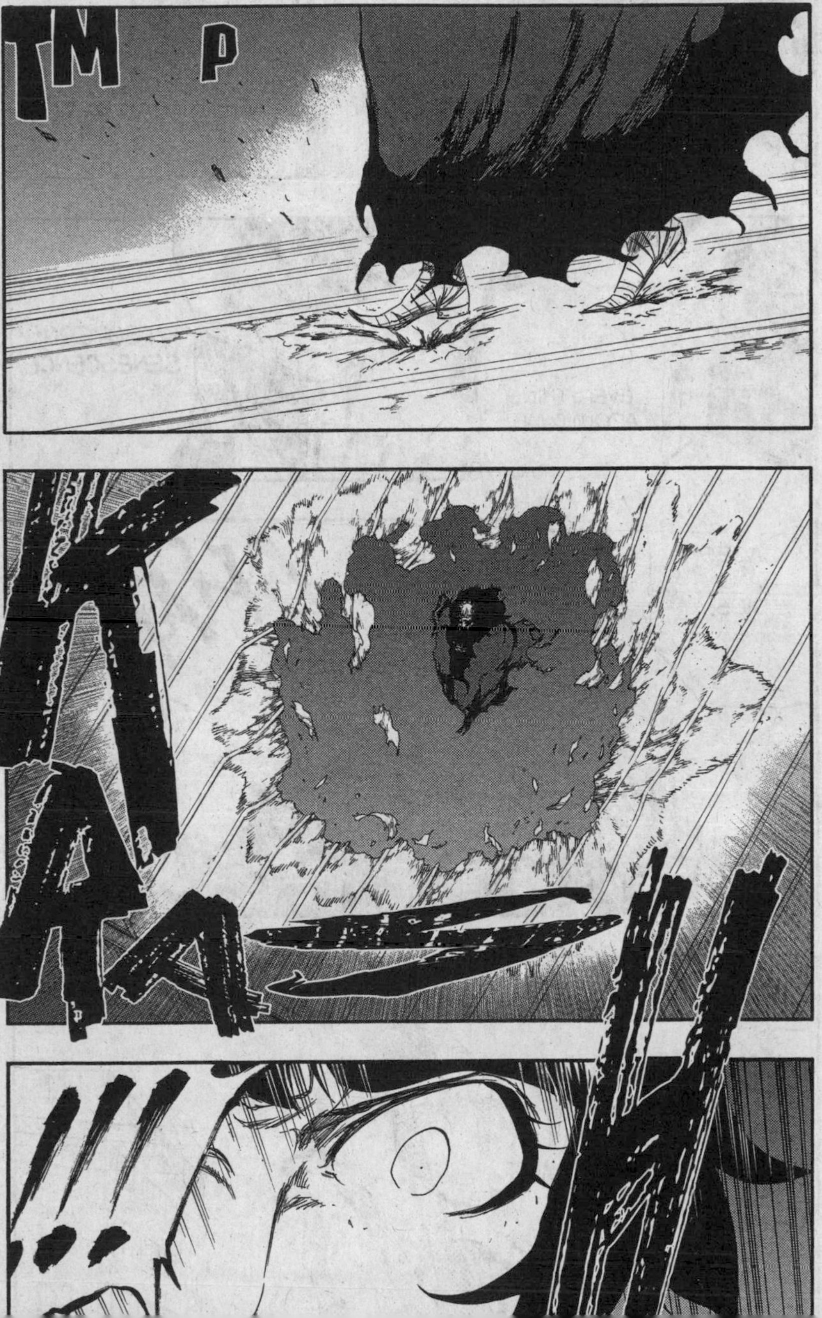
TMP
!!!

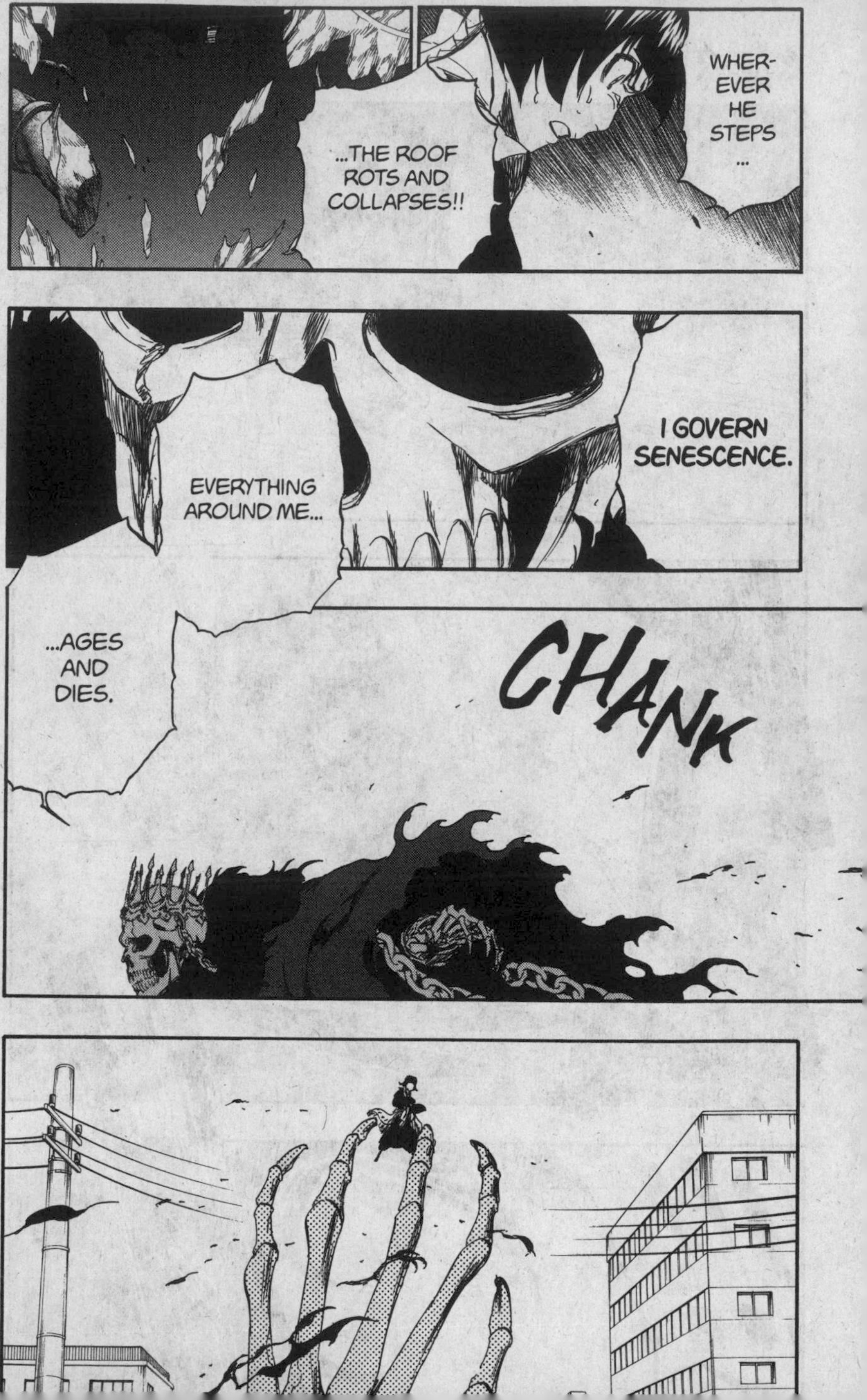
WHER-EVER HE STEPS ...
...THE ROOF ROTS AND COLLAPSES!!
I GOVERN SENESCENCE.
EVERYTHING AROUND ME...
...AGES AND DIES.
CHANK

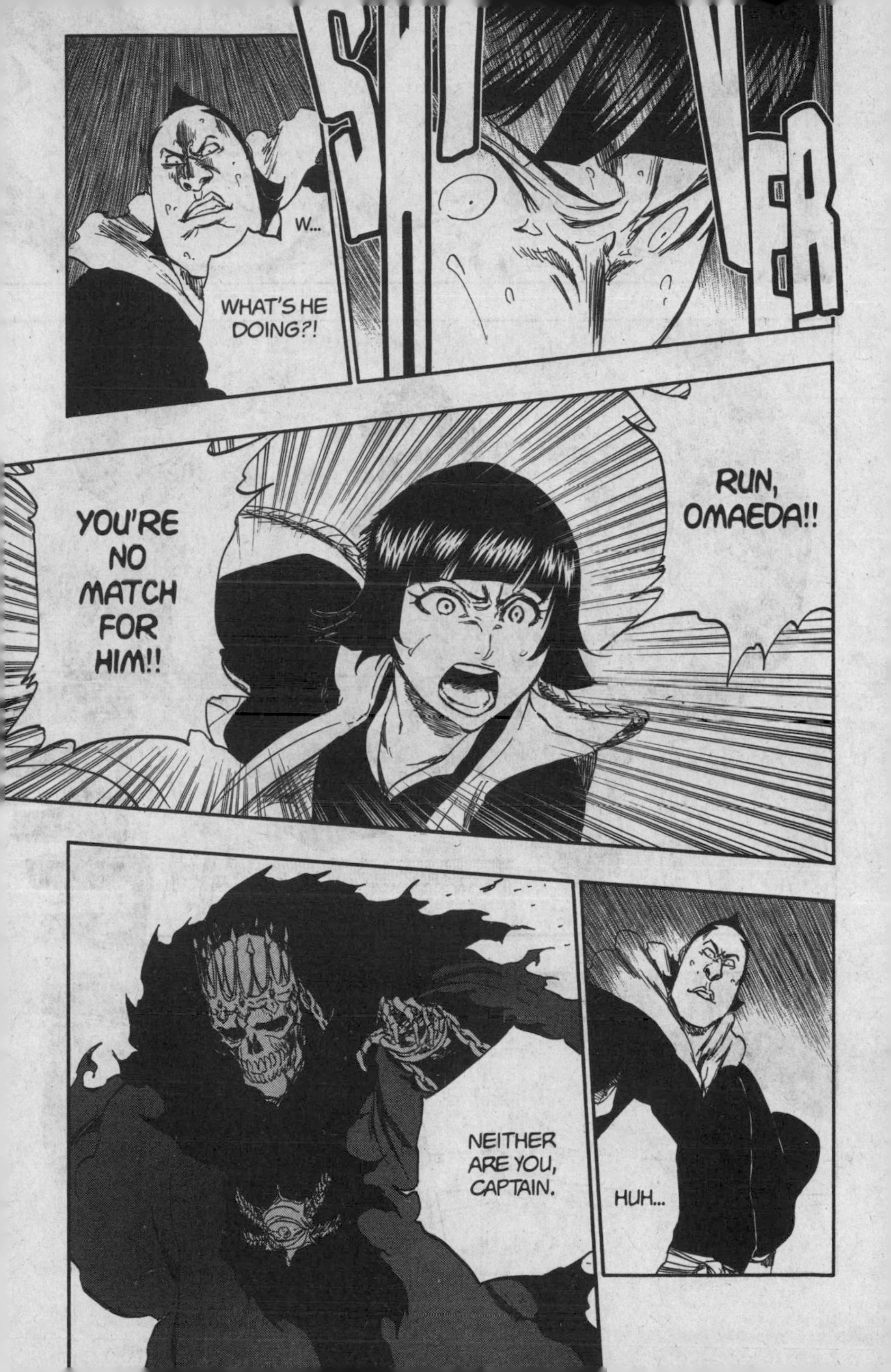
SHIVER
W...
WHAT'S HE DOING?!
RUN, OMAEDA!!
YOU'RE NO MATCH FOR HIM!!
HUH...
NEITHER ARE YOU, CAPTAIN.

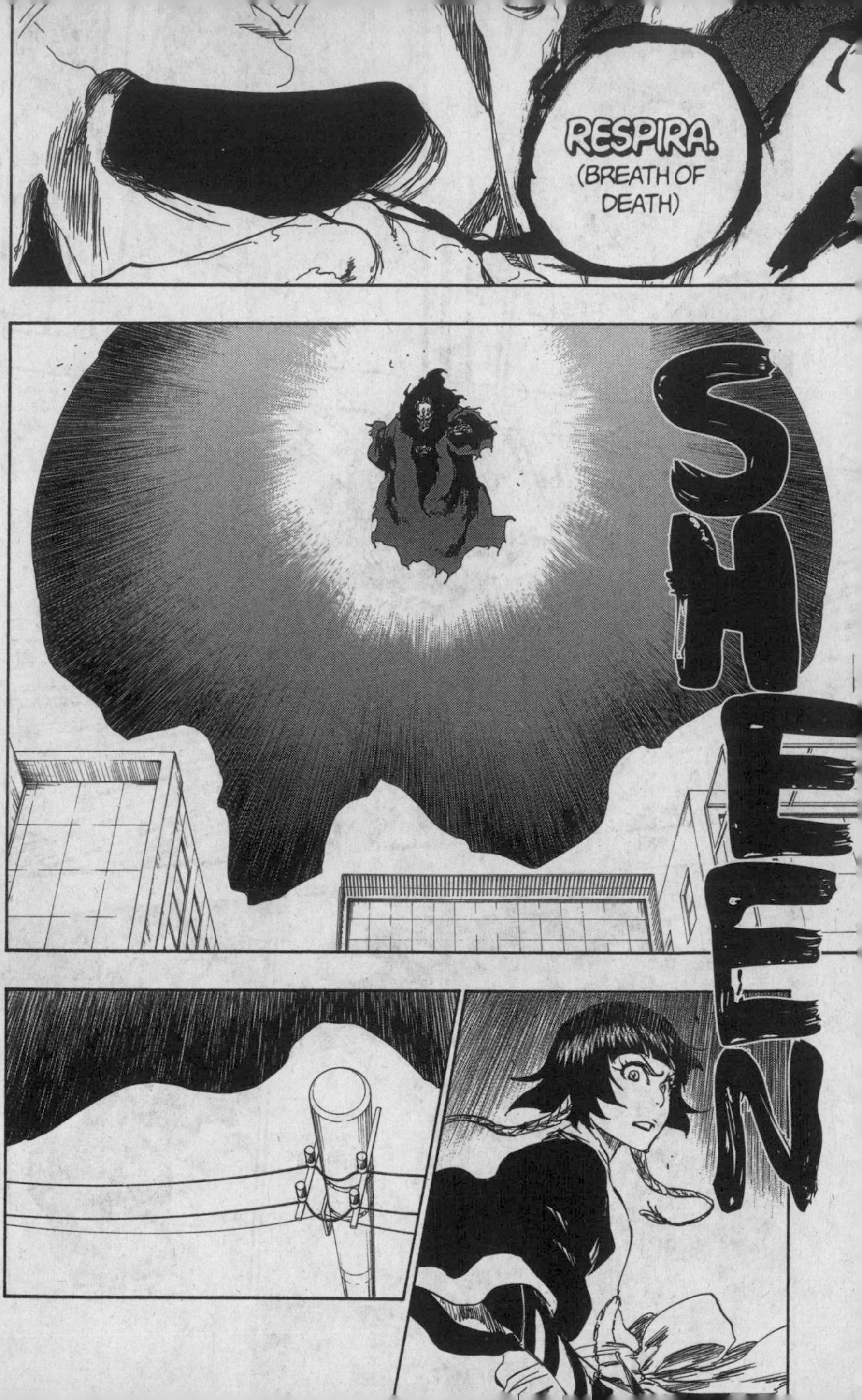
RESPIRA.
(BREATH OF DEATH)
SHEEN

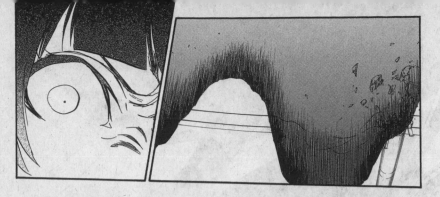

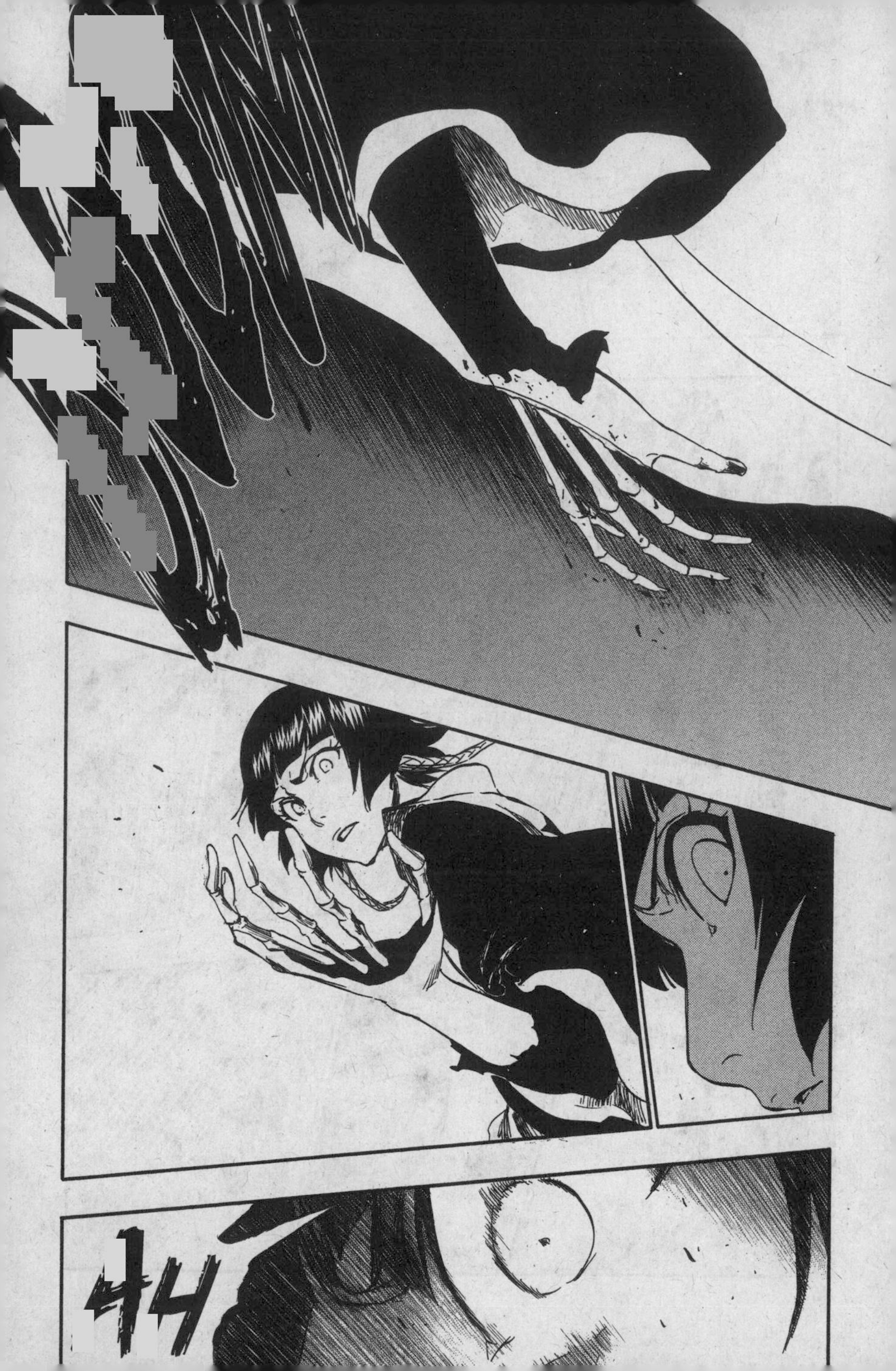

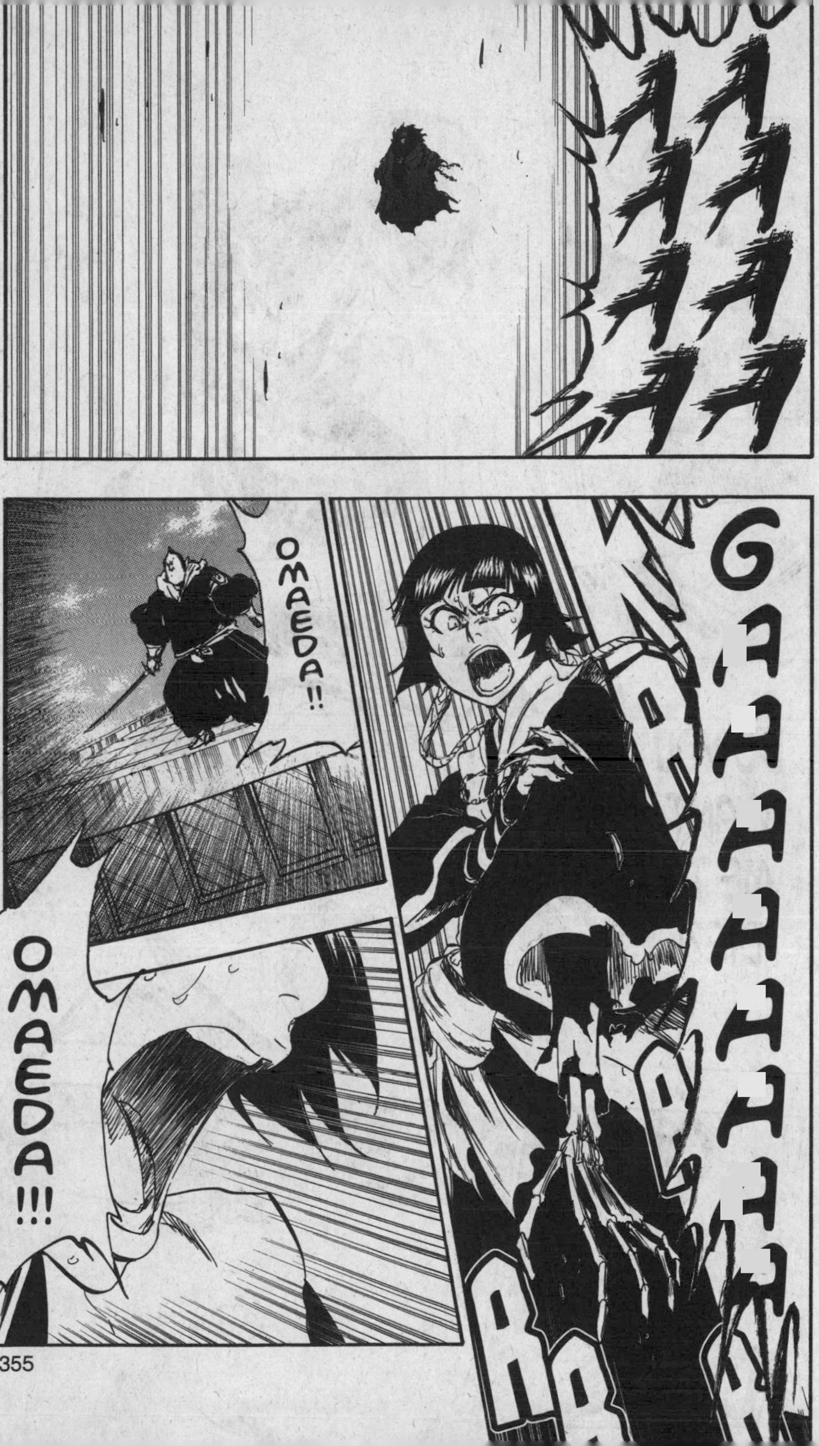
OMAEDA!!
OMAEDA!!!

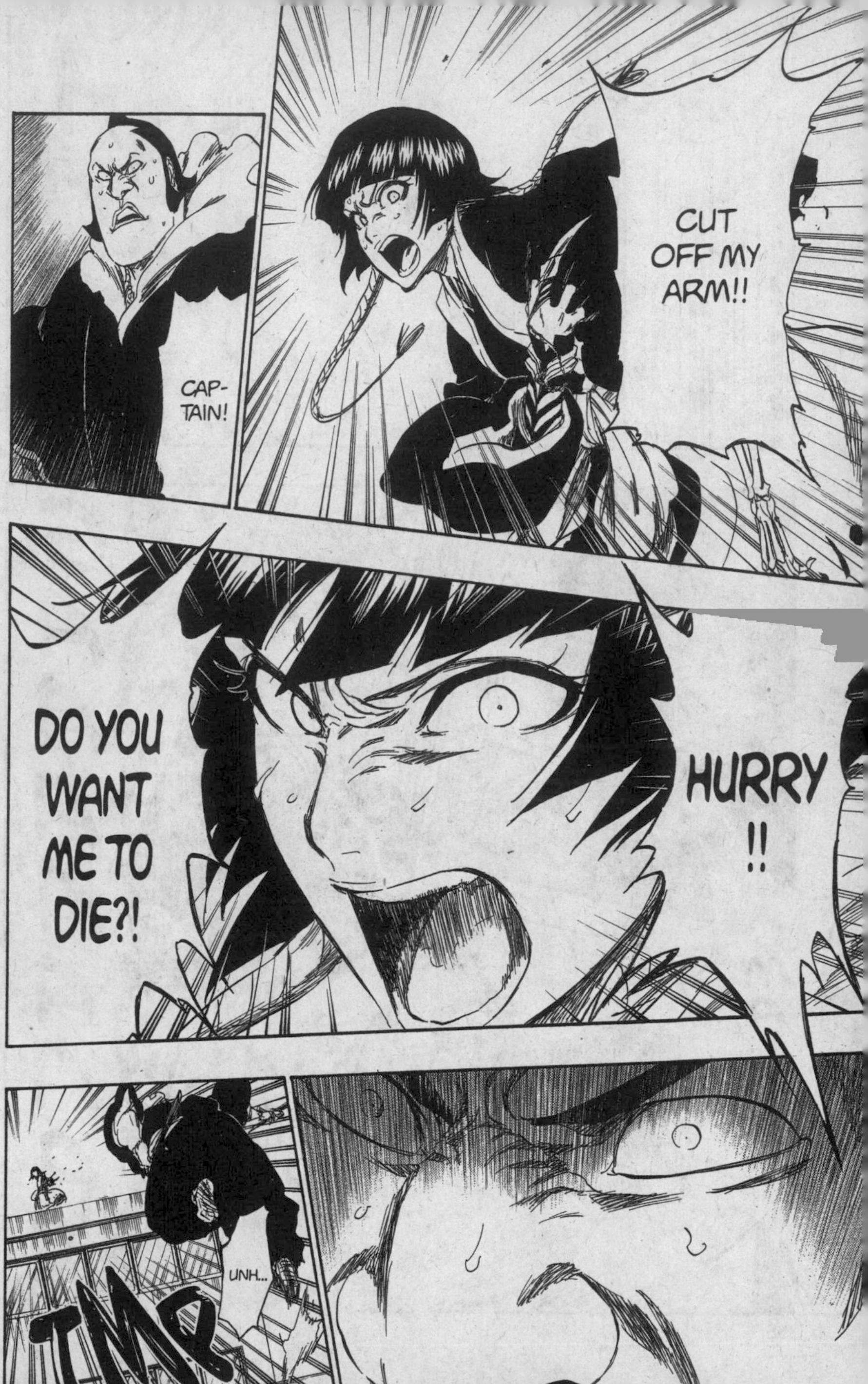
CUT OFF MY ARM!!
CAP-TAIN!
HURRY !!
DO YOU WANT ME TO DIE?!
UNH...
TMP

RATS!!

WHOOF

THUD

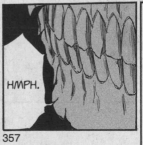

HMPH.

...

WOOOOOOOO

HOW AMUSING.

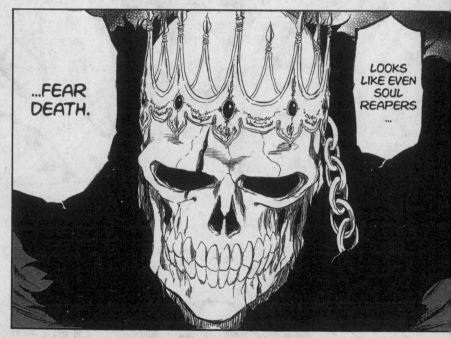

...FEAR DEATH.

LOOKS LIKE EVEN SOUL REAPERS ...

...!

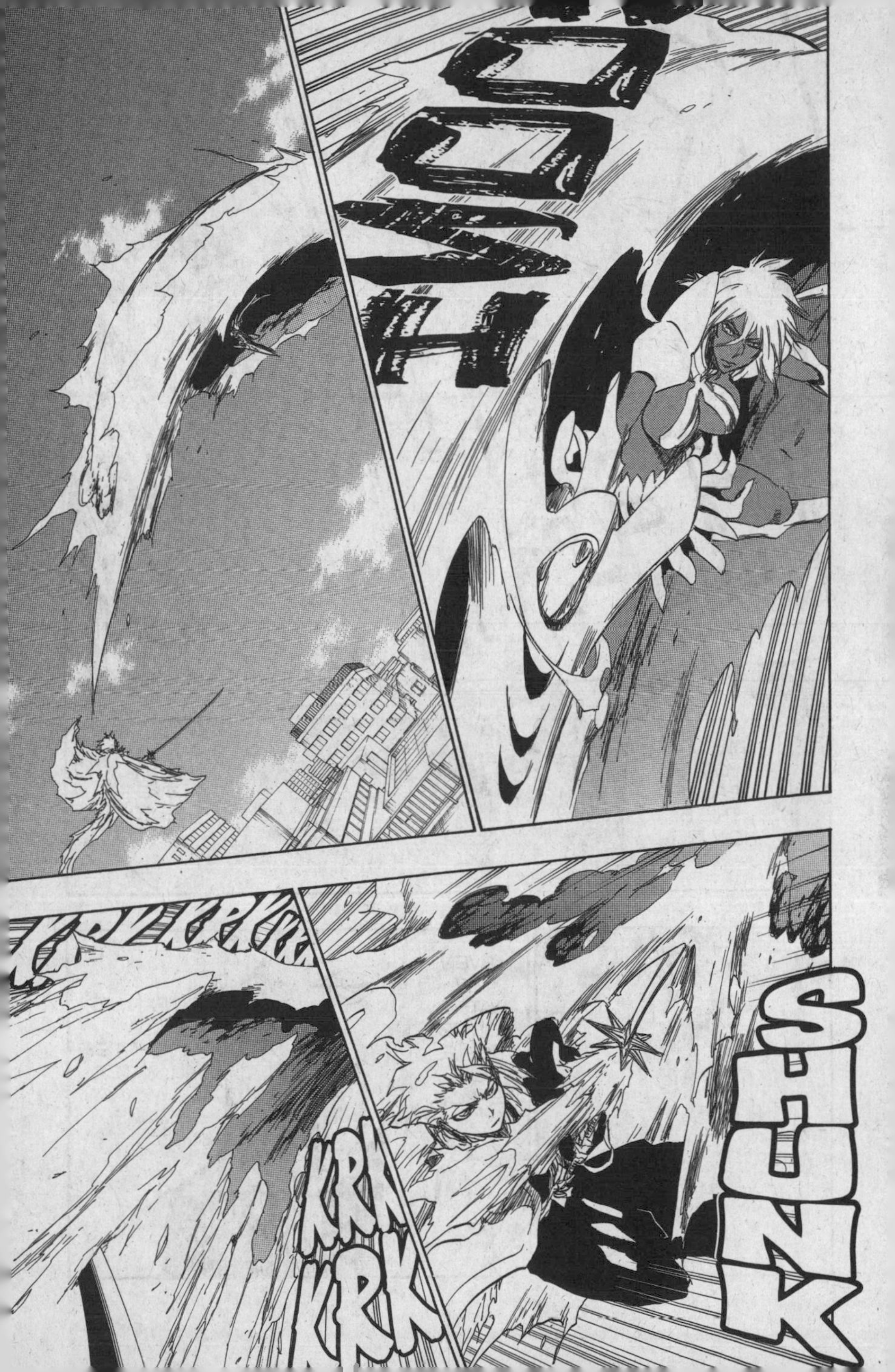
FOOM
SHUNK
KRK KRK

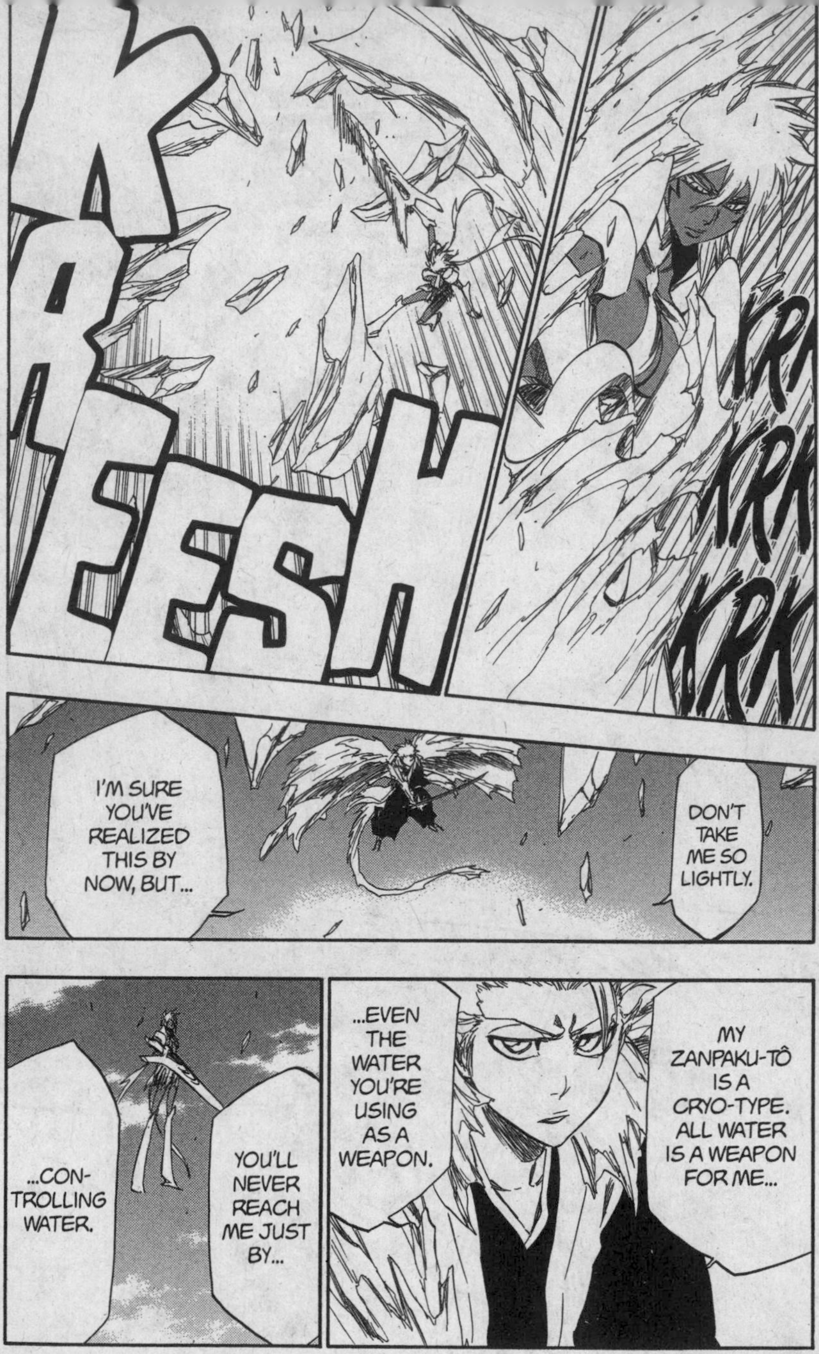
DON'T TAKE ME SO LIGHTLY.
I'M SURE YOU'VE REALIZED THIS BY NOW, BUT...
MY ZANPAKU-TÔ IS A CRYO-TYPE. ALL WATER IS A WEAPON FOR ME...
...EVEN THE WATER YOU'RE USING AS A WEAPON.
YOU'LL NEVER REACH ME JUST BY...
...CON-TROLLING WATER.

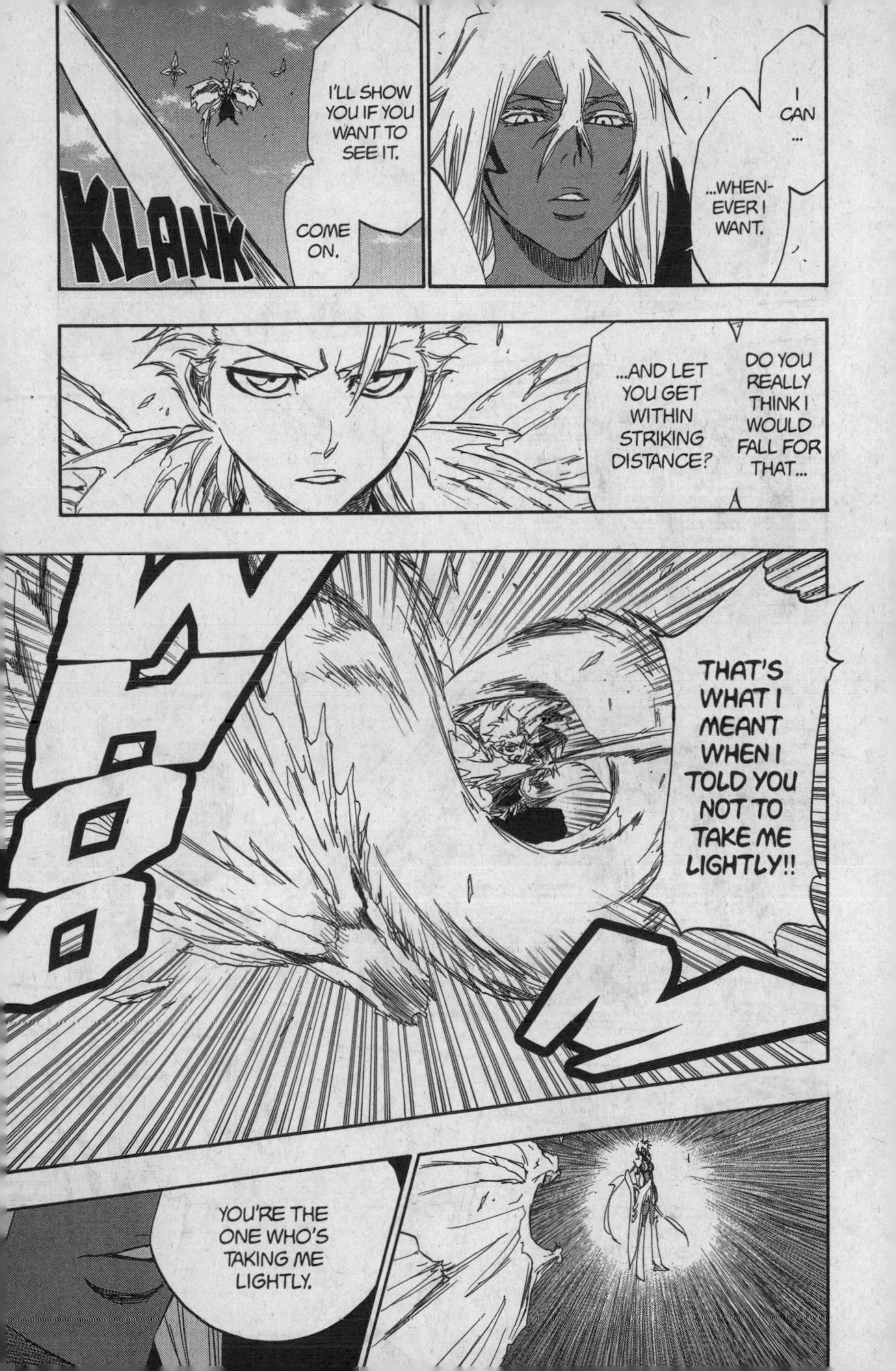
I CAN ...
...WHEN-EVER I WANT.
I'LL SHOW YOU IF YOU WANT TO SEE IT.
COME ON.
KLANK
DO YOU REALLY THINK I WOULD FALL FOR THAT...
...AND LET YOU GET WITHIN STRIKING DISTANCE?
THAT'S WHAT I MEANT WHEN I TOLD YOU NOT TO TAKE ME LIGHTLY!!
YOU'RE THE ONE WHO'S TAKING ME LIGHTLY.

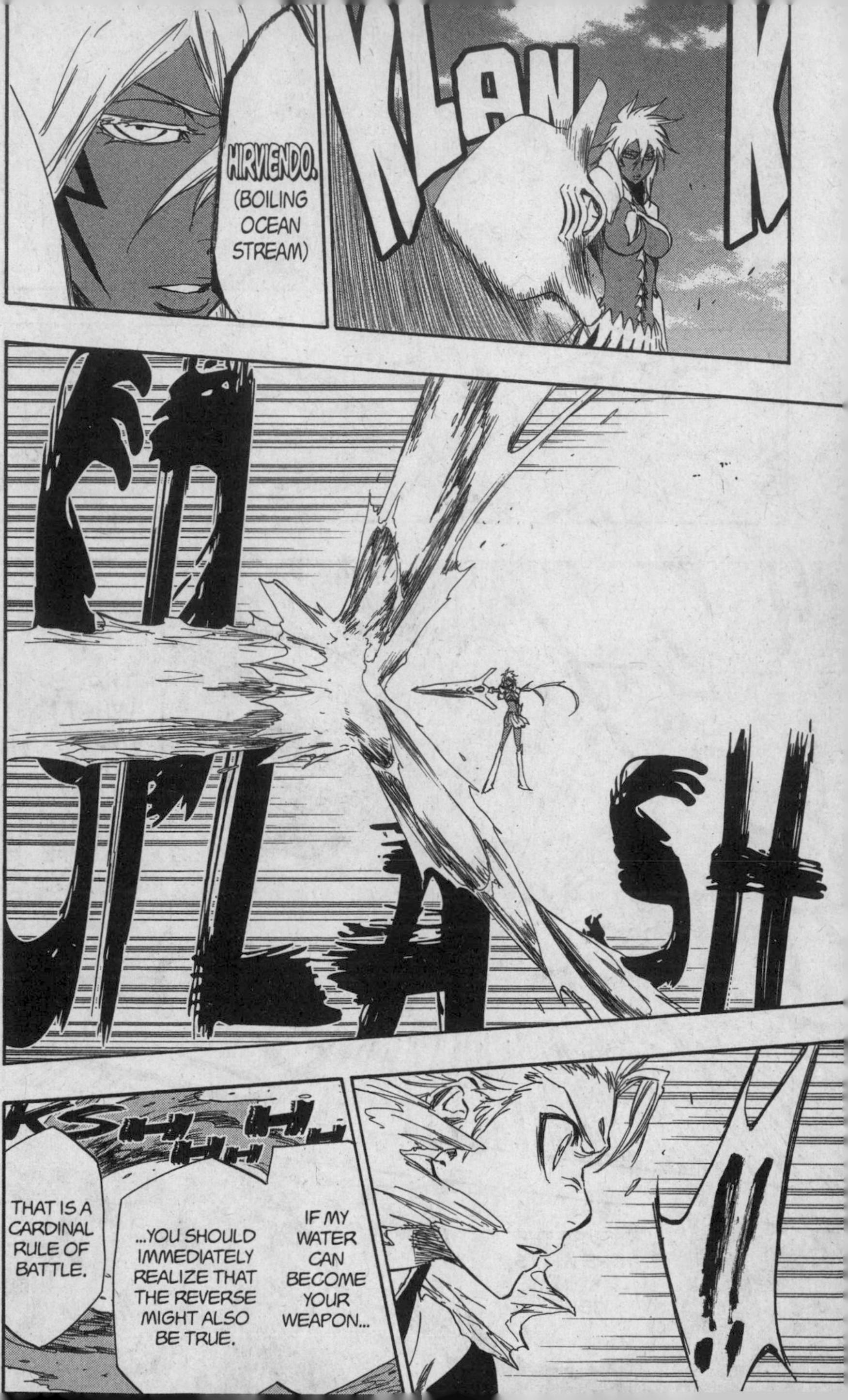
KLANK
HIRVIENDO.
(BOILING OCEAN STREAM)
SPLASH
!!
KSHHHHH...
IF MY WATER CAN BECOME YOUR WEAPON...
...YOU SHOULD IMMEDIATELY REALIZE THAT THE REVERSE MIGHT ALSO BE TRUE.
THAT IS A CARDINAL RULE OF BATTLE.

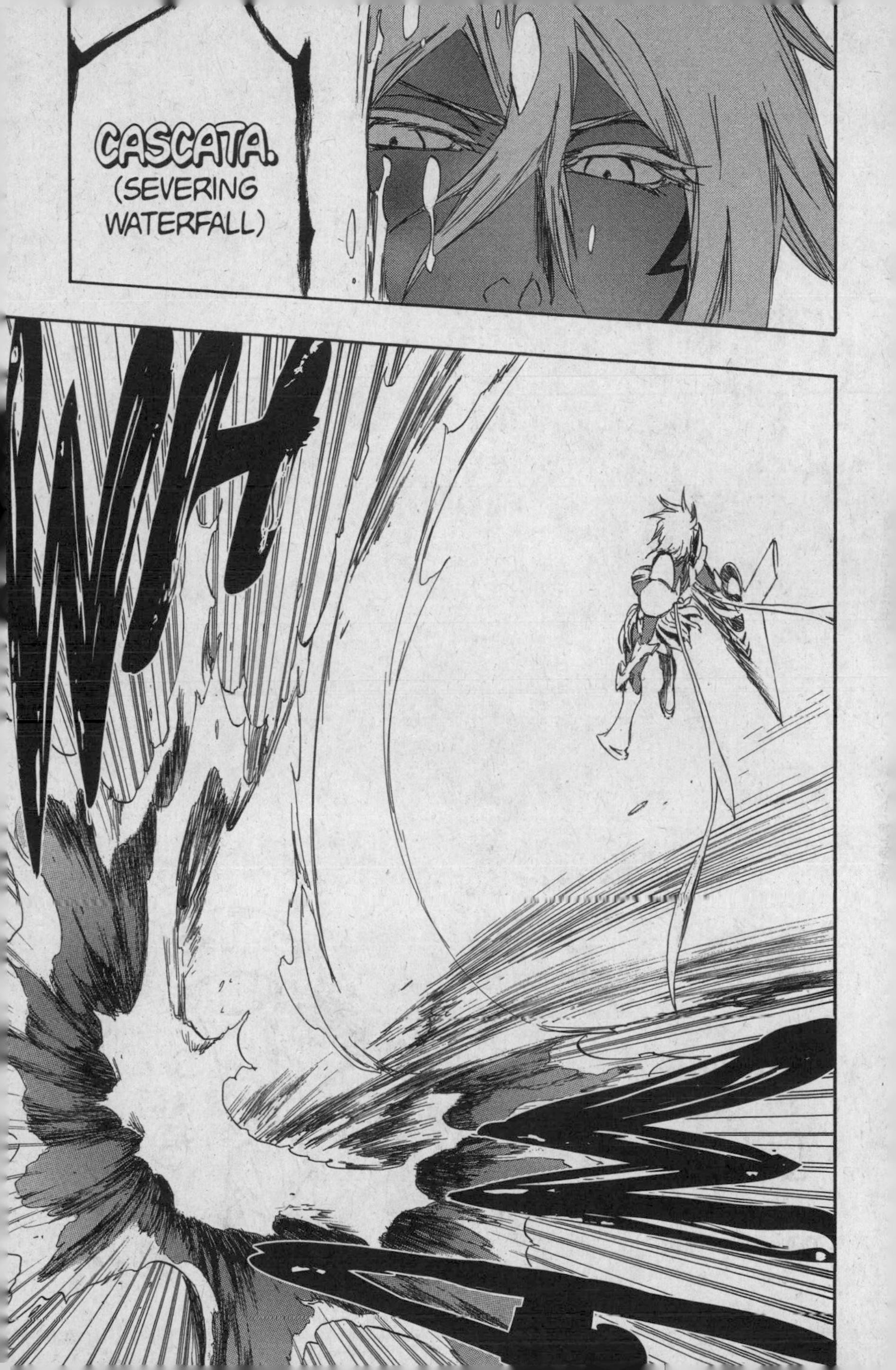
CASCATA.
(SEVERING WATERFALL)

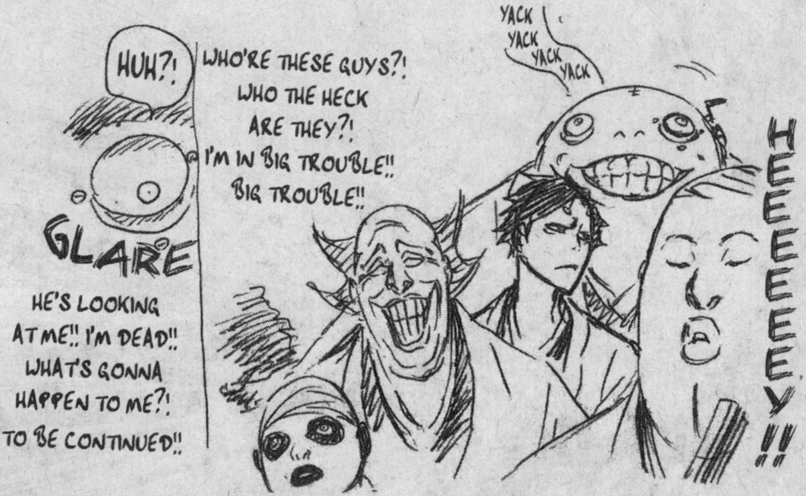
YACK YACK YACK YACK
HEEEEEEEY!!
WHO'RE THESE GUYS?! WHO THE HECK ARE THEY?! I'M IN BIG TROUBLE!! BIG TROUBLE!!
HUH?!
GLARE
HE'S LOOKING AT ME!! I'M DEAD!! WHAT'S GONNA HAPPEN TO ME?!
TO BE CONTINUED!!

358. King of the Clouds

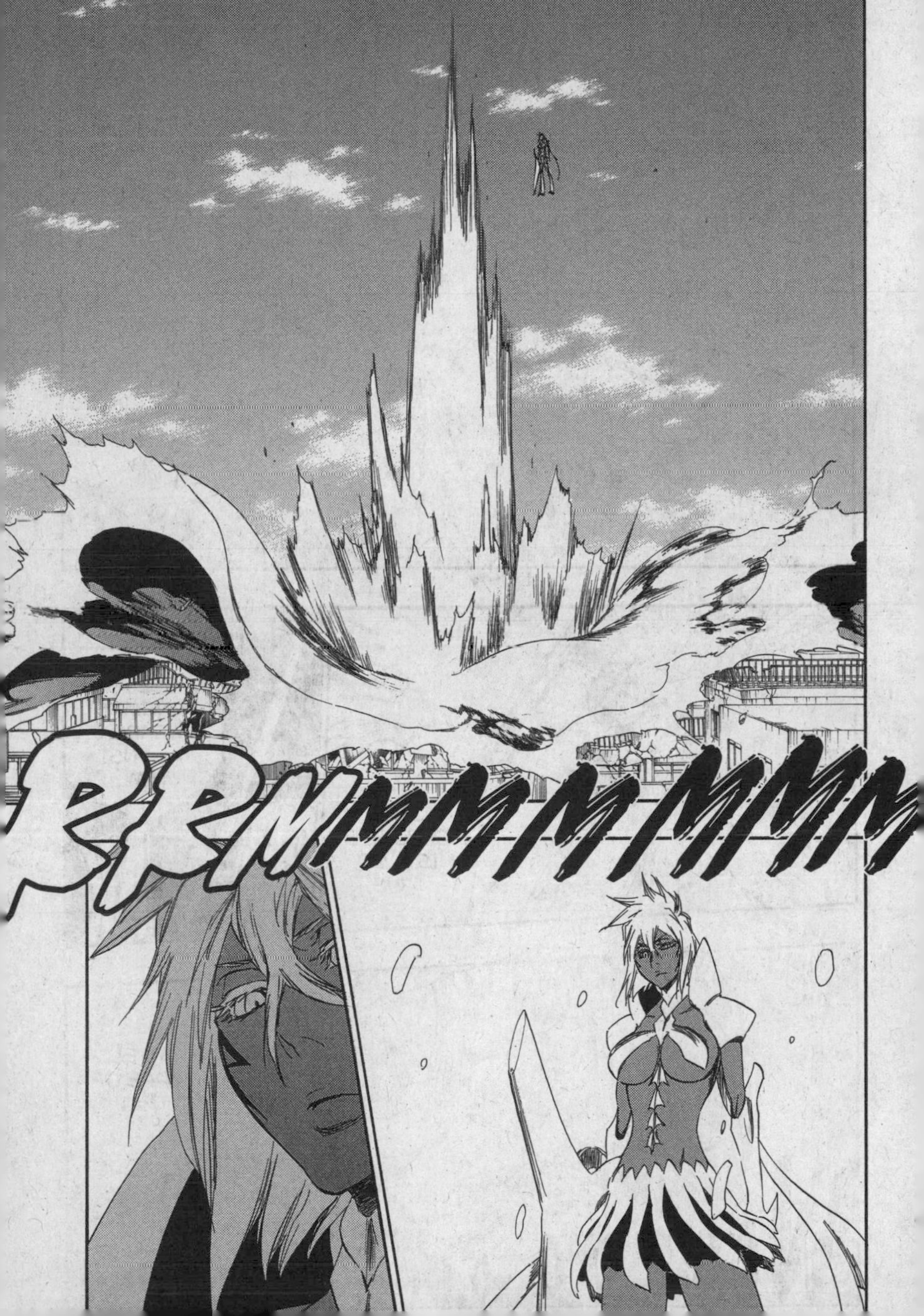
RRMMMMMMMMMMM

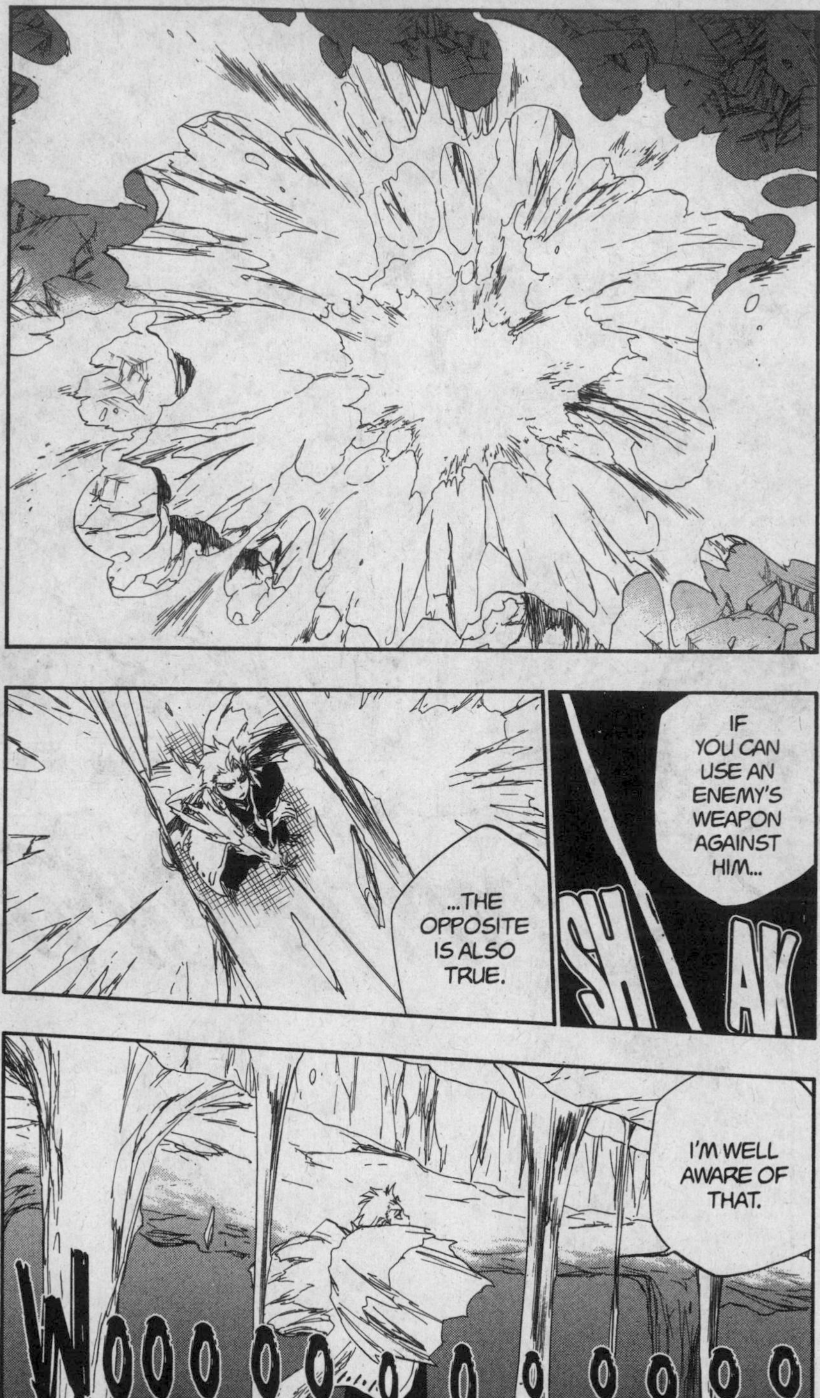
IF YOU CAN USE AN ENEMY'S WEAPON AGAINST HIM...
SHAK
...THE OPPOSITE IS ALSO TRUE.
I'M WELL AWARE OF THAT.
WOOOOOOOOOOOO

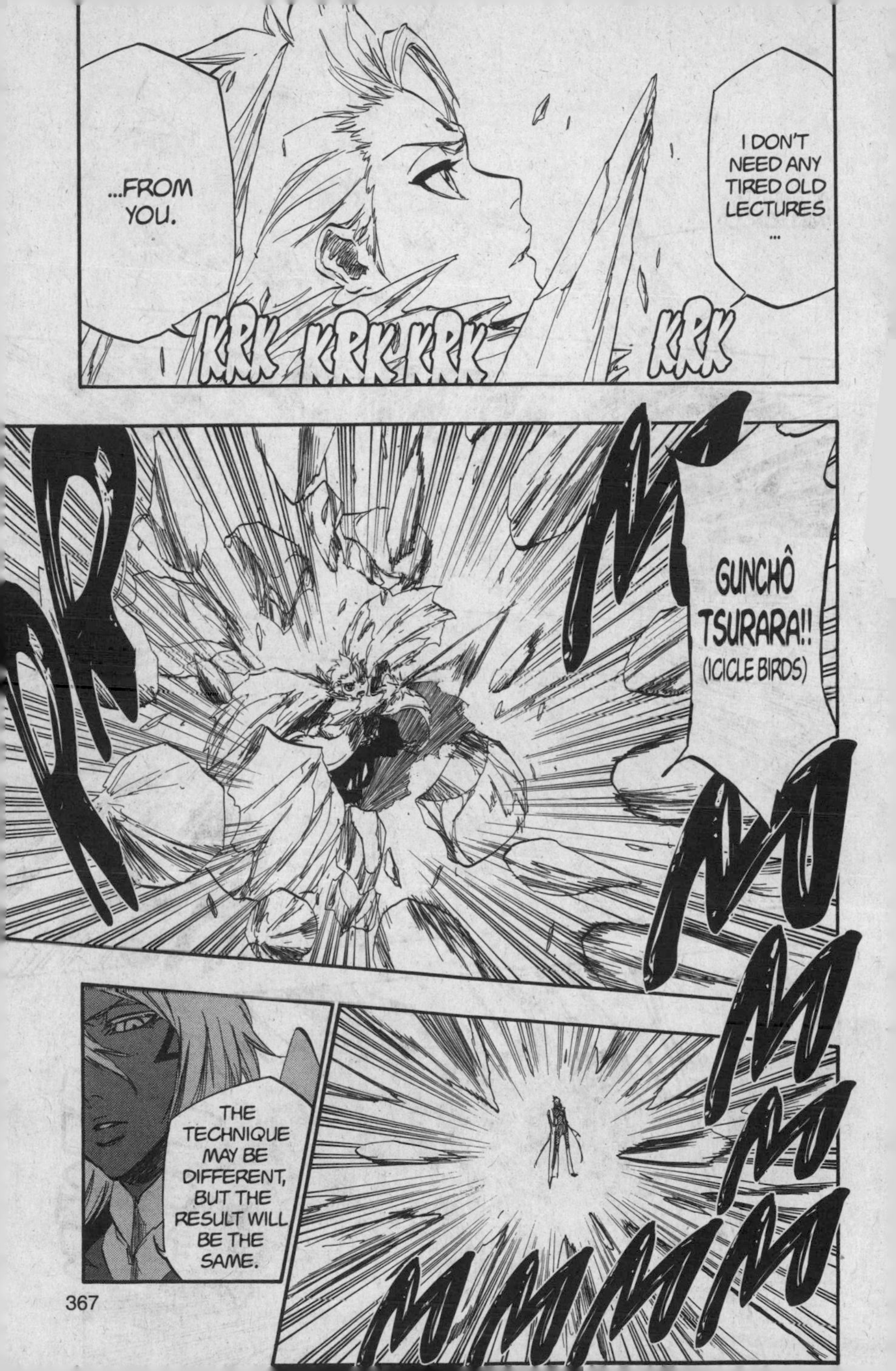
I DON'T NEED ANY TIRED OLD LECTURES ...
...FROM YOU.
KRK
KRK KRK KRK
GUNCHÔ TSURARA!! (ICICLE BIRDS)
THE TECHNIQUE MAY BE DIFFERENT, BUT THE RESULT WILL BE THE SAME.

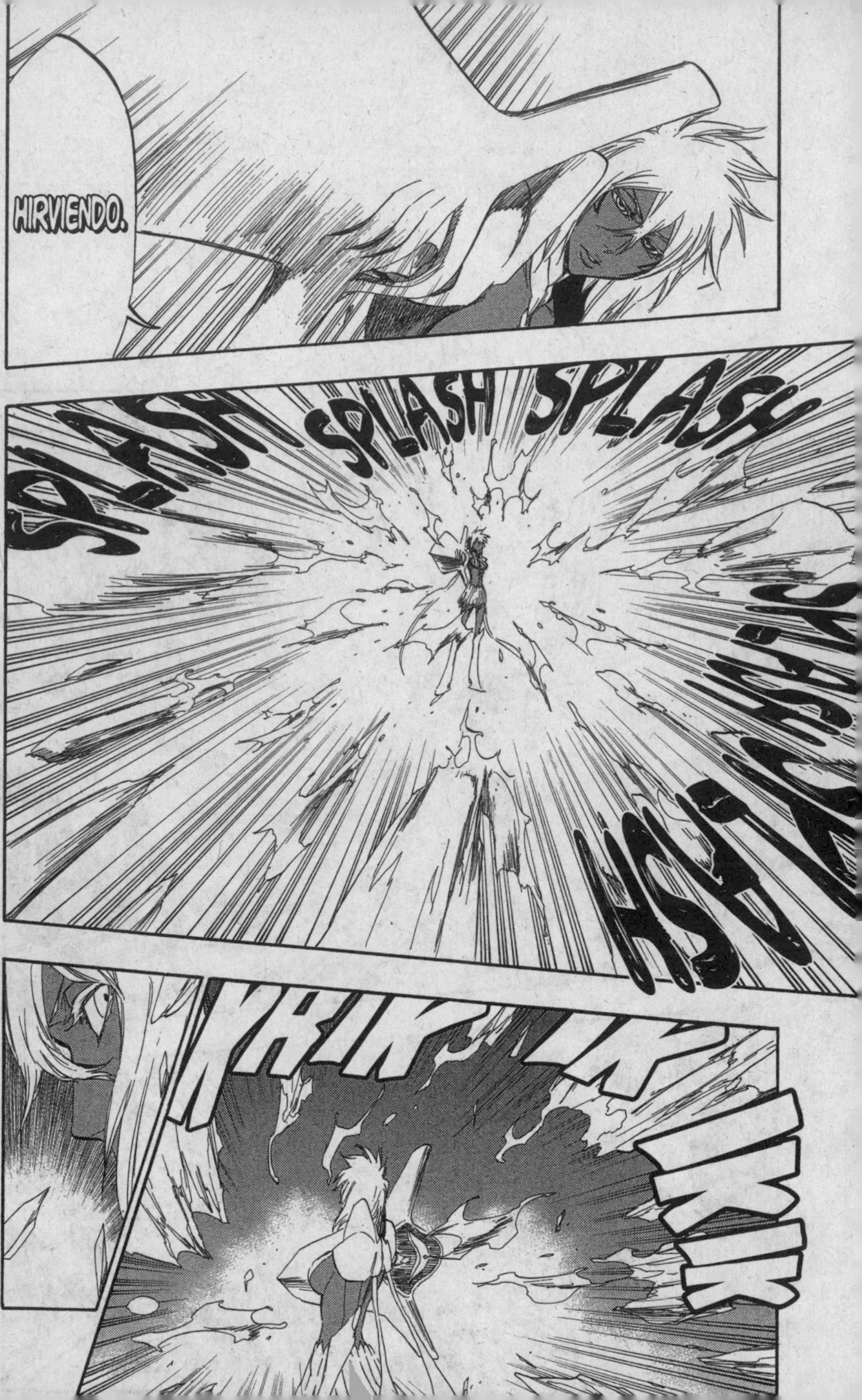
HIRVIENDO.
SPLASH SPLASH SPLASH SPLASH
SPLASH
KRIK KRIK

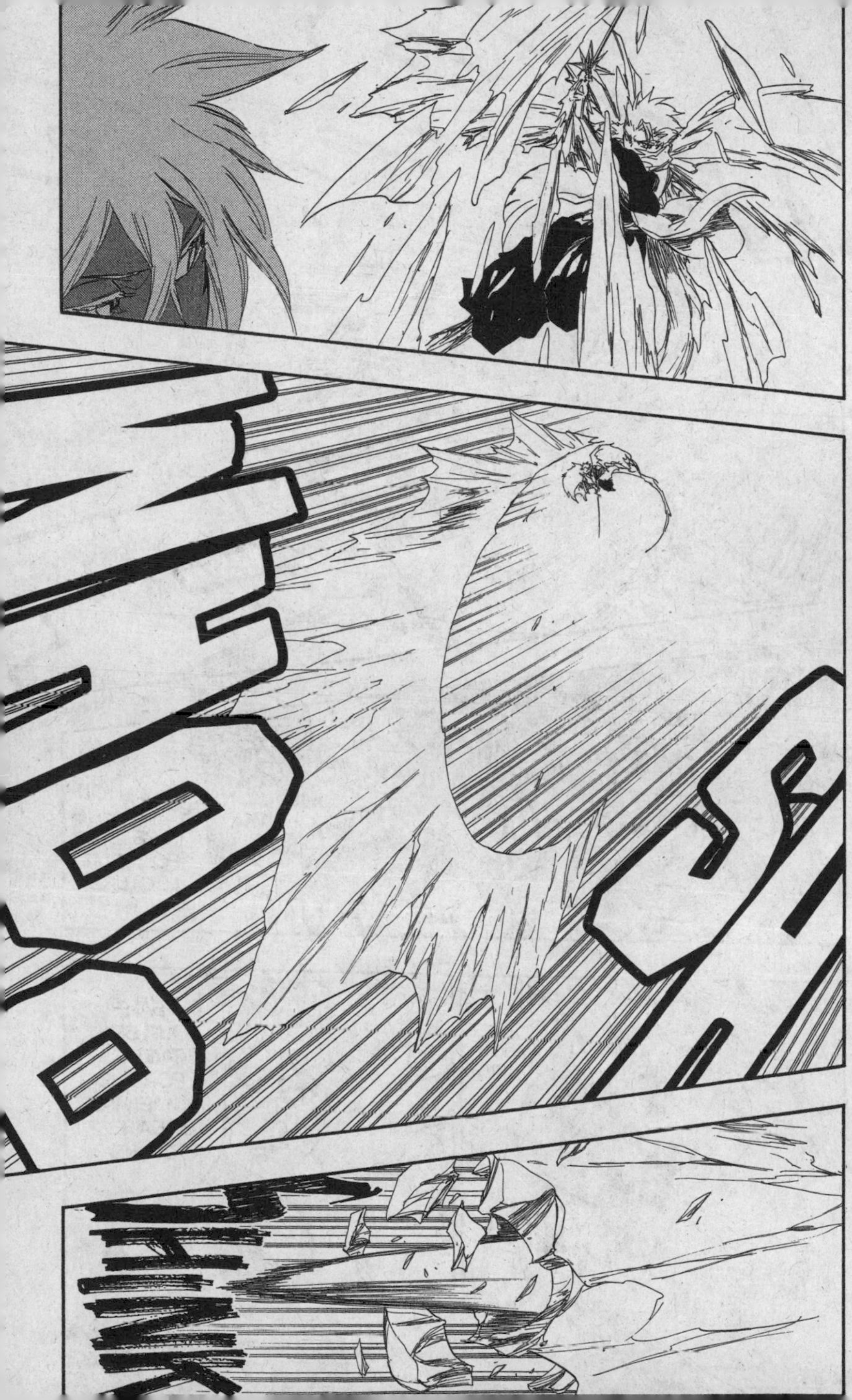

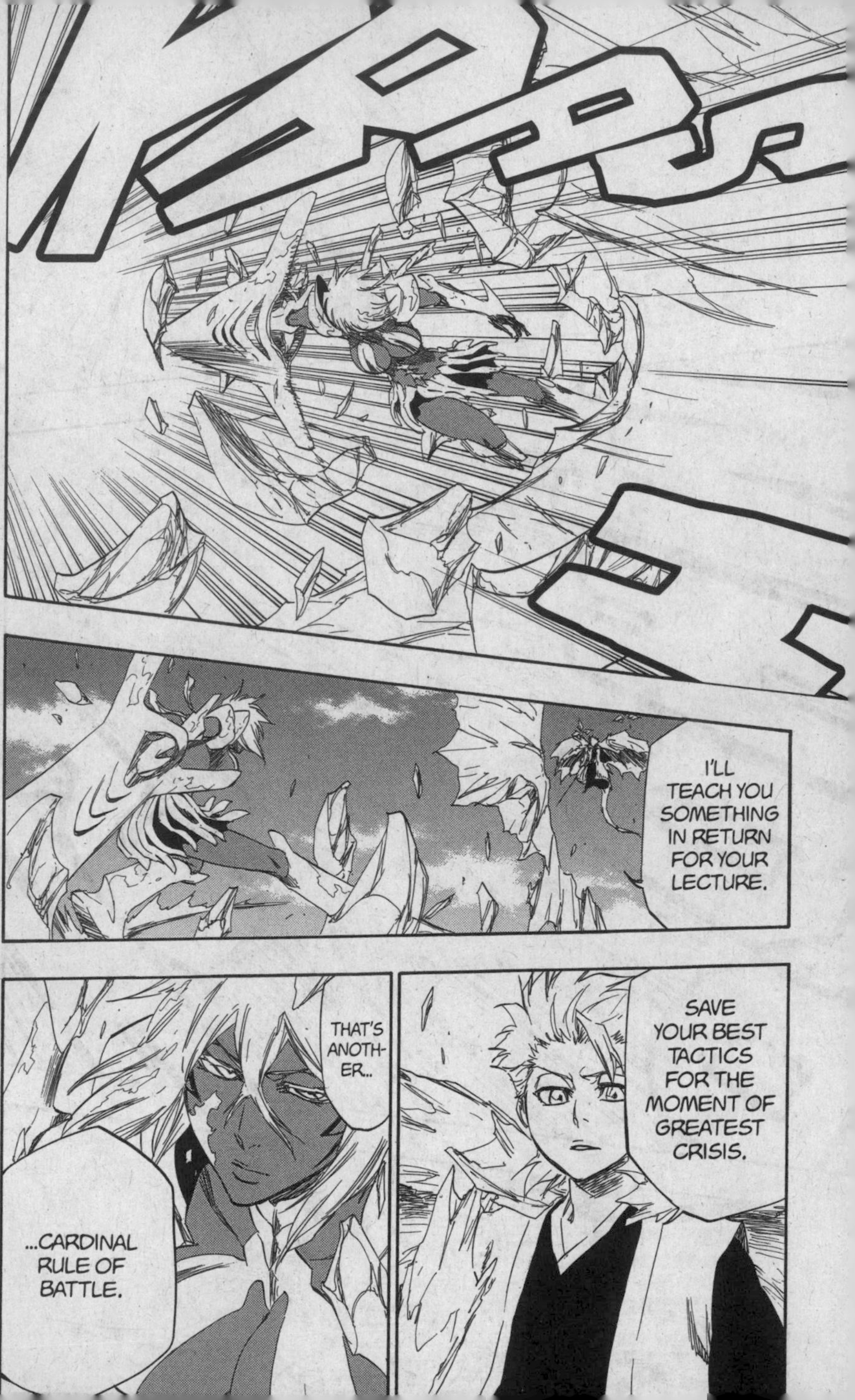
I'LL TEACH YOU SOMETHING IN RETURN FOR YOUR LECTURE.
SAVE YOUR BEST TACTICS FOR THE MOMENT OF GREATEST CRISIS.
THAT'S ANOTHER-ER...
...CARDINAL RULE OF BATTLE.

BLEACH358. King of the Clouds

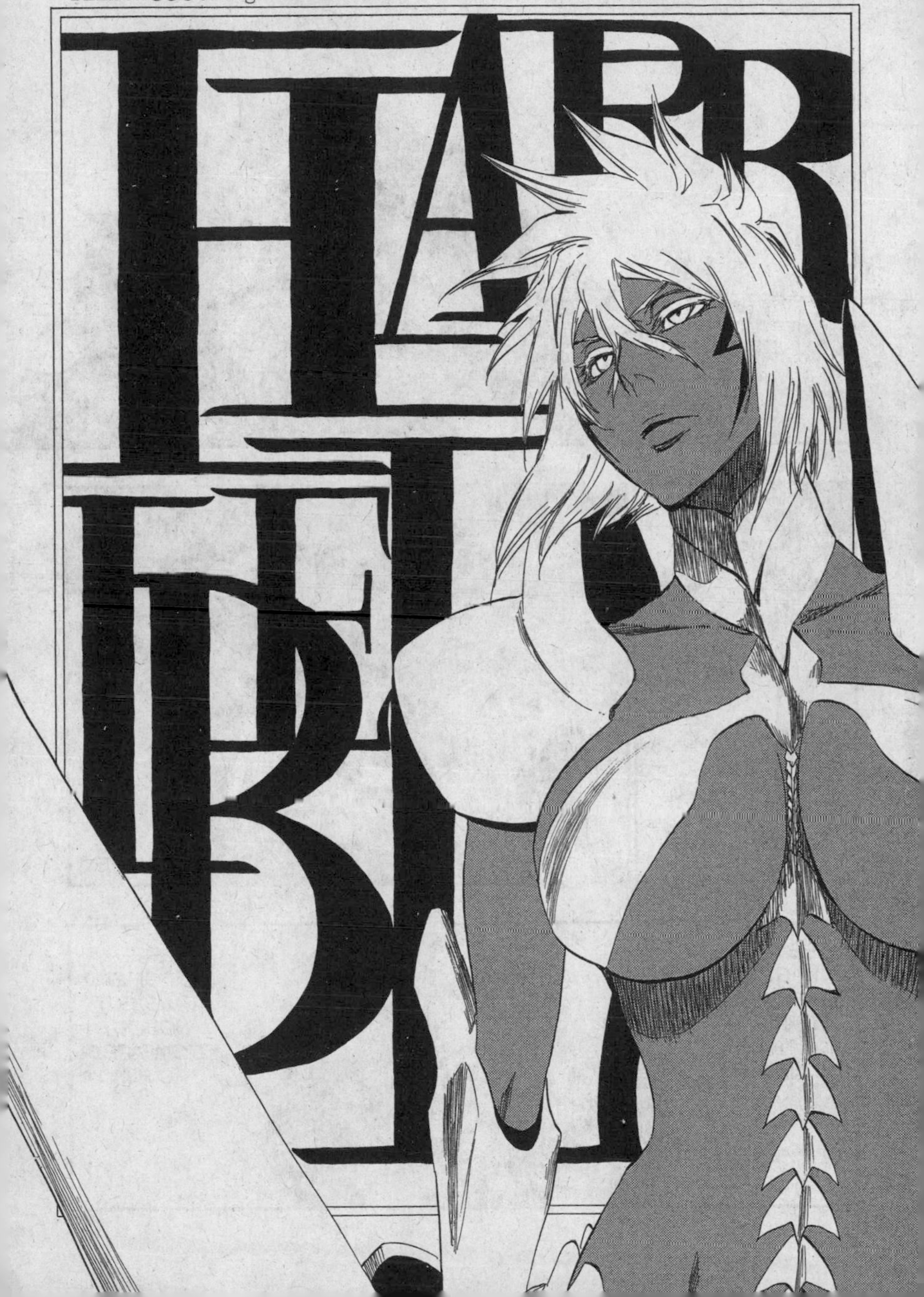

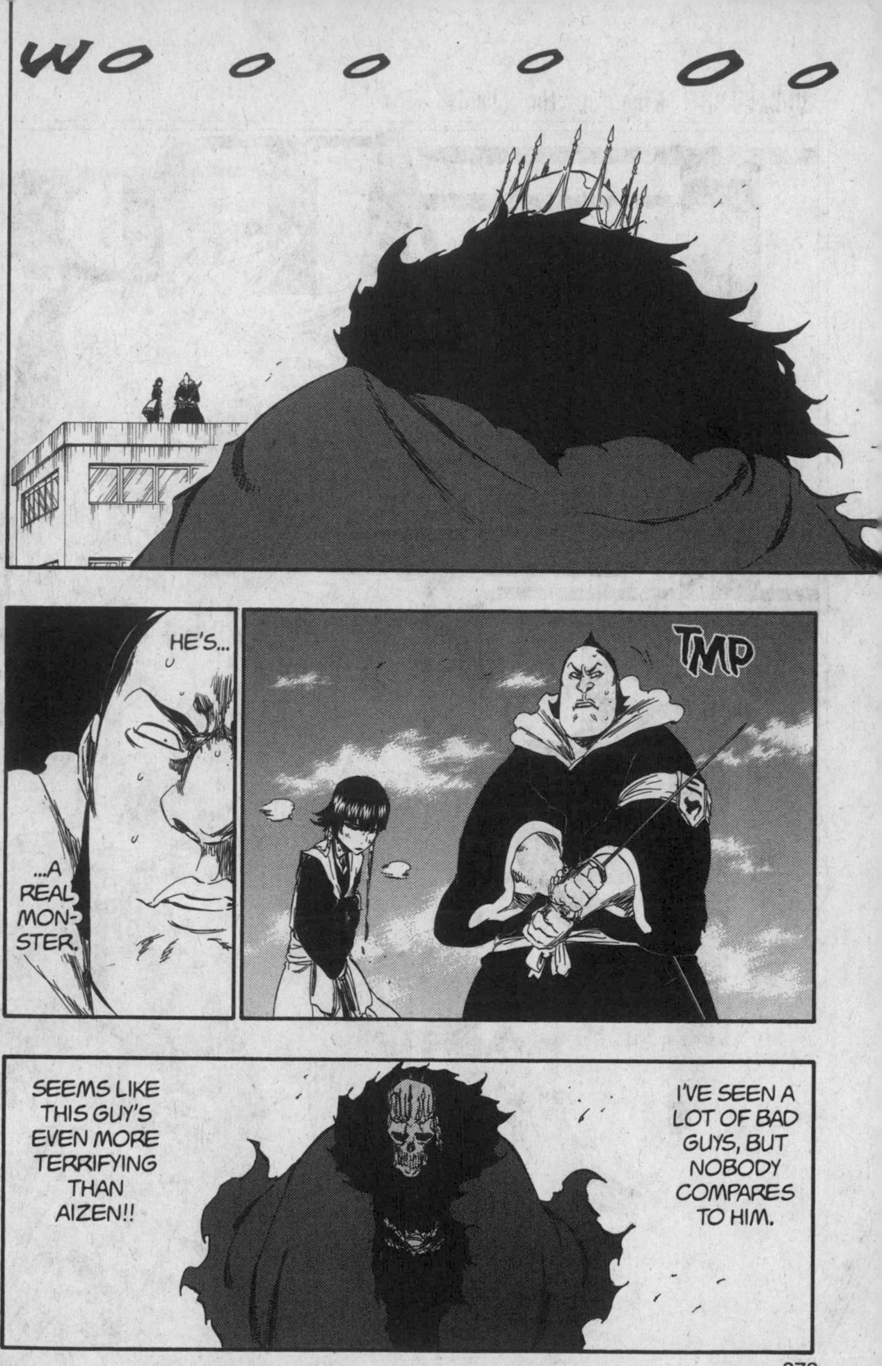
WOOOOOO
TMP
HE'S...
...A REAL MON-STER.
I'VE SEEN A LOT OF BAD GUYS, BUT NOBODY COMPARES TO HIM.
SEEMS LIKE THIS GUY'S EVEN MORE TERRIFYING THAN AIZEN!!

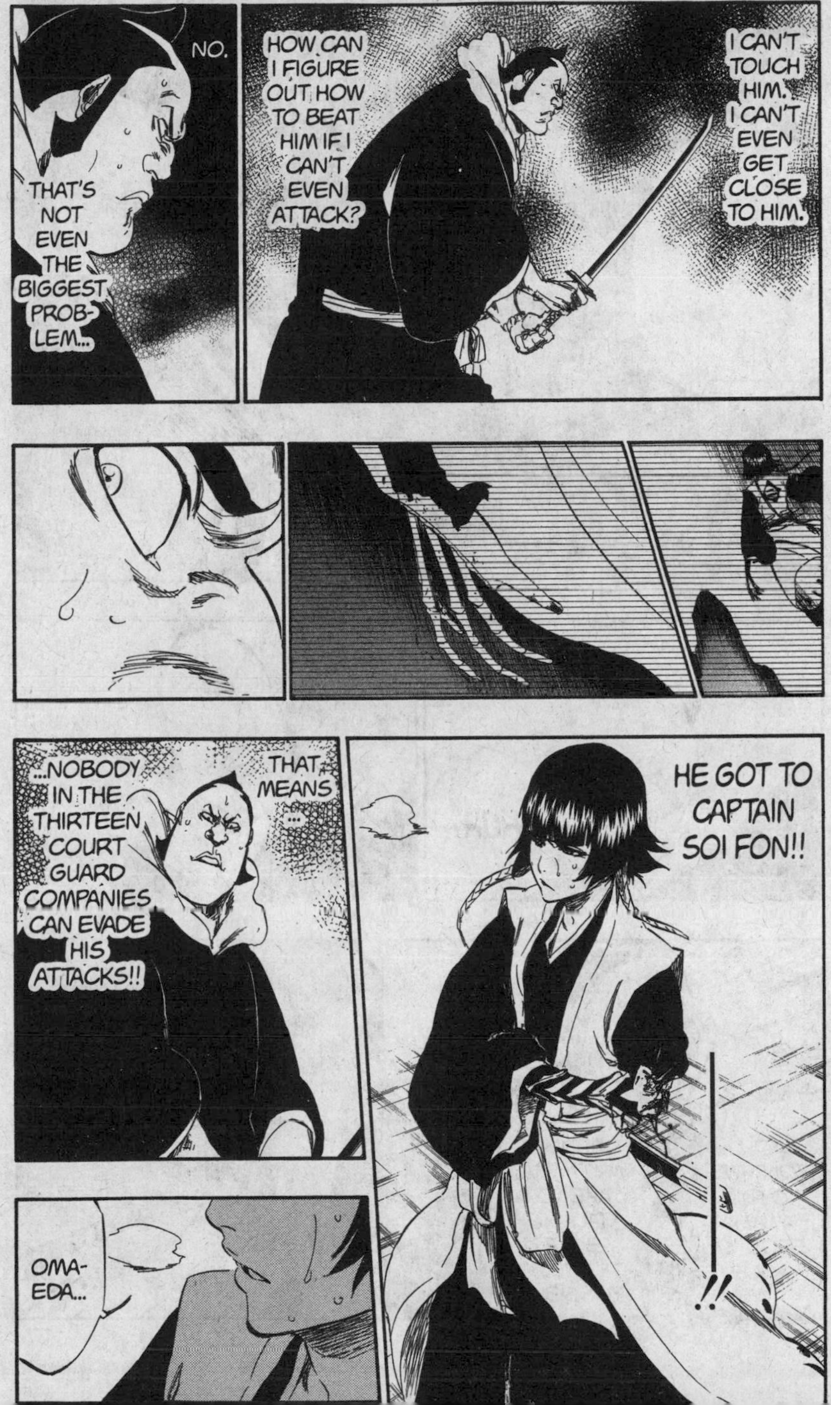
I CAN'T TOUCH HIM. I CAN'T EVEN GET CLOSE TO HIM.
HOW CAN I FIGURE OUT HOW TO BEAT HIM IF I CAN'T EVEN ATTACK?
NO.
THAT'S NOT EVEN THE BIGGEST PROB-LEM...
HE GOT TO CAPTAIN SOI FON!!
!!
THAT MEANS...
...NOBODY IN THE THIRTEEN COURT GUARD COMPANIES CAN EVADE HIS ATTACKS!!
OMA-EDA...

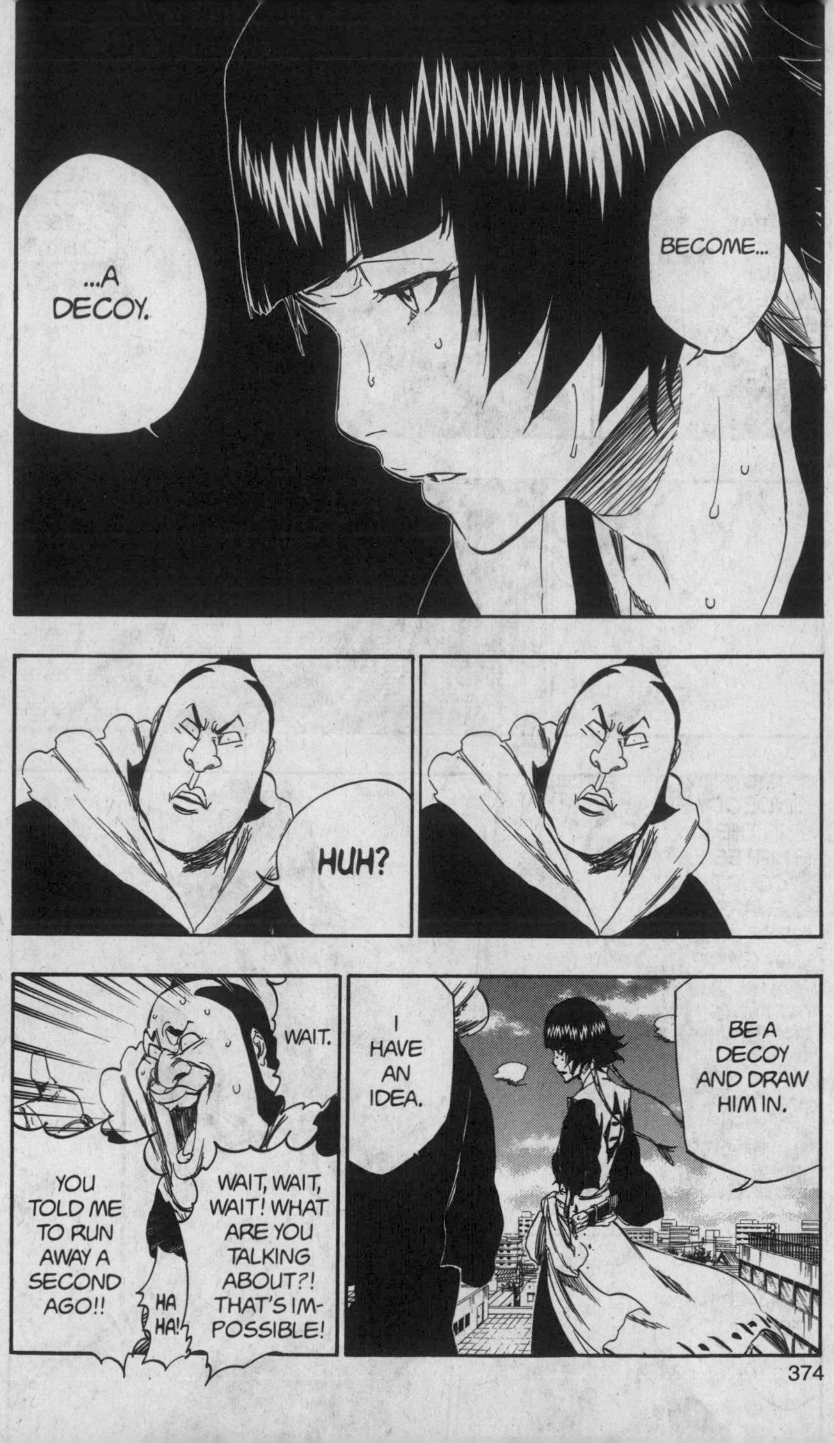
BECOME...
...A DECOY.
HUH?
BE A DECOY AND DRAW HIM IN.
I HAVE AN IDEA.
WAIT.
WAIT, WAIT, WAIT! WHAT ARE YOU TALKING ABOUT?! THAT'S IM-POSSIBLE!
YOU TOLD ME TO RUN AWAY A SECOND AGO!!
HA HA!

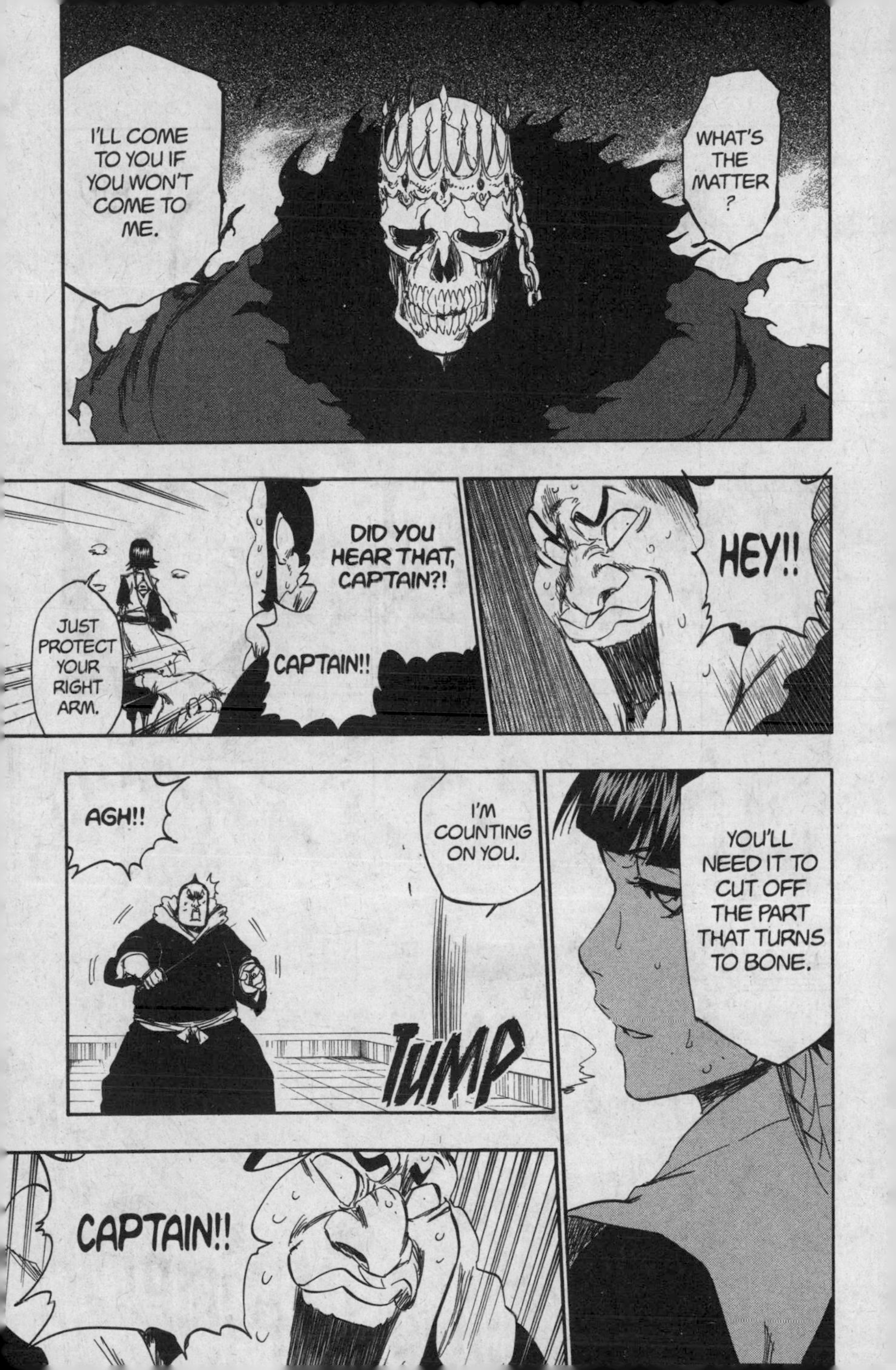
WHAT'S THE MATTER?
I'LL COME TO YOU IF YOU WON'T COME TO ME.
HEY!!
DID YOU HEAR THAT, CAPTAIN?!
CAPTAIN!!
JUST PROTECT YOUR RIGHT ARM.
YOU'LL NEED IT TO CUT OFF THE PART THAT TURNS TO BONE.
I'M COUNTING ON YOU.
AGH!!
TUMP
CAPTAIN!!

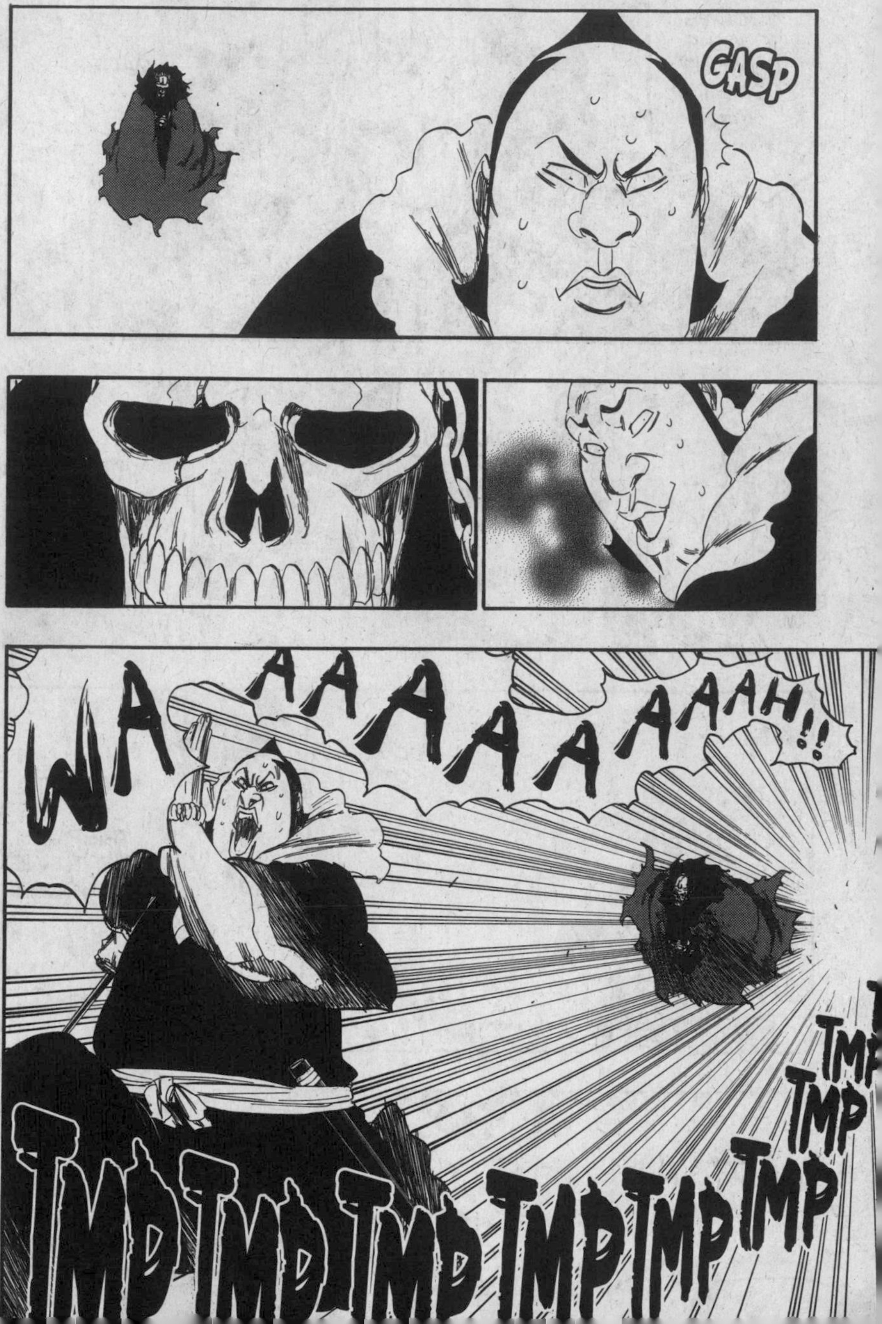
GASP
WAAAAAAAAAAH!!
TMP TMP TMP TMP TMP TMP TMP TMP TMP

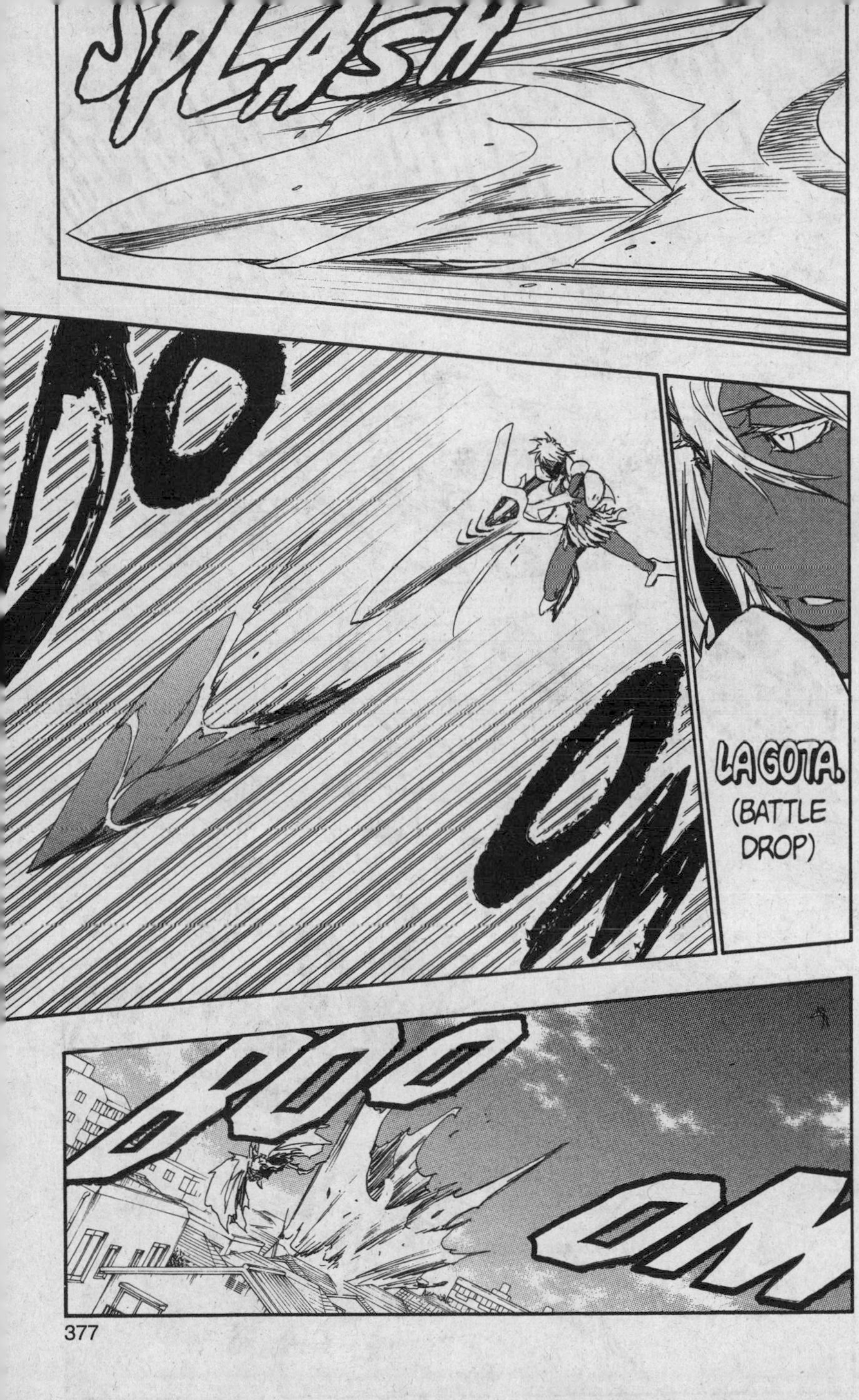
SPLASH
DOOM
LA GOTA.
(BATTLE DROP)
FWOOM

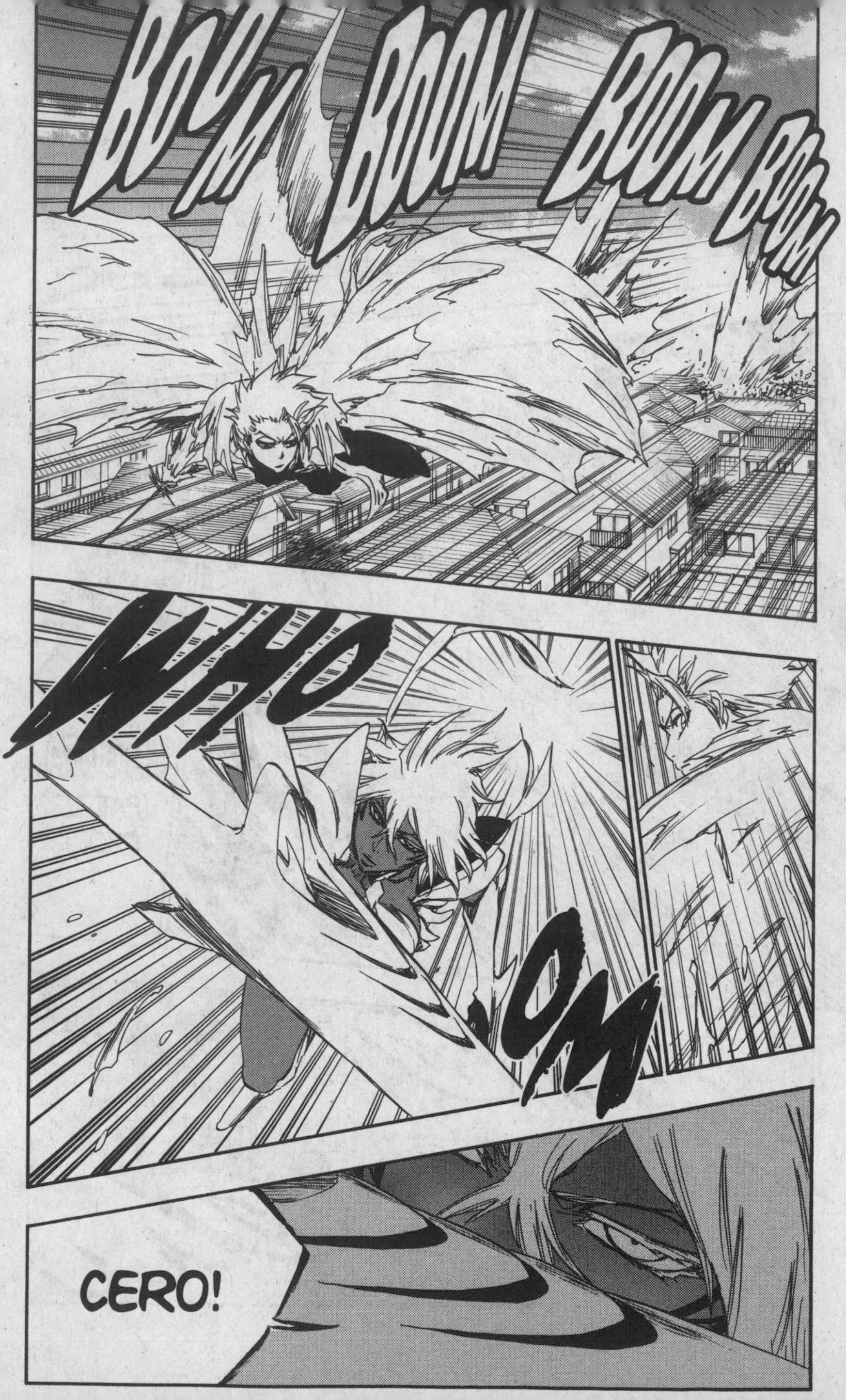

BOOM BOOM BOOM BOOM BOOM
WHOOM
CERO!

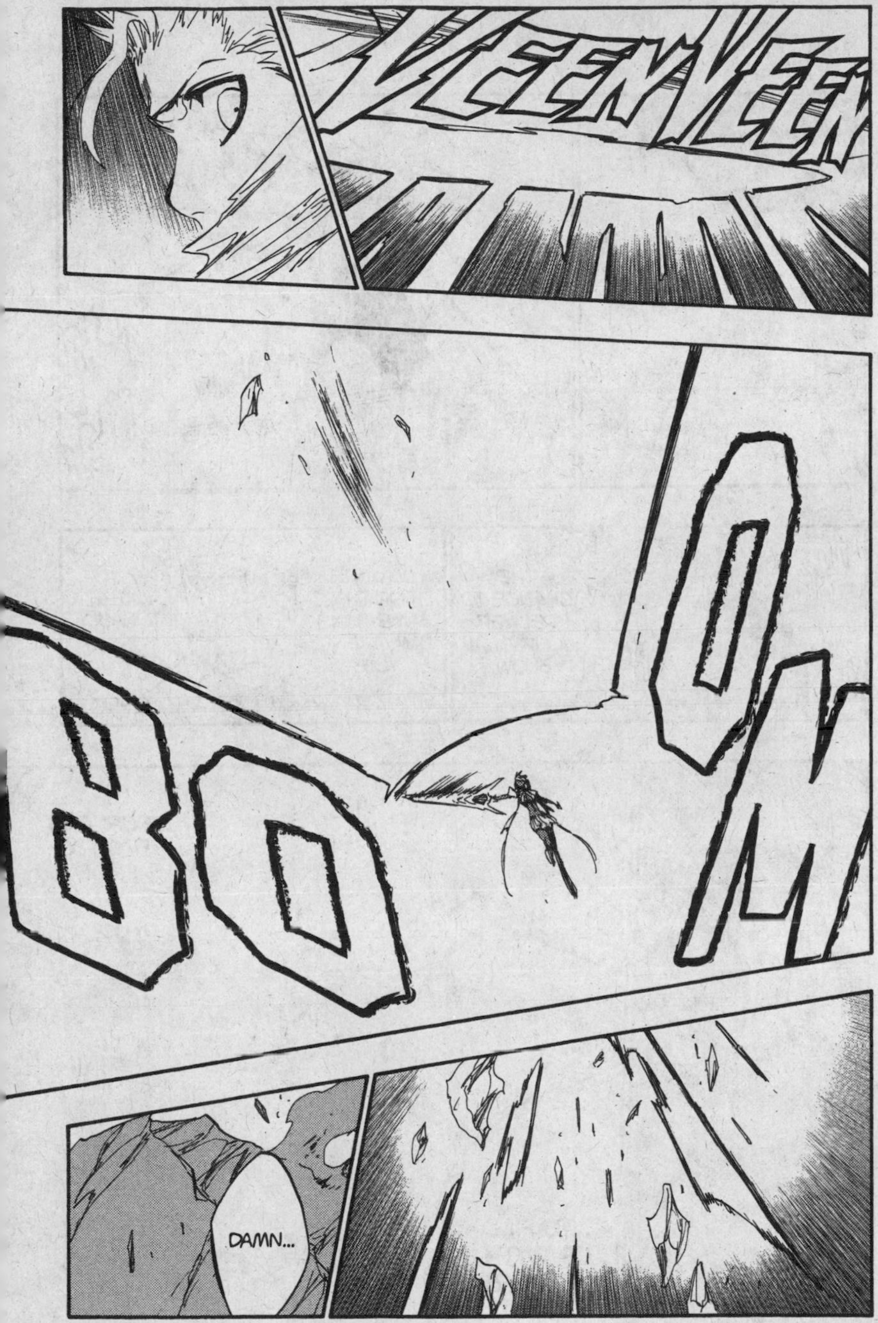
VEEN VEEN
BOOM
DAMN...

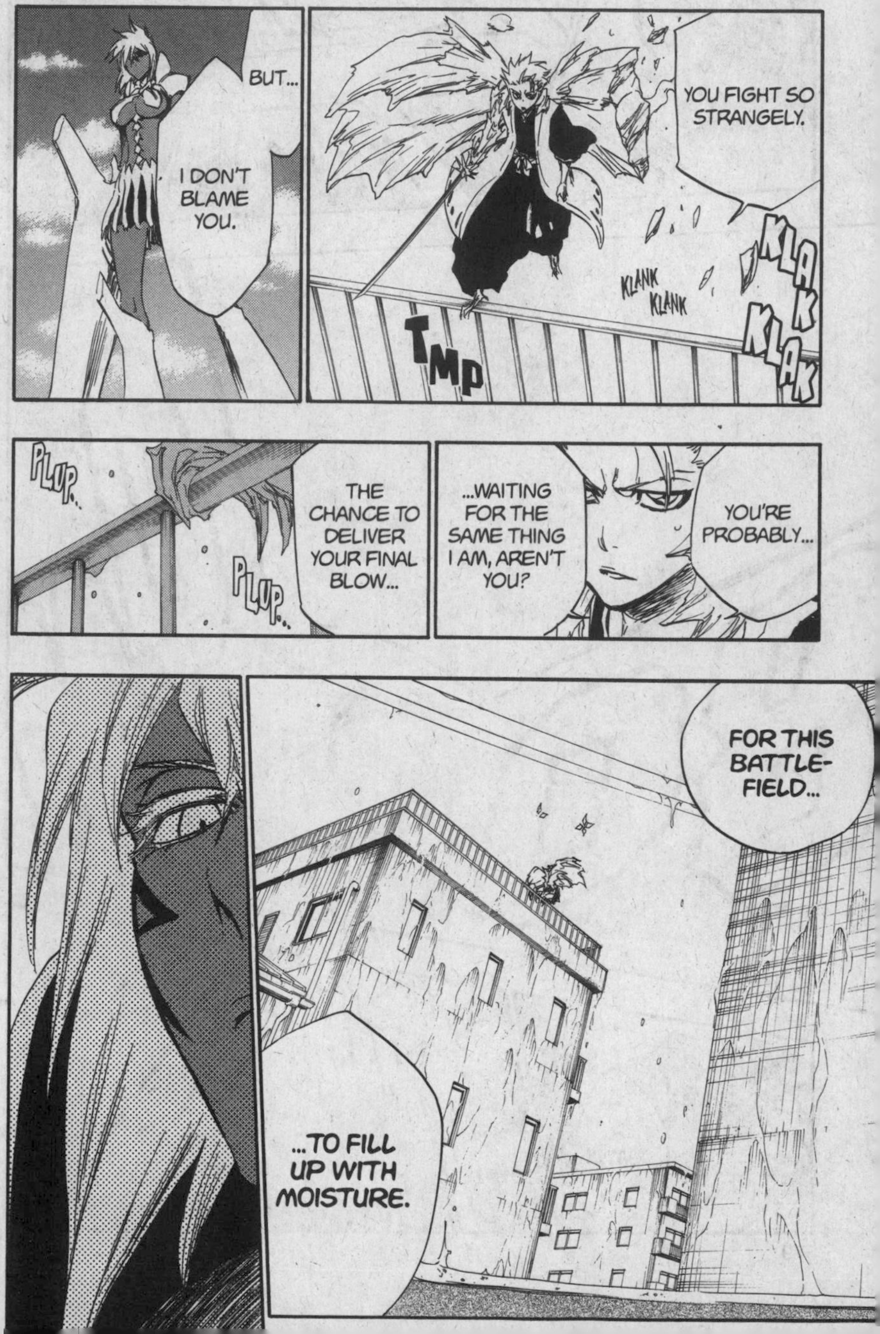
YOU FIGHT SO STRANGELY.
KLAK KLAK
KLANK KLANK
TMP
BUT...
I DON'T BLAME YOU.
YOU'RE PROBABLY...
...WAITING FOR THE SAME THING I AM, AREN'T YOU?
THE CHANCE TO DELIVER YOUR FINAL BLOW...
PLUP..
PLUP..
FOR THIS BATTLE-FIELD...
...TO FILL UP WITH MOISTURE.

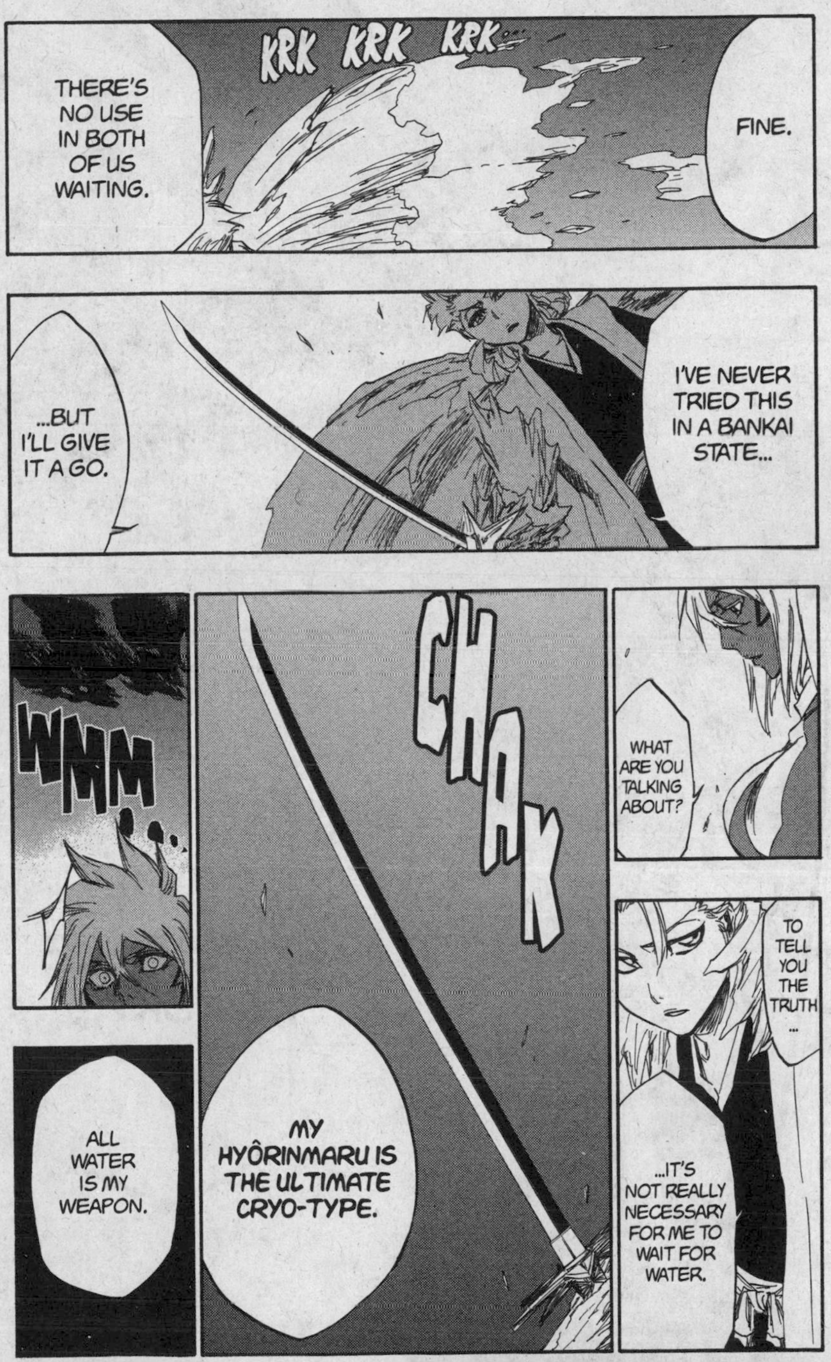
KRK KRK KRK...
FINE.
THERE'S NO USE IN BOTH OF US WAITING.
I'VE NEVER TRIED THIS IN A BANKAI STATE...
...BUT I'LL GIVE IT A GO.
WHAT ARE YOU TALKING ABOUT?
TO TELL YOU THE TRUTH...
...IT'S NOT REALLY NECESSARY FOR ME TO WAIT FOR WATER.
CHAK
MY HYÔRINMARU IS THE ULTIMATE CRYO-TYPE.
WMM
ALL WATER IS MY WEAPON.

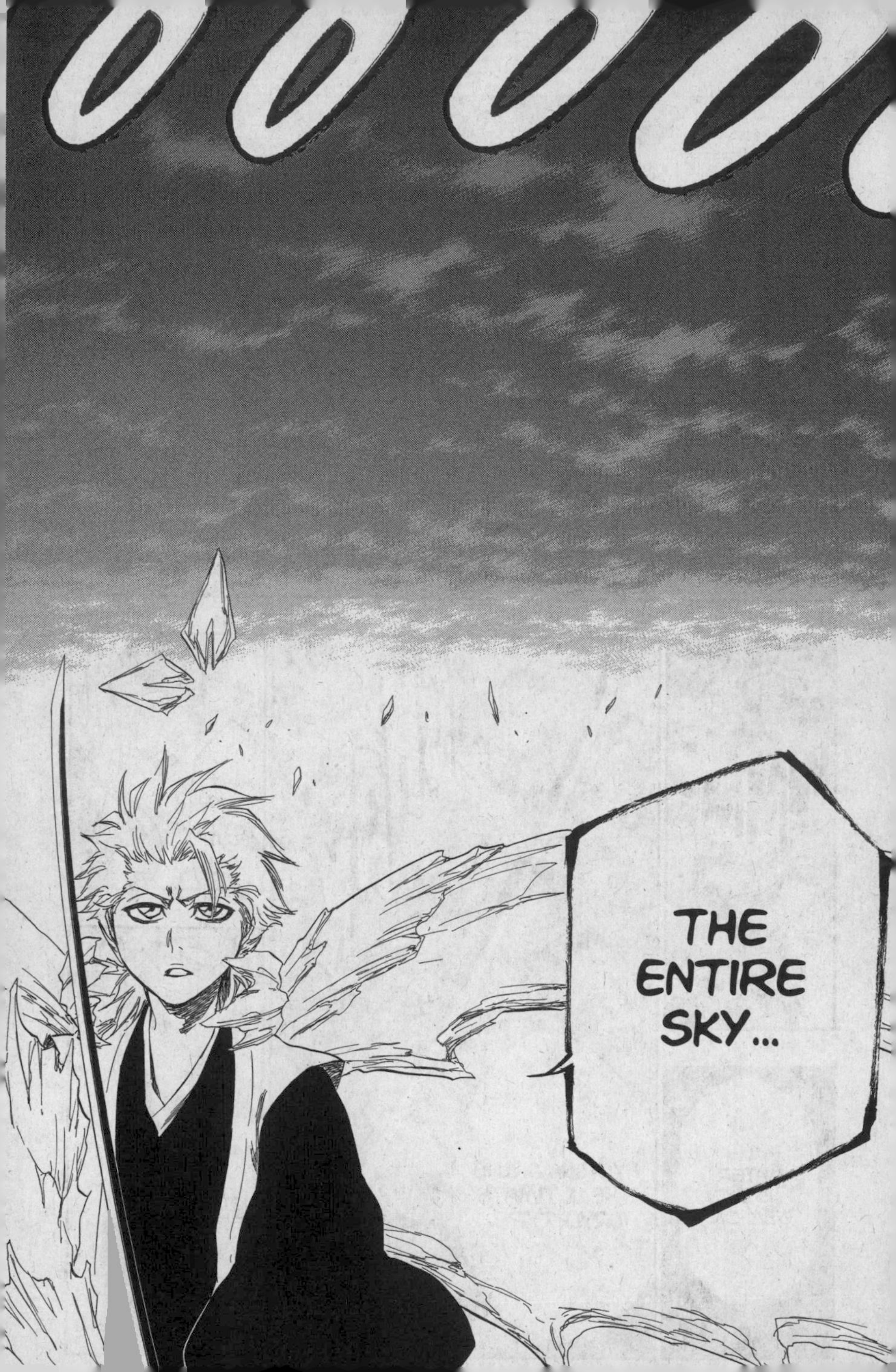
THE ENTIRE SKY...

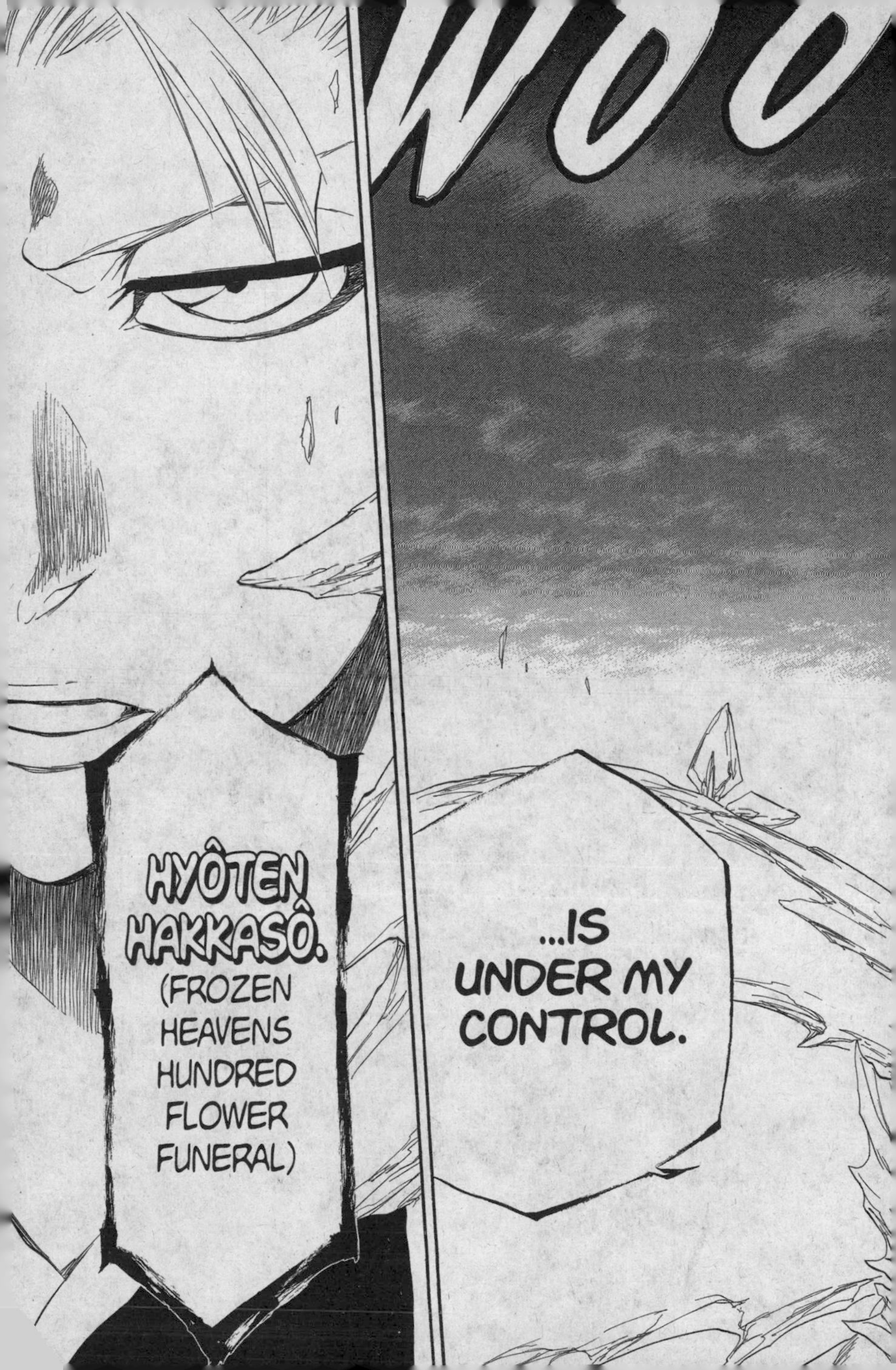
WOO
...IS UNDER MY CONTROL.
HYÔTEN HAKKASÔ. (FROZEN HEAVENS HUNDRED FLOWER FUNERAL)

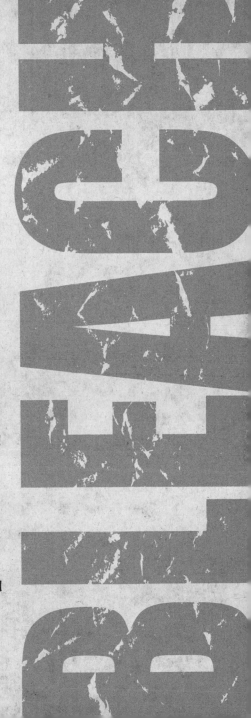

My editor, who had a perm, shaved his head. The following week a new editor was assigned to me: now I had two editors. The following week my new editor shaved his head. That same week I got a perm.

With the way things are going, I'm worried either Ichigo or I will end up with a shaved head due to some kind of accident.

-Tite Kubo, 2009

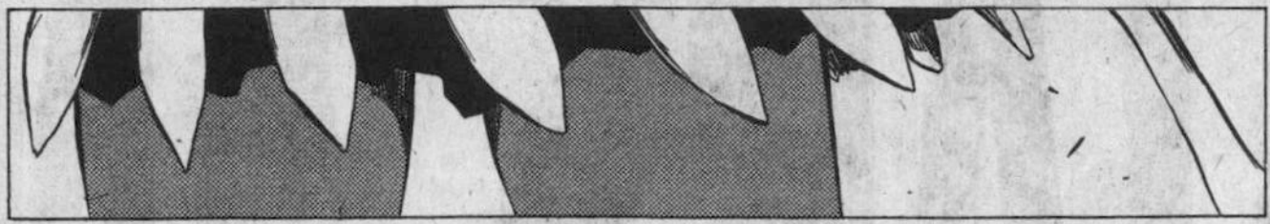

No world exists without sacrifice.
Do we not realize that we call
this hell where ash floats
upon a sea of blood, the world

BLEACH 42

SHOCK OF THE QUEEN

Shonen Jump Manga

STARS AND

スターク

Stark

Soi Fon

砕蜂

京樂春水

Shunsui Kyoraku

plot

When high school student Ichigo Kurosaki meets Soul Reaper Rukia Kuchiki his life is changed forever. Soon Ichigo is a soul-cleansing Soul Reaper too, and he finds himself having adventures, as well as problems, that he never would have imagined. Now Ichigo and his friends must stop renegade Soul Reaper Aizen and his army of Arrancars from destroying the Soul Society and wiping out Karakura as well.

Though Ichigo defeats Ulquiorra and saves Orihime, the battle between the Thirteen Court Guard Companies and the Espadas in Karakura rages on! Despite their wounds, the captains each challenge a high-ranking Espada! Now it's Kyoraku vs. Stark, Soi Fon vs. Barragan, and Hitsugaya vs. Halibel! Who will win, and who will perish in these deadly duels?!

BLEACH ALL

Halibel

Barragan

Toshiro Hitsugaya

日番谷冬獅郎

STORIES

BLEACH 42

SHOCK OF THE QUEEN

Contents

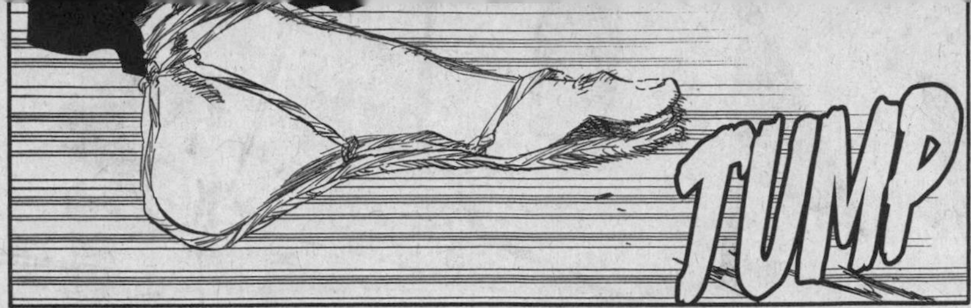
TUMP

359. The Frozen Obelisk

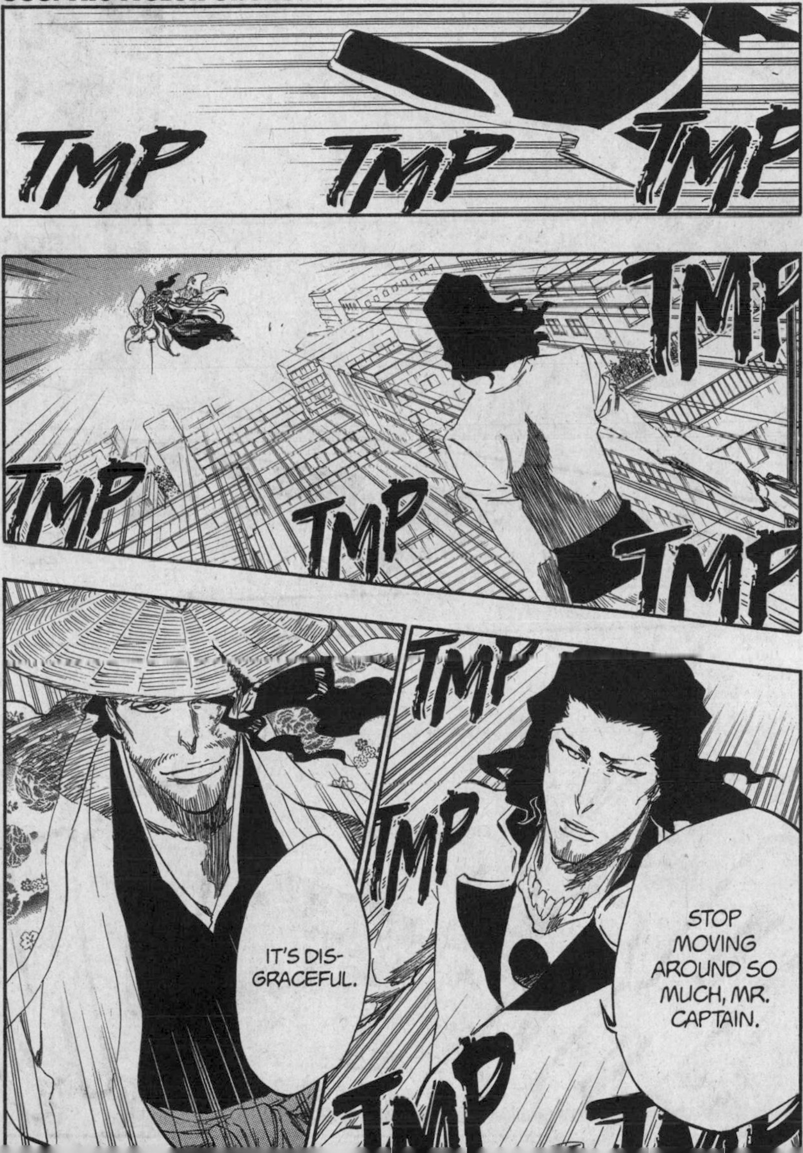
TMP
TMP
TMP
TMP
TMP
TMP
TMP
TMP
TMP
TMP
TMP
STOP MOVING AROUND SO MUCH, MR. CAPTAIN.
IT'S DIS-GRACEFUL.
TMP

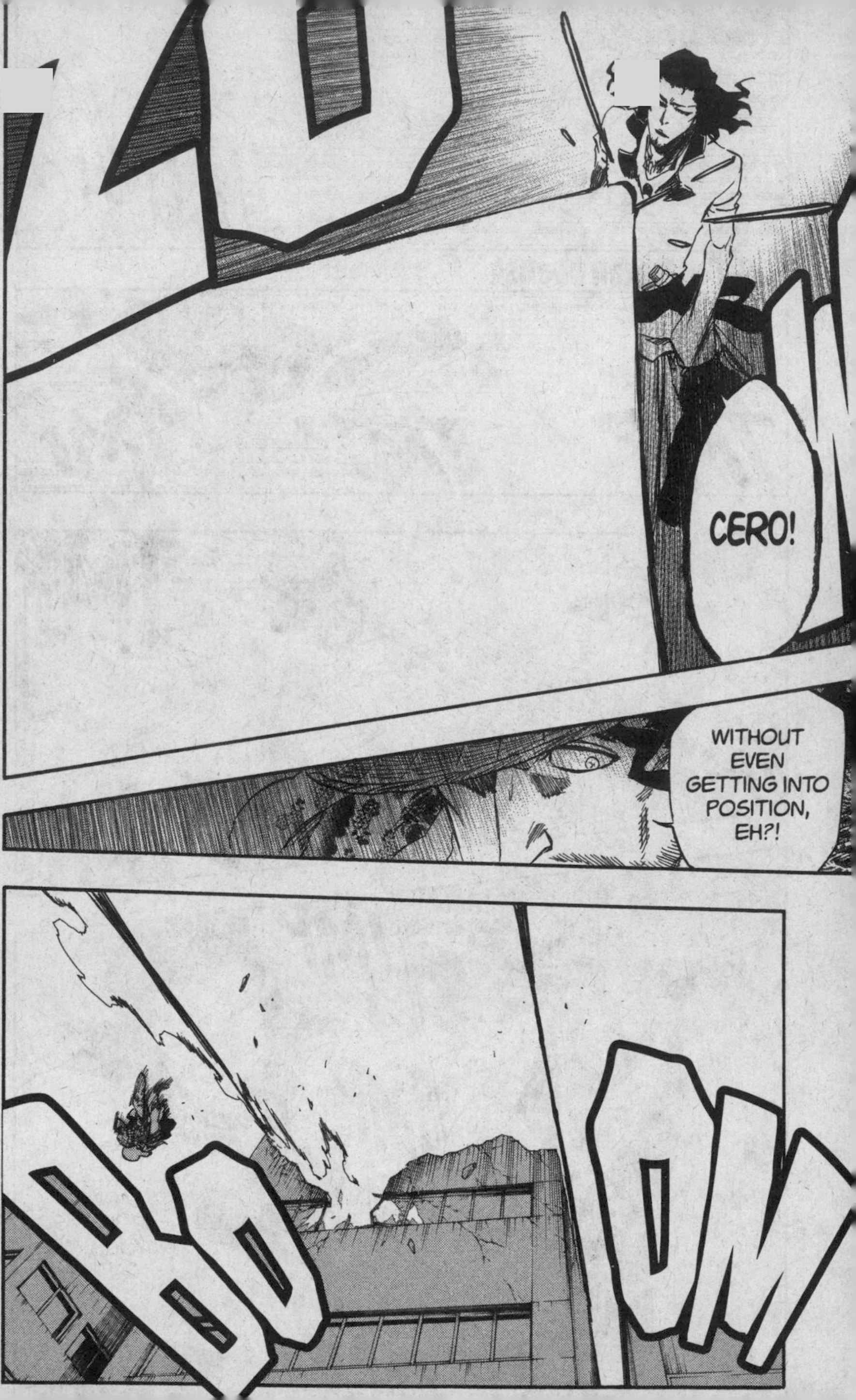
CERO!
WITHOUT EVEN GETTING INTO POSITION, EH?!

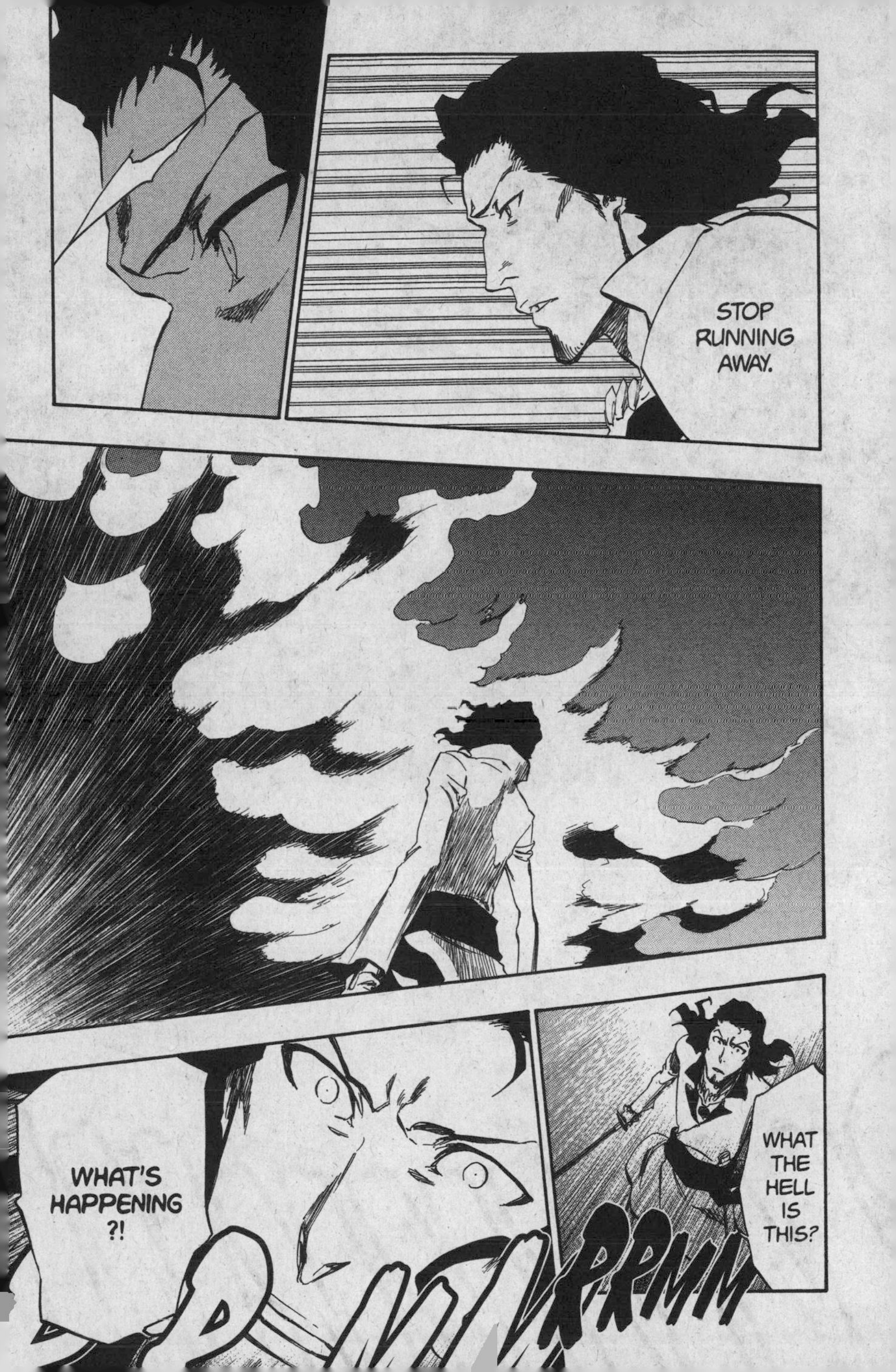
STOP RUNNING AWAY.
WHAT THE HELL IS THIS?
WHAT'S HAPPENING ?!
DMMRRMM

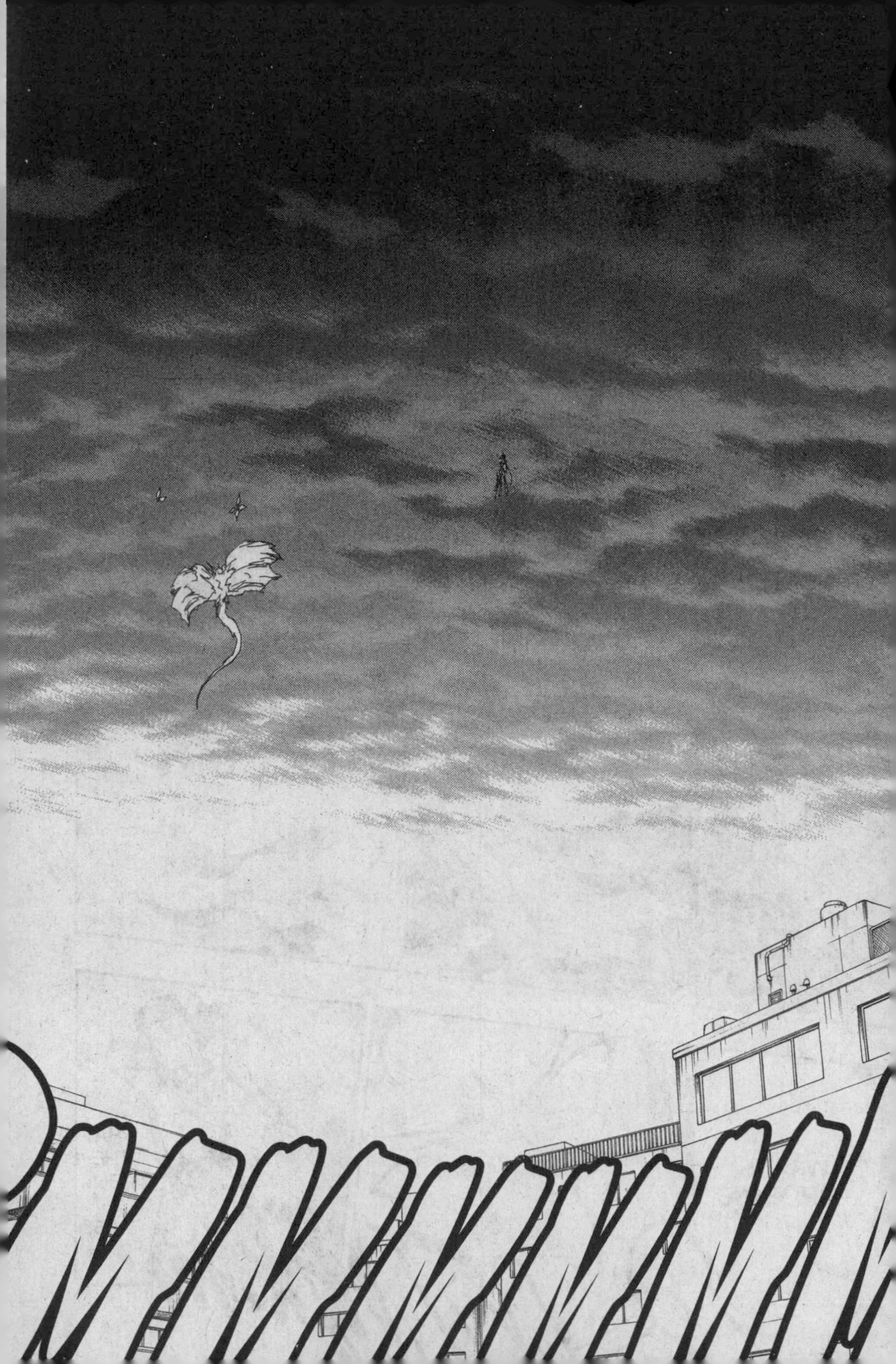

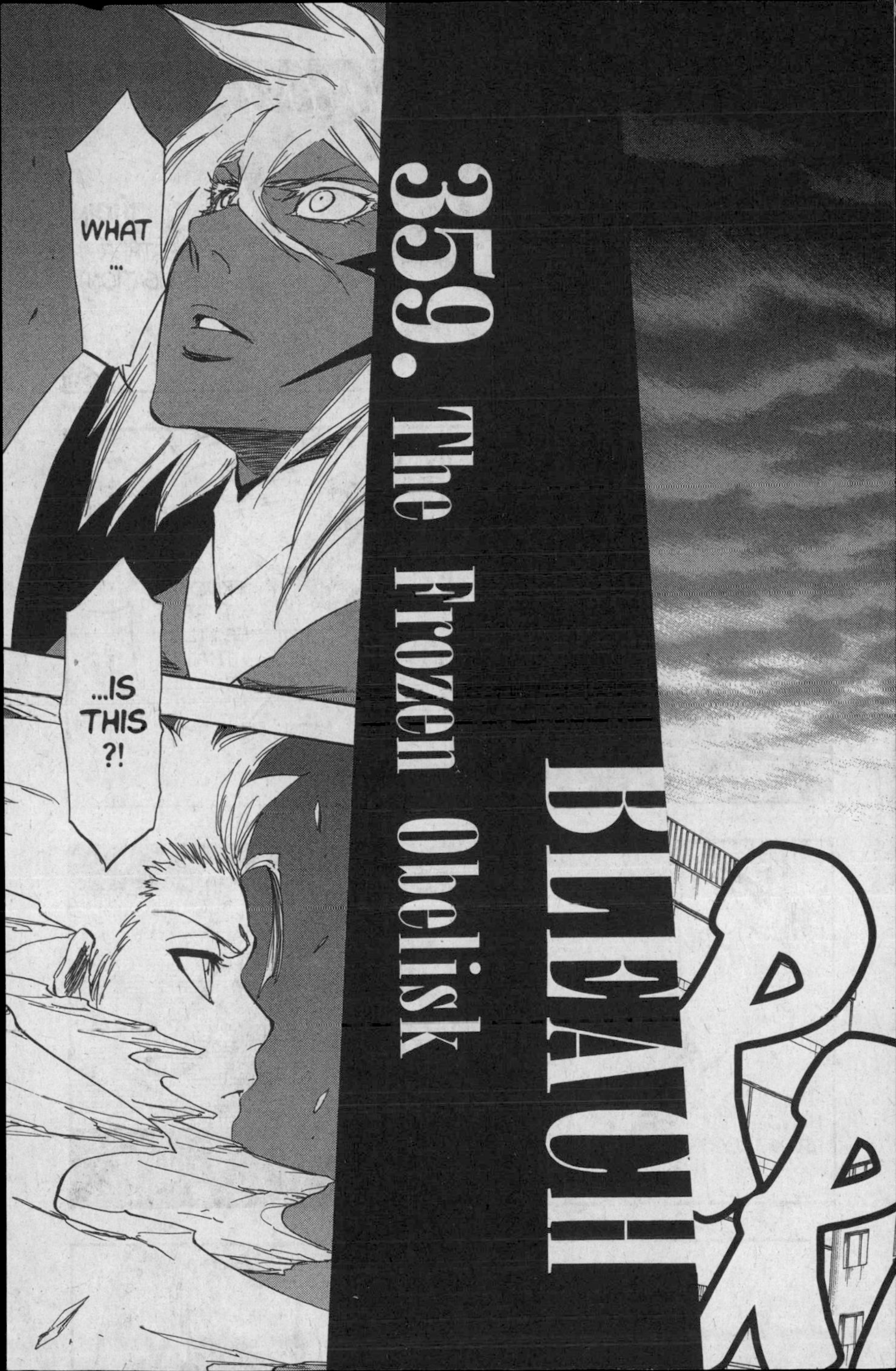
BLEACH
359. The Frozen Obelisk
WHAT ...
...IS THIS ?!

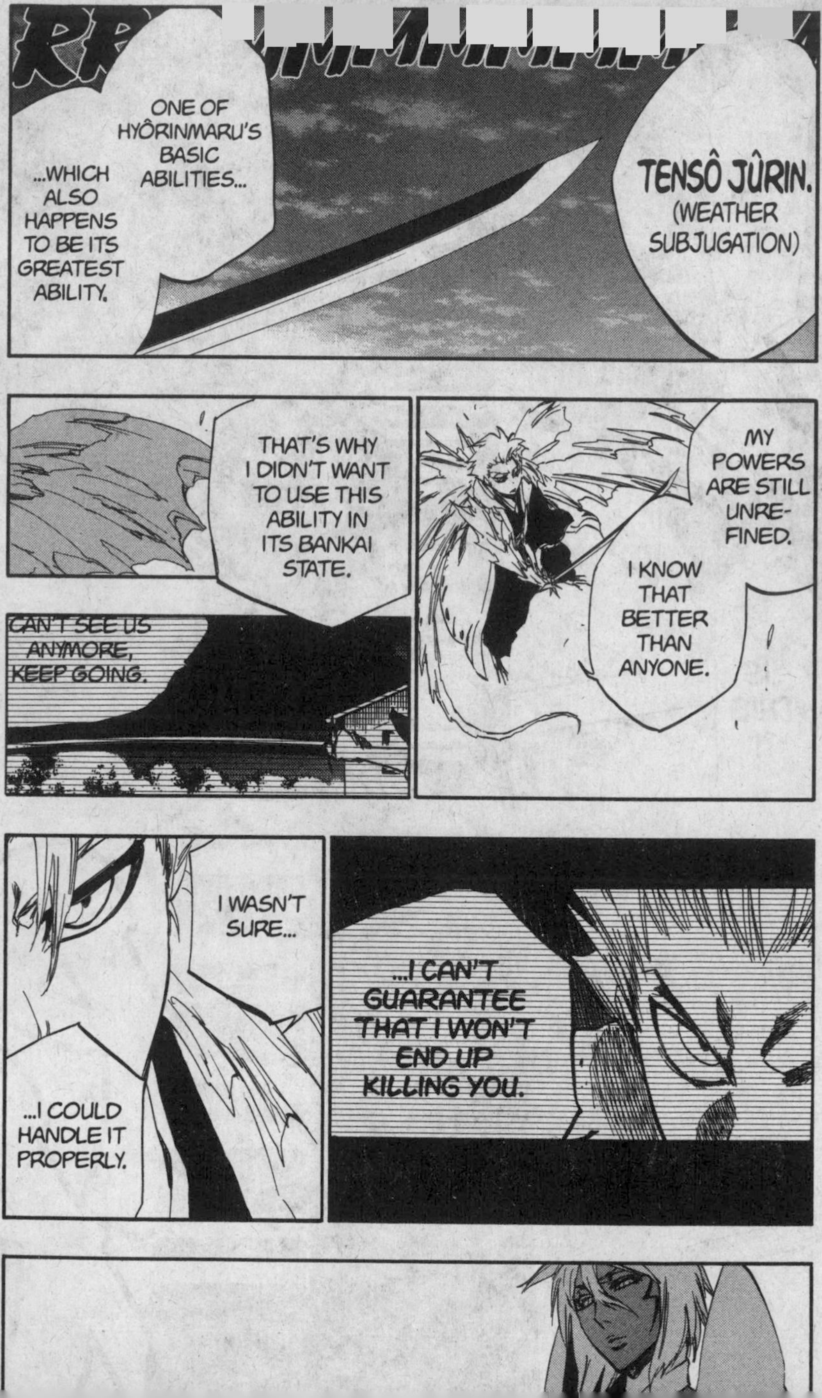
ONE OF HYÔRINMARU'S BASIC ABILITIES...
...WHICH ALSO HAPPENS TO BE ITS GREATEST ABILITY.
TENSÔ JÛRIN. (WEATHER SUBJUGATION)
THAT'S WHY I DIDN'T WANT TO USE THIS ABILITY IN ITS BANKAI STATE.
CAN'T SEE US ANYMORE, KEEP GOING.
MY POWERS ARE STILL UNREFINED.
I KNOW THAT BETTER THAN ANYONE.
I WASN'T SURE...
...I COULD HANDLE IT PROPERLY.
...I CAN'T GUARANTEE THAT I WON'T END UP KILLING YOU.

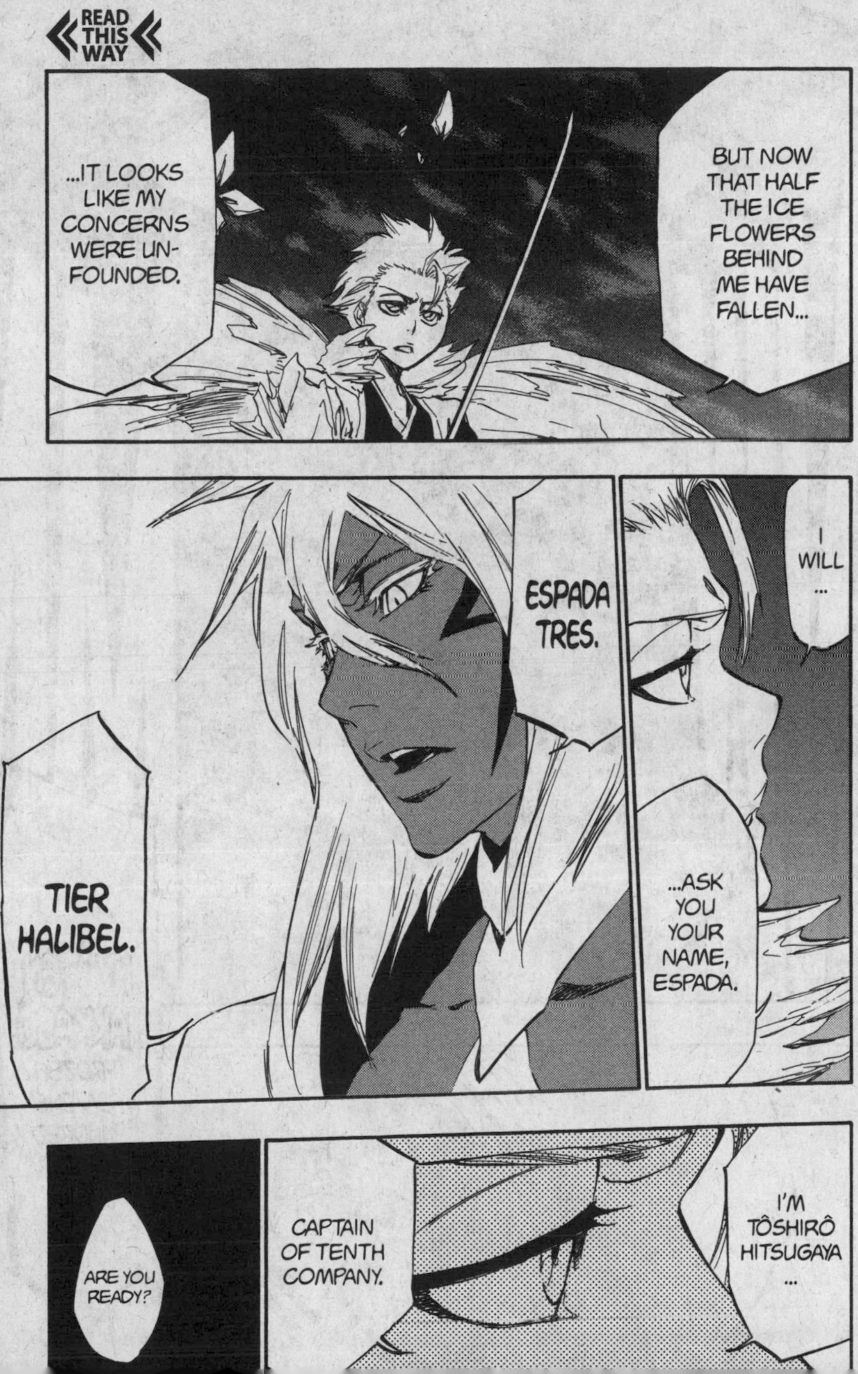
READ THIS WAY
BUT NOW THAT HALF THE ICE FLOWERS BEHIND ME HAVE FALLEN...
...IT LOOKS LIKE MY CONCERNS WERE UN-FOUNDED.
I WILL...
...ASK YOU YOUR NAME, ESPADA.
ESPADA TRES.
TIER HALIBEL.
I'M TÔSHIRÔ HITSUGAYA...
CAPTAIN OF TENTH COMPANY.
ARE YOU READY?

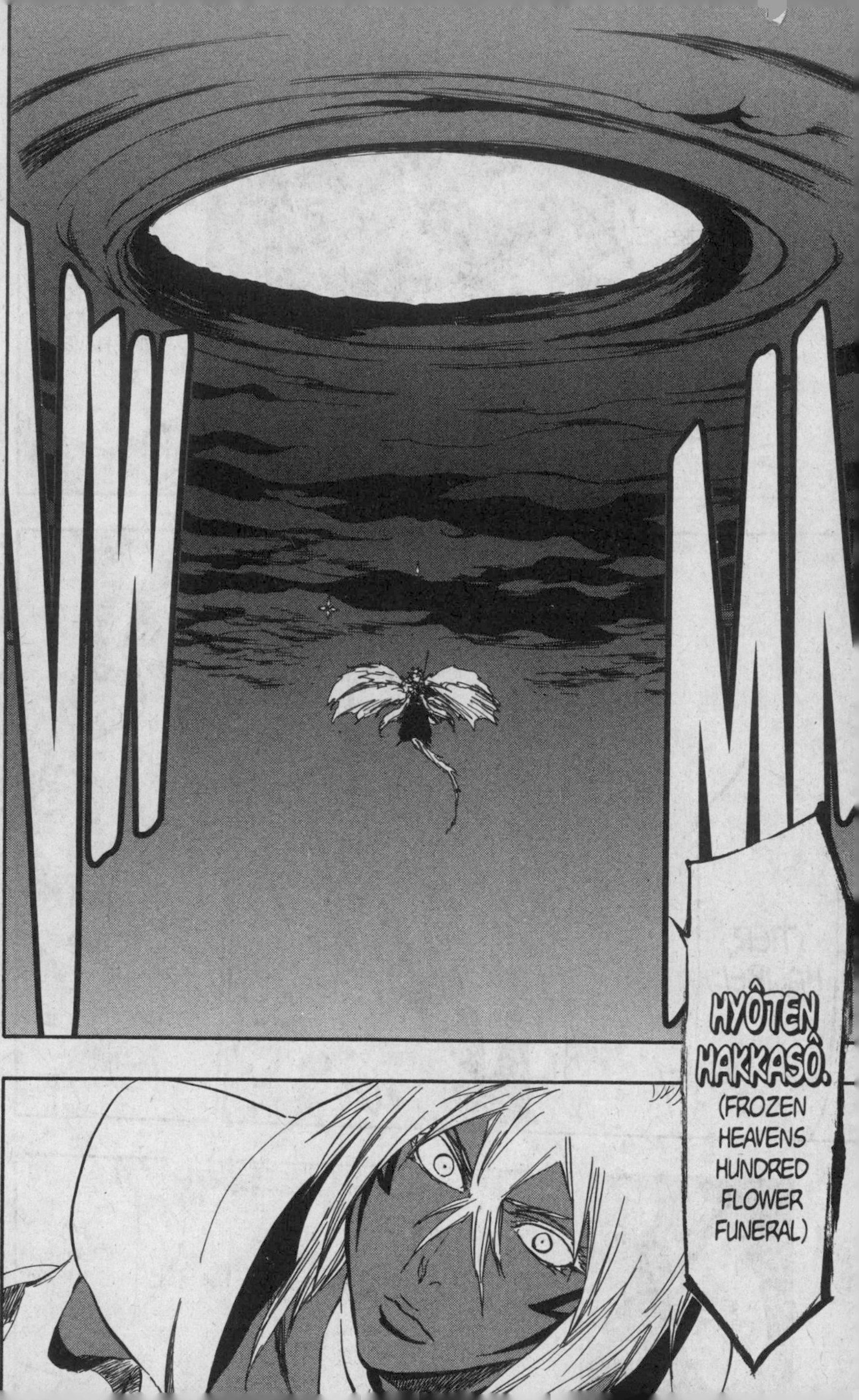
HYÔTEN HAKKASÔ.
(FROZEN HEAVENS HUNDRED FLOWER FUNERAL)

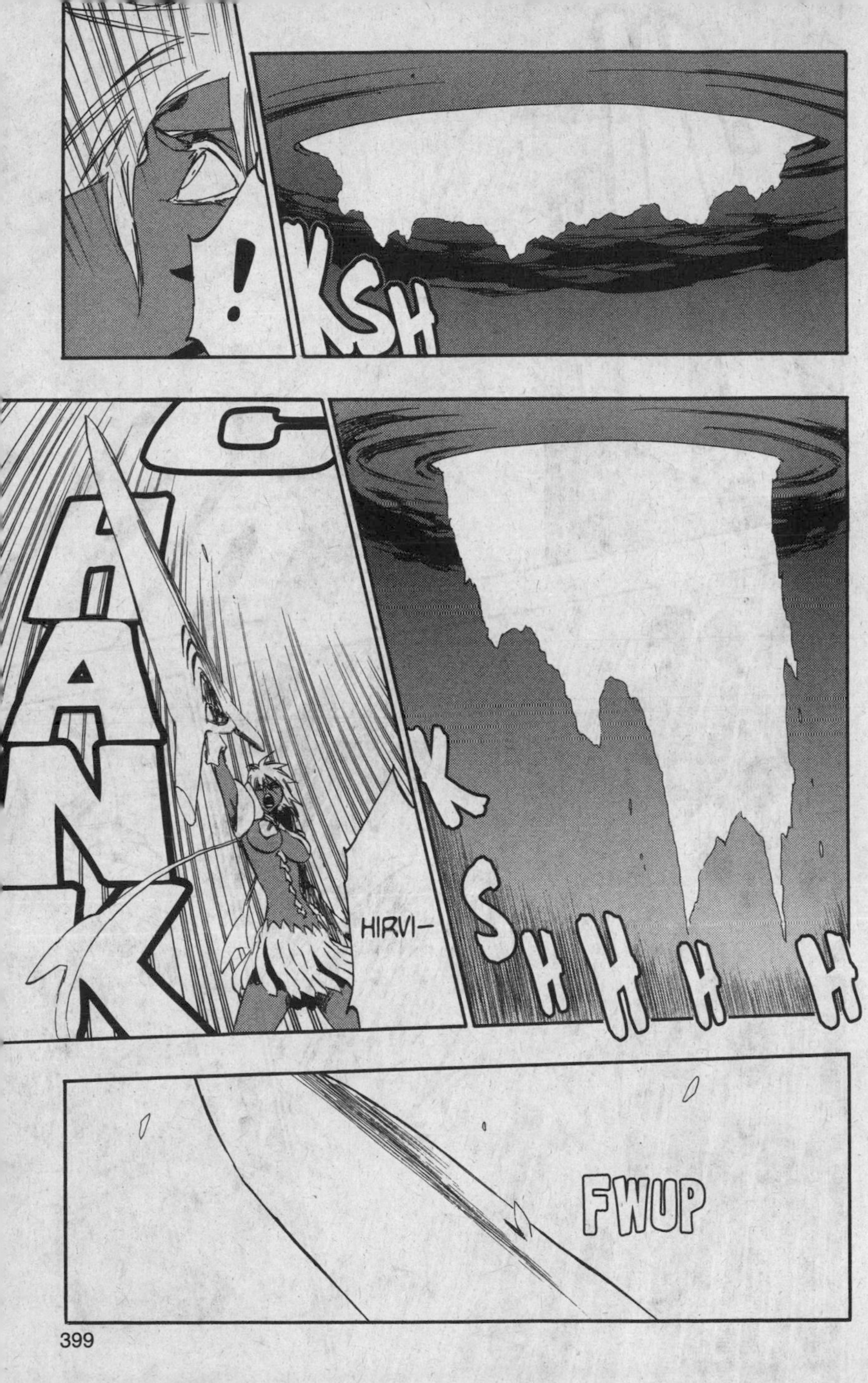
KSH
!
KSHHHHH
HIRVI–
CHANK
FWUP

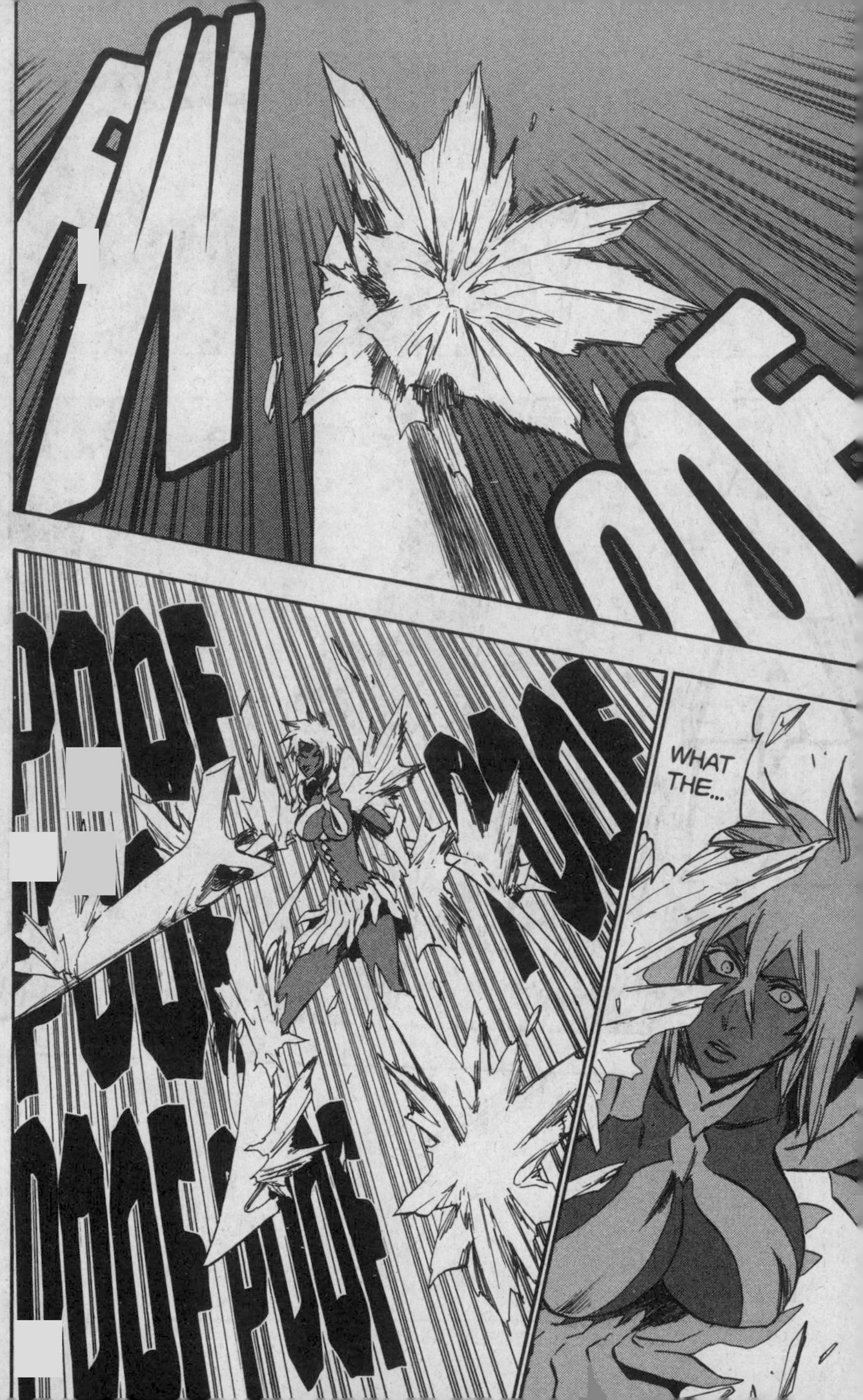
WHAT THE...

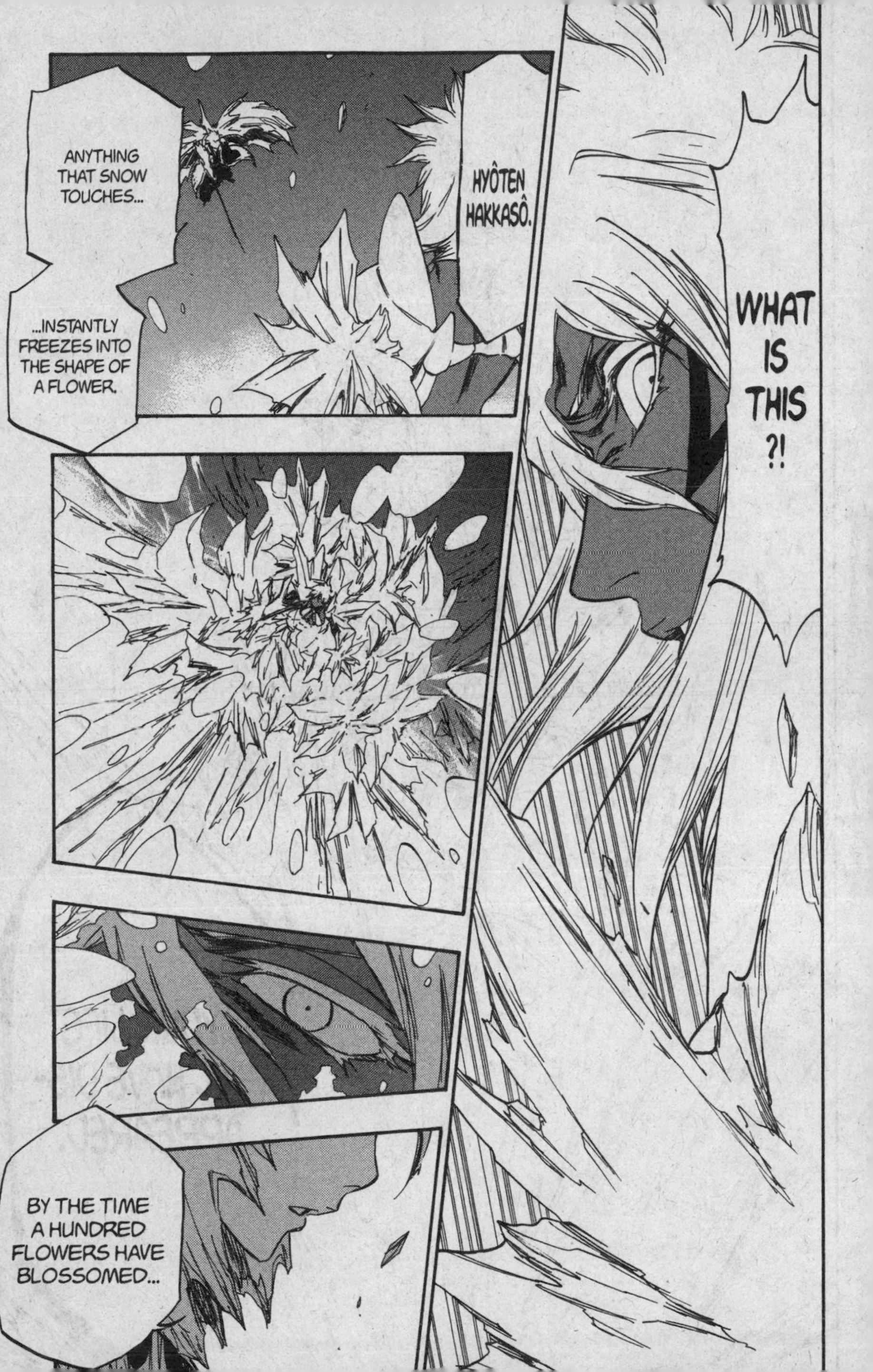
WHAT IS THIS ?!
HYÔTEN HAKKASÔ.
ANYTHING THAT SNOW TOUCHES...
...INSTANTLY FREEZES INTO THE SHAPE OF A FLOWER.
BY THE TIME A HUNDRED FLOWERS HAVE BLOSSOMED...

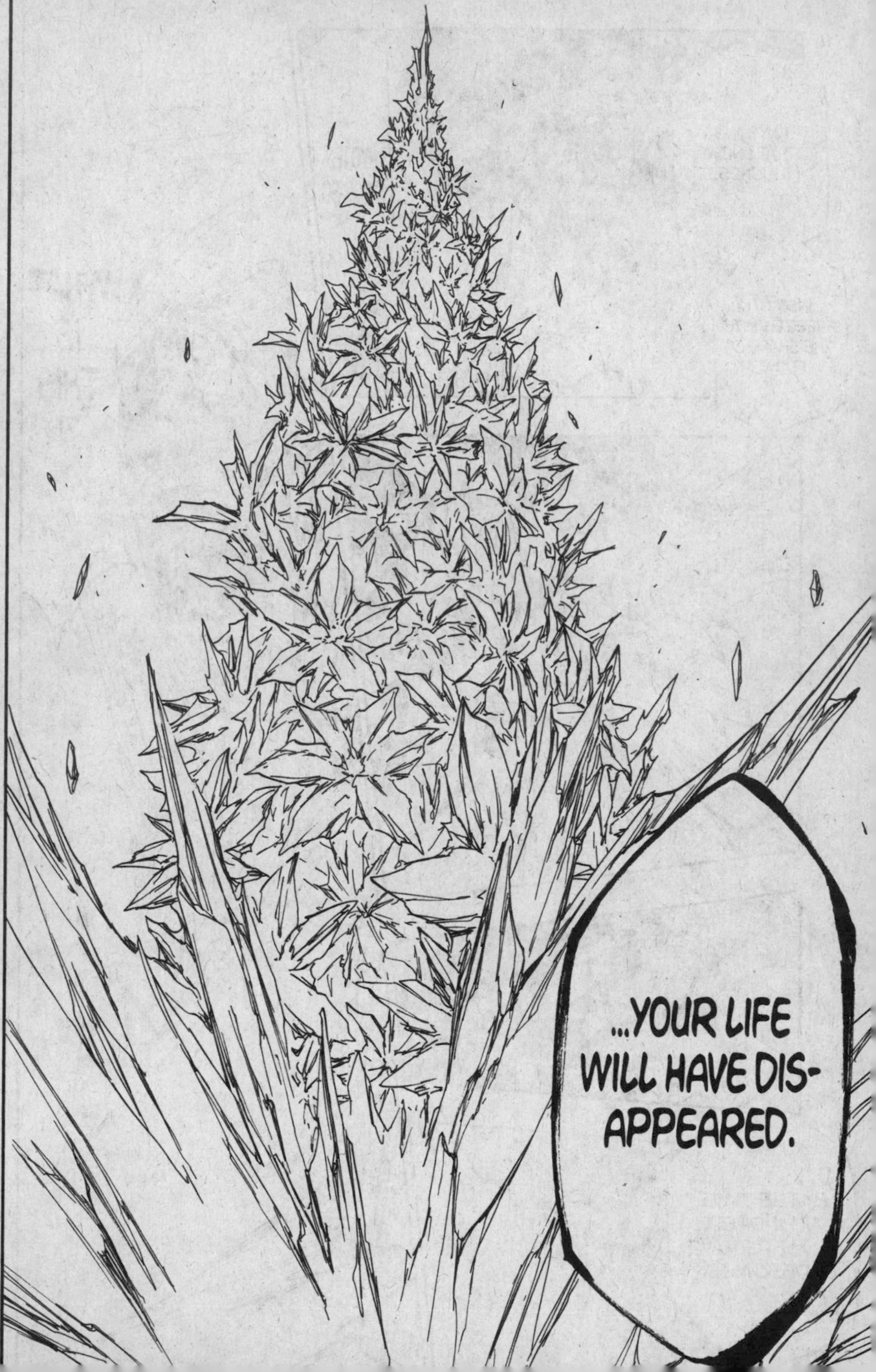
...YOUR LIFE WILL HAVE DIS-APPEARED.

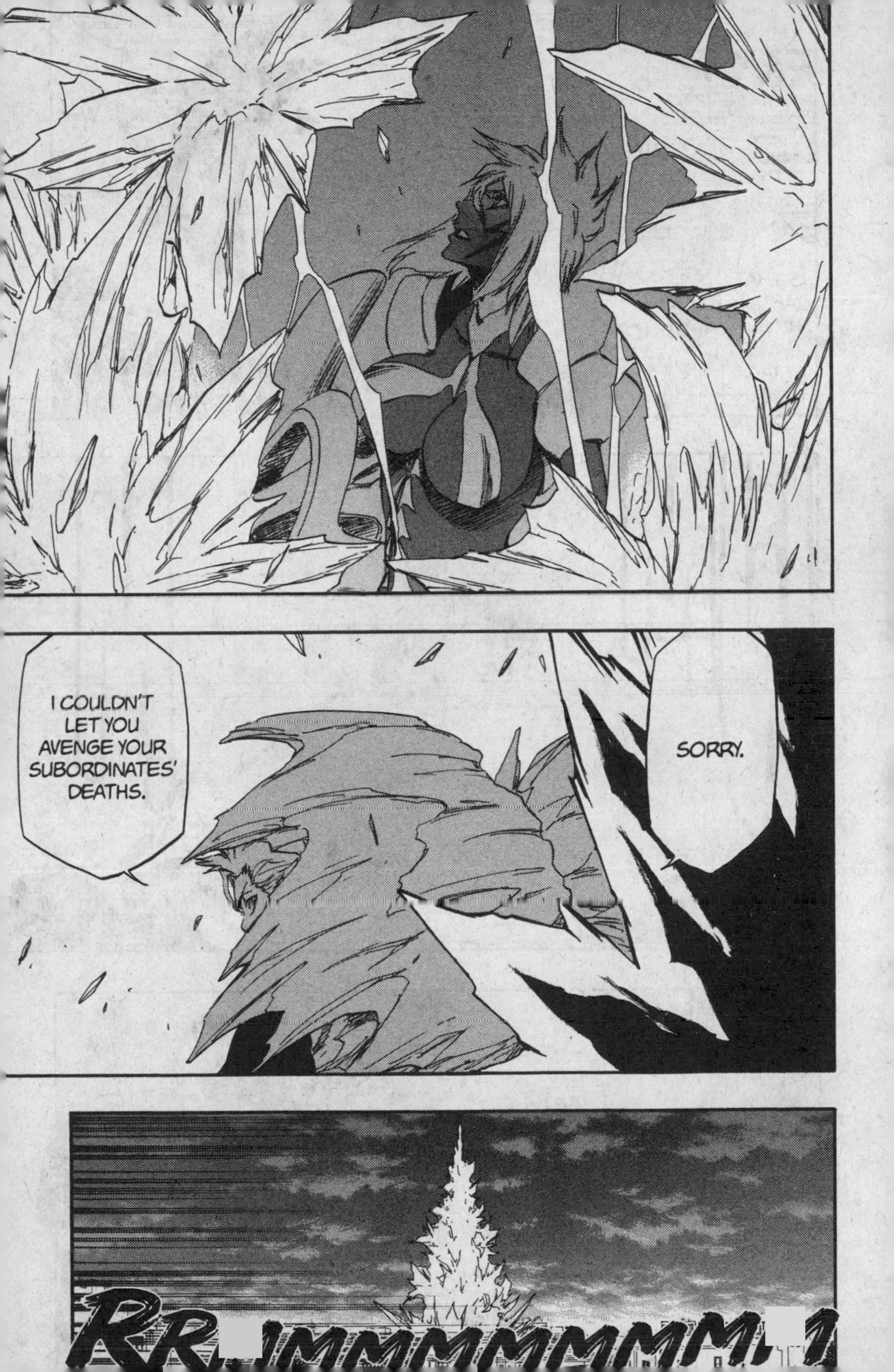
SORRY.
I COULDN'T LET YOU AVENGE YOUR SUBORDINATES' DEATHS.
RR MMMMMMMMM

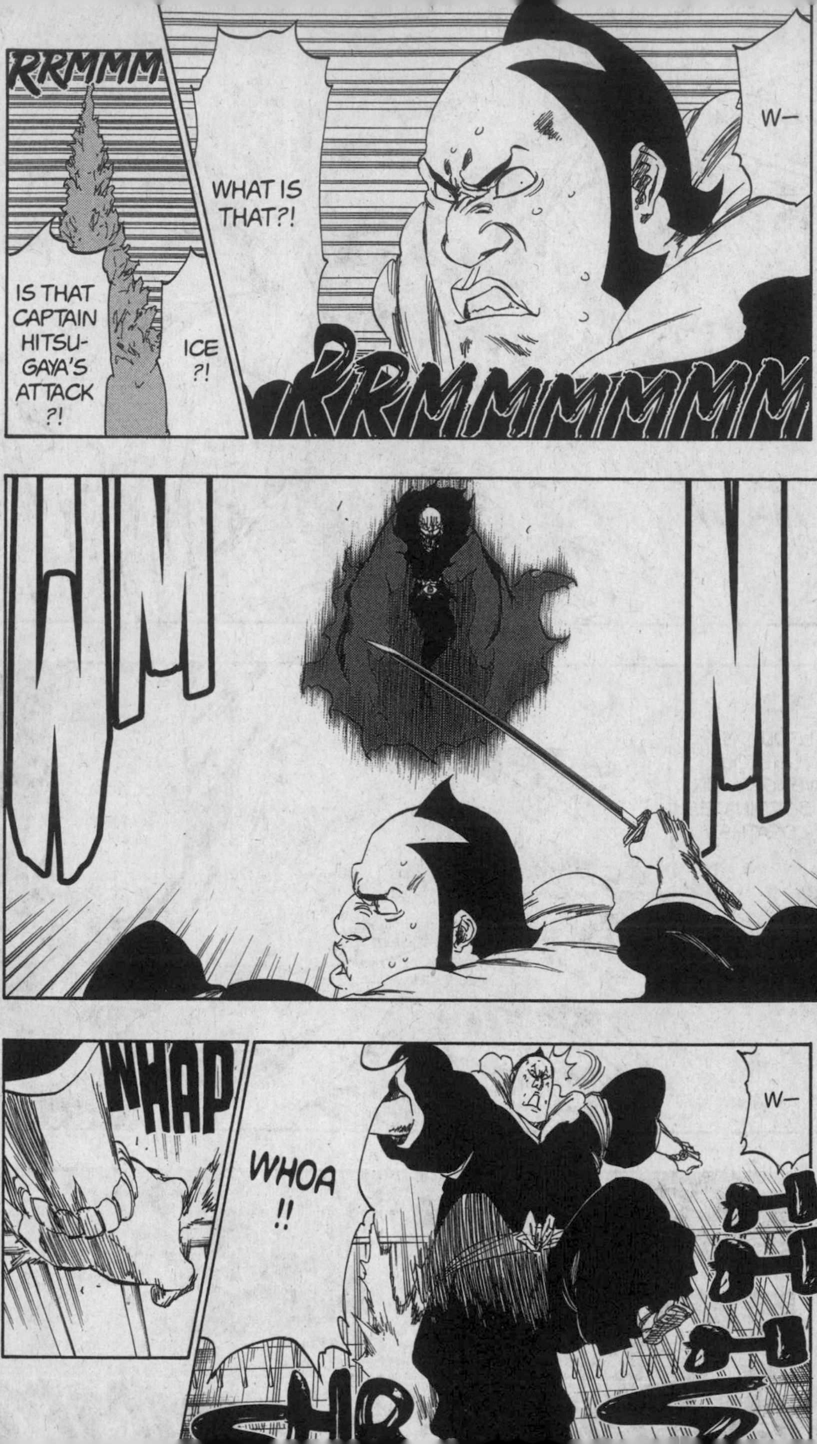
W—
WHAT IS THAT?!
ICE ?!
RRMMMMMMMM
RRMMM
IS THAT CAPTAIN HITSU-GAYA'S ATTACK ?!
WM
M
W—
WHOA !!
SHR
S
WHAP

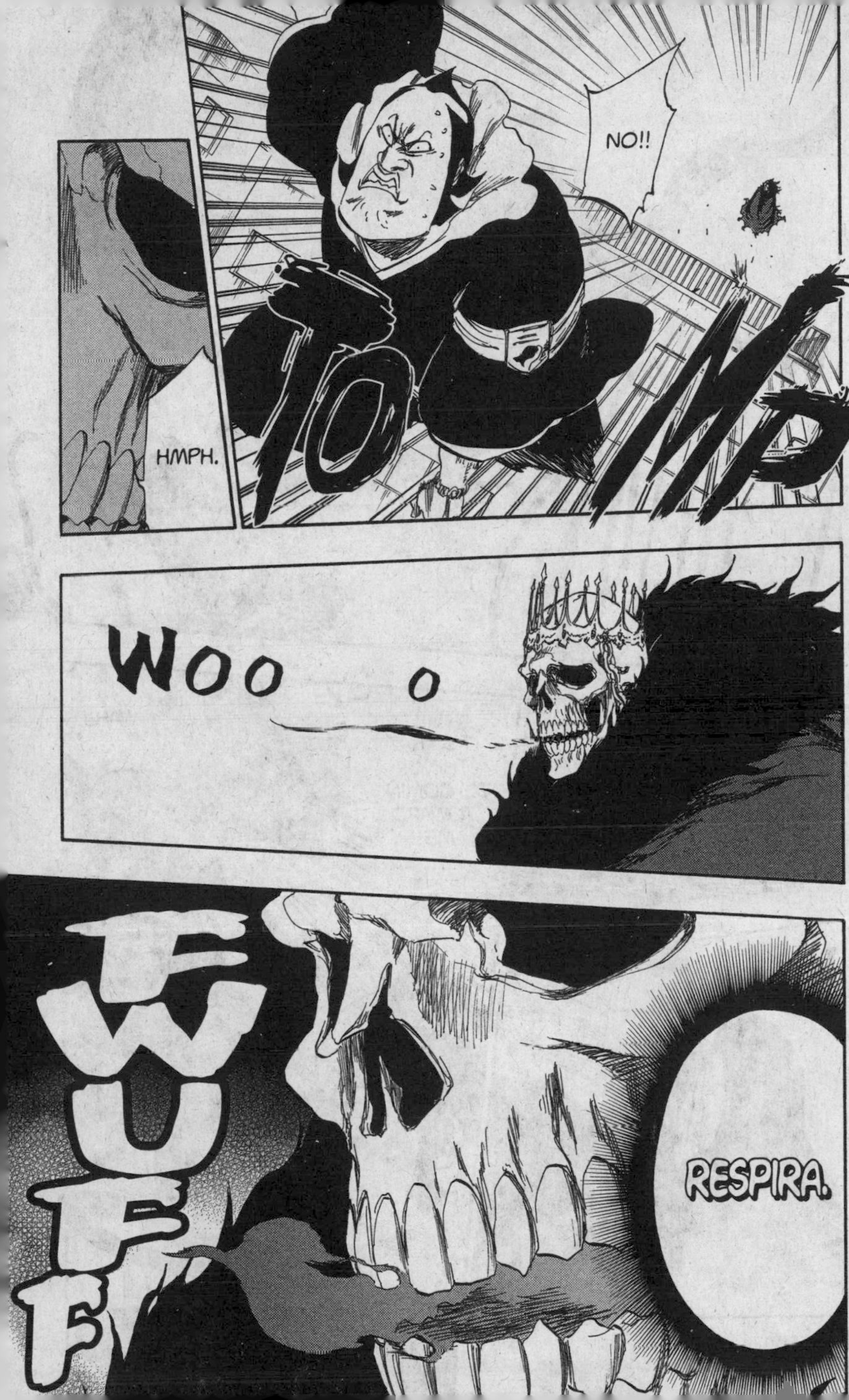
NO!!
TOOMP
HMPH.
WOO O
RESPIRA.
FWUFF

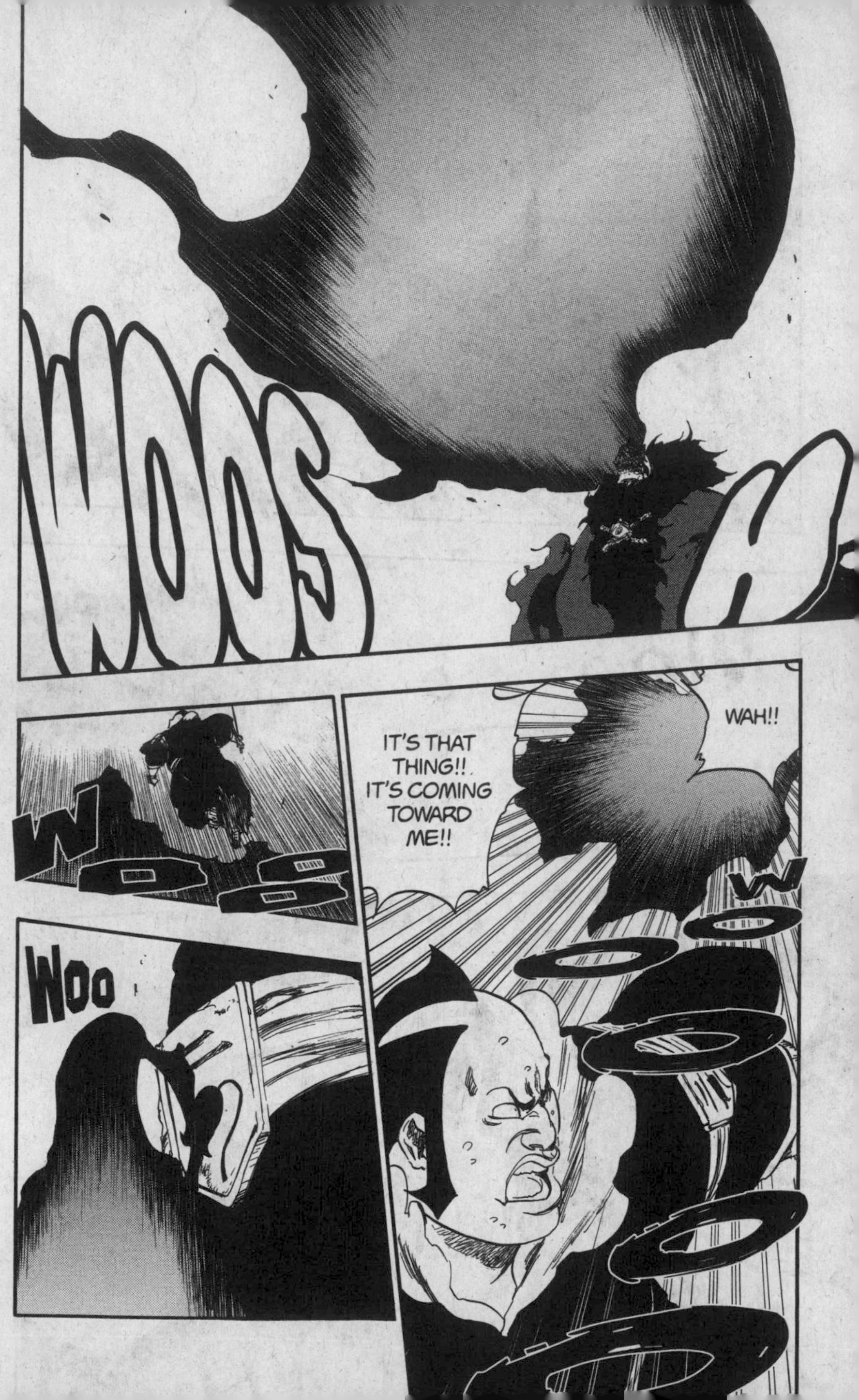
WOOSH
WAH!!
IT'S THAT THING!! IT'S COMING TOWARD ME!!
WOOOO
WOOS
WOO

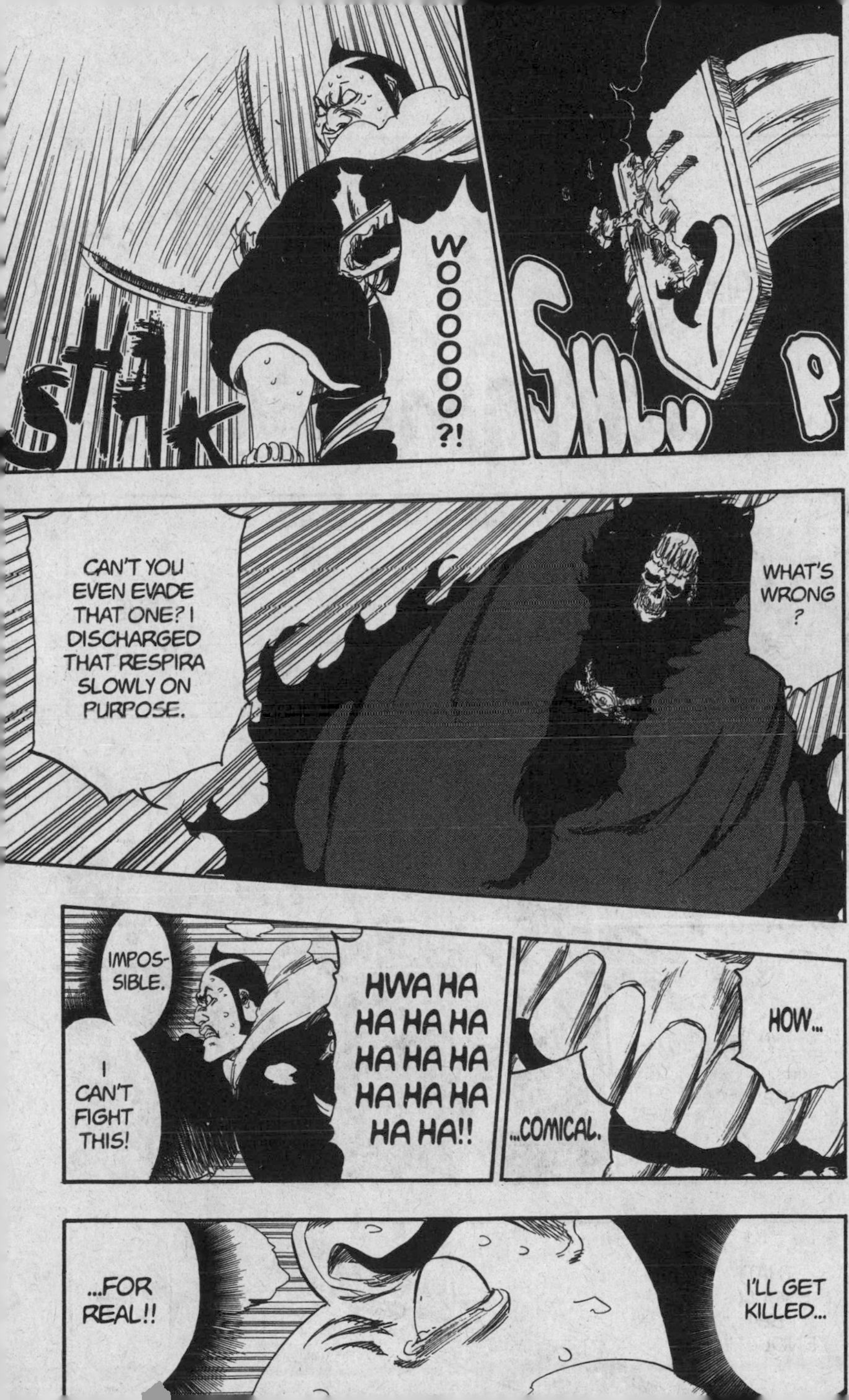
SHLUP
WOOOOOOO?!
SHAK
WHAT'S WRONG?
CAN'T YOU EVEN EVADE THAT ONE? I DISCHARGED THAT RESPIRA SLOWLY ON PURPOSE.
HOW...
...COMICAL.
HWA HA HA HA HA HA HA HA HA HA HA HA HA HA HA!!
IMPOS-SIBLE.
I CAN'T FIGHT THIS!
I'LL GET KILLED...
...FOR REAL!!

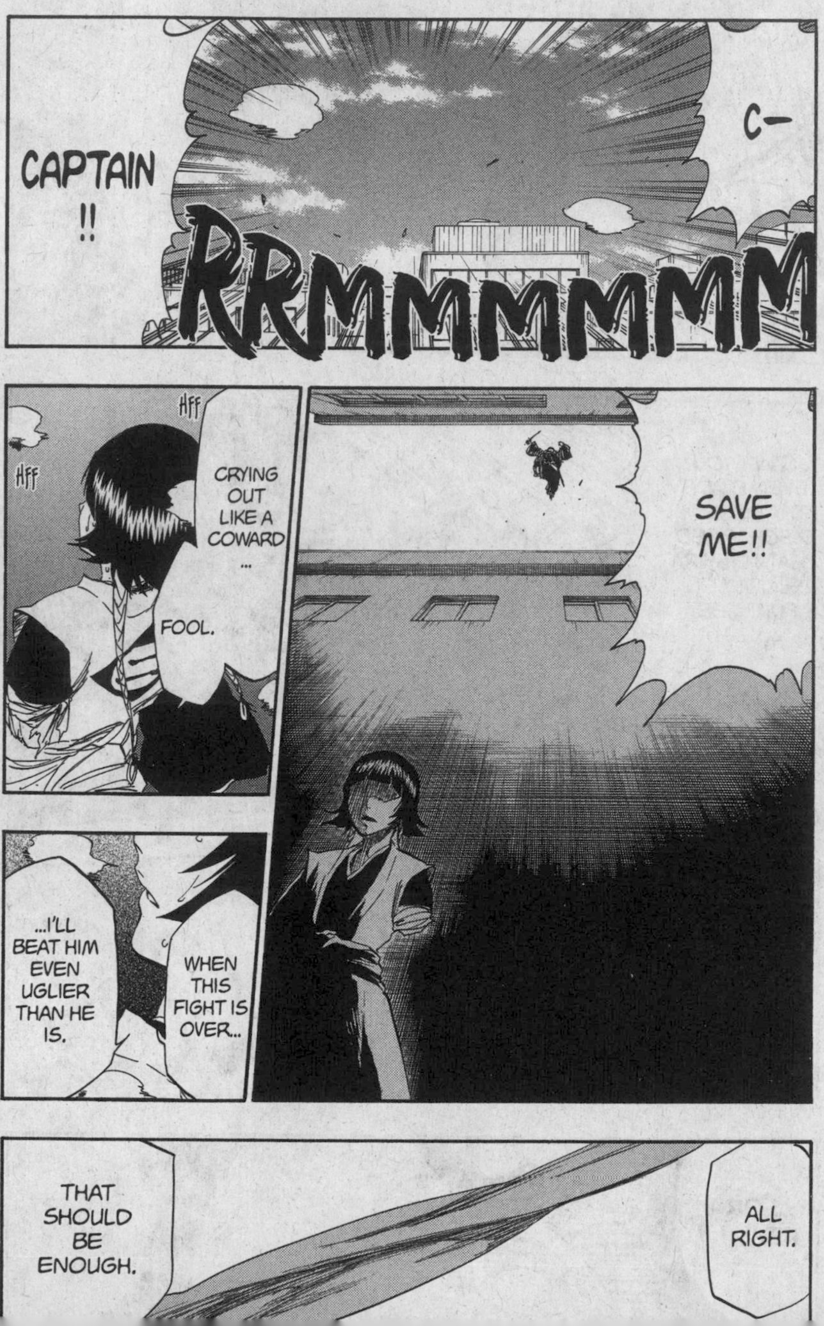
C—
CAPTAIN !!
RRMMMMMM
SAVE ME!!
HFF
HFF
CRYING OUT LIKE A COWARD...
FOOL.
WHEN THIS FIGHT IS OVER..
...I'LL BEAT HIM EVEN UGLIER THAN HE IS.
ALL RIGHT.
THAT SHOULD BE ENOUGH.

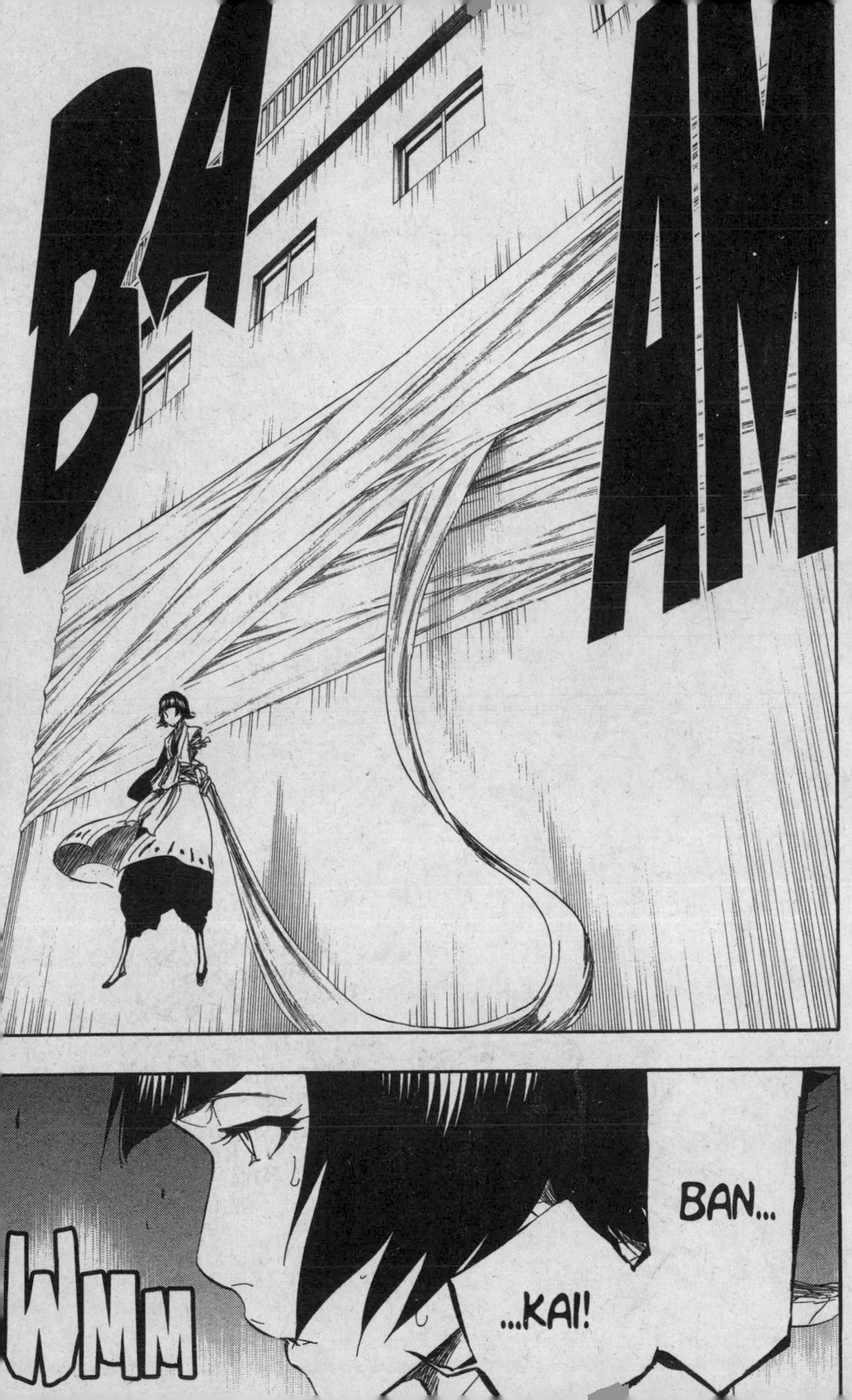
BA-AM
BAN...
...KAI!
WMM

VEEN

SUMMARY!

KON, WHO WAS SENT TO THE SOUL SOCIETY ALONG WITH THE CITY AS PART OF THE THIRTEEN COURT GUARD COMPANIES' "KARAKURA SWITCH PLAN" (TENTATIVE TITLE), IS FOUND BY THE MEMBERS OF THE RESEARCH AND DEVELOPMENT DEPARTMENT WHO HAVE COME TO INVESTIGATE THE SCENE!

WHAT WILL HAPPEN TO KON?! WE WON'T FORGET ABOUT YOU!!

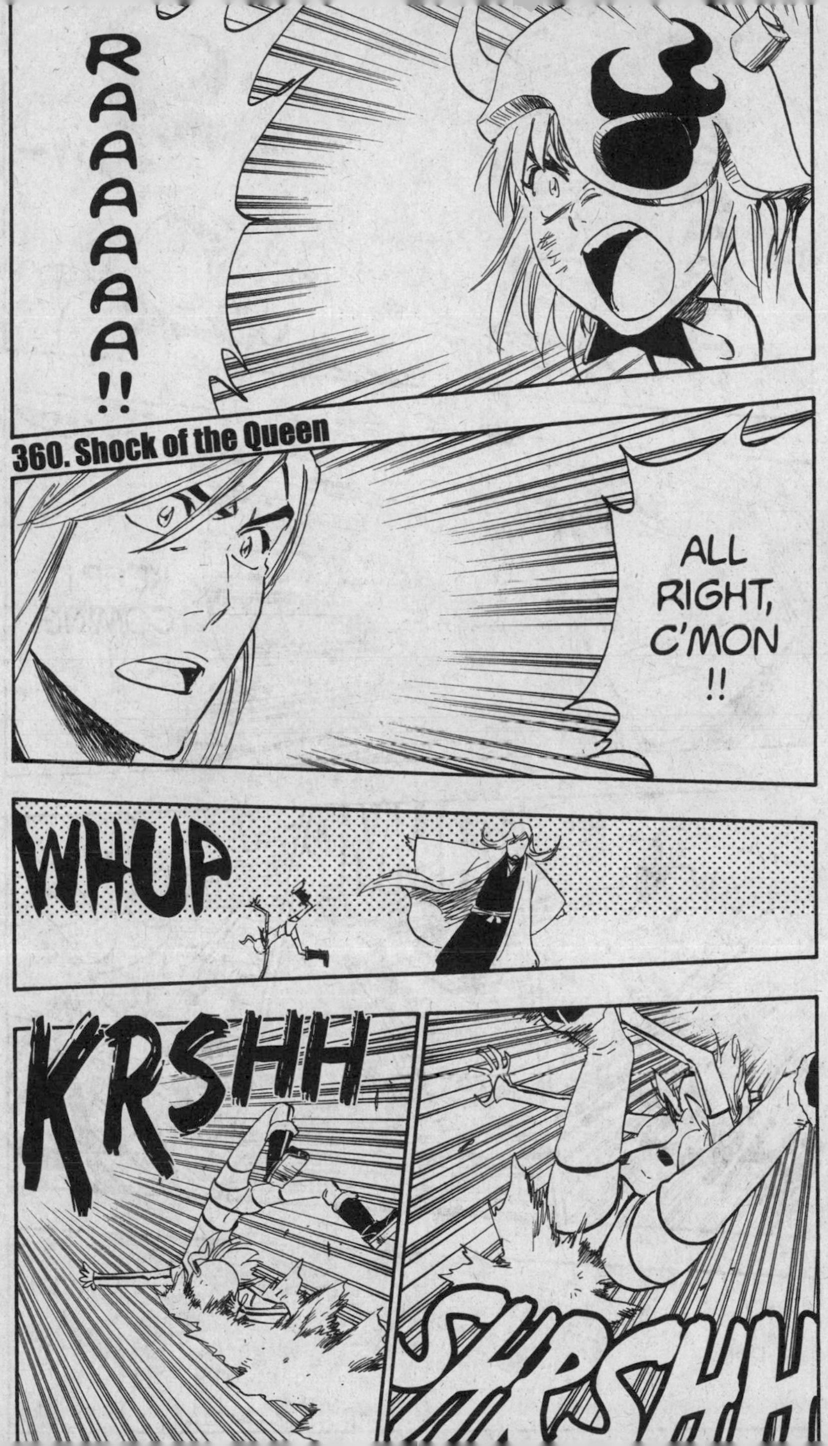
RAAAAAA!!
360. Shock of the Queen
ALL RIGHT, C'MON!!
WHUP
KRSHH

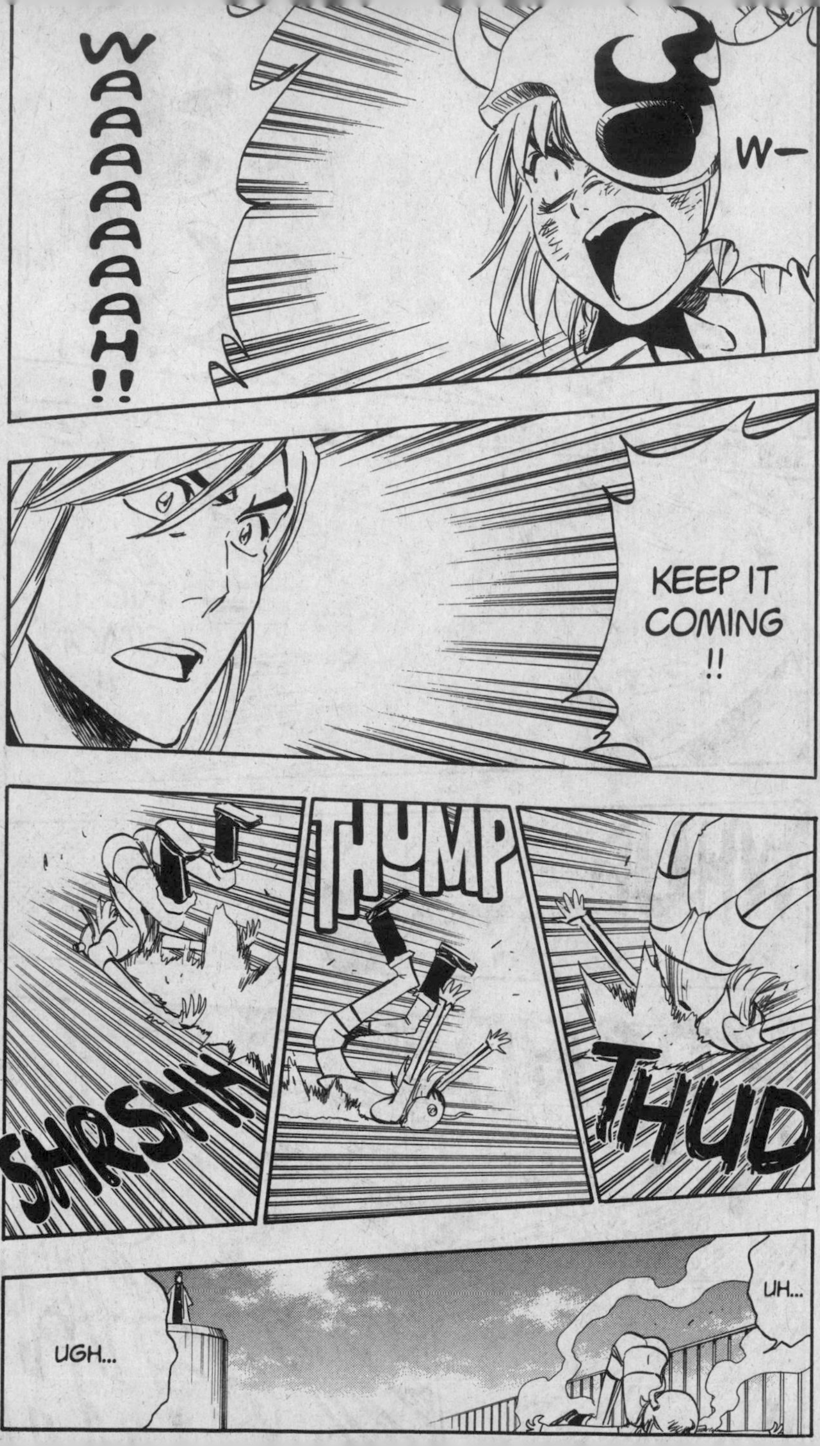
W—
WAAAAAAAAH!!
KEEP IT COMING !!
THUD
THUMP
SHRSH
UH...
UGH...

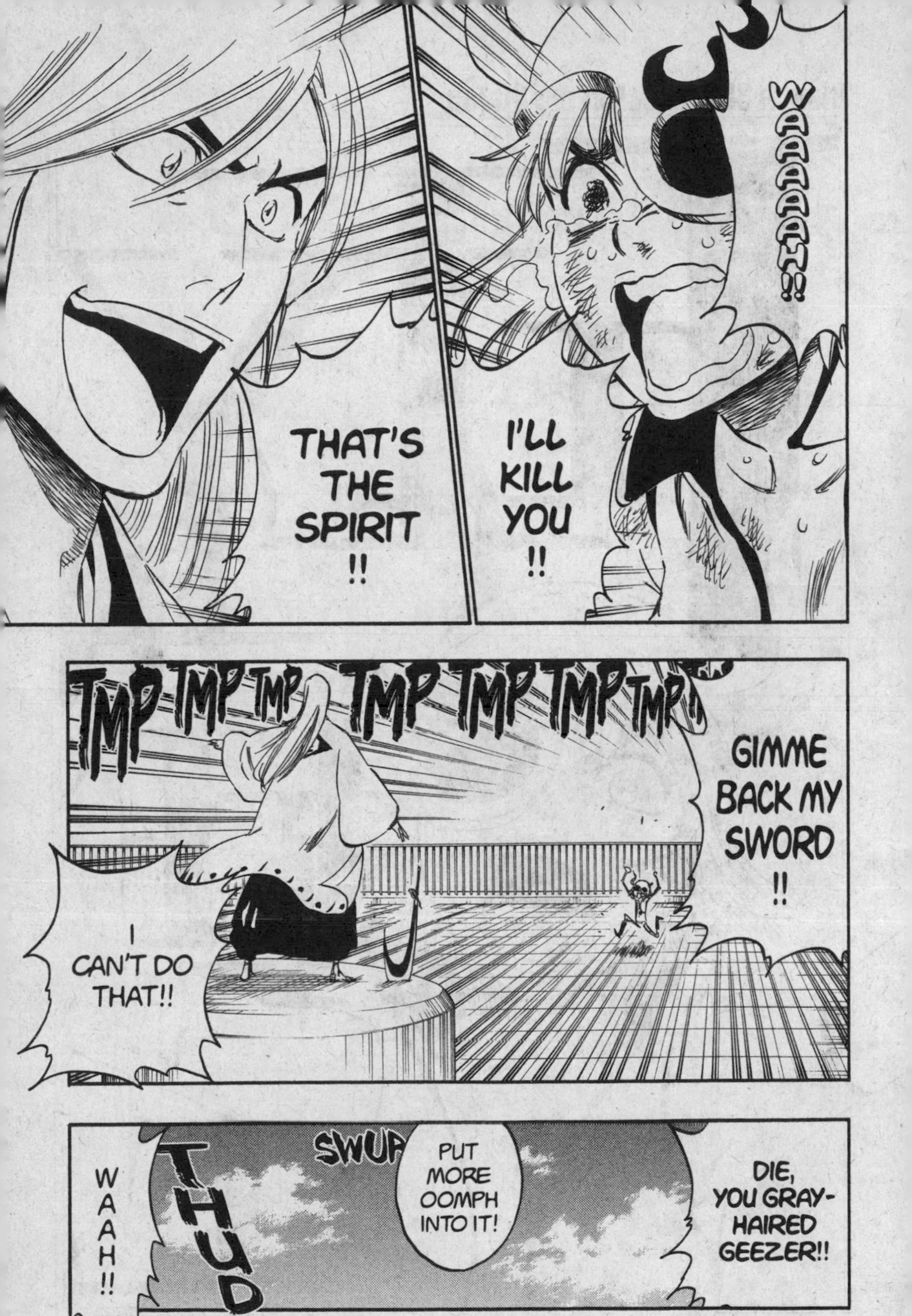
WAAAAAH!!
I'LL KILL YOU!!
THAT'S THE SPIRIT!!
TMP TMP TMP TMP TMP TMP TMP TMP
GIMME BACK MY SWORD!!
I CAN'T DO THAT!!
DIE, YOU GRAY-HAIRED GEEZER!!
PUT MORE OOMPH INTO IT!
SWUP
THUD
WAAH!!

Bleach 360. Shock of the Queen

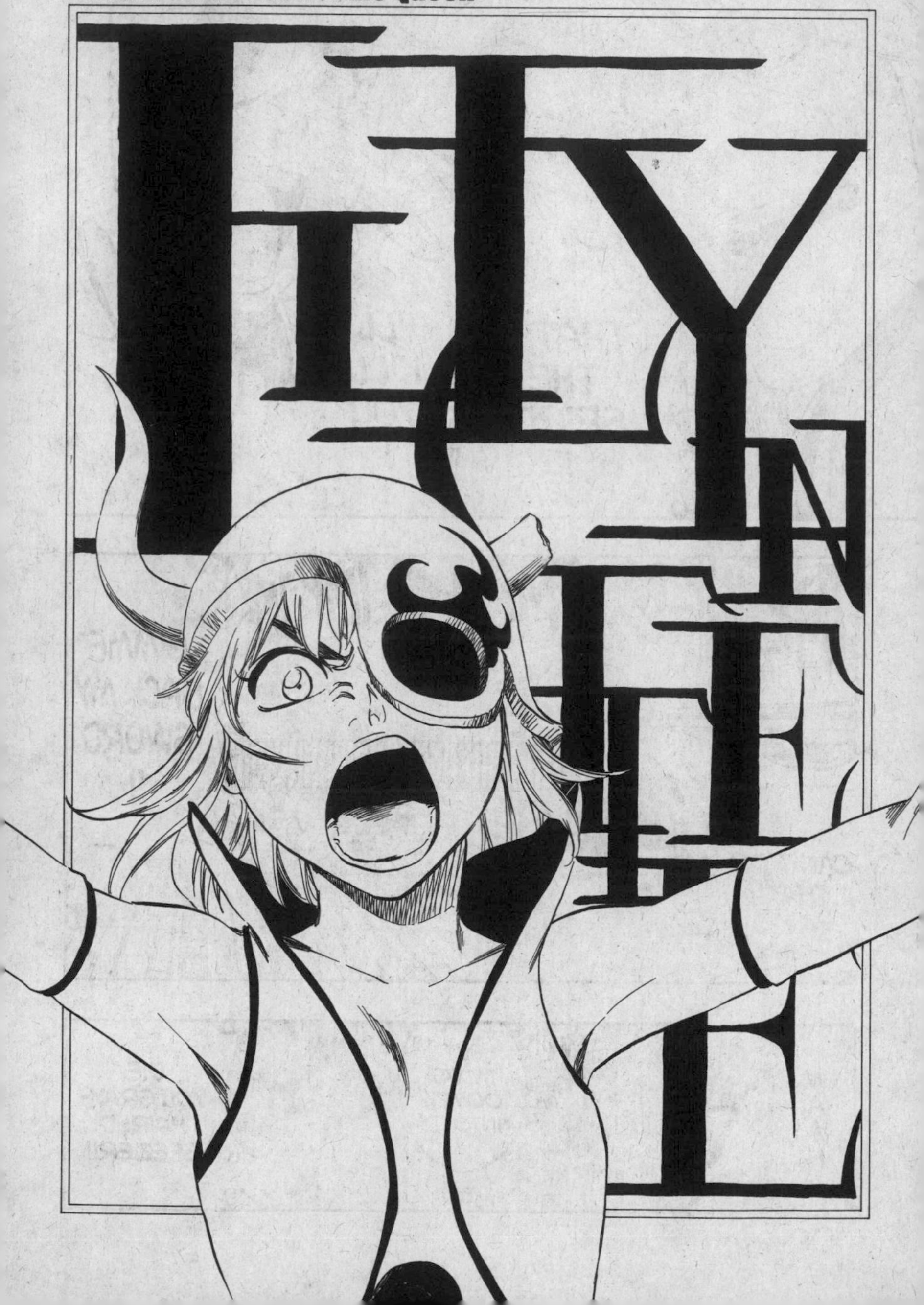

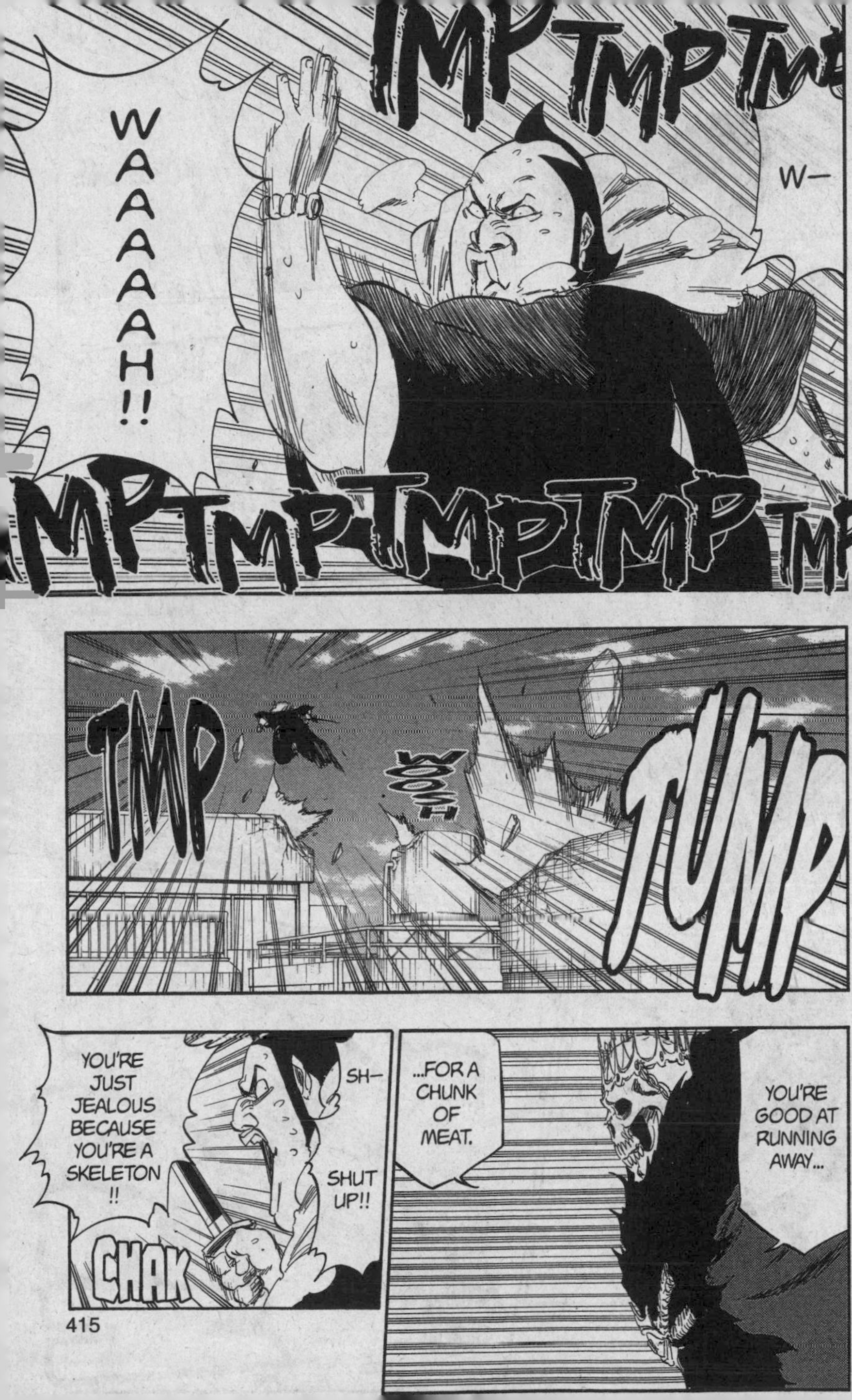
IMP TMP TM
W—
WAAAAAAH!!
MP TMP TMP TMP TMP TMP
TUMP
WOOSH
TMP
YOU'RE GOOD AT RUNNING AWAY...
...FOR A CHUNK OF MEAT.
SH—
SHUT UP!!
YOU'RE JUST JEALOUS BECAUSE YOU'RE A SKELETON!!
CHAK

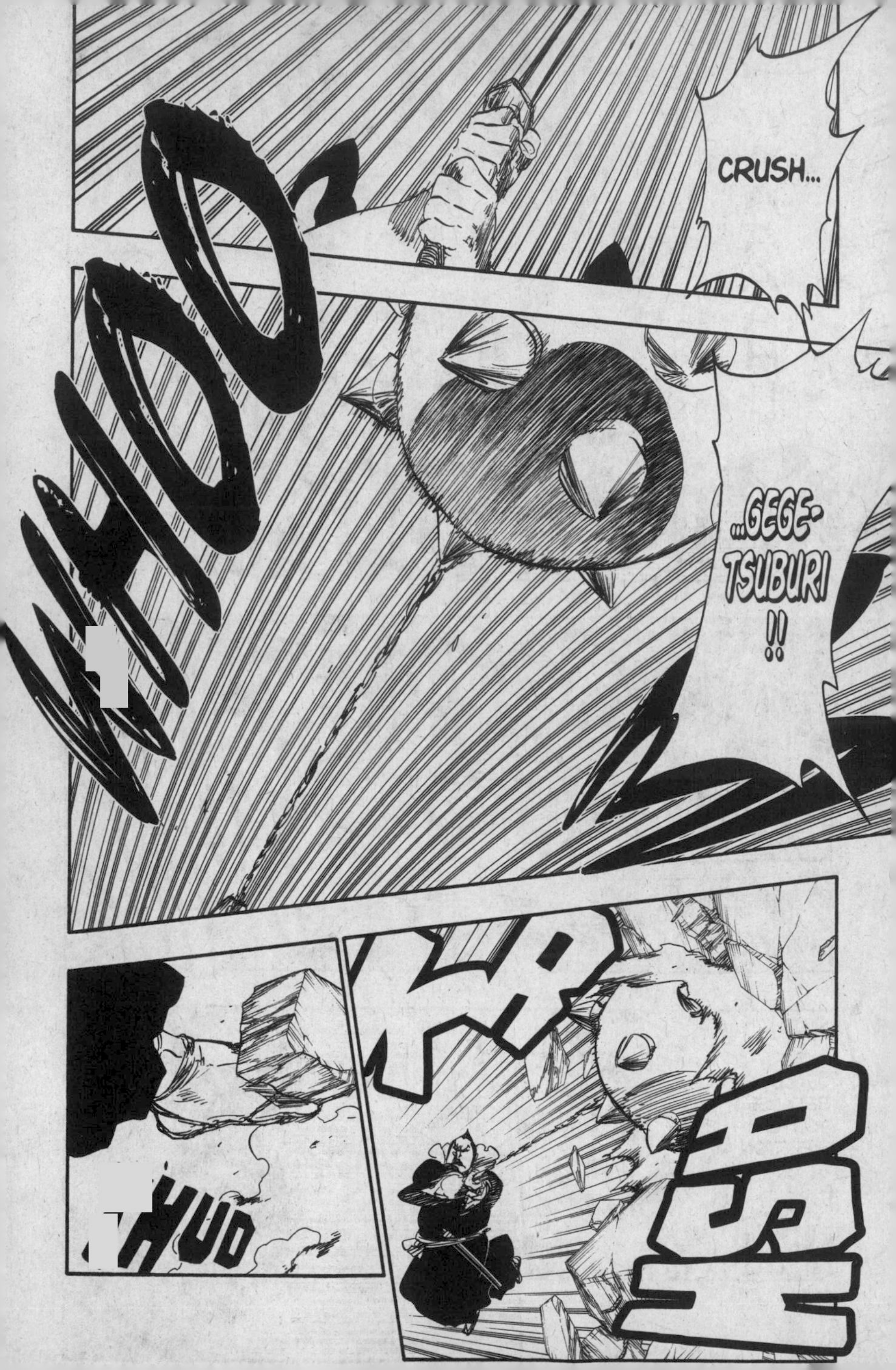
CRUSH...
...GEGE-TSUBURI !!

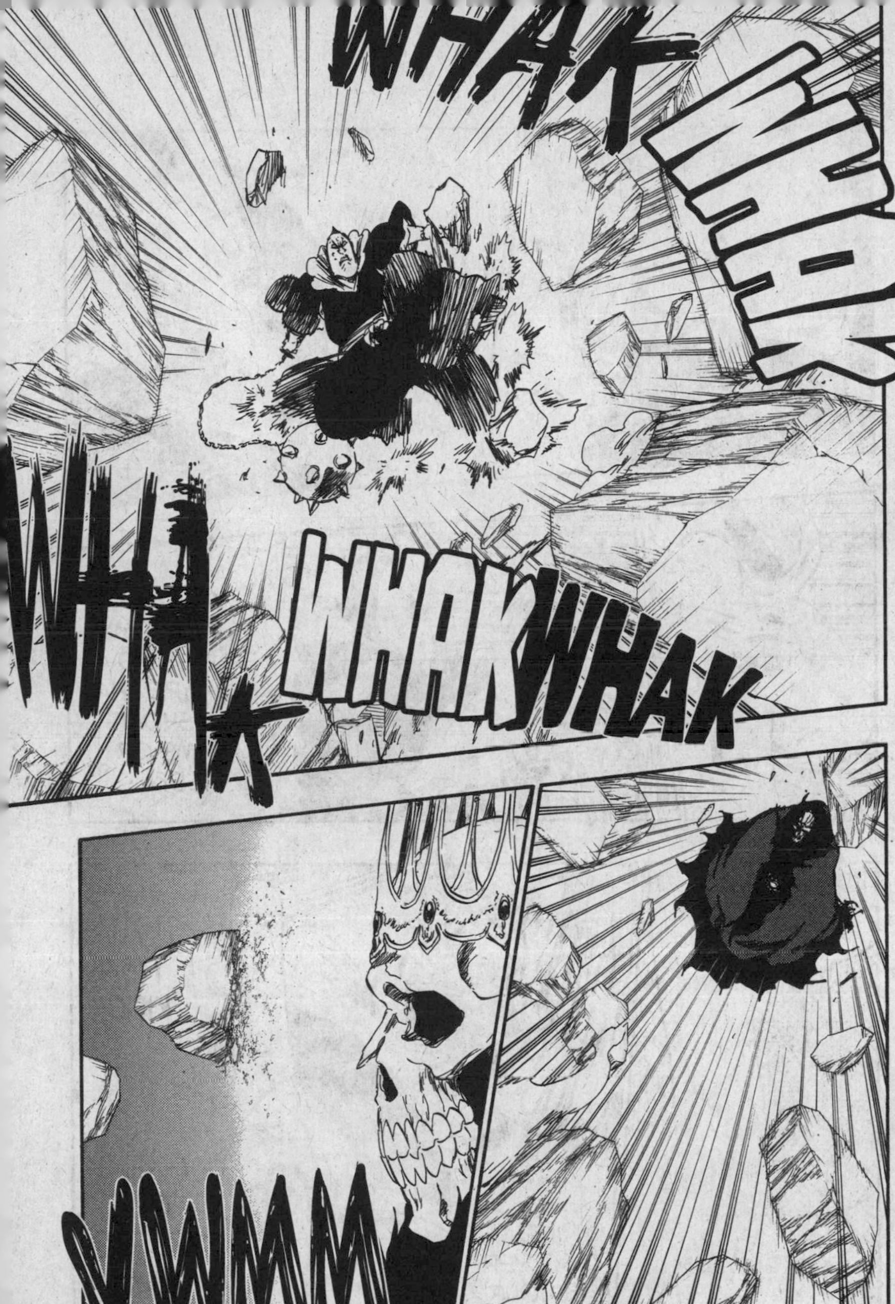
WHAK
WHAK
WHAK
WHAK WHAK
VWMMM

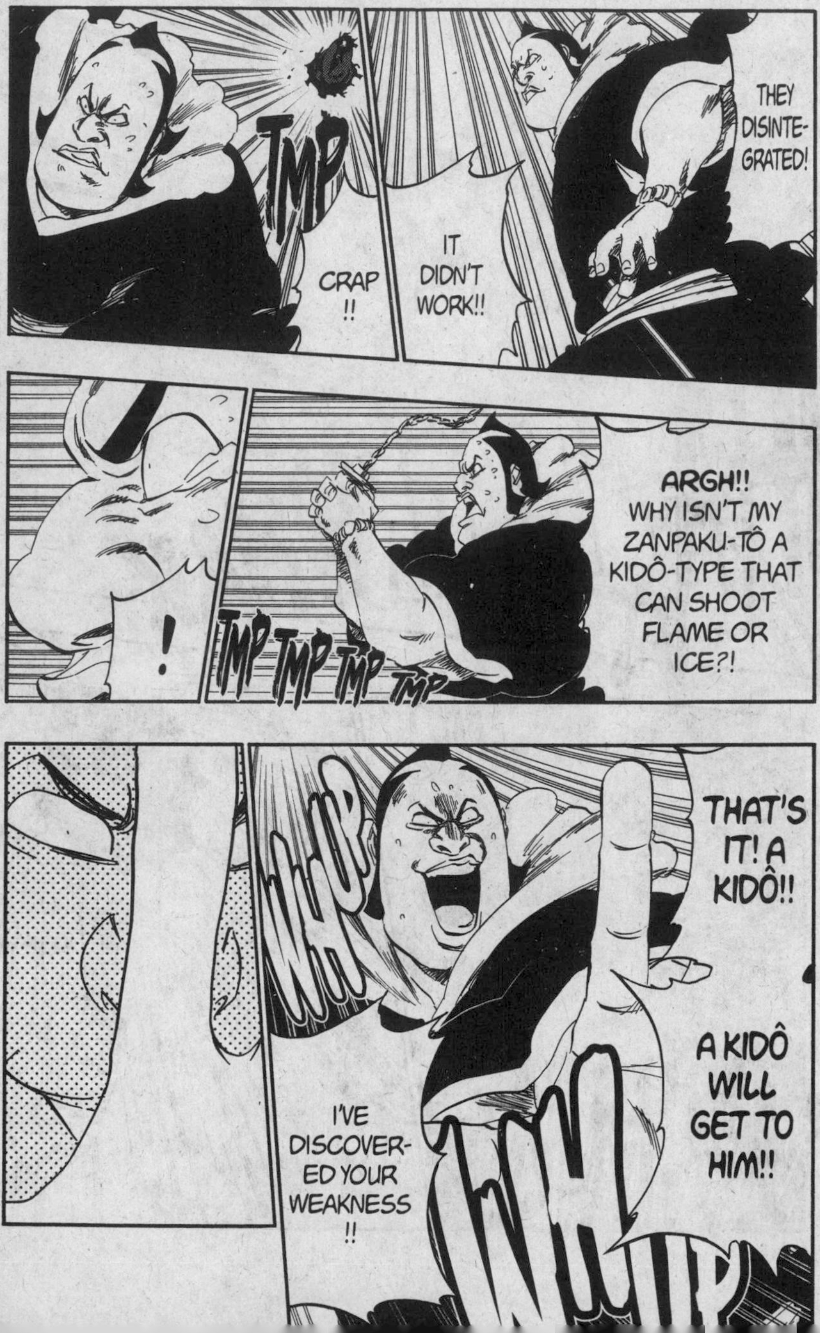
THEY DISINTE-GRATED!
IT DIDN'T WORK!!
TMP
CRAP !!
ARGH!! WHY ISN'T MY ZANPAKU-TÔ A KIDÔ-TYPE THAT CAN SHOOT FLAME OR ICE?!
TMP TMP TMP TMP
!
THAT'S IT! A KIDÔ!!
A KIDÔ WILL GET TO HIM!!
I'VE DISCOVER-ED YOUR WEAKNESS !!

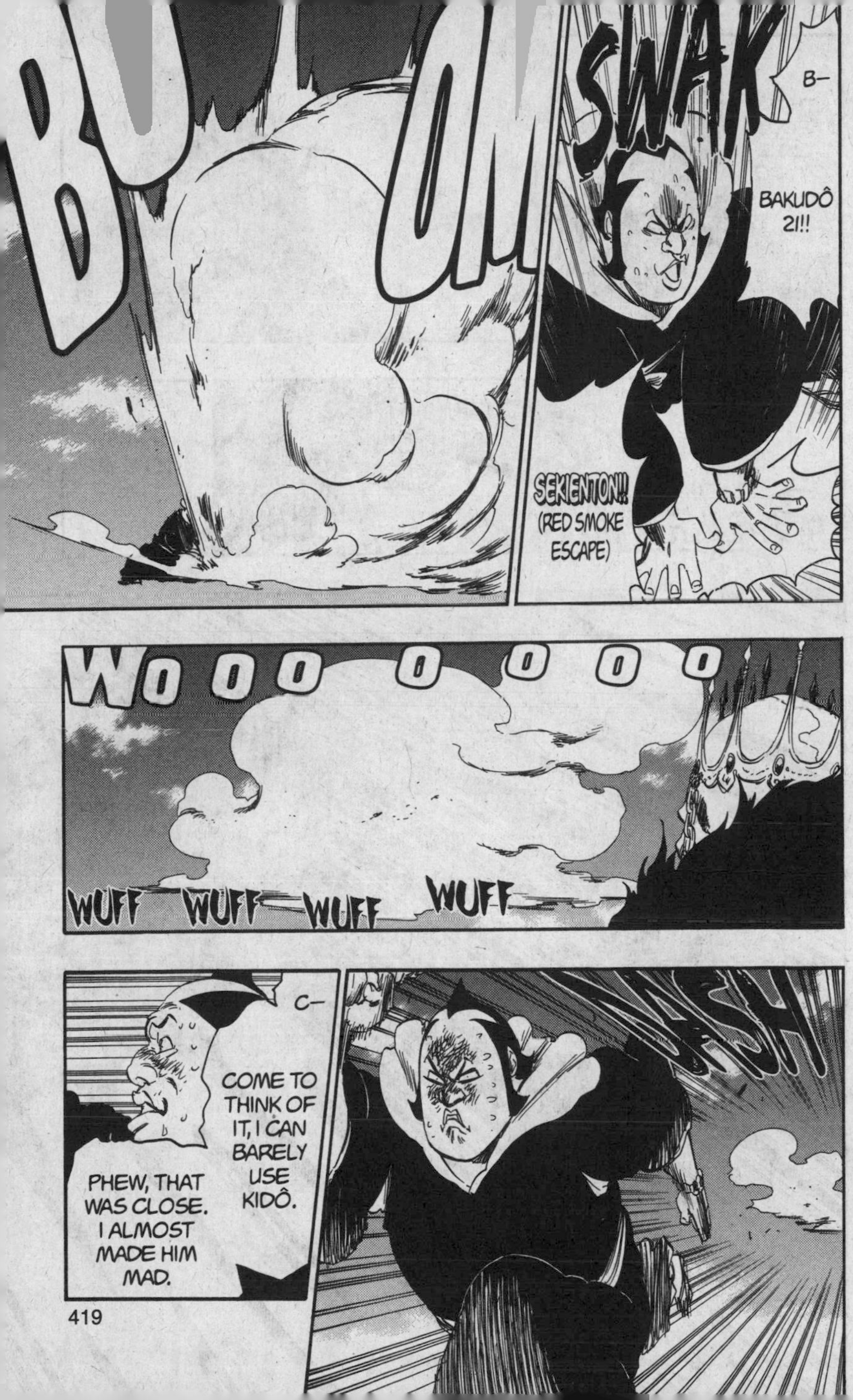
B—
SWAK
BAKUDÔ 21!!
SEKIENTON!!
(RED SMOKE ESCAPE)
BOOM
WOOOOOOO
WUFF WUFF WUFF WUFF
C—
COME TO THINK OF IT, I CAN BARELY USE KIDÔ.
PHEW, THAT WAS CLOSE. I ALMOST MADE HIM MAD.

...THAT'S ABOUT ALL HE CAN DO.

LOOKS LIKE...

HMPH.

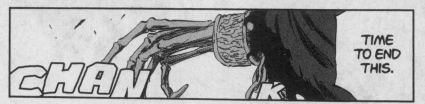

CHAN

TIME TO END THIS.

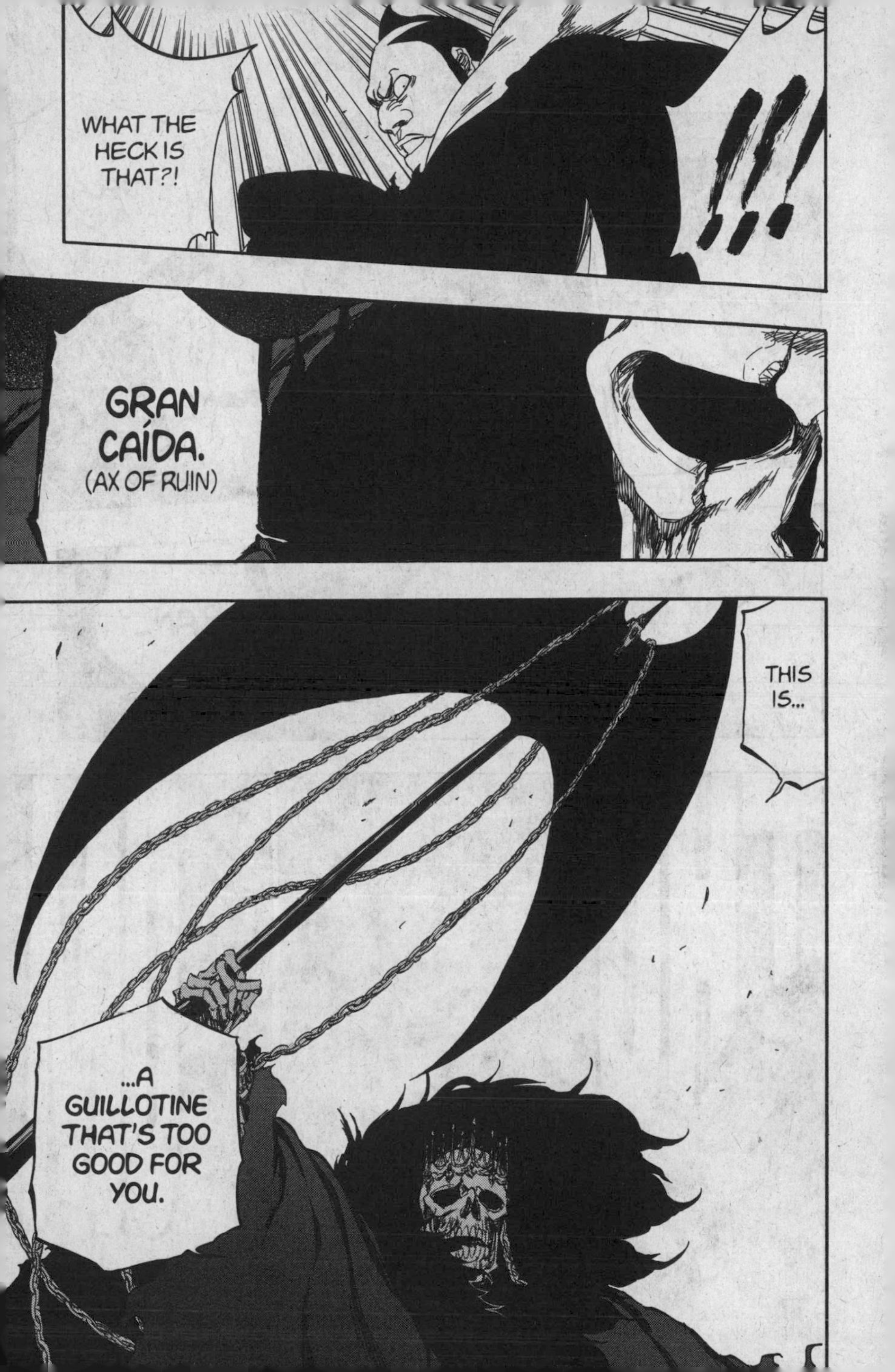
WHAT THE HECK IS THAT?!
!!
GRAN CAÍDA.
(AX OF RUIN)
THIS IS...
...A GUILLOTINE THAT'S TOO GOOD FOR YOU.

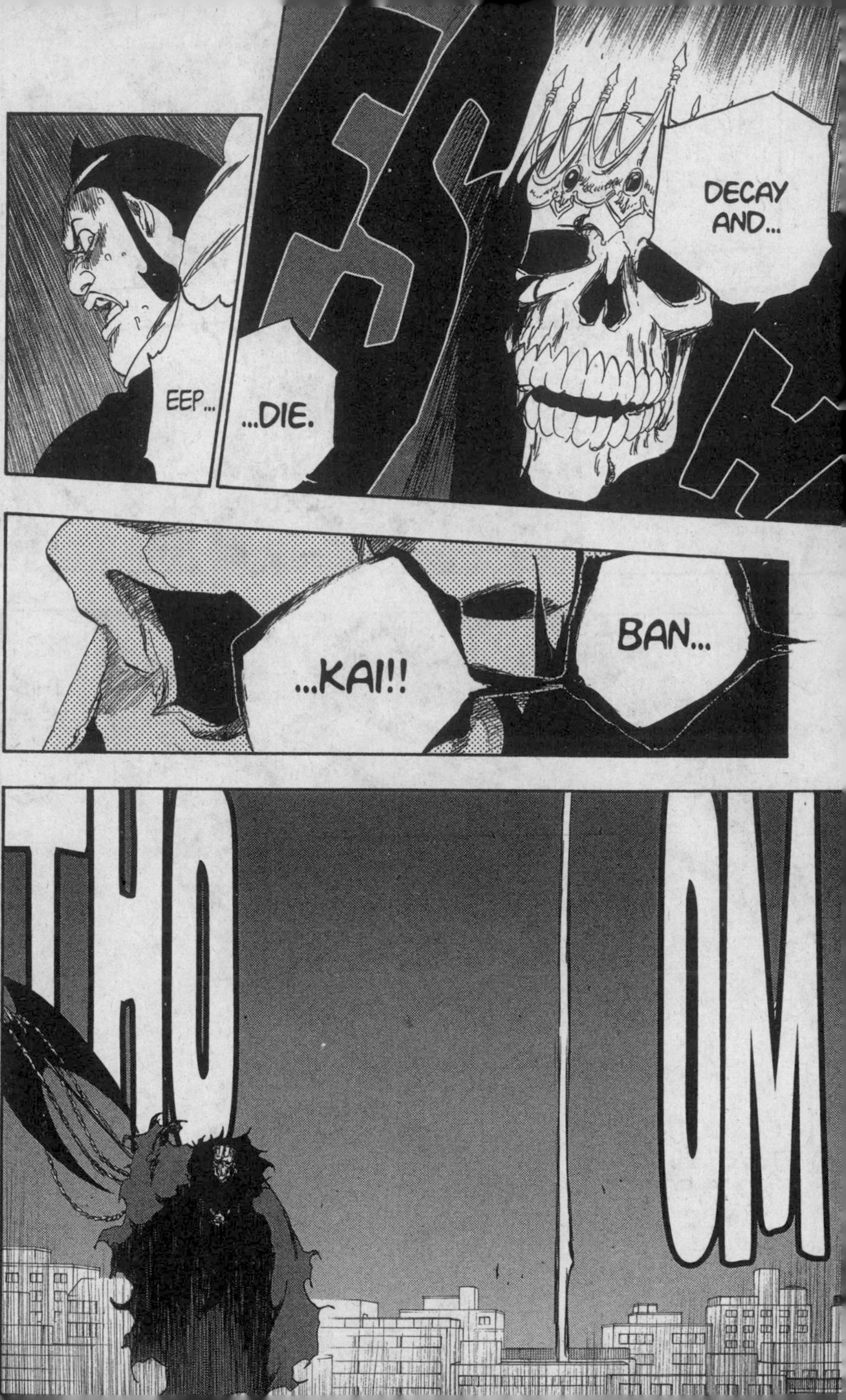
DECAY AND...
...DIE.
EEP...
BAN...
...KAI!!
THOOM

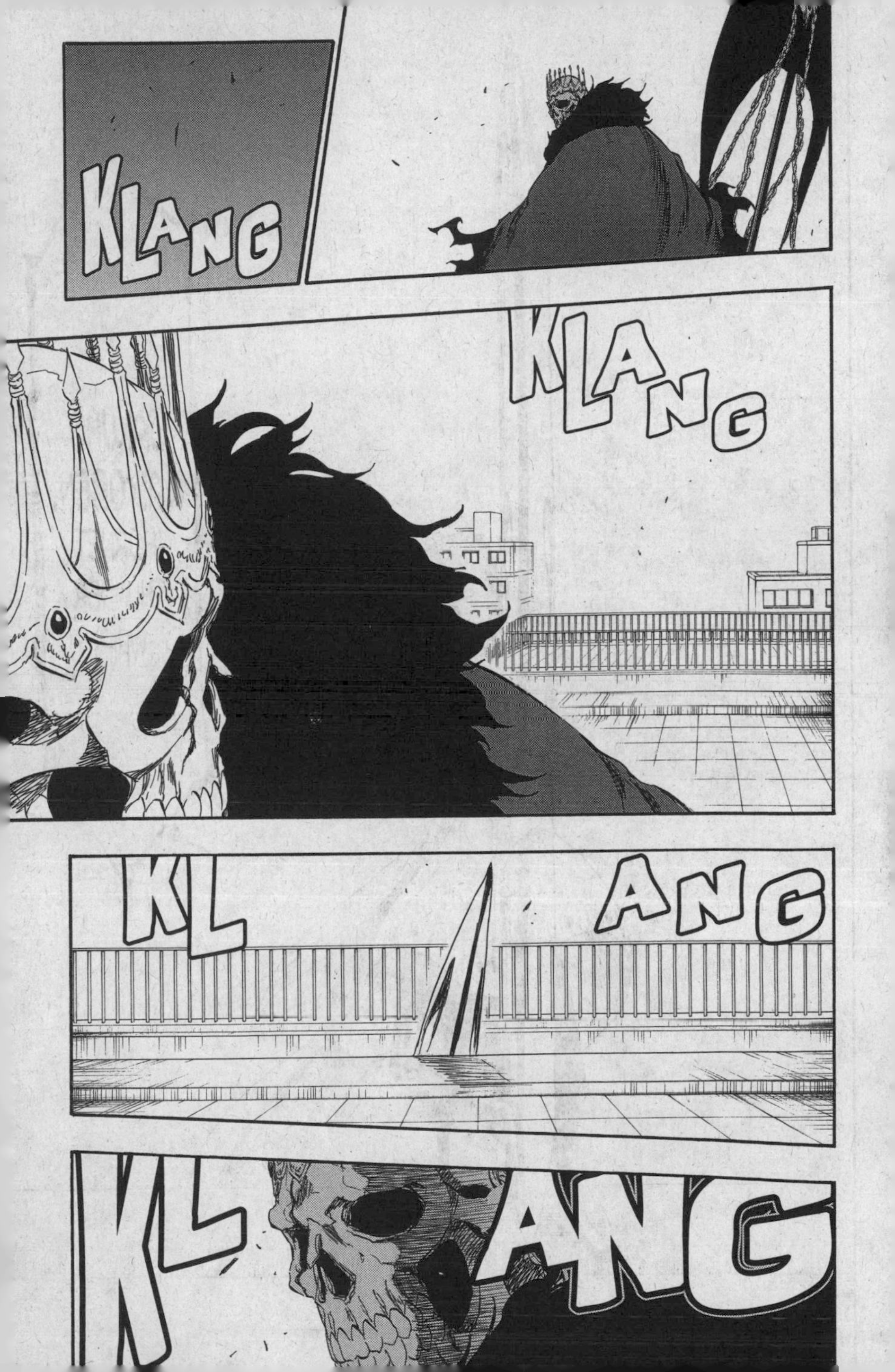
KLANG
KLANG
KL ANG
KL ANG

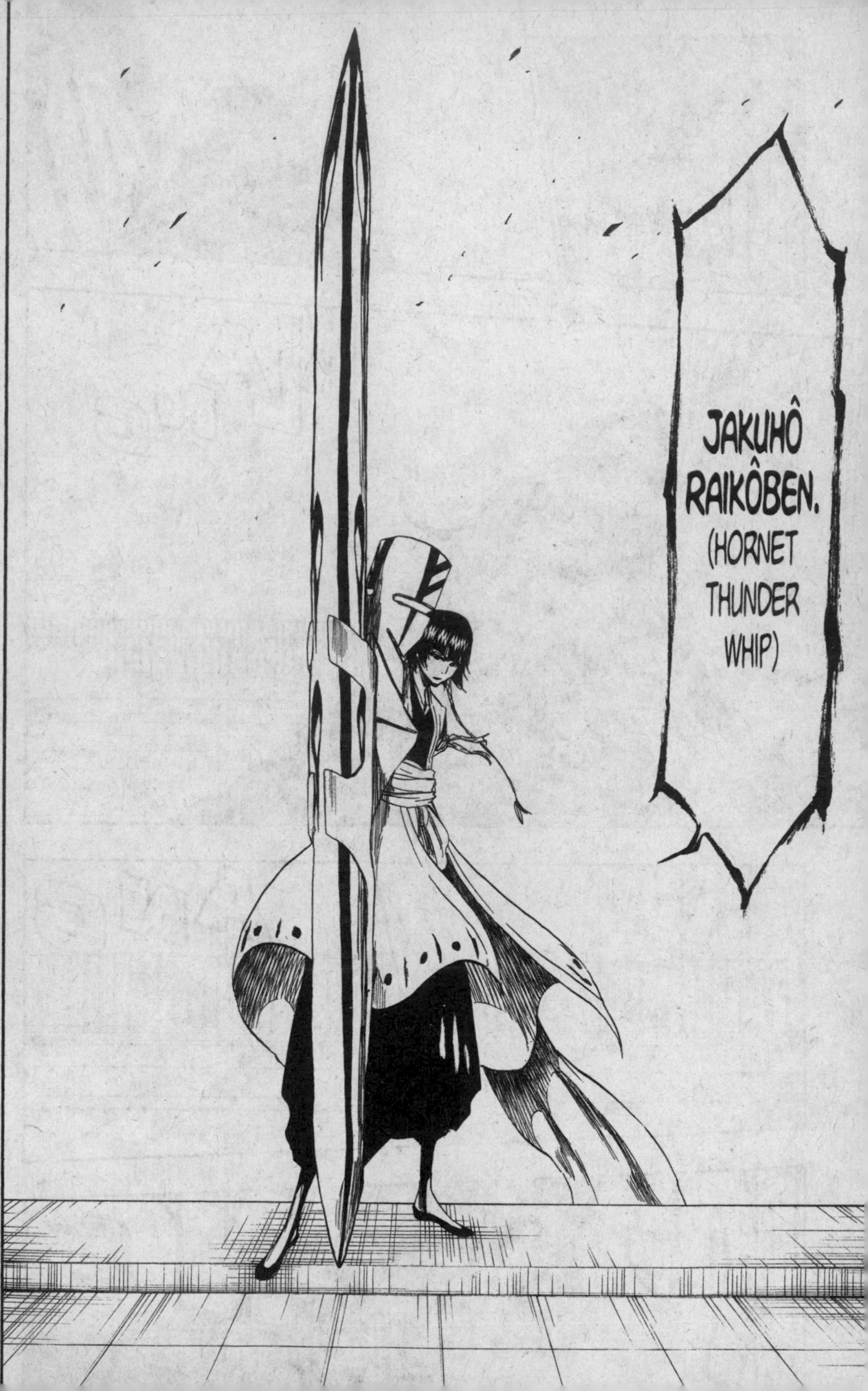
JAKUHÔ RAIKÔBEN. (HORNET THUNDER WHIP)

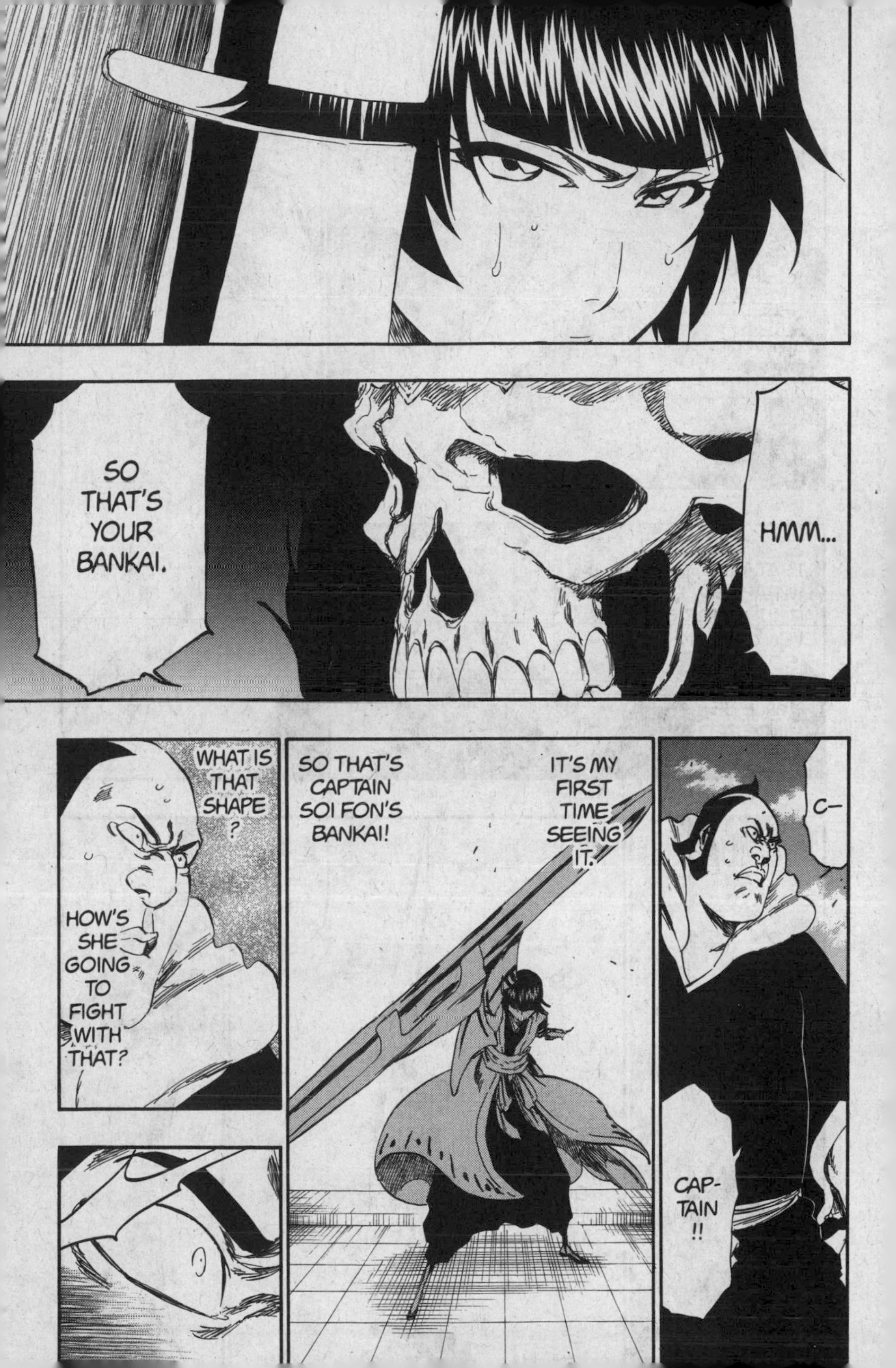
HMM...
SO THAT'S YOUR BANKAI.
C—
CAP-TAIN!!
IT'S MY FIRST TIME SEEING IT.
SO THAT'S CAPTAIN SOI FON'S BANKAI!
WHAT IS THAT SHAPE?
HOW'S SHE GOING TO FIGHT WITH THAT?

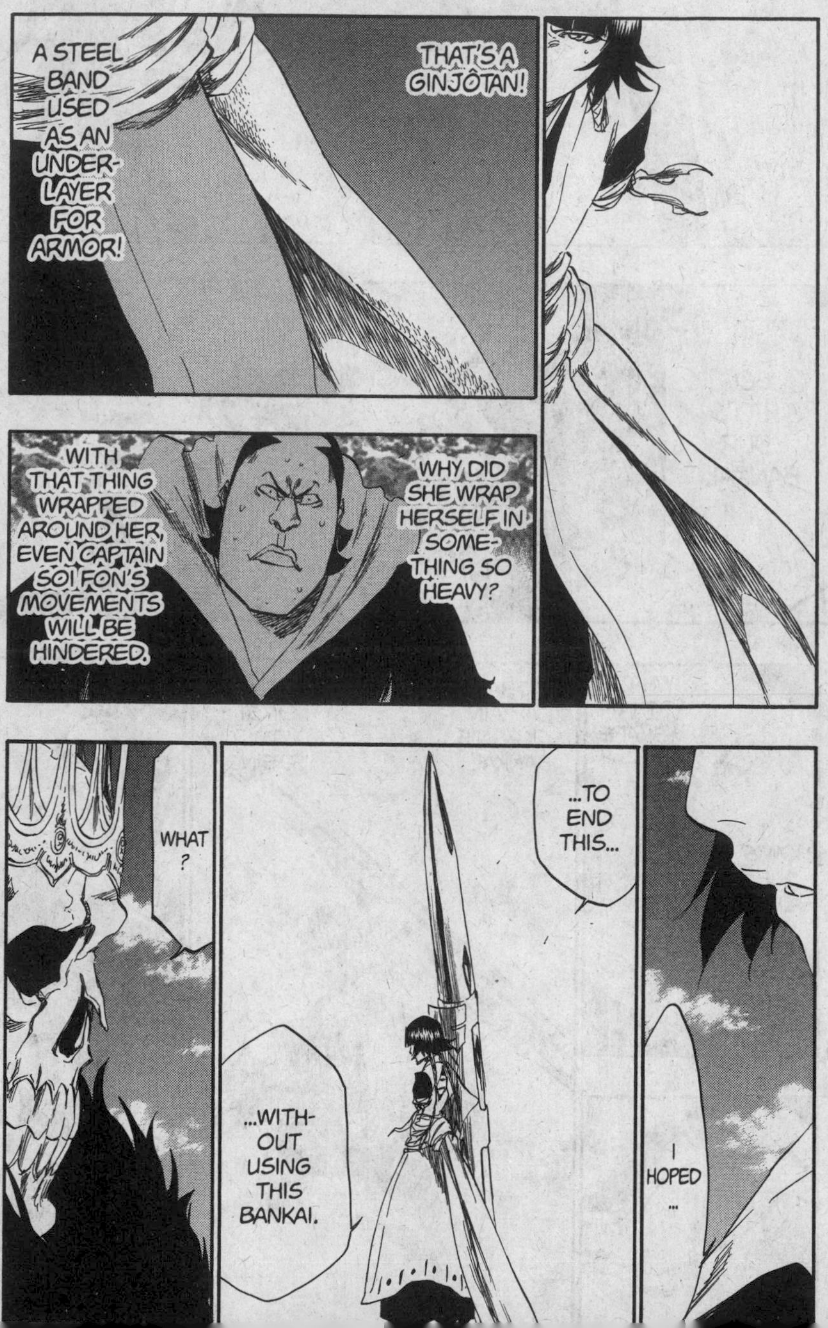
THAT'S A GINJÔTAN!
A STEEL BAND USED AS AN UNDER-LAYER FOR ARMOR!
WHY DID SHE WRAP HERSELF IN SOME-THING SO HEAVY?
WITH THAT THING WRAPPED AROUND HER, EVEN CAPTAIN SOI FON'S MOVEMENTS WILL BE HINDERED.
I HOPED ...
...TO END THIS...
...WITH-OUT USING THIS BANKAI.
WHAT ?

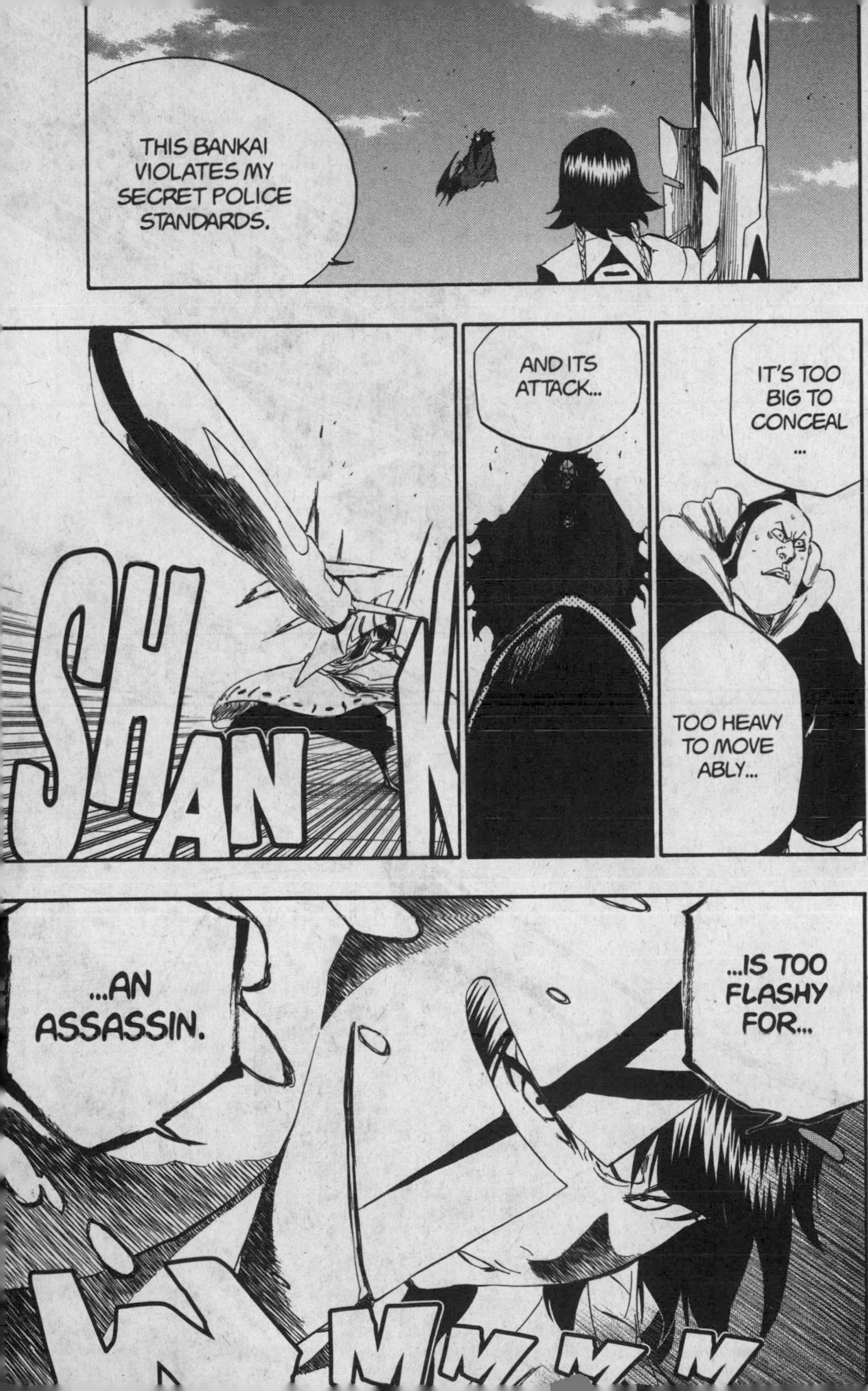
THIS BANKAI VIOLATES MY SECRET POLICE STANDARDS.
IT'S TOO BIG TO CONCEAL ...
TOO HEAVY TO MOVE ABLY...
AND ITS ATTACK...
SHANK
...IS TOO FLASHY FOR...
...AN ASSASSIN.
MMMMM

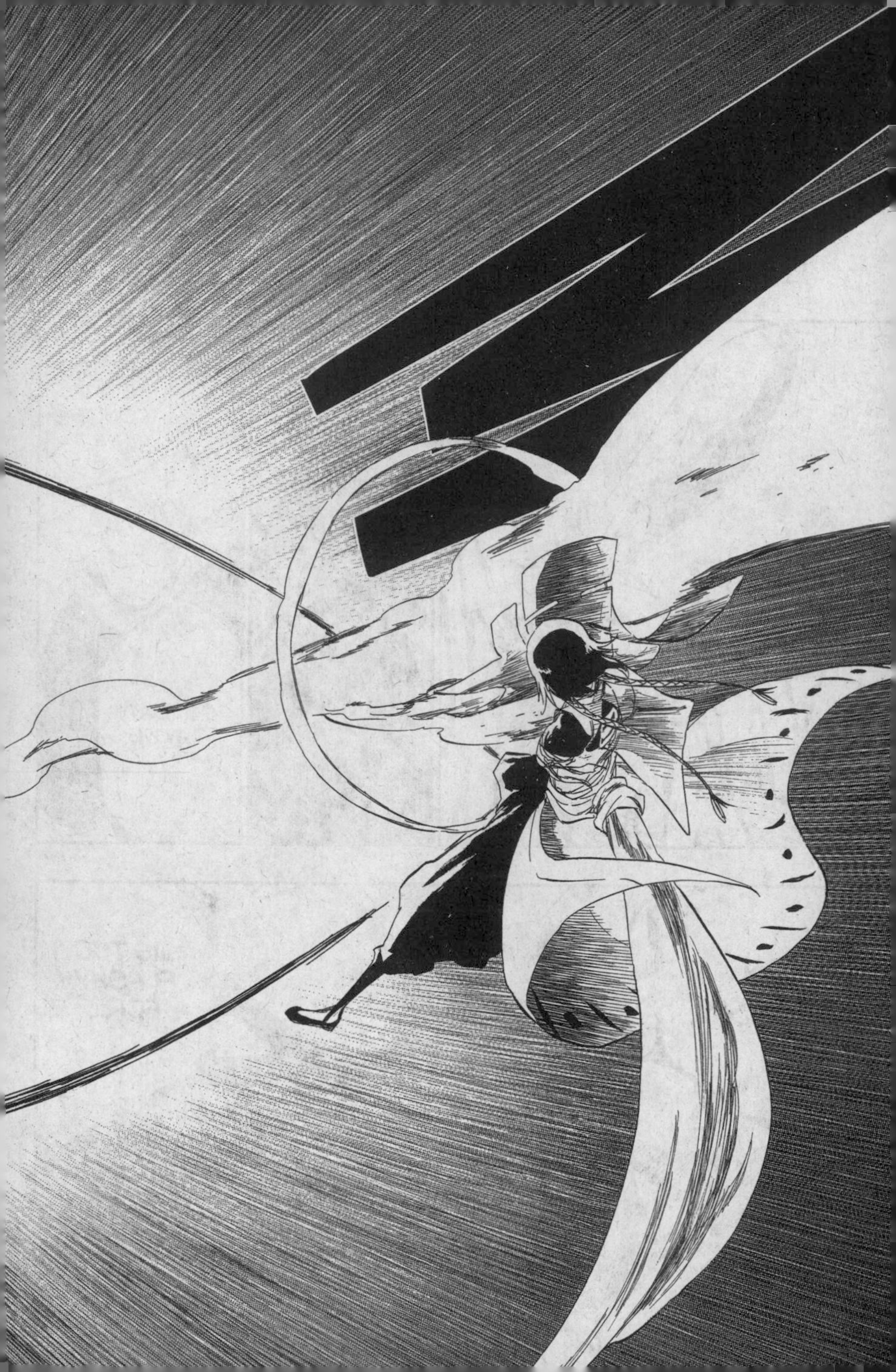

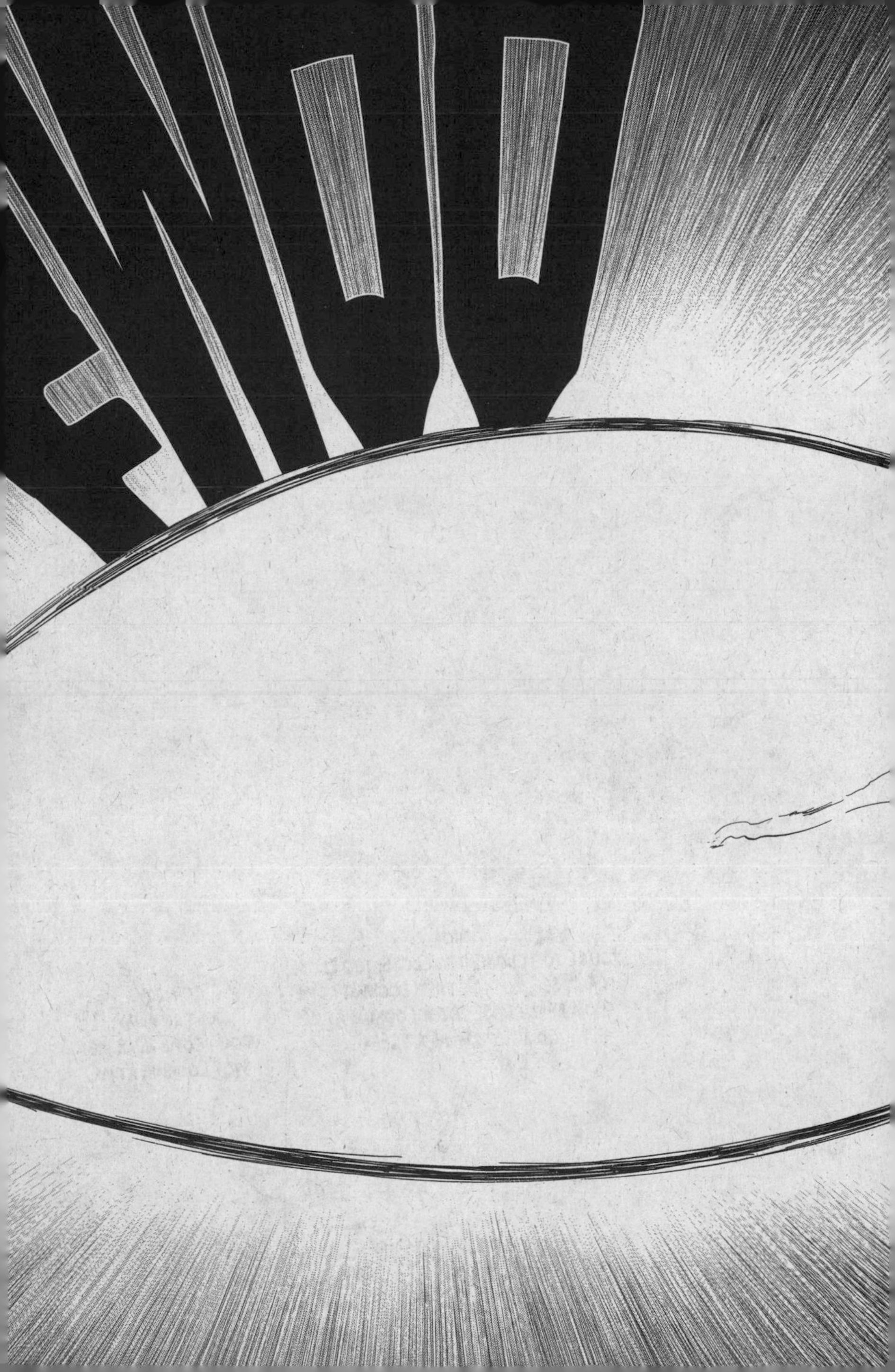

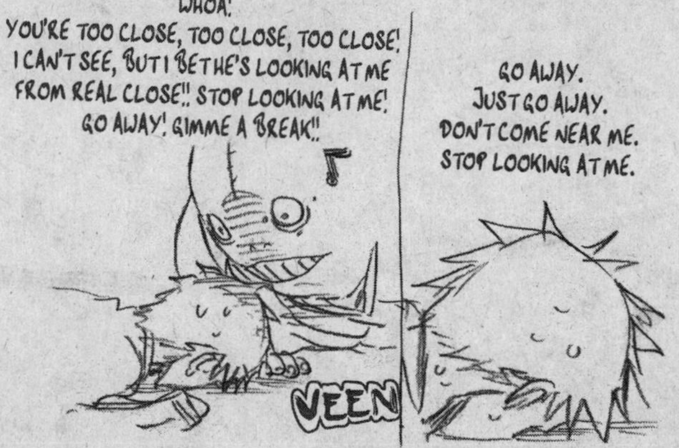
GO AWAY.
JUST GO AWAY.
DON'T COME NEAR ME.
STOP LOOKING AT ME.
WHOA!
YOU'RE TOO CLOSE, TOO CLOSE, TOO CLOSE!
I CAN'T SEE, BUT I BET HE'S LOOKING AT ME FROM REAL CLOSE!! STOP LOOKING AT ME!
GO AWAY! GIMME A BREAK!!
VEEN

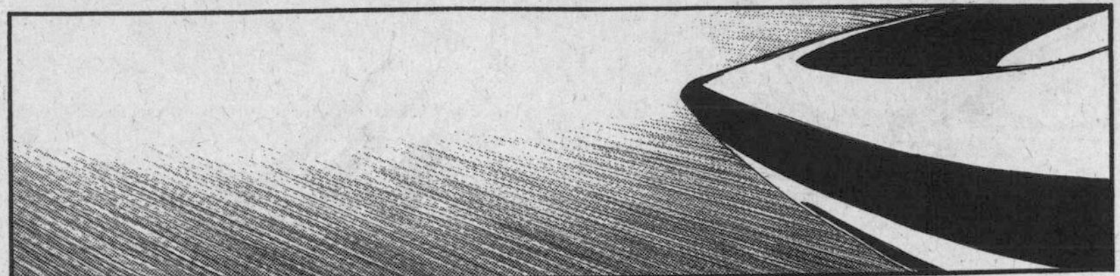

361. I Hate Loneliness, But It Loves Me

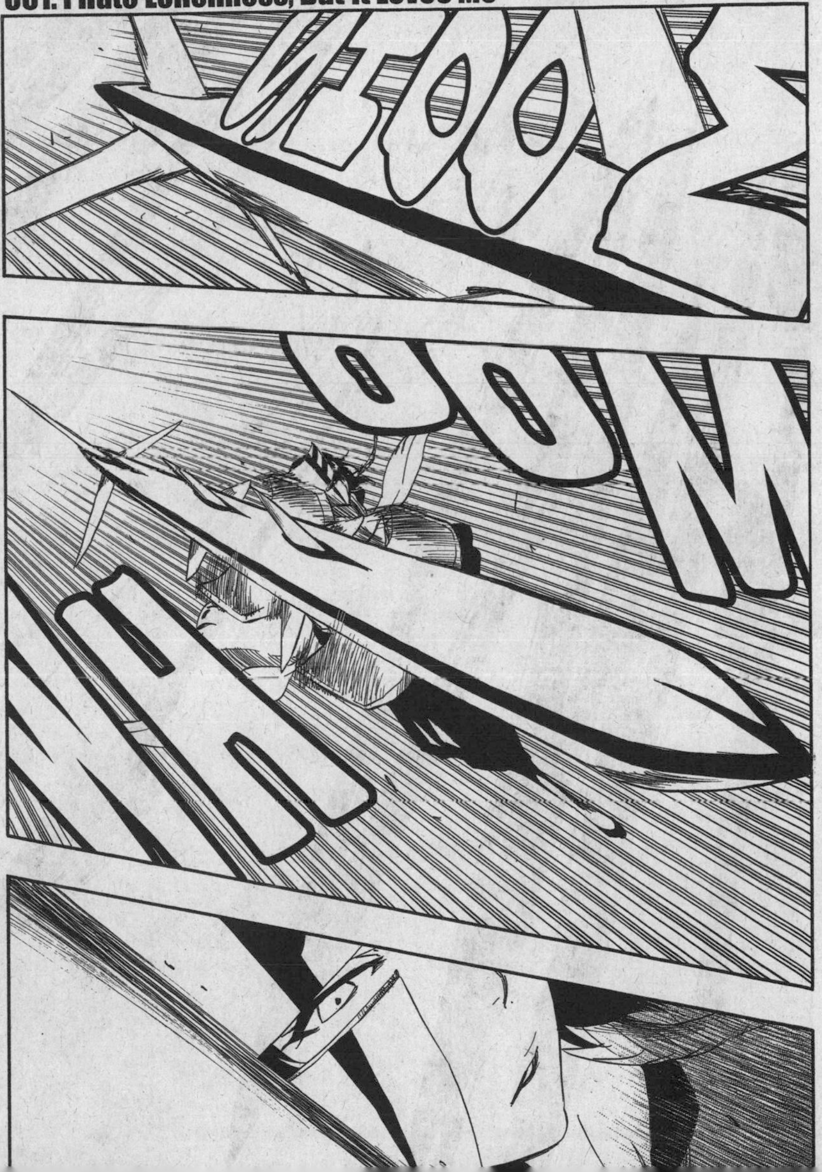

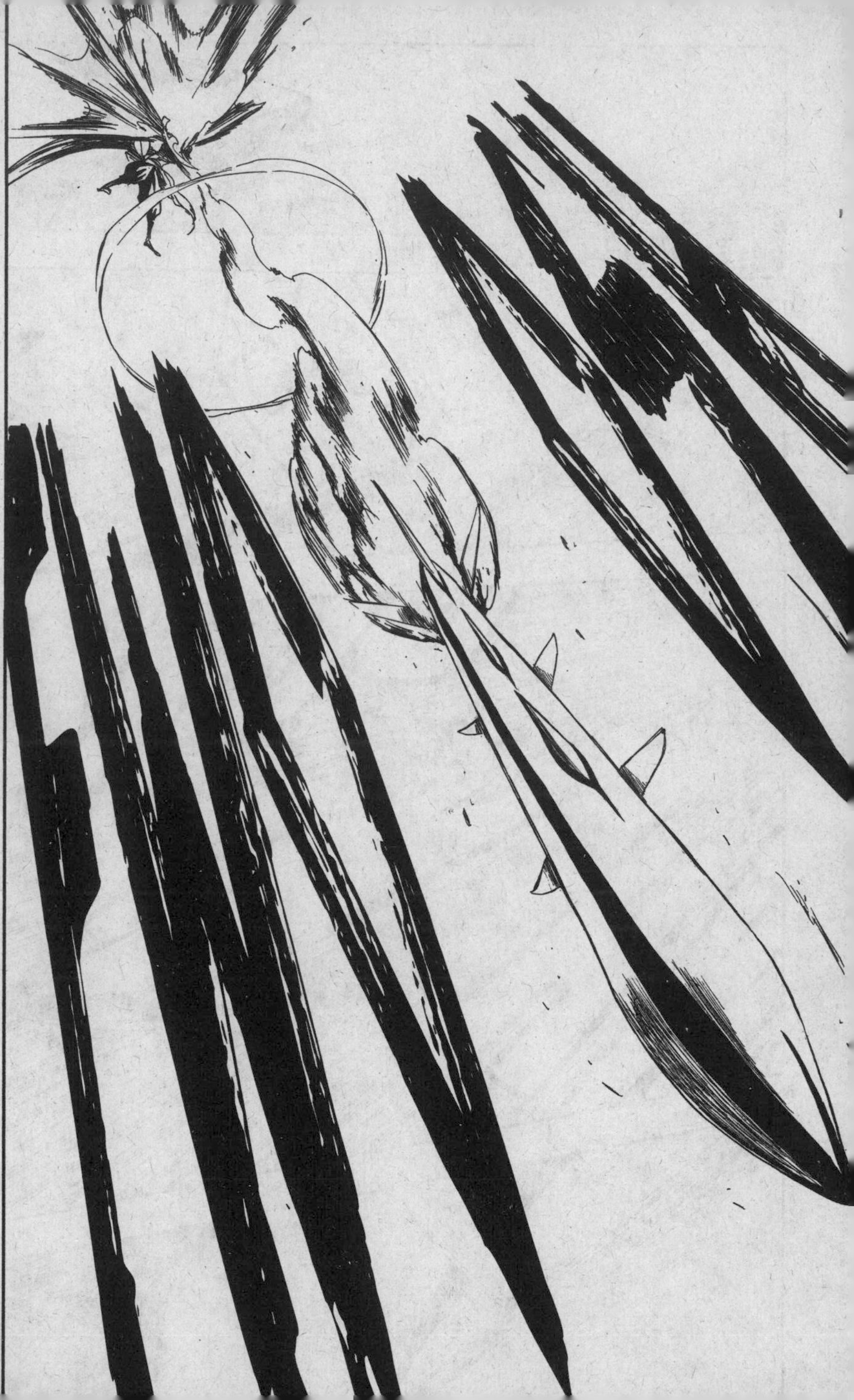

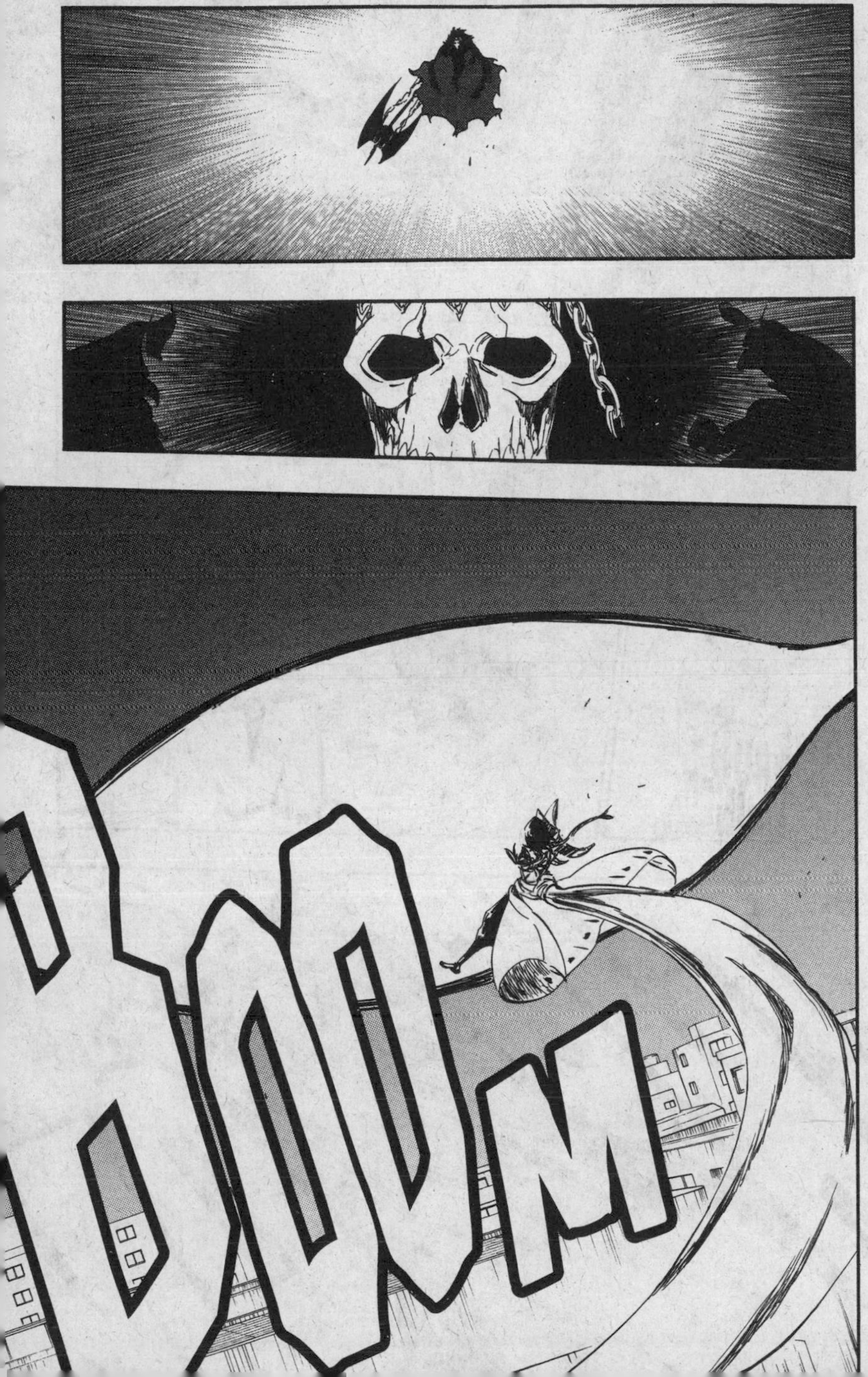
BOOM

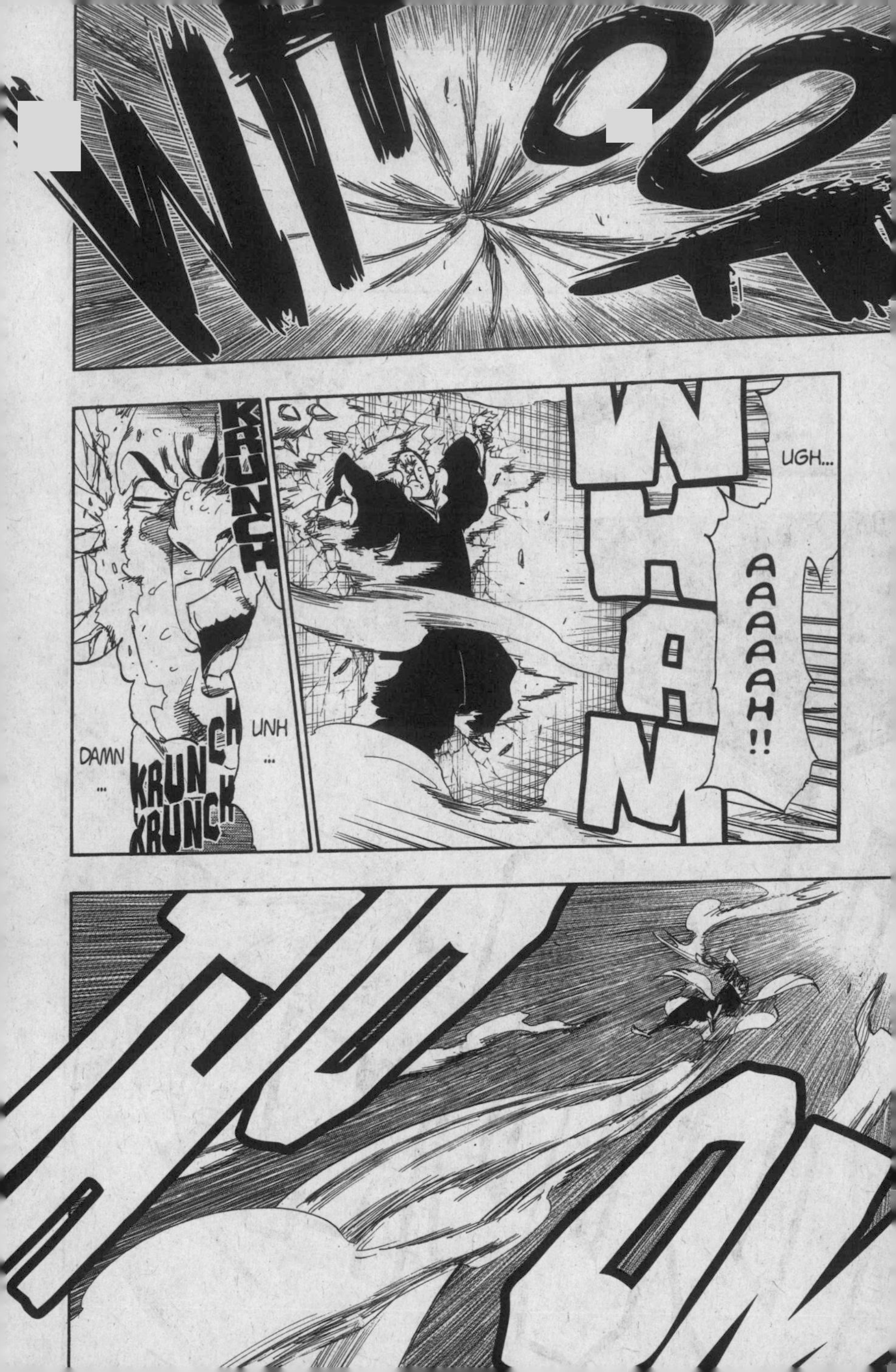
WHAM
UGH...
AAAAAH!!
KRUNCH
UNH...
KRUNCH
KRUNCH
KRUNCH
DAMN...

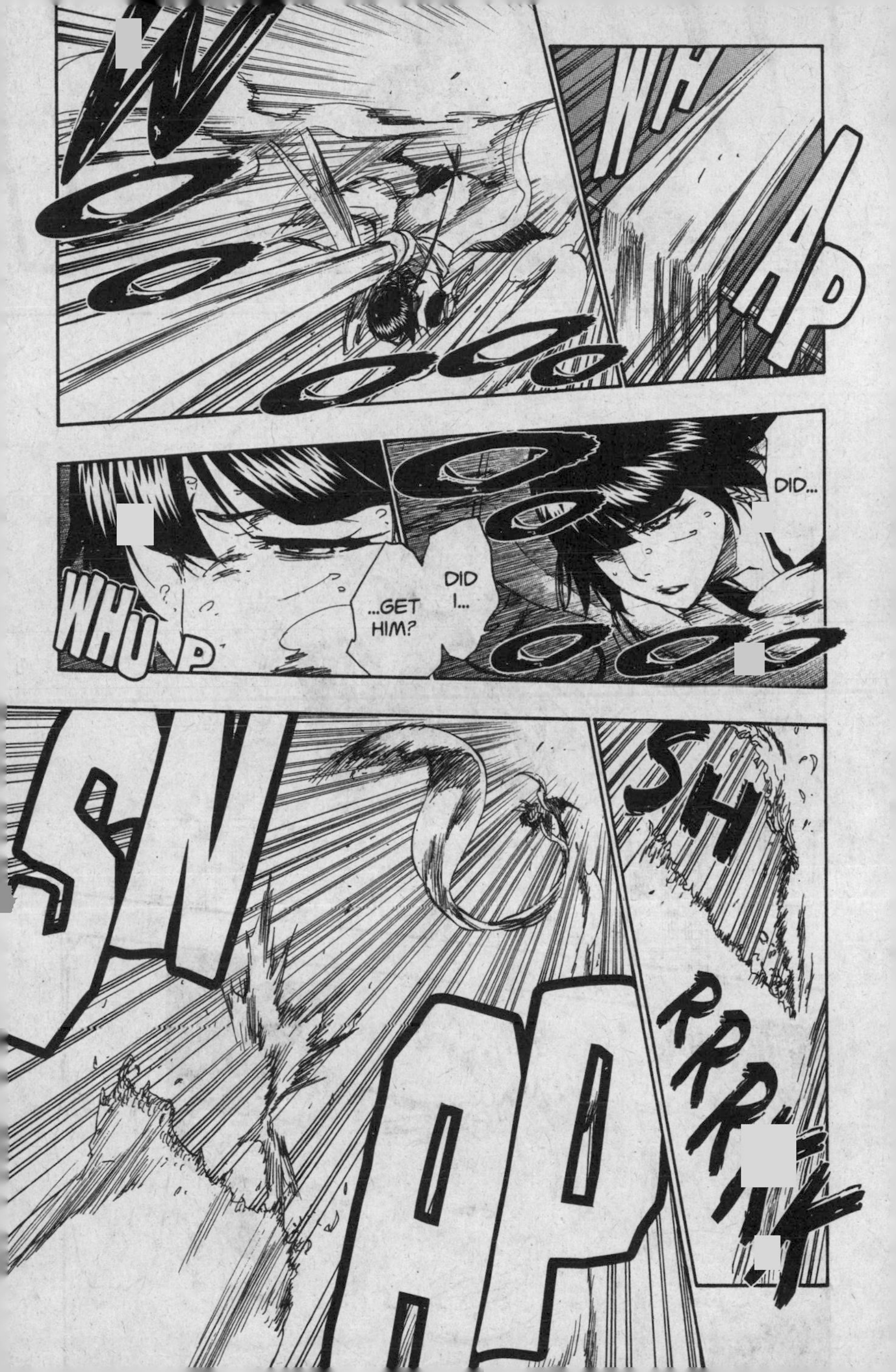

WHAP
DID...
DID I...
...GET HIM?
WHUP
SHRRRRK
SNAP

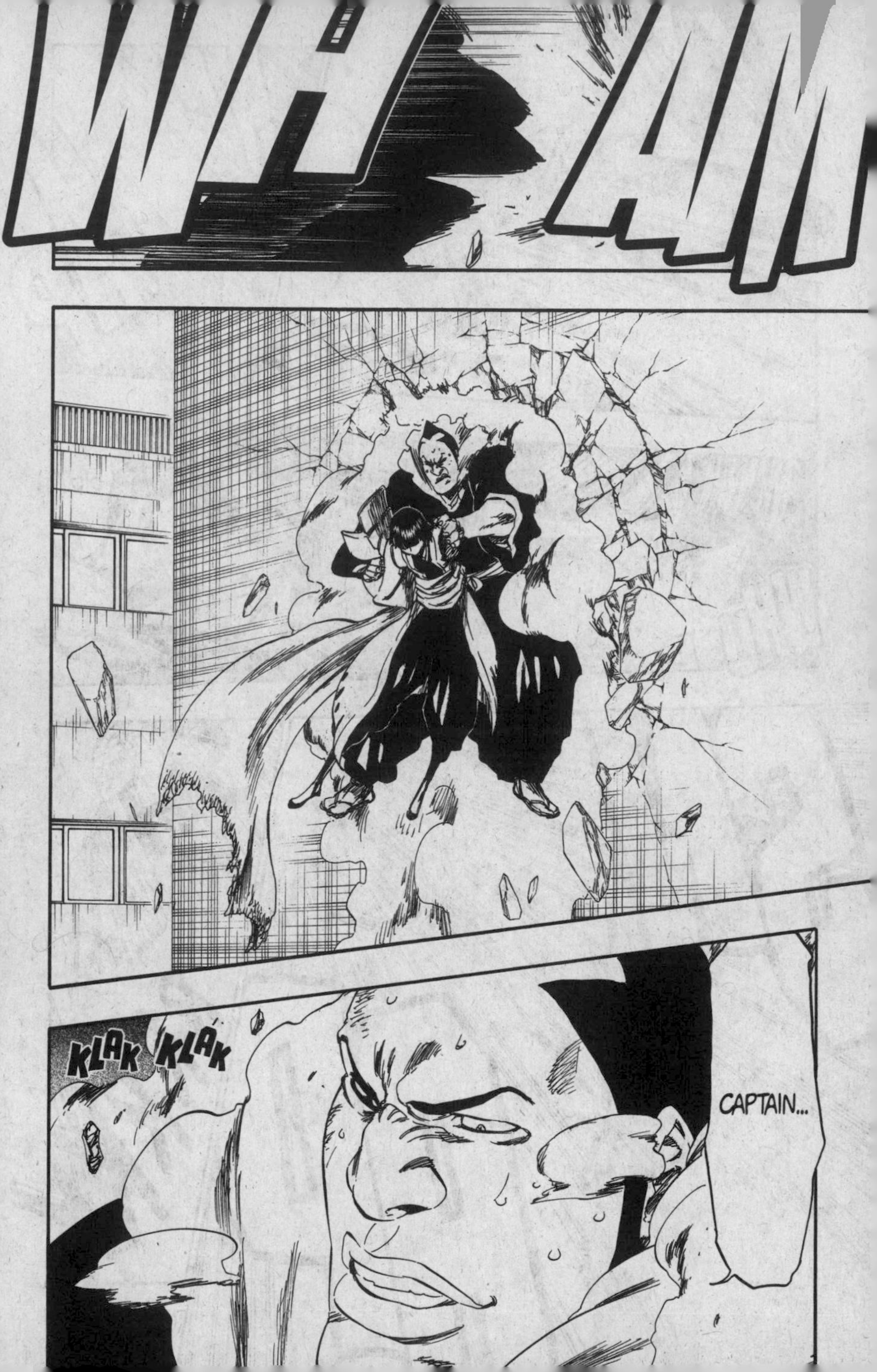
WHAM
KLAK KLAK
CAPTAIN...

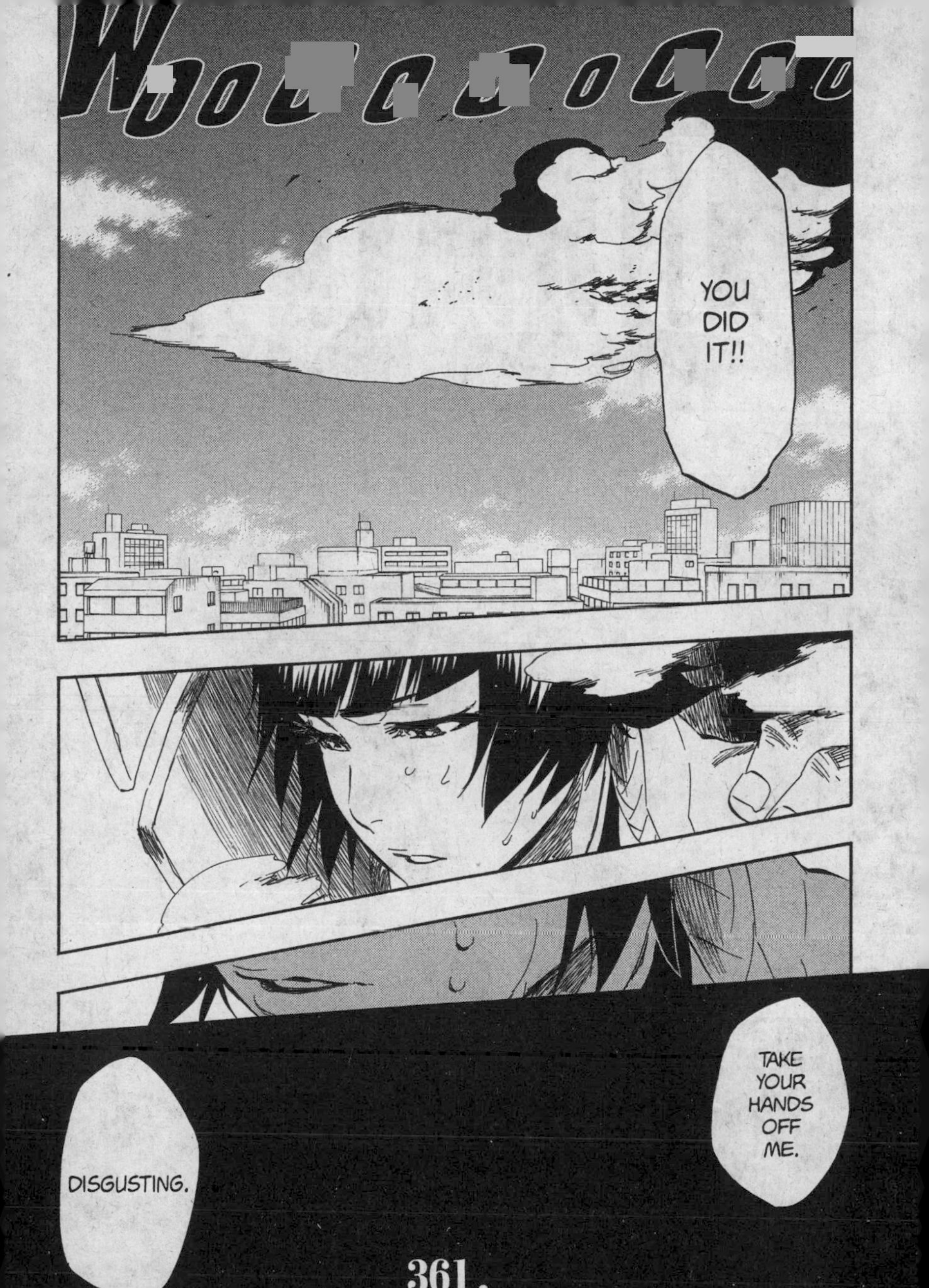
YOU DID IT!!
TAKE YOUR HANDS OFF ME.
DISGUSTING.

361. I Hate Loneliness But It Loves Me

BLEACH

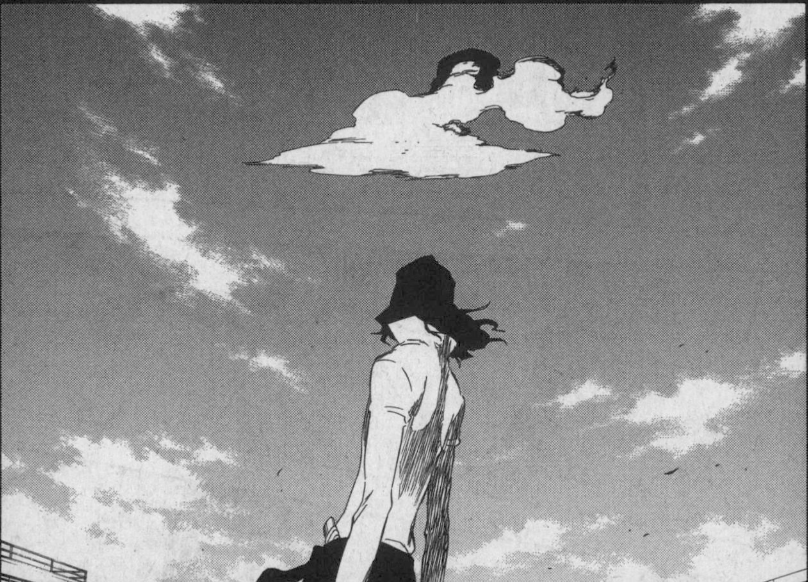

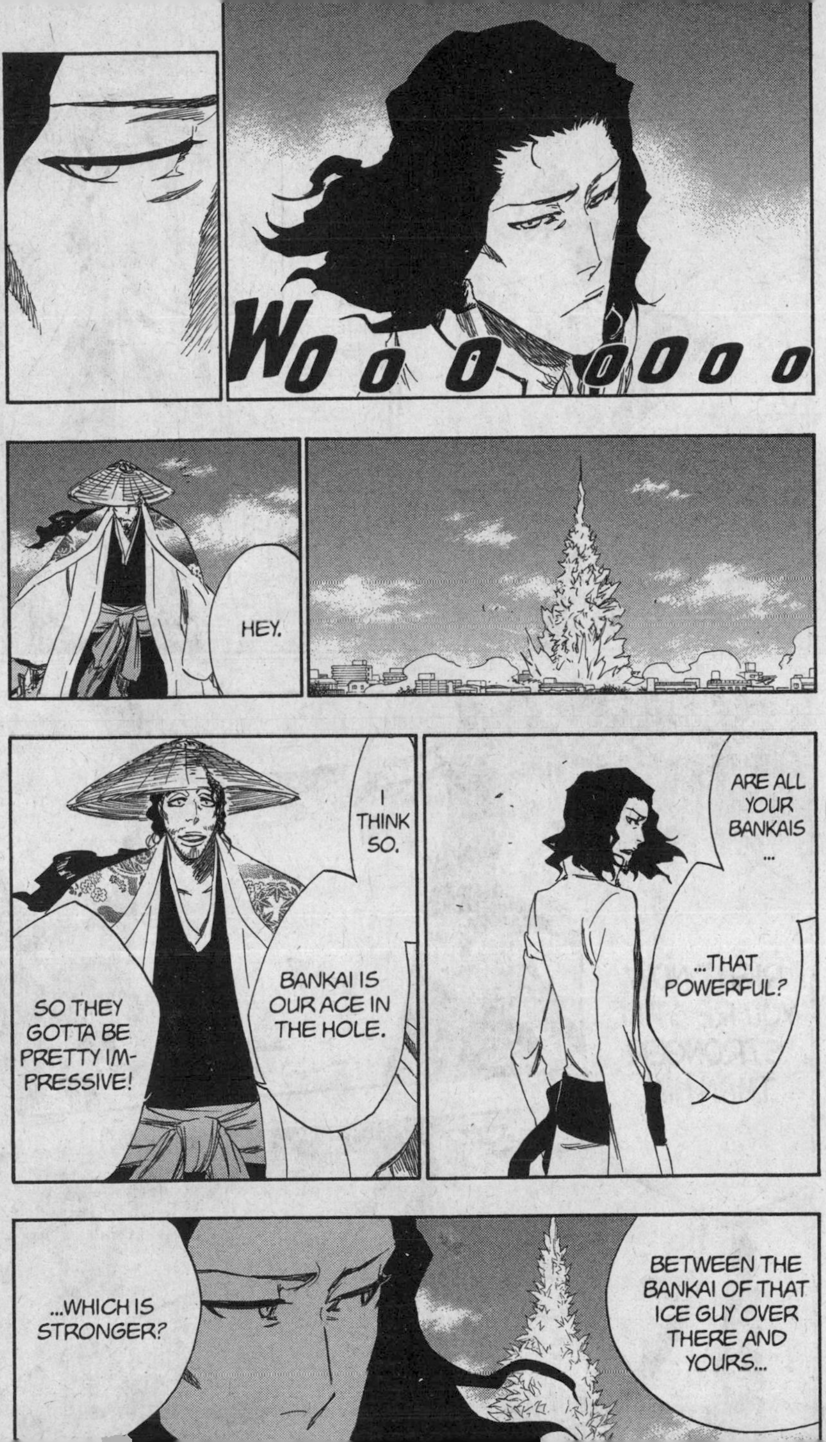
WOOOOOOO
HEY.
ARE ALL YOUR BANKAIS ...
...THAT POWERFUL?
I THINK SO.
BANKAI IS OUR ACE IN THE HOLE.
SO THEY GOTTA BE PRETTY IMPRESSIVE!
BETWEEN THE BANKAI OF THAT ICE GUY OVER THERE AND YOURS...
...WHICH IS STRONGER?

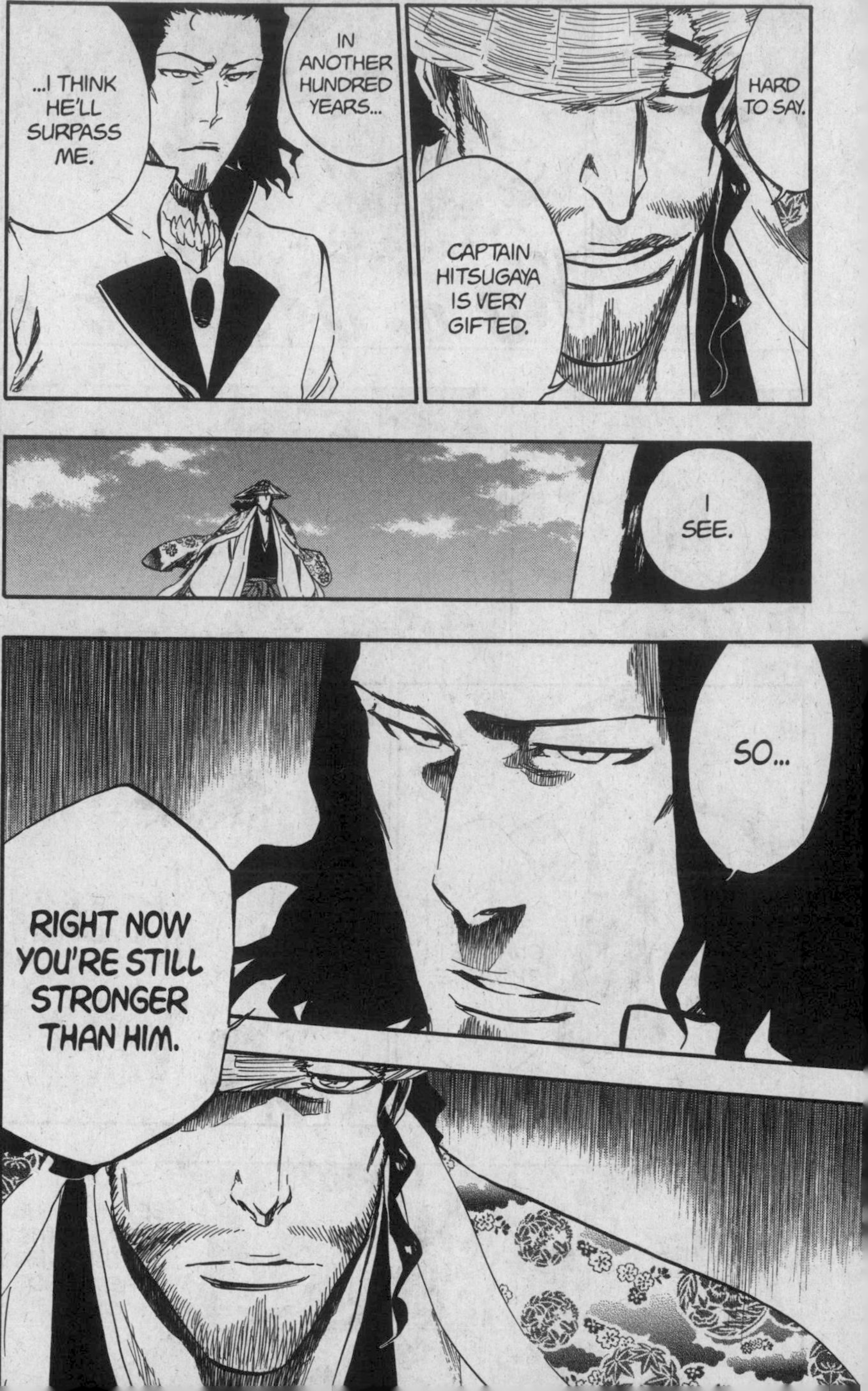
HARD TO SAY.
CAPTAIN HITSUGAYA IS VERY GIFTED.
IN ANOTHER HUNDRED YEARS...
...I THINK HE'LL SURPASS ME.
I SEE.
SO...
RIGHT NOW YOU'RE STILL STRONGER THAN HIM.

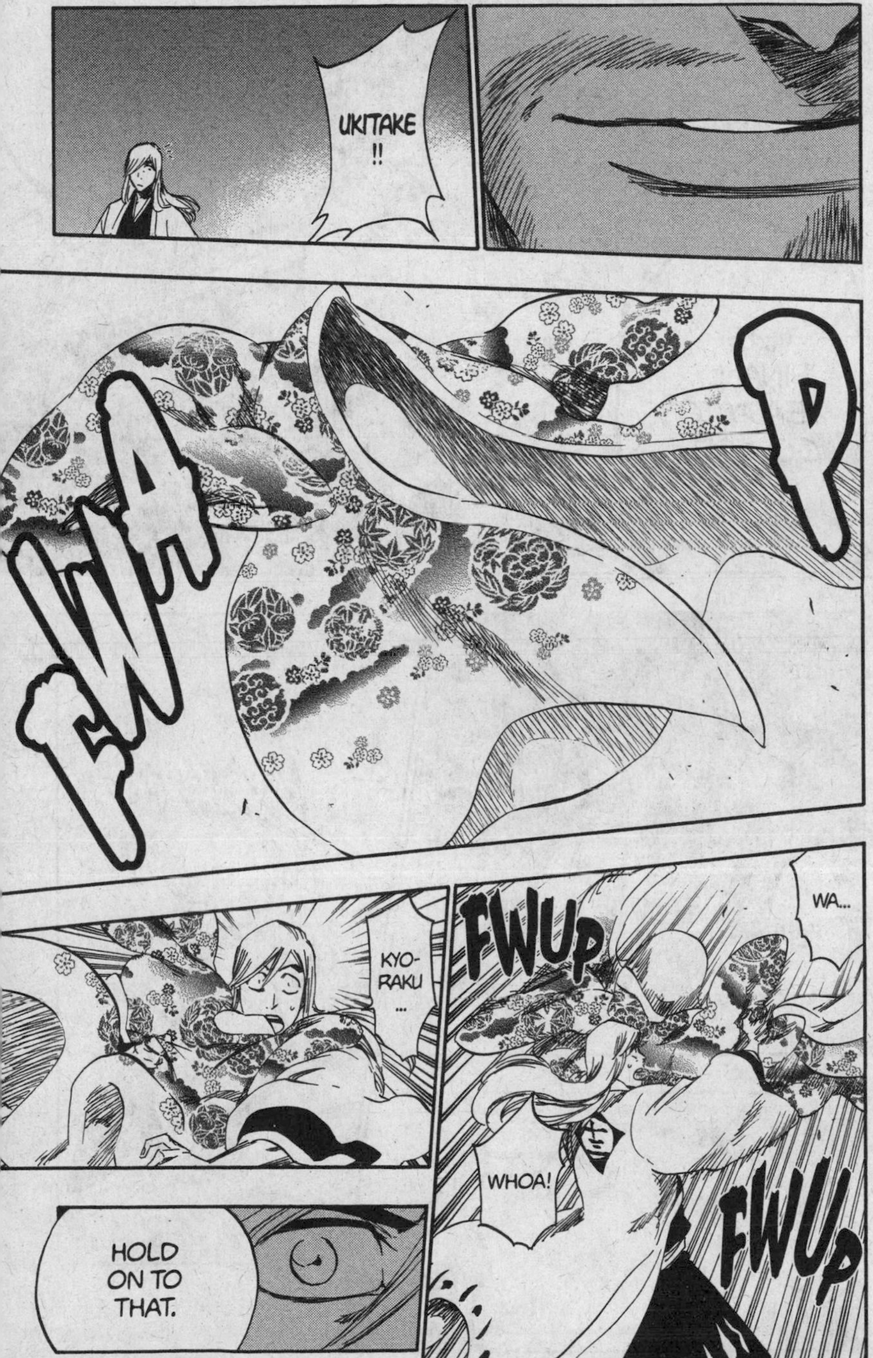
UKITAKE !!
FWAP
WA...
FWUP
WHOA!
FWUP
KYO-RAKU ...
HOLD ON TO THAT.

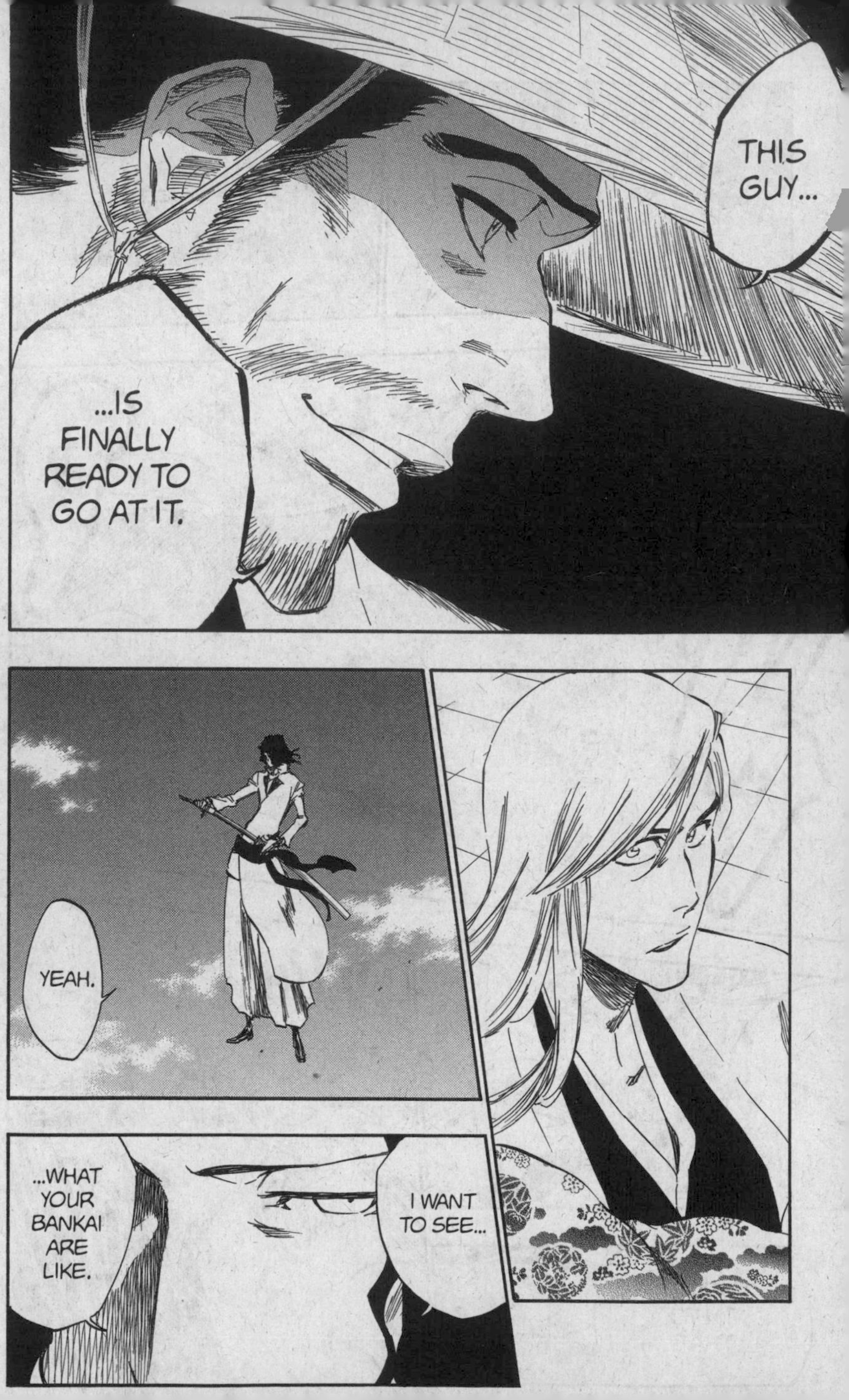
THIS GUY...
...IS FINALLY READY TO GO AT IT.
YEAH.
I WANT TO SEE...
...WHAT YOUR BANKAI ARE LIKE.

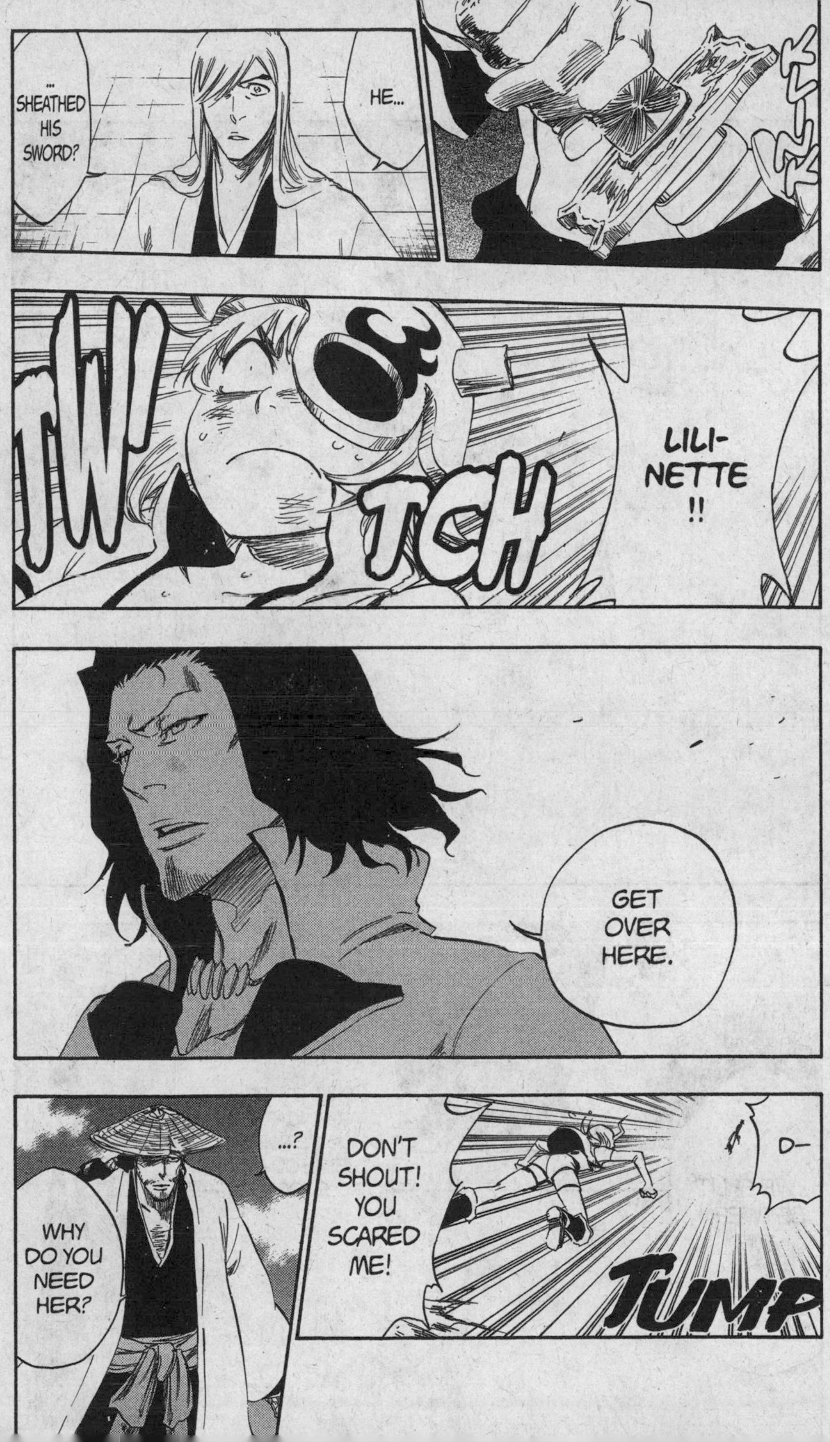
HE...
... SHEATHED HIS SWORD?
LILI-NETTE !!
TWITCH
GET OVER HERE.
D—
DON'T SHOUT! YOU SCARED ME!
JUMP
...?
WHY DO YOU NEED HER?

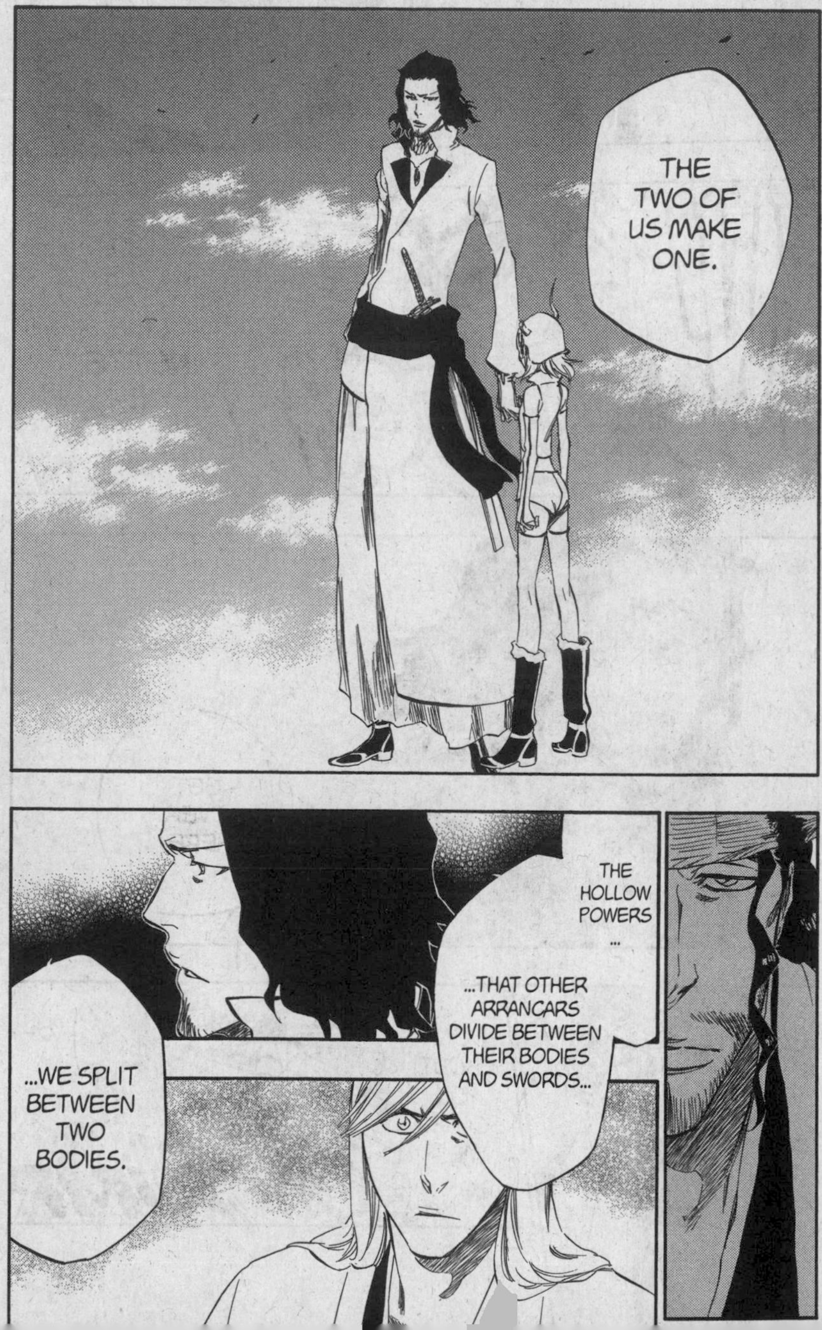
THE TWO OF US MAKE ONE.
THE HOLLOW POWERS ...
...THAT OTHER ARRANCARS DIVIDE BETWEEN THEIR BODIES AND SWORDS...
...WE SPLIT BETWEEN TWO BODIES.

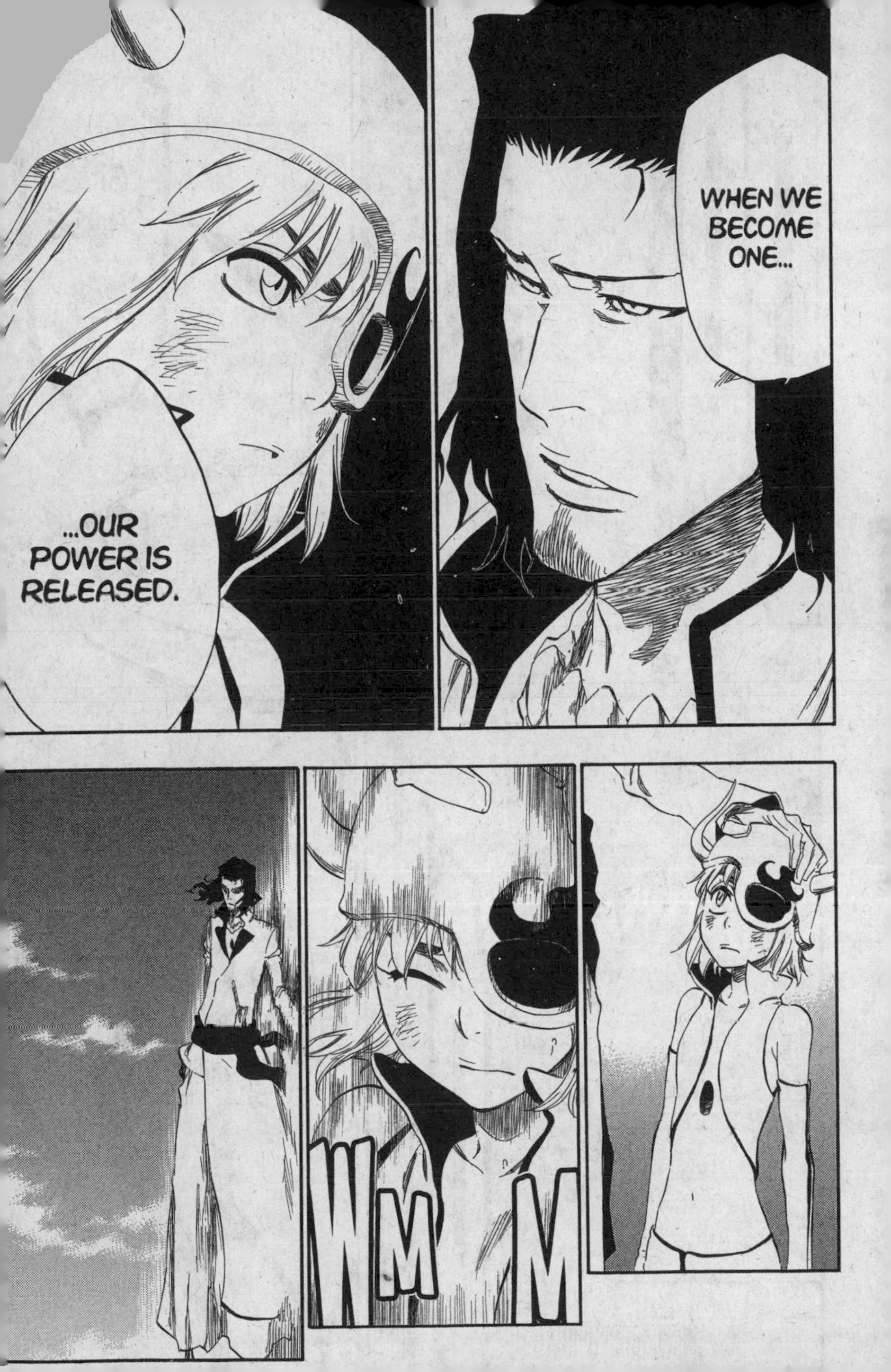
WHEN WE BECOME ONE...
...OUR POWER IS RELEASED.
WMM

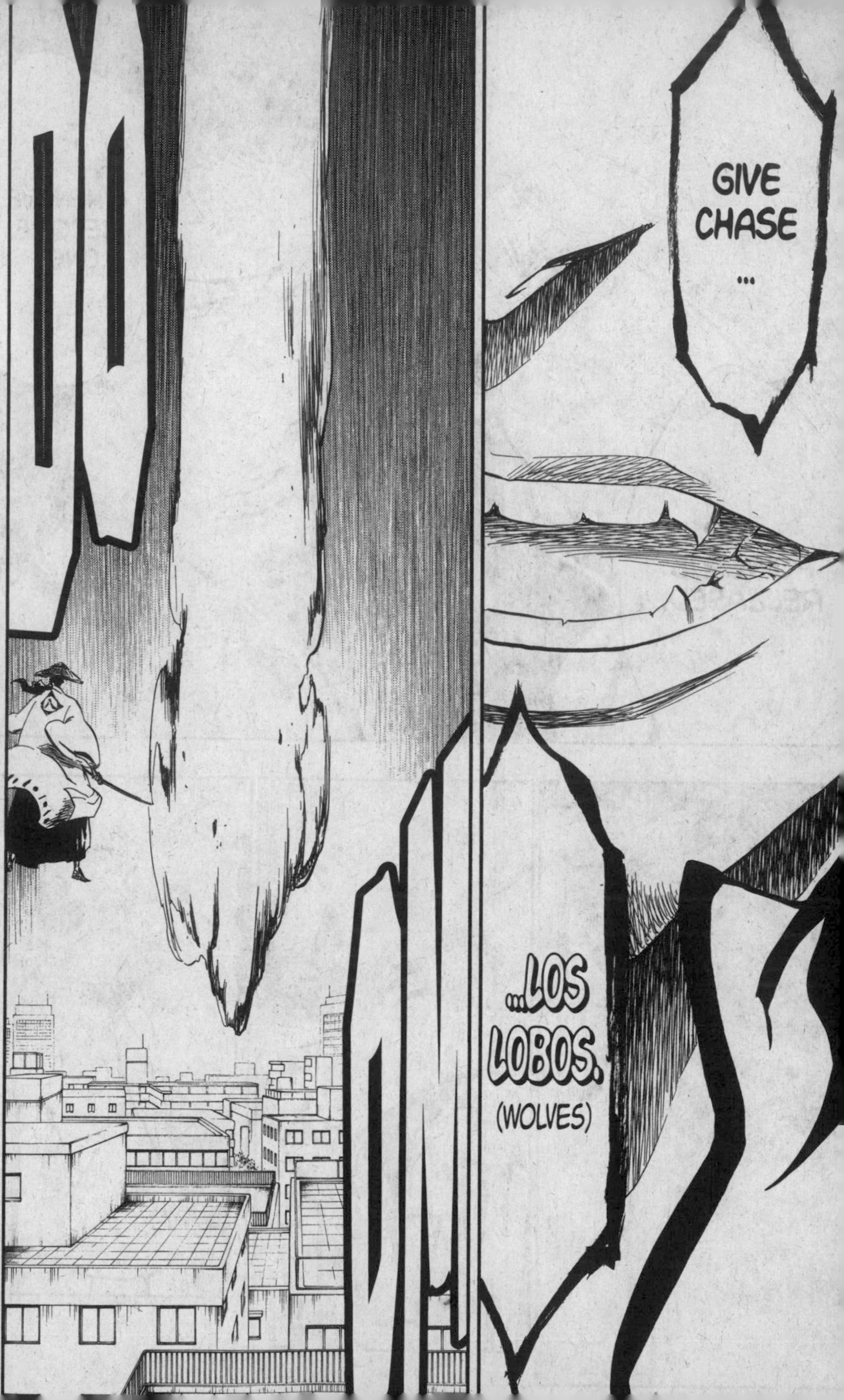
GIVE CHASE ...
...LOS LOBOS.
(WOLVES)

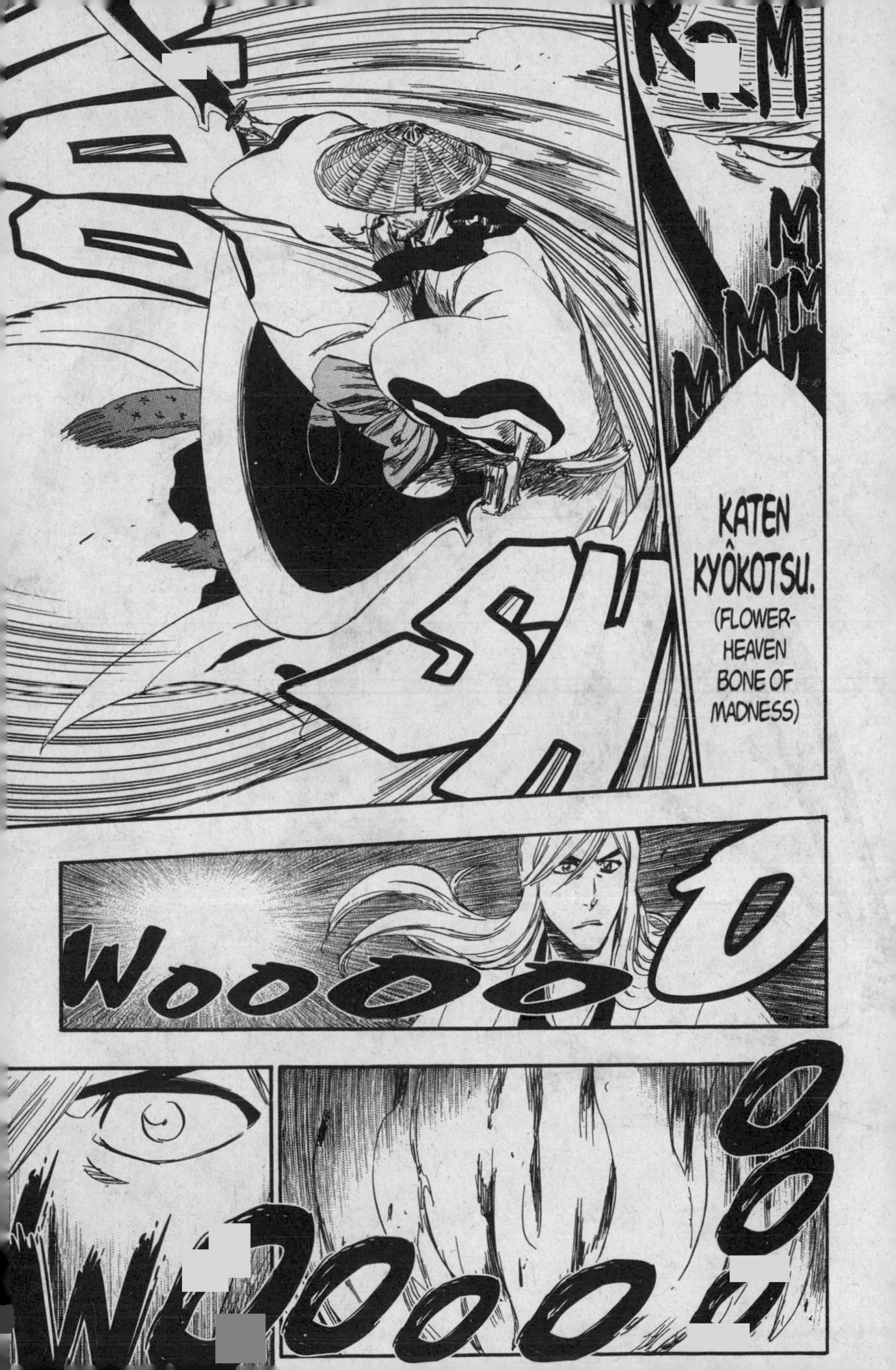
KATEN KYÔKOTSU.
(FLOWER-HEAVEN BONE OF MADNESS)
WOOOOO

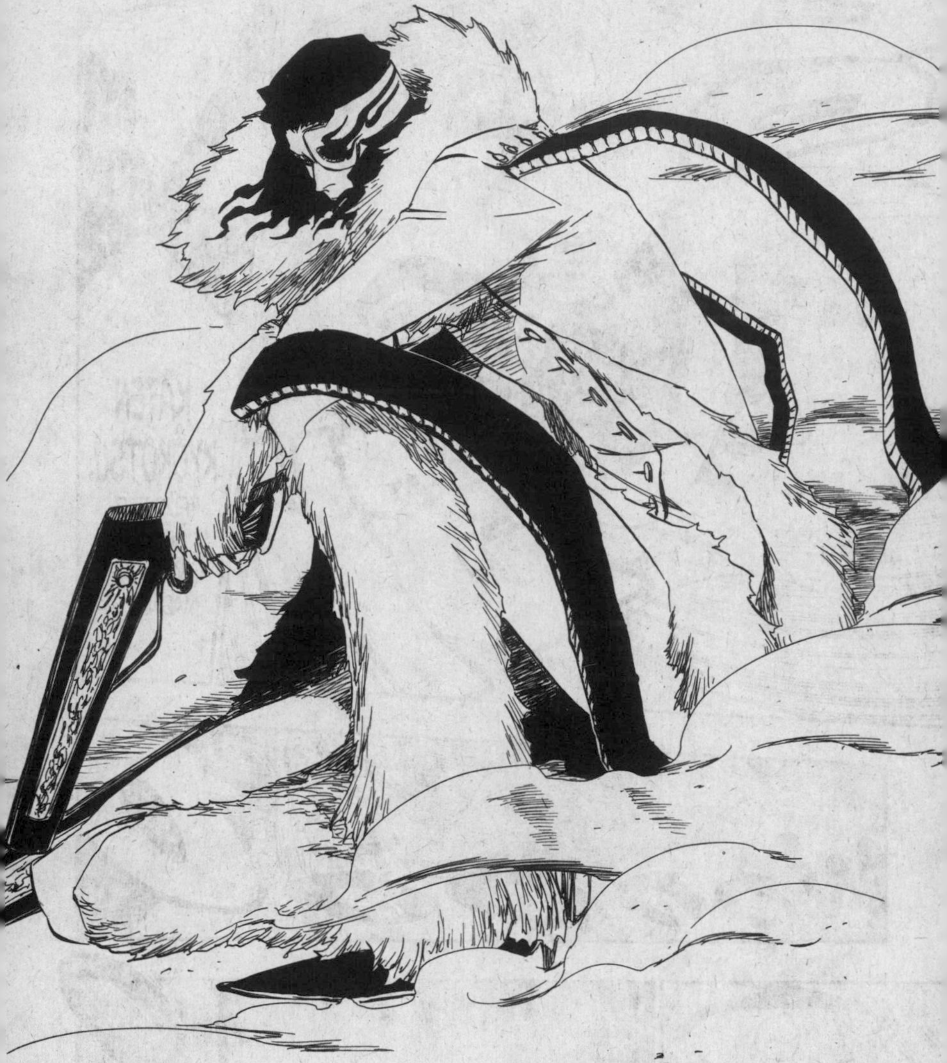

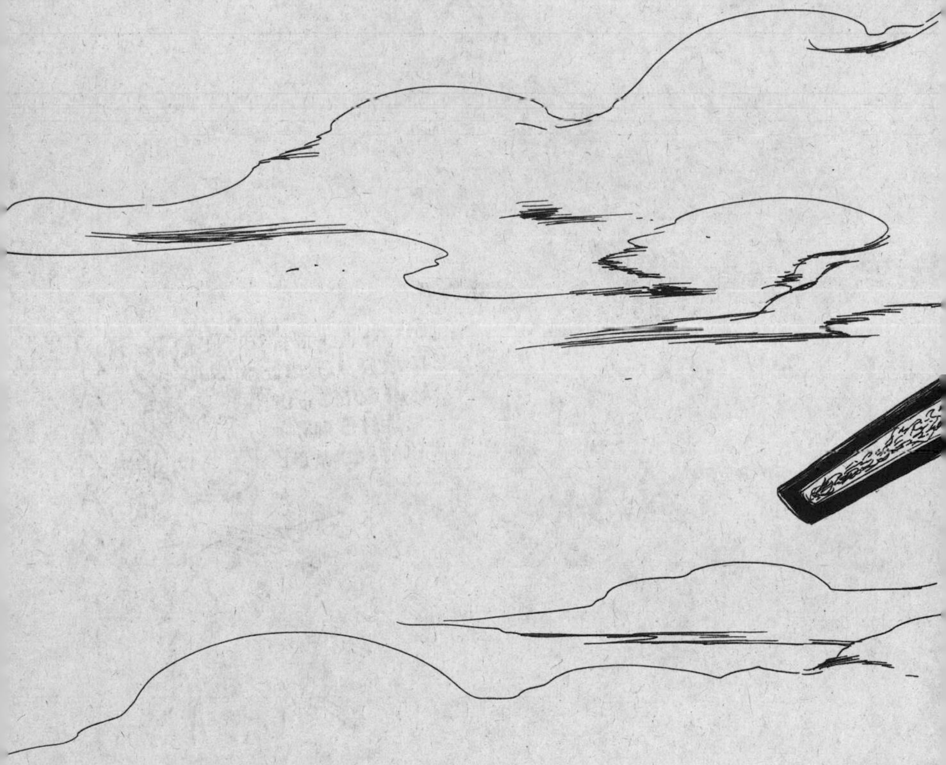

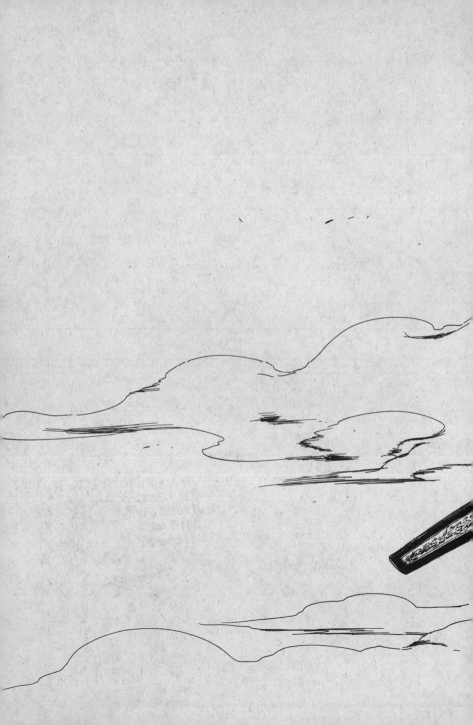

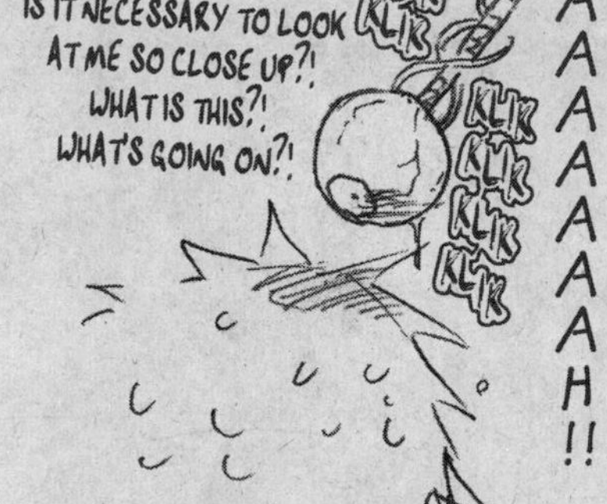
WHAT THE HECK IS THIS?! IS IT NECESSARY TO LOOK AT ME SO CLOSE UP?! WHAT IS THIS?! WHAT'S GOING ON?!
KLIK KLIK
KLIK KLIK KLIK KLIK
AAAAAAAAH!!

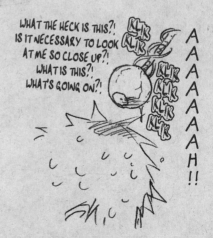

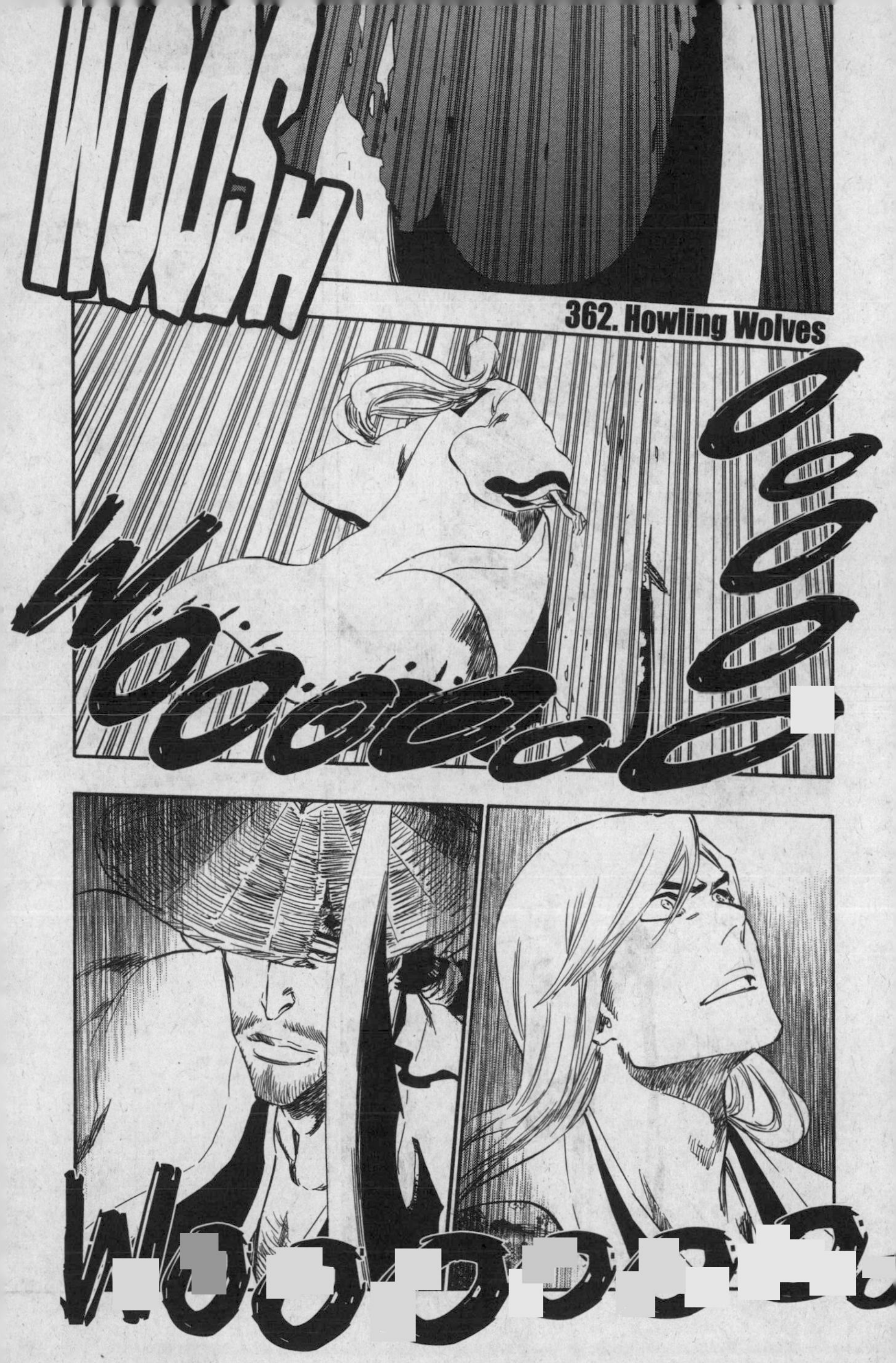
WOOSH
362. Howling Wolves

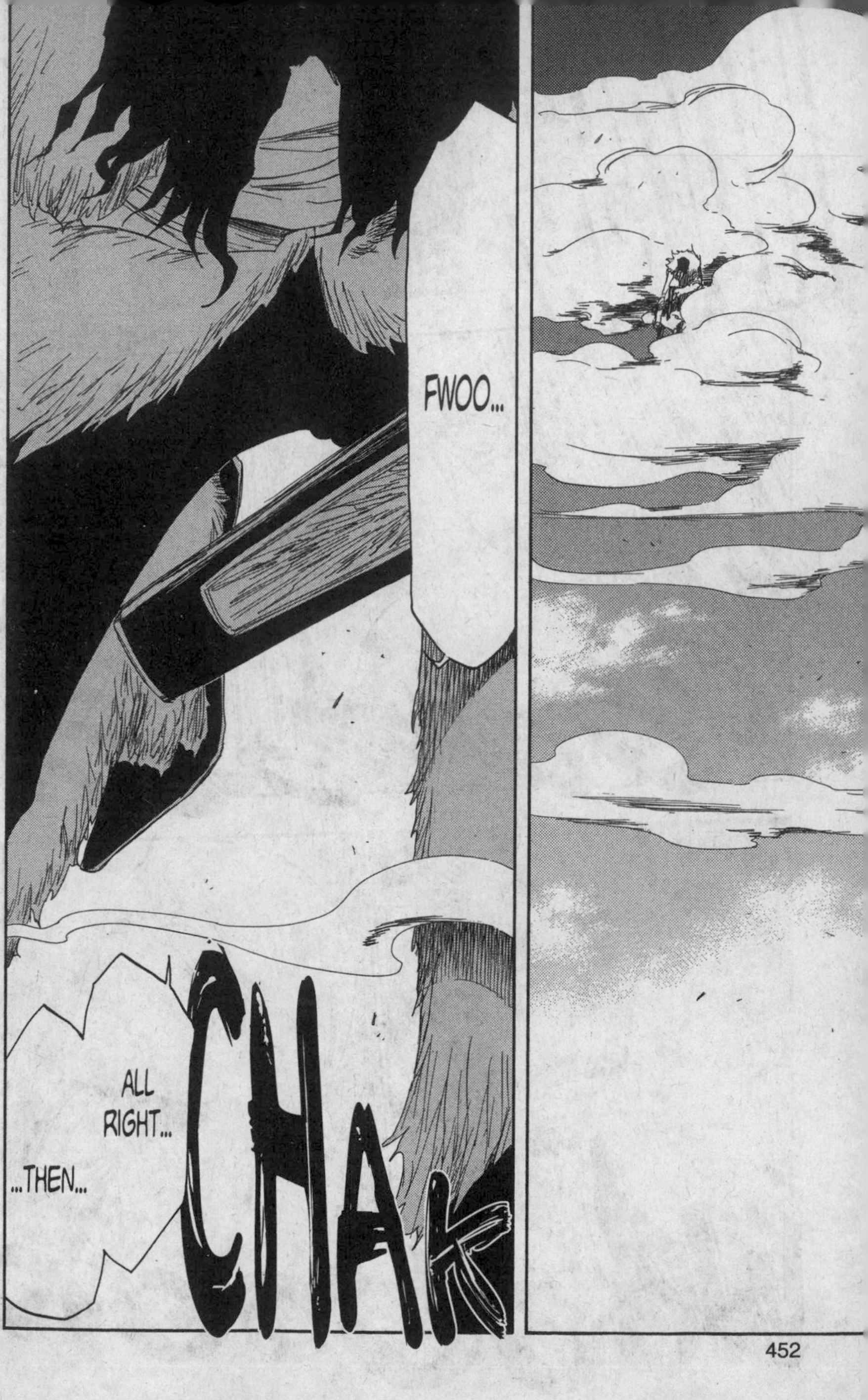
FWOO...
ALL RIGHT...
...THEN...
CHAK

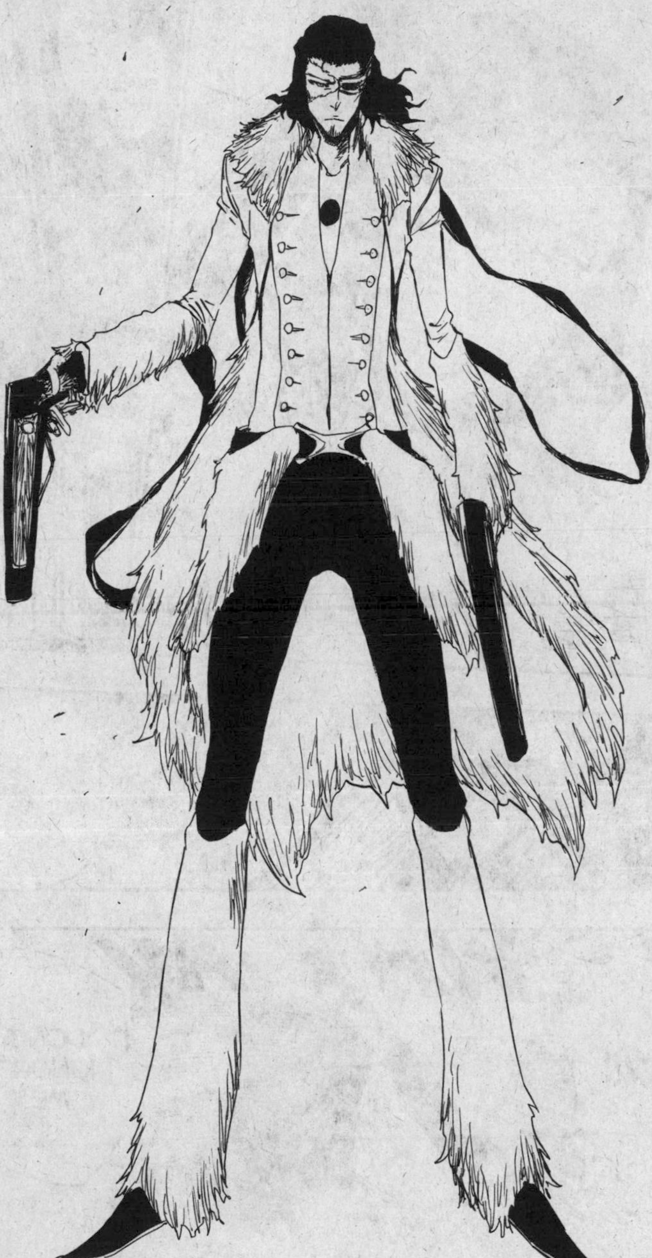

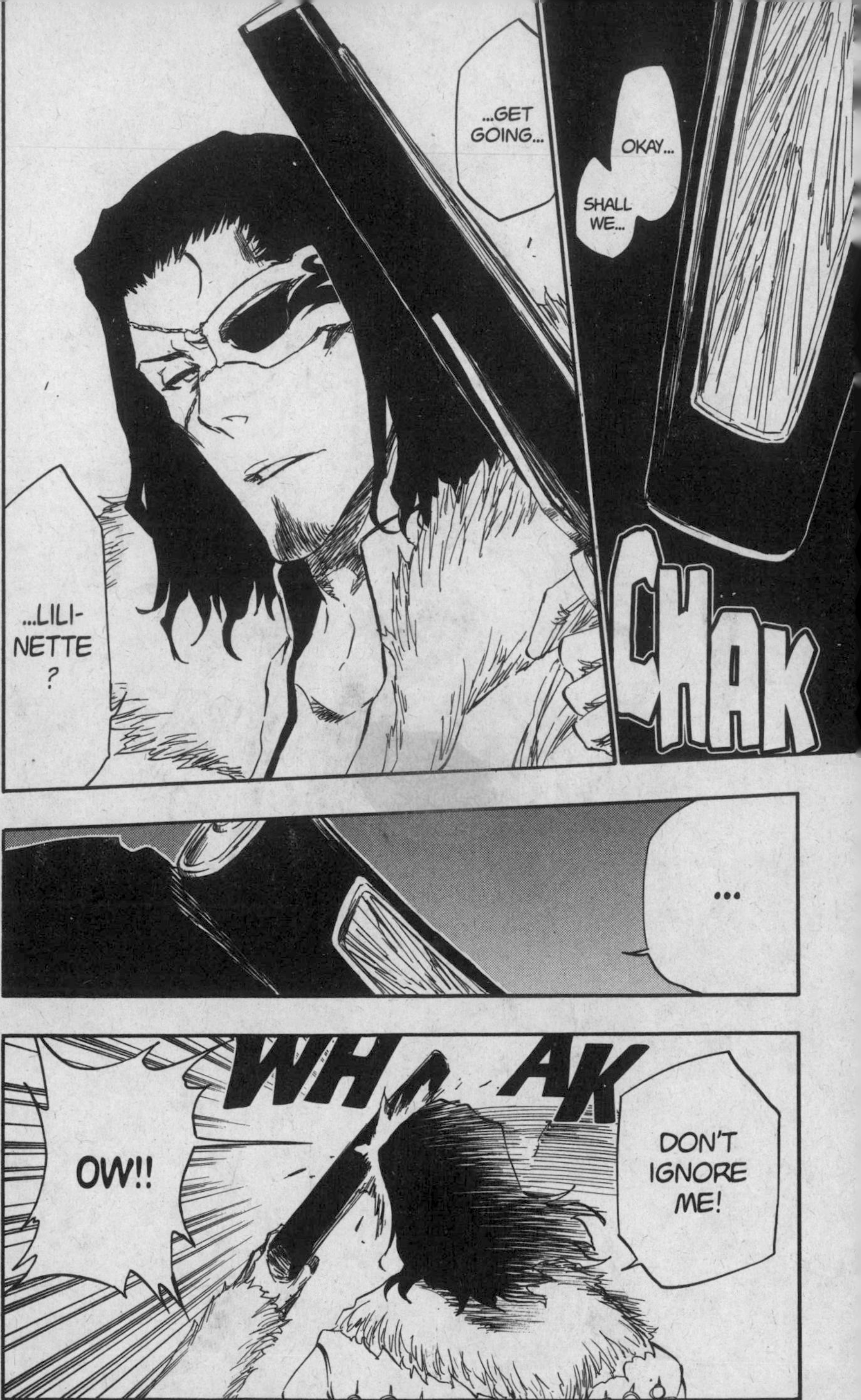
OKAY... SHALL WE...
CHAK
...GET GOING...
...LILI-NETTE ?
...
WH AK
DON'T IGNORE ME!
OW!!

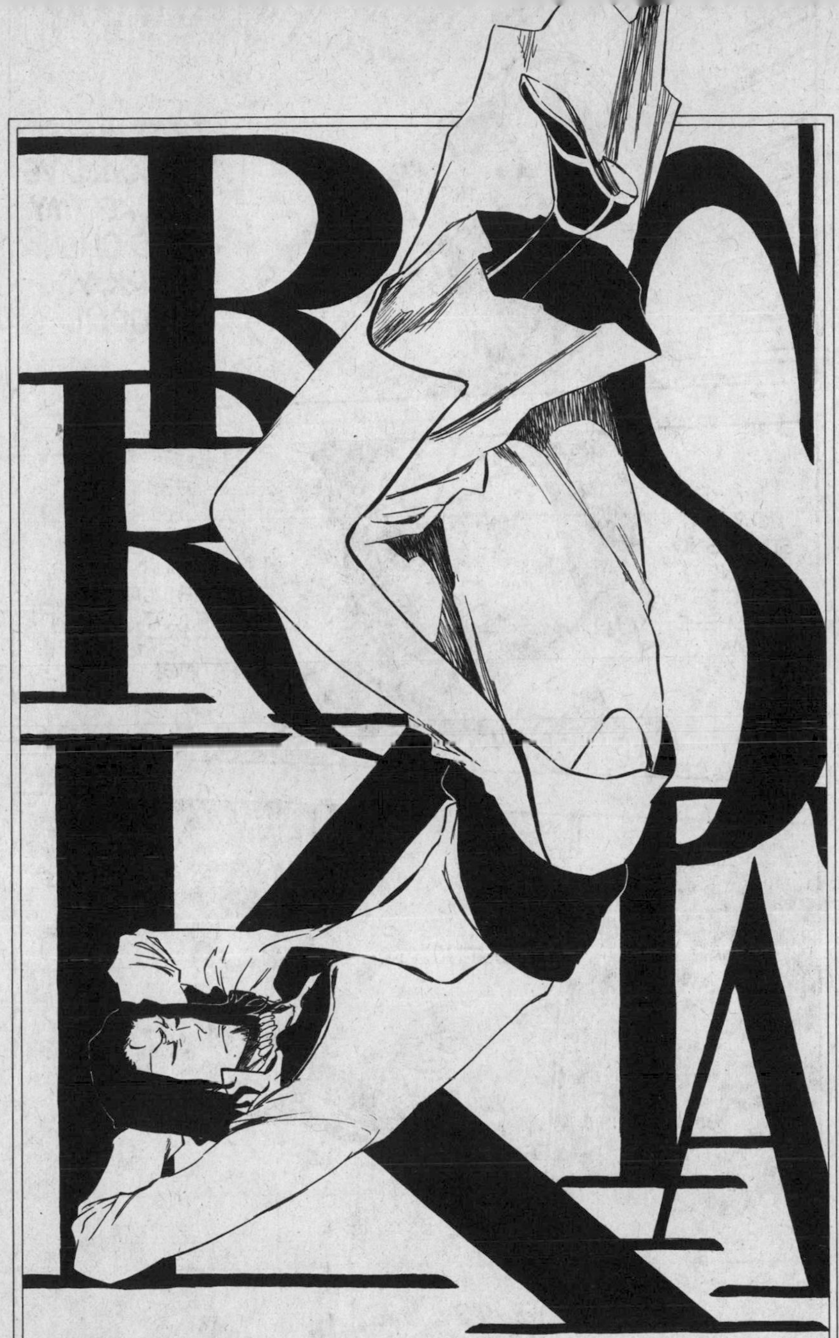

BLEACH 362. Howling Wolves

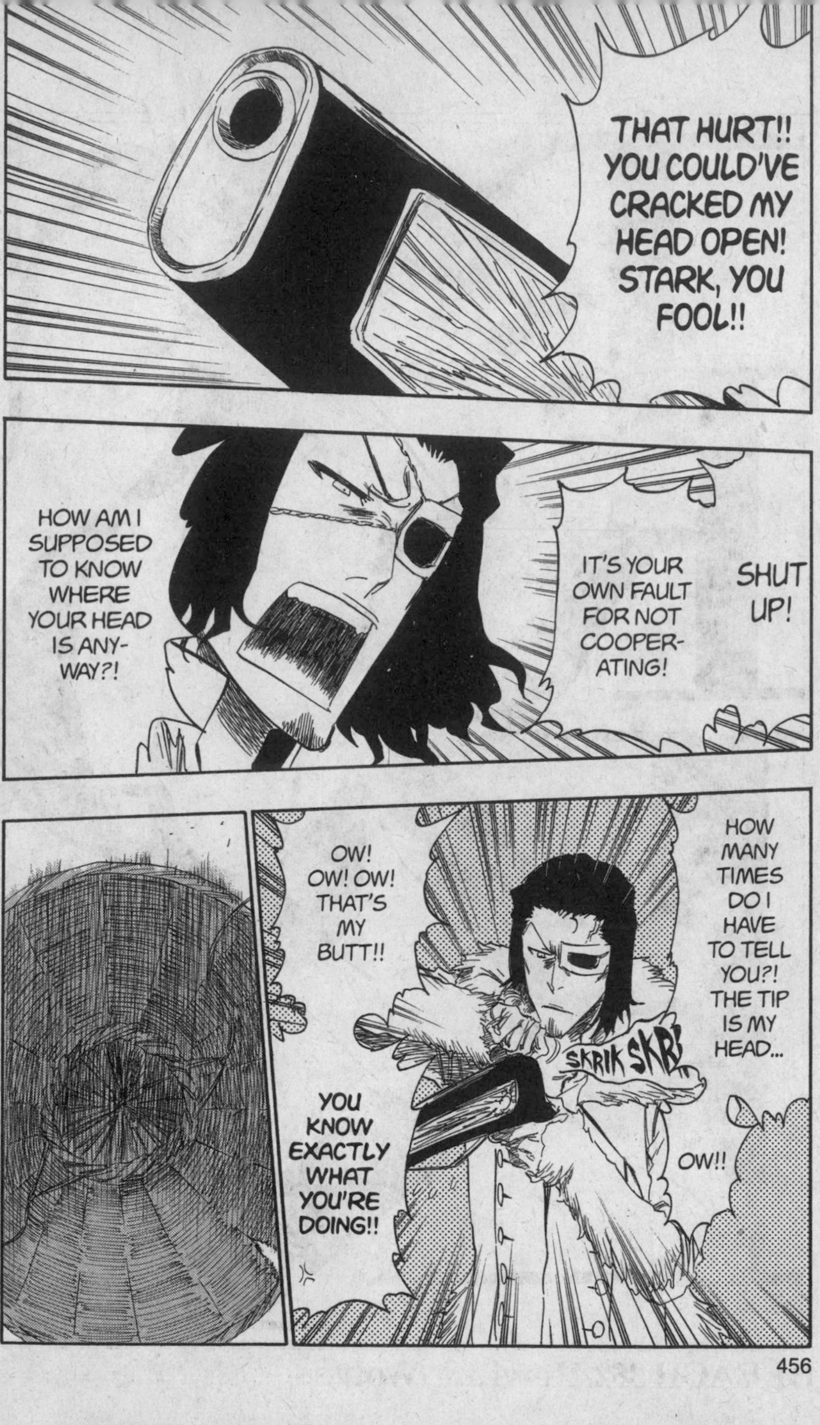
THAT HURT!! YOU COULD'VE CRACKED MY HEAD OPEN! STARK, YOU FOOL!!
SHUT UP!
IT'S YOUR OWN FAULT FOR NOT COOPERATING!
HOW AM I SUPPOSED TO KNOW WHERE YOUR HEAD IS ANYWAY?!
HOW MANY TIMES DO I HAVE TO TELL YOU?! THE TIP IS MY HEAD...
OW!!
SKRIK SKRI
OW! OW! OW! THAT'S MY BUTT!!
YOU KNOW EXACTLY WHAT YOU'RE DOING!!

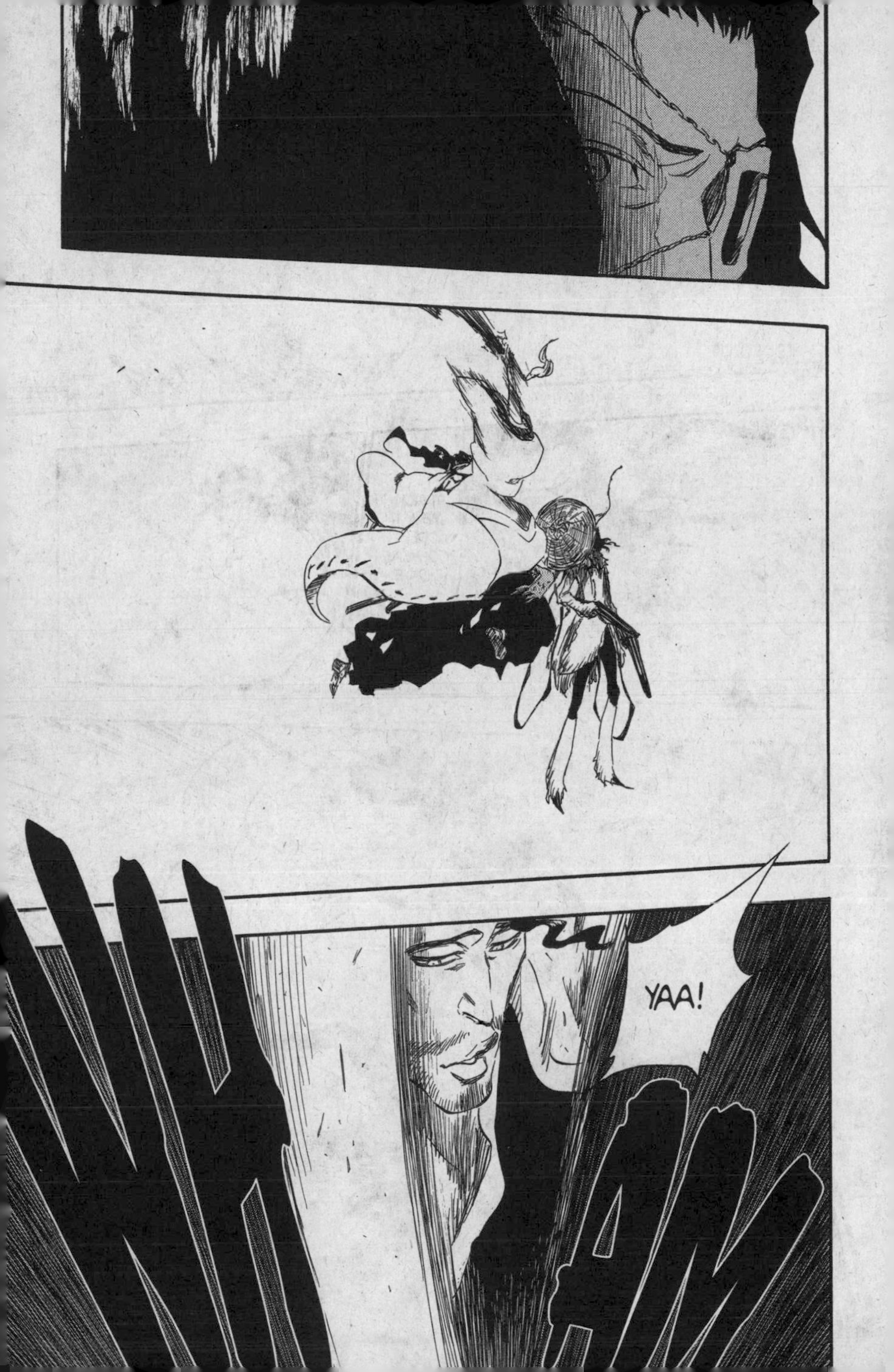
YAA!

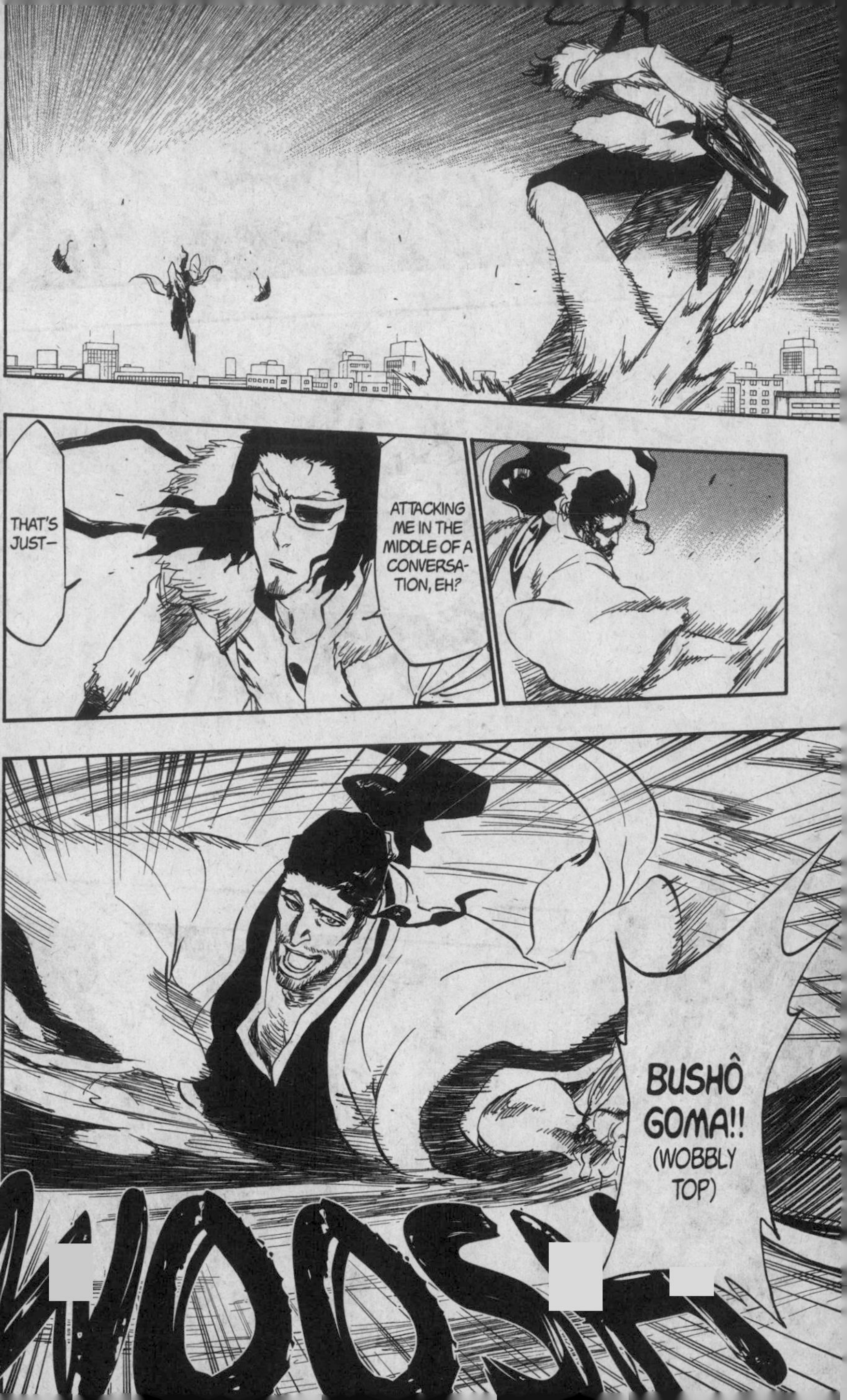
ATTACKING ME IN THE MIDDLE OF A CONVERSATION, EH?
THAT'S JUST—
BUSHÔ GOMA!! (WOBBLY TOP)
WOOSH

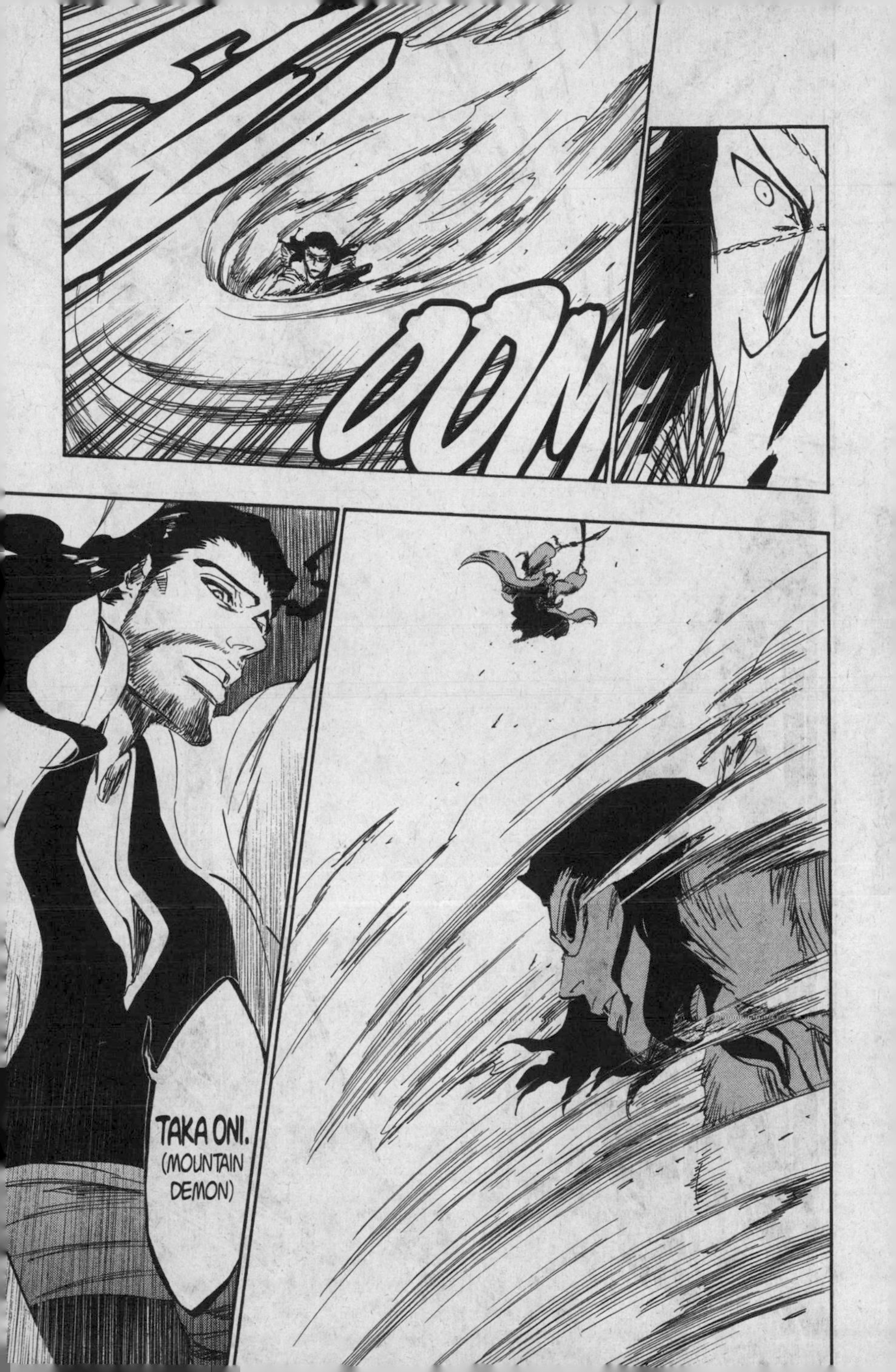

OOM!
TAKA ONI.
(MOUNTAIN DEMON)

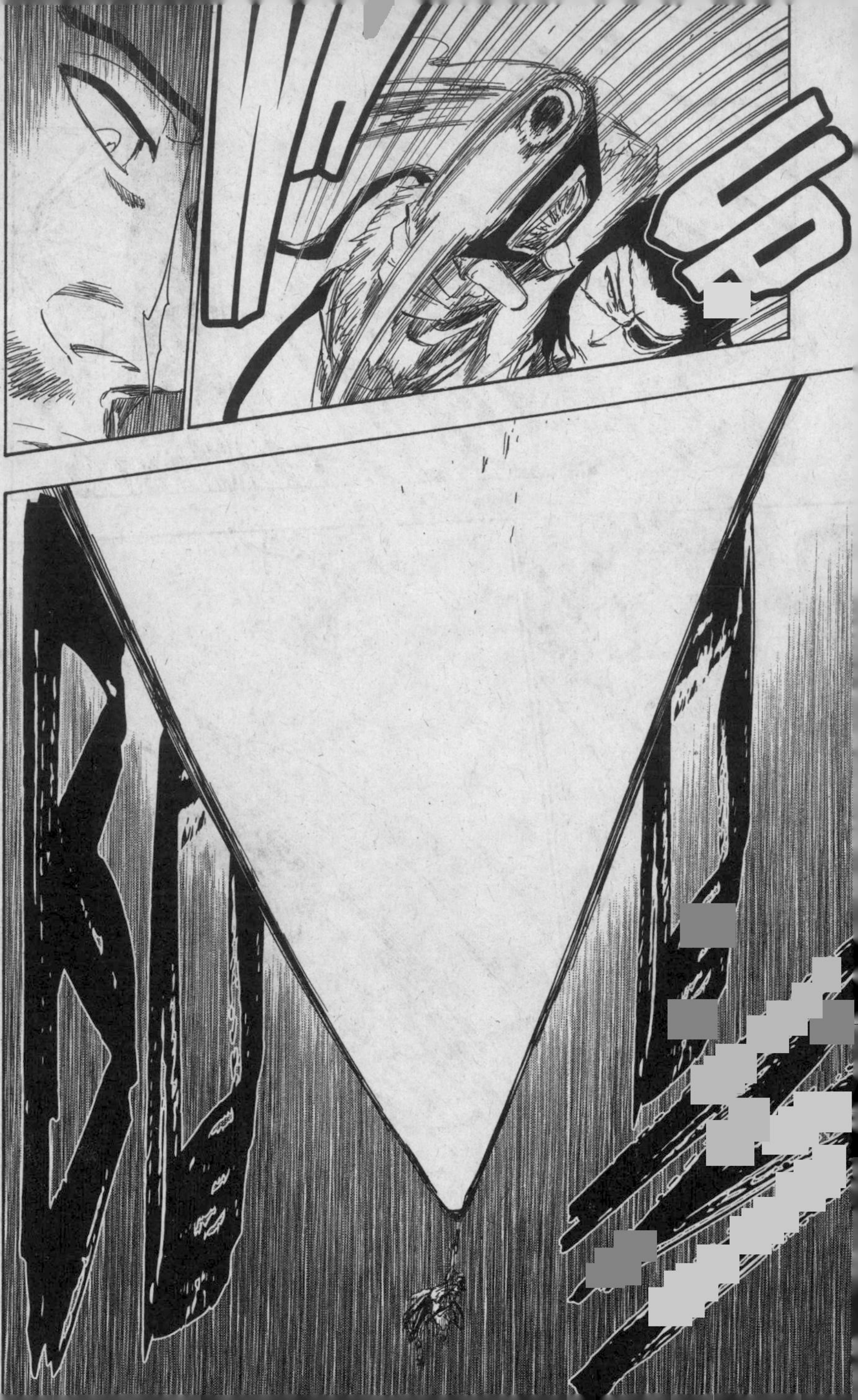

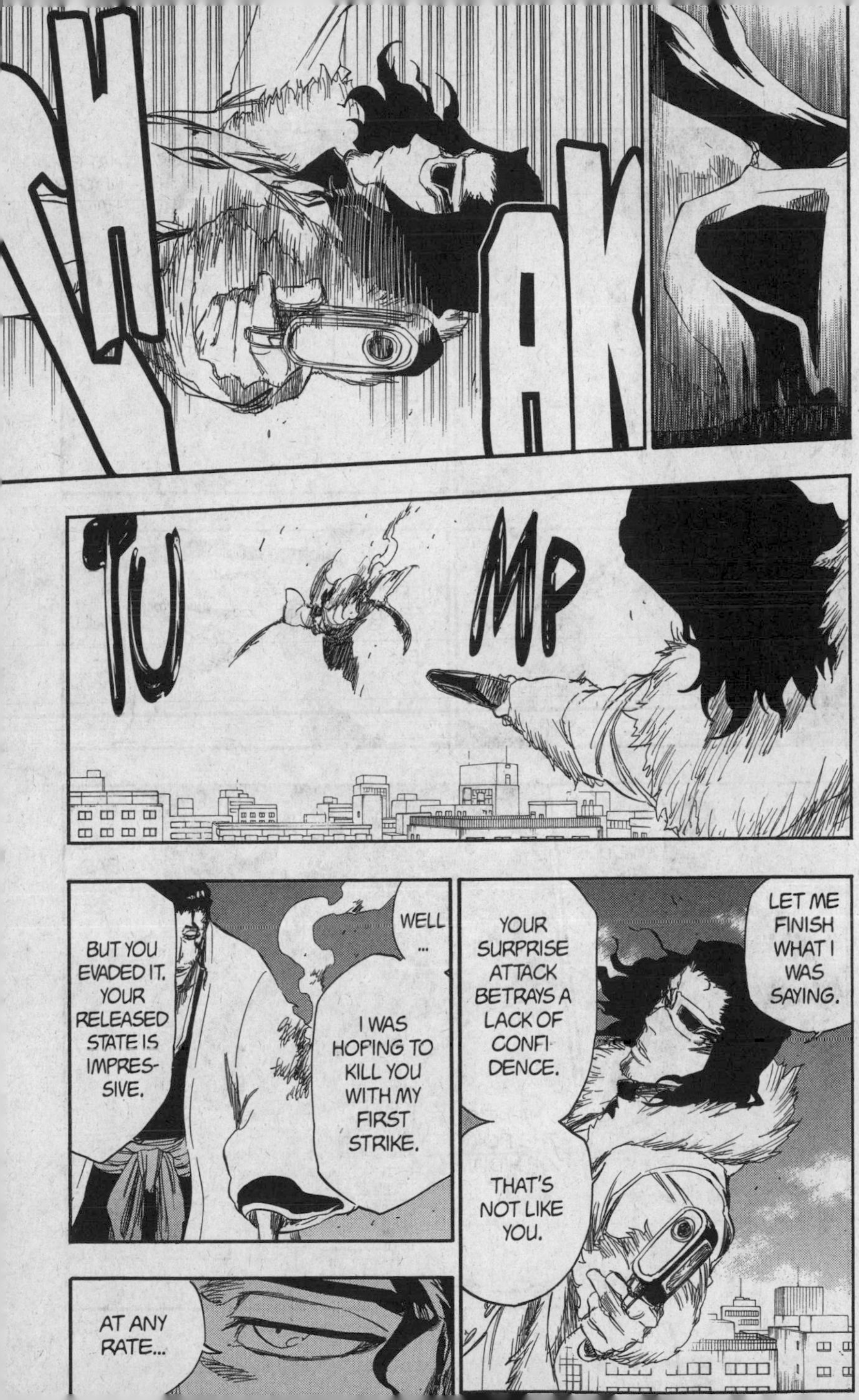
LET ME FINISH WHAT I WAS SAYING.
YOUR SURPRISE ATTACK BETRAYS A LACK OF CONFIDENCE.
THAT'S NOT LIKE YOU.
WELL ...
I WAS HOPING TO KILL YOU WITH MY FIRST STRIKE.
BUT YOU EVADED IT. YOUR RELEASED STATE IS IMPRESSIVE.
AT ANY RATE...

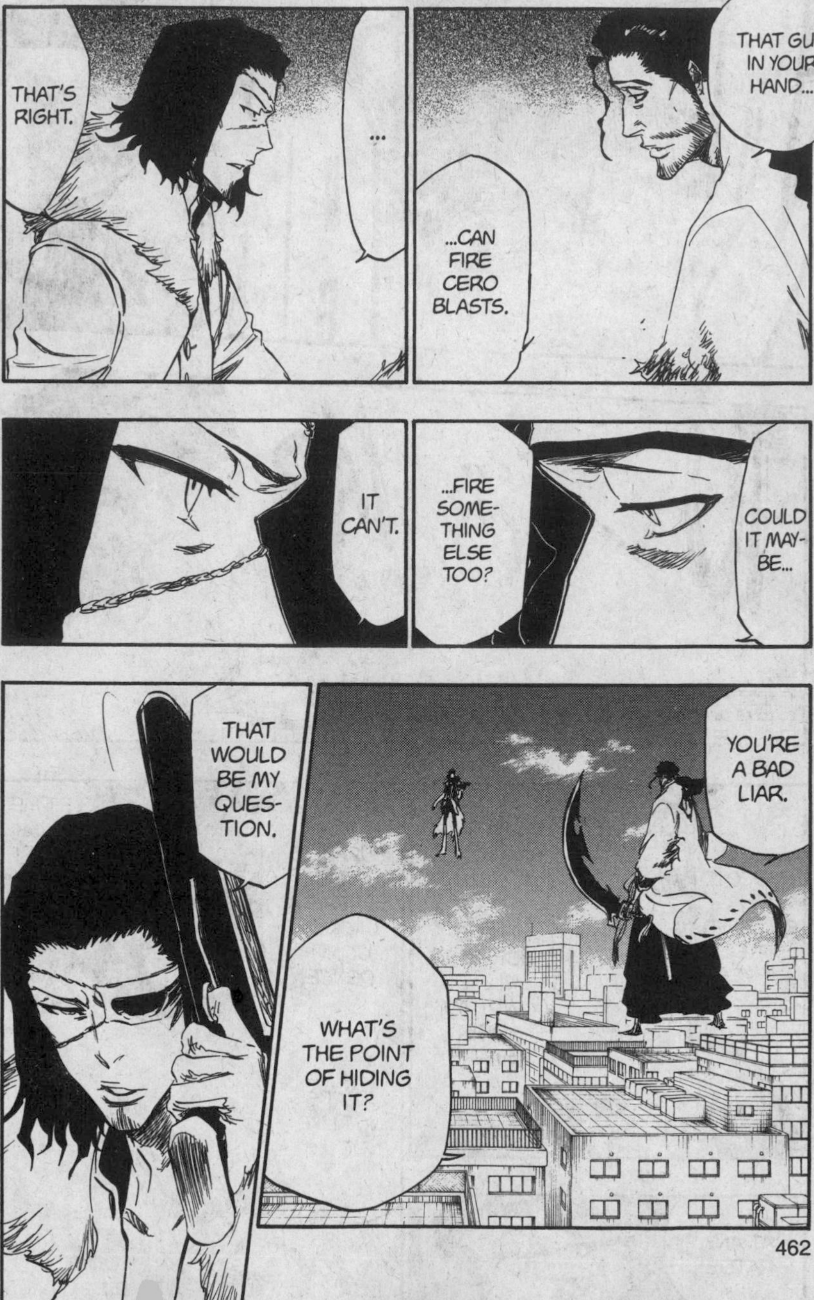
THAT GUN IN YOUR HAND...
...CAN FIRE CERO BLASTS.
...
THAT'S RIGHT.
COULD IT MAYBE...
...FIRE SOMETHING ELSE TOO?
IT CAN'T.
YOU'RE A BAD LIAR.
WHAT'S THE POINT OF HIDING IT?
THAT WOULD BE MY QUESTION.

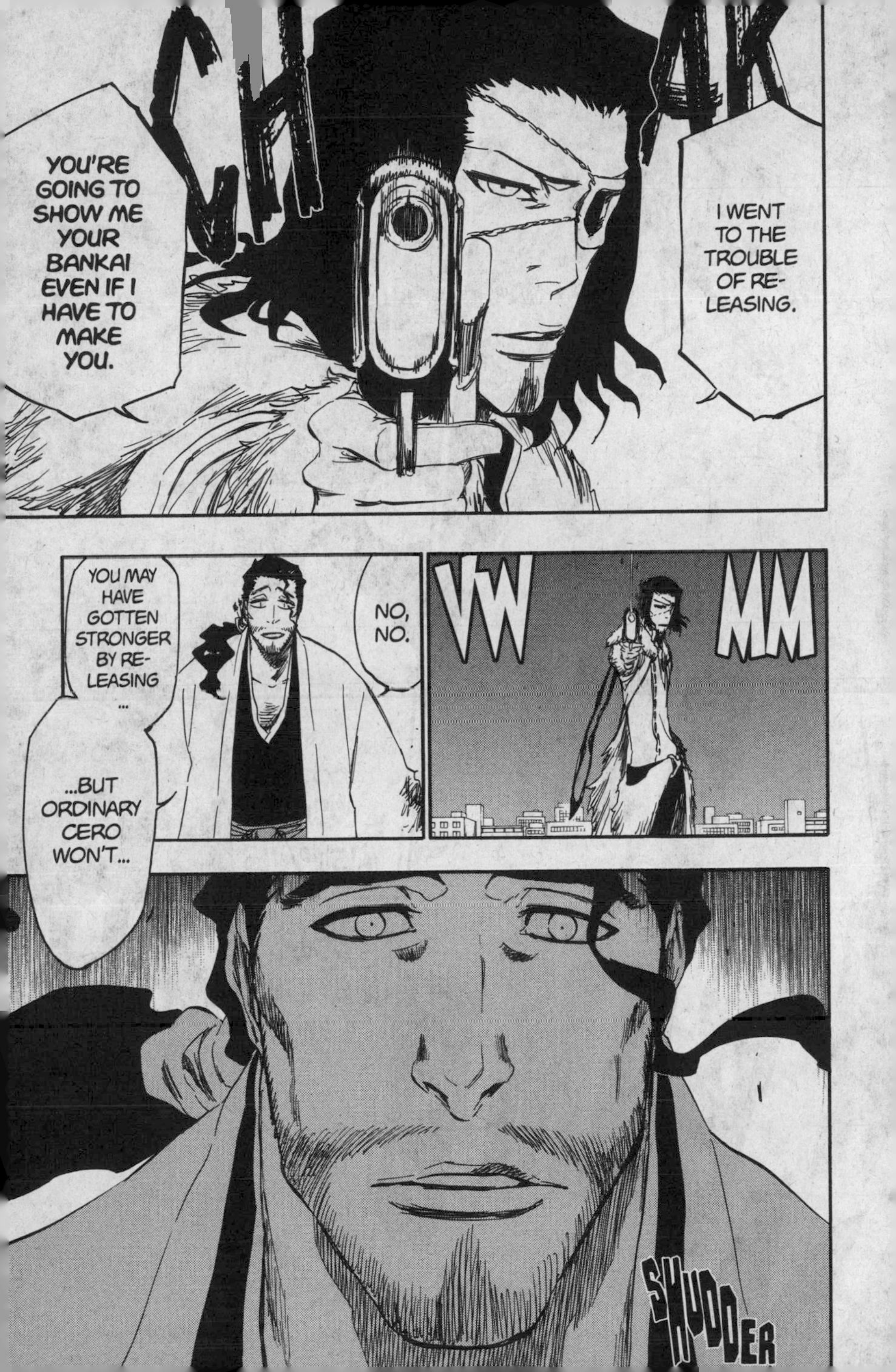
CHAK
I WENT TO THE TROUBLE OF RE-LEASING.
YOU'RE GOING TO SHOW ME YOUR BANKAI EVEN IF I HAVE TO MAKE YOU.
VWMM
NO, NO.
YOU MAY HAVE GOTTEN STRONGER BY RE-LEASING ...
...BUT ORDINARY CERO WON'T...
SHUDDER

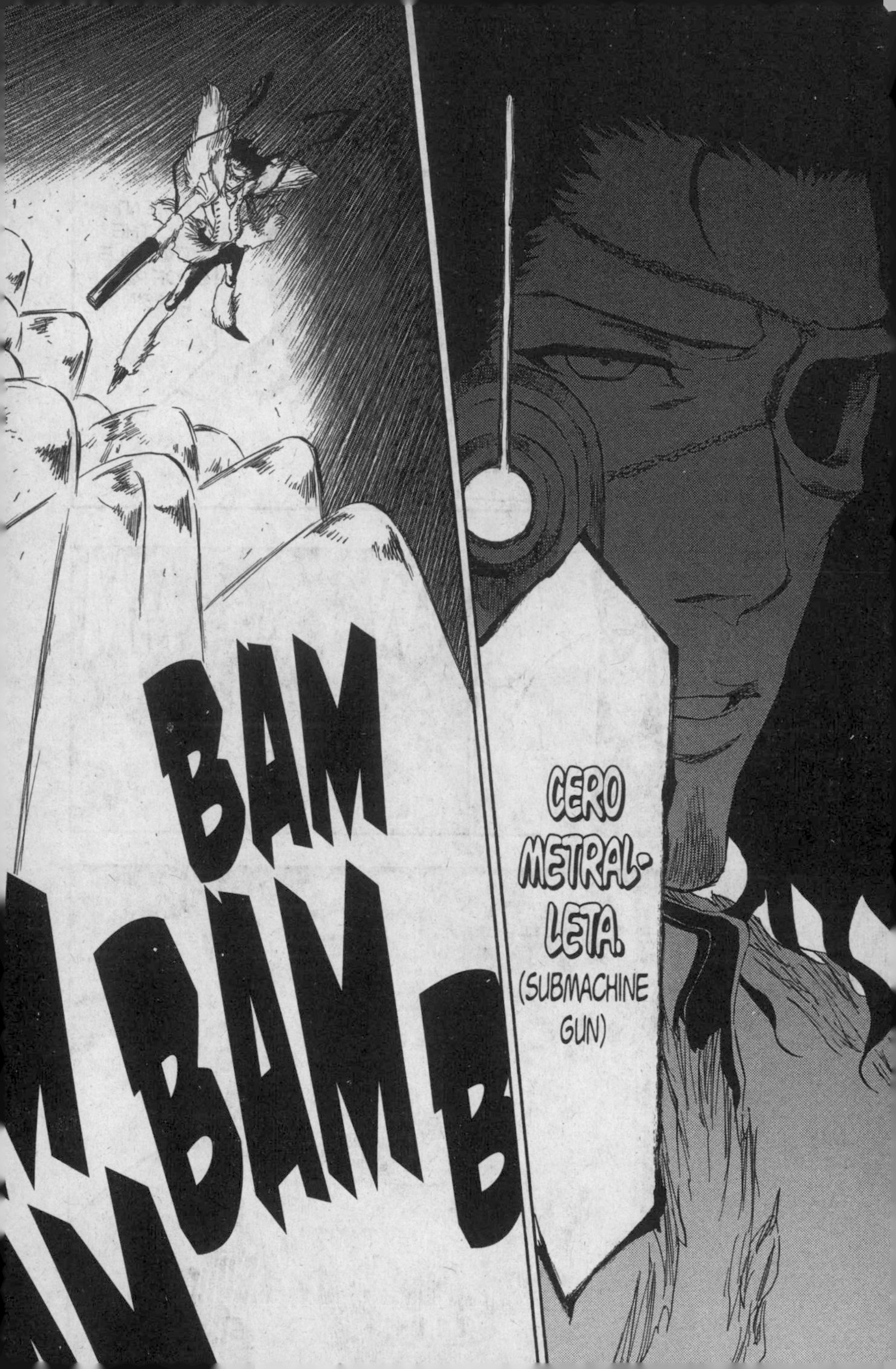
CERO METRAL-LETA.
(SUBMACHINE GUN)
BAM
BAM BAM B

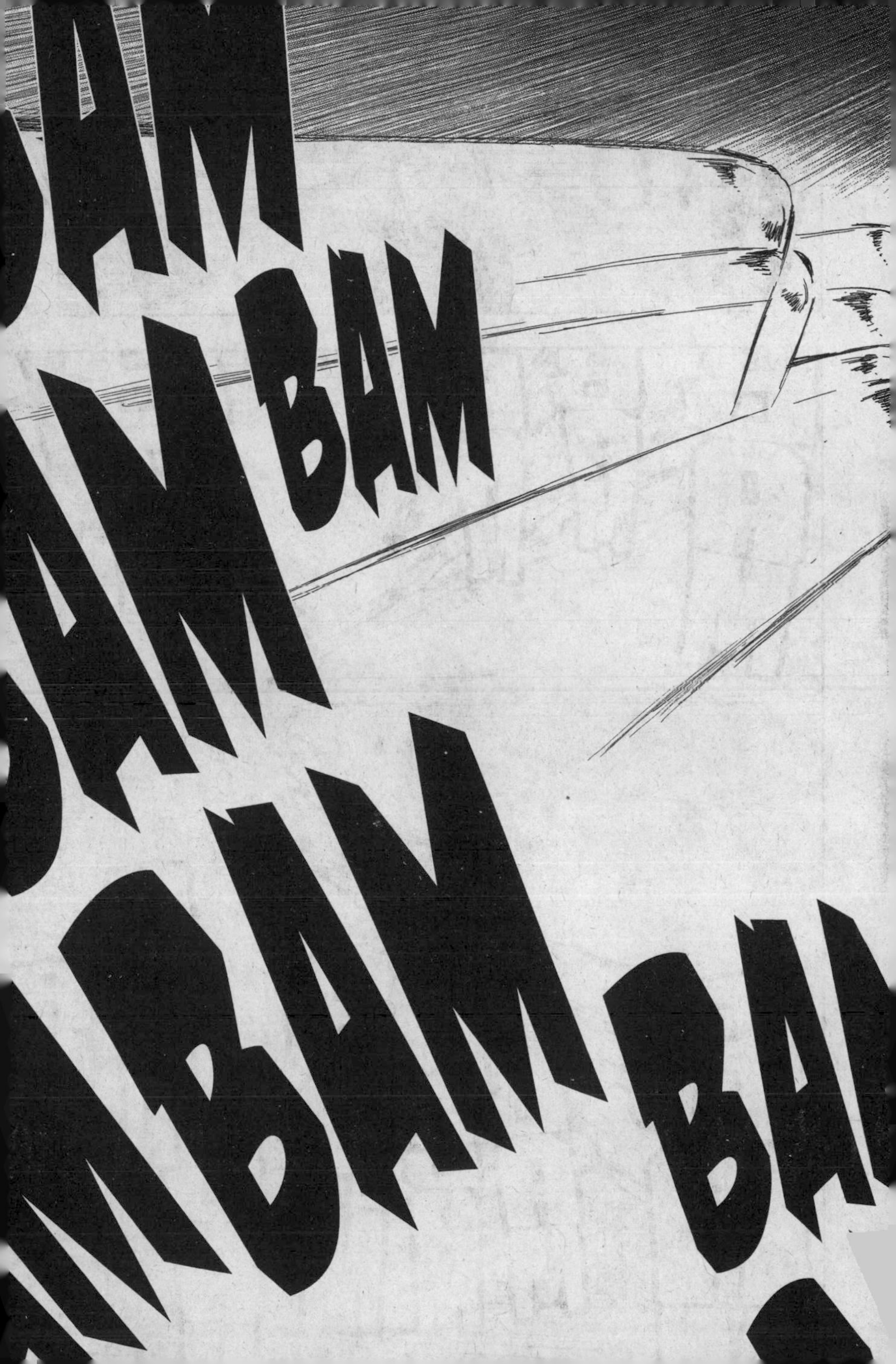
BAM
BAM

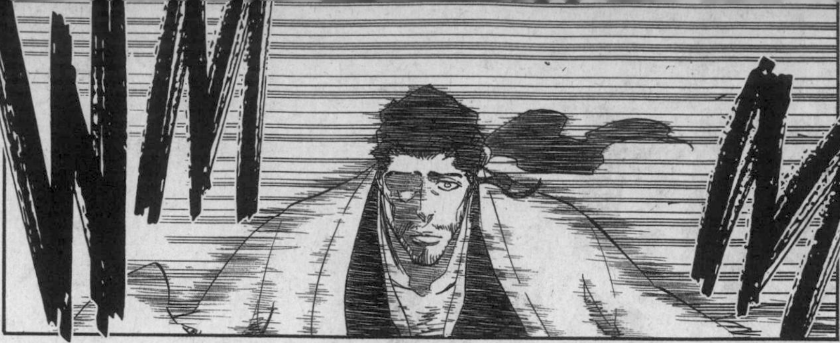

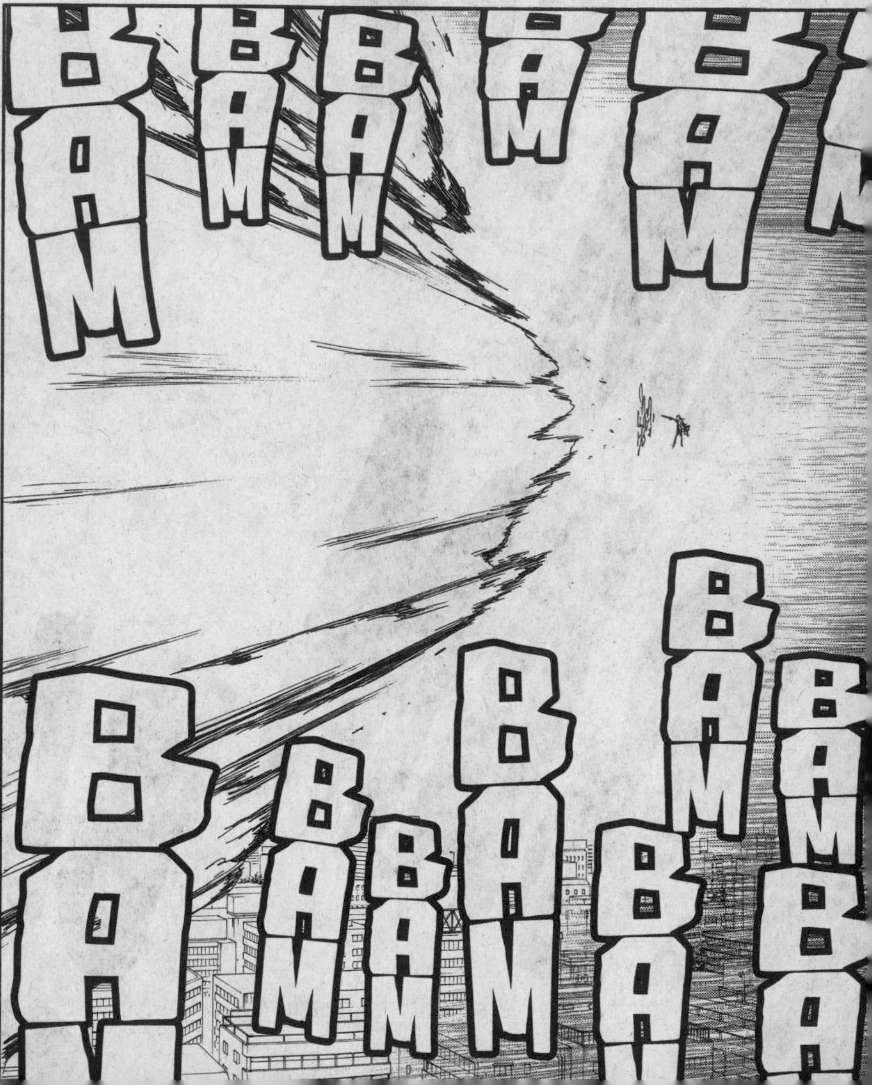
BAM
BAM
BAM
BAM
BAM
BAM
BAM
BAM
BAM
BAM
BAM
BAM
BAM
BAM

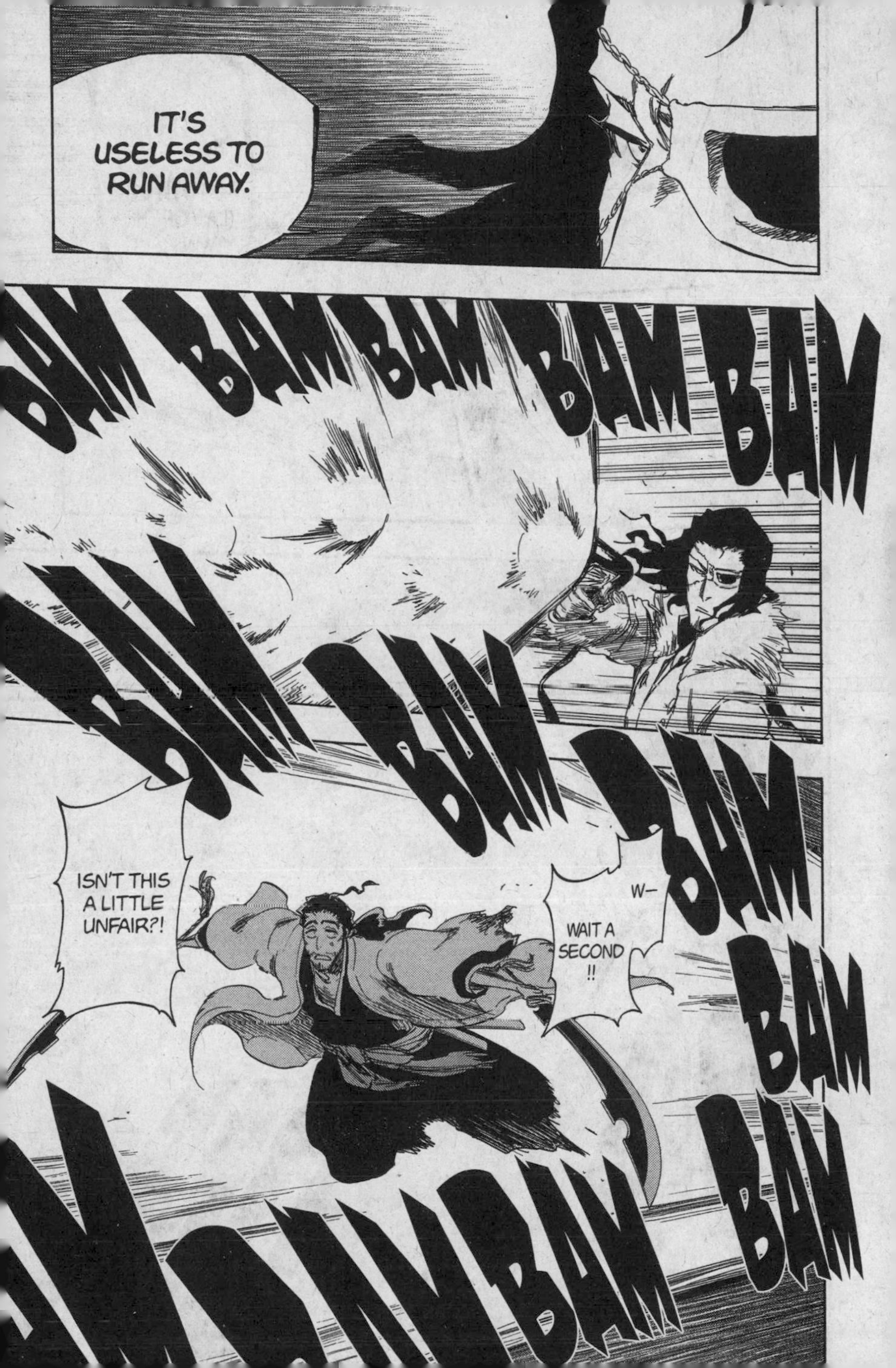
IT'S USELESS TO RUN AWAY.
BAM BAM BAM BAM BAM BAM BAM
BAM BAM BAM BAM BAM BAM BAM BAM BAM BAM BAM
W— WAIT A SECOND!!
ISN'T THIS A LITTLE UNFAIR?!

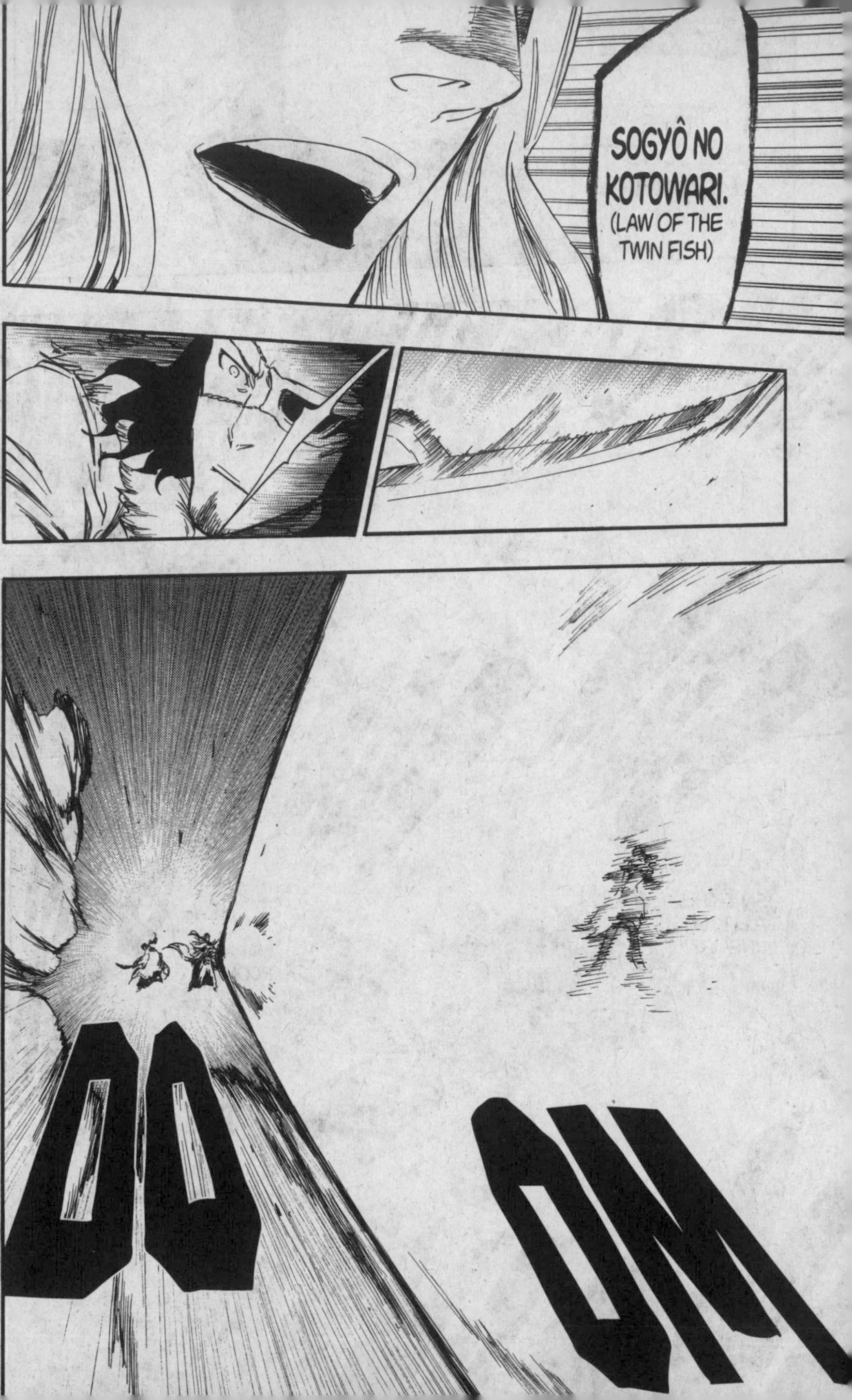
SOGYÔ NO KOTOWARI.
(LAW OF THE TWIN FISH)
DOOM

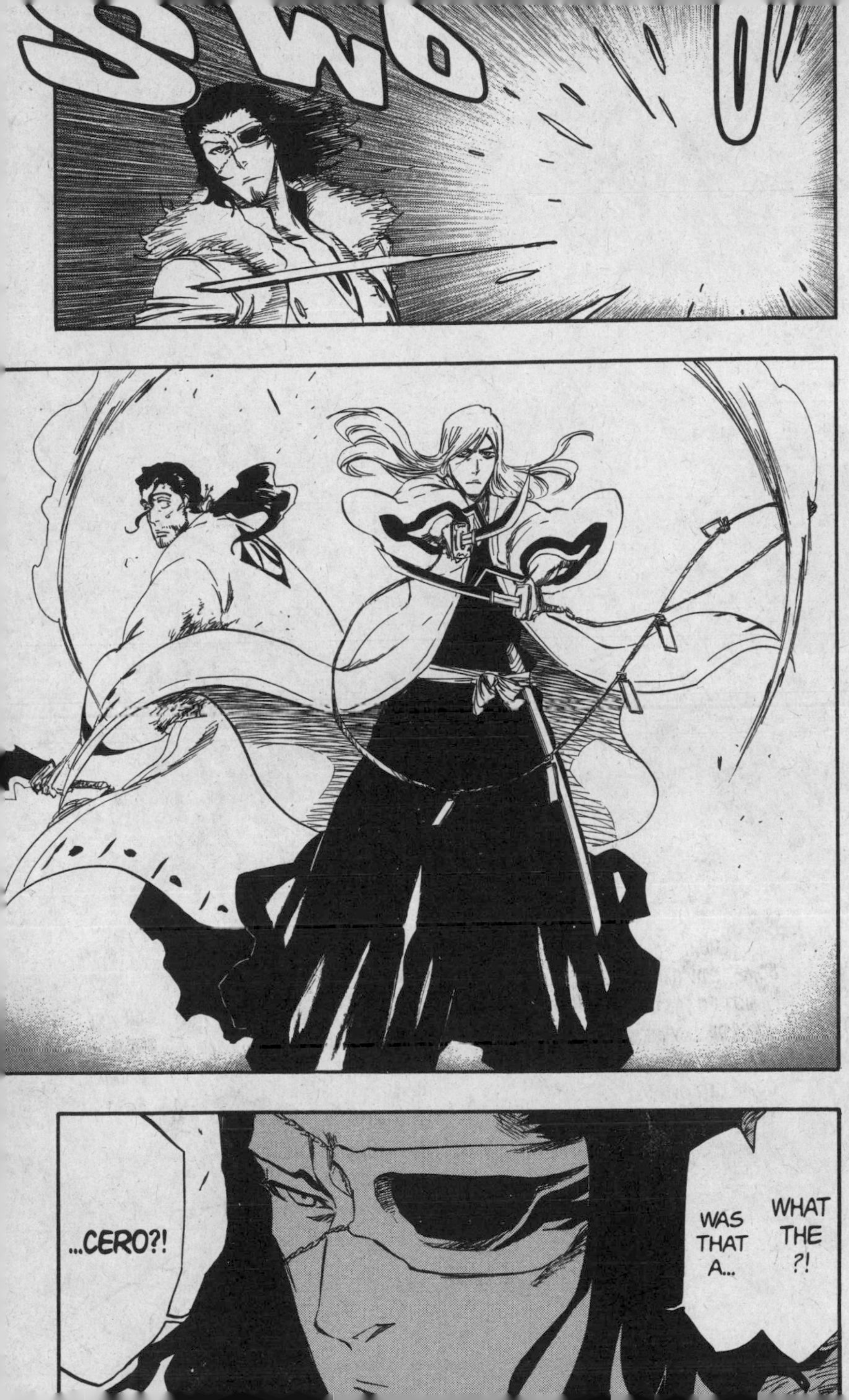
SWOO
WHAT THE ?!
WAS THAT A...
...CERO?!

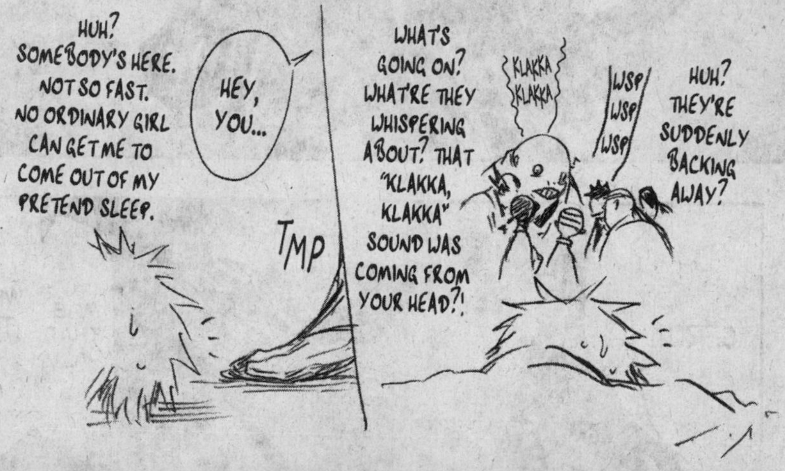
HUH? THEY'RE SUDDENLY BACKING AWAY?
WSP WSP WSP
KLAKKA KLAKKA
WHAT'S GOING ON? WHAT'RE THEY WHISPERING ABOUT? THAT "KLAKKA, KLAKKA" SOUND WAS COMING FROM YOUR HEAD?!
HEY, YOU...
TMP
HUH? SOMEBODY'S HERE. NOT SO FAST. NO ORDINARY GIRL CAN GET ME TO COME OUT OF MY PRETEND SLEEP.

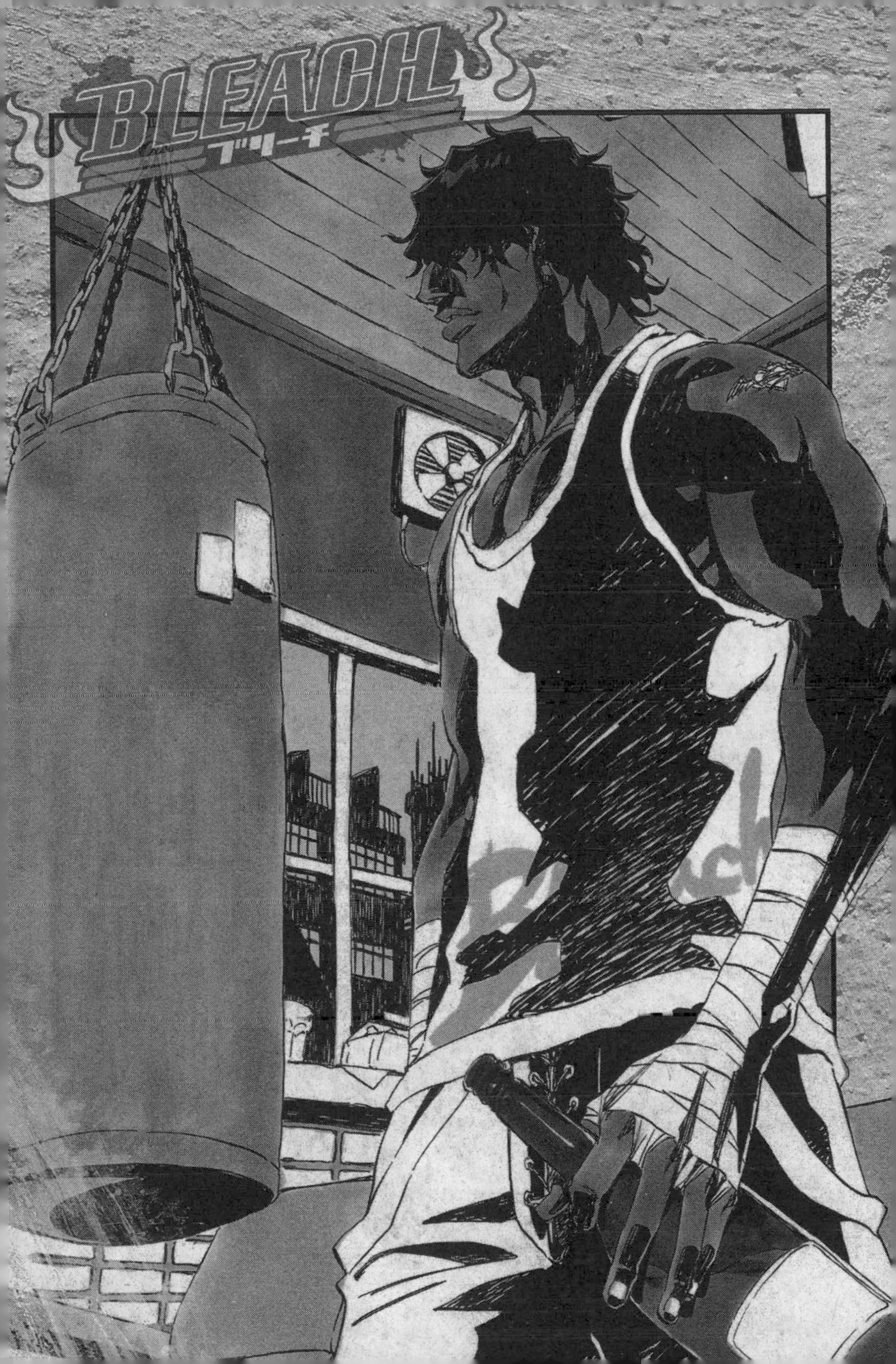
BLEACH
ブリーチ

BLEACH
ブリーチ

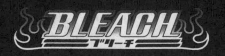

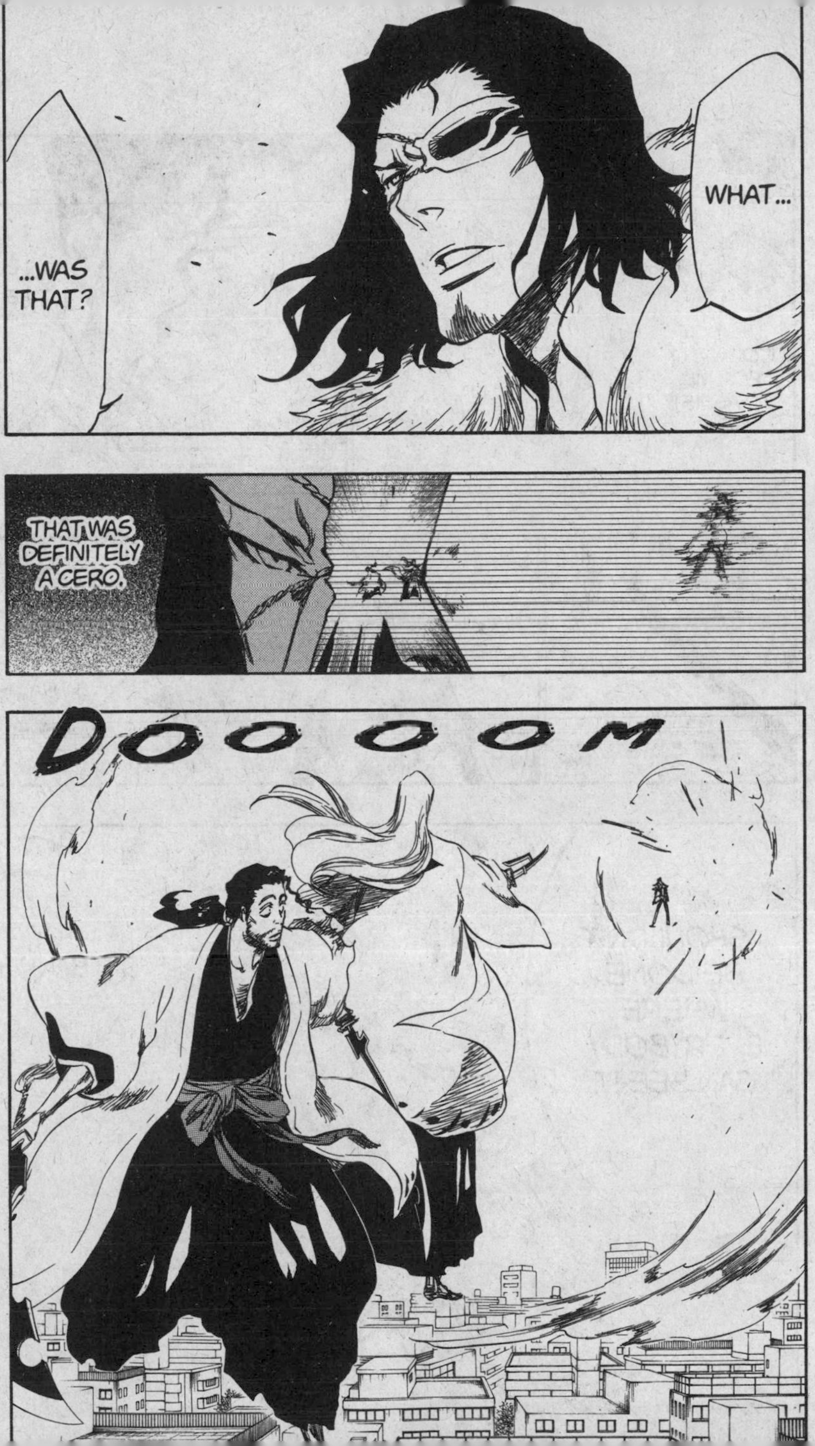
WHAT...
...WAS THAT?
THAT WAS DEFINITELY A CERO.
DOOOOOM

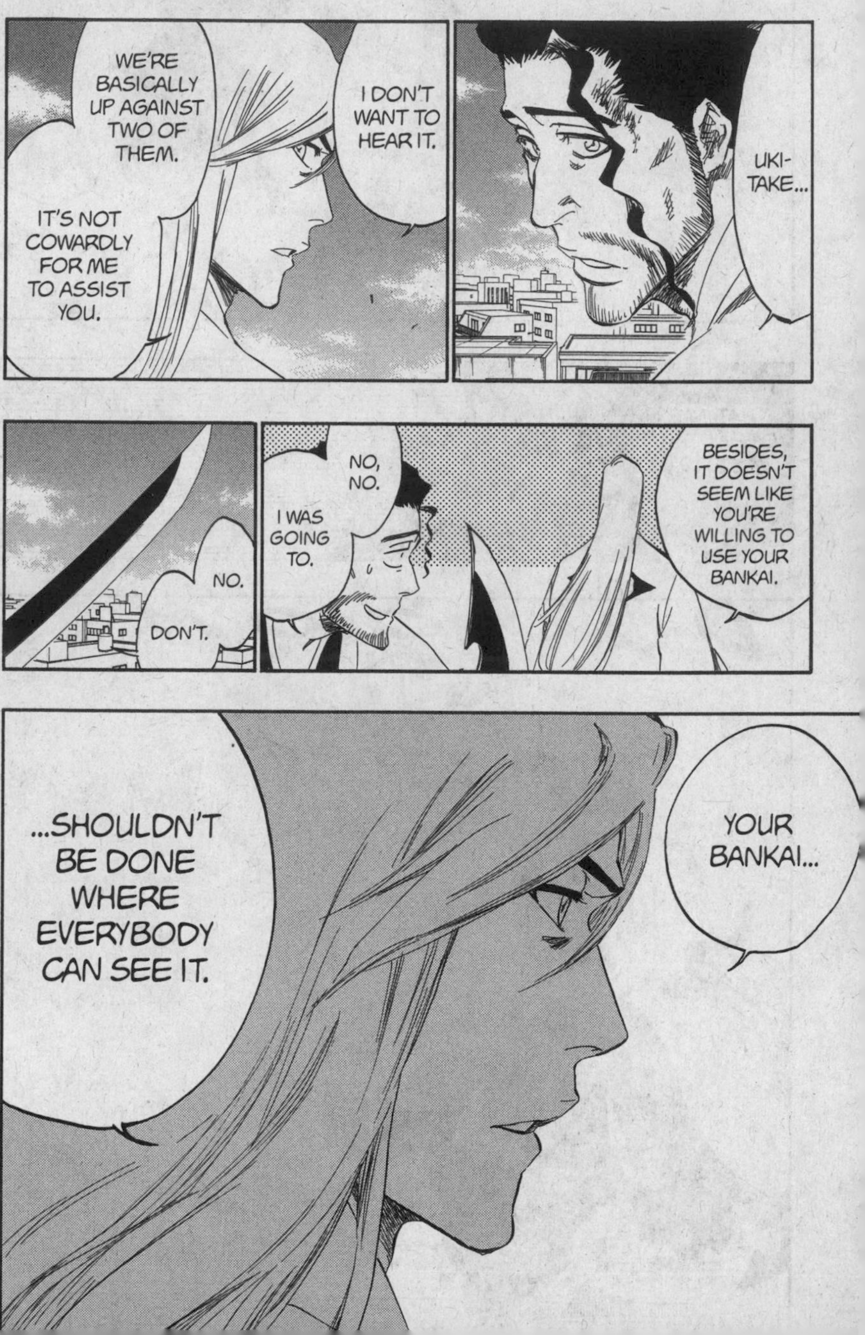
UKI-TAKE...
I DON'T WANT TO HEAR IT.
WE'RE BASICALLY UP AGAINST TWO OF THEM.
IT'S NOT COWARDLY FOR ME TO ASSIST YOU.
BESIDES, IT DOESN'T SEEM LIKE YOU'RE WILLING TO USE YOUR BANKAI.
NO, NO.
I WAS GOING TO.
NO.
DON'T.
YOUR BANKAI...
...SHOULDN'T BE DONE WHERE EVERYBODY CAN SEE IT.

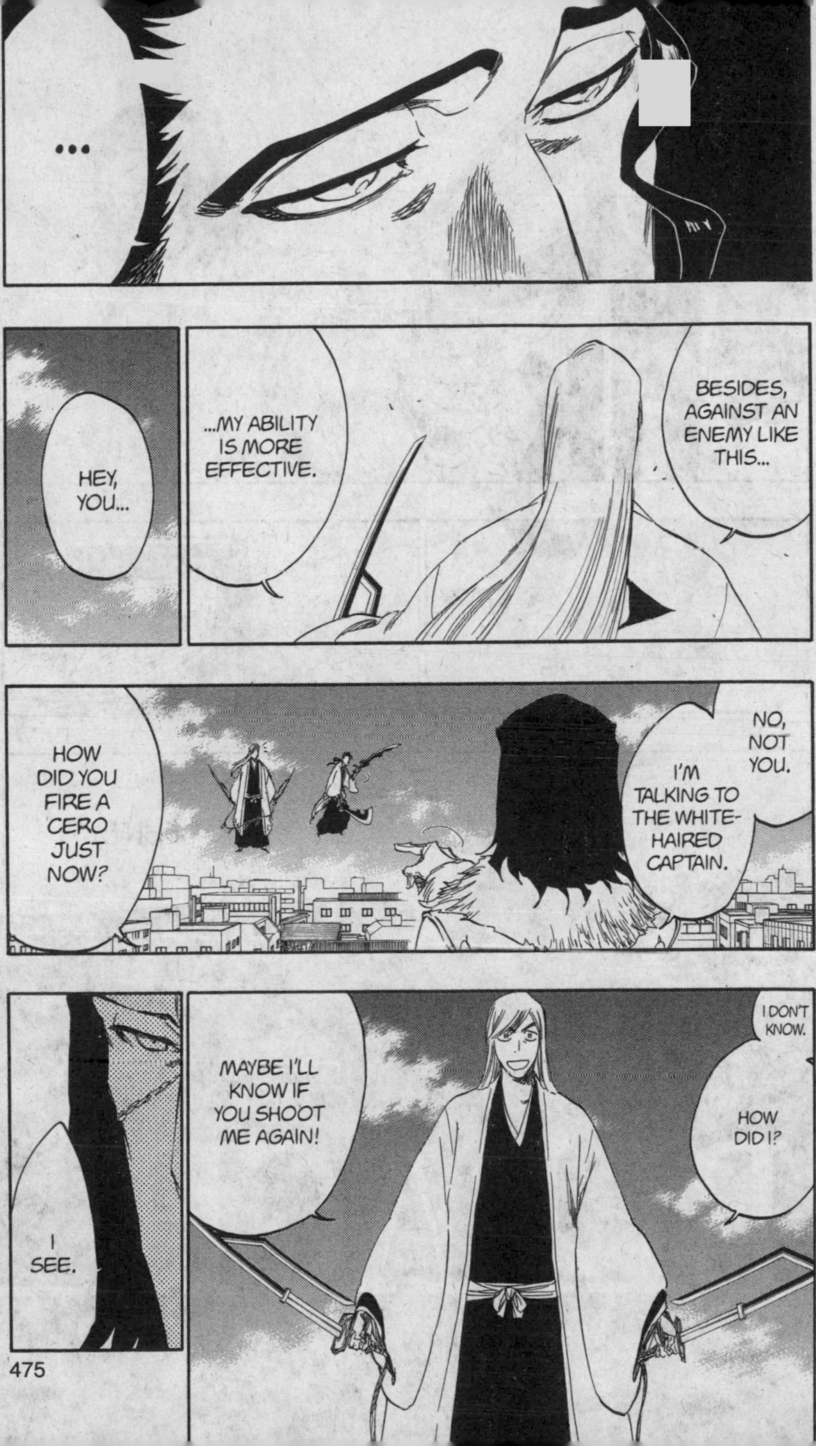
...
BESIDES, AGAINST AN ENEMY LIKE THIS...
...MY ABILITY IS MORE EFFECTIVE.
HEY, YOU...
NO, NOT YOU.
I'M TALKING TO THE WHITE-HAIRED CAPTAIN.
HOW DID YOU FIRE A CERO JUST NOW?
I DON'T KNOW.
HOW DID I?
MAYBE I'LL KNOW IF YOU SHOOT ME AGAIN!
I SEE.

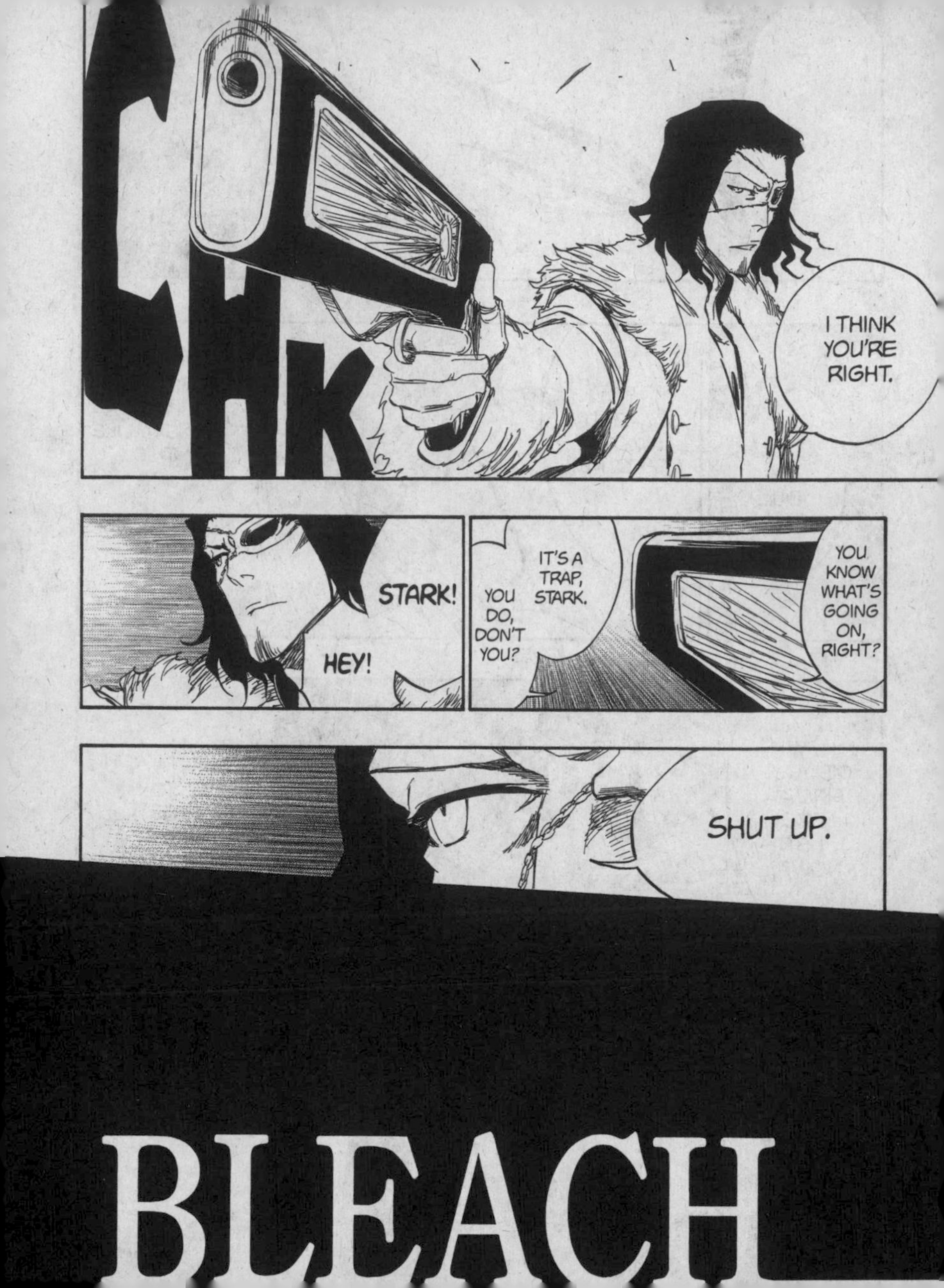
CHK
I THINK YOU'RE RIGHT.
YOU KNOW WHAT'S GOING ON, RIGHT?
IT'S A TRAP, STARK.
YOU DO, DON'T YOU?
STARK!
HEY!
SHUT UP.
BLEACH

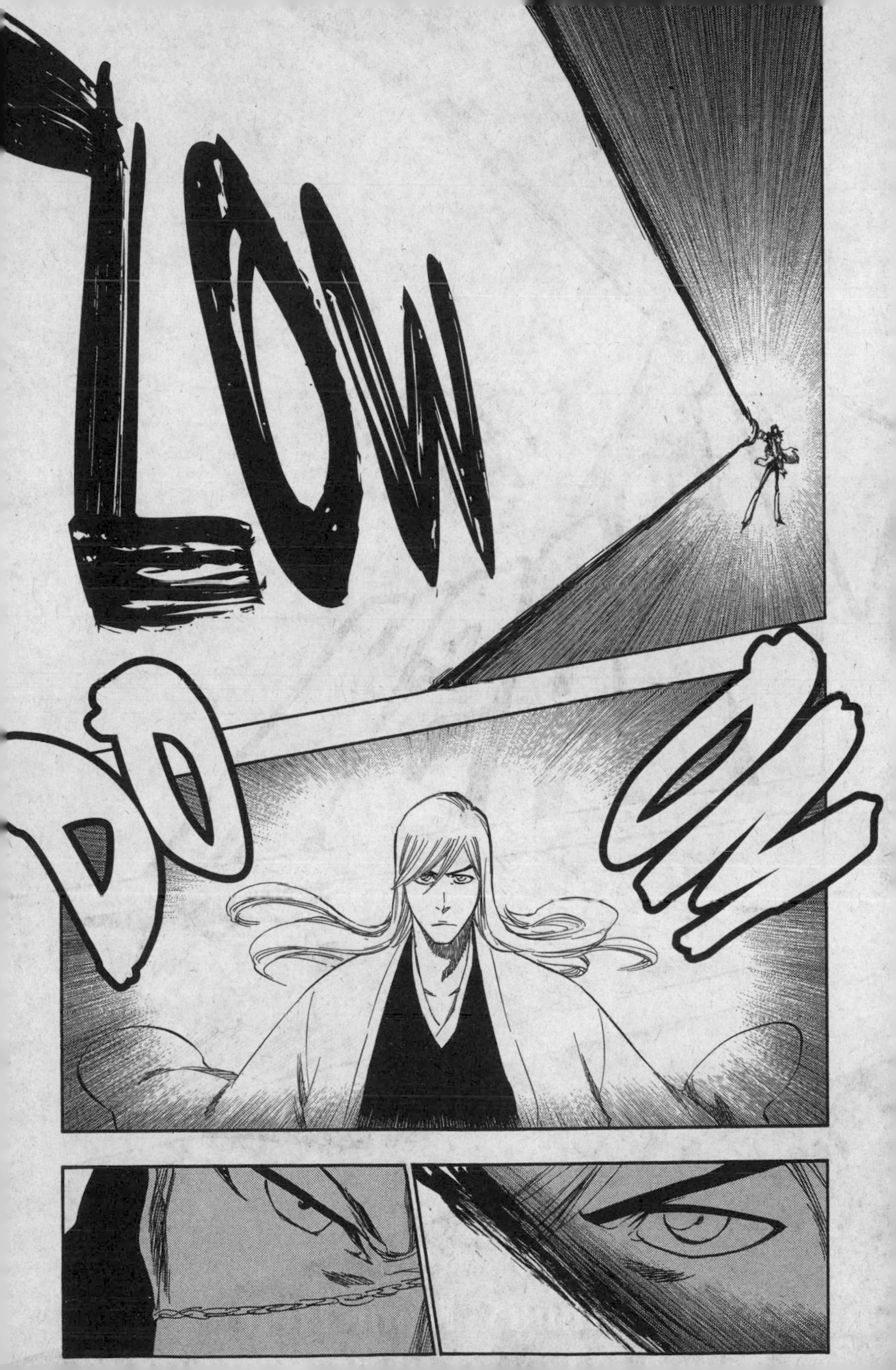

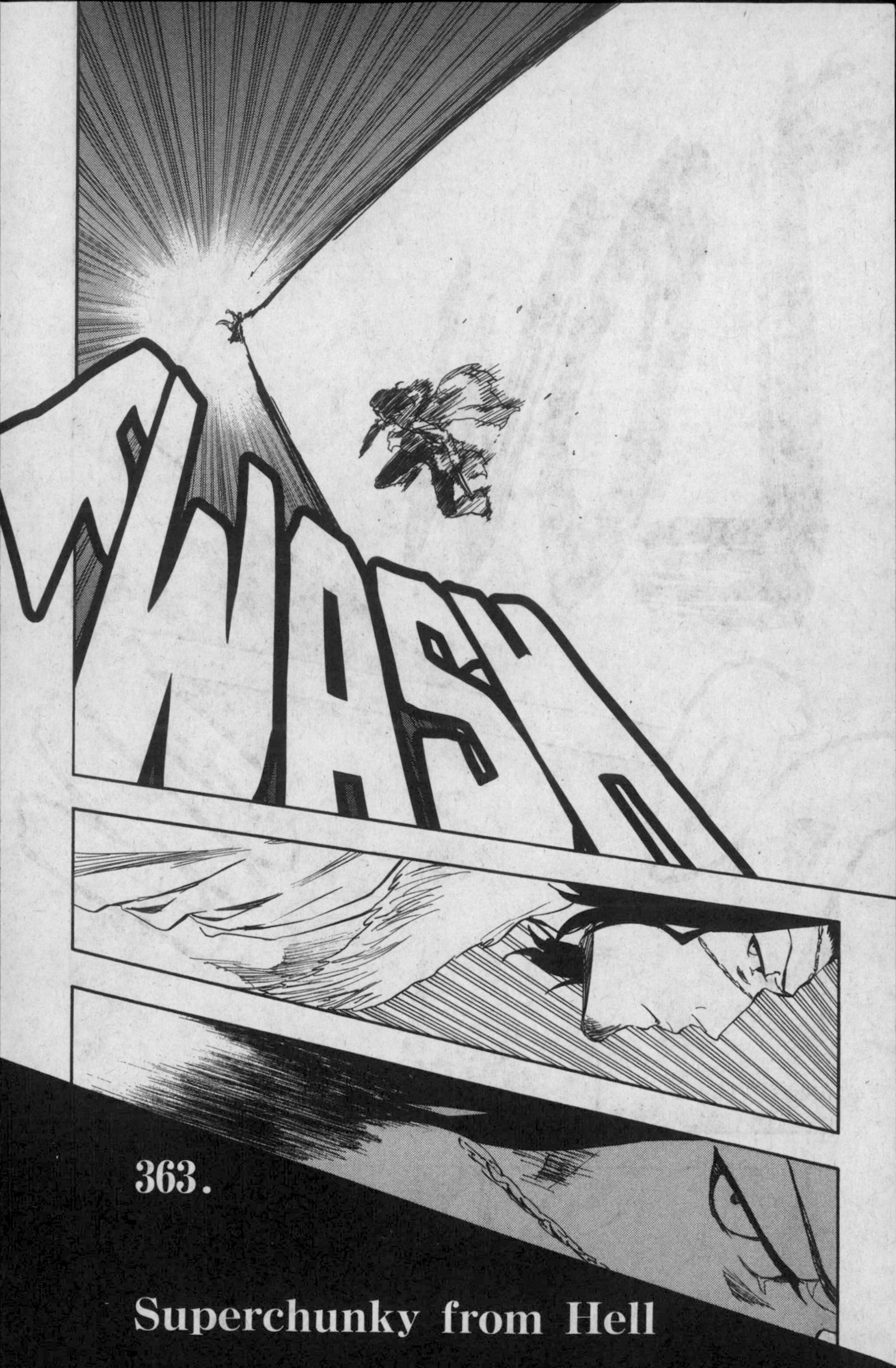
363.
Superchunky from Hell

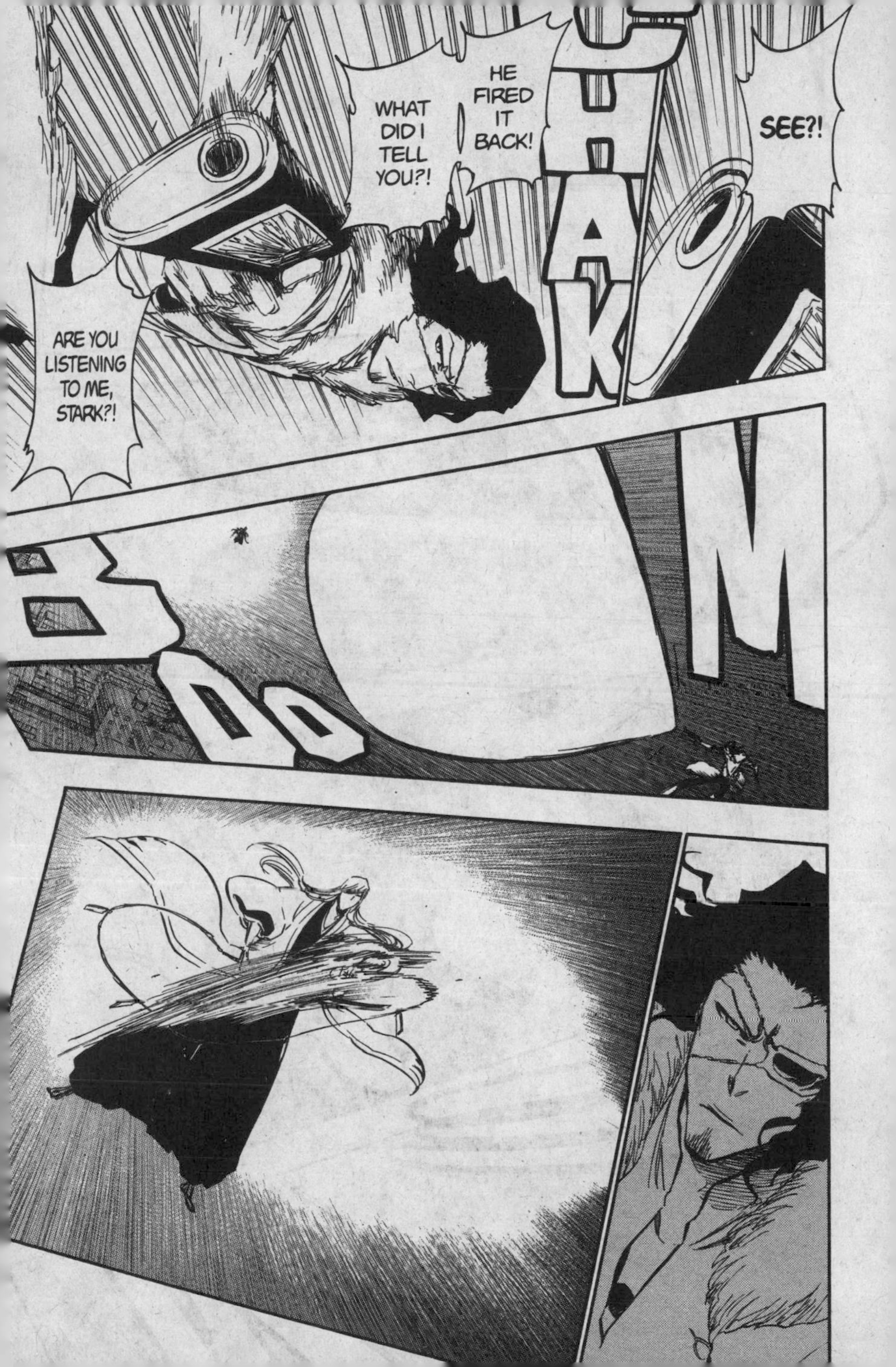
SEE?!
HE FIRED IT BACK!
WHAT DID I TELL YOU?!
ARE YOU LISTENING TO ME, STARK?!

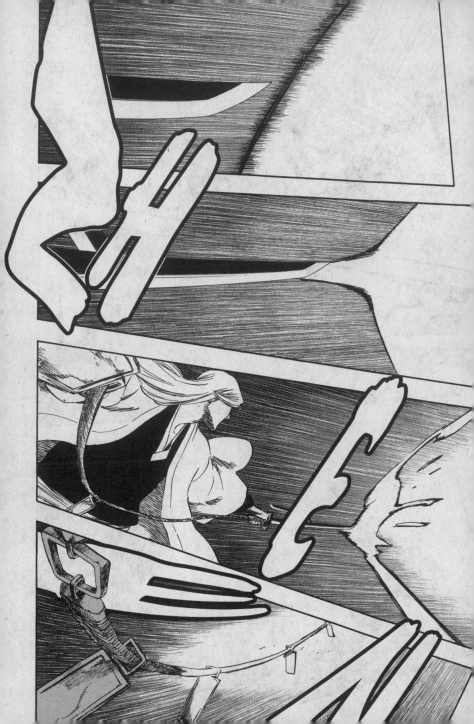

READ THIS WAY

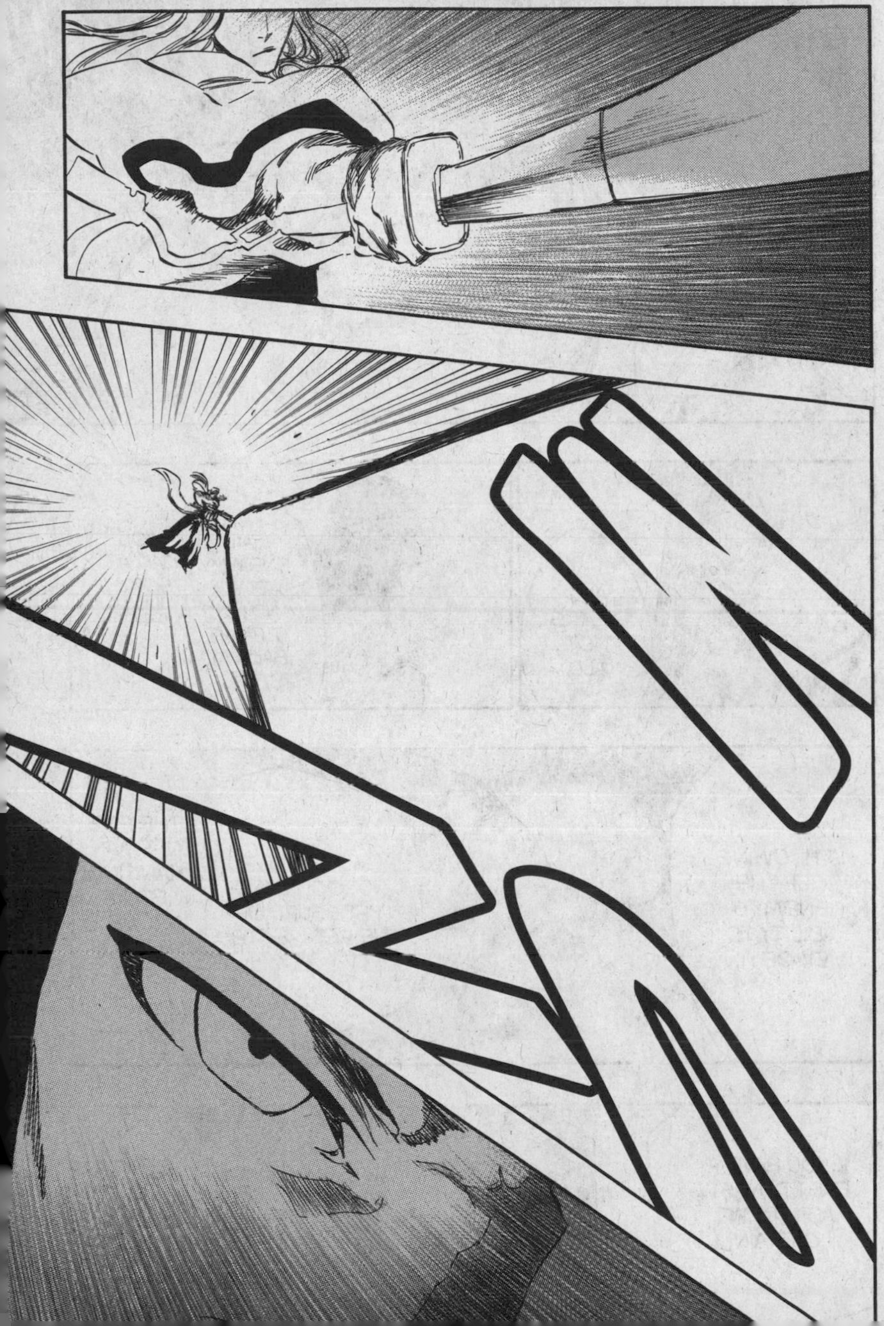

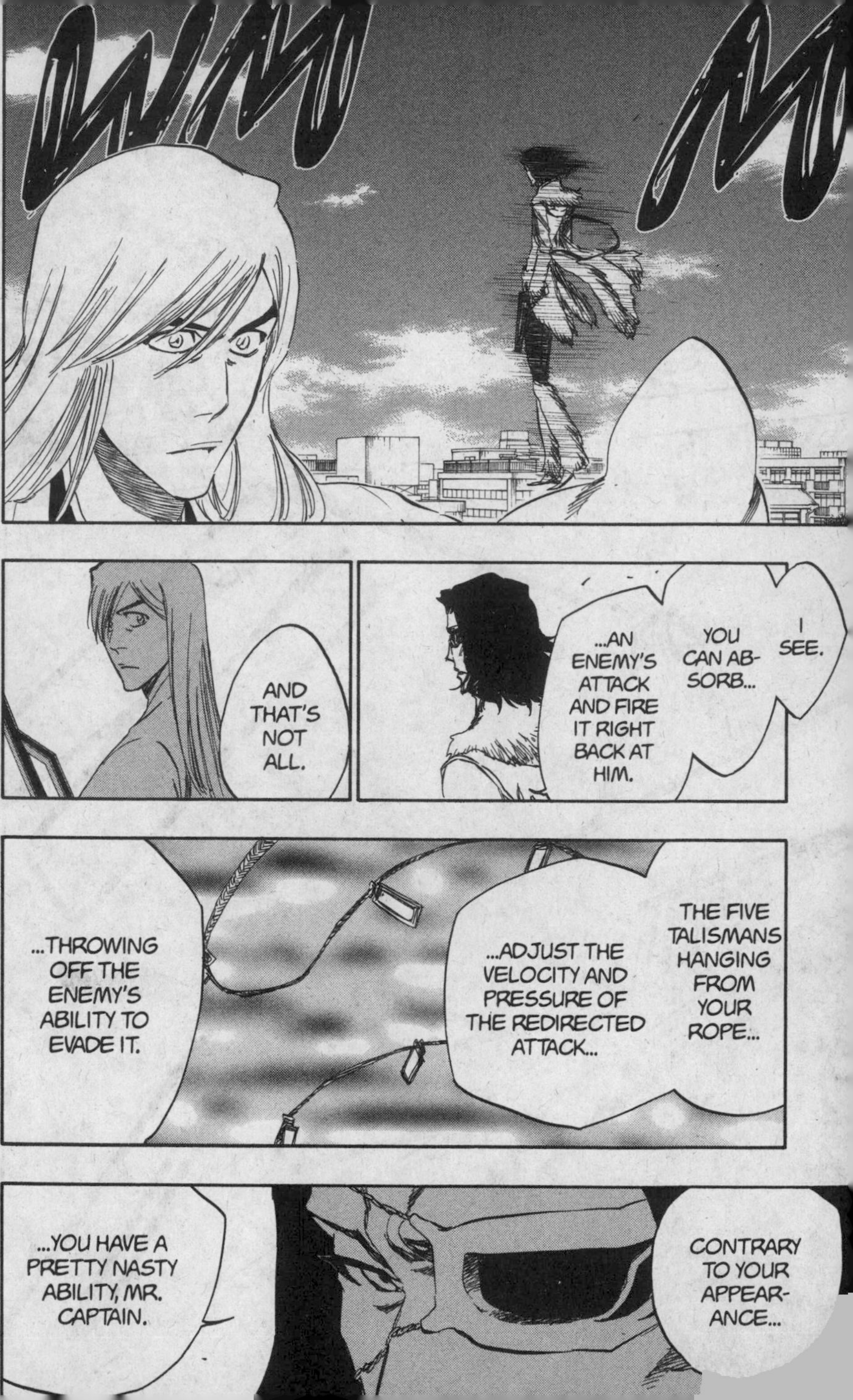
I SEE.
YOU CAN ABSORB...
...AN ENEMY'S ATTACK AND FIRE IT RIGHT BACK AT HIM.
AND THAT'S NOT ALL.
THE FIVE TALISMANS HANGING FROM YOUR ROPE...
...ADJUST THE VELOCITY AND PRESSURE OF THE REDIRECTED ATTACK...
...THROWING OFF THE ENEMY'S ABILITY TO EVADE IT.
CONTRARY TO YOUR APPEARANCE...
...YOU HAVE A PRETTY NASTY ABILITY, MR. CAPTAIN.

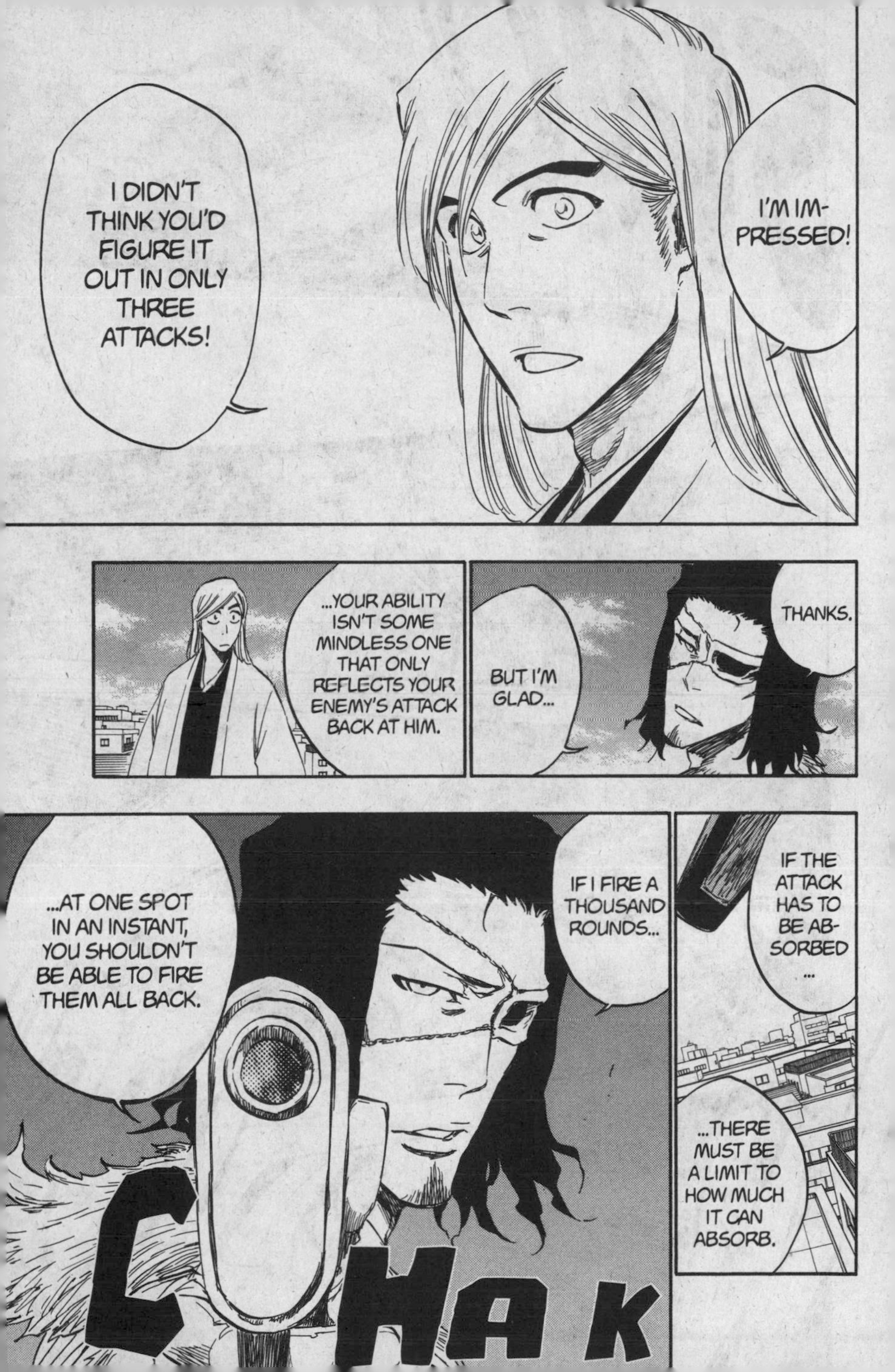
I'M IM-PRESSED!
I DIDN'T THINK YOU'D FIGURE IT OUT IN ONLY THREE ATTACKS!
THANKS.
BUT I'M GLAD...
...YOUR ABILITY ISN'T SOME MINDLESS ONE THAT ONLY REFLECTS YOUR ENEMY'S ATTACK BACK AT HIM.
IF THE ATTACK HAS TO BE AB-SORBED ...
...THERE MUST BE A LIMIT TO HOW MUCH IT CAN ABSORB.
IF I FIRE A THOUSAND ROUNDS...
...AT ONE SPOT IN AN INSTANT, YOU SHOULDN'T BE ABLE TO FIRE THEM ALL BACK.
CHAK

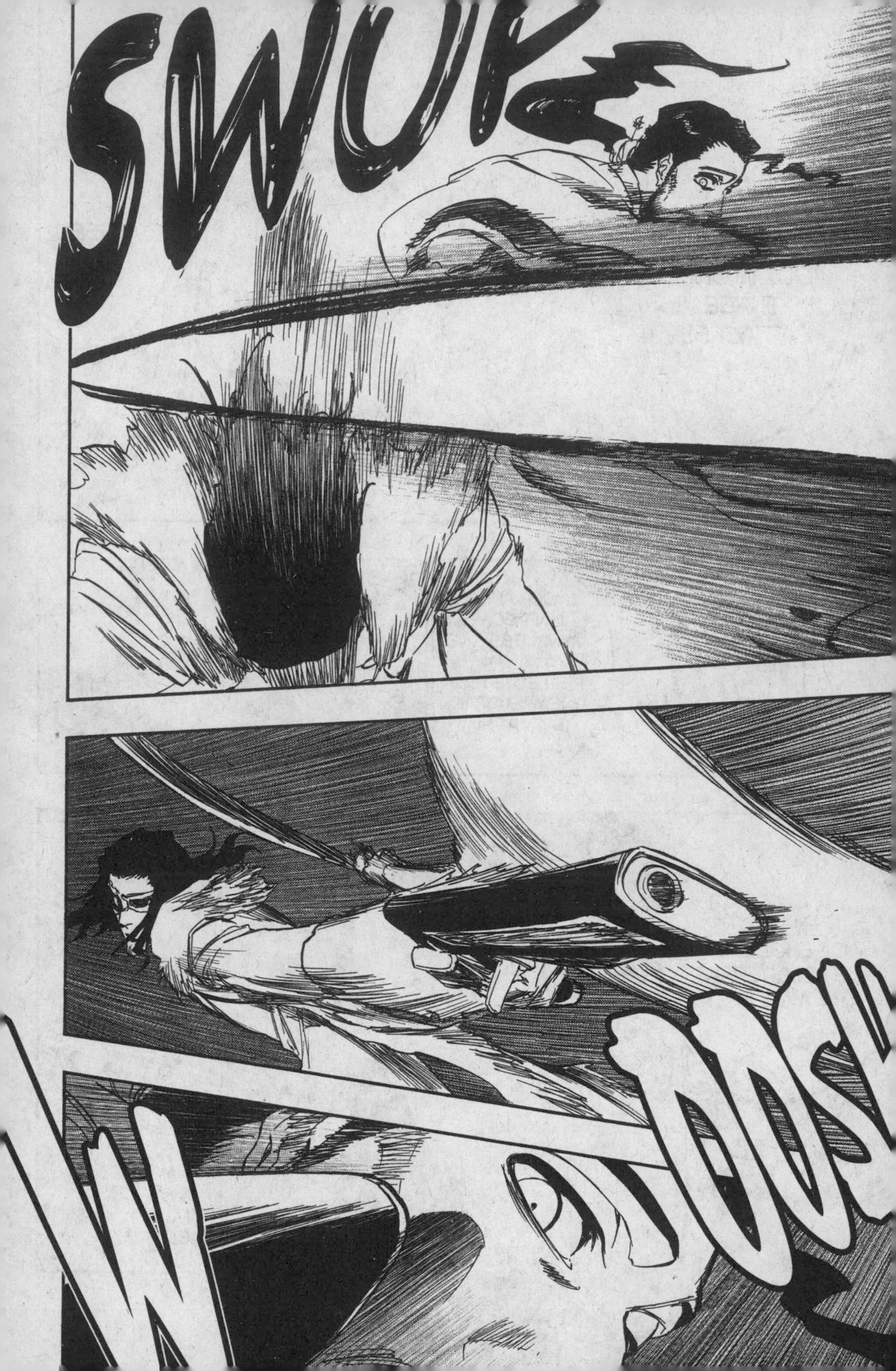
SWOP

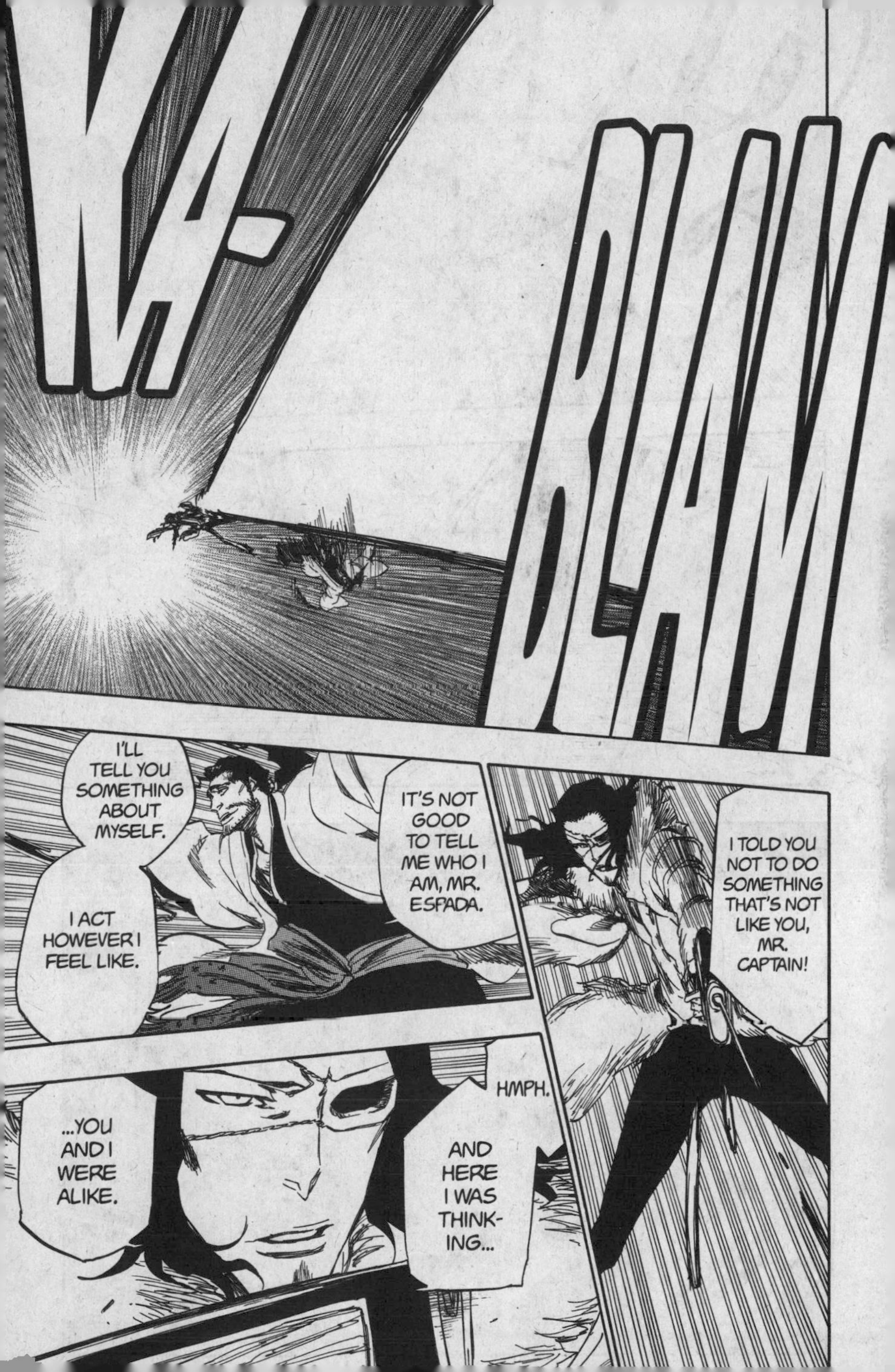
KA-
BLAM
I TOLD YOU NOT TO DO SOMETHING THAT'S NOT LIKE YOU, MR. CAPTAIN!
IT'S NOT GOOD TO TELL ME WHO I AM, MR. ESPADA.
I'LL TELL YOU SOMETHING ABOUT MYSELF.
I ACT HOWEVER I FEEL LIKE.
HMPH.
AND HERE I WAS THINKING...
...YOU AND I WERE ALIKE.

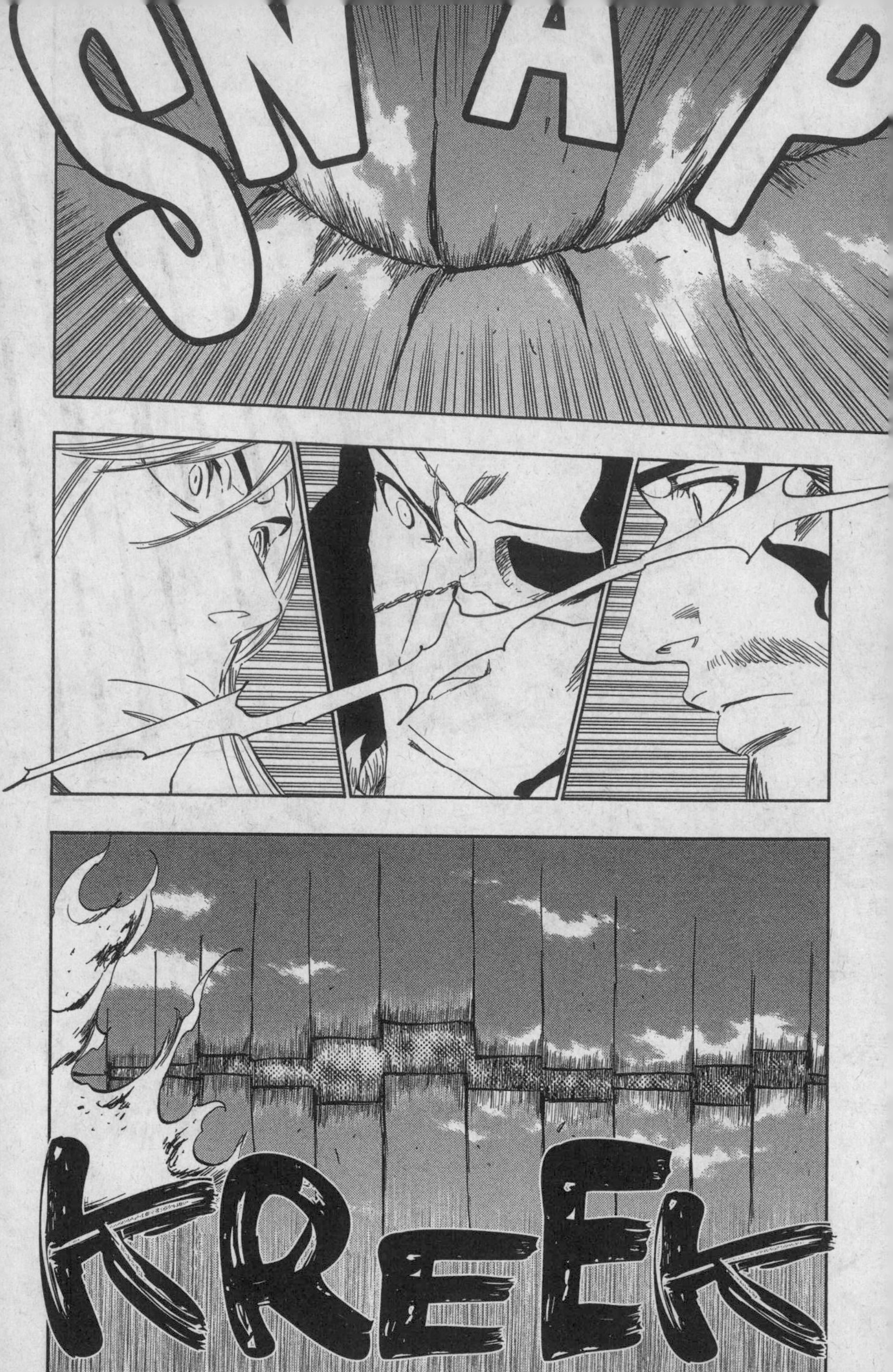
SNAP
KREEK

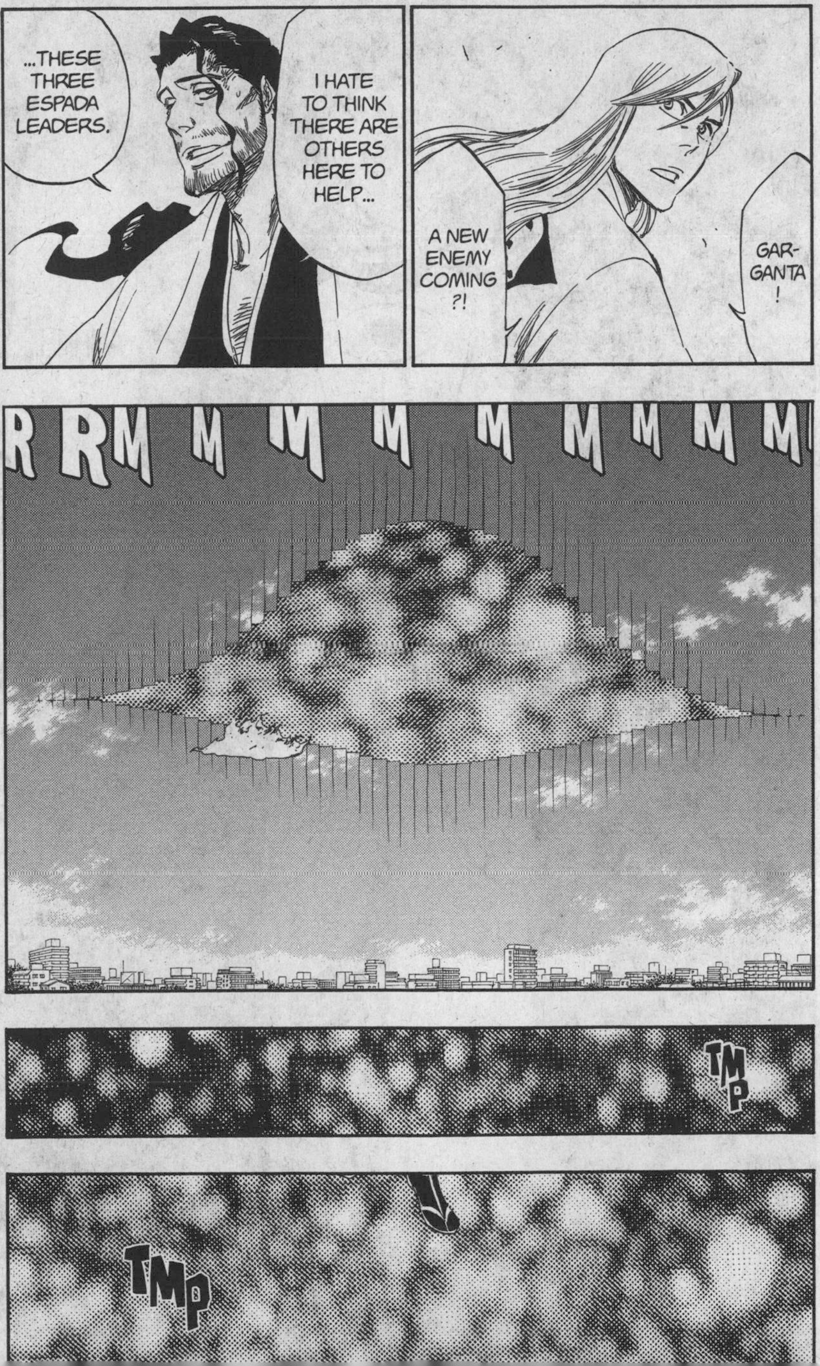
GAR-GANTA!
A NEW ENEMY COMING?!
I HATE TO THINK THERE ARE OTHERS HERE TO HELP...
...THESE THREE ESPADA LEADERS.
RRMMMMMMMMM
TMP
TMP

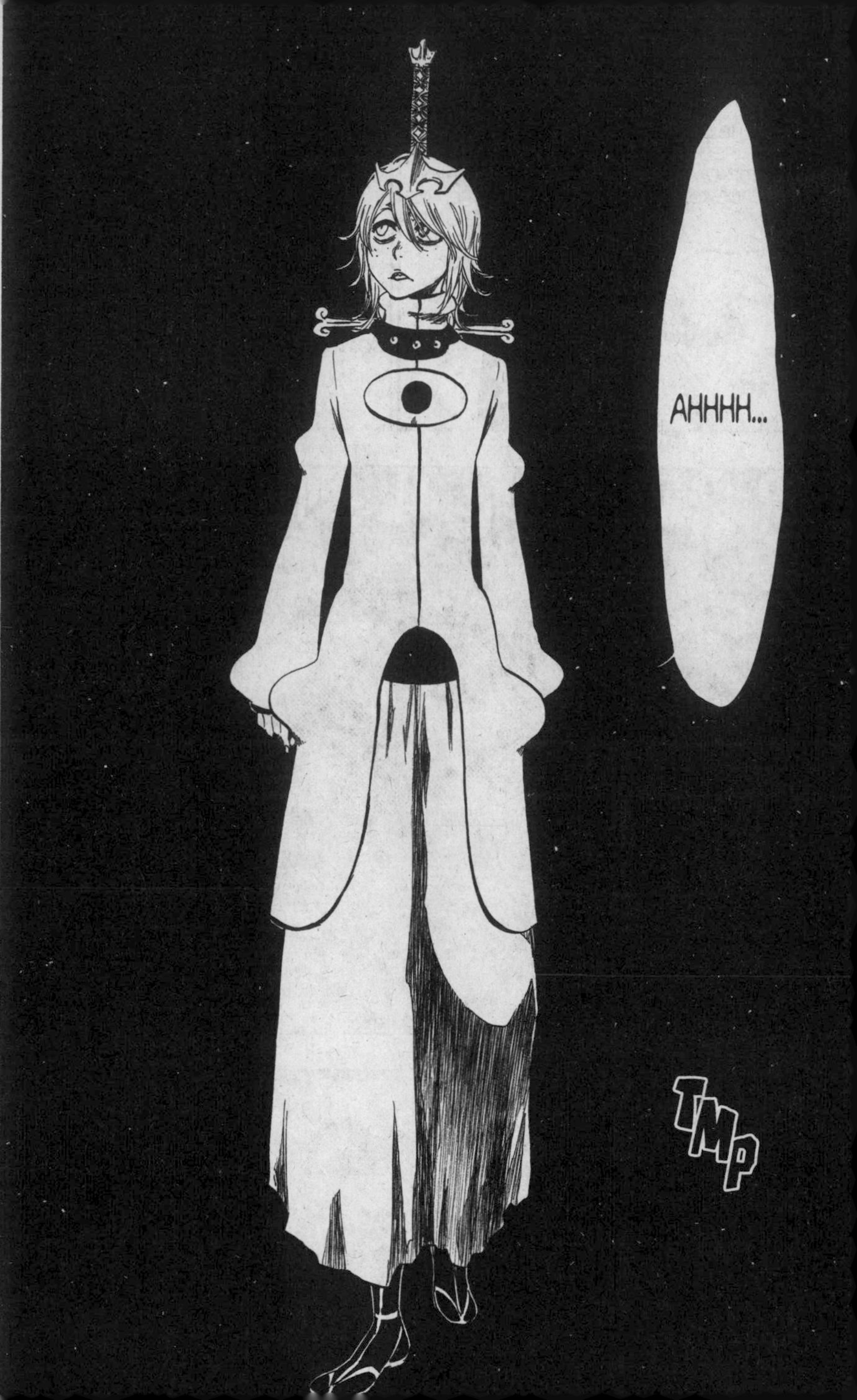
AHHHH...
TMP

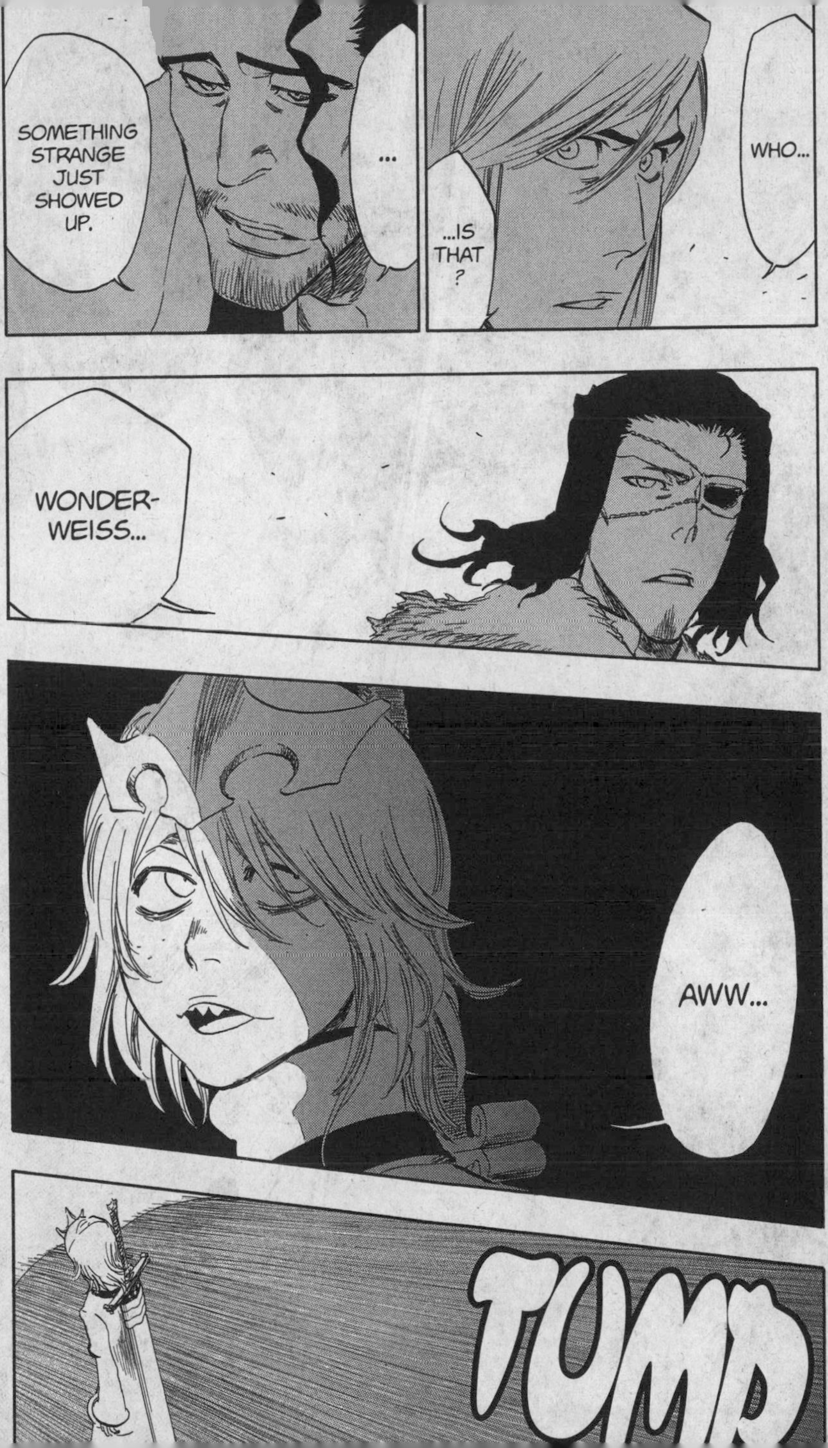
WHO...
...IS THAT?
...
SOMETHING STRANGE JUST SHOWED UP.
WONDER-WEISS...
AWW...
TUMP

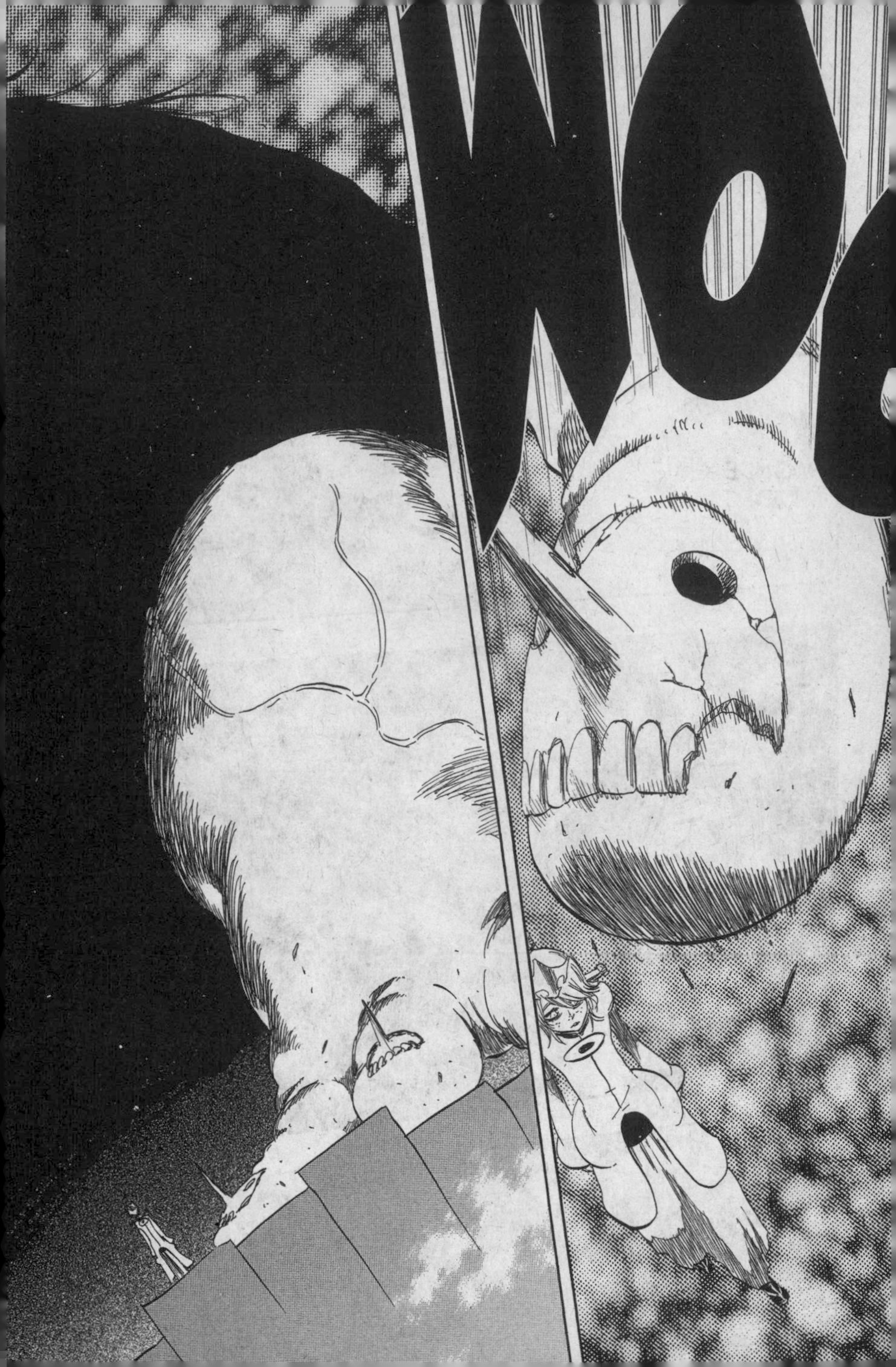
WO

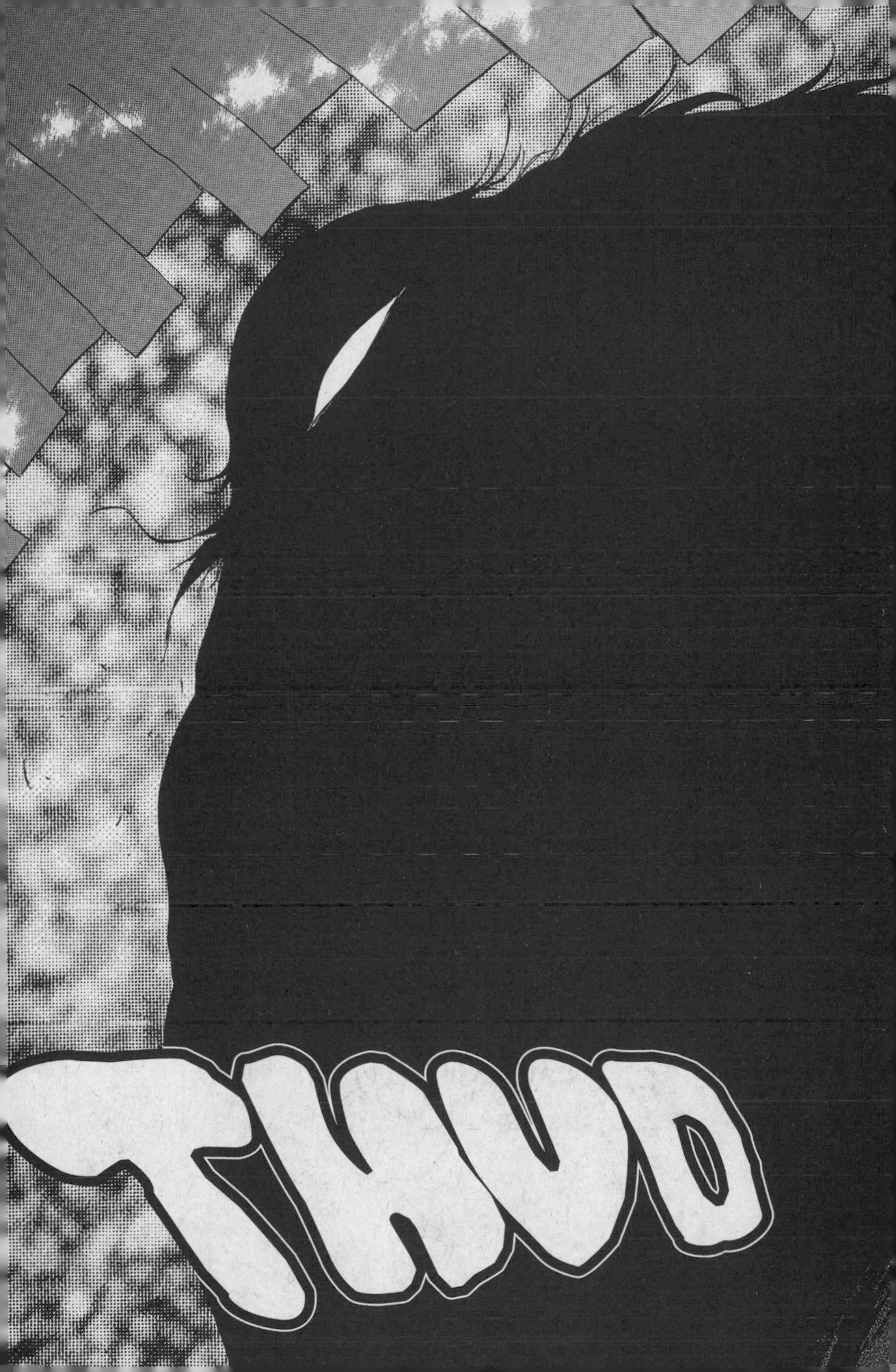
THUD

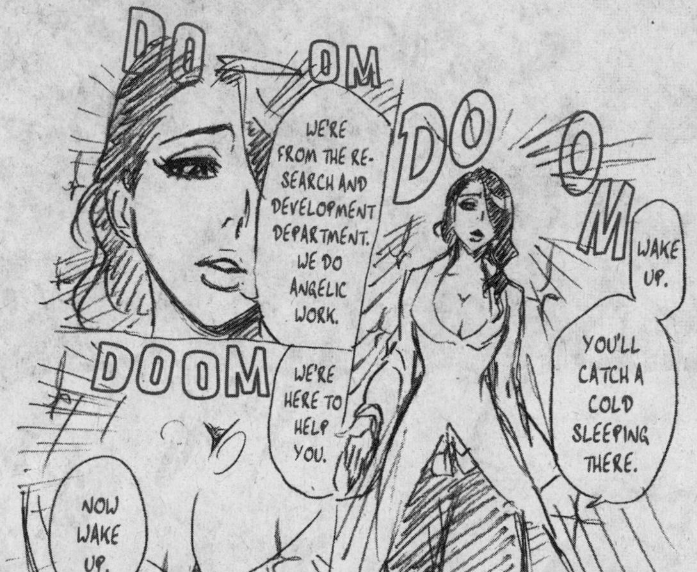
DO OM
WAKE UP.
YOU'LL CATCH A COLD SLEEPING THERE.
DO OM
WE'RE FROM THE RESEARCH AND DEVELOPMENT DEPARTMENT. WE DO ANGELIC WORK.
DOOM
WE'RE HERE TO HELP YOU.
NOW WAKE UP.

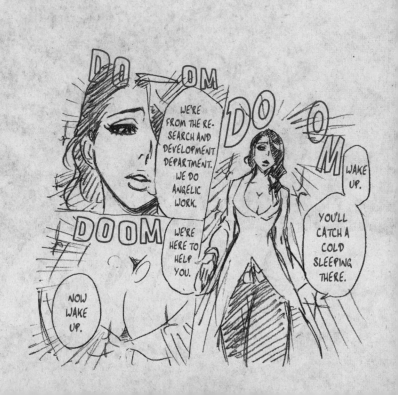

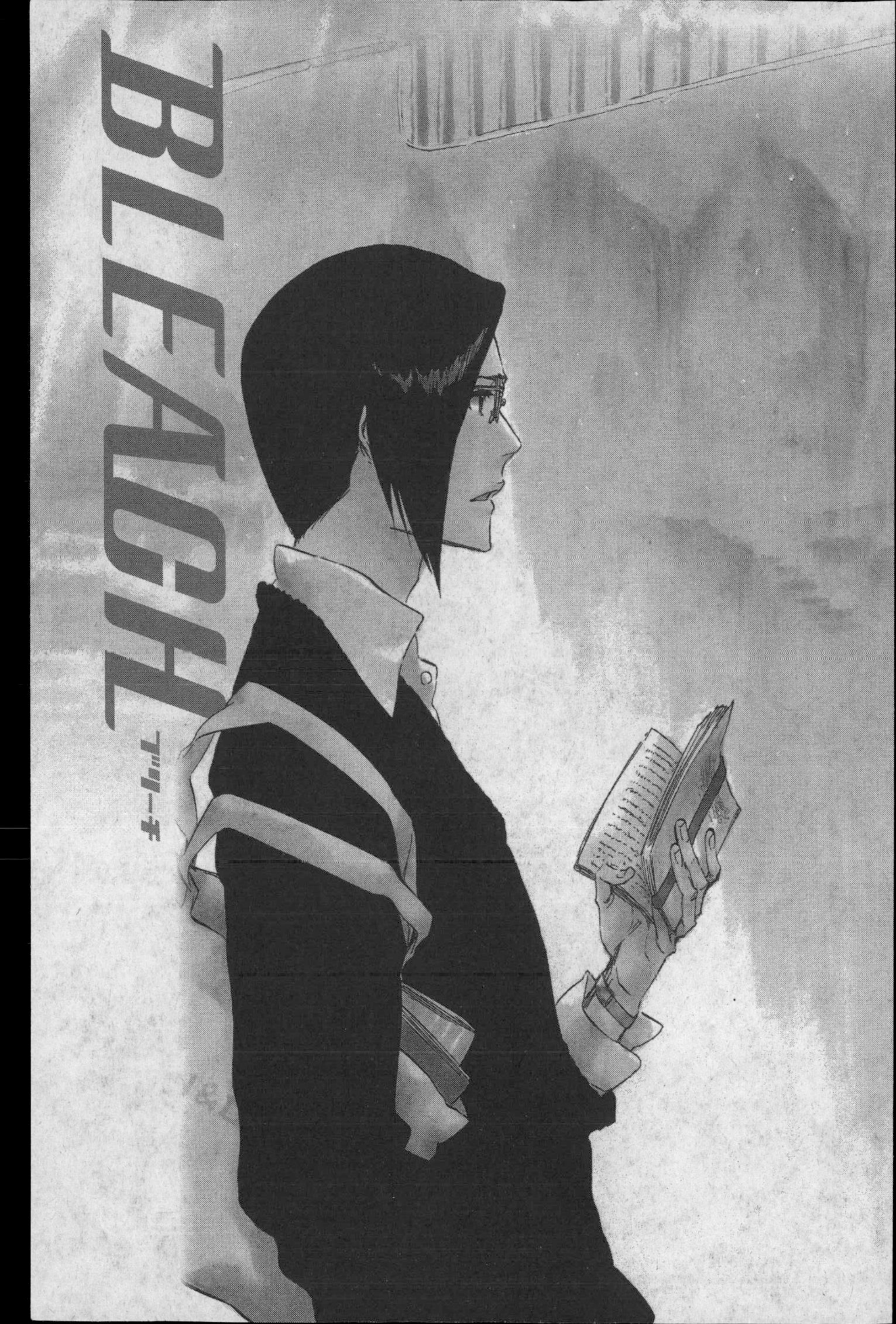
BLEACH
ブリーチ

BLEACH
ブリーチ

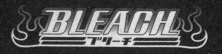

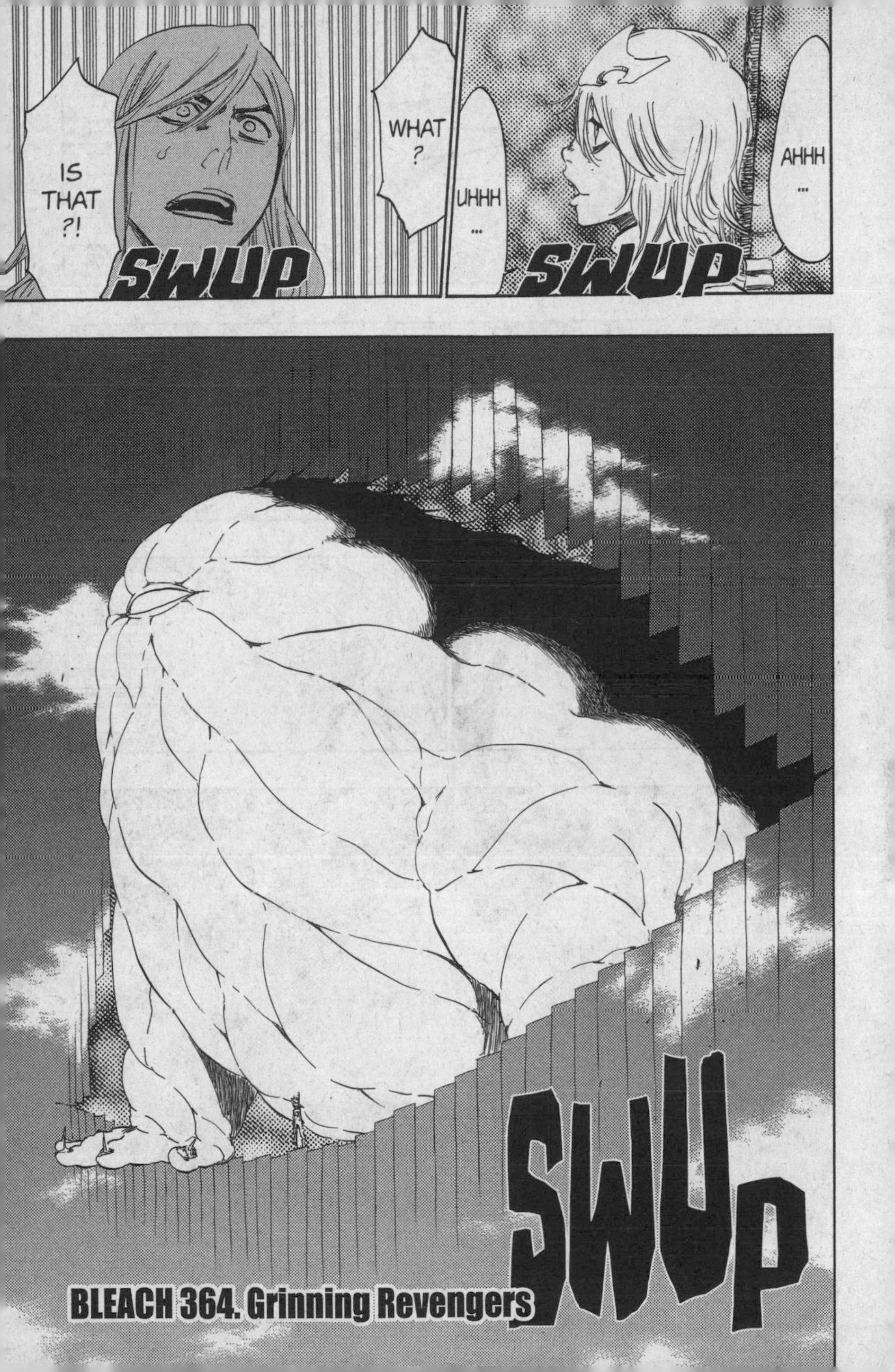
AHHH ...
UHHH ...
SWUP
WHAT ?
IS THAT ?!
SWUP
SWUP

BLEACH 364. Grinning Revengers

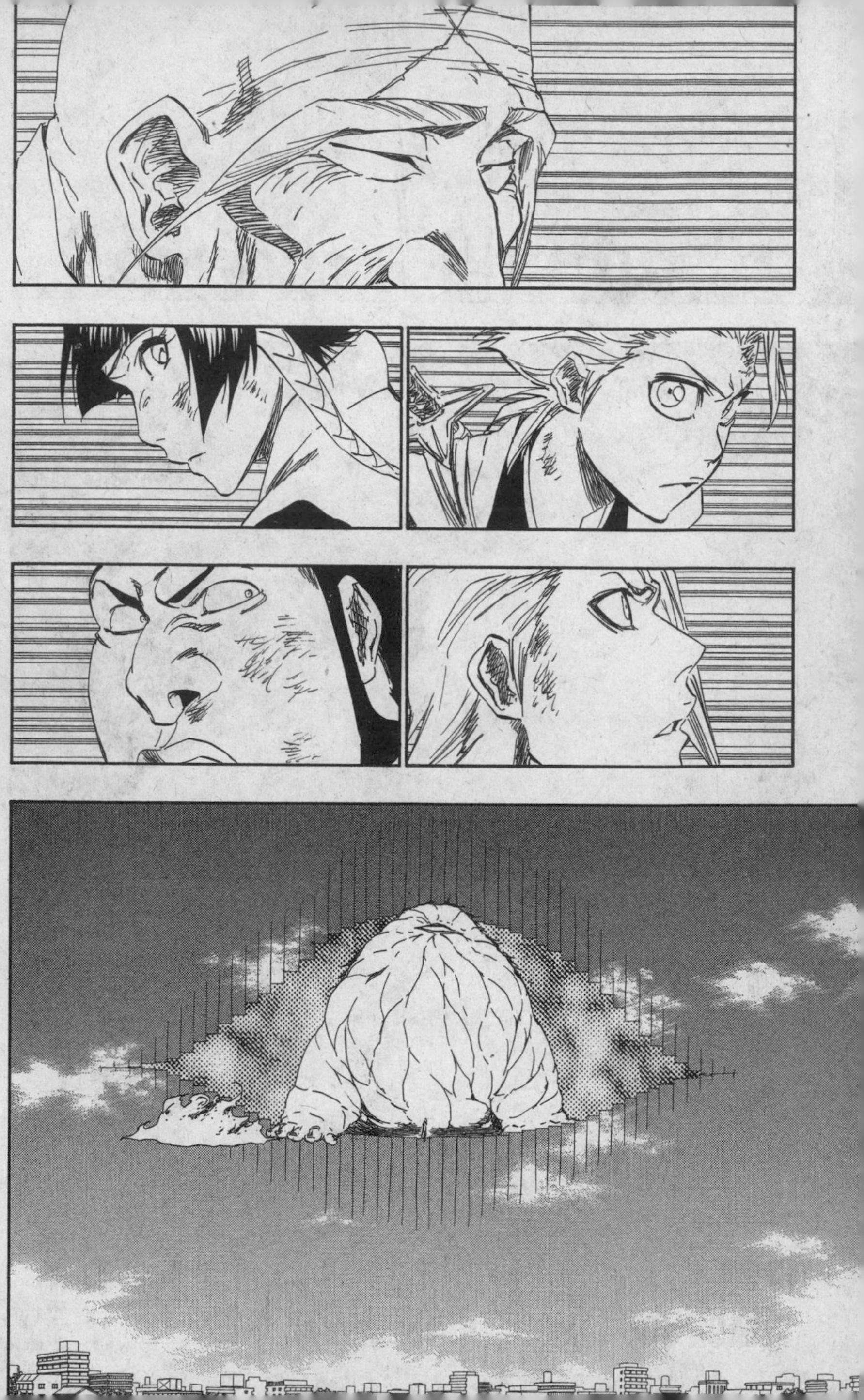

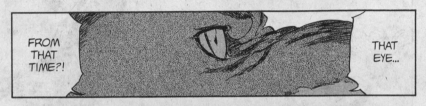

FROM
THAT
TIME?!

THAT
EYE...

TUMP

AHHH...

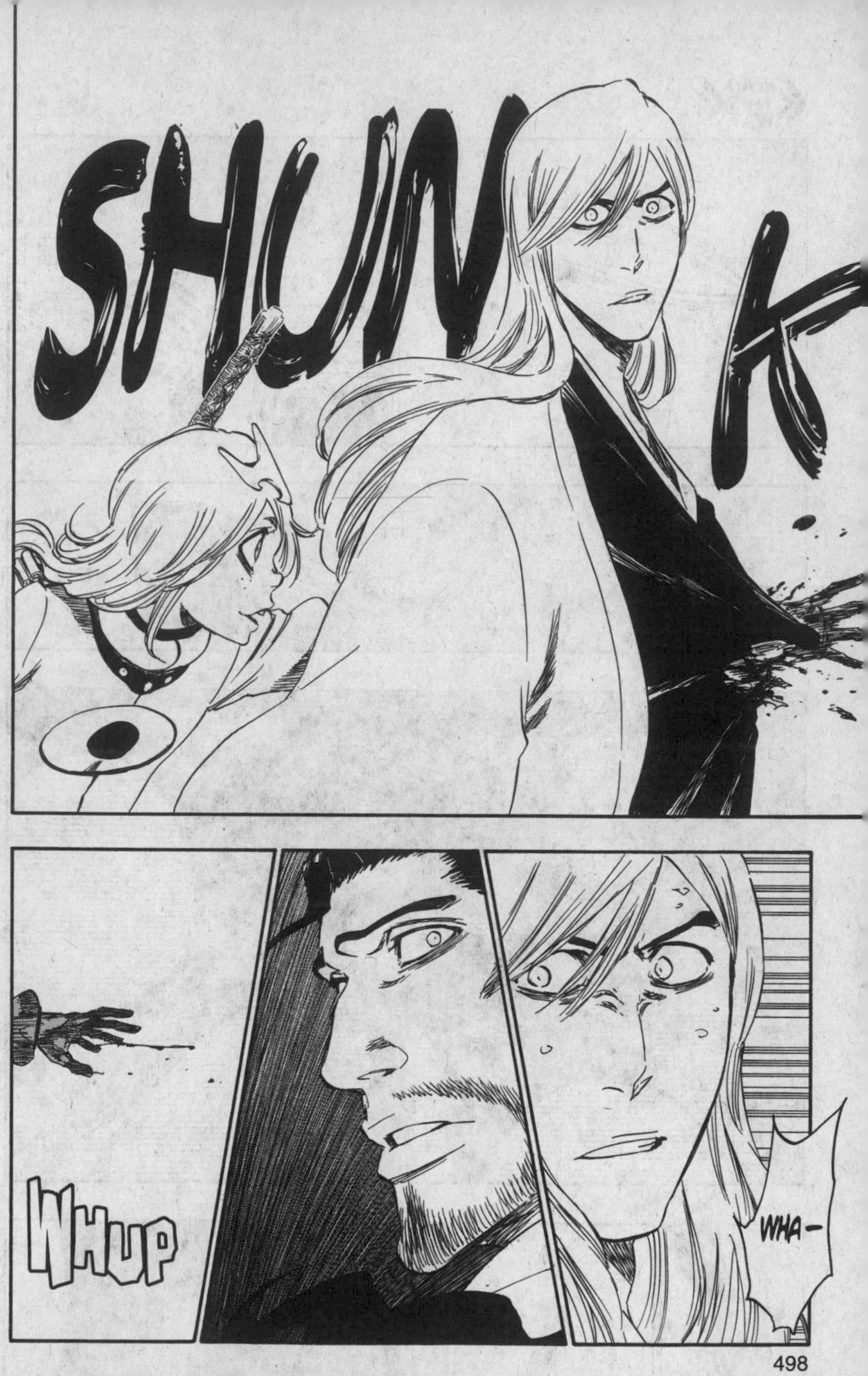
SHUNK
WHA-
WHUP

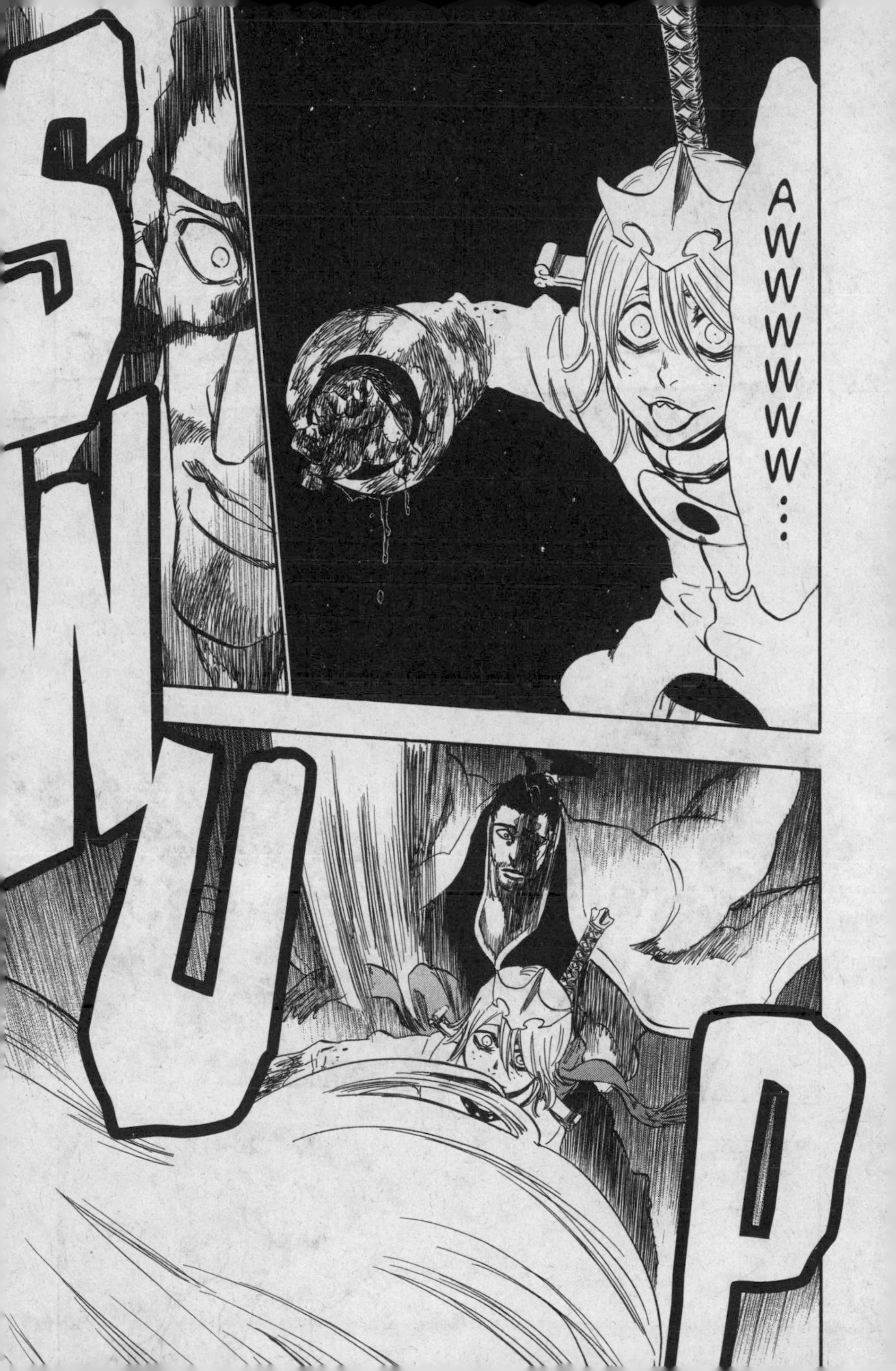
AWWWWWWW...

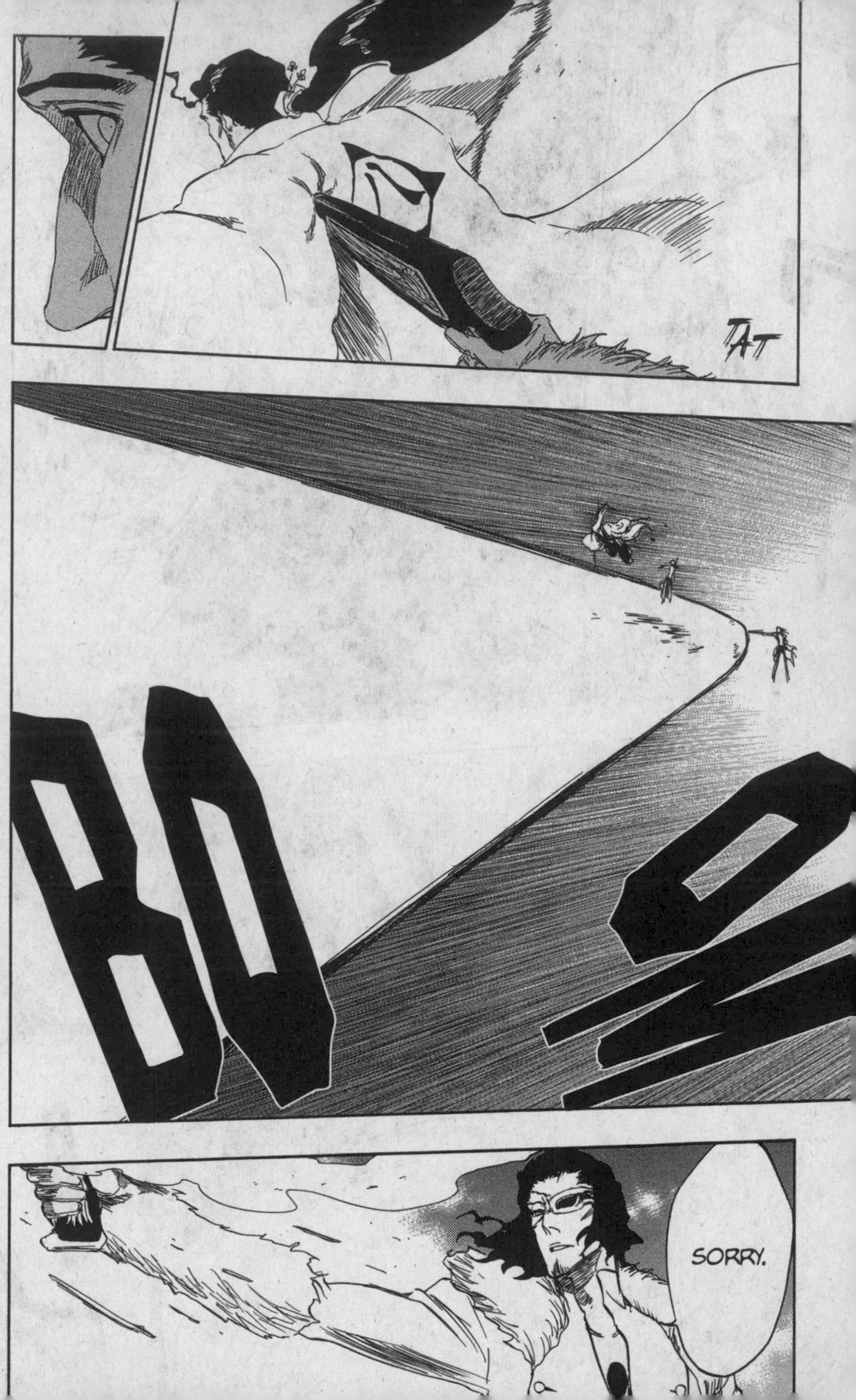
TAT
BOOM
SORRY.

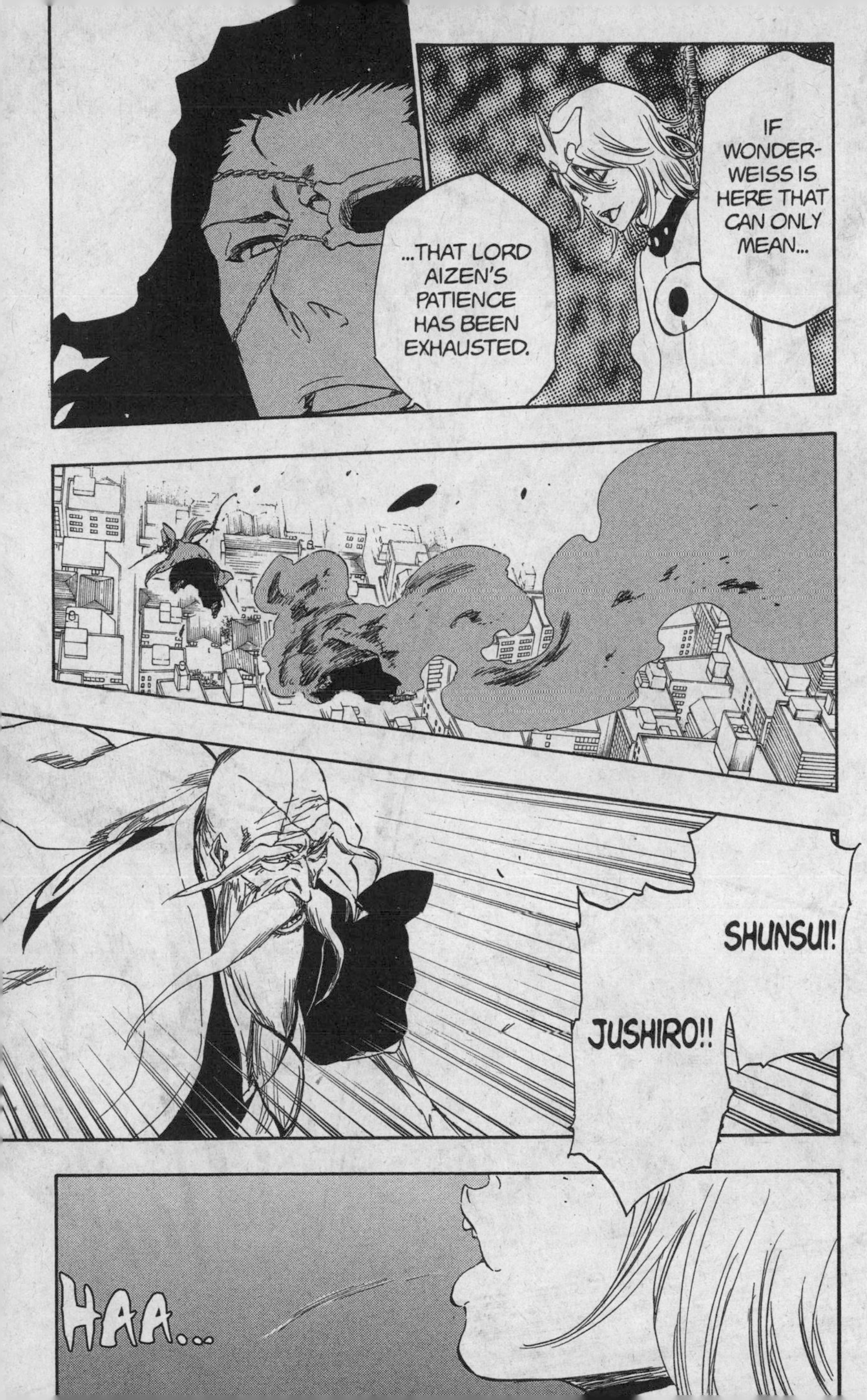
IF WONDER-WEISS IS HERE THAT CAN ONLY MEAN...
...THAT LORD AIZEN'S PATIENCE HAS BEEN EXHAUSTED.
SHUNSUI!
JUSHIRO!!
HAA...

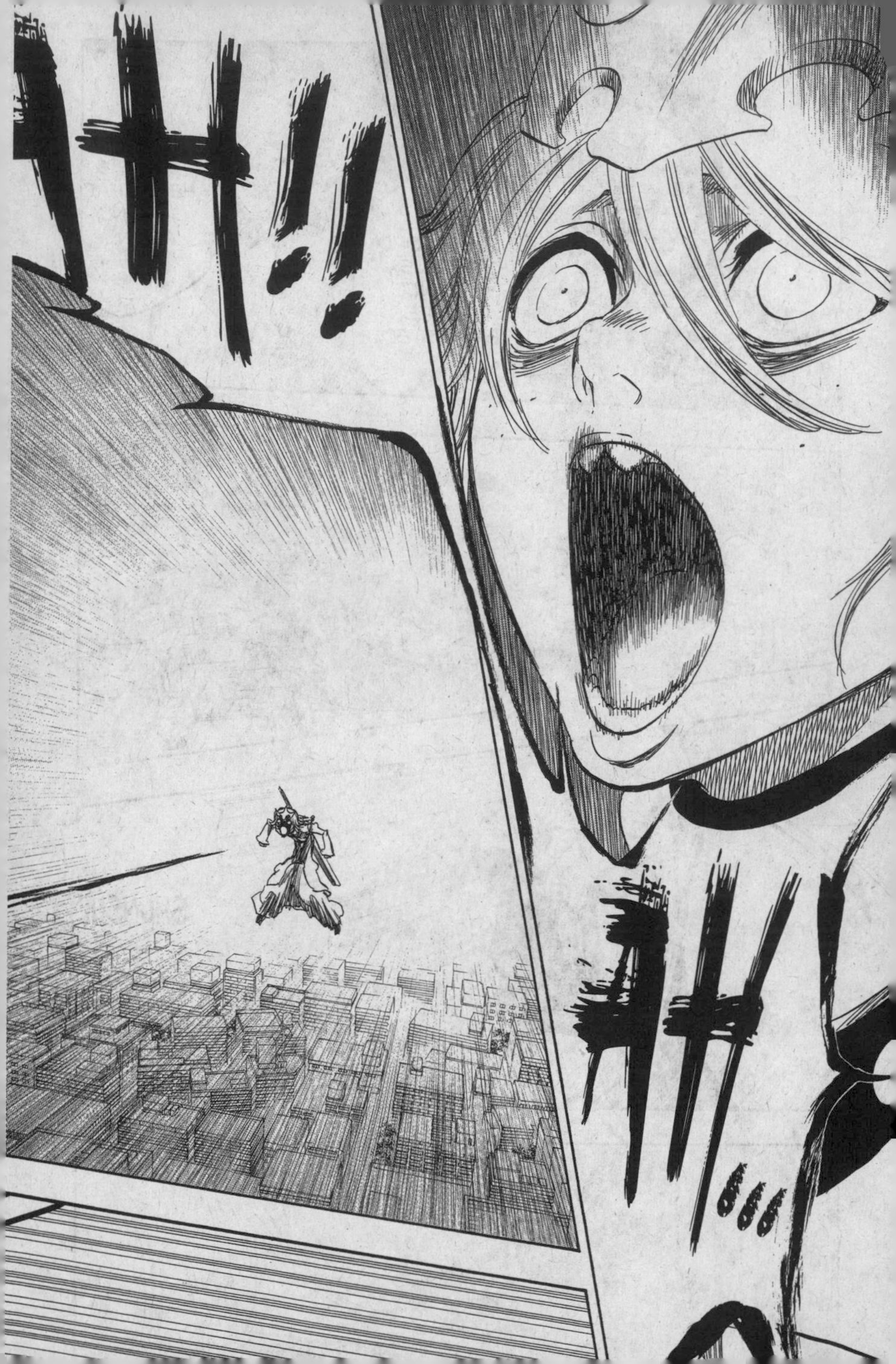
AH!!
AH

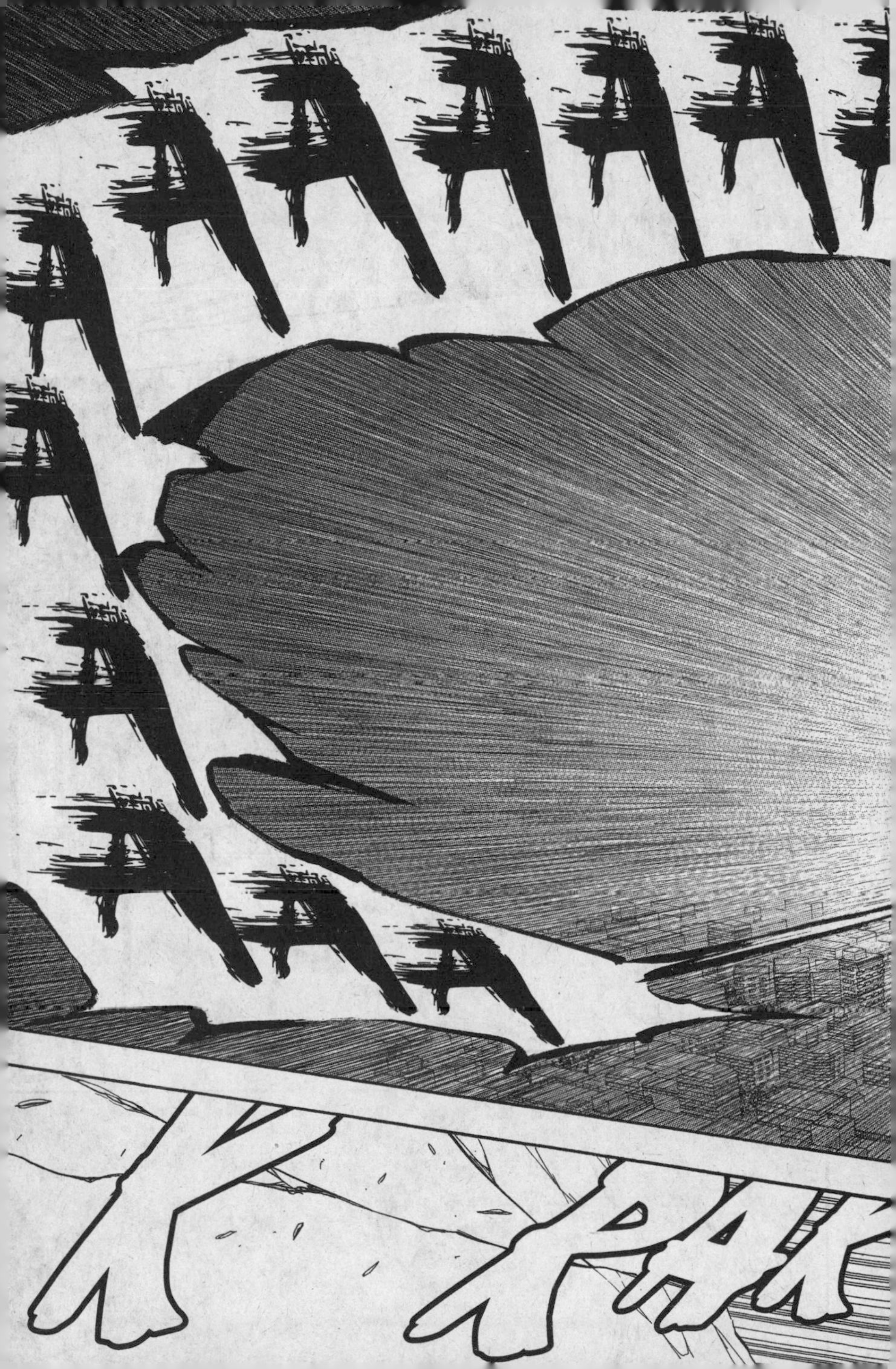
AAAAAAAAAAAA
PAK

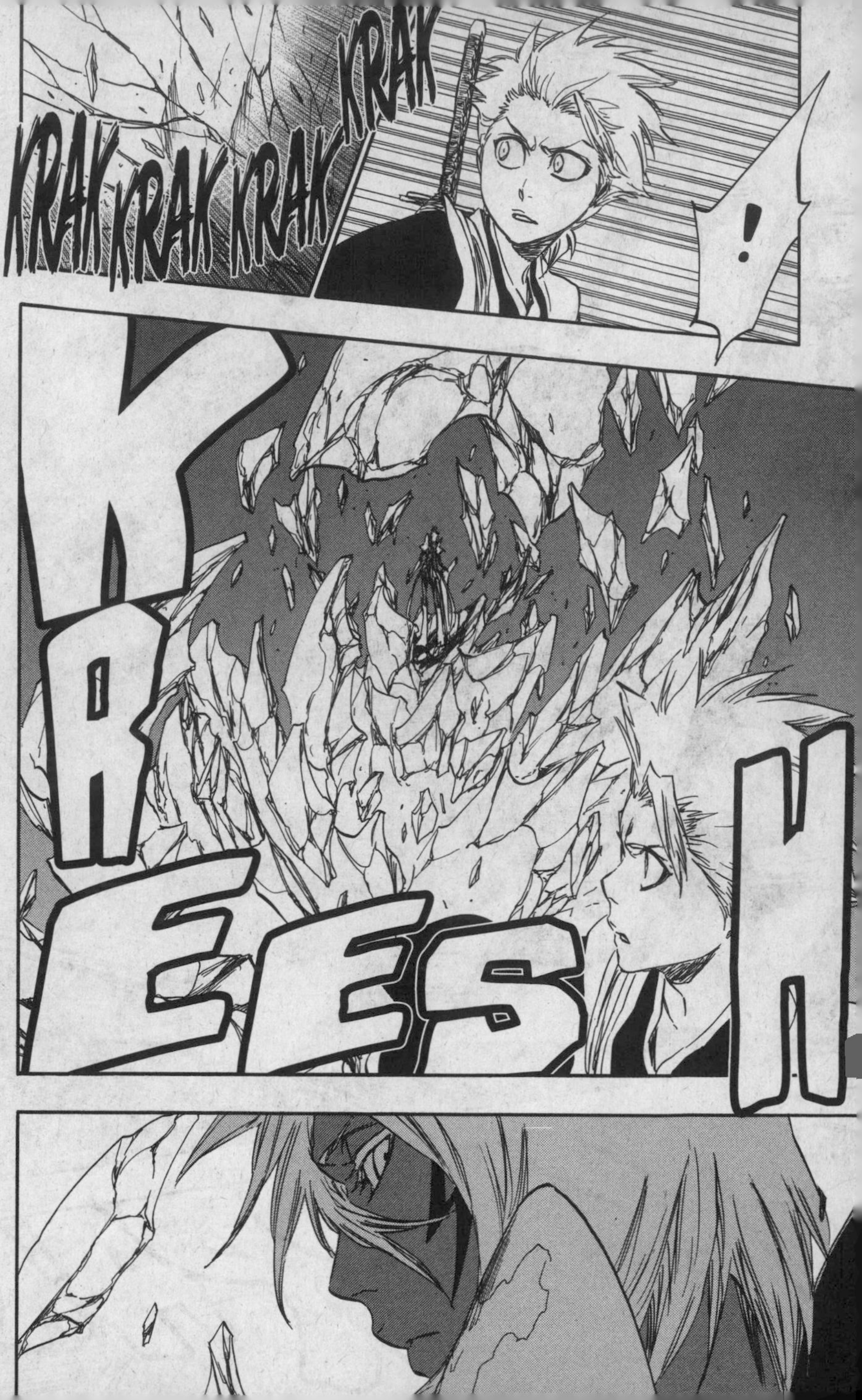
KRAK KRAK KRAK KRAK
!
KREESH

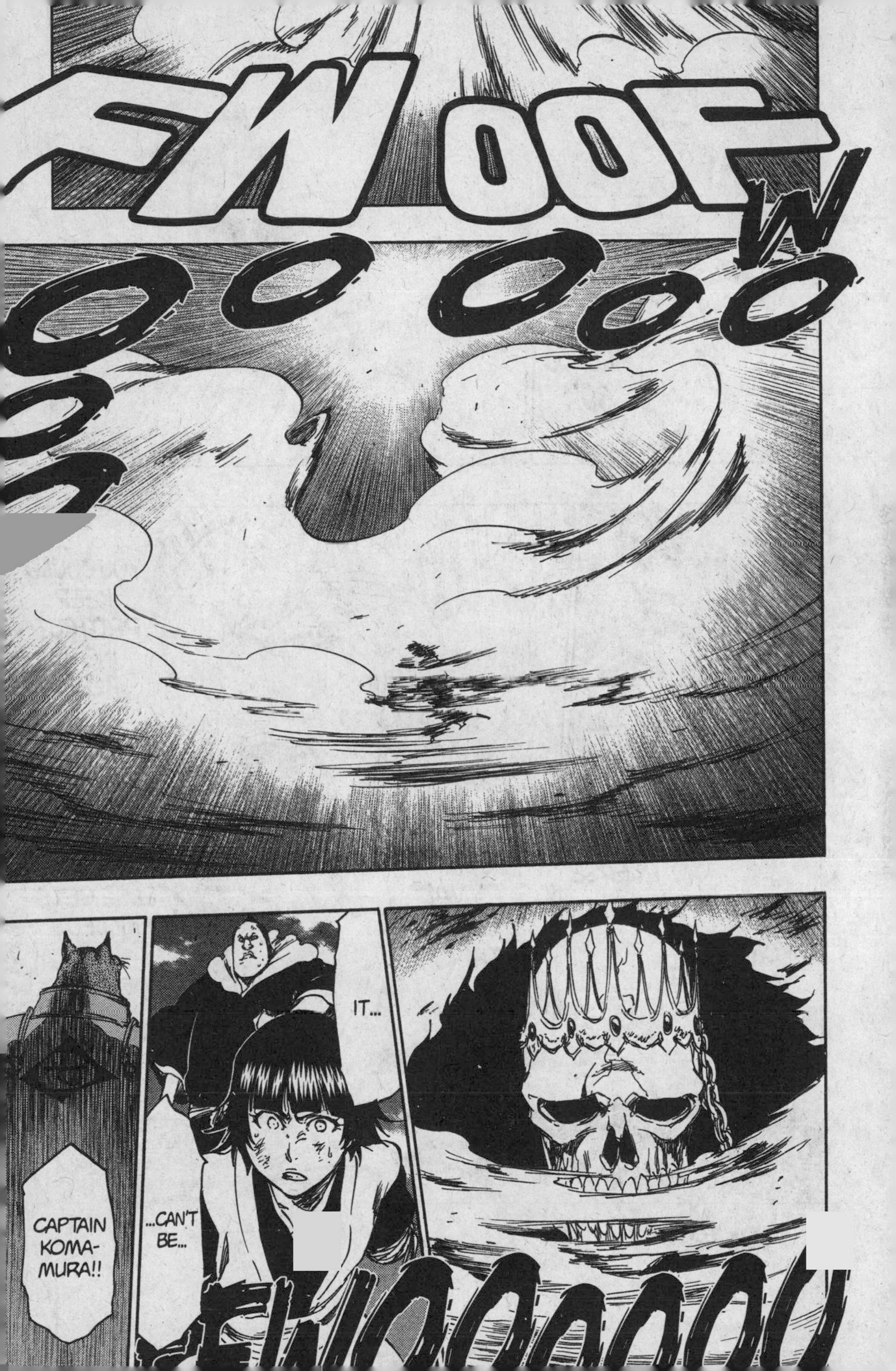
IT...
...CAN'T BE...
CAPTAIN KOMAMURA!!

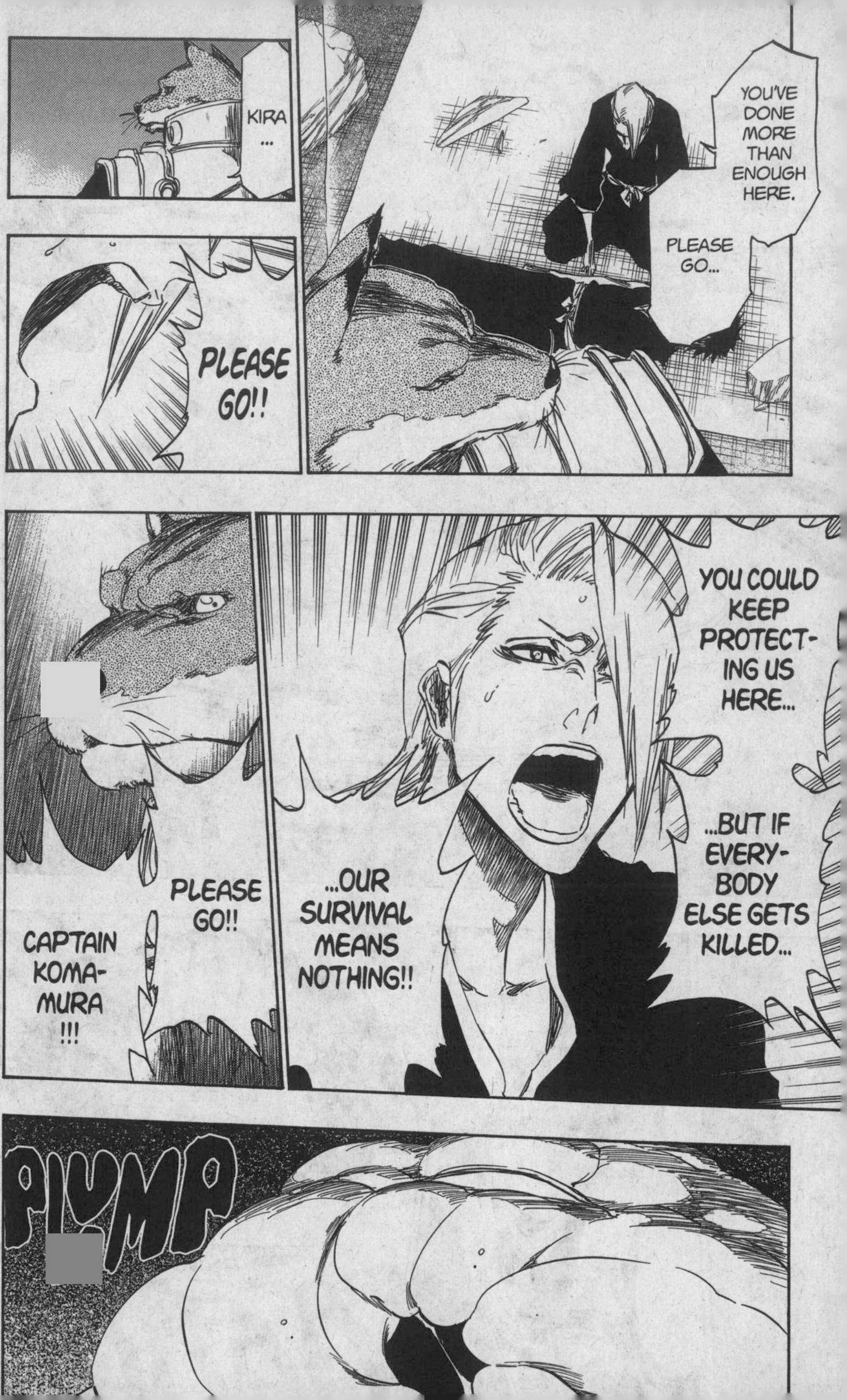
YOU'VE DONE MORE THAN ENOUGH HERE.
PLEASE GO...
KIRA ...
PLEASE GO!!
YOU COULD KEEP PROTECTING US HERE...
...BUT IF EVERYBODY ELSE GETS KILLED...
...OUR SURVIVAL MEANS NOTHING!!
PLEASE GO!!
CAPTAIN KOMAMURA!!!
PLUMP

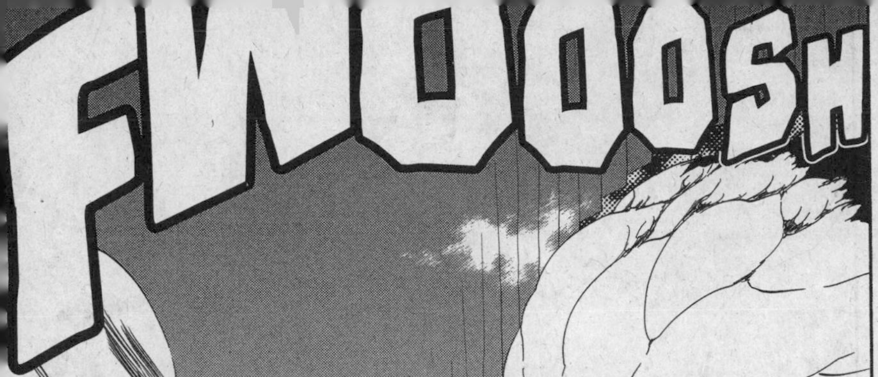
FWOOOSH

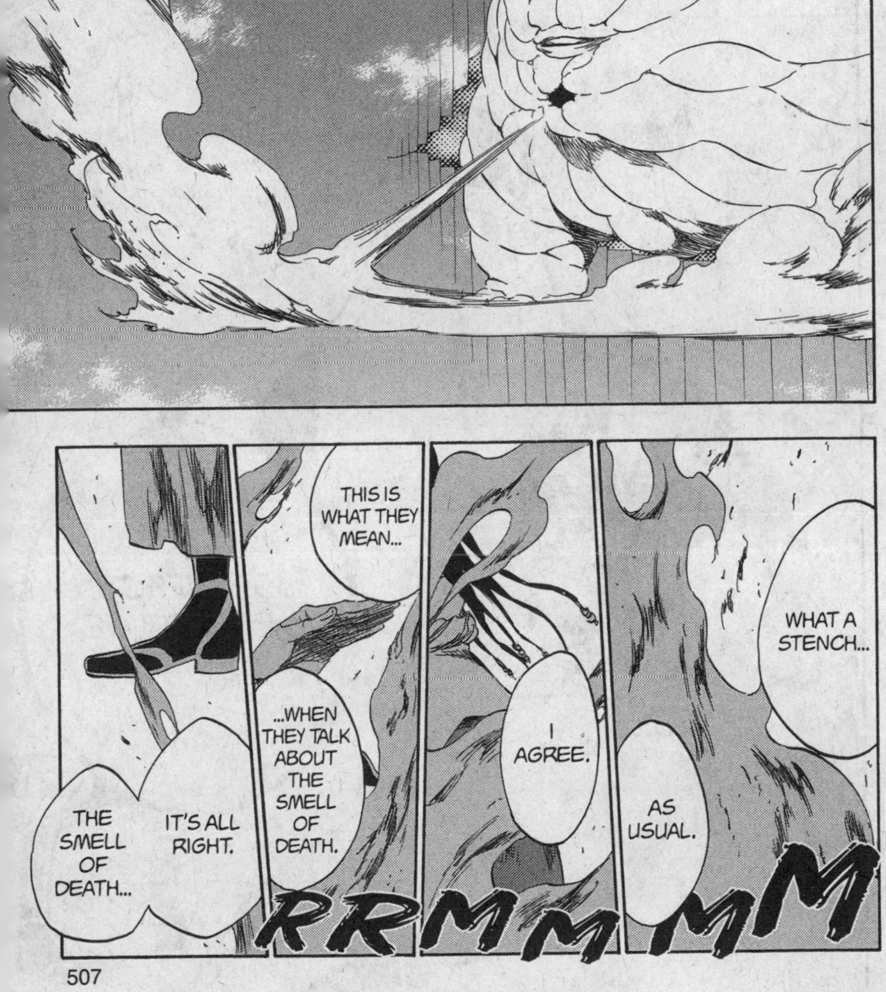
WHAT A STENCH...
AS USUAL.
I AGREE.
THIS IS WHAT THEY MEAN...
...WHEN THEY TALK ABOUT THE SMELL OF DEATH.
IT'S ALL RIGHT.
THE SMELL OF DEATH...
RRMMMMM

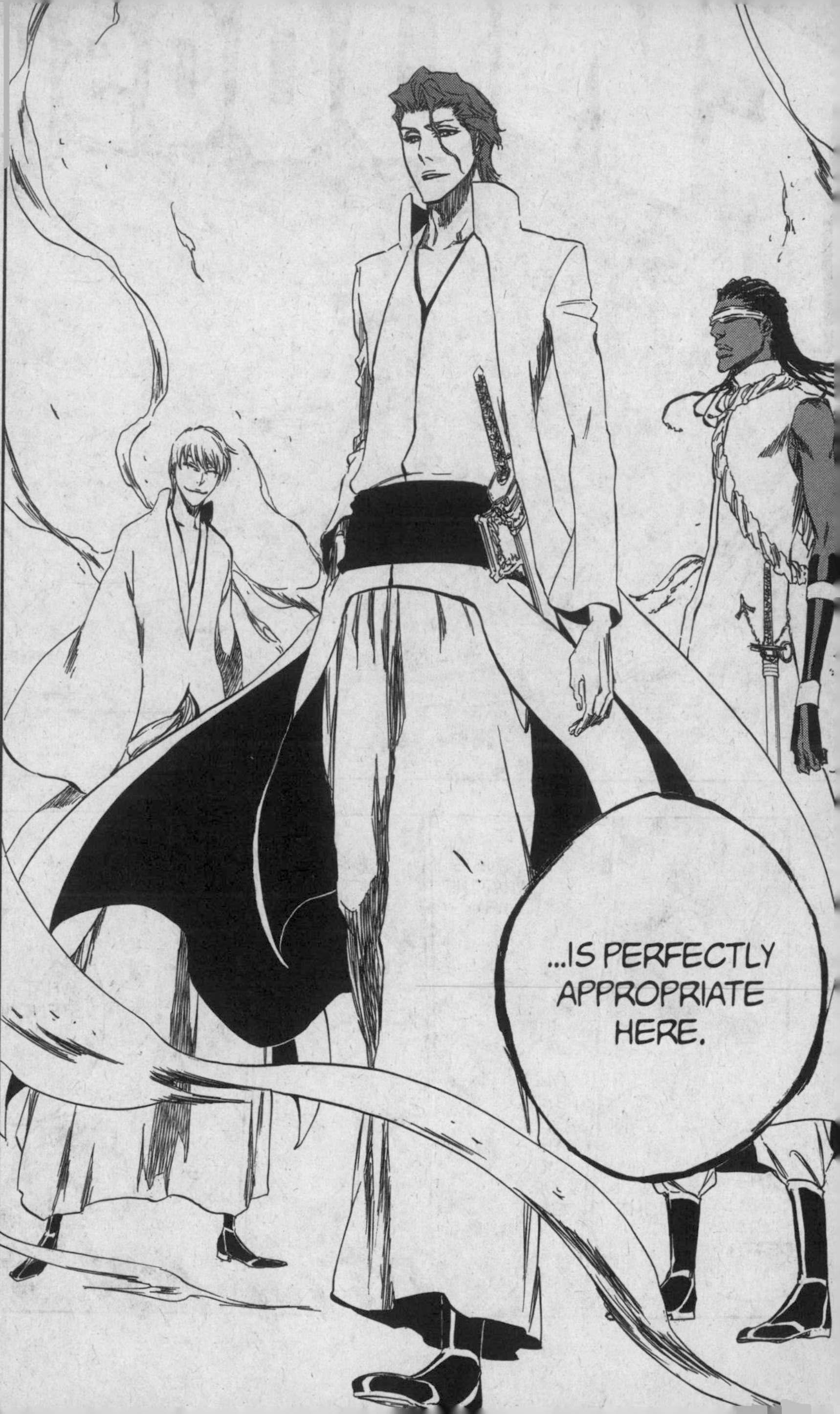
...IS PERFECTLY APPROPRIATE HERE.

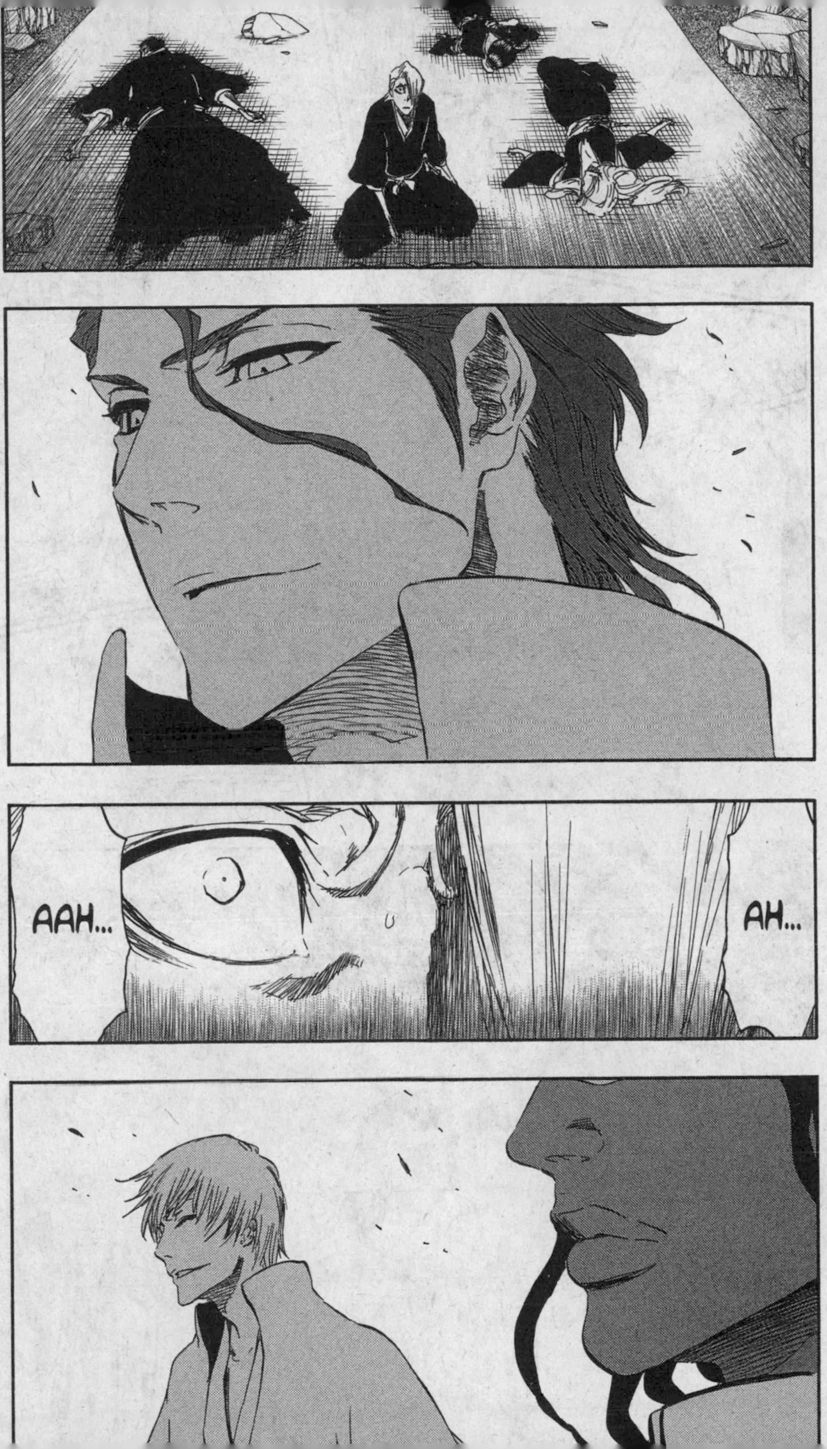
AH...
AAH...

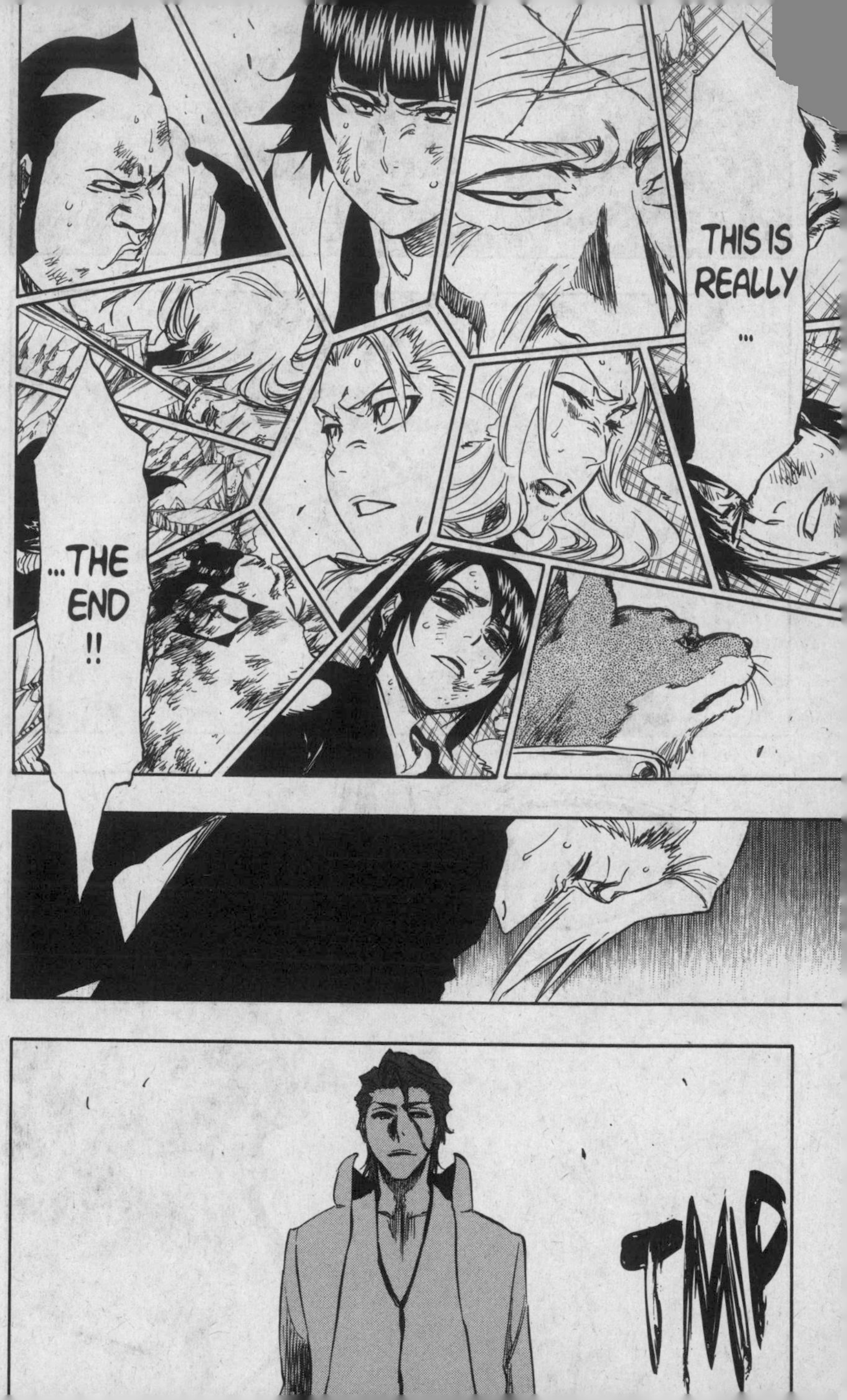
THIS IS REALLY ...
...THE END !!
TMP

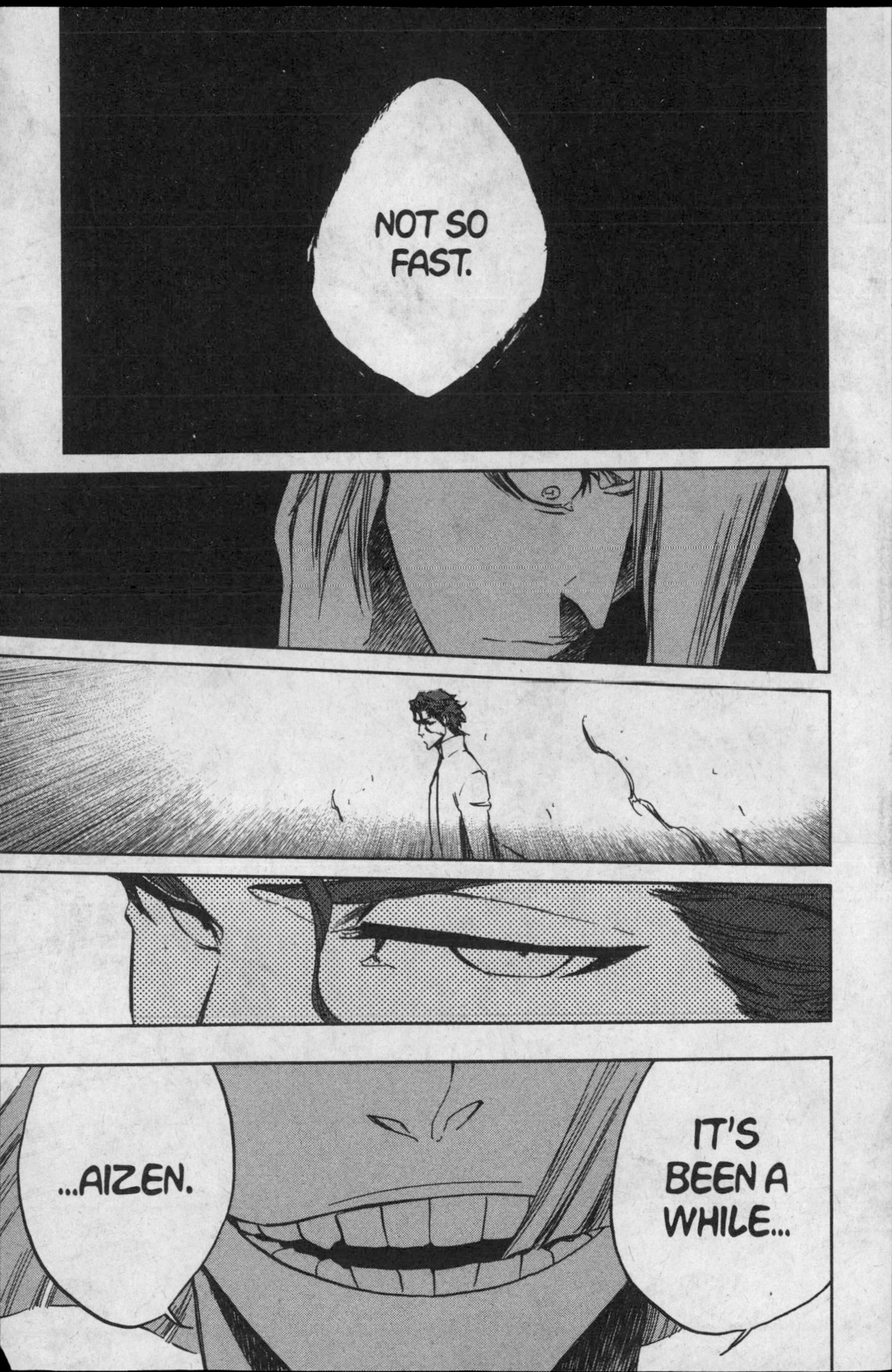
NOT SO FAST.
IT'S BEEN A WHILE...
...AIZEN.

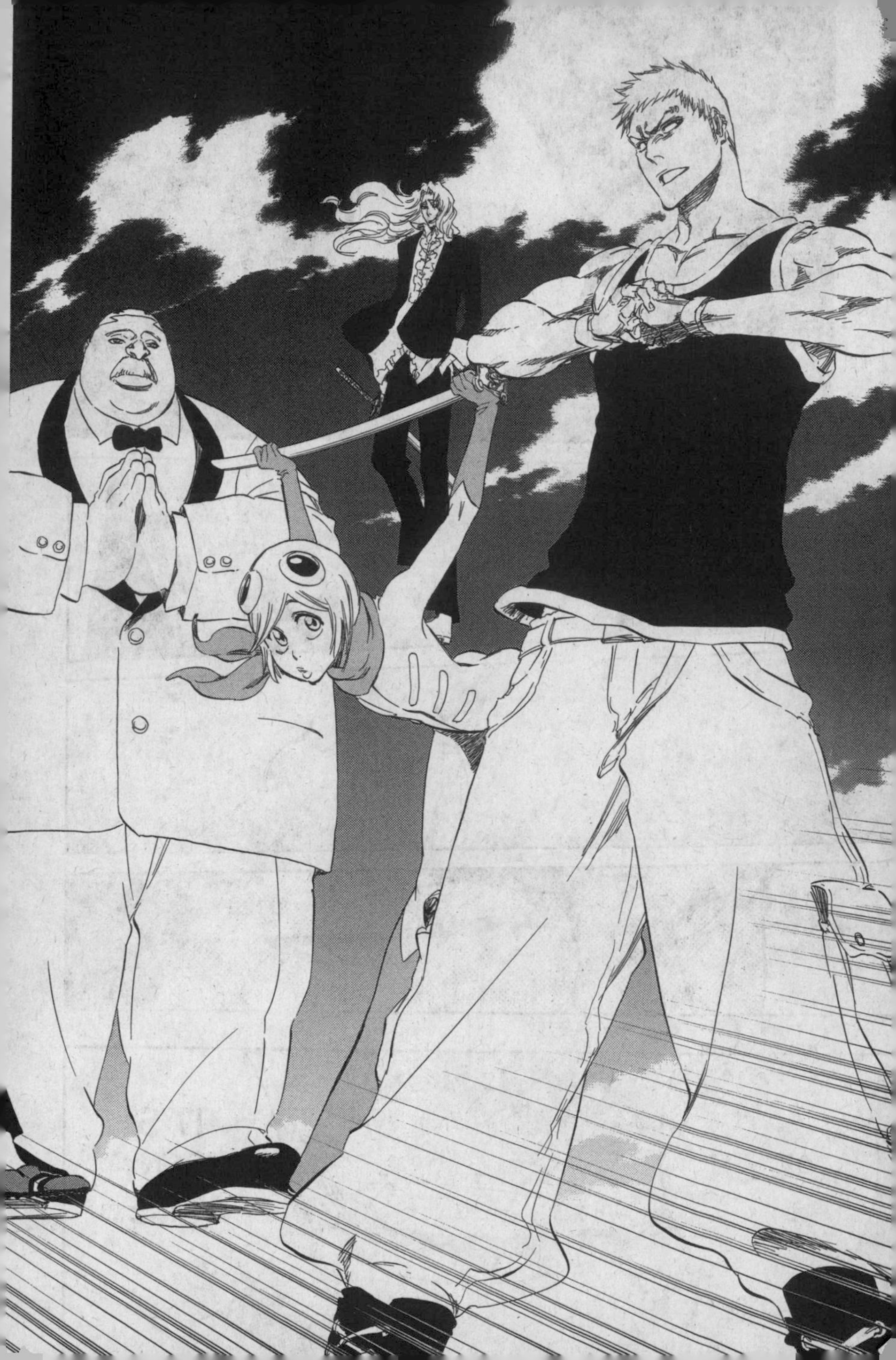

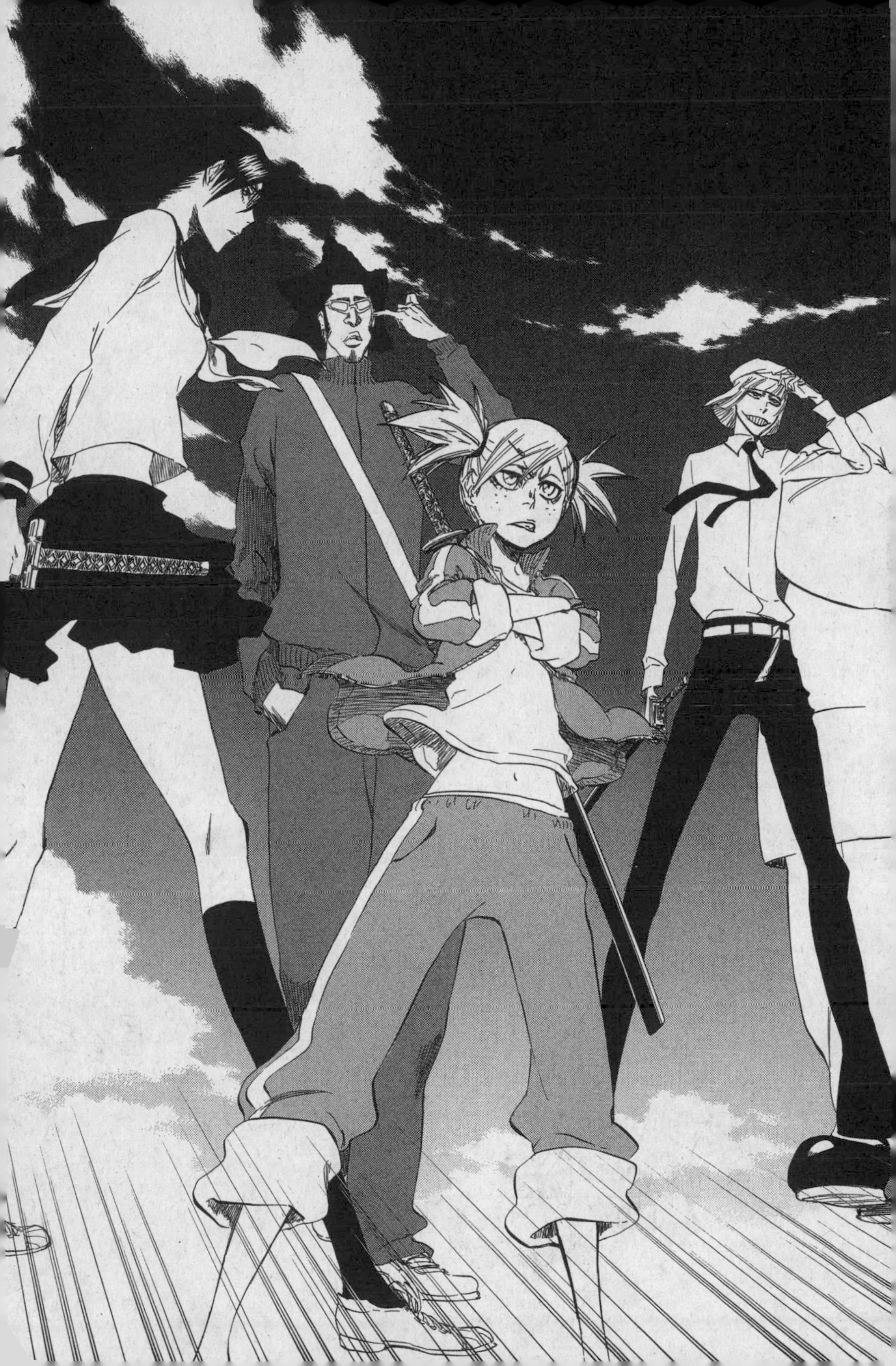

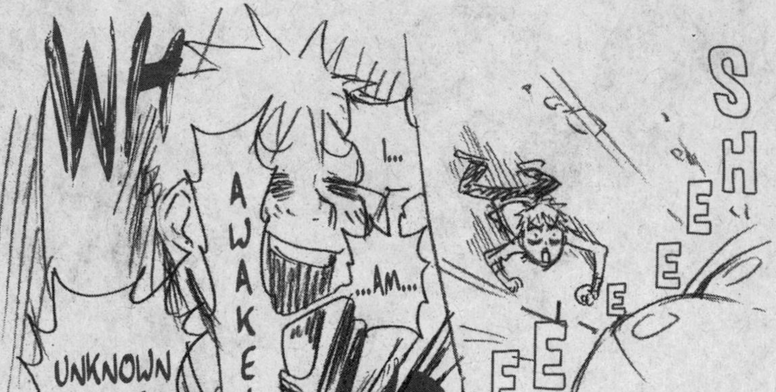
SHEEEEEN
I...
...AM...
AWAKE!
WHUP
UNKNOWN BOOB LADY!!

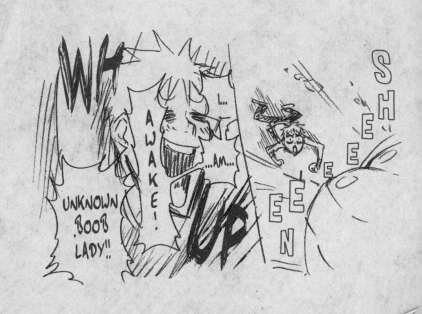

365. Whose Side Are We On

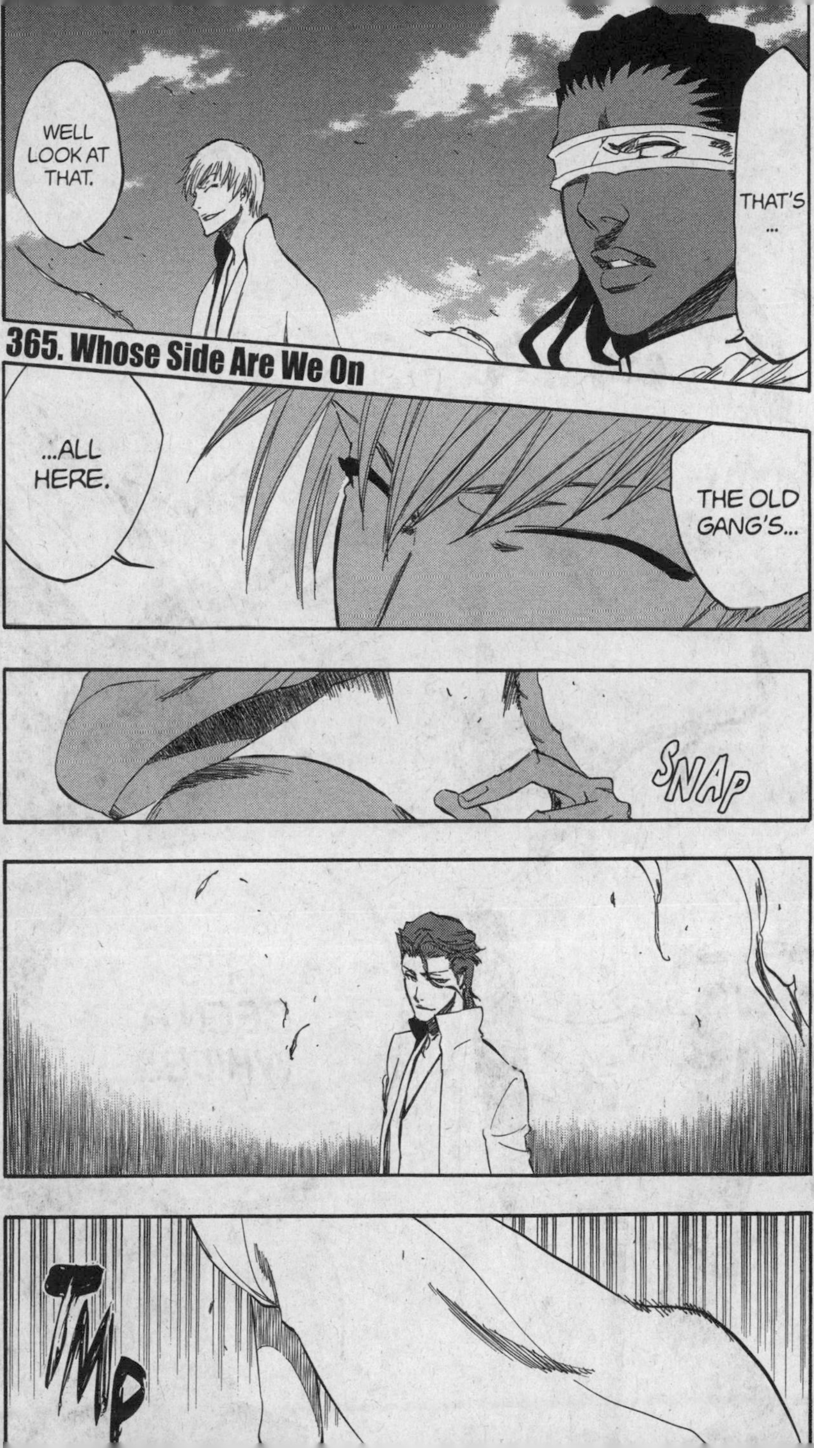
THAT'S ...
WELL LOOK AT THAT.
THE OLD GANG'S...
...ALL HERE.
SNAP
TMP

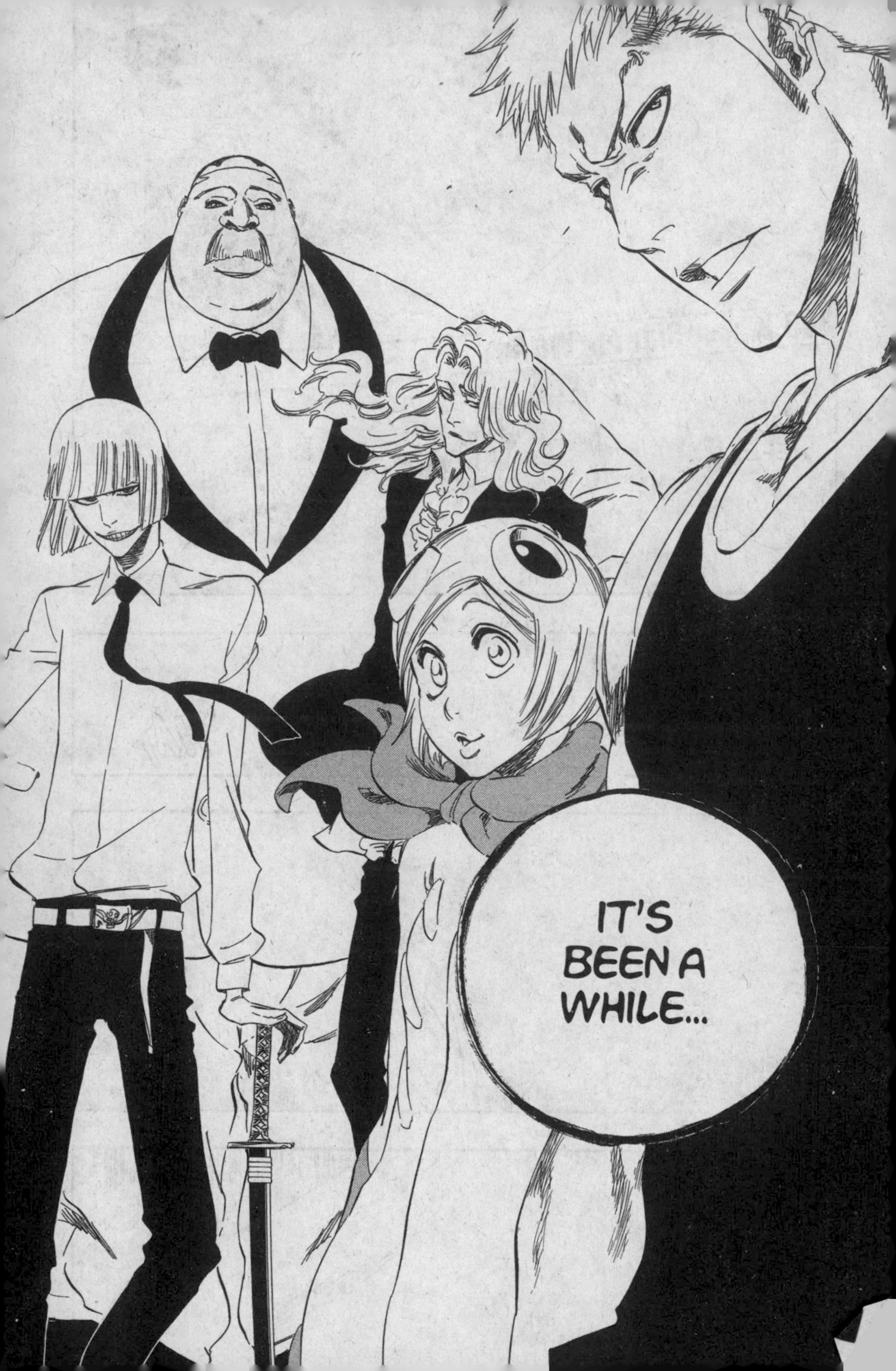
IT'S BEEN A WHILE...

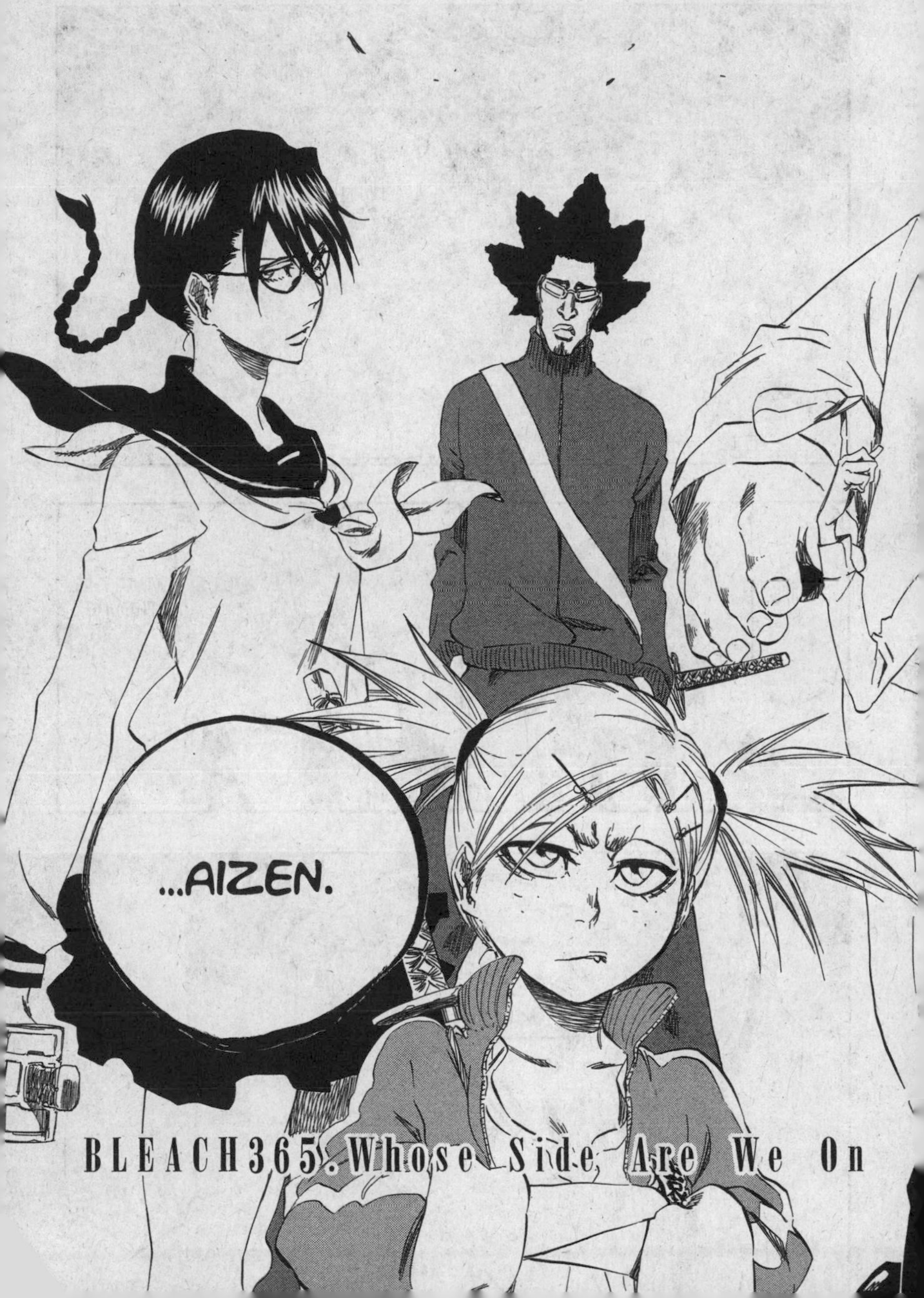
...AIZEN.
BLEACH365. Whose Side Are We On

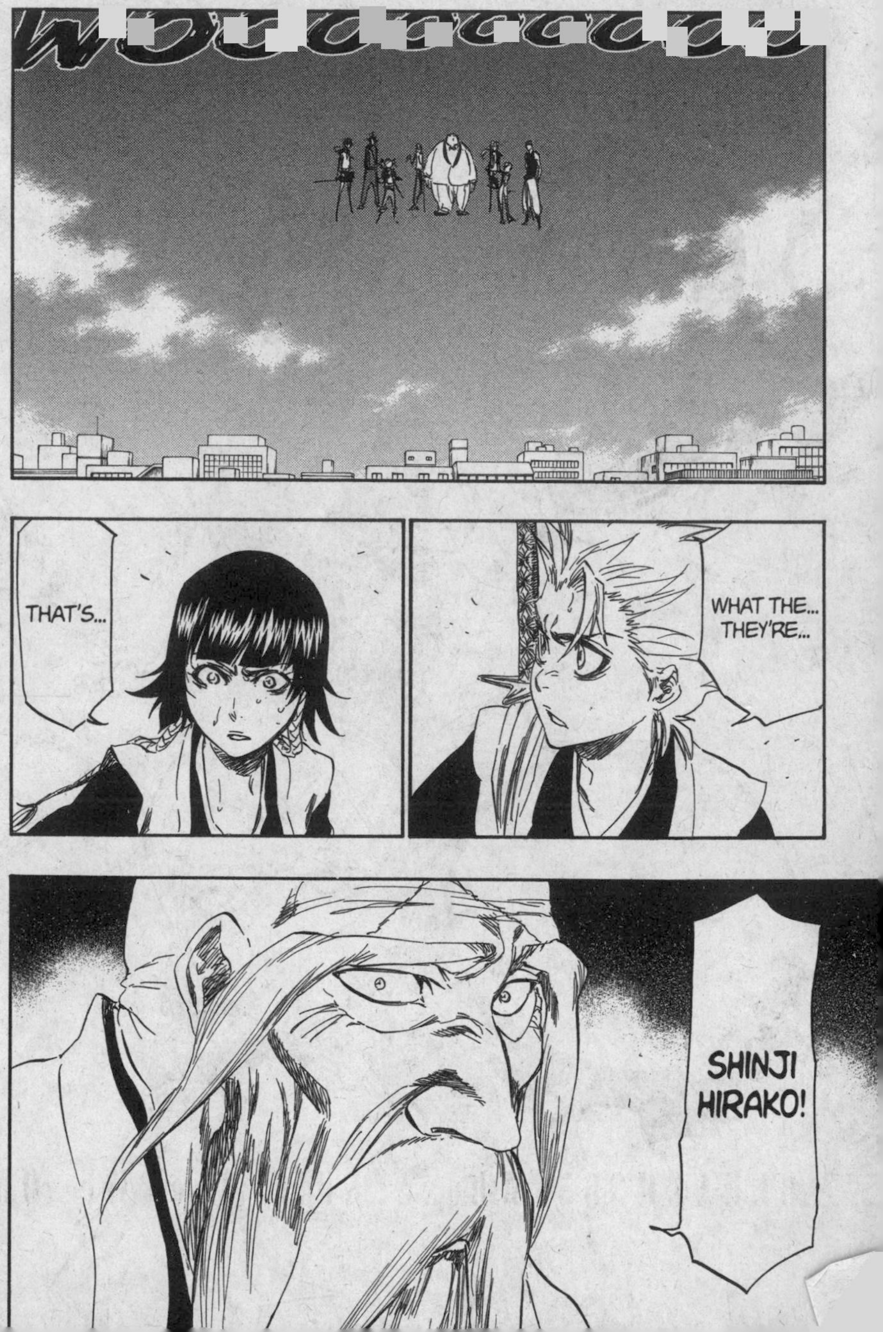
WHAT THE... THEY'RE...
THAT'S...
SHINJI HIRAKO!

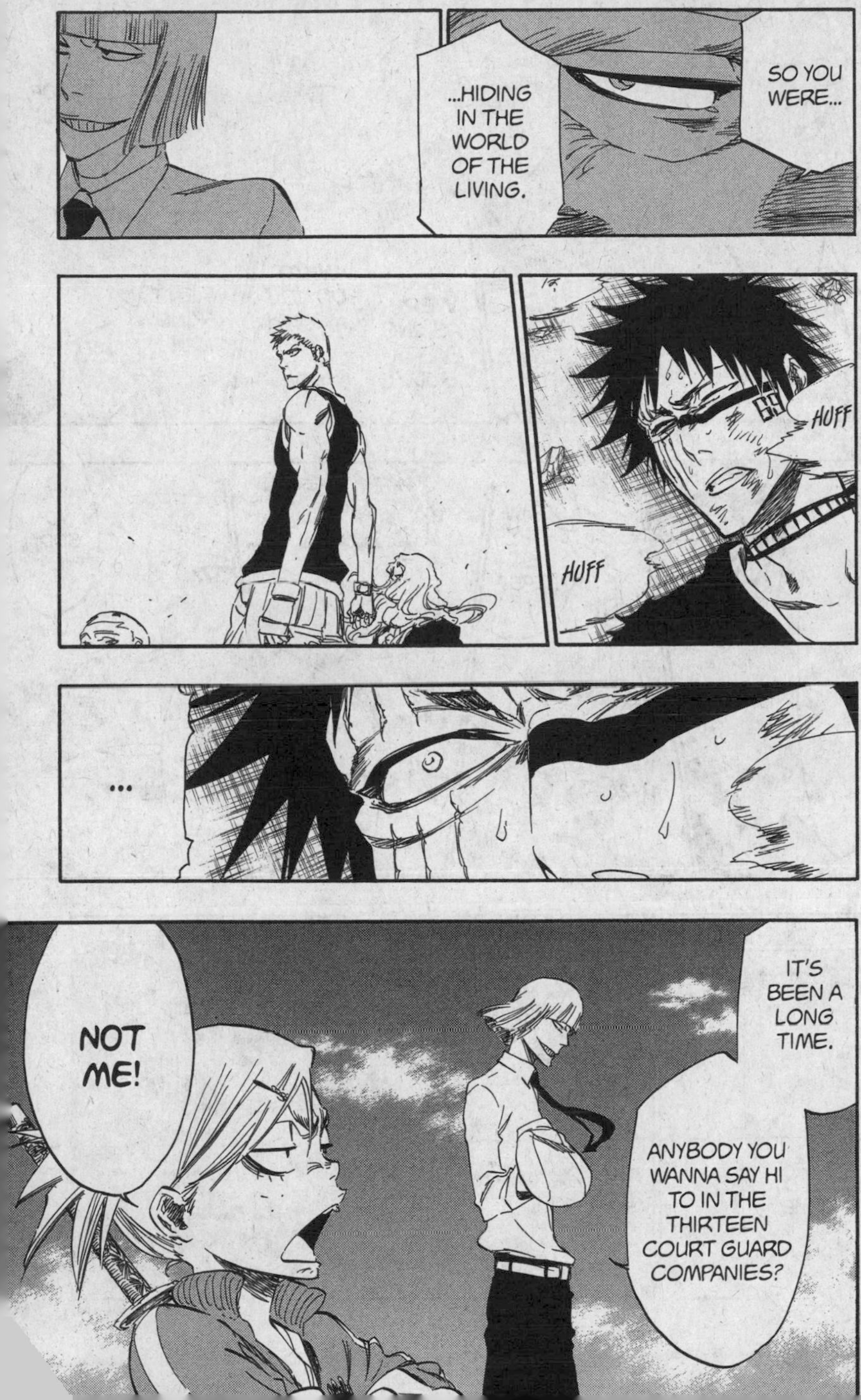
SO YOU WERE...
...HIDING IN THE WORLD OF THE LIVING.
HUFF
HUFF
...
IT'S BEEN A LONG TIME.
ANYBODY YOU WANNA SAY HI TO IN THE THIRTEEN COURT GUARD COMPANIES?
NOT ME!

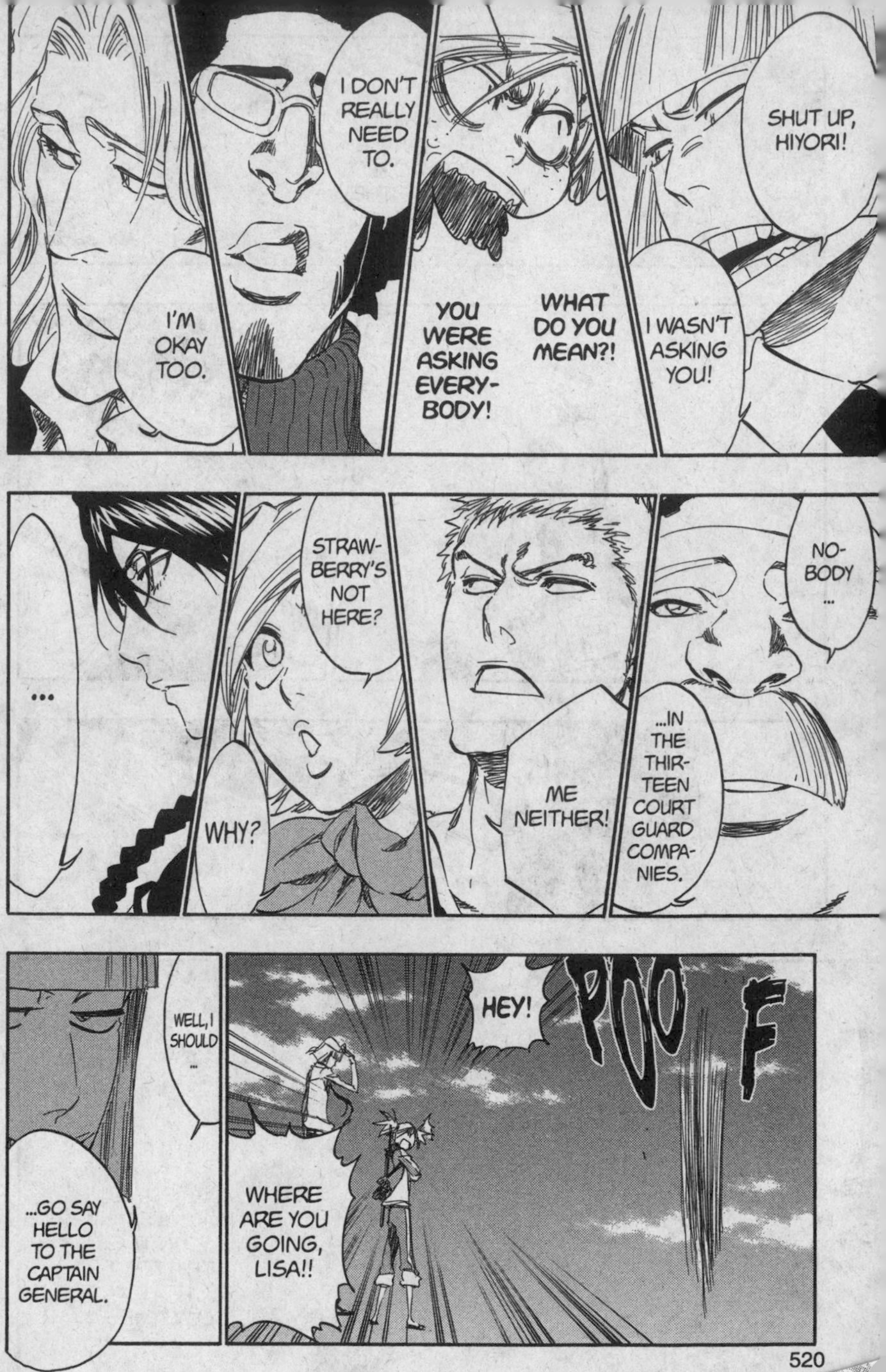
SHUT UP, HIYORI!
I WASN'T ASKING YOU!
WHAT DO YOU MEAN?!
YOU WERE ASKING EVERY-BODY!
I DON'T REALLY NEED TO.
I'M OKAY TOO.
NO-BODY ...
...IN THE THIR-TEEN COURT GUARD COMPA-NIES.
ME NEITHER!
STRAW-BERRY'S NOT HERE?
WHY?
...
POOF
HEY!
WHERE ARE YOU GOING, LISA!!
WELL, I SHOULD ...
...GO SAY HELLO TO THE CAPTAIN GENERAL.

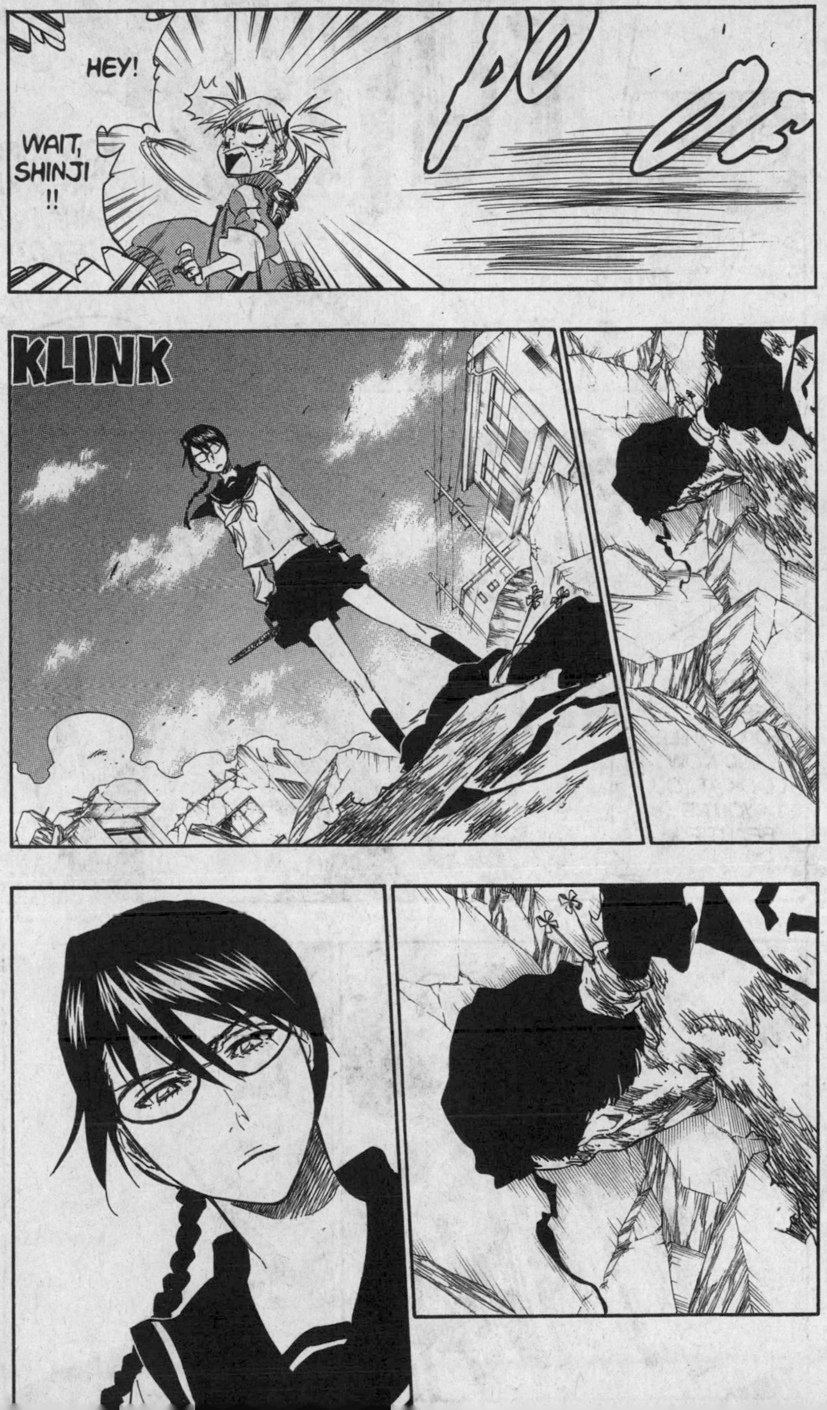
DOOF
HEY!
WAIT, SHINJI !!
KLINK

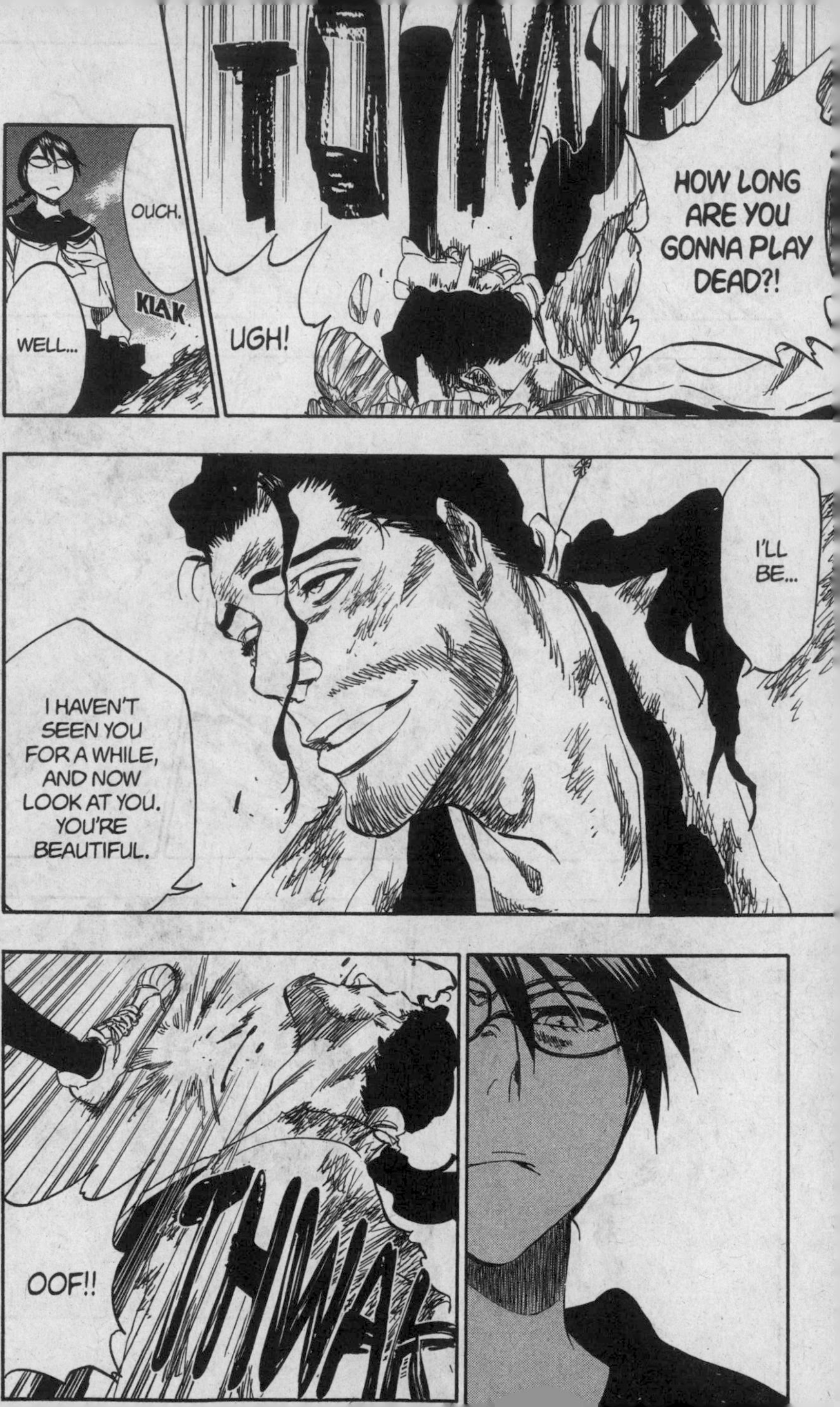
HOW LONG ARE YOU GONNA PLAY DEAD?!
UGH!
OUCH.
KLAK
WELL...
I'LL BE...
I HAVEN'T SEEN YOU FOR A WHILE, AND NOW LOOK AT YOU. YOU'RE BEAUTIFUL.
OOF!!

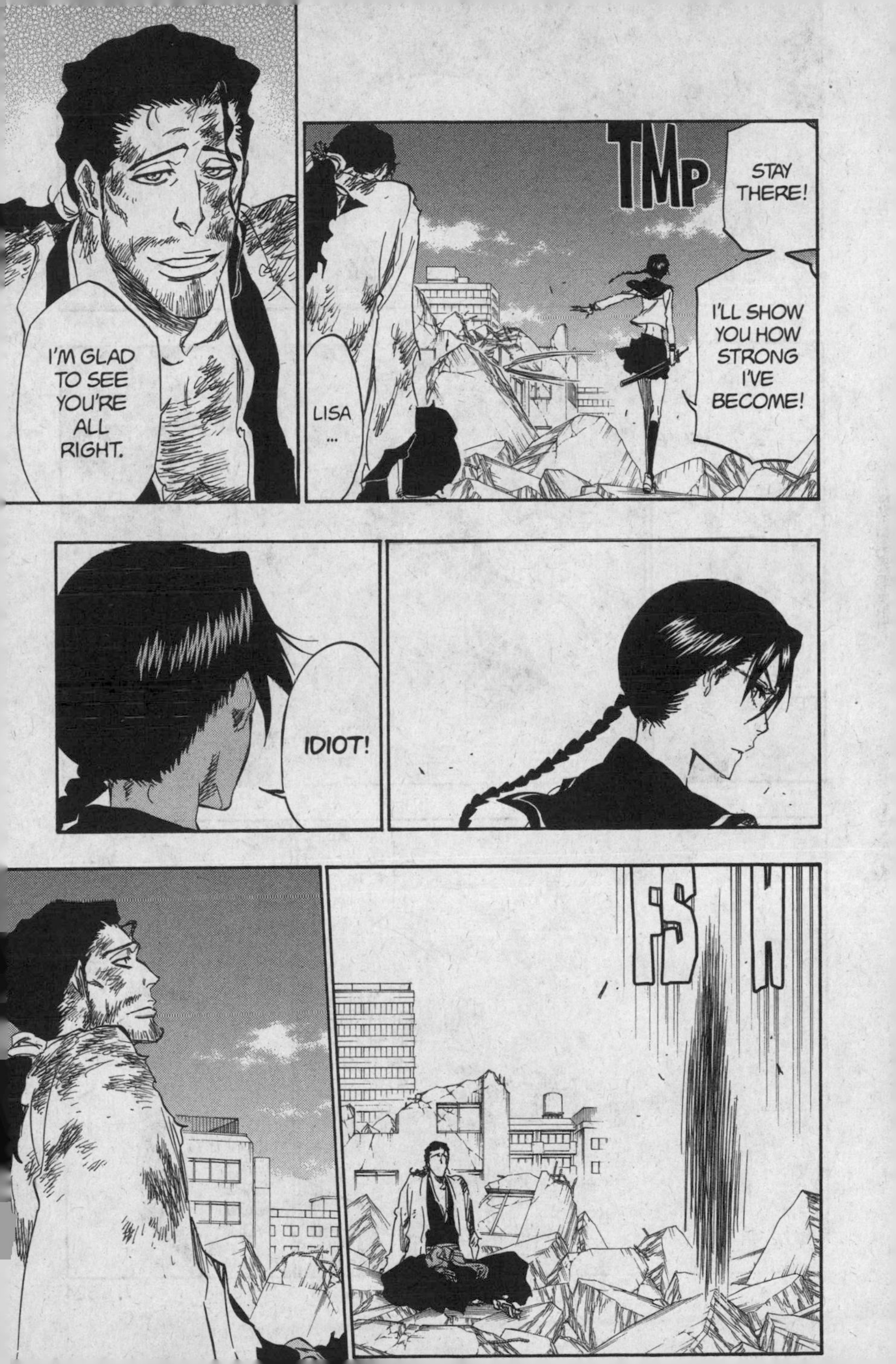
TMP
STAY THERE!
I'LL SHOW YOU HOW STRONG I'VE BECOME!
LISA ...
I'M GLAD TO SEE YOU'RE ALL RIGHT.
IDIOT!

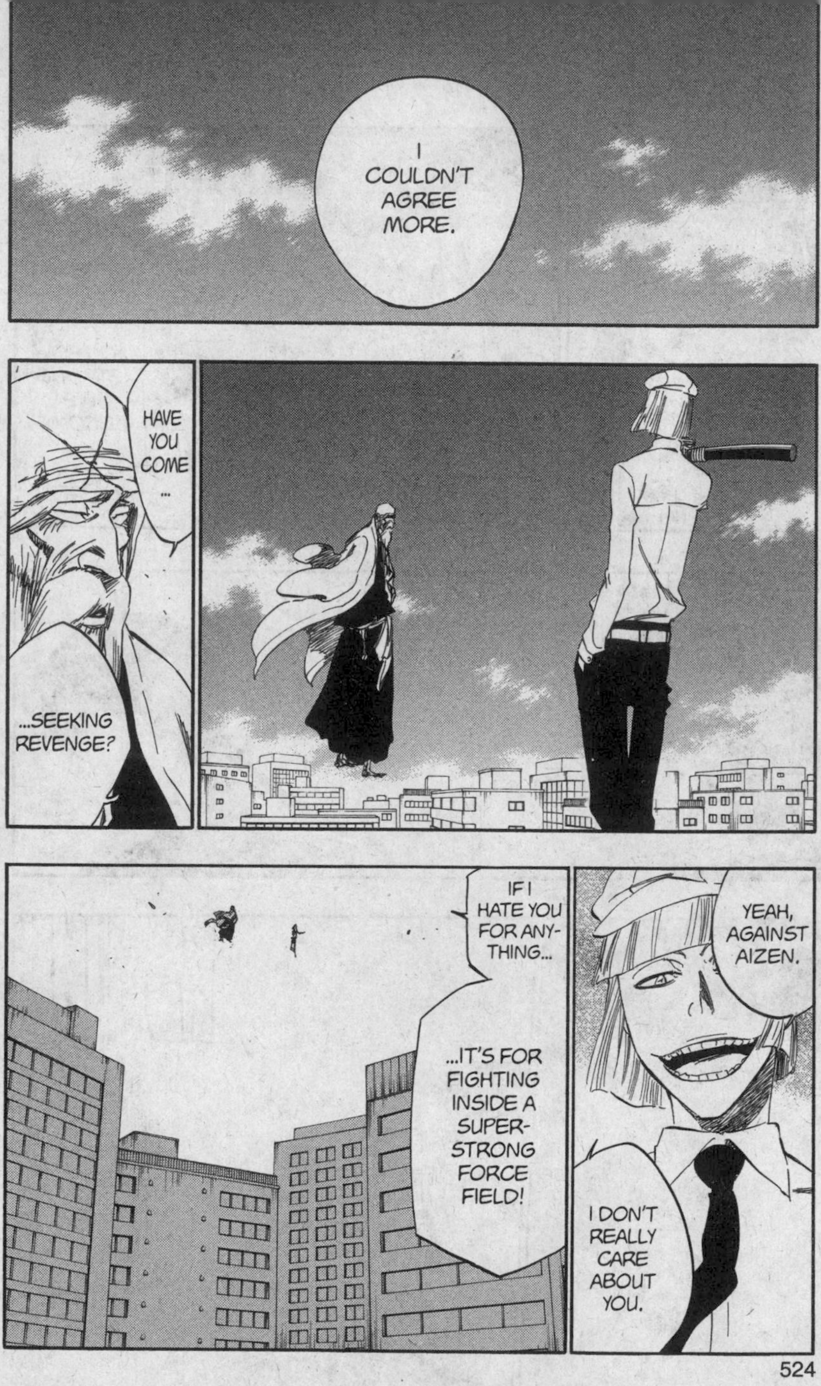
I COULDN'T AGREE MORE.
HAVE YOU COME ...
...SEEKING REVENGE?
YEAH, AGAINST AIZEN.
I DON'T REALLY CARE ABOUT YOU.
IF I HATE YOU FOR ANY-THING...
...IT'S FOR FIGHTING INSIDE A SUPER-STRONG FORCE FIELD!

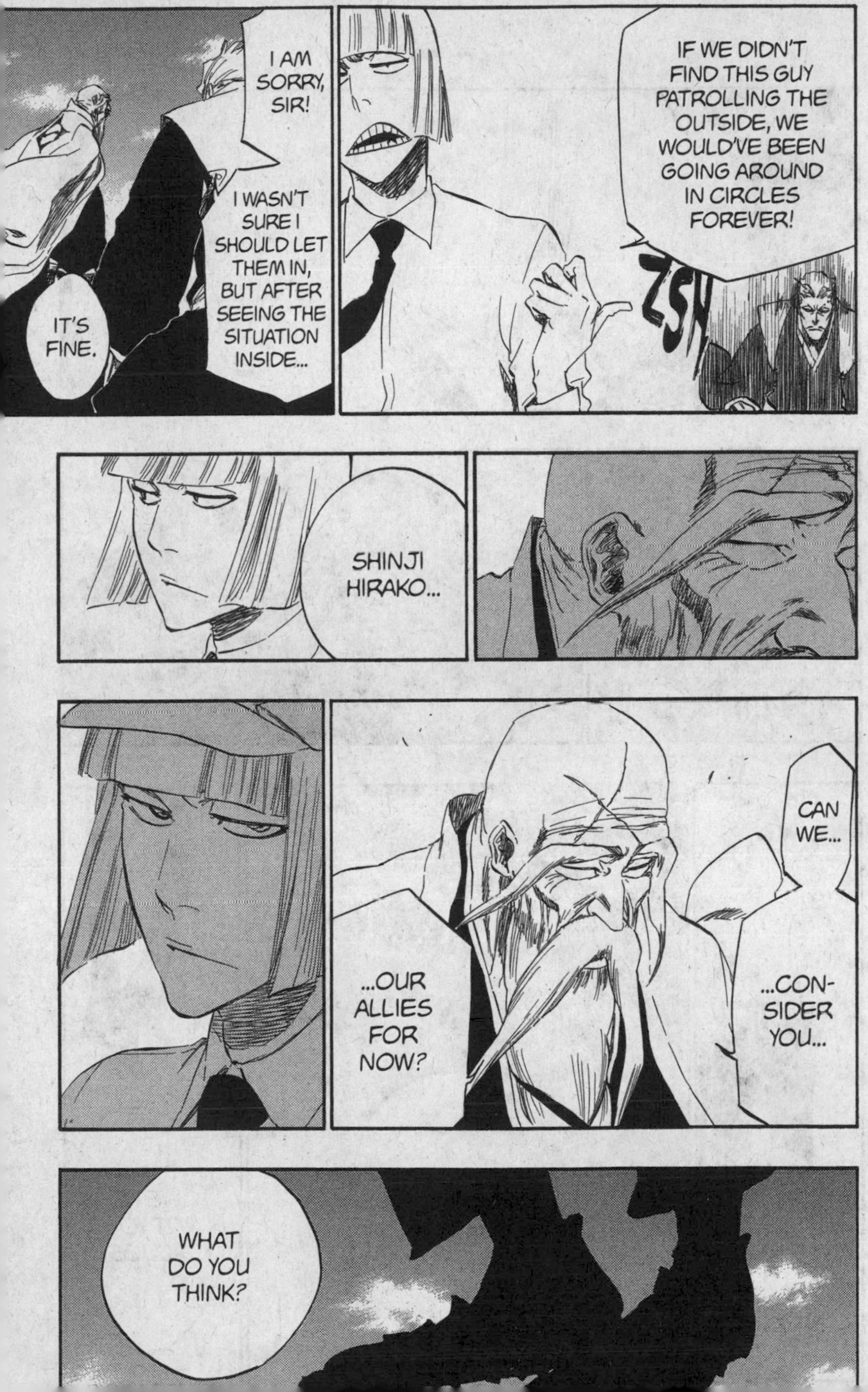
IF WE DIDN'T FIND THIS GUY PATROLLING THE OUTSIDE, WE WOULD'VE BEEN GOING AROUND IN CIRCLES FOREVER!
ZSH
I AM SORRY, SIR!
I WASN'T SURE I SHOULD LET THEM IN, BUT AFTER SEEING THE SITUATION INSIDE...
IT'S FINE.
SHINJI HIRAKO...
CAN WE...
...CON- SIDER YOU...
...OUR ALLIES FOR NOW?
WHAT DO YOU THINK?

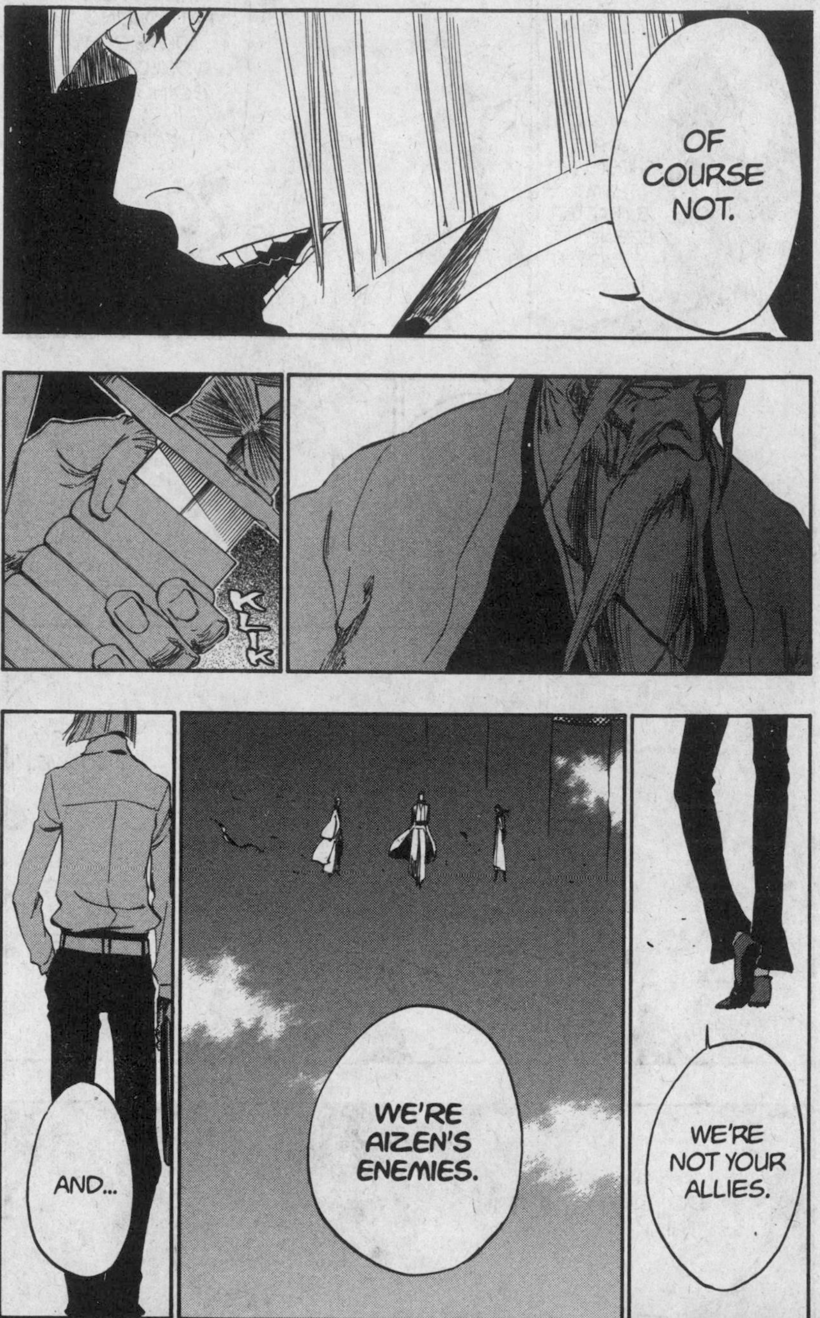
OF COURSE NOT.
KLIK
WE'RE NOT YOUR ALLIES.
WE'RE AIZEN'S ENEMIES.
AND...

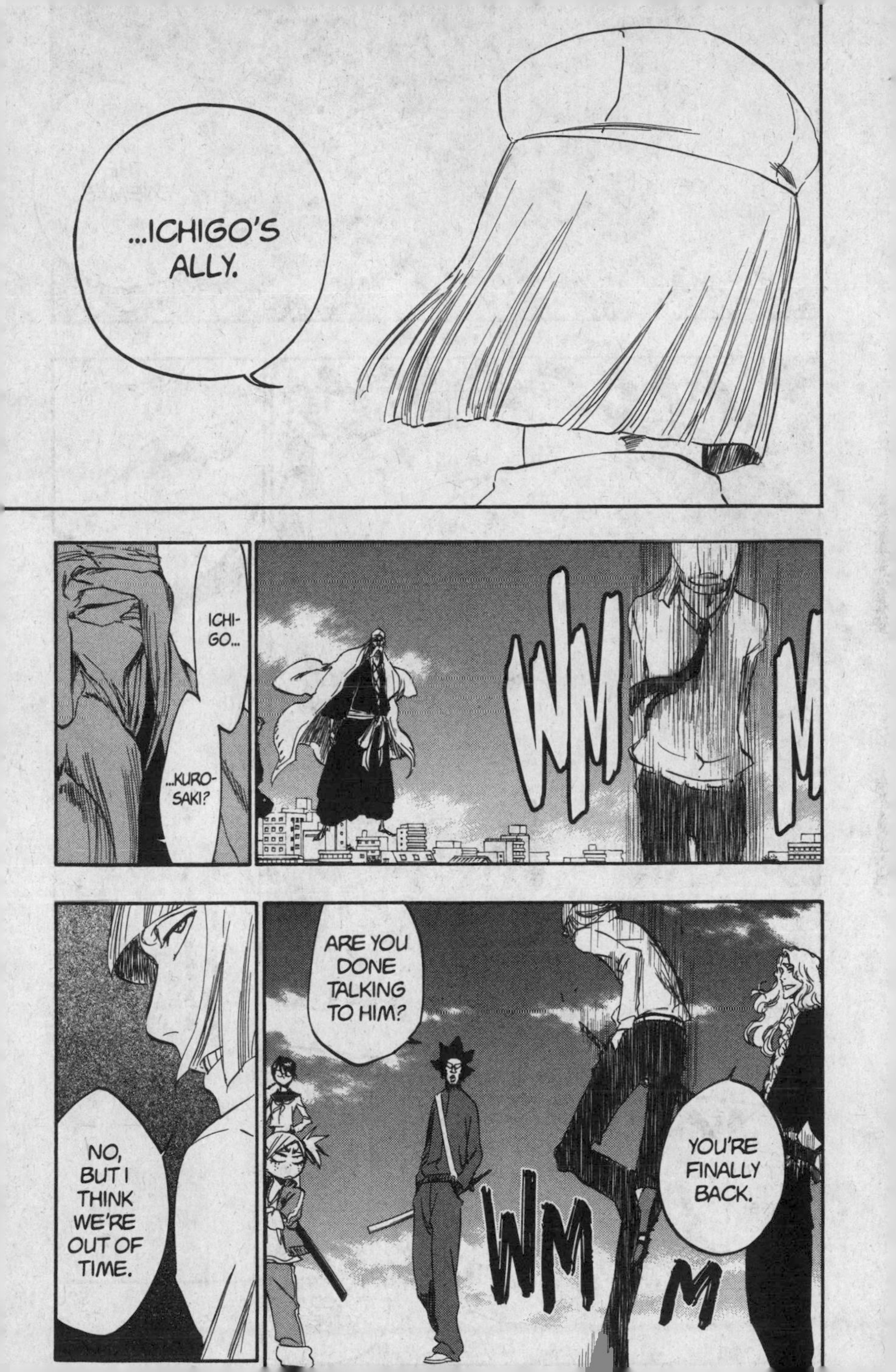
...ICHIGO'S ALLY.
WM
M
ICHI-GO...
...KURO-SAKI?
YOU'RE FINALLY BACK.
ARE YOU DONE TALKING TO HIM?
WM
M
NO, BUT I THINK WE'RE OUT OF TIME.

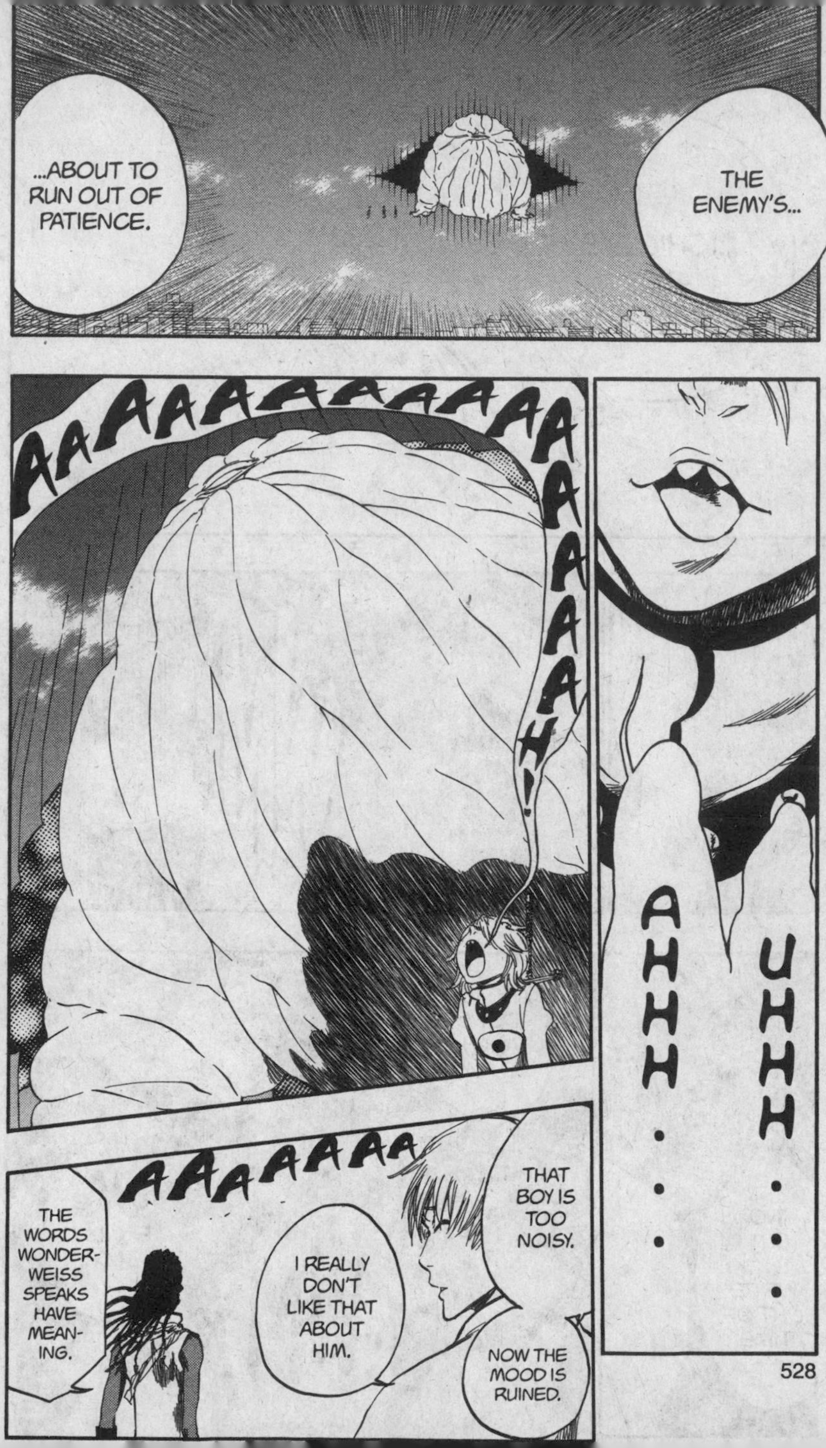
THE ENEMY'S...
...ABOUT TO RUN OUT OF PATIENCE.
UHHH...
AHHH...
AAAAAAAAAAAAAAAAAAAH!
AAAAAAAA
THAT BOY IS TOO NOISY.
NOW THE MOOD IS RUINED.
I REALLY DON'T LIKE THAT ABOUT HIM.
THE WORDS WONDER-WEISS SPEAKS HAVE MEAN-ING.

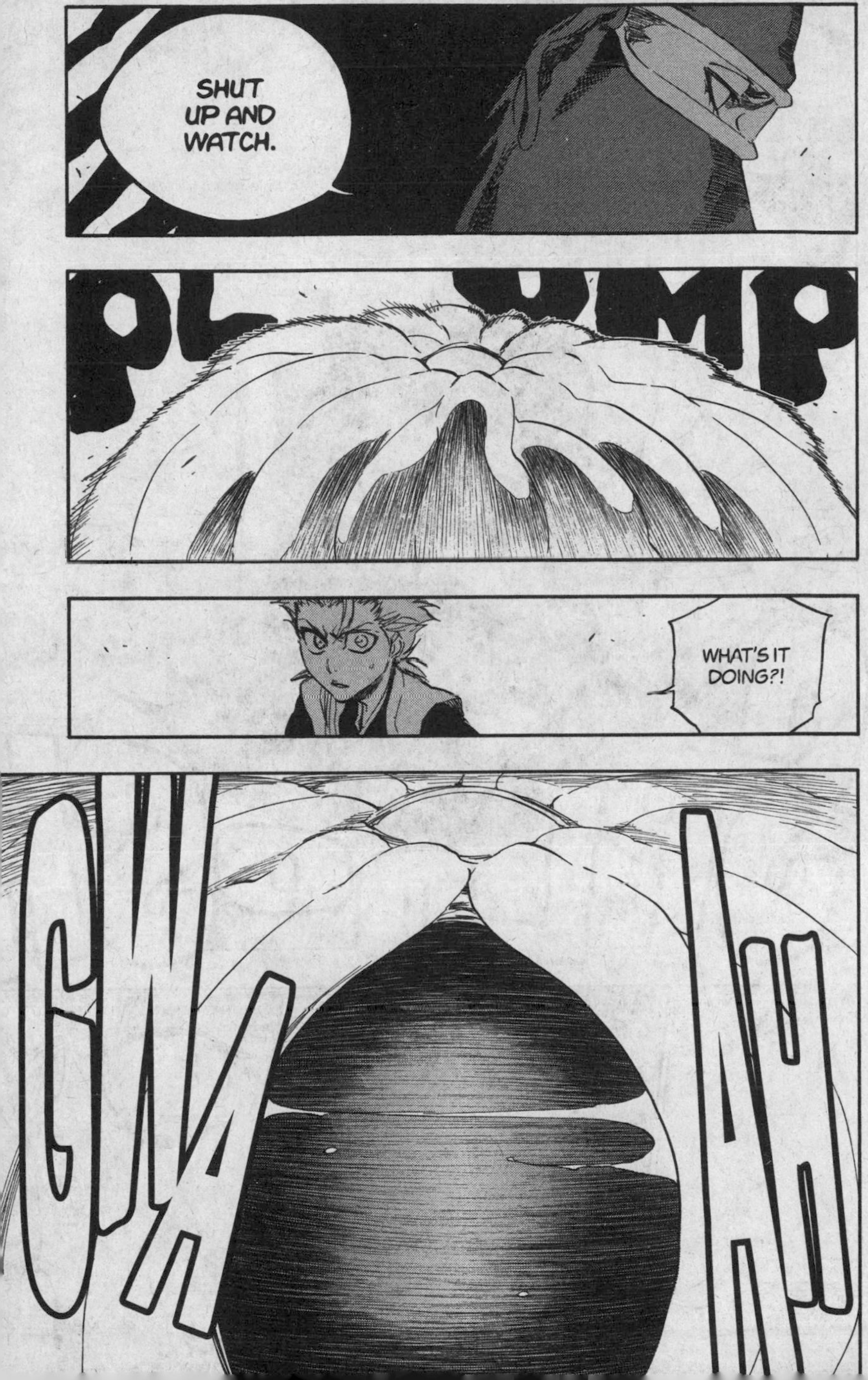
SHUT UP AND WATCH.
PLUMP
WHAT'S IT DOING?!
GWAAH

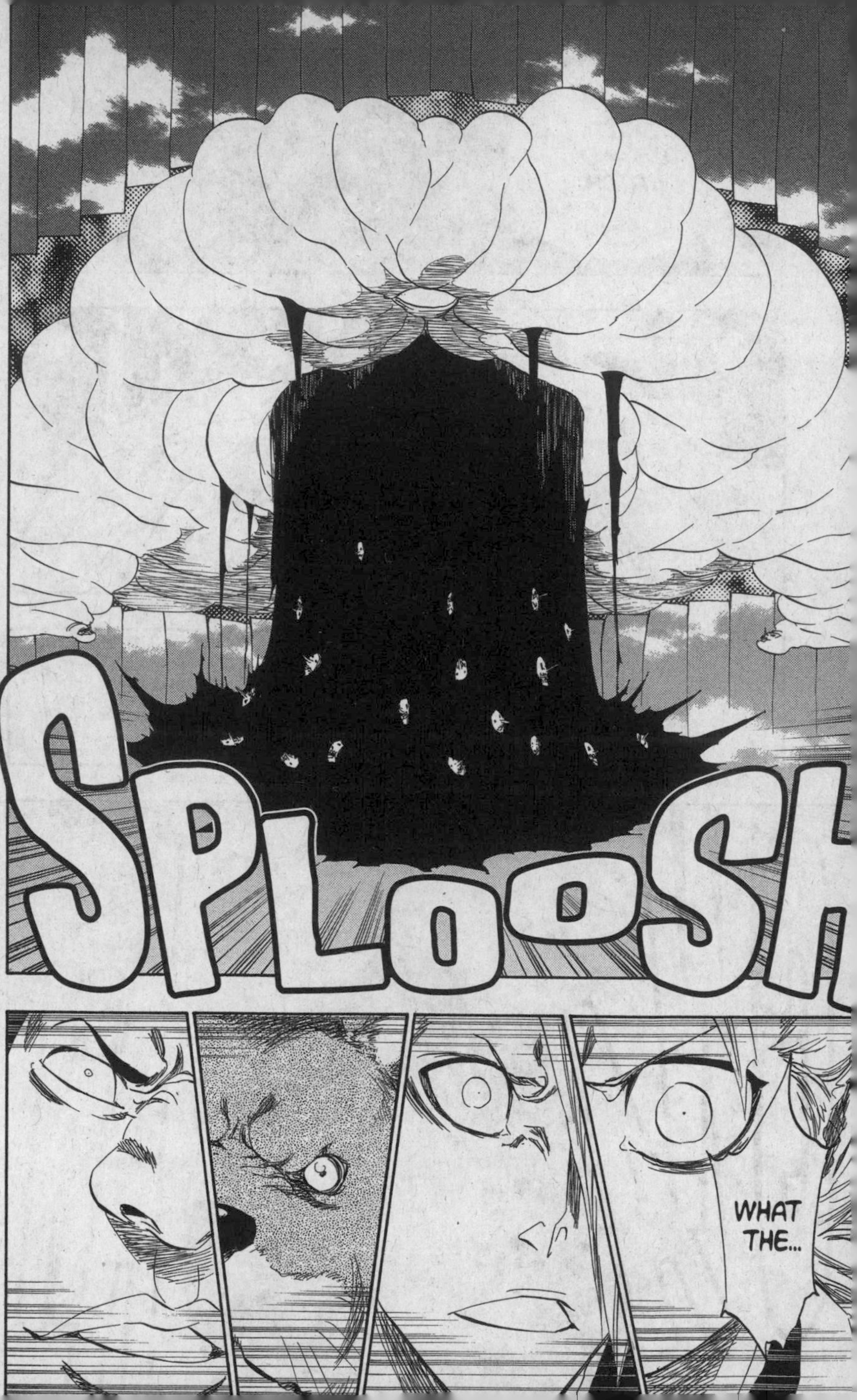
SPLOOSH
WHAT THE...

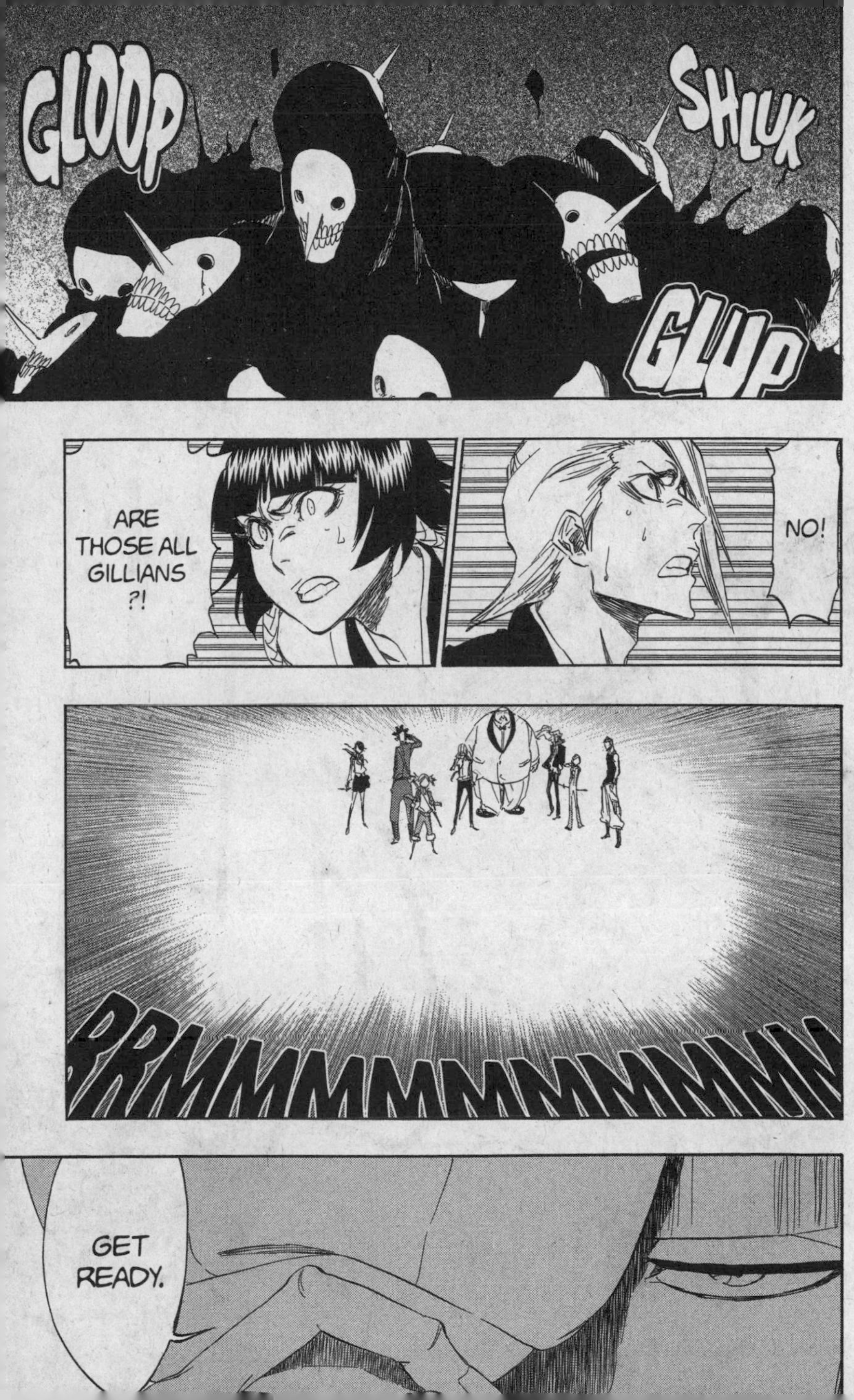
SHLUK
GLOOP
GLUP
NO!
ARE THOSE ALL GILLIANS ?!
BRMMMMMMMMMMMM
GET READY.

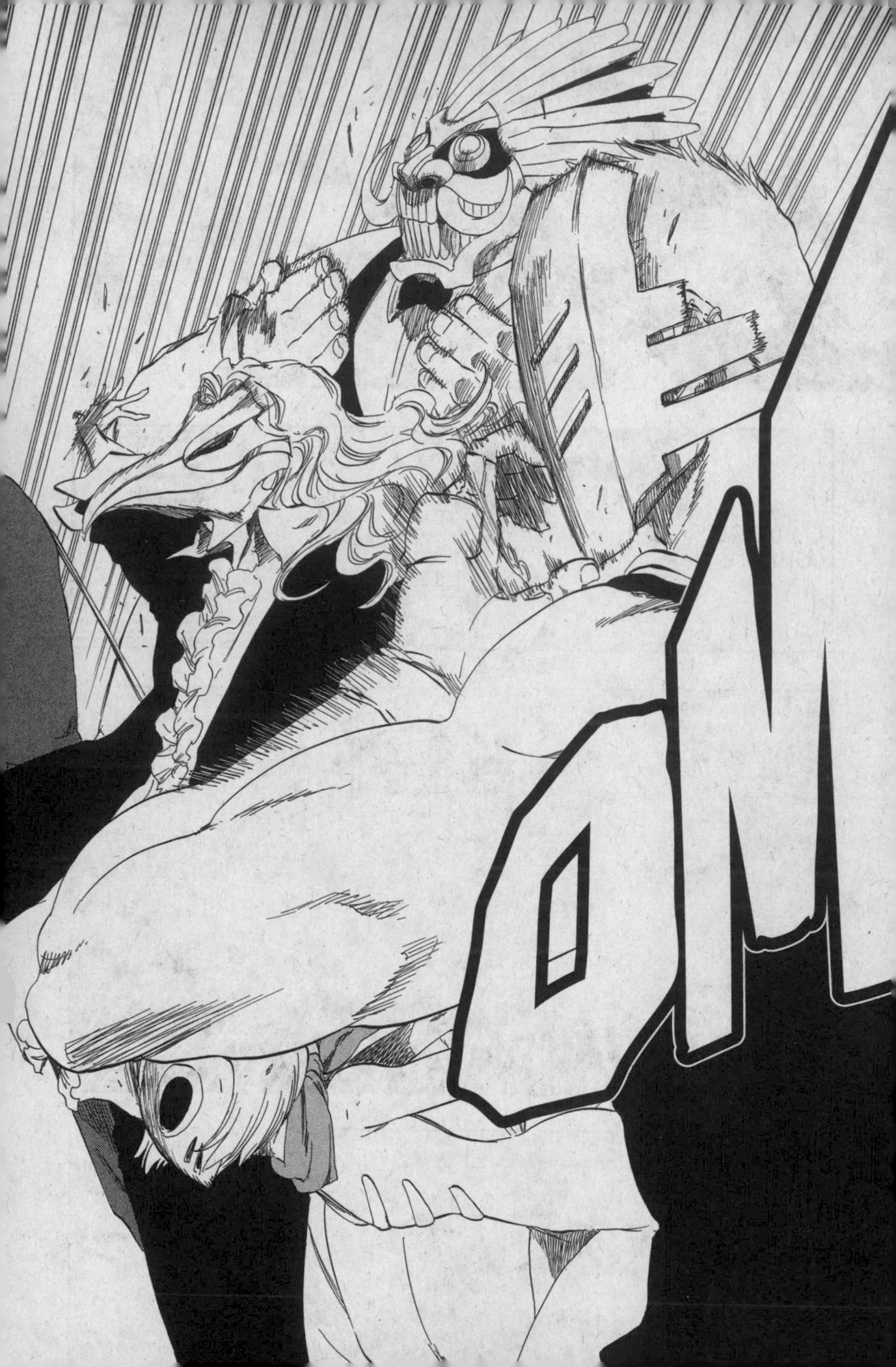
OM

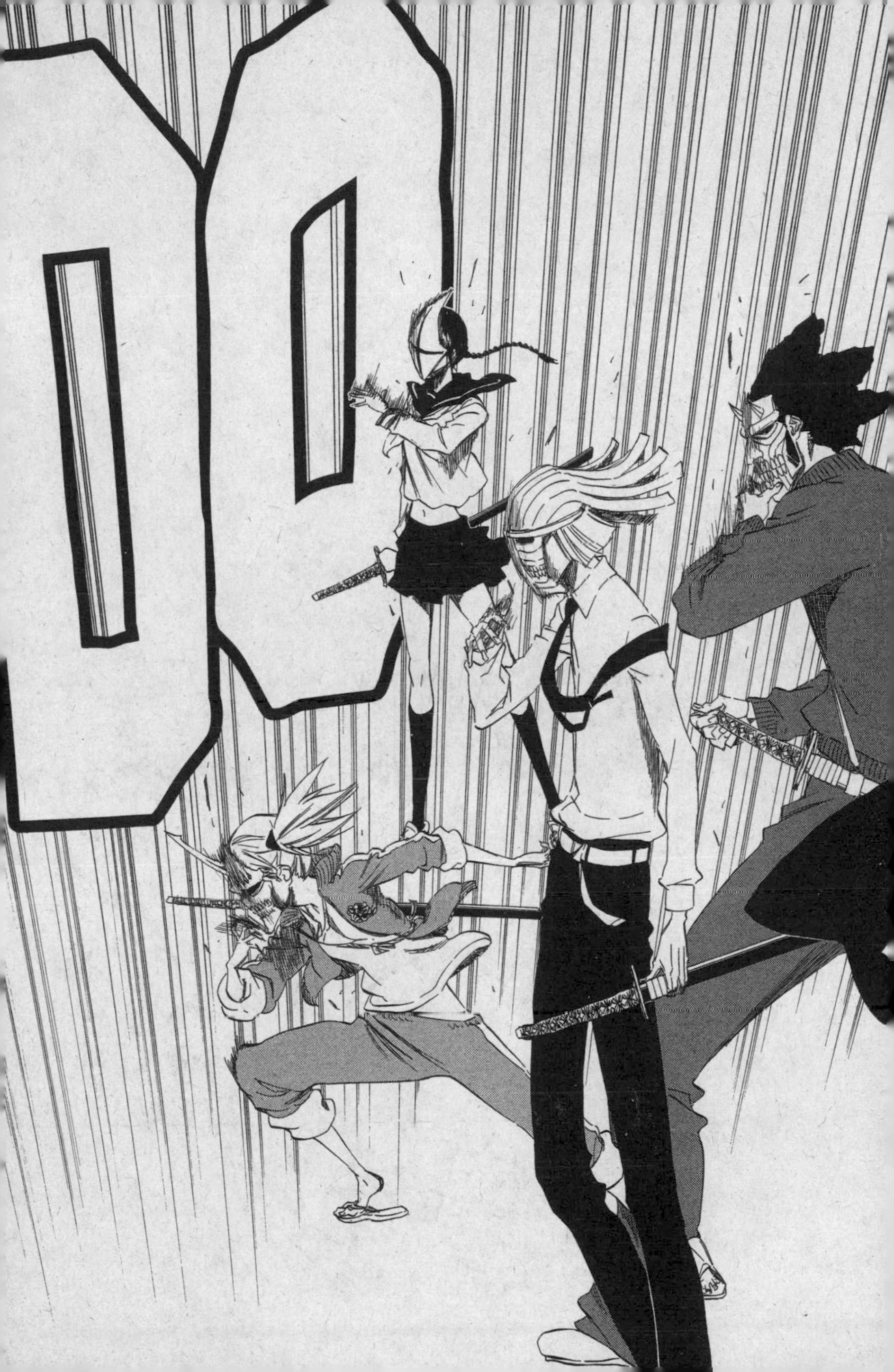

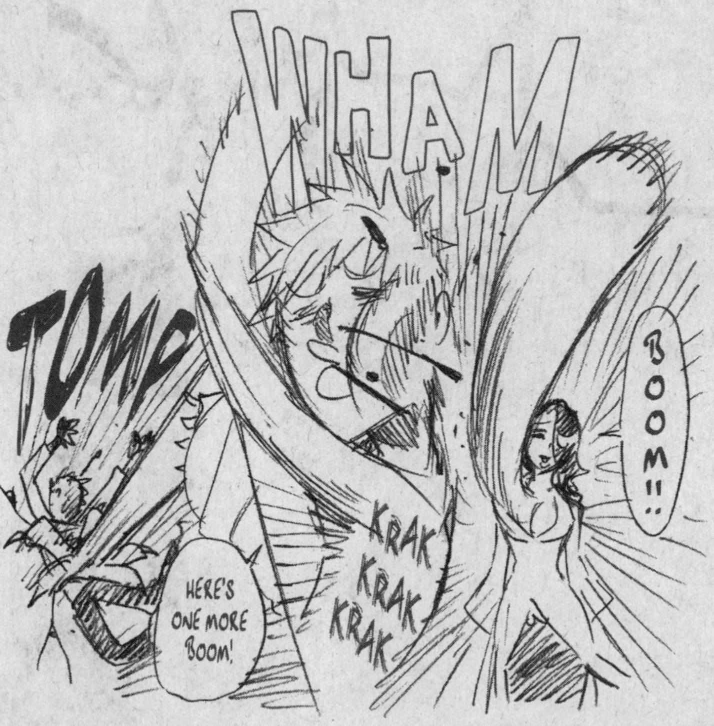
BOOM!!
WHAM
KRAK KRAK KRAK
HERE'S ONE MORE Boom!
TOMP

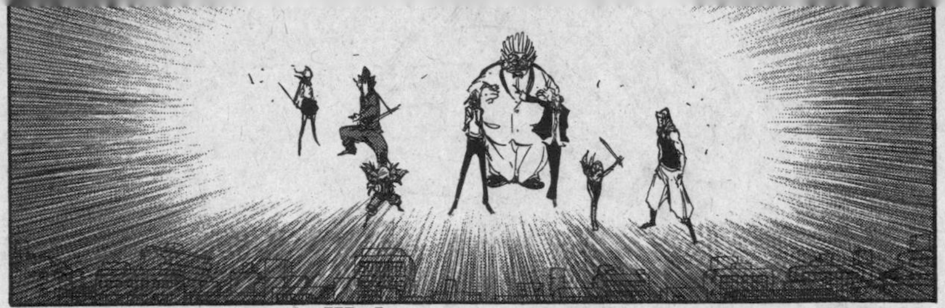

366. The Revenger's High

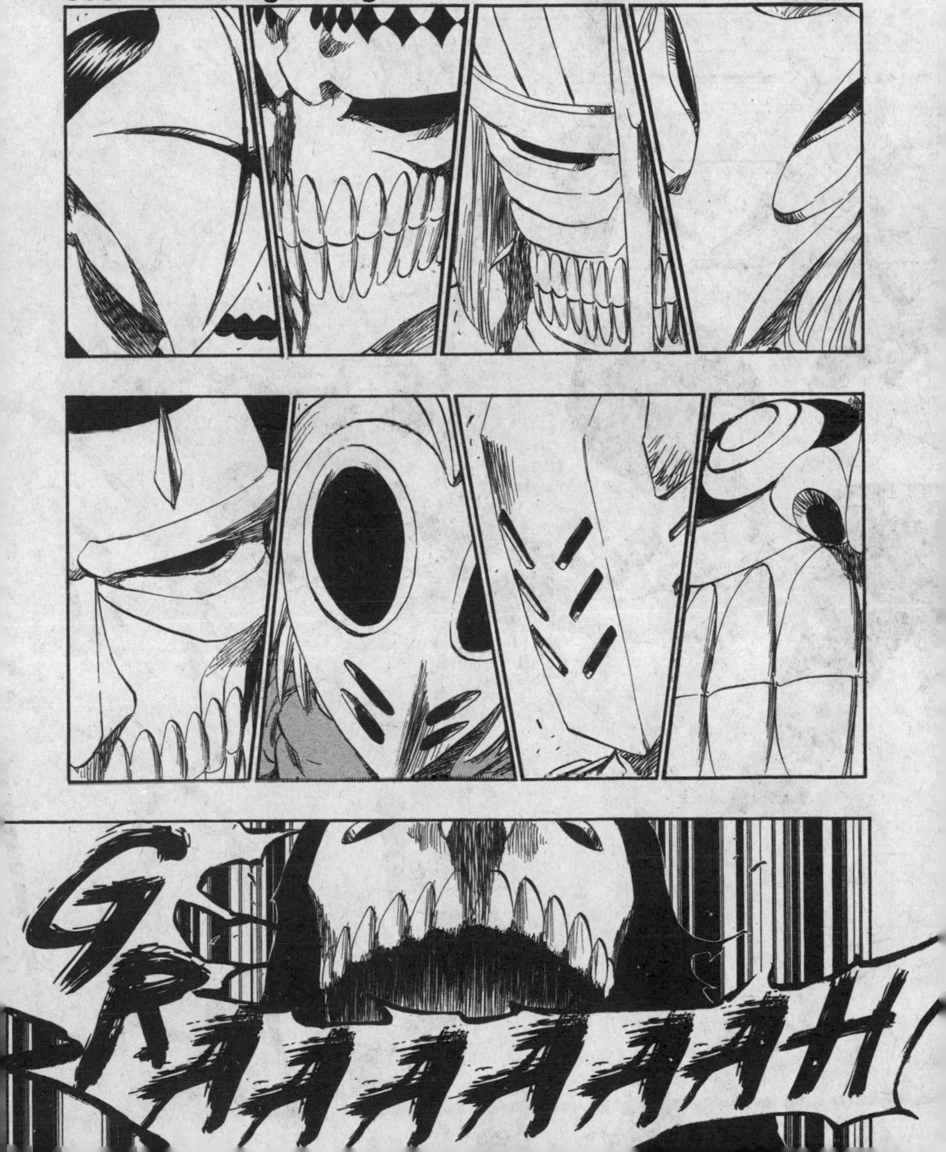
GRRAAAAAAAAAH

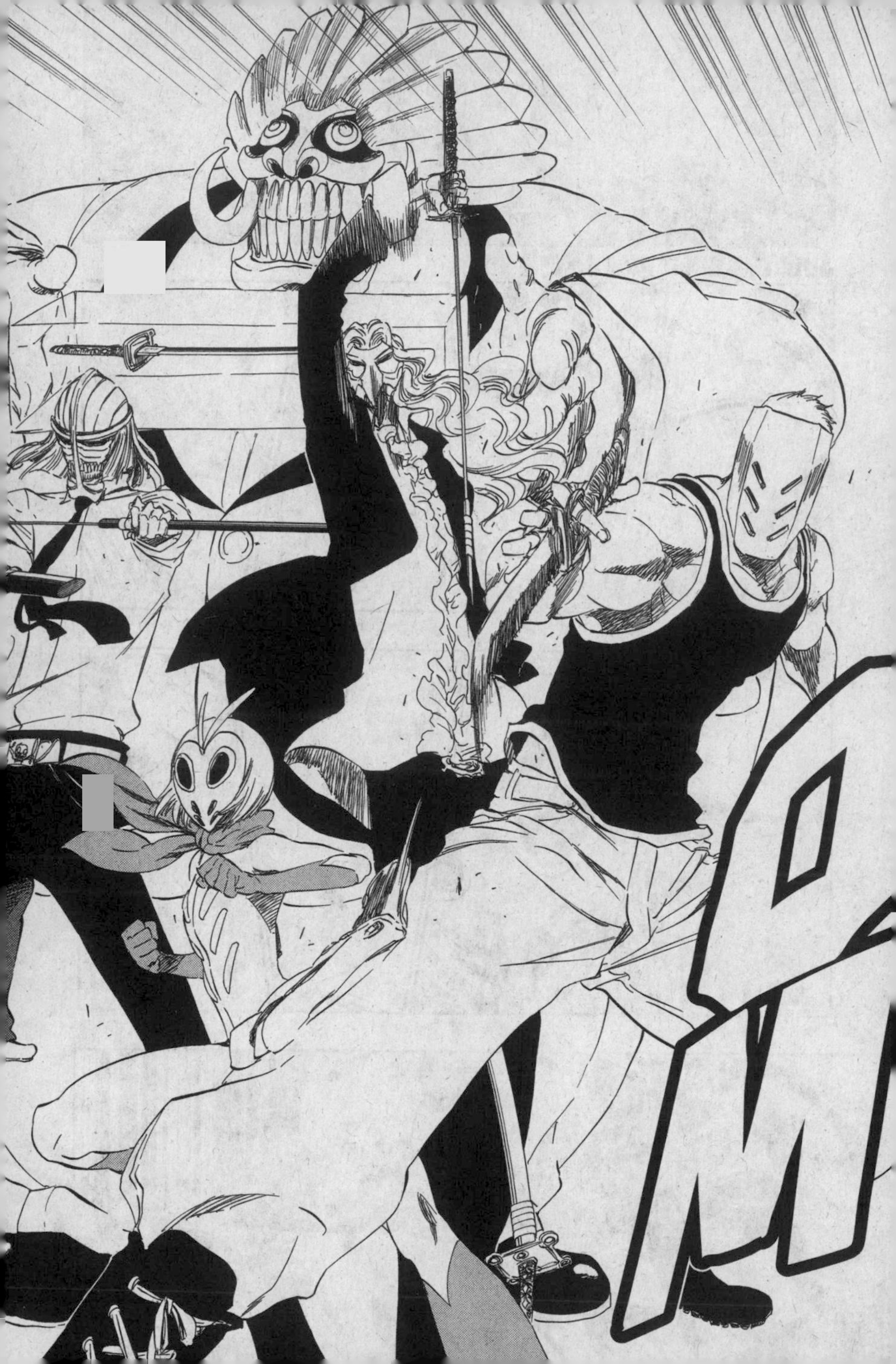

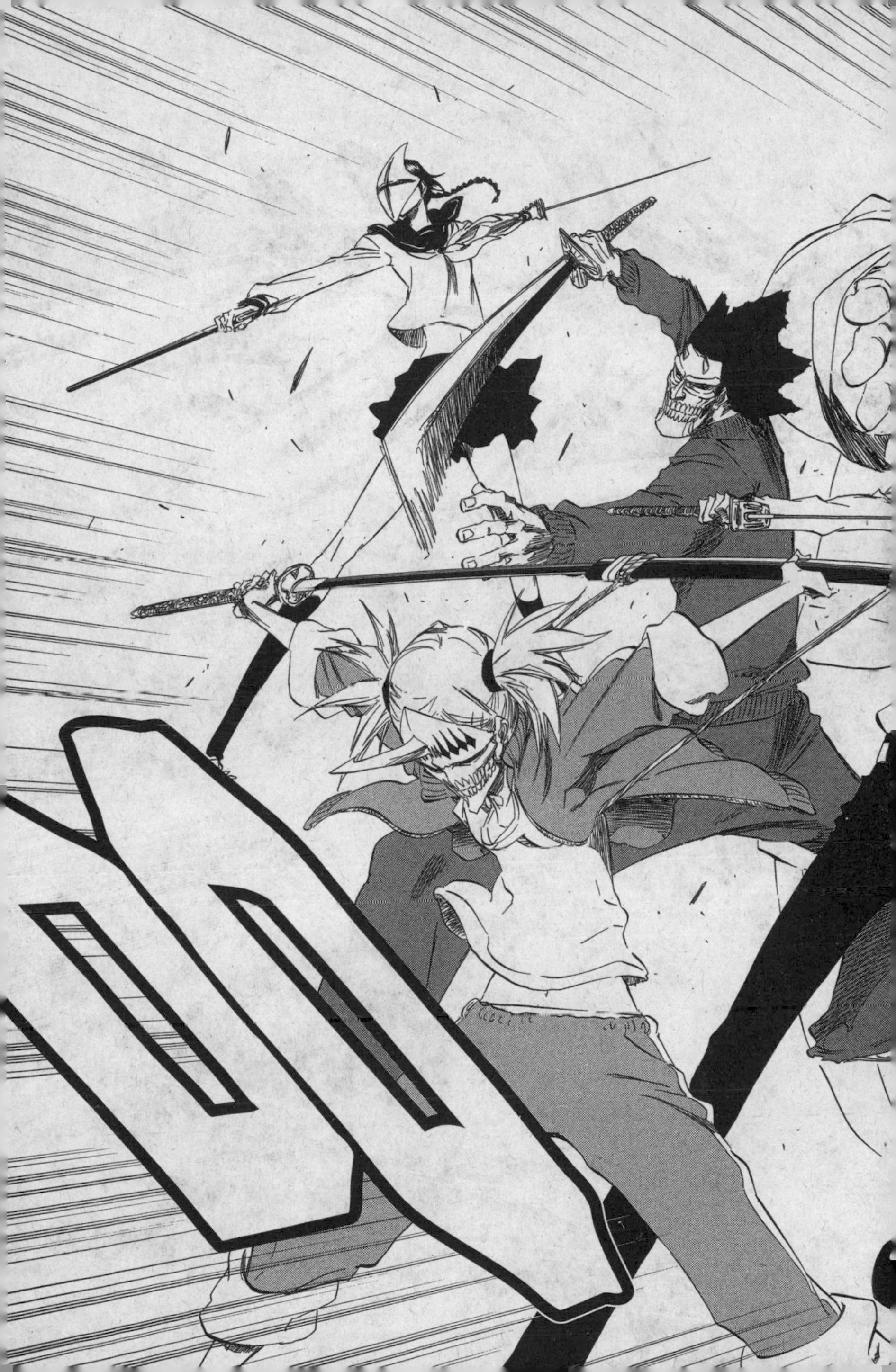

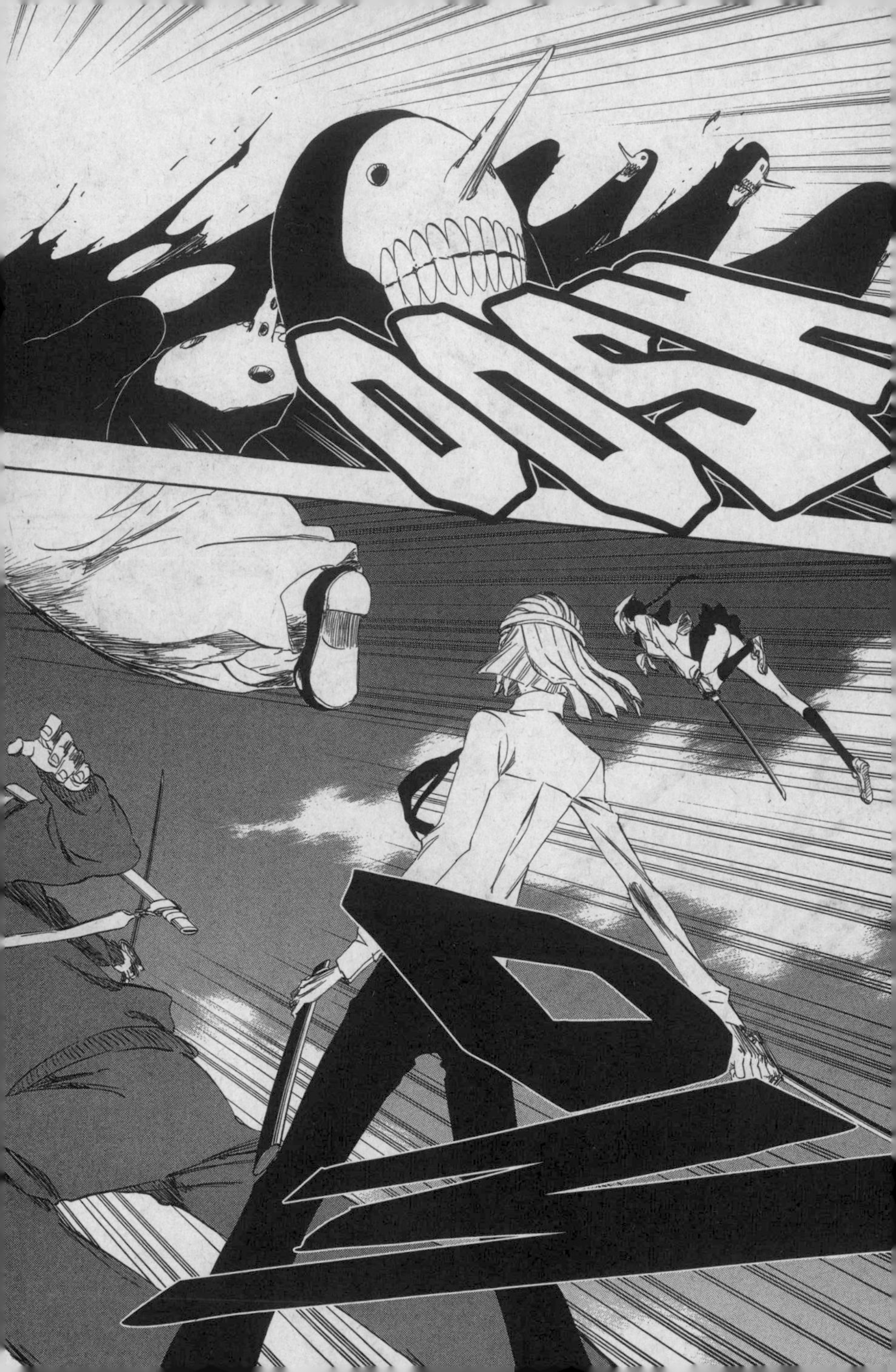

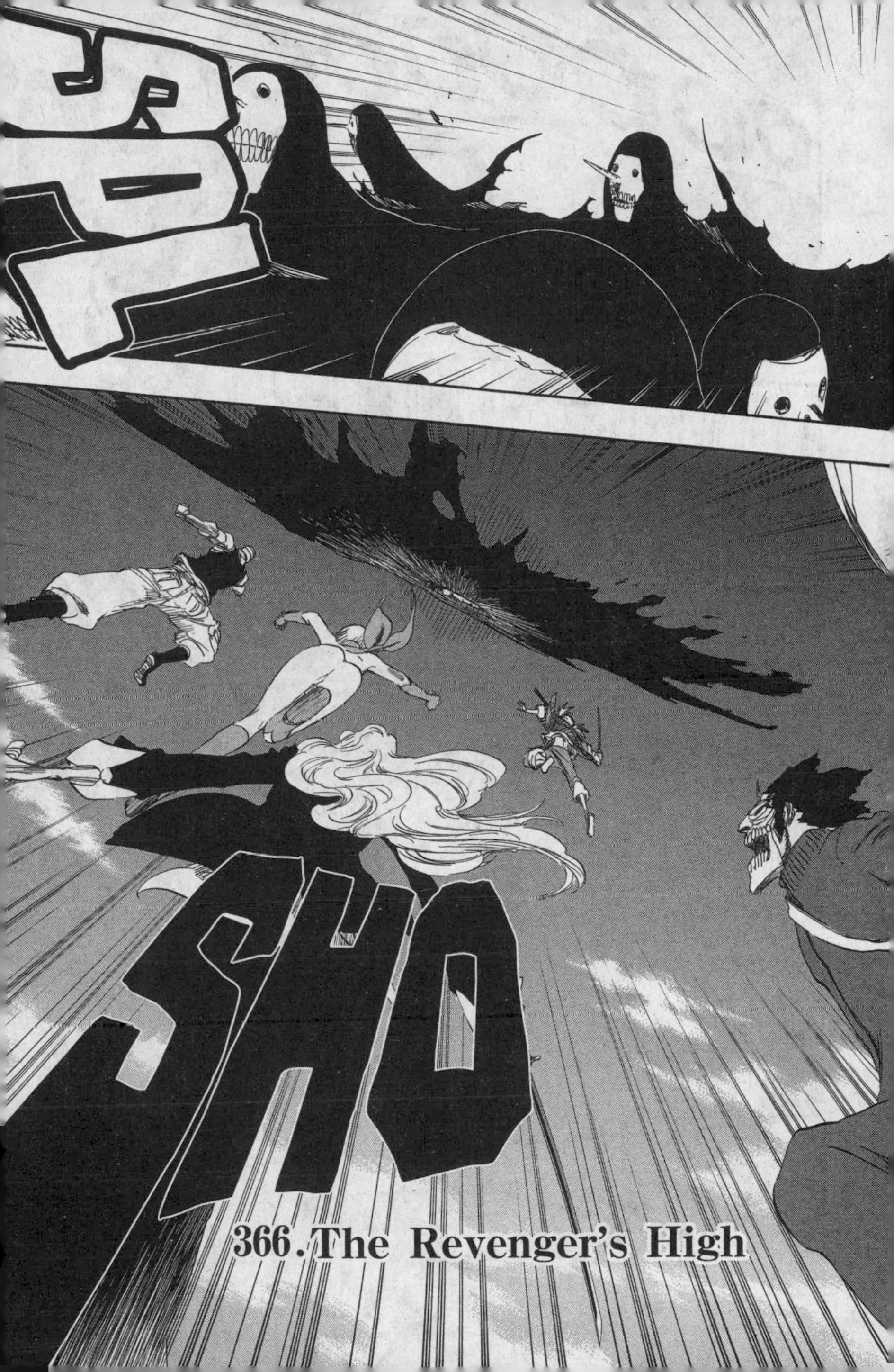

ZOO
SHOO

366. The Revenger's High

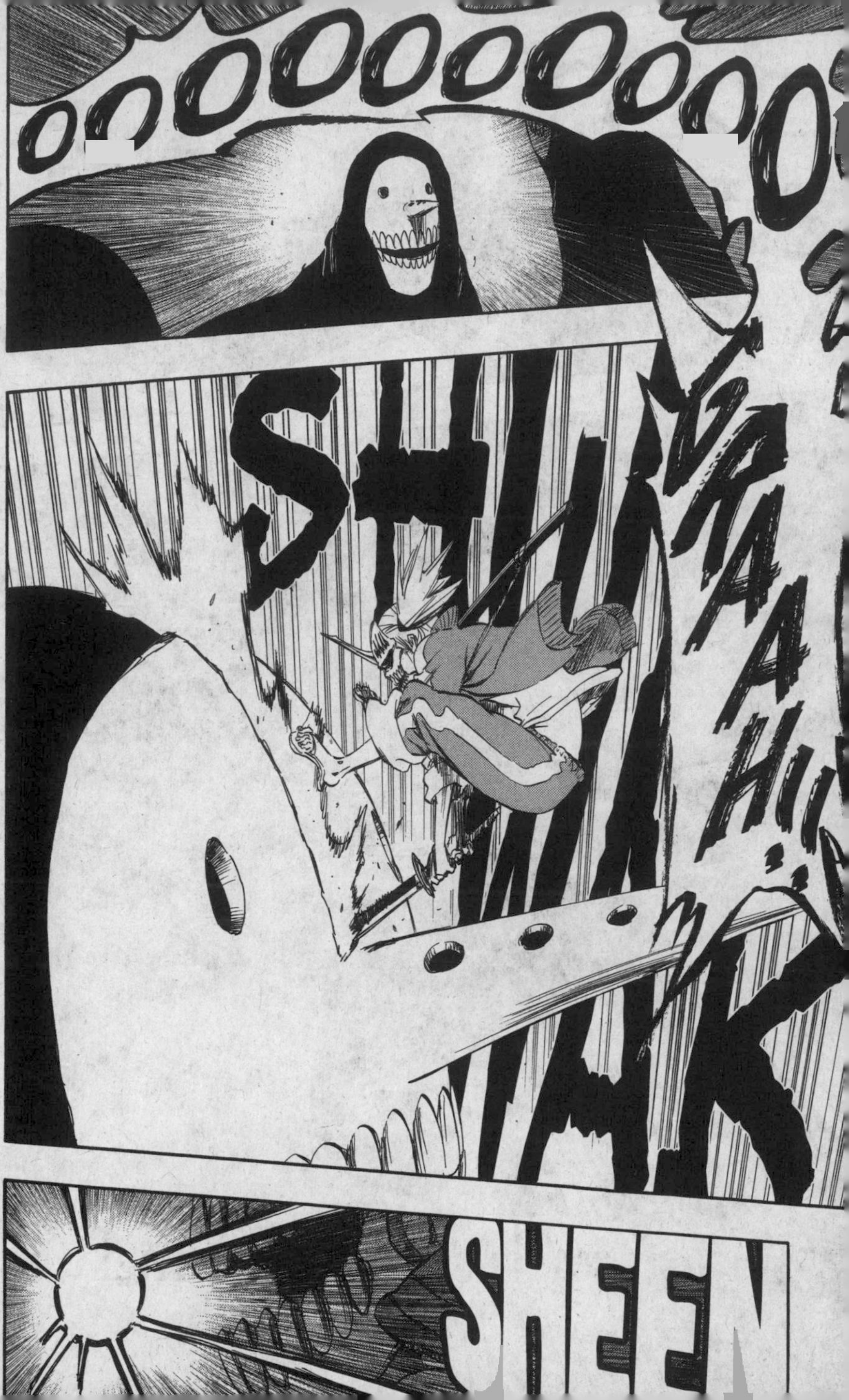
SHEEN

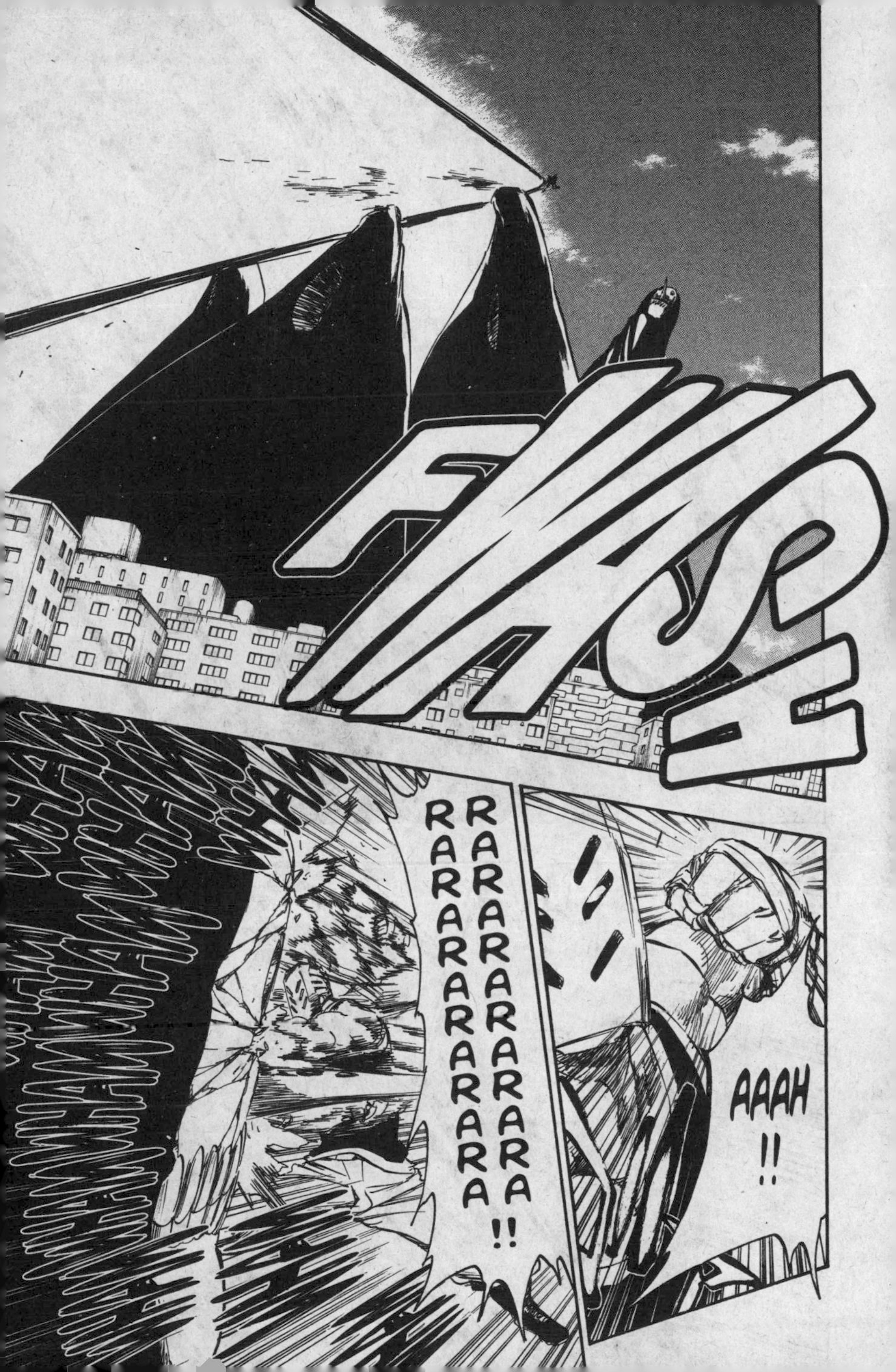
FWSH
RARARARARARA
RARARARARARA!!
AAAH!!

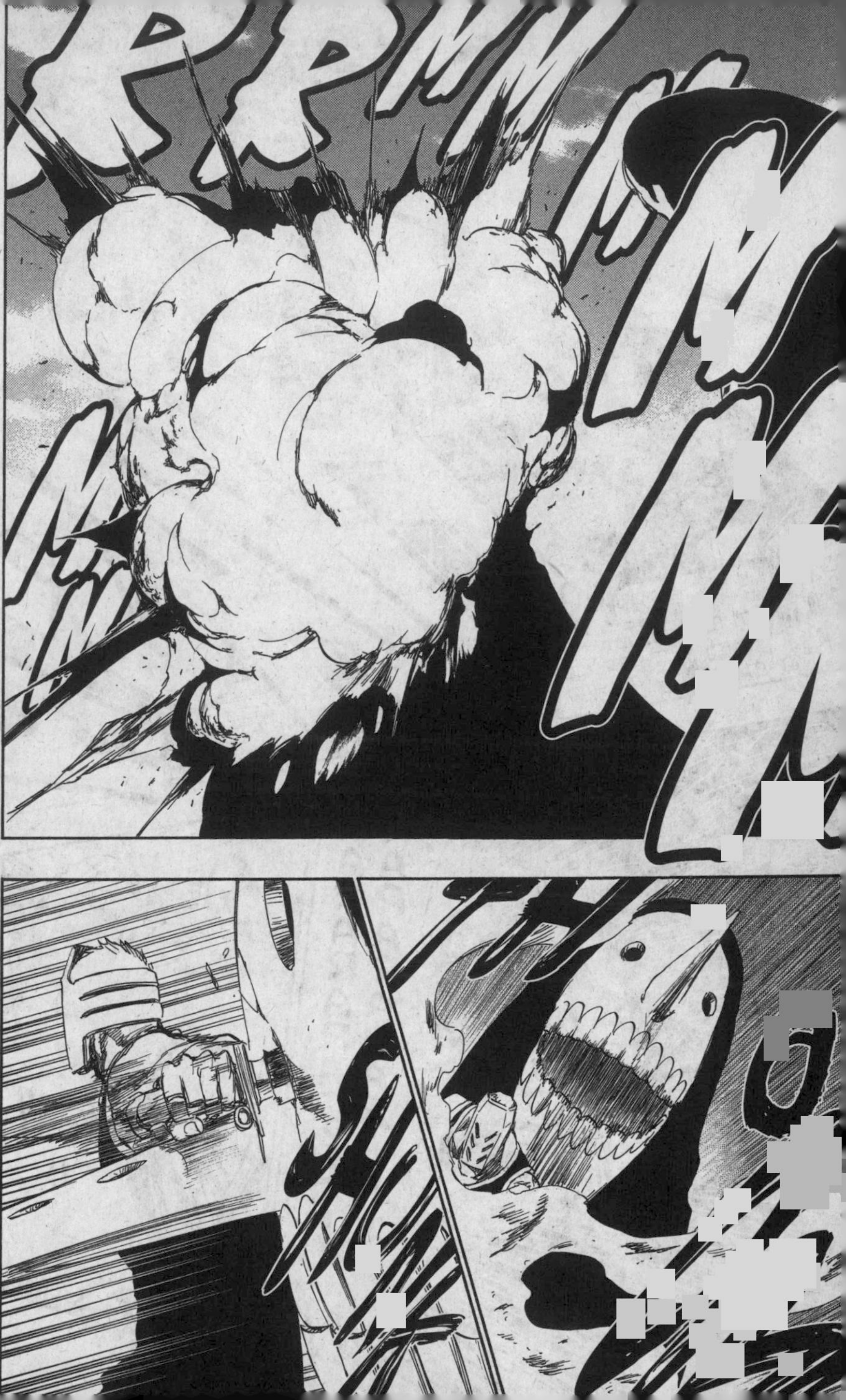

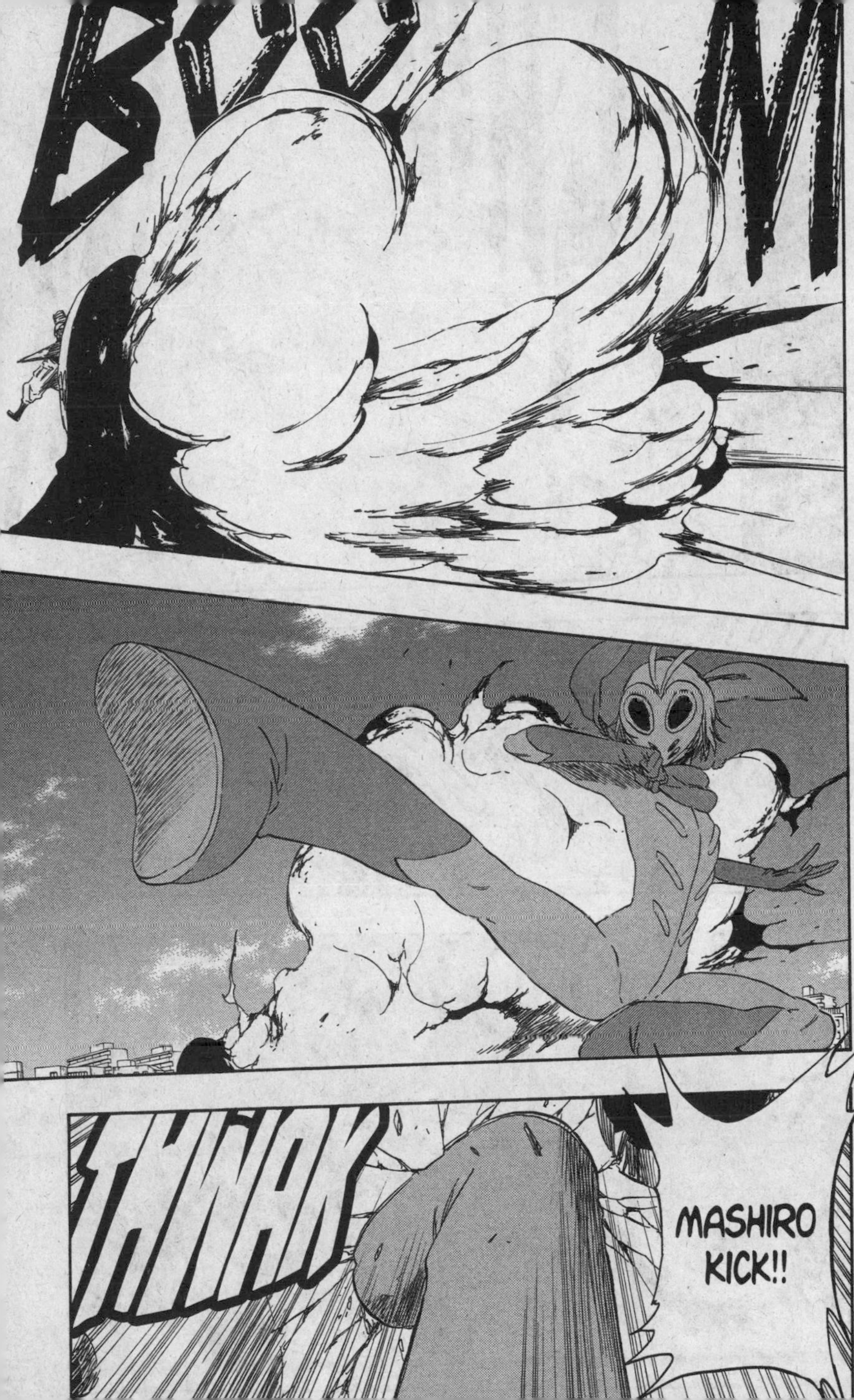
BOOM
THWAK
MASHIRO KICK!!

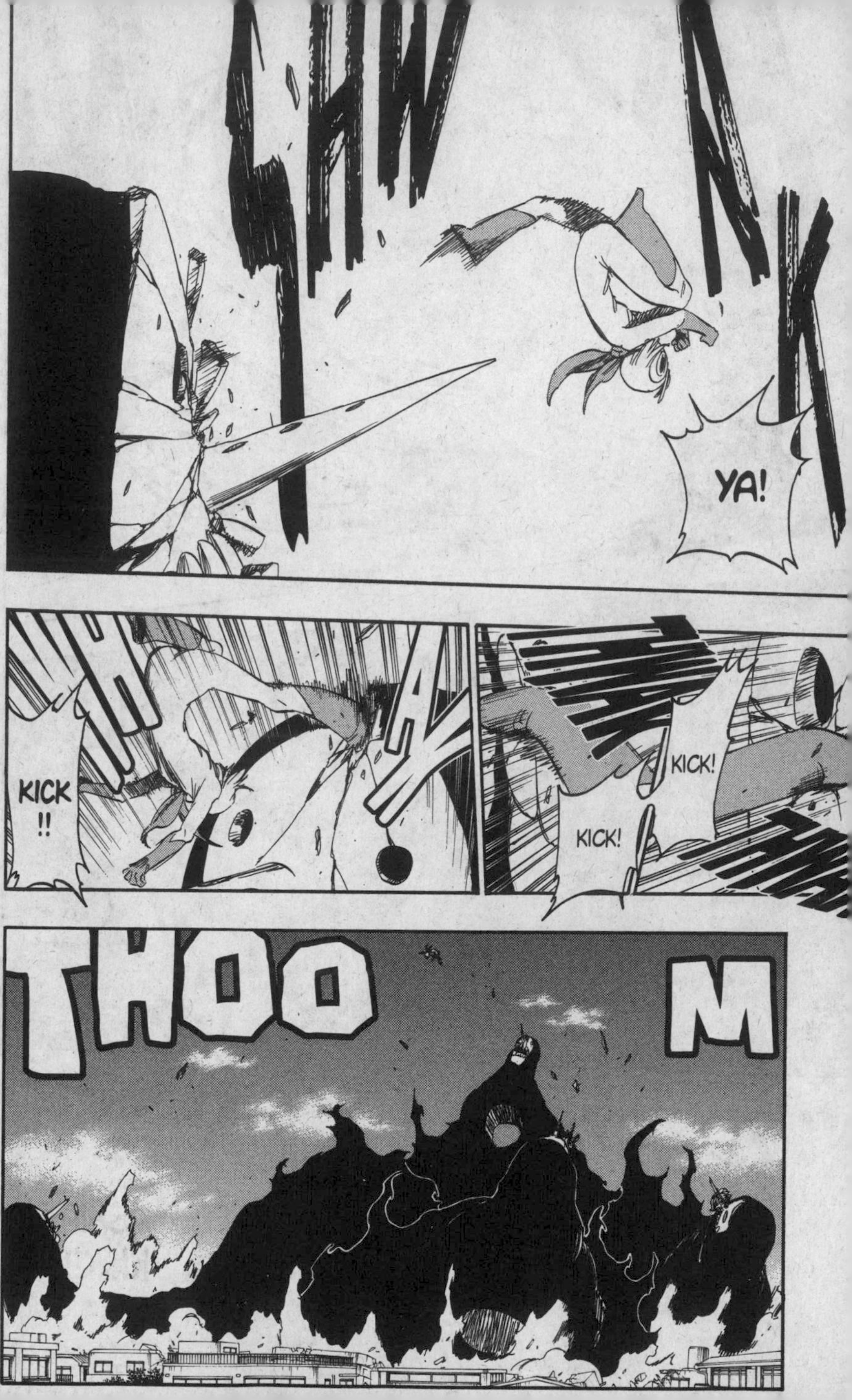
CHW
R
K
YA!
KICK!
KICK!
KICK
!!
THOO
M

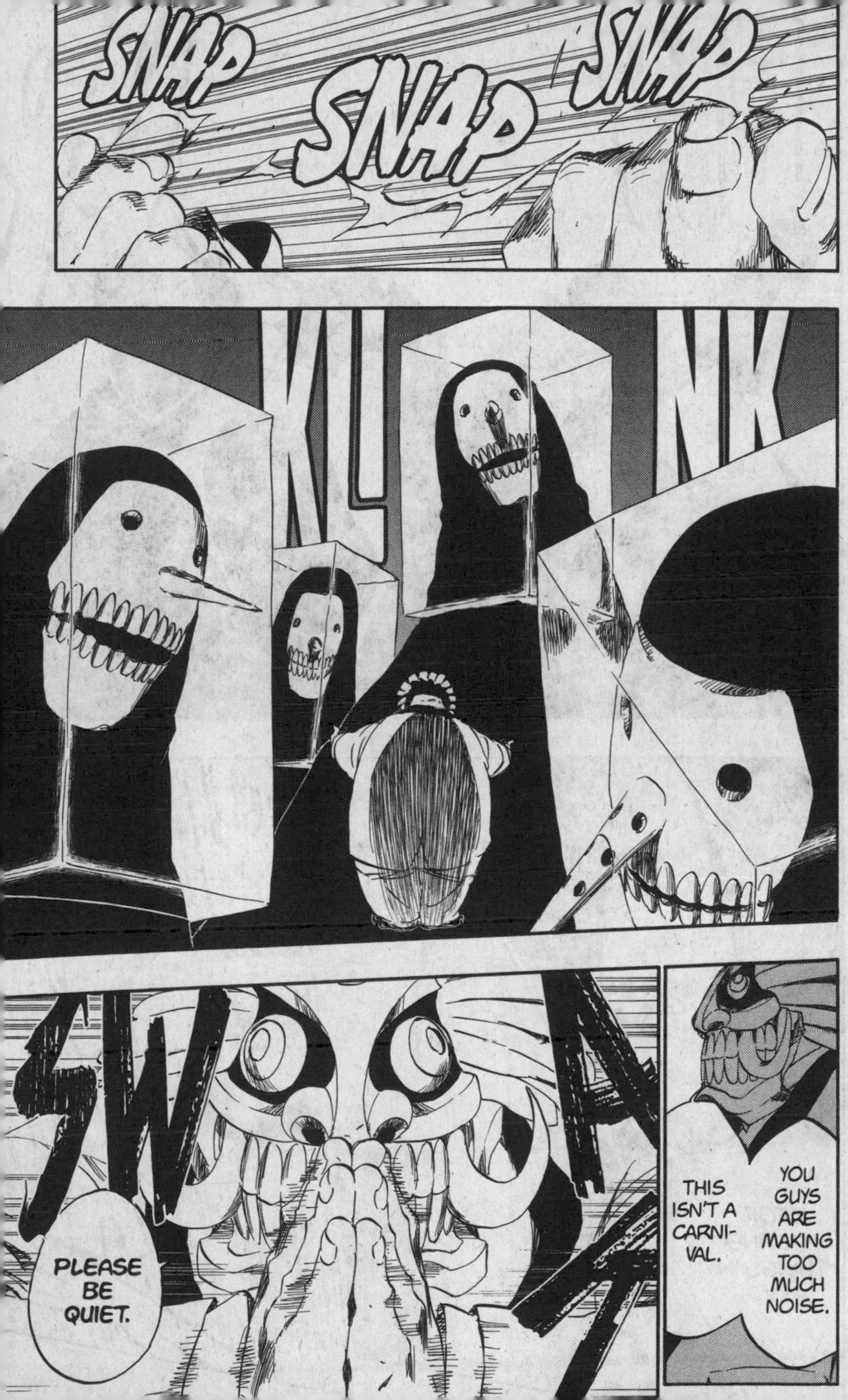
SNAP
SNAP
SNAP
YOU GUYS ARE MAKING TOO MUCH NOISE.
THIS ISN'T A CARNI-VAL.
PLEASE BE QUIET.

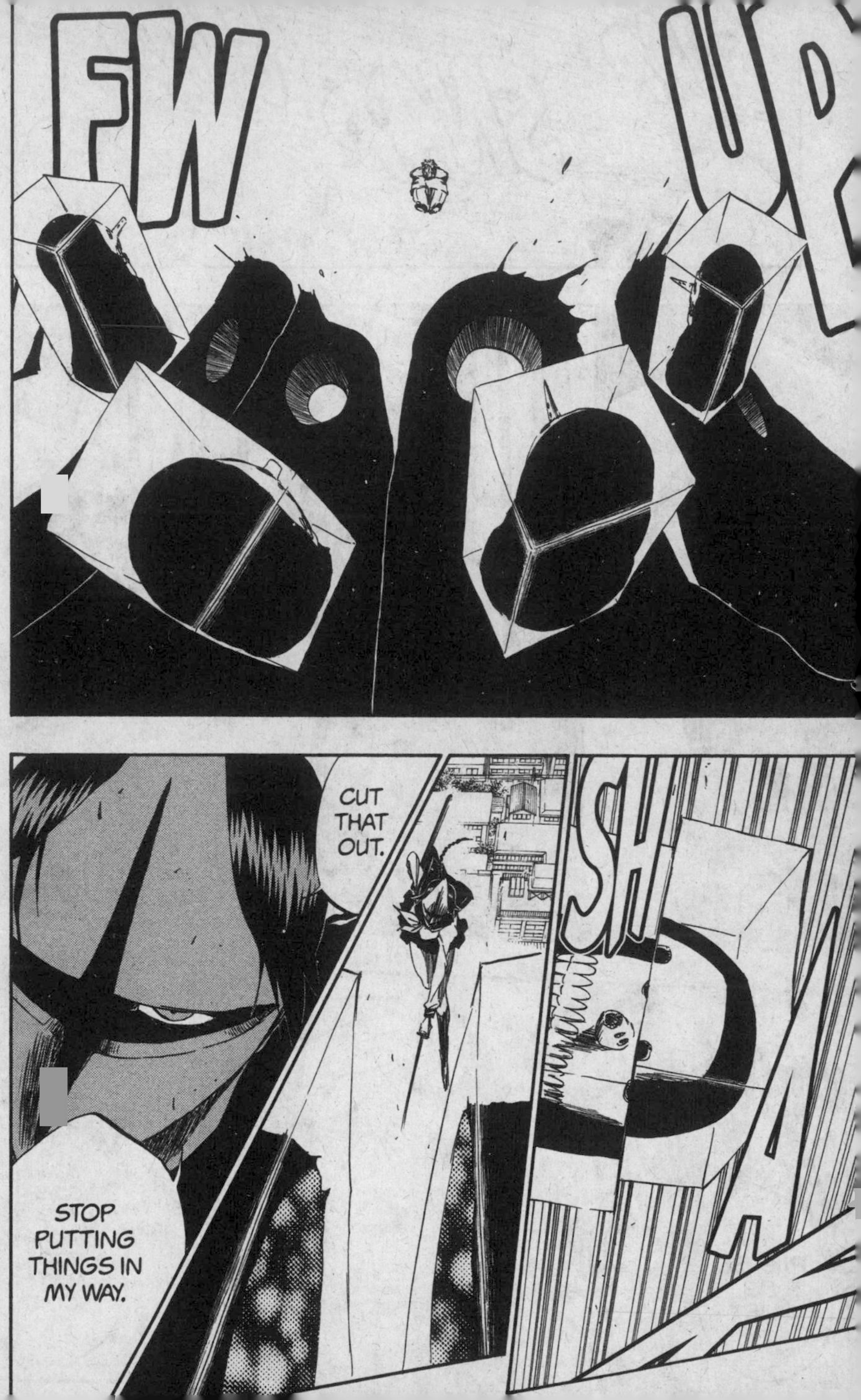
CUT THAT OUT.
STOP PUTTING THINGS IN MY WAY.

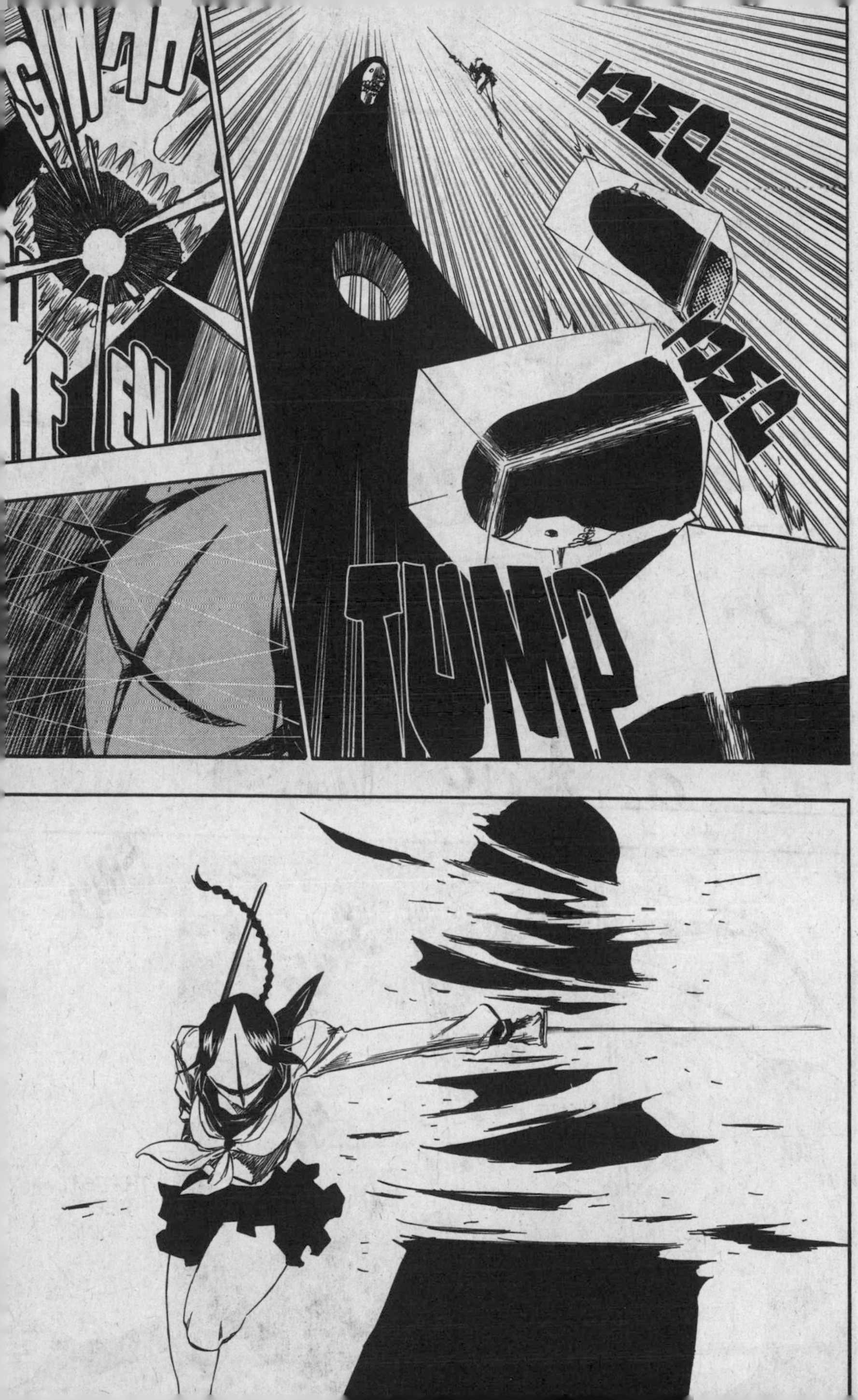
TUMP

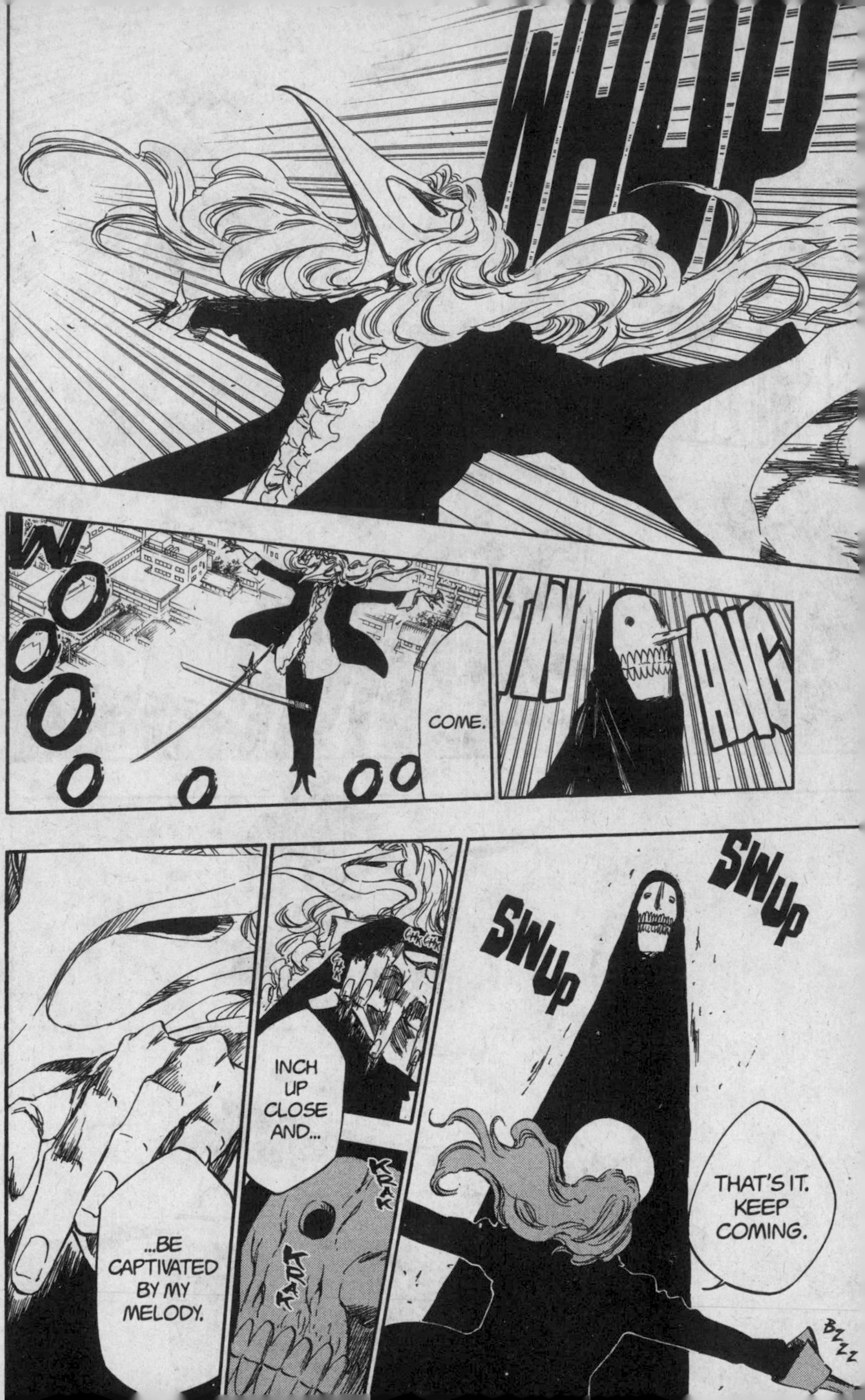
WHIP
TWANG
WOOOOOOOOO
COME.
SWUP
SWUP
THAT'S IT. KEEP COMING.
BZZZ
INCH UP CLOSE AND...
KRAK
KRAK
...BE CAPTIVATED BY MY MELODY.

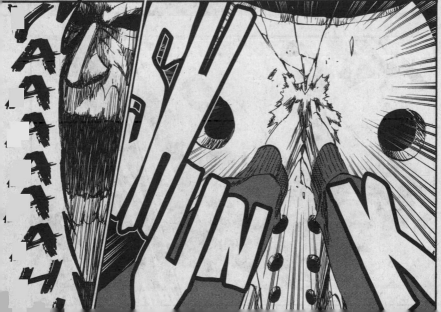

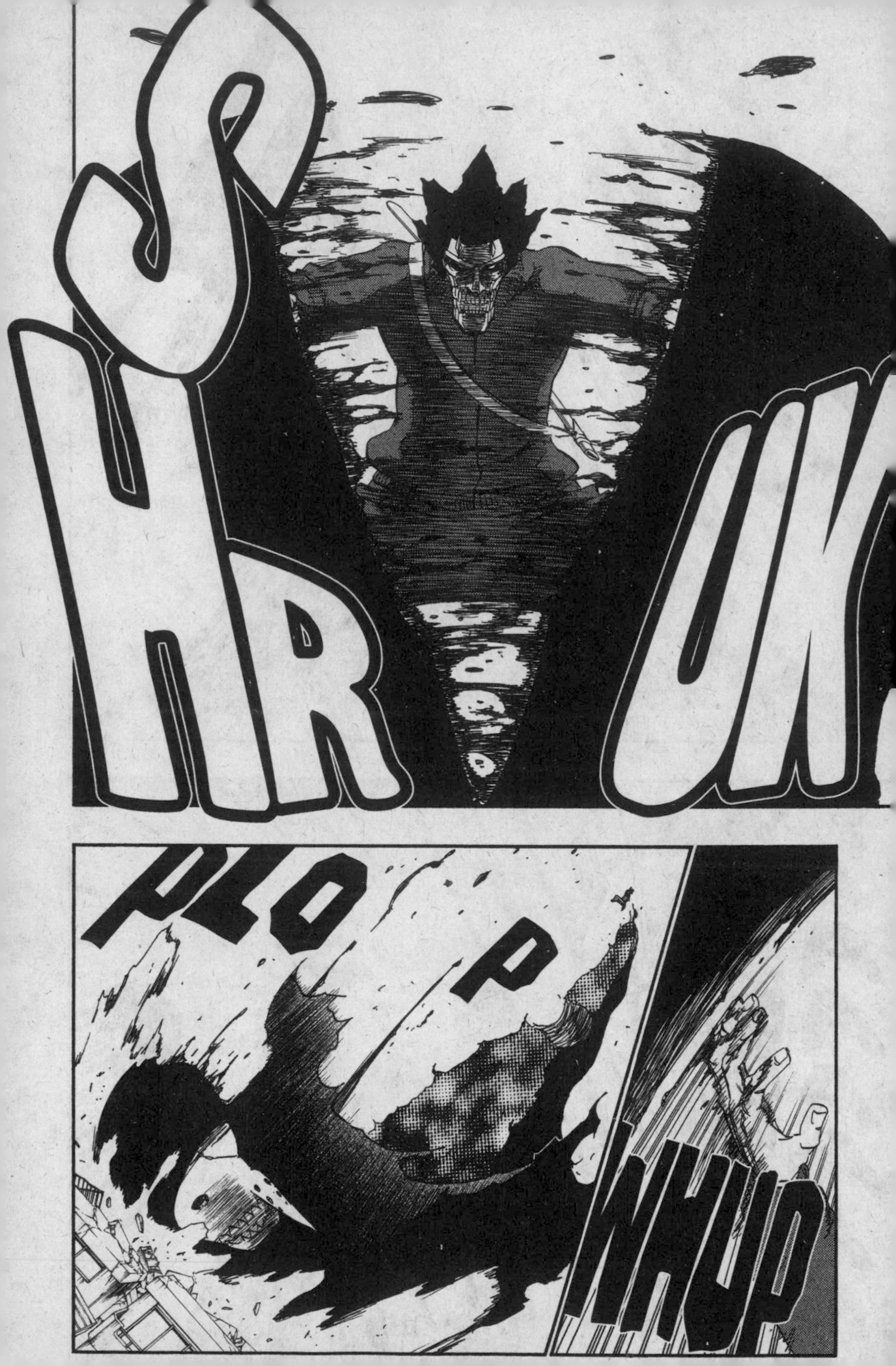
SHRUN
WHUP
PLOP

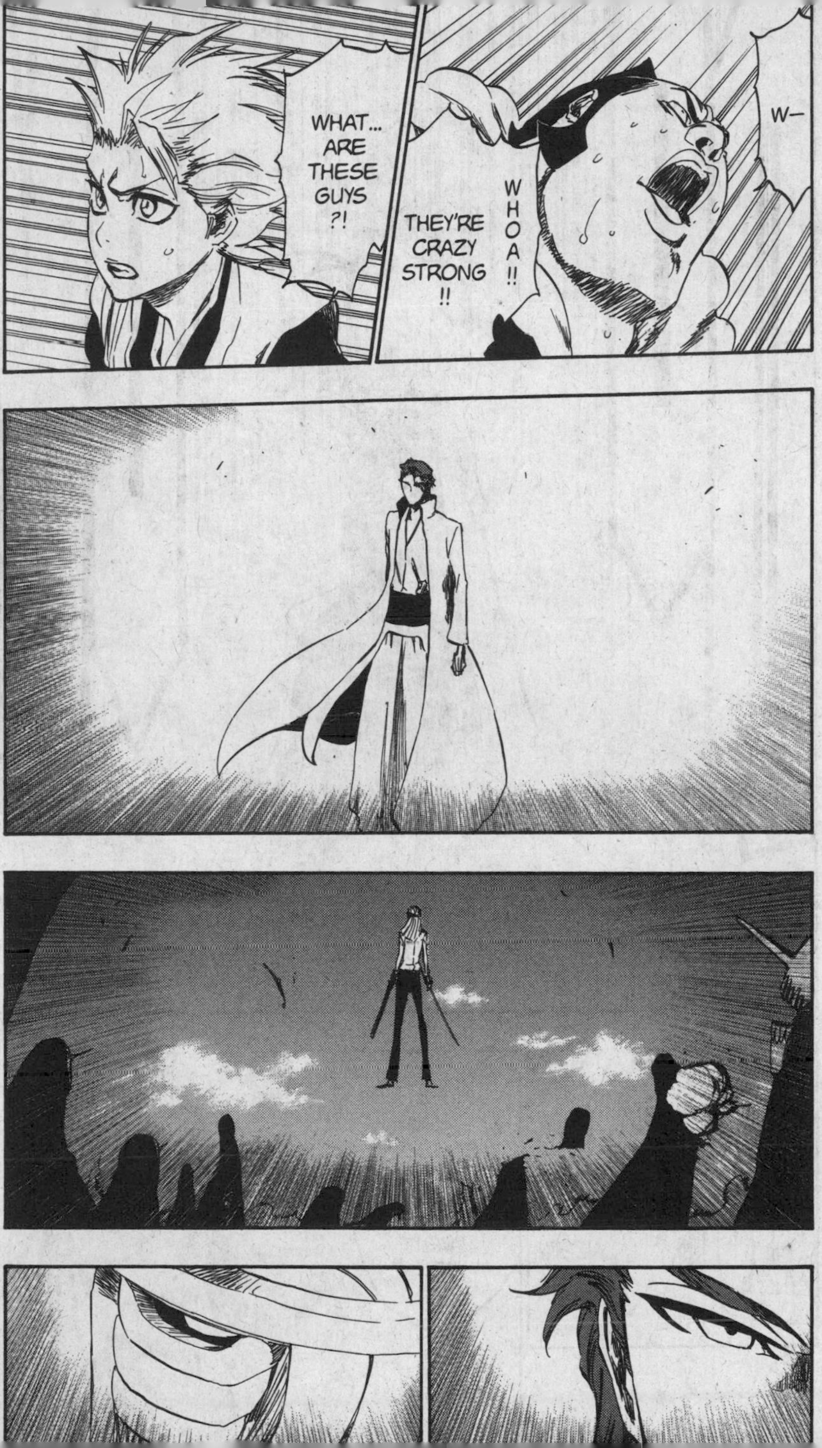
W—
WHOA!!
THEY'RE CRAZY STRONG!!
WHAT... ARE THESE GUYS?!

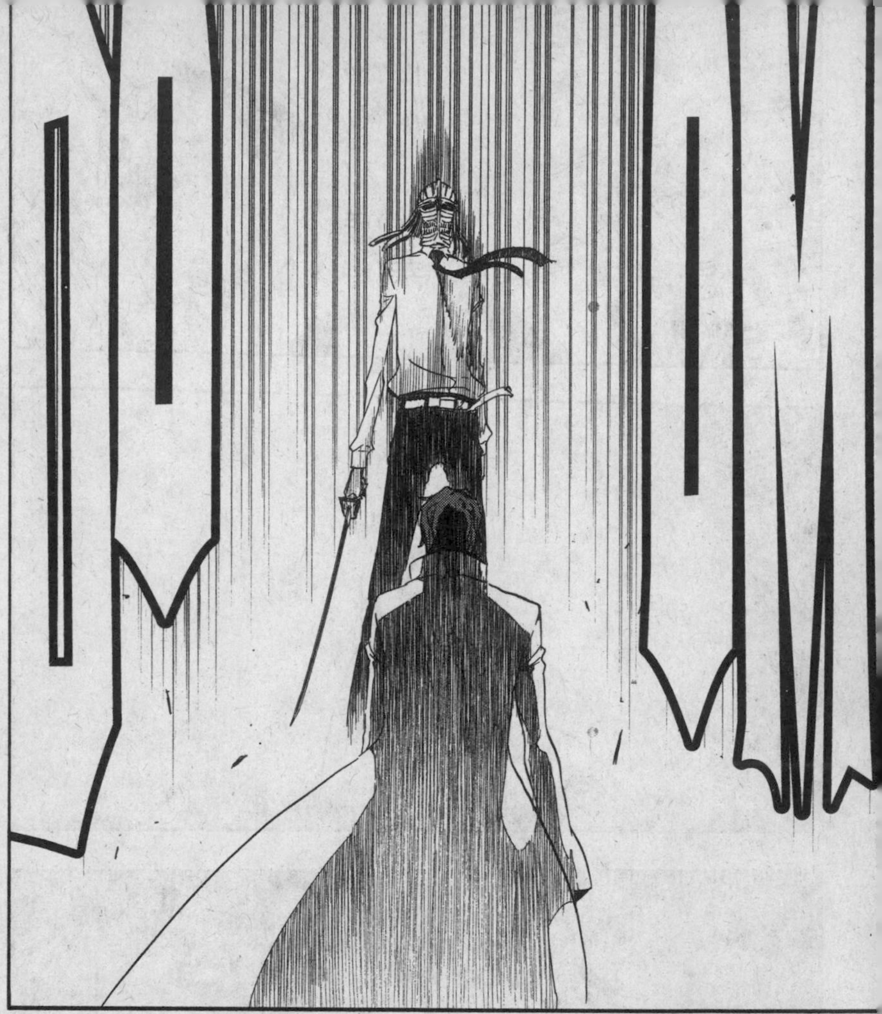

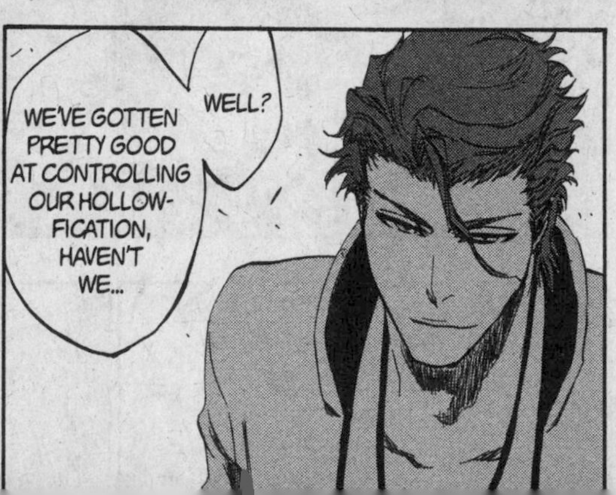
WELL?
WE'VE GOTTEN PRETTY GOOD AT CONTROLLING OUR HOLLOW-FICATION, HAVEN'T WE...

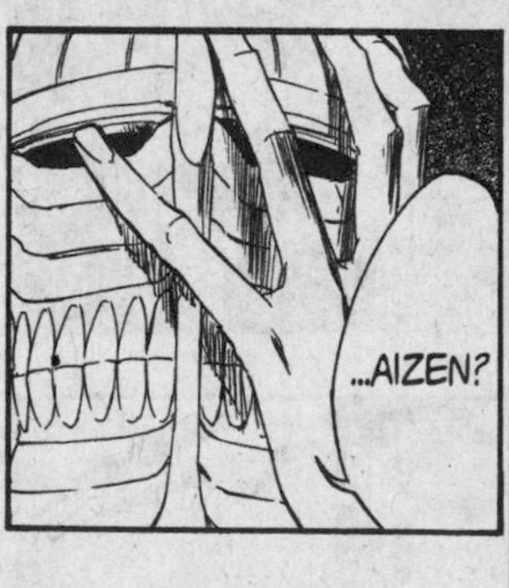
...AIZEN?

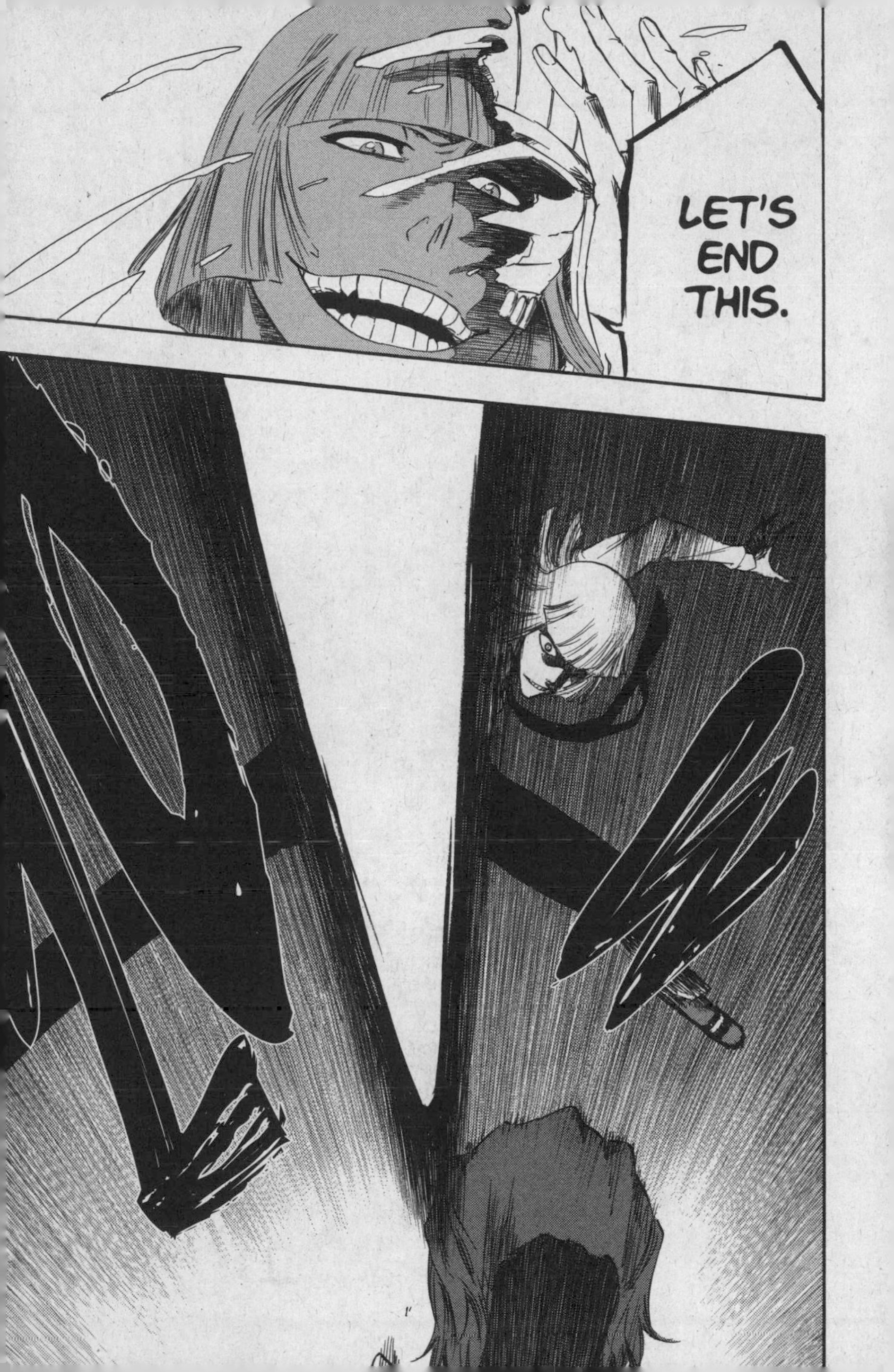
LET'S END THIS.

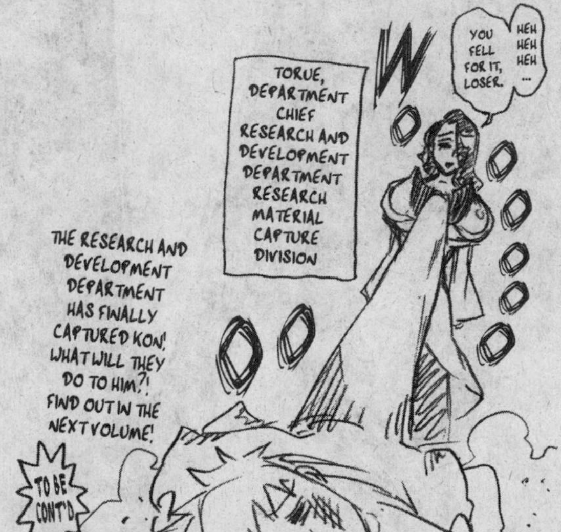
HEH HEH HEH ...
YOU FELL FOR IT, LOSER.
W
TORUE, DEPARTMENT CHIEF RESEARCH AND DEVELOPMENT DEPARTMENT RESEARCH MATERIAL CAPTURE DIVISION
THE RESEARCH AND DEVELOPMENT DEPARTMENT HAS FINALLY CAPTURED KON! WHAT WILL THEY DO TO HIM?! FIND OUT IN THE NEXT VOLUME!
TO BE CONT'D

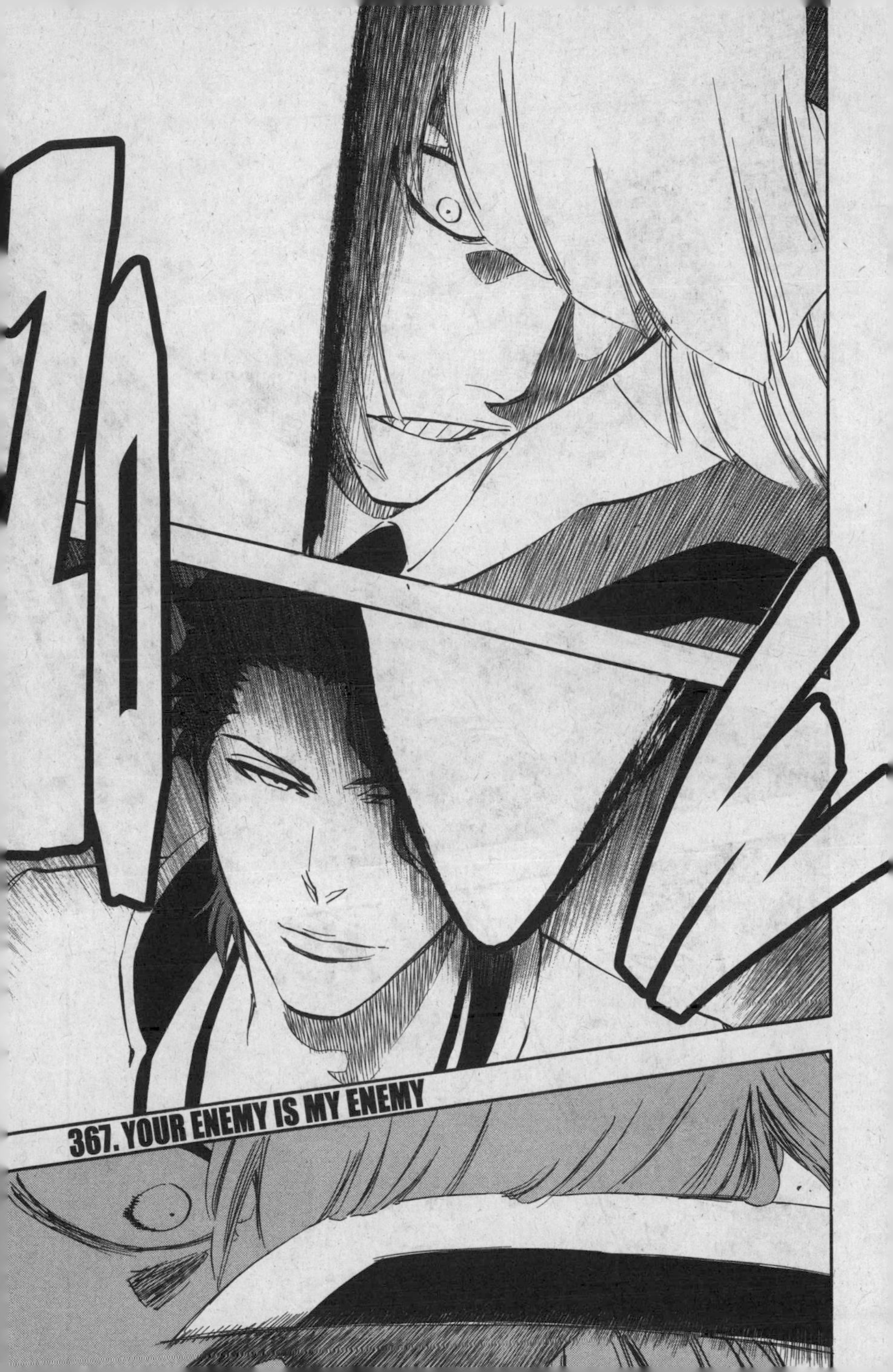
367. YOUR ENEMY IS MY ENEMY

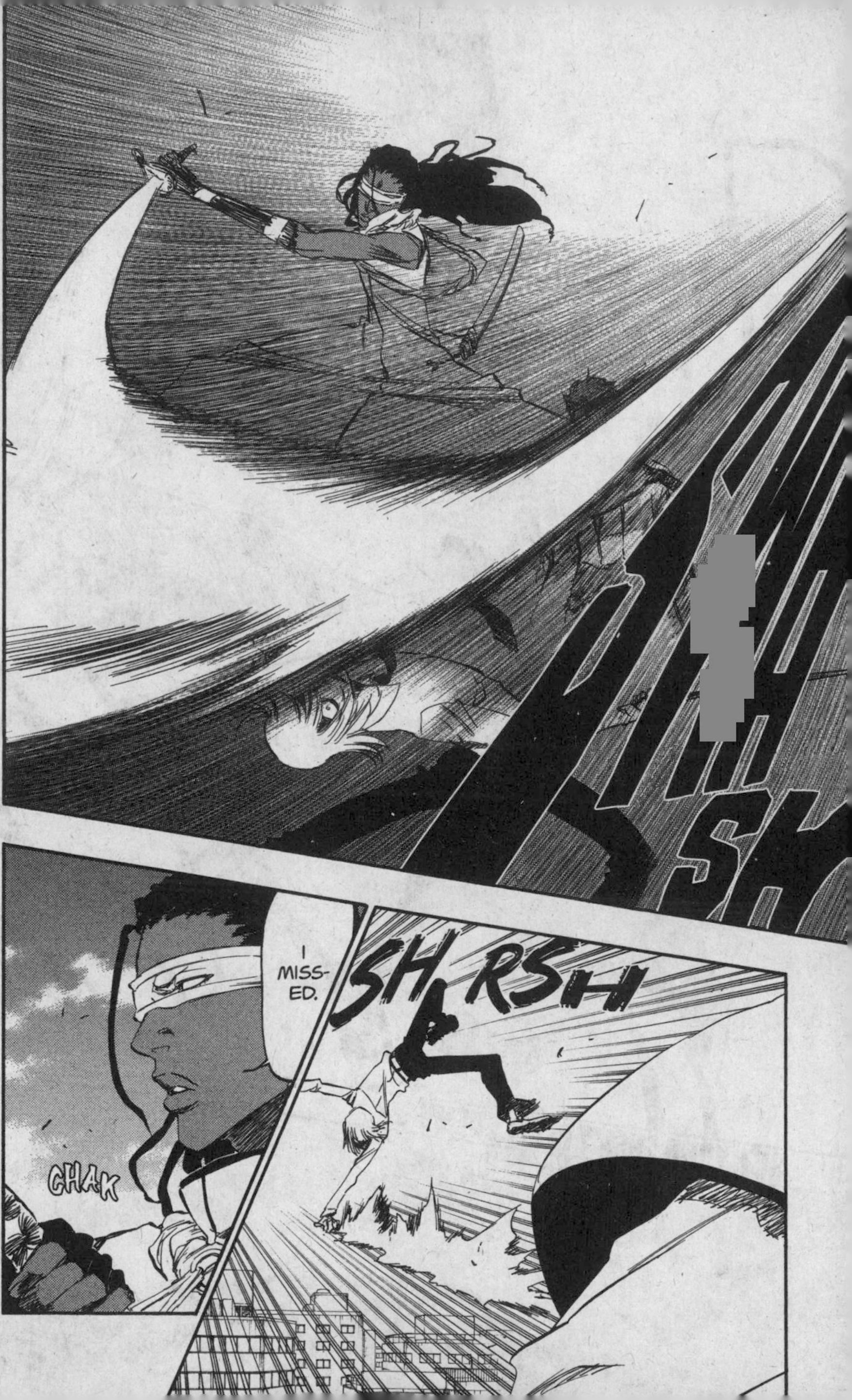

SHRSH
I MISSED.
CHAK

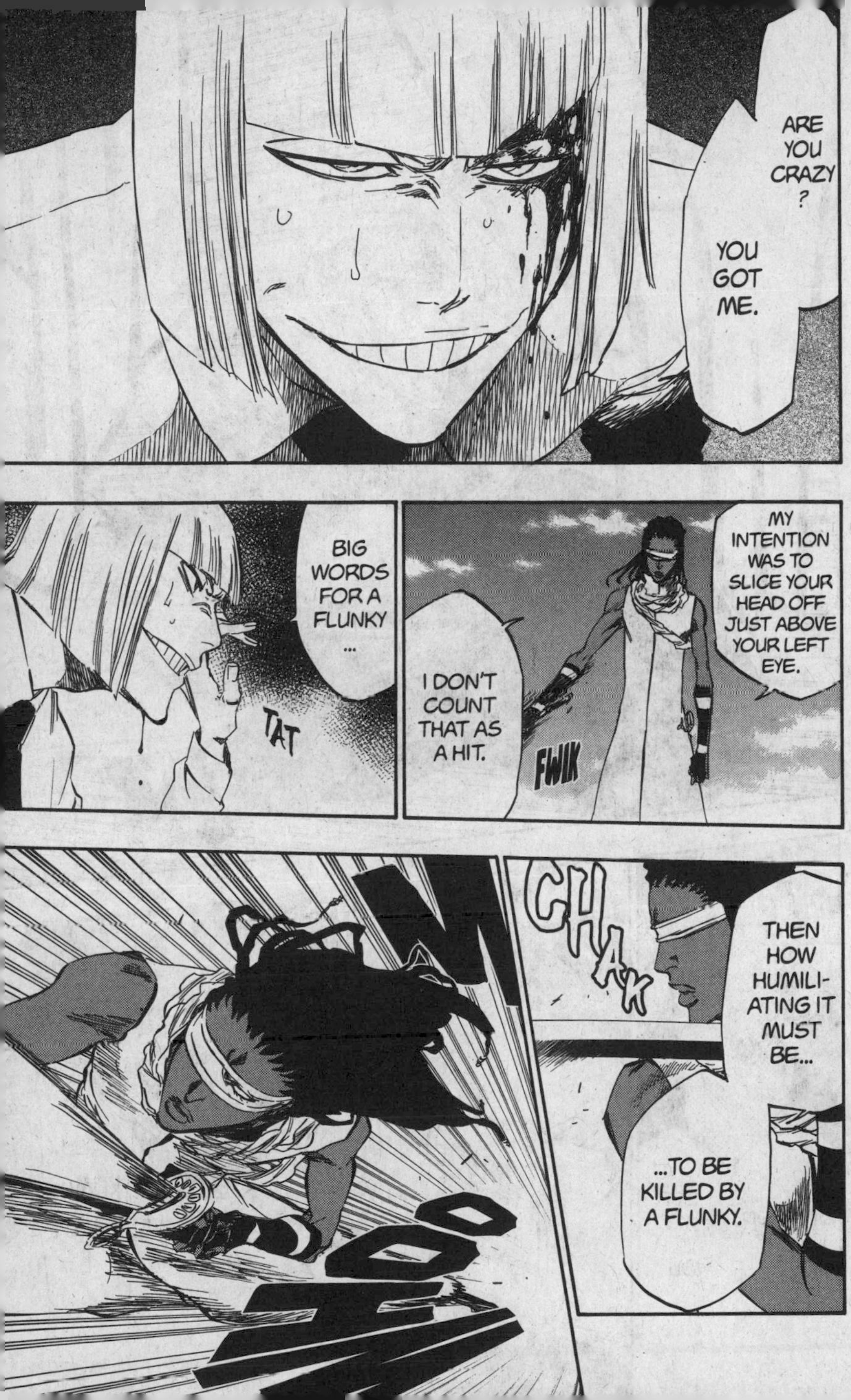
ARE YOU CRAZY?
YOU GOT ME.
MY INTENTION WAS TO SLICE YOUR HEAD OFF JUST ABOVE YOUR LEFT EYE.
I DON'T COUNT THAT AS A HIT.
FWIK
BIG WORDS FOR A FLUNKY...
TAT
CHAK
THEN HOW HUMILI-ATING IT MUST BE...
...TO BE KILLED BY A FLUNKY.

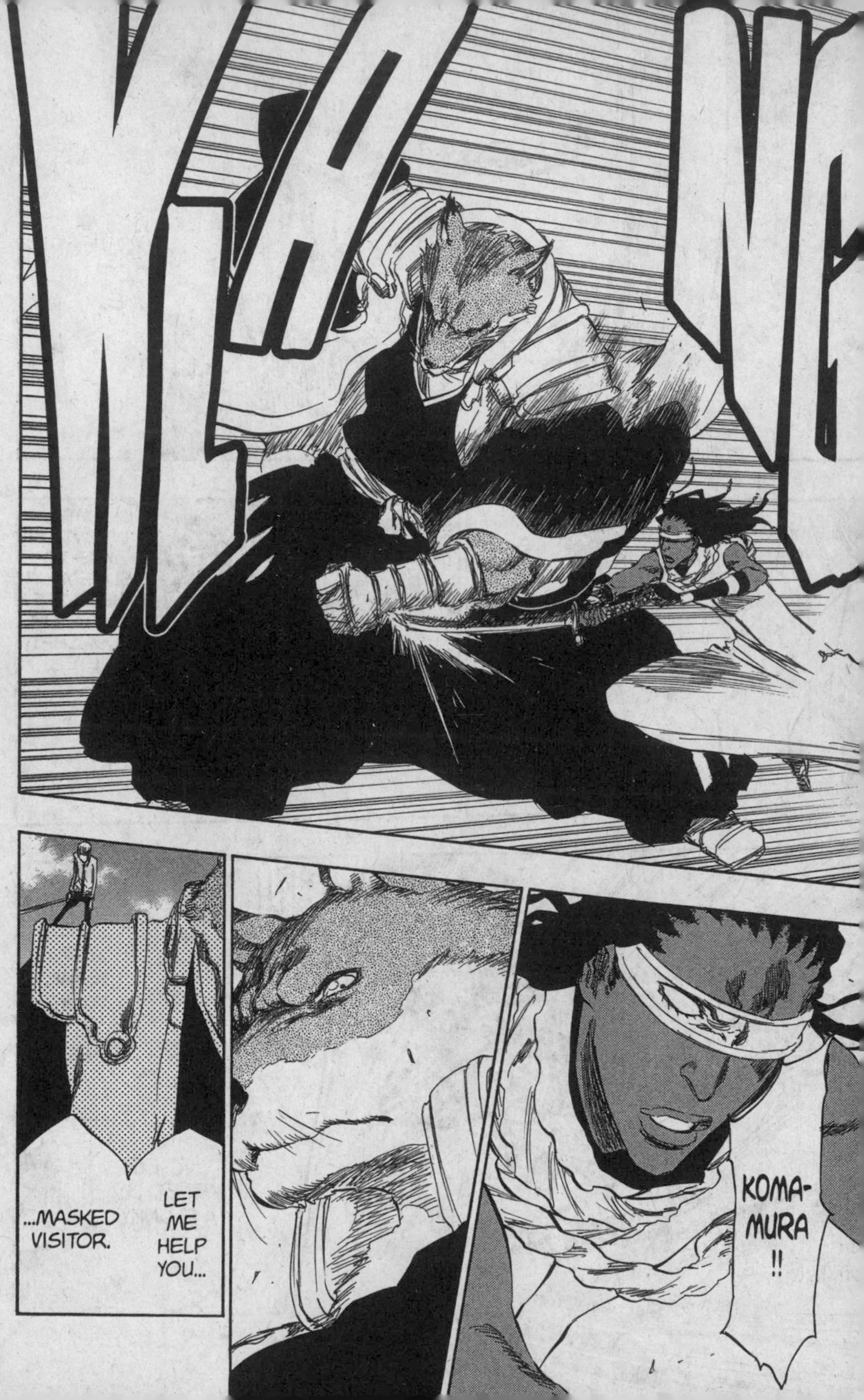
KOMA-
MURA
!!
LET ME HELP YOU...
...MASKED VISITOR.

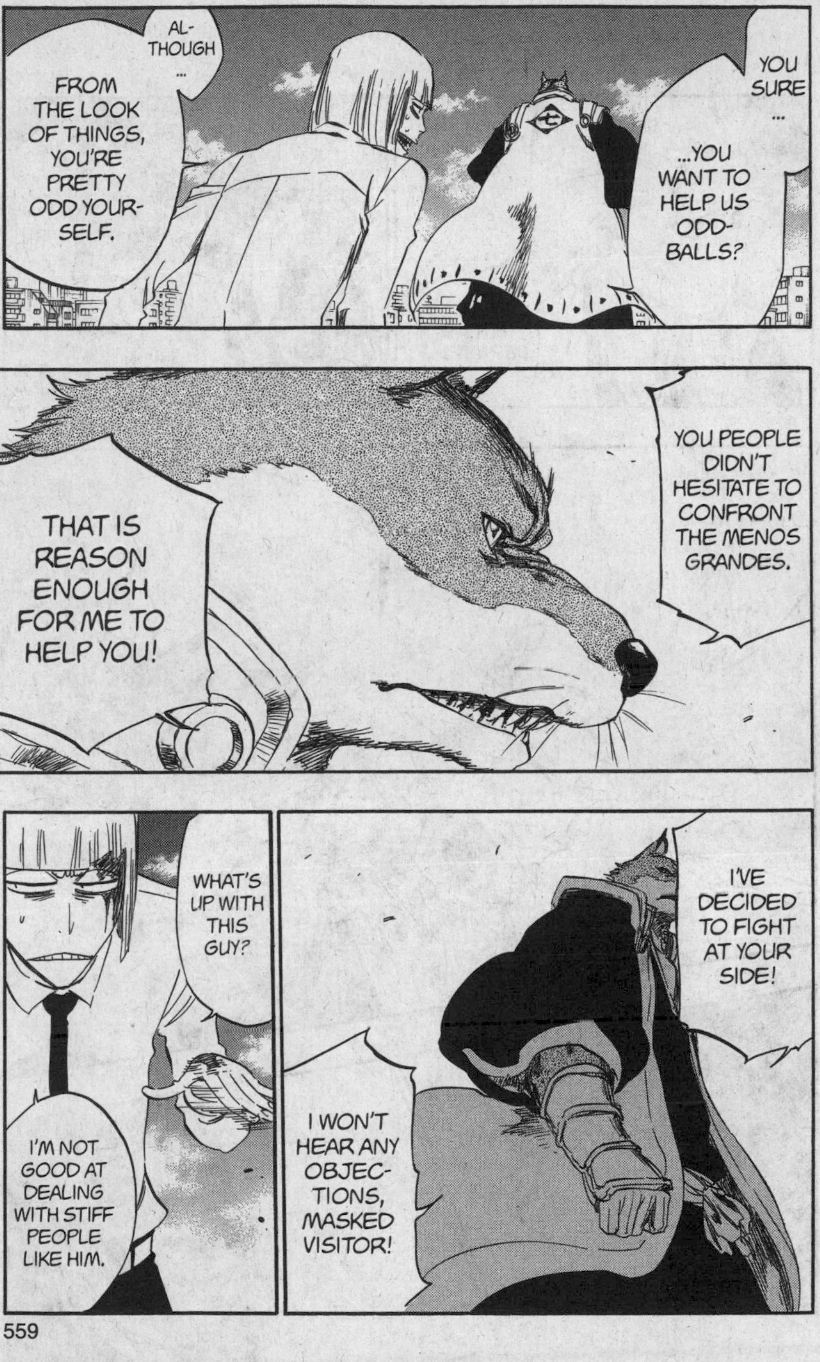
YOU SURE ... ...YOU WANT TO HELP US ODDBALLS?
ALTHOUGH ...
FROM THE LOOK OF THINGS, YOU'RE PRETTY ODD YOURSELF.
YOU PEOPLE DIDN'T HESITATE TO CONFRONT THE MENOS GRANDES.
THAT IS REASON ENOUGH FOR ME TO HELP YOU!
I'VE DECIDED TO FIGHT AT YOUR SIDE!
I WON'T HEAR ANY OBJECTIONS, MASKED VISITOR!
WHAT'S UP WITH THIS GUY?
I'M NOT GOOD AT DEALING WITH STIFF PEOPLE LIKE HIM.

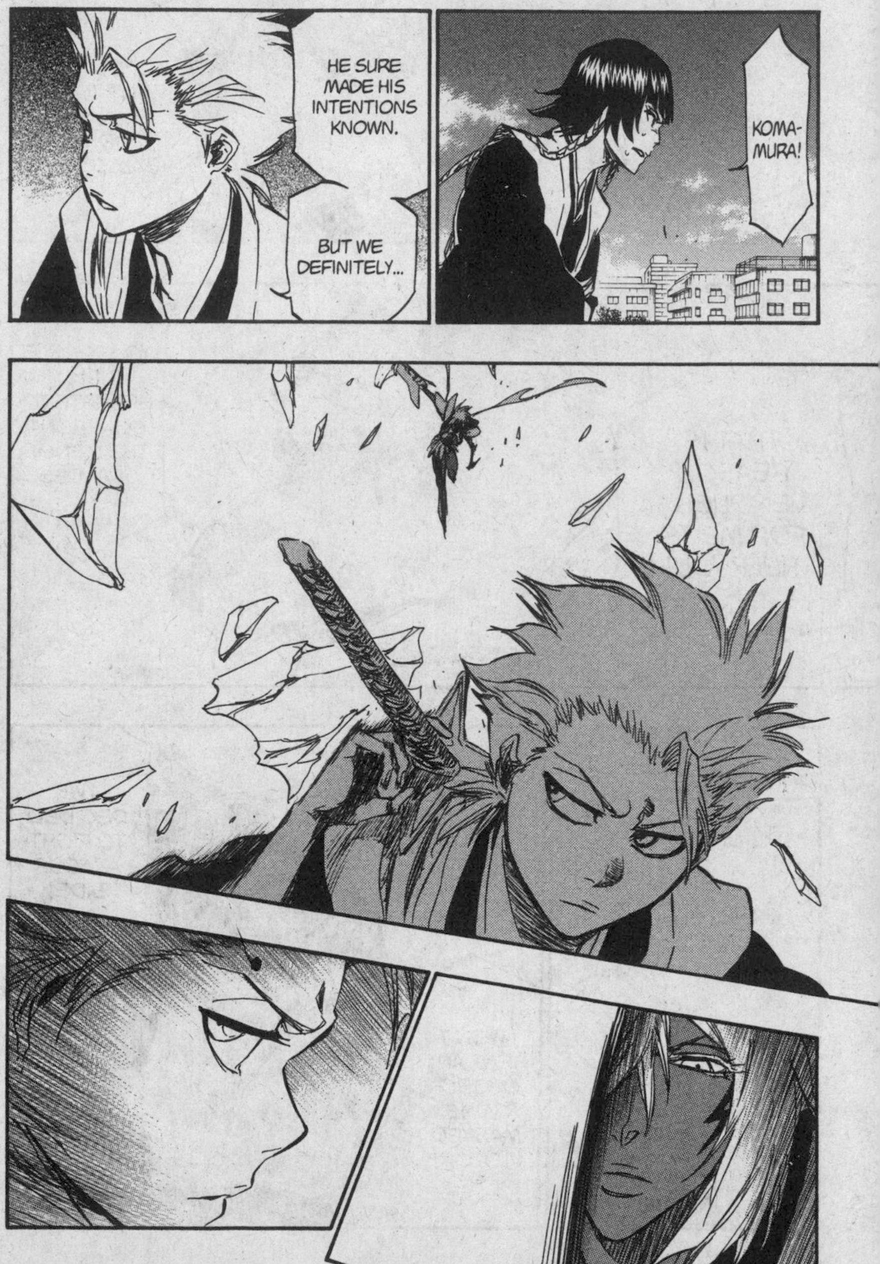
KOMA-
MURA!
HE SURE MADE HIS INTENTIONS KNOWN.
BUT WE DEFINITELY...

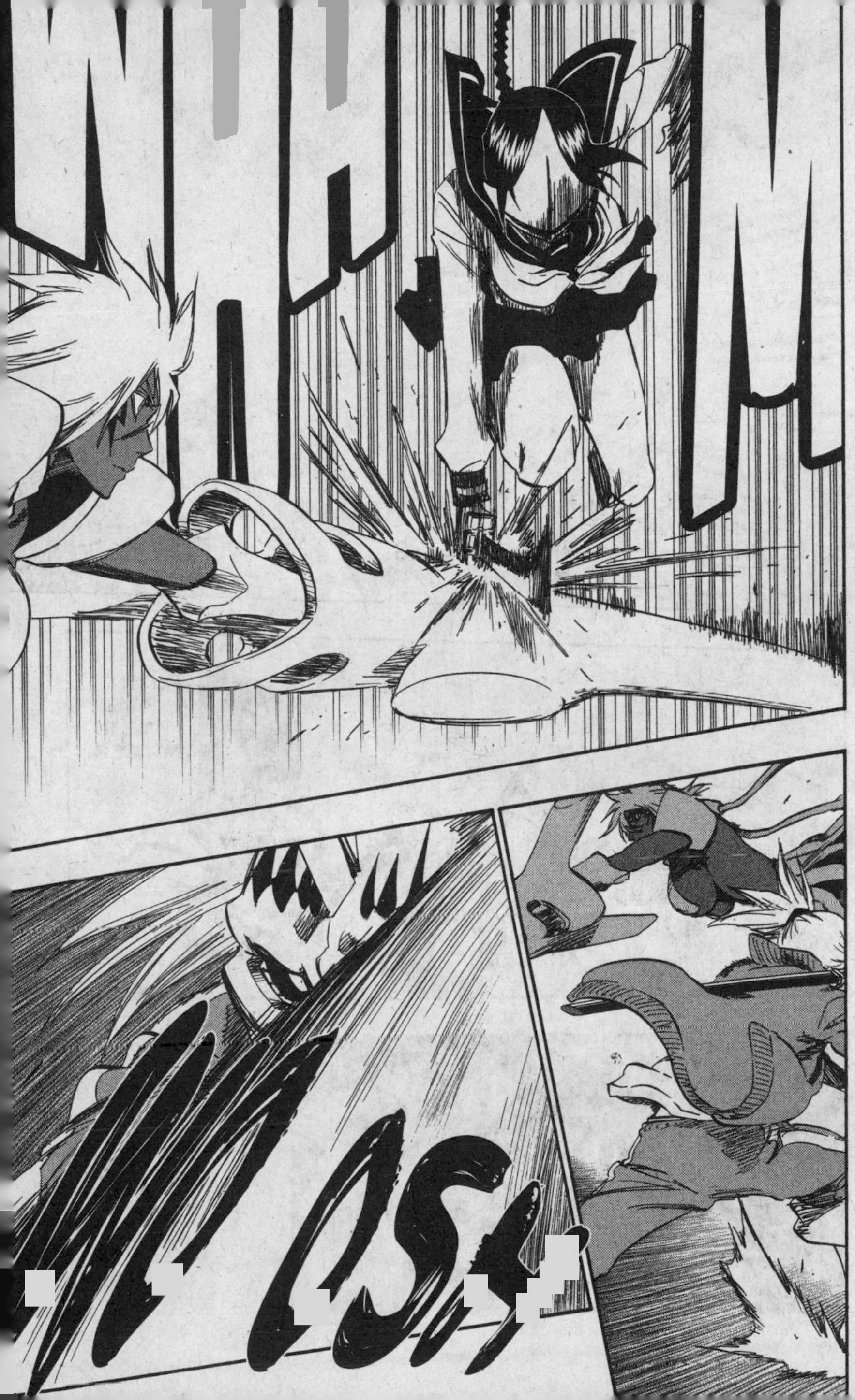

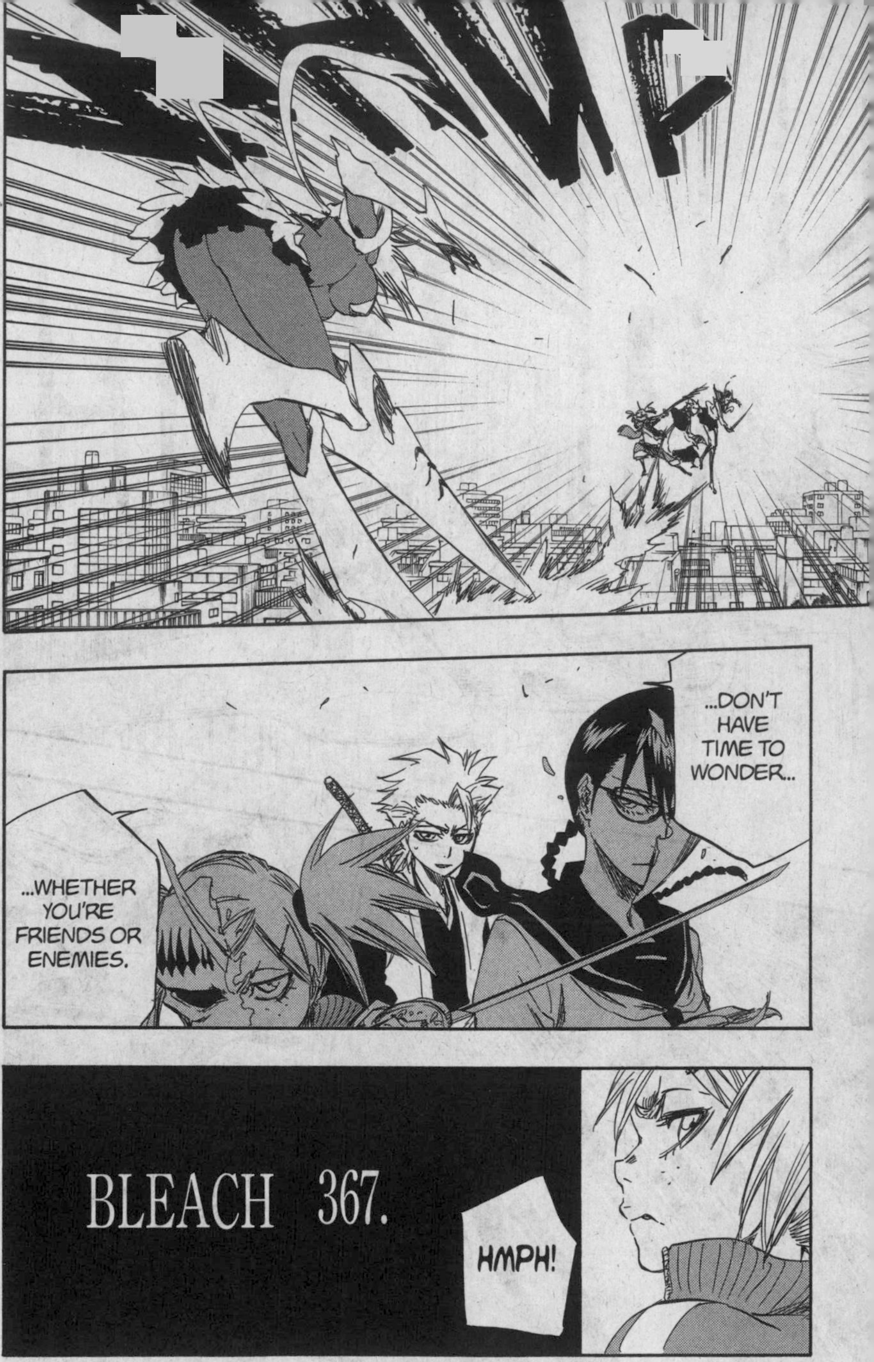
...DON'T HAVE TIME TO WONDER...
...WHETHER YOU'RE FRIENDS OR ENEMIES.
HMPH!
BLEACH 367.

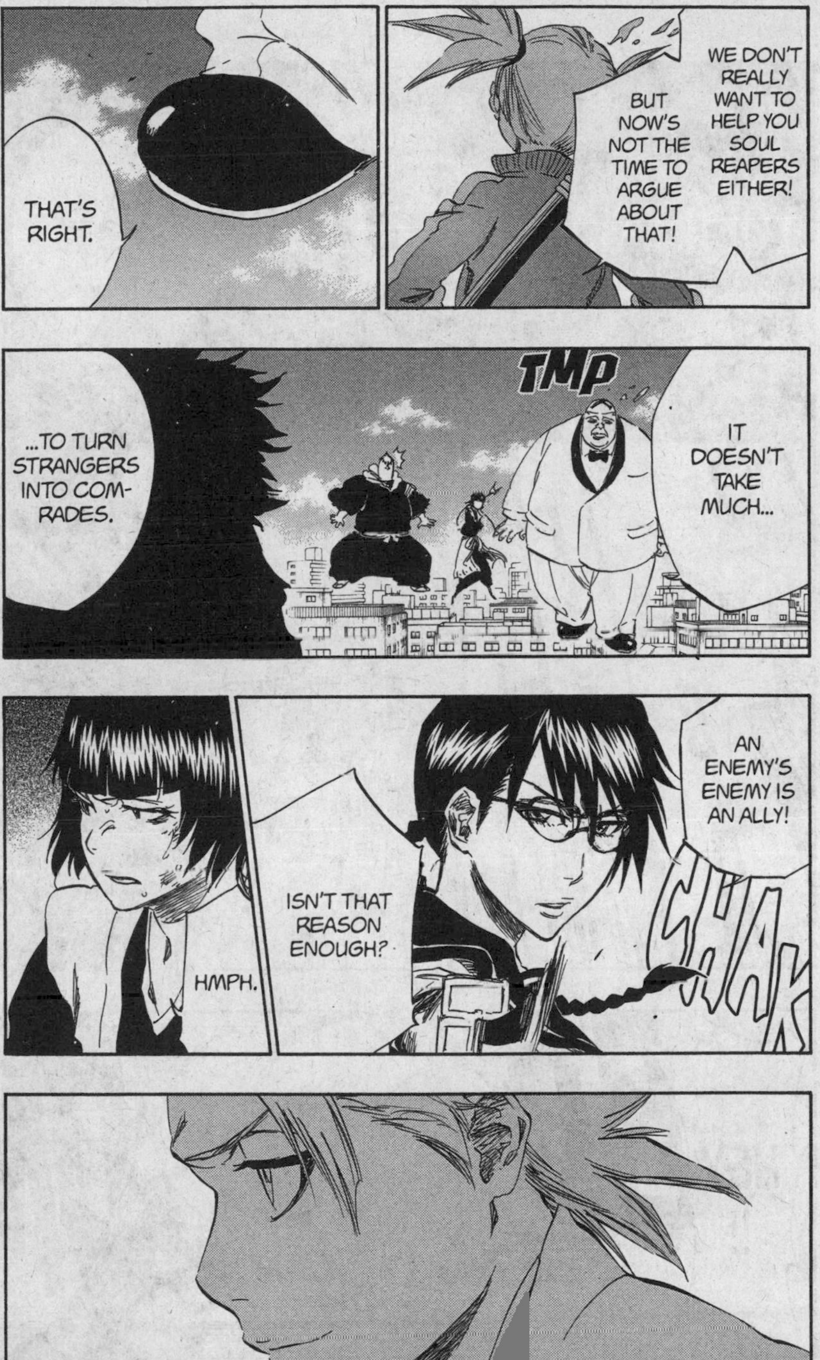
WE DON'T REALLY WANT TO HELP YOU SOUL REAPERS EITHER!
BUT NOW'S NOT THE TIME TO ARGUE ABOUT THAT!
THAT'S RIGHT.
TMP
IT DOESN'T TAKE MUCH...
...TO TURN STRANGERS INTO COM-RADES.
AN ENEMY'S ENEMY IS AN ALLY!
CHAK
ISN'T THAT REASON ENOUGH?
HMPH.

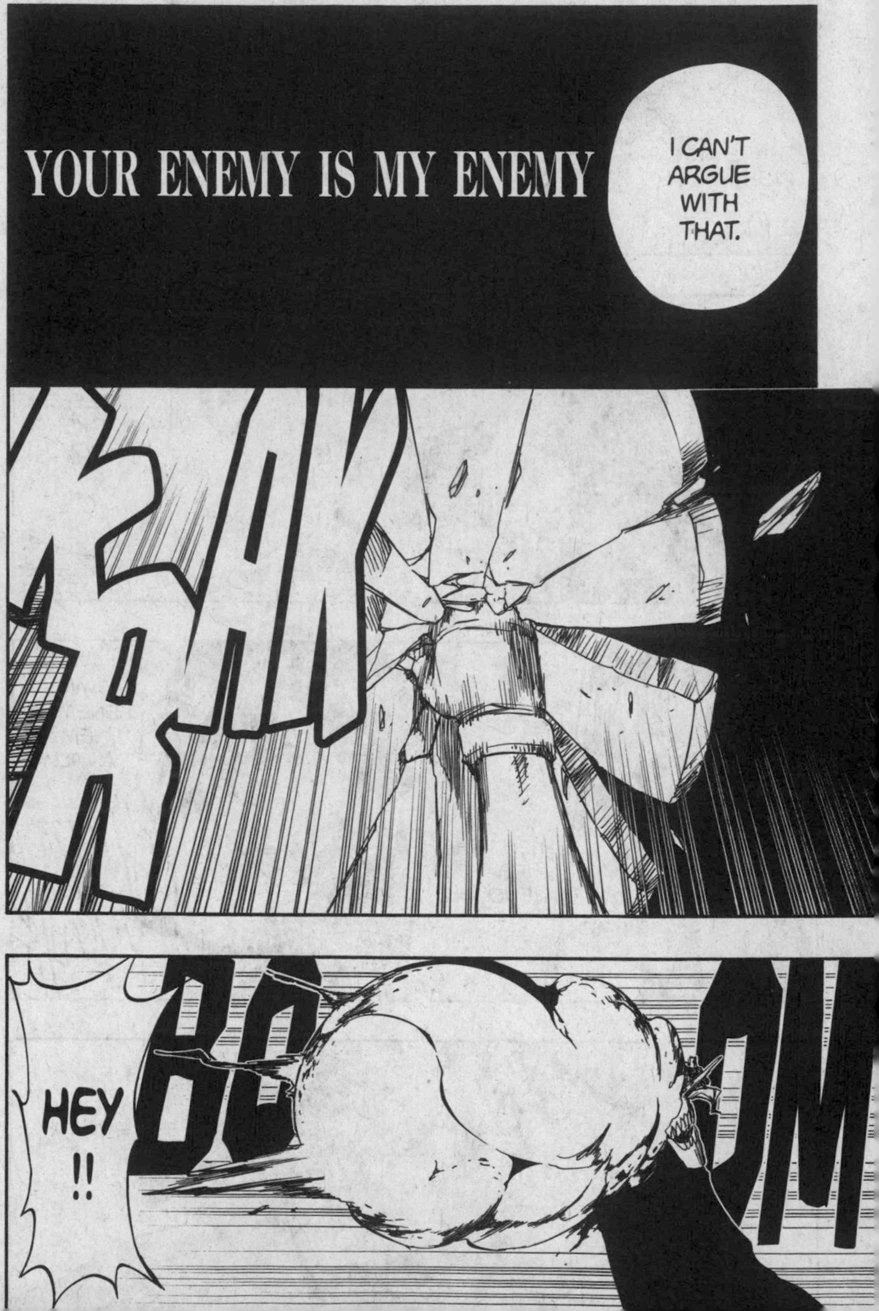
YOUR ENEMY IS MY ENEMY
I CAN'T ARGUE WITH THAT.
KRAK
BOOM
HEY!!

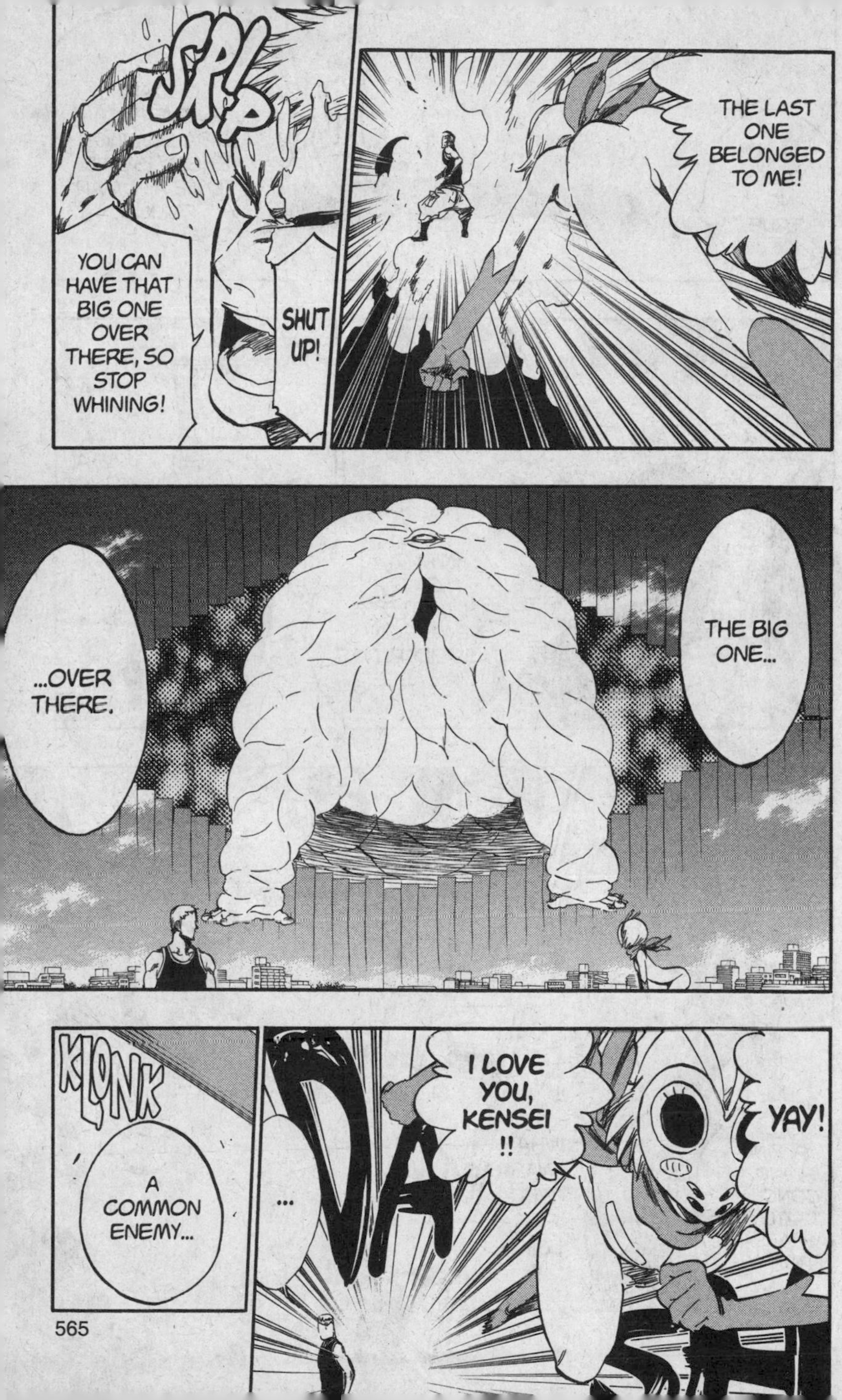
THE LAST ONE BELONGED TO ME!
YOU CAN HAVE THAT BIG ONE OVER THERE, SO STOP WHINING!
SHUT UP!
THE BIG ONE...
...OVER THERE.
YAY!
I LOVE YOU, KENSEI !!
...
KLONK
A COMMON ENEMY...

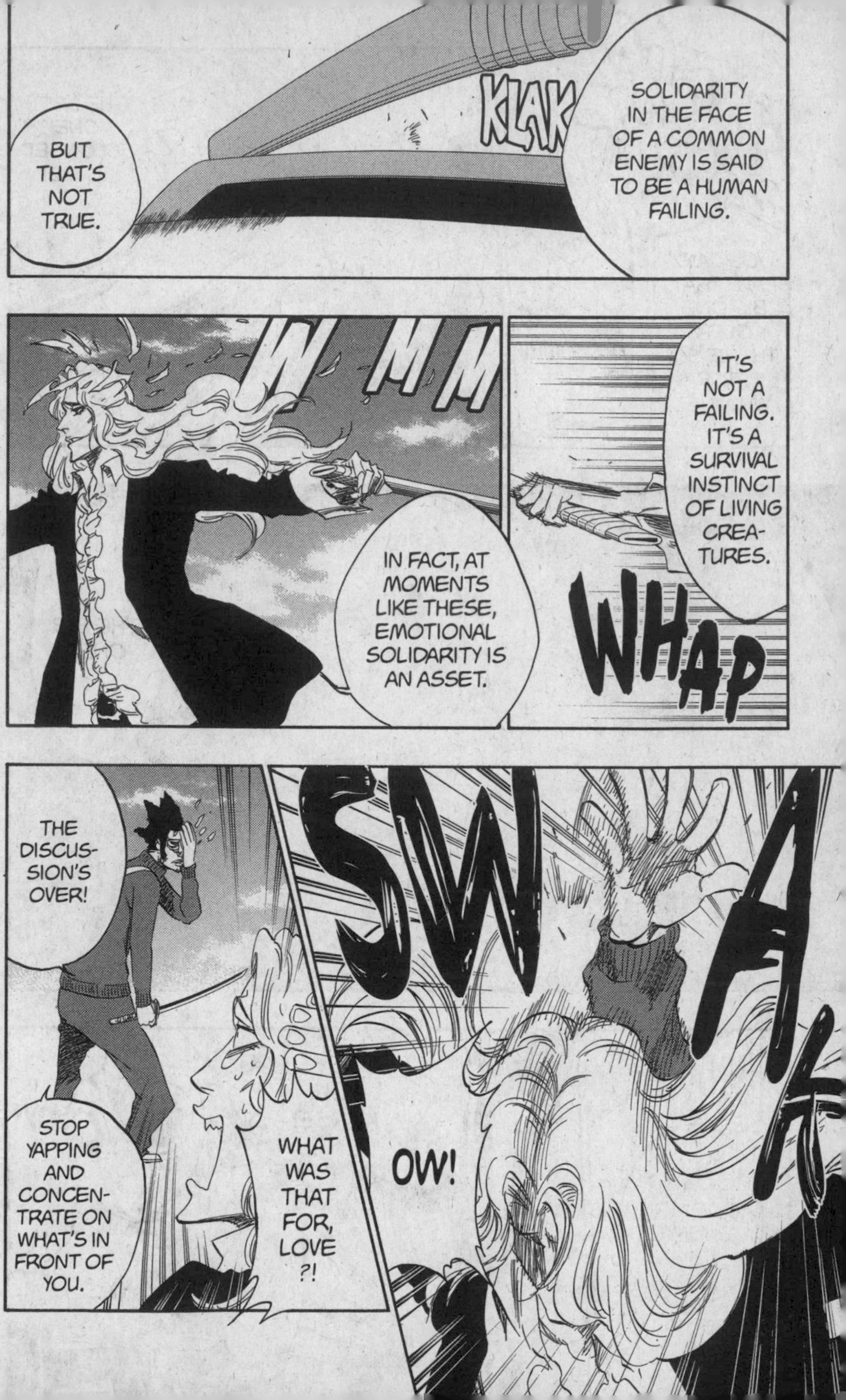
SOLIDARITY IN THE FACE OF A COMMON ENEMY IS SAID TO BE A HUMAN FAILING.
KLAK
BUT THAT'S NOT TRUE.
IT'S NOT A FAILING. IT'S A SURVIVAL INSTINCT OF LIVING CREATURES.
WHAP
WMM
IN FACT, AT MOMENTS LIKE THESE, EMOTIONAL SOLIDARITY IS AN ASSET.
SWA
OW!
WHAT WAS THAT FOR, LOVE?!
THE DISCUSSION'S OVER!
STOP YAPPING AND CONCENTRATE ON WHAT'S IN FRONT OF YOU.

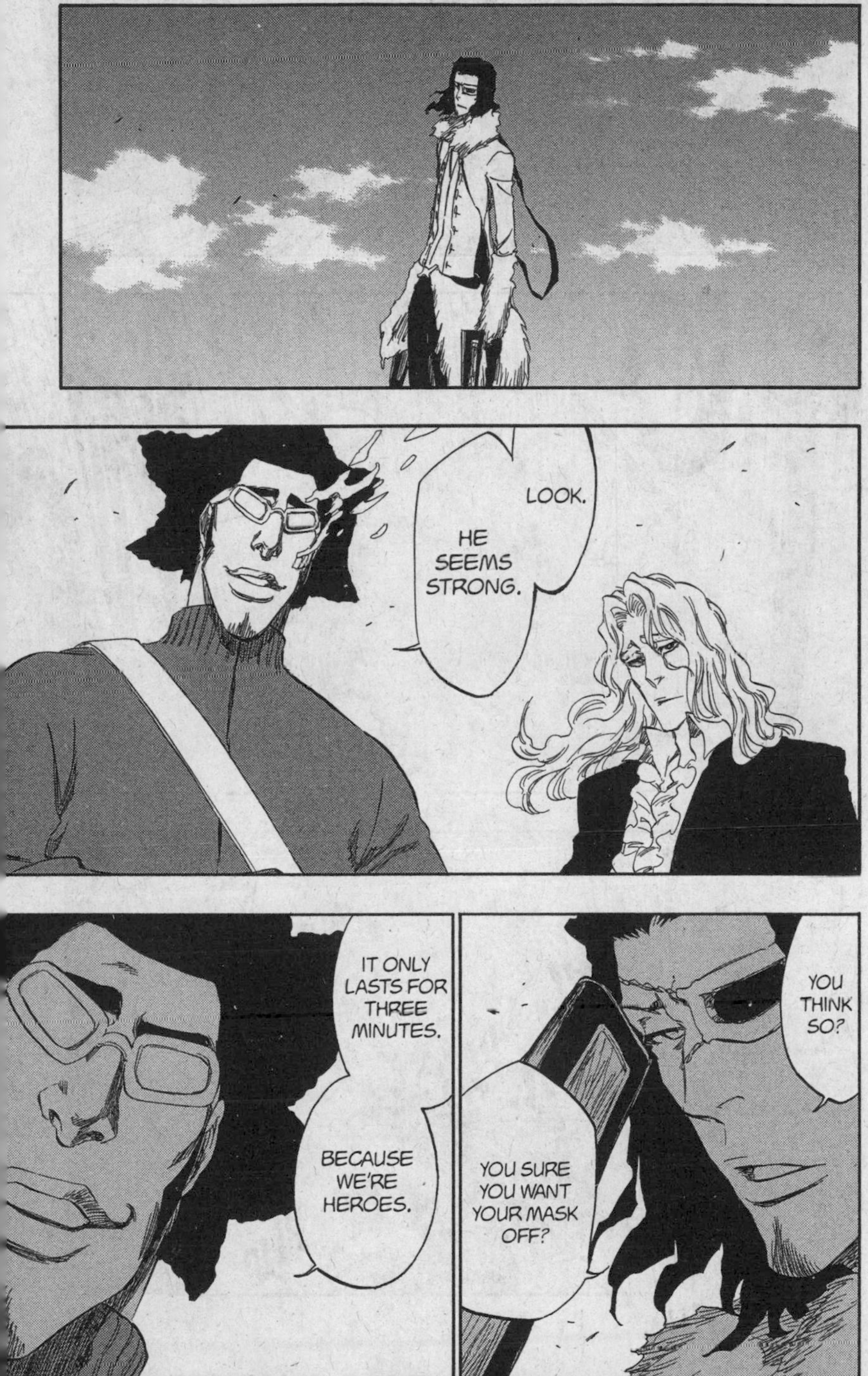
LOOK. HE SEEMS STRONG.
YOU THINK SO?
YOU SURE YOU WANT YOUR MASK OFF?
IT ONLY LASTS FOR THREE MINUTES.
BECAUSE WE'RE HEROES.

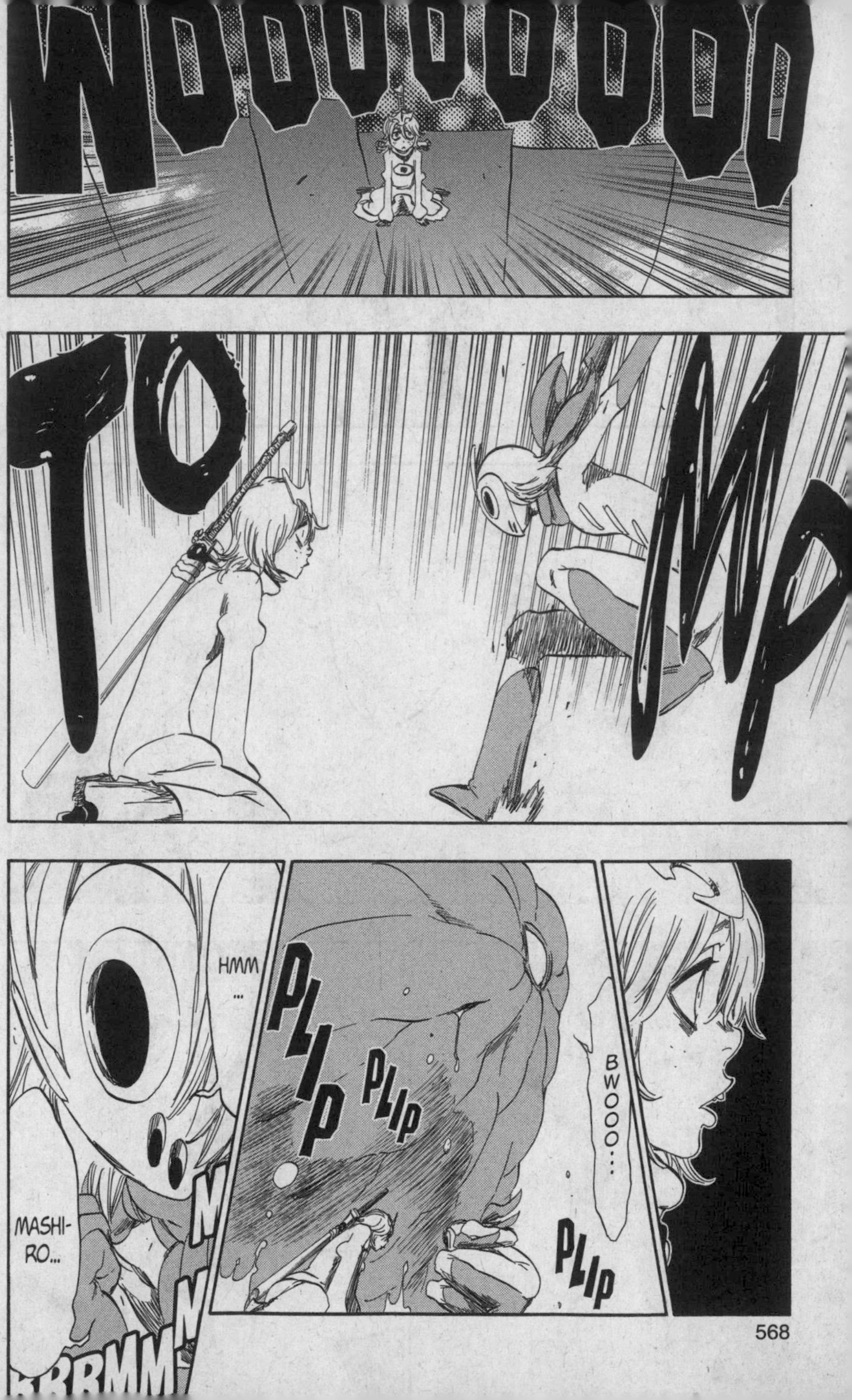
WOOOOOOOO
TOMP
BWOOO....
PLIP
PLIP
PLIP
HMM...
MASHIRO...
MM
KRRMMM

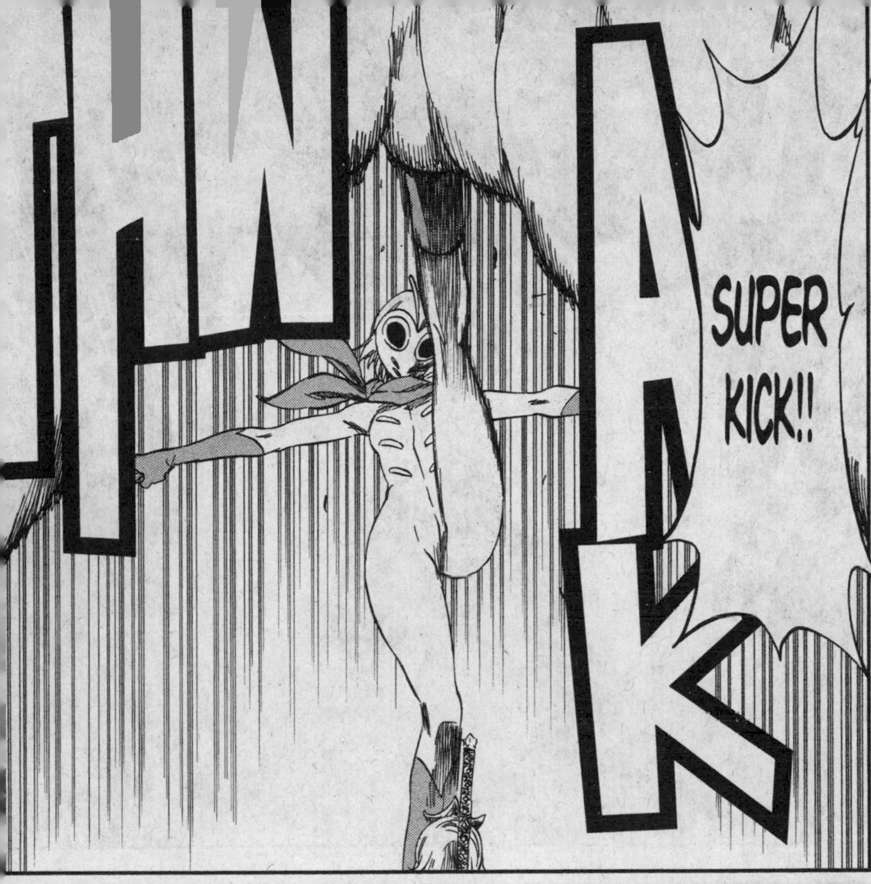
THWACK
SUPER KICK!!
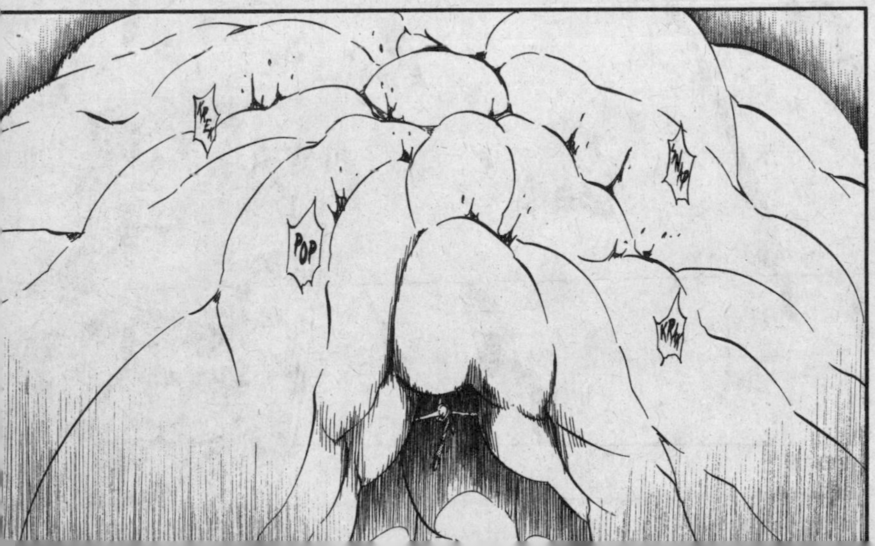
SNAP
KREK
POP

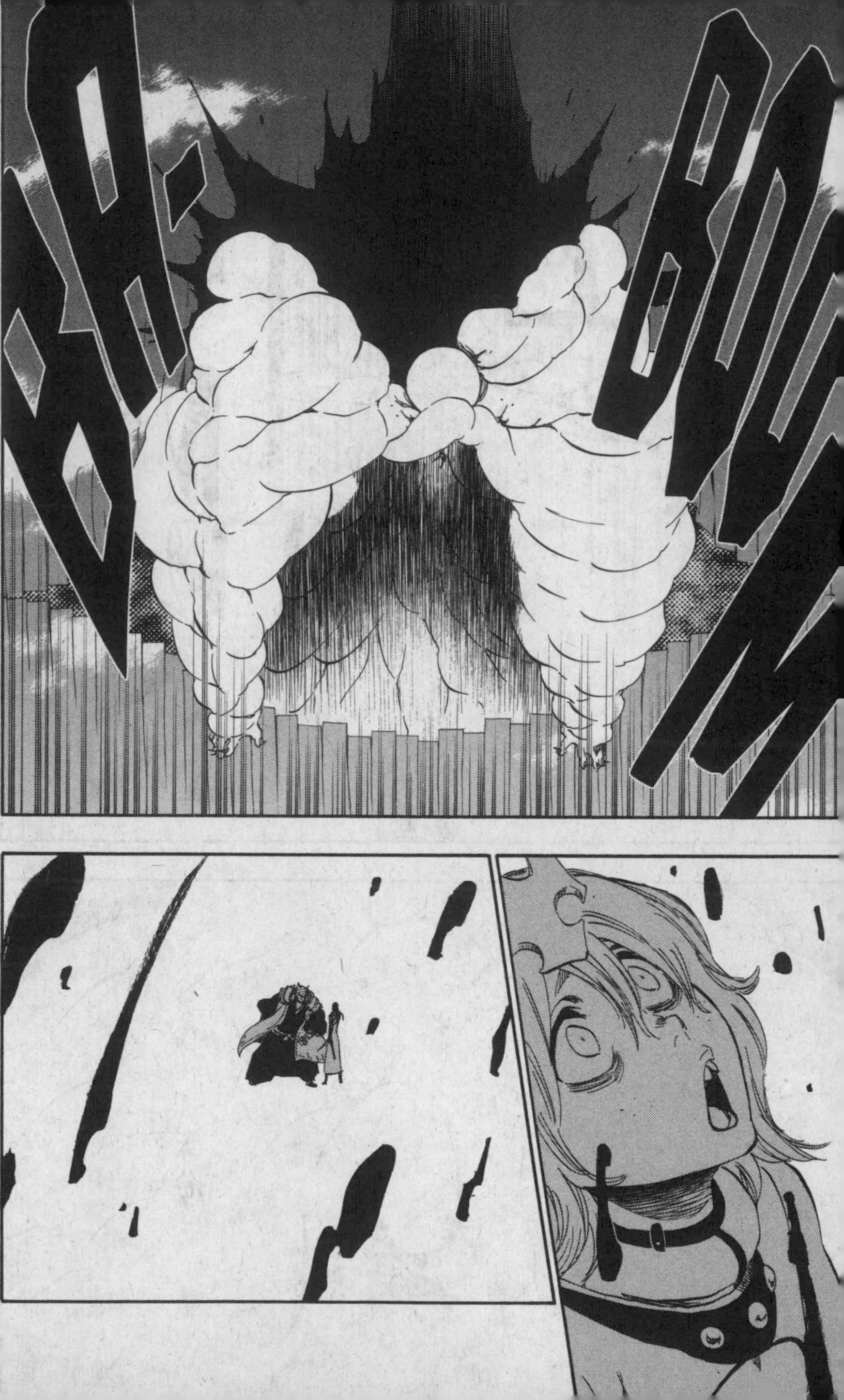

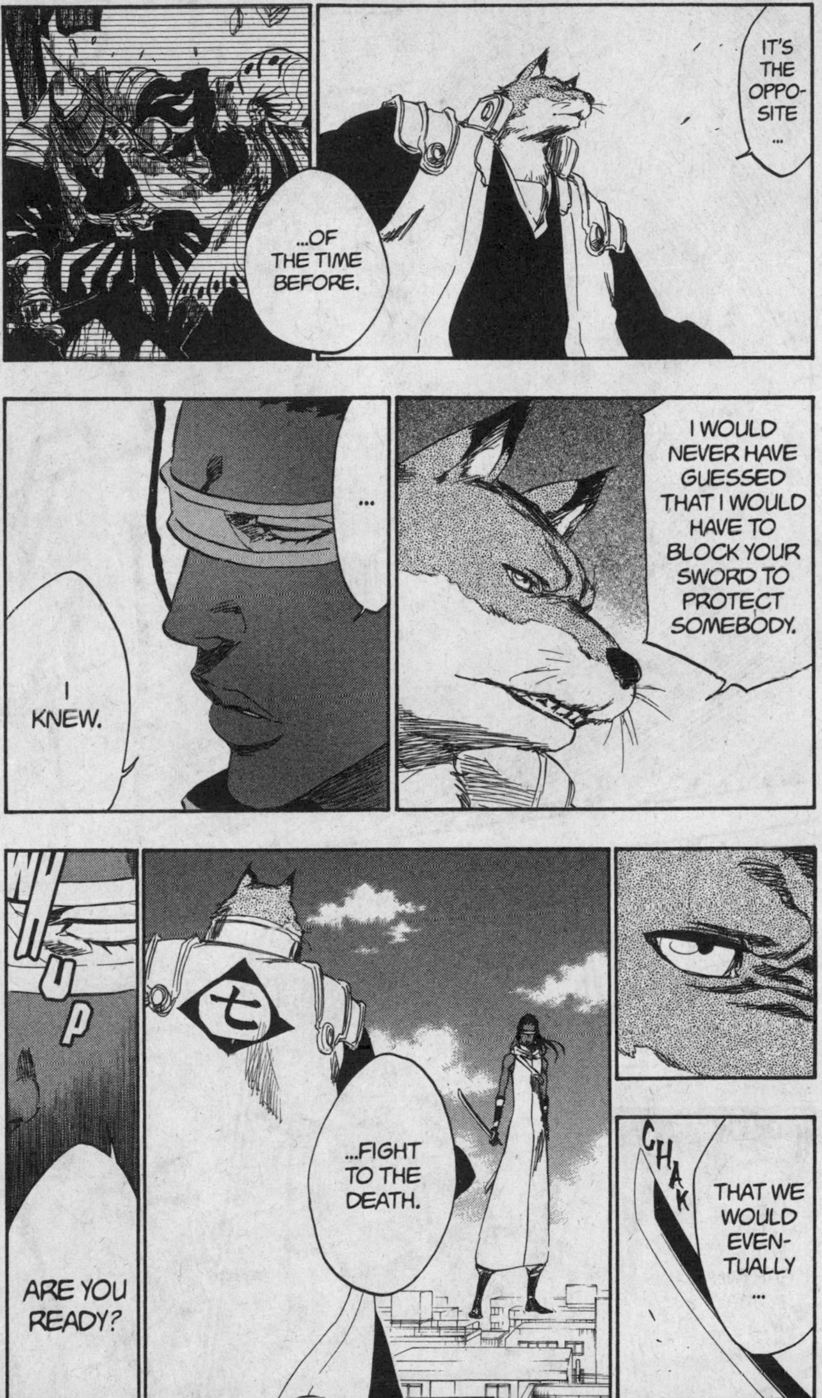
IT'S THE OPPO-SITE...
...OF THE TIME BEFORE.
I WOULD NEVER HAVE GUESSED THAT I WOULD HAVE TO BLOCK YOUR SWORD TO PROTECT SOMEBODY.
...
I KNEW.
CHAK
THAT WE WOULD EVEN-TUALLY...
...FIGHT TO THE DEATH.
WHUP
ARE YOU READY?

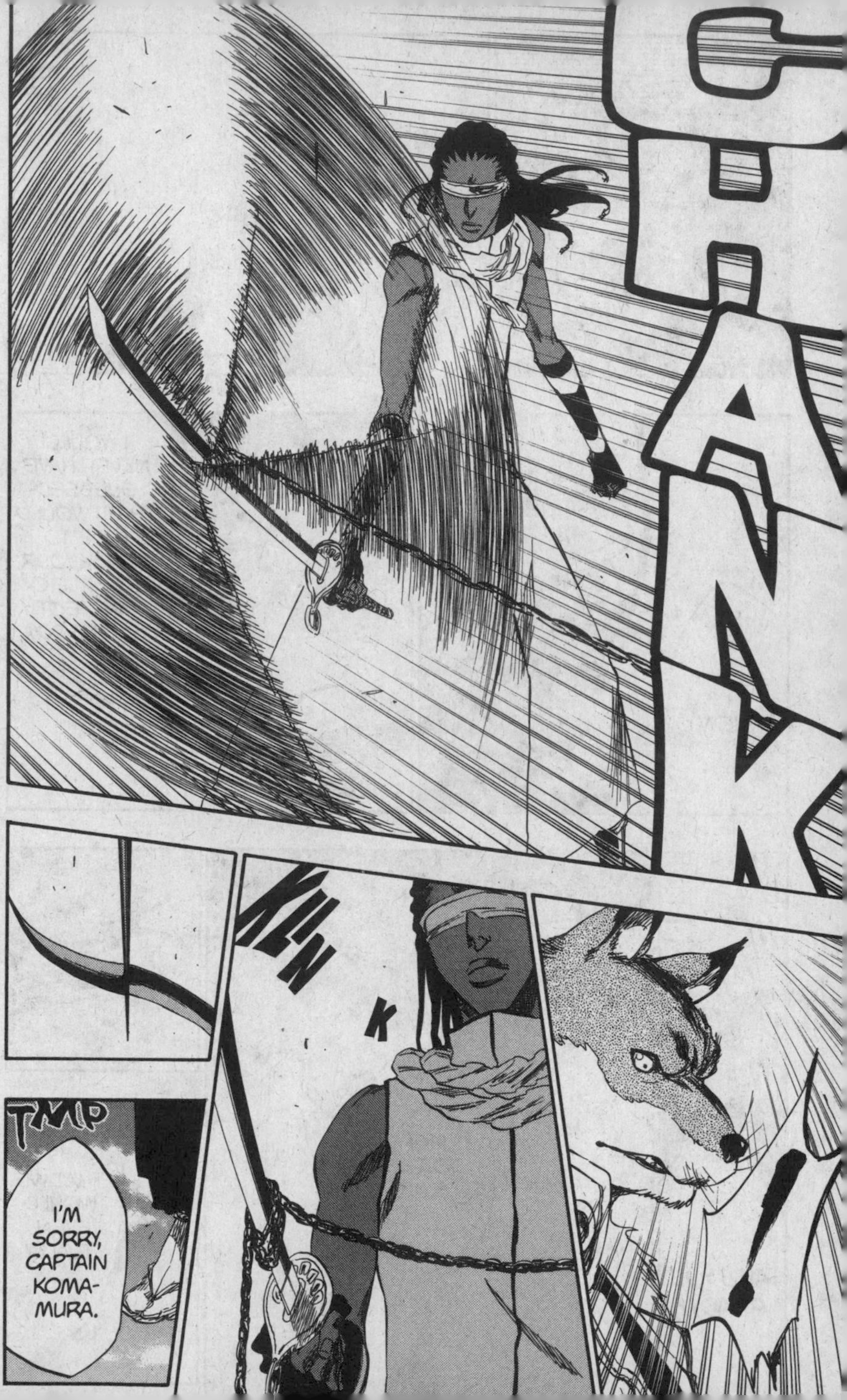
CHANK!
KLINK
TMP
I'M SORRY, CAPTAIN KOMAMURA.
!!

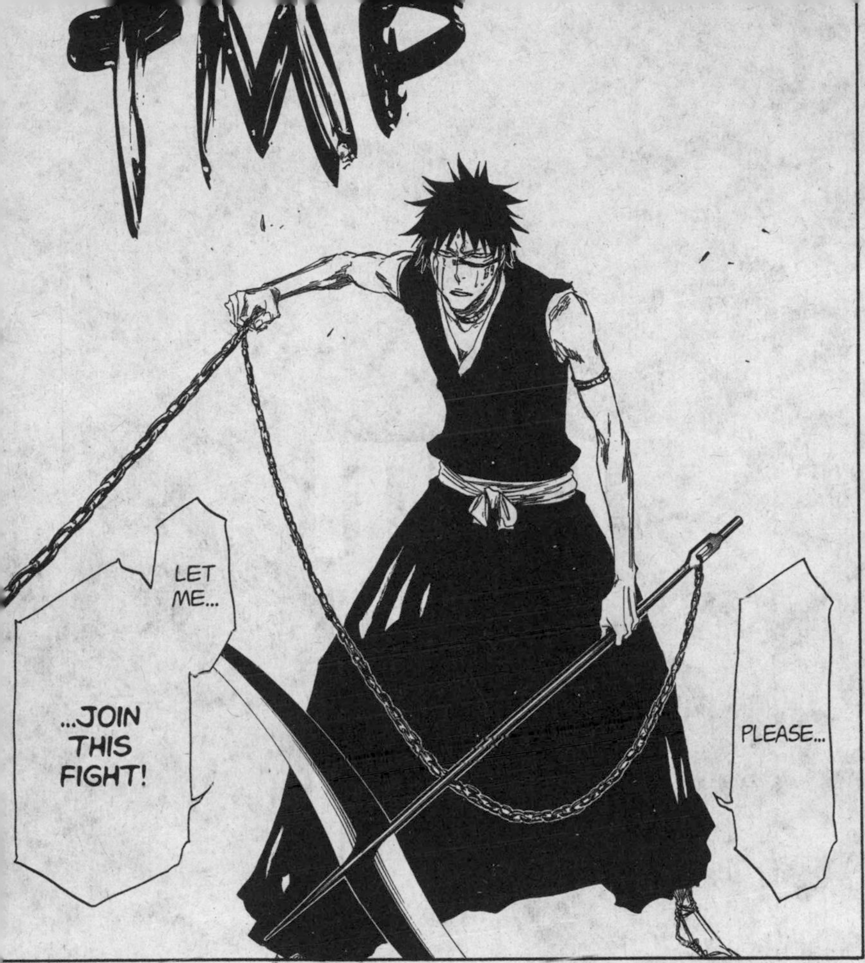
TMP
PLEASE...
LET ME...
...JOIN THIS FIGHT!
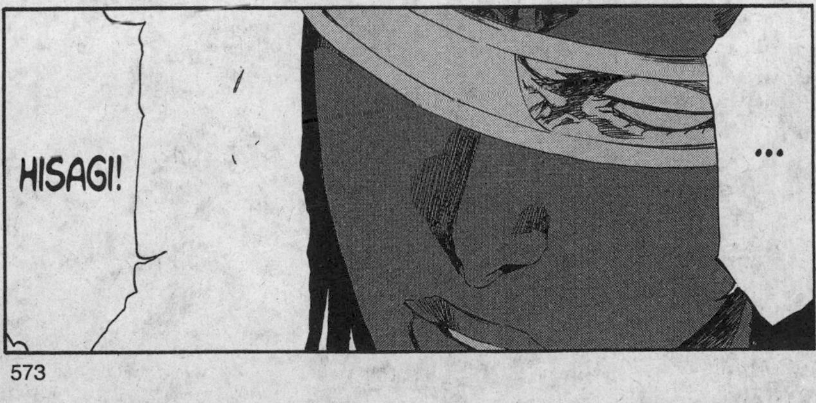
...
HISAGI!

CONTINUED IN BLEACH 43

Next Volume Preview

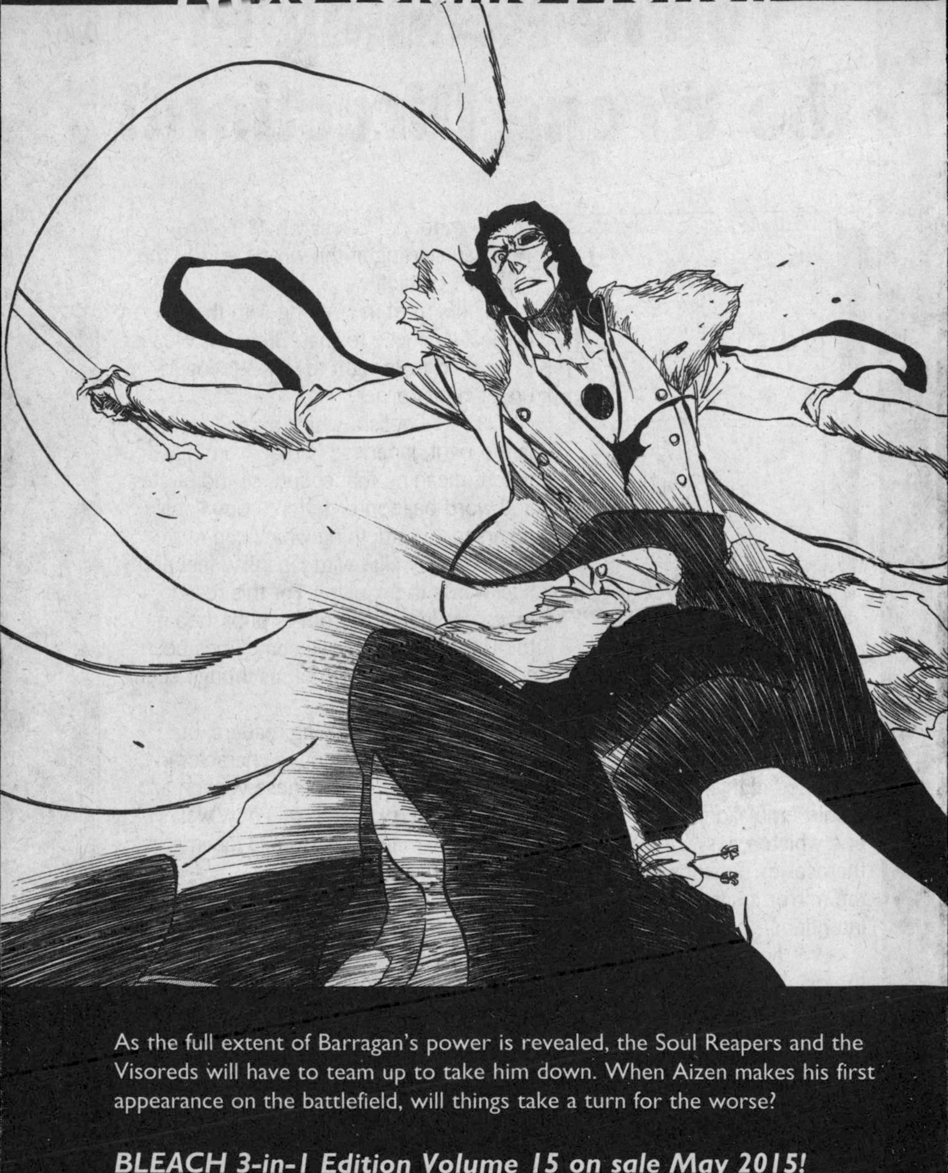

As the full extent of Barragan's power is revealed, the Soul Reapers and the Visoreds will have to team up to take him down. When Aizen makes his first appearance on the battlefield, will things take a turn for the worse?

BLEACH 3-in-1 Edition Volume 15 on sale May 2015!

You're Reading in the Wrong Direction!!

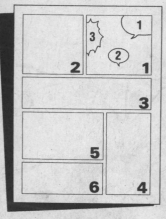

Whoops! Guess what? You're starting at the wrong end of the comic!

…It's true! In keeping with the original Japanese format, **Bleach** is meant to be read from right to left, starting in the upper-right corner.

Unlike English, which is read from left to right, Japanese is read from right to left, meaning that action, sound effects and word-balloon order are completely reversed… something which can make readers unfamiliar with Japanese feel pretty backwards themselves. For this reason, manga or Japanese comics published in the U.S. in English have sometimes been published "flopped"—that is, printed in exact reverse order, as though seen from the other side of a mirror.

By flopping pages, U.S. publishers can avoid confusing readers, but the compromise is not without its downside. For one thing, a character in a flopped manga series who once wore in the original Japanese version a T-shirt emblazoned with "M A Y" (as in "the merry month of") now wears one which reads "Y A M"! Additionally, many manga creators in Japan are themselves unhappy with the process, as some feel the mirror-imaging of their art skews their original intentions.

We are proud to bring you Tite Kubo's **Bleach** in the original unflopped format. For now, though, turn to the other side of the book and let the adventure begin…!

—Editor